BRINGING INTERNATIONAL FUGITIVES TO JUSTICE

Extradition and Its Alternatives

A novel and robust framework for the operational and legal analysis of recovering fugitives abroad, *Bringing International Fugitives to Justice* addresses how States, working alone, in cooperation, or with third-party intervention, strive to secure the custody of fugitives in order to bring them to justice – for prosecution or punishment purposes – while evaluating the lawfulness of those pursuit efforts. The book introduces redefined terms and new concepts to add precision to the discourse; sets forth comprehensive typologies, including of extradition arrangements and impediments; and provides a mapping to account for the full range of means and methods – extradition, collateral and remedial approaches to extradition, and full-scale and fallback alternatives to extradition – by which international fugitives can be retrieved. The study considers the judicial, diplomatic, and policy consequences of reliance on the more aggressive or controversial alternatives, proffering recommendations that, if adopted, could facilitate the recovery of fugitives while minimizing associated risks.

DAVID A. SADOFF, J.D., PH.D., most recently was General Counsel at the Rome-based International Development Law Organization. Previously, he served as the first Nepal Country Director for the ABA Rule of Law Initiative; in various legal or policy positions with the U.S. National Security Council, the CIA, and the U.S. Department of State; and as a Litigation Associate with Crowell & Moring LLP. He is also a Senior Research Fellow with the Centre for International Sustainable Development Law.

BRINGING INTERNATIONAL FUGITIVES TO JUSTICE

Extradition and Its Alternatives

DAVID A. SADOFF

CAMBRIDGE
UNIVERSITY PRESS

CAMBRIDGE
UNIVERSITY PRESS

One Liberty Plaza, 20th Floor, New York, NY 10006, USA

Cambridge University Press is part of the University of Cambridge.

It furthers the University's mission by disseminating knowledge in the pursuit of education, learning, and research at the highest international levels of excellence.

www.cambridge.org
Information on this title: www.cambridge.org/9781107129283

First published 2016

Printed in the United Kingdom by Clays, St Ives plc

A catalogue record for this publication is available from the British Library.

Library of Congress Cataloging-in-Publication Data
Sadoff, David A., author.
Bringing international fugitives to justice: extradition and its alternatives / David A. Sadoff
New York, NY: Cambridge University Press, 2016. | Based on author's thesis (doctoral – Université de Genève, 2014) issued under title: Bringing fugitives to justice under international law.
LCCN 2016024589 | ISBN 9781107129283 (hardback)
LCSH: Criminal procedure (International law) | Extradition | BISAC: LAW / International.
LCC KZ7398 .S23 2016 | DDC 345/.052–dc23
LC record available at https://lccn.loc.gov/2016024589

ISBN 978-1-107-12928-3 Hardback

CONTENTS

ACKNOWLEDGMENTS

This has been a protracted and challenging project that would not have been possible without the generous contributions of many people. I begin by thanking University of Geneva Law Professor Robert Kolb, whose outstanding teaching and passion for public international law inspired my interest in this field. I also wish to acknowledge the editorial team at Cambridge University Press, led by John Berger, for their professionalism, dedication, and attention to detail. I owe my parents, Robert and Joan Sadoff, an immeasurable debt of thanks for the values of fairness and justice they championed and modeled. Finally, I extend my deepest gratitude to my dear wife Claudia and our three children, Haley, Rachel, and Jake, to whom I collectively dedicate this book. Their patience – even indulgence – was greatly appreciated, but it was their love and encouragement that gave me the fortitude to complete this work.

ACRONYMS AND ABBREVIATIONS

A.C.	Appeal Cases (U.K.)
ACHPR	African Charter of Human and Peoples' Rights (1981)
ACHR	American Convention on Human Rights (1969)
ADR	Alternative Dispute Resolution
AFB	Air Force Base
AG	Attorney General
AJIL	AMERICAN JOURNAL OF INTERNATIONAL LAW
AP I	Additional Protocol I (1977) to the Geneva Conventions of August 12, 1949
ASIL	American Society of International Law
A.T.S.	AUSTRALIAN TREATY SERIES
AU	African Union
B&H	Bosnia and Herzegovina
BHRC	Butterworths Human Rights Cases
B.Y.B.I.L.	BRITISH YEAR BOOK OF INTERNATIONAL LAW
CARICOM	Caribbean Community
CAT	Convention against Torture and other Cruel, Inhuman or Degrading Treatment or Punishment (U.N.) (1984)
CCE	Continuing Criminal Enterprise (U.S.)
CERD	International Convention on the Elimination of All Forms of Racial Discrimination (U.N.) (1966)
C.F.R.	CODE OF FEDERAL REGULATIONS (U.S.)
CIS	Commonwealth of Independent States
C.J.	Chief Judge
C.L.R.	COMMONWEALTH LAW REPORTS
CoE	Council of Europe
Conc.	Concurrent
CRM	*Criminal Resource Manual* (U.S. DoJ)
C.R.S.	Congressional Research Service (U.S.)
CSCE	Conference on Security and Co operation in Europe
CSM	Convention on Special Missions (U.N.) (1969)
CTIA	CONSOLIDATED TREATIES & INTERNATIONAL AGREEMENTS
DEA	Drug Enforcement Administration (U.S.)

DHS	Department of Homeland Security (U.S.)
D.L.R.	DOMINION LAW REPORTS (Canada)
DoD	Department of Defense (U.S.)
DoJ	Department of Justice (U.S.)
D.R.	DECISIONS AND REPORTS (law reporter)
DS	Diplomatic Security (U.S. Department of State)
DWA	Deportation with Assurances (U.K.)
EAW	European Arrest Warrant
ECHR	European Convention for the Protection of Human Rights and Fundamental Freedoms (more commonly known as the European Convention on Human Rights) (1950)
ECJ	European Court of Justice
ECOSOC	Economic and Social Council (U.N.)
ECOWAS	Economic Community of West African States
ECtHR	European Court of Human Rights
EEC	European Economic Community
EEZ	Exclusive Economic Zone
EHRR	EUROPEAN HUMAN RIGHTS REPORTS
EJIL	EUROPEAN JOURNAL OF INTERNATIONAL LAW
E.T.S.	EUROPEAN TREATY SERIES
EUROJUST	E.U.'s Judicial Cooperation Unit
EUROPOL	European Union's law enforcement agency
EWHC	England and Wales High Court of Justice
FAM	*Foreign Affairs Manual* (U.S. Department of State)
FARRA	Foreign Affairs Reform and Restructuring Act of 1998 (U.S.)
FCO	Foreign and Commonwealth Office (U.K.)
FED. R. CRIM. PR.	FEDERAL RULES OF CRIMINAL PROCEDURE (U.S.)
FIDH	International Federation for Human Rights
F.R.E.	Federal Rules of Evidence (U.S.)
F.R.G.	Federal Republic of Germany (West Germany)
FSB	Federal Security Service of the Russian Federation (a KGB successor)
FSIA	Foreign Sovereign Immunities Act (U.S.)
FTCA	Federal Tort Claims Act (U.S.)
GC I	Geneva Convention for the Amelioration of the Condition of the Wounded and Sick in Armed Forces in the Field of August 12, 1949
GC II	Geneva Convention for the Amelioration of the Condition of Wounded, Sick and Shipwrecked Members of Armed Forces at Sea of August 12, 1949
GC III	Geneva Convention Relative to the Treatment of Prisoners of War of August 12, 1949

GC IV	Geneva Convention Relative to the Protection of Civilian Persons in Time of War of August 12, 1949
GRU	Foreign Intelligence Directorate of the Russian Armed Forces
HCP	High Contracting Party
H.L.	House of Lords (U.K.)
HRC	Human Rights Committee (ICCPR implementing body)
HRW	Human Rights Watch
IAC	International Armed Conflict
IAJC	Inter-American Juridical Committee
ICAO	International Civil Aviation Organization
ICC	International Criminal Court
ICCPR	International Covenant on Civil and Political Rights (U.N.) (1966)
ICE	Immigration and Customs Enforcement (agency of U.S. DHS)
ICHRP	International Council on Human Rights Policy
ICJ	International Court of Justice (U.N.)
ICRC	International Committee of the Red Cross
ICTR	International Criminal Tribunal for Rwanda
ICTY	International Criminal Tribunal for the former Yugoslavia
IDF	Israeli Defense Forces
IELR	INTERNATIONAL ENFORCEMENT LAW REPORTER
IFOR	Implementation Force (NATO Operation in the Balkans, Dec. 1995–Dec. 1996)
IGO	Intergovernmental Organization
IHL	International Humanitarian Law
IHRR	INTERNATIONAL HUMAN RIGHTS REPORTS
IIL	Institute of International Law
ILA	International Law Association
ILC	International Law Commission (U.N.)
ILM	INTERNATIONAL LEGAL MATERIALS
ILR	INTERNATIONAL LAW REPORTS
IMAC	Federal Act on International Mutual Assistance in Criminal Matters (Switz.)
INA	Immigration and Naturalization Act (U.S.)
INLR	IMMIGRATION AND NATIONALITY LAW REPORTS
I.N.S.	Immigration and Naturalization Service (U.S.)
Inter-Am. C.H.R.	Inter-American Court of Human Rights
INTERPOL	International Criminal Police Organization
IPP	Internationally Protected Person
IRA	Irish Republican Army
IRC	Islamic Revolutionary Committee (Iran)
IRS	Internal Revenue Service (U.S.)

ITLOS	International Tribunal for the Law of the Sea
KB	King's Bench (U.K.)
KGB	Komitet Gosudarstvennoy Bezopasnosti [Committee for State Security] (U.S.S.R.) (1954–91)
LCO	Lure and Capture Operation
MLAA	Mutual Legal Assistance Agreement
MLAT	Mutual Legal Assistance Treaty
MOU	Memorandum of Understanding
NATO	North Atlantic Treaty Organization
NIAC	Non-International Armed Conflict
NSC	National Security Council (U.S.)
NZLR	New Zealand Law Reports
OAS	Organization of American States
OAU	Organization of African Unity
OECD	Organisation of Economic Co-operation and Development
OIA	Office of International Affairs (U.S. DoJ)
O.J.	*Official Journal* (League of Nations)
OJC	*Official Journal* (C Series) (publication of the E.U.)
OJEC	*Official Journal of European Communities*
OSCE	Organization for Security and Co-operation in Europe
PA	Palestinian Authority
PAW	Provisional Arrest Warrant
P.C.	Judicial Committee of the Privy Council (U.K.)
PCA	Permanent Court of Arbitration
PCIJ	Permanent Court of International Justice (League of Nations) (1922–46)
PKK	Kurdistan Worker's Party
P.L.	Public Law (U.S.)
QB	Queen's Bench (U.K.)
RIAA	Reports of International Arbitral Awards
RICO	Racketeer Influenced and Corrupt Organizations Act (U.S.)
RPE	Rules of Procedure and Evidence
R.S.C.	Royal Statutes of Canada
SCSL	Special Court for Sierra Leone
SDO	Seizure and Delivery Operation
SFOR	Stabilization Force (NATO Operation in the Balkans, Dec. 1996–Dec. 2004)
SIS	Secret Intelligence Service (a/k/a MI-6) (U.K.)
SOFA	Status of Forces Agreement
STL	Special Tribunal for Lebanon
T.I.A.S.	Treaties and Other International Acts Series (U.S.)
TRIAL	Track Impunity Always (a non-governmental organization)

T.S.	Treaty Series
UCMJ	Uniform Code of Military Justice (U.S.)
UDHR	Universal Declaration of Human Rights (1948)
UFAP	Unlawful Flight to Avoid Prosecution (type of U.S. federal crime)
UNCAC	United Nations Convention against Corruption (2003)
UNCHR	United Nations Commission on Human Rights (1946–2006) (succeeded by the Human Rights Council)
UNGA	United Nations General Assembly
UNHCHR	United Nations High Commissioner for Human Rights
UNHCR	United Nations High Commissioner for Refugees
UNODC	United Nations Office of Drugs and Crime
UNSC	United Nations Security Council
U.N.T.S.	United Nations Treaty Series
USAF	United States Air Force
U.S.C.	United States Code
USCS	United States Customs Service
USCG	United States Coast Guard
VCCR	Vienna Convention on Consular Relations (1963)
VCDR	Vienna Convention on Diplomatic Relations (1961)
VFA	Visiting Forces Agreement
WLR	Weekly Law Reports (U.K.)

TABLE OF CASES

International

Commissions of Enquiry

The Red Crusader, Comm'n of Enquiry (Den. v. U.K.), Mar. 23, 1962, 582–83

Committee against Torture

Agiza v. Sweden, Commc'n No. 233/2003, U.N. Doc. CAT/C/34/D/233/2003, May 20, 2005, 420

Alan v. Switzerland, Commc'n No. 21/1995, U.N. Doc. CAT/C/16/D/21/1995, May 8, 1996, 293–94

Arana v. France, Commc'n No. 63/1997, U.N. Doc. CAT/C/23/D/63/1997, June 5, 2000, 438, 447

Elmi v. Australia, Commc'n. No. 120/1998, U.N. Doc. CAT/C/22/D/120/1998, May 25, 1999, 431–32

G.R.B. v. Sweden, Commc'n No. 83/1997, U.N. Doc. CAT/C/20/D/83/1997, May 15, 1998, 441

Khalsa, et al. v. Switzerland, Commc'n No. 336/2008, U.N. Doc. CAT/C/46/D/336/2008, May 26, 2011, 294, 432

Ktiti v. Morocco, Commc'n No. 419/2010, U.N. Doc. CAT/C/46/D/419/2010, July 5, 2011, 295

Núñez Chipana v. Venezuela, Commc'n No. 110/1998, U.N. Doc. CAT/C/21/D/110/1998, Nov. 10, 1998, 293, 294

S.S.S. v. Canada, Commc'n No. 245/2004, U.N. Doc. CAT/C/35/D/245/2004, Nov. 16, 2005, 441

Human Rights Chamber for Bosnia and Herzegovina

Bensayah v. Bosnia & Herzegovina, Case No. CH/02/9499, Decision on Admissibility and Merits, H.R. Ch. for Bosnia & Herzegovina, Apr. 4, 2003, 393, 398, 438, 448

Human Rights Committee (HRC)

International Arbitral Claims Commissions

International Court of Justice (ICJ)

International Criminal Tribunal for Rwanda (ICTR)

International Criminal Tribunal for the former Yugoslavia (ICTY)

International Tribunal for the Law of the Sea (ITLOS)

Permanent Court of Arbitration (PCA)

Deserters of Casablanca (Fr. v. Ger.), PCA Award, Hague Ct. Rep. (Scott) 110, May 22, 1909, 528

Savarkar Case (Fr. v. Gr. Br.), PCA Award, Hague Ct. Rep. (Scott) 276, Feb. 24, 1911, 36–37, 126, 459, 468, 470, 471, 542

Permanent Court of International Justice (PCIJ)

Certain German Interests in Upper Polish Silesia, Case Concerning, Merits (Ger. v. Pol.), 1926 P.C.I.J. (ser. A) No. 7 (May 25, 1925), 140

Chorzów Factory, Indemnity (Ger. v. Pol.), 1928 P.C.I.J. (ser. A) No. 17 (Sept. 13, 1928), 582

Chorzów Factory, Jurisdiction (Ger. v. Pol.), 1927 P.C.I.J. (ser. A) No. 9 (July 26, 1927), 581

SS "Lotus" (Fr. v. Turk.) 1927 P.C.I.J. (ser. A) No. 10 (Sept. 7, 1927), 61, 66, 70, 74, 78, 96, 140, 468–69, 514

Special Court for Sierra Leone (SCSL)

Taylor, Prosecutor v., Case No. SCSL-2003-01-I, App.Ch., Decision on Immunity from Jurisdiction, May 31, 2004, 244, 386

Regional

African Commission on Human and Peoples' Rights (ACHPR)

Modise v. Botswana, Commc'n No. 97/93, (2000) AHRLR 25, Nov. 6, 2000, 397, 427, 432

Rencontre Africaine pour la Defense des Droits de l'Homme (RADDHO) v. Zambia, Commc'n No. 71/92, (2000) AHRLR 321, Oct. 1996, 421

European Commission of Human Rights

Altmann (Barbie) v. France, Appl. No. 10689/83, Eur. Comm'n of Hum. Rgts. 37 D.R. 225, July 4, 1984, 271–72, 442, 443, 451, 452

Amekrane v. U.K., Appl. No. 5961/72, Eur. Comm'n of Hum. Rts., 44 C.D. 101, Oct. 11, 1973, 584

Bonnechaux v. Switzerland, Appl. No. 8224/78, Eur. Comm'n of Hum. Rts., 18 D.R. 100, Dec. 5, 1979, 235–36

Lynas v. Switzerland, Appl. No. 7317/75, Eur. Comm'n of Hum. Rts., 6 D.R. 141, Oct. 6, 1976, 529

Ramirez Sánchez v. France, Appl. No. 28780/95, Eur. Comm'n of Hum. Rts., 86 D.R. 155, June 24, 1996, 468, 519

European Court of Human Rights (ECtHR)

European Court of Justice (ECJ)

Inter-American Court of Human Rights (Inter-Am. C.H.R.)

Inter-American Juridical Committee

Domestic

Argentina

Australia

Austria

Belgium

Botswana

Brazil

Burma (now Myanmar)

Canada

Chile

Colombia

El Salvador

France

Germany

Greece

Guatemala

Hungary

India

Ireland

Israel

Italy

Japan

Mauritius

Netherlands

New Zealand

Palestine

Philippines

Scotland

South Africa

Spain

Sweden

Switzerland

United Kingdom

United States

Venezuela

Zimbabwe

TABLE OF TREATIES

TABLE OF MUNICIPAL AUTHORITIES

Costa Rica
  Constitution, Nov. 7, 1949, art. 31, 427–28
Cyprus
  Constitution, Aug. 16, 1960, 237

Dominica
  Extradition Act, Act No. 6 of 1981, Feb. 19, 1981, art. 7(1), 199, 313
Dominican Republic
  Ley No. 278-98, July 29, 1998, 239
  Ley No. 489-69 (1969), 239

El Salvador
  Constitution, Dec. 15, 1983, 178, 236, 311

France
  Penal Code, Law No. 2004-204, Mar. 9, 2004, 198
    art. 17, 3
    art. 694, 85–86
    art. 689, 79–80, 82

Georgia
  Constitution, Aug. 24, 1995, art. 13(4), 238
Germany
  Basic Law (Constitution) of the F.R.G. (Grundgesetz), May 8, 1949, 238
  Code of Crimes against International Law (CCAIL or Völkerstrafgesetzbuch), June 26, 2002, 91
  Penal Code of 1871 (Strafgesetzbuch), May 15, 1871, 76
    § 3, 79–80
    § 4, 79–80
    § 7, 83
Gibraltar
  Aliens Order in Council, Aug. 30, 1873, 444

Honduras
  Immigration Act, Decreto Número 208-2003, Mar. 3, 2004, art. 3(23), 398

India
  Extradition Act, Act No. 34 of 1962, Sept. 15, 1962
    § 3(4), 269
    § 30, 289
    § 34C, 310
  Penal Code, Act No. 45 of 1860, Oct. 6, 1860, § 4, 79–80

Introduction

This book concerns the often dramatic,[1] yet at times incongruous, world of capturing and delivering international fugitives from justice. This topical and dynamic subject lies at the crossroads of law and politics, of municipal[2] and international law, and of law enforcement and individual rights. This subject also gives rise to the full spectrum of inter-State[3] relations, running the gamut from diplomatic cooperation to political hostility to armed conflict; involves extraterritorial conduct that bores to the heart of State sovereignty; and implicates a diverse array of public

1 Discussed herein, for example, are undercover operations, forcible seizures, and military interventions. A U.S. judge described the facts of one such case as "present[ing] elements one might expect to encounter in a grade-B film scenario – an organized underworld conspiracy to import massive quantities of heroin into the United States, and American agents kidnapping the leading perpetrators from South America to bring them to trial." *United States ex rel. Lujan v. Gengler*, 510 F.2d 62, 63 (2d Cir. 1975) (Kaufman, C.J.), *cert. denied*, 421 U.S. 1001 (1975).

2 The words "municipal," "domestic," "national," and "State," when used as modifiers of such terms as "officials," "legislation," or "courts," are intended to be interchangeable throughout.

3 The term "State" refers to nation-states and appears in upper case (unless quoting a source in lower case) to distinguish it from those sub-national entities of the same name: "state" (*e.g.*, California, United States, or Bihar, India). "Under international law, a state is an entity that has a defined territory and a permanent population, under the control of its own government, and that engages in, or has the capacity to engage in, formal relations with other such entities." American Law Inst., Restatement (Third) of the Foreign Relations Law of the United States § 201 (1987), May 14, 1986 [hereinafter Restatement (Third)]. Some scholars have added other, or re-characterized existing, criteria for Statehood, such as legal independence and formal acceptance Statehood by the international community, *e.g.*, Michael Ross Fowler & Julie Marie Bunck, Law, Power, and the Sovereign State: The Evolution and Application of the Concept of Sovereignty 36–61 (1995); and/or a willingness to observe international law and a certain degree of civilization. James Crawford, Brownlie's Principles of Public International Law 134 (8th ed. 2012) [hereinafter Crawford, Brownlie's Principles]. From a legal perspective, all States are treated herein as equal regardless of their relative political, military, or economic strength.

international law fields, encompassing, *inter alia*, immigration law, treaty law, human rights law, and criminal law.

a Nature and Purpose

The nature of this inquiry can best be mapped via a generic fact pattern. Suppose a crime such as corporate fraud or manslaughter has been perpetrated *on* State A's territory, or weapons or narcotics have been illegally trafficked *into* State A, or a violation of State A's laws such as currency counterfeiting or bribery has taken place *outside* its boundaries, or other unlawful conduct has occurred in *virtual space*, such as cybertheft or the unauthorized Internet posting of classified government documents of State A. Following a criminal investigation, a prosecutor from State A charges the crime's chief suspect under State A's domestic law based on testimonial, physical, documentary, and/or forensic evidence. Before the charged individual can be arrested, however, he[4] travels to a neighboring country, State B, of which he is a national.[5] (Alternatively, he may have committed the crime abroad or have fled to

[4] The use of "he" or "his" in definitions, hypothetical examples, or non-case-specific legal analysis, whether in reference to a fugitive, government official, or otherwise, is intended strictly for shorthand convenience, and accordingly is to be understood as gender neutral.

[5] For present purposes, a "national" is "a natural person upon whom [a State] has conferred its nationality . . . in conformity with international law." Draft Conv. on Research in Int'l Law of the Harvard Law School, "Jurisdiction with Respect to Crime," 29 AJIL 435, 473 (Supp. 1935) (not formally adopted by States) [hereinafter Harvard Research]. According to the International Court of Justice (ICJ), nationality has "as its basis a social fact of attachment, a genuine connection of existence, interests and sentiments, together with the existence of reciprocal rights and duties," and therefore much latitude exists for States claiming a fugitive as one of its own. *Nottebohm Case* (Liech. v Guat.), Second Phase, Judgment [1955] I.C.J. Rep. 4, 23 (Apr. 6). For example, the Japanese Government decided to treat Alberto Fujimori as a Japanese national, because, consistent with Japanese legislation, his father was a Japanese national at the time of Alberto's birth, notwithstanding the fact that Alberto had served as the President of Peru. Arnd Düker, *The Extradition of Nationals: Comments on the Extradition Request for Alberto Fujimori*, 4 German L.J. 1165, 1167–68 (2003). Nationality can arise as a function of birth or naturalization. A national of a given State is generally, but not necessarily, also a "citizen" of that State; the distinction, where it exists, tends to lie in citizens possessing certain additional political rights, such as the right to vote and to stand for elected office, or even eligibility to apply for certain State jobs. *See, e.g*, "Appeals Court: No Birthright Citizenship for American Samoa," *AP*, June 5, 2015 (reporting on a U.S. appellate court ruling that birth alone in the unincorporated U.S. territory of American Samoa conferred U.S. nationality but not U.S. citizenship, and thereby denied the plaintiff eligibility to apply for a position as a law enforcement officer in California, which required the latter).

State B after escaping from police custody or from prison in State A but before either receiving or completing his sentence.)

State A submits official requests to State B, first to locate and provisionally arrest[6] and later to extradite (*i.e.*, in essence, cooperatively deliver) the fugitive, seeking his return to face criminal charges (or to potentially receive and/or serve out a prison sentence). State B law enforcement authorities find, apprehend, and temporarily detain the fugitive, but he does not consent to return to State A, and is not otherwise accidentally or fortuitously returned. State B may choose to extradite him, but also may refuse on one of many grounds, including that, under its domestic law, State B is barred from extraditing one of its own nationals.[7]

Despite a number of recent and meaningful improvements to the international extradition system (discussed in Chapter 4.f), there remain many impediments that can obstruct, or at least complicate or delay, the transfer of known or alleged criminals from one State to another for the purpose of bringing them to justice.[8] In circumstances whereby extradition is either (i) *unavailable* – whether because it has been unsuccessfully pursued or, because under the circumstances, including the absence of an extradition treaty and/or a bilateral political climate non-conducive to

[6] A "provisional arrest" is *the temporary arrest of a fugitive made on an emergency basis at the behest of a pursuing State (or international criminal tribunal) prior to but in anticipation of an extradition (or surrender) request.*

[7] In May 2011, while on the tarmac awaiting departure of his flight from New York to Paris, Dominique Strauss-Kahn, then-President of the International Monetary Fund (IMF) and a prominent French politician with presidential aspirations, was arrested by U.S. law enforcement authorities on charges of rape and sexual assault of a chambermaid at a Manhattan hotel. Angelique Chrisafis, *et al.*, "Dominique Strauss-Kahn Charged with Sex Attack on New York Hotel Maid," *The Guardian*, May 15, 2011. Had the plane taken off an hour earlier and not landed until it had reached French territory, however, in all likelihood his extradition to the U.S. would have been barred, as under the applicable bilateral extradition treaty, France has no obligation to extradite one of its nationals (Treaty on Extradition, U.S.-Fr., Apr. 23, 1996, art. 3(1)), and French statutory law prohibits the extradition of its own nationals, as determined at the date of the offense for which the extradition is requested. Fr. Code of Crim. Proc., art. 696–4, *adopted by* Law No. 2004–204, Mar. 9, 2004, art. 17. *See* discussion of this impediment to extradition in Chapter 6.a.

[8] These impediments will be examined in Chapters 5–7. "Bring to justice" is defined herein as *a law enforcement action with the end result of: (i) prosecuting an individual for a charged crime; or (ii) punishing an individual whose guilt has been established but has yet to pay his debt to society, whether by incarceration, re-incarceration (in the event of a prison escape), or other legally sanctioned means.*

extradition,[9] it is reasonably anticipated that it will be denied if sought[10] – or (ii) *undesirable* – whether because its procedures are deemed too onerous or time-consuming, its outcome too uncertain or sub-optimal,[11] and/or more expeditious or predictable means are preferred[12] – which lawful recourses, including remedial or collateral approaches, or alternatives, to extradition,[13] does a State have for bringing a charged or convicted individual ultimately to justice?[14]

In a nutshell, this book aims to present a novel and robust framework for the operational and legal analysis of recovering fugitives

[9] For example, Israel and its Arab neighbors lack extradition arrangements with one another, Israel Ministry of Foreign Affairs, Bilateral Treaties Database, updated to Feb. 24, 2014, *available at* http://mfa.gov.il/MFA/AboutTheMinistry/LegalTreaties/Pages/Bilateral-Treaties.aspx (last visited on May 27, 2016), and otherwise have been disinclined politically to cooperate in such law enforcement matters.

[10] Sometimes, the host State will make clear in advance that any request for extradition of a given individual will be denied. For example, British officials warned that Sarah Ferguson, the Duchess of York, would not be extradited to Turkey for charges related to her covert filming of a documentary in Turkish orphanages. Bruce Zagaris, *Turkish Gov't Pursues Criminal Charges against Duchess of York*, 28 IELR 88 (2012). But a State may, for reasons of principle or in combination with political pressure, still choose to submit an extradition request.

[11] *See* Keith R. Fisher, *In Rem Alternatives to Extradition for Money Laundering*, 25 LOY. L.A. INT'L & COMP. L. REV. 409 (2003) ("the person who is prosecutable for the money laundering offense is rarely the person law enforcement really wants, the one at the top of the pyramid of unlawful activity; . . . [r]ather, the prosecutable person is likely to be someone farther down the criminal food chain, someone who can be sacrificed, if need be, without doing more than inconveniencing the criminal enterprise, and then only slightly.").

[12] *See* ETHAN A. NADELMANN, COPS ACROSS BORDERS: THE INTERNATIONALIZATION OF U.S. CRIMINAL LAW ENFORCEMENT 398–99 (1993) [hereinafter NADELMANN, COPS] (recognizing that States may pursue fugitives by means other than by extradition even when the State in which the fugitive is located is willing to extradite).

[13] The term "alternatives to extradition" herein *refers expansively to all measures, methods, and mechanisms, whether ultimately regarded as lawful or unlawful, that: (i) fall outside the extradition regime; (ii) aim to bring a fugitive to justice fully or partially, directly or indirectly; and (iii) do not entail a fugitive's delivery as a function of sheer fortuity.*

[14] Although rare, a State may choose not to actively seek the custody of fugitives and therefore pursue neither extradition nor one of its alternatives. For example, until 1982, with one notable exception (*i.e.*, the requested extradition of naturalized U.S. citizen Hermine Braunsteiner Ryan in 1973 for multiple counts of murder committed while she was a guard at the Lublin Concentration Camp in Poland), the Federal Republic of Germany did not seek extradition from the United States of former Nazis, as it was reluctant to prosecute Ukrainians, Lithuanians, and other individuals not of German origin and who acted beyond the territorial borders of Nazi Germany during World War II. James W. Moeller, *United States Treatment of Alleged Nazi War Criminals: Int'l Law, Immigration Law, and the Need for Int'l Cooperation*, 25 VA. J. INT'L L. 793, 810 & n.86 (1985).

abroad.[15] It addresses how States – whether working alone, in cooperation, or with the assistance of third parties – strive to secure the custody of fugitives for the purpose of prosecution or punishment,[16] while evaluating the propriety of those pursuit efforts under international law where applicable.

At the same time, this book in no way purports to suggest that the extradition system is broken or hollow – indeed, it serves an indispensable function, operates reasonably well in most instances,[17] continues to

[15] Even if a pursuing State ultimately succeeds in bringing a fugitive to justice, however, the potential future injury and damage he can cause, directly or through his agents, does not necessarily cease, even if sentenced for life. A fugitive could escape from incarceration, including with the help of associates or while on a furlough or during a conjugal visit; he could eventually be set free early based on a grant of amnesty or a political deal struck, and return to a life of crime; he could wreak havoc from his prison cell through agents he still controls (a major Mexican drug kingpin, Joaquín Guzmán (a/k/a El Chapo), was indicted in 1994 with operating his cartel from prison through his brother, *see* Bruce Zagaris, *Mexico Arrests El Chapo with Help from the United States*, 30 IELR 175, 176 (2014)); or his associates could seek his release through blackmail, ransom, or violence. *See, e.g.*, Mary Anne Weaver, "Terrorist's Extradition Ends Greek Legal Battle," *Wash. Post*, Oct. 4, 1976, at 24 (discussing how Rolf Pohle, a member of West Germany's Baader-Meinhof group, was set free after only eighteen months of a six-and-half-year prison term as ransom for a West Berlin mayoralty candidate who had been kidnapped by the group); Note, *The Abu Daoud Affair*, 11 J. Int'l L. & Econ. 539, 540 (1977) ("[o]n March 1, 1973, members of Black September seized the Saudi Arabian Embassy in Khartoum, killing the American Ambassador and two others when their demand for [Abu] Daoud's release was not met.").

[16] Criminal punishment frequently, but not always, consists of a prison term; other possibilities include fines, forfeitures, curfews, discharges, community service, hard labor, or the death penalty. For simplicity sake and because extradition treaties characteristically call for conduct punishable by some form of prison sentence or deprivation of liberty, imprisonment is the presumed type of criminal sentence at issue for present purposes. In addition, to be clear, a reference in this discourse to "punishment" in the context of "prosecution or punishment" means that a fugitive would serve out whatever period is stipulated under, or remains of, an imposed prison sentence based on a criminal conviction rather than, say, be penalized arbitrarily on account of his political views.

[17] *See* Richard Downing, Recent Development, *The Domestic and Int'l Legal Implications of the Abduction of Criminals from Foreign Soil*, 26 Stan. J. Int'l L. 573, 577 (1989–90). Extradition's potential effectiveness can be exemplified by Colombia, which extradited an average of more than 130 alleged offenders per year between 2002 and 2010 mostly on drug trafficking charges in the U.S. and, at least partly as a result, witnessed a much improved security environment on the ground. Hannah Stone, "With Extradition Law, Honduras Outsources Justice to U.S.," *Insightcrime.org*, Jan. 30, 2012, *available at* www.insightcrime.org/news-analysis/with-extradition-law-honduras-outsources-justice-to-us (last visited on May 27, 2016). It should not be overlooked, however, that effecting an arrest in connection with to an extradition request can present its own set of risks. For example, in May 2010, when, pursuant to a U.S. extradition request, Jamaican police sought to apprehend Christopher (Dudus) Coke, the leader of Tivoli Gardens in West

represent the generally preferred means of bringing fugitives to justice,[18] and its very threat can have powerful, even mortal, consequences.[19] Similarly, there is no intention here to imply that alternatives – such as informal law enforcement cooperation or a lure and capture operation – should displace extradition altogether, but rather acknowledges that in today's world neither extradition nor its alternatives alone will suffice.[20] The two must co-exist while serving complementary functions.

Indeed, while recognizing the additional risks and legal complications that alternatives to extradition can impose and while seeking to mitigate those risks (*see* recommendations in the Conclusion), this book adopts an agnostic posture regarding the relative policy desirability of extradition or its alternatives in a given instance. Likewise, while this book adopts the vantage point of law enforcement in tracking down fugitives and holding them accountable, the legal analysis strives to be balanced, and accordingly is neither ideologically pro- nor anti-fugitive in its orientation.

With that perspective in mind, it is hoped this book will contribute to the work of government officials who handle international law enforcement

Kingston, a "garrison community" that he effectively controlled, the assault resulted in the deaths of no fewer than seventy-four persons while failing to locate Coke, who was only discovered adventitiously a month later at a roadblock disguised as a woman. Mattathais Schwartz, *A Report At Large: A Massacre in Jamaica*, The New Yorker, Dec. 2011, at 64, 69.

18 Nadelmann, Cops, *supra* n.12, at 398.

19 *See* Stone, *supra* n.17 ("former [Honduran] Security Minister Alfredo Landaverde, who was assassinated on the streets of Tegucigalpa in December [2011], had spoken out in favor of extradition in one of his last public appearances"; and "[i]n Colombia, many lives were lost as powerful drug traffickers fought to prevent the government allowing extradition in the 1980s and 90s, with traffickers famously declaring: 'Better a grave in Colombia than a prison in the U.S.'"). *See generally* Lord Inglewood, Chairman, House of Lords, Select Comm. on Extradition Law, Extradition: U.K. Law and Practice, 2d Report of Sess., 2014–15, HL Paper 126, Mar. 10, 2015 ("Extradition will always be a complex, sensitive and potentially controversial issue. In many instances, the stakes are high on a personal and, occasionally, international level.").

20 *See* Bruce Swartz, Dep'y Asst. AG, in Testimony before the Crim. Justice, Drug Policy, and Human Resources Subcomm. of the House Gov't Reform Comm. on Oct. 1, 2003 ("Solving the Extradition Problem") ("Although important and effective, formal extradition is not the only mechanism available for obtaining the international surrender of fugitives."); David P. Warner, *Challenges to Int'l Law Enforcement Cooperation for the U.S. in the Middle East and North Africa: Extradition and Its Alternatives*, 50 Vill. L. Rev. 479, 507 (2005) (observing that "[e]xtradition and its alternatives are tools that enable governments to locate, apprehend and return fugitives to face justice. In the context of the Middle East and North Africa, the focus must be on the alternatives given a dearth of bilateral extradition treaties between the United States and countries throughout the region.").

matters, principally those hailing from foreign affairs and justice ministries. The aim is to assist such officials when contemplating extradition or one of its alternatives to ensure they make informed, sound, and lawful decisions by appreciating the full range of options available and their corresponding implications.[21] This book also should prove beneficial to policy and legal scholars, analysts, and students with an interest in international law enforcement; legal practitioners and human rights lawyers representing fugitives; private investigators, bail bondsmen, and bounty hunters; and policymakers, journalists, diplomats, prosecutors, judges, judicial clerks, and immigration officials focused on or managing fugitive cases.

b Scope

Beyond the nature and purpose of this inquiry, it is also critical to set clear parameters governing its scope, specifically with regard to the types of players and crimes at issue, the geographic coverage, and the sources and character of applicable law. In the present context, subjects of interest must be *natural* persons – not States[22] or juridical persons such as businesses or organizations. In addition, the subject must be a convicted or alleged criminal who is "wanted" by law enforcement, rather than a mere suspect,[23] a material witness in an investigation,[24] a prisoner of war (POW) not otherwise accused of a violation of international

[21] This analysis does not purport to address individual remedial measures for fugitive defendants, such as the dismissal of an indictment, the reversal of a conviction, or monetary relief under domestic laws, *e.g.*, *Sosa v. Álvarez-Machaín*, 542 U.S. 692 (2004) (addressing liability under the Federal Tort Claims Act (FTCA) and the Alien Tort Statute (ATS)). Likewise, this analysis does not address remedies for the victims of underlying criminal acts. *See generally* Ilaria Bottigliero, Redress for Victims of Crimes Under International Law (2004).

[22] Accordingly, suits brought in the United States under the Foreign Sovereign Immunities Act (FSIA), Oct. 21, 1976 28 U.S.C. § 1602 *et seq.* (2012), lie outside the scope of this inquiry as they concern *State* liability; *e.g.*, *Frolova v. U.S.S.R.*, 761 F.2d 370 (7th Cir. 1985) (per curiam).

[23] When suspects are involved, States typically invoke mutual legal assistance treaties (MLATs) or mutual legal assistance agreements (MLAAs), which typically authorize the collection of evidence, the taking of witness statements, the provision of data, the return of property, and the like. *E.g.*, Mutual Legal Assistance Treaty, Braz.-Cuba, May 21, 2008, Decree 6,462.

[24] A witness in a criminal trial, however, can become a fugitive to the extent he flees the jurisdiction to avoid giving testimony, and thereby is charged with a crime himself. Black's Law Dictionary 741 (9th ed. 2009) (defining a fugitive from justice to include a "witness in a criminal case who flees, evades, or escapes . . . the giving of testimony, especially by fleeing the jurisdiction or by hiding.").

humanitarian law,[25] or a missing person.[26] Convicted criminals include those who have escaped from police custody or prison before receiving or serving out their assigned sentences, while alleged ones have been charged with a crime (or the functional equivalent thereof[27]), whether

[25] POW transfers are principally governed by the Geneva Conv. Relative to the Treatment of Prisoners of War (GC III), Aug. 12, 1949, art. 12, 6 U.S.T. 3316, T.I.A.S. No. 3364, 75 U.N.T.S. 135 ("Prisoners of war may only be transferred by the Detaining Power to a Power which is a party to the Convention and after the Detaining Power has satisfied itself of the willingness and ability of such transferee Power to apply the Convention.").

[26] Because the focus of this study is on fugitives, it does not address the numerous circumstances in which a State might try to obtain custody over *non-fugitives* to meet various national interests, such as: (i) to return persons illegally seeking immigration (*e.g.*, *Sale v. Haitian Centers Council*, 509 U.S. 155 (1993) (discussing seizures of Haitian boat people on the high seas and returned to Haiti)); (ii) to arrange for a prospective prisoner exchange of one's own spies or other government assets (*e.g.*, in 1964, Greville Wynne, a British spy convicted of espionage by the Soviet Union, was exchanged for Conon Molody, better known as Gordon Lonsdale in the United States, who spied for the Soviets and was convicted to a fifteen-year sentence (AP, "Greville Wynne, Spy for Britain in the Soviet Bloc, Is Dead at 71," *N.Y. Times*, Mar. 2, 1990)); (iii) to serve the language and cultural needs of national spy schools (*see* Justin McCurry, "North Korea's Kidnap Victims Return Home after 25 Years," *The Guardian*, Oct. 16, 2002 (discussing how in the late 1970s and early 1980s more than a dozen Japanese nationals were seized by and taken back to North Korea presumably to train its spies in Japanese culture and language)); or (iv) to impede progress on an enemy weapons program (*e.g.*, Germany's Werner Heisenberg, who had been appointed director of the Kaiser-Wilhelm Institute, a nuclear research facility in Berlin, and was instrumental to its atomic weapons program, was considered as a target for capture). KAI BIRD & MARTIN J. SHERWIN, AMERICAN PROMETHEUS: THE TRIUMPH AND TRAGEDY OF J. ROBERT OPPENHEIMER 222 (2005).

[27] To be "charged" does not necessarily mean an individual has been indicted; "[a]n accusation of a crime supported by an arrest warrant [or an intent to prosecute] is sufficient." M. CHERIF BASSIOUNI, INTERNATIONAL EXTRADITION: UNITED STATES LAW AND PRACTICE 888 (6th ed. 2014) (citing *In re Assarsson*, 687 F.2d 1157, 1162 (8th Cir. 1982)). Swedish law is a notable exception; under that system, the national prosecutor, which conducts both the investigation and prosecution, seeks extradition after the preliminary investigation is over but only formally charges an individual after completing the investigation, including an interrogation on Swedish soil. This provision played out in the highly publicized case in which Sweden successfully sought the approved extradition from the United Kingdom of Julian Assange, the founder and editor-in-chief of Wikileaks, a "whistleblower" website responsible for disclosing hundreds of thousands of classified U.S. Government documents, for *pre-indictment* questioning by Swedish prosecutors in connection with one count of unlawful coercion, two counts of sexual molestation, and one count of rape in Stockholm in August 2010, unrelated to his organization's mission or actions, as alleged by two Swedish women who were serving as Wikileaks volunteers. The fact that Mr. Assange was subject to extradition prior to formal indictment was little more than a function of an unusual feature of the Swedish

in public or secret proceedings, and whether as its author, an accomplice, or a co-conspirator.

The subject could be a national of the State seeking his physical custody, of the State in which he is currently located, or even of a third State. The subject must be pursued because of his individual actions – not solely as the agent or representative of, or merely because of an affiliation with, a government.[28] In addition, this book does not address the extradition or any alternative means of securing the custody of minors (*i.e.*, those under the age of majority, typically eighteen), as not only do they represent a negligible percentage of the fugitive population, but also because special protective rules typically apply to them.[29] Furthermore,

criminal law system, wherein indictment only follows a second round of suspect questioning. It is also significant that the prosecutors had identified the legal violations when they issued the extradition request, which reflects a more advanced stage than mere suspect questioning. Furthermore, a European Arrest Warrant (EAW) (discussed *infra*, beginning in Chapter 4.c) was issued by Swedish prosecutors only after it had been subject to independent scrutiny by a Swedish court. The U.K. Supreme Court found that, under the operative EAW system, the Swedish prosecutor was equivalent to a "judicial authority," such as a judge, capable of issuing the arrest warrant. *Assange v. The Swedish Prosecution Auth.* [2012] UKSC 22, *on appeal from* [2011] EWHC 2849 (Admin). Mr. Assange, a then-forty-year-old Australian, had been arrested by British authorities in December 2010, eventually granted bail, and then resided on an estate under house arrest, and later at the Ecuadorean Embassy as a diplomatic asylee in London pending his extradition. Bruce Zagaris, *British Appellate Court Affirms Assange's Extradition to Sweden*, 28 IELR 14, 14–16 (2012). In March 2015, in the face of an extradition impasse and to avoid certain charges under investigation exceeding their statutes of limitations, Swedish prosecutors agreed to question Assange and obtain his DNA in London rather than holding out for his transfer to Sweden. Stephen Castle, "Swedes Offer to Question Assange in London," *INYT*, Mar. 14–15, 2015, at 4.

28 Ethan A. Nadelmann, *The Evolution of United States Involvement in the Int'l Rendition of Fugitive Criminals*, 25 N.Y.U. J. Int'l L. & Pol. 813, 882 (1993) [hereinafter Nadelmann, *Int'l Rendition*].

29 Some States, for example, refuse to extradite on the grounds that the alleged offender is a minor. *See* Sibylle Kapferer, Dep't of Int'l Protection, U.N. High Comm'r for Refugees, Legal and Protection Policy Research Series, *The Interface Between Extradition and Asylum*, PPLA/2003/05, Nov. 2003, ¶ 112 & n.212 (citing Belgium and Spain as examples). Others impose conditions that require compliance with certain minimum standards; *e.g.*, Extradition Act of Canada, Royal Statutes of Canada (R.S.C.) June 17, 1999, § 47, as *amended*, July 19, 2005 (the Minister may refuse an extradition request if he is satisfied that: "(c) the person was less than eighteen years old at the time of the offense and the law that applies to them in the treaty over which the extradition partner has jurisdiction is not consistent with the fundamental principles governing the Youth Crim Justice Act"); Switz., Federal Act on Int'l Mutual Assistance in Crim. Matters [IMAC], Mar. 20, 1981, art. 33, *as amended* (unofficial translation), *reprinted in* 20 ILM 1339 (1981) (where extradition is requested, juveniles under eighteen "shall, if possible, be repatriated by the juvenile authorities. The same applies for persons between 18 and 20 if extradition could

as this inquiry is concerned with securing the custody of *persons*, it does not address the often closely related legal issues regarding the lawfulness of a seizure and/or the admissibility of physical evidence found in the possession, or on the property, of an accused.[30]

As for the protagonist of this inquiry, the focus is on *States* seeking the return of a fugitive abroad. This means that, while some limited discussion will ensue with respect to the direct, support, or collateral roles of (i) international criminal tribunals,[31] (ii) U.N. peacekeeping missions,[32] (iii) regional organizations,[33] and (iv) sub-national entities such as U.S. states and Canadian provinces, such treatment will be largely by way of contrast with the role of States and exceptionally with respect to any relevant legal commentary or case law issued.[34] When States pursue a fugitive, they may rely on their own "State officials" (*i.e.*, government employees) or, alternatively, on "State agents" who constitute *any non-State officials contracted on behalf of a national government to undertake a specific task, project, or mission whose conduct during such time is attributable to that*

endanger their mental development or social rehabilitation."). Other international instruments also may have direct relevance to extradition or its alternatives; for example, with respect to Article 38 of the Convention on the Rights of the Child (CRC), the Committee on the Rights of the Child adopted a General Comment noting, *inter alia*, that "States shall refrain from returning a child in any manner whatsoever to the borders of a State where there is a real risk of underage recruitment, including recruitment not only as a combatant but also to provide sexual services for the military or where there is a real risk of direct or indirect participation in hostilities, either as a combatant or through carrying out other military duties." Comm. on the Rights of the Child (CRC), Gen. Cmt. No. 6, *Treatment of Unaccompanied and Separated Children Outside Their Country of Origin*, U.N. Doc. CRC/GC/2005/6, ¶ 28, Sept. 1, 2005.

30 *See, e.g., Brulay v. United States*, 383 F.2d 345 (9th Cir. 1967) (addressing the admissibility of amphetamine tablets found in the defendant's car in Mexico absent a search warrant).

31 *E.g.*, the International Criminal Court (ICC), the International Criminal Tribunal for Rwanda (ICTR), or the Nazi war tribunals at Nuremberg (the initial International Military Tribunal (IMT) for the major war criminals and the subsequent Nuremberg Military Tribunal (NMT) for lesser war criminals).

32 *E.g.*, UNOSOM I or II (Somalia) or UNMIL (Liberia), including any endowed with arrest and detention authority and operating on behalf of an international criminal tribunal.

33 *E.g.*, the Caribbean Community (CARICOM), the European Economic Community (EEC), or the NATO-led Implementation Force (IFOR) in Bosnia and Herzegovina.

34 In fact, for a number of crimes no international forum has jurisdiction to prosecute alleged perpetrators, so the responsibility for such criminal prosecutions falls by default to States. *See* Margaret L. Satterthwaite, *The Legal Regime Governing Transfer of Persons in the Fight against Terrorism*, N.Y.U. Public Law and Legal Theory Working Papers, Paper 192, May 1, 2010, at 1 n.1 (discussing terrorism crimes).

State.[35] State agents could include paid or unpaid private citizens[36] or even State officials of another government while acting in their personal capacity.

Actual or alleged criminal conduct germane to this inquiry broadly consists of violations of municipal or international law enforceable by municipal courts (civilian and military alike[37]), whether: (1) implicating individual or corporate rights or public interests (a) in a single State (such as burglary or trespassing) or (b) across two or more States (such as transborder narcotics trafficking or "childnapping"[38]); or (2) constituting offenses against the world community itself (such as crimes against

[35] The applicable test for State attribution, as initially set forth by the ICJ in the 1986 *Nicaragua Case* is "effective control." *Case Concerning Military and Paramilitary Activities in and against Nicaragua* (Nicar. v. U.S.) Merits, [1986] I.C.J. Rep. 14, ¶¶ 109–15 (June 27). The ICJ distinguished "effective control" from the upper bound of "complete dependence" (reserving the latter standard when proving that a given group is a *de facto* government organ under Article 4 of the ILC's *Responsibility of States for Int'lly Wrongful Acts with Commentaries* (Draft), Dec. 12, 2001, Annex to UNGA Res. 56/83, U.N. GAOR, 56th Sess., Supp. No. 10, at 43, U.N. Doc. A/56/10 (2001) [hereinafter ILC, *State Responsibility*]), while expressly rejecting the less demanding "overall control" test, as articulated in *Prosecutor v. Tadic,* Case No. IT-94-1-A, ¶¶ 137–45, App. Ch., July 15, 1999, at least for purposes of finding State responsibility. *Case Concerning the Application of the Conv. on the Prevention and Punishment of the Crime of Genocide* (Bosn. & Herz. v. Serb. & Mont.), (2007) I.C.J. Rep. 1, ¶¶ 391–94, 399–407 (Feb. 26). The "effective control" test entails the strict requirement that a non-State actor must be operating "on the instructions of, or under the direction or control" of a State with respect to each individual operation. *Id.* ¶ 398 (quoting ILC, *State Responsibility, supra,* art. 8).

[36] For example, over a century ago, in 1909, a "private individual who was acting under the direction of a German police officer" and who allegedly self-identified as a German police officer, lured a Swiss resident named Göntsch across the border into Germany ostensibly "to search for a lost child," where he was then arrested for espionage. Lawrence Preuss, *Kidnaping of Fugitives from Justice on Foreign Territory,* 29 AJIL 502, 506 (1935). After the Swiss lodged a protest, Göntsch was returned and the German police officer who directed the action was "later censured and dismissed for his part in the incident." *Id.*

[37] Violations under military law include those related to military absenteeism and desertion, but, as such, may fall within the military offense exclusion recognized in many extradition treaties (*see* Chapter 5.a.iii).

[38] "Childnappers" are parents who take their *own* child away, usually from a divorced or separated spouse with whom the child is residing, contrary to the terms of a court-imposed custody order or arrangement, often but not necessarily by crossing State borders. The recovery of such parental offenders is challenging, in part, because few States recognize such conduct as an extraditable crime (*see* Chapter 5.a.i) and, in part, because the perpetrators often return to States of their own nationality (which may have a law prohibiting the extradition of their own nationals, as addressed in Chapter 6.a). *See* U.S. Dep't of State, *Foreign Affairs Manual,* Vol. 7 – Consular Affairs, Other Extradition Matters, 7 FAM 1640, 1647, *updated* Feb. 18, 2011. As a result, the Hague Convention on the Civil Aspects of International Child Abduction, outlines a constructive and creative approach for the recovery of the *unlawfully seized child,* rather than of the perpetrator

humanity[39] or piracy[40]).[41] More traditional labels, such as "international offenses" and "transnational crimes," have been avoided in outlining the crimes covered herein, as such labels have come to assume multiple meanings and consequently have sown confusion.[42] In any event, the

parent himself, and thereby serves the best interests of the child while vitiating any wrongful gains, even if the offending parent is not ultimately subject to prosecution or punishment. The Hague Conv. on the Civil Aspects of Int'l Child Abduction, Oct. 25, 1980, T.I.A.S. No. 11,670, 1343 U.N.T.S. 89. Instances exist, however, of extradition based on the crime of childnapping. *See, e.g.*, "Eileen Clark Extradition: 'Final Step in a Very Painful Time,'" *BBC News*, July 5, 2014 (discussing the case of a woman who fled from the United States with her three children to Oxford, United Kingdom, in 1998, but whose challenge against an extradition order failed).

39 Rome Statute of the Int'l Criminal Court (ICC), July 17, 1998, art. 7(1), 2187 U.N.T.S. 3, U.N. Doc. A/CONF.183/9 (1998), *reprinted in* 37 ILM 999 (defining "crimes against humanity" as such acts as murder, torture, rape, and enslavement, among others, "when committed as part of a widespread or systematic attack directed against any civilian population, with knowledge of the attack").

40 Sea piracy, which peaked in the decade between 1812 and 1823 due to conditions leading to a "market for illegal commerce in the North Atlantic," G. Edward White, *The Marshall Court and Int'l Law: The Piracy Cases*, 83 AJIL 727, 729 (1989), recently resurfaced after nearly a couple of hundred years of relative dormancy. There was a spike in pirate attacks between 2007 and 2009 off the coast of Somalia, resulting in over 140 incidents in Somalia and the Gulf of Aden in the first half of 2009 alone. "State of Crime and Criminal Justice Worldwide": Report of the Secretary-General, Feb. 1, 2010, Twelfth U.N. Congress on Crime Prevention and Crim Justice, April 12–19, 2010, U.N. Doc. A/CONF. 213/3, at 3 [hereinafter UNODC, 2010 Crime Report]. Notably, however, the frequency of sea piracy worldwide abruptly declined after 2012, with reports of 264 attacks recorded worldwide in 2013, a 40% drop from the 2011 peak. ICC Int'l Maritime Bureau, *Piracy and Armed Robbery against Ships: Report for the Period 1-Jan. – 31 Dec. 2013* (Jan. 2014). Piracy will be addressed elsewhere in this book, including in the discussion of universal jurisdiction (Chapter 2.c.ii) and the lawfulness of undertaking unilateral actions where *hostis humani generis* crimes are implicated (Chapter 12.c.iv).

41 While some may question the role of domestic courts in prosecuting offenses against the world community, such crimes are not limited to the jurisdiction of international tribunals. A number of States, notably Austria, France, Germany, and Israel, have passed legislation permitting them to hold Nazi war criminals accountable, *e.g.*, Nazi and Nazi Collaborators (Punishment) Law, 57 Aug. *9, 1950, 57 Sefer Ha-Chukkim* 281, Aug. 9, 1950, while other States have prosecuted violations arising out of international armed conflicts on their native soil, such as Croatia, Iraq, and Serbia. For example, after more than six years, Croatia secured the extradition from Australia of dual Australian-Serbian national Dragan Vasiljkovic, who was wanted for alleged war crimes – *i.e.*, torturing and killing Croat combatants and civilians along with a foreign journalist – while commanding a Serbian paramilitary outfit during the armed conflict in the former Yugoslavia, for which the ICTY also retains jurisdiction. Lanai Vasek, "Croatia Bid for Dragan Vasiljkovic Extradition Approved," *The Australian*, Nov. 17, 2012.

42 *See* Cyrille Fijnaut, *Transnat'l Crime and the Role of the United Nations in Its Containment through Int'l Cooperation: A Challenge for the 21st Century*, 8 Eur. J. Crim. L. & Crim. Just.

point here is not to classify crimes into defined categories,[43] but rather to underscore how virtually any domestically or universally recognized crime conceivably *could* be the trigger for an extradition request or an alternative approach to recovering a fugitive,[44] and in fact this book considers the full panoply of crimes rather than limiting itself to one type as some analyses do.

The geographic coverage relevant to this inquiry is global:[45] it is not confined to a single State or region or to some particular collection of States with shared interests (*e.g.*, the British Commonwealth), and the intention is that its analysis, conclusions, and policy prescriptions will be generally applicable and of interest to States *writ large*, mindful that no single treatment can fully capture all nuanced variations across State law and practice worldwide. Consistent with that caveat, this book places a special emphasis on the United States,[46] which has entered into the

119, 120 (2000) (characterizing the term "transnational crime" as "misleading"); *cf. Questions Relating to the Obligation to Prosecute or Extradite* (Belg. v. Sen.) [2012] I.C.J. Rep. 471, 477 (July 20) (Abraham, J., Sep. Op.) (doubting the "legal relevance" of the term "international crimes"). *Compare* ILC, *State Responsibility, supra* n.35, art. 19 (defining "international crimes" as only those which a State - not an individual - can commit) *with* M. Cherif Bassiouni & Edward M. Wise, aut dedere aut judicare: The Duty to Extradite or Prosecute in International Law 6 n.11 (1995) (defining "international offenses" broadly as an offense of international concern).

43 Indeed, some crimes are not prone to neat categorization. For example, money laundering could occur strictly within the territory of a single State (rather than be transacted cross-border), while manslaughter may implicate the interests of two States (rather than one) where, say, the perpetrator is a foreign diplomat. Depending on the circumstance, torture may qualify either as a domestic law violation implicating rights in a single State or as an international law violation constituting an offense against the world community. In addition, terrorism may implicate only one's State's interests, as in the case of domestic terrorism, or it could be the product of foreign government financing or other material support, thereby imbuing it with an international complexion.

44 This is not to suggest that differences between those offenses expressly criminalized by international treaty and strictly domestic offenses are not meaningful in the extradition context. One legal scholar noted that the former, by contrast with the latter, may give rise to universal jurisdiction, are more likely to be treated as exceptions to the political offense exclusion, and fully allow for the operation of the *aut dedere aut judicare* principle. *See* Yoram Dinstein, *Some Reflections on Extradition*, 36 Ger. Y.B. Int'l L. 46, 57–58 (1993). (All referenced concepts are discussed *infra*.)

45 "Like pollution, commerce, and war, criminal activity knows no territorial bounds." Edward M. Morgan, *Criminal Process, Int'l Law, and Extraterritorial Crime*, 38 U. Toronto L.J. 245, 245 (1988).

46 For those less familiar with the U.S. legal system, a brief overview of several critical features may prove instructive: (i) the United States operates under a federalist system of government that divides jurisdiction over its laws between its fifty individual states and the federal government, so a fugitive could be indicted by a state or federal prosecutor, tried in a state or federal court, and sentenced to serve in a state or federal prison; only the

most extradition treaties of any State,[47] has been a leading exponent of bold and/or innovative approaches or alternatives to extradition, and has generated a disproportionately large body of law in this field, although concededly its jurisprudence is not uniformly followed.

In addition, all the means and methods discussed for bringing a fugitive to justice involve the fugitive's presence in another State's sovereign territory or at least non-sovereign territory/international space.[48] This inquiry, therefore, is not concerned with either intra-State

federal government, however, may request extradition from or process extradition to another State, so in such instances, the federal government must represent a state's interests, 18 U.S.C. §§ 3183 (2012) (covering not only states, but also any U.S. "Territory, District, or Possession"); DoJ, *U.S. Attorneys' Manual*, Chapter 9–15.100 (2d ed. 2007–3 Supp.); there is also a Uniform Code of Military Justice (UCMJ) that governs U.S. military law, 10 U.S.C. § 821 (2012); (ii) the U.S. Supreme Court does not hear appeals as a matter of right (with one exception that is not applicable here), but rather must agree to hear a case based on a so-called petition for a *writ of certiorari*; only about eighty cases on average are heard by the U.S. Supreme Court each year, or about 1% of all cases petitioned (STEPHEN BREYER, MAKING OUR DEMOCRACY WORK: A JUDGE'S VIEW 229 (2010)), so in practice U.S. Courts of Appeals are most frequently the final arbiters; there are twelve geographic appellate courts (numbered by circuit) covering ninety-four judicial districts, plus a U.S. Court of Appeals for the Federal Circuit that handles specialized cases; and (iii) the United States is a dualist system, so when its executive enters into an international treaty, those provisions do not automatically take effect as U.S. law, but rather must first be adopted in one form or another into U.S. legislation; within the hierarchy of U.S. law, treaties are regarded on par with U.S. statutes but both are subordinate to the U.S. Constitution. JOHN M. ROGERS, INTERNATIONAL LAW AND UNITED STATES LAW 76 (1999). Where a statute and treaty are mutually inconsistent, the one that last came into effect prevails. *See Whitney v. Robertson*, 124 U.S. 190, 194 (1888) (applying the "last-in-time" rule). To the extent possible, U.S. courts are to interpret U.S. law so as to avoid violating principles of public international law, *Murray v. Schooner Charming Betsy*, 6 U.S. (2 Cr.) 64, 102 (1804), but public international law controls only by default "where there is no treaty and no controlling executive or legislative act or judicial decision." *The Paquete Habana*, 175 U.S. 677, 700 (1900).

47 *See* n.51 in Chapter 4.

48 This inquiry dispenses with such Latin terms as *terra nullius*, *res nullius*, and *res communis*, as their meanings have become somewhat confused or conflated over time in legal discourse. *See* KATHRYN MILUN, THE POLITICAL UNCOMMONS: THE CROSS-CULTURAL LOGIC OF THE GLOBAL COMMONS 57–70 (2011) (discussing and comparing these terms and their definitions); *cf.* MALCOLM N. SHAW, PUBLIC INTERNATIONAL LAW 492, 533–34 (6th ed. 2008) (distinguishing *terra nullius*, which technically stands for territory in which international law does not recognize a sovereign, from its cousin *res communis*, which constitutes territory that is "generally not capable of being reduced to sovereign control" from space denominated for the time being as the "common heritage of mankind"). Besides, the point here is only to emphasize that there are some places that, whether or not they are potentially susceptible to sovereign acquisition or whether or not they represent

relations (*e.g.*, as between two Canadian provinces or between two American states[49] or the removal of a defendant between U.S. federal districts for the purpose of assigning trial court jurisdiction),[50] with relationships between a sub-national entity and another State,[51] or between a State and an international tribunal, except to the limited extent of illustrating such dynamics by comparison or contrast.

The final scope consideration is the source and nature of laws that will be examined. This inquiry takes an inclusive approach to legal sources,[52] factoring in not only conventional or treaty law[53] and

part of the global commons, *are not recognized by the international community as currently subject to sovereign ownership or control*. Accordingly, examples of "non-sovereign territory/international space" for present purposes include: (i) the high seas; (ii) Antarctica (*see* SHAW, *supra*, at 536 (discussing that continent as having competing territorial claims by seven States but that each claimant State is a party to the Antarctic Treaty, Dec. 1, 1959, art. IV(2), 402 U.N.T.S. 571, which suspended all such claims during the duration of the treaty)); (iii) unclaimed islands outside of territorial waters; (iv) airport international zones; (v) various lands between the border posts of sovereign States (*e.g.*, "Namibia: Congolese Refugees Trapped in No-Man's Land," July 23, 2009, *available at* www.irinnews.org/news/2009/07/23/congolese-refugees-trapped-no-mans-land (last visited on Apr. 29, 2016) (describing the location of Congolese refugees as "between the border posts of Buitepos in Namibia and Mamuno in Botswana"); and arguably (vi) failed States (defined at n.171 in Chapter 12).

49 Although some cases examined in this study involve offenses prosecuted in U.S. state courts, in each instance inter-State relations were implicated; *e.g.*, *Kasi v. Commw. of Virginia*, 508 S.E.2d 57 (Va. 1998) (a Virginia trial court convicted Mir Aimal Kasi, a Pakistani national, of capital murder and related crimes in connection with his shooting of five CIA employees outside CIA Headquarters in Fairfax County, Virginia), *cert. denied*, 527 U.S. 1038 (1999). *See generally* JAMES A. SCOTT, THE LAW OF INTERSTATE RENDITION: A TREATISE 2–4 (1983) (highlighting "seven fundamental points of difference" regarding the "methods of demanding, arresting and surrendering fugitives from justice" between the international norms and those of the U.S. domestic system).

50 *See* Alexander Holtzoff, *Removal of Defendants in Federal Criminal Procedure*, 33 CAL. L. REV. 230, 230 (1945).

51 Notably, in the United States, extradition is governed by federal law, 18 U.S.C. § 3181 *et seq.* (2012), which does not empower states to engage in the extradition of fugitives with foreign countries. *See supra* n.46.

52 *See* Statute of the ICJ, Apr. 18, 1946, art. 38 (recognizing as applicable sources of law in rendering its decisions "international conventions," "international custom," "general principles of [international] law," and (as subsidiary means) "judicial decisions and the teachings of the most highly qualified publicists of the various nations").

53 These encompass both bilateral and multilateral treaties, whether they are aimed at crime suppression, extradition, human rights protection, or otherwise. Such documents must, of course, actually qualify as treaties (versus, say, resolutions, declarations, or guidelines), must have entered into force, and must take account of any reservations or understandings invoked by a given State party, although even if

customary international law,[54] but also general principles of international law,[55] judicial opinions[56] (from international tribunals, domestic courts,[57] and arbitral panels alike), the writings of

a State has only signed but not yet ratified a treaty, it is still expected to "refrain from acts which defeat the object and purpose of a treaty." Vienna Conv. on the Law of Treaties (VCLT), May 23, 1969, art. 18(a), 1155 U.N.T.S. 332, *reprinted in* 8 ILM 679. The treaty also must not be invalid (*e.g.*, Treaty on the Basic Relations between Japan and the Repub. of Korea, June 22, 1965, art. II, *reprinted in* 2 JAPAN'S FOREIGN RELATIONS-BASIC DOCUMENTS 569–72 ("It is confirmed that all treaties or agreements concluded between the Empire of Japan and the Empire of Korea on or before August 22, 1910, are already null and void.") (referencing a series of bilateral treaties of 1905, 1907, and 1910)), must not violate peremptory norms, VCLT, *supra*, art. 53, and must not be established on *ultra vires* grounds.

54 Customary international law was formerly known as the "law of nations." *See Siderman de Blake v. Repub. of Arg.*, 965 F.2d 699, 714 (9th Cir. 1992), *cert. denied*, 507 U.S. 1017 (1993); Michael Akehurst, *Jurisdiction in Int'l Law*, 46 B.Y.B.I.L. 145, 212 (1972–73) [hereinafter Akehurst, *Jurisdiction*] ("'The law of nations' is a translation of the Latin *ius gentium*, which did not mean international law in the modern sense, but those rules of municipal law which were common to all peoples."). Customary international law is defined as the "general and consistent practice of states followed by them from a sense of legal obligation." RESTATEMENT (THIRD), *supra* n.3, § 102(2); *accord North Sea Continental Shelf Cases* (F.R.G. v. Den., F.R.G. v. Neth.) [1969] I.C.J. Rep. 3, ¶¶ 71–73 (Feb. 20). Customary international law, which depends on the consent of States (in Latin known as *jus dispositivum*), binds all States (even those not committed via specific treaty obligations), except any that persistently have objected to the norm. RESTATEMENT (THIRD), *supra* n.3, § 102, cmt. d. "The law of nations 'may be ascertained by consulting the works of jurists, writing professedly on public law; or by the general usage and practice of nations; or by judicial decisions recognizing and enforcing that law.'" *Filártiga v. Pena-Irala*, 630 F.2d 876, 880 (2d Cir. 1980) (quoting *United States v. Smith*, 18 U.S. (5 Wheat.) 153, 160–61 (1820)).

55 *See* CRAWFORD, BROWNLIE'S PRINCIPLES, *supra* n.3, at 37 (citing examples including "consent, reciprocity, equality of states . . . the legal validity of agreements, good faith, domestic jurisdiction, and the freedom of the seas").

56 This analysis will review case law mainly from courts in the State where the fugitive is found (typically to challenge his extradition or deportation) and in the State that has successfully secured his custody (usually to challenge the court's personal jurisdiction or application of the specialty rule, discussed in Chapters 13.a.i and 7.c.ii, respectively).

57 Decisions of national courts "have been an important source for material on . . . extradition[; h]owever the value of these decisions varies considerably, and many present a narrow national outlook or rest on a very inadequate use of the sources." CRAWFORD, BROWNLIE'S PRINCIPLES, *supra* n.3, at 41. *See also* Harvard Research, *supra* n.5, at 444 ("[T]he materials which are clearly of the greatest significance for the work of codification are found in the national legislation on penal law and penal procedure and in the adjudications of national courts. If it is true . . . that 'international law is, in one sense, merely a summary of what governments claim as their rights or recognize as the rights of others' . . . it follows certainly that an adequate statement of the international law of penal jurisdiction must rest primarily upon a foundation built of materials from the cases, codes and statutes of national law.")

publicists,[58] and even soft law.[59] With the notable exception of immigration law, as discussed in Chapter 10, the focus of this study is on criminal as opposed to civil law.

While this book addresses domestic law in a myriad of respects (*e.g.*, constitutional or statutory bars to extradition), the thrust of the legal analysis is based on *international law* standards.[60] Accordingly, this

(citation omitted). *See also* Akehurst, *Jurisdiction*, *supra* n.54, at 216 ("International law sometimes incorporates rules of municipal law. For instance, a treaty between States may provide that some question related to the subject-matter of the treaty shall be governed by some system of municipal law.").

[58] *See* Crawford, Brownlie's Principles, *supra* n.3, at 43 (including not only eminent jurists like de Vattel, but also by analogy such substantially authoritative sources as the ILC's *Draft Articles on State Responsibility* and the Harvard Research drafts).

[59] "Soft law" herein means "[g]uidelines, policy declarations, or codes of conduct that set standards of conduct that are not legally binding." Black's Law Dictionary, *supra* n.24, at 1519. In short, such legal pronouncements are exhortatory rather than mandatory in character. U.N. General Assembly (UNGA) declarations represent a unique breed; while not binding on member States, as such pronouncements are recommendatory only, there is a strong expectation that members will abide by such pronouncements and "insofar as the expectation is gradually justified by State practice, a declaration may by custom become recognized as laying down rules binding upon States." Stephen M. Schwebel, *The Effect of Resolutions of the U.N. General Assembly on Customary Int'l Law*, 73 ASIL Proc. 301, 304 (1979) (quoting a 1962 memorandum issued by the U.N. Office of Legal Affairs and transmitted to the UNGA).

[60] International law is constantly evolving, with standards that originally were based on comity ripening into customary practice and with treaties ultimately consecrating widespread norms. Accordingly, this study examines international law as it exists *today*. *Accord Filártiga*, 630 F.2d at 881 ("Thus it is clear that courts must interpret international law ... as it has evolved and exists among the nations of the world today.").

It is worth briefly examining the interplay between municipal law and international law. As a general rule, "[a] state cannot plead provisions of its own law or deficiencies in that law in answer to a claim against it for an alleged breach of its obligations under international law." Crawford, Brownlie's Principles, *supra* n.3, at 51. Courts are expected to "bring internal law into conformity with obligations under international law," *id.* at 35, and to the extent possible to interpret domestic law consistent with its international obligations. *Charming Betsy*, 6 U.S. (2 Cr.) at 118; Restatement (Third), *supra* n.3, § 114; *Polites v. Commw.*, High Ct., Austl., Apr. 10, 1945, 70 C.L.R. 60, 68–69, *reprinted in* 19 ALJ 92 ("every effort should be made" to construe domestic statutes so they are consistent with Australia's international obligations); *Legal Opinion on the Decision of the Supreme Court of the United States in the* Alvarez-Machain Case, OAS Res. CJI/Res.II-15/92, Inter-Am. Juridical Comm., OEA/ser. G/CI, Doc.No. 2302/92, ¶ 7, Sept. 1, 1992, *reprinted in* 13 Hum. Rts. L.J. 395 (1992); ("[I]t is unquestionably a rule of international law that the provisions of the internal law of a state may not be invoked by such state to avoid complying with its international obligations."); *Questions Relating to the Obligation to Prosecute or Extradite* (Belg. v. Sen.), [2012] I.C.J. Rep. 422, ¶ 113 (July 20) ("Senegal cannot justify its breach of the obligation provided for in Article 7, paragraph 1, of the Convention against

analysis is not concerned as a *legal matter* with instances in which a State intentionally, negligently, or unwittingly violates solely its own domestic law in effecting the transfer of a fugitive to another State.[61] In addition, although this inquiry explores statutes and jurisprudence from both common law and civil law jurisdictions, our focus is strictly on *public* international law; therefore, commercial and property law,[62] as well as

Torture by invoking provisions of its internal law, in particular by invoking the decisions as to lack of jurisdiction rendered by its courts in 2000 and 2001, or the fact that it did not adopt the necessary legislation pursuant to Article 5, paragraph 2, of that Convention until 2007."). At the same time, however, in dualist (versus monist) States, such as the United States and the United Kingdom, international law can become relegated to subordinate status. For example, under U.S. law, "[i]n their character as law of the United States, rules of international law and provisions of international agreements of the United States are subject to the Bill of Rights and other prohibitions, restrictions, and requirements of the Constitution, and cannot be given effect in violation of them. However, failure of the United States to carry out an obligation on the ground of its unconstitutionality will not relieve the United States of responsibility under international law." RESTATEMENT (THIRD), *supra* n.3, ch. 2, Intro. Note at 40; § 111 cmt. a (citations omitted). *See also Reid v. Covert*, 354 U.S. 1, 18 (1957) ("This Court has also repeatedly taken the position that an Act of Congress [*i.e.*, federal legislation], which must comply with the Constitution, is on a full parity with a treaty, and that, when a statute which is subsequent in time is inconsistent with a treaty, the statute to the extent of conflict renders the treaty null."); *FTC v. Compagnie de Saint-Gobain-Pont-a-Mousson*, 636 F.2d 1300, 1323 (D.C. Cir. 1980) (U.S. courts are "obligated to give effect to an unambiguous exercise by Congress of its jurisdiction to prescribe even if such an exercise would exceed the limitations imposed by international law."); *cf. Eichmann v. Attorney General of the Gov't of Israel*, Sup. Ct., Isr., May 29, 1962, *reprinted in* 36 ILR 277, 280 (E. Lauterpacht ed. 1968) (where a conflict exists between municipal and international law, "it is the duty of the Court to give preference to and apply the laws of the local Legislature" under the presumption "that the Legislature strives to adjust its laws to the principles of international law which have received general recognition ... [b]ut where a contrary intention clearly emerges from the statute itself, that presumption loses its force and the Court is enjoined to disregard it").

61 For example, despite the Bosnian Supreme Court having released Algerian individuals suspected by the United States of terrorism on the basis of insufficient evidence against them, Bosnian executive branch officials seized them and handed them over to U.S. authorities. Human Rights Watch, *World Report 2003, available at* www.hrw.org/legacy/wr2k3/europe5.html (last visited on May 27, 2016).

62 This inquiry will not touch on property rights or *in rem* actions (*e.g., United States v. Saccoccia*, 58 F.3d 757, 784 (1st Cir. 1995) *cert. denied*, 517 U.S. 1105 (1996)), except to the extent of seizing or freezing a fugitive's assets with the ultimate objective of bringing him to justice (*see* Chapter 9.a), rather than merely seeking to "deal a genuine blow to [a] criminal enterprise." Fisher, *supra* n.11.

most other types of private international law,[63] do not figure into the analysis.

c Significance

The issue of securing the custody of fugitives has become increasingly important in recent years due largely to three international developments. First, the global prospects for and incidence of crime, particularly of a transborder character,[64] are greater than ever before.[65] The world is vastly more inter-connected through telecommunications, improved transportation links, and advanced transactional mechanisms. In addition, commercial markets are expanding, fueled by greater opportunities for trade and profit and the more rapid and efficient movement of goods, services, and capital. This also means that criminals today can more easily harm one State's interests while acting from another State's territory through counterfeiting, financial fraud, and cybercrime,[66] among other activities. Moreover, the advent of certain transborder crimes can precipitate still others; for example, narcotics trafficking can lead to such attendant crimes as murder to protect cartel profits, money laundering to dispose of unlawful revenues, and robbery to support individual drug addictions.[67]

[63] One notable exception to this general rule is an examination of the role of professional bondsmen acting beyond national boundaries so as to prevent the companies employing or contracting them from forgoing the posted bail (*see* Chapter 3.b).

[64] The value of transnational organized crime has been estimated at 3.6 percent of the global economy. Council on Foreign Relations, *The Global Regime for Transnat'l Crime*, Issue Brief, June 25, 2013, at 1.

[65] Louise Shelley, "The Globalization of Crime and Terrorism," IIP Digital, June 5, 2008, *available at* http://iipdigital.usembassy.gov/st/english/publication/2008/06/20080608103639xjyrrep4.218692e-02.html#axzz49x7s6R4l (last visited on May 27, 2016); Neil Boister, An Introduction to Transnational Criminal Law 287–88 (2012). In fairness, not all types of crimes are on the rise. Property crimes throughout much of Europe, for example, have declined in recent years, probably due in part to target hardening. UNODC, 2010 Crime Report, *supra* n.40, at 3.

[66] *See, e.g.*, Mike Nizza, "British Hacker Closer to Facing Trial in America," *The Lede*, July 30, 2008 (describing how U.S. prosecutors sought to secure custody over and try British national Gary McKinnon for hacking into computers belonging to NASA, the U.S. Department of Defense, and elsewhere within the U.S. Government in 2001–02 from London). *See generally* Marc Goodman, "A Cybercrime Tsunami," *The Economist: The World in 2016*, Nov. 2015, at 154–55 (discussing the prospect of "a tsunami of criminal activity on the horizon" in the form of cybercrime, costing businesses an estimated US $2 trillion per year by 2019).

[67] Crimes involving narcotics are decidedly on the rise. The rate of drug-related crimes in nineteen countries that collect long-term data almost doubled between 1995 and 2008. UNODC, 2010 Crime Report, *supra* n.40, at 3.

Second, criminals today have more available safe havens[68] and greater physical mobility,[69] including porous international

[68] A "safe haven" is defined herein as *a State that provides legal protection to individuals or groups residing within its jurisdictional control while they carry out unlawful operations and/or evade the reach of overseas law enforcement.* Specific safe havens are sought by criminals *as operating bases* for one or more of three essential reasons: (i) the harboring State politically sympathizes with the criminal's aims; (ii) the harboring government is unable or unwilling to control the criminal conduct either because of a weak police force or collusion by its officers (for example, drug cartels have notoriously operated in Colombia with effective impunity); and/or (iii) the harboring State lacks the legal regime to treat such conduct as "criminal" (for example, the United Kingdom only enacted legislation criminalizing cartel activity in 2003, *see* Bruce Zagaris, *U.S. Extradition from the U.K. Engenders Controversies*, 21 IELR 312, 312–14 (2005), so until then cartels were not deemed unlawful). Convicted or accused criminals also seek out safe havens *when they are on the run* (*e.g.*, as indictees not yet arrested, custodial or prison escapees, or bail jumpers) to States where they are not wanted for prosecution or punishment and that are believed will not ultimately extradite them to the pursuing State, whether for legally grounded reasons, political enmity, lack of inter-State reciprocity, or otherwise. Christopher A. Donesa, Note, *Protecting Nat'l Interests: The Legal Status of Extraterritorial Law Enforcement by the Military*, 41 Duke L.J. 867, 869–70 n.11 (1991). The number of potential safe havens has almost quadrupled since 1945, when only fifty-one States existed versus approximately 200 today. It is also the case that not enough States are parties to multilateral conventions that try to suppress crimes, and so those that are not can become appealing safe havens for actual or alleged criminals; for instance, the hijackers of a Kuwaiti aircraft were able to escape because Algeria was not a party to relevant treaties and so was under no obligation to extradite or punish. Antonio Cassese, *The Int'l Community's 'Legal' Response to Terrorism*, 38 Int'l & Comp. L.Q. 589, 593 (1989). Safe havens, however, are not necessarily permanent. They can lose their status in the event political leadership changes, whether through election, retirement, death, or a *coup d'etat. E.g.*, Marc Lacey, "U.S. Fugitives Worry About a Cuba Without Castro," *N.Y. Times*, May 12, 2007, at A3 (noting that for the roughly seventy U.S. fugitives residing in Cuba, their fate may turn on the successor to their aging protector Fidel Castro); Theodore Schleifer, "U.S. Eyes Extradition of Fugitives Living in Cuba: New Relationship Could Bring Old Fugitives to Justice," *CNN*, Apr. 16, 2015 (the U.S. government expressed an interest in extradition cooperation from Cuba in the broader context of normalizing political relations with Cuba, particularly following the U.S. decision to remove Cuba from a list of State sponsors of terrorism). Safe havens also can disappear when two States that have historically never entered into an extradition treaty decide to do so. For example, until 1990, Canada and the Philippines had no extradition treaty between them, and therefore in 1986 when Philippine national Rodolfo Pacificador fled the Philippines after the overthrow of President Ferdinand Marcos, he chose Canada, but not long after their bilateral extradition treaty was executed, Pacificador was arrested. Bruce Zagaris, *Philippine Extradition Request to Canada Raises Human Rights Issues*, 14 IELR 12, 12–13 (1998). In addition, a State may have second thoughts about providing refuge to a fugitive, such as when a fugitive violates the conditions stipulated for his protective treatment. *E.g.*, David D. Kirkpatrick, "Niger Hands Qaddafi Son Over to Libya," *INYT*, Mar. 7, 2014, at 3.

[69] *Foster v. Minister for Customs and Justice*, High Ct., Austl., Aug. 3, 2000, 200 C.L.R. 442, 474. It is interesting to note that as far back as the 1930s, a U.S. appellate court judge made an observation that resonates today: "The rapid advancement and progress in intercommunications amongst nations, and the ease with which a criminal can flee from the

borders,[70] than in times past, and consequently can more easily evade detection and arrest.[71] One reasonably would expect such mobility and evasiveness to result in a growing pool of international fugitives. While such statistical data are difficult to pin down, one meaningful proxy measure is the number of INTERPOL[72] "Red Notices"[73] issued for

country of his crime and seek an asylum in another country, the lessening of national barriers, all tend to minimize the fact that crime has always been considered a local matter." *United States ex rel. Donnelly v. Mulligan*, 74 F.2d 220, 221 (2d Cir. 1934) (Manton, J.).

70 Neil Boister, *The Trend to "Universal Extradition" over Subsidiary Universal Jurisdiction in the Suppression of Transnat'l Crime*, 2003 Acta Juridica 287, 288 (2003).

71 Some fugitives employ a variety of clever techniques to evade detection for years. For example, Vazquez Mendoza, wanted by the United States for armed robbery- and murder-related charges, managed to remain free for almost six years; "[h]e avoided cell phones and modern communications, severed ties to relatives and started a new family under a stolen name. He lived simply in some remote areas of Mexico, protected from the police by neighbors, dense vegetation and terrain best traversed on burro or horse." Bruce Zagaris, *Mexico Arrests Mexican National on U.S. Extradition Warrant for Murder of DEA Agent*, 16 IELR 902, 903 (2000). Others frequently change their identities, phone numbers, and addresses, and reside in places like Costa del Sol, Spain, where they can blend into the tourist crowd. Bruce Zagaris, *Spain Arrests Alleged Colombian Drug Lord*, 30 IELR 416, 417 (2014).

72 INTERPOL, which stands for the International Criminal Police Force, is "the world's largest international police organization, with 190 member countries." INTERPOL website, *available at* www.interpol.int/About-INTERPOL/Overview (last visited on Apr. 29, 2016). The organization is based in Lyon, France, has seven regional offices, and each of its members maintains a National Central Bureau staffed by its own law enforcement officers. INTERPOL "work[s] to ensure that police around the world have access to the tools and services necessary to do their jobs effectively. [They] provide targeted training, expert investigative support, relevant data and secure communications channels. This combined framework helps police on the ground understand crime trends, analyse information, conduct operations and, ultimately, arrest as many criminals as possible." *Id.*

73 A Red Notice is a posting circulated by INTERPOL to national police forces of concern that a particular individual is wanted for arrest by an INTERPOL member State. It is the closest equivalent to an international arrest warrant that exists today. More precisely, the Red Notice, by contrast with other colored INTERPOL-issued notices that serve corresponding functions, is an efficient mechanism for alerting the international law enforcement community to the identity and possible whereabouts of a fugitive and requesting his arrest and provisional detention pending a formal extradition request. *U.S. Attorneys' Manual, supra* n.46, § 611. While Red Notices are frequently taken seriously, some governments regard them as a notice to locate a fugitive but not necessarily arrest him absent an extradition request. Nadelmann, *Int'l Rendition, supra* n.28, at 819. In certain instances, the Red Notices may be ignored altogether. *See* AFP, "Niger Will Not Extradite Kadhafi Son," Feb. 12, 2012 (Niger was unwilling to arrest and extradite Saadi Qaddafi, son of slain Libyan leader Moammar Qaddafi, despite INTERPOL having issued a Red Notice for his arrest); Peter Baker, "Prayer Breakfast Includes Russian Fugitives," *Wash. Post*, Feb. 5, 2005, at A5 ("U.S. officials said they saw no reason to honor the Interpol red notices" with respect to Russian indictees and partners of billionaire Mikhail Khodorkovsky, Mikhail Brudno and Vladimir Dubov, who attended a prayer breakfast with U.S. President George W. Bush at the White House). Some criticism has been directed in recent years against certain States for

wanted persons, which increased six-fold over the span of a decade, from 1,378 in 2003, to 3,126 in 2008, to 8,857 in 2013.[74] While these figures may possibly be explained by other variables, this noteworthy surge strongly suggests a rising tide of fugitives.

Third, progressively since World War II and particularly since the 1970s with the "internationalization of drug enforcement," the global demand for tracking down and bringing fugitives to justice has increased.[75] States have asserted more expansive and innovative grounds for extraterritorial jurisdiction (discussed in Chapter 2.c.iii) and for exploring alternative means to extradition to secure their physical custody abroad (examples can be found in Chapters 9–13). This trend is exemplified by the spate of model treaties on international law enforcement cooperation adopted by the United Nations General Assembly between 1985 and the early 1990s;[76] by the growing number of multilateral crime suppression treaties related to terrorism, drug trafficking, and other forms of illegal conduct; and by the spawning of specialized criminal tribunals (*e.g.*, the ICTY, ICTR, and hybrid courts).

In March 2003, the Grand Chamber of the European Court of Human Rights (ECtHR) summed up the overall importance of this subject, including its contributing factors, when it stated: "As movement about the world becomes easier and crime takes on a larger international dimension, it is increasingly in the interest of all nations that suspected offenders who flee abroad should be brought to justice."[77]

misusing Red Notices for political ends, such as demonizing dissidents. Fair Trials Int'l, *Written Submission to INTERPOL's Working Group on the Processing of Information*, June 10, 2015, *available at* www.fairtrials.org/wp-content/uploads/GTI-Submission_Fair-Trials-2.pdf (last visited on May 27, 2016); Istanbul Decl. and Resolutions adopted by the OSCE Parliamentary Ass'y at the Twenty-Second Annual Sess., Istanbul, June 29–July 3, 2013.

74 *INTERPOL Annual Report 2013*, at 58, *available at* www.interpol.int/News-and-media/Publications2/Annual-reports2 (last visited on May 27, 2016). Another way to view these data is to consider that of the 8,857 Red Notices issued in 2013, 1,749 resulted in arrests, *id.* at 59, or virtually 20% of the total, which represented more than all the Red Notices issued only ten years earlier. *Id.*

75 Nadelmann, Cops, *supra* n.12, at 403.

76 *See, e.g.*, U.N. Model Agreement on the Transfer of Foreign Prisoners and Recommendations for the Treatment of Foreign Prisoners, Nov. 29, 1985, U.N. Doc. A/CONF.121/22/Rev.1 (1986); U.N. Model Treaty on Extradition, Dec. 14, 1990, UNGA Res. 45/116, Annex, 45 U.N. GAOR Supp. (No. 49A), at 212, U.N. Doc. A/45/49 (1990), *reprinted in* 30 ILM 1407; U.N. Model Treaty on Mutual Assistance in Criminal Matters, Dec. 14, 1990, U.N. Doc. A/RES/45/117, *as amended by* UNGA Res. 53/112; U.N. Model Treaty on the Transfer of Proceedings in Criminal Matters, Dec. 14, 1990, U.N. Doc. A/RES/45/118; and U.N. Model Treaty on Supervision of Offenders Conditionally Sentenced or Released, Dec. 14, 1990, U.N. Doc. A/RES/45/119.

77 *Öcalan v. Turkey (Merits)*, Appl. No. 46221/99, Gr. Ch., 37 EHRR 10, ¶ 88, May 12, 2005. This need has been recognized by domestic courts as well. *E.g., United States*

d Methodology and Challenges

This book adheres to the following six-part methodology. In Part I, it addresses the two foundational elements, namely, the definition and explication of core terms and a discussion of the principles and dynamics underlying subject matter jurisdiction (pertinent to the prosecution scenario alone). Part I also treats as a background matter the various methods in which fugitives return, or are returned, to the State interested in their prosecution or punishment without any substantial effort on the part of that State or otherwise through mere fortuity, so as to distinguish such scenarios from the active pursuit of fugitives via extradition or one of its alternatives, which is the thrust of this inquiry.

In Part II, this book focuses on extradition, its aims, legal status, various applications (ranging from bilateral extradition treaties to the comity of nations[78]), mechanics (*i.e.*, the step-by-step extradition process), adaptability, and recent developments. This examination describes the nature and operation of extradition as the principal vehicle for securing the custody of a fugitive abroad and sets the stage for a comprehensive typological analysis, undertaken over three chapters, of its own impediments and challenges that help explain why States choose to entertain alternatives to extradition in their pursuit of fugitives.

Part III explores the means by which a State can seek to obtain extradition, whether by revamping its approach, creating incentives or disincentives to change the posture of the State in whose territory the fugitive resides, or seeking external engagement. Such efforts do not qualify as *bona fide* alternatives to extradition, as extradition itself remains the ultimate objective.

In Part IV, this study catalogues, describes, and evaluates for their legality under international law standards what are termed herein as *fallback* alternatives to extradition (those of second-order preference), which comprise partial or redirected means limited to merely locating or arresting a fugitive or those that result specifically in returning the

v. Cotroni, Sup. Ct., Can., [1989] 48 C.C.C. (3d) 193, 215 ("The investigation, prosecution, and suppression of crime for the protection of the citizen and the maintenance of peace and public order is an important goal of all organized societies. The pursuit of that goal cannot realistically be confined within national boundaries. That has long been the case, but it is increasingly evident today.").

78 "International comity is said to describe those actions between States based solely on goodwill or courtesy." *Harksen v. President of the Repub. of So. Afr. and Others*, Case CCT 41/99, Const. Ct., So. Afr., Mar. 30, 2000, (2000) (2) SA 825, *reprinted in* 132 ILR 529, 557 n.1 (E. Lauterpacht, *et al.*, eds. 2008).

fugitive to another State's judiciary or to an international criminal tribunal to face prosecution.

Part V explores *full-scale* alternatives to extradition, meaning those whose end result would functionally achieve what extradition seeks, namely, the physical return to one's own jurisdiction of a fugitive overseas to face prosecution or punishment in one's own judicial system. Such alternatives fall into one of three categories: those that (i) rely on domestic immigration laws, (ii) capitalize on informal law enforcement cooperation, or (iii) are undertaken unilaterally.

Part VI considers the implications of the *full-scale* alternatives outlined in Part V, which, generally being more controversial, give rise to key questions of personal jurisdiction and individual standing, diplomatic recourse (including legal remedies), and policy consequences bilaterally and for world public order. The Conclusion summarizes the content of the discourse, draws some high-level observations, and advances a set of recommendations designed to rectify some of the problem areas encountered.

An inquiry of this type faces several major challenges. To begin, the subject matter defies simple classification, is ever evolving, is often characterized by inconsistent State practice, and much of it is based ultimately on voluntary cooperation. In addition, the coverage is broad in terms of both geographical expanse and the nature of criminals, spanning billionaires to those operating on the margins of society and from war criminals to conscientious objectors. Furthermore, by focusing on alternatives to extradition, this inquiry raises a host of diverse issues, ranging from privileges and immunities to immigration, from State sovereignty to State responsibility, and from diplomacy to the use of force.

Finally, this area of law is so deeply suffused with politics to the point where the two often become inseparably co-mingled and the law itself at times can be difficult to isolate as an independent variable.[79] Examples of politics figuring into this arena can be found with respect to extradition avoidance,[80] as the real or alleged motivational force behind an

[79] *See* Sari Horwitz & Jia Lynn Yang, "Snowden Extradition May be Complicated Process if Criminal Charges are Filed," *Wash. Post*, June 19, 2013 ("'The dirty little secret about extradition law is it's really about 90 percent politics and only 10 percent law.'") (quoting Stephen I. Vladeck, Associate Dean at American Univ.'s Washington College of Law and a professor of national security law).

[80] *See, e.g.*, David M. Herszenhorn, "Russia Warns Citizens about Extradition and U.S. Justice," *IHT*, Sept. 4, 2013, at 2 (the Russian Foreign Ministry remarkably issued a travel advisory to its citizens warning those wanted by U.S. law enforcement to forgo visiting countries that have an extradition treaty with the United States).

extradition request,[81] as a disinclination to extradite to a given State,[82] as a response to extradition approvals[83] or denials,[84] and in the context of alternatives to extradition.[85]

[81] *See, e.g.*, C.J. Chivers, "In Swiss Court, Russian Avoids Extradition to the U.S.," *N.Y. Times*, Dec. 30, 2005, at A8 (after the United States sought the extradition from Switzerland of Russia's former Nuclear Energy Minister, Yevgeny Adamov, on fraud and money laundering charges, Russia "reacted ... viscerally, insisting that Mr. Adamov was chosen for prosecution by the United States in hopes of prying nuclear secrets from him.").

[82] *See, e.g.*, AP, "Escaped IRA Gunman Savors Liberty in Dublin," *L.A. Times*, June 24, 1990 (Irish "Prime Minister Charles Haughey's Fianna Fail party, political heirs of the Irish nationalist heroes who wrested independence from Britain in the 1920s, is opposed to handing Irish people [including IRA gunmen] over to the British."); Francis Robles, "U.S. Investigates Brother from Ecuador with Ties to Campaigns," *N.Y. Times*, Mar. 28, 2014, at A4 (discussing speculation that the U.S. Government's decision to deny Ecuador's request for the extradition of brothers Roberto and William Isaias may have been influenced by the political contributions they made in the United States to Barack Obama's re-election campaign, to the Democratic Party, and to U.S. Sen. Robert Menendez (D.-N.J.), chair of the Senate Foreign Relations Committee).

[83] *See, e.g.*, Bruce Zagaris, *German Arrest and Extradition of Rwandan Chief Protocol Officer to France Produces Diplomatic Tensions with Rwanda*, 25 IELR 1, 1 (2009) (in November 2008, when, pursuant to a request by France, Germany arrested and extradited Rose Kabuye, "the chief protocol officer for the Rwandan government on French charges that she participated in the 1994 assassination of then Rwandan president 'President Juvenal Habyarimana," Rwanda responded by expelling Germany's Ambassador to Kigali).

[84] *See, e.g.*, Michael D. Shear, "Obama Cancels Visit to Putin as Snowden Adds to Tensions," *N.Y. Times*, August 7, 2013 (within a week of Russia's granting political asylum to Edward Snowden, on August 1, and thereby thwarting efforts to bring him to justice, Barack Obama cancelled a presidential summit scheduled for September with his counterpart Vladimir Putin to discuss a broad range of issues of mutual interest).

[85] For example, from the beginning of its history, the United States was opposed to the seizure of sailors from its ships by the British navy, many of whom were British deserters and faced military trials upon their return. Their seizure was a chronic source of conflict, so when the *HMS Leopard* attacked the *USS Chesapeake* in 1807 and abducted sailors from her crew, U.S. President Thomas Jefferson ordered an embargo on trade with Great Britain. But abductions did not end, and that practice became one of the causes of the War of 1812. Christopher H. Pyle, Extradition, Politics, and Human Rights 265 (2001). (Admittedly, treaty-based extradition was not then an available recourse between the United States and Great Britain, as the Jay Treaty, which established such bilateral law enforcement cooperation, had lapsed that very year, and only would have recognized extraditions for the crimes of murder or forgery, anyway. Nevertheless, the two States' tense political relations at the time help explain the British resort to such aggressiveness, and the physical seizures at issue undoubtedly constituted an alternative to what could otherwise have been a cooperative approach to international law enforcement.) *See* other examples of anticipated or actual political impact arising from unilateral alternatives to extradition at n.17 in Chapter 12.

PART I

Background Context

1

Core Terminology

A Fresh Look

Part I examines three topics that, in the aggregate, provide the necessary backdrop for the operational and legal analysis of extradition and its alternatives. This chapter proffers terminology and accompanying definitions essential to undergirding the discourse, as well as identifies commonly used vernacular that arguably should be avoided. Chapter 2 discusses subject matter jurisdiction and its various underlying principles for extending a State's extraterritorial reach to bring a fugitive to justice. Chapter 3 focuses on the various ways in which a fugitive returns, or is returned, to a State interested in his custody but without having to undertake any effort of its own or in which the fugitive otherwise is delivered by mere fortuity – so-called "silver platter" scenarios.

With respect to terminology, we first must understand the meaning of "international fugitive from justice," as that individual's status, conduct, and custody lies at the center of this inquiry. We also require a label for the State that wants to prosecute or punish a fugitive but over whom it lacks custody or control, as well as for the State within whose territory the fugitive is located. In addition, we need vocabulary for identifying States once they are or have been engaged in extradition or the cooperative delivery of fugitives for law enforcement purposes. Moreover, the term "rendition" has regrettably lost its bearings in the popular lexicon and therefore requires clarification, and there is a need to discuss some internal differentiation and new reference terms for States when unilateral operations are being or have been undertaken. Furthermore, because the term "extradition" tends to be characterized superficially without fully accounting for its integral nuances, a more precise definition is herein supplied.

A closer look at the term "summary extradition," as well as the often conflated terms "*de facto* extradition" and "disguised extradition," is also warranted. Further, a terminological distinction should be drawn between the functionally similar but contextually oppositional terms "extradition" and "surrender." Finally, two new terms, "lure and capture operation" (a substitute for a "lure") and "seizure and delivery operation" (a replacement for an extraterritorial "abduction" or "kidnapping") are introduced. This section seeks to provide robust definitions and explications for each of these core terms while justifying any departure from conventional usage. Additional terms are introduced and definitions provided in later chapters; all defined terms can be found in the Glossary.

a "International Fugitive from Justice"

When exactly is an individual regarded as an international fugitive from justice? A clear definition is important not only so there is no misunderstanding about who is being pursued (or safeguarded, as the case may be) and whether particular treaty provisions or municipal laws apply to such persons, but also because whether an individual qualifies as a fugitive from justice may be relevant to certain domestic judicial considerations, including statutes of limitations, speedy trial obligations, and the right to appeal.[1] No single authoritative definition of the term "international fugitive from justice" exists, however; and, indeed, those advanced often contain material differences, particularly with respect to the element of motivation or awareness of the individual subject to governmental pursuit.[2]

The term "international fugitive from justice" is herein defined as *a person formally charged with a crime, or a convicted criminal whose punishment has not yet been determined or fully served, who is currently outside the territorial jurisdiction and beyond the custody or control of the State (or the custody or control of the international criminal tribunal) pursuing him.*[3] This definition, which adopts the perspective of the

[1] *E.g., United States v. Fowlie*, 24 F.3d 1059 (9th Cir. 1994) (statute of limitations analysis); *United States v. Blanco*, 861 F.2d 774 (2d Cir. 1988) (speedy trial analysis); *Degen v. United States*, 517 U.S. 820 (1996) (right to appeal analysis).

[2] *Compare Rodriguez v. Comm'n on Elections*, G.R. No. 120099, Sup. Ct., Phil. (en banc), July 24, 1996 (adopting a definition with a motivational element that includes "not only those who flee after conviction to avoid punishment but likewise those who, after being charged, flee to avoid prosecution") *with United States v. Steinberg*, 478 F. Supp. 29, 32 (N.D. Ill. 1979) ("if, after the commission of a crime within a state, the person who allegedly committed it leaves the state, *no matter for what purpose, with what motive, or under what belief*, he becomes, from the time of such leaving, within the Constitution and laws of the United States, a fugitive from justice.") (emphasis supplied).

[3] Because "there is no prerequisite that the relator be a fugitive in order to seek his extradition," M. Cherif Bassiouni, International Extradition: United States Law and Practice 831 (5th ed. 2007), how narrowly or broadly the term "fugitive" is defined is not determinative of whether extradition can be pursued.

seeking State's law enforcement authorities, rather than that of the individual at issue, or of the State within whose territory he currently resides, or even a disinterested third State, is worthy of some elaboration:

- Although the term "fugitive" colloquially connotes "one who flees or tries to escape," stemming from the Latin *fugere*, meaning "to flee,"[4] the subject may not necessarily have committed a crime (*e.g.*, he may have been charged on erroneous or prejudicial evidence), may not be aware that he is under pursuit by law enforcement authorities, and may not have left a jurisdiction at all.[5]
- The subject must be, or is reasonably believed to be, outside the territory of the State seeking him and beyond its custody or control (or that of an international criminal tribunal, as the case may be);[6] this factor is what imbues the term with its *international* dimension.
- This term is flexible with respect to the relative physical freedom of the subject individual; he could be at large and his specific whereabouts unknown (as is most common), held in detention or confinement by another State (when not acting on behalf of a State that actively seeks his physical recovery, residing openly under the protection of a "safe haven" State or a State otherwise unwilling to arrest the subject, or even located in non-sovereign territory/international space.[7]
- A fugitive *from justice* is an individual wanted by law enforcement authorities for an actual or alleged criminal violation, and therefore, depending on the circumstances and the applicable law, can be distinguished from other types of fugitives, such as fugitive soldiers (those evading military requirements), fugitive debtors (those escaping financial obligations), fugitive slaves (those seeking freedom from physical constraints), and individuals trying to avoid private retribution.

[4] Webster's New World Dictionary 544 (1988). *E.g., Appleyard v. Commw. of Massachusetts*, 203 U.S. 222, 222–23 (1906) (defining a fugitive as one who commits or is charged with a crime in one state and then "leaves it") (municipal case).

[5] For example, a fugitive may have committed the crime at issue beyond the borders of the State pursuing him and simply remained there following the crime. *See* 6 Marjorie M. Whiteman, Digest of International Law 768 (1968) ("The English High Court of Justice, King's Bench Division, held that it is not essential to the concept of 'fugitive' that the accused have fled from the country in which he was alleged to have committed the crime") (citations omitted).

[6] *See* Paul Michell, *English-Speaking Justice: Evolving Responses to Transnat'l Forcible Abduction after* Alvarez-Machain, 29 Cornell Int'l L.J. 383, 390 & n.24 (1996).

[7] This concept is defined at n.48 of the Introduction.

- The subject must have been at least criminally charged (or its functional equivalent); it is not sufficient if he is still merely a suspect under investigation, a material witness in a criminal case,[8] or one whose name appears on a "no-fly" list;[9] and it is of no matter whether the charge was issued publicly or in secret.
- To the extent that the subject was earlier convicted, it makes no difference to this definition whether he was tried *in absentia* or personally appeared in court; whether the convict represented himself or was represented by counsel; or whether as judge, judicial panel, or jury determined his conviction.
- The subject could have relocated to the sovereign or non-sovereign territory in which he is physically present: (i) prior to or contemporaneously with the crime, (ii) after the crime was committed but before charges were brought,[10] (iii) after charges were brought but before being apprehended,[11] (iv) after being apprehended but before or during the trial proceedings, whether during bail or while subject to (evidently insecure) police custody, or (v) after incarceration as a prison escapee.

[8] Under U.S. law, a person who flees a state jurisdiction with the intent to avoid giving testimony in a state criminal proceeding where the underlying offense is punishable by death or constitutes a felony in the relevant jurisdiction is considered a "fugitive," 18 U.S.C. 1073 (2012), but that law is not intended to apply in cases where the person flees to another country. DoJ, *U.S. Attorneys' Manual*, CRM 1780 (Fugitive Felon Act) (2d ed. 2007–3 Supp.).

[9] For example, in August 1989, when Ruben Zuno-Arce, brother-in-law of former Mexican President Luis Echeverria, voluntarily flew from Mexico to San Antonio, Texas, on a business trip, he was arrested some hours after his arrival at a supermarket following surveillance. Notably, Zuno-Arce had not been charged with any crime; rather, he was on a "special list of people believed to be drug traffickers" and was wanted as a "material witness" in the 1985 murder of Drug Enforcement Administration (DEA) agent Enrique Camarena Salazar. Paul Lieberman, "Camarena Case Spotlight Shifts to L.A. Unit's Tactics," *L.A. Times*, May 7, 1990, at A1, A23; Henry Weinstein, "Man Seized in Camarena Case is Kin to Ex-Leader," *L.A. Times*, Aug. 12, 1989.

[10] *See, e.g.*, Whiteman, *supra* n.5, at 768 ("It is apparently contended by Mylonas that since no charges were outstanding in Greece at the time he came to the United States from that country he is therefore not a fugitive seeking asylum and is therefore not subject to the provisions of the [U.S.-Greece] Extradition Treaty. We know of no requirement in international extradition that the individual being sought must have been charged with the offense at the time he left the country which subsequently seeks his extradition.").

[11] Whether following or in anticipation of an indictment a subject fled a State's jurisdiction and was living in secret versus left at a leisurely pace and was living openly could be a relevant factor regarding the appearance of guilt or innocence and for such purposes as tolling time under speedy trial laws (*see supra* n.1), but would not be pertinent to his status as a fugitive.

- The state of mind or motivation of the individual being pursued is irrelevant; he may be in active post-crime flight to avoid capture;[12] he may have crossed an international border unaware that it came on the heels of another's commission of a crime;[13] he may be innocent and yet trying to avoid undeserved punishment because of possible feared misidentification, discrimination, or a case of "guilt by association"; or he may have committed the crime in question yet be unaware that he has been charged and an arrest warrant has been issued[14] (possibly because of a secret indictment).[15]
- The subject must be the ongoing object of pursuit by a State's law enforcement authorities;[16] accordingly, a criminal case must not have been closed, and to the extent the subject has been convicted, his sentence must remain incomplete, including that in the meantime no amnesty has been imposed on the crime(s) at issue,[17] nor has any presidential pardon been granted.
- The length of time the subject has been at large beyond the jurisdiction, custody, and control of the State during its pursuit is immaterial to this

[12] It is notable that, under at least some domestic laws, it is an independent crime to avoid prosecution, custody, or confinement after conviction. *E.g.*, 18 U.S.C. § 1073 (2012) ("Whoever moves or travels in interstate or foreign commerce with intent . . . to avoid prosecution, or custody or confinement after conviction, under the laws of the place from which he flees . . . shall be fined under this title or imprisoned not more than five years, or both.").

[13] Even if captured and tried, such persons may be exonerated at trial or on appeal, and thus any cross-border travel following the commission of a crime would have been purely coincidental. Consequently, unless the individual was a convict who later escaped from incarceration, the use of the term "fugitive offender," which is commonly encountered in the literature, should be avoided as prejudicial and as inconsistent with the legal principle of "innocent until proven guilty."

[14] A State need not show that an alleged offender fled to avoid prosecution or that he was even aware of the charges against him. *White v. Armontrout*, 29 F.3d 357, 359 (8th Cir. 1994) (municipal case).

[15] For example, in August 1999, Austrian plainclothes police officers arrested General Momir Talić, chief of staff of the Bosnian Serb Army, while he was attending a conference at the National Defense Academy in Vienna, unaware that he had been charged in a secret indictment by the ICTY with crimes against humanity for his actions during the 1992–95 Bosnian war. Marlise Simons, "Top Bosnian Serb Officer Arrested for U.N. Tribunal," *N.Y. Times*, Aug. 26, 1999, at A10 (international criminal tribunal case). Secret (or sealed) indictments are discussed at Chapter 9.a.

[16] Michell, *supra* n.6, at 390 & n.24. Among of the most wanted international fugitives today are Ayman al-Zawahiri (terrorism) and Joseph Kony (genocide).

[17] For example, in 1968 France granted amnesty to all crimes committed in connection with the civil upheaval in Algeria in the early 1960s. Axel Knabe, *Double Jeopardy Case Highlights Inconsistencies in Int'l Criminal Law*, 25 IELR 143, 143 (2009).

definition – it could be mere hours or many years[18] – unless, of course, the interested State's domestic statute of limitations corresponding to the crime has run,[19] and the person has thereby lost his criminal status.[20]

- The perspective of State(s) in which the person of interest has (have) nationality, and the State(s) where the crime was committed, or any other State, apart from the one seeking his custody are not relevant to this definition, and therefore this definition is fundamentally subjective.[21]

For shorthand convenience, unless otherwise indicated, any reference to "fugitive" in this study should be understood to constitute an "international fugitive from justice" based on the foregoing definition.

b "Pursuing State" and "Host State"

Labels are required for both the State seeking custody of a fugitive and the State within whose territory a fugitive is presently located. To simplify matters, terms are used herein that identify the relationship between those States whether they are engaged in an extradition *or* a non-extradition exercise. Such uniform terminology is particularly helpful when referring to a State that seeks both extradition and deportation (of an unlawful alien), whether concurrently or sequentially.[22] In the

18 U.S. national George Wright had been at large for forty-one years, living pseudonymously in a seaside village outside of Lisbon with his Portuguese wife before a New York–New Jersey joint task force on fugitives identified him through a fingerprint match in 2011 and the United States requested his extradition. Wright had escaped a New Jersey state prison in August 1970 while serving a sentence for murdering a gas station owner and then, in 1972, while dressed as a priest, led the dramatic hijacking of a Delta Airlines plane eventually to Algiers and demanded the unprecedented sum of US $1 million from an FBI agent he insisted appear dressed in a bathing suit. James Barron, "A Long Life Spent on the Lam," *IHT*, Sept. 30, 2011, at 2.

19 This assumes that the clock did not toll on account of the fugitive's effort to evade detection by law enforcement authorities, as some States do not apply a time bar in instances where an individual has fled from justice. *E.g.*, 18 U.S.C. § 3290 (2012).

20 The fact that an extradition request may be denied by the State in whose territory the fugitive is located based on its interpretation that the statute of limitations has run on the underlying crime does not itself have to alter the subject's fugitive status from the legal perspective of the State seeking his custody. For example, just because a Portuguese court ultimately denied the U.S. extradition request for George Wright reportedly in part on the grounds that the statute of limitations on his murder conviction had run (Barry Hatton, "Portugal Refuses to Send U.S. Fugitive Home," *AP*, Nov. 17, 2011), did not require the United States to remove Wright from its list of wanted fugitives.

21 *See Michell, supra* n.6, at 390 & n.24.

22 *See, e.g.*, "Turkey Revokes Passport of Cleric Based in the U.S.," *INYT*, Feb. 5, 2015, at 5 (reporting that Turkey had just revoked the passport of religious cleric and self-exile

extradition context, the terms typically used to designate these States are the "requesting" (or at times "requisitioning" or "petitioner") State and the "requested" State, respectively.[23] In addition to being inapposite in the non-extradition context, there may be times when those labels can even become *reversed in meaning*, as when the State where the fugitive is located (now in effect the *requesting* State) chooses to reach out to and inquire with a State to which he could be extradited (now in effect the *requested* State), say, because the State where the fugitive is located has no interest itself in prosecuting and yet wants to see justice done.[24]

Alternatively, and typically in the non-extradition context, most scholars and practitioners rely on the terms "forum" (or "prosecuting") State and "asylum" (or "refuge") State to refer, respectively, to the State where a future prosecution will be held and the State that currently has jurisdiction over the subject individual.[25] The use of these terms is not advisable. The term "forum" suggests that that State will provide the prosecution forum in a given case, but in fact the fugitive might never be tried in that State's courts (let alone be transferred at all) and, moreover, there could be multiple States seeking recovery of a fugitive and it is uncertain which, if any, will eventually prevail. Besides, when a State seeks a fugitive to serve out an unfinished sentence, rather than to face prosecution, there would be no role for a judicial "forum" at all. Similarly, the term "asylum" State could generate confusion to the extent that the State is inferred to be providing asylum to a fugitive seeking political refuge or other

Fethullah Gülen, now residing in rural Pennsylvania, "in a push for his deportation," even while awaiting word on his extradition based on an arrest warrant issued by a Turkish court in December 2014).

23 Exceptionally, the European Arrest Warrant (EAW) system (discussed at the beginning of Chapter 4.c) uses the term "issuing State" instead of "requesting State" and "executing State" instead of "requested State." Notwithstanding the treatment herein, the terms, "requesting State" and "requested State," continue to be relevant and accurate when discussing extradition processes, procedures, or relations *exclusively*. The "requesting State" is defined as *the State that seeks physical custody over a fugitive from the State with jurisdiction over him and submits a request for his extradition to that end*, while the "requested State" is defined as *the State with jurisdiction over a fugitive and from which his physical custody is sought via an extradition request.*

24 *See* Claire Mitchell, *The Scope and Operate of the Obligation (Part 2) of* Aut Dedere, aut Judicare: *The Extradite or Prosecute Clause in Int'l Law*, IHEID, Graduate Inst. Publications Online, 2009, ¶ 17, *available at* http://books.openedition.org/iheid/302 (last visited on May 27, 2016) ("if a State does not wish to prosecute the alleged offender itself, it is not precluded from actively seeking another State who is willing to [do so].").

25 *E.g.*, Manuel R. Garcia-Mora, *Criminal Jurisdiction of a State over Fugitives Brought from a Foreign Country by Force or Fraud: A Comparative Study*, 32 Ind. L.J. 427 (1957).

protection, and may even imply a non-national (or non-resident) status of the fugitive, which, again, may not bear out factually.

Accordingly, let us substitute these sets of terms with "pursuing" State and "host" State,[26] and thereby eliminate these unnecessary sources of confusion. A "pursuing State" is to be understood herein as *a State that seeks the prosecution or punishment of a fugitive, prior to any delivery into its own territory, custody or control, whether within or outside the extradition context.* The term "pursuing" directly and functionally links a State in question to the fugitive, regardless of the means of acquisition, intended destination, or ultimate success, while allowing for the possibility that there could be multiple States concurrently seeking the fugitive for charges under their respective domestic laws and, in that case, each could equally be called a "pursuing" State.

The "host State" is to be understood as *the State, other than that of a pursuing State, within whose territory a particular fugitive is currently located, however temporarily, whether within or outside the extradition context.* The term is intended to be neutral, without giving any hint as to the relationship of the fugitive to that State apart from his physical presence, and is not necessarily accompanied by any protection, service, or other benefit.[27] By contrast with "pursuing States," of which there could be one or more in play, in the case of the "host State" there can be only one at any given point in time with regard to a specific fugitive. Accordingly, the term has a convenient variable quality to it such that the fugitive's status can, and does, change when he is, say, on foreign business travel or a passenger on an aircraft that has stopped temporarily in another State's territory for refueling.[28] "Asylum State" does not connote such flexibility.

[26] To this author's knowledge, these terms have not been used before in tandem in this context, although the individual terms can be found sprinkled throughout the international law literature in one reference or another when discussing such varied topics as the "right of hot pursuit" (discussed in Chapter 11.b), refugee matters, and consent to another State's exercise of the use of force on one's territory. New York University Law Professor Margaret Satterthwaite has referred to the "nation where the suspect has taken refuge" as the "host state," but continued to refer to the State with interest in the fugitive's custody as the "requesting state" or "transferring state." Margaret L. Satterthwaite, *The Legal Regime Governing Transfer of Persons in the Fight against Terrorism*, N.Y.U. Public Law and Legal Theory Working Papers, Paper 192, May 1, 2010, at 3, 6.

[27] Indeed, the nationality or immigration status of the fugitive makes no difference as to the designation of the "host" State. The fugitive could be a native-born citizen, a naturalized citizen, a refugee or asylee, a resident alien, a temporary visitor, or even a denaturalized citizen pending deportation.

[28] For example, in the *Savarkar Case* (Fr. v. Gr. Br.), PCA Award, Hague Ct. Rep. (Scott) 276, Feb. 24, 1911, HAGUE CT. REP. 276 (J.B. Scott ed. 1916), when Vinayak Damodar

The denomination of "host State" also avoids any confusion arising from another common term, "territorial State," which refers to *the State where the actual or alleged underlying crime was committed*[29] (*see* discussion of subject matter jurisdiction in Chapter 2.c), rather than to the State where the fugitive is currently located. While the term "custodial State" is also facially appealing, it could imply that the State had physical custody of the accused, but in many instances a request from a pursuing State will be issued before the individual of interest has been located and detained by law enforcement authorities.

c "Transferor State" and "Transferee State"

A pursuing State, once successful, *could* transform into a "forum" (or "adjudicating") State, but for several reasons that terminology is still not recommended. First, as noted above, the term "forum State" assumes that the aim is to seek a fugitive's prosecution, but that is not always the case, as he could be sought for re-incarceration following a prison escape. Second, even if the fugitive is to be prosecuted, the counterpart term "asylum State" (or "requested State") is no longer as useful or accurate, as his delivery and its aftermath have now rendered that term obsolete. Third, the terms "forum State" and "asylum State" fail to distinguish whether the delivery was carried out cooperatively or unilaterally, and in doing so sacrifice some degree of clarity, particularly in the context of specialty (*see* Chapter 7.c.ii) and post-transfer issues (*see* Chapter 13).

To fully address these vernacular concerns while maximizing precision and flexibility, two new terms are proposed. The "transferor State" is herein defined as *the State that is effecting or has effected the cooperative law enforcement delivery of a fugitive by any means into the jurisdiction, custody, or control of another State or an international criminal tribunal.* The counterpart term, "transferee State," is defined as *the State into whose territory, custody, or control a fugitive is being or has been cooperatively delivered by another State or an international criminal tribunal for law enforcement purposes.*[30] These terms encompass not only all forms of

Savarkar, an Indian revolutionary charged with murder, escaped while his ship was docked in Marseilles in the course of an England-to-India voyage, the host State when he was arrested along the port was France, even though Indian Army military police were responsible for escorting him.

[29] Antonio Cassese, International Criminal Law 281 (2003).

[30] Deportation operates under a distinct legal regime and accordingly embraces a specialized set of terms, "Removing State" and "Receiving State," addressed in

extradition but also any informal law enforcement cooperation, cover both intermediate and ultimate destination deliveries, and apply both during and after any such movement of a fugitive between States.[31]

d "Rendition," "Rendering State," and "Rendered State"

Primarily in connection with the U.S. Global War on Terrorism, the term "rendition" has embedded itself in the public consciousness. Unfortunately, however, its meaning has been glossed, if not obfuscated, by the term's most extreme and popular[32] variation – "extraordinary rendition."[33] Because "rendition" is subject to varying understandings and because it has no strict definition under international law,[34] the

Chapter 10.a. As unilateral operations by their nature are not cooperative, they, too, require a separate terminology: "Rendering State" and "Rendered State" (*see* the next section).

[31] To the extent that an international criminal tribunal, rather than a State, effects the transfer of a fugitive under these circumstances, the term "transferor Tribunal" is recommended, and where the recipient of such a State surrender is an international criminal tribunal, it can be referred to as the "transferee Tribunal." (*See* Glossary).

[32] *See* OUP, Oxford Dictionaries website, "Rendition," *available at* https://books.google.com/books?id=anecAQAAQBAJ&pg=PA1504&lpg=PA1504&dq=oxford+dictionaries+%22rendition%22&source=bl&ots=TZiugviNBP&sig=zw4aUtrcgy43iZpzFx4oSjVWuXo&hl=en&sa=X&ved=0ahUKEwi4q4S53LTMAhVIWD4KHWzdBrsQ6AEIOjAF#v=onepage&q=oxford%20dictionaries%20%22rendition%22&f=false (last visited on Apr. 29, 2016) ("The Oxford English Corpus has shown a steady increase in examples throughout the last decade, with a particular rise in the phrase *extraordinary rendition*, which is now the most common collocate of *rendition* by far") (emphasis in original).

[33] This term is defined on pp. 41–42 *infra*.

[34] *Compare* U.K. Parliament, Foreign Affairs Comm., Human Rights Annual Report 2008, Chapter 2: Rendition [hereinafter Hum. Rts. Ann. Rep. 2008] (referring to it as "a political term of art"); *with* E.P. AUGHTERSON, THE LAWS OF AUSTRALIA: JURISDICTIONAL ENFORCEMENT, § 11.10, Part A, at 7 (1995) (noting that the term "rendition," by contrast with "extradition," has "been used in relation to the return of persons between states and territories within a federal system.") *with* MICHAEL FORDE & KIERAN KELLY, EXTRADITION LAW AND TRANSNATIONAL CRIMINAL PROCEDURE 5 (4th ed. 2012) ("under a common understanding . . . two or more states affected enact virtually identical legislation, which provides for handing over those who are sought by the other state or states" citing, by example, the arrangement of the Nordic States since 1962) *with* David B. Ottaway & Don Oberdorfer, "Administration Alters Assassination Ban; In Interview, Webster Reveals Interpretation," *Wash. Post*, Nov. 4, 1989, at A1, A4 (describing use of the term "rendition" by Judge William H. Webster, CIA Director, in 1989, as a "new term" contained in a DoJ legal opinion issued in June 1989, referring to the act of capturing and bringing back to the United States a criminal suspect particularly aimed at allowing the CIA or FBI to seize a terrorist in countries like Lebanon where there is no longer any rule of law or capacity to provide law enforcement or assistance); *and with* Simona Granata, Note, *Review of Judgments and Decisions Delivered in 2005 and 2006 by the European*

positing of a clear and helpful meaning is warranted. "Rendition" herein refers flexibly to *the involuntary physical transfer of an individual of interest by officials or agents of a State from one location or jurisdiction to another for any law enforcement, military, or intelligence purpose.*[35] (An "international rendition" would entail such an involuntary physical transfer *specifically between two States for any law enforcement, military, or intelligence purpose, or between a State and an international criminal tribunal.*)

Notably, under this definition, "rendition" is a neutral term that is not intended to imply necessarily either lawfulness or unlawfulness, as the specific conduct at issue could be positively or negatively sanctioned. Although this definition precludes transfers under immigration law (a separate terminology applies in that instance; see Chapter 10), it does flexibly permit transfers for military or intelligence purposes (although those lie outside the present discourse). By contrast with some common definitions, a rendition need not result in a change of custody between States, but can rather involve the cross-jurisdictional transfer by a single State with retained custody, or simply the relocation of an individual within the territorial borders of the *same* State.

Renditions that result in the individual's transfer to pursuing State territory or into pursuing State custody or control are known herein as "strategic," and *those that result in the individual's transfer to any other location, including into a third State's custody or control, whether on an intermediate basis or as a final destination*, are referred to in this discourse as "tactical."[36] Renditions may be carried out pursuant to extradition or non-extradition proceedings, although the more specific

Court of Human Rights on Subjects Relevant to Int'l Law, 16 ITAL. Y.B. INT'L L. 283, 290 (2006) (renditions are "*unlawful* inter-State transfers of prisoners") (emphasis in original).

35 Although this author has not found any fully satisfactory definition in the literature, for the general notion *see* Michael John Garcia, *Renditions: Constraints Imposed by Laws on Torture*, C.R.S. Report No. 7–5700, Sept. 8, 2009 ("The surrender of a fugitive from one State to another") (citing BLACK'S LAW DICTIONARY 1298–99 (7th ed. 1999)); JORDAN PAUST, ET AL., INTERNATIONAL CRIMINAL LAW 436 (2d ed. 2000) ("when an individual is surrendered by a requested country to a requesting state"); Michell, *supra* n.6, at 388 n.15 (rendition does not include where a State intervenes to evacuate its own nationals from another state because the intent there is protection, not prosecution).

36 An "intermediate rendition" is defined as *the initial and temporary physical transfer of a fugitive to third State territory, custody, or control, where the aim is subsequently to transfer him to pursuing State territory, custody, or control.* All intermediate renditions, therefore, are "tactical" in character, but not all "tactical renditions" qualify as "intermediate."

operational term (*e.g.*, extradition, prisoner exchange, *ad hoc* transfer) is generally used. Note that all renditions constitute operations, but not all operations constitute renditions.

Apart from the "strategic" versus "tactical" distinction above, the term "rendition" can be seen to encompass three operational variants: formal, semi-formal, and informal.[37] Although seldom separated out, such terminological differentiation recognizes noteworthy contrasts that lie within the overall meaning of the term and lends precision to their application in a given context. "Formal rendition" refers to *any rendition carried out pursuant to a formal written agreement between States or between a State and an international criminal tribunal.* These include any transfers undertaken via an extradition treaty or a specialized bilateral agreement (*e.g.*, SOFA).

"Semi-formal rendition" refers to *any rendition handled through an ad hoc, non-treaty-based arrangement that nevertheless involves some legal process.* These renditions would include extradition via comity or reciprocity; arrangements authorized by and executed under domestic law; political arrangements in which fugitive prisoners are exchanged; and certain facilitated operations by a third State while the person is being transited through its territory.

"Informal rendition" refers to *any rendition handled absent any legal process.* Informal rendition can be sub-divided based on the nature of participation into four types: (i) *unilateral*, when conducted by pursuing State officials or agents without the participation, knowledge, or consent of the host State; (ii) *consensual*, when conducted exclusively by pursuing State officials or agents, but *with* the prior consent of the host State, often via a "wink and a nod"; (iii) *surrogate*, when conducted exclusively by host State officials or agents at the pursuing State's behest; and (iv) *joint*, when conducted by pursuing and host State officials or agents working together. In all of these instances except the unilateral scenario, there is some degree of cooperation (or complicity, as the case may be) on the part of the host State. Defined in this disaggregated manner, contrary to some legal commentary, "informal renditions" may well entail operations beyond unilateral abductions alone.

[37] *Cf.* Satterthwaite, *supra* n.26, at 6 n.20 (indicating that while her article defines the term "rendition" only to encompass informal transfers, the author acknowledges that other scholars use the term to refer to both formal and informal transfers); John F. Murphy, Punishing International Terrorists: The Legal Framework for Policy Initiatives 36 (1985) (rendition can consist of both formal and informal transfers).

To the extent a pursuing State informally renders a fugitive by unilateral means, terminology is required to denominate the two States involved, independent of the "transferor State" and "transferee State" which apply only in the context of *cooperative* deliveries.[38] The term "rendering State" is used herein to refer to *a pursuing State that unilaterally is transferring or has transferred a fugitive from host State territory into its own territory, custody, or control.* A "rendered State" refers to its mirror image, that is, *the former host State from whose territory a pursuing State unilaterally is transferring or has transferred a fugitive into its own territory, custody, or control.*[39]

There are also two other well-known variants of "rendition" that merit mention, if only to eliminate potential confusion. The first, "extraordinary rendition," is not relevant to this discourse. An "extraordinary rendition" refers to *"the extra-judicial transfer of persons from one jurisdiction or State to another, for the purposes of detention and interrogation outside the normal legal system, where there [is] a real risk of torture or cruel, inhuman or degrading treatment."*[40] As this book is not concerned with mere

[38] The use of "transferor State" and "transferee State" in the unilateral rendition context could prove problematic and confusing, as the pursuing State would in effect play both the role of the transferor State and the transferee State under such a scenario.

[39] Concededly, the "rendered State" is not technically the object of the rendering – the fugitive is – but alternative formulations are cumbersome, the use of the word "State" distinguishes it from the rendered "individual," and the context and meaning is clear enough. Separately, as the definition of "rendition" does not encompass *deliveries made by serendipity or at the initiative of the host State or an international criminal tribunal or by a private party, including one or more government officials operating in a non-official capacity or* ultra vires, *or those in which a fugitive arrives on his own volition, even if acting upon innocently mistaken information or representations*, the beneficiary State requires a specialized label to capture such scenarios; the recommended term is "fortuitously acquiring State." Because such a State may elect not to grant demands for the fugitive's return to the State from which he came, the former host State may determine that the fortuitously acquiring State has effectively ratified the physical transfer and accordingly take retaliatory or other adverse measures against it. *See* Chapter 13.b.

[40] This definition was first adopted by the ECtHR in *Ahmad and Others v. U.K.*, Appl. Nos. 24027/07, 11949/08, 36742/08, 66911/09, and 67354/09, 56 EHRR, Apr. 10, 2012 (final issued on Sept. 24, 2012), and was later embraced by the U.K. Intelligence and Security Committee, and then again by the Grand Chamber of the ECtHR in *El-Masri v. Former Yugoslav Repub. of Macedonia*, Appl. No. 39630/09, 57 EHRR, Dec. 13, 2012. *See also* Hum. Rts. Ann. Rep. 2008, *supra* n.34, Ch. 2: Rendition, ¶ 11 ("The phrase 'Extraordinary Rendition' is generally used to describe activities involving the clandestine and deliberate transfer of terrorist subjects to foreign countries for interrogation using torture [or] inhuman or degrading treatment in order to gain intelligence for the 'war against terrorism'. The process exists entirely outside normal, formal extradition proceedings. It is also referred to as 'torture by proxy' or 'outsourcing torture'") (supplied by the House of Commons Library). By contrast, according to former senior CIA legal counsel John Rizzo, an "extraordinary rendition" "just

criminal suspects *or* with any intended post-fugitive-delivery scenario, apart from prosecution or from punishment for those who have yet to serve their full, legally authorized sentence,[41] such operations necessarily lie outside the scope of this inquiry.

The second related term, "irregular rendition" (or its functional equivalent "irregular seizure"),[42] is a slippery and overbroad term that has no discernible legal significance, and thereby is dispensed with in the present treatment.[43] The term appears to refer obliquely to the universe of renditions that are not conventionally configured. It is unclear whether the term is intended to include only unlawful methods (in which case it should simply say so) or perhaps less conventionally exercised but still lawful ones as well (but then why mix the two?).[44] At a minimum, however, the term would appear to embrace extraordinary renditions, which are not relevant to this inquiry. It is also at least arguable that such unconventional methods, which presumably include some combination of informal renditions[45] when taken in the aggregate,

amounts to a pejorative redundancy" as "it is a practice [*i.e.*, rendition] that has been employed through the years in extraordinary circumstances, including "outside normal judicial processes such as extradition." JOHN RIZZO, COMPANY MAN: THIRTY YEARS OF CONTROVERSY AND CRISIS IN THE CIA 259–60 (2014).

41 Two well-known alleged examples of extraordinary rendition cases include those of: (i) Maher Arar, a Canadian citizen, who was transferred from U.S. to Syrian custody on suspicion of having a connection to terrorism, Bruce Zagaris, *Canada Protests Deportation of Canadian Citizen to Syria*, 20 IELR 10 (2004); and (ii) Khaled El-Masri, a German citizen who was seized by U.S. officials or agents while on holiday in Macedonia and taken to Afghanistan. Bruce Zagaris, *ACLU Sues Former CIA Director on Extraordinary Rendition*, 22 IELR 56–57 (2006).

42 *E.g., United States v. Sobell*, 142 F. Supp. 515, 522 (S.D.N.Y. 1956), *aff'd*, 244 F.2d 520 (2d Cir.), *cert. denied*, 355 U.S. 873 (1957), *reh'g denied*, 355 U.S. 920 (1958).

43 One treatise author has defined "irregular rendition" as when an "individual [is] taken from one country to another as a criminal suspect against [his] free will and without consent of the country from which [he is] taken." PAUST, *supra* n.35, at 436. Several problems arise with such a definition, including, for instance, whether the word "taken" refers solely to seizures but not to lures, whether the person taken could be an indictee or someone who had been previously convicted of a crime but escaped before his sentence was completed rather than strictly a "suspect," and whether a State's acquiescence after the fact would negate its "irregular" status.

44 *See* Paul Arnell, Male Captus Bene Detentus *in Scotland*, THE JURIDICAL REV. 251, 254 n.19 (2004) (the term implies wrongful conduct, but it could still be lawful but just not follow extradition procedures).

45 *See* Abraham Abramovsky, *Extraterritorial Abductions: America's "Catch and Snatch" Policy Run Amok*, 31 VA. J. INT'L L. 151, 155 (1991) (defining "irregular rendition" as "an apprehension that receives the tacit approval or acquiescence of the country from which the defendant is rendered" versus an "abduction," which operates absent any consultation with a responsible representative of a host State).

are not so uncommon in practice.[46] Furthermore, it is far more desirable to treat each case on an individual basis in evaluating its lawfulness than to characterize it as "irregular," and thereby in effect cast doubt as to the propriety of such conduct on its face.

e "Extradition" and "Summary Extradition"

Another term that warrants a close examination at this juncture is "extradition."[47] That term has been subject to multiple definitions,[48] none of which has assumed a position of unquestioned primacy, and each of which regrettably is not entirely precise or complete. This study proposes a new definition that seeks to rectify those defects. The following definition of (*de jure*) "extradition" will be used throughout this discourse: *a cooperative law enforcement process by which the physical custody of a person: (i) charged with committing a crime or (ii) convicted of a crime whose punishment has not yet been determined or fully served, is formally transferred, directly or indirectly, by authorities of one State to those of another at the request of the latter for the purpose of prosecution or punishment, respectively.*[49]

Let us now unpack this definition to appreciate its essential elements and dimensions, as a proper definition should account for each of them.

46 *See* Ethan A. Nadelmann, Cops Across Borders: The Internationalization of U.S. Criminal Law Enforcement 437 (1993) ("Some Justice Department officials have claimed that . . . 'irregular rendition' is largely a misnomer because rendition of fugitives by means other than an extradition treaty is neither illegal nor unusual"); J.E. Baker, In the Common Defense: National Security Law for Perilous Times 165 (2007) ("Informal processes of transfer are the prevalent method for obtaining custody over fugitives abroad").

47 The term first officially surfaced in the late 1700s in France. Forde & Kelly, *supra* n.34, at 1 (1791 in France); Ivor Stanbrook & Clive Stanbrook, Extradition: Law and Practice 4 (2d ed. 2000) (1781 in a treaty between Louis XVI of France and Prince-Bishopric of Basel); Christopher L. Blakesley, Terrorism, drugs, International Law, and the Protection of Human Liberty: A Comparative Study of International Law, Its Nature, Role, and Impact in Matters of Terrorism, Drug Trafficking, War, and Extradition 171–72 (1992) [hereinafter Blakesley, Comparative Study] (although the term was not used until the late 18th century, the concept was around long before).

48 Curiously, in none of the international or regional conventions obligating States to "extradite or prosecute" under the principle known as *aut dedere aut judicare* (discussed in Chapters 2.c.ii and 9.c) is the term "extradite" ever defined. Mitchell, *supra* n.24, ¶ 5.

49 This definition specifically pertains to "*international* extradition," as extradition also can occur domestically within a given State between sub-national entities.

- Extradition constitutes a process, means, or legal device[50] – it does not itself render underlying acts or omissions unlawful,[51] confirm the guilt of the extradited individual (who of course ultimately may be exonerated at trial)[52], or constitute punishment for an offense.[53]
- Extradition is to be used exclusively for criminal law enforcement purposes,[54] rather than for diplomatic, military, intelligence collection,[55] immigration, or other reasons, such as the enforcement of *civil* judgments.[56]

50 Most definitions refer to extradition as a "process," *see, e.g.*, American Law Inst., Restatement (Third) of the Foreign Relations Law of the United States, May 14, 1986, Subchapter B (Extradition), Intro. Note, at 556–57 [hereinafter Restatement (Third)]; Arvinder Sambei & John R.W.D. Jones, Extradition Law Handbook 1 (2005), or a "legal device." M. Cherif Bassiouni, *Unlawful Seizures and Irregular Rendition Devices as Alternatives to Extradition*, 7 Vand. J. Transnat'l L. 25, 25 (1973) [hereinafter Bassiouni, *Unlawful Seizures*]. Despite colloquial usage to the contrary and reliance by some States on the non-intuitive term "passive extradition" (*see* Glossary), the act of extradition itself is carried out in one direction by the transferor State. That is to say the transferee State does not extradite *per se*, but rather is the custodial recipient of the extraditee.

51 *See* Whiteman, *supra* n.5, at 753 ("Extradition treaties do not, of course, make acts crimes.").

52 *E.g.*, "Portillo Found Not Guilty," *Central American Politics Blogspot*, May 10, 2011, *available at* http://centralamericanpolitics.blogspot.com/2011/05/portillo-found-not-guitly.html (last visited on May 27, 2016) (after his extradition from Mexico, former Guatemalan President Alfonso Portillo (2000–04) was exonerated by a Guatemalan court on embezzlement charges due reportedly to false testimony by the prosecution's two key witnesses).

53 *See United States ex rel. Oppenheim v. Hecht*, 16 F.2d 955, 956 (2d Cir.) ("extradition is not punishment for crime, though such punishment may follow extradition"), *cert. denied*, 273 U.S. 769 (1927).

54 According to a leading expert, extradition is one of eight recognized forms of inter-State law enforcement cooperation; the other seven are: (i) legal assistance; (ii) execution of foreign penal sentences; (iii) recognition of foreign penal judgments; (iv) transfer of criminal proceedings; (v) freezing and seizing of assets deriving from criminal conduct; (vi) intelligence and law enforcement information-sharing; and (vii) regional and sub-regional "judicial spaces" (*e.g.*, the E.U., OAS, and the League of Arab States). M. Cherif Bassiouni, Introduction to International Criminal Law 333 (2003). Other forms of cross-border cooperation arguably could include joint planning operations, skills transfers and resource burden-sharing, harmonizing laws and policies, and advocacy and networking activities.

55 *See, e.g.*, Bruce Zagaris, *British Appellate Court Allows Algerian Pilot Held on U.S. Extradition Charges to Pursue Compensation Claims*, 24 IELR 132, 132–33 (2008) (discussing how in February 2008 after Lotfi Raissi, the first individual formally accused of a connection to the September 11, 2001, attacks on the United States, was released from extended detention and sought compensation, a British appeals court found that the United States had subverted the extradition process to "secure his presence" in the United States for the purpose of investigating the terrorist attacks rather than prosecuting him for the offenses on which his extradition was based).

56 Whiteman, *supra* n.5, at 727.

- The aim of an extradition must specifically be to bring a person to trial, or to have him serve a criminal sentence previously meted out[57] (or possibly have the punishment determined first, in the event he escaped between conviction and sentencing), rather than to, say, solely interrogate him, remove him from the field of operations, or punish him arbitrarily.[58]
- The person whose custody is being transferred must have been charged or convicted[59] of a crime (in the latter instance whose punishment has not yet been determined or fully served)[60], rather than being a mere suspect in a crime[61] or wanted for questioning as a material witness.[62]
- Extradition must stem from some type of punishable conduct,[63] although typically minor offenses do not qualify;[64] it is not limited to

[57] *See* MICHAEL ABBELL, EXTRADITION TO AND FROM THE UNITED STATES 47 (2010) (discussing U.S. law and the limited purposes that extradition must serve); *e.g.*, Mary Anne Weaver, "Terrorist's Extradition Ends Greek Legal Battle," *Wash. Post*, Oct. 4, 1976, at 24 (Rolf Pohle, a member of the West German Baader-Meinhof terrorist group, was extradited by Greece to West Germany in order to complete five years of a six-and-a-half-year prison term).

[58] A number of definitions of "extradition," while otherwise accurate, remain incomplete by failing to reference the objective of this cooperative law enforcement mechanism. In addition, in connection with its request, the pursuing State typically will represent its competence to prosecute or punish the subject individual, but such capacity is not a definitional requirement and may, as a factual matter, not bear out. This is one flaw in the definition propounded by the U.S. Supreme Court in an opinion rendered more than a century ago. *See Terlinden v. Ames*, 184 U.S. 270, 289 (1902) ("The surrender by one nation to another of an individual accused or convicted of an offense outside of its own territory, and within the territorial jurisdiction of the other, which, *being competent to try and to punish him*, demands his surrender") (emphasis supplied).

[59] CLIVE NICHOLLS, ET AL., EDS., THE LAW OF EXTRADITION AND MUTUAL ASSISTANCE 17 (2d ed. 2007). Sometimes a dispute will arise regarding whether a person has been formally charged. *E.g., Emami v. U.S. Dist. Ct.*, 834 F.2d 1444 (9th Cir. 1987). Many extraditions involve the transfer of convicted persons who have since escaped from prison or have been tried *in absentia* and found guilty of the charges lodged against them.

[60] *See* FORDE & KELLY, *supra* n.34, at 1 ("Extradition may be loosely defined as a formal process based on international agreement whereby a person in one country, who is wanted in another country to stand trial *or to be sentenced, or to serve imprisonment or other punishment there*, is handed over by the authorities in the former country to officials in the latter") (emphasis supplied).

[61] BLAKESLEY, COMPARATIVE STUDY, *supra* n.47, at 171.

[62] NICHOLLS, *supra* n.59, at 17; *see also* n.24 in the Introduction and n.8 in Chapter 1.

[63] *E.g.*, U.N. Model Treaty on Extradition, Dec. 14, 1991, art. 2, UNGA Res. 45/116, Annex, 45 U.N. GAOR Supp. (No. 49A), at 212, U.N. Doc. A/45/49 (1990), *reprinted in* 30 ILM 1407.

[64] *See* RESTATEMENT (THIRD), *supra* n.50, § 475, cmt. c ("Extradition is generally granted only for serious crimes, usually those punishable in both the requesting and the requested state by imprisonment for one year or more"); *e.g.*, Katherine Shaver, "A Murder's Long Shadow," *Wash. Post*, Sept. 29, 2007 (discussing how Sol Sheinbein, who was charged with the misdemeanor of obstructing a police investigation related to his son Samuel's

common crimes, and may include ones that might likewise fall within the jurisdiction of international criminal tribunals, such as war crimes or crimes against humanity.[65]

- Extradition takes place between functioning States[66] – *not* between a State and either a sub-national entity (*e.g.*, municipality, state, county, or province)[67] or a supranational body (including an international or regional tribunal),[68] let alone between any two such non-State entities *or* involving an entity no longer recognized as a State by the international community.[69]
- It is a cooperative mechanism that calls upon States to work in a coordinated manner,[70] and is therefore not based on unilateral efforts to transfer an individual's custody;[71] sometimes, it even involves

murder charge, may not be subject to extradition for such a relatively minor crime). *See* discussion of extraditable crimes in Chapter 5.a.i.

65 Barbara M. Yarnold, International Fugitives: A New Role for the International Court of Justice 12 (1991).

66 Even where a State's sovereignty is compromised due to military occupation or other foreign control, extradition may still obtain. *E.g.*, 18 U.S.C. 3185 (2012) (Fugitives from Country Under Control of United States into the United States); *In re Kraussman*, 130 F. Supp. 926, 928–29 (D. Conn. 1955).

67 Hong Kong presents an anomaly. Although the United States and Hong Kong executed an extradition treaty in December 1996, Agreement Between the United States of America and the Gov't of Hong Kong for the Surrender of Fugitive Offenders, Dec. 20, 1996, T.I.A.S. 98–121, the unprecedented agreement was struck while Hong Kong was still under the control of the United Kingdom (its ninety-nine-year territorial lease did not end until July 1, 1997), the People's Republic of China (PRC) authorized the arrangement, and Hong Kong holds a unique status within the PRC as a Special Administrative Region (SAR) with an unusually high degree of autonomy.

To the extent that historical instances exist in which a U.S. state directly, albeit improperly, arranged for the direct transfer of a fugitive from a foreign State, these would be more properly characterized as semi-formal renditions as opposed to extraditions.

68 *See* discussion of the term "surrender" at pp. 52–54. Notably, the June 2003 Agreement on Extradition between the European Union and the United States, June 25, 2003, S. Treaty Doc. 109–14, operates as a "framework agreement" that cals upon individual E.U. member States to amend or supplement, as needed, their respective bilateral treaties with the United States to make them consistent with the provisions set forth in the E.U.-U.S. Extradition Agreement. Accordingly, extradition does not take place between the E.U. and the United States, but rather between individual E.U. itself member States and the United States.

69 Whiteman, *supra* n.5, at 769.

70 *See* Valerie Epps, *The Development of the Conceptual Framework Supporting Int'l Extradition*, 25 Loy. L.A. Int'l & Comp. L. Rev. 369, 372 (2003) (characterizing extradition in one sense as "an agreement [by the host State] to operate as the police force and the initial judicial hearing officer for the requesting [pursuing] state.").

71 *See* James W. Moeller, *United States Treatment of Alleged Nazi War Criminals: Int'l Law, Immigration Law, and the Need for Int'l Cooperation*, 25 Va. J. Int'l L. 793, 803 (1985)

negotiated compromises in which the extradition is made on a conditional basis.[72]

- Extradition entails the government-to-government transfer[73] between the *authorities* of two States,[74] as opposed to the *States* themselves, as a charged person or convicted criminal technically could be turned over to pursuing State officials within host State territory, in non-sovereign territory/international space, or even inside the geographical borders of a third State.[75]
- An extradition request need not be made by the authorities of the fugitive's homeland or country of residence, as is often assumed because it is the most common scenario, but rather could be made by

(extradition requires a request by one State and the return by another). By contrast, deportation or exclusion procedures, undertaken pursuant to a State's domestic laws, entail the unilateral removal of an individual from that State's territory with only passive participation, in principle, on the part of the receiving State. *See* n.59 and accompanying text in Chapter 10. Unilateral alternatives to extradition, as shall be seen in Chapter 12, likewise take place absent inter-State cooperation.

72 *See* Dutch Extradition Law (1967), Act of Mar. 9, 1967, Stb. 139, art. 4(2), *reprinted in* BERT SWART & ANDRE KLIP EDS., INTERNATIONAL CRIMINAL LAW IN THE NETHERLANDS 267–86 (1997) (providing for conditional extradition); Michael Plachta, *The Lockerbie Case: The Role of the Security Council in Enforcing the Principle* Aut Dedere Aut Judicare, 12 EJIL 125, 130 & n.15 (2001) (noting how extraditions can arise out of compromises); *e.g.*, Bruce Zagaris, *Mexico Extradites Mexican National Wanted for Murdering U.S. Drug Agent*, 21 IELR 137, 137–38 (2005) (in January 2005, U.S. prosecutors agreed to recommend that any prospective sentence include the possibility of parole, in connection with the extradition of Augustin Vásquez Mendoza, a Mexican national suspected of conspiring to murder an undercover U.S. drug agent in Arizona in 1994, in order to accommodate a Mexican Supreme Court ruling that barred the extradition of individuals facing life sentences abroad). Conditional extradition is defined herein as *the host State's agreement to extradite a fugitive to a pursuing State only on one or more stipulated conditions (e.g., that he be retried in the event of a prior* in absentia *conviction or that a host State national serve any imposed sentence in his own country).*

73 A fugitive's voluntary return through *private* arrangements, alternatives to extradition does not qualify as extradition. STANBROOK & STANBROOK, *supra* n.47, at 60.

74 *See* SIR ROBERT JENNINGS & SIR ARTHUR WATTS, EDS., 1 OPPENHEIM'S INTERNATIONAL LAW 960 (9th ed. 1992) (describing extradition as the handing over of a fugitive between the respective police authorities of the two States).

75 *See* Donna E. Arzt, *The Lockerbie 'Extradition by Analogy' Agreement: 'Exceptional Measure' or Template for Transnat'l Criminal Justice?*, 18 AM. U. INT'L L. REV. 163, 167–68 (2002) (discussing the *Lockerbie Case*, where an extradition was effected between Dutch and Scottish authorities, allowing for the criminal prosecution of two Libyan nationals before a Scottish judicial panel in a courtroom on a former NATO airfield in the Netherlands; this was notably "the first time that a national civilian court had ever conducted an entire criminal trial in the territory of another sovereign country."). Failure to account for this factor is a common oversight in many definitions of extradition.

the authorities of *any State* with subject matter jurisdiction wishing to prosecute, and/or punish the subject individual.[76]

- It is not necessary, no matter how common, that extradition be effected via a treaty, whether bilateral or multilateral;[77] it may also occur by means of comity, reciprocity, or other agreements or arrangements, even possibly indirectly.[78]
- Extradition consists solely of a physical transfer; while it typically entails an arrest of an individual beforehand, such antecedent action is not technically part of the extradition process itself,[79] nor is the prosecution, sentencing, and/or punishment that may follow.[80]
- Extradition must entail a *formal* transfer of custody in which an individual is physically passed through means and channels officially established and intended for that purpose.[81]
- Extradition is triggered by a request from a pursuing State,[82] reflecting its national interest, and thereby marking an important distinction

[76] *E.g.*, AP, "E.U. Court Rules for Extradition of British Hacker to U.S.," *IHT*, Aug. 28, 2008 (discussing the case of British national Gary McKinnon who, by virtue of a U.S. extradition request, in the words of his counsel, faced "the prospect of prosecution and imprisonment thousands of miles away from his family in a country in which he has never set foot.").

[77] *See* the variety of extradition and extradition-like vehicles discussed in Chapter 4.c.

[78] An "indirect extradition" is an *extradition between States that lack diplomatic relations with one another, and therefore all related communications and the physical transfer itself occur via an intermediary party.* For example, in the *Pan Am 103/Lockerbie Case* (discussed extensively in Chapter 8.c), the United States and the United Kingdom submitted an extradition request to Libya with whom they lacked diplomatic relations via the Belgian Embassy in Tripoli to turn over two Libyan suspects in the bombing (Fhimah and al-Megrahi). Plachta, *supra* n.72, at 126.

[79] This is a superfluous feature of the Restatement (Third)'s definition: "Extradition is the process by which a person charged with or convicted of a crime under the law of one state is *arrested* in another state and returned for trial or punishment." Restatement (Third), *supra* n.50, at 556–57 (emphasis supplied).

[80] Geoff Gilbert, Responding to International Crime 5 (2006).

[81] Many definitions of "extradition" omit this requisite element. *Informal law enforcement* transfers of fugitives are addressed in Chapter 11 as a full-scale alternative to extradition.

[82] *See* Jennings & Watts, *supra* n.74, at 959 (extradition is granted only if asked for); Whiteman, *supra* n.5, at 727; *Fong Yue Ting v. United States*, 149 U.S. 698, 709 (1893); *Stevenson v. United States*, 381 F.2d 142, 144 (9th Cir. 1967) ("[A] demand in some form by the one country upon the other is required, in order to distinguish extradition from the unilateral act of one country, for its own purposes, deporting or otherwise unilaterally removing unwelcome aliens"); Conv. on Legal Aid and Legal Relations in Civil, Family and Crim. of the Commonwealth of Independent States, Jan. 22, 1993, art. 56 (extradition obligations require an underlying "request"). Some States draw a distinction between so-called "active" and "passive" extradition; under that construct, an "active extradition" is the *extradition process undertaken by, and from the perspective of, a* pursuing *State,*

with immigration-based procedures, which are generally precipitated by, or at least must be legally justified based on, host State concerns.[83]

The term "summary," as used in such contexts as trials, convictions, and executions, generally means shortened in time or immediate, as distinct from occurring within the ordinary course. Consistent with that usage, a "summary extradition" (or alternatively referred to as a "simplified extradition procedure") is, in effect, a short-cut that bypasses much of the typical legal process associated with this particular law enforcement modality.[84]

Perhaps surprisingly, subjects do not always insist on an extradition hearing, such as when they expect opportunities or benefits in the pursuing State, such as more favorable judicial treatment, a shorter prospective length or preferred conditions of incarceration, or where they are keen to prove their innocence. A fugitive also may consent to an expeditious extradition in order to be closer to family or friends in the pursuing State at issue, or because he does not have the funds (or does not choose to spend them) with respect to challenging the extradition.[85]

"Summary extradition" is defined herein simply as *an expedited or abbreviated extradition, which may be formally or informally executed.*[86] Accordingly, a summary extradition need not have nefarious motives or

commencing with the submission of an extradition request, while *"passive extradition"* is *the extradition process undertaken by, and from the perspective of, the* host *State, commencing with the receipt of an extradition request.*

83 *See* discussion of removal procedures in Chapter 10.

84 *See* Stanbrook & Stanbrook, *supra* n.47, at 60.

85 *See, e.g.*, Bruce Zagaris, *Turkey Requests Iraqi Extradition of Two Islamists for 2003 Attack*, 21 IELR 356, 356–57 (2005) (counsel for two Turkish Islamists detained at Abu Ghraib prison in Iraq and sought by Turkey argued for their return to Turkey); Coggle Gibbons, "Deuss in Court Again Amid Extradition Moves," *Bermuda Sun*, Oct. 18, 2006 (in October 2006, following his legal defeat in contesting extradition, oil executive and banker John Deuss voluntarily returned through official channels from Bermuda to his native Netherlands to face charges related to the diversion of public funds into his private bank account).

86 *See* CoE, Comm. of Ministers, *Recommendation No. R (80) 7 to Member States Concerning the Practical Application of the European Conv. on Extradition*, adopted June 27, 1980, *available at* CoE, *Extradition: European Standards – Explanatory Notes and Minimum Standards*, Dec. 2006, at 162 ("With a view to expediting extradition and keeping the period of provisional arrest as short as possible, consideration should be given to the use of a summary procedure enabling the rapid surrender of the person sought without following ordinary extradition procedures, provided that the person concerned consents to it"); *e.g.*, Treaty on Extradition, U.S.-Mex., May 4, 1978, art. 18, 31 U.S.T. 5059, T.I.A.S. 9656, *reprinted in* 17 ILM 1058 (1978) (if a person consents to extradition, he may be extradited on an expedited or summary basis without the need for further proceedings); Thailand Extradition Act 2551 (C.E. 2008), § 28 ("If the extradition case is in the course of proceeding at any court and the person expresses consent before the court for extradition, the trial

be executed arbitrarily. The most common type is a consented return in which the transfer occurs expeditiously,[87] dispensing with the production of documentation or an extradition hearing.[88] As a general rule, the consent must be informed, which means the subject needs to be advised in advance of the conditions and consequences of his consent;[89] for example, his consent may or may not be retractable[90] and he may or may not be entitled to preserve his treaty-based defenses for use at criminal trial, notably including the right to invoke the specialty provision.[91] Nor is consent necessarily an automatic ticket to summary extradition, as the host State may harbor concerns about the permissibility of the extradition itself and therefore insist on a court hearing.[92]

f "*De Facto* Extradition" and "Disguised Extradition"

"*De facto* extradition," by contrast with *de jure* extradition (discussed *supra*), can be defined as follows: *a State's formal or informal exercise of non-extradition-related laws, authorities, or administrative procedures*

proceeding at the court shall not be required and the order of detention for extradition shall be issued under Section 22.").

[87] *See, e.g.*, Conv. Drawn up on the Basis of Article K.3 of the Treaty on European Union, on Simplified Extradition Procedure between the Member States of the E.U., Mar. 30, 1995, art. 11, *O.J.C.* 78 [hereinafter Simplified Procedure Conv.] (extradition to occur within twenty days of consent provided).

[88] A consented extradition is to be distinguished from a *waiver* of formal extradition proceedings in which, where an applicable treaty provides for it – and most contemporary ones do – and the fugitive signs an affidavit to that effect, he relinquishes *all* treaty-based rights and technically returns outside of the extradition context. Ronald J. Hedges, *Int'l Extradition: A Guide for Judges*, at 8–10 (Fed. Judicial Center 2014); *e.g.*, *Soapa Case*, Sup. Ct., Arg., Mar. 1928, 150 *Fallos* 316, *reprinted in* [1927–28] 4 ANN. DIG. PUB. INT'L L. CASES 347, 347 (A.D. McNair & H. Lauterpacht eds. 1931) ("the affected party could validly waive, for his personal advantage, as he has done, the requirements of that [extradition] proceeding, as such waiver does not affect the public order nor infringe upon the rights of third parties.").

[89] *See* CoE Comm. of Experts on the Operation of European Convs. on Co-operation in Crim. Matters, Summ. Report of the 56th mtg. of the PC-OC, May 12–14, 2009, ¶ 69 (requiring free and informed consent).

[90] *E.g.*, Simplified Procedure Conv., *supra* n.87, art. 7(4) (consent cannot be revoked).

[91] *Compare* Treaty on Extradition, U.S.-Mexico, May 4, 1978, art. 18, 31 U.S.T. 5059, T.I.A.S. 9656, *reprinted in* 17 ILM 1058 (1978) (specialty provision inapplicable in connection with summary extradition) *with* Agreement Between the United States of America and the Government of Hong Kong for the Surrender of Fugitive Offenders, Dec. 20, 1996, art. 18, T.I.A.S. 98-121 (to the extent required by the requested party's [host State's] domestic law, the specialty provision applies).

[92] *Macedonia Law on Int'l Cooperation on Crim. Matters, Official Gazette of the RM No.* 124/2010, Sept. 20, 2010, art. 72(1) (requiring public prosecutor's opinion on the matter).

that yields the delivery of a fugitive directly or indirectly to a State with a law enforcement interest in him. Therefore *de facto* extradition is a neutral term that does not necessarily connote either lawfulness or unlawfulness or characterize benificently or nefariously a State's motivations (which cannot always be ascertained in any event), but merely indicates that the functional upshot of extradition[93] has been achieved by means that were designed for other purposes.[94]

De facto extradition can occur in the presence or absence of an extradition treaty,[95] as a legitimate contingency option when extradition has failed or is reasonably expected to fail (for example, where no other State is willing to receive an alien subject to removal and the host State has complied with all other applicable international legal obligations), or as a deliberate bypass of an otherwise available but undesirable extradition procedure. It is most often effected under a State's immigration laws, but also sometimes pursuant to other law enforcement authorities or procedures (*e.g.*, a cross-border handover of a fugitive between cooperating law enforcement officials or the host State configuring a fugitive's airline flight schedule to ensure he lands in pursuing State territory).

Disguised extradition[96] is a term closely associated but not co-extensive with *de facto* extradition, although the two terms often are conflated.[97]

[93] By way of illustration, when the United States deported Mousa Mohammed Abu Marzook (Abu Marzook), the then-political leader of Hamas, to Jordan in May 1997 because Jordan agreed to receive him unconditionally and had no intention of prosecuting or punishing him (Neil MacFarquhar, "Jordan to Let Terror Suspect Held in U.S. Into Kingdom," *N.Y. Times*, May 1, 1997), that delivery did *not* constitute *de facto* extradition.

[94] For example, in February 1983, absent an extradition treaty between France and Bolivia, Bolivia relied on its domestic removal authorities to deport Klaus Barbie to France, where he was wanted for crimes against humanity for his Gestapo activities in Lyon. "Barbie Case May Open Old Wounds in France," *The Milwaukee Journal*, Feb. 9, 1983, at 9; Richard Bernstein, "As the Trial of Barbie Begins, France Also Is Being Judged," *N.Y. Times*, May 11, 1987.

[95] Satyadeva Bedi, Extradition: A Treatise on the Laws Relevant to the Fugitive Offenders Within and With the Commonwealth Countries 407 (2002).

[96] This term appears to have been first used in 1860. *See* Ivan Anthony Shearer, Extradition in International Law 78 n.2 (1971) (dating the term "*extradition déguisée*" to a French court judgment of that year (citing André Decocq, *La livraison des délinquants en dehors du droit commun de l'extradition*, Revue Critique de Droit International Privé 411 (1964)).

[97] *See, e.g.*, M. Cherif Bassiouni, International Extradition and World Public Order 133 (1974) [hereinafter Bassiouni, World Public Order] (defining "disguised extradition" as "[t]he process by which a person is placed in such a condition that he falls or is likely to fall under the control of authorities of a state which has an interest in subjecting that person to its jurisdictional control"); Terry Richard Kane, *Prosecuting Int'l Terrorists in United States Courts: Gaining the Jurisdictional Threshold*, 12 Yale J. Int'l L.

"Disguised extradition" is rather best understood *as a subset of* de facto *extradition that entails a purposeful circumvention of extradition laws or treaties by the host State to deliver a fugitive directly or indirectly to a State with a law enforcement interest in him, most commonly via immigration laws.*[98] Indeed, the word "disguised" implies such a hidden motive, and the case law overall reflects that understanding. This concept will be discussed more extensively in Part V in connection with full-scale alternatives to extradition.

g "Surrender"

"Surrender"[99] is a term often used synonymously with "extradition." There are two problems with such treatment. First, "surrender" is a broader and looser term than "extradition," as the former could be used to describe not only extraditions, but also other types of semi-formal or informal renditions or even deportations. Second, even assuming the two terms were functionally equivalent, they operate in distinctive contexts.[100] "Surrender" is a term that properly applies in instances

294, 333 (1987) (a State engages in "disguised extradition" when it employs legal procedures other than extradition to transfer a fugitive from its territory into the hands of another state's authorities). These definitions of "disguised extradition" fit squarely the more expansive concept of *de facto* extradition as defined herein.

98 *See* Shearer, *supra* n.96, at 78 (true disguised extradition occurs when the vehicle of deportation is used with the prime motivation of extradition, not just incidentally); Ian Leigh, *Nat'l Courts and Int'l Intelligence Cooperation, in* International Intelligence Cooperation and Accountability 244 (Hans Born, *et al.*, eds. 2011) (defining disguised extradition as "deportation with an ulterior motive"); UNGA, *Expulsion of Aliens*, U.N. Doc. A/CN.4/565, July 10, 2006, at 278 ("the term 'disguised extradition' may have a negative connotation since it implies an ulterior motive which may indicate an abuse of right or bad faith"); Paul O'Higgins, 27 Modern L. Rev. 521, 522 (1964) ("cases in which by the use of a power, with which it has been vested for another and different purpose, the state may give effect to a request for the surrender of a fugitive criminal which it is not otherwise lawfully authorized to do.").

99 At the opposite end of the spectrum from surrender are bilateral *non-surrender* agreements, including the approximately five dozen entered into by the United States to date to prohibit the surrender or transfer by any means of any current or former government officials, employees, military personnel or nationals of the other party to any international tribunal for any purpose, except one established by the UNSC. Chet J. Tan, Jr., *The Proliferation of Bilateral Non-Surrender Agreements among Non-Ratifiers of the Rome Statute of the Int'l Criminal Court*, 19 Am. U. Int'l L. Rev. 1115 (2004).

100 *See* Cassese, *supra* n.29, at 361 ("while one may speak of *extradition* of the accused from one State to another, it is more appropriate to speak of *transfer* of the accused from a State to an international criminal tribunal") (emphasis in original); Robert Kolb, *The Exercise of Criminal Jurisdiction over Int'l Terrorists, in* Enforcing International Law Norms against Terrorism 259 (Andrea Bianchi ed. 2004)

when the physical custody of an individual is transferred "vertically" from a State to an international criminal tribunal, such as the ICTY or ICC, as opposed to "horizontally" to another State.[101] Indeed, that distinction was found to be meaningful by the European Court of Human Rights when it denied a claim that an individual might suffer a flagrant denial of his fair trial rights, because such rights would only be implicated under an "extradition" scenario, which did not apply in the case of a State "surrender" to the ICTY.[102]

As these tribunals have no police forces of their own,[103] they must rely on State cooperation to hand over charged persons or escaped convicts in cases falling within their jurisdiction.[104] The constitutive documents for these tribunals notably never use the term "extradition," but instead rely principally on the word "surrender" and occasionally "transfer."[105] Differences between "surrender" (or "transfer") in the international criminal tribunal

(distinguishing "extraditions" between States from "surrenders" by States to international criminal tribunals).

101 Michael Plachta, *European Arrest Warrant: Revolution in Extradition?*, 11 Eur. J. Crime, Crim. L. and Crim. J. 178, 192 (2003).

102 *See Naletilić v. Croatia*, Appl. No. 51891/99, 29 EHRR, May 4, 2000, *reprinted in* 121 ILR 209 ("The Court recalls that exceptionally, an issue might be raised under Article 6 of the Convention by an *extradition* decision in circumstances where the applicant risks suffering a flagrant denial of a fair trial. However, it is not an act in the nature of an extradition which is at stake here, as the applicant seems to think. Involved here is the *surrender* to an international court which, in view of the content of its Statute and Rules of Procedure, offers all the necessary guarantees including those of impartiality and independence") (emphasis supplied).

103 *See* Cassese, *supra* n.100, at 355 (these tribunals lack the necessary enforcement agencies to "seize evidentiary material, compel witnesses to give testimony, search the scenes where crimes have allegedly been committed, or execute arrest warrants.").

104 *E.g., Ntakirutimana v Reno*, 184 F.3d 419 (5th Cir. 1999) (approving the surrender of a fugitive to the ICTR), *cert. denied*, 120 S. Ct. 977 (2000).

105 *E.g.*, Rome Statute of the Int'l Criminal Court (ICC), July 17, 1998, art. 102(a), 2187 U.N.T.S. 3, U.N. Doc. A/CONF.183/9 (1998), *reprinted in* 37 ILM 999 (defining "surrender" as the delivery of a person from a State to the Court pursuant to the Statute; *id.*, art. 102(b) (defining "extradition" as the delivery of a person between States pursuant to treaty or domestic legislation). All related documents, including the UNSC resolutions establishing the tribunals, the implementing Rules of Procedure and Evidence (RPE), and the Secretary-General's Reports by which the Secretariat presented the Statutes to the UNSC, consistently rely on the terms "surrender" and "transfer." *See also* Jackson Nyamuya Maogoto, State Sovereignty and International Criminal Law: Versailles to Rome 167 (2003) ("'Transfer' is a new regime in international law introduced by the ICTY Statute to circumvent legal and political bottlenecks inherent in the extradition regime governing inter-State relations" as it is "envisaged that the normal questions raised by extradition requests – the fairness of the proceeding and legitimacy of the charges – should not arise").

context and "extradition" in the bilateral State context are explored in Chapter 2.c.iv. To avoid confusion between these terms in their particularized settings, this discourse will refrain from any reference to "extradition" in the international criminal tribunal context and from any reference to "surrender" when discussing cases that involve State-to-State transfers.[106]

h "Lure and Capture Operation"

The *U.S. Attorneys' Manual* defines a "lure" as "involv[ing] a subterfuge to entice a criminal defendant to leave a foreign country so that he or she can be arrested in the United States, in international waters or airspace, or in a third country for subsequent extradition, expulsion, or deportation to the United States."[107] While this term, a simple noun, is understandable on its face and its definition certainly elaborates upon its function, there is merit in casting the term as an express operational activity to avoid any doubt as to its nature while, at the same time, capturing its actual, limited purpose (*i.e.*, apprehension).[108]

In addition, this definition, which was written within a specific geographic and bureaucratic context, does not fully satisfy the required elements for present purposes, namely: (i) it must be adapted for international applicability, (ii) the targeted individual may not be a "criminal defendant," (iii) the definition should reflect the types of participants who could engage in the subterfuge, and (iv) it fails to reflect the possibility that the fugitive could be lured to travel to another part of the host State – not necessarily to pursuing State territory, international space, or a cooperating third State.[109] Accordingly, a definition for a new

[106] It should be noted that, exceptionally, the European Arrest Warrant (EAW) (addressed initially in Chapter 4.c) has adopted the term "surrender" or "execution" when discussing State-to-State extraditions. That usage has proved misleading. Plachta, *supra* n.101, at 192.

[107] DoJ, *U.S. Attorneys' Manual*, § 9-15.630 (2d ed. 2007–3 Supp.). *Accord* NADELMANN, *supra* n.46, at 443–4 (describing lures as moving "fugitives from their foreign havens to other countries in which cooperative law enforcement officials would then arrest them and extradite or deport them.").

[108] In principle, a lure need not have as its object an individual's capture; it could, instead, seek to remove someone from one location to another (for example, so as not to be available as a witness or an interfering influence), or it may be used to entrap or embarrass a person, solely entice him into a particular business transaction, or lead him into a risky or dangerous situation.

[109] While atypical, such a scenario could occur where a fugitive were viewed as being more easily captured or arrested, say, outside the capital city or near an unprotected border area, rather than in another State's territory.

term, to be referred to as a "lure and capture operation," or LCO, is hereby proposed: *a deceptive activity in which a pursuing State and/or host State officials or agents entice a fugitive to travel to another location or jurisdiction with the consequential intention of apprehending him.*

Per terminology specific to this analysis, *strategic* LCOs occur when the operation results in the fugitive's relocation directly to pursuing State territory, custody, or control (even if ostensibly to non-sovereign territory/international space whereas if it results in his transfer to another (final or intermediate) destination or into another's custody or control, it would be designated a *tactical* lure. Where State destinations are concerned, *tactical* LCOs tend to be more common than strategic ones because it is generally easier to entice a fugitive to a State where they are not wanted for prosecution or punishment than to a State where they know or suspect they are.

Four varieties of LCOs can be discerned which track the types of informal renditions discussed *supra*: (i) *unilateral*, when conducted by pursuing State officials or agents without the participation, knowledge, or consent of the host State (*see* Chapter 12); (ii) *consensual*, when conducted exclusively by pursuing State officials or agents but with the prior consent of the host State (*see* Chapter 11); (iii) *surrogate*, when conducted exclusively by host State officials or agents at a pursuing State government's behest (*see* Chapter 11); and (iv) *joint*, when conducted by both pursuing and host State officials or agents working together (*see* Chapter 11).

i "Seizure and Delivery Operation"

When discussing the informal capture in, and transborder movement of fugitives from, foreign State territory by or at the behest of pursuing State officials or agents, courts and scholars alike often rely on such terms as extraterritorial "abduction" or "kidnapping."[110] Such nomenclature, we submit, is affirmatively unhelpful: not only is there wide inconsistency in the way these terms are defined, but they also tend to be incomplete

[110] *E.g.*, Andrew B. Campbell, Note, *The* Ker-Frisbie *Doctrine: A Jurisdictional Weapon in the War on Drugs*, 23 VAND. J. TRANSNAT'L L. 385, 409 (1990). The phrase "snatch and grab operations" is also sometimes invoked to describe this particular conduct. That terminology has a regrettably casual tone that additionally is unclear regarding whether the fugitive ultimately is to be delivered into the custody of a State or even whether the purpose is limited to detention, and therefore is avoided herein.

and/or misleading, in addition to being essentially pre-determinative of the unlawfulness of the conduct, which may not always bear out in reality.

With respect to inconsistency across definitions, some legal authorities focus on the capture of the fugitive while others are concerned with his movement or transfer.[111] Another source of inconsistency is whether the lack of consent referenced in many definitions denotes that of the fugitive or that of the State where the conduct occurs.[112] Moreover, some definitions of "abduction" are limited in scope to forcible actions while others are open to non-forcible conduct, by which is generally meant deception or fraud.[113]

These definitions also tend to be potentially misleading or incomplete. The use of the term "removal," as found in several leading definitions,[114]

111 *Compare* Bassiouni, World Public Order, *supra* n.97, at 124 ("Abduction is characterized by the following: agents of one state acting under the color of law unlawfully *seize* the body of a person within the jurisdiction of another state without its consent.") (emphasis supplied) *with* Abraham D. Sofaer, *Terrorism, the Law, and the National Defense*, 126 Mil. L. Rev. 95, 109–10 (1989) ("The forcible, unconsented *removal* of a person by agents of one State from the territory [or jurisdiction] of another State.") (emphasis supplied).

112 *Compare* Bedi, *supra* n.95, at 393 ("Abduction is the process by which a person is removed *without his consent* from the jurisdiction of one state to another by force, threat of force, or by fraud, trickery or deception") (emphasis supplied) *with* Philip B. Heymann & Ian Heath Gershengorn, *Pursuing Justice, Respecting the Law, in* Principles and Procedures for a New Transnational Criminal Law: Documentation of an International Workshop in Freiburg, May 1991, at 121 (Albin Eser & Otto Lagodny eds. 1992) (abductions occur "when agents of one state acting under color of law unlawfully seize a person within the jurisdiction of another state *without that state's consent*") (citing Bassiouni) (emphasis supplied).

113 *Compare* Sofaer, *supra* n.111, at 109–10 ("The *forcible*, unconsented removal of a person by agents of one State from the territory [or jurisdiction] of another State") (emphasis supplied) *with* Bedi, *supra* n.95, at 393 ("Abduction is a process by which a person is removed without his consent from the jurisdiction of one state to another by force, threat of force, *or by fraud, trickery or deception*") (emphasis supplied) *and* Black's Law Dictionary 4 (9th ed. 2009) ("Abduction" has been defined as "The act of leading someone away by force or fraudulent persuasion."). The very notion of a "non-forcible abduction" (*e.g.*, fraud) seems oxymoronic, as any reasonably understood definition of "abduction" ought to entail some form of physical force, restraint, or incapacitation. Moreover, the use of the term "fraud" in this context is unfortunate, as there is a significant difference between a fraud perpetrated against a law-abiding citizen for profit and a public deception undertaken by law enforcement officers to bring a criminal to justice; the former is a clear violation of the law while the latter serves an important public function, and yet the term "fraud" is conceptually broad enough to embrace both circumstances.

114 *E.g.*, Jackson Nyomuya Maogoto, Battling Terrorism: Legal Perspectives on the Use of Force and the War on Terror 65 (2005) ("the forcible, unconsented *removal* of a person by agents of one state from the territory of another state.") (emphasis supplied).

is potentially confusing, as that word, as discussed in Chapter 10.a, is now sometimes used to specifically denote deportations and exclusions. As for the nonconsensual character of such an action, to the extent that it refers to the host State (versus the fugitive), it is unclear whether the consent must be *ex ante* or can be *ex post*, or if an official protest by the executive branch of government is required to invalidate an implied consent. Furthermore, it remains ambiguous whether "forcible" conduct is presumed to include the *threat* of force as well. Perhaps most importantly, the terms "abduction" and "kidnapping" unfairly prejudge the lawfulness of the conduct in question. They are loaded terms that by definition imply a violation of law, if they do not say as much expressly,[115] while such terms are additionally commonly associated with pecuniary or other non-law enforcement motives (*e.g.*, ransom).

For all of the aforementioned reasons, these terms are not used in this discourse; instead, a term is needed that will be clearer and more consistent, specify the dual purpose of the activity to both apprehend and transfer, prove flexible to account for a variety of situations (including standard arrests), and signal legal neutrality. To those ends, the following alternative term is proffered: "seizure and delivery operation," or SDO, means *the capture or arrest of a fugitive effected in territory other than that of a pursuing State carried out by pursuing State and/or host State officials or agents with the intended subsequent delivery of that fugitive to pursuing State territory, custody, or control.*

There are five types of SDOs, the first four of which occur within host State territory and duplicate those discussed in the LCO context above: (i) unilateral, (ii) consensual, (iii) surrogate, and (iv) joint. A fifth variant, simply called an "international arrest," *occurs when a fugitive is apprehended by pursuing State authorities on non-sovereign territory/international space.*[116] An SDO is generally "strategic" in that such operations tend to be directed back to a pursuing State's territory or into its custody or control, but could be "tactical" in the sense of arranging for the temporary or intermediate delivery into a third State's territory, custody, or control.

* * * * *

[115] *Cf.* Daniel Statman, *Targeted Killing*, 5 THEORETICAL INQUIRIES IN LAW, No. 1, at 179 (2004) ("In choosing the term 'targeted killing' rather than 'assassination,' I have sought to avoid the negative moral connotation that is almost inherent in the latter.").

[116] This treatment is consistent with Harvard Law Professor Philip Heymann's definition of "international arrest" as occurring when no violation of territorial sovereignty is involved. Heymann & Gershengorn, *supra* n.112, at 137 n.211.

Armed with new terms and definitions, our analysis of the ways in which States pursue fugitives overseas can be more precise and targeted. Before exploring those specific forms of pursuit and the extent of their lawfulness, however, it is essential to understand why and how States assert extraterritorial jurisdiction over crimes and the legal effect of such assertions.

2

Subject Matter Jurisdiction

This chapter begins by examining the foundational concept of jurisdiction, including its inextricable relationship with the principle of sovereignty. It then discusses and distinguishes the two types of jurisdiction required by a State to effectively hold a fugitive judicially accountable, namely, "personal jurisdiction" (*i.e.*, over an individual) and "subject matter jurisdiction" (*i.e.*, over an offense). This chapter next focuses in depth on subject matter jurisdiction, in particular exploring its territorial and extraterritorial dimensions, how it is asserted, how competing jurisdictional claims are resolved, and recent efforts to extend State extraterritorial reach in the criminal arena. Finally, it considers the concept of *concurrent* jurisdiction, as exhibited by certain international criminal tribunals, by way of illustrative contrast. (*Personal* jurisdiction will be discussed in detail in Chapter 13.a.i.)

a Concept of Jurisdiction

In common parlance, jurisdiction refers variously to geographic boundaries; governmental, supranational, or judicial structures or powers; or even certain people, positions, or procedures.[1] Where jurisdiction is a function specifically of international law, however, the term is most usefully defined as "the power of a sovereign to affect the rights of persons, whether by legislation, executive decree, or by the judgment of a court."[2] Alternatively phrased, jurisdiction confers on a State the "legal

[1] B.J. George, Jr., *Extraterritorial Application of Penal Legislation*, 64 Mich. L. Rev. 609, 609 (1966). *See generally* Michael Akehurst, *Jurisdiction in Int'l Law*, 46 B.Y.B.I.L. 145, 145 (1972–73) ("[T]he word 'jurisdiction' is used by different writers to denote a wide variety of different things.").

[2] Iain A. Cameron, The Protective Principle of International Criminal Jurisdiction 3 (1994) (quoting Beale).

power or competence to exercise governmental functions"[3] and thereby affect legal interests.[4]

The concept of jurisdiction is intertwined with that of State sovereignty. Indeed, jurisdiction is properly viewed as an expression or dimension of sovereignty[5] and arguably "one of [its] most jealously guarded aspects."[6] While the term "sovereignty" is subject to multiple interpretations,[7] and is not a boundary-free concept,[8] this analysis is concerned with sovereignty in the sense of a State possessing legal personality and competence along with the various rights and powers attendant to that status – such as the rights to acquire title to and dispose of territory, the rights to internally govern and administer, and various historic or prescriptive rights to ownership or passage – that rely on customary law rather than on the consent of another State.[9]

Sovereignty supplies the general legal basis upon which a State has primacy not only over who comes within or leaves its borders, but also over the control and treatment of all persons inside its

[3] Luc Reydams, Universal Jurisdiction: International and Municipal Legal Perspectives 3 (2003).

[4] *See* IIL, 19th Comm'n (Maarten Bos, Rapporteur), *Draft Resolution on the Extraterritorial Jurisdiction of States*, art. 1(1), *reprinted in* 65 Y.B. Inst. Int'l L. 174 (1993) [hereinafter IIL, *Draft Resolution*] (defining "jurisdiction" as a State's authority to subject persons (natural or juridical) and things to its legal order").

[5] *See* Cameron, *supra* n.2, at 3 (jurisdiction under international law is "an aspect or an ingredient or a consequence of sovereignty") (quoting Frederick Mann)). A State with sovereignty over a piece of land may, however, cede jurisdiction over that land to another State without abdicating its ownership. *E.g.*, Agreement between the United States and Cuba for the Lease of Lands for Coaling and Naval Stations, Feb. 23, 1903, T.S. No. 418, 6 Bevans 113, art. III.

[6] Cameron, *supra* n.2, at 6.

[7] The term variously may "mean status in international relations as a dependent part of another country; or degree of political freedom that might be termed de facto independence; or degree of legal freedom that might be termed de jure independence." Michael Ross Fowler & Julie Marie Bunck, Law, Power, and the Sovereign State: The Evolution and Application of the Concept of Sovereignty 6–7 (1995). In fact, such ambiguity has led at least two legal commentators to characterize sovereignty as "a somewhat misty concept clouded by a fog of contested assumptions and unresolved questions." *Id.* at 32.

[8] *See* Josef L. Kunz, *The Nottebohm Judgment*, 54 AJIL 536, 545 (1960) ("Any *a priori* or unlimited political concept of sovereignty must, with inescapable logic, lead to the non-existence of international law as law. Sovereignty is, therefore, essentially a *relative* notion.") (emphasis in original).

[9] *Cf.* Covey T. Oliver, *The Jurisdiction (Competence) of States*, *in* International Law: Achievements and Prospects 307 (Mohammed Bedjaoui ed. 1991) (jurisdiction "is overwhelmingly sourced in customary international law").

boundaries,[10] including, for example, the right to confer or waive an individual's immunity[11] (discussed more extensively in Chapter 6.b) and the right to control a foreign national while he is physically within its sovereign space.[12] But it is not only about a State's jurisdiction over individuals; "as a proxy for state power, jurisdiction also defines another species of legal relationship, namely that of the state to other sovereigns."[13] Indeed, this broad jurisdictional power accorded to sovereign States or its corollary restriction on those lacking sovereignty in a given instance is at times expressly echoed in multilateral conventions.[14]

A State's sovereign power logically extends to how actual or alleged offenders found on its territory are managed, notably including any

[10] *See* R. Stuart Phillips, *The Political Offence Exception and Terrorism: Its Place in the Current Extradition Scheme and Proposal for Its Future*, 15 DICKINSON J. INT'L L. 337, 338 (1997); *SS "Lotus"* (Fr. v. Turk.) 1927 P.C.I.J. (ser. A) No. 10, at 18 (Sept. 7, 1927), *reprinted in* ANN. DIG. PUB. INT'L L. CASES 153 (No. 98) (H. Lauterpacht ed. 1938) [hereinafter *Lotus Case*] ("the first and foremost restriction imposed by international law upon a State is that . . . it may not exercise its power in any form in the territory of another State."). This notion is captured by the Latin expression *quid quid est in territorio est etiam de territorio* – a State has supreme authority over all individuals and property within its boundaries.

[11] *See Schooner Exchange v. McFaddon*, 11 U.S. (7 Cr.) 116, 137 (1812) (nations, including the United States, have agreed to accept certain limitations on their territorial jurisdiction due to the "common interest impelling [sovereign nations] to mutual intercourse, and an interchange of good offices with each other," including "the exemption of the person of the sovereign from arrest or detention within a foreign territory."); *In re Doe*, 860 F.2d 40, 45–46 (2d Cir. 1988) (discussing the right of the Government of the Philippines to waive former head-of-State immunity for Ferdinand and Imelda Marcos).

[12] *See, e.g.*, Letter from Ernest A. Gross, State Dep't Legal Adviser, to The Hon. Samuel Dickstein, N.Y. Sup. Ct. Justice, Aug. 18, 1948, "Position on Status of Mrs. Oksana Kasenkina," *reprinted in Dep't of State Bull.*, Vol. 19, No. 478, Pub. No. 3267, Aug. 29, 1948, at 261–62 ("It is the view of the United States Government that there is no basis under international law . . . for considering that [Soviet national] Mrs. Kosenkina [sic] is in any manner subject to the control or the authority of the Soviet Government so long as she remains in this country.").

[13] Anthony J. Colangelo, *Constitutional Limits on Extraterritorial Jurisdiction: Terrorism and the Intersection of Nat'l and Int'l Law*, 48 HARV. INT'L L.J. 121, 126 (2007); *accord* IIL, *Draft Resolution, supra* n.4, art. 2(2).

[14] *E.g.*, CHARTER OF THE UNITED NATIONS, June 26, 1945, arts. 2(1), 2(4) and 2(7) [hereinafter U.N. CHARTER] (the exercise of extraterritorial jurisdiction in the territory of another State without the latter's consent is forbidden under international law); Inter-Am. Conv. against Terrorism, June 3, 2002, art. 19, OAS Res. 1840 (XII-O/02), OAS No. A-66 ("Nothing in this Convention entitles a state party to undertake in the territory of another state party the exercise of jurisdiction or performance of functions that are exclusively reserved to the authorities of that other state party by its domestic law.").

criminal law enforcement-related activity.[15] Accordingly, a State is prohibited in principle from "perform[ing] outside its territory acts auxiliary to prosecution and trial of an offense (*e.g.*, arresting suspects, collecting evidence, inspecting sites, deposing witnesses, serving documents) unless explicitly authorized by [the host State]."[16] With few self-imposed exceptions – consisting mainly of certain privileges and immunities granted to individuals or missions,[17] concessions to supranational bodies,[18] rights conveyed via treaty,[19] *ad hoc* certifications,[20] or other agreements – a

[15] *See* LYAL S. SUNGA, THE EMERGING SYSTEM OF INTERNATIONAL CRIMINAL LAW: DEVELOPMENTS IN CODIFICATION AND IMPLEMENTATION 251 (1997); Neil Boister, *The Trend to 'Universal Extradition' over Subsidiary Universal Jurisdiction in the Suppression of Transnat'l Crime*, 2003 ACTA JURIDICA 287 (2003) (international law considers national criminal jurisdiction to be coterminous with sovereignty); B.J. George Jr., *Immunities and Exceptions*, *in* 1 INTERNATIONAL CRIMINAL LAW: CRIMES 107 (2d ed. M. Cherif Bassiouni ed. 1999); *Wilson v. Girard*, 354 U.S. 524, 529–30 (1957) ("A sovereign nation has exclusive jurisdiction to punish offenses against its laws committed within its borders, unless it expressly or impliedly consents to surrender its jurisdiction."). The reluctance of States to allow the application of foreign criminal laws in their territories stands in stark contrast to States' general willingness to permit their courts to apply foreign law to *private* disputes involving a foreign element. CAMERON, *supra* n.2, at 6.

[16] REYDAMS, *supra* n.3, at 3. *Cf.* Akehurst, *supra* n.1, at 148 (no usurpation of sovereign powers occurs when foreign-deployed diplomats seize someone attempting to burglarize their embassy and hand him over to the police).

[17] A.R. Carnegie, *Jurisdiction over Violations of the Laws and Customs of War*, 39 B.Y.B.I.L. 402, 402 (1963); HUGH M. KINDRED & PHILLIP M. SAUNDERS, EDS., INTERNATIONAL LAW: CHIEFLY AS INTERPRETED AND APPLIED IN CANADA 598 (7th ed. 2006) (recognizing the immunities States have accorded foreign diplomats).

[18] In recent years States increasingly have conferred criminal jurisdiction over individuals to certain supranational bodies. For example, the European Court of Human Rights (ECtHR) and other regional human rights tribunals may find a State in violation of its ECHR treaty obligations if it were to extradite or deport an individual to another State where the person's human rights were not expected to be respected. *See* examples in Chapters 7.e and 10.d. In addition, States are obligated to surrender individuals wanted for prosecution to the UNSC-established ICTY and ICTR. UNSC Res. 827, U.N. SCOR, 48th Year, 3217th mtg. (May 25, 1993) at 1, U.N. Doc. S/RES/827 (1993), *reprinted in* 32 ILM 1203 [ICTY Resolution]; and UNSC Res. 955, U.N. SCOR, 49th Year (Nov. 8, 1994), U.N. Doc. S/INF/50 (1994), *reprinted in* 33 ILM 1602 [ICTR Resolution].

[19] *See, e.g., United States v. Shiroma*, 123 F. Supp. 145, 149 (D. Haw. 1954) (Japan ceded criminal jurisdiction of its sovereign territory via treaty to the United States: "Under Article 3 of the Treaty of Peace, Japan which previously had full sovereignty over Okinawa transferred a part of that sovereignty, while retaining the residue. That portion of the sovereignty which gives the United States 'the right to exercise all and any powers of administration, legislation and jurisdiction' under Article 3 may be labeled 'de facto sovereignty.' The residue or 'residual sovereignty' retained by Japan is the traditional 'de jure sovereignty.'").

[20] *See, e.g., United States v. Robinson*, 843 F.2d 1, 4 (1st Cir.) (finding the 1986 certification by Panama's Director General of Consular and Shipping Affairs authorizing the United

State has virtually unfettered authority over all persons and property within its territory, including through the exercise of its police and immigration powers.[21] It is therefore the host State in the first instance that must determine how to deal with a fugitive found on its territory.[22] "Among the many problems concerning the limits of the sovereignty of States, few are as difficult or as much disputed as that which concerns the extent of the right of a State to exercise its criminal jurisdiction as it pleases."[23]

Viewed from an international law perspective, jurisdiction generally consists of three types of government powers or competencies: prescriptive, enforcement, and adjudicative.[24] The ***prescriptive*** power allows the

States not only "to board, inspect, search, seize and escort the vessel to the United States" but also "to prosecute the persons aboard the vessel" as sufficient basis under international law for the exercise of U.S. jurisdiction), *cert. denied*, 488 U.S. 834 (1988).

21 *Cf.* Valerie Epps, *The Development of the Conceptual Framework Supporting Int'l Extradition*, 25 Loy. L.A. Int'l & Comp. L. Rev. 369, 372 (2003) (extradition exists as a means to recover an actual or alleged offender precisely because a sovereign may not exercise law enforcement power on another sovereign's territory unless it consents). In a novel development, without conceding their host country law enforcement powers and prerogatives as such, France and Italy have stretched the conventional bounds of this legal standard. To date, Chinese police, donning Chinese police uniforms, have been deployed in Milan, Paris, and Rome in a cooperative arrangement to assist Chinese tourists in contacting authorities, reporting crimes, and raising their sense of security while traveling abroad, while at the same time sharing data with their host country counterparts. Barry Neild & Cristiana Moisescu, "Chinese Police to Patrol Streets of Rome to Protect Tourists," *CNN*, May 3, 2016, *available at* www.cnn.com/2016/05/03/travel/chinese-police-italy-rome-milan-tourists/ (last visited on May 27, 2016).

22 *See* Satyadeva Bedi, Extradition: A Treatise on the Laws Relevant to the Fugitive Offenders Within and With the Commonwealth Countries 392 (2002) (turning over fugitives from justice is a matter in which a State regulates its conduct according to its discretion, as each State has sole power of the execution of its laws within its domain). Sovereignty operates, in effect, as a two-edged sword, as while conferring on individual States such powerful jurisdictional authorities, it also offers criminals an opportunity to evade arrest by exploiting legal differences between States and any lack of cooperation between them. For example, Edward Snowden, the NSA contractor who shared classified U.S. Government surveillance program information with journalists, considered seeking refuge in Ecuador specifically in order to thwart his extradition, given that State's defiant posture against cooperation with the United States. James Pomfret & Lidia Kelly, "U.S. Warns Countries against Snowden Travel," *Reuters*, U.S. Ed., June 23, 2013 (noting that Ecuador is a "member [] of the ALBA bloc, an alliance of leftist governments in Latin America that pride themselves on their 'anti-imperialist' credentials.").

23 Carnegie, *supra* n.17, at 402. *Accord* Kwame Frimpong, *Punishing Offences Committed Abroad: Practical (National) Relevance or Theoretical Claim*, *in* Principles and Procedures for a New Transnational Criminal Law: Documentation of an International Workshop in Freiburg, May 1991, at 29–30 (Albin Eser & Otto Lagodny eds. 1992).

24 American Law Inst., Restatement (Third) of the Foreign Relations Law of the United States, May 14, 1986, § 401 [hereinafter Restatement (Third)]; Ivor

State to formulate and promulgate laws, regulations, or rules "applicable to the activities, relations, or status of persons, or the interests of persons in things."[25] For present purposes, such authority addresses matters including prohibited conduct;[26] extradition; deportation; and the capture, treatment, and punishment of criminals.[27] Of particular significance in this analysis, such *substantive* authority also may establish (based on principles discussed *infra*) what is known as "subject matter jurisdiction" that in effect recognizes a nexus between the State and the underlying crime in order to confer adjudicative competency on that State's courts.[28] *Such legislation or regulation ensures that once the fugitive is arrested and transferred, he can face prosecution in that pursuing State's courts for such crimes.*[29]

Stanbrook & Clive Stanbrook, Extradition: Law and Practice 111 n.1 (2d ed. 2000); Edmund S. McAlister, Note, *The Hydraulic Pressure of Vengeance:* United States v. Alvarez-Machain *and the Case for a Justifiable Abduction*, 43 DePaul L. Rev. 449, 453 (1994). Not all international law scholars, however, recognize the adjudicative power.

25 Restatement (Third), *supra* n.24, § 401(a); *e.g., United States v. Crews*, 605 F. Supp. 730, 734 (S.D. Fla. 1985) ("As a matter of international law, any country may exercise its jurisdiction to prescribe, *i.e.*, it may apply its body of law, to its citizens anywhere in the world."). Accordingly, U.S. courts cannot adjudicate cases involving violations of *foreign* criminal law unless the U.S. Congress also has enacted a law that provides for prescriptive jurisdiction over that crime. *United States v. Hudson & Goodwin*, 11 U.S. (7 Cr.) 32, 34 (1812).

26 *E.g.*, U.S., Omnibus Diplomatic Security and Antiterrorism Act of 1986, Pub. L. 99–399, Aug. 27, 1986, § 1202(a), 100 Stat. 896, *codified as amended at* 18 USC. § 2331 (2012) [hereinafter U.S. Omnibus Act of 1986] (extending "Extraterritorial Jurisdiction Over Terrorist Acts Abroad against United States Nationals," to include the offenses of homicide, attempt or conspiracy with respect to homicide, and serious bodily injury).

27 Extraterritorial *prescription* does not necessarily give rise to co-extensive extraterritorial *enforcement* authority (*see* discussion *infra*). While the U.S. Congress, for example, may have intended the reach of a criminal statute to extend beyond U.S. borders, this does not mean that federal law enforcement officers were thereby granted unfettered authority to conduct operations in the sovereign territory of other States to enforce those laws. Sean D. Murphy, 2 United States Practice in International Law, 2002–04, at 214 (2006). *See also* Joshua Robinson, Note, *United States Practice Penalizing Int'l Terrorists Needlessly Undercuts Its Opposition to the Passive Personality Principle*, 16 B.U. Int'l L.J. 487, 493 (1998) (it is essential to distinguish between "the *legislative* act of promulgating [a statute] and the *executive* act of asserting jurisdiction under it.") (emphasis in original).

28 Colangelo, *supra* n.13, at 126; *e.g., United States v. Sobell*, 142 F. Supp. 515, 522 (S.D.N.Y. 1956), *aff'd*, 244 F.2d 520 (2d Cir.), *cert. denied*, 355 U.S. 873 (1957), *reh'g denied*, 355 U.S. 920 (1958).

29 Philip B. Heymann & Ian Heath Gershengorn, *Pursuing Justice, Respecting the Law, in* Principles and Procedures for a New Transnational Criminal Law: Documentation of an International Workshop in Freiburg, May 1991, at 137 (Albin Eser & Otto Lagodny eds. 1992).

The ***enforcement*** power is a State's authority to "induce or compel compliance or to punish noncompliance" with those laws or other prescribed mandates.[30] "Jurisdiction to enforce generally entails some exercise of executive power – whether by police, prosecutorial or military action."[31] This could involve such illustrative actions as collecting taxes, inspecting ships, expropriating property from another State, requesting extradition,[32] or (more controversially) unilaterally pursuing the return of international fugitives from justice.[33] Consistent with the principle of sovereignty discussed above, as a general rule, "[a] State may not exercise jurisdiction to enforce in the territory of another State without the other State's express consent thereto."[34] *The extent of lawfulness of a State's enforcement measures within another's sovereign territory lies at the heart of this inquiry.*

The ***adjudicative*** power signifies a State's authority to assert judicial control or process over persons or things;[35] when this authority is exercised with respect to persons it is commonly known as "personal jurisdiction,"[36] and addresses *procedurally* whether a court (or administrative agency) may hear a case against a person brought before it.[37] As discussed more extensively in Chapter 13.a.i, personal jurisdiction functionally amounts to physical custody, and while some States permit *in absentia* trials, U.S. courts generally are prohibited from doing so unless waived by the defendant.[38] *Securing physical custody over a fugitive in*

30 Restatement (Third), *supra* n.24, § 401(c).

31 Colangelo, *supra* n.13, at 126.

32 *See* Boister, *supra* n.15, at 296 (once a State establishes its subject matter jurisdiction over a crime, extradition allows it to lawfully seek the custody of an actual or alleged criminal in another jurisdiction).

33 *E.g., Authority of the Federal Bureau of Investigation to Override Int'l Law in Extraterritorial Law Enforcement Activities*, 13 Op. Off. Legal Counsel 163, U.S. DoJ (1989) (authorizing FBI agents to pursue fugitives overseas).

34 IIL, *Draft Resolution, supra* n.4, art. 3(4). *Accord* Cameron, *supra* n.2, at 93 (customary international law prohibits one State's exercise of enforcement jurisdiction in the territory of another State, although noting that subpoena power may or may not constitute such exercise); *cf.* Robinson, *supra* n.27, at 495 (in the course of enforcement on another State's sovereign territory, a pursuing State's national law or mandate must be construed in conformity with international law).

35 Restatement (Third), *supra* n.24, § 401(b).

36 Colangelo, *supra* n.13, at 126.

37 *See* Cameron, *supra* n.2, at 14 (distinguishing between procedural and substantive competence).

38 *See* Rule 43, Fed. R. Crim. Pr., Title IX (with few express exceptions or unless waived, requiring the presence of the defendant at the initial appearance, initial arraignment, the plea, all trial stages, and sentencing). As for what qualifies as a waiver, *see, e.g.*, Restatement

order to assert personal jurisdiction is precisely why States enter into extradition arrangements or pursue alternative methods.

These three sets of jurisdictional powers correspond only roughly to the branches of government to which they are associated.[39] Accordingly, while the legislature makes laws and is in fact the principal branch involved in prescription, the executive branch or the courts also can participate on this front.[40] Likewise, while the executive branch is predominantly responsible for a State's enforcement functions, the courts can exercise such power as well.[41] And although the courts exercise primary adjudicatory powers, executive branch agencies sometimes play such a role, too.[42] It is therefore advisable to speak of the authorities exercised rather than the corresponding governmental branches when discussing State jurisdiction.[43]

These jurisdictional authorities need not be mutually co-extensive,[44] but in any event the enforcement and adjudicative competencies cannot exceed or deviate from what has been prescribed.[45] These forms of State jurisdiction operate with greater conviction when dealing with persons, things, or property within the State's own territory than extraterritorially,[46] but must in any event comply with the norms and standards of international law.[47] Furthermore, although such jurisdictional authority

(Third), *supra* n.24, § 422, cmt. c(iii) ("the accused will be deemed to have waived his right to be present, if he flees after the trial has begun, or if he must be removed from the courtroom because he creates a disturbance.").

39 *See id.*, § 401 cmt. a ("Although the aspects of jurisdiction here set forth resemble the traditional division of governmental authority into legislative, judicial, and executive powers, the exercise of jurisdiction does not fit neatly into such categories.").

40 *See id.* § 401(a) (States can prescribe jurisdiction "by legislation, by executive act or order, by administrative rule or regulation, or by determination of a court.").

41 *See id.* § 401(c) (States can enforce jurisdiction "through the courts or by use of executive, administrative, police, or other nonjudicial action.").

42 Louis Henkin, et al. International Law: Cases and Materials 1046 (3d ed. 1993).

43 Cameron, *supra* n.2, at 4.

44 A State is not obliged to exercise its prescriptive jurisdiction to the fullest extent allowed by international law; even if it does so, it may choose not to provide for the same level of enforcement competence. *Id.* at 14.

45 *See* Restatement (Third), *supra* n.24, § 431, cmt. a; *Lotus Case, supra* n.10 (despite the physical presence of a French ship officer on Turkish territory, Turkey could not enforce its law against him absent prescriptive jurisdiction); *Rivard v. United States*, 375 F.2d 882, 885 (5th Cir. 1967).

46 Stanbrook & Stanbrook, *supra* n.24, at 111; Colangelo, *supra* n.13, at 126.

47 For example, were a national statute to permit the expropriation of aliens' property without just compensation or allow a State's own nationals to counterfeit the currency of another State, that would constitute a violation of international law. Akehurst, *supra* n.1, at 188.

falls within the exclusive domain of each State, such jurisdiction can be, and sometimes is, conceded or waived, whether expressly or impliedly.[48]

b Requirements for State Criminal Jurisdiction

To bring a fugitive to justice, and thereby enforce applicable laws, a State must have both subject matter jurisdiction over the crime (a function of prescriptive authority) *and* personal jurisdiction over the individual of interest (a form of adjudicative authority).[49] The first establishes a relationship between the State and the crime; the second ensures a connection between the State and the individual of interest.

Meeting one of these requirements alone will not suffice. Accordingly, a State cannot bring a charged individual to justice, even if it has secured effective control over him through an extradition request or some alternative means,[50] so long as it lacks a recognized connection to the underlying crime; for example, absent a sufficient State nexus to the territory where the crime occurred or to the nationality of the perpetrator(s) or the victim(s).[51] Likewise, satisfying subject matter jurisdiction by itself does not allow a State to fully exercise its laws vis-à-vis a fugitive where no personal jurisdiction exists,[52] typically due to lack of physical custody,[53] but also possibly to other factors, such as a fugitive's presence obtained

48 *E.g., Smallwood v. Clifford*, 286 F. Supp. 97, 100 (D.D.C. 1968). Such consent can be communicated in *ad hoc* instances as well as via treaties. *See, e.g., Robinson*, 843 F.2d 1 (upholding the conviction of two Panamanian crew members stopped by the USCG on the high seas for possession of 20 tons of marijuana on the ground that Panama had agreed to the U.S. prosecution); *Wilson v. Girard*, 354 U.S. 524 (1957) (upholding the conviction by a Japanese court of a member of the U.S. armed forces for the murder of a Japanese woman where it was deemed a waiver when the U.S. Government turned him over to the Government of Japan to face prosecution).

49 McAlister, *supra* n.24, at 453.

50 Sometimes, States assert jurisdiction against the property of absent persons (*e.g.*, ships or bank accounts), Kindred & Saunders, *supra* n.17, at 598, but such actions are beyond the scope of this inquiry.

51 *Goldstone Co. v. Payne*, 94 F.2d 855, 857 (2d Cir. 1938). Under U.S. law at least, to the extent subject matter jurisdiction is in doubt, a federal court is expected to raise the issue at oral argument and solicit views from the parties. *In re Recticel Foam Corp.*, 859 F.2d 1000, 1002 (1st Cir. 1988). The specific grounds on which subject matter jurisdiction can be established are discussed *infra*.

52 Kindred & Saunders, *supra* n.17, at 598; *Rankin v. Howard*, 633 F.2d 844, 848 (9th Cir. 1980), *cert. denied*, 451 U.S. 939 (1981).

53 *See* Kindred & Saunders, *supra* n.17, at 598; Abraham Abramovsky & Steven J. Eagle, *United States Policy in Apprehending Alleged Offenders Abroad: Extradition, Abduction or Irregular Rendition?*, 57 Or. L. Rev. 51, 53–54 (1977). If a State lacks physical custody, its courts could still conceivably exercise personal jurisdiction where they had some other

via an invalid extradition treaty, in breach of an applicable treaty,[54] or through outrageous governmental conduct.[55] *In absentia* criminal proceedings present an interesting twist on the matter of personal jurisdiction, and while many States permit their use,[56] as a practical matter, absent physical custody of an accused, no punishment can obtain.[57]

c Subject Matter Jurisdiction: Scope and Dynamics

Although obtaining personal jurisdiction is essential to bringing international fugitives to justice and, indeed, is the *raison d'être* for an extradition request or the exercise of one of its alternatives, in the

form of custody or control over an individual, such as when that individual were temporarily held by another State operating at the adjudicating State's direction.

[54] *Ford v. United States*, 273 U.S. 593 (1927); *Cook v. United States*, 288 U.S. 102 (1932). Gen. Manuel Noriega of Panama sought to divest the federal district court's jurisdiction over his person on the grounds that he was a POW under Articles 82, 84, 85, 87, 99, 22, and 118 of GC III, but the court rejected that contention under the operative facts. *United States v. Noriega*, 746 F. Supp. 1506, 1525–29 (S.D. Fla. 1990), *aff'd*, 117 F.3d 1206 (11th Cir. 1997).

[55] *See United States v. Toscanino*, 500 F.2d 267, 275 (2d Cir.) (a federal court "must divest itself of jurisdiction over the person of a defendant where it has been acquired as the result of the government's deliberate, unnecessary and unreasonable invasion of the accused's constitutional rights."), *reh'g denied*, 504 F.2d 1830 (1974), *motion to dismiss denied on remand*, 398 F. Supp. 916 (E.D.N.Y. 1975). Other bases for lack of personal jurisdiction exist under domestic law; for example, U.S. courts martial have no personal jurisdiction over American civilians overseas for crimes they committed during peacetime. *Reid v. Covert*, 354 U.S. 1, 35 (1957).

[56] *See* Anne Klerks, *Trials in absentia in Int'l (Criminal) Law*, LL.M Thesis, Tilburg Univ., June 2008, *available at* http://arno.uvt.nl/show.cgi?fid=81103 (last visited on May 1, 2016) ("In the civil law tradition, trials *in absentia* are usually a normal part of the criminal system. However, this does not mean that all civil law traditions allow for trials *in absentia*. Whether a State allows for trials *in absentia* depends on the national law of the State and often on the severity of the crime concerned. For instance, Germany does not allow for trials *in absentia* at all. However, the French Code of Criminal Procedure permits trials *in absentia* for felony cases, under the condition that when the suspect is captured, he has the right to a retrial. Moreover, several States of the European Union, including the Netherlands, allow for trials *in absentia*. In countries that have a common law tradition, trials *in absentia* are however 'not an ordinary part of the criminal system.'").

[57] In some cases, the criminal defendant simply refuses to appear in court, although he has been provided a full and fair opportunity to do so and remains within the control of the prosecuting State. Although technically qualifying as an *in absentia* trial, personal jurisdiction is nevertheless fully satisfied. In other instances, the defendant remains at large, and while the State proceeds with a criminal trial, cognizant all the while of protecting the defendant's due process rights, the State would not be in a position to subject a convicted individual to imprisonment.

context of this inquiry we must first clarify the nature and scope of subject matter jurisdiction, not only to further distinguish it from personal jurisdiction (as the two terms are often confused[58]), but also to better appreciate its dynamics and limitations and because this prescriptive element is the proper triggering mechanism for all the law enforcement efforts that may follow. This discussion of subject matter jurisdiction is strictly relevant to the pursuit of fugitives who have allegedly committed crimes and are being sought for prosecution rather than for those who have already been convicted of a crime and are being sought for punishment.

"States have developed and apply different types of rules regulating the *spatial scope* of their respective criminal laws."[59] Subject matter jurisdiction can be justified on either a territorial or extraterritorial[60] basis, but in any event, that exercise must not be unreasonable.[61] If a crime is committed on a pursuing State's soil, even if the perpetrator then flees to another State, that pursuing State can set out a *territorial* claim over the crime.[62] If, by contrast, the crime occurs within another State's territory, a pursuing State must make its case based on an *extraterritorial* ground to claim jurisdiction over the conduct at issue. At times, there may be competing demands by two or more States for subject matter jurisdiction.[63] We will now briefly identify, describe, and assess the relative strength of each available ground for subject matter jurisdiction.

[58] One important difference between them is that while a fugitive can consent to *personal* jurisdiction, he cannot consent to *subject matter* jurisdiction, as the latter is a State's prerogative alone.

[59] Cameron, *supra* n.2, at 16 (emphasis supplied).

[60] Extraterritoriality was not always recognized as a legitimate basis for jurisdiction. Sambei, Arvinder & John R.W.D. Jones, Extradition Law Handbook 1–2 (2005); *e.g.*, *The Apollon*, 22 U.S. (9 Wheat.) 362 (1824) (stressing that a nation's domestic laws do not extend beyond its territory).

[61] *See* Restatement (Third), *supra* n.24, § 403, cmt. a ("The principle that an exercise of jurisdiction on one of the bases indicated . . . is nonetheless unlawful if it is unreasonable . . . has emerged as a principle of international law"); *id.* § 403(2) (reasonableness is evaluated according to certain criteria, including notably: "(g) the extent to which another state may have an interest in regulating the activity; and (h) the likelihood of conflict with regulation by another state"); *e.g.*, *United States v. Vasquez-Velasco*, 15 F.3d 833, 841 (9th Cir. 1994) (holding the extraterritorial application of 18 U.S.C. § 1959 (2012), which penalizes violent crimes committed in aid of a racketeering enterprise, to be reasonable under international law).

[62] Boister, *supra* n.15, at 290.

[63] How such a conflict is resolved will depend to a large extent on any applicable treaty provisions. *See* sub-section c.iii *infra* on de-confliction.

i Territorial Jurisdiction

Territoriality is a universally recognized and generally dispositive basis for subject matter jurisdiction, authorizing the State within whose territory a crime allegedly occurred (the *locus delicti commissi*) to exercise its prescriptive reach over that crime.[64] This jurisdictional ground is rooted in the principle of national sovereignty,[65] and accepts that when an individual violates the domestic laws of another State, he is legally accountable to that State for any such acts or omissions, even if he has no domicile or residency there.[66]

For criminal jurisdictional claims based on territory, one must logically understand the full extent of a State's territorial domain.[67] To begin, a State's territory comprises: (i) the land and water areas within its borders, (ii) its internationally defined territorial seas,[68] and (iii) earth

64 *See* RESTATEMENT (THIRD), *supra* n.24, § 402, cmt. c ("The territorial principle is by far the most common basis for the exercise of jurisdiction to prescribe, and it has generally been free from controversy."); *Lotus Case, supra* n.10; Rüdiger Wolfrum, *The Decentralized Prosecution of Int'l Offences Through National Nat'l Courts, in* WAR CRIMES IN INTERNATIONAL LAW 233 (Yoram Dinstein & Mala Tabory eds. 1996). It is noteworthy that, until the early 1990s, there had been no case in which the Botswanan courts determined they had jurisdiction over an offense committed in a foreign country, as exemplified by *Ngwenya v. State*, Crim. Appl. No. 202, Botsw., 1983 (unreported), *discussed in* Frimpong, *supra* n.23, at 35.

65 RESTATEMENT (THIRD), *supra* n.24, § 402(1)(a) and cmt. c (1987); STANBROOK & STANBROOK, *supra* n.24, at 112; Note, *Extraterritorial Jurisdiction and Jurisdiction Following Forcible Abduction: A New Israeli Precedent in Int'l Law*, 72 MICH. L. REV. 1087, 1089 (1974) [hereinafter Note, *Israeli Precedent*].

66 REYDAMS, *supra* n.3, at 3; SIR ROBERT JENNINGS & SIR ARTHUR WATTS, EDS., 1 OPPENHEIM'S INTERNATIONAL LAW 901 (9th ed. 1992) ("The fact that every state exercises territorial supremacy over all persons on its territory, whether they are its nationals or aliens, excludes the exercise of the power of foreign states over its nationals in the territory of another state."); *United States v. Burns*, Sup. Ct., Can., Feb. 15, 2001, [2001] 1 S.C.R. 283 (4th) 1 ("individuals who choose to leave Canada leave behind Canadian law and procedures and must generally accept the local law, procedure and punishments which the foreign state applies to its own residents"). Before the territorial principle was recognized, States relied on the personality of laws whereby an individual was governed by the national law wherever he happened to reside. ANTONIO CASSESE, INTERNATIONAL CRIMINAL LAW 278 (2003).

67 "[S]tatehood is inconceivable in the absence of a reasonably defined geographical base. The frontiers of such an entity need not be established beyond dispute, nor is there any prescribed minimum of territory for the existence of a state, but some piece of land is essential before one can accept the establishment and continuation of a state." Malcolm N. Shaw, *Territory in Int'l Law, in* TITLE TO TERRITORY 3 (Malcolm N. Shaw ed. 2005) [hereinafter Shaw, *Territory*]; *accord* SURYA P. SHARMA, TERRITORIAL ACQUISITION, DISPUTES AND INTERNATIONAL LAW 2 (1997).

68 Territorial sea extends up to 12 nautical miles from a State's coast. Third U.N. Conv. on the Law of the Sea, Dec. 10, 1982, art. 3, U.N. Doc. A/CONF.62/122 & Corr.1–8, 1833

subjacent and air space superjacent to all such geographical surfaces.[69] In addition, two or more States can agree to share sovereignty over a particular piece of territory.[70]

Territory is also defined to encompass, albeit today only on a *constructive* basis,[71] a State's nationally registered or flagged vessels[72] – whether sea-faring, airborne, or aloft in outer space[73] (sometimes

U.N.T.S. 3, *reprinted in* 21 ILM 1261 [hereinafter Law of the Sea Conv.]; Antiterrorism and Effective Death Penalty Act of 1996, art. 901(a), Pub. L. 104–132, 110 Stat. 1214, 1317 (1996), *reprinted at* 18 USC. § 7 note (2012) (enacting U.S. Presidential Proclamation No. 5928, Dec. 27, 1988, 3 C.F.R. § 547 (1988) (declaring that territorial seas extend 12 miles from coast)). The concept of territory includes "islands, islets, rocks, and (in certain circumstances) reefs" within a State's territorial waters. JAMES CRAWFORD, BROWNLIE'S PRINCIPLES OF PUBLIC INTERNATIONAL LAW 203 (8th ed. 2012) (citations omitted). In addition, States often recognize a "contiguous zone" to the territorial sea, also known as an "exclusive economic zone" (EEZ), which extends from 12 to 24 nautical miles from the coast, in which a State may exercise certain prescribed rights, including for exploration, exploitation, and conservation, to prevent the infringement of immigration, fiscal, and other laws within its territory or its territorial sea and to punish infringement of such laws committed within its territory and its territorial sea. *See* Shaw, *Territory, supra* n.67, at 30; Conv. on the Territorial Sea and the Contiguous Zone, Apr. 29, 1958, art. 24, 15 U.S.T. 1606, 516 U.N.T.S. 205; *e.g.*, U.S. Presidential Proclamation No. 7219, Aug. 2, 1999, 64 Fed. Reg. 48701. The contiguous zone or EEZ, however, does *not* qualify as State territory. *United States v. Romero-Galue*, 757 F.2d 1147, 1149 n.1 (11th Cir. 1985). While as a general rule the "freedom of the high seas" prohibits any sovereign claim over them, as a narrow exception, the high seas adjacent to territorial waters of coastal States may be subject to that State's sovereignty. *Anglo-Norwegian Fisheries Case* (U.K. v. Nor.) [1951] I.C.J. Rep. 116 (Dec. 18). *Cf.* Marvin C. Ott, *Deep Danger: Competing Claims in the South China Sea*, CURRENT HISTORY, Sept. 2011 (discussing the PRC's official assertion of territorial sovereignty over the entire South China Sea in overreaching terms).

69 This follows from the Latin maxim, *cujus est solum est usque ad caelum et ad inferos*, or "he who owns the surface has title both to the airspace above and the subsoil below."

70 *See, e.g.*, Prot. Respecting the New Hebrides, Aug. 6, 1914 (joint sovereignty between the United Kingdom and France over the New Hebrides islands); Agreement Concerning the Boundary between Nejd and Kuwait, Dec. 2, 1922 (Saudi Arabia and Kuwait agreed that a defined territory between them would be joint and common and they would share equal rights in it).

71 Historically, a State's foreign-based facilities or vessels on the high seas were often treated as if they were the actual territory of that State. 6 MARJORIE M. WHITEMAN, DIGEST OF INTERNATIONAL LAW 744 (1968); *e.g.*, *United States v. Archer*, 51 F. Supp. 708, 709 (S.D. Cal. 1943) (a consulate, even if the building is not owned by the U.S. Government, it is still "a part of the territory of the United States of America.").

72 *See* Conv. on Int'l Civil Aviation [Chicago Conv.], Annex 9 (1944), *as amended*, Dec. 7, 1944, 15 U.N.T.S. 295, art. 17, ("Aircraft have the nationality of the State in which they are registered."); Law of the Sea Conv., *supra* n.68, art. 91(1) ("States shall have the nationality of the State whose flag they are entitled to fly.").

73 Terry Richard Kane, *Prosecuting Int'l Terrorists in United States Courts: Gaining the Jurisdictional Threshold*, 12 YALE J. INT'L L. 294, 298 (1987).

referred to as "floating territoriality" or "constructive territoriality"[74]). In such instances, only one national flag may be used per vessel,[75] there must be (at least in principle) a genuine link between the State and the vessel,[76] and such jurisdictional primacy cannot be presumed and remains unresolved as a matter of international law when such vessels are found in another State's territorial waters or air space.[77] Other forms of a State's "constructive" territory include its embassies,[78] consular

[74] Elizabeth R.P. Bowen, Note, *Jurisdiction over Terrorists Who Take Hostages: Efforts to Stop Terror-Violence against United States Citizens*, 2 Am. U. J. Int'l L. & Pol'y 153, 179 (1987); George, *supra* n.1, at 613; Cameron, *supra* n.2, at 18.

[75] *See* Conv. on Int'l Civil Aviation, *supra* n.72, art. 18 (no dual registration permitted). A ship on the high seas that flies more than one State flag "may be treated as a ship without nationality" and a Stateless ship "may be boarded and seized on the high seas." Malcolm Shaw, International Law 613 [hereinafter Shaw, International Law] (citing, *inter alia*, *Molvan v. Attorney-General for Palestine* [1948] A.C. 351 (P.C.), in which the U.K.'s Judicial Committee of the Privy Council found lawful the seizure of a Stateless ship by the British Navy).

[76] *Nottebohm Case* (Liech. v Guat.), Second Phase, Judgment [1955] I.C.J. Rep. 4 (Apr. 6); Law of the Sea Conv., *supra* n.68, art. 91; *M/V Saiga (No. 2)* (St. Vincent v. Guinea), ITLOS Case No. 2, July 1, 1999, *reprinted in* 38 ILM 1323 (1999). This requirement was intended to address flags of convenience offered by States like Liberia and Panama. Shaw, International Law, *supra* n.75, at 611–12.

[77] *See* Draft Conv. on Research in Int'l Law of the Harvard Law School, "Jurisdiction with Respect to Crime," art. 4, 29 AJIL 435 (Supp. 1935) [hereinafter Harvard Research]; Bart DeSchutter, *Problems of Jurisdiction in the Int'l Control and Repression of Terrorism, in* International Terrorism and Political Crimes 382 n.10 (M. Cherif Bassiouni ed. 1975). *Cf.* Chooi Fong, *Some Legal Aspects of the Search for Admission into other States of Persons Leaving the Indo-Chinese Peninsula in Small Boats*, 52 B.Y.B.I.L. 53 (1982) ("In this field there are two conflicting theories, the one stating that the ship is a floating piece of State territory and the other that a ship is only the property of a State at a place where no local jurisdiction exists. Neither theory is accepted by the majority of specialists on international law. The generally accepted view is that a merchant ship in the open sea is subject not to territorial jurisdiction but to the jurisdiction of the State of the flag."). For an historical case, *see Chung Chi Cheung v. R.* [1939] A.C. 160 (P.C.) (rejecting the notion of floating jurisdiction at least in criminal matters; where a crime was committed on a Chinese-flagged vessel in Hong Kong territorial waters then under U.K. sovereignty, the accused was prosecuted under Hong Kong law on the ground that "a public ship in foreign waters is not, and is not treated as, territory of her own nation.").

[78] *See* Alfred P. Rubin, "U.S. Embassies are Not U.S. Territory," Opinion, *N.Y. Times*, Mar. 1, 1984 ("As a matter of international law, an embassy is not 'territory' of the sending state; it is territory of the receiving state that is accorded, through various treaties and customs, some immunities from host-country law."); U.S. Dep't of State website, Discover Diplomacy, "What Is a U.S. Embassy?," *available at* http://diplomacy.state.gov/discoverdiplomacy/diplomacy101/places/170537.htm (last visited on May 1, 2016) ("While *diplomatic spaces remain the territory of the host state*, an embassy or consulate represents a sovereign state. International rules do not allow representatives of the host country to enter an embassy without permission – even to put out a fire – and designate an attack on an embassy as an attack on the country it represents.") (emphasis supplied).

premises, and military facilities abroad,[79] in addition to any overseas territory for which an agreement establishes some right of use or ownership, such as leased land, a trusteeship,[80] or occupied territory pursuant to an unconditional surrender (*e.g.*, Berlin following World War II).[81]

Territorial claims of criminal jurisdiction become more complicated when an offense begins (or is conceived) on one State's territory but is consummated (or its effects are experienced) on another's. Does, for instance, the criminal act of murder occur only on the territory of State A from which a sniper shoots a cross-border bullet, only on the territory of State B where the human target is mortally wounded, or on both States' territories? Cybercrimes – whether cyberspace is exploited for fraudulent, pornographic, stalking, terrorist, or other criminal purposes – pose a particular jurisdictional challenge.[82]

79 Boister, *supra* n.15, at 290 n.9. But there are limits as to what constitutes a military facility abroad for territorial purposes. *See, e.g., United States v. Morton*, 314 F. Supp.2d 509, 512–15 (D. Md. 2004) (finding no subject matter jurisdiction in a case involving a civilian accused of sexual misconduct with a minor while visiting a U.S. Government housing facility off the premises of Ramstein AFB, which, while the land was "reserved or acquired for the use of the United States," it was not under the "exclusive or concurrent jurisdiction" of the United States, and therefore did not qualify as a "special maritime and territorial jurisdiction" of the United States pursuant to 18 USC. § 7(3) (2012)).

80 U.N. Charter, *supra* n.14, Chap. XII.

81 *See* Hans Smit, *The Panama Canal: A Nat'l or Int'l Waterway?*, 76 Colum. L. Rev. 965 (1976) (the Panama Canal Zone was transferred to the United States under the Hay-Bunau-Varilla Convention of 1903 and the United States exercised its rights there as if it were the territorial sovereign); Sunga, *supra* n.15, at 300 (the Nuremberg and Tokyo trials were conducted in territory occupied by the Allies, who were entitled to occupy Germany and Japan pursuant to terms of unconditional surrender; thus, the Allies were in a position to apprehend and prosecute the offenders on the spot through the tribunals themselves or through thousands of subsequent trials in the occupied zones). The Geneva Conventions of 1949 provide guidance in cases of military occupation: "The penal laws of the occupied territory shall remain in force, with the exception that they may be repealed or suspended by the Occupying Power in cases where they constitute a threat to its security or an obstacle to the application of the present Convention. Subject to the latter consideration and to the necessity for ensuring the effective administration of justice, the tribunals of the occupied territory shall continue to function in respect of all offences covered by the said laws." Geneva Conv. Relative to the Protection of Civilian Persons in Time of War (GC IV), Aug. 12, 1949, art. 64(1), 6 U.S.T. 3516, T.I.A.S. No. 3365, 75 U.N.T.S. 287.

82 *See* Armando A. Cottim, *Cybercrime, Cyberterrorism and Jurisdiction: An Analysis of Article 22 of the COE Conv. on Cybercrime*, Eur. J. Legal Studies, Issue 6 (2010), *available at* http://cadmus.eui.eu/handle/1814/15118 (last visited on May 1, 2016) ("The Convention on Cybercrime points the way toward cooperation with respect to criminalizing certain behaviours and pursuing those responsible. It does not, however, resolve the issues of international jurisdiction.").

There are no uniform answers to these issues; rather, States vary in their approach, each generally recognizing and applying one of the following three doctrines. First, there is the so-called "subjective territorial principle," where a State stakes a jurisdictional claim to prosecute a crime that commenced or a portion of which occurred within its territory, even though the crime was concluded or its effects felt elsewhere.[83]

A second approach is the "objective territorial principle" (occasionally referred to as the "effects doctrine" or "qualified territorial principle"), wherein a State chooses to assert jurisdiction over a crime that, while commenced elsewhere, was completed or resulted in injury or damage within its territory,[84] even in instances where the chief offender never set

[83] David Freestone, *Int'l Cooperation against Terrorism and the Development of Int'l Law Principles of Jurisdiction, in* Terrorism and International Law 43 n.4 (Rosalyn Higgins & Maurice Flory eds. 1997); Cameron, *supra* n.2, at 53–54 (preferring the label "initiatory jurisdiction" to avoid confusion between the differential American and British understandings of the term "subjective territorial"). Many States are prepared to assert territorial jurisdiction over a crime even if the lion's share occurred elsewhere so long as part of the offense occurred within its territory. *E.g.*, N.Z. Crimes Act, Pub. Act 43, Nov. 1, 1961, § 7; Crim. Justice Act, 1993 (England and Wales), July 27, 1993 § 2; Conv. for the Suppression of Illicit Traffic in Dangerous Drugs, June 26, 1936, § 2, 198 L.N.T.S. 299 (1939) [hereinafter Dangerous Drugs Conv.]; *Libman v. The Queen*, Sup. Ct., Can., [1985] 2 S.C.R. 178.

[84] Freestone, *supra* n.83, at 43–44 & n.4; Cameron, *supra* n.2, at 54 (preferring the label "terminatory jurisdiction"); Note, *Israeli Precedent, supra* n.65, at 1089 & n.11; Adelheid Puttler, *Extraterritorial Application of Criminal Law: Jurisdiction to Prosecute Drug Traffic Conducted by Aliens Abroad, in* Extraterritorial Jurisdiction in Theory and Practice 106–07 (Karl M. Meessen ed. 1996); Geoff Gilbert, *Extradition, in* The Harvard Research in International Law: Contemporary Analysis and Appraisal 416–20 (John P. Grant & J. Craig Barker eds. 2007) (noting that the entire commission of the crime could have taken place within the territory of the non-prosecuting State); *United States v. MacAllister*, 160 F.3d 1304, 1308 (11th Cir. 1998) (this principle "applies where the defendant's actions either produced some effect in the United States, or where he was part of a conspiracy in which any conspirator's overt acts were committed within the United States' territory."). A prime example can be found in the famous *Lotus Case*. A collision occurred on the high seas between a French ship, the *SS Lotus*, and a Turkish ship, the *Boz-Kourt*, which resulted in the death of eight passengers and crew on the Turkish vessel. The French officer in charge (Demons) was put on trial in Turkey charged with criminal negligence. France argued that the Turkish exercise of jurisdiction was contrary to international law and the parties submitted the dispute to the PCIJ. The main issue facing the Court was whether Turkey had jurisdiction to try Demons for a crime committed outside Turkish territory. A divided court ruled (on the President's deciding vote) that Turkey had jurisdiction under the objective territoriality principle in that his crime of negligence had been consummated on a Turkish vessel, which constituted Turkish territory. *Lotus Case, supra* n.10.

foot on the prosecuting State's territory.[85] As a U.S. Court of Appeals observed some fifty years ago: "All the nations of the world recognize 'the principle that a man who outside of a country willfully puts in motion a force to take effect in it is answerable at the place where the evil is done.'"[86] In a case involving strictly criminal consequences within a State's territory, however, it is generally expected not only that the effect on the prosecuting State would be "primary, direct, and substantial,"[87] but also that criminal intent can be established.[88]

The third approach is the "ubiquity principle" (often associated with Germany where it originated), which provides maximum latitude to

[85] *E.g.*, AP, "U.S. Citizen Pleads Guilty to Defaming Thai King," *IHT*, Oct. 11, 2011, at 4 (Thailand asserted territorial jurisdiction over Joe Gordon, a Thai-born American, who pled guilty to charges under Thai law prohibiting insults of its king (lèse-majesté) for translating excerpts of a nationally banned biography of King Bhumibol Adulyadej entitled *The King Never Sleeps*, and posting them on an online blog and by providing links to the translation to two other Internet sites, even though the actual effects on Thai territory were based entirely on Internet access in Thailand); Bruce Zagaris, *Australia Extradites Alleged Software Pirate to U.S.*, 23 IELR 189, 189–90 (2007) (in early 2007, Australia extradited a British national, Hew Raymond Griffiths, residing in Bateau Bay, Australia, on criminal copyright infringement charges as leader of a prominent Internet software piracy group called DrinkOrDie; significantly, while he argued he had never physically been in the United States, Australia still found that the United States had territorial jurisdiction by virtue of his violation of U.S. laws). Firm jurisdictional basis exists even if an accused was part of a conspiracy but never actually entered the territory in question and relied instead on agents, innocent or otherwise, to consummate the crime. *E.g., Noriega*, 746 F. Supp. at 1513.

[86] *Rivard*, 375 F.2d at 887 (citations omitted).

[87] Third Restatement, *supra* n.24, § 402(1)(c) and cmt. d; *accord* Puttler, *supra* n.84, at 107; Boister, *supra* n.15, at 294 & n.36. *See also* IIL, *Draft Resolution, supra* n.4, art. 2(4) ("Under international law, the territorial jurisdiction of a State extends to activities performed outside the State's territory ('effects doctrine'), provided the effect is a significant one relating to the State's public order or interest."); R.Y. Jennings, *Extraterritorial Jurisdiction and the United States Antitrust Laws*, 33 B.Y.B.I.L. 146, 159 (1957) (if it were permissible to base objective territorial jurisdiction on more or less remote repercussions of an act wholly performed in another territory, then there would be virtually no limit to a State's territorial jurisdiction).

[88] For example, if a Dutch drug dealer intended to bring cannabis into Germany by giving it to German citizens who then smuggled it in for him, the test would be met, but if he sold cannabis to Germans in the Netherlands and did not care where they consumed it or what they did with it, then there would be an insufficient nexus. Puttler, *supra* n.84, at 106. *See also United States v. Columba-Colella*, 604 F.2d 356, 359 (5th Cir. 1979) ("Assume . . . that persons or their agents conspire to rent a boat in Miami, sail it beyond United States coastal waters, and load it with a cargo of illegal drugs. Then, *en route* to a United States port but while still on the high seas, the conspirators are apprehended. This country may under the objective territorial theory apply its drug laws to punish them if it can establish intent to violate those laws.") (finding no basis for subject matter jurisdiction in the case at bar).

States, with subscribers flexibly accepting either conduct or effects as a basis for a territorial claim of jurisdiction.[89]

We must also consider whether a State can claim jurisdiction over inchoate crimes, *i.e.*, those that *intend* to cause damage or injury on a State's territory, such as conspiracy to defraud or attempted murder (even if hatched elsewhere), but that do not actually materialize.[90] Although such crimes are more difficult to prove and many international conventions are silent as to their applicability,[91] some judicial support, including in the United Kingdom[92] and the United States,[93] exists for the exercise of jurisdiction over such crimes by the uninjured State.

[89] *See* Christopher L. Blakesley & Otto Lagodny, *Finding Harmony Amidst Disagreement over Extradition, Jurisdiction, the Role of Human Rights, and Issues of Extraterritoriality in Int'l Criminal Law*, 24 Vand. J. Transnat'l L. 1, 15 (1991) ("The German principle of ubiquity provides that a crime is deemed to have occurred in the place where the perpetrator acted or in the place where the statutorily proscribed harm occurred.") (citing German Penal Code, *see infra* n.113)); Cameron, *supra* n.2, at 54–55. The United States has liberalized its conception of territorial jurisdiction over the years by gradually coming to accept a position closely approximating the ubiquity doctrine, permitting prosecutions of individuals responsible for either a material element of an offense abroad or a criminal result on U.S. territory. Christopher L. Blakesley, Terrorism, Drugs, International Law, and the Protection of Human Liberty: A Comparative Study of International Law, Its Nature, Role, and Impact in Matters of Terrorism, Drug Trafficking, War, and Extradition 198–99 (1992) [hereinafter Blakesley, Comparative Study].

[90] *See* Restatement (Third), *supra* n.24, § 402, cmt. d ("Cases involving intended but unrealized effect are rare, but international law does not preclude jurisdiction in such instances, subject to the principle of reasonableness. When the intent to commit the proscribed act is clear and demonstrated by some activity, and the effect to be produced by the activity is substantial and foreseeable, the fact that a plan or conspiracy was thwarted does not deprive the target state of jurisdiction to make its law applicable.").

[91] *E.g.*, Dangerous Drugs Conv., *supra* n.83.

[92] In 1991, the Judicial Committee of the Privy Council ruled that the Governor of Hong Kong had jurisdiction to order the extradition to the United States of an individual charged with conspiracy to import heroin into the United States. The individual had agreed to supply heroin while he was in Thailand but was arrested in Hong Kong, when he went to collect payment there, even though there was no overt act in furtherance of the conspiracy in Hong Kong. The Court reasoned that "there is nothing in precedent, comity, or good sense that should inhibit the common law from regarding a conspiracy abroad as an offense if it was intended to result in a criminal offense in England even though no overt act took place there." *Liangsiriprasert v. United States* [1991] 1 A.C. 225 (P.C.), [1990] 2 All E.R. 866, 878 (Lord Griffiths). *Accord R. v. Sansom, et al.* [1991] 2 WLR 366, 366 (CA).

[93] *E.g.*, *United States v. Winter*, 509 F.2d 975, 982–83 (5th Cir. 1975) (where an individual committed an act in furtherance of a conspiracy on U.S. territory, the court had jurisdiction even though the co-conspirators were arrested on the high seas and had not yet entered U.S. territory); *Noriega*, 746 F. Supp. at 1513 (international law now recognizes "a mere showing of *intent* to produce effects in this country, without requiring proof of an overt act or effect within the United States.") (emphasis in original) (citing *United States v. Wright-Barker*, 784 F.2d 161, 168 (3d Cir. 1986)).

Territoriality boasts a number of advantages that commend it as a jurisdictional base:[94] (i) non-territorial States generally wish to honor the principles of territorial sovereignty and the equality of States, and not interfere in the internal affairs of the State where an offense occurred;[95] (ii) the territorial State is typically most affected by the criminal conduct at issue and therefore tends to be more willing to invest the time, money, and human resources necessary to investigate and prosecute a case;[96] (iii) the territorial State generally has the greatest interest in deterring the further commission of such crime;[97] (iv) it is frequently the case that the accused will be identified and arrested on the territory where the alleged crime occurred and that material evidence and witnesses will be more easily produced and accessed in the territorial State; and (v) the accused often stands an improved prospect of having his rights protected and understanding the local language, while the judge and jury normally will better reflect local views, values, and standards regarding the crime.[98]

At the same time, however, the territorial principle suffers from several challenges, some of which have been referenced above. To begin, it is not always clear within whose territory an actual or alleged crime was committed, as, say, certain vessels or buildings may belong to one State but be located within another's territory, or certain tracts of land may be co-owned by two States or leased by one State but owned by another. In addition, when a crime is initiated on one State's territory but consummated on another, or a crime was intended to injure a State but never came to fruition, there could be multiple competing claims of jurisdiction over that crime.[99] Furthermore, there could be political unwillingness on the part of territorial State prosecutors to pursue claims against individuals if it could implicate certain public officials in the underlying crime.[100] Finally, an accused may be more likely to enjoy official immunity or amnesty under the territorial State's laws than under those of a non-territorial State.[101]

[94] Notably, under the Conv. on the Prevention and Punishment of the Crime of Genocide, Dec. 9, 1948, art. VI, 78 U.N.T.S. 277, *reprinted in* 28 ILM 763 [hereinafter Genocide Conv.], persons accused must be brought before the national court where the act was performed.

[95] Gilbert, *supra* n.84, at 416 & n.6; Note, *Israeli Precedent, supra* n.65, at 1089.

[96] Gráinne Mullan, *The Concept of Double Criminality in the Context of Extraterritorial Crimes*, 1997 Crim. L. Rev. 17, 17 (1997).

[97] Note, *Israeli Precedent, supra* n.65, at 1089; Cassese, *supra* n.66, at 279.

[98] Cassese, *supra* n.66, at 279.

[99] Blakesley, Comparative Study, *supra* n.89, at 199.

[100] *Id.*

[101] Cassese, *supra* n.66, at 280.

ii Extraterritorial Jurisdiction

As a great many crimes do not occur on the territory of a State that may wish to prosecute an alleged offender, States seek to establish extraterritorial reach for their criminal laws.[102] Under international law, States have reasonably wide latitude to establish criminal laws with the "spatial scope" to cover events or conduct occurring overseas[103] and then to authorize their courts to adjudicate such crimes[104] – and all States to some extent exercise such discretion.[105] Beginning in 1935 with the

[102] *See* Stanbrook & Stanbrook, *supra* n.24, at 113 (under U.K. law, an extraterritorial offense means "an offense against U.K. law although it occurred entirely outside the U.K. and its territorial waters"); *EEOC v. Arabian Am. Oil Co.*, 499 U.S. 244, 248 (1991) ("Congress has the authority to enforce its laws beyond the territorial boundaries of the United States."); Destruction of Aircraft or Aircraft Facilities, 18 U.S.C. § 32(b)(1) (2012) ("Whoever willfully performs an act of violence against any individual on board any civil aircraft registered in a country other than the United States while such aircraft is in flight, if such aircraft is likely to endanger the safety of that aircraft . . . shall be fined under this title or imprisoned not more than twenty years, or both. There is jurisdiction over an offense under this subsection if a national of the United States was on board, or would have been on board, the aircraft; an offender is a national of the United States; or an offender is afterward found in the United States.").

[103] *See Lotus Case*, *supra* n.10, at 19 (States have a "wide measure of discretion which is only limited in certain cases by prohibitive rules."); *In re Extradition of Demjanjuk*, 612 F. Supp. 544, 555 (D.C. Ohio 1985) (citing the *Lotus Case*).

[104] Wolfrum, *supra* n.64, at 233; Boister, *supra* n.15, at 290. States have even been known, through constitutional or legislative amendment, to create express exceptions to the principle of non-retroactivity of their criminal laws, in order to establish jurisdiction over certain offenses, sometimes to bring their laws into conformity with international treaty obligations. *See, e.g., Questions Relating to the Obligation to Prosecute or Extradite* (Belg. v. Sen.) [2012] I.C.J. Rep. 422, ¶¶ 28, 31 (July 20) (in 2007, to implement measures necessary to observe its obligations under the CAT, Senegal amended Article 9 of its Constitution and made a variety of changes to its criminal laws to allow for the prosecution and sentencing of persons for genocide, crimes against humanity, and war crimes even though such conduct did not constitute a crime under Senegalese law at the time they occurred, but where they were considered criminal offenses under then-prevailing general principles of international law).

[105] Cameron, *supra* n.2, at 12. Traditionally, civil law States have been more inclined than common law States to exercise extraterritorial jurisdiction. Ilias Bantekas & Susan Nash, International Criminal Law 179 (2d ed. 2003). Under U.S. law, where a statute is silent as to its extraterritorial application, the rebuttable presumption is that it was *not* intended to have such reach; accordingly, U.S. courts examine statutes to determine whether that intention is explicit or "may be inferred from the nature of the offenses and Congress' other legislative efforts to eliminate the type of crime involved." *Kiobel v. Royal Dutch Petroleum Co.*, 133 S. Ct. 1659 (2013) (no rebuttable presumption of extraterritoriality under the Alien Tort Statute). *See also Morrison v. Austl. Nat'l Bank Ltd.*, 561 U.S. 247 (2010) (no cause of action permitted for foreign plaintiffs suing foreign and American defendants under section 10(b) of the Securities Exchange Act of 1934 for securities fraud perpetrated on a foreign stock exchange); *United States v. Zehe*, 601 F.

seminal, albeit unofficial, Harvard Research Draft Convention on Jurisdiction with Respect to Crime,[106] four bases for extraterritorial jurisdiction have been recognized to some extent over the years;[107] they will be identified, described, and explicated throughout the remainder of this section.

Active Personality Principle. Under this basis, a pursuing State may assert extraterritorial jurisdiction over its own nationals (and at times even residents[108]) for crimes they committed abroad,[109] even if not punishable under the law of the territorial State or elsewhere,[110] and even if the accused is also a national of the territorial State itself (*i.e.*, a dual citizen).[111] According to this principle, as a well-established ground for subject matter jurisdiction,[112] a State need not demonstrate

Supp. 196, 200 (D. Mass. 1985) (finding "strong congressional intent to apply the Espionage Act to the extraterritorial acts of noncitizens both from the face of the statute and from the nature of the crime of espionage."); *United States v. Benitez*, 741 F.2d 1312 (11th Cir. 1984) (finding applicable statutes prohibiting the theft of government agent credentials and assault and attempted murder of DEA agents to have extraterritorial application based on the nature of the crime), *cert. denied*, 471 U.S. 1137 (1985).

106 Harvard Research, *supra* n.77. Although the Harvard Research draft is not official text, it is useful nonetheless as it represents a synthesis of State practice that continues to be relied on today. SUNGA, *supra* n.15, at 251. States and scholars alike have since accepted these Harvard Research draft principles as proper and defensible grounds for asserting jurisdiction. Patrick L. Donnelly, Note, *Extraterritorial Jurisdiction Over Acts of Terrorism Committed Abroad: Omnibus Diplomatic Security and Anti-terrorism Act of 1986*, 72 CORNELL L. REV. 599, 601 (1987).

107 Many international treaties do not preclude the application of criminal jurisdiction exercised in accordance with national laws; thus, to the extent such statutes or regulations are not contrary to international law, they can be treated as complementary principles, and prosecution may be independently based on them. DeSchutter, *supra* n.77, at 386.

108 Hassan Poorbafrani & Masoud Zamani, *A Comparative Critique of Regulating the Personal and the Passive Personality Principles in the Iranian Penal System*, 3 ELEC. J. ISLAMIC & MIDDLE EASTERN L. 117, 122 (2015), *available at* http://papers.ssrn.com/sol3/papers.cfm?abstract_id=2713296 (last visited on May 1, 2016) (identifying by example Denmark, Finland, and Liberia).

109 *See, e.g., Public Prosecutor v. Antoni*, Sup. Ct., Swed., 1960, *reprinted in* 32 ILR 140 (E. Lauterpacht ed. 1966) hereinafter *[Antoni Case]* ("every crime committed by a Swedish citizen may be punished, even if committed abroad").

110 Wolfrum, *supra* n.64, at 233; CASSESE, *supra* n.66, at 281.

111 *Kawakita v. United States*, 343 U.S. 717 (1952).

112 Nationality as an established or at least optional basis for extraterritorial jurisdiction can be found in case law, *e.g., United States v. Wright-Barker*, 784 F.2d 161, 167 n.5 (3d Cir. 1986) (international law recognizes subject matter jurisdiction based on "nationality – as applied to nationals, wherever located.") as well as in a number of international treaties, such as the U.N. Conv. against Torture and Other Cruel, Inhuman or Degrading Treatment or Punishment, Dec. 10, 1984, art. 5(1), UNGA Res. 39/46 Annex, U.N. GAOR, 39th Sess.,

substantial harm to its domestic interests when justifying its application.[113] That said, the active personality principle (sometimes referred to as the "personal principle") is not often invoked[114] and its application in practice is not altogether standardized.[115]

Indeed, such practice historically has varied considerably as between civil law and common law States, with the former, as a general rule, much more prone to apply the principle and the latter only recently beginning to appreciate the principle's appeal.[116] That said, common law countries have been inclined to assert the active personality principle particularly in instances where: (i) serious offenses, such as murder or manslaughter, are committed by its nationals abroad;[117] (ii) a State's own security or governmental functions are put at risk by its nationals overseas;[118] and (iii) due to economic or cultural factors, developing countries are perceived as unable to suppress certain crimes in which a developed State's nationals are directly engaged.[119]

Several justifications have been advanced to support the active personality principle: (i) to ensure one's own nationals "comply with its [domestic] law, whether at home or abroad, regardless of what is provided for

Supp. No. 51, U.N. Doc. E/CN.4/1984/72, Annex (1984), 1465 U.N.T.S. 85, *reprinted in* 23 ILM 1027 [hereinafter CAT]; the Conv. on the Physical Protection of Nuclear Material, Mar. 3, 1980, art. 8(1)(b), IAEA Doc. C/225, 1456 U.N.T.S. 101, *reprinted in* 18 ILM 1419 (1980); and the U.N. Conv. against Illicit Traffic in Narcotic Drugs and Psychotropic Substances, Dec. 20, 1988, art. 4(1)(c), U.N. Doc. E/CONF/82/15 (1988), *reprinted in* 28 ILM 493 (1989). Domestic legislation likewise frequently authorizes jurisdiction expressly over nationals who allegedly committed crimes abroad. *E.g.*, France, Code de Procédure Penale, Mar. 9, 2004, art. 689, *adopted by* Law No. 2004–204 [hereinafter Fr. Penal Code]; German Penal Code (Strafgesetzbuch), §§ 3 and 4 [hereinafter Ger. Penal Code]; India Penal Code, Act. No. 45 of 1860, Oct. 6, 1860, § 4 (3d ed. Raju 1965).

113 Boister, *supra* n.15, at 291.

114 Its infrequent use derives mainly from the fact that in such instances States have no compelling reason to pursue prosecution against such individuals. *Id.* at 292.

115 *See* Gilbert, *supra* n.84, at 417 (wide variations in use); Cassese, *supra* n.66, at 282 (no uniformity of application with respect to whether the alleged offender must possess the nationality of the pursuing State at the time when the crime occurred or when the criminal proceedings were instituted).

116 Freestone, *supra* n.83, at 44 n.5; Gilbert, *supra* n.84, at 417; Sambei & Jones, *supra* n.60, at 2.

117 Stanbrook & Stanbrook, *supra* n.24, at 113–14 (discussing U.K. treatment).

118 *See* discussion of the protective principle *infra*.

119 *E.g.*, U.K. Sexual Offences (Conspiracies and Incitement) Act, 1996, § 7(2) (regarding sex tourism with minors).

[abroad]";[120] (ii) to prevent a State from becoming a safe haven for its own nationals who commit crimes overseas and then return to their home country;[121] (iii) to hold criminally accountable nationals to the extent they owe allegiance to their State, in part because of the protections it extends to them;[122] and (iv) to help neutralize any negative reputational light such criminal acts may cast on the State of their nationality.[123] One criticism historically directed at this principle had been that it did not apply to the population of *non-nationals*. Yet, in recent years the active personality doctrine has at times expanded to encompass resident or domiciled aliens,[124] as well as those who have since become nationals even if they were foreigners at the time the crime was committed.[125]

Passive Personality Principle. By direct contrast with active personality, which focuses on a national who is the alleged *offender* of a crime overseas, passive personality allows a State to claim extraterritorial jurisdiction over a national who is the *victim* of a crime committed abroad.[126] Along with the universal principle (discussed *infra*), the passive personality principle is arguably the most controversial basis of jurisdiction,[127] and traditionally was strongly disfavored by the United States[128] and other

[120] Cassese, *supra* n.66, at 281.

[121] Gilbert, *supra* n.84, at 417.

[122] *E.g., Antoni Case, supra n.109, reprinted in*, 32 ILR 140. This rationale goes hand-in-hand with the limitation imposed by many civil law countries not to extradite their own nationals. Sambei & Jones, *supra* n.60, at 2; Boister, *supra* n.15, at 291.

[123] Blakesley, Comparative Study, *supra* n.89, at 63.

[124] Note, *Israeli Precedent, supra* n.65, at 1090 & n.14; *e.g.*, U.K. War Crimes Act, May 9, 1991, § 1(2) (permitting extraterritorial jurisdiction over crimes by habitual residents in addition to nationals). *See generally* Wolfgang Friedmann, The Changing Structure of International Law 235–36 (1984) (domicile as a potential basis for jurisdiction); *cf.* Restatement (Third), *supra* n.24, § 402 cmt. e ("International law has increasingly recognized the right of a state to exercise jurisdiction on the basis of domicile or residence, rather than nationality, especially in regard to 'private law' matters such as the laws of wills and succession, divorce and family rights, and, in some cases, liability for damages for injury.").

[125] Cassese, *supra* n.66, at 282.

[126] Donnelly, *supra* n.106, at 601. Because of its requirement that there exist one or more victims, this principle has no utility regarding so-called "victimless" crimes such as drug smuggling. Boister, *supra* n.15, at 293.

[127] Restatement (Third), *supra* n.24, § 402 cmt. g; Robinson, *supra* n.27, at 487 *et seq.*

[128] The U.S. Government vigorously opposed this principle throughout much of its history. In one celebrated case in the late 1880s, when a Mexican court convicted an American national for libel against a Mexican national based on a newspaper article published in Texas, U.S. Secretary of State Bayard wrote to his Mexican counterpart: "A sovereign has jurisdiction of offenses which take effect within his territory, although concocted or commenced outside of it; but the right is denied of any foreign sovereign to punish a citizen of the United States for an offense consummated on our soil in violation of our

Western States,[129] although a number of States have long found this principle acceptable.[130] However, with the increased incidence of, and intolerance for, such pernicious offenses as international terrorism,[131] torture,[132] hostage-taking,[133] crimes against humanity,[134] and genocide, many States have come to adopt legislation and enter into treaties that authorize such subject matter jurisdiction[135] while, at the same time, not contesting others' assertions on this ground.[136]

The growing appeal of this principle stems from a perception that States increasingly need to intervene out of a duty to protect their nationals living, working, studying, or traveling abroad, especially as many are targeted precisely because of their citizenship;[137] and territorial

laws, even though the offense be against a subject or citizen of such sovereign." *Cutting Case* (1887), *reprinted in* 2 John Bassett Moore, A Digest of International Law 23–24 (1906). It is telling that the ALI's previous Restatement on Foreign Relations likewise did not recognize this principle. American Law Inst., Restatement (Second) of the Foreign Relations Law of the United States, § 30(2)(1965).

129 Donnelly, *supra* n.106, at 602; Freestone, *supra* n.83, at 44–45.

130 *See* Harvard Research, *supra* n.77, at 578 (identifying the following countries as claiming passive personality jurisdiction in one guise or another since at least the mid-1930s: Albania, Brazil, China, Cuba, Czechoslovakia, Estonia, Finland, Greece, Guatemala, Italy, Japan, Latvia, Lithuania, Mexico, Monaco, Peru, Poland, Rumania, San Marino, the Soviet Union, Sweden, Switzerland, Turkey, Uruguay, Venezuela, and Yugoslavia).

131 In response to international terrorism, France embraced the passive personality principle in 1975, Fr. Penal Code, *supra* n.112, art. 689(1); in June 1987, Israel requested the extradition of Mahmoud El-Abed Ahmad, a non-Israeli national charged with bombing a bus full of civilians in Israeli-occupied territory, *Ahmad v. Wigen*, 726 F. Supp. 389, 398 (E.D.N.Y. 1989), *aff'd*, 910 F.2d 1063 (2d Cir.), *stay denied*, 111 S. Ct. 23 (1990); and the United States adopted the principle in its Antiterrorism and Effective Death Penalty Act of 1996, Pub. L. 104–132, Apr. 24, 1996, § 443(a).

132 *E.g.*, CAT, *supra* n.112, art. 5(1).

133 *E.g.*, Int'l Conv. against the Taking of Hostages, Dec. 17, 1979, art. 5(1)d, UNGA Res. 34/146 (XXXIV), 34 U.N. GAOR Supp. (No. 46), at 245, U.N. Doc. A/34/46 (1979), 1316 U.N.T.S. 205, T.I.A.S. No. 11081, *reprinted in* 18 ILM 1456 [hereinafter New York Conv.].

134 *E.g.*, "Argentina Generals Get Life," *BBC News*, Dec. 6, 2000 (discussing a case in which Argentina Gen. Carlos Guillermo Suarez Mason was convicted *in absentia* in Italy for the kidnapping and murder of eight Italian nationals in Argentina during its "Dirty War").

135 Wolfrum, *supra* n.64, at 233; Freestone, *supra* n.83, at 45.

136 For example, the United Kingdom, which exceptionally does not endorse the passive personality principle for its own use, is willing to accommodate other States' invocation of jurisdiction on this ground in compliance with the terms of an international treaty. *See Rees v. Sec'y of State for the Home Dep't* [1986] 1 A.C. 937 (H.L.), [1986] 2 All E.R. 321 (the U.K. House of Lords conceded to Germany's invocation of jurisdiction on passive personality grounds where one of its diplomats was kidnapped in Bolivia under the terms of the 1979 Hostage-Taking Convention).

137 The passive personality principle is "increasingly accepted as applied to terrorist and other organized attacks on a state's nationals by reason of their nationality."

States cannot always be counted on to demonstrate the judicial capacity and/or political will to hold violators accountable.[138]

Reasons for resistance to this principle include: (i) its tendency to undercut the sovereignty of the State where the alleged crime occurred, and thereby foster, rather than minimize, inter-State jurisdictional conflicts;[139] (ii) relatedly, it may be viewed as tantamount to a "vote of no confidence" in other States' criminal law systems and their capacity to effectively bring offenders to justice;[140] (iii) its prospects for prosecutorial abuse through States' selective enforcement to protect their nationals abroad;[141] and (iv) its questionable utility in light of the substantial overlap with the "protective principle" (discussed *infra*), which has comparatively more international support.[142]

The operation of this principle varies widely among States. Virtually no State applies the passive personality principle in unfettered form;[143] each imposes some kind of conditionality or limitation.[144] For instance, some require dual criminality (discussed *infra*), in which the offense must be cognizable in the State where the crime was committed as well as in the State asserting passive personality jurisdiction.[145] Others adopt a

Restatement (Third), *supra* n.24, § 402 cmt. g. Consistent with this trend, Harvard Law professor Philip Heymann has developed a variant of this principle to address those persons targeted by an attack specifically because of their nationality. Designated as the "Targeted Passive Personality Principle," it combines the protective principle (discussed *infra*) and the passive personality principle. Heymann & Gershengorn, *supra* n.29, at 119. This ground is particularly appropriate for invocation involving terrorist attacks, as the crime against the individual is really one directed against the State and intended to cause fear in all of its citizens, thereby imbuing the victim's State with a strong interest in punishing the perpetrator. *Id.* at 119–20.

138 A number of States since the mid-1970s (*e.g.*, France and Sweden) have come to expressly adopt the passive personality principle as they believe that a State should prosecute terrorists for crimes perpetrated against its nationals when the State with primary responsibility for such prosecution has failed to do so. Donnelly, *supra* n.106, at 602–03. *See also* U.S. Omnibus Act of 1986, *supra* n.26, 100 Stat. at 896–97 (U.S. legislation).

139 Gilbert, *supra* n.84, at 418, 419.

140 *Id.* at 419.

141 DeSchutter, *supra* n.77, at 382–83 & n.13.

142 Boister, *supra* n.15, at 293.

143 Poorbafrani & Zamani, *supra* n.108, at 129.

144 DeSchutter, *supra* n.77, at 382–83 & n.13. The passive personality principle, much like the active personality principle, is subject to temporality concerns regarding specifically when an individual acquires his nationality, as such timing will have a bearing on the principle's application.

145 For example, under German law, jurisdiction is available for "crimes committed abroad against a German if such conduct is punishable by the law of the place where it occurred." Ger. Penal Code, *supra* n.112, § 7.

deferential posture vis-à-vis the territorial State, limiting the assertion of jurisdiction to instances where its nationals were victims of crimes abroad that implicated national security.[146] Still others insist that this principle must meet a minimum threshold of punishment;[147] make exceptions for a serious violation of international law, such as a war crime or crime against humanity;[148] or constitute an act where the pursuing State has a compelling national interest, such as in combating terrorism or hostage-taking.[149]

At the same time, it is not unheard of for a State to expand the application of this principle by treating residents on par with nationals or to encompass inchoate crimes within its scope.[150] In addition, some States, to the extent possible, try to couple any assertion of the passive personality principle with another jurisdictional basis, typically the protective principle, so that passive personality need not carry the full jurisdictional burden alone.[151]

[146] Under French law, "every alien who is either a principal or accomplice in a crime (as opposed to a "delit" or misdemeanor) committed outside French territory may be prosecuted and adjudged on the basis of French law, if the victim of the crime is a French national"; however, this jurisdiction is "subsidiary to that of the country in which the offense occurs, except in cases involving national security." Christopher L. Blakesley, *A Conceptual Framework for Extradition and Jurisdiction over Extraterritorial Crime*, 1984 Utah L. Rev. 685, 714 (1984).

[147] Italian law provides for jurisdiction over acts committed by foreigners abroad that injure Italian citizens, provided the offense is punishable under Italian law by perpetual hard labor or imprisonment for one year or more. Italian Penal Code, Royal Decree No. 1398, Oct. 19, 1930, art. 10, *as amended.*

[148] Argentina imposes a dual criminality requirement in connection with the assertion of jurisdiction on passive personality grounds *unless* the offense is regarded as an international crime. *E.g., The Priebke Extradition Case,* Case No. 16.063/94, Sup. Ct., Arg., Nov. 2, 1995, *summarized in* 1998 Y.B. Int'l Human. L. 341 (war crime at issue).

[149] Restatement (Third), *supra* n.24, § 402 cmt. g; *e.g., United States v. Yunis,* 924 F.2d 1086 (D.C. Cir. 1991) (a State may punish non-nationals for crimes committed against its nationals outside of its territory, at least where the State has a particularly strong interest in the crime) (prosecuted under the Hostage-Taking Act); *Benitez,* 741 F.2d at 1316 (passive nationality principle invoked to approve the prosecution of a Colombian citizen convicted of shooting U.S. drug agents in Colombia).

[150] Israel, Knesset, Penal Law (Offenses Committed Abroad), 5716 (1955), § 7(a), *Sefer Ha-Chukkim* 7, 10 Laws of the State of Israel (L.S.I.) 7, *as amended.*

[151] Even in the case of terrorist acts against U.S. nationals, the passive personality principle has usually been adopted in conjunction with others. Boister, *supra* n.15, at 292–93 & n.28; Blakesley, Comparative Study, *supra* n.89, at 201–02; *e.g., United States v. Layton,* 509 F. Supp. 212 (N.D. Cal.), *cert. denied,* 452 U.S. 972 (1981).

Protective Principle. A third basis for extraterritorial jurisdiction is the so-called "protective principle," also occasionally labeled the "security principle"[152] or the "principle of the injured forum."[153] Under this principle, which derives from its sovereign status,[154] a State may choose to prosecute non-nationals who commit crimes abroad that threaten the integrity or security of the State or endanger or undermine its essential governmental institutions or functions, or public interests.[155] While neither conduct need occur nor effects be felt on the jurisdictional State's territory,[156] its fundamental purpose is to "safeguard the political independence of the State," rather than to promote a State's policies or interests overseas[157] or to protect nationals abroad from any possible harm.[158]

Its rationale derives from the twin concerns of self-protection[159] and inadequate State legislation elsewhere to penalize conduct on its territory that adversely affects another State's vital interests.[160] Examples of such qualifying conduct, which need not arise out of a state of armed conflict,[161] include treason, espionage, crimes against the peace, attacks on diplomats, counterfeiting State seals or currency, forgery of official documents, and perjury before a diplomatic or consular officer.[162]

This principle, which traces its origins back to the Italian Renaissance but was not always embraced by common law countries,[163] is widely

152 Sambei & Jones, *supra* n.60, at 3.

153 Cameron, *supra* n.2, at 2–3 n.1.

154 Sambei & Jones, *supra* n.60, at 3; Boister, *supra* n.15, at 295.

155 Restatement (Third), *supra* n.24, § 402(3); Wolfrum, *supra* n.64, at 233; Cameron, *supra* n.2, at 2; *e.g., United States v. Pizzarusso*, 388 F.2d 8 (2d Cir. 1968).

156 Gilbert, *supra* n.84, at 420; *e.g., United States v. Biermann*, 678 F. Supp. 1437, 1444 (N.D. Cal. 1988).

157 Puttler, *supra* n.84, at 109.

158 Heymann & Gershengorn, *supra* n.29, at 118.

159 *Nusselein v. Belgian State*, Ct. of Cassation, Feb. 27, 1950, [1950] *Pasicrisie belge* 448, *reprinted in* 17 ILR 136 (H. Lauterpacht ed. 1956).

160 Note, *Israeli Precedent, supra* n.65, at 1090–91; Cameron, *supra* n.2, at 31–32.

161 *See In re Bayot*, Ct. of Cassation (Crim. Ch.), Fr., Feb. 22, 1923, *reprinted in* 2 Ann. Dig. Pub. Int'l L. Cases 109, 109 (No. 54) [1923–24] (J.F. Williams & H. Lauterpacht eds. 1933) (application of a criminal code provision embodying the protective principle "does not depend upon the continuance of the state of war with the enemy nation on whose behalf the offence was committed.").

162 *See* Restatement (Third), *supra* n.24, § 402 cmt. f; *e.g., Archer*, 51 F. Supp. 708 (convicting an alien who committed perjury before a U.S. vice consul in Mexico in connection with an application for a non-immigrant visa); *Columba-Colella*, 604 F.2d at 358 ("A state/nation is competent, for example, to punish one who has successfully defrauded its treasury, no matter where the fraudulent scheme was perpetrated.").

163 Note, *Israeli Precedent, supra* n.65, at 1090–91.

recognized by States today, as reflected in statutes[164] and international treaties[165] alike. That said, the principle is generally viewed as a basis of last resort[166] and is applied most commonly with such offenses as terrorism, drug trafficking, and illegal immigration.[167] State practice varies considerably and turns largely on the types of security and other threats States face, as well as their overall attitude toward human rights.[168] For instance, while most States specify germane crimes in their domestic statutes,[169] other States leave such provisions open-ended;[170] and while certain States recognize only intentional crimes under the protective principle, others authorize jurisdiction for mere negligence.[171]

Problems associated with the protective principle mainly consist of those that apply to extraterritorial jurisdictional bases *writ large*,

[164] *E.g.*, U.S. Omnibus Act of 1986, *supra* n.26 (granting jurisdiction to federal courts over the killing of any U.S. national if intended to coerce, intimidate, or retaliate against a government or civilian population); Fr. *Penal Code, supra* n.112, at art. 694 (conferring jurisdiction over foreigners who outside French territory commit acts either as a perpetrator or an accomplice against the security of the State); Isr., Knesset, Mar. 21, 1972, *Sefer Ha-Chukkim* 52, 32 L.S.I. 63 (1978), *as amended* (extending jurisdiction over offenses committed abroad which, had they been committed in Israel, harmed or were intended to harm the State of Israel, its security, property, or economy, or its transport or communication links with other countries).

[165] *E.g.*, Int'l Conv. for the Suppression of Counterfeiting Currency, Apr. 20, 1929, 112 L.N.T.S. 371 (1931).

[166] Stanbrook & Stanbrook, *supra* n.24, at 120. This jurisdictional principle was notably invoked in a series of French cases arising out of World War I (*e.g., In re Urios*, Ct. of Cassation (Crim. Ch.), Fr., 1920 (in French Algeria), *reprinted in* [1919–22] 1 Ann. Dig. Pub. Int'l L. Cases 107 (No. 70) (J.F. Williams & H. Lauterpacht eds. 1932)); and by Israel with regard to Adolf Eichmann, who was prosecuted for crimes committed against Jews during World War II before Israel was founded as a State, on the rationale that there is a close nexus between the Jewish people and the State of Israel. Gilbert, *supra* n.84, at 422. Otherwise, States infrequently have exercised jurisdiction over non-nationals acting abroad to the detriment of the security of the State, despite statutory authorizations that a State may invoke such jurisdiction. Even during Germany's Third Reich, the National Socialist (Nazi) regime refrained from invoking the protective jurisdiction provided for under German law, despite opportunities to do so. Note, *Israeli Precedent, supra* n.65, at 1094–95.

[167] *E.g., Rivard*, 375 F.2d 882; *Pizzarusso*, 388 F.2d 8; *United States v. Rodriguez*, 182 F. Supp. 479 (S.D. Cal. 1960), *aff'd in part sub nom. Rocha v. United States*, 288 F.2d 545 (9th Cir.), *cert. denied*, 366 U.S. 948 (1961).

[168] Cameron, *supra* n.2, at 50.

[169] *E.g.*, Fr. Penal Code, *supra* n.112, art. 694 (identifying crimes directed against the security of France, counterfeiting seal or currency of France, and those against French diplomatic or consular officers or missions).

[170] Gilbert, *supra* n.84, at 419 n.30; Cameron, *supra* n.2, at 49–50.

[171] Austria, France, and Luxembourg each require the element of intent for all protective principle offenses, while Germany and the Netherlands do not. Cameron, *supra* n.2, at 49 & n.66.

including: (i) the potential for multiple State assertions of jurisdiction and consequential conflicts, as well as the possibility of triggering double jeopardy (discussed *infra*) if the same offender were to be prosecuted in multiple States for the same offense; (ii) the accused could be prosecuted for conduct not punishable in the State where his acts occurred, raising questions about how fair it would be to expect him to be aware of all non-obvious yet relevant criminal laws in that State; and (iii) the defendant might well suffer from language barriers, ignorance regarding host State legal procedures, and delays in collecting evidence and rounding up witnesses.[172] In addition, because defining a State's vital interests and determining what is required to reasonably maintain its security is subject to significant discretion, the applicable scope could be expanded *in extremis* and thereby prove abusive.[173]

Universal Principle. This principle affords jurisdiction to *any* State to prosecute a criminal violation[174] even when: (i) committed within a foreign territory, (ii) involving non-nationals as perpetrator(s) and victim(s), *and* (iii) lacking any protective interest on the part of the State, but which, given the seriousness and broadly condemned character of the crime, nevertheless constitutes an offense against the international community itself.[175] In effect, "certain offenses may be punished by any State because the offenders are common enemies of all mankind and all nations have an equal interest in their apprehension and punishment."[176] The offenses at issue constitute violations of *erga omnes* obligations[177]

172 *Id.* at 32–34.

173 *See* Boister, *supra* n.15, at 295 (noting problems arising from over-inclusive claims such as those implicating economic interests); Note, *Israeli Precedent, supra* n.65, at 1097 (arguing that Israel has pushed the limits on this principle and set a new standard by authorizing jurisdiction merely for an individual's membership in an organization rather than for any acts themselves directed at Israel's security).

174 Universal jurisdiction applies generally to crimes, but "international law does not preclude the application of non-criminal law on this basis, for example, by providing a remedy in tort or restitution for victims of piracy." Restatement (Third), *supra* n.24, § 404 cmt. b.

175 Helen Duffy, The 'War on Terror' and the Framework of International Law 99–100 (2005); DeSchutter, *supra* n.77, at 383 (discussing specific grave breaches of an international character).

176 *In re Extradition of Demjanjuk*, 612 F. Supp. 544, 556 (D.C. Ohio 1985) (citations omitted). Such crimes tend to include those directed against the international public order (*delicta juris gentium*). Robert Kolb, *The Exercise of Criminal Jurisdiction over Int'l Terrorists, in* Enforcing International Law Norms against Terrorism 249 n.80 (Andrea Bianchi ed. 2004).

177 *Erga omnes obligations* refer to those "[o]bligations in whose fulfilment all states have a legal interest because their subject matter is of importance to the international community as a whole. It follows from this that the breach of such an obligation is of concern not

upon which a State may rely to invoke universal jurisdiction to repress and punish criminal conduct.[178] The "idea is to cast the widest net of jurisdiction possible for those limited number of offenses that qualify."[179]

Crimes generally regarded as satisfying this standard, as reflected in international agreements and resolutions, include piracy,[180] slave trade,[181] aircraft hijacking,[182] hostage-taking,[183] grave breaches (*i.e.*, the most serious war crimes) of the Geneva Conventions of 1949 and Additional Protocol I of 1977,[184] apartheid,[185] torture,[186]

only to the victimized state but also to all the other members of the international community. Thus, in the event of a breach of these obligations, every state must be considered justified in invoking (probably through judicial channels) the responsibility of the guilty state committing the internationally wrongful act." "Erga Omnes Obligations," Oxford Reference, *available at* www.oxfordreference.com/view/10.1093/oi/authority.20110803095756413 (last visited on May 1, 2016).

178 Kolb, *supra* n.176, at 249 n.80; Int'l Council on Hum. Rts. Policy, *Hard Cases: Bringing Human Rights Violators to Justice Abroad: A Guide to Universal Jurisdiction*, at 4–5 (Switzerland 1999) [hereinafter ICHRP].

179 Freestone, *supra* n.83, at 44.

180 *Piracy jure gentium* has long been recognized as a crime against all States under international law, Stanbrook & Stanbrook, *supra* n.24, at 120, evidenced in part by the Conv. on the High Seas, Apr. 29, 1958, art. 14, 13 U.S.T. 2312, 450 U.N.T.S. 82, T.I.A.S. No. 5200 ("All States shall co-operate to the fullest possible extent in the repression of piracy on the high seas or in any other place outside the jurisdiction of any State."); Law of the Sea Conv., *supra* n.68, art. 100 (same).

181 Restatement (Third), *supra* n.24, § 404; Sambei & Jones, *supra* n.60, at 3.

182 Heymann & Gershengorn, *supra* n.29, at 115; Freestone, *supra* n.83, at 44 & n.8. Numerous international agreements exist that seek to suppress hijacking and attacks on aircraft, notably including the Conv. for the Suppression of Unlawful Seizure of Aircraft, Dec. 16, 1970, U.N. Doc. A/C.6/418/Corr.1, Annex II, 860 U.N.T.S. 105, 22 U.S.T. 1641, *reprinted in* 10 ILM 133 (1971) [hereinafter Hague Hijacking Conv.]; and the Conv. for the Suppression of Unlawful Acts against the Safety of Civil Aviation, Sept. 23, 1971, U.N. Doc. A/C.6/418/Corr.2, Annex III, 974 U.N.T.S. 177, 24 U.S.T. 564, *reprinted in* 10 ILM 1151.

183 New York Conv., *supra* n.133, art. 1. Although hostage-taking *per se* is absent from the list of crimes subject to universal jurisdiction in the Restatement (Third), *supra* n.24, it arguably is captured by reference to the "hijacking of aircraft" and by "perhaps certain [other] acts of terrorism." *Id.* § 404.

184 Gilbert, *supra* n.60, at 423 n.61; Sambei & Jones, *supra* n.60, at 3; Donnelly, *supra* n.106, at 602. Not all States, including the United States, have ratified Addt'l Prot. I to the Geneva Convs. of August 12, 1949, and Relating to the Protection of Victims of Int'l Armed Conflicts of June 8, 1977 [AP I], U.N. Doc. A/32/144 (1977) Annex I, *reprinted in* 16 ILM 1391, and therefore are not bound by its provisions but nevertheless would be obligated to honor any specific provisions deemed to constitute customary international law.

185 Int'l Conv. on the Suppression and Punishment of the Crime of Apartheid [Apartheid Conv.], Nov. 30, 1973, art. 5, UNGA Res. 3068 (XXVIII), U.N. GAOR, 28th Sess., Supp. No. 30, at 75, U.N. Doc. A/9030 (1973), 1015 U.N.T.S. 243, *reprinted in* 13 ILM 50 (1977).

186 CAT, *supra* n.112; Sambei & Jones, *supra* n.60, at 3; Colangelo, *supra* n.13, at 130.

and crimes against humanity.[187] Other inarguably egregious crimes of an international nature[188] that appear currently to lack consensus to pass muster under the universality principle include genocide[189] and terrorism,[190] although the list of qualifying crimes continues to evolve.[191]

[187] Duffy, *supra* n.175, at 99–100; ICHRP, *supra* n.178, at 1–2; Rome Statute of the Int'l Crim. Ct., July 17, 1998, 2187 U.N.T.S. 3, U.N. Doc. A/CONF.183/9 (1998), *reprinted in* 37 ILM 999 [hereinafter ICC Statute]; Statute of the Int'l Tribunal for the Prosecution of Persons Responsible for Serious Violations of Int'l Humanitarian Law Committed in the Territory of the Former Yugoslavia since 1991, May 25, 1993, adopted by UNSC Res. 827, U.N. Doc. S/25704, at 36, Annex (1993) and S/25704/Add.1 (1993), U.N. Doc. S/RES/827 (1993), *as amended* [hereinafter ICTY Statute]. The Restatement (Third), however, does not expressly include "crimes against humanity" on its list of crimes subject to universal jurisdiction. Restatement (Third), *supra* n.24.

[188] Crimes subject to universal jurisdiction and "crimes against international law" are not necessarily equivalent terms, although they are at times treated synonymously. Some crimes fall within one category but not the other, Gilbert, *supra* n.84, at 423 n.61, and what constitutes a "universal" crime is not settled or static. Heymann & Gershengorn, *supra* n.29, at 112.

[189] It is unclear whether genocide should qualify as a crime subject to universal jurisdiction. By its own terms, the Convention on Genocide does not contemplate genocide as a universal crime. Genocide Conv., *supra* n.94, art. VI ("Persons charged with genocide or any of the other acts enumerated in Article 3 shall be tried by a competent tribunal of the State in the territory of which the act was committed, or by such international penal tribunal as may have jurisdiction with respect to those Contracting Parties which shall have accepted its jurisdiction."). *But see* Donnelly, *supra* n.106, at 603–04 (acknowledging that the United States has not ratified the Convention, but the author still would add genocide to the list of qualifying crimes); Restatement (Third), *supra* n.24, § 404; ICHRP, *supra* n.178, at 4; ICC Statute, *supra* n.187; ICTY Statute, *supra* n.187.

[190] "[P]erhaps certain acts of terrorism" should be subject to universal jurisdiction but not all, Restatement (Third), *supra* n.24, § 404, leaving unclear which ones. *See also* Note, *Israeli Precedent, supra* n.65, at 1099–1100 (noting the lack of current recognition); Kolb, *supra* n.176, at 277 (pointing out unsuccessful efforts to date of the U.N. Working Group to draft a comprehensive convention on international terrorism). Some courts have ruled negatively on this proposition. *See, e.g., Tel-Oren v. Libyan Arab Repub.*, 726 F.2d 774 (D.C. Cir. 1984) (upholding case dismissal for lack of subject matter jurisdiction, ruling that terrorist attacks do not violate the law of nations or other federal law), *cert. denied*, 470 U.S. 1003 (1985). A major reason for the reluctance in elevating terrorism to universal crime status is the lack of an agreed-upon meaning of terrorism. Heymann & Gershengorn, *supra* n.29, at 116–17; Donnelly, *supra* n.106, at 603–04. Finally, even at the national legislative level, governments have struggled with how to define and criminalize terrorism. Heymann & Gershengorn, *supra* n.29, at 116–17. In any event, the definition of terrorism "must [first] be accepted at the international level since the crime envisaged should be international in nature and not merely criminalized at the national level." Kolb, *supra* n.176, at 276.

[191] *See* Note, *Israeli Precedent, supra* n.65, at 1099 (noting the lack of consensus at present in treating as "universal crimes" the "use of explosives to cause a common danger, traffic in

The logic undergirding application of this principle is as follows: (i) to broadly signal intolerance for certain heinous types of conduct;[192] (ii) to bolster deterrence against such conduct by maximizing the number of potential prosecutorial forums and thereby minimizing available safe havens;[193] and (iii) to combat impunity where the territorial State or another State with an extraterritorial nexus to the crime either does not have applicable domestic legislation on the books or the capacity or will to enforce those laws.[194]

An early example of universal jurisdiction arose in the seventeenth century with respect to piracy, a crime that occurred on the high seas (*i.e.*, beyond any single nation's territorial reach[195]) and that threatened all nations alike.[196] Today, universal jurisdiction is recognized under customary international law (for crimes like piracy) and/or international conventions[197] (*e.g.*, concerning hostage-taking and aircraft

narcotics or pornography, injury to submarine cables, crimes against the public health, and injury to international means of communication").

[192] *See* ICHRP, *supra* n.178, at 16 (showing that "serious human rights violations are a concern of everyone").

[193] Sunga, *supra* n.15, at 252; Kolb, *supra* n.176, at 250; Note, *Israeli Precedent, supra* n.65, at 1100 (noting the difficulty in measuring the deterrent effect); ICHRP, *supra* n.178, at 11.

[194] Win-Chiat Lee, *Terrorism and Universal Jurisdiction, in* Intervention, Terrorism, and Torture: Contemporary Challenges to Just War Theory 209 (Steven P. Lee ed. 2007); ICHRP, *supra* n.178, at 1–2. For any number of reasons, there may be a failure to prosecute such heinous crimes of international concern. For example, a State's judiciary may not be fully competent; it could be politically inexpedient to pursue prosecution of one of its own officials; the judges could be subject to threats or intimidation by parties sympathetic to the accused; or seeking justice may compromise reconciliation efforts.

[195] *Cf. United States v. Wright-Barker*, 784 F.2d 161, 166 (3d Cir. 1986) (although no State may assert *territorial* jurisdiction over the high seas, States may assert *extraterritorial* jurisdiction over domestic law violations occurring on the high seas consistent with their constitutional and international law commitments).

[196] The genesis of universal jurisdiction are a matter of dispute. *Compare* Note, *Israeli Precedent, supra* n.65, at 1091 (universal jurisdiction originated with piracy when a menace existed to international commerce) *with* Sunga, *supra* n.15, at 253 ("universal jurisdiction arose out of ancient customs and laws of war, which provided that certain acts, such as the use of certain prohibited weapons or the subjection of civilians to murder or rape, pose such a serious affront to the honor of the military profession that perpetrators could be tried anywhere, regardless of the *locus delictum* or nationality of the offender").

[197] Duffy, *supra* n.175, at 100; Gilbert, *supra* n.84, at 424. To establish universal jurisdiction by convention, the treaty must both specify certain conduct as constituting a crime and contain an agreement of the parties to apply universal jurisdiction to that offense. Puttler, *supra* n.84, at 110–11.

hijacking). Although broadly accepted as a *bona fide* jurisdictional principle, because application of universal jurisdiction is rarely, if ever, mandatory[198] and because few States are prone to prosecute cases in which they have no clear national interest at stake, it has been asserted infrequently.[199] Examples can be found, however, in the courts of Spain[200] and Belgium,[201] although in recent years both States have

198 One of the rare arguable exceptions is for "grave breaches" of war crimes under the Geneva Conventions of 1949 and AP I of 1977. *See* Francesco de Sanctis, *The Practice of Nat'l and Int'l Courts on Transnat'l Seizure: Is a Fair Balance Between Human Rights and Accountability Possible?*, 22 NETH. Q. HUM. RTS. 529, 540 n.53 (2004).

199 SUNGA, *supra* n.15, at 254; *United States v. Yousef*, 927 F. Supp. 673, 681–82 (S.D.N.Y. 1996) (arguing that "while courts have discussed universality as a basis of jurisdiction, in practice, it has never been used as the sole basis for the United States to assert jurisdiction over a defendant." (quoting defendant's brief)). *See also* Tom Gede, *Universal Jurisdiction: The German Case against Donald Rumsfeld*, 8 ENGAGE 41, 41 (June 3, 2007) ("On April 27, 2007, the German Federal Prosecutor General announced that she would not commence an investigation against former U.S. Defense Secretary Donald Rumsfeld and others for international human rights violations associated with the handling of prisoners at Abu Ghraib in Iraq and Guantánamo Bay in Cuba. For the second time within the last two years, the Federal Public Prosecutor's office declined to commence an investigation against Rumsfeld, based upon a criminal accusation filed by German human rights lawyer Wolfgang Kaleck, on behalf of the Center for Constitutional Rights (CCR) and other organizations and individuals. Kaleck argued for, among other things, the application of Germany's Code of Crimes against International Law (CCAIL), a controversial law adopted in 2002 that purports to extend Germany's domestic criminal law jurisdiction to crimes against international law, specifically genocide, crimes against humanity and war crimes.").

200 Spain's first prosecution under universal jurisdiction commenced in January 2005 and was directed against Adolfo Scilingo, a former Argentine naval officer who had been charged with committing acts of genocide, torture, and crimes against humanity during Argentina's "Dirty War." Jason McClurg, *Argentine Naval Officer Tried in Spain for Genocide*, 21 IELR 151 (2005). Although it is widely believed that Spain's attempt to bring to justice Gen. Auguste Pinochet, former President of Chile, was based on an assertion of universal jurisdiction, in fact, it was under the passive personality principle because the crimes he was alleged to have committed were against *Spanish* nationals during his regime in the 1970s. Win-Chiat Lee, *supra* n.194, at 204.

201 Belgium has been the most active exponent of universal jurisdiction to date, although as shown below, its domestic law authorizing universal jurisdiction has been subject to significant dilution over the past decade. In 2001, Belgium successfully prosecuted Sisters Maria Kisito and Gertrude, two Benedictine nuns, for complicity in the commission of genocide in Rwanda in 1994 under a 1999 domestic law that authorized Belgian courts to exercise universal jurisdiction in cases related to genocide and crimes against humanity, Anthony Sammons, *The 'Under-Theorization' of Universal Jurisdiction: Implications for Legitimacy on Trials of War Criminals by National Nat'l Courts*, 21 BERKELEY J. INT'L L. 111, 138 (2003); "Special Report: Judging Genocide," *The Economist*, June 16, 2001, at 23–24. In 2005, Belgium successfully prosecuted two prominent Rwandan businessmen, Samuel Ndashyikirwa and Etienne Nzabonimana, for war crimes also connected to the 1994 genocide in Rwanda but under an amended domestic law that permitted trials for war crimes even when committed by foreigners outside of Belgium so long as the persons

significantly reined in their domestic universal jurisdiction legislation.[202]

Universal jurisdiction has been the subject of pointed criticism. It faces many of the same challenges seen in other extraterritorial contexts, namely, exposing an accused to an unfamiliar legal and linguistic environment, and complicating access to evidence and witnesses.[203] This jurisdictional base, however, introduces additional problems, including: (i) undermining the principle of State sovereignty and thereby setting a dangerous precedent that could later be exercised on a reciprocal basis against the State asserting jurisdiction;[204] (ii) creating political tensions with other, more interested governments,[205] particularly where the State claiming jurisdiction is viewed as having either unfair judicial standards, ulterior motives, or unusually strict sentencing;[206] (iii) burdening a

charged resided in Belgium, "Two Rwandans Guilty over Genocide," *BBC News*, June 29, 2005. In 2006, on behalf of Chadians living in Belgium, Belgium prosecuted the former Chadian leader Hissène Habré *in absentia* on charges of torture and crimes against humanity; the case was allowed to proceed on a "grandfathered" basis. Bruce Zagaris, *Senegal Allows Habre to Stay Pending African Union Decision*, 22 IELR 59, 59–60 (2006).

202 "On 13 March 2014, Spain adopted new legislation restricting its universal jurisdiction law. Henceforth, Spanish jurisdictions are competent to investigate genocide, crimes against humanity and war crimes in three cases: the suspect is a Spanish citizen; the suspect habitually resides in Spain; or the suspect is a foreigner, present on Spanish territory, whose extradition has been denied. These new requirements do not apply to crimes of terrorism, and crimes connected to such an offence." TRIAL, ECCHR, and FIDH, *Universal Jurisdiction Annual Review 2015: Make Way for Justice*, at 33, *available at* www.fidh.org/IMG/pdf/trial-ecchr-fidh_uj_annual_review_2014.pdf (last visited on May 2, 2016). In August 2003, Belgium amended its universal jurisdiction law, permitting jurisdiction of Belgian courts over international crimes only "if the accused is Belgian or has his primary residence in Belgium; if the victim is Belgian or has lived in Belgium for at least three years at the time the crimes were committed; or if Belgium is required by treaty to exercise jurisdiction over the case." HRW, *Belgium: Universal Jurisdiction Law Repealed*, Aug. 1, 2003, *available at* www.hrw.org/news/2003/08/01/belgium-universal-jurisdiction-law-repealed (last visited on May 2, 2016).

203 Note, *Israeli Precedent*, *supra* n.65, at 1101; Boister, *supra* n.15, at 308–09 (observing that criminal laws vary too much across States for individuals to be able to necessarily understand and comply with them).

204 Gary J. Bass, *The Adolf Eichmann Case: Universal and National Jurisdiction*, *in* Universal Jurisdiction: National Courts and the Prosecution of Serious Crimes under International Law 78 (Stephen Macedo ed. 2004).

205 The assertion of universal jurisdiction may embroil that State in a diplomatic confrontation with one or more other States. *Id.*

206 *See* Oscar Schachter, *Int'l Law in Theory and Practice*, 179 Rec. des Cours 263–64 (1982-V) (querying whether the possible absence of any link between the State exercising universal jurisdiction and the person over whom it is exercised requires more extensive safeguards for individual protection); Kolb, *supra* n.176, at 278 (noting the risk of an unfair trial).

domestic court system with what could well amount to a lengthy and complex set of proceedings with no discernible benefit to the local population;[207] and (iv) triggering a resented international imbalance to the extent that this principle were to consistently play out with developed States trying repressive or corrupt officials from developing ones.[208]

An important variant on universal jurisdiction, especially in the extradition context, is a principle known as ***subsidiary universal jurisdiction***. This arises when the State that arrests an alleged offender on its territory chooses to prosecute that person in its courts, even if that State has no other nexus to the crime, the alleged perpetrators, any victims, or its national interests, provided that no other State entitled to exercise jurisdiction insists on or is deemed worthy of doing so.[209] This concept is referred to as "subsidiary"[210] because the prosecuting State is in effect acting on behalf of the territorial State, as well as possibly others, given the absence or rejection of an extradition request; and is "universal" in the sense that there is no other recognized basis for the assertion of jurisdiction[211] and *any* custodial State could therefore exercise jurisdiction. The custodial component is what gives rise to this specialized form of jurisdiction.[212]

This particular brand of jurisdiction confusingly goes by many names. It is sometimes known as the "Custodial (or Representative) Principle of Jurisdiction," as "Vicarious (or Sound) Administration of Justice," or as "Secondary (or Last Resort) Universal Jurisdiction."[213] Regardless of its

207 Bass, *supra* n.204, at 78.

208 ICHRP, *supra* n.178, at 17–28.

209 Carnegie, *supra* n.17, at 405.

210 There is a second subsidiary basis for jurisdiction called the "Distribution of Competence Principle." Under that principle, the territorial State waives its claim to prosecute or punish an alleged offender by requesting *his* State of nationality (or domicile) to do so on its behalf. Cameron, *supra* n.2, at 18. The principle tends to operate with respect to minor offenses like street traffic violations that are of negligible judicial interest to the territorial State, or in instances where the territorial State would prefer that the offender's State of nationality (or domicile) manage the punishment, such as when the offense may call for a stiffer prison sentence in the State of nationality. *Id.* at 83; D. Oehler, Internationales Strafrecht 138–40 (2d ed. 1983).

211 The use of the term "universal" could be viewed as a misnomer because such jurisdiction could derive from a bilateral treaty. Rosalyn Higgins, *The Legal Bases of Jurisdiction, in* Extra-territorial Application of Laws and Responses Thereto 94–95 (Cecil J. Olmstead ed. 1984).

212 *See Arrest Warrant of 11 April 2000* (D.R.C. v. Belg.), [2002] I.C.J. Rep. 3 (Feb. 14) (President Guillaume's Op.) (*obiter dictum*) (stressing the custodial element).

213 *E.g.*, DeSchutter, *supra* n.77, at 381 (discussing "Sound Administration of Justice"); Boister, *supra* n.15, at 305 (referring to "representative or vicarious administration of justice").

label, however, it functions the same, with the custodial State "stepping into the shoes" of another State[214] and, representing its interests, prosecutes the alleged offender but virtually always in cases where the custodial State also treats the conduct at issue as criminal. This principle arises out of the notion of solidarity among States to bring criminals to justice,[215] and generally operates pursuant to a treaty provision[216] authorizing a custodial State to proceed with prosecution in the event it cannot or chooses not to extradite.[217]

A *mandated* counterpart to subsidiary universal jurisdiction, commonly known by the Latin expression *aut dedere aut judicare*,[218] which *would contractually obligate the host State either to extradite a fugitive to a pursuing State or to undertake good faith measures toward adjudicating the fugitive under its own judicial system*,[219] will be discussed more extensively in Chapter 9.c as a fallback alternative to extradition.

214 Gilbert, *supra* n.84, at 423.

215 Puttler, *supra* n.84, at 113.

216 A custodial State sometimes applies this principle in its domestic law absent a treaty but most States seek international treaty support (generally pursuant to a crime suppression or extradition treaty) for what may be a controversial assumption of jurisdiction from the perspective of the territorial State. Boister, *supra* n.15, at 305.

217 *See, e.g., Universal Jurisdiction (Austria) Case*, Sup. Ct., Aus., May 29, 1958, *reprinted in* 28 ILR 341, 342 (1963) (finding that Austrian courts had subsidiary universal jurisdiction under its domestic law to prosecute a Yugoslav national for crimes alleged to have been committed in Yugoslavia where Austria was unwilling to extradite him to Yugoslavia on political offense exclusion grounds).

218 *Aut dedere aut judicare* is understood to mean "one must deliver or adjudicate." The concept originated with Hugo Grotius, the seventeenth-century Dutch international jurist, as *aut dedere aut punire*, which called for punishment by the host State as an alternative to transferring a fugitive, and has since been updated to reflect the concept of judging conduct via trial versus certain punishment. M. Cherif Bassiouni, Introduction to International Criminal Law 334 (2003) [hereinafter Bassiouni, Introduction]. Also, while no letter "j" existed in classical Latin, M. Cherif Bassiouni & Edward M. Wise, Aut Dedere aut Judicare: The Duty to Extradite or Prosecute in International Law xii–xiii n.7 (1995), and so sometimes the term *judicare* is rendered with an "i" as *iudicare*, this book adopts the modern-era spelling. Some scholars, *e.g.*, Kolb, *supra* n.176, at 247, prefer *aut dedere aut prosequi* as a more precise formulation of the term (*i.e.*, "prosecute" versus "adjudicate").

219 An example of *aut dedere* can be found in the case of Mohammed Hamadei, a 22-year-old Lebanese man whom the United States charged, *inter alia*, with hostage-taking and aircraft sabotage in connection with a June 1985 TWA airplane hijacking that resulted in the murder of U.S. Navy diver Robert Stethem. After the West German Government denied his extradition to the United States, the host State agreed to prosecute him, leading to his conviction. Heymann & Gershengorn, *supra* n.29, at 145.

Scholarly difference of opinion persists regarding whether *aut dedere* is a specific manifestation or "sub-species"[220] of universal jurisdiction or, alternatively, should not be regarded as a form of universal jurisdiction at all. At bottom, because the *aut dedere* concept shares the single most significant defining characteristic with universal jurisdiction – namely, the absence of any other recognized nexus between the State and the crime – the noted differences (*e.g.*, right vs. duty,[221] universal application vs. limited application to States parties to conventions, and a broad vs. narrow range of applicable crimes) represent minor variations by comparison.[222] As University of Geneva Law Professor Robert Kolb succinctly summed it up, *aut dedere is* a form of universal jurisdiction that is: (i) relative (dependent on States parties to, and the purpose of, the underlying convention), (ii) compulsory (pursuant to a convention-dictated duty), and (iii) subsidiary (applicable only when the person of interest has not been extradited).[223]

iii Establishing, De-conflicting, and Extending Jurisdiction

This sub-section addresses three critical aspects of jurisdiction: how States prescribe jurisdiction over crimes, how competing State claims of subject matter jurisdiction are resolved, and in what ways – and why – the United States (among others) has sought to extend the scope of its criminal jurisdiction.

States take direction either from: (i) international conventions that authorize them to assert jurisdiction over certain crimes premised on one or more of the principles outlined above,[224] or (ii) customary international law principles that permit State courts through domestic

220 Duffy, *supra* n.175, at 99 & n.141.

221 *See* Claire Mitchell, *The Scope and Operation of the Obligation (Part 2) of* Aut Dedere, aut Judicare*: The Extradite or Prosecute Clause in Int'l Law*, IHEID, Graduate Inst. Publications Online, 2009, at ¶ 13, *available at* http://books.openedition.org/iheid/249 (last visited on May 17, 2016) (distinguishing universal jurisdiction, as permissive, from the *aut dedere* principle, as compulsory).

222 Kolb, *supra* n.176, at 249–54

223 *Id.* at 253–54.

224 *See* Robinson, *supra* n.27, at 488 (subject matter jurisdiction can be supported by overlapping bases). For example, in Israel's request for the extradition of Mahmoud El-Abed Ahmad (*see Ahmad v. Wigen*, 726 F. Supp. 389 (E.D.N.Y. 1989), *aff'd*, 910 F.2d 1063 (2d Cir.), *stay denied*, 111 S. Ct. 23 (1990)), where Ahmad was charged with bombing a bus full of civilians in Israeli-occupied territory, Israel premised its jurisdictional claim on both passive personality and protective principles. Heymann & Gershengorn, *supra* n.29, at 143.

legislation to prescribe subject matter jurisdiction where no prohibition exists.[225] While under the classical rule, a State could assert criminal jurisdiction without necessarily presenting a legitimate nexus to the conduct in question (*i.e.*, the burden of proof lay with a challenger),[226] today States must affirmatively set forth a reasonably close or significant connection.[227] By and large, the territorial and extraterritorial principles outlined above readily justify jurisdiction.[228]

Sometimes two or more States will each claim subject matter jurisdiction over a given act or incident. In such cases of so-called "concurrent jurisdiction,"[229] a situation recognized by international law,[230] de-confliction is required to determine which State has primacy.[231] Some treaties provide a priority consideration,[232] yet many others do not,[233] and no pre-determined hierarchy exists.[234] Often, the territoriality principle

[225] DeSchutter, *supra* n.77, at 380–81.

[226] As set forth in the *Lotus Case*, there was no principled limit to the nature and scope of criminal jurisdiction a State could claim, although such an invocation could be challenged as a violation of international law. Stanbrook & Stanbrook, *supra* n.24, at 111; DeSchutter, *supra* n.77, at 380–81.

[227] Boister, *supra* n.15, at 290; Puttler, *supra* n.84, at 105–06.

[228] *See* Yvonne G. Grassie, Note, *Federally Sponsored Int'l Kidnapping: An Acceptable Alternative to Extradition?*, 64 Wash. U.L.Q. 1205, 1209–10 (1986) (applicable principles "make a finding of subject matter jurisdiction relatively perfunctory in most cases").

[229] This term is not to be confused with the other type of concurrent jurisdiction (discussed *infra*) that refers to competing claims of jurisdiction between a State and the ICTY or ICTR.

[230] *See* Restatement (Third), *supra* n.24, § 403, cmt. d; *Laker Airways Ltd. v. Sabena, Belgian World Airlines*, 731 F.2d 909, 922 (D.C. Cir. 1984) ("Because two or more states may have legitimate interests in prescribing governing law over a particular controversy ... jurisdictional bases are not mutually exclusive ... Thus, under international law, territoriality and nationality often give rise to concurrent jurisdiction.").

[231] *See* Boister, *supra* n.15, at 291 (this can be "as much a political as it is a legal problem.").

[232] *See, e.g.*, Conv. for the Suppression of Unlawful Acts against the Safety of Maritime Navigation, Mar. 10, 1988, art. 11(5), IMO Doc. Sua/Con/15/Rev.1, *reprinted in* 27 ILM 668 (1988) ("[I]n selecting the State to which the offender or alleged offender is to be extradited," States parties shall "pay due regard to the interests and responsibilities of the State Party whose flag the ship was flying at the time of the commission of the offence.").

[233] *See, e.g.*, Hague Hijacking Conv., *supra* n.182 (offering no provision establishing priority of claims in event of concurrent jurisdiction regarding a hijacking); Joseph J. Lambert, Terrorism and Hostages in International Law 163 (1990) (noting that even the State with territorial jurisdiction over the offense has no priority claim and that "priority would seem to depend solely on custody").

[234] Cassese, *supra* n.66, at 348 ("There are no general international rules determinative of this matter, just as there are no international customary rules designed to resolve the question of concurrent jurisdiction of two or more States, by giving pride of place to one legal ground of national jurisdiction ... over another such ground"); *cf.* Christopher Blakesley, *Extraterritorial Jurisdiction, in* 2 International Criminal Law: Procedure

prevails over the others,[235] but that assumes the territorial State has the capacity to effectively and fairly adjudicate the matter,[236] which is not always the case. In addition, some exceptions to this rule exist,[237] and the territorial State may always waive or concede criminal jurisdiction. Ultimately, however, concurrent claims tend to be resolved through consultation or negotiation[238] and are generally based on a "reasonableness" standard[239] that applies with respect to each of the jurisdictional bases,

AND ENFORCEMENT MECHANISMS 82 (2d ed. M. Cherif Bassiouni ed. 1999) ("Thus, it is far from clear that the bases of jurisdiction are hierarchical. Attempting to establish a hierarchy is highly problematical.").

235 *See* IIL, *Draft Resolution, supra* n.4, art. 9(1) ("the jurisdiction of that State shall prevail which shows the closest territorial link with the adressee [sic] of the two orders."); Agreement on Illicit Traffic by Sea, Implementing Article 17 of the U.N. Conv. against Illicit Traffic in Narcotic Drugs and Psychotropic Substances, Jan. 31, 1995, art. 3(4), E.T.S. No. 156 ("The flag State has preferential jurisdiction over any relevant offence committed on board its vessel."). Eighteenth-century Italian jurist Cesare Beccaria, among others, has argued for the primacy of the territorial principle on two grounds: (i) as State laws vary, one should only be punished in a place where one has infringed the law; and (ii) as crime constitutes a violation of the social contract, it is only just that he be punished where the contract was breached. CASSESE, *supra* n.66, at 278. The more a crime can be localized to the territory of a State, the less need there is for that State to rely on the protective principle or any other principle of extraterritoriality to take jurisdiction over it. CAMERON, *supra* n.2, at 52.

236 *See* "Trial for International Crimes," OAS Res. 1/03, Preamble, Oct. 24, 2003 ("[T]he principle of territoriality must prevail in the case of a jurisdictional conflict, provided that there are adequate, effective remedies in that state to prosecute such crimes and guarantee the application of rules of due process for the alleged perpetrators, and that there is an effective will to bring them to justice."). For example, concerns remain about transferring jurisdiction from the ICTR to Rwandan domestic courts, including how effectively they can protect witnesses, the adequacy of working conditions for defense counsel, and the prospect that those convicted for life imprisonment could be placed in solitary confinement. Robert Mugabe, "U.N. Urges ICTR to Transfer Genocide Suspects to Rwanda," *The New Times*, Dec. 17, 2008.

237 For example, "the jurisdiction of a State acting upon a binding decision of the Security Council of the United Nations always prevails over the jurisdiction of a State not so acting." IIL, *Draft Resolution, supra* n.4, art. 9(2).

238 *See id.*, art. 9(4) ("States shall seek to avoid conflicts of jurisdiction by any other means at their disposal, such as self-restraint and consultations"); *e.g.*, Conv. on Combating Bribery of Foreign Public Officials in Int'l Business Transactions, Dec. 18, 1997, art. 4(3), *reprinted in* 37 ILM 1 (1998) ("When more than one party has jurisdiction over an alleged offence described in this Convention, the Parties involved shall, at the request of one of them, consult with a view to determining the most appropriate jurisdiction for prosecution.").

239 *See* RESTATEMENT (THIRD), *supra* n.24, § 421 (noting a reasonableness standard applies when States exercise subject matter jurisdiction); McAlister, *supra* n.24, at 467–68 (States are limited to "reasonable" exercises of extra-territorial jurisdiction); *e.g., Noriega*, 746 F. Supp. at 1513–15. Reasonableness is understood to mean that asserting subject matter

except possibly the universal principle.[240] In effect, each State's claim is measured and compared against others according to the significance and proximity of the nexus established between the State and the crime.[241]

Over the past three decades, triggered by increasing globalization and a spike in international terrorism against their nationals abroad,[242] some States, most notably the United States, have extended the reach of their extraterritorial criminal jurisdiction.[243] In a series of federal statutes in the 1980s – the Aircraft Sabotage Act (1984), the Omnibus Diplomatic Security and Antiterrorism Act (1986), and the Hostage-Taking (1988) – the U.S. Congress sought to raise the prospects of bringing a class of criminals to justice by expressly extending U.S. subject matter jurisdiction, primarily through the liberalized use of the passive personality principle, for certain crimes committed *against U.S. citizens* abroad. This stream of legislation represented a deviation from historical American practice, which had relied predominantly on territoriality and active personality principles in its assertions of subject matter jurisdiction.[244]

Such federal statutes operate on several fronts to: (i) fill in legal gaps that had previously precluded U.S. courts from prosecuting such violators as a function of subject matter jurisdiction; (ii) exert greater pressure on host States either to extradite or prosecute such violators; (iii) impress

jurisdiction will "not conflict with another state's significant interest." RESTATEMENT (THIRD), *supra* n.24, § 403 cmt. a.

240 *Compare id.* § 423 (treating universal jurisdiction as an exception to the reasonableness standard) *with* Schachter, *supra* n.206, at 240–42 (treating all forms of extra-territorial jurisdiction under the reasonableness standard).

241 *See* IIL, *Draft Resolution*, *supra* n.4, art. 9(1) ("Failing such [a territorial] link, the jurisdiction of the State most directly involved shall prevail.").

242 *See* David M. Kennedy, *et al.*, *The Extradition of Mohammed Hamadei*, 31 HARV. INT'L L.J. 5, 6 (1990) (according to the U.S. Department of State, 30–35% of worldwide incidents over a then-recent period were directed against U.S. citizens and interests).

243 Donnelly, *supra* n.106, at 599.

244 *Id.* In a recent, widely reported application of two statutes with longer established extraterritorial reach – the 1970 Racketeer Influenced and Corrupt Organizations (RICO) Act and the 1961 International Travel Act (which prohibits interstate or foreign travel or the use of U.S. mail to engage in certain criminal activities), the United States issued a mass indictment in May 2015 of fourteen senior officials of FIFA, soccer's global governing body, for corrupt practices. The U.S. DoJ "claim[ed] the right to go after anyone who uses its banking system (including indirectly, using 'correspondent' banks to clear payments) or plans an illegal scheme on its soil. Some of the accused FIFA officials and marketing executives allegedly discussed or engaged in palm-greasing while in America. Several banks and branches that handled transactions are American, and some of the implicated associations and marketing companies have offices there." "America's Legal Reach: The World's Lawyer," *The Economist*, June 6, 2015, at 50.

upon foreign judges that Congress is amenable to the passive personality principle and thereby spur them to rule favorably in cases involving extraditions to the United States; and (iv) signal to actual or would-be terrorists that the United States is committed to bringing the full weight of its law enforcement machinery on them and, in doing so, deter such actions.[245]

At the same time, the United States has supported the drafting and ratification of multilateral crime suppression treaties that authorize greater latitude for extraterritorial jurisdiction over transborder crimes to foster extradition.[246] One consequence of this phenomenon is that "[a]s States make increasingly broad claims to extraterritorial legislative jurisdiction (and where those claims enjoy a degree of acceptance), of necessity it becomes more likely that more than one State will have potential judicial jurisdiction to try an offender."[247]

iv Contrast with Concurrent Jurisdiction of the ICTY/ICTR

To underscore the dynamics of *State* criminal jurisdiction, while eliminating any potential confusion with a distinctive jurisdictional model that goes by the same term ("concurrent jurisdiction"), it is useful to describe and distinguish the rules and modalities governing the International Criminal Tribunal for the former Yugoslavia (ICTY) and the International Criminal Tribunal for Rwanda (ICTR).

At times, a State is requested to surrender a fugitive to an international criminal tribunal that has levied charges against him.[248] A half-century after the International Military Tribunal (IMT) at Nuremberg that litigated war crimes claims against major Nazi officers arising out of World War II[249] – the first modern-era court for international crimes of its

[245] Heymann & Gershengorn, *supra* n.29, at 103, 142–45.

[246] Boister, *supra* n.15, at 311.

[247] Colin Warbrick, *Recent Developments in U.K. Extradition Law*, 56 Int'l & Comp. L.Q. 199, 206 (2007).

[248] When an international criminal tribunal prosecutes an international law claim it is known as *direct* enforcement. By contrast, when a State decides not to surrender a fugitive to an international tribunal, but rather to prosecute him in its own domestic courts or transfer him to another State's courts, it is called *indirect* enforcement of international law. Bassiouni, Introduction, *supra* n.218, at 333.

[249] That Tribunal, along with its counterpart in Tokyo, the International Military Tribunal for the Far East (IMTFE), were distinct from today's international criminal tribunals in that they were held on occupied territory in Germany and Japan, respectively, and the

kind[250] – a number of others have sprouted up. For simplicity sake, we can classify them into three bundles.

First, there are the two tribunals (ICTY and ICTR) established in the 1990s by the U.N. Security Council (UNSC) to address specific conflicts in the former Yugoslavia and Rwanda, respectively. Second, there is the International Criminal Court (ICC), which was created by treaty in 1998, operates worldwide, and relies on the principle of "complementary" jurisdiction.[251] Because complementary jurisdiction is heavily deferential to national courts, it is not so distinctive and therefore does not warrant

fugitives were surrounded by Allied forces. Consequently, those Tribunals did not depend so heavily on other States to provide law enforcement cooperation as today's do. *See* Kenneth J. Harris & Robert Kushen, *Surrender of Fugitives to the War Crimes Tribunals for Yugoslavia and Rwanda: Squaring Int'l Legal Obligations with the U.S. Constitution*, 7 Crim. L.F. 561, 561–62 (1996).

250 *See* Andreas O'Shea, Amnesty for Crime in International Law and Practice 104 (2002) ("The earliest known example would seem to be an international military tribunal established by the Holy Roman Empire in 1474 in Breisach, Germany, to try Peter von Hagenbach for crimes against 'the laws of God and man' consisting of raping, killing and pillaging the property of innocent civilians.").

251 Under complementary jurisdiction national courts are accorded presumptive priority. As the late Professor Antonio Cassese summarized its operation, the international tribunal "must generally defer to national courts, except when these courts are not in a position to do justice in a proper and fair way, and in addition the case is of sufficient gravity to warrant the [Tribunal's] stepping in." Cassese, *supra* n.66, at 353. The rationale behind this approach lies with respect for State sovereignty, concern for inundating the ICC with a worldwide caseload, and recognition that national courts can more readily locate and secure evidence and witnesses. *Id.* at 351. Like other international treaties, the Rome Statute establishing the ICC applies only to States that have either ratified or acceded to its terms. Accordingly, when the ICC issues an order requesting that a State arrest and surrender a fugitive for the purpose of prosecution under Article 89, only States Parties are obligated to comply. Geert-Jan Alexander Knoops, Surrender to International Criminal Courts: Contemporary Practice and Procedures 15 (2002). A narrow exception exists for a State to optionally declare the non-applicability of war crimes regarding one's own nationals or on own territory for up to seven years after the Statute has taken effect with respect to that State. ICC Statute, *supra* n.187, art. 124. Per Article 89, the failure to comply may result in a finding to that effect by the Court and a referral to the Assembly of States Parties (or, alternatively, to the UNSC to the extent that it referred the matter). Compliance entails taking immediate steps to arrest the subject and surrender him to the Tribunal, unless it needs to consult with the Court first or another justifiable circumstance arises under Article 89 that is handled immediately. *But see* Norimitsu Onishi, "Omar al-Bashir, Leaving South Africa, Eludes Arrest Again," *INYT*, June 15, 2015, at 1 (discussing how the South African Government allowed Sudanese President Omar Hassan al-Bashir, who was wanted for violations of war crimes, crimes against humanity, and genocide in connection with suppressing an insurgency in Darfur, to flee Johannesburg while attending an African Union meeting "just hours before a South African court ruled that the government was legally required to arrest him and hand him over to international prosecutors, despite the

elaborated treatment herein. Third, there are (or have been) various *ad hoc* or "hybrid" tribunals, including in Cambodia, Kosovo, Sierra Leone, East Timor, and Lebanon, that are limited to single countries or conflicts and are governed by domestic as well as international law and/or adjudicated by panels consisting of mixed domestic and international judges.[252] The statutes forming these relatively new tribunals establish a jurisdictional relationship strictly with the host State's courts, and thus are not addressed in this analysis.[253]

The ICTY and ICTR are unique in that they were created as subsidiary judicial organs of the UNSC pursuant to its Chapter VII enforcement power under the U.N. Charter.[254] In essence, the UNSC determined that the situations in the former Yugoslavia and Rwanda constituted a "threat to international peace and security" and therefore took "measures . . . to give effect to [those] decisions"[255] by establishing courts that, in holding criminals publicly accountable, could help minimize the incidence of serious wartime violations by serving as a deterrent and restore peace.[256] Notably, these Tribunals do *not* constitute supranational bodies to which

fact that South Africa is a member of the ICC and a South African high court had issued an order prohibiting al-Bashir from leaving the country").

252 Duffy, *supra* n.175, at 103–06. In addition, in August 2012, "Senegal and the [African Union] signed an agreement to establish a special court in the Senegalese justice system with African judges appointed by the AU presiding over [former Chadian leader Hissène Habré's] trial and any appeals." Bruce Zagaris, *Senegal and Chad Sign Cooperation Agreement to Facilitate Habre's Trial*, 29 IELR 309 (2013). International human rights tribunals, such as the European Court of Human Rights and Inter-American Court of Human Rights, are not relevant on this score because they are designed to judge the extent to which *States* comply with their international obligations to uphold human rights standards, rather than to evaluate whether an *individual* has committed a crime.

253 *E.g.*, Statute of the Special Tribunal for Lebanon (STL), UNSC Res. 1664 (2006), Mar. 29, 2006, art. 4, U.N. Doc. S/RES/1757 (STL has primacy over Lebanese domestic courts).

254 Knoops, *supra* n.251, at 17; de Sanctis, *supra* n.198, at 542. Although not established as a subsidiary judicial organ of the UNSC, the Special Tribunal for Lebanon (STL), like the ICTY and ICTR, was formally created by the UNSC (by Res. 1757 (2007)), after the speaker of the Lebanese parliament refused to convene the parliament to ratify the January 23, 2007, agreement struck between the United Nations and the Lebanese Government, and subsequently a majority of Lebanese MPs petitioned the U.N. Secretary-General for the UNSC to establish the Tribunal. Special Tribunal for Lebanon website, "Creation of the STL," *available at* www.stl-tsl.org/en/about-the-stl/creation-of-the-stl (last visited on May 2, 2016).

255 U.N. Charter, *supra* n.14, arts. 39 and 41.

256 *See* ICTY Statute, *supra* n.187; Statute of the Int'l Tribunal for the Prosecution of Persons Responsible for Genocide and Other Serious Violations of Int'l Humanitarian Law Committed in the Territory of Rwanda and Rwandan Citizens Responsible for Genocide and Other Such Violations Committed in the Territory of Neighbouring States, between 1 January 1994 and 31 December 1994, Nov. 8, 1994, adopted by UNSC Res. 955, U.N. SCOR,

States have conceded or transferred criminal jurisdiction,[257] but rather UNSC sub-organs with unprecedented concurrent jurisdictional authority that can mandate cooperation to secure the presence of alleged offenders in furtherance of a treaty interest to restore and maintain international peace and security.[258]

Consequently, when ICTY or ICTR trial chambers issue an order to a State for a "natural person"[259] to be identified and located, arrested and detained, and/or surrendered or transferred, or for any other form of prosecutorial assistance at any stage of the proceedings,[260] that order is to be treated as an extension of UNSC enforcement authority[261] and is to be acted upon "without undue delay."[262] (Although such an order is compulsory, a responding State may first ensure the authenticity of the order or indictment, or reconfirm that the person arrested is the same one identified on the warrant.[263])

The ICTY's and ICTR's authority to mandate State cooperation technically extends only to U.N. member States on account of several articles of the U.N. Charter, which variously require them to carry out decisions

49th Sess., 3453d mtg. at 3, U.N. Doc. S/RES/955 (1994), *as amended, reprinted in* 33 ILM 1598 [hereinafter ICTR Statute].

[257] Although one could plausibly read the U.N. Secretary-General's Report as intending to make a Tribunal Order equivalent to the legal and moral authority of a UNSC resolution, it is questionable whether the UNSC could delegate its authority in this respect. A more reasonable reading is that the UNSC created a subsidiary organ in the context of a Chapter VII enforcement measure. Kenneth S. Gallant, *Securing the Presence of Defendants before the Int'l Tribunal for the Former Yugoslavia: Breaking with Extradition*, 5 Crim. L.F. 557, 560–66 (1994). *See also* Knoops, *supra* n.251, at 14–15; Mark Brkljacic, Note, *The Dangers of State Sponsored and Court Ratified Abduction*, 5 J. Int'l L. & Prac. 117, 131–32 (1996).

[258] *See* Harris & Kushen, *supra* n.249, at 564–65 (U.N. member obligations to render assistance derive from Chapter VII of the U.N. Charter).

[259] "Natural persons" in this context comprise not only nationals of U.N. member States, but also of non-member States and even of *de facto* entities exercising government functions, whether recognized as a State or not. Gallant, *supra* n.257, at 559 n.5.

[260] *Report of the Secretary-General pursuant to Paragraph 2 of Security Council Resolution 808* (1993), ¶ 125, U.N. Doc. S/25704 & Add.1, 125 (May 3, 1993), *reprinted in* 32 ILM 1163 (1993).

[261] *Id.* ¶ 126.

[262] Int'l Tribunal for the Prosecution of Persons Responsible for Serious Violations of Int'l Humanitarian Law Committed in the Territory of the Former Yugoslavia since 1991, RPE, Feb. 11, 1994, *as amended*, 29(2)(e), U.N. Doc. IT/32/Rev.7 (1996), [hereinafter ICTY RPE]; Int'l Crim. Trib. for Rwanda, RPE June 29, 1995, art. 28, U.N. Doc. ITR/3/REV.1 (1995) [hereinafter ICTR RPE].

[263] Gallant, *supra* n.257, at 586–87.

of the UNSC in general, to execute UNSC decisions specifically for the maintenance of international peace and security, and to meet such obligations even if duties under other international agreements should conflict with those under the U.N. Charter.[264] Accordingly, each of the 193 sovereign States that are U.N. members today (including the most recent addition of South Sudan in July 2011 but excluding the Vatican City, which has its own *sui generis* status) is subject to this duty. Although a non-U.N. member State or a non-State territory (such as Palestine) would not be legally obligated to comply with an ICTY or ICTR order, such a State or territory could still be penalized by the UNSC to the extent its non-cooperation were deemed to be a "threat to international peace and security."[265]

U.N. member States must give legal effect to these obligations.[266] Dualist States, like the United States and Germany, must adopt implementing domestic legislation, consistent with their constitutions, to authorize the surrender of fugitives to these tribunals upon request.[267] That legislation must prevail over any other national law, including those related to extradition or domestic prosecution, which could otherwise obstruct or impede such cooperation with one of the tribunals.[268] Absent such required deference to the ICTY and ICTR, States would be far less likely to actively seek out and surrender fugitives who, in turn, might well continue to wield power or influence in that State whether because of their former positions, personal wealth, and/or high-level contacts.[269]

264 U.N. Charter, *supra* n.14, arts. 25, 48, 49, and 103.

265 *Id.*, Chapter VII and art. 2(6); Knoops, *supra* n.251, at 14–15.

266 *See* Harris & Kushen, *supra* n.249, at 567 (this requirement is based on UNSC resolutions (827, 955), the Statutes (arts. 28 and 29), and the Secretary-General's Report). In fact, all States have promulgated some kind of pre-surrender procedure, most typically a judicial hearing. *Id.* at 568.

267 *See, e.g.*, 18 USC. § 3181 *et seq.* (2012) based on legislation executed in February 1996. The U.S. approach was somewhat unconventional. In 1995, U.S. President Bill Clinton entered into an executive agreement with the ICTR, which provided that the United States "agrees to surrender to the Tribunal ... persons ... found in its territory whom the Tribunal has charged with or found guilty of a violation or violations within the competence of the Tribunal." Agreement on the Surrender of Persons, U.S.-ICTR, Jan. 24, 1995, art. 1(1), T.I.A.S. 12601. A year later, the U.S. Congress passed implementing legislation. National Defense Authorization Act for Fiscal Year 1996, Pub. L. 104–106, Feb. 10, 1996, § 1342, Stat. 186, 486 (1996). The validity of this so-called "Congressional-Executive Agreement" was challenged as it authorized the surrender of individuals absent a treaty. *See Ntakirutimana v. Reno*, 184 F.3d 419 (5th Cir. 1999) (upholding constitutionality of the Agreement), *cert. denied*, 120 S. Ct. 977 (2000).

268 ICTY RPE, *supra* n.262, Rule 58; ICTR RPE, *supra* n.262, Rule 58.

269 Gallant, *supra* n.257, at 564.

A prime illustration of such cooperation occurred in May 2007, when pursuant to an arrest warrant and surrender order, the Serbian Government captured Zdravko Tolimir and transferred him to the ICTY. As a senior intelligence and security officer to the chief of staff of the Bosnian Serb military forces, who had been implicated in the killing of approximately 8,000 Bosnian Muslims in Srebenica in July 1995, Tolimir was then regarded as the third highest-ranking fugitive in the Balkans.[270] About a year later, in July 2008, the Serbian Government surrendered to the ICTY Radovan Karadžić, the former Bosnian Serb leader who had been indicted for genocide, crimes against humanity, and war crimes because of the "ethnic cleansing" of non-Serbs he perpetrated during the 1992–95 Bosnian War; Karadžić had been an ICTY fugitive for thirteen years.[271] Other types of cooperation may include a State seconding prosecutors or judges to the ICTY or ICTR, supplying a tribunal with evidence or intelligence, or offering financial rewards for information leading to the arrest of fugitives sought by a Tribunal.[272]

Although under their statutes, the ICTY and ICTR "shall have primacy over national courts" and "may formally request national courts to defer to the[ir] competence,"[273] the judge-made rules that fleshed out those pronouncements do not require all relevant cases to be tried by these tribunals and, indeed, even contemplate the tribunals *turning over cases to national courts* in appropriate instances.[274] Accordingly, the ICTY may claim primacy over a national court in only three instances: (i) where a national court either intentionally or unwittingly devalues the seriousness of an international crime by treating it as an ordinary crime; (ii) where a national court appears to lack independence or impartiality or its proceedings otherwise are intended to "shield the accused from individual criminal responsibility"; and (iii) the case at

270 Bruce Zagaris, *Serbia Arrests and Surrenders No. Three War Crimes Suspect to ICTY*, 23 IELR 313, 313–14 (2007).

271 Peter Finn, "Karadzic Extradited to The Hague to Face War Crimes Charges," *Wash. Post*, July 30, 2008, at A9.

272 *E.g.*, Bruce Zagaris, *U.S. Renews Rewards for the Arrest of Men Suspected of War Crimes During Rwanda Genocide*, 24 IELR 335, 336 (2008) (discussing how the U.S. Government renewed its rewards program in May 2008 by offering up to US $5 million for information leading to the arrest of a fugitive wanted by the ICTR).

273 ICTY Statute, *supra* n.187, art. 9; ICTR Statute, *supra* n.256, art. 8.

274 ICTY RPE, *supra* n.262, Rule 11 *bis*; ICTR RPE, *supra* n.262, Rule 11 *bis*. In recent years, due to mounting workloads and a recognition of more efficient and impartial national courts, the tribunals have been increasingly amenable to national court jurisdiction. Cassese, *supra* n.66, at 351.

issue is closely related to others under the jurisdiction of the tribunal or could have significant legal or factual bearing on other investigations or proceedings.[275] A somewhat different standard applies to the ICTR.[276]

The dynamic involving a State's surrender of a fugitive to one of these two tribunals can be distinguished in several respects from the extradition exercise carried out between States. To begin, as discussed above, States and the Tribunals do not operate on a level plane; the tribunals have international legal primacy over States regarding prosecutorial access to fugitives in what can be characterized as a "vertical" relationship.[277] In addition, such transfers are not based strictly on reciprocity; rather, transfers tend to move predominantly in the direction of the tribunals.[278] Moreover, surrenders to the ICTY and ICTR are subject less to legal technicalities and operate more informally in connection with the manner in which they are effected than is the case with inter-State extraditions.[279]

Furthermore, the rules governing surrenders to the tribunals dispense with any recognition of national sovereignty or prerogatives that could potentially thwart the turnover of a fugitive. This point is manifest in several respects. First, the *aut dedere* principle is inapposite, as a State has no choice regarding whether to transfer a fugitive or prosecute him in its own courts; the decision is mandatorily pre-struck in favor of transfer

[275] ICTY RPE, *supra* n.262, Rule 9.

[276] ICTR RPE, *supra* n.262, Rule 9 ("Where it appears to the Prosecutor that crimes which are the subject of investigations or criminal proceedings instituted in the courts of any State: (i) Are the subject of an investigation by the Prosecutor; (ii) Should be the subject of an investigation by the Prosecutor considering, *inter alia:* (a) The seriousness of the offences; (b) The status of the accused at the time of the alleged offences; (c) The general importance of the legal questions involved in the case; or (iii) Are the subject of an indictment in the Tribunal, the Prosecutor may apply to the Trial Chamber designated by the President to issue a formal request that such court defer to the competence of the Tribunal.").

[277] de Sanctis, *supra* n.198, at 542.

[278] Harris & Kushen, *supra* n.249, at 585; Louis Klarevas, *The Surrender of Alleged War Criminals to Int'l Tribunals: Examining the Constitutionality of Extradition Via Congressional-Executive Agreement*, 8 UCLA J. INT'L L. & FOR. AFF. 77, 112 (2003).

[279] For example, the ICTY rejected a preliminary motion raised by a defendant that he had been unlawfully surrendered under the legislation of the host State, arguing that as the surrender request was issued to the FRY but was made by the Government of Serbia, and because the latter lacked the competence to carry out the transfer, there was an abuse of process. The trial chamber found that the defendant's rights had not been "egregiously breached" and that the transfer had been handled consistent with the procedural provisions of the ICTY, which in any event prevail over any domestic legal impediment to the surrender of a fugitive. *Prosecutor v. Milosević*, Case No. IT-99–37-PT, Tr. Ch., Decision on Prelim. Motions, Nov. 8, 2001.

even while the tribunals' constituitive documents allow for "concurrent" domestic jurisdiction.[280]

Second, as will be shown when discussing the nature of extradition in Chapter 4.d, whereas a State may inquire as to the motivation or merits of an extradition request, especially by independently insisting on *prima facie* (or other standard of) evidence, surrenders to the ICTY or ICTR adopt the so-called "rule of non-inquiry,"[281] which amounts to taking at face value the determination of a tribunal judge regarding the propriety of a surrender request and any post-delivery treatment.[282]

Third, while a State contemplating whether to extradite might rely on any number of discretionary substantive or procedural legal grounds to reject a request from another State, no such bases are relevant or acceptable in the ICTY/ICTR surrender context.[283] For example, if a State

280 The UNSC and tribunals have dispensed with the *aut dedere* formula, as the model of sovereign equality and reciprocity is inadequate to deal with offenses within the tribunals' subject matter jurisdiction, such as violations of international humanitarian law. "In many instances the crimes have been committed by persons working on behalf of state policy, in the name of state policy, or in the name of a group aspiring to state or government status. The requirement that a state prosecute if it does not extradite is insufficient where there is reason to suspect that such a prosecution will not be conducted in good faith. Without the support of a legal obligation to transfer defendants and without the muscle of the Security Council, neither the Tribunal nor the concerned states are likely to try many defendants charged with humanitarian crimes in the former Yugoslavia." Gallant, *supra* n.257, at 570.

281 For purposes of definition in the present context, the "rule of non-inquiry" refers to *the principle in which a State's executive deems it inappropriate to ascertain the motive behind another State's request for the custodial transfer of a fugitive, and/or to examine another State's legal standards or procedures for handling a fugitive post-delivery, and therefore is prepared to transfer a fugitive without scrutiny.*

282 Under the ICTY and ICTR statutes and rules, there is no requirement that the tribunals transmit to the arresting State a statement of the evidence against the accused; at best, the warrant and confirmed indictment will be proof that a tribunal judge has determined that a *prima facie* case exists. Harris & Kushen, *supra* n.249, at 586. Although no exceptions are facially permitted, in practice it is up to the States themselves to minimize the risk of a clash between their domestic and international legal obligations by streamlining the surrender process and by imposing an evidentiary threshold lower than the usual national standard. Maogoto, *supra* n.114, at 169. Some States, however, have retained domestic evidentiary safeguards; *e.g.*, the United States imposes a "reasonable basis" standard, and both Australia and New Zealand allow their respective Attorneys-General to refuse requests in exceptional cases. *Id.* at 171.

283 ICTY Statute, *supra* n.187, art. 29; ICTY RPE, *supra* n.262, Rule 58; ICTR RPE, *supra* n.262, art. 58. *See also* Maogoto, *supra* n.114, at 167–68; *Third Annual Report of the Int'l Tribunal for the Prosecution of Persons Responsible for Serious Violations of Int'l Humanitarian Law Committed in the Territory of the Former Yugoslavia Since 1991*, U.N. GAOR, 51st Sess., pt. 2, U.N. Docs. A/51/292, S/1996/665 (1996).

might rule out extradition where its own national is the subject of the request[284] or where domestic law applies a strict time bar for a given crime,[285] a State may not deny an ICTY or ICTR trial court order on such bases.[286] Indeed, it was the express intention of the UNSC in creating these tribunals to overcome such domestic legal barriers to the transfer of fugitives.[287]

Fourth, extradition and surrender to the ICTY or ICTR also differ in principle in terms of the weight of enforcement and political leverage they comparatively exert. States may impose sanctions or exact other penalties on one another for the failure to extradite a wanted fugitive, as well as "jawbone" and engage in exchanges, but ultimately States are limited in the muscle they can flex. By contrast, because the ICTY and ICTR were established under UNSC auspices, the UNSC, at the behest of a tribunal president,[288] in appropriate circumstances may verbally condemn non-cooperation, apply economic or diplomatic incentives to encourage cooperation regarding an arrest and surrender order, or even intervene with the use of force or sanctions when a State fails to cooperate.[289]

[284] *See* Knoops, *supra* n.251, at 12 (a constitutional prohibition on the extradition of nationals does not preclude surrender to the ICTY). *But see* Jovan Kovacic, "U.S. Envoy Warns Serb President to Aid Tribunal," *Boston Globe*, Nov. 8, 1996, at A2; Harris & Kushen, *supra* n.249, at 570–71 & n.22 (noting that the Bosnian Serbs nevertheless raised the nationality exception to extradition to justify refusal to cooperate with the ICTY).

[285] Harris & Kushen, *supra* n.249, at 573 (limitations of time do not apply to tribunal prosecutions and should not be a valid basis for denying a surrender request; indeed, the non-applicability of such limitations to many violations of IHL is recognized as emerging customary law, and is enshrined in the U.N. Conv. on the Non-Applicability of Statutory Limitations to War Crimes and Crimes against Humanity, Nov. 26, 1968, UNGA Res. 2391 (XXIII), 754 U.N.T.S. 73 (1968)).

[286] U.S. Agreements with the Tribunals reflect this reality. *See* Michael Abbell, Extradition to and from the United States 179–80 (2010) (noting that U.S. agreements with the ICTY and ICTR, while modeled on standard U.S. extradition treaties with other States, omit references to the "nationality of requested person, political offenses, military offenses, specialty, lapse of time, *non bis in idem*, and dual criminality" as inapplicable).

[287] Harris & Kushen, *supra* n.249, at 573.

[288] ICTY RPE, *supra* n.262, Rules 7 *bis*, 59, 61; ICTR RPE, *supra* n.262, Rules 10, 59, and 61 (if within a reasonable time after an arrest warrant has been transmitted to the State, no report is made on action taken, this shall be deemed a failure to execute the warrant of arrest and the tribunal may notify the UNSC accordingly).

[289] Michael P. Scharf, *The Tools for Enforcing Int'l Criminal Justice in the New Millennium: Lessons from the Yugoslavia Tribunal*, 49 DePaul L. Rev. 925, 927–28 (2000); Mary Alice Kovac, *Apprehension of War Crimes Indictees: Should the U.N. Outsource Private Actors to Catch Them?*, 51 Cath. U. L. Rev. 619, 648 (2002).

Sometimes, the threat of such UNSC measures can be enough to coax a State into complying with its obligations,[290] but that threat has not been invoked often.[291] (In addition, certain supranational bodies can foster compliance by host States with tribunal requests through the offer of incentives or disincentives,[292] or through direct cooperation via a peacekeeping mission.[293]) Notwithstanding their powerful legal mandate for prompting States to arrest and surrender fugitives found within their territory, however, the ICTY and ICTR have not always fared well with regard to State cooperation.[294]

* * * * *

[290] *E.g.*, Maogoto, *supra* n.114, at 216 (in January 1995, several African states, including Kenya, agreed to hand over to the ICTR those who had taken part in the Rwandan genocide, but later on, Kenyan President Moi stated that he would refuse to cooperate with the ICTR and that he would prevent them from seeking out suspects in his country; ICTR Prosecutor Goldstone then sent him a letter warning him that his refusal would be regarded as a breach of Kenya's obligations under international law and a matter for the UNSC to consider; President Moi soon retracted his statement).

[291] *See* Cassese, *supra* n.66, at 350.

[292] For example, in 2006, on account of Serbia's non-cooperation with the ICTY, the European Union (E.U.) stalled negotiations with Serbia over joining the E.U. as a member State; Serbia's interest in membership evidently helped prompt its arrest and surrender of Zdravko Tolimir, after which the membership talks were quickly resumed. Bruce Zagaris, *Serbia Arrests and Surrenders No. Three War Crimes Suspect to ICTY*, 23 IELR 313 (2007).

[293] *See* Evelyn Leopold, "U.N. Council Readies Resolution on New Bosnia Force," *Reuter EC Rep.*, Dec. 15, 1995; Harris & Kushen, *supra* n.249, at 562–63 n.3 (the NATO peacekeeping force in Bosnia (IFOR, later known as SFOR) was obligated to arrest and surrender tribunal-designated fugitives under the General Framework Agreement of 1995; NATO announced that it would detain indicted war criminals who came into contact with the peacekeeping force in the execution of its assigned tasks in order to assure the transfer of these persons to the tribunal).

[294] *See* Walter Gary Sharp, Sr., *In Search of Peace and Justice: War Criminals at Large in the Former Yugoslavia*, 32 Int'l Law. 489, 489–90 (1998) (the ICTY has had difficulty apprehending many suspected war criminals due in large part to the international community's unwillingness to actively search for and arrest war criminals within Yugoslavia); Bruce Zagaris, *Rwanda Prosecutor Calls on Surrounding Countries to Cooperate with ICTR*, 21 IELR 32 (2005) (in October 2004, ICTR prosecutor Hassan Jallow urged countries still harboring fourteen important genocide suspects to arrive and transfer them to the ICTR and fulfill their legal obligations to cooperate with the ICTR); Bruce Zagaris, *Int'l Criminal Tribunal for the Former Yugoslavia (ICTY) Focuses on Remaining Fugitives*, 23 IELR 437 (2007) (the ICTY Office of the Prosecutor has maintained that the international community has not done enough to arrest key fugitive leaders, particularly Mladić and Karadžić and transfer them to the tribunal); Colette Retif, *By What Means Justice? The Acceptance of Secret Indictments in the United States and in Int'l Law*, 13 Pace Int'l L. Rev. 233, 234 (2001).

This chapter focused on subject matter jurisdiction as a condition precedent for a pursuing State court to adjudicate criminal charges against a fugitive. The next chapter turns briefly to an examination of those circumstances in which fugitives come into the custody of a pursuing State due to sheer fortuity. Such scenarios are treated in the background context because, beginning in Part II, this book addresses the wide variety of ways in which States *actively* seek the custody of fugitives abroad.

3

"Silver Platter" Scenarios

As a final preliminary matter before exploring the various means and methods by which States attempt to bring fugitives to justice, it is essential to recognize that, on many occasions, a fugitive returns, is returned, or his return is substantially facilitated – to pursuing State territory, custody, or control effortlessly or adventitiously (from its perspective), whether or not an extradition request is pending. For the purposes of this inquiry, such instances are called "silver platter"[1] scenarios because of the sheer fortuity with which a pursuing State acquires a sought-after fugitive. This chapter explores how and why such scenarios occur and evaluates the legal implications arising therefrom.

More specifically, such scenarios may take place: (i) based on an error or misunderstanding by the fugitive, an international criminal tribunal, or the host State, including via deportation while innocent of the receiving State's law enforcement interest in the fugitive; (ii) intentionally by the fugitive but in reliance on personal motivations unrelated to law enforcement measures or pressures;[2] (iii) deliberately by the host State in reversing an initial extradition denial when prompted by

[1] This term may be more familiar to many in another criminal procedural context, namely, when under U.S. law, evidence is admissible in a federal court even if obtained unlawfully so long as it was collected by a *state* police officer and no federal officer participated in or requested the search. The U.S. Supreme Court ultimately rejected this concept in *Elkins v. United States*, 364 U.S. 206 (1960). In an alternative guise, this term can refer to evidence seized by *foreign* governments and provided to federal agents without federal government participation, including as a joint venture, that would be deemed admissible and not subject to the exclusionary rule, *United States v. Janis*, 428 U.S. 433, 455 (1976); *United States v. Mount*, 757 F.2d 1315, 1317 (D.C. Cir. 1985), unless the circumstances surrounding the seizure were sufficient to "shock the judicial conscience." *Rochin v. People of Calif.*, 342 U.S. 165, 172 (1952) (Frankfurter, J.). The meaning of this term as used herein should not be confused with either of these like-named U.S. evidentiary concepts.

[2] Scenarios in which a fugitive's decision to return is responsive to law enforcement measures or pressures are discussed herein under Part IV (fallback alternatives) and Part V (negotiated returns or LCOs).

exogenous, non-law enforcement-related factors; or (iv) by private actors, including government officials acting in their personal capacity or *ultra vires*, regardless of motivation.[3]

Such scenarios are worth addressing for at least three reasons. First, it is important to distinguish such methods of inter-State fugitive delivery from genuine alternatives to extradition (addressed in Parts IV and V), especially as they have been erroneously conflated with such alternatives in the international law literature. Second, States occasionally try to dress up undercover seizure operations to appear as if they had been carried out by private actors, and thus it is essential to understand this motivation and its legal implications. Third, although these scenarios are relatively straightforward, they nevertheless give rise to a few lawfulness issues that warrant an analysis, particularly related to the extent to which "private" actions may entail State responsibility and whether the accidental inter-State delivery of a fugitive can be reversed at the request of the transferor State.

As for scope, once a fugitive has been arrested, any decision he takes to waive extradition and cooperatively submit to pursuing State jurisdiction would fall beyond the parameters of the instant discussion, and instead shall be treated as a form of consented "summary extradition."[4] By contrast, the *host State's* decision to transfer a fugitive to pursuing State territory, custody, or control, once he has been detained, could still qualify as a "silver platter" scenario, as it could appear nevertheless to occur by happenstance from the standpoint of the pursuing State at issue, as discussed below.

[3] Although a fugitive's whereabouts may be confirmed without any effort on the part of the pursuing State, that information, albeit welcome from a law enforcement optic, would not itself constitute a "silver platter" scenario, which requires the fugitive's physical delivery to pursuing State territory, custody, or control.

[4] To the extent a fugitive waives his right to an extradition hearing, a fugitive (or his counsel) could contend that the subject was mentally impaired when he made the decision, and therefore was not aware of its full implications; and/or that he had not been appointed a lawyer or had not been properly advised of his right to one before agreeing to return (at least where such factors apply under domestic law). *See, e.g.*, AP, Greg Pallone, "'Shawshank' Fugitive on Lam Since 1959 now Fighting Extradition," *Bay News 9* [Brevard County, Fla.], May 14, 2015, *available at* http://www.baynews9.com/content/news/baynews9/news/article.html/content/news/articles/cfn/2015/5/14/shawshank_fugitive_fl.html (last visited on May 27, 2016) (discussing the case of Frank Freshwater who waived his right to an extradition hearing in Florida, but his counsel sought reconsideration on several grounds, including that his client was allegedly under stress when he made his decision to return to Ohio and did not appreciate its upshot) (municipal case example).

a Action by the Fugitive

A fugitive could return to pursuing State territory, custody, or control on his own accord via private (*i.e.*, non-official) channels or arrangements in one of four ways. First, he could do so knowingly and voluntarily – and not in response to any law enforcement pressure applied by a pursuing State – with the full expectation of arrest and prosecution or punishment by presenting himself at a pursuing State's border, port, or embassy or other such overseas installation.

Second, he could be aware of a pending indictment and warrant for his arrest but nevertheless be willing to assume the risk of capture and detention in the interest of some overriding potential benefit. Third, although aware of a pending charge, he may simply fail to account for a scheduled or unscheduled stopover on pursuing State territory in connection with his private or business travel.[5] Fourth, he could return by virtue of an innocent mistake or unintentional misinformation (official or otherwise) that led him to believe that a particular pursuing State was not seeking his arrest (for a crime he may or may not have committed) or that his crime is not extraditable.[6] A pursuing State may lawfully arrest a fugitive who returns to its territory under any of these scenarios.[7]

As a matter of nomenclature, upon a fugitive's return on his own volition under any of the scenarios listed above, or when he is delivered by private actors, including by government officials operating *ultra vires*[8]

[5] While overlooking a *scheduled* stopover on pursuing State territory would certainly constitute an error or miscalculation on the part of the fugitive, and while one cannot fairly judge him by the same standard regarding an *unscheduled* stopover, in either event the pursuing State at issue is a fortuitous beneficiary. The fact that a pursuing State maintains updated information at its ports of entry and exploits such opportunities for arrest where they arise does not foreclose classification as a "silver platter" scenario. By contrast, however, monitoring a fugitive's travel to a *cooperating third State*, whether scheduled or unscheduled, and communicating with that third State about his prospective capture and follow-on activity, is treated herein as a fallback alternative to extradition (*see* Chapter 9.b).

[6] Excluded from this list would be scenarios, for example, in which a pursuing State sought to conceal its interest in a fugitive through a secret (or sealed) indictment, tried to lure him under false pretenses, threatened to seek his extradition unless he returns on his own, or deliberately misinformed him of his fugitive status or whether the offense for which he is wanted is extraditable. Each of these scenarios is discussed elsewhere.

[7] Mark Brkljacic, Note, *The Dangers of State Sponsored and Court Ratified Abduction*, 5 J. Int'l L. & Prac. 117, 129–30 (1996).

[8] In Latin, *ultra vires* means "beyond the power or authority." A separate legal consideration is whether a given *ultra vires* act even though unauthorized, can be attributable to a State. When an official acts outside of his legal authority, whether his conduct is attributable to

or in their private capacity[9] (*see* discussion *infra*), a pursuing State shall be referred to herein as a "fortuitously acquiring State" to distinguish it from: (i) a "transferee State" (in the case of extraditions, informal cooperative deliveries, and all transfers, including accidental ones, by another State or an international criminal tribunal), (ii) a "receiving State" (in the case of immigration law-based), or (iii) a "rendering State" (in the case of unilaterally arranged deliveries from host State territory).

A fugitive may voluntarily return to the territory or otherwise submit to the custody or control of a pursuing State to knowingly face arrest and prosecution or punishment. A fugitive may choose such a course of action outside extradition channels for any number of reasons. He may, for instance, wish to erase any doubt regarding his innocence once and for all;[10] may perceive that extradition is inevitable given the relative weakness of his legal arguments and/or the likelihood that his asylum application in the host State will be denied;[11] when the host State is contemplating prosecution, he might well prefer to be tried in a pursuing State where he understands the language or expects to be more humanely treated,[12] receive a shorter

a State depends on if he acted with apparent authority as a competent official or used powers or means at his disposal derivative of that capacity. ILC, *Responsibility of States for Int'lly Wrongful Acts with Commentaries* (Draft), Dec. 12, 2001, art. 7, Annex to UNGA Res. 56/83, U.N. GAOR, 56th Sess., Supp. No. 10, at 43, U.N. Doc. A/56/10 (2001) [hereinafter ILC, *State Responsibility*].

9 For a case example analyzing this element, *see Youmans Claim* (U.S. v. Mex.), Gen. Claims Comm'n, 4 RIAA 110, 116 (1926) ("we do not consider that the participation of the [Mexican] soldiers in the murder at Angangueo can be regarded as acts of soldiers committed in their private capacity when it is clear that at the time of the commission of these acts the men were on duty under the immediate supervision and in the presence of a commanding officer.").

10 *See* J. David Goodman, "Prosecutor Says Qaddafi Son May Turn Himself In," *IHT*, Oct. 29–30, 2011, at 5 (in indirect discussions with ICC prosecutors, Seif al-Islam el-Qaddafi, the ex-Libyan dictator's son, considered possibly turning himself in to prove his innocence, although he never did so).

11 *E.g.*, Bruce Zagaris, *Former Turks and Caicos Premier Continues to Battle Extradition from Brazil*, 29 IELR 323 (2013) (reporting how former Turks and Caicos Islands (TCI) Premier Michael Misick had agreed to voluntarily return to TCI following the second denial of his asylum application, "but contingent on his traveling on a private chartered flight his family would provide.").

12 For example, in November 1964, Mordechai Luk, an Israeli national believed to be a double agent for Egyptian and Israeli intelligence services, volunteered to return to Israel to face military desertion and espionage charges (for which he was ultimately convicted on six counts) after Egyptian agents unsuccessfully attempted to transport him drugged in a specially fitted trunk to Cairo via aircraft from Rome. AP, "Italy Balks Air Abduction of Man in a Trunk," *N.Y. Times*, Nov. 18, 1964, at 1; "Italy Expels Egyptian Envoys Accused in Trunk Abduction Attempt," *N.Y. Times*, Nov. 19, 1964, at 1; "Israel

prison sentence,[13] and/or better conditions of incarceration;[14] or he may simply miss his family or friends, is tired of being on the run, or has a powerful hankering to be back in familiar surroundings.

For example, in 1994, after seven years on the lam, reportedly "roam[ing] throughout Eastern Europe and the Middle East," Stig Bergling, "one of Sweden's most notorious Cold War spies" who had "escaped from prison during a conjugal visit" in 1987, voluntarily returned to Sweden with his wife on the grounds that "they were homesick for their families."[15] In another instance, Ronnie Biggs, the mastermind behind the 1963 "Great Train Robbery" in the United Kingdom who later escaped from prison and made a home for himself in Brazil, and who had withstood a U.K. extradition request only four years earlier, voluntarily returned to the United Kingdom in May 2001, claiming, "I am a sick man. My last wish is to walk into a Margate pub as an Englishman and buy a pint of bitter."[16]

A fugitive may be aware of a pending indictment against him in a pursuing State, but is nevertheless willing to risk arrest by returning to that State's territory based on a favorable benefit-cost calculation.[17] Some fugitives opt to travel to pursuing State territory well aware of the risk of arrest in order to visit with family or friends; obtain medical care; attend a wedding or funeral; join a government delegation; or explore a potentially lucrative business

'Trunk Man' Found Guilty of Spying; to be Sentenced Today," *Jewish News Archive*, Sept. 10, 1965. Under the circumstances, it is presumed he believed that he would be more humanely treated by an Israeli court than by an Egyptian one.

13 This could occur either because of a longer average sentence assigned to the same offense in the host State or because of the opportunity for a plea bargain based on cooperation with pursuing State law enforcement authorities.

14 Some jails are reputed to be particularly unpleasant, such as Bologna's "notoriously overcrowded Dozza jail." Bruce Zagaris, *Former UBS Wealth Management Head Agrees to Extradition to the U.S.*, 30 IELR 50, 50-51 (2014) (extradition case example).

15 Margalit Fox, "Stig Bergling, Swedish Cold War Spy Who Escaped, Dies at 77," *INYT*, Feb. 3, 2015, at 2.

16 BBC News, "Timeline: Ronnie Biggs," *available at* http://news.bbc.co.uk/2/hi/uk/8014189.stm (last visited on May 4, 2016) (noting that Biggs returned on board a private jet chartered by *The Sun* (U.K.) newspaper and was arrested immediately upon his arrival in London); "Brazilian Court Won't Extradite 'Great Train Robbery' Fugitive," *N.Y. Times*, Nov. 13, 1997.

17 This could include an instance where the fugitive had been accidentally misinformed by a host or pursuing State official that the conduct for which he is wanted *is* an extraditable offense.

venture. For example, in October 2011, Joe Gordon, a Thai-born U.S. citizen living in Colorado who had translated part of a banned biography of Thai King Bhumibol Adulyadej (entitled *The King Never Sleeps* by Paul Handley) and then posted that translated text on an Internet blog in contravention of Thailand's strict *lèse majesté* law (§ 112 of the Criminal Code) against insulting the monarchy, was arrested when he voluntarily returned to Bangkok for medical treatment, bypassing any need for the Thai Government to request his extradition.[18]

A fugitive may be aware of a criminal charge against him, but either overlooked a scheduled, or was caught off-guard by an unscheduled, stopover on pursuing State territory in the course of his discretionary travel. A fugitive may be on business or personal air or sea travel[19] that entails a scheduled intermediate stop within pursuing State territory while *en route* to a third-State destination. There also may be an unscheduled or emergency stopover within pursuing State territory due to such factors as inclement weather, a cabin altercation, a mechanical problem, or a passenger stroke or heart attack. To the extent that a pursuing State can merely keep its border and port officials informed of this possibility (presumably through updated computer databases), arrests can be effected absent any directed effort on the part of the pursuing State at issue to even monitor a fugitive's movements, let alone prompt or entice his return.

A fugitive may be unaware of pending criminal charges against him in the pursuing State at issue and, absent any purposeful actions on the part of that State to deceive or coax him,[20] returns to that State's territory entirely innocent of the ensuing consequences. This lack of

[18] AP, "U.S. Citizen Pleads Guilty to Defaming Thai King," *IHT*, Oct. 11, 2011, at 4 (the defendant was sentenced to five years but it was halved to two-and-a-half years due to his guilty plea).

[19] Deportations operate under a distinct dynamic, as either the fugitive himself is permitted to select the destination (in which case he is highly unlikely to opt for a State that has pending criminal charges against him) or the removing State places him on an aircraft or ship intended for a destination of its choosing (in which case fugitive conduct would not be at issue). In one case, in June 1994, the United States apprehended Jairo Trujillo, a narcotics trafficker, in Miami, Florida, during a stopover on an airplane trip from the United Kingdom to Colombia (his native country) following his deportation, where the United States had not requested extradition nor was there any express or implicit evidence that the United States had sought that particular routing in order to arrest him. *See United States v. Trujillo*, 871 F. Supp. 215, 217–21 (D. Del. 1994).

[20] Where a given pursuing State has issued a sealed (or secret) indictment to conceal its law enforcement interest in the fugitive, any return by that fugitive because he is unaware of the risk involved would not constitute a "silver platter" scenario, but rather is addressed herein as a "fallback alternative to extradition."

awareness may be a function of the fact that he lives as a recluse without a phone number or mailing address and so could not be contacted by law enforcement authorities; he may have been misinformed by family or friends as to his non-fugitive status; or he may naïvely believe that, because of the lapse of time, he is no longer on law enforcement's radar screen or the statute of limitations for his offense has elapsed. As a result, he may innocently return to the territory of a State interested in his prosecution or punishment and be arrested upon his arrival.

A fugitive may choose to return to pursuing State territory after being inadvertently misinformed about his non-fugitive status or the non-extraditability of his offense by pursuing State officials. Under this scenario, pursuing State officials could erroneously but innocently lead a fugitive to believe that he is not actually wanted by law enforcement or that the offense for which he *is* wanted is non-extraditable (*e.g.*, it is only a misdemeanor), and consequently he decides to return home. In a case arising out of such an innocent error, a U.K. court reasoned that such a return was essentially voluntary and did not establish a basis either for illegality or for finding that the court lacked personal jurisdiction over the defendant.[21]

b Action by Private Actor(s)[22]

In general, there are three types of private actors who might physically seize a fugitive and then make him available to a pursuing State: (i) paid individuals such as bounty hunters[23] or private investigators who tend to

[21] *Walker v. Governor of HM Prison Nottingham* [2002] EWHC 39.

[22] Sometimes, the facts remain unclear as to whether a seizure was perpetrated by private volunteers or by paid agents of a pursuing State. In cases where an actor's identity or status cannot be ascertained with any degree of certainty – a so-called indeterminate party – the law can do little else but treat him as a private individual, because it would be unfair to merely presume he was operating under the effective control of a particular State. For example, in July 1984, three Israelis and a Nigerian diplomat seized at gunpoint Umara Dikko, a Nigerian exile who was among his own government's most wanted fugitives. Dikko was drugged and placed in a shipping crate labeled diplomatic baggage at London's Stansted Airport. The Governments of Nigeria and Israel denied any involvement in the matter. The four men were arrested and charged with kidnapping. Jo Thomas, "Britain Charges Three Israelis and Nigerian in Kidnapping of Exile," *N.Y. Times*, July 11, 1984, at A4.

[23] In America's Old West, bounty hunters acted as *de facto* freelance deputy sheriffs, collecting rewards for bringing back fugitives. "Putnam County," *Time*, Aug. 8, 1983, at 58.

work for bail bondsmen[24] or creditors;[25] (ii) unpaid volunteers whose participation, whether via a physical return or a location tip-off, has a political, community security, principle-driven, or other non-pecuniary motivation; and (iii) pursuing or host State officials acting *ultra vires* (whether alone or in cooperation with law enforcement officials of another State, and whether or not their actions are ultimately deemed attributable to a State[26]) or in their personal capacities.[27]

A bounty hunter or private investigator may capture and return a fugitive on behalf of a private person or entity. These cases involve paid individuals who tend to work for creditors or, more likely, bail bondsmen who have posted bail on behalf of criminal defendants as a financial guarantee that they will not flee during court proceedings. If and when a defendant does skip bail, the bail bondsmen must recover him or forfeit an often-substantial sum. For example, in September 1981, with the prodding of Florida state prosecutors, an insurance company that had posted bail hired two bounty hunters to seize Canadian businessman Sidney Jaffe from his home in Toronto and return him to Florida to face land fraud charges. Jaffe was taken against his will to

[24] Although no reliable statistics exist, the use of bounty hunters to locate and retrieve fugitives abroad is believed "to occur with some frequency," at least in the U.S. context. MICHAEL ABBELL, EXTRADITION TO AND FROM THE UNITED STATES 382 (2010).

[25] Creditors most typically are involved in cases involving financial fraud or embezzlement. *See, e.g.*, Paul O'Higgins, *Unlawful Seizure and Irregular Extradition*, 36 B.Y.B.I.L. 279, 305 (1960) (Joseph Lamb was seized by agents of his creditors and hurried on board a British ship in Rotterdam and sailed back to England to face charges of embezzlement and fraudulent bankruptcy).

[26] A distinction must be drawn between a State being held responsible *ex post facto* for its rogue officials' conduct and its own foreknowledge and intentionality regarding that conduct. Even when *ultra vires* acts are found to be imputable to a State, however, such fugitive deliveries still constitute "silver platter" scenarios. To the extent, however, that an *ultra vires* act by one or more pursuing State officials is ultimately found to be imputable to a State, that State may be subjected to greater diplomatic pressure to return a recovered fugitive.

[27] Simply because a fugitive is delivered on a "silver platter" by private actors does not necessarily mean that a fortuitously acquiring State will accept the individual; in some cases, the fugitive will be returned from where he came, perhaps to demonstrate that the fortuitously acquiring State itself was not responsible for an extraterritorial seizure. *See, e.g.*, "Abducted Rhodesian Freed; Returns from South Africa," *N.Y. Times*, Sept. 3, 1964, at 6 (discussing how three white men had kidnapped Dennis Higgs, a British national living in Lusaka (then part of Northern Rhodesia, today Zambia), and brought him to a park in Johannesburg, South Africa, where he was wanted on charges of being an accessory to murder, and how South Africa returned him to Lusaka and indicated plans to seek his extradition through proper channels).

Ontario, driven across the border at Niagara Falls, and then flown from a local airport to Florida.[28] Similarly, in June 2003, infamous American bounty hunter Duane Lee "Dog" Chapman and two associates sought out and captured Andrew Luster, the Max Factor (cosmetics company) heir indicted for multiple rapes in California while living under an assumed name in Puerto Vallarta, Mexico.[29]

Such cross-border seizure actions violate the domestic law of the host State, and individual bounty hunters can be either caught while in country by law enforcement officers[30] or later sought by the former host State via extradition on kidnapping, wrongful detention, deprivation of liberty, or similar charges (or even request the fortuitously acquiring State to indict him under its own laws[31]), but such underlying conduct does *not* implicate either international law or State responsibility.

One or more concerned citizens or politically motivated persons may tip off law enforcement authorities about a suspicious individual or take direct action themselves. These cases are distinguished by the fact that the action in support of law enforcement is undertaken without a request for, or the receipt of, financial compensation. For example, in the spring of 1997, Mexican immigration officers received "two or three calls" from "tipsters" indicating that Ernesto López, an escaped murderer from a U.S. prison who had been on the lam for 35 years, "was a foreigner

[28] *See Jaffe v. Boyles*, 616 F. Supp. 1371, 1373 (W.D.N.Y. 1985) (Accredited Surety & Casualty posted bail bonds totaling US $137,000 to secure Jaffe's release from confinement pending trial proceedings; by the time the trial was scheduled, however, Jaffe had fled to Canada and refused to return; attempts at his extradition failed; Accredited ordered two of its agents, Timm Johnsen and Daniel Kear, to kidnap Jaffe and return him to Florida); Kristofer R. Schleicher, *Transborder Abductions by American Bounty Hunters – the* Jaffe *Case and a New Understanding Between the United States and Canada*, 20 GA. J. INT'L & COMP. L. 489, 489 (1990).

[29] Bruce Zagaris, *U.S. Detains Bounty Hunter on 2003 Mexican Kidnaping Charges*, 22 IELR 432, 432–33 (2006) [hereinafter Zagaris, *Bounty Hunter*].

[30] For example, in October 1986, American bounty hunters Jesse and Coantha Mendez tried to seize Jeffrey S. Clair, who was wanted on fraud charges in Houston, Texas, on behalf of a company that had posted a US $50,000 bond to guarantee his appearance at trial, but because of an automobile accident in which they were involved during the operation, Canadian police discovered the seizure and arrested the bounty hunters. Howard Kurtz, "For U.S. Bounty Hunters, National Boundaries are Little or No Constraint," *Wash. Post*, May 15, 1987, at A23.

[31] *See, e.g.*, Zagaris, *Bounty Hunter, supra* n.29, at 432–33 (noting that, upon his return to the United States with Andrew Luster, at the behest of the Mexican Government, U.S. authorities arrested Duane Chapman and charged him with "deprivation of liberty"; ironically, when he was released on bail, Chapman did not return for his scheduled court hearing in July 2003).

apparently living illegally in Mexico" and consequently was captured, transferred, and returned to prison.[32] In another example, in February 1963, French police received an anonymous tip from a person self-identified with the Organization of the Secret Army (OAS), a right-wing French terrorist organization that opposed Algerian independence, regarding the specific whereabouts in central Paris of Antoine Argoud, a former French Army colonel and active OAS member, who had most recently been in Munich. Based on the tip, Argoud, who had been charged with attempting to assassinate President de Gaulle, was promptly located roped up and bruised in the back of a van near French police headquarters.[33]

A host or pursuing State official could act *ultra vires* or in his personal capacity to deliver a fugitive. Precedent exists for law enforcement officers acting without their own government's knowledge, authority, or direction, or possibly in direct contravention of official policy or instruction, in bringing or luring a fugitive to pursuing State territory. In March 1920, for instance, on their own (unofficial) initiative, a U.S. Department of Justice official and two Internal Revenue (tax) agents pursued and seized in British territorial waters Charles Vincenti, a U.S. citizen and the president of a Baltimore liquor company, for the crime of shipping large quantities of liquor to the Bahamas in connection with Prohibition,[34] and returned him initially to Miami; the U.S. Government subsequently acknowledged that the arrest had been unlawful and released Vincenti.[35]

[32] AP, "Murderer Convicted of 1956 Crime Back in Texas After Escape," *Lubbock Avalanche-Journal*, June 27, 1987.

[33] "1963: Argoud Charged Over de Gaulle Plot," On This Day: February 27, *BBC News*, *available at* http://news.bbc.co.uk/onthisday/low/dates/stories/february/27/newsid_2515000/2515735.stm (last visited on May 4, 2016); Ivan A. Shearer, Extradition in International Law 74 & n.5 (1971).

[34] The Prohibition Era in the United States took place during the 1920s and early 1930s, during which the manufacture, sale, transportation, importation, and exportation of alcoholic beverages was prohibited due to social and health concerns about alcoholic consumption and intoxication. Prohibition commenced a year after the 18th amendment to the U.S. Constitution was ratified on January 16, 1919, and ended when that amendment was repealed on December 5, 1933, by ratification of the 21st amendment. Const. of the United States, Sept. 17, 1787, arts. 18 and 21, *as amended*.

[35] *See* 1 Digest of Int'l Law 624 (Green H. Hackworth ed. 1940); Michael H. Cardozo, *When Extradition Fails, Is Abduction the Solution?*, 55 AJIL 127, 132 (1961) (the U.S. Government apologized and explained that the officials had "acted on their own initiative and without the knowledge or approval of this government."). To the extent that the officials acted with apparent authority or used means at their disposal as officials to carry out this seizure, at least under contemporary international law standards, their actions would be imputable to the U.S. Government. *See supra* n.8.

In April 1990, among those responsible for seizing and returning to the United States Humberto Álvarez-Machaín, a Guadalajara-based medical doctor accused of participating in the torture and murder of a Drug Enforcement Administration (DEA) agent in Mexico, were "two current policemen" in addition to civilians and some former military police officers who collectively were referred to as the "Wild Geese" acting *ultra vires* or in their personal capacity on behalf of the DEA.[36] In an apparent example of an *ultra vires* operation, in January 2005, the Venezuelan Vice President announced that "five Venezuelan National Guardsmen and three police officers had been detained on suspicion of participating in the [December 2004] kidnapping" of Rodrigo Granda, a Venezuelan national and FARC leader who was taken across the border into Colombia.[37]

Under international law, responsibility for unlawful conduct generally extends to government agents or others acting under color of law rather than to private volunteers.[38] That is because international law is concerned primarily with limiting *State* conduct, not that of individuals acting in their personal capacity, which is typically handled instead through domestic legislation.[39]

36 Christopher H. Pyle, Extradition, Politics, and Human Rights 282–83 (2001).

37 Bruce Zagaris, *Venezuela Recalls Ambassador to Protest Kidnapping Colombian Rebel Leader*, 21 IELR 96, 96–97 (2005). This incident led to the recalling of the Venezuelan Ambassador to Colombia, the suspension of bilateral trade relations, and the demand of a public apology from the Colombian President. *Id.*

38 *See* Satyadeva Bedi, Extradition: A Treatise on the Laws Relevant to the Fugitive Offenders Within and With the Commonwealth Countries 394 (2002) (State responsibility only arises through official complicity); Cardozo, *supra* n.35, at 132; Jeffrey J. Carlisle, *Extradition of Gov't Agents as a Municipal Law Remedy for State-Sponsored Kidnapping*, 81 Cal. L. Rev. 1541, 1556 (1993) ("[A]ctions by private individuals in a foreign country which are not on behalf of a state do not involve a foreign sovereign's exercise of authority. Accordingly, cross-border abductions by private citizens do not give rise to a violation of international law since '[i]nternational responsibility is incurred only through official complicity.'") (quoting Lawrence Preuss, *Kidnaping of Fugitives from Justice on Foreign Territory*, 29 AJIL 502, 507 (1935)).

39 M. Cherif Bassiouni, International Extradition and World Public Order 126 (1974); Alona E. Evans, *The Apprehension and Prosecution of Offenders: Some Current Problems, in* Legal aspects of International Terrorism 197 (Alona E. Evans & John F. Murphy eds. 1978). Indeed, liability can befall the private volunteer under domestic law. *See Kear v. Hilton*, 699 F.2d 181 (4th Cir. 1983) (the bail bondsman who seized Sidney Jaffe and took him across the border from Canada into the United States was deemed extraditable under Canadian law for kidnapping); *Villareal & Hernandez v. Hammond*, 74 F.2d 503 (5th Cir. 1934) (Villareal, a bounty hunter, seized a bond defaulter named López in Mexico and forcibly returned him to the United States; as a result he was charged with kidnapping under Mexican law, and the United States eventually extradited Villareal to

While generally no State responsibility obtains in instances involving conduct by a private actor, in cases where the State is found to have encouraged or sponsored the wrongful act, such as through posting a bounty for a fugitive's capture;[40] where a private individual has been empowered with authority of the State to act on its behalf;[41] where the State has effective control over the actions of the private individual;[42] or where governmental personnel do not take adequate measures to prevent certain conduct,[43] such actions can be imputed to the State. In addition, it is even possible, as noted above, for State imputability to obtain where a government official undertakes unauthorized or *ultra vires* actions,[44]

Mexico to face those charges); ETHAN A. NADELMANN, COPS ACROSS BORDERS: THE INTERNATIONALIZATION OF U.S. CRIMINAL LAW ENFORCEMENT 450 (1993).

[40] *See* Perry John Seaman, Note, *Int'l Bountyhunting: A Question of State Responsibility*, 15 CAL. W. INT'L L.J. 397, 405 (1985); *e.g., United States v. Caro-Quintero, et al.*, 745 F. Supp. 599, 609 (C.D. Cal. 1990) (a State-advertised capture reward was deemed tantamount to State sponsorship when U.S. DEA agents paid Mexican individuals US $20,000 for their role in seizing Humberto Álvarez-Machaín and returning him to the United States to face criminal charges) *aff'd sub nom. United States v. Álvarez-Machaín*, 946 F.2d 1466 (9th Cir. 1991), *rev'd on other grounds*, 504 U.S. 655 (1992).

[41] *See* ILC, *State Responsibility, supra* n.8, art. 5 (State responsibility obtains when the "conduct of a person or entity which is not an organ of the State under article 4 but which is empowered by the law of that State to exercise elements of the governmental authority, provided the person or entity is acting in that capacity in the particular instance," such as a privatized corporation that retains public or regulatory functions); Seaman, *supra* n.40, at 406–07.

[42] *See* ILC, *State Responsibility, supra* n.8, art. 8 (State responsibility obtains when "conduct of a person or group of persons if acting on the instructions of, or under the direction or control of, that State carrying out the conduct."). Regarding the second part, the ILC Commentary stresses that "[s]uch conduct will be attributable to the state only if it directed or controlled the specific operation and the conduct complained of was an integral part of the operation." *Id.* at 104. For further discussion on this point, *see* n.35 in the Introduction.

[43] "Although private individuals are not regarded as state officials so that the state is not liable for their acts, the state may be responsible for failing to exercise the control necessary to prevent such acts. This was emphasized in the *Zafiro* case between Great Britain and the United States in 1925. *Earnshaw, et al. Claim* (a/k/a *Zafiro* Case) (Gr. Br. v. U.S.), Gen. Claims Comm'n, 6 RIAA 160 (1925). The tribunal held the latter responsible for the damage caused by the civilian crew of a naval ship in the Philippines, since the naval officers had not adopted effective preventative measures." MALCOLM N. SHAW, PUBLIC INTERNATIONAL LAW 789 (6th ed. 2008).

[44] *See supra* n.8; *Caire Claim* (Fr.-Mex.), Claims Comm'n, 5 RIAA 516, 530 (1929) (officials "have acted at least to all appearances as competent officials or organs or they must have used powers or methods appropriate to their official capacity"); SHAW, *supra* n.43, at 786 ("The state may also incur responsibility with regard to the activity of its officials in injuring a national of another state, and this activity need not be one authorised by the authorities of the state."); JAMES CRAWFORD, BROWNLIE'S PRINCIPLES OF PUBLIC INTERNATIONAL LAW 549 (8th ed. 2012).

and/or if the State fails to repudiate such actions[45] or in effect "acknowledges and adopts the conduct in question as its own."[46]

Circumstances may nevertheless dictate that a State, even where not technically at fault, determine for political, diplomatic, comity, or other reasons, that it should return a fugitive taken by a private individual. For example, "in the *Blair* case, the abduction from the United States evidently was handled by a British private investigator not acting on government orders, and yet the victim was in due course returned to the United States."[47] A privately seized fugitive has even been returned based on the threat of force exercised by an interested third State. While in Turkey, a gang of ruffians seized Martin Koszta, a Hungarian revolutionary sought by Austria, and took him on board an Austrian warship. The captain of a U.S. warship, who believed Koszta was entitled to U.S. protection because he had filed for U.S. citizenship, "demanded Koszta's release and prevailed after threateningly swinging his guns in line with the Austrian vessel."[48]

Because of international law's focus on *State* conduct, a State may try to mislead others or the world community at large into believing that private volunteers perpetrated a legally questionable act when in fact the State was the force behind it. This occurred when Israel tried to initially justify the seizure of Adolf Eichmann, a German Nazi SS officer and architect of the Holocaust, off a street in Buenos Aires in 1960 by claiming it had been the handiwork of private volunteers, although it was later shown that the true perpetrators, Mossad agents, had operated "with the connivance of the Israeli government."[49] Likewise, in August 1973, to save face, South Korea initially claimed (but later recanted) that it had nothing to do with

[45] *See* Frederick A. Mann, *Reflections on the Prosecution of Persons Abducted in Breach of Int'l Law, in* International Law at a Time of Perplexity: Essays in Honour of Shabtai Rosenne 408 (Yoram Dinstein ed. 1989) ("a police officer whose acts are not repudiated by his government always acts as an agent of the state").

[46] ILC, *State Responsibility, supra* n.8, art. 11. *See* Michael Akehurst, *Jurisdiction in Int'l Law*, 46 B.Y.B.I.L. 145, 148 n.1 (1972–73) ("Seizure by a private individual [of a fugitive in another State's territory] is not a breach of international law, but the State ratifies the act and assumes responsibility for it by keeping the individual in its custody").

[47] Cardozo, *supra* n.35, at 132.

[48] *Id.* at 134.

[49] Bassiouni, *supra* n.39, at 126–27. *See also* O'Higgins, *supra* n.25, at 296 ("If in fact [volunteers] meant that [the captors] were private citizens acting on their own initiative Israel would not be liable for their actions; on the other hand, if the kidnappers were private citizens acting with the connivance of the Israeli authorities, or were Israeli officials who had volunteered for the particular assignment offered to them by the Israeli authorities, then Israel was internationally liable for their actions.").

the seizure of Kim Dae Jung, a spokesperson for South Korea's opposition political party, from a Tokyo hotel room, but rather it had been privately and unofficially perpetrated by then-First Secretary of the South Korean Embassy in Japan, Kim Dong Woon.[50]

c Action by the Host State or an International Criminal Tribunal

The host State or an international criminal tribunal could deliver a fugitive to a pursuing State: (i) proactively absent an extant extradition request; (ii) intentionally for reasons independent of a pending extradition request, or (iii) accidentally as a function of error, confusion, or misunderstanding in connection with an extradition or transfer or request thereof. The most salient legal question under this set of scenarios is whether the erroneous return of a fugitive is recognized as reversible under international law.

The host State or an international criminal tribunal may propose, unprompted, to transfer a fugitive to a pursuing State. Even before a pursuing State has requested a fugitive's return, the host State or an international criminal tribunal, by sheer coincidence, could propose to turn over an individual for whom a State has an as yet unannounced law enforcement interest. This may occur, for example, due to foreign policy reasons, to offload a politically problematic individual, or pursuant to a procedural rule for a national court referral from an international criminal tribunal, and is premised on the fact that the transferee State has yet to seek a provisional arrest by the host State or request that INTERPOL post a Red Notice for his arrest, let alone propound an extradition request itself.

For example, in the early 1980s, the United States encouraged Israel to seek the extradition under its Nazis and Nazi Collaborators (Punishment) Act (for "crimes of murdering Jews") of John Demjanjuk – a Ukrainian-born U.S. citizen living in Ohio who was then believed to be the infamous "Ivan the Terrible" from the Treblinka Concentration Camp responsible for the deaths of thousands of Jews in 1942–43 – rather than deporting him to the U.S.S.R.[51] In May 1997, after a U.S. trial court had earlier

[50] In early November 2007, the South Korean Government issued a formal apology for the incident, acknowledging for the first time that its intelligence agency had been involved. AP, "Seoul to Apologize for Kim Abduction in Tokyo in 1973," *The Japan Times*, Oct. 28, 2007.

[51] Pyle, *supra* n.36 at 235–62. Given Israel's reluctance, Demjanjuk was eventually transferred to Germany in 2009 and tried and convicted there in May 2011 of being an

approved the extradition to Israel of Mousa Mohammed Abu Marzook, a specially designated global terrorist, and then Israel dropped its extradition request, the U.S. reportedly inveigled upon Jordan to take him; as a result, he was deported there.[52] And in September 2005, pursuant to Rule 11 *bis* of the RPE, the ICTY referred the case of Radovan Stankovič to Bosnia and Herzegovina (B&H) authorities for trial, and accordingly handed over the accused without B&H having to request his transfer.[53]

The host State may respond favorably to a pending extradition request, following an original denial, with the change driven solely by exogenous pressures. The host State may choose to extradite a fugitive only on account of third-party pressure to amend or reinterpret its domestic laws or policies otherwise impeding extradition. For example, Croatia, which had just joined the E.U. in July 2013, and strictly in connection thereof had "amended its laws in line with the bloc's standards," was now in a position to reverse its initial rejection of extradition to Germany of Josip Perković, "a ranking Yugoslav secret service official in the 1980s" wanted for "allegedly masterminding the murder of a Yugoslav dissident there in 1983."[54]

A host State official acting under color of law may return or order the return of a fugitive by error, confusion, or misunderstanding in connection with a requested or executed transfer or extradition. A government official (or private individuals or entities with delegated governmental authority[55]) may be unaware of the limits of his (or their) authority with regard to a transfer or extradition, may not have heard

accessory to over 28,000 murders at the Nazi Concentration Camp in Sobibor, Poland. Jack Ewing & Alan Cowell, "Demjanjuk Convicted of Role in Nazi Death Camp," *N.Y. Times*, May 12, 2011. Although he was sentenced to five years in prison, he was released pending appeal and died a free man in Bavaria at the age of ninety-one. AP, "John Demjanjuk, Convicted Nazi Death Camp Guard, Dies Aged 91," *The Guardian*, Mar. 17, 2012.

52 "Militant Ejected by U.S. Meets with Jordan King," N.Y. Times, May 14, 1997, at A11.

53 Olympia Bekou, *Rule 11 Bis: An Examination of the Process of Referrals to Nat'l Courts in ICTY Jurisprudence*, 33 Fordham Int'l L.J. 723 (2009).

54 AP, "Court Orders Extradition of Ex-Spy Chief to Germany," *INYT*, Jan. 9, 2014, at 3.

55 For example, in a domestic U.S. case in May 2005, four days before Violet Armour and her daughter Deborah Castillo were scheduled to appear in a Florida court to challenge their extradition to St. Thomas, one of the U.S. Virgin Islands, to face charges of embezzlement and forgery, the Corrections Corporation of America (CCA), a private company authorized to manage the county jail, mistakenly released the pair into the custody of Virgin Islands Justice Department officials before the Governor of Florida had signed the warrant for their inter-state extradition. Bruce Zagaris, *Florida County Jail Surrenders to U.S.V.I. Detained Persons Fighting Extradition Without Hearing*, 21 IELR 270, 270–72 (2005).

about a controlling domestic court decision denying extradition, or simply may be confused about underlying factual circumstances or applicable extradition procedures.

For example, in 1866, the Governor-General of Canada issued a warrant to transfer Monsieur Lamirande to France to face a forgery charge, which was promptly executed, unaware that a Canadian court was still reviewing his *habeas corpus* petition (and which a day later was in fact granted).[56] In November 1970, officers of a USCG ship, on orders from headquarters, unaware of a valid claim to U.S. citizenship by Simonas Kudirka, a Lithuanian radio operator working aboard a Soviet trawler who had dramatically jumped across a ten-foot gap between the two vessels while in U.S. territorial waters in order to seek asylum in the United States, was mistakenly returned to the Soviet trawler on a Soviet assertion that he had stolen the equivalent of US $2,000 from the ship's purse.[57] In July 1991, the Government of Jamaica sought an emergency *writ of habeas corpus* to release Richard Morrison, who had been indicted on narcotics trafficking charges in Florida, after he had been extradited to the United States due to a clerical error while his appeal to the U.K. Privy Council was still pending.[58]

In such instances, a pursuing State is under no customary international law obligation to rectify the situation by transferring the fugitive back to the host State,[59] unless possibly fraud or deception was used to induce the mistaken transfer.[60] This principle was articulated by the Permanent Court of Arbitration (PCA) in the classic 1911 *Savarkar Case*. In that case, a British Indian named Vinayak Damodar Savarkar escaped custody from a steamship while docked in Marseilles, France, during a voyage to India where he was to face prosecution for allegedly abetting a murder.

[56] Alpheus Todd, Parliamentary Government in the British Colonies 291–92 (2d ed. 2006).

[57] AP, "Soviets Reportedly Free Sailor Who Jumped Ship," *Watertown Daily Times*, Aug. 30, 1974, at 1; Vladistav Krasnov, Soviet Defectors: The KGB Wanted List 125 (1986); Terry Richard Kane, *Prosecuting Int'l Terrorists in United States Courts: Gaining the Jurisdictional Threshold*, 12 Yale J. Int'l L. 294, 333 (1987).

[58] *Gov't of Jamaica v. United States*, 770 F. Supp. 627 (M.D. Fla. 1991).

[59] Bedi, *supra* n.38, at 398. For example, in the *Morrison* case in Jamaica just discussed, the U.S. federal district court ruled that the United States did not need to return him to Jamaica as the United States had done nothing unlawful and there was no violation of Jamaican law with respect to the extradition proceedings. *Gov't of Jamaica*, 770 F. Supp. at 633.

[60] O'Higgins, *supra* n.25, at 311.

Although the British Indian police from the ship gave chase, it was a French policeman who captured and mistakenly returned him into British custody. While France subsequently requested his return, the PCA found no basis in international law for such restitution. The tribunal reasoned as follows:

> there is no rule of international law imposing, in circumstances such as those which have been set out above, any obligation on the Power which has in its custody a prisoner, to restore him because of a mistake committed by the foreign agent who delivered him up to that Power.[61]

* * * * *

This chapter has addressed those scenarios, while rather uncommon, in which a pursuing State acquires the custody or control of a wanted fugitive due to entirely fortuitous circumstances. The next chapter turns to the *most common* means relied upon by States to recover fugitives: extradition.

[61] *Savarkar Case* (Fr. v. Gr. Br.), PCA Award, Hague Ct. Rep. (Scott) 276, Feb. 24, 1911.

PART II

Extradition and Its Impediments

4

Extradition

The focus of Part II is on extradition. The extradition process between States represents not only the most legally and politically preferred method of rendering fugitives, but also the most ancient[1] and popular[2] law enforcement cooperation modality.[3] This chapter seeks a baseline understanding of extradition, including its aims, legal status, types, and mechanics; assesses its capacity to adapt to today's changing needs and challenges; and examines its overall effectiveness and trend lines. Chapters 5, 6, and 7 then systematically explore this modality's obstacles and limitations.

1 Extradition, which ranks as the world's oldest vehicle for international cooperation in penal matters, IVOR STANBROOK & CLIVE STANBROOK, EXTRADITION: LAW AND PRACTICE 1 (2d ed. 2000), traces its known origins to the Jewish scriptures when, in approximately 1350 BCE, the Benjamite tribe refused to extradite men who had gang-raped a Levite concubine, which led to war between Israel and the Benjamite tribe. M. CHERIF BASSIOUNI, INTERNATIONAL EXTRADITION: UNITED STATES LAW AND PRACTICE 4–5 (6th ed. 2014) [hereinafter BASSIOUNI, U.S. EXTRADITION]. The first recorded extradition treaty occurred almost as far back, to the time of the Biblical Moses, in the mid-13th century BCE, when an Egyptian Pharoah (Ramses II) and a Hittite monarch (Hattushilish III; the spelling of which varies) entered into a peace treaty following a war over control of Syria that also constituted perhaps history's oldest diplomatic document. That treaty notably contained a provision for the reciprocal return of criminals, although in reality, political enemies. *Id.* at 5; Theo Vogler, *Perspectives on Extradition and Terrorism, in* INTERNATIONAL TERRORISM AND POLITICAL CRIMES 391 (M. Cherif Bassiouni ed. 1975); Geoff Gilbert, *Extradition, in* THE HARVARD RESEARCH IN INTERNATIONAL LAW: CONTEMPORARY ANALYSIS AND APPRAISAL 247 (John P. Grant & J. Craig Barker eds. 2007) [hereinafter Gilbert, *Extradition*].

2 *See* American Law Inst., RESTATEMENT (THIRD) OF THE FOREIGN RELATIONS LAW OF THE UNITED STATES, May 14, 1986 (1987), Subchapter B, Intro. Note, at 557 [hereinafter RESTATEMENT (THIRD)] ("The practice of extradition is the most widespread example of cooperation among states in criminal matters.").

3 For a list of other law enforcement cooperation modalities, *see* n.54 in Chapter 1.

a Aims

Extradition is premised on the underlying principles of sovereign respect and equality,[4] reciprocity,[5] and comity.[6] Extradition is not an end in itself but rather an important means[7] to such specific ends as the following:

- Preventing impunity by disallowing charged (or convicted) persons to avoid prosecution (or punishment) merely by fleeing to or remaining in a "safe haven" State;[8]

[4] *See* Melanie M. Laflin, Note, *Kidnapped Terrorists: Bringing Int'l Criminals to Justice Through Irregular Rendition and Other Quasi-Legal Options*, 26 J. Legis. 315, 316 (2000) (the practice of extradition developed as sovereign entities grew to respect the territorial integrity of other nations); Kenneth S. Gallant, *Securing the Presence of Defendants before the Int'l Tribunal for the Former Yugoslavia: Breaking with Extradition*, 5 Crim. L.F. 557, 567 (1994) (equality is a hallmark of extradition); *cf.* Patrick M. Haggan, Note, *Gov't Sponsored Extraterritorial Abductions in the New World Order: The Unclear Role of Int'l Law in United States Courts and Foreign Policy*, 17 Suffolk Transnat'l L. Rev. 438, 441 n.15 (1994) (a principal reason States execute extradition treaties is to protect their sovereignty).

[5] Gallant, *supra* n.4, at 567; *e.g.*, Switz., Federal Act on Int'l Mutual Assistance in Crim. Matters, Mar. 20, 1981, art. 8(1), *as amended* (unofficial translation), *reprinted in* 20 ILM 1339 (1981) [hereinafter Swiss IMAC] ("As a rule, a request shall be granted only if the requesting State guarantees reciprocity."). At times, partner States maintain unequal standards, which can generate domestic resentment in the State whose extradition requests are or are perceived to be subject to a less favorable standard. A well-known example occurred in the context of the U.S.-U.K. extradition treaty (2003) in which the U.K. Government no longer required evidentiary proof in support of U.S. extradition requests, whereas the United States continued to require probable cause from the United Kingdom. Treaty on Extradition, U.S.-U.K., Mar. 31, 2003, art. 8.3(c).

[6] Gallant, *supra* n.4, at 567; Hersch Lauerpacht, 3 International Law: Being the Collected Papers of Hersch Lauterpacht 223 (E. Lauterpacht ed. 1977).

[7] M. Cherif Bassiouni, Introduction to International Criminal Law 335 (2003) [hereinafter Bassiouni, Introduction].

[8] *See* Robert Cryer, et al., An Introduction to International Criminal Law and Procedure 79 (2d ed. 2010) (extradition helps to "expunge safe havens"); Geoff Gilbert, Responding to International Crime 5 (2006) [hereinafter Gilbert, International Crime] (extradition helps prevent fugitives from evading justice). *Cf. Liangsiriprasert v. United States* [1991] 1 A.C. 225, 244 (P.C.), [1990] 2 All E.R. 866 (Lord Griffiths) ("To put the matter bluntly, it is no direct concern of English society if a crime is committed in another country. It was for this reason that the law of extradition was introduced between civilized nations so that fugitive offenders might be returned for trial in the country against whose laws they had offended.").

- Strengthening law enforcement and crime prevention both in the pursuing State at issue[9] and the host State;[10]
- Serving the interests of international cooperation and stability by promoting the use of agreements to transfer custody, and in so doing diminishing political tensions and the likelihood of territorial invasion or war;[11] and
- Safeguarding in principle various procedural rights and basic protections of an accused under both host and pursuing State law.[12]

The aims of extradition have changed significantly over time, reflecting a shifting focus on the international community's criminal and political priorities.[13] From ancient times[14] stretching through the Middle Ages

[9] Ilias Bantekas & Susan Nash, International Criminal Law 179 (2d ed. 2003); Kyle M. Medley, Note, *The Widening of the Atlantic: Extradition Practices Between the United States and Europe*, 68 Brook. L. Rev. 1213, 1217 (2002–03).

[10] *See* Matthew W. Henning, Note, *Extradition Controversies: How Enthusiastic Prosecutions Can Lead to Int'l Incidents*, 22 B.C. Int'l & Comp. L. Rev. 347, 350 (1999) (a fugitive might commit a crime while harbored in the host State); *Soering v. U.K.*, Appl. No. 14038/88, 11 EHRR 439, 468, July 7, 1989. Host State law enforcement also can be enhanced by extradition in instances where its "courts and prisons are no match for drug lords who can bribe or intimidate judges and witnesses, and run their empires from jail cells using mobile phones." "Extradition in Latin America: How to Handle a Drug Gang," *The Economist*, Nov. 21, 2015, at 35 (adding by example that "[i]n 1991 Colombian kingpin Pablo Escobar was confined to a 'jail' called the Cathedral, featuring a football field, Jacuzzi, waterfall and prostitutes"). At the same time, however, the host State could develop a dependency on extradition to address crime within its territory such that the incentive to take measures to improve its own criminal justice system abates and thereby the domestic laws designed to protect its own population do not become effective. *Id.* at 35–36.

[11] *See* Bantekas & Nash, *supra* n.9, at 179; Mark Brkljacic, Note, *The Dangers of State Sponsored and Court Ratified Abduction*, 5 J. Int'l L. & Prac. 117, 117 (1996); Henning, *supra* n.10, at 350 (extradition helps to avoid bilateral tensions); *United States v. Álvarez-Machaín*, 504 U.S. 655, 672 n.4 (1992) (Stevens, J., dissenting op.) ("Extradition treaties prevent international conflict by providing agreed-upon standards so that the parties may cooperate and avoid retaliatory invasions of territorial sovereignty."), *on remand*, 971 F.2d 310 (9th Cir. 1992), *reprinted in* 31 ILM 902 (1992).

[12] Lyal S. Sunga, The Emerging System of International Criminal Law: Developments in Codification and Implementation 257 (1997); Gilbert, International Crime, *supra* n.8, at 5; Ethan A. Nadelmann, Cops Across Borders: The Internationalization of U.S. Criminal Law Enforcement 398 (1993) [hereinafter Nadelmann, Cops] (because extradition procedures tend to be written and detailed, they allow "for both judicial evaluation and executive oversight of all requests").

[13] Valerie Epps, *The Development of the Conceptual Framework Supporting Int'l Extradition*, 25 Loy. L.A. Int'l & Comp. L. Rev. 369, 374 (2003).

[14] For example, an agreement between Ancient Rome and Syria provided for the enforced return of Hannibal, Stanbrook & Stanbrook, *supra* n.1, at 3, a Carthaginian military

until the early part of the nineteenth century, decisions to extradite typically amounted to gestures of courtesy or personal friendship or were driven by alliance-building interests between sovereign rulers and involved predominantly political opponents, religious refugees, or military deserters,[15] rather than being based on formal treaties with an eye to cooperation toward the suppression of common crimes or those of an international character, as is the case today.[16]

commander who fought against the Roman Empire during a period of its expansion in the Mediterranean.

[15] *See* J. Richard Barnett, *Extradition Treaty Improvements to Combat Drug Trafficking*, 15 GA. J. INT'L & COMP. L. 285, 285 n.1 (1985) (citing ancient Egypt, Chaldean, and Chinese civilizations); Vogler, *supra* n.1, at 392; M. Cherif Bassiouni, *The Political Offense Exception in Extradition Law and Practice, in* INTERNATIONAL TERRORISM AND POLITICAL CRIMES 398 (M. Cherif Bassiouni ed. 1975) ("Historically, extradition was the means resorted to for the surrender of political offenders"); STANBROOK & STANBROOK, *supra* n.1, at 4 (citing the Anglo-Danish and Anglo-Dutch Treaties of 1661 and 1662, respectively, as examples of the Restoration Government of England entering into treaties with European states to secure the return of those alleged of committing regicide); EDWARD M. WISE, ET AL., INTERNATIONAL CRIMINAL LAW: CASES AND MATERIALS 462 n.* (3d ed. 2009) ("A 1788 consular convention between France and the U.S. obligated the parties to surrender deserting sailors.").

[16] R. Stuart Phillips, *The Political Offence Exception and Terrorism: Its Place in the Current Extradition Scheme and Proposal for Its Future*, 15 DICKINSON J. INT'L L. 337, 339 (1997); ALUN JONES & ANAND DOOBAY, JONES AND DOOBAY ON EXTRADITION AND MUTUAL ASSISTANCE 5 (2005); Henri Labayle, *Terrorism and Extradition: A French Perspective, in* TERRORISM AND INTERNATIONAL LAW 185 (Rosalyn Higgins & Maurice Flory eds. 1997); Yvonne G. Grassie, Note, *Federally Sponsored Int'l Kidnapping: An Acceptable Alternative to Extradition?*, 64 WASH. U.L.Q. 1205, 1207 (1986). Scattered exceptions during this period, however, existed, notably including: (i) a 1303 extradition treaty between England's Edward I and the King of France, which focused on the criminal process rather than on political opponents, JONES & DOOBAY, *supra*, at 5; and (ii) the 1794 Treaty on Amity, Commerce and Navigation between the United States and England, Nov. 19, 1794, 8 Stat. 116 (1795), 12 U.S.T. 13, T.S. No. 105 (named after chief U.S. negotiator John Jay), which concededly recognized only murder and forgery as grounds for extradition and provided no specific procedure for extradition. Barnett, *supra* n.15, at 298. Interestingly, when the first reported case arose under the Jay Treaty – the 1799 case of Jonathan Robbins accused by the British of murder during the mutiny of a British ship (*Holmes v. Jennison*, 39 U.S. (14 Pet.) 540 (1840)) – he was arrested and imprisoned without a hearing and turned over to the British despite his claim that he was a U.S. citizen who had been impressed into service by the British navy. This case generated much controversy because he was deprived of his procedural and substantive rights. As a result, the Jay Treaty was allowed to lapse in 1807 and, for the next four decades, with the exception of the so-called Webster-Ashburton Treaty with Britain (formally entitled, "Boundaries, Slave Trade, Extradition," Aug. 9, 1842, 8 Stat. 572, T.S. No. 119, 12 T.I.A.S. 82) that encompassed seven offenses, the United States had no extradition treaties in effect with any country. Benjamin N. Bedrick, Note, *United States Extradition Process: Changes in Law to Address Constitutional Infirmity*, 15 DICKINSON J. INT'L L. 385, 387–88 (1997); STANBROOK & STANBROOK, *supra* n.1, at 4; Ethan A. Nadelmann, *The Evolution of United*

By the 1830s, as the political refugee population had grown as a function of liberation movements and those fleeing "despotic regimes in Central and Eastern Europe,"[17] coupled with the rise of common criminals due to increased trade, industrial production, and a greater accumulation of wealth, States began to appreciate the importance of distinguishing between political and all other types of "criminals" subject to extradition requests.[18] In 1834, an extradition treaty (between Belgium and France) for the first time treated political crimes (*délit politique*) as an invalid basis for extradition,[19] although even then, only a year later, "Austria, Prussia, and Russia engaged [one another] to deliver up persons guilty of high treason, armed rebellion or acts against the security of the throne or the government."[20]

Domestic extradition statutes based on the modern approach favoring international cooperation toward crime suppression came to be embraced in the legislation of Belgium, France, and Switzerland, in 1833, 1834, and 1834, respectively.[21] From about the mid-twentieth century, extradition treaties and statutes have introduced human rights as an additional priority,[22] paying greater heed to individual freedom from arbitrary arrest, maltreatment, and abuse of process.[23]

b Status

Extradition is based on the sovereign prerogatives of the States concerned.[24] Under either customary international law or general

States Involvement in the Int'l Rendition of Fugitive Criminals, 25 N.Y.U. J. Int'l L. & Pol. 813, 821 (1993).

17 Stanbrook & Stanbrook, *supra* n.1, at 4.

18 *Id.* at 5; Epps, *supra* n.15, at 375–76; Ann Powers, *Justice Denied? The Adjudication of Extradition Applications*, 37 Tex. Int'l L.J. 277, 281 (2002).

19 Epps, *supra* n.13, at 376; Stanbrook & Stanbrook, *supra* n.1, at 5; Christopher H. Pyle, Extradition, Politics, and Human Rights 82 (2001).

20 Vogler, *supra* n.1, at 392.

21 *Id.*; Stanbrook & Stanbrook, *supra* n.1, at 5; Sir Robert Jennings & Sir Arthur Watts, eds., 1 Oppenheim's International Law 954 & n.5 (9th ed. 1992); Pyle, *supra* n.19, at 81–82 (Belgium was the first State to address political offenses in a national statute (Oct. 1, 1833), just after winning its independence from the Netherlands).

22 Silvia Borelli, *The Rendition of Terrorist Suspects to the United States: Human Rights and the Limits of Int'l Cooperation, in* Enforcing International Law Norms against Terrorism 333 (Andrea Bianchi ed. 2004).

23 Epps, *supra* n.13, at 376–77.

24 *See* Christopher L. Blakesley, Terrorism, Drugs, International Law, and the Protection of Human Liberty: A Comparative Study of International Law, Its

principles of international law, there is no inherent obligation on the part of the host State to extradite a fugitive,[25] even in instances involving serious war crimes or crimes against humanity.[26] Thus, a host State is under no international legal duty[27] to extradite a fugitive absent some affirmative commitment entered into with the pursuing State, generally expressed through treaties,[28] although in most cases it may still do so on a voluntary basis through, say, comity (discussed *infra*).[29] Indeed, some treaties explicitly indicate that States are *not* obligated to grant

NATURE, ROLE, AND IMPACT IN MATTERS OF TERRORISM, DRUG TRAFFICKING, WAR, AND EXTRADITION 172 (1992) [hereinafter BLAKESLEY, COMPARATIVE STUDY] (when a State decides to extradite an individual, it can be seen as either exercising its sovereignty or conceding some part of it). Some have argued, however, that with the March 1992 decision by the UNSC to exhort "with more than rhetorical condemnation" Libya to extradite two intelligence officers, "sovereign authority within the extradition system is no longer absolute." Christopher C. Joyner & Wayne P. Rothman, *Libya and the Aerial Incident at Lockerbie: What Lessons for Int'l Law?*, 14 MICH. J. INT'L L. 222, 260 (1993).

[25] *See* RESTATEMENT (THIRD), *supra* n.2, Subchapter B, Intro. Note, at 557 ("[T]he network of treaties has not created a principle of customary law requiring extradition, and it is accepted that states are not required to extradite except as obligated to do so by treaty.") (citation omitted); Yoram Dinstein, *Some Reflections on Extradition*, 36 GER. Y.B. INT'L L. 46, 48 (1993); *Daya Singh Lahoria v. Union of India and Others*, Sup. Ct., India, Apr. 17, 2001, (2001) 4 SCC 516, *reprinted in* 125 ILR 530, 534 (E. Lauterpacht, *et al.*, eds. 2004) ("There is no rule of international law which imposes any duty on a State to surrender a fugitive in the absence of an extradition treaty."); *Factor v. Laubenheimer*, 290 U.S. 276, 287 (1933); *The State (Duggan) v. Tapley*, Sup. Ct., Ir., [1952] I.R. 62, *reprinted in* 18 ILR 336 (1951).

[26] *See* David M. Kennedy, *et al.*, *The Extradition of Mohammed Hamadei*, 31 HARV. INT'L L.J. 5, 12 & n.34 (1990) (the view that general international law imposes an obligation to extradite in cases of crimes against peace or humanity or in cases of war crimes has not gained wide acceptance).

[27] Of course, States may be obligated to extradite as a function of *domestic* legislation.

[28] BLAKESLEY, COMPARATIVE STUDY, *supra* n.24, at 186; Brkljacic, *supra* n.11, at 130; HELEN DUFFY, THE 'WAR ON TERROR' AND THE FRAMEWORK OF INTERNATIONAL LAW 107 & n.180 (2005); BANTEKAS & NASH, *supra* n.9, at 179.

[29] The existence of an extradition treaty, while binding the States parties to transfer custody of fugitives "under certain circumstances," "does not purport to limit the discretion of the two sovereigns to [extradite] fugitives for reasons of comity, prudence, or even as a whim." *United States v. Najohn*, 785 F.2d 1420, 1422 (9th Cir.) (per curiam), *cert. denied*, 479 U.S. 1009 (1986). The United States, for example, allows for comity as a basis for extradition on an exceptional and conditional basis, as follows: "The provisions of this chapter shall be construed to permit, in the exercise of comity, the surrender of persons, other than citizens, nationals, or permanent residents of the United States, who have committed crimes of violence against nationals of the United States in foreign countries without regard to the existence of any treaty of extradition with such foreign government if the Attorney General certifies, in writing, that—(1) evidence has been presented by the foreign government that indicates that had the offenses been committed in the United States, they would constitute crimes of violence as defined under section 16 of this title; and (2) the offenses charged are not of a political nature." 18 U.S.C. § 3181(b) (2012).

extradition requests.[30] The corollary to this rule is that a pursuing State has no *a priori* right to have an individual of interest extradited into its custody. Accordingly, a fugitive's State of nationality is under no general duty to request his extradition.[31] Customary international law, however, imposes limitations on the host State's *decision to extradite*, to the limited extent that fundamental human rights could be violated.[32]

Extradition decisions "are a combination of national and international law,"[33] heavily influenced by any applicable treaties and by the status of diplomatic relations between the concerned States, but ultimately determined by the host State's domestic law and its political

30 *E.g.*, Conv. on Offences and Certain Other Acts Committed on Board Aircraft, Sept. 14, 1963, art. 16, U.N. Doc. A/C.6/418/Corr.1, Annex II, 704 U.N.T.S. 219, 20 U.S.T. 2941, ICAO Doc. 8364, *reprinted in* 2 ILM 1042, 1045 (1963).

31 When sixty-nine South African nationals held in Harare, Zimbabwe, sought their government's intervention by insisting that South Africa request their extradition home, rather than allowing them to be extradited to Equatorial Guinea, where the men had already been convicted of crimes and were awaiting sentence, the Pretoria High Court (in June 2004) and the Constitutional Court of South Africa (in August 2004) each ruled that South Africa could not be forced to request their return, although South Africa was obligated to try to shield them from a potential death penalty and unacceptable conditions of detention through diplomatic representations. *Kaunda and Others v. The President of the Repub. of So. Afr.*, Case CCT 23/04, Const. Const. Ct., So. Afr., Aug. 4, 2004, [2005] (4) SA 235 (Chaskalson, C.J.). Seeking extradition, however, can effectively impose a duty on a prosecutor's office to the extent that domestic "speedy trial" requirements demand a good faith effort to try to secure the custody of a fugitive through extradition, at least where it might be plausibly granted. *E.g., United States v. Pomeroy*, 822 F.2d 718, 720–22 (8th Cir. 1987) (dismissing an indictment on speedy trial grounds where the United States knew of defendant's whereabouts in a Canadian prison for two years but failed to seek his extradition and thereby bring him to trial in the United States, even though Canada ultimately could have denied such a request).

32 *See* Donna E. Arzt, *The Lockerbie 'Extradition by Analogy' Agreement: 'Exceptional Measure' or Template for Transnat'l Criminal Justice?*, 18 Am. U. Int'l L. Rev. 163, 173 (2002); Kennedy, *supra* n.26, at 12 & n.35; Duffy, *supra* n.28, at 107. This restriction is discussed more extensively in Chapter 7.e.

33 *Tsebe and Another v. Minister of Home Affairs and Others*, Case Nos. 27682/10, 51010/10, So. Gauteng High Ct., Johannesburg, So. Afr., Sept. 22, 2011, 1 All SA 83, ¶ 112. *See also Daya Singh Lahoria v. Union of India and Others*, *supra* n.25, 534–35 ("The law of extradition, therefore, is a dual law. It is ostensibly a municipal law; yet it is part of international law also, inasmuch as it governs the relations between two sovereign States over the question of whether or not a given person should be handed over by one sovereign State to another sovereign State."); Joanna Harrington, *The Role for Human Rights Obligations in Canadian Extradition Law*, 43 Can. Y.B. Int'l L. 45, 45 (2005); Gregor Haas, *State Security Interests in the French Extradition Procedure, in* National Security and International Criminal Justice 193 (Herwig Roggemann & Petar Šarčević eds. 2002).

objectives.[34] The Constitutional Court of the Republic of South Africa (RSA) in 2000 elucidated this dynamic between international and domestic law as follows:

> An extradition procedure works both on an international and a domestic plane. Although the interplay of the two may not be severable, they are distinct. On the international plane, a request from one foreign State to another for the extradition of a particular individual and the response to the request will be governed by the rules of public international law. At play are the relations between States. However, before the requested State may surrender the requested individual, there must be compliance with its own domestic laws. Each State is free to prescribe when and how an extradition request will be acted upon and the procedures for the arrest and surrender of the requested individual. Accordingly, many States have extradition laws that provide domestic procedures to be followed before there is approval to extradite.[35]

[34] "Treaties may provide for the rendition of criminal fugitives between states, but it is for municipal law to determine whether the fugitive is to be surrendered in accordance with the extradition treaty." John Dugard & Christine van den Wyngaert, *Reconciling Extradition with Human Rights*, 92 AJIL 187, 188 (1998). *See also* Thomas E. Carbonneau, *The Provisional Arrest & Subsequent Release of Abou Daoud by French Authorities*, 17 Va. J. Int'l L. 495, 496 (1977); David Freestone, *Int'l Cooperation against Terrorism and the Development of Int'l Law Principles of Jurisdiction, in* Terrorism and International Law 45–46 (Rosalyn Higgins & Maurice Flory eds. 1997). *Cf.* Note, *The Abu Daoud Affair*, 11 J. Int'l L. & Econ. 539, 559 (1977) (summarizing the findings of a "conceptual framework" analysis conducted by Professor M. Cherif Bassiouni in 1969 in which of the key factors driving extradition decisions, "national interest" was the most important).

It is not uncommon that a State must confront the question whether domestic or international law prevails when the two are in direct conflict in the extradition context. *See* Ivan A. Shearer, Extradition in International Law 115 (1971) ("in *civil law systems* international law is generally of superior force to municipal law. Thus, in the event that an extradition treaty should impose an obligation on these countries to extradite a national [for example] this obligation must be discharged, notwithstanding the contrary provisions of municipal law.") (emphasis supplied). But that is not always the case. For example, in February 1999 the Israeli Supreme Court held that Samuel Sheinbein, a U.S. national who had committed murder and fled to Israel and claimed Israeli citizenship from birth through his father, should not be extradited to the United States to face prosecution, as Israel needed to honor its domestic law denying nationals from extradition even in the face a 1962 extradition treaty with the United States and a long history of cooperation between the two countries. Jesse Hallee, *The Sheinbein Legacy: Israel's Refusal to Grant Extradition as a Model of Complexity*, 15 Am. U. Int'l L. Rev. 667, 673–76 (2000).

[35] *Harksen v. President of the Repub. of So. Afr.and Others*, Case CCT 41/99, Const. Ct., So. Afr., Mar. 30, 2000, (2000) (2) SA 825, ¶ 4, *reprinted in* 132 ILR 529, 557 (E. Lauterpacht, *et al.*, eds. 2008) [hereinafter *Harksen Case*]. One could draw an analogy between extradition and diplomatic immunities based on the way they operate between, and are jointly governed by, international and domestic legal authorities.

Extradition defies straightforward legal categorization. In one sense, it falls within the field of international criminal law, as extradition is a cooperative law enforcement mechanism for States to bring individuals to justice and figures into a wide range of treaties to that end,[36] but it nevertheless occupies a unique, if uncertain, place within the sphere of public international law.[37] Although extraditions have certain attributes of a criminal proceeding – *e.g.*, the accused has been indicted and arrested, may be held in pretrial confinement or let out on bail, prosecutors are involved, and the liberty of the accused is at stake[38] – extradition is not a criminal proceeding *per se*.[39] Indeed, at extradition hearings in the U.S., neither the U.S. Federal Rules of Evidence,[40] the Federal Rules of Criminal Procedure,[41] nor the Sixth Amendment to the U.S. Constitution[42] apply, and many of the protections associated with criminal proceedings (*e.g.*, application of the hearsay rule and the opportunity to present affirmative defenses) are not observed.[43]

[36] *See* BANTEKAS & NASH, *supra* n.9, at 179 (classifying extradition law as a branch of international criminal law).

[37] *See* Haas, *supra* n.33, at 193 (extradition is commonly treated as its own particular legal field).

[38] John G. Kester, *Some Myths of United States Extradition Law*, 76 GEO. L.J. 1441, 1446 (1998).

[39] *See United States ex rel. Oppenheim v. Hecht*, 16 F.2d 955, 956 (2d Cir.) ("Extradition proceedings are not in their nature criminal, even if the relator is a criminal"), *cert. denied*, 273 U.S. 769 (1927); *United States v. Fernandez-Morris*, 99 F. Supp.2d 1358, 1366 (S.D. Fla. 1999); Dinstein, *supra* n.25, at 47 ("Extradition proceedings in the requested State have 'decidedly criminal consequences,' although they are not criminal proceedings in the technical sense. Such proceedings must not be confused with a trial culminating with a verdict as to whether the alleged offender is guilty or not guilty. The sole issue is whether or not the alleged offender should be surrendered to the requesting State for trial and/or punishment there."). *But see* BLAKESLEY, COMPARATIVE STUDY, *supra* n.24, at 193 (an extradition hearing is a criminal proceeding as the accused will be incarcerated immediately, and if found extraditable will be sent to trial in the requesting State).

[40] FED. R. EVID. 1101(d)(3) (2015) and accompanying Advisory Comm. notes.

[41] FED R. CRIM. P. 1(a)(5)(A) (2014) (formerly Rule 54(b)(5)); *e.g.*, *Romeo v Roache*, 820 F.2d 540 (1st Cir. 1987) (per curiam).

[42] The Sixth Amendment, which guarantees the right to the assistance of counsel in all criminal prosecutions, does not apply to extradition proceedings, because such proceedings are conducted under "civil rules"; indeed, "[n]o jury will sit, no elements of the offense will be adjudicated in a speedy and public trial, the accused will not be confronted by the witnesses against them, jeopardy does not attach … and so on." *DeSilva v. DiLeonardi*, 181 F.3d 865, 868 (7th Cir. 1999).

[43] *See Quinn v. Robinson*, 783 F.2d 776 (9th Cir. 1984), (admitting hearsay evidence), *cert. denied*, 479 U.S. 882 (1986); Kester, *supra* n.38, at 1443–45; BLAKESLEY, COMPARATIVE STUDY, *supra* n.24, at 282 (alibi claims and defenses are irrelevant in an extradition hearing); *e.g.*, *Hooker v. Klein*, 573 F.2d 1360 (9th Cir.) (insanity defense impermissible),

c Vehicles

This chapter now turns to a consideration of the full range of extradition and extradition-like vehicles – some of which do not follow standard extradition procedures but nevertheless fall within the broad definition of "extradition" as set forth in Chapter 1[44] – beginning with the most formal types and loosely progressing toward the least formal.[45]

The first and most common vehicle is the ***bilateral extradition treaty***,[46] in which two States[47] negotiate mutually agreeable and generally reciprocal terms governing the extradition of fugitives between them.[48] Many States

cert. denied, 439 U.S. 932 (1978); *Eain v. Wilkes*, 641 F.2d 504, 511 (7th Cir.) ("An accused in an extradition hearing has no right to contradict the demanding country's proof or to pose questions of credibility as in an ordinary trial, but only to offer evidence which explains or clarifies that proof."), *cert. denied*, 454 U.S. 894 (1981).

44 Each of these vehicles satisfies the indicia of extradition.

45 A common misconception is that bilateral treaties provide the exclusive means by which an extradition can be authorized and effected. As this section will reveal, extraditions can be lawfully carried out under other agreements, pursuant to domestic law, or via reciprocity or comity. *See Harksen Case, supra* n.35, 132 ILR at 557, ¶ 3 (the absence of an extradition treaty between South Africa and the F.R.G. was "no bar to the extradition of requested individuals."). The modern system of extradition often depends on an *ad hoc* network of bilateral treaties supplemented by an increasing number of modern single crime multilateral conventions. Freestone, *supra* n.34, at 45.

46 Barbara M. Yarnold, International Fugitives: A New Role for the International Court of Justice 13 (1991). Most treaties are bilateral because specific criminal needs necessitate the creation of tailored treaties between States. Laflin, *supra* n.4, at 316–17. Extradition treaties tend to be self-executing (versus executory) and therefore do not require implementing legislation. 6 Marjorie M. Whiteman, Digest of International Law 734 (1968); Aimée J. Buckland, *Offending Officials: Former Gov't Actors and the Political Offense Exception to Extradition*, 94 Cal. L. Rev. 423, 432 n.74 (2006). Self-executing treaties take effect as domestic law immediately upon ratification. John E. Nowak, et al., Constitutional Law § 6.7 (4th ed. 1986).

47 In an apparent exception, in October 2009, the United States and a group of States – the European Union (E.U.) – ratified a framework extradition agreement that was signed in June 2003, and thereby took a step toward modernizing the underlying bilateral extradition treaties the United States had with each of the E.U.'s twenty-seven member States. Digest of United States Practice in International Law 2009, at 45–49 (Elizabeth R. Wilcox ed. 2009). Significantly, that treaty does not contemplate or allow extraditions between the United States and the E.U. *per se. See* n.68 in Chapter 1.

48 *E.g.*, Extradition Agreement between South Africa and the Federation of Rhodesia and Nyasaland, Nov. 19, 1962, No. 6592, 458 U.N.T.S. 60 (1963). Bilateral extradition treaties can be supplemented by memoranda of understanding (MOUs) or protocols to build upon originally agreed provisions. For example, the U.S.-Australia Extradition Treaty added a 1990 Protocol obligating the United States to extradite for offenses that meet its criminality requirements and are punishable by imprisonment of more than one year in prison. Protocol Amending the Extradition Treaty between the U.S. and Australia of May

have entered into scores of bilateral extradition treaties, such as the United States,[49] while others have demonstrated less inclination, or have had less success, in doing so, such as Argentina,[50] the People's Republic of China[51] and the Philippines.[52]

While States are obligated to perform in good faith under any treaty to which they have ratified or acceded (per the principle of *pacta sunt servanda*[53]), the host State may always choose at its prerogative to unilaterally waive a treaty right or entitlement to which it is due (at least none which would violate an international human rights law standard) and extradite a fugitive.[54] In addition, international law, in principle, does not bar host and pursuing States from jointly agreeing to work outside the extradition treaty, or otherwise not in precise conformity with its terms, to effect the physical transfer of a fugitive, so long as they do not incidentally violate an independent treaty right accorded a third State or

14, 1974, dated Sept. 4, 1990, 1992 A.T.S. No. 43 (1995). In addition, bilateral treaties do not have to take effect for both State parties simultaneously; the timing depends on when the treaty is ratified and comes into effect in each State. Bassiouni, U.S. Extradition, *supra* n.1, at 95.

49 18 U.S.C. § 3181 note (2012) (listing all U.S. extradition agreements current through January 3, 2012, and comprising approximately 60% of the world's States). The number of estimated bilateral treaties worldwide is over 1,000, Bassiouni, Introduction, *supra* n.7, at 351 n.73, so the number of U.S. bilateral extradition treaties represents just over 10% of all those worldwide. No other State has so many. Kester, *supra* n.38, at 1489. Notably absent from the list of U.S. bilateral extradition treaties include those with such major States as Indonesia, PRC, Russia, and Saudi Arabia.

50 Clarissa F. Dias & Hung-En Sung, *Argentina in* 2 Crime and Punishment around the World: The Americas 18 (Janet P. Stamatel & Hung-En Sung, eds. 2010) (Argentina maintains eighteen bilateral extradition treaties).

51 To date, the PRC has signed extradition treaties with thirty-nine countries, mostly from the developing world. "China Signs Extradition Treaties with 39 Nations," *China Daily*, Mar. 20, 2015. One impediment has been fears in developed States about the PRC's death penalty and whether its judicial system would dispense fair rulings. David Lague, "China Urges Western Nations to Enter Extradition Treaties," *N.Y. Times*, May 29, 2007, at A3.

52 Veronica Uy, "RP Extradition Treaty with only 10 States," *Inquirer* (Manila), Feb. 4, 2010 (Philippines has only ten extradition treaties, based on information provided by J. Edward Malaya, the head of the Office of Legal Affairs within the Philippines' Dep't of Foreign Affairs).

53 Vienna Conv. on the Law of Treaties (VCLT), May 23, 1969, art. 26, 1155 U.N.T.S. 332, *reprinted in* 8 ILM 679. This principle has acquired customary international law status and therefore applies equally to non-parties to the VCLT. Phillips, *supra* n.16, at 339.

54 *Gluckman v. Henkel*, 221 U.S. 508 (1910). For example, the specialty and dual criminality principles, discussed in Chapters 7.c.ii and 5.a.ii, respectively, *infra*, may be waived to permit extradition. *United States v. Saccoccia*, 58 F.3d 754 (1st Cir. 1995), *cert. denied*, 517 U.S. 1105 (1996); Edward M. Wise & Ellen S. Podgor, International Criminal Law: Cases and Materials 350–51 (2000 & Supp. 2003).

a protected human right owed to the fugitive.[55] Another advantage of the bilateral treaty approach is that States can tailor the terms and provisions to accord with their specific political relations, national interests, and criminal legal systems.[56]

Bilateral treaties, however, are subject to a number of drawbacks, notably including the heavy investment of resources required to execute them,[57] the fact that they bind only two States at a time,[58] their lack of uniformity,[59] the need to keep them periodically updated in line with new circumstances or contemporary legal standards,[60] and complications that may affect their status that arise out of such political developments as severed diplomatic relations[61] and State succession.[62] Furthermore, it is not always clear whether a bilateral treaty necessarily trumps conflicting domestic law.[63]

[55] *See generally SS "Lotus"* (Fr. v. Turk.) 1927 P.C.I.J. (ser. A) No. 10 (Sept. 7, 1927), *reprinted in* ANN. DIG. PUB. INT'L L. CASES 153 (No. 98) (H. Lauterpacht ed. 1938), and as discussed at nn.63–65 and accompanying text in Chapter 11.

[56] Gilbert, *Extradition, supra* n.1, at 248–49; BASSIOUNI, INTRODUCTION, *supra* n.7, at 351–52; NADELMANN, COPS, *supra* n.12, at 410.

[57] *See* BASSIOUNI, INTRODUCTION, *supra* n.7, at 351–52 (describing bilateral treaty practice as "lengthy, cumbersome and costly").

[58] *See Case Concerning Certain German Interests in Upper Polish Silesia (Merits)* (Ger. v. Pol.), 1926 P.C.I.J. (ser. A). No. 7, ¶ 82 (May 25, 1925) ("A treaty only creates law as between the States which are parties to it").

[59] YARNOLD, *supra* n.46, at 13–14.

[60] Gilbert, *Extradition, supra* n.1, at 248–49. Indeed, sometimes, a bilateral treaty is rarely, if ever employed, in part at least because it has not been updated for a long time and might only reference a select number of crimes. *See, e.g.*, David P. Warner, *Challenges to Int'l Law Enforcement Cooperation for the U.S. in the Middle East and North Africa: Extradition and Its Alternatives*, 50 VILL. L. REV. 479, 485 & n.30 (2005) (citing by way of example the U.S.-Egyptian extradition treaty of 1934, which "apparently neither country has invoked to seek a fugitive's extradition.").

[61] *E.g., Argento v. Horn*, 241 F.2d 258 (6th Cir. 1957), *cert. denied*, 355 U.S. 818, *reh'g denied*, 355 U.S. 885 (1957).

[62] *E.g., Extradition (Jurisdiction) Case*, Sup. Ct. of the Reich (in Crim. Matters), Aug. 13, 1936, *reprinted in* [1935–37] 8 ANN. DIG. & REP. PUB. INT'L L. CASES 348, 349 (No. 165) (H. Lauterpacht ed. 1941) ("The extradition treaties concluded between France and the German States are extinguished in consequence of the law of January 30, 1934, regulating the reorganisation of the German Empire, by virtue of which Germany has become a Unitarian State, while the German States have ceased to exist in their capacity as subjects of international law. There is no agreement between Germany and France to the effect that these treaties shall remain in force."). That said, in most instances, newly independent States inherit extradition laws from their predecessors. *E.g., Sabatier v. Dabrowski*, 586 F.2d 866 (1st Cir. 1978) (Canada succeeded to the 1842 U.S.-Gr. Br. extradition treaty).

[63] Although as a general rule of international law, reliance on domestic law is not a legitimate defense to the breach of a binding international obligation, SHEARER, *supra*

A second type of vehicle is the ***multilateral extradition treaty***.[64] While no globally applicable extradition treaty yet exists,[65] the United Nations has drafted a Model Treaty on Extradition[66] that serves as a useful framework for the crafting of multilateral and bilateral extradition treaties alike.[67] There are, however, a number of regionally- or sub-regionally-based extradition treaties or protocols in effect today, including (in chronological order below):

(i) Montevideo Convention on Extradition (Inter-American) (1933);[68]

n.34, at 195, some States treat their constitutions as superior to treaty law, Michael Abbell, Extradition to and from the United States 58–59 (2010) (discussing U.S. law) and domestic legislation is sometimes accorded a priority over a treaty commitment. *See, e.g., Geisser v. United States*, 554 F.2d 698 (5th Cir. 1977), *reprinted in* 61 ILR 443 (1981); *Royal Gov't of Greece v. Governor of Brixton Prison, ex parte Kotronis* [1971] A.C. 250 (H.L.) (the United Kingdom did not allow the extradition of Kotronis, based on statutory law, despite the wording of a treaty that required his extradition). *See also* n.60 in the Introduction and *supra* n.34 and accompanying text in this chapter.

64 As with the case of bilateral treaties, States can work out supplemental or clarifying provisions or protocols under a multilateral convention to govern the operation of extraditions between any two or more States. For example, in November 2006, the United Kingdom and Russia executed an MOU to facilitate their extradition arrangements under the 1957 European Extradition Convention to which both were parties. The impetus for this MOU was to address Russia's frustration with British court denials of Russian extradition requests for high-profile nationals such as Boris Berezovsky (former oligarch) and Ahmed Zakayev (Chechen leader). In particular, the MOU enabled prosecutors to cooperate directly with each other with respect to extradition requests to ensure they are correctly prepared and include supporting evidence. Bruce Zagaris, *Russia and U.K. Sign Agreement to Facilitate Extradition*, 23 IELR 17 (2007).

65 Stanbrook & Stanbrook, *supra* n.1, at 18.

66 U.N. Model Treaty on Extradition Dec. 14, 1991, UNGA Res. 45/116, Annex, 45 U.N. GAOR Supp. (No. 49A), at 212, U.N. Doc. A/45/49 (1990), *reprinted in* 30 ILM 1407 (1991). *See* Gilbert, *Extradition, supra* n.1, at 249 (commenting that the U.N. Model Treaty is the closest the international community has come to establishing a universal extradition treaty).

67 *See* Bantekas & Nash, *supra* n.9, at 192–93 (observing its similarity to the 1957 European Convention on Extradition); Roger S. Clark, *United Nations Model Treaties on Cooperation in the Criminal Process*, 18 Commw. L. Bull. 1544, 1544 (1992) (describing the Model Treaty as "a kind of international formbook"); *id.* at 1545 (noting that the Model Treaty "captures the state of the art in drafting extradition treaties and is based largely on Australia's recent extensive negotiating experience in this field").

68 Montevideo Conv. on Extradition, Dec. 26, 1933, 49 Stat. 3111, *reprinted in* 28 AJIL 65 (1934). This treaty, entered into among twenty States in the Americas, remains valid today, and operates effectively as a backfill where States parties do not or cannot otherwise proceed under another bilateral or collective extradition treaty. *Id.*, art. 21. It has not been invoked to date by the United States. Bassiouni, U.S. Extradition, *supra* n.1, at 96.

(ii) Arab League Extradition Agreements (1952 and 1983);[69]
(iii) European Convention on Extradition (1957);[70]
(iv) Convention on Judicial Cooperation among Certain African States (1961);[71]
(v) Nordic Cooperation Agreement (1962), comprising Denmark, Finland, Iceland, Norway, and Sweden, which addresses extradition;[72]
(vi) Benelux Extradition Convention (1962) consisting of Belgium, the Netherlands, and Luxembourg;[73]
(vii) Inter-American Convention on Extradition (1981);[74]

[69] Arab League Extradition Agreement (1952), Sept. 14, 1952, League of Arab States, Collection of Treaties and Agreements, (1978) (ratified by only Egypt, Jordan, and Saudi Arabia); Arab League Agreement on Extradition and Judicial Cooperation ("Riyadh Agreement"), Apr. 6, 1983, *available at* www.refworld.org/docid/3ae6b38d8.html (last visited on Aug. 15, 2016) (ratified by 16 States and incorporates the 1952 Agreement).

[70] Eur. Conv. on Extradition, Dec. 13, 1957, E.T.S. No. 24. The Convention, which has four additional protocols to date, was executed through the Council of Europe (CoE), and all of its forty-seven members are parties to the Convention. Gilbert, *Extradition, supra* n.1, at 250–51. The Convention represents the largest collection of States subscribing to a single extradition treaty and has yielded more extraditions than any other treaty of its kind. Stanbrook & Stanbrook, *supra* n.1, at 18; Thomas F. Muther, Jr., *The Extradition of Int'l Criminals: A Changing Perspective*, 24 Denv. J. Int'l L. & Pol'y 221, 223 (1995). Non-CoE member States may accede to the Convention, few reservations have been introduced, and the Convention has provided model language for a number of bilateral extradition agreements. Bassiouni, U.S. Extradition, *supra* n.1, at 23–24. Despite its remarkable success, this Convention has been largely superseded by the Council Framework Decision of June 2002 adopted by the Council of the European Union (E.U.) and the related European Arrest Warrant (EAW) (discussed *infra*), but as to States, like Switzerland, that have not signed on to the Council Framework Decision, their obligations under the European Convention remain in effect. Note, Swiss Delegation to Council of the European Union, "Article 95 of the Schengen Convention, Eur. Arrest Warrant (EAW)," Apr. 20, 2009.

[71] Conv. on Judicial Cooperation of the Organization Communale Africaine et Malgache (OCAM), Sept. 12, 1961, *available at Journal Officiel de la é Malgache*, Dec. 23, 1961, at 2242 (consisting of 12 of France's former African colonies).

[72] Agreement Concerning Co-operation (Den.-Fin.-Ice.-Nor.-Swe.), Mar. 23, 1962, 434 U.N.T.S. 145 (1962) ("Helsinki Treaty" or "Nordic Extradition Treaty"). This treaty is not self-executing but rather requires each State party to enact implementing legislation, and in 2005 the member States built upon this platform by establishing a Nordic Arrest Warrant modeled on the EAW. Bassiouni, U.S. Extradition, *supra* n.1, at 40.

[73] Benelux Conv. on Extradition and Mutual Assistance in Criminal Matters, June 27, 1962, 616 U.N.T.S. 120 (1968) (Helsinki Treaty or). Most of its provisions track those found in the European Convention on Extradition. Bassiouni, U.S. Extradition, *supra* n.1, at 38.

[74] Inter-Am. Conv. on Extradition, Feb. 25, 1981, OAS T.S. No. 60, *reprinted in* 20 ILM 723 (1981). Notably, this Convention indicates that it shall "not supersede" earlier bilateral or multilateral treaties entered into by State parties unless otherwise expressed. *Id.*, art. 33. Accordingly, the 1933 Montevideo Convention on Extradition is still technically in effect.

(viii) Extradition Treaty among the African States of Benin, Ghana, Nigeria, and Togo (1984);[75]
(ix) Convention on Legal Aid and Legal Relations in Civil, Family and Criminal Cases of the Commonwealth of Independent States (CIS) (1993);[76]
(x) ECOWAS Convention on Extradition (1994);[77] and
(xi) Southern African Development Community (SADC) Protocol on Extradition (2002).[78]

Mulitlateral treaties, which can stand alone or replace or supplement existing bilateral treaties,[79] have the benefits of encompassing a large number of States, resource efficiency, and consistency across State practice through harmonization across otherwise disparate bilateral arrangements and national laws.[80] Their primary disadvantage lies in the fact that, to accommodate the interests of a number of diverse States, the terms of such treaties tend to be more generalized with greater dilution or more limited application.[81] In addition, some States find their own legal systems are not compatible with a

See supra n.68. In addition, some regional customary laws apply in the Inter-American context. *Asylum Case* [1950] I.C.J. Rep. 266, 316 (Nov. 20).

75 Extradition Treaty between the People's Republic of Benin, Republic of Ghana, Federal Republic of Nigeria, and the Republic of Togo, Dec. 10, 1984, *reprinted in* Immigration and Refugee Board of Canada, *Ghana: Extradition Treaties with Neighbouring Countries during 1985–1986*, Sept. 1, 1989, GHA2129.

76 Adopted in Minsk, Jan. 22, 1993 (Articles 56–71 relate to extradition), Info. Doc. No. 1 of Apr. 2005, Hague Conf. on Private Int'l Law (HCCH), *available at* http://nbe.gov.ge/files/documents/MINSKI.pdf (last visited on May 5, 2016).

77 ECOWAS Conv. on Extradition, A/PI/8/94, Aug. 6, 1994, *available at* www.unodc.org/tldb/pdf/Burkina-Faso/BKF_Convention.pdf (last visited on May 5, 2016). The Convention was signed by all ECOWAS member States; a Protocol was added in 2005 to establish a regional criminal investigative bureau known as the CIIB.

78 Southern African Development Community (SADC), Prot. on Extradition, Oct. 3, 2002, *available at* www.sadc.int/documents-publications/show/Protocol_on_Extradiction.pdf (last visited on May 5, 2016) (comprising fourteen member States).

79 *See* Warner, *supra* n.60, at 484 (discussing how because the highly dated but still valid 1934 U.S.-Egyptian extradition treaty (in which Egypt as the party is even referred to as the "Ottoman Empire") only includes eight crimes or types of crimes as the basis for extradition, the States could nevertheless carry out an extradition between them on a crime unlisted in the extradition treaty but covered by a multilateral treaty to which they are both parties, such as narco-terrorism financing under the 1988 U.N. Convention against Illicit Traffic in Narcotics and Psychotropic Substances).

80 Bassiouni, U.S. Extradition, *supra* n.1, at 22.

81 Nadelmann, Cops, *supra* n.12, at 410 (observing that such treaties tend to settle on the lowest common denominator of cooperation).

multilateral approach,[82] and as is the case with their bilateral counterparts, it remains unclear whether multilateral extradition treaties or *domestic legislation* trumps in the event of a conflict.[83] Multilateral conventions generally indicate in the text whether they defer to or prevail over conflicting provisions found in *bilateral treaties*.[84]

A third vehicle available to States is to enter into ***bilateral or multilateral non-extradition treaties that nevertheless contain provisions expressly intended to authorize extradition on a surrogate basis*** where: (i) an extradition treaty does not otherwise exist or is circumstantially inapplicable between two States, and (ii) such a treaty is required by the host State to carry out an extradition. These multilateral treaties, while providing a basis for extradition to proceed, including in instances that might otherwise be barred on account of an outdated or scope-circumscribed bilateral extradition treaty,[85] may be limited in their applicability and contain lacunae.[86]

82 The United States, for instance, has largely steered clear of multilateral extradition agreements for additional reasons, including "the relative complexity of the U.S. legal system, with its common law traditions, federal distribution of jurisdiction, and highly intricate rules of evidence, none of which has been particularly well suited to multilateral extradition arrangements with the majority of foreign states in which civil law traditions dominate." *Id.*

83 *See supra* n.63.

84 WHITEMAN, *supra* n.46, at 770; *e.g.*, Eur. Conv. on Extradition, *supra* n.70, art. 28 (superseding existing bilateral treaties but permits future ones to supplement its provisions); Conv. for the Suppression of Unlawful Acts against the Safety of Maritime Navigation, Rome, Mar. 10, 1988, art. 11(7), IMO Doc. Sua/Con/15/Rev.1, *reprinted in* 27 ILM 668, 680 [Maritime Navigation Conv.] ("With respect to the offences as defined in this Convention, the provisions of all extradition treaties and arrangements applicable between States Parties are modified as between States Parties to the extent that they are incompatible with this Convention.").

85 For example, in November 2011, Guatemala authorized the extradition to the United States of former Guatemalan President Alfonso Portillo (2000–04) on money laundering charges, but needed to rely on the U.N. Convention against Corruption (UNCAC) rather than the U.S.-Guatemala Extradition Treaty, which dated to 1903 and contained only a limited number of extraditable offenses, despite a 1940 supplement treaty that added narcotics offenses. Ignacio Martinez-Arrieta & Bruce Zagaris, *Guatemalan President Authorizes Extradition of Former President to the United States on Money Laundering Charges*, 28 IELR 16, 16–18 (2012).

86 *See* Antonio Cassese, *The Int'l Community's 'Legal' Response to Terrorism*, 38 INT'L & COMP. L.Q. 589, 593–95 (1989) (observing that most multilateral treaties treat terrorist-type acts from treatment as political offenses and thereby exempt them from extradition); *e.g.*, U.N. Conv. against Corruption, Oct. 31, 2003, art. 44(2), Annex to UNGA Res. 58/4, U.N. Doc. A/58/422 [hereinafter UNCAC] (obligating each signatory State to extradite a requested defendant but only with respect to transnational corruption, and therefore not implicating simple domestic corruption).

Examples include the Convention for the Suppression of Unlawful Seizure of Aircraft (1970);[87] the Inter-American Convention to Prevent and Punish Torture (1985);[88] the Convention for the Suppression of Unlawful Acts against the Safety of Maritime Navigation (1988);[89] the U.N. Convention against Illicit Traffic in Narcotic Drugs and Psychotropic Substances (1988);[90] the Council of Europe (CoE) Agreement on Illicit Traffic by Sea, Implementing Article 17 of the above U.N. Convention (1995);[91] the Inter-American Convention against the Illicit Manufacturing of and Trafficking in Firearms, Ammunition, Explosives, and Other Related Materials (1997);[92] the Inter-American Convention against Terrorism (2002);[93] the U.N. Convention against Corruption (UNCAC) (2003);[94] and the Protocol Amending the European Convention for the Suppression of Terrorism (2003).[95]

Fourth, there are ***bilateral or mulilateral non-extradition treaties or agreements that stipulate to extradition-like or custodial transfer arrangements between them regarding actual or alleged***

[87] Conv. for the Suppression of Unlawful Seizure of Aircraft, Dec. 16, 1970, art. 8.3, U.N. Doc. A/C.6/418/Corr.1, Annex II, 860 U.N.T.S. 105, 22 U.S.T. 1641, 10 ILM 133 (1971).

[88] Inter-Am. Conv. to Prevent and Punish Torture, Dec. 9, 1985, art. 13, OAS T.S. No. *reprinted in* 25 ILM 519 (1986).

[89] Maritime Navigation Conv., *supra* n.84, Mar. 10, 1988, art. 11(2).

[90] U.N. Conv. against Illicit Traffic in Narcotic Drugs and Psychotropic Substances, Dec. 20, 1988, art. 6(3), U.N. Doc. E/CONF/82/15 (1988), *reprinted in* 28 ILM 493 (1989) ("If a Party which makes extradition conditional on the existence of a treaty receives a request for extradition from another Party with which it has no extradition treaty, it may consider this Convention as the legal basis for extradition in respect of any offence to which this article applies. The Parties which require detailed legislation in order to use this Convention as a legal basis for extradition shall consider enacting such legislation as may be necessary."). That Convention, *inter alia*, established extradition relations between the United Kingdom and the United Arab Emirates (UAE) in a case that arose in 2001. *Lodhi v. Governor of HMP Brixton and the Gov't of UAE* [2001] EWHC 178 (Admin).

[91] Agreement on Illicit Traffic by Sea, Implementing Article 17 of the U.N. Conv. against Illicit Traffic in Narcotic Drugs and Psychotropic Substances, Jan. 31, 1995, E.T.S. No. 156.

[92] Inter-Am. Conv. against the Illicit Manufacturing of and Trafficking in Firearms, Ammunition, Explosives, and Other Related Materials, Nov. 14, 1997, art. XIX(3), OAS Doc. A-63 ("If a State Party that makes extradition conditional on the existence of a treaty receives a request for extradition from another State Party with which it does not have an extradition treaty, it may consider this Convention as the legal basis for extradition with respect to any offense to which this article applies.").

[93] Inter-Am. Conv. against Terrorism, June 3, 2002, OAS Res. 1840 (XII-O/02), OAS No. A-66.

[94] UNCAC, *supra* n.86, art. 44(2).

[95] Prot. Amending the Eur. Conv. for the Suppression of Terrorism (2003), May 15, 2003, art. 3(2) E.T.S. No. 190, (not yet in force).

offenders.[96] These instruments may include wartime or post-conflict treaties, general law enforcement cooperation agreements, and other specialized conventions. Historic examples include: the Treaty of Amiens (1802) between France, Great Britain, Holland, and Spain;[97] the Treaty of Versailles (1919) at the end of World War I;[98] the Havana Convention Relating to Consular Agents (1928);[99] and the U.S.-Japan Security Treaty (1951).[100] Modern

[96] While Mutual Legal Assistance Treaties (MLATs) or Mutual Legal Assistance Agreements (MLAAs), like extradition treaties, typically authorize the transfer of persons in custody, such transfers tend to be temporary, involve witnesses (versus criminal defendants) to testify or assist in investigations, and require their consent and return. *See, e.g.*, Agreement between the Gov't of the Hong Kong Special Admin. Region of the People's Repub. of China and the Gov't of the Repub. of Finland Concerning Mutual Legal Assistance in Crim. Matters, Oct. 4, 2007, art. 15(1), as found in Hong Kong Legislation, Chap. 525Y, Gazette No. E.R. 2 of 2012 ("A person in custody in the Requested Party whose presence is requested in the Requesting Party as a witness pursuant to this Agreement shall, if the Requested Party consents, be transferred from the Requested Party to the Requesting Party for that purpose, provided the person consents and the Requesting Party has guaranteed the maintenance in custody of the person and his subsequent return to the Requested Party.").

[97] Definitive Treaty of Peace between the French Republic, his Majesty the King of Spain and the Indies, and the Batavian Republic (on the one Part); and his Majesty, the King of the United Kingdom of Great Britain and Ireland (on the other Part) [Treaty of Amiens], Mar. 25, 1802, *available at* http://www.napoleon-series.org/research/government/diplomatic/c_amiens.html (last visited on May 5, 2016) ("It is agreed that the contracting parties, upon requisitions made by them respectively, or by their ministers, or officers duly authorized for that purpose, shall be bound to deliver up to justice persons accused of murder, forgery, or fraudulent bankruptcy, committed within the jurisdiction of the requiring party, provided that this shall only be done in cases in which the evidence of the crime shall be such, that the laws of the place in which the accused persons shall be discovered, would have authorized the detaining and bringing him to trial, had the offence been committed there.").

[98] Treaty of Peace Between the Allied and Associated Powers and Germany [Treaty of Versailles], June 28, 1919, art. 228, T.S. No. 4, *reprinted in* 11 Martens Nouveau Recueil (ser. 3d) 323 ("The German Government shall hand over to the Allied and Associated Powers, or to such one of them as shall so request, all persons accused of having committed an act in violation of the laws and customs of war, who are specified either by name or by the rank, office or employment which they held under the German authorities.").

[99] Havana Conv. Relating to Consular Agents, Feb. 20, 1928, art. 19, 155 L.N.T.S. 291 (obligating consuls "to deliver, upon the simple request of the local authorities" fugitives who have sought asylum in their consulates).

[100] U.S.-Japan Security Treaty, Sept. 8, 1951, T.I.A.S. No. 2491, *as discussed* in *Wilson v. Girard*, 354 U.S. 524 (1957) (finding that the U.S. Government's decision to return an American serviceman into the custody of the Government of Japan on a charge of murder was authorized under a security treaty versus an extradition treaty between the United States and Japan).

examples include the CARICOM Arrest Warrant Treaty (2008)[101] and the New Nikerie ("Nieuw Nickerie") cooperation agreement concluded in May 2008 between the neighboring States of Guyana and Suriname, intended to combat cross-border crime and address other law enforcement issues of common concern, including the apprehension of fugitives from justice, despite the absence of a bilateral extradition treaty.[102]

Such instruments also include Status of Forces Agreements (SOFAs) and Visiting Forces Agreement (VFAs).[103] Significantly, these instruments are not viewed as following, and do not in fact follow, standard extradition procedures,[104] yet still operate to yield the return of a fugitive. Under a modern-day SOFA or VFA, it is generally incumbent upon a foreign military force (whether that of an individual State or a military alliance like the North Atlantic Treaty Organization (NATO)) to return one of its members charged with an offense committed within host State territory to host State custody to face criminal prosecution.[105] Even in instances

[101] CARICOM Arrest Warrant Treaty (2008), art. IX, *available at* www.oas.org/juridico/mla/en/treaties/en_caricom_arrest_warrant_treaty_2008.pdf (last visited on May 5, 2016) (providing for a transfer procedure between ratifying States with or without the consent of the individual of interest).

[102] "Guyana-Suriname Meet to Discuss Cross-Border Crimes," *Island Journal*, Mar. 10, 2010; "Guyana-Suriname-Security-CARICOM Neighbours Discussing Cross-Border Crimes," *Antigua Observer*, Mar. 9, 2010; "Extradition Treaty Needed in Guyana/Suriname Crime Fight – Hinds," *Guyana Times Int'l*, Aug. 11, 2011.

[103] *E.g.*, Agreement under Article VI of the Treaty of Mutual Cooperation and Security between the United States of America and Japan, Regarding Facilities and Areas and the Status of U.S. Armed Forces in Japan, Jan. 19, 1960, art. XVII(5) ("(a) The military authorities of the United States and the authorities of Japan shall assist each other in the arrest of members of the United States armed forces, the civilian component, or their dependents in the territory of Japan and in handing them over to the authority which is to exercise jurisdiction in accordance with the above provisions."). In addition, the U.S.-Republic of China (Taiwan) executive agreement authorizes the extradition of military persons between them. *Starks v. Seamans*, 334 F. Supp. 1255 (E.D. Wis. 1971).

[104] Two of the major differences between SOFAs and extradition treaties are that the former entails neither a judicial determination before transfer nor the possibility of a refusal by the executive based on discretionary grounds. M. Cherif Bassiouni, 2 International Criminal Law: Multilateral and Bilateral Enforcement Mechanisms 297–98 (3d ed. 2008) [hereinafter Bassiouni, Enforcement Mechanisms].

[105] North Atlantic Treaty Organization (NATO) Status of Forces Agreement (SOFA), June 19, 1951, art. VII, 199 U.N.T.S. 67, 4 U.S.T. 1792, T.I.A.S. 2846 (authorities of receiving and sending States shall assist each other in the arrest of members of a force or civilian component or their dependents in the territory of the receiving State and in handing them over to the authority with jurisdiction). That said, during the pendency of the proceedings, a SOFA or VFA may allow the individual to remain in the custody of the foreign military force. *See, e.g.*, Bruce Zagaris, *U.S. Refuses Philippine Request for Marines*

where the individual serviceman finds his way back to his home country during criminal proceedings, the foreign military force is generally obligated, upon host State request, to transfer him back to host State custody.[106]

For example, in October 2011, the United States handed over a soldier from its Second Infantry Division stationed in the Republic of Korea (RoK) to South Korean authorities on charges of breaking into a woman's motel room, raping her, and stealing her money; he was later sentenced to ten years in prison.[107] Likewise, in the 1972 U.S. landmark case of *Holmes v. Laird*,[108] two U.S. Army servicemen unsuccessfully contended that they should not be turned over to West German authorities, pursuant to the NATO SOFA, to face punishment based on convictions for attempted rape while stationed in West Germany, on the grounds that the trial procedures followed were unfair.[109]

Fifth, States at times have resorted to ***case-specific arrangements to authorize an extradition or other form of custodial transfer***.[110] For example, in 2006, to compensate for the absence of a bilateral extradition

Accused of Rape, 22 IELR 94 (2006) (discussing a case in the Philippines in which four U.S. Marines were charged in the rape of a twenty-two-year-old Filipina but remained in U.S. custody in the course of the proceedings pursuant to the applicable VFA). Earlier SOFAs dating back to the 1940s or 1950s sometimes provided more expansive rights to the foreign military force. *See, e.g.*, Agreement Under Article IV of the Mutual Defense Treaty between the United States of America and the Republic of Korea, Regarding Facilities and Areas and the Status of United States Armed Forces in the Republic of Korea [U.S.-ROK SOFA], July 9, 1966, T.I.A.S. 6127 (South Korea unilaterally waived criminal jurisdiction in certain limited cases).

106 Where a U.S. serviceman, being held in U.S. custody pending criminal proceedings by the host country, is mistakenly transferred to the United States or returns to the United States without authorization and resists U.S. attempts to return him to the host country pursuant to SOFA obligations, courts consistently have held that the serviceman may be returned, but not necessarily under formal extradition procedures. ABBELL, *supra* n.63, at 182–83; *e.g.*, *Williams v. Rogers*, 449 F.2d 513 (8th Cir. 1971) (USAF Staff Sgt. Bernard Williams stationed at Clark AFB in the Philippines was inadvertently transferred to an AFB in North Dakota in November 1969 during the pendency of a trial for the forcible abduction of a Filipino woman; the court ruled that he must be returned to the custody of the Philippines pursuant to the Military Bases in the Philippines Agreement, as amended), *cert. denied*, 405 U.S. 926 (1972).

107 Choe Sang-Hun, "10 Years for U.S. Soldier in South Korea Rape Case," *IHT*, Nov. 2, 2011, at 3.

108 459 F.2d 1211 (D.C. Cir.), *cert. denied*, 409 U.S. 869 (1972), *reprinted in* 60 ILR 35 (1981).

109 John Quigley, *The Rule of Non-Inquiry and the Impact of Human Rights on Extradition Law*, 15 N.C. J. INT'L L. & COMM. REG. 401, 416–17 (1990); BASSIOUNI, ENFORCEMENT MECHANISMS, *supra* n.104, at 296–97.

110 This practice is more likely to be followed by common law States that, as a rule, do not extradite absent a treaty or some type of diplomatic correspondence. SHEARER, *supra*

treaty, the United Kingdom and Rwanda signed a time-sensitive MOU to authorize the transfer of four men accused of murdering and otherwise aiding and abetting the murder of Tutsis in Rwanda in 1994, who were the subject of an extradition request by the Rwandan Government to the United Kingdom.[111] Similarly, in September 1998, the United Kingdom and the Netherlands executed a specialized, *ad hoc* bilateral treaty that in effect authorized the physical transfer of two Libyan defendants to a Scottish court on Dutch territory that the Dutch Government agreed could be used for the singular purpose of the *Lockerbie* criminal trial (discussed at Chapter 8.c).[112]

Sixth, certain States also have established ***cooperative, non-treaty-based schemes to facilitate inter-State extraditions***. Perhaps the best known of these is the European Union's (E.U.'s) Framework Decision that, while binding on member States, did not require ratification and therefore does not qualify as a treaty.[113] The Framework Decision in June 2002 set up the system of European Arrest Warrants (EAWs) (discussed more extensively *infra*) that operates much like that of the physical transfer of a fugitive within a given State,[114] "based on the principle of mutual recognition as opposed to that of mutual cooperation."[115]

Similar to the Framework Decision, the Scheme Relating to the Rendition of Fugitive Offenders within the Commonwealth of 1966 – which was subject to an interim overhaul in April 1990 and then renamed the London Scheme for Extradition within the Commonwealth in November 2002 – also did not require ratification, and therefore is not

n.34, at 28 (citing the United States and British Commonwealth countries); Barnett, *supra* n.15, at 298 n.98.

111 Bruce Zagaris, *U.K. Arrests Four Rwanda Genocide Suspects for Potential Extradition*, 23 IELR 89, 89–91 (2007).

112 Agreement Concerning a Scottish Trial in the Netherlands, Neth.-U.K., Sept. 18, 1998, *reprinted in* 38 ILM 926 (1999). One legal commentator (Prof. Bert Swart) reportedly coined the expression "extradition by analogy" to describe that arrangement. Arzt, *supra* n.32, at 178 n.54.

113 CoE Framework Decision on the European Arrest Warrant & the Surrender Procedures between Member States, June 13, 2002, art. 34, 2002/584/JHA, OJEC 1–20, L190/1 of July 18, 2002 [hereinafter Framework Decision on the EAW]. The EAW's validity as a framework decision (versus a convention) was challenged by a group of Belgian lawyers but upheld by the European Court of Justice (ECJ) in May 2007. *Advocaten voor de Weeld VZW v. Leden van de Ministerraad*, Case C-303/05, ECJ, Gr. Ch., May 3, 2007.

114 Gilbert, *Extradition*, *supra* n.1, at 251–52; Bassiouni, Introduction, *supra* n.7, at 350–51.

115 Bassiouni, U.S. Extradition, *supra* n.1, at 25.

technically accorded treaty status. Rather, it operates through the adoption of patterned domestic legislation based on guidelines propounded for the extradition between member States of the Commonwealth and its dependencies.[116]

In addition, there is a special bilateral arrangement known as the "backing of warrants" between particularly close neighboring States with a long history of cooperation: Australia and New Zealand.[117] Significantly, this arrangement is based on reciprocal domestic legislation – not on a treaty.[118] It provides for the presumptive issuance of an arrest warrant and extradition order by a judge of the host State (with no contemplated executive branch role) on behalf of the pursuing counterpart State, unless that judge finds that doing so would be unjust or oppressive.[119]

Seventh, a number of States have fashioned ***domestic laws that set forth available contingency arrangements, albeit without legal obligation, to authorize and process extraditions*** in instances where no extradition treaty exists with a given pursuing State.[120] Examples include Australia's Extradition (Foreign States) Act No. 76 of 1966 (but was repealed in 1988),[121] Colombian Penal Code

[116] Gilbert, *Extradition, supra* n.1, at 252–53. This scheme has been characterized as being "based on the reciprocal legislation approach." Bassiouni, U.S. Extradition, *supra* n.1, at 39.

[117] Australia Extradition Act, 1988, *as amended*, Part III, Attorney-General's Department.

[118] *See, e.g., In re Ellis* and *In re Gilligan* (Applications for Writs of Habeas Corpus) [2001] 1 A.C. 84 (H.L.) (Lord Steyn) ("There is no extradition treaty between the United Kingdom and the Republic of Ireland. The process for rendition between the two countries of persons accused and convicted is modelled on the backing of warrants system long familiar to English law. Historically, magistrates in England only had local jurisdiction and a warrant was valid only in the jurisdiction of the issuing magistrate. A fresh warrant had to be obtained if an accused went to another county. In due course the practice developed that where an accused left the jurisdiction where a warrant was issued a justice who had jurisdiction in the area where the accused was residing would endorse the warrant so that it could be executed in that jurisdiction.") (describing the system while it was still in effect).

[119] Until 2003, a comparable arrangement existed between the United Kingdom and the Republic of Ireland, Backing of Warrants (Republic of Ireland) Act 1965, *available at* http://www.legislation.gov.uk/ukpga/1965/45/pdfs/ukpga_19650045_en.pdf (last visited on May 5, 2016), but was repealed by reciprocal domestic legislation, including the U.K. Extradition Act 2003, Nov. 20, 2003, § 218(a), *available at* http://www.legislation.gov.uk /ukpga/2003/41/contents (last visited on May 6, 2016).

[120] *See* Muther, *supra* n.70, at 223 n.16; Abbell, *supra* n.63, at 376 (such arrangements at times require reciprocity); Jennings & Watts, *supra* n.21, at 952 n.10.

[121] Australia's Extradition (Foreign States) Act No. 76 of 1966 (repealed by Act. No. 5 of 1988); *e.g., R. v. MacDonald*, Ontario High Ct., Aug. 25, 1982, [1983] 40 O.R. (2d) 39, *reprinted in* 101 ILR 281 (in November 1981, absent a bilateral extradition treaty, Canada sought the extradition of Robert Daniel MacDonald under an extradition arrangement

(2000),[122] the Republic of South Africa's Act 77 of 1996,[123] Switzerland's Act on International Mutual Criminal Assistance of 1981 (IMAC),[124] and Thailand's Act on Mutual Assistance in Criminal Matters (1992).[125]

Eighth, States sometimes proceed with extraditions barring a treaty, cooperative scheme, or domestic statute, based on the principle of ***reciprocity***.[126] Reciprocity derives from sovereign equality and the principle that State A is willing to extradite to State B so long as State B is committed to extradite to State A under equivalent circumstances in the future.[127] For some States, such as Argentina, Austria, Belgium, Japan,[128] Peru, Spain, and Thailand,[129] reciprocity is a required legislative condition for extradition absent a treaty or other written arrangement. The requirement of reciprocity also may derive from a judicial ruling,

pursuant to this Australian statute under which he was apprehended and surrendered to Canada to stand trial on narcotics charges).

122 Colombian Penal Code, Law No. 599 of 2000, July 24, 2000, art. 9 ("in the absence of public treaties the Government may offer or grant extradition in conformity with the procedure laid down in the Code of Penal Procedure.").

123 RSA, Act 77 of 1996, Nov. 20, 1996, § 3(a) (1996) ("Any person accused or convicted of an extraditable offence committed within the jurisdiction of a foreign State which is not a party to an extradition agreement shall be liable to be surrendered to such foreign State, if the President has in writing consented to his or her being so surrendered.").

124 Swiss IMAC, *supra* n.5.

125 Laflin, *supra* n.4, at 321; Thongbai Thongpao, "Commentary: Extradition Procedures Must Not be Ignored," *Bangkok Post*, Mar. 21, 1999, *available at* 1999 WL 8496140.

126 For example, "[i]n 1872, the French Minister of Justice issued a *circulaire*, which stated that reciprocity was a permissible basis for extradition absent a treaty, and that in such circumstances the practice was to be governed by the applicable rules of international law." Bassiouni, U.S. Extradition, *supra* n.1, at 8.

127 Kennedy, *supra* n.26, at 18 n.73; *e.g., Italian Nat'l Re-Extradition Case*, Fed. Sup. Ct. (Crim. Div.), FRG, Oct. 16, 1970, *reprinted in* 70 ILR 374; *In re Richard Eckermann*, Sup. Ct. of Justice, Guat., May 28, 1929, 26 *Gaceta de los Tribunales* 992, *reprinted in* [1929–30] 5 Ann. Dig. Pub. Int'l L. Cases 293, 294 n.2 (No. 189) (H. Lauterpacht ed. 1935) (in 1929, the Guatemalan Ministry of Foreign Relations agreed to grant the extradition of a former German officer for his role in ordering the murder of a suspected inflitrator into a secret organization (the Black Army) where no extradition treaty existed between Guatemala and Germany but where "[t]he Government of Germany ha[d] offered reciprocity in cases which may occur in the future.").

128 Japan, Law of Extradition, Law No. 68 of 1953, art. 3(2), *as amended* (requiring that, absent a bilateral extradition treaty, the requesting State must assure "that it would honor a request of the same kind made by Japan.").

129 Thailand Extradition Act, § 9 ("The Government of Thailand may consider the extradition for legal proceedings or conviction according to the judgment [with regard to a] criminal offense . . . (2) If there exists no mutual treaty and the Requesting State commits to assist Thailand in the same manner when requested.").

as occurred in September 2004, when Mexico's Supreme Court of Justice opined that Mexico would only extradite a fugitive where the pursuing State can provide assurances that it will abide by the reciprocity principle should Mexico require extradition.[130]

Finally, absent any of the above arrangements, host States may elect to extradite a requested fugitive on the grounds of ***comity*** – a courteous or good will gesture extended *ex gratia, i.e.*, with no legal obligation attached.[131] States that extradite on the basis of comity typically do so pursuant to domestic law[132] and tend to regard as criminal the underlying fugitive's conduct.[133]

Extradition documentation requirements are generally the same for comity as under a treaty but handled via a diplomatic note.[134] A problem with reliance on comity is that many of the protections afforded the subject of an extradition under an extradition treaty do not necessarily apply.[135] Another problem is that some States do not allow, or are less comfortable with, a non-treaty approach to extradition, although, under some circumstances, this defect can be remedied via the expedited adoption of an *ad hoc* MOU or ratification of an extradition treaty.[136]

[130] Rodrigo Labardini, *Mexican Supreme Court Requires Extradition Reciprocity Assurances*, 22 IELR 7 (2006). In response to that ruling, the United States sent Mexico a diplomatic note to satisfy the reciprocity requirement because it otherwise was not reflected in the U.S.-Mexico Extradition Treaty. *Id.*

[131] Richard Downing, Recent Development, *The Domestic and Int'l Legal Implications of the Abduction of Criminals from Foreign Soil*, 26 STAN. J. INT'L L. 573, 577 (1989–90). For example, in 1956, U.S. military authorities in Germany requested the transfer for trial of Sgt. Frank Koveleskie, who was charged in Frankfurt with armed robbery, assault with a dangerous weapon, false official statement, and desertion, and who was being held by Swiss authorities in Basel. Both the United States and Switzerland agreed that their bilateral extradition treaty did not apply under the circumstances, but nevertheless the Swiss transferered him under an act of comity. WHITEMAN, *supra* n.46, at 744–45.

[132] BLAKESLEY, COMPARATIVE STUDY, *supra* n.24, at 191; Roberto Iraola, *Foreign Extradition, Provisional Arrest Warrants, and Probable Cause*, 43 S.D. L. REV. 347, 348 n.3 (2006); JENNINGS & WATTS, *supra* n.21, at 955.

[133] *E.g., Fiocconi v. United States*, 462 F.2d 475 (2d Cir.) (the Italian Government agreed to extradite two French citizens found in Italy via comity where narcotics crimes of which they were indicted in Massachusetts were not identified as extraditable under the U.S.-Italy Extradition Treaty, but where the offenses were regarded as crimes under Italian law), *cert. denied*, 409 U.S. 509 (1972), *reprinted in* 51 ILR 272 (1978).

[134] BLAKESLEY, COMPARATIVE STUDY, *supra* n.24, at 191.

[135] *E.g., United States v. Vreeken*, 803 F.2d 1085 (10th Cir. 1986). *But see Fiocconi*, 462 F.2d 475 (specialty rule still applied in extradition via comity).

[136] For example, in February 2007, faced with criticism for handing over ten rebels of the Rassemblement du Peuple Rwandais" (Assembly of Rwandese People) to Rwanda absent any legal instrument, Uganda quickly ratified *ex post facto* an extradition treaty that had

d Mechanics

This chapter now pivots from vehicles to mechanics, and examines how extradition operates as a procedural matter under State municipal law, policy, and practice.[137] The key source for municipal extradition law is the statute, but pertinent constitutional provisions,[138] human rights law obligations,[139] or administrative rules otherwise applicable to criminal proceedings[140] also can prove dispositive or provide supplementary guidance. Domestic statutes governing extradition are estimated to exist in only about half the States worldwide.[141] Of those with extradition statutes, there is wide variety regarding almost every aspect of how States process extraditions, including, for instance, evidentiary standards imposed (*i.e.*, the quantum of proof required), the application of specific human rights safeguards, whether an extradition treaty is required, and the interplay of decision-making between the executive and judicial branches of government.[142]

With regard to the last point, while most States have a mixed system in which both the judiciary and the executive play a material role,[143]

been signed in 2006. Bruce Zagaris, *Uganda Agrees to Sign Extradition Treaty with Rwanda*, 23 IELR 212 (2007).

[137] A State's domestic extradition process is governed by its internal laws and policies. Laflin, *supra* n.4, at 317. International law affords States wide latitude in terms of determining which crimes to treat as extraditable and when to refuse extradition requests, at least when consistent with States' treaty commitments. Jennings & Watts, *supra* n.21, at 957.

[138] Some States, for example, have constitutional bars to the extradition of their own nationals. *See* Chapter 6.a.

[139] *See* Jennings & Watts, *supra* n.21, at 960 & n.6 (stressing that in some instances a State need not even be a party to a human rights convention and still be required to comply with its provisions where they are regarded as customary international law, such as respect for family life); *e.g.*, *Russell v. Fanning*, Sup. Ct., Ir., [1988] I.R. 505, *reprinted in* 79 ILR 134 (1989); *Soering*, *supra* n.10 (ruling that the United Kingdom was prohibited from extraditing Jens Soering to Virginia to possibly face the death penalty for a double murder, under Article 3 of the ECHR, under a newly-fashioned legal theory labelled the "death row phenomenon"). Human rights considerations relevant to extraditions are discussed at length in Chapter 7.e.

[140] *E.g.*, *In re Alvarez*, Sup. Ct., Chile, Aug. 26, 1959, *reprinted in* 30 ILR 390 (1966).

[141] Bassiouni, Introduction, *supra* n.7, at 348.

[142] *Id.*; Dugard & van den Wyngaert, *supra* n.34, at 188.

[143] *See* Blakesley, Comparative Study, *supra* n.24, at 192 (observing that both branches are needed, given that State sovereignty, international cooperation, and individual liberties are all implicated) (citing France and Austria as examples); Bantekas & Nash, *supra* n.9, at 179–80 (most States prefer a hybrid system, citing Canada, the United Kingdom, and the United States). In some hybrid cases, the court's opinion is binding if a person is declared non-extraditable, but if declared extraditable, the

a fraction of States mandate that the executive exercise exclusive control,[144] while others contemplate a mere advisory role for the courts.[145] The executive need not always take the form of a president, prime minister, or minister; in the case of France, for example, the Conseil d'État (the Council of State) is that nation's supreme administrative body (endowed with both administrative and court functions) for such purposes.[146] It may also be the case that the executive takes undue liberties by effecting an extradition that is out of compliance with domestic law, as occurred when the Government of Serbia decided to surrender Slobodan Milosević, the former Yugoslav President, to the ICTY, in defiance of a Serbian court order suspending the government's decree to extradite him pending consideration of its constitutionality.[147]

To complicate matters, a State's practice may vary depending on its particular treaty partners,[148] or its law may be in a state of evolution.[149]

Executive can reverse the decision. This approach is followed by the United States, the British Commonwealth countries, and others. Matthew A. Muir, *A Guide to the Law and Practice of Int'l Extradition*, in 4A MODERN LEGAL SYSTEMS CYCLOPEDIA 4A.160.7 (Kenneth Robert Redden ed. 1989). A number of States' laws provide an opportunity for a wanted person to have the lawfulness of his extradition determined by the courts. JENNINGS & WATTS, *supra* n.21, at 960; *e.g.*, Int'l Comm'n of Jurists, Richard Plender, "The Ugandan Crisis and the Right of Expulsion under International Law," 9 *The Review: Int'l Comm'n of Jurists* 19, 78 (Dec. 1972) (the Costa Rican Supreme Court held unconstitutional the extradition of an individual by the executive branch that was decided without recourse to extradition proceedings in the courts).

144 Although historically this was often the case, SHEARER, *supra* n.34, at 198, few states still provide for exclusive executive control. *Id.*; BLAKESLEY, COMPARATIVE STUDY, *supra* n.24, at 192 & n.89 (citing as examples Ecuador, Panama, Portugal, and some Eastern European countries).

145 *See* BLAKESLEY, COMPARATIVE STUDY, *supra* n.24, at 192 & n.90 (citing Belgium as an example); *e.g., In re Garcia-Setien*, Ct. of Cassation, Belg., Apr. 8, 1963, *reprinted in* 43 ILR 244 (1971).

146 ANDREW HEYWOOD, POLITICS 366 (4th ed. 2013).

147 Peter Finn, "Serb Leaders Hand Over Milosevic for Trial by War Crimes Tribunal; Tribunal Lives up to Its Promise," *Wash. Post*, June 29, 2001, at A1 (international criminal example).

148 For example, U.S. extradition treaties in the early part of the twentieth century sometimes barred the extradition of its own nationals and sometimes did not. *See Valentine v. United States ex rel. Neidecker*, 299 U.S. 5, 7–8 (1936) (Hughes, C.J.) (noting that while extradition treaties with Great Britain (1794) and Italy (1868) allowed for the extradition of nationals, treaties with France (1909, the one at issue) and with the Netherlands expressly restricted such a practice).

149 French law, for example, has morphed over the decades in phases, beginning with the Conseil d'Etat, which had no authority to reconsider a governmental decision based on a 1927 law, but today may reconsider any governmental decision regarding extradition. Haas, *supra* n.33, at 204–07.

Common law and civil law States traditionally have tended to divide along several fault lines, with the former generally requiring a treaty or at least legislative authorization to extradite, imposing a *prima facie* or probable cause evidentiary requirement (discussed more *infra*),[150] and being freely willing to extradite their own nationals, while civil law States typically have adopted the opposite positions.[151] Despite the foregoing, as States' domestic laws are becoming more standardized and courts often cite as persuasive authority other States' domestic rulings, State practice divergences between common law and civil law traditions are less stark than they once were.[152]

We now turn to the conventional mechanics of extradition – how it is pursued, processed, and authorized. For illustrative purposes, this treatment relies centrally on U.S. extradition law,[153] which is governed by both applicable extradition treaties and federal statutes.[154] While some variation exists across State municipal laws, the U.S. approach[155] comprehensively outlines the general sequence of steps involved and can thereby provide a helpful and reasonably representative portrait of the step-by-step operation of extradition.[156]

[150] The United Kingdom only abandoned its insistence on the *prima facie* evidentiary rule in 1990 when it acceded to the 1957 European Convention on Extradition. STANBROOK & STANBROOK, *supra* n.1, at 9.

[151] BASSIOUNI, INTRODUCTION, *supra* n.7, at 350; STANBROOK & STANBROOK, *supra* n.1, at 5–6; ABBELL, *supra* n.63, at 41–43 (discussing U.S. law).

[152] BASSIOUNI, INTRODUCTION, *supra* n.7, at 348–49; STANBROOK & STANBROOK, *supra* n.1, at 6 (citing dual criminality and specialty as examples of increasingly common features found in domestic laws across a diverse set of States).

[153] Significantly, in 1979, the United States shifted primacy for extradition implementation from the Department of State to the Department of Justice, which, with an institutional mission focused on law enforcement, elevated extradition as a governmental priority. ABBELL, *supra* n.63, at 15–16 NADELMANN, COPS, *supra* n.12, at 402 (viewing this shift as the single most important reason for an increase in U.S. extraditions).

[154] Tomislav Z. Kuzmanovic, Note, *The Artukovic Case: Do the Means Justify the End?*, 6 WIS. INT'L L.J. 155, 159–60 (1987). The principal governing federal statute is 18 U.S.C. § 3181 *et seq.* (2012).

[155] For a useful, step-by-step approach under U.S. extradition law, in particular *see* ABBELL, *supra* n.63. *See also* Declaration of Andre M. Surena, Asst. Legal Adviser for Law Enforcement and Intelligence, in *Gill & Sandhu v. Imundi*, 747 F. Supp. 1028 (S.D.N.Y. 1990).

[156] The extradition law of the Philippines, for example, is almost identical to that of the United States, even though the Philippines did not enter into its first extradition treaty until 1977 (with Indonesia). Severino H. Gaña, Jr., *Extradition and Legal Assistance: The Philippine Experience*, Resource Materials Series No. 57, Visiting Experts' Papers, 114th Int'l Training Course, U.N. Asia and Far East Inst. for the Prevention of Crime and the Treatment of Offenders (UNAFEI) (2000).

Step 1: Pursuing State Prepares Underlying Materials. When the United States is the pursuing State, the first step is for a state prosecutor (regarding a state crime) or the Office of the Attorney General (regarding a federal crime) to prepare a request in which all evidence must be duly certified and authenticated under the proper state or federal seal, respectively. The package, together with any required representations, is sent to the Office of International Affairs (OIA) within the U.S. Department of Justice (DoJ), where it is reviewed for legal conformity with the requirements of any applicable extradition treaty.[157] Once approved (and, where appropriate, translated), the package is sent to the U.S. Department of State for dispatch to the U.S. embassy in the host State with instructions to request extradition.[158]

Step 2: Pursuing State Submits Request. The pursuing State submits its extradition request,[159] typically addressed via diplomatic channels[160] (switching now to the United States as the *host* State) to the U.S. Secretary of State who heads the U.S. Department of State. In instances of urgency, flight risk, or concerns about a criminal investigation being compromised, a pursuing State may seek a provisional arrest warrant (PAW), directly or via INTERPOL, that would allow for the immediate arrest of a fugitive and his detention for a period of time (typically forty-five to sixty days), pending preparation and submission of a formal request for extradition coupled with

[157] Where no applicable extradition treaty exists, a pursuing State most likely would compile materials and make representations either: that are required under a governing extradition-like vehicle, that the host State reasonably would expect before rendering an extradition determination, or that the host State specifically has demanded in connection with an extradition request.

[158] DoJ, *U.S. Attorneys' Manual*, Chapter 9–15.230 thru 9–15.300 (2d ed. 2007–3 Supp.) (Int'l Extradition and Related Matters); BLAKESLEY, COMPARATIVE STUDY, *supra* n.24, at 222–23.

[159] In certain circumstances, the host State may even encourage a pursuing State to file an extradition request. *See, e.g.*, Peter Baker & Randal C. Archibald, "U.S. Asks for Arrest of Mexican Kingpin Who was Freed in American's Murder," *N.Y. Times*, Aug. 15, 2013, at A6 (during his visit to Washington to discuss law enforcement cooperation, Mexican Attorney General Jesús Murillo Karam apparently privately suggested to U.S. Attorney General Eric Holder that the United States request the extradition of Rafael Caro-Quintero, who had been released early from a Mexican prison after serving twenty-eight years for the torture and murder of DEA Agent Enrique Camarena and who the United States still sought for other crimes).

[160] Diplomatic channels are the typical form of submission for extradition requests around the world, but some treaties dispense with this formality, such as the Benelux Conv. on Extradition and Mutual Assistance in Crim. Matters (Belg., Lux., Neth.), June 27, 1962, 616 U.N.T.S. 120 (1968).

supporting evidence.[161] It is rare for a pursuing State to reconsider its interest in extradition after the fugitive, has been so detained and temporarily imprisoned by the host State.[162]

Step 3: Department of State Examines Request. The documentation accompanying the request must meet certain requirements to be considered complete: (i) a valid treaty authorizing extradition between the United States and the pursuing State at issue must exist (in all but one exceptional instance[163]); (ii) an arrest warrant in the pursuing State at issue has been issued; (iii) subject matter jurisdiction is established;[164] (iv) any offenses identified in the arrest warrant are listed or treated as extraditable under the applicable treaty; (v) sufficient evidence exists to prove (against a probable cause standard) that the individual named in the arrest warrant is the same person as is being sought for extradition;[165]

[161] JENNINGS & WATTS, *supra* n.21, at 960 & n.3; *e.g., Provisional Arrest for Extradition Case*, Fed. Sup. Ct. in Criminal Matters, F.R.G., Jan. 29, 1965, *reprinted in* 45 ILR 378 (1972); *Kissel v. Ministère Public*, Super. Ct. of Justice (Chamber of Arraignments), Lux., May 13, 1980, *reprinted in* 73 ILR 665 (1987); Treaty on Extradition, U.S.-Italy, Oct. 13, 1983, art. XII, 35 U. S.T. 3023, T.I.A.S. 10837, S. Treaty Doc. No. 20, 98th Cong., 2d Sess., 130 Cong. Rec. S8573–74 (daily ed. June 28, 1984); Gov't of Canada, Public Prosecution Service of Canada, Federal Prosecution Service Deskbook, Chap. 41, "Extradition: Provisional Arrest." As a general rule, it is prudent that such PAWs not be made public prematurely as their existence "could alert the fugitive or his confederates, friends, or family, enabling the fugitive to flee and/or avoid apprehension." U.S. Dep't of State, *Foreign Affairs Manual*, Vol. 7 – Consular Affairs, Other Extradition Matters, 7 *FAM* 1648 ("Public Inquiries About Extradition"). Although such provisional arrest requests are most commonly issued via diplomatic channels, some exceptions have been created, as found under the U.S.-Italy Extradition Treaty. BLAKESLEY, COMPARATIVE STUDY, *supra* n.24, at 222–23. Only very occasionally are such requests rejected. *E.g.*, Bruce Zagaris, *U.S. Denies Venezuelan Provisional Arrest Request for Alleged Terrorist*, 21 IELR 275, 275–77 (2005) (in May 2005, the United States turned down Venezuela's request for a PAW regarding Luis Posada Carilles who had been charged with terrorist crimes, including the explosion of a Cuban airliner).

[162] *E.g.*, "Militant Ejected by U.S. Meets with Jordan King," *N.Y. Times*, May 14, 1997, at A11 (describing how, for security reasons, Israel "dropped a request" for the extradition of Mousa Mohammed Abu Marzook, the political head of Hamas, after he had been imprisoned in Jordan at Israel's request on "suspicion of terrorism").

[163] "[W]ithout regard to the existence of a treaty" on the basis of comity, and with Attorney General certification, the U.S. may extradite "persons, other than citizens, nationals or permanent residents of the United States, who have committed crimes of violence against nationals of the United States in foreign countries." 18 U.S.C. § 3181(b) (reflecting 1996 legislative).

[164] Neil Boister, *The Trend to 'Universal Extradition' over Subsidiary Universal Jurisdiction in the Suppression of Transnat'l Crime*, 2003 ACTA JURIDICA 287, 296 (2003). *See* discussion in Chapter 2.c.

[165] ABBELL, *supra* n.63, at 40–41, 94–99; BLAKESLEY, COMPARATIVE STUDY, *supra* n.24, at 193–94 & n.98. Unlike the United States, many States do not insist on a probable cause standard.

and (vi) any offenses charged also would amount to a crime if they had been committed in the United States (a concept known as dual or dual criminality, which is discussed more extensively in Chapter 5.a.ii).[166]

If upon its review, the Office of the Legal Adviser at the Department of State deems the package incomplete, any treaty conditions are unfulfilled, authenticity questions arise, or there are any doubts that the evidence was obtained in good faith,[167] the request is returned to the pursuing State at issue via a diplomatic note indicating the defects.[168] If the package is satisfactory, it is forwarded to the Department of Justice.[169]

Step 4: Department of Justice Reviews Request. The Office of International Affairs (OIA) at the Department of Justice undertakes a similar screening of the request and accompanying documentation for validity and completeness. If any defects are detected, the package is returned to the State Department and from there back to the pursuing State; if satisfactory, the package is forwarded to the Office of the United States Attorney[170] for the federal district (*e.g.*, Southern District of Florida, Eastern District of New York) where the fugitive has been found or is believed to be located.[171]

Step 5: United States Attorney's Office Files Complaint; Judge Grants Arrest Warrant and Arrest is Effected. Assuming the subject has not already been detained under a PAW, after reviewing the extradition request, and provided the assigned Assistant United States Attorney (AUSA)[172] concurs that the request is *bona fide* and without defect, and the subject is extradition-worthy, the AUSA prepares and files

[166] Kuzmanovic, *supra* n.154, at 159–60; *e.g., In re Extradition of Platko*, 213 F. Supp.2d 1229 (S.D. Cal. 2002).

[167] *Cf. In re Saifi* [2001] 4 All E.R. 168 (English Divisional Court holding it would be unfair and unjust to return the applicant to India on the ground that the evidence supporting the extradition request appeared to have been obtained in bad faith).

[168] *See* Blakesley, Comparative Study, *supra* n.24, at 223–24 (incomplete filing); Jennings & Watts, *supra* n.21, at 959 (unmet conditions).

[169] Kuzmanovic, *supra* n.154, at 159–60; Sean D. Murphy, 1 United States Practice in International Law, 1999–2001, at 332 (2002) [hereinafter Murphy, U.S. Practice, 1999–2001].

[170] The United States Attorney (U.S. Attorney) is the head of the prosecutor's office for a given federal district, and is not to be confused with the U.S. Attorney General, who heads the Department of Justice as the nation's chief law enforcement officer.

[171] Kuzmanovic, *supra* n.154, at 159–60. Challenges on improper venue grounds are unusual. Ronald J. Hedges, *Int'l Extradition: A Guide for Judges* 4 (Fed. Judicial Center 2014).

[172] An AUSA is a federal prosecutor who has been assigned the case on behalf of the United States Attorney whose Office has jurisdiction.

a complaint regarding the offenses charged. The complaint must be made under oath and provide supporting evidence.[173] At the same time, the AUSA seeks an arrest warrant from a magistrate judge[174] or a federal district court judge (sitting as a magistrate judge.[175])[176]

Upon the judge's review of the complaint, he may then agree to issue an arrest warrant.[177] If so, this generally leads to the fugitive's arrest by the U.S. Marshal's Service, the federal judiciary's law enforcement body, assuming he can be located. In addition, the extradition subject typically is informed that an arrest warrant has been sought for him,[178] unless a decision has been made to keep the indictment secret (*see* Chapter 9.a).

Step 6: Initial Appearence; Extradition Hearing is Scheduled if not Waived. Once the subject is arrested, he is brought before a magistrate for a so-called Initial Appearance, at which time the subject is formally informed of the sought extradition and related charges and advised of his rights; the subject also may then seek bail so as to avoid serving time in prison pending extradition proceedings. Assistance of counsel may be considered (*i.e.*, in cases where the subject is indigent) and an extradition hearing is scheduled along with interim case management conferences in some cases.[179]

Alternatively, the subject may elect to waive extradition proceedings altogether, in which case he would return to pursuing State territory outside the extradition regime;[180] or consent to extradition by forgoing

173 Abbell, *supra* n.63, at 25–26.

174 "U.S. magistrates are judicial officers appointed by U.S. district court judges in the respective districts to assist them in certain proceedings and are not judges appointed under Article III of the U.S. Constitution. Their appointment, tenure, and jurisdiction is spelled out in 28 U.S.C. §§ 631, 636 (2012). The role of the magistrate judge is established by 18 U.S.C. § 3184 (2012)." Powers, *supra* n.18, at 284 n.48.

175 *See In re Extradition of Howard*, 996 F.2d 1320, 1325 (1st Cir. 1993) (ruling by an extradition judge is not a "district court" decision as such, as he does not act in the capacity of an "Article III judge" under the U.S. Constitution).

176 *Id.*; Murphy, U.S. Practice, 1999–2001, *supra* n.169, at 332.

177 *See* Abbell, *supra* n.63, at 30–31 (traditionally, a federal judge could only issue an arrest warrant if the person of interest could "reasonably and in good faith" be found in the court's jurisdiction, but by virtue of two amendments over the past quarter-century, Pub. L. 100–690, § 7087 (1988) and Pub. L. 101–647, § 1605 (1990), a U.S. judge can now issue an arrest warrant even when the fugitive's whereabouts in the United States is not known or if the person is believed to be shortly entering the United States).

178 *Id.* at 25–26.

179 Kuzmanovic, *supra* n.154, at 159–60; Murphy, U.S. Practice, 1999–2001, *supra* n.169, at 332; Hedges, *supra* n.171, at 6.

180 U.S. extradition treaties do not always provide for a waiver, and in such instances a request can be denied. *See* Hedges, *supra* n.171, at 9 & n.34. One reason a fugitive

only his specific right to an extradition hearing, in which case he would sign an Affidavit of Consent for Extradition and return pursuant to the applicable extradition treaty, recognizing that all of its requirements have been met, but preserving the right to invoke treaty-based defenses at the criminal trial.[181]

Step 7: Judge Holds Extradition Hearing. A person may not be involuntarily extradited without first having the option of an evidentiary hearing, as mandated by the due process clause of the U.S. Constitution, as a person's liberty is at stake.[182] That hearing is more akin to a preliminary hearing than a full-scale trial[183] and is not intended to adjudicate the individual's guilt or innocence with respect to the underlying charge(s),[184] but rather merely to determine whether all the conditions of the extradition treaty have been satisfied, particularly that the individual is who he is purported to be, that the charged offenses are extraditable, that there is probable cause to show that he committed those offenses, and that the same offenses are punishable under U.S. law.[185] Issues may surface at this stage to challenge the court's personal jurisdiction, question the admissibility of inculpatory evidence, and/or object to one or more charges on the grounds of specialty (discussed *infra*), but such efforts do not generally succeed.[186]

might opt for such an all-out waiver is if he believes that, in exchange for such cooperation under domestic law, he can obtain a reduced sentence. *E.g., Austl. High Court Overturns Sentence Due to Non-Insistence on Rule of Specialty*, 16 IELR 904, 905 (2000) (a fugitive called for resentencing in line with credit due to having waived extradition rights as to thirty-nine charges).

181 Hedges, *supra* n.171, at 8–9. A fugitive's consent to extradition to a particular pursuing State does not have to be honored by the host State, which could, for example, elect to extradite him to another pursuing State, based on the criteria spelled out in the applicable extradition treaty or, where such criteria are not provided, on selection factors discussed in Chapter 7.d.

182 Const. of the United States, Sept. 17, 1787, amend. V (no person shall "be deprived of life, liberty, or property, without due process of law"). This clause applies even to aliens unlawfully present in the United States. *Zadvydas v. Davis*, 533 U.S. 678, 693 (2001). *See also* Blakesley, Comparative Study, *supra* n.24, at 193; *Caplan v Vokes*, 649 F.2d 1336 (9th Cir. 1981).

183 Kuzmanovic, *supra* n.154, at 161 & n.42 (not a "full dress trial"); *Merino v. U.S. Marshal*, 326 F.2d 5, 12 (C.D. Cal. 1963).

184 Steven Lubet & Jan Stern Reed, *Extradition of Nazis from the United States to Israel: A Survey of Issues in Transnat'l Criminal Law*, 22 Stan. J. Int'l L. 1, 7–9 (1986); *e.g., Collins v. Loisel*, 259 U.S. 309, 316 (1922); *Jimenez v. Aristeguieta*, 311 F.2d 547, 556 (5th Cir. 1962).

185 Stephen Dycus, et al., Counterterrorism Law 512–13 (2007); Kuzmanovic, *supra* n.154, at 162; *United States v. Fernandez-Morris*, 99 F. Supp.2d 1358, 1361 (S.D. Fla. 1999).

186 *See generally* Bassiouni, U.S. Extradition, *supra* n.1, at 879–926 (discussing extradition hearings in the United States).

"Although there is no explicit statutory basis for ordering discovery in extradition proceedings, the extradition court has the inherent power to order such discovery procedures as law and justice require."[187] Any documents and other evidence, including that which would ordinarily be deemed excludable, such as hearsay, are admissible to support extradition so long as they are authenticated;[188] their evidentiary significance, reliability, and weight are not a matter for the hearing judge to assess. Significantly, "self-incriminating statements of accomplices are sufficient to establish probable cause in an extradition hearing."[189] Although the extradition subject may be represented by private counsel at an extradition hearing,[190] the subject may only introduce explanatory evidence designed to question probable cause – *not* exculpatory evidence or any other intended to rebut the government's case[191] – and has no right to cross-examine witnesses.[192] Under prevailing convention, the pursuing State's interests are represented by the U.S. Attorney's Office.[193]

Step 8: Judge Certifies Extraditability Finding to the Secretary of State. Should the judge finds that the subject may be extradited in compliance with U.S. law, including its treaty commitments, he then certifies that ruling, together with the produced evidence, to the U.S. Secretary of State.[194] If, however, the judge does *not* find that the evidence supports extradition, he will not so

[187] *Oen Yin-Choy v. Robinson*, 858 F.2d 1400, 1407 (9th Cir. 1988).

[188] 18 U.S.C. § 3190 (2012); Kuzmanovic, *supra* n.154, at 161 & n.42; Dycus, *supra* n.185, at 512; Lubet & Reed, *supra* n.184, at 7–9 (noting use of modified rules of evidence); *Fernandez-Morris*, 99 F. Supp.2d at 1361. Indeed, the government need not call any witnesses if it so chooses. Lubet & Reed, *supra* n.184, at 7 (observing that a case can be presented through "documents, depositions, and affidavits" alone).

[189] *Zanazanian v. United States*, 729 F.2d 624, 627 (9th Cir. 1984).

[190] Dycus, *supra* n.185, at 512–13; *Sindona v. Grant*, 461 F. Supp. 199, 204 (S.D.N.Y. 1978) (representation by private counsel permitted), *rev'd on other grounds*, 619 F.2d 167 (2d Cir. 1980).

[191] *Fernandez-Morris*, 99 F.Supp.2d at 136; Lubet & Reed, *supra* n.184, at 7–9. *See also supra* n.43 and accompanying text.

[192] *Messina v. United States*, 728 F.2d 77 (2d Cir. 1984).

[193] Abbell, *supra* n.63, at 24–25. "Until the mid-1970s . . . extradition cases were so rare that U.S. prosecutors hardly ever handled them. Foreign nations pursuing a person in the United States were required to hire a private attorney to track down the fugitive and gain a court order to have him sent back for trial." David Lauter, "There's No Place to Hide: Extraditions Have Tripled, and It's Only the Beginning," *Nat'l L.J.*, Nov. 26, 1984, at 1. By dispensing with the need for private representation of foreign government interests and relying instead on Department of Justice attorneys to perform that function, the cost incurred no longer operates as a deterrent. Abbell, *supra* n.63, at 16–17.

[194] *Id.* at 44.

certify [195] and there is no opportunity for the U.S. Government to appeal,[196] although it may file a revised or supplemental extradition request at the behest of the pursuing State at issue[197] or submit a separate extradition complaint seeking a *de novo* hearing to relitigate issues of fact and law.[198]

Step 9: Individual May File a *Habeas Corpus* Petition and, if Denied, Seek an Emergency Order Staying Extradition. Because a judge's certification of extraditability does not qualify as a final order, the subject of the extradition has no legal right to appeal any part of the ruling.[199] That said, the subject still has an opportunity to seek relief collaterally to the extent that he may petition for a writ of *habeas corpus*, contending that he has been unlawfully detained,[200] but such petitions are narrowly confined[201] and impose the burden of proof on the petitioner rather than on the government.[202] If the petition to a U.S. district court is

[195] Kuzmanovic, *supra* n.154, at 162.

[196] Abbell, *supra* n.63, at 45–46.

[197] Kuzmanovic, *supra* n.154, at 162–63.

[198] Such a *de novo* hearing "is permissible and does not violate principles of res judicata or double jeopardy." *Ahmad v. Wigen*, 726 F. Supp. 389, 397 (E.D.N.Y. 1989) (citing *Collins v. Loisel*, 262 U.S. 426, 429–30), *aff'd*, 910 F.2d 1063 (2d Cir.), *stay denied*, 111 S. Ct. 23 (1990).

[199] *Collins v. Miller*, 252 U.S. 364, 369 (1920); Kuzmanovic, *supra* n.154, at 162–63; *In re Extradition of Howard*, 996 F.2d at 1325. By contrast, under French law, a fugitive found to be extraditable does have the right to appeal certain aspects of the decision to the Conseil d'État, but only those relating to the question of whether the decision to extradite was made under proper procedures and conditions. Blakesley, Comparative Study, *supra* n.24, at 275. In addition, the French Minister of Justice may order judicial review of a decision to extradite "to assure the unity of decisions and the interpretation of extradition treaties and domestic law." *Id.* Under Australian law, "[t]he person or foreign country [*i.e.*, the pursuing State] can seek review of the magistrate's determination as to the person's eligibility for surrender to the Federal Court of Australia within 15 days of the magistrate's order." Austl. Gov't, Attorney-General's Dep't., Int'l Crime Cooperation Div., *Fact Sheet 2 – Overview of the Extradition Process.*

[200] "The sole mechanism for review of a magistrate's order approving extradition is a collateral habeas corpus proceeding." *Ahmad*, 726 F. Supp. at 395 (citing *Collins*, 252 U.S. at 369). *Accord* Lubet & Reed, *supra* n.184, at 7–9; Abbell, *supra* n.63, at 45–46 Exceptionally, at least under Canadian law, *habeas* petitions also can be used to defeat *deportation* orders. *In re Shepherd and Minister of Employment & Immigration*, Ontario Ct. of App., [1989] 70 O.R. (2d) 765.

[201] *Fernandez v. Phillips*, 268 U.S. 311, 312 (1925).

[202] *See Skaftouros v. United States*, 667 F.3d 144, 158 (2d Cir. 2011) ("[C]ollateral review of an international extradition order should begin with the presumption that both the order and the related custody of the fugitive are lawful. We therefore hold that ... the petitioner must prove by a preponderance of the evidence that he is 'in custody in violation of the Constitution or laws or treaties of the United States.'") (citations omitted).

denied, it may be elevated to the corresponding U.S. circuit court or the subject may seek an emergency order to stay extradition.[203]

Step 10: Secretary of State Makes Final Decision Regarding Extradition. The ultimate call on whether an individual should be extradited lies with the executive,[204] specifically the U.S. Secretary of State[205] (or the Deputy Secretary by delegated authority) who is "not bound by the judicial record"[206] and can therefore review a judicial determination to extradite *de novo*,[207] and the Secretary's decision itself is not reviewable by a court. That discretionary review takes place only after all judicial proceedings have occurred and generally accounts for

[203] Kuzmanovic, *supra* n.154, at 162–63. In many States, after exhausting domestic remedies, an individual might well seek judicial relief in a supra-national tribunal like the European Court of Human Rights or the Inter-American Commission on Human Rights. (Because the United States has never ratified the American Convention on Human Rights (ACHR), the Commission, which was established under the ACHR, has no competence to hear claims brought by individuals against the United States.) Although it is rare for a State to deliberately ignore a tribunal's ruling, whether a final judgment or an interim measure, it can happen. *See, e.g., Trabelsi v. Belgium*, Appl. No. 140/10, [2014] ECHR 893 ¶¶ 150–51, Sept. 4, 2014 (discussing Belgium's disregard for an interim measure imposed by the ECtHR to prevent the extradition of Nizar Trabelsi, a Tunisian national, to the United States where, if convicted, he could face life imprisonment without the possibility of parole, in violation of Article 3 of the ECHR).

[204] *See Chicago & Southern Air Lines, Inc. v. Waterman S.S. Corp.*, 333 U.S. 103, 111 (1948) ("[T]he very nature of executive decisions as to foreign policy is political, not judicial. Such decisions are wholly confided by our Constitution to the political departments of the government, Executive and Legislative . . . They are decisions of a kind for which the Judiciary has neither aptitude, facilities nor responsibility and have long been held to belong in the domain of political power not subject to judicial intrusion or inquiry.") In a rare instance of deferral to the judiciary, in March 2010, the Jamaican Prime Minister Bruce Golding decided to let a court determine the extraditability to the United States of Jamaican national Christopher "Dudus" Coke following U.S. criticism directed at Jamaica's handling of the case. Bruce Zagaris, *Jamaican Prime Minister Will Allow Court to Decide U.S. Extradition Request*, 26 IELR 225 (2010).

[205] 18 U.S.C. § 3184 (2012); Abbell, *supra* n.63, at 45–46. Notably, in 1995, a federal court judge ruled that the U.S. statutory scheme for international extraditions was unconstitutional to the extent that it violated the separation of powers doctrine by "confer[ring] upon the Secretary the authority to review the legal determinations of federal extradition judges." *Lobue v. Christopher*, 893 F. Supp. 65, 68 (D.D.C. 1995), *vacated*, 82 F.3d 1081 (D.C. Cir. 1996). That ruling was, however, struck down on jurisdictional grounds.

[206] Lubet & Reed, *supra* n.184, at 7–9; *e.g., In re Doherty*, 786 F.2d 491, 499 (2d Cir. 1986).

[207] Where a U.S. court opines that an individual may be extradited, the U.S. Secretary of State may refuse to do so but would have to rationalize such a refusal; however, if the court has denied extradition, the Executive is bound not to extradite that individual. Blakesley, Comparative Study, *supra* n.24, at 280. By contrast, the U.K. Home Secretary may grant extradition over a high court's opposition.

humanitarian and foreign policy considerations,[208] such as the age and health of the individual, whether he likely would be tortured or suffer from inhuman or degrading treatment upon delivery, whether the request is intended as a ruse to try him for another crime, or whether he would likely be prosecuted or punished for his political beliefs or on other impermissible grounds.[209]

Significantly, no *habeas* review is available to individuals once they have been slated for extradition by the U.S. Secretary of State, including claims that they are likely to face torture in the pursuing State.[210] In the event the determination is to deny extradition, the pursuing State may request extradition again, even multiple times, either on new facts or different charges.[211]

Step 11: Secretary of State Issues Extradition Warrant, Possibly with Conditions, and the Individual is Extradited. In rendering a decision favoring extradition, the Secretary of State may add conditions,[212] such as that a new trial must be held rather than reliance on an *in absentia* verdict, that the trial must be held in a civilian versus an extraordinary court,[213] that the individual cannot be re-extradited or deported to a specified third State,[214] or that upon conviction the

208 Abbell, *supra* n.63, at 46–47.

209 Borelli, *supra* n.22, at 333–34; *e.g.*, *Eain*, 641 F.2d at 518 ("The determination in this case whether or not the request for extradition on common crimes amounts to a subterfuge by Israel to punish petitioner for a political offense is ... a decision within the sole province of the Secretary of State.").

210 *See Mironescu v. Costner*, 480 F.3d 664 (4th Cir. 2007) (holding that while a Secretary of State's extradition decision is not foreclosed to *habeas* review on account of the rule of non-inquiry, such review is barred based on the plain language of the Foreign Affairs Reform and Restructuring Act (FARRA) of 1998, *codified at* 8 U.S.C. § 1231 note (2012), which authorizes courts to review claims under the Convention against Torture and Other Cruel, Inhuman or Degrading Treatment or Punishment (CAT) only in connection with final immigration-related *removal* orders, discussed in Chapter 10.d.ii); *Garcia v. Thomas*, 683 F.3d 952 (9th Cir. 2012) (en banc) (disallowing a *habeas* challenge to an extradition ruling by the Secretary of State on substantive grounds; challenge is permitted only where the Secretary failed to make the requisite determination under the FARR).

211 Blakesley, Comparative Study, *supra* n.24, at 280; *e.g.*, *Ruiz-Massieu v. Reno*, 91 F.3d 416, 418 (3d Cir. 1996) (seeking extradition four times, each unsuccessfully).

212 *See United States v. Kin-Hong*, 110 F.3d 103, 110 (1st Cir. 1997) (noting that, by contrast, the U.S. judiciary is not authorized to attach conditions).

213 *Cf. In re Gatti*, Ct. of App. of Grenoble, Fr., (Chambre des Mises en Accusation), Jan. 13, 1947, *reprinted in* [1947] 14 Ann. Dig. & Rep. Pub. Int'l Cases 145, 145 (No. 70) (H. Lauterpacht ed. 1951).

214 *E.g.*, *Emami v. U.S. Dist. Ct.*, 834 F.2d 1444, 1454 (9th Cir. 1987) (discussing how "the State Department alone has the power to condition the extradition of Emami on an agreement with Germany not to deport Emami to Iran.").

individual must be returned to the United States to serve out his sentence.[215] At any rate, once the Secretary of State decides that the requested extradition should proceed, he then issues a warrant for extradition to the U.S. Marshals Service.[216] The Secretary of State also then authorizes the pursuing State to dispatch representatives to physically transfer the extradition subject out of the United States;[217] the failure to effect that transfer within the prescribed two-month time frame could result in the subject's release.[218]

Step 12 (Provisional): U.S. Government May Take Steps to Address Speciality Concerns in Transferee State. Generally, once the individual has physically been delivered into pursuing State territory, the extradition process is over; however, one important exception exists. Under the recognized customary law principle known as "specialty" (discussed in Chapter 7.c.ii), which is addressed in virtually every extradition treaty today, a transferee State may only try an extraditee for those offenses specifically set forth in its request[219] and that were the subject of review and approval by the host State.[220] The extraditee may not be prosecuted for any other offenses that pre-existed the physical transfer, typically in the context of a superseding indictment, unless it is a lesser included offense or the express consent of the transferor State has been obtained.[221] In such instances, the United States may monitor trial proceedings in the transferee State to ensure this condition is strictly honored (or may otherwise hear from the extradited individual or a third party

[215] Abbell, *supra* n.63, at 48.

[216] Dycus, *supra* n.185, at 512–13; Kuzmanovic, *supra* n.154, at 162.

[217] Lubet & Reed, *supra* n.184, at 7–9.

[218] 18 U.S.C. § 3188 (2012); Abbell, *supra* n.63, at 131 (noting that nearly all post-1960s U.S. extradition treaties either authorize or mandate release in such circumstances). This issue is discussed further in Chapter 5.b.

[219] *United States v. Abello-Silva*, 948 F.2d 1168, 1172–74 (10th Cir. 1991), *cert. denied*, 506 U.S. 835 (1992).

[220] *See* Borelli, *supra* n.22, at 336 (noting that specialty is designed to protect the rights of the extraditee as well as the rights of the host State).

[221] Extradition treaties frequently allow a transferee State to charge a fugitive with additional offenses related to the underlying crime after extradition has occurred so long as the transferor State consents. *E.g.*, Eur. Conv. on Extradition, *supra* n.73, art. 14. One potential problem is that the transferor State's *executive* authorities alone would typically grant such consent. Borelli, *supra* n.22, at 336 (noting the absence of any former host State judicial scrutiny in that determination). The March 2003 U.S.-U.K. Extradition Treaty expressly provides that either State may waive the specialty provision. Treaty on Extradition, U.S.-U.K., Mar. 31, 2003, art. 18(1).

about concerns in this regard) and request the fugitive's return absent compliance.[222]

e Adaptability

For all of its procedural formality and apparent cumbersomeness, the extradition process does not *necessarily* amount to a slow, rigid, and regimented exercise. In fact, it possesses a number of notably flexible features that can facilitate and even accelerate such inter-State custodial transfers. This section examines those factors that contribute to this modality's adaptability.

First, while an extradition often takes months or even years to ultimately authorize and carry out, such a process can be ***expedited*** – sometimes known as a "simplified extradition procedure" or "summary extradition"[223] – typically but not always effected with the consent of the detainee. The Convention on Simplified Extradition Procedure (1995)[224] provides that where the individual of interest is informed of the simplified procedure and what it means, has access to counsel, and both he and the host State consent to extradition, formal procedures can be dispensed with and delays and expenses avoided.[225]

The Inter-American Convention on Extradition (1981) likewise allows for such a procedure on one of two possible grounds: when domestic law does not proscribe it or when the detainee provides written consent after being informed of his rights.[226] Such prompt transfer is permitted under

[222] An illustration of such post-extradition oversight can be found in a November 2005 case in which a Lisbon High Court granted extradition to India of gangster Abu Salem on eight charges, including the 1993 Mumbai explosions. Once in India, Salem was additionally charged with making extortionary calls to a Delhi-based businessman; given that that new charge was a capital offense, and violated the principle of specialty (especially since India had given an "executive assurance" that it would not charge Salem with any crime that would entail more than 25 years or the death penalty if convicted), the Portuguese High Court in September 2011 ordered termination of the extradition and requested his return to Lisbon. "Portuguese Court Cancels Extradition of Abu Salem," *The Asian Age* (India), Sept. 27, 2011.

[223] *See* definition in Chapter 1.e. *See, e.g.*, Bruce Zagaris, *Spain Arrests Isabel Perón on Argentine Extradition Warrant for Crimes against Humanity*, 23 IELR 87 (2007) (noting that Spanish law has a simplified extradition procedure whereby a fugitive can waive extradition and be transferred rapidly to a particular pursuing State).

[224] Conv. Drawn up on the Basis of Article K.3 of the Treaty on European Union, on Simplified Extradition Procedure between the Member States of the E.U., Mar. 30, 1995, *O.J.C.* 78 [hereinafter Simplified Procedure Conv.].

[225] *Id.*; Bantekas & Nash, *supra* n.9, at 195–96.

[226] Inter-Am. Conv. on Extradition, *supra* n.74, art. 21.

the U.S.-Mexico and U.S.-Romania Extradition Treaties, for example, so long as the detainee consents.[227] A fugitive may wish to forfeit his right to an extradition hearing for such reasons as impatience in seeking vindication on the merits of the criminal charges, forgoing potentially steep expenditures on legal representation, prompt reunification with his family in the pursuing State, or the avoidance of continued detention in the host State.[228]

Albeit rare, expedited extradition can take place even absent a fugitive's consent. One variant of summary extradition has been referred to as "conditional release."[229] Under this procedure, host State officials release to pursuing State authorities "a suspect already under arrest in [the host State] on other charges. [In effect,] the suspect is 'lent' to the [pursuing State] for prosecution on the condition that [he] will be returned for prosecution in [the host State] at the end of [any] sentence. This procedure is much faster than a formal extradition, and has proven so successful, that [U.S.] DEA sometimes designs operations to bring suspects to [a State receptive to this approach] so they can be arrested [there] and turned over to U.S. authorities quickly."[230]

For example, in April 2007, the U.S. Embassy in Panama City sent a diplomatic note to the Panamanian Ministry of Foreign Affairs seeking the "conditional release" of Jesús Ernesto Mondragón García and José Alfonso Núñez Gutiérrez, two Mexican nationals wanted for narcotics trafficking charges. While a U.S.-Panama Extradition Treaty existed, the United States did not invoke that authority to secure their custody. Instead, the Government of

227 Treaty on Extradition, U.S.-Mex., May 4, 1978, art. 18, 31 U.S.T. 5059, T.I.A.S. 9656, *reprinted in* 17 ILM 1058 (1978); *e.g., In re Munguia*, 294 F. Supp.2d 893, 895–96 (S.D. Tex. 2003) (finding that the summary extradition provision was satisfied); Treaty on Extradition, U.S.-Rom., Sept. 10, 2007, art. 18, S. Treaty Doc. 110–11, 2 CTIA 351 (2007) [hereinafter U.S.-Rom. Extradition Treaty].

228 *See, e.g.*, Neil MacFarquhar, "Jordan to Let Terror Suspect Held in U.S. Into Kingdom," *N.Y. Times*, May 1, 1997 (Mousa Mohammed Abu Marzook ("Abu Marzook"), the political leader of Hamas, who had been held in New York City for months on accusations of terrorism and immigration violations, eventually agreed not to continue fighting extradition to Israel so as not to endure possible "endless detention in Manhattan.").

229 This term is defined in this particular context as *a variant of summary extradition in which an individual in host State custody or confinement is transferred to a pursuing State on the condition that he be returned to the host State for its own law enforcement purposes as soon as the adjudicatory proceedings and any resulting sentencing have concluded.*

230 U.S. Embassy Panama Cable, No. 08PANAMA704, Aug. 26, 2008, "Panamanian Security Cooperation: Irreplaceable?," ¶ 17, *available at* https://wikileaks.org/plusd/cables/08PANAMA704_a.html (last visited on May 5, 2016) (classified SECRET but posted on the Internet).

Panama acceded to the U.S. request for their "conditional release" and, upon a challenge from the defendants that the physical transfer had occurred in contravention of the treaty, a U.S. federal district court (MD. Fla.) rejected the motion, ruling that Panamanian officials presumably had determined that the extradition treaty provisions had been satisfied when the defendants were released.[231]

Second, extradition proceedings can be ***held in secret***.[232] Such an approach is most likely to occur in cases involving violent criminals with powerful organizational connections. The concern with public disclosure in such cases would be that their comrades or collaborators (*e.g.*, from the Taliban, a drug cartel, or a mafia family) might take precipitous action to break the detainee out of prison, negotiate for his release, exert heavy pressure on the host government, or otherwise try to scuttle his extradition. For example, in October 2005, Haji Baz Mohammad, one of the world's most wanted drug kingpins with alleged ties to the Taliban, was transferred into U.S. custody after months of secret extradition proceedings following his January 2005 arrest in Kandahar.[233]

Third, State judiciaries have pronounced that extradition provisions found in treaties or municipal statutes ought to be ***construed liberally*** to serve the purpose for which they were written. For example, in 1988, the U.K. House of Lords adopted the view that the then-operative U.K. domestic extradition statute should be interpreted generously to facilitate extraditions.[234] Similarly, U.S. courts, including the Supreme Court, have articulated the need to interpret U.S. bilateral extradition treaties with an eye to transferring fugitives to face prosecution or punishment for their alleged or actual crimes.[235]

[231] Bruce Zagaris, *U.S. District Court Denies Standing to Challenge Extradition from Panama*, 24 IELR 49 (2008).

[232] Exceptionally, a State like Portugal treats extradition proceedings behind closed doors on a routine basis. Hatton, *supra* n.20.

[233] Robert D. McFadden, "Drug Suspect in Afghan Ring is Sent to U.S.," *N.Y. Times*, Oct. 25, 2005, at B1. For much the same logic, governments may maintain secrecy regarding whether an extradition actually took place, as demonstrated by the U.S. Government's unwillingness to confirm whether Mexico had extradited Colombian drug trafficker Harold Mauricio Poveda-Ortega (known as "The Rabbit") after being captured in Mexico City in 2010 following an undercover investigation that infiltrated his operations and found that he had delivered about 150 tons of cocaine to Mexico since 2000, much of it intended for the United States. Ginger Thompson, "To Infiltrate Drug Cartels, U.S. Agents Aided Traffickers," *IHT*, Jan. 10, 2012, at 5.

[234] *R. v. Governor of Ashford. ex parte Postlethwaite* [1988] A.C. 924, 946–47 (H.L.).

[235] *Laubenheimer*, 290 U.S. at 298; *Villareal*, 74 F.2d at 505.

Furthermore, a Belgian court ruled that it had "no authority to review the regularity of an extradition granted by a foreign Government" in a case where the Netherlands extradited an individual to Belgium based on its request that occurred sixteen days after his arrest despite a requirement in the applicable bilateral extradition treaty that such requests be made within two weeks of arrest.[236] In the same spirit, the Supreme Court of the German Reich in 1936 pronounced: "There is no generally recognised principle of international law to the effect that extradition is unlawful if granted for acts for which prescription [*i.e.*, a time bar] has taken place according to the law of the extraditing State as distinguished from that of the requesting State."[237]

Fourth, in some States, including the United States, extradition treaties may ***apply retroactively***.[238] This means that, unless expressly limited or treated as such as a matter of domestic practice, extradition treaty provisions may have effect even on crimes committed before the treaty came into force or while the treaty was suspended.[239] It is possible, therefore,

[236] *Geldof v. Meulemeester & Steffen*, Court of Cassation, Belg., Feb. 20, 1961, [1961] *Pasicrisie belge*, 674 [French text], *reprinted in* 31 ILR 385 (E. Lauterpacht ed. 1966).

[237] Extradition (Jurisdiction) Case, Sup. Ct. of the Reich (in Crim. Matters), *supra* n.62, at 350 (affirming German court jurisdiction despite France's extradition of an individual whose crime under French law had been time barred).

[238] For the United States, *see* ABBELL, *supra* n.63, at 83–84 (noting that most pre-1970 U.S. bilateral extradition treaties are silent regarding retroactivity, but that U.S. courts have ruled that where they are silent, they are to be construed as having retroactive effect); *e.g.*, U.S.-Rom. Extradition Treaty, *supra* n.227, 2 CTIA at 371 ("This Treaty shall apply to offenses committed before as well as after the date it enters into force."). For other States' practices, *see generally* Bruce Zagaris, *U.S. Efforts to Extradite Persons for Tax Offenses*, 25 LOY. L.A. INT'L & COMP. L. REV. 653, 667 (2003) (citations omitted) ("Importantly, countries vary in the application of the treaty or national law provisions on retroactivity."); *e.g.*, Dan Harrison, "Push for Hungarian War Crimes Extradition," *Sydney Morning Herald*, Mar. 29, 2012 (despite Hungary's passage in 1945 of retroactive legislation rendering "war crimes" a violation of national law, an Australian federal court found that Charles Zentai could not be extradited to Hungary pursuant to an extradition request on a charge of "war crimes," as such an offense did not exist in November 1944 when the defendant allegedly beat a Jewish teenager to death and threw his body in the Danube River, and the applicable extradition treaty required that the offense in question must have been recognized as an offense in the requesting State at the time the acts or omissions constituting the offense occurred).

[239] *E.g.*, *Markham v. Pitchess*, 605 F.2d 436, 437–38 (9th Cir. 1979) (the United States can enter into a treaty that applies to crimes already committed), *cert. denied*, 447 U.S. 904 (1980); *Gallina v Fraser*, 177 F. Supp. 856 (D. Conn. 1959), *aff'd*, 278 F.2d 77 (2d Cir.), *cert. denied*, 364 U.S. 851 (1960) (treaty suspension case). *See generally* ABBELL, *supra* n.63, at 61–62 (distinguishing between treaty suspension and abrogation).

that while a crime would not have been deemed extraditable at the time it was committed, it may become so, even years later, by virtue of an extradition request under a presently operative treaty that recognizes such conduct as extraditable so long as the underlying conduct was deemed criminal under the municipal law of both States at the time of commission.[240] As extradition treaties do not render conduct criminal,[241] they do not violate *ex post facto* laws.[242]

Fifth, extradition proceedings ***need not forestall prompt apprehension*** of the fugitive. Even before it submits an extradition request, a pursuing State can seek the host State's cooperation in provisionally arresting the fugitive.[243] This common feature of extradition treaties incidentally can help prevent the fugitive from hearing about a pursuing State's law enforcement interest in him and, while the various extradition proceedings play out through diplomatic channels, take the opportunity to hide away or take refuge in another State.[244]

Sixth, some municipal laws and international agreements ***permit the extradition of a fugitive for the temporary and limited purpose of standing trial*** for charged offenses in a particular pursuing State, even though he is already serving a criminal sentence in the host State.[245] This

[240] *See* Blakesley, Comparative Study, *supra* n.24, at 276 (underlying conduct must already be criminalized in both States); *e.g.*, *In re Colman*, Ct. of App. of Paris, Fr. (Chambre des Mises en Accusation), Dec. 5, 1947, *reprinted in* [1947] 14 Ann. Dig. & Rep. Pub. Int'l Cases 139 (No. 67) (H. Lauterpacht ed. 1951) ("The offender cannot invoke the principle of the non-retroactivity of laws. He has no right not to be surrendered for facts which were not provided for, at the time of the consummation of the offence, by the Franco-Belgian Convention . . . as long as both French and Belgian law render criminal and punish the offences at the time when they were committed.").

[241] *See* n.51 and accompanying text in Chapter 1.

[242] *E.g.*, *United States ex rel. Oppenheim v. Hecht*, 16 F.2d 955, 956 (2d Cir.), *cert. denied*, 273 U.S. 769 (1927); *Wright v. Court of Appeals*, G.R. No. 113213, Sup. Ct., Phil., Aug. 15, 1994, 235 SCRA 346 (1994). While this principle may seem to run counter to the U.S. Constitution's prohibition on Congress passing an *ex post facto* law, a treaty executed by the executive branch is not the same thing as Congress adopting legislation. In addition, the Constitution's due process protections found in the 5th and 14th amendments (the former in the federal context, the latter in the state context) do not apply to extraditions involving foreign nationals abroad, as the term "the people" or "persons" in those amendments refers specifically to U.S. citizens or those who have developed ties to the United States. *Johnson v. Eisentrager*, 339 U.S. 763, 785 (1950) (5th amendment); *United States v. Verdugo-Urquidez*, 494 U.S. 259, 265 (1990) (14th amendment).

[243] *See supra* n.161 and accompanying text.

[244] Shearer, *supra* n.34, at 200–02.

[245] *E.g.*, London Scheme for Extradition within the Commonwealth, Nov. 2002, art. 16(2)(b)(i), LMM (90)32 (authorizing "the temporary extradition of the person to stand trial in the requesting country on condition that, following trial and sentence, the person is returned to

practice is a form of "conditional release" but distinct from the circumstance in which a State temporarily releases a criminal defendant from either pre-trial custody to expedite extradition or detention pending an extradition decision.

The benefit of such flexibility is that an accused in a pursuing State can be prosecuted while witnesses are still alive, their memories fresh, and other evidence available, rather than risking a trial potentially years later with insufficient evidence after the subject has fully served his existing sentence in the host State.[246] In addition, were the fugitive part of a criminal enterprise, he might be willing to assist with the investigation or prosecution of other enterprise members when returned to stand trial.[247] In September 2008, for example, when indicted for involvement in terrorist attacks in Casablanca in 2003, Hassan el Haski, a native Moroccan then serving a fifteen-year prison sentence in Spain for his role in the Madrid terrorist bombings of 2004, was temporarily extradited by Spain to Morocco for this purpose.[248]

Seventh, flexibility is also apparent with respect to seeking the extradition of fugitives for ***crimes not expressly itemized or covered by the applicable extradition treaty***. How an offense is denominated is not normally determinative; rather, many courts tend to examine the underlying conduct itself and query whether, for dual criminality purposes (discussed in Chapter 5.a.ii), the two sets of domestic laws are "substantially analogous" and "directed at the same basic evil."[249] Additionally, at times, the host State will agree to extradite a fugitive even when the crime at issue is neither listed in the extradition treaty nor substantially

the requested country to serve his or her sentence"); Framework Decision on the EAW, *supra* n.113, art. 5(3) ("where a person who is the subject of a European arrest warrant for the purposes of prosecution is a national or resident of the executing Member State, surrender may be subject to the condition that the person, after being heard, is returned to the executing Member State in order to serve there the custodial sentence or detention order passed against him in the issuing Member State."); Murphy, U.S. Practice, 1999–2001, *supra* n.169, at 329 (in September 2000 the State Department lauded the virtues of such a practice in seeking Senate confirmation of its extradition treaties with Belize, Paraguay, South Africa, and Sri Lanka, each of which contained such a provision).

246 Murphy, U.S. Practice, 1999–2001, *supra* n.169, at 330.

247 *Id.*

248 Al Goodman, "Spain to Extradite Convicted Train Bomber," *CNN.com/Europe*, Sept. 23, 2008, *available at* www.cnn.com/2008/WORLD/europe/09/23/spain.terror/ (last visited at May 27, 2016).

249 *Peters v. Egnor*, 888 F.2d 713, 719 (10th Cir. 1989). In the United States, for example, in trying to gauge whether a particular conduct qualifies as a crime, a U.S. federal court may evaluate not only the law of the individual state where the crime was committed, but also federal law and the law of the majority of U.S. states. Abbell, *supra* n.63, at 28–29

analogous, but where it nevertheless exists at common law.[250] Furthermore, as noted above, simply because a crime is not itemized or otherwise eligible for extradition in a treaty does not prevent States from mutually choosing to waive that particular provision and proceed outside the treaty context, say, as a matter of reciprocity or comity.[251]

Eighth, under some State laws, including the United States, a pursuing State ***can, under certain circumstances, renew an extradition request following a denial.*** For those States, "[t]here is no double jeopardy prohibition against such a renewed request, nor is a finding of non-extraditability *res judicata* to a second proceeding. Nevertheless, findings of fact made by a judge cannot be overturned by another judge of the same jurisdiction without new facts to support a different finding."[252] It is also true, however, that for most States, once an extradition request has been denied, a new submission may not be made with respect to the same offense(s).[253]

Ninth, the ***validity of extradition treaties is generally upheld even when State status is in transition or there is a radical or revolutionary change in the government of a State.***[254] Accordingly, municipal courts

250 *E.g.*, Bruce Zagaris, *Trinidad Magistrate Orders Extradition of Three Suspects to U.S. in JFK Airport Terrorism Plot*, 23 IELR 375, 375–76 (2007) (in August 2007, a Trinidad & Tobago (T&T) magistrate judge ordered three men – Abdul Kair, Kareem Ibrahim, and Abdel Nur – extradited to the United States on charges they conspired to sabotage jet fuel storage tanks and fuel lines at New York City's Kennedy International Airport, despite the fact that the T&T Extradition Act did not recognize an offense of conspiracy to commit terrorism, because the magistrate found that such an offense existed at common law).

251 *See* pp. 151–52.

252 Bassiouni, U.S. Extradition, *supra* n.1, at 991 (citing, *e.g.*, *Hooker v. Klein*, 573 F.2d 1360 (9th Cir.), *cert. denied*, 439 U.S. 932 (1978)).

253 *E.g.*, Nicaragua, Code of Crim. Proc., Nov. 13, 2001, art. 359 ("If extradition of a person is denied on its merits, the request may not be repeated for the same crime.").

254 *See Perlin v. Superintendent of Prisons*, Sup. Ct., Palestine, Nov. 16, 1942, 9 Law Reports of Palestine 683 (1942), *reprinted in* 10 Ann. Dig. & Rep. Pub. Int'l L. Cases 328, 329 (H. Lauterpacht ed. 1945) ("It seems to be settled practice in International Law that treaties and international agreements are not affected by a change in government, or in the form of government of one of the contracting parties, and remain in force until denounced by the new government or they expire by effluxion of time. Thus, if a State changes its form of government from a monarchial to a republican one, treaties to which it was a party still remain in force."); *In re Escudero*, Cámara Federal, Arg., Sept. 4, 1939, 67 *Jurisprudencia Argentina* 797, *reprinted in* [1938–40] 9 Ann. Dig. & Rep. Pub. Int'l L. Cases 408, 408 (No. 155) (H. Lauterpacht ed. 1942) (an Argentinian court granted extradition to Spain pursuant to their bilateral extradition treaty notwithstanding a radical change of government between the Republican government that requested the extradition and the Nationalists who had since acquired control of Spanish territory and to whom the prisoner was delivered).

tend to confirm the applicability of extradition treaties to former colonies or territories of States parties notwithstanding the fact that the concerned State's independence has since been attained (*e.g.*, Singapore or Lebanon).[255]

Extradition treaty validity likewise has been affirmed in cases involving States that are the legacy of a split-up (*e.g.*, Czech Republic or Serbia)[256] where the erstwhile parent State had been a treaty partner, as well as for newly consolidated States (*e.g.*, Yugoslavia after World War I) that have succeeded a predecessor State that had been an original treaty partner, at least when both current States concerned can demonstrate (usually via an exchange of diplomatic notes) that they regard the treaty as remaining in effect.[257] Furthermore, extradition treaties have been upheld as valid in instances where long-term leased territory has been returned to its original owner. In the case of Hong Kong to the PRC, for example, a U.S. appellate court found no objection to extradition where an individual charged with economic crimes in Hong Kong prior to the reversion date (July 1, 1997) was to be transferred to the PRC only after Hong Kong was restored to the PRC following the U.K.'s ninety-nine-year territorial lease.[258]

[255] Abbell, *supra* n.63, at 59 & n.15; *e.g.*, *Shehadeh, et al. v. Comm'r of Prisons, Jerusalem* Sup. Ct., Palestine, Oct. 31, 1947, *reprinted in* (Lebanon's change from a Mandate to an independent Republic since its execution of an extradition agreement was no defense to an extradition request, given that Lebanon's international obligations remained intact).

[256] Abbell, *supra* n.63, at 60 & n.16; *e.g.*, *Platko*, 213 F. Supp.2d 1229 (upholding a decision to deny *habeas* relief for Jaroslava Lorie Kastnerova from a decision that she should be extradited to the Czech Republic to face fraud charges, despite the fact that the applicable extradition treaty was the one concluded in July 1925 between the United States and Czechoslovakia, where evidence existed that the United States and the Czech Republic both considered that treaty to be in effect).

[257] *E.g.*, *Ivancevic v. Artukovic*, 211 F.2d 565 (9th Cir. 1954) (treating Yugoslavia as the successor-in-interest to Serbia with which the United States had entered into an extradition treaty in 1901, given that the United States and Yugoslavia, which had no direct extradition treaty between them, acted in such a manner to suggest their acceptance of the U.S.-Serbian treaty's continuing effect).

[258] The Court ruled that despite the fact that the fugitive defendant could not be tried and punished by the British Crown Colony before the reversion date, "the [U.S.] Senate was well aware of the reversion when it approved a supplementary [extradition] treaty with the United Kingdom in 1986"; "[t]he [U.S.] President . . . recently executed a new treaty with the incoming government of Hong Kong [the HKSAR], containing the same guarantees . . . [as] the earlier treaties"; and "governments of [U.S.] treaty partners often change, sometimes by ballot, sometimes by revolution or other means, and the possibility or even certainty of such change does not itself excuse compliance with the terms of the agreement embodied in the treaties between the countries." *United States v. Kin-Hong*, 110 F.3d 103, 106 (1st Cir. 1997). *See also Cheng Na-Yuet v. Hueston*, 734

Tenth, extradition ***can operate even during an international armed conflict*** between the parties to that conflict, notwithstanding generally applicable restrictions against transferring a "protected person," so long as such transfer is "in pursuance of [an] extradition treat[y] concluded before the outbreak of hostilities" with respect to "offences against ordinary criminal law."[259]

f Developments

In recent years, substantial progress has been made to harmonize and improve the extradition process,[260] as well as build greater reliance on its use.[261] These critical developments, which "have helped enhance effectiveness, minimize arbitrariness, and safeguard essential human rights protection,"[262] can be loosely categorized as follows: (i) the introduction of new or revised bilateral or multilateral treaties that address extradition;

F. Supp. 988, 993–94 (S.D. Fla. 1990) (no denial of extradition for a kidnapping offense for which the maximum penalty was life imprisonment in Hong Kong, even though the fugitive's prison term extended past the reversion date to the PRC, and Chinese law allowed for the death penalty in cases of kidnapping offenses).

259 Geneva Conv. Relative to the Protection of Civilian Persons in Time of War (GC IV), Aug. 12, 1949, art. 45(5), 6 U.S.T. 3516, T.I.A.S. No. 3365, 75 U.N.T.S. 287.

260 To provide a general sense of the scale of extradition requests issued by States and their approximate "yield" (percentage of granted extraditions), consider that in 2012, some States like Barbados, El Salvador, Nigeria, and Singapore each sought extradition in fewer than five cases, while other States like Algeria, Australia, Greece, and Israel each sought extradition in ten–fifty cases, while others like Armenia, Azerbaijan, and Mexico each sought extradition in 51–100 cases, while still others like Germany, Poland, and Russia each sought extradition in over 400 cases. UNODC, Statstics on Outgoing Requests for Extradition, 2010–2012, *available at* www.unodc.org/unodc/en/data-and-analysis/statistics/crime.html (last visited on May 27, 2016). Annual yields varied considerably that year as well, with Mexico registering about a 13% rate, Ireland a 32% rate, Armenia a 66% rate, and Germany an 88% rate. *Id.*

261 Bantekas & Nash, *supra* n.9, at 192. With respect to the United States, since 1970, "U.S. negotiators have sought to maximize the number of offences for which a treaty partner will extradite; to narrow as much as possible the 'political offense' exception, especially in negotiations with close allies; to accommodate the extraterritorial reach of U.S. and foreign criminal laws and jurisdictional notions; to persuade foreign governments to extradite their nationals, or else ensure vicarious prosecution at the request of the U.S. government; to reconcile U.S. capital punishment laws with the insistence of foreign governments that fugitives delivered by them not be executed; and, more generally, to clear up confusions and needless obstacles that have hobbled extradition relations under the older treaties." Nadelmann, Cops, *supra* n.12, at 410. The watershed decade for increase in U.S. extraditions was the 1970s. *Id.* at 401.

262 Duffy, *supra* n.28, at 108.

(ii) the facilitation of extradition through streamlined or more permissive domestic laws; (iii) the liberalization of host State decision-making with respect to extradition requests; and (iv) the advent of more effective regional extradition cooperation.[263]

New or Revised Treaties. In recent years, there have been a number of noteworthy developments on the bilateral extradition treaty front. In 2006, African neighbors Uganda and Rwanda signed an extradition treaty (ratified in 2007); this was particularly significant because Uganda was the subject of an ICC investigation and Rwanda was the locus of genocide, and each had fugitives within its borders who had fled from the other State.[264]

Over the past decade, the PRC has begun to negotiate extradition treaties with Western States, beginning with France, Portugal, and Spain;[265] and the Republic of South Africa has adopted a more proactive approach to extradition treaties.[266] In February 2012, the Russian Justice Minister and U.S. Attorney General met to discuss negotiating a first-ever Russia-U.S. extradition treaty,[267] although this has yet to reach fruition. Furthermore, in July 2003, the United States and the

263 In addition, some States have undertaken bilateral coordination efforts outside of the treaty context to foster extradition. *See, e.g.*, U.S. Dep't of State, 2014 International Narcotics Control Strategy Report (INCSR), Country Report on El Salvador (undated), *available at* www.state.gov/j/inl/rls/nrcrpt/2015/vol1/238968.htm (last visied on May 6, 2016) ("Under the Partnership for Growth bilateral assistance initiative between the United States and El Salvador, the two countries consult regularly to promote extraditions as a tool for combating crime.").

264 Bruce Zagaris, *Uganda Agrees to Sign Extradition Treaty with Rwanda*, 23 IELR 212, 212–13 (2007). In October 2009, Rwanda also agreed to execute an extradition treaty with Burundi. James Karuhanga, "Rwanda-Burundi to Sign Extradition Treaty," Oct. 15, 2009, *The New Times* (Rwanda).

265 Bruce Zagaris, *Proposed France-China Extradition Treaty Raises Human Rights Issues*, 23 IELR 96 (2007); Bruce Zagaris, *PRC Promotes Negotiation of Extradition Treaties*, 23 IELR 296 (2007).

266 As of December 8, 2010, the RSA had ratified thirteen bilateral extradition treaties, another three had been signed but not yet ratified, and seven had been negotiated but not yet signed. RSA, Dep't of Justice and Constitutional Development, "Extradition and Mutual Legal Assistance in Criminal Matters Treaties," *available at* www.justice.gov.za/ilr/mla.html (last visited on May 6, 2016).

267 "Russia Proposes Entering into Extradition Treaties with United States," Russian Legal Information Agency (RAPSI), Feb. 15, 2012, *available at* www.rapsinews.com/judicial_news/20120210/260104596.html (last visited on May 6, 2016). In 1999, the United States and Russia executed a mutual legal assistance treaty regarding criminal matters, but that treaty does not address extradition. Treaty between the United States and the Russian Federation on Mutual Legal Assistance in Crim. Matters, June 17, 1999, T.I.A.S. 13046.

E.U. entered into an extradition agreement – an unprecedented law enforcement cooperation initiative (along with an MLAT) between those two entities – intended to guide the revision of bilateral extradition treaties between the United States and individual E.U. members.[268]

In addition, some States, notably the United States, have made a concerted effort to modernize their bilateral extradition treaties by streamlining procedures, improving efficiency, and facilitating transfers. Examples include: (i) in 2003, the United States and the United Kingdom revised their extradition treaty, replacing the 1972 baseline treaty (as supplemented in 1985) that, *inter alia*, lowered the evidentiary standard required of U.S. extradition requests,[269] redefined more flexibly extraditable offenses, and eliminated any time bar;[270] (ii) in 1996, the United States executed virtually identical updated extradition treaties with six former British colonies that now comprise the Organization of Eastern Caribbean States (OECS) – Antigua and Barbuda, Dominica, Grenada, St. Kitts and Nevis, St. Lucia, and St. Vincent and the Grenadines – that had previously operated under U.S.-U.K. extradition treaties, particularly in order to improve cooperation in international narcotics-related law enforcement;[271] and (iii) in 2001, the United States executed extradition treaties with Belize, Paraguay, South Africa, and Sri Lanka that included, for instance, a provision allowing for the unrestricted extradition of

268 Agreement on Extradition between the European Union and the United States, June 25, 2003 Treaty Doc. 109–14,. The E.U.-U.S. Extradition Agreement can be more accurately characterized as a "master-model agreement" or "framework agreement" that "removes the legislative and certification requirements and simplifies the documentation in order to expedite the extradition process." Bassiouni, U.S. Extradition, *supra* n.1, at 32. *See also supra* nn.47 and 68 and accompanying text.

269 The resulting differential standard became a source of controversy in the United Kingdom. *See supra* n.5. Not only were the evidentiary requirements no longer reciprocal between the two States, but also the United States could now seek preventive detention abroad without first establishing sufficient evidence to justify a criminal charge in the United States. Such preventive detention was requested, for example, in the case of Lofti Raissi, an Algerian national suspected of involvement in training the pilots from the September 11, 2001, attacks on U.S. soil.; he was held by U.K. authorities at the request of the United States but then was released after five months when the United States proved unable to muster the evidence necessary to support an extradition request. Duffy, *supra* n.28, at 135 & n.317.

270 *Id.* at 133 n.305; Bruce Zagaris, *Senate Foreign Relations Committee Holds Hearings on Four Treaties*, 22 IELR 38 (2006).

271 Marian Nash Leich, *Contemporary Practice of the United States Relating to Int'l Law*, 92 AJIL 44, 44–47 (1998).

nationals and a broader definition of dual criminality that no longer relied on itemized crimes in the treaty.[272]

On the multilateral front, over the past twenty years States have executed new treaties or revised existing ones (whether through amendments or protocols) to promote or facilitate extradition, or have pursued the ratification of signed treaties, sometimes with the encouragement of the U.N. Security Council.[273] Examples of such developments include the amended European Convention on Extradition (1996),[274] the Protocol amending the European Convention on the Suppression of Terrorism (2003),[275] and the Additional Protocol to the SAARC Regional Convention on Combating Terrorism (2004).[276]

Streamlined or More Permissive Legislative or Constitutional Text. Over the past two decades, a number of States have recognized the need for reform or in fact have revised their domestic legislation or amended constitutional provisions governing extradition in order to streamline the process and allow for greater cooperation in bringing fugitives to justice. Some prominent examples include:

- In 2003, the United Kingdom revamped its Extradition Act, which, *inter alia*, established a two-tiered system for evaluating requests and set up a simplified appeals process;[277]
- Israel amended its Penal Act in 1999 to close a domestic extradition law loophole that was conspicuously exposed through a Supreme

[272] Murphy, U.S. Practice, 1999–2001, *supra* n.169, at 329–30.

[273] *E.g.*, UNSC Res. 1373, Sept. 28, 2001, U.N. Doc. S/Res/1373 (2001) (urging States to ratify existing anti-terrorism treaties).

[274] Simplified Procedure Conv., *supra* n.224. Under this amended Convention, States not party to the 1957 Convention became eligible to join, and the definition of an extraditable offense was liberalized to entail imprisonment of at least one year in a pursuing State and at least six months in the host State. Bantekas & Nash, *supra* n.9, at 196–97.

[275] Prot. Amending the Eur. Conv. on the Suppression of Terrorism, *supra* n.95 (not yet in force).

[276] Addt'l Prot. to the SAARC Regional Conv. on Suppression of Terrorism, Jan. 6, 2004 SAARC/SUMMIT.12/SC.29/27.

[277] "The legislation was brought in by the Blair government in a bid to speed up and simplify extradition procedures in a post 9/11 world where criminal conduct was becoming increasingly cross-border and multi-jurisdictional and serious crimes such as terrorism, people trafficking, internet pornography, money laundering and large-scale fraud were becoming ever more 'globalized.'" Chatherine Heard, *Fair Trials Int'l's Policy Paper: A Brief Review of U.S.-U.K. Extradition Under the Extradition Act of 2003 From a Human Rights Perspective*, 25 IELR 2 (2009).

Court decision earlier the same year that had permitted *non-resident* Israeli citizens to avoid extradition;[278]

- El Salvador enacted a constitutional amendment in July 2000 to allow the extradition of its nationals;[279]
- The Australian Attorney-General issued a Department Review paper in 2005 expressing the need for domestic legal reform to ensure that "Australia can extradite to and from a large number of countries and can grant extradition for a wider range of offences. The process must also be more responsive and streamlined in order to prevent lengthy delays and offer appropriate safeguards";[280]
- In 2008, to expedite narcotics-related extradition requests, Guatemala passed a law establishing specialized courts to serve this function;[281] and
- In January 2012, Honduras passed and ratified a constitutional reform permitting the extradition of Honduran nationals on drug trafficking, terrorism-related, or organized crime charges, thereby reversing a thirty-year-old blanket prohibition on the extradition of its nationals.[282]

Liberalized Host State Decision-Making. We also have recently witnessed the extradition of certain kinds of individuals who had been

[278] By a three–two decision, the Israeli Supreme Court reversed a lower court ruling that had granted a U.S. request for the extradition of an American teenager named Samuel Sheinbein for co-committing a violent murder in the United States. The case turned on the issue of Sheinbein's citizenship. While he was a resident of Maryland, he was nevertheless deemed to have Israeli citizenship from birth through his Israeli father. The Supreme Court found that Israel's 1978 Penal Law that prohibited the extradition of Israeli nationals trumped Israel's international obligations under a 1962 U.S.-Israel Extradition Treaty. In response, the Israeli Knesset (parliament) amended that statute to prevent foreign criminals who are not Israeli residents from finding a safe haven in Israel. Dina Kraft, "After Sheinbein, Parliament Approves New Extradition Bill," *AP*, Apr. 19, 1999, at 2.

[279] Const. of El Salvador, Dec. 15, 1983, *amended in* 2003 (Eng.), *available at* http://confinder.richmond.edu/admin/docs/ElSalvador1983English.pdf (last visited on May 6, 2016); U.S. Department of State, *Third Report on Int'l Extradition Pursuant to Section 3203 of the Emergency Supplemental Act, 2000, as Enacted in Public Law 106–246 Relating to Plan Colombia* (2002).

[280] Australia, Attorney-General's Dep't, *A New Extradition System – A Review of Australia's Extradition Law and Practice*, Dec. 2005, at 6.

[281] Hannah Stone, "With Extradition Law, Honduras Outsources Justice to U.S.," *Insightcrime.org*, Jan. 30, 2012, *available at* www.insightcrime.org/news-analysis/with-extradition-law-honduras-outsources-justice-to-us (last visited on May 6, 2016).

[282] *Id.* (noting additionally that Honduras then had the highest murder rate in the world and that the Honduras "Congress voted on the bill in a closed session, with tight security measures").

historically off-limits. For example, it has been rare for presidents or heads of State to be the subject of extraditions, primarily due to political considerations, insufficient evidence, statutes of limitations, and immunity laws.[283] Yet in October 2006, Mexico authorized the extradition to Guatemala of the latter's former President, Alfonso Portillo (2000–04), on embezzlement charges (although he was not actually transferred for two more years)[284] and seven years later, in May 2013, Guatemala extradited him to the United States based on charges of conspiracy to launder money.[285] Likewise, in September 2007, the Chilean Supreme Court ultimately decided to extradite former Peruvian President Alberto Fujimori (1990–2000) back to Peru to face corruption and human rights charges.[286]

Another type of individual that generally had not been susceptible to extradition is a State's own military officers,[287] but by way of departure, in March 2006, Uruguay authorized the extradition to Chile of three Uruguayan military officers charged with participation in the assassination of a Chilean chemist who had been prepared to testify at trial involving the homicide of a former Chilean diplomat.[288]

[283] *E.g.*, AP, "Spain: Extradition of Isabel Peron to Argentina is Rejected by Court," *N.Y. Times*, Apr. 29, 2008 (on evidentiary and statute of limitations grounds Spain refused to extradite Isabel Martínez de Perón, a former Argentine President, on charges of human rights abuses and crimes against humanity stemming from the work of right-wing death squads that abducted and murdered left-wing activists during her 1974–76 rule). The issue of immunity is discussed more extensively as an impediment to extradition in Chapter 6.b.

[284] Bruce Zagaris, *Mexico Authorizes Extradition of Former Guatemalan President for Embezzlement*, 23 IELR 19 (2007). Notably, however, when former President Portillo was put on trial, he was exonerated of all charges in May 2011 due to insufficient evidence and freed. "Guatemala Ex-President PortilloCleared of Wrongdoing," *BBC News*, May 10, 2011, *available at* www.bbc.com/news/world-latin-america-13351194 (last visited on May 6, 2016).

[285] Bruce Zagaris, *Guatemala Extradites Former President to U.S. on Money Laundering Charges*, 29 IELR 282 (2013).

[286] *See* Megan Haas, *Fujimori Extaditable!: Chilean Supreme Court Sets Int'l Precedent for Human Rights Violations*, 39 U. Miami Inter-Am. L. Rev. 373, 373–74 (2008) (marking "the first time that a court has ordered a former Latin American president back to his country to stand trial for grave violations of human rights committed during his mandate"). Fujimori was later convicted and sentenced to twenty-five years in prison on corruption, bribery, and human rights charges. Simon Romero, "Peru's Ex-President Convicted of Rights Abuses," *N.Y. Times*, Apr. 7, 2009.

[287] The historically low incidence of military officer extraditions as a function of immunity is examined in Chapter 6.b *infra*.

[288] *See* Bruce Zagaris, *Uruguay to Extradite Three Military Officials to Chile*, 22 IELR 228, 228–29 (2006) (the officers were believed to be involved in the assassination of Eugenio

Furthermore, within the past decade, some States have authorized extraditions that to date had been unprecedented in their respective domestic experience. Examples include:

(i) in October 2005, Pakistan extradited for the first time Taliban fugitives to Afghanistan – a total of fourteen, including Taliban spokesmen Abdul Latif Hakimi;[289]
(ii) in January 2007, newly installed Mexican President Felipe Calderón authorized the extradition for the first time of top-level drug traffickers to the United States, which was all the more remarkable because fifteen of them were secretly delivered at once;[290]
(iii) in May 2007, the United Kingdom transferred its first individual – Syed Hashmi, a/k/a "Fahad" – to the United States on terrorism-related charges, namely, material support to a foreign terrorist organization, al-Qaida;[291]
(iv) in April 2010, a Swiss court for the first time approved an extradition request arising out of tax evasion charges;[292]
(v) in April 2014, the German extradition to the United States of Italian national Romano Pisciotti for participating in a conspiracy to fix prices and suppress competition in the marine hose industry represented the first extradition to the United States involving an antitrust charge;[293] and
(vi) in May 2014, Honduras extradited its first alleged drug trafficker to the United States (Carlos Arnoldo Lobo).[294]

Berrios in the 1990s; Berrios had been taken from Chile in 1991 to avoid his providing testimony in the trial for the 1976 homicide of former diplomat Orlando Letelier).

289 Bruce Zagaris, *Pakistan Extradites Pakistan Fugitives to Afghanistan*, 22 IELR 6, 6–7 (2006) (noting, however, that that this occurred only after repeated complaints by Afghanistan that Taliban guerrillas were using Pakistan as a staging ground for attacks).

290 Rodrigo Labardini, *Mexico Extradites Fugitives to U.S. in 'Historic Delivery,'* 23 IELR 119 (2007) (noting by contrast that Mexico had extradited a total of only eight fugitives from 1978–1994, and only thirteen on average per year from 1996–2000).

291 AP, "Britain Extradites Terrorism Suspect," *Wash. Post*, May 27, 2007, at A18.

292 Bruce Zagaris, *Swiss Highest Court Affirms Extradition to Germany for Tax Evasion*, 26 IELR 277 (2010) (related to a German national indicted with evading value-added taxes (VAT) with respect to the state of Hamburg).

293 U.S. DoJ, *First Ever Extradition on Antitrust Charge*, Press Release 14–340, Apr. 4, 2014.

294 AP, "Honduras Makes First Extradition of Suspected Drug Trafficker to U.S.," *New Europe*, May 9, 2014, *available at* www.neweurope.eu/article/honduras-makes-first-extradition-suspected-drug-trafficker-us-1/ (last visited on May 27, 2016).

In addition, the EAW has served as the inspiration and model for two other regional initiatives to streamline extradition procedures. In December 2005, the Nordic States plus two non-E.U. member States entered into their own arrest warrant system,[309] and in July 2008, fifteen Caribbean Community (CARICOM) member States executed an Arrest Warrant Treaty that expressly seeks to reduce costs and delays in processing extraditions between them while improving the effectiveness of its law enforcement efforts targeted against transnational criminals.[310] Although the CARICOM arrest warrant system has yet to come into force, it nevertheless represents an important development in principle toward greater cooperation and harmonization on extradition matters.

* * * * *

This chapter has focused on extradition: what it is, how it operates, why it is valued, and where it appears to be headed. While extradition offers the international community an important and proven cooperative means to deter and punish crime, and while it possesses certain flexible features and continues to evolve as a mechanism, the next three chapters now turn to the various impediments that at times thwart or discourage extradition and prompt States to consider and pursue other methods for securing the custody of a fugitive abroad.

Submission to the Extradition Review Panel on the European Arrest Warrant, Dec. 21, 2010; "Lithuania Shocked as Austria Frees Ex-KGB Man," *Euronews*, July 17, 2011 (Austria diplomats claimed the EAW issued by Lithuania was "too vague" to justify the continued detention of Mikhail Golovatov, a former commander of the KGB's Alpha Group who was allegedly responsible for storming state television studios on January 13, 1991, resulting in the death of fourteen persons).

309 Conv. on Surrender for Crime between Nordic States [Nordic Arrest Warrant], Dec. 15, 2005.

310 CARICOM Arrest Warrant Treaty, *supra* n.101. *See also* Twelfth U.N. Congress on Crime Prevention and Crim. Justice, Salvador, Braz., Apr. 12–19, 2010, ¶ 12.

5

Impediments I

Legal Standards and Governmental Factors

This and the next two chapters comprehensively explore the rich panoply of limitations and impediments to extradition, or what one legal commentator has referred to as the "field of defences, exceptions and exemptions."[1] Despite extradition's adaptability and ever-improving effectiveness and efficiency, this cooperative law enforcement modality remains riddled with "formidable barriers"[2] that impede its overall potential for success and its application in a variety of circumstances.[3] *The use of the term "impediments" is not intended to be pejorative, but to be viewed neutrally as those grounds relied upon for denying extradition, as many of these barriers actually reflect important societal values or afford significant protections to fugitives, such as dual criminality, specialty, and the political offense exclusion.* In this chapter, the focus will be on the general *legal* standards and *governmental* factors pertaining to extradition. In Chapter 6 the focus shifts to extradition bars based on *individual* status and circumstances, and Chapter 7 concentrates on *inter-State* relations and sensitivities that tend to thwart extradition.

It is worth cataloguing these constraints for at least three reasons. First, we should appreciate the vast variety of ways in which extraditions can be

1 Bert (A.H.J.) Swart, *Refusal of Extradition and the United Nations Model Treaty on Extradition*, 23 NETH. Y.B. INT'L L. 175, 179 (1992).

2 Neil Boister, *The Trend to 'Universal Extradition' over Subsidiary Universal Jurisdiction in the Suppression of Transnat'l Crime*, 2003 ACTA JURIDICA 287, 296–304 (2003).

3 Such impediments can and do arise even when a valid extradition treaty exists with a friendly State. Philip B. Heymann & Ian Heath Gershengorn, *Pursuing Justice, Respecting the Law*, *in* PRINCIPLES AND PROCEDURES FOR A NEW TRANSNATIONAL CRIMINAL LAW: DOCUMENTATION OF AN INTERNATIONAL WORKSHOP IN FREIBURG, MAY 1991, at 42 (Albin Eser & Otto Lagodny eds. 1992). However, where a court determines that extradition must not proceed on account of certain charges, that determination does not necessarily prevent the fugitive from being extradited on other, non-barred charges. *E.g., Barapind v. Enomoto*, 400 F.3d 744, 748–49 (9th Cir. 2005).

undermined, affording States[4] a veritable potpourri of ready bases or rationalizations, as the case may be, for refusing requests.[5] Second, this exercise underscores why alternatives to extradition are at times sought and cannot be discounted. Third, the process of identifying and evaluating the operation of these impediments is tantamount in a very real sense to a lawfulness analysis for extradition itself.

This chapter examines four broad types of impediments that fall within the domain of legal standards and governmental factors, namely: (i) the inherent nature and scope of the offense (*e.g.*, dual criminality and specified offense exclusions), (ii) prescription, (iii) evidentiary standards, and (iv) the realities of governmental procedures and processing (such as improper filings, undue influence, and delays). A fifth, catch-all type arguably could be added to reflect those situations in which a State chooses not to extradite out of a general sense of fairness,[6] sometimes justified under the notion of "interests of justice"[7] or on the ground of ensuring compliance with the public order (*ordre public*); however, denials based on such abstract language or logic are almost always captured by one of the other specific grounds described in this Part.

[4] In this and Chapters 6 and 7, while a reference to the term "State" most often will signify a government's executive branch, it also may denote its legislature or judiciary.

[5] Extradition denials may have significant diplomatic consequences. For example, in July 2007, the Russian prosecutor general formally notified British prosecutors that Russia would not extradite Andrei K. Lugovoi, the former KGB officer sought by the United Kingdom in connection with the murder of ex-KGB officer Alexander Litvinenko. In response, Britain expelled four mid-ranking Russian diplomatic officials unconnected to the Litvinenko case and stated it would temporarily cease talks aimed at streamlining visa applications for Russian citizens. A few days later, Russia retaliated by expelling four British diplomats from its territory and announced plans to tighten visa requirements on British Government officials' travel to Russia and to suspend counterterrorism cooperation. Andrew E. Kramer, "Russia Orders 4 British Diplomats Home in Poisoning Case," *N.Y. Times*, July 20, 2007, at A10.

[6] *See, e.g.*, Extradition Act of Canada, Royal Statutes of Canada (R.S.C.), June 17, 1999, § 44(1)(a), *as amended*, July 19, 2005 [hereinafter Canada Extradition Act] (Canada may refuse extradition where it "would be unjust or oppressive having regard to all the relevant circumstances"); *Gov't of the Repub. of So. Afr. v. Dewani (No. 2)* [2014] EWHC 153 (Admin), [2014] WLR (D) 41 (holding that it could be "unjust and oppressive" to extradite an individual deemed to be unfit to plead without considering whether an undertaking should be required from the pursuing State to permit his return to the host State if found, after a reasonable period of treatment in the pursuing State, that he was likely to remain unfit to plead).

[7] *See* Alan Travis, "Home Secretary Theresa May Overhauls Extradition Laws," *The Guardian*, Feb. 6, 2013 ("[U.K. Home Secretary Theresa] May has met the demands of extradition law reformers by tabling amendments to introduce a 'forum bar', which will allow British courts to block an extradition request if they believe it is in the *interests of justice* for the defendant to stand trial in the U.K.") (emphasis supplied).

a Inherent Nature and Scope of Offense

This section first examines the notion and significance of an extraditable offense and its close relative, the concept of dual (or double) criminality. That analysis is followed by an assessment of three particular types of exclusions commonly referenced in extradition treaties and statutes: those related to political, military, and fiscal offenses.

i Extraditable Offense

To qualify as an extraditable offense, a State must both have criminalized the conduct at issue *and* recognize it as extradition-worthy. For conduct to be criminalized, it must appear in a State's or a sub-national entity's[8] criminal code, or be designated elsewhere as a criminal offense within the body of its domestic laws.[9] This requirement derives in essence from the Latin maxim *nulla poena sine lege*[10] – *i.e.*, there can be no punishment absent applicable criminal law. It is not enough that the conduct has been criminalized only by another State (or other sub-national entities),[11] or even that it constitutes a civil wrong or contractual breach.[12] There also may be limits on whether certain conduct can be properly criminalized; for example, many State constitutions or criminal codes prohibit the use of *ex post facto* legislation that would retroactively criminalize conduct;[13]

[8] In federal systems, even if federal law itself does not criminalize certain conduct, state or provincial law may do so and, where relevant, that is enough to meet the extraditable offense standard. *E.g., Scott v. State of Israel*, Sup. Ct. sitting as a Ct. of Crim. App., Isr., Jan. 29, 1970, *reprinted in* 48 ILR 188 (1975).

[9] Christopher L. Blakesley, Terrorism, Drugs, International Law, and the Protection of Human Liberty: A Comparative Study of International Law, Its Nature, Role, and Impact in Matters of Terrorism, Drug Trafficking, War, and Extradition 224 & n.246 (1992); *e.g.*, Switz., Federal Act on Int'l Mutual Assistance in Crim. Matters, Mar. 20, 1981, art. 35, *as amended* (unofficial translation) [hereinafter Swiss IMAC] (offence must be punishable under the law of Switzerland).

[10] Boister, *supra* n.2, at 297 & n.57; Robert Cryer, et al., An Introduction to International Criminal Law and Procedure 74 (2d ed. 2010).

[11] *See* Ethan A. Nadelmann, *The Evolution of United States Involvement in the Int'l Rendition of Fugitive Criminals*, 25 N.Y.U. J. Int'l L. & Pol. 813, 815 (1993) (noting that the U.S. Government may not prosecute an individual for conduct in violation only of foreign law).

[12] Ivor Stanbrook & Clive Stanbrook, Extradition: Law and Practice 22 (2d ed. 2000).

[13] *See infra* n.29; Const. of the United States, Sept. 17, 1787, art. I, § 10, *as amended* ("No State shall ... pass any ... ex post facto Law"). For a national Supreme Court opinion regarding whether this principle constitutes a rule of customary international law, *see Attorney General of the Gov't of Israel v. Eichmann*, Crim. Case No. 40/61, Dist.

and States may even set restrictions regarding how far back in time offenses occurred in order to qualify as extraditable.[14]

The second prong requires that the criminal conduct at issue be regarded as warranting extradition. International law affords States maximum latitude in determining which crimes to designate as extraditable or non-extraditable. Sometimes, for political, cultural, or moral reasons, or possibly because of their country's particular experience with crime, a State simply has not yet come to view a particular offense as extraditable. For example, the United States did not recognize parental abductions of one's own children as an extraditable offense until 1998.[15] In 2005, Japan released former U.S. chess champion Bobby Fischer from custody, despite an American extradition request, partially on the grounds that the trade sanctions violation for which the United States sought his custody did not qualify in Japan as an extraditable crime.[16] In 1952, a Swiss court denied extradition to Italy of an Italian national for the crime of carrying arms without a license, which was not then recognized as an extraditable crime under Swiss statutory law.[17]

Ct. of Jerusalem, Isr., Dec. 12, 1961, *reprinted in* 36 ILR 5, *aff'd sub nom., Eichmann v. Attorney General of the Gov't of Israel*, Sup. Ct., Isr., May 29, 1962, *reprinted in* 36 ILR 277, 281 (E. Lauterpacht ed. 1968) (observing that this principle "in so far as it negates penal legislation with retroactive effect, has not yet become a rule of customary international law."). The Israeli Supreme Court went even further, however, noting that *ex post facto* laws can arguably be validated where, for example, the statutory crimes are regarded "as having always borne the stamp of international crimes, banned by the law of nations and entailing individual criminal responsibility." *Id.*, 36 ILR at 287.

14 For example, Colombia has set a temporal threshold for the commission of an extraditable crime (*i.e.*, no earlier than December 16, 1997) specifically with regard to extraditions to the United States. Under the U.S.-Colombia Extradition Treaty, U.S. authorities may not prosecute suspects for crimes committed before December 16, 1997, the day when the Colombian Constitutional Court authorized the resumption of extraditions, which had been barred since 1991. Bruce Zagaris, *Colombian Supreme Court Inquires About Potential U.S. Violations of Extradition Terms*, 21 IELR 222 (2005).

15 In 1998, the U.S. Congress passed legislation in which "parental kidnapping" was to be construed as a form of "kidnapping" generally as it appeared in any U.S. extradition treaty. Extradition Treaties Interpretation Act of 1998, Pub. L. 105–323, Oct. 30, 1998, § 203, *codified as* 18 U.S.C. § 1204 (2012).

16 Bruce Zagaris, *Iceland Grants Bobby Fischer Citizenship and Japan Deports Him to Iceland*, 21 IELR 186 (2005) (the U.S. trade sanctions were imposed because Fischer had accepted a US $3.3 million fee to play an exhibition chess match in Yugoslavia in 1992; in March 2005, in lieu of his extradition to the United States, Japan deported him to Iceland, where the latter's Parliament had recently granted him citizenship).

17 *In re Nappi*, Trib. Féd. Suisse, Jan. 23, 1952, *reprinted in* 19 ILR 375, 375 (1957) (the court did, however, grant extradition for the crime of robbery arising out of the same underlying facts).

In addition, given the time and expense associated with extradition, the vast majority of States do not find it worthwhile to recognize crimes as extraditable when they are considered minor offenses (*i.e.*, those punishable by a *de minimis* prison sentence, typically under twelve months).[18] Furthermore, an individual's violation of the terms of parole, bail, or a court order, his escape from prison, or his failure to attend a sentencing hearing, are generally considered non-extraditable offenses.[19] Moreover, under some extradition statutes and treaties, where the lion's share of the conduct constituting the extraditable offense occurs *within its own territory*,[20] or is otherwise simply more suitably

[18] Sir Robert Jennings & Sir Arthur Watts, eds., 1 Oppenheim's International Law 957 (9th ed. 1992); Stanbrook & Stanbrook, *supra* n.12, at 8; Valerie Epps, *The Development of the Conceptual Framework Supporting Int'l Extradition*, 25 Loy. L.A. Int'l & Comp. L. Rev. 369, 374 (2003). There is less consensus, but mounting pressure, with respect to granting extradition in instances where there are multiple offenses each of which individually fall short of the requisite penalty threshold for extradition but where, in combination, they exceed that threshold. Boister, *supra* n.2, at 299.

[19] Blakesley, *supra* n.9, at 217; *e.g., United States v. Antonakeas*, 255 F.3d 714, 717–18 (9th Cir. 2001) (the German Government denied a U.S. extradition request for a convicted individual on a charge of failing to appear at his sentencing hearing).

[20] *See, e.g.*, Terry Richard Kane, *Prosecuting Int'l Terrorists in United States Courts: Gaining the Jurisdictional Threshold*, 12 Yale J. Int'l L. 294, 333–34 (1987) (describing how Sweden rejected an extradition request from the F.R.G. in 1975 for the surviving members of the Baader-Meinhoff Gang, a West German-based terrorist organization, after their lethal attack on the West German Embassy in Stockholm on the basis that the offense was non-extraditable); *R. v. Bow Street Metropolitan Magistrate and Others, ex parte Pinochet Ugarte (No. 3)* [2001] 1 A.C. 147 (H.L.), [1999] 2 WLR 827, 828 (in the celebrated case of Spain's extradition request for Gen. Auguste Pinochet, the U.K. House of Lords ruled that because "*extraterritorial torture* did not become a crime in the United Kingdom until . . . 29 September 1988 . . . all the alleged offences [of torture or murder or the conspiracy thereof] which did not occur in Spain were crimes for which [Pinochet] could not be extradited.") (emphasis supplied); U.N. Model Treaty on Extradition, Dec. 14, 1991, art. 4(f), UNGA Res. 45/116, Annex, 45 U.N. GAOR Supp. (No. 49A) at 212, U.N. Doc. A/45/49 (1990), *reprinted in* 30 ILM 1407 [hereinafter U.N. Model Extradition Treaty] (citing as an optional ground for refusing extradition where "the offence for which extradition is requested is regarded under the law of the requested State as having been committed in whole or in part within that State."). This ground tends to be found in older extradition treaties or domestic statutes, and sometimes further requires that the *locus delicti* must have been pursuing State territory. Satyadeva Bedi, Extradition in International Law and Practice 175–78 (1968) (citing by way example the U.S.-RSA Extradition Treaty, Dec. 18, 1947, art. 1, 2 U.S.T. 884); República de Panamá, por la cual se Aprueba el Codigo Penal, Nov. 17, 1922, art. 11, *reprinted in Gaceta Oficial*, Número 4049, Dec. 8, 1922 [Spanish text]).

adjudicated in another forum,[21] the host State may treat the offense in question as non-extraditable.

ii Dual Criminality

Dual (or double) criminality refers to a condition precedent for extradition by which both the pursuing and host States have criminalized the same or substantially similar conduct.[22] In essence, the dual criminality requires that the two States involved in an extradition each find that the conduct at issue constitutes a criminal offense under their respective domestic laws. Although extraditable offenses and dual criminality are closely related concepts, and therefore at times are conflated or treated as interchangeable by courts and scholars, these concepts are distinct and merit separate discussion.

The former term relates to the host State's determination regarding which offenses are to be treated as extraditable *under its domestic law*,[23] while the latter term focuses on the *relationship* of the two sets of laws to verify whether a proper identity can be established between them. In practical terms, if either State's law does not recognize certain conduct as a penal offense (*i.e.*, the crime is not extraditable), then by logical implication dual criminality cannot obtain. Indeed, this is frequently the reason why dual criminality fails; however, it also could fall short due to sufficiently material differences in their respective characterization of a given extraditable offense.

Dual criminality is so fundamental to, and of such common usage in, extradition law that it is widely considered to be a rule of customary

[21] *See* Clive Nicholls, et al., eds., The Law of Extradition and Mutual Assistance 106 (2d ed. 2007); *e.g.*, Bruce Zagaris, *Trinidadian Court Denies U.S. Extradition on Piarco Airport Case*, 28 IELR 22, 22–23 (2012) (denial decision based on judgment that extradition to the United States would be "unjust, oppressive, and unlawful" as the appropriate forum to hear the claims was Trinidad & Tobago (T&T), in part because that is where the alleged crimes were committed and T&T was most affected by the underlying actions).

[22] *See* Jennings & Watts, *supra* n.18, at 958 (noting the need for at least "substantial similarity" between the offenses in both States); Stanbrook & Stanbrook, *supra* n.12, at 20. Of course, if the fugitive happens to flee to pursuing State territory and is arrested there, the dual criminality requirement no longer applies as extradition itself has become moot. Boister, *supra* n.2, at 297.

[23] Sometimes, States agree in the context of a multilateral treaty to designate a certain act as an extraditable offense under their municipal laws. *E.g.*, Conv. on Combating Bribery of Foreign Public Officials in Int'l Business Transactions, Dec. 18, 1997, art. 10(1), *reprinted in* 37 ILM 1 ("Bribery of a foreign public official shall be deemed to be included as an extraditable offence under the laws of the Parties").

international law.[24] As such, whether or not it appears in a particular treaty, States are obligated to honor the principle as an implicit condition unless expressly (or jointly) waived.[25] Under the conventional rule of dual criminality, to the extent that the two States' laws themselves do not treat the conduct as essentially the equivalent crime[26] – that is, the host State would not treat the conduct at issue the same way the pursuing State would if it had occurred within host State territory[27] – then the dual criminality requirement would not be met and extradition would not be expected to proceed.[28] Likewise, where a pursuing State's law is deemed to be invalid, say, on account of its prohibited retroactive application, dual criminality would not be satisfied.[29]

Traditionally, dual criminality was established by examining whether the extraditable offense at issue was set forth in a bilateral extradition treaty in "list" or "enumerated" form.[30] Under this so-called "objective" or "*in concreto*" approach to dual criminality, the determination turned

[24] Stanbrook & Stanbrook, *supra* n.12, at 19–20; Helen Duffy, The 'War on Terror' and the Framework of International Law 136 & n.321 (2005).

[25] *See* Blakesley, *supra* n.9, at 224 (dual criminality is "always required either by explicit provision or implicitly as part of extradition law in general"); Silvia Borelli, *The Rendition of Terrorist Suspects to the United States: Human Rights and the Limits of Int'l Cooperation*, *in* Enforcing International Law Norms against Terrorism 336 (Andrea Bianchi ed. 2004). As with the case of extraditable offenses, dual criminality rests on the maxim *nulla poena sine lege* with reciprocity the effective guarantor of compliance. Ilias Bantekas & Susan Nash, International Criminal Law 181 (2d ed. 2003).

[26] *E.g., Cotroni v. Attorney-General of Canada*, Sup. Ct., Can., Oct. 23, 1974, [1976] 1 S.C.R. 219, *reprinted in* 69 ILR 218 (1974); *R. v. Governor of Pentonville Prison, ex parte Budlong and Another* [1980] 1 All E.R. 701, [1980] 1 WLR 1110; *In re Tang Yee-Chun*, 674 F. Supp. 1058 (S.D.N.Y. 1987). Notably, dual criminality is not undercut by a fugitive's assertion of an alibi or affirmative defense. *Hu Yau-Leung v. Soscia*, 649 F.2d 914 (2d Cir. 1981).

[27] Stanbrook & Stanbrook, *supra* n.12, at 20; Borelli, *supra* n.25, at 336.

[28] Perhaps more dramatically, a conviction and sentence based on an extradition lacking dual criminality could be vacated. *E.g., United States v. Anderson*, 472 F.3d 662 (9th Cir. 2006).

[29] *E.g., Denmark (Collaboration with the Enemy) Case*, Fed. Sup. Ct., Braz., May 21, 1947, 4 *Boletim da Sociedade Brasileira de Direito Internacional* 128, *reprinted in* 14 Ann. Dig. & Rep. Pub. Int'l L. Cases 146, 146–47 (No. 71) (H. Lauterpacht ed. 1951) [hereinafter *Collaboration with the Enemy Case*] (denying an extradition request, in part, because Denmark's treason law was enacted in June 1945 but was improperly applied to offenses that occurred during German occupation before its enactment).

[30] *See* Michael Abbell, Extradition to and from the United States 64 (2010) (in the United States, until 1970, extradition crimes were defined in a list that grew from only two in the Jay Treaty of 1794 (murder and forgery, *see* n.16 in Chapter 4) to more than thirty by 1970 (in, for example, the Treaty on Extradition, U.S.-N.Z., Jan. 12, 1970, T.I.A.S. 7035, 22 U.S.T. 1).

on the extent to which a one-to-one correspondence could be shown between the States' laws with regard to the denomination and the specific elements of the offense.[31] Where either a crime was not itemized or no such unity could be demonstrated, a State was under no obligation to extradite.[32]

Perhaps not surprisingly, that approach proved to be overly rigid and lost its appeal as definitions for the same crime sometimes diverged or where proof of a crime hinged on a single element.[33] In other cases, it might be unclear whether the nomenclature assigned to a given offense and the underlying conduct at issue corresponded to one another,[34] and the host State would not necessarily be well-positioned to inquire into the substantive criminal law of the pursuing State at issue to confirm equivalency.[35] In addition, as State criminal codes introduce new offenses or revise the definitions of existing ones, executed bilateral extradition treaties could become obsolete in certain respects, and keeping them current would entail frequent and onerous updating.[36]

While the list system can still be found in some older bilateral extradition treaties, beginning in the 1970s, for the most part States adopted

[31] Boister, *supra* n.2, at 297; *e.g.*, Treaty on Extradition, U.S.-Austl., May 14, 1974, art. II, *reprinted in* Igor I. Kavass, 1 Extradition Laws and Treaties: United States (2000 & Supp. 2004); *The State (Furlong) v. Kelly*, Sup. Ct., Ir., [1971] I.R. 132.

[32] Blakesley, *supra* n.9, at 212; David Freestone, *Int'l Cooperation against Terrorism and the Development of Int'l Law Principles of Jurisdiction, in* Terrorism and International Law 46 (Rosalyn Higgins & Maurice Flory eds. 1997); Richard Downing, Recent Development, *The Domestic and Int'l Legal Implications of the Abduction of Criminals from Foreign Soil*, 26 Stan. J. Int'l L. 573, 576 (1989–90); *e.g.*, *Liangsiriprasert v. United States* [1991] 1 A.C. 225 (P.C.), [1990] 2 All E.R. 866, 871 (discussing how the 1922 U.S.-Siam [now Thailand] Extradition Treaty did not contemplate extradition for narcotics offenses); *United States v. Fiocconi*, 462 F.2d 475 (2d Cir. 1972) (the U.S.-Italy Extradition Treaty of 1868, as amended, did not regard the conspiracy to import heroin as a ground for extradition).

[33] *See* Stanbrook & Stanbrook, *supra* n.12, at 22; *e.g.*, *In re Gerber*, Fed. Sup. Ct., F.R.G. Apr. 11, 1957, *reprinted in* 24 ILR 493, 495 (H. Lauterpacht & E. Lauterpacht eds. 1961) ("It is generally recognized both in doctrine and in jurisprudence, that extradition is permissible in cases in which, according to German law, the breaking of the peace of a private home and causing damage to property are merely constituents of the offence of burglary, whereas according to Swiss law they are independent criminal offences").

[34] Stanbrook & Stanbrook, *supra* n.12, at 8.

[35] Bantekas & Nash, *supra* n.25, at 181.

[36] *Id.*; Boister, *supra* n.2, at 298–99 & n.67; Downing, *supra* n.32, at 576. For example, because until the early 1970s U.S. list-based extradition treaties did not include any reference to the crime of *conspiracy* to commit other extraditable offenses and to such inchoate crimes as aiding and abetting or attempt, Abbell, *supra* n.30, at 67–68, all pre-existing U.S. extradition treaties would need to be updated accordingly.

a replacement methodology called the "no-list," "eliminative," or "minimum penalty" approach.[37] This modern substitute removed the objective methodology, dispensing with a set of itemized offenses or the need for identical denominations or definitions of a crime, and introduced a dose of flexibility into the dual criminality calculus by assessing the general comparability of the underlying conduct.[38] This new, "subjective" or "*in abstracto*" approach examines the *character* or *gravamen* of the offense to ensure that, labels and elements notwithstanding, the two States each have laws that criminalized essentially equivalent conduct.[39]

In general, this more functional approach additionally establishes a threshold based on the seriousness or gravity of a crime, most typically by assigning a minimum level of punishment a crime must yield.[40] Most applicable treaties and municipal laws have set as a lower bound a crime that carries a one-year/twelve-month prison sentence;[41] others have set

[37] *See* Blakesley, *supra* n.9, at 212; Stanbrook & Stanbrook, *supra* n.12, at 8; Duffy, *supra* n.24, at 108 & n.187; Abbell, *supra* n.30, at 65–66 (referencing a "straight dual criminality method"). However, some earlier exceptions existed. *See, e.g., Collins v. Loisel*, 259 U.S. 309, 312 (1921) ("The law does not require the name by which the crime is described in the two countries shall be the same; nor that the scope of the liability shall be coextensive, or, in other respects, the same in the two countries. It is enough if the particular act charged is criminal in both jurisdictions."); *Gallina v Fraser*, 177 F. Supp. 856 (D. Conn. 1959) (authorizing extradition of the fugitive based on the gravamen of the offense, not on the denomination of the crime).

[38] Duffy, *supra* n.24, at 108; Treaty on Extradition, U.S.-RSA, Sept. 16, 1999, art. 2(3), 2 U.S.T. 884 [hereinafter U.S.-RSA Extradition Treaty] (noting the irrelevancy for dual criminality purposes whether the offense falls within same category of offences or is denominated by the same terminology); *e.g., United States v. Sensi*, 879 F.2d 888, 893 (D.C. Cir. 1989) (mail fraud under U.K. and U.S. law was deemed close enough to satisfy dual criminality even though under U.K. law one must additionally show that an item was successfully stolen); *In re Russell*, 789 F.2d 801, 804 (9th Cir. 1986) (conspiracy under Australian and U.S. law was regarded as analogous despite the fact that Australian law, unlike U.S. law, did not require an overt act).

[39] Boister, *supra* n.2, at 297; Borelli, *supra* n.25, at 337.

[40] Stanbrook & Stanbrook, *supra* n.12, at 8; Abbell, *supra* n.30, at 68–69.

[41] Abbell, *supra* n.30, at 69 & n.64; *e.g.*, Treaty on Extradition, U.S.-U.K., Mar. 31, 2003 (minimum one-year imprisonment); PRC, Extradition Law, Order of the President No. 42, adopted at the 19th Meeting of the Standing Committee of the Ninth National People's Congress, Dec. 28, 2000, art. 7(2) [PRC Extradition Law] ("punishable by a fixed term of imprisonment for one year or more or by any other heavier criminal penalty"); Framework Decision on the European Arrest Warrant & the Surrender Procedures Between Member States, June 13, 2002, art. 2(1), 2002/584/JHA, OJEC 1–20, L190/1 of July 18, 2002 [hereinafter Framework Decision on the EAW] (warrant issued for acts punishable "by a custodial sentence or a detention order for a maximum period of at least 12 months").

a higher minimum sentence[42] or in certain circumstances abandoned such a threshold altogether.[43] (For those whose extradition has been requested to serve out all or the remainder of an imposed sentence, rather than to face prosecution, a temporal threshold likewise often is set for the length of imprisonment left to be served, typically measured on the order of months.[44]) Key advantages to this approach are that extradition treaties do not require frequent updating,[45] and they embrace a potentially far greater number of extraditable crimes.[46]

Modern State practice with respect to dual criminality possesses other flexible features. Domestic law and the applicable treaty may not require that an inquiry be conducted to examine the partner State's domestic law to verify dual criminality.[47] In addition, States generally permit reformulated charges during bilateral proceedings so long as they also are extraditable crimes and are based on the same underlying facts.[48] Furthermore, States often use multilateral treaty negotiations as an opportunity to bring broader international recognition for specified

[42] *E.g.*, Japan, Law of Extradition, art. 2(3) and (4), Law No. 68 of 1953, *as amended* (requiring an offense for which extradition is requested to be punishable by death, by life imprisonment, or by a maximum term of three years or more by the laws of Japan and by the laws of the pursuing State); Inter-Am. Conv. on Extradition, Feb. 25, 1981, art. 3, OAS T.S. No. 60, *reprinted in* 20 ILM 723 (1981) (penalty must be at least two years).

[43] Most U.S. extradition treaties since 1977 allow for the discretionary extradition of related offenses to one that is extraditable even if the related ones do not meet the minimum sentence term so long as all other requirements for extradition are met. ABBELL, *supra* n.30, at 69; *e.g.*, U.S.-RSA Extradition Treaty, *supra* n.38, art. 2(7).

[44] *See, e.g.*, PRC Extradition Law, *supra* n.41, art. 7(2) ("period of sentence that remains to be served by the person sought is at least six months at the time when the request is made."); Inter-Am. Conv. on Extradition, *supra* n.42, art. 3(3) (at least six months); Sweden, Extradition for Crim. Offences Act (1957:668), Dec. 6, 1957, § 4(1), *as amended* (at least four months); Framework Decision on the EAW, *supra* n.41, art. 2(1) (at least four months).

[45] Boister, *supra* n.2, at 299.

[46] *Id.*

[47] STANBROOK & STANBROOK, *supra* n.12, at 21 n.7 (such an inquiry is not required under U.K. extradition law, except possibly to confirm that a violation of the other State's law calls for a minimum period of imprisonment); *e.g.*, *In re Nielsen* [1984] A.C. 606 (H.L.), *reprinted in* 74 ILR 458.

[48] STANBROOK & STANBROOK, *supra* n.12, at 62; *e.g.*, Ignacio Martinez-Arrieta, *U.S. Seeks Singaporeans Extradition for Export Control Violations with Iran*, 28 IELR 57, 58 (2012) (although the bilateral extradition treaty did not recognize export control violations as an extraditable offense, by reframing the charge as a conspiracy to defraud, the same result could obtain).

crimes,[49] and when States cannot forge a workable international consensus on the meaning of a particular crime, such as "terrorism,"[50] they may choose to rely on surrogate violations of law undertaken incidentally for which clear definitions exist, such as hostage taking, murder, arson, or sabotage.[51]

Moreover, in recent years, some bilateral or multilateral extradition instruments have allowed for the concept's limited or discretionary application,[52] which would allow the host State to grant extradition as

[49] *E.g.*, U.N. Conv. against Corruption, Oct. 31, 2003, art. 16(1), Annex to UNGA Res. 58/4, U.N. Doc. A/58/422 [hereinafter UNCAC].

[50] In 1938, the League of Nations drafted the Convention for the Prevention and Punishment of Terrorism (CPPT), the first treaty that designated terrorism as an international offense. L. of N. Doc. C.546.M.383.1937.V., Nov. 16, 1937, *reprinted in* 19 *O.J.* 23 (1938). Under that Convention, terrorism was defined broadly as "criminal acts directed against a state and intended or calculated to create a state of terror in the minds of particular persons, or a group of persons or the general public," *id.*, art. 1(2), but the Convention never entered into force. Since then, efforts by the United Nations to draft a single broad definition of terrorism acceptable to all States, such as that found in the CPPT, have failed. *See* Theo Vogler, *Perspectives on Extradition and Terrorism, in* International Terrorism and Political Crimes 391–92 (M. Cherif Bassiouni ed. 1975) (no existing convention or internal law mentions "terrorism" as an extraditable offense in large part because of the difficulty distinguishing terrorist acts and political crimes (*political delictum*)). *But see* Framework Decision on the EAW, *supra* n.41, art. 2(2) (treating "terrorism" as a punishable offense as defined by the host State's law). A proposed convention that defines terrorism can be found at Int'l Law Ass'n (ILA), *Draft Single Conv. on the Legal Control of Int'l Terrorism*, ILA Report of the 59th Conference, art. 1(j), at 497–504 (1982). The late Judge and Professor Antonio Cassese concluded that, at least with respect to times of peace (versus armed conflict) "international law defines and regulates international terrorism" by the following five factors: it "(i) is an action normally criminalized in national legal systems; (ii) is transnational in character, i.e., not limited in its action or implications to one country alone; (iii) is carried out for the purpose of coercing a state or international organization to do or refrain from doing something; (iv) uses for this purpose two possible modalities: either spreading terror among civilians or attacking public or eminent private institutions or their representatives; and (v) is not motivated by personal gain but by ideological or political aspirations." Antonio Cassese, *The Multifaceted Criminal Notion of Terrorism in Int'l Law*, 4 J. Int'l Crim. Just. 933, 957 (2006).

[51] Jackson Nyomuya Maogoto, Battling Terrorism: Legal Perspectives on the Use of Force and the War on Terror 58 (2005).

[52] Blakesley, *supra* n.9, at 239 (recent U.S. extradition treaties specifically provide for discretion to extradite in the face of the dual criminality requirement); Cryer, *supra* n.10, at 75 & n.25 (with respect to extradition among Nordic States, dual criminality is not required except regarding extradition of nationals and where political offenses are at issue); *e.g.*, Framework Decision on the EAW, *supra* n.41, art. 2(2) (no verification of dual criminality is required so long as one of the enumerated offenses is punishable by the host State "by a custodial sentence or a detention order for a maximum period of at least three years," as defined by the host State); UNCAC, *supra* n.49, art. 44(2)-(3).

a matter of volition even if the offense charged by a pursuing State were not prosecutable under the host State's own law.[53] At least in the United States (a federal republic), even where dual criminality cannot be established through a federal law or a law in the U.S. state of jurisdiction, dual criminality still can be satisfied if the conduct is generally recognized as criminal throughout the United States if it is found in a majority of state statutes.[54] In at least one State (Argentina), so long as the offense at issue is deemed to be an *international crime*, it automatically satisfies the dual criminality standard.[55]

Modern State practice is not uniform concerning whether justifications (*e.g.*, self-defense) or excuses (*e.g.*, insanity) should be accounted for in determining whether a given offense is punishable. States like Germany and Russia, for example, which maintain an *in concreto* approach, factor in such considerations when determining whether dual criminality has been satisfied, while States like Belgium and Switzerland, for example, which take an *in abstracto* approach, choose to rely on whether the underlying conduct is punishable regardless of such factors.[56] To complicate matters further, some States adopt a variable understanding, in which their approach could depend on which State they are interacting with or whether they are extraditing under the *aut dedere aut judicare* principle (discussed in Chapter 9.c).[57]

Finally, States are splintered with respect to their practice regarding the moment in time when the dual criminality principle is triggered. Some States maintain that the reference point is when the extradition request is made;[58] others hold the reference point to be when the *decision* on the extradition request is issued;[59] while still others believe the reference

[53] *E.g.*, *In re Assarsson*, 687 F.2d 1157, 1163–64 (8th Cir. 1982).

[54] *See* n.65 *infra*.

[55] *The Priebke Extradition Case*, Case No. 16.063/94, Sup. Ct., Arg., Nov. 2, 1995, *summarized in* 1998 Y.B. Int'l Human. Rts. L. 341 (involving the extradition of a German national to Italy where a war crime was held to constitute an international crime).

[56] Eur. Comm. on Crime Problems (CDPC), *Note on Dual Criminality,* in Concreto *or* in Abstracto, PC-OC (2012) 02 Final, May 11, 2012, at 2.

[57] *See* Michael Plachta, *Council of Europe Experts Discuss Double (Dual) Criminality in the Context of Extradition*, 30 IELR 495, 496–97 (citing Georgia in the former instance and Sweden in the latter).

[58] *E.g.*, Treaty on Extradition, Austl.-Ger., Apr. 14, 1987, art. 2(1).

[59] *See* Plachta, *supra* n.57, at 496–97 (citing Sweden and Switzerland in the context of COE Workshop I on the Application of the Double Criminality Principle, held in Strasbourg on May 20, 2014).

point is as early as when the alleged criminal act was committed,[60] or even espouse an undifferentiated approach.[61]

Notwithstanding this flexibility, dual criminality can remain an impediment to extradition for either of two significant reasons. First, some conduct may not satisfy dual criminality as the pursuing and host States do not classify the same or similar conduct as *criminal*. This may be a function of definitional conflicts over a particular type of conduct (such as terrorism);[62] result from a decision by some States to address a particular social ill through reliance on administrative measures versus criminal punishment;[63] arise out of a State's interpretation of a domestic law at variance with its definition as set forth in a multilateral convention;[64] or because some conduct defies a shared perception as to its criminality or seriousness, such as assisted suicide, euthanasia, abortion, homosexuality, adultery, marital rape, or computer hacking.[65]

Along these lines, State legislatures have promulgated specialized criminal laws that simply lack counterparts elsewhere. For example, the

[60] *E.g., R. v Bow Street Metropolitan Magistrate and Others, ex parte Pinochet Ugarte (No. 3)* [2001] 1 A.C. 147 (H.L.), 2 WLR 827, 837 (Lord Browne-Wilkinson); *Hackstetter v. State of Israel*, Sup. Ct. sittng as a Ct. of Crim. App., Isr., Jan. 9, 1972, *reprinted in* 51 ILR 331 (1972).

[61] *See* Plachta, *supra* n.57, at 496 (citing Georgia as taking into account all three reference points).

[62] *See supra* n.50 (definition of terrorism); Vogler, *supra* n.50, at 391 (noting lack of a universally accepted definition of "terrorism").

[63] *See* Boister, *supra* n.2, at 303 & n.97 (citing by way of example differences between the way neighboring Germany and the Netherlands treat the possession and supply of marijuana, thwarting law enforcement cooperation between them on that score).

[64] *See* Robert Kolb, *The Exercise of Criminal Jurisdiction over Int'l Terrorists, in* ENFORCING INTERNATIONAL LAW NORMS AGAINST TERRORISM 270–71 (Andrea Bianchi ed. 2004); *e.g.*, Belgium, The Act of June 16, 1993 Concerning the Punishment of Grave Breaches of the Geneva Convs. of 12 August 1949 and Their Addt'l Prots. I and II of 18 June 1977, *reprinted in O.J.* at 17751–17755, Aug. 5, 1993, *as amended* by the Act of 10 February 1999 (allowing for the prosecution of grave breaches of the Geneva Conventions in the non-international armed conflict (NIAC) context despite the fact that international treaties only recognize the prosecution of grave breaches in *international armed conflicts* (IACs)).

[65] STANBROOK & STANBROOK, *supra* n.12, at 20 & n.3; BLAKESLEY, *supra* n.9, at 225; *e.g.*, Linda Friedman Ramirez & Nicole Mariani, *U.S. Magistrate Denies Extradition to Ireland for Role in Assisted Suicide*, 24 IELR 88, 88–89 (2008) (in October 2007, a federal magistrate from a West Virginia court denied an Irish extradition request for George David Exoo pursuant to the 1983 U.S.-Ireland Extradition Treaty for assisted suicide on the ground that no such conduct was criminalized by federal law, by West Virginia state law, or by a *majority* of state jurisdictions (only twenty-five of fifty; therefore, one short) to reflect general recognition within the United States).

United States over the years has had many requests for extradition rejected involving such offenses as wire or mail fraud,[66] perjury unconnected to a judicial proceeding,[67] obstruction of justice,[68] continuing criminal enterprise (CCE),[69] violations under the Racketeer Influenced and Corrupt Organizations (RICO) Act,[70] the use of a telephone to facilitate the commission of a drug felony,[71] desertion of a naval vessel,[72] and assault on a federal agent.[73] By way of illustration, in March 2008, the Appellate Commission of the U.K. House of Lords denied extradition to the United States of Ian Norris for conspiring to fix prices in the U.S. carbon industry because the United Kingdom did not recognize, as the United States did, participation in a cartel alone (absent aggravating factors) as a crime under either its statutory or common law.[74]

Second, in addition to establishing dual criminality with respect to the offense itself, the pursuing and host States also may need to mutually recognize the jurisdictional basis for the charged conduct, known as "special use" of dual criminality.[75] This principle could surface where

[66] *E.g., In re Lamar* Alberta Sup. Ct., [1940] 1 D.L.R. 701, 706-07 (no wire or mail fraud equivalent recognized under Canadian law); *Sensi*, 879 F.2d 888 (mail fraud unaccompanied by theft rendered it non-extraditable). To remove this obstacle, U.S. extradition treaties sometimes expressly indicate that proof of use of mails or interstate transportation, whose purpose is to establish federal jurisdiction, should not be a factor in determining whether dual criminality exists. *E.g.*, Treaty on Extradition, U.S.-Jam., June 14, 1983, S. Treaty Doc. No. 98–18 (1984), art. 2(3)(b).

[67] *E.g., Eisler v. United States*, 170 F.2d 273 (D.C. Cir. 1948) (Britain refused extradition to the United States because perjury was only cognizable as a crime in Britain when committed in the course of judicial proceedings).

[68] *E.g., United States v. Kashoggi*, 717 F. Supp. 1048 (S.D.N.Y. 1989) (Switzerland refused to extradite the subject for obstruction of justice, but agreed to extradite under other offenses).

[69] Colombian drug traffickers have challenged extradition on the ground that the CCE is uniquely American, but U.S. courts have shown some leeway to prosecutors on this score. Boister, *supra* n.2, at 297 n.61; *e.g., United States v. Lehder-Rivas*, 668 F. Supp. 1523 (M.D. Fla. 1987).

[70] In an instance where a foreign court allowed the extradition of a fugitive to the United States under the RICO Act, *see Sudar v. United States*, [1981] 25 S.C.R. (3d) 183 (finding the dual criminality requirement was satisfied on account of the fact that the underlying conduct charged under the RICO Act involved murder, arson, and extortion, which were recognized as crimes in Canada).

[71] *E.g., United States v. Khan*, 993 F.2d 1368, 1372–73 (9th Cir. 1993).

[72] Downing, *supra* n.32, at 576.

[73] *Id.*

[74] Bruce Zagaris, *U.K. National Wins Partial Victory in Resisting U.S. Extradition Request*, 24 IELR 175 (2008).

[75] Heymann & Gershengorn, *supra* n.3, at 137–38; U.N. Model Extradition Treaty, *supra* n.20, art. 4(e) (citing as an optional ground for refusing extradition where "the offence for which extradition is requested has been committed outside the territory of either Party

the host State does not recognize, say, the passive personality principle as a ground for extraterritorial jurisdiction, where a pursuing State laid a jurisdictional claim to a fugitive on the sole basis that he had criminally wronged a pursuing State national.[76] For example, in 1985, a U.S. judge denied France's extradition request on a narcotics conspiracy charge, despite both States having criminalized such conduct, where the United States did not find that France had sufficient territorial basis to claim subject matter jurisdiction as the fugitive "neither conspired with anyone in France nor performed any overt acts in France. There is absolutely no evidence to demonstrate that [he] intended to cause any detrimental effects in France. Under these circumstances it would be clearly unreasonable for a court in this country to exercise jurisdiction over [him]."[77] In recent years, however, application of the "special use" rule appears to be receding.[78]

iii Specified Offense Exclusions (Political, Military, Fiscal)

This sub-section addresses three types of offenses – political, military, and fiscal[79] – that may be singled out for exclusionary treatment, and when recognized as such, extradition is generally denied. Of these, the

and the law of the requested State does not provide for jurisdiction over such an offence committed outside its territory in comparable circumstances.").

[76] In 1977, France justified its refusal to extradite to either West Germany or Israel Abu Daoud, who allegedly participated in the massacre of Israeli athletes during the 1972 Munich Olympics, on the grounds that at the time French law did not regard this conduct as a crime, even if French nationals had been the victims, as France did not amend its Penal Code to recognize passive personality jurisdiction until 1975 and the court was unwilling to apply that new basis for jurisdiction retroactively. Sidney Liskofsky, *The Abu Daoud Case: Law or Politics*, 7 Isr. Y.B. Hum. Rts. 66 (1977) (discussing the ruling of the *Chambre d'Accusation* of the Paris Ct. of App., including its twenty-minute hearing only four days after the accused had been arrested, and the decision to release him to Algeria where he was received as a hero).

[77] *Repub. of France v. Moghadam*, 617 F. Supp. 777, 788 (N.D. Cal. 1985). Similarly, under U.K. legislation, an extradition to a Category 1 or Category 2 territory can be barred where a "significant part of the conduct alleged to constitute the extradition offence is conduct in the United Kingdom," and in light of the circumstances, the "interests of justice" would so dictate. U.K. Extradition Act 2003, Nov. 20, 2003, §§ 19B & 83A, *available at* www.legislation.gov.uk/ukpga/2003/41/contents (last visited on May 6, 2016).

[78] Boister, *supra* n.2, at 298 & n.66 (citing the need to suppress transnational crime).

[79] Historically, a *religious* offense exclusion was at times also recognized. *E.g.*, Montevideo Conv. on Extradition, Dec. 26, 1933, art. 3(f), 49 Stat. 3111, *reprinted in* 28 AJIL 65 (1934).

political offenses exclusion has been the most controversial and litigated.[80]

Political Offenses. A standard provision found in municipal extradition statutes as well as in bilateral and multilateral extradition treaties[81] (albeit spanning varied interpretations and qualified by specified exceptions discussed *infra*) is the exclusion for "political offenses" – *i.e.*, conduct consisting directly or indirectly of a political character.[82] This exclusion (sometimes referred to as an "exception") is focused on the political nature of the *offense*, rather than on the political motivations for the capture, or any expected politically prejudicial treatment, by a pursuing State of a political dissident, anti-government activist, or secessionist.[83] (These latter concerns are treated as a human rights law matter and are addressed in Chapter 7.e.)

Despite its frequent usage, the political offense exclusion has yet to assume customary international law status or to emerge as a general principle of international law,[84] but rather operates as

[80] It has been observed that, despite all the significant change in extradition law and practice over the past century, three trends remain constant from debates held in this field dating to 1880: "the appropriateness of the nationality defence," "the application of the 'rule' of non-inquiry," *and a still sharp divide on the "political offenses exception."* Nicholas Kasirer, *Defenses, Exceptions and Exemptions to Extradition*, 62 INT'L REV. PENAL L. 91, 91–92 (1991) (emphasis supplied).

[81] *See* M. Cherif Bassiouni, *The Political Offense Exception in Extradition Law and Practice, in* INTERNATIONAL TERRORISM AND POLITICAL CRIMES 399 (M. Cherif Bassiouni ed. 1975) [hereinafter Bassiouni, *Political Offense Exception*]; D. Cameron Findlay, *Abducting Terrorists Overseas for Trial in the United States: Issues of Int'l and Domestic Law*, 23 TEX. INT'L L.J. 1, 11 (1988) ("nearly all" bilateral and international conventions contain this exception). As Sir Hersch Lauterpacht observed more than seventy years ago: "in the legislation of modern states there are few principles so universally adopted as that of non-extradition of political offenders." Hersch Lauterpacht, *Laws of Nations and the Punishment of War Crimes*, 21 B.Y.B.I.L. 58, 88 (1944). *E.g.*, U.N. Model Extradition Treaty, *supra* n.20, art. 3(a); Dominica, Extradition Act, Act 6 of 1981, Feb. 19, 1981, art. 7(1) (no extradition permitted if the alleged crime is of a political character).

[82] The "indirect" reference protects from extradition persons who support an act, whether they are aware or unaware of its underlying political purpose or nature. ABBELL, *supra* n.30, at 117–18. This concept is discussed *infra*.

[83] *See, e.g.*, Bruce Zagaris, *English Court Denies Russian Extradition Request for Chechen Official*, 20 IELR 12 (2004) (discussing the United Kingdom's refusal in November 2003 to extradite Akhmed Zakayev, a Chechen rebel leader, to Russia to face charges of false imprisonment and murder, among others, partly on the ground that the prosecution was viewed as politically motivated).

[84] *See* Aimée J. Buckland, *Offending Officials: Former Gov't Actors and the Political Offense Exception to Extradition*, 94 CAL. L. REV. 423, 440 n.121 (2006) (noting that former Soviet bloc States do not include this provision in their extradition treaties); STANBROOK &

a "reservation"[85] that can be invoked to deny extradition. As the exclusion suffers from a lack of an agreed definition, its provisions are typically generic (leaving it to courts to sort out its meaning based on the pertinent facts as evaluated against their national laws and policies), and while substantially similar, many legal authorities contain express caveats or limitations to ensure that it does not become over-inclusive.[86] This exclusion is particularly relevant with respect to alleged acts of terrorism, as such offenses are frequently claimed to be politically motivated,[87] and sometimes the exclusion thwarts extraditions even between close allies with shared political systems and jurisprudential traditions.[88]

STANBROOK, *supra* n.12, at 65 n.1 (this provision is less a general principle of international law and more an exception to the general treaty obligation to extradite).

[85] R. Stuart Phillips, *The Political Offence Exception and Terrorism: Its Place in the Current Extradition Scheme and Proposal for Its Future*, 15 DICKINSON J. INT'L L. 337, 340 n.25 (1997) (noting that, as a technical matter, the political offense exclusion is a "reservation," as the detainee bears the evidentiary burden of bringing himself within its protective embrace); STANBROOK & STANBROOK, *supra* n.12, at 65 n.1 (describing it as "a reservation of the freedom which absent a treaty the territorial sovereign would in any case be able to exercise"). The use of the term "reservation" in this context is not to be confused with its distinctive meaning under the Vienna Conv. on the Law of Treaties (VCLT), May 23, 1969, arts. 19–23, 1155 U.N.T.S. 332, *reprinted in* 8 ILM 679.

[86] Stipulated exceptions can be found, by way of example, in the following conventions and domestic laws: Eur. Conv. on Extradition, Dec. 13, 1957, art. 3(3), E.T.S. No. 24 (excluding from political offense coverage the assassination or attempted assassination of a head of State or a member of his family); U.N. Model Extradition Treaty, *supra* n.20, art. 3 & n.8 (allowing for discretionary exclusions, including for "serious offences involving an act of violence against the life, physical integrity or liberty of a person"); Canada Extradition Act, *supra* n.6, § 46(2) (excluding murder or manslaughter; inflicting serious bodily harm; sexual assault; kidnapping, abduction, hostage-taking or extortion; using explosives, incendiaries, devices or substances in circumstances in which human life is likely to be endangered or serious bodily harm or substantial property damage is likely to be caused; and an attempt or conspiracy to engage in, counselling, aiding or abetting another person to engage in, or being an accessory after the fact in relation to, the conduct above).

[87] Boister, *supra* n.2, at 300 & n.79; *e.g.*, "Arabs Negotiate Over 5 Hijackers," *N.Y. Times*, Dec. 23, 1973, at 3 (in December 1973, Arab militants attacked a Pan Am airliner at the Rome airport, killing thirty-two persons, then hijacked a Lufthansa plane and flew to Athens, where they demanded the release of two Palestinians imprisoned there, and finally flew to Kuwait. Despite extradition requests from Italy, Morocco, West Germany, and the United States, Kuwait refused to turn over the militants to any of the pursuing States, treating the underlying acts as having a "political character," and instead transferred them to the Arab Liberation Movement).

[88] *See, e.g.*, Boister, *supra* n.2, at 300 & n.75 (citing as an example the U.S. refusal to extradite to the U.K. Irish Republican Army (IRA) individuals believed to have participated in terrorist acts in Northern Ireland).

The political offense exclusion emerged largely as a by-product of the American and French Revolutions and democratic movements and popular political uprisings of the nineteenth century that sought to bring down monarchies and oppressive rulers.[89] With these winds of change, extradition law, which until then had been largely focused on securing the custody of political and religious dissidents and military deserters,[90] came to recognize that such individuals had a right to actively pursue political change, even if some laws might be broken incidentally.[91] After all, many of the new liberal democracies of the 1800s had themselves only recently acquired power through rebellious conduct.[92] Correspondingly, the law needed to protect such individuals from States that, it was feared, sought their return to prosecute or punish them – and worse, possibly under unfair or discriminatory circumstances – specifically for their anti-government actions.[93]

In 1833, Belgium became the first State to introduce the political offense exclusion into its national law;[94] the same year, Belgium and France executed an extradition treaty that contained a "political offenses" provision;[95] by the end of the nineteenth century the notion had become widespread.[96] Significantly, the political offense exclusion preserves the independent right of States to grant asylum[97] for perceived political

[89] *See* Phillips, *supra* n.85, at 340 (these revolutionary ideas curried sympathy with its protagonists and the exclusion was intended to protect them from retribution); Findlay, *supra* n.81, at 11; Bassiouni, *Political Offense Exception, supra* n.81, at 400.

[90] *See* pp. 131–32 in Chapter 4.

[91] *See Quinn v Robinson*, 783 F.2d 776, 793 (9th Cir. 1986), *cert. denied*, 479 U.S. 882 (1986); Stanbrook & Stanbrook, *supra* n.12, at 66 (noting that legal violations went hand-in-hand with standing up to tyranny and it seemed unfair to return those seeking political freedom to their oppressors); Duffy, *supra* n.24, at 109; Yvonne G. Grassie, Note, *Federally Sponsored Int'l Kidnapping: An Acceptable Alternative to Extradition?*, 64 Wash. U.L.Q. 1205, 1207 (1986).

[92] Phillips, *supra* n.85, at 341 & n.34 (singling out Russia as the exception, which punished political offenders with death).

[93] Duffy, *supra* n.24, at 109–10; Colm Campbell, *Extradition to Northern Ireland: Prospects and Problems*, 52 Mod. L. Rev. 585, 586–87 (1989).

[94] Phillips, *supra* n.85, at 340 (Belgian Extradition Act of 1833).

[95] Stanbrook & Stanbrook, *supra* n.12, at 66 (the treaty language referred to a "political offense or an offense connected with a political offense").

[96] Bassiouni, *Political Offense Exception, supra* n.81, at 398–99.

[97] "Asylum accorded by a State to persons in its territory is generally referred to as territorial asylum. Asylum accorded in other places, most notably on the premises of an embassy or a legation, is referred to as extraterritorial or, more particularly, diplomatic asylum." Atle Grahl-Madsen, *Territorial Asylum, in* 1 Encyclopedia of Public International Law 283–84 (Rudolf Bernhardt ed. 1992). An example of the "diplomatic" variety occurred in May 2002 when three North Koreans entered the U.S. consulate in Shenyang, PRC,

oppression (*see* Chapter 6.c),[98] keeps States from interfering in others' domestic political struggles via extradition,[99] and affords States broad discretion over such potentially sensitive matters.[100]

Political offenses essentially come in three varieties: (i) pure, (ii) relative, and (iii) indirect. The *pure* form consists of those prototypical political acts, including treason, sedition, subversion, espionage, and conspiracy to overthrow the government, which are directed exclusively at the State, typically do not entail physical violence or the commission of a common crime, and leave private interests unaffected.[101] Such acts might involve, for example, delivering protest speeches, printing and disseminating subversive pamphlets, and surveilling government operations. Although exceptions exist (especially with a crime like espionage[102]), there is broad international consensus that such pure offenses fall squarely within the exclusion and therefore should not be subject to extradition.[103]

Consistent with this view, the Brazil Supreme Court denied an extradition request from Denmark for Danish nationals who allegedly supplied German occupation forces during World War II with "used and new machines and boats," partly on the grounds that "[t]he crime of assisting the enemy in time of war is a political one *lato sensu* [in a broad,

seeking asylum. Elisabeth Rosenthal, "North Korean Migrants Pull U.S. into a Diplomatic Mess," *N.Y. Times*, May 12, 2002, at 4. Another example occurred when Ecuador granted Wikileaks founder Julian Assange diplomatic asylee status in its embassy in London while he was the subject of an extradition request by Sweden regarding sexual molestation-related charges. Bruce Zagaris, *Ecuador Grants Asylum to Assange*, 28 IELR 403, 403–05 (2012).

98 *See* Bantekas & Nash, *supra* n.25, at 186; Stanbrook & Stanbrook, *supra* n.12, at 7; *id.* at 83 (citing the example of an Italian court granting asylum to the murderer of King Alexander I of Yugoslavia in Marseilles in 1934). "It is possible for a person to have been declared as non-extraditable on the basis of the 'political offense exception' and to thereafter seek asylum. The latter may or may not be granted. The two determinations are made in different legal processes using different legal standards and having different review processes and standards." M. Cherif Bassiouni, International Extradition: United States Law and Practice 180 (6th ed. 2014).

99 Duffy, *supra* n.24, at 110; Bantekas & Nash, *supra* n.25, at 186; Campbell, *supra* n.93, at 586–87; *e.g.*, *Quinn*, 783 F.2d at 792–93.

100 Stanbrook & Stanbrook, *supra* n.12, at 67.

101 Phillips, *supra* n.85, at 342 & n.42; Grassie, *supra* n.91, at 1207; Stanbrook & Stanbrook, *supra* n.12, at 69–70; Bassiouni, *Political Offense Exception, supra* n.81, at 405–07.

102 Bassiouni, *Political Offense Exception, supra* n.81, at 406–07 (noting varying interpretations).

103 Phillips, *supra* n.85, at 342.

as opposed to, strict sense] because it is a crime against the State in its supreme function, namely its external defence and its sovereignty."[104]

A *relative* political offense, by contrast, assumes a hybrid character, consisting of an act driven by a political agenda or occurring within a political context *and* one that manifests at least in part as a common crime affecting private interests.[105] The hijacking of a commercial aircraft or the bombing of a popular hotel to cast greater international attention on the plight of a disenfranchised people illustrates this variant.

Finally, the *indirect* form (or *delite connexe*[106]) of a political offense consists of a common crime not committed against the prevailing political order itself, but rather in connection with or in support of an act that itself constitutes a political offense. This can be exemplified where a person steals or lends money to help another afford a truck that would be driven into an embassy compound to protest that government's policies.[107]

Whether political offenses, particularly the relative ones, are treated as exclusion-eligible turns largely on which of several judicial tests is applied to determine which offenses warrant protection for their political significance.[108] The three major tests are: (i) the "political incidence" (or "political disturbance") test, (ii) the "injured rights" test, and (iii) the "predominant motive" (or "mixed Continental") test.

The United States and the United Kingdom are most closely associated with the first of these, the political incidence test,[109] which purports to

[104] *Collaboration with the Enemy Case, supra* n.29, 14 Ann. Dig. & Rep. Pub. Int'l L. Cases at 146–47.

[105] Grassie, *supra* n.91, at 1208; Phillips, *supra* n.85, at 342–43; Bassiouni, *Political Offense Exception, supra* n.81, at 408.

[106] Vogler, *supra* n.50, at 393.

[107] *Id.; e.g., Bourke v. Attorney General* Sup. Ct., Ir., [1972] I.R. 36, [1973] I.L.T.R. 33 (accepting petitioner's argument that he, a non-Communist, but who purely out of friendship assisted fellow inmate George Blake, a Soviet spy, escape from a British prison, should be subject to the political offense exclusion and therefore not be extradited back to the United Kingdom on the basis that his offense was connected to Blake's "political offense" of espionage).

[108] Another key factor turns out to be domestic political or foreign relations pressures, which can trigger invocation of the political offense exclusion, possibly on pretextual grounds. *See* Heymann & Gershengorn, *supra* n.3, at 139; Abraham D. Sofaer, *The Political Offense Exception and Terrorism*, 15 Denv. J. Int'l L. & Pol'y 125, 128–29 (1986).

[109] Buckland, *supra* n.84, at 441 (noting it is also referred to as the Anglo-American "incidence" test); Bassiouni, *Political Offense Exception, supra* n.81, at 414–15 (observing that many Latin American countries also subscribe to this approach).

examine the extent to which: (i) a criminal act was committed by a member of a group that was part of a "temporally and spatially limited"[110] political conflict, uprising, or disturbance "related to the struggle of individuals to alter or abolish the existing government in their country"[111] or to seek political asylum from governmental oppression,[112] and (ii) the act itself was incidental to or in furtherance of that conflict.[113]

Under this test, extradition is typically denied when the act – even including for such heinous crimes as murder[114] and terrorism[115] – was undertaken in some measure while directly engaged in, or as part of, a political struggle.[116] The exclusion generally has not been applied,

110 *Quinn*, 783 F.2d at 817.

111 *Id.* Notably, anarchist crimes are not covered. *See, e.g., In re Meunier* [1894] 2 QB 415, 419 (granting extradition to France of an anarchist accused of detonating a bomb that killed two persons; the court reasoned that "there must be two or more parties in the state, each seeking to impose the Government of their own choice on the other," but anarchists did not have a party and advocated the *absence* of government); Treaty on Extradition, U.S.-Braz., Jan. 13, 1961, art. V(6)(b), 15 U.S.T. 2093, T.I.A.S. No. 5691 (exempting from political offense exclusion "[c]riminal acts which constitute clear manifestations of anarchism or envisage the overthrow of the bases of all political organizations").

112 *E.g., R. v. Governor of Brixton Prison, ex parte Kolczynski* [1955] 2 QB 540, 1 All E.R. 31, *reprinted in* 21 ILR 240 (1954) (finding seven Polish nationals entitled to be released from custody on the basis of the political offense exclusion where they had overpowered the captain and other crew members on a Polish fishing trawler in the North Sea and brought the vessel to an English port for the purpose of seeking political asylum in England).

113 Manuel R. Garcia-Mora, *Crimes Against Humanity and the Principle of Nonextradition of Political Offenders*, 62 Mich. L. Rev. 927 (1964); *Van Duc Vo v. Benov*, 447 F.3d 1235 (9th Cir. 2006).

114 In the British case establishing this legal test, England denied extradition to Switzerland of Angelo Castioni on a charge of murdering a member of the State Council of a Swiss canton. *In re Castioni*, 1 QB 149, 166 (1890).

115 U.S. courts have famously refused to extradite IRA terrorists to the United Kingdom on political offense grounds. *E.g., In re Mackin*, 80 Cr.Misc. 1, 1988 U.S. Dist. LEXIS 7201 (S.D.N.Y. Aug. 13, 1981), *appeal dismissed*, 668 F.2d 122 (2d Cir. 1981); *McMullen v. I.N.S.*, 658 F.2d 1312 (9th Cir. 1981), *review denied*, 788 F.2d 591 (9th Cir. 1986); *In re Doherty*, 599 F. Supp. 270 (S.D.N.Y. 1984), *aff'd*, 786 F.2d 491 (2d Cir. 1986). This impediment was pointedly addressed in a Supplemental Treaty between the United States and the United Kingdom, "by excluding from the scope of the political offense exception serious offenses typically committed by terrorists, e.g., aircraft hijacking and sabotage, crimes against diplomats, hostage taking, and other heinous crimes such as murder, manslaughter, malicious assault, and certain serious offenses involving firearms, explosives, and damage to property." *Letters of Transmittal to the U.S. Senate*, United Kingdom-United States: Extradition Treaty Supplement Limiting Scope of Political Offenses to Exclude Acts of Terrorism, June 25, 1985, *reprinted in* 24 ILM 1104 (1985).

116 The concept is flexible as it can be applied even when the offense and its political character are arguably attenuated. *E.g., United States v. Pitawanakwat*, 120 F. Supp.2d

however, in cases involving acts committed at a time of revolution but undertaken outside the specific context of that struggle,[117] or when the acts were not directed against the State, but against a political party in a time of peace.[118]

Recent application of this test has not always been consistent, as evidenced by the varying perspectives adopted by U.S. courts. The U.S. Court of Appeals for the Seventh Circuit and the U.S. District Court for the Southern District of New York (S.D.N.Y.), for example, have ruled that acts indiscriminately targeting civilians cannot be "political" (as the conduct must be directed against the State), while the U.S. Court of Appeals for the Ninth Circuit disagreed.[119] The Seventh Circuit has taken a narrow view that the political uprising must be limited to traditional military insurrections, a position rejected by the S.D.N.Y., while the Ninth Circuit has insisted that the uprising be undertaken by a group on its own land against its own government (as opposed to, say, suppressing terrorist operations abroad).[120] It is generally agreed, however, that, while under this test

921, 931, 938 (D. Or. 2000) (denying extradition on political offense grounds for the crimes of illegal weapons possession and endangering lives by discharging a weapon because the accused was initially involved as part of a broader protest aimed at the Canadian Government in support of sovereignty by native peoples).

117 *E.g.*, *Ornelas v. Ruiz*, 161 U.S. 502 (1896) (in the only U.S. Supreme Court case to date to address the political offense exclusion, extradition to Mexico was authorized of Mexican bandits who had raided a Mexican border town during a time of revolutionary activity because they were not engaged in combat with Mexican Governmental forces when the raid occurred).

118 *E.g.*, *In re Campora*, Sup. Ct., Chile, Sept. 24, 1957, *reprinted in* 25 ILR 518 (1957) (allowing the extradition to Argentina of Guillermo Patricio Kelly and others for murder, robbery, and other offenses in connection with a raid perpetrated on a local Communist Party headquarters in Buenos Aires, rather than on the Government of Argentina itself, and that took place during a time of tranquility).

119 *Compare Eain v. Wilkes*, 641 F.2d 504 (7th Cir. 1981) (not applying the political offense exclusion in the context of a PLO bombing in a crowded Israeli market that was not aimed at overthrowing a government), *cert. denied*, 454 U.S. 894 (1981), *and Ahmad v. Wigen*, 726 F. Supp. 389 (S.D.N.Y. 1989) (granting the extradition of a Palestinian who firebombed a civilian bus as IHL prohibits violence directed at civilians), *aff'd*, 910 F.2d 1063 (2d Cir.), *stay denied*, 111 S. Ct. 23 (1990), *with Quinn*, 783 F.2d 776 (9th Cir.) (although ruling in favor of extradition, pronouncing that civilian bombing tactics aside, the fact that insurgents are trying to change their government is what matters, so politically legitimate) (*dicta*).

120 *Compare Eain*, 641 F.2d at 519 (7th Cir.) (casting doubt on the existence of political conflict between the PLO and Israel as there were no "ongoing battles between contending armies" and the PLO is "dispersed in nature") *with Doherty*, 599 F. Supp. at 275 (S.D.N.Y.) (rejecting "the notion that the political offense exception is limited to actual armed insurrections of more traditional and overt military hostilities.") *with Quinn*, 783 F.2d at 813 (9th Cir.) ("the word 'uprising' means exactly that: it refers to a people *rising up*, in

a court may occasionally consider the political motivation behind the *act*, it cannot be the primary or sole factor.[121] In addition, the U.S. Congress has carved out a number of exceptions to the political offense exclusion.[122]

The second approach, known as the "injured rights" test, originated in French courts and maintains that political offenses are those that must directly harm the rights of a State's political organization, regardless of any underlying political agenda or motive.[123] Accordingly, where a crime adversely impacts only private, commercial, or minority political party interests, or where an individual commits an otherwise common crime but claims it was undertaken pursuant to a political objective, such offenses would *not* qualify as an exclusion to extradition under this test. For example, when German national Richard Eckermann had a suspected spy killed who was trying to join a secret, anti-Communist organization in Germany called the Black Army, and there was no detriment to the State government itself and the act was not aimed at changing the government,

their own land, against the government of that land. It does not cover terrorism or other criminal conduct exported to other locations.") (emphasis in original).

121 *Eain*, 641 F.2d at 504; *Quinn*, 783 F.2d 776; *In re Gonzalez*, 217 F. Supp. 717 (S.D.N.Y. 1963) (noting that courts occasionally look at the intentions of alleged perpetrators).

122 *See* ABBELL, *supra* n.30, at 120–23 & n.352 (referencing such exceptions as "murder or attempted murder of a Head of State or member of his family," "offenses for which the U.S. has an obligation to prosecute or grant extradition pursuant to a multilateral convention," "specifically listed offenses and types of offenses: murder, unlawful detention, kidnapping, etc.," and "offenses specifically prohibited from consideration as political offenses by multilateral convention").

123 *See In re Gatti*, Ct. of App. of Grenoble, Fr., (Chambre des Mises en Accusation), Jan. 13, 1947, *reprinted in* [1947] 14 ANN. DIG. & REP. PUB. INT'L CASES 145, 145–46 (No. 70) (H. Lauterpacht ed. 1951) ("In brief, what distinguishes the political crime from the common crime is the fact that the former only affects the political organisation of the state, the proper rights of the state, while the latter exclusively affects rights other than those of the state. The fact that the reasons of sentiment which prompted the offender to commit the offence belong to the realm of politics does not itself create a political offence. *The offence does not derive its political character from the motive of the offender but from the nature of the rights it injures.*") (emphasis supplied) (granting extradition to the Republic of San Marino for one of its nationals who tried to murder a member of a Communist cell); *In re Colman*, Ct. of App. of Paris, Fr. (Chambre des Mises en Accusation), Dec. 5, 1947, *reprinted in* [1947] 14 ANN. DIG. & REP. PUB. INT'L CASES 139 (No. 67) (H. Lauterpacht ed. 1951) ("[I]n a country occupied by the enemy (in time of war), collaboration with the latter excludes the idea of a criminal action against the political organization of the state which characterizes the political offense.") (permitting extradition to Belgium for crimes of collaboration with the enemy, including assassination). Belgian courts have taken this standard a step further and held categorically that actions that endanger innocent people who are not involved in the political conflict do not qualify as political crimes. Phillips, *supra* n.85, at 348 n.100.

the Supreme Court of Justice of Guatemala ruled that the political offense exclusion was not satisfied and extradited him.[124]

The third approach, known by several labels, including the "political predominance" and "predominant motive" test,[125] was developed by Swiss courts[126] and subsequently has been adopted by most continental European States, including France,[127] and evidently such East Asian States as Thailand and South Korea.[128] The thrust of this largely discretionary-based test is to assess the comparative weight of the political and criminal aspects of the offense.[129]

Courts applying this test essentially examine three factors: (i) whether the act was politically driven, (ii) whether the act and political ends were proximately related, and (iii) whether the political dimension of the act predominates over, or is proportionally greater compared with, its common crime dimension.[130] The test also considers whether the means

124 Bassiouni, *Political Offense Exception, supra* n.81, at 406.

125 Findlay, *supra* n.81, at 12–13 (labeling it the "predominance test"); Phillips, *supra* n.85, at 346 (referring to the "predominant motive" test).

126 Bassiouni, *Political Offense Exception, supra* n.81, at 423–24; *e.g., In re Vogt*, Trib. Féd. Suisse, Jan. 26, 1924, *reprinted in* 2 ILR 285 (1933); *In re Kaphengst*, Trib. Féd. Suisse, Oct. 17, 1930, *reprinted in* 5 Ann. Dig. Pub. Int'l L. Cases 292 (H. Lauterpacht ed. 1935); *In re Ockert*, Trib. Féd. Suisse, Oct 20, 1933, *reprinted in* 7 Ann. Dig. & Rep. Int'l Law Cases 369 [1933–1934] (H. Lauterpacht ed.) (1940) (political offenses were defined as "those acts which have the character of an ordinary crime appearing on the list of the extraditable offenses, but which, because of the attendant circumstances, in particular because of the motive and the object, are of a predominantly political complexion").

127 Phillips, *supra* n.85, at 348.

128 *See* AP, "Thailand Not to Extradite Vietnamese Dissident," *Pravda* (Eng. version), Apr. 3, 2007 (discussing Thai Appeals Court decision not to extradite Vietnamese dissident Ly Tong, a veteran of the South Vietnamese Air Force, on political offense grounds where he had violated Vietnam's airspace by hijacking a twin-engine airplane and dropping 50,000 anti-Communist leaflets over Ho Chi Minh City); Choe Sang-Hun, "South Korean Court Rejects Extradition in Attack on Shrine," *N.Y. Times*, Jan. 4, 2012, at A6 (when a South Korean court opposed the extradition to Japan of Chinese national Lui Qiang who, in November 2012, had thrown a gasoline bomb at the Japanese Yasukuni Shrine in Seoul to protest the Japanese Government's refusal to apologize and compensate for wrongs committed against women sexual slaves during World War II, the thrust of the rationale for that ruling stemmed from the principle of not extraditing political prisoners).

129 Bassiouni, *Political Offense Exception, supra* n.81, at 409, 411–12; Blakesley, *supra* n.9, at 266.

130 *See* Bassiouni, *Political Offense Exception, supra* n.81, at 424 (citing *In re V.P. Wassilief*, Trib. Féd. Suisse, July 13, 1908 (unreported)) (extraditing individual who had murdered a local police chief at the behest of the Russian Revolutionary Socialist Party trying to overthrow the Czar); *e.g., In re Kavic, Bjelanovic & Arsenijevic*, Trib. Féd. Suisse, Apr. 30, 1952, *reprinted in* 19 ILR 371 (1957) (No. 80) (denying Yugoslavia's extradition request on political offense exclusion grounds where three Yugoslav nationals, while serving as crew members on a civilian aircraft restrained persons, endangered the safety of those on board

were disproportionate to the ends sought; in such cases the political offense exclusion is often deemed void.[131] Thus, courts tend to reject the political offense exclusion where there is a taking of life and/or a more efficient alternative means was available to achieve the political objective sought.[132]

Despite the fact that in principle all official actions taken by *current or former government officials* while in power are or were political in nature, such conduct only rarely qualifies in practice for the political offense exception, including with respect to cases of electoral fraud and political corruption.[133] This logic lies primarily with: (i) their lack of an historic claim to the exclusion, which was fundamentally intended to benefit insurgents and dissidents outside the government against unfair or oppressive rule; (ii) the need to hold such individuals accountable for their offenses while representing, presumably in good faith, the people and their interests; and (iii) their access to other forms of protection, such as political asylum, petitioning for a stay, *non-refoulement*,[134] and reliance on non-discrimination provisions.[135]

and wrongfully appropriated property in order to divert the aircraft to Switzerland to seek political asylum).

131 Stanbrook & Stanbrook, *supra* n.12, at 77 (where pursue political ends but indiscriminately then exclusion not applied); Vogler, *supra* n.50, at 393–94 (means versus ends must be evaluated); *e.g.*, *Ktir v. Ministère Public Fédéral*, Trib. Féd. Suisse, 1961, *reprinted in* 34 ILR 143 (the means employed must be the only means available to accomplish the end pursued).

132 *See, e.g.*, *In re Peruzov*, Trib. Féd. Suisse, 1951, *reprinted in* 18 ILR 38 (the murder of a fascist in Italy in December 1945 long after hostilities had ceased was not subject to the political offense exclusion because the means used were not considered proportional to the end sought, namely, the suppression of fascism). *But see In re Holder and Kerkow*, Ct. of App. of Paris, Fr., Apr. 14, 1975 (unreported), *reprinted in* 1975 Dig. U.S. Prac. Int'l L. 168 (a French court denied a U.S. extradition request for two Americans who had hijacked a plane to Algeria and extorted US $500,000 from the airplane; the court held that the exclusion applied because the hijackers had made passing reference to Angela Davis and Eldridge Cleaver, who were leaders of the Black Panthers, a Black empowerment and anti-government organization, and had asked to be taken to Hanoi in Communist Vietnam).

133 Boister, *supra* n.2, at 300–01; Buckland, *supra* n.84, at 449; *e.g.*, *Ordinola v. Hackman*, 478 F.3d 588, 598 (4th Cir. 2007) (*dicta*).

134 *Non-refoulement* is an international legal principle that prohibits the expulsion or return, including via extradition, of an individual to another State if he is reasonably expected to be mistreated there. *See* U.N. High Comm'r for Refugees, *UNHCR Note on the Principle of Non-Refoulement*, Nov. 1997 (citing U.N. Exec. Comm. Conclusion No. 25, ¶ (b); U.N. Docs. A/AC.96/694, ¶ 21; A/AC.96/660, ¶ 17; A/AC.96/643, ¶ 15; A/AC.96/609/Rev.1, ¶ 5). The term lacks a uniform scope, but for present purposes it prohibits return in particular if the individual is likely to face torture; cruel, inhuman, or degrading treatment or punishment; extrajudicial execution; enforced disappearance; or deprivation of freedom on improper grounds. This term is further discussed in Chapters 6.c, 7.e, and 10.d.

135 Buckland, *supra* n.84, at 425, 448, 450; *e.g.*, *Suarez-Mason*, 694 F. Supp. 676 (N.D. Cal. 1988).

Although the political offense exclusion remains a significant barrier to extradition, due to increasing frustration over its inconsistent application, particularly with respect to acts of terrorism,[136] its reach has been markedly circumscribed in recent years in a number of crime suppression and extradition treaties, U.N. documents, and domestic extradition statutes. More specifically, the political offense exclusion has not figured into such terrorism-related instruments as the 1977 European Convention on the Suppression of Terrorism,[137] the 1998 International Convention on the Suppression of Terrorist Bombings,[138] the 1999 International Convention for the Suppression of the Financing of Terrorism,[139] and the International Convention for the Suppression of Acts of Nuclear Terrorism,[140] while being omitted from UNSC Resolution 1373 in 2001 (addressing acts of terrorism).[141]

A similar eliminative dynamic on the political offense exclusion has played out in treaties and legislation alike regarding such other heinous crimes as genocide,[142] torture,[143] extrajudicial killings,[144] war crimes and crimes against humanity,[145] enforced disappearances,[146] and assassinations or attempted assassinations of heads of State or members of their families (sometimes referred to as *clause d'attentat*[147]).[148]

[136] Duffy, *supra* n.24, at 109–10 & n.190; Grassie, *supra* n.91, at 1208; Stanbrook & Stanbrook, *supra* n.12, at 15 ("strict application could be highly inexpedient and unjust").

[137] Jan. 27, 1977, E.T.S. No. 90.

[138] Jan. 9, 1998, U.N. Doc. A/Res/52/164 (1997), *reprinted in* 37 ILM 249 (1998).

[139] Dec. 9, 1999, U.N. Doc. A/Res/54/109 (1999), *reprinted in* 39 ILM 270 (2000) [hereinafter Anti-Terrorism Financing Conv.].

[140] Apr. 13, 2005, U.N. Doc. A/RES/59/290, *available at* https://treaties.un.org/doc/db/Terrorism/english-18-15.pdf (last visited on May 9, 2016).

[141] Sept. 28, 2001, U.N. Doc. S/Res/1373 (2001), ¶ 3(g).

[142] Conv. on the Prevention and Punishment of the Crime of Genocide, Dec. 9, 1948, art. 7, 78 U.N.T.S. 277, *reprinted in* 28 ILM 763.

[143] U.N. Conv. against Torture and Other Cruel, Inhuman or Degrading Treatment or Punishment [CAT], Dec. 10, 1984, art. 8, UNGA Res. 39/46 Annex, U.N. GAOR, 39th Sess., Supp. No. 51, U.N. Doc. E/CN.4/1984/72, Annex (1984), 1465 U.N.T.S. 85, *reprinted in* 23 ILM 1027.

[144] U.N., *Principles on the Effective Prevention and Investigation of Extra-Legal, Arbitrary and Summary Executions*, Principle 18, E.S.C. Res. 1989/65, Annex, 1989 U.N. ESCOR Supp. (No. 1) at 52, U.N. Doc. E/1989/89 (1989).

[145] Addt'l Prot. to the Eur. Conv. on Extradition, Oct. 15, 1975, E.T.S. No. 86.

[146] Int'l Conv. for the Protection of all Persons from Enforced Disappearance, Dec. 20, 2006, UNGA Res. 61/177, U.N. Doc. A/61/448.

[147] This provision is also sometimes referred to as the "Belgian clause" as it was first set forth in Belgian legislation in 1856. S. Prakash Sinha, Asylum and International Law 178 (1971).

[148] *See* Phillips, *supra* n.85, at 341 (noting the rise in anarchist activity in the 1890s that helped popularize this exception); Stanbrook & Stanbrook, *supra* n.12, at 82 (observing that the trend was extended to cover diplomatic representatives); *e.g.*, Treaty of

Furthermore, the 2003 U.K. Extradition Act,[149] the 1999 U.S.-RSA Extradition Treaty,[150] and the 2002 Framework Decision on the EAW[151] have rolled back or dispensed altogether with a role for the political offense exclusion.

Military Offenses. The military offense exclusion permits the host State to withhold extradition on the ground that the offense for which extradition is sought is a pure military crime in the sense that it violates a State's military law (or military code) for which no ordinary criminal law counterpart exists. The exclusion consists of any offense committed by a member of a State's military (or an embedded civilian) that occurs on a military base or facility or that occurs in the course of his military service,[152] but does *not* include any crime also cognizable under ordinary criminal law[153] or any violation of international humanitarian law or international criminal law.[154] The most common examples include mutiny, desertion, insubordination, and neglect of duty.

Extradition, U.S.-Venez., Jan. 19 and 22, 1922, art. 3, 43 Stat. 1698, T.S. 675, 49 L.N.T.S. 435; *In re Pavelić*, Ct. of App. of Turn, Italy, Nov. 23, 1934, *reprinted in* [1933–34] ANN. DIG. NO. 158 (involving assassins of King Alexander of Yugoslavia).

149 U.K. Extradition Act 2003, *supra* n.77, Chap. 41.

150 U.S.-RSA Extradition Treaty, *supra* n.38, art. 4 (itemizing multiple exceptions to the application of the political offense exclusion, including for murder, abduction, and hostage-taking, as well as for aiding and abetting, attempt, and conspiracy in relation to such offenses).

151 Framework Decision on the EAW, *supra* n.41.

152 BLAKESLEY, *supra* n.9, at 263 & n.412.

153 In September 2008, a Thai court denied the extradition to the United States of Iranian national Jamshid Ghassemi under the charge of attempting to purchase and export twelve accelerometers to Iran in violation of U.S. trade sanctions against Iran. While the court decision was not made public, one argument reportedly made by his counsel relied on the military offense exclusion provision of the 1991 U.S.-Thai Extradition Treaty. His counsel contended that Ghassemi, a military officer, had acted under orders of a superior officer. Were that the actual basis for the extradition denial, it would be a misreading of the exclusion, as export control violations are decidedly within the scope of ordinary criminal law. "Thai Court Refuses U.S. Extradition Request for Export Defendant," *ExportLawBlog*, posted by Clif Burns, Sept. 25, 2008, *available at* www.exportlawblog.com/archives/398 (last visited on May 9, 2016). More likely, however, the extradition was estopped due to a lack of dual criminality, as the United States was the only State that then had imposed trade sanctions against Iran.

154 For example, consider the case of accused Croatian war criminal Dragan Vasilijković, who was accused of personally killing civilians and instructing others to commit murder during his tenure as commander of Serbian paramilitary forces and who was the subject of a Croatian extradition request to Australia. In his defense, he contended that normal Croatian criminal laws did not apply during a war, that conduct that would be illegal during peacetime may not be unlawful during armed conflict, that his

This exclusion was less relevant until the 1970s, when bilateral extradition treaties started to treat dual criminality more flexibly, including for pure military offenses; before then, when extraditable crimes were itemized, pure military offenses generally were not listed among them.[155] Although the exclusion is widely found in such extradition instruments as the European Convention on Extradition,[156] bilateral extradition treaties,[157] and the U.N. Model Treaty on Extradition,[158] not many cases arise under this exclusion and in any event States are largely disinclined to extradite when pure military offenses are at issue.[159]

Fiscal Offenses. Traditionally, the idea of extraditing a fugitive to face charges in another State for such *fiscal* offenses as tax evasion, non-payment of customs duties, or currency or foreign exchange control violations was disfavored.[160] This view, which stemmed from a discomfort, in effect, with enforcing *foreign fiscal, tax, or revenue laws*[161] – versus often related but distinct *economic* crimes such as

actions were intended to prevent POWs from escaping, and that his acts were not so grave as to violate the Geneva Conventions. An Australian Deputy Chief Magistrate rejected his arguments, ordering the extradition to proceed. To the extent Vasilijković was considered a protected person under the Geneva Conventions, however, it could affect the events for which he were punished and the severity of the penalty; and his military rank (captain) would factor into the determination of command responsibility. Bruce Zagaris, *Accused Croatian War Criminal Loses Effort to Block Australian Extradition Hearing*, 23 IELR 54, 55 (2007).

155 Charles Doyle, "Extradition To and From the United States: Overview of the Law and Recent Treaties," C.R.S. Report for Congress, No. 98-958 A, Aug. 3, 2007, at 6; *cf.* Abbell, *supra* n.30, at 126–27 (noting that all U.S. extradition treaties after 1978 include a provision barring extradition for pure military offenses).

156 Eur. Conv. on Extradition, *supra* n.86, art. 4 ("Extradition for offences under military law which are not offences under ordinary criminal law is excluded from the application of this Convention.").

157 *E.g.*, Treaty on Extradition, U.S.-Belize, Mar. 30, 2000, art. 4(4), T.I.A.S. 13089, S. Treaty Doc. 106-38 ("The executive authority of the Requested State may refuse extradition for offenses under military law which are not offenses under ordinary criminal law."); Treaty on Extradition, Switz.-Isr., Dec. 31, 1958, art. 3(2), 77 U.N.T.S. 305 (1958).

158 U.N. Model Extradition Treaty, *supra* n.20, art. 3(c).

159 Bantekas & Nash, *supra* n.25, at 189; Douglas W. Jones & David L. Raish, *American Deserters and Draft Evaders: Exile, Punishment, or Amnesty*, 13 Harv. Int'l. L.J. 88 (Winter 1972) (discussing the non-extradition by Sweden and Canada of U.S. military deserters); David A. Tate, *Draft Evasion and the Problem of Extradition*, 32 Albany L. Rev. 337 (1968).

160 Stanbrook & Stanbrook, *supra* n.12, at 9; Boister, *supra* n.2, at 301 & n.87; Keith R. Fisher, In Rem *Alternatives to Extradition for Money Laundering*, 25 Loy. L.A. Int'l & Comp. L. Rev. 409, 412 & n.17 (2003).

161 Bantekas & Nash, *supra* n.25, at 189.

currency counterfeiting, money laundering, and embezzlement – was manifested in a range of bilateral and multilateral extradition instruments, including, for example, the 1990 U.S.-Switzerland Extradition Treaty[162] and the European Convention on Laundering, Search, Seizure and Confiscation of the Proceeds From Crime.[163]

While some States, including Switzerland, continue to maintain this policy,[164] there has been considerable movement in recent decades, generated in part by the growth in global financial crime, to treat such offenses as extraditable.[165] That said, as such fiscal offenses can be specialized, the rules governing dual criminality could continue to obstruct extraditions except for those States with close economic bonds[166] or where treaties expressly rule out any such interpretative leeway.[167]

b Prescription

Extradition also can be impeded due to statutes of limitations and discretionary time bars applicable under domestic law. Multilateral

162 Treaty on Extradition, U.S.-Switz., Nov. 14, 1990, art. 3(a)&(b), S. Treaty Doc. 104–9 (permitting the host State to deny extradition for acts that are exclusively violations of currency, trade, or economic policy, or that are intended exclusively to reduce taxes or duties).

163 Conv. on Laundering, Search, Seizure and Confiscation of the Proceeds from Crime, Nov. 8, 1990, art. 18(1)(d), E.T.S. No. 141 (parties may refuse cooperation where a fiscal offence is involved).

164 *See, e.g.*, Swiss IMAC, *supra* n.9, art. 3(3).

165 *See* Abbell, *supra* n.30, at 73–74 Geoff Gilbert, *Extradition, in* The Harvard Research in International Law: Contemporary Analysis and Appraisal 256–57 (John P. Grant & J. Craig Barker eds. 2007); *e.g.*, *Prushinowski v. Samples*, 734 F.2d 1016 (4th Cir. 1984); *e.g.*, Second Addt'l Prot. to the Eur. Conv. on Extradition, Mar. 17, 1978, art. 2, E.T.S. No. 98 [hereinafter Second Addt'l Prot.]; Anti-Terrorism Financing Conv., *supra* n.139, art. 13 ("States Parties may not refuse a request for extradition... on the sole ground that it concerns a fiscal offence."); U.N. Conv. against Transnational Organized Crime, Nov. 15, 2000, art. 16(15), U.N. GAOR, 55th Sess., 62d Plen. Mtg., Annex I, U.N. Doc. A/RES/55/25; London Scheme for Extradition within the Commonwealth, Nov. 2002, art. 2(4)(a) LMM (90)32 [hereinafter London Scheme]; Treaty on Extradition, Austl.-Mex., June 22, 1990, art. 4, 1991 A.T.S. No. 13 (1995).

166 Gilbert, *supra* n.165, at 257–58.

167 *E.g.*, Second Addt'l Prot., *supra* n.165, art. 2(2) ("Extradition may not be refused on the ground that the law of the requested Party does not impose the same kind of tax or duty or does not contain a tax, duty, customs or exchange regulation of the same kind as the law of the requesting Party.").

conventions,[168] bilateral treaties,[169] cooperative schemes,[170] and municipal statutes[171] alike generally prohibit extradition where prosecution or punishment is disallowed on account of the passage of time since the underlying crime occurred[172] or the individual became unlawfully at large, respectively.[173] Variation exists, however, as to the applicable law: the host State's alone, the pursuing State's alone, either, or both.[174] Where either State's law has been (or would be deemed) violated on account of a time bar, it follows that no dual criminality (*see supra*) would obtain. Increasingly, however, no statute of limitations applies as a basis for denying extradition,[175] or applies only on a discretionary matter where extradition would be deemed "unjust" and/or "oppressive" in light of the lapse of time.[176]

168 *E.g.*, Inter-Am. Conv. on Extradition, *supra* n.42, art. 4(2) ("the prosecution or punishment [of a fugitive] is barred by the statute of limitations according to the laws of the requesting State or the requested State prior to the presentation of the request for extradition.").

169 *E.g.*, U.S.-RSA Extradition Treaty, *supra* n.38, art. 8 ("Extradition shall not be granted when the prosecution has become barred by lapse of time according to the laws in the Requesting State.").

170 *E.g.*, London Scheme, *supra* n.165, art. 13(b)(iii).

171 *E.g.*, Sweden, Extradition for Crim. Offences Act (1957:668), Dec. 6, 1957, § 10(2), *as amended*.

172 For example, in July 1979, had West Germany's parliament, the Bundestag, decided not to lift the State's statute of limitations on ordinary murder, genocide, war crimes, and crimes against humanity, Nazi war crimes would have been barred from prosecution in West German courts effective December 31, 1979. 2 International Crime and Punishment: Selected Issues 15–17 (Sienho Yee ed. 2004).

173 Blakesley, *supra* n.9, at 262. *See generally* Stanbrook & Stanbrook, *supra* n.12, at 148 (noting that statutes of limitations are designed "to protect an accused from dilatoriness or incompetence by the requesting state").

174 Typically, if the statute of limitations has run under either State's law, then extradition is barred. *Id.* at 141; Blakesley, *supra* n.9, at 262. In more historic U.S. extradition treaties, only the prescriptive law of the host State mattered, but examples exist of only the pursuing State's law or both as well. Abbell, *supra* n.30, at 105–07.

175 *See id.* at 3–52 (characterizing prescriptive bars as disfavored); *e.g.*, Treaty on Extradition, U.S.-Jordan, Mar. 28, 1995, art. 6, S. Treaty Doc. 104-3 ("The decision whether to grant the request for extradition shall be made without regard to the provisions of the law of either Contracting State concerning lapse of time."); Fourth Addt'l Prot. to the Eur. Conv. on Extradition, Sept. 20, 2012, art. 1(2) ("Extradition shall not be refused on the ground that the prosecution or punishment of the person claimed would be statute-barred according to the law of the requested Party.").

176 In June 2007, a U.K. court denied extradition to the United States of Stanley Tollman, a hotelier charged with bank fraud and tax evasion, partly on the ground that his extradition would have been regarded as "unjust and oppressive," given the significant passage of time (approximately a dozen years) since the alleged commission of the offenses. Bruce Zagaris, *U.K. Court Denies U.S. Extradition Request for Former Hotel Owner, Citing Prosecutors' Delays*, 23 IELR 358, 358–59 (2007) (the U.K. court cited to

Where statutes of limitations are in effect, the total number of years since the crime occurred may need to be recalculated to reflect any "tolling" of the time period based on relevant circumstances, such as wartime, the need to obtain foreign evidence, or a person's flight from justice.[177] Absent express application, States tend to rely upon a statute of limitations corresponding to the analogically closest substantive offense to the one for which the individual has been charged.[178] Treaty and persuasive authority alike exists for the proposition that statutes of limitations should not apply to war crimes or crimes against humanity, and thereby not bar extraditions in such cases.[179]

To illustrate how such cases can play out, consider the following examples. In December 1931, a Belgian Court of Appeal denied a request for extradition by Italy for a convicted Italian national because Belgium's statute of limitations for the underlying crime had run on

§ 82 of Extradition Act 2003, also finding that, if extradited, Tollman would be unable to continue caring for his ailing wife). *See also Kakis v. Gov't of the Repub. of Cyprus* [1978] 2 All E.R. 634, 1 WLR 779 (H.L.) (extradition was deemed unjust where there was a prolonged delay since the commission of the crime); STANBROOK & STANBROOK, *supra* n.12, at 140 (under U.K. law, no time bar is imposed on serious offenses with a few exceptions like sexual violations).

177 *E.g.*, 18 U.S.C. § 3288 (2012) (wartime suspension); 18 U.S.C. § 3292 (2012) (allow prosecutors time to collect evidence abroad); 18 U.S.C. § 3290 (2012) (persons fleeing from justice). *See also* Bruce Zagaris, *Court of Appeal Affirms and Overturns Extradition Request to Korea on Bribery Charges*, 24 IELR 269 (2008) (U.S. court tolled the time period on a five-year statute of limitations related to a bribery charge to authorize the extradition to South Korea of Man-Soek Choe); *In re Assarsson*, 687 F.2d at 1160–63 (finding that the district court did not err in tolling the clock on the statute of limitations because, although the fugitive had been living openly in Illinois with full knowledge of Swedish authorities, the material fact was that he had fled Sweden with the intent to avoid arrest or prosecution).

178 *See, e.g., In re Requested Extradition of Suarez-Mason*, 694 F. Supp. 676, 686–87 (N.D. Cal. 1988) (Argentina charged the accused with twenty-four counts of unlawful deprivation of freedom; kidnapping was found to be the closest analog, and applying the U.S. statute of limitations on kidnapping (five years), per the terms of the treaty, extradition was barred as more than five years had elapsed since the charges had been filed).

179 *See* U.N. Conv. on the Non-Applicability of Statutory Limitations to War Crimes and Crimes Against Humanity, Nov. 26, 1968, art. 4, UNGA Res. 2391 (XXIII), 754 U.N.T.S. 73 (1968) (parties agreeing to eliminate time bars to war crimes, crimes against humanity, and genocide under their domestic law); Eur. Conv. on the Non-Applicability of Statutory Limitations to Crimes Against Humanity and War Crimes, Jan. 25, 1974, Eur. T.S. No. 82; *Fédération Nationale des Déportés et Internés Résistants et Patriotes and Others v. Barbie*, Ct. of Cassation (Crim. Ch.), Fr., Oct. 6, 1983, *reprinted in* 78 ILR 125, 135 (1988); Rome Statute of the Int'l Crim. Court (ICC), July 17, 1998, art. 29, 2187 U.N.T.S. 3, U.N. Doc. A/CONF.183/9 (1998), *reprinted in* 37 ILM 999; Princeton Univ, *Princeton Principles on Universal Jurisdiction* (updated as of July 2001), Principle 6.

account of the protracted nature of criminal proceedings in the Italian courts.[180] In November 1997, Brazil's Supreme Court unanimously denied a U.K. request for the extradition of Ronnie Biggs, a perpetrator of the 1963 "Great Train Robbery" (that constituted a record haul at the time), due to the fact that his crime and his 1965 prison escape were time-barred under Brazil's twenty-year statute of limitations.[181] And in November 2011, with respect to a convicted murderer named George Wright who had escaped from a New Jersey prison in 1970 and then was on the lam for forty-one years, a Portuguese court refused to extradite him to the United States ostensibly, in part, because the Portuguese statute of limitations on murder had expired.[182]

c Evidentiary Standards

One of the stiffest obstacles to extradition, at least among common law States, can be meeting the host State's evidentiary standard.[183] The purpose of that standard is to show the likelihood that the accused in fact committed the crime(s) for which he has been charged[184] or that one sentenced *in absentia* actually committed the crime(s) for which he was convicted.[185]

Wide variety exists across States in this regard.[186] Some State courts have adopted a "rule of non-inquiry," and therefore do not deem it

[180] *In re Addis*, Ct. of App. of Brussels, Belg., Dec. 19, 1931, *reprinted in* Ann. Dig. Pub. Int'l L. Cases 306, 306–07 (No. 166) (H. Lauterpacht ed. 1938).

[181] "Brazilian Court Won't Extradite 'Great Train Robbery' Fugitive," *N.Y. Times*, Nov. 13, 1997.

[182] Barry Hatton, "Portugal Refuses to Send U.S. Fugitive Home," *AP*, Nov. 17, 2011 (although the court proceedings were secret and therefore no judicial opinion is available, Wright's lawyer represented that part of the judge's rationale was that the Portuguese statute of limitations on murder had expired).

[183] Bantekas & Nash, *supra* n.25, at 183–84.

[184] *See* Abbell, *supra* n.30, at 101 (most recent U.S. extradition treaties require only "an authenticated or certified copy of the sentence or judgment of conviction and proof that the requested person is the person to whom the judgment or sentence refers"); Grassie, *supra* n.91, at 1206.

[185] In cases of *in absentia* convictions, probable cause is not necessarily established merely by the fact that there has been a conviction; rather, courts scrutinize the evidence to determine at least a reasonable probability that the subject individual is guilty of the crime. *E.g., United States v. Fernandez-Morris*, 99 F. Supp.2d 1358, 1366 (S.D. Fla. 1999) (finding no probable cause to believe the U.S. national subject committed fraud, illegal association, and breach of trust in Bolivia as had been found when he was tried *in absentia*).

[186] Bantekas & Nash, *supra* n.25, at 180.

appropriate to examine other States' legal standards or procedures, let alone ascertain the motive behind an extradition request.[187] Most civil law States do not insist that *any* evidence be propounded in connection with an extradition hearing;[188] instead, they may simply ask for proof of a *bona fide* indictment or arrest warrant, dual criminality, and the fact that the person before the court is the same as the subject of the extradition request.[189] Others may leave themselves the option of requiring some degree of evidentiary proof of a crime.[190]

A number of States with common law traditions require that a pursuing State set forth sufficient evidence to meet a *prima facie*,[191] or (lower) probable cause,[192] or (lower still) reasonable probability,[193] standard. These amount, in effect, to screening devices for a host State to ensure it has grounds to believe the extradition subject did commit or

[187] *Id.; e.g., Ahmad v. Wigen*, 910 F.2d 1063, 1066–67 ("The interests of international comity are ill-served by requiring a foreign nation such as Israel to satisfy a United States District Judge concerning the fairness of its laws and the manner in which they are enforced."), *stay denied*, 111 S. Ct. 23 (1990).

[188] *See* Gilbert, *supra* n.165, at 261 (noting that such evidentiary standards are "alien to civil law states' investigation-prosecution procedure").

[189] *See* Blakesley, *supra* n.9, at 218 (citing France); Duffy, *supra* n.24, at 110–11 & n.195. This approach is exemplified by the Eur. Conv. on Extradition, *supra* n.86, art. 12, which embraces a civil law approach and requires no evidence.

[190] *See* Gilbert, *supra* n.165, at 262 n.58 (citing by example Germany and Scandinavian countries); *e.g.*, Steven Lee Myers, "Rebuffing Russia, Denmark Frees Chechen Envoy It Detained," *N.Y. Times*, Dec. 4, 2002 (the Danish Ministry of Justice denied a Russian extradition request for Akhmed Zakayev, an alleged Chechen rebel leader, for lack of "sufficient credible evidence").

[191] Jennings & Watts, *supra* n.18, at 958–59; Bantekas & Nash, *supra* n.25, at 183–84; Gilbert, *supra* n.165, at 262 n.58 (citing Israel as an example of a State imposing a *prima facie* evidentiary standard); Boister, *supra* n.2, at 302 & nn.92–94; *e.g., United States v. Sheppard*, Sup. Ct., Can., [1977] May 5, 1976, 2 S.C.R. 1067, *reprinted in* 71 ILR 510 (1987). A *prima facie* standard is relatively high, as it calls for evidence sufficient to convict the individual for the crime charged. *See* American Law Inst., Restatement (Third) of the Foreign Relations Law of the United States, May 14, 1986 (1987), § 476 cmt. B (stating that while U.S. law and treaties require a showing of probable cause, "[i]n Great Britain and states following the British model, the standard is stricter, equivalent to a prima facie case").

[192] Duffy, *supra* n.24, at 110 & n.195; Blakesley, *supra* n.9, at 217–18; Jennings & Watts, *supra* n.18, at 958 n.6 (noting that a number of U.S. bilateral extradition treaties contain "probable cause" evidentiary requirements); *e.g., United States ex rel. Argento v. Jacobs*, 176 F. Supp. 877 (N.D. Ohio 1959). Probable cause calls for evidence showing reasonable grounds to believe that the individual committed the crime but not necessarily enough to convict him of it. *In re Extradition of Marzook*, 924 F. Supp. 565 (S.D.N.Y. 1996).

[193] A reasonable probability is a relatively low standard defined as "a probability sufficient to undermine confidence in the outcome." *Dyson v. Dormire*, 2009 U.S. Dist. LEXIS 90211 (E.D. Mo. Sept. 1, 2009).

could well have committed the offense in question[194] and not transfer him merely "on the word of a prosecutor, coupled with conclusory allegations and unsubstantiated, unreliable evidence"[195] or because "extradition is not warranted simply by a showing of [an] in absentia conviction."[196] Some common law States apply differential evidentiary standards depending on the identity of the pursuing State at issue.[197]

Few States demand evidence in cases where the accused freely consents to extradition.[198] States may determine that despite ample inculpatory evidence overall, where the evidence fails to meet one element of the crime, the request for extradition may be rejected based on insufficient evidence.[199] Evidence could be inadequate for any number of reasons, including, for example, if witness statements are unsworn or incomplete,

194 Duffy, *supra* n.24, at 110–11 & n.195; *e.g.*, Bruce Zagaris, *U.S. Trial Court Denies Extradition Request on Murder Charges*, 27 IELR 512, 513 (2011) (denying the extradition request by Argentina of Robert Guillermo Bravo for murder and attempted murder charges based on inadequate evidence); Renee Dopplick, "International Laws Aid Fujimori's Extradition," *Inside Justice* (blog), Feb. 19, 2006, *available at* www.insidejustice.com/author/renee/page/21/ (last visited on May 9, 2016) (Japan "felt that Peru's 700-page extradition request [for Alberto Fujimori, former President of Peru] failed to provide sufficient evidence.").

195 *Fernandez-Morris*, 99 F. Supp.2d 1358; *accord In re Extradition of Platko*, 213 F. Supp.2d 1229, 1237–41 (S.D. Cal. 2002); Bruce Zagaris, *Court of Appeal Affirms and Overturns Extradition Request to Korea on Bribery Charges*, 24 IELR 269 (2008) (discussing a case in April 2008 where the U.S. Court of Appeals for the Ninth Circuit overturned an extradition order with respect to one of two bribery charges levied against Man-Soek Choe, a Korean citizen and resident of Los Angeles, where an insufficient basis existed to establish probable cause in Korea's request for extradition; the charge in question was that Choe paid off Mr. Hwang, a member of the National Assembly, to use his influence to win a contract bid for a particular company, but there was no evidence presented that Choe promised Hwang a reward, that Choe gave him anything, or that they even met – just conclusory allegations).

196 *Argento v. Jacobs*, 176 F. Supp. at 879.

197 For example, Australia requires *prima facie* evidence from other Commonwealth countries, maintains a separate system with New Zealand, and may rely on reciprocity and mutual understanding with countries with which it has no extradition treaty. Matthew Groves, *Review of Australian Extradition Law*, 30 Crim. L.J. 337, 338 (2006).

198 *E.g.*, U.S.-RSA Extradition Treaty, *supra* n.38, art. 19.

199 The March 2004 Tokyo High Court denial of a U.S. request for the extradition of Japanese scientist Takashi Okamoto on economic espionage and related charges is illustrative. Although Dr. Okamoto admitted to taking certain genetic material out of a disease research institute in Cleveland, Ohio, he did so late at night, and had an accomplice who pled to a lesser charge, the judge ruled there was no probable cause to believe he had intended to benefit his new employer, the Institute of Physical and Chemical Research (RIKEN), a Japanese Government-funded institute – an essential element of economic espionage. Tetsuya Morimoto, *First Japanese Denial of U.S. Extradition Request: Economic Espionage Case*, 20 IELR 288 (2004).

there is no opportunity to cross-examine them, or their statements are suspiciously identical.[200] Fraud cases are notoriously challenging because it is often difficult to demonstrate criminal intent, and therefore extradition requests can be denied for failure to show that element.[201]

An extradition hearing is not generally considered tantamount to even an abbreviated criminal trial, as it does not purport to try an individual for his guilt or innocence on the merits.[202] Rather, its limited purpose, which is much more akin to that of a domestic committal hearing,[203] is merely to determine whether, under the host State's municipal law, an individual can and should be extradited to a pursuing State to face prosecution or punishment.[204] While rare, however, it is possible that a reviewing State court may overreach its mandate and choose "to try the case instead of confining [itself] to ascertaining whether the evidence submitted ... was sufficient to justify the fugitive's apprehension and commitment for trial," and in so doing reach the conclusion that the evidence falls short of the applied standard.[205]

[200] *E.g.*, Alan Cullison and Nicole Lundeen, "Austrian Court Denies U.S. Request to Extradite Dmytro Firtash," *Wall St. J.*, World News, May 1, 2015 (denying the extradition of a Ukrainian billionaire to the United States on bribery charges due in part to concerns about the lack of evidence stemming from the U.S. prosecutors' reliance on "two anonymous witnesses to try to prove Mr. Firtash's complicity in the bribery scheme [while not providing] the full transcript of their testimonies or [making] the witnesses available for questioning"). It is not uncommon for such opinions also to express reservations about the political motivation of the extradition request. *See id.* and Chapter 7.e.i regarding prosecutorial discrimination.

[201] *E.g.*, Bruce Zagaris, *South African Court Rejects Zimbabwe Extradition Request*, 27 IELR 966, 966–67 (2011).

[202] *See* p. 160 in Chapter 4; Jennings & Watts, *supra* n.18, at 958–59; Duffy, *supra* n.24, at 110–11. *Contra R. v. Governor of Brixton Prison, ex parte Levin* [1997] A.C. 741 (H.L.) (the House of Lords held that since extradition proceedings are of a criminal character, the committing magistrate was entitled to apply regular domestic rules of criminal evidence and procedure).

[203] Gilbert, *supra* n.165, at 261.

[204] In the event the subject of an extradition skips bail and flees the jurisdiction, this can be seen by courts as circumstantial evidence of guilt, even if there is no direct proof of his motivation for having done so. *Cf. United States v. Green*, 25 F.3d 206, 210 (3d Cir. 1994) ("We have held in the past that '[e]vidence of a defendant's flight after a crime has been committed is admissible to prove his consciousness of guilt.").

[205] *See* Charles Cheney Hyde, *The Extradition Case of Samuel Insull Sr. in Relation to Greece*, 28 AJIL 307, 311 (1934) (discussing the 1932 case of Samuel Insull Sr. in which the Greek Court of Appeals investigated the merits of the charges against him in a trial-like manner, rather than merely determining if enough evidence existed, in contravention of the terms of the applicable extradition treaty) (relying on a November 1933 letter from the U.S. Minister to Greece to the Greek Minister of Foreign Affairs complaining about Greece's unwillingness to extradite Samuel Insull Sr. on larceny-related charges).

By and large, much less evidence is required by host States, even under rigorous screening tests, than would be necessary to render a guilty verdict.[206] Accordingly, pursuing States need not have completed their investigations into the underlying facts before deciding to seek extradition,[207] and even may choose to withhold certain types of collected evidence for strategic reasons.[208] In addition, the host State typically need not comply with the evidentiary rules applicable to criminal trials,[209] thus permitting the introduction, for example, of hearsay testimony,[210] while affirmative defenses (such as entrapment[211]) advanced by the accused are not considered admissible.[212]

Despite such procedural flexibility[213] and a general trend toward a loosening of the standard,[214] reliance on an evidentiary requirement

[206] Duffy, *supra* n.24, at 110.

[207] *Id.* at 110–11 & n. 195.

[208] *Id.* at 110; M. Cherif Bassiouni, International Extradition and World Public Order 179–81 (1974) [hereinafter Bassiouni, World Public Order].

[209] *See* n.39 in Chapter 4 and accompanying text; Jennings & Watts, *supra* n.18, at 958–59.

[210] *E.g., Rice v. Ames*, 180 U.S. 371, 375–76 (1901); *In re Extradition of Marzook*, 924 F. Supp. 565 (S.D.N.Y. 1996) (considering properly authenticated documents notwithstanding their hearsay content).

[211] Under U.S. law, the government may rely on decoys to ensnare criminals and simply offering him an opportunity to commit a crime is not deemed sufficient to defeat a prosecution on an entrapment defense. Paul Marcus, *Presenting, Back From the [Almost] Dead, the Entrapment Defense*, College of William & Mary Law School Faculty Publications, 1995, at 243, *available at* http://scholarship.law.wm.edu/cgi/viewcontent.cgi?article=1612&context=facpubs (last visited on May 28, 2016). Rather, something more is required. *See United States v. Gendron*, 18 F.3d 955, 961 (1st Cir. 1994) ("[a]n 'inducement' consists of an 'opportunity' *plus* something else – typically, excessive pressure by the government upon the defendant or the government's taking advantage of an alternative, non-criminal type of motive") (emphasis in original).

[212] *E.g.*, Bruce Zagaris, *Trinidad Magistrate Orders Extradition of Three Suspects to U.S. in JFK Airport Terrorism Plot*, 23 IELR 375 (2007) (discussing the case in which Trinidad & Tobago ordered the extradition of Abdul Kair, Kareem Ibrahim, and Abdel Nur to the United States on charges that they conspired with a former airport cargo worker to sabotage jet fuel storage tanks and fuel lines at New York's Kennedy International Airport over an objection that they were entrapped by a confidential U.S. informant into plotting the attack).

[213] *E.g.*, Bruce Zagaris, *Colombian Supreme Court Inquires About Potential U.S. Violations of Extradition Terms*, 21 IELR 222, 223 (2005) (U.S. prosecutors were allowed to introduce pre-December 17, 1997, evidence to prove Fabio Ochos, a founder of the Medellín cartel, was guilty of crimes commissioned after December 17, 1997, in order to show, *inter alia*, opportunity, motive, intent, preparation, knowledge, and pattern of conduct, even though an amendment to the 1991 Colombian Constitution expressly prohibited the extradition of its nationals for offenses committed on or before December 17, 1997).

[214] *E.g.*, Framework Decision on the EAW, *supra* n.41, arts. 58(3) and 91(2) (addressing surrenders to the ICC).

undoubtedly can confound an extradition request, which can be exacerbated in one of several scenarios. First, for those States that insist on *prima facie* evidence, that standard can be particularly challenging to meet.[215] Indeed, some civil law States may even be unwilling to submit their evidence to a common law State whose courts insist on a *prima facie* (or probable cause) standard before agreeing to extradite a fugitive.[216] Plus, some cases require physical evidence or witnesses that are only available in another State and the transportation or shipment for hearing purposes can prove prohibitively expensive or logistically complicated.[217] And in older cases, notably those that date back decades, it can be difficult to even locate the requisite witnesses and physical and scientific data to meet the host State's applicable evidentiary standard.[218]

In addition, to the extent the host State court finds that certain inculpatory evidence was gathered unlawfully (*e.g.*, through confessions or information elicited via duress or torture,[219] or data collected from an

[215] *See* BANTEKAS & NASH, *supra* n.25, at 183–84; Gilbert, *supra* n.165, at 261 (citing the Home Office, *A Review of the Law and Practice of Extradition in the United Kingdom*, Report of an Interdepartmental Working Party, Criminal Justice Department, Home Office, May 1982, ¶ 4.6, in which the British Government recognized that the most common cause of failure of applications under extradition treaties was the *prima facie* requirement); Richard Goldberger, *It's Just not Cricket: Is the Principle of Reciprocity Being Honored in the U.S.-U.K. Extradition Treaty?*, 29 CARDOZO L. REV. 819, 839 n.135 (2007) (noting that in 1978, the then-Anglo-Spanish Extradition Treaty lapsed because not a single Spanish request had been granted mainly due to the *prima facie* requirement).

[216] Boister, *supra* n.2, at 302 & nn.92–94.

[217] *See id.* at 302 & nn.92–94 (citing by example *In re Reyat's Application for a Writ of Habeas Corpus*, CO/1157/88, MWC, QB Div., Mar. 22, 1989 (unreported), in which Canada had to fly witnesses to Hong Kong from Japan to take evidence to establish a *prima facie* case for an extradition from the U.K.).

[218] *See* BASSIOUNI, WORLD PUBLIC ORDER, *supra* n.208, at 179–81; *e.g., Jacobs*, 176 F. Supp. 877 (finding lack of probable cause in a case where the underlying crime occurred in 1922, an *in absentia* conviction took place in Italy in 1931, and an extradition request was lodged in 1959); Bruce Zagaris, *Canadian Supreme Court Denies Appeal of Extradition for WWII War Crimes*, 24 IELR 109, 109–10 (2008) (Canadian Federal Court Justice James O'Reilly expressed concerns more than six decades later about the sufficiency of the evidence that defendant Michael Seifert had committed the atrocities attributed to him at the Bolzano prisoner camp during World War II).

[219] *E.g., RB (Algeria) (FC) and Another v. Sec'y of State State for the Home Dep't* [2009] UKHL 10 (concerns expressed about whether evidence obtained via torture would be used by the prosecution in Jordan); *In re Saifi* [2001] 4 All E.R. 168 (a U.K. court refused to return a person to India because of concern that witness testimony had been procured via duress); Robert Jackson & Juanita Darling, "U.S. Judge Won't Extradite Former Mexico Official," *L.A. Times*, June 23, 1995, at A1, A17 (denying a Mexican request for

unauthorized wiretap), was the product of plea bargaining,[220] is based primarily on unreliable witness testimony[221] or on discriminatory intent,[222] or there are signs of bad faith or corrupt prosecutors or police,[223] that court may not treat the evidence as admissible and thereby find the evidentiary standard for granting extradition has not been satisfied.

d Governmental Procedures and Processing

Among the principal factors impeding or deterring extradition in terms of governmental procedures and processing are: (i) ineffective or disempowered investigators, overreaching prosecutors, corrupt bureaucrats (from the executive and judicial branches alike), and decision-shy, intimidated, or unavailable judges; (ii) the often excessive time, heavy expense, and ultimate uncertainty involved in such matters; (iii) improper filing and paperwork; (iv) an array of timing issues; and (v) the failure to comply with host State domestic law.

extradition of Mexico's former Deputy Attorney General on murder charges on the grounds that the witness statements against him were obtained via torture).

220 *E.g.*, Shirley Christian, "Chile Indicates It Won't Turn Over Two to the U.S. in Letelier Case," *N.Y. Times*, June 15, 1987, at A10 ("In 1979, the Chilean Supreme Court rejected the United States' request to extradite two [Chilean intelligence officers] on the ground that the evidence against them had been obtained through plea bargaining, which is not acceptable under Chilean jurisprudence."). *See generally* "America's Legal Reach: The World's Lawyer," *The Economist*, June 6, 2015, at 50 ("European judicial systems discourage plea-bargaining because of the risk that suspects will not so much sing as compose, inventing stories that implicate others.").

221 *E.g., Gramenos v. Jewel Cos., Inc.*, 797 F.2d 432, 440 (7th Cir.) (the probable cause evidentiary requirement was not met where the testimony of the government's chief witness was deemed unreliable and unpersuasive and the credibility of the second key government witness was questioned), *cert. denied*, 481 U.S. 1028 (1987).

222 In both 1998 and 2004, the Government of Israel denied Poland's requests for the extradition of Salomon Morel, a naturalized Israeli citizen and Holocaust victim who had headed a Soviet prison camp at the tail end of World War II that allegedly brutalized Nazi and other German inmates, partly on the basis that the evidence against him was developed "during a time of virulent anti-Semitism, and directed against a Jewish citizen." *Letter from State of Israel, Office of the State Attorney, to the Gov't of Poland*, June 6, 2005, found on Poland's Institute of National Remembrance website, *available at* https://ipn.gov.pl/en/news/2006/response-by-the-state-of-israel-to-the-application-for-the-e (last visited on May 9, 2016).

223 *E.g., In re Saifi* [2001] 4 All E.R. 168 (ruling it was unfair to return the applicant to India on the ground that the evidence supporting the request for extradition was obtained in bad faith).

Investigators, Prosecutors, Bureaucrats, and Judges. The incapacity of a host State police force or other criminal investigative body to locate the whereabouts of a fugitive within its territory can ultimately stymie extradition, as such a transfer cannot occur without first finding and arresting the fugitive. Some host State law enforcement agencies, despite the best intentions, are simply not up to the task, as they lack the requisite skills and resources to hunt down wanted persons.[224] A related concern is when a police force is not empowered or authorized to arrest a top-level political leader (*e.g.*, Gen. Manuel Noriega while serving as *de facto* leader of Panama).[225] Moreover, prosecutorial misconduct can result in a scuttled extradition where, for instance, due process rights have been violated on account of a "breach of a valid prosecutor-defendant agreement."[226]

Some host States are hamstrung on account of corruption within their bureaucratic ranks to the extent they are susceptible to bribes, threats, payoffs, kickbacks, or favors, or simply harbor political sympathies.[227] Examples abound of such behavior or reasonable concerns thereof and include the following:

- In 1959, when West Germany finally sought the extradition from Argentina of Josef Mengele, the Nazi doctor responsible for conducting horrific scientific experiments on prisoners at the Auschwitz Concentration Camp, he disappeared before he could be arrested and resurfaced later in Paraguay, most likely based on an inside tip from a sympathetic Argentine official.[228]

[224] Jonathan A. Gluck, *The Customary Int'l Law of State-Sponsored Int'l Abduction and United States Courts*, 44 Duke L.J. 612, 613 n.8 (1994); Downing, *supra* n.32, at 576 (citing Lebanon as an example).

[225] Downing, *supra* n.32, at 576.

[226] *Plaster v. United States*, 720 F.2d 340 (4th Cir. 1983) (resulting in a U.S. extradition denial to Germany).

[227] Bassiouni, World Public Order, *supra* n.208, at 179–81; Melanie M. Laflin, Note, *Kidnapped Terrorists: Bringing Int'l Criminals to Justice Through Irregular Rendition and Other Quasi-Legal Options*, 26 J. Legis. 315, 318 (2000) (noting rampant bribery and corruption in Latin America influencing States' refusal to comply with extradition treaties).

[228] Gary J. Bass, *The Adolf Eichmann Case: Nat'l Jurisdiction*, *in* Universal Jurisdiction: National Courts and the Prosecution of Serious Crimes under International Law 87 (Stephen Macedo ed. 2004). Tellingly, throughout the post-World War II era, Argentina maintained a secret anti-Semitic order that, until it was acknowledged and repealed in 2005, barred Jews fleeing the Holocaust from entering Argentina. Monte Reel, "In South America, a 'Last Chance' to Hunt

- In the 1970s, after fleeing the United States for the Bahamas, Robert Vesco, a Wall Street financier who had stolen hundreds of millions of dollars from mutual fund investors, bribed Bahamian officials into not extraditing him.[229]
- For years until 1997, narcotics traffickers paid Mario Ruiz Massieu, Mexico's top anti-drug enforcement official and director of the Institute for Combating Drugs in Mexico (INCD), along with his agents, millions of dollars to allow illegal trafficking operations to proceed without interference.[230]
- "There is ample circumstantial evidence that an effort is underway to obstruct the extradition [in 1988] from the U.S. of CPT [Captain] Alvaro Rafael Saravia, the cashiered [dismissed] Salvadoran Air Force Officer charged with complicity in the March 24, 1980 assassination of Archbishop Oscar Arnulfo Romero," including the apparent collusion of an administrative law judge.[231]
- In May 2013, a Colombian Government official with access to U.S. requests for the extradition of alleged Colombian drug traffickers (Freddy Mauricio Tellez-Buitrago), and a Colombian criminal defense attorney (Adriana Gonzalez-Marquez) were extradited to the United States on charges of stealing sensitive information about U.S. extradition requests and selling it to a Colombian drug trafficker, and thereby obstructing justice.[232]

Governmental processing impediments likewise can occur when judges are unwilling to rule on extradition based on a purported

Down Nazi War Criminals," *Wash. Post*, Dec. 6, 2007, at A20. It was the knowledge of Mengele's escape that, a year later, led a Jewish West German prosecutor, Fritz Bauer, to provide Israel with newly acquired information that Adolf Eichmann was in Buenos Aires because he feared that if he told the West German Government, a Nazi sympathizer would tip off Eichmann or otherwise prevent his extradition. Bass, *supra*, at 80.

229 Michael R. Pontoni, *Authority of the United States to Extraterritorially Apprehend and Lawfully Prosecute Int'l Drug Traffickers and Other Fugitives*, 21 Cal. W. Int'l L.J. 215, 215–16 (1990–91); Ronald J. Ostrow, "FBI Gets OK for Overseas Arrests," *L.A. Times*, Oct. 13, 1989, at 1.

230 Rishi Hingoraney, *Int'l Extradition of Mexican Narcotics Traffickers: Prospects and Pitfalls for the New Millennium*, 30 Ga. J. Int'l & Comp. L. 331, 349–50 (2002).

231 "The Saravia Extradition and the D'Aubuisson Mafia," U.S. Dep't of State Cable, San Salvador 13183, Oct. 3, 1988 (declassified).

232 Bruze Zagaris, *Colombia Extradites Gov't Official and Criminal Defense Attorney to U.S. for Corruption Related to Extradition*, 29 IELR 331 (2013).

lack of jurisdiction or justiciability. In November 2005, for example, a Senegalese court (the *Chambre d'accusation* of the Dakar Court of Appeal) ruled that it was incompetent to opine on a Belgian request to extradite Hissène Habré, Chad's former leader, concerning charges of torture, war crimes, and crimes against humanity during his political tenure (1982–90), on the grounds that Habré was subject to immunity for acts committed as head of State in the exercise of his official functions.[233] That ruling, however, was rejected both by the African Union's (AU's) Assembly of Heads of State and Government by Decision 127 (VII) in July 2006, which mandated that Senegal prosecute him, and by the ICJ when it found in July 2012 that "the Republic of Senegal must, without further delay, submit the case of Mr. Hissène Habré to its competent authorities for the purpose of prosecution, if it does not extradite him."[234]

Finally, judges may be the targets of intimidation or even of homicide, such that it becomes difficult for them to carry out their jobs either because they are unwilling to risk their lives for the proper dispensation of justice or because, frankly, their ranks have been diminished and there are few left to conduct the work of the judiciary. For instance, in November 1990, in connection with announcing changes to help protect his nation's judges from assassination, the Colombian Justice Minister reported that "250 judges and magistrates [had been] killed by drug traffickers and other criminals and that 84 percent of cases [had been] dropped during the investigative stages, often when the judges ordering the investigations [were] killed or bribed."[235]

[233] Bruce Zagaris, *Senegal Allows Habre to Stay Pending African Union Decision*, 22 IELR 59, 59–60 (2006) [hereinafter Zagaris, *Senegal*].

[234] *Questions Relating to the Obligation to Prosecute or Extradite* (Belg. v. Sen.) [2012] I.C.J. Rep. 422, ¶¶ 23, 122(6) (July 20) (basing the decision specifically on text found in the CAT). Notably, the Dakar Court of Appeal ruling followed ones in July 2000 and in March 2001 in which Senegal's Court of Appeal and its Court of Cassation (*i.e.*, its highest court), respectively, ruled that Habré could not be adjudicated in Senegal for acts allegedly carried out in Chad for the Courts' lack of jurisdiction. *Id.* ¶¶ 17–18.

[235] Ken Dermota, "Colombia Gets Plan to Protect Its Judges," *Wash. Times*, Nov. 21, 1990, at A7.

Time, Expense, and Uncertainty. While a routine extradition request generally takes a number of months on average to process[236] – although in exceptional instances, such as when the individual consents or when a particularly dangerous, well-networked criminal is involved, it may take only a matter of days[237] – more legally complicated or politically charged cases can take significantly longer. Some extraditions can take two or three years to process,[238] while

[236] *See, e.g.*, Canada, Dep't of Justice, "Federal Involvement in the Case of Ernest Fenwick MacIntosh," Oct. 25, 2013 ("Over the past decade, most requests have taken between six and twenty months from the time the prosecutors have decided to seek an extradition, to the time the fugitive is returned to Canada."); U.K. Parliament, "The U.K.'s block opt-out of pre-Lisbon criminal law and policing measures – European Scrutiny Committee," Nov. 7, 2013, ¶ 109, *available at* www.publications.parliament.uk/pa/cm201314/cmselect/cmeuleg/683/68321.htm (last visited on May 28, 2016) ("On average, it takes approximately three months to extradite someone under an EAW. An extradition under Part 2 of the Extradition Act 2003, which is to say extradition to non-E.U. countries, takes approximately ten months."); UNODC, Implementation Review Group, *Implementation of Chapter IV (Int'l Cooperation) of the United Nations Conv. against Corruption: Thematic Report Prepared by the Secretariat*, U.N. Doc. No. CAC/COSP/IRG/2011/CRP.6, Sept. 2, 2011, ¶ 18 ("As to the average duration of extradition proceedings, two States parties provided information pointing to substantial differences in this regard, with one State party mentioning an average length of two to three months and the other of seven months.").

[237] *E.g.*, Bruce Zagaris, *Panama Extradites Alleged Colombia Drug Lord to the U.S.*, 20 IELR 89, 89–90 (2004) (in January 2004, only four days after a joint U.S.-Panamanian law enforcement operation captured Arcangel de Jesus Henao Montoya, an alleged Colombian drug lord and one of its most suspected cocaine traffickers to the United States, he was extradited).

[238] *E.g.*, Bruce Zagaris, *Australia Extradites Alleged Software Pirate to U.S.*, 23 IELR 189, 189–90 (2007) (in early 2007, following approximately a three-year detention, Australia extradited to the United States a British national, Hew Raymond Griffiths, on criminal copyright infringement-related charges "as the leader of one of oldest and most prominent Internet software piracy groups called DrinkOrDie"); Andreas F. Lowenfeld, *Ahmad: Profile of an Extradition Case*, 23 N.Y.U. J. Int'l L. & Pol. 723, 724, 748 (1991) (for over three years until October 1990, Mahmoud El-Abed Ahmad, an Abu Nidal terrorist, was in detention pending extradition from the United States to Israel); AP, "Suspected Arms Trafficker Flown to NYC," *CBS New York*, Nov. 17, 2010, *available at* http://newyork.cbslocal.com/2010/11/17/suspected-arms-trafficker-flown-from-bangkok-to-nyc/ (last visited on May 28, 2016) (after more than two-and-a-half years, in November 2010, the Thai Government extradited to the United States Viktor Bout, "a Russian arms trafficking suspect accused of arming failed states and insurgents across the Third World since the 1990s").

others extend to five to ten years[239] or in extreme cases even decades.[240]

Such delay is largely a function of a multi-step legal process designed to protect national interests and individual rights alike.[241] Extradition might require a series of hearings; the supplemental request for and evaluation of evidence; recurring diplomatic channel communications between the host and pursuing States; numerous motions, appeals, and petitions at various levels, including in some instances the possible referral to a human rights tribunal for review;[242] bureaucratic discussions and in-fighting on strategic issues; and sensitive deliberation over discretionary calls.[243]

239 *E.g.*, Edmund S. McAlister, Note, *The Hydraulic Pressure of Vengeance:* United States v. Alvarez-Machain *and the Case for a Justifiable Abduction*, 43 DePaul L. Rev. 449, 475 n.197 (1994) (it took nine years and six court cases before Joseph Doherty was extradited from the United States to Ireland); Sandra Dibble, *Arellano Felix Cartel Leader Extradited to U.S.*, S.D. Union-Tribune, Apr. 29, 2011 (after nine years of litigation and appeals, Mexico extradited a leader of the Arellano-Felix Organization, Tijuana's dominant drug cartel, to the United States to face a RICO prosecution); Bruce Zagaris, *Interpol Issues Red Notice for Ex-Comverse Chief Wanted for Fraud*, 22 IELR 384, 385–86 (2006) (after almost five years, in 1993, Israel extradited to the United States Eddie Antar, founder of defunct electronics chain Crazy Eddie, Inc.); Bruce Zagaris, *Mexico Extradites Alleged Drug King Quintero-Payan to U.S.*, 26 IELR 270 (2010) (alleged Mexican drug kingpin Juan Jose Quintero-Payan fought extradition to the United States for eight years, although he finally reached the United States in April 2010); Bruce Zagaris, *Canada Extradites Schreiber to Germany*, 25 IELR 410, 410–11 (2009) (Karlheinz Schreiber, accused of fraud and bribery in connection with arms contracts, was extradited to Germany after a ten-year legal battle to stay in Canada, in part by threatening to disclose a scandal about a former Canadian prime minister).

240 *E.g.*, Tomislav Z. Kuzmanovic, Note, *The Artukovic Case: Do the Means Justify the End?*, 6 Wis. Int'l L.J. 155, 155 (1987) (Andrija Artuković, a Croatian politician known as the "Himmler of the Balkans," because he set up and operated concentration camps and committed war crimes against Jews, Roma, Serbs, and other minorities, was extradited from the United States to Yugoslavia after thirty-five years of litigation when he was eighty-six years old).

241 The Canadian justice system, for example, is notorious for offering a "protracted extradition process and lengthy appeals," encouraging a number of fugitives to relocate there to "escape justice for years." Doug Struck, "Fugitives From Other Places Go to Canada to Escape the Heat," *Wash. Post*, Oct. 29, 2005, at A14.

242 For example, the ECtHR ultimately cleared Abu Hamza al-Masri's extradition to the United States to face terrorist-related charges, despite his prospective lengthy incarceration in a maximum security U.S. prison if convicted. Alan Cowell & John F. Burns, "Britain Is Allowed to Send 5 Terror Suspects to U.S.," *IHT*, Apr. 11, 2012, at 6.

243 *See* Alona E. Evans, *Acquisition of Custody over the Int'l Fugitive Offender—Alternatives to Extradition: A Survey of United States Practice*, 40 B.Y.B.I.L. 77, 94 (1964) ("Delay [is] always present in a proceeding involving decision-making by various agencies – the extradition commissioner, the courts if the accused petitions for habeas corpus and

Sometimes, a pursuing State will submit successive extradition requests that over time are intended to present more compelling inculpatory evidence, or seek to accommodate host State requirements about the nature of the trial or potential punishment awaiting an extraditee,[244] or attempt to capitalize on newly introduced liberal legal reforms in the host State (*e.g.*, relaxed evidentiary standards) or changed factual circumstances in the pursuing State at issue (*e.g.*, the reduced risk of persecution due to new political leadership).

In addition, where international terrorism, piracy, or other such crimes are implicated, national intelligence services may wish to interrogate the extradition subject before he is transferred into the custody of law enforcement, thereby postponing extradition.[245] Delays for this or any other reason can operate to effectively deny an extradition altogether to the extent the subject of the extradition dies or becomes physically or mentally incapacitated in the meantime, and in the latter instance no longer becomes eligible for prosecution or punishment.[246]

Beyond the temporal considerations that can discourage some States from *pursuing* extradition, the costs associated with locating, arresting, detaining, processing, litigating, and ultimately transferring individuals can often be steep and thereby may serve as a deterrent to *host* States.

appeals are taken, and the Secretary of State"); McAlister, *supra* n.239, at 475 n.197; Bassiouni, World Public Order, *supra* n.208, at 179–81; Downing, *supra* n.32, at 576 n.22; Evert Clark & Nicholas Horrock, Contrabandista! 177–231 (1973).

244 *E.g.*, Bruce Zagaris, *Britain Agrees to Extradite Algerian to France on Terrorism Charges*, 22 IELR 58 (2006) (in 2001, the British High Court had ruled that Britain could not grant France's request for the extradition of Rashid Ramda a/k/a Abu Fares, an alleged member of the Groupe Islamique Armé, the Algerian militant organization that has sought to overthrow the Algerian Government and install an Islamic State, because he would be "subject to inhumane and degrading treatment" and a rigged trial in France; however, the British Home Secretary issued an extradition order in April 2005 on the basis that Abu Fares would receive a fair trial).

245 *E.g.*, Bruce Zagaris, *Turkey Requests Iraqi Extradition of Two Islamists for 2003 Attack*, 21 IELR 356, 356–57 (2005) (noting that the Turks, Americans, Iraqis, and even Israelis may wish to obtain intelligence from Burhan Kus and Sadettin Aktas, Turkish Islamists detained by the Iraqis in 2005, that could potentially delay their extradition to Turkey on charges related to their participation in a 2003 terrorist attack in Istanbul).

246 For example, Australian businessman Christopher Charles Skase, who fled to the Spanish island of Majorca, was sought throughout the 1990s by the Australian Government on charges related to business improprieties in connection with the Qintex company he owned and managed, but in August 2001, while proceedings with Dominica (a State in which he had become a citizen in 1998) were still underway, he died of stomach cancer and so succeeded in evading extradition. James Morton & Susanna Lobez, "Our Criminals on Parade," *The Australian*, Oct. 17, 2009. This circumstance illustrates *in extremis* the adage, "justice delayed is justice denied."

Unlike in the past,[247] host States today absorb these expenses, including legal fees and discovery, which can prove financially onerous.[248] As a result, some States limit their extradition-related activity to strictly high-profile, criminally egregious, and/or politically significant cases.[249]

Costs can mount, especially when extradition subjects are wealthy and willing to pay for top-tier legal counsel to represent their interests and explore every conceivable legal angle for as long as necessary to avoid extradition.[250] Even after all the time, money, and effort expended on extradition, however, the final result cannot necessarily be predicted; such uncertainty itself can dissuade would-be pursuing States from filing an extradition request in the first instance.[251]

Improper Filing and Paperwork. The simple erroneous filing of an extradition request can result in a denial. A misfiling may occur when the request is not submitted in written form or through diplomatic channels, at least where an applicable extradition treaty so dictates.[252] In addition, treaty-based extradition procedures can be complex[253] and may entail specialized domestic requirements of which pursuing State officials are not necessarily aware.[254] Moreover, an extradition request may need to

[247] Traditionally, all costs associated with apprehending, securing and transmitting a fugitive were to be paid by the requesting State. ABBELL, *supra* n.30, at 53. For example, "in 1939 [the U.S. state of] Nebraska asked the Department of State to withdraw its request for the extradition of a fugitive [Harry Fahrenbruch] from Mexico because of the expense to the [s]tate of maintaining an agent at the border for several weeks pending a decision as to whether the fugitive should be surrendered." Evans, *supra* n.243, at 95 & n.2 (1964).

[248] M. Cherif Bassiouni, *Unlawful Seizures and Irregular Rendition Devices as Alternatives to Extradition*, 7 VAND. J. TRANSNAT'L L. 25, 63–64 (1973); Downing, *supra* n.32, at 576–77 n.22 (costs include counsel hired for these proceedings and discovery expenses).

[249] *See* ETHAN A. NADELMANN, COPS ACROSS BORDERS: THE INTERNATIONALIZATION OF U.S. CRIMINAL LAW ENFORCEMENT 460 (1993); *cf.* Epps, *supra* n.18, at 374 ("Petty criminals are not often subject to extradition, in part because extradition is an expensive process and application of a cost-benefit analysis reveals that petty criminals are simply not worth pursuing.").

[250] *E.g.*, David Henry, "Marc Rich, "Fugitive Commodities Trader in 1980s, Dies at 78," *Bloomberg News*, June 26, 2013, *available at* www.bloomberg.com/news/articles/2013-06-26/marc-rich-fugitive-commodities-trader-in-80s-dies-78 (last visited on May 28, 2016) ("Rich, who held U.S., Spanish and Israeli citizenship at various times, [and whose assets were estimated at over US $1.5 billion], spent about two decades dodging a team of U.S. [M]arshals and international executives who operated under the code-name Otford Project. The group was tasked with bringing Rich back to the U.S.").

[251] Downing, *supra* n.32, at 576–77 n.22.

[252] IVAN A. SHEARER, EXTRADITION IN INTERNATIONAL LAW 207 (1971).

[253] DUFFY, *supra* n.24, at 108.

[254] *See* SHEARER, *supra* n.252, at 207–08 & n.5 (citing to *In re Ribeiro*, Sup. Ct. of Justice, Colom., July 2, 1958, *reprinted in* 26 ILR 525 (1963)) (an extradition request was denied

be sufficiently specific regarding the nature of the crime, the identity of the fugitive, and the underlying criminal offense, or it may be rejected.[255]

Further, the underlying arrest warrant must have been issued by a pursuing State court with applicable subject matter jurisdiction and with the authority to enforce the warrant,[256] and the arrest warrant itself on which the extradition request is based must be authentic[257] and non-defective.[258] Even when the filing itself is proper, post-extradition administrative errors can trigger an extradition subject's release from detention.[259]

Timing Issues. Late timing or undue delay in meeting *procedural* requirements or deadlines,[260] whether express or discretionary, also can obstruct an extradition. This can occur in one of several ways. First, the host State may deny a request in politically sensitive cases where expedited dispatch of the matter (typically via release or deportation) by the

where the pursuing State failed to assert that the offense was not time-barred, as required under municipal law).

255 *E.g., Malary v. Haiti*, Case 11.335, Inter-Am. C.H.R., OEA/ser. L/V/II.111, Doc. 20 rev. at 296, ¶ 88, Dec. 4, 2000 (referencing the case of Emmanuel Constant, the leader and founder of the FRAPH, a right-wing paramilitary group formed in 1993, implicated in the murder of Guy Malary whose extradition from the United States to Haiti was denied based on a "defective" factual submission).

256 *E.g., Sacirbey v. Guccione*, 589 F.3d 52 (2d Cir. 2009) (treating the issue as a matter of first impression and resulting in a grant of the defendant's petition for a writ of *habeas corpus*).

257 *E.g.*, Bruce Zagaris, *Senegalese Court Denies Belgian Extradition Request for Habré*, 28 IELR 86, 86–87 (2012) (citing as one ground for denying Belgium's extradition request that the copy of the international arrest warrant supporting the request was not authentic).

258 *E.g.*, H.R.S. Ryan, *Ex parte John Anderson*, 6 Queen's L.J. 382, 387 (1981) (discussing an historic case in Upper Canada in 1860, before the U.S. Civil War and the end of slavery in the United States, in which the United States, on behalf of the state of Missouri, sought the extradition from Canada under the Webster-Ashburton Treaty of escaped slave John Anderson on the grounds of "willfully, maliciously and feloniously stab[ing] and kill-[ing]" a woman, but the failure of the warrant to indicate that this act had been committed with "malice aforethought and thereby constituted murder" was deemed by the court to be invalid, and the defendant was released from custody).

259 For example, after France extradited an ETA terrorist, Maite Aranalde, to Spain in August 2009, and the French Court of Appeals had "mislaid" the applicable arrest warrant, a Spanish High Court judge granted Aranalde's release on bail. Bruce Zagaris, *Spanish Judge Tries to Re-Arrest Missing ETA Terrorist After French Judicial Error*, 25 IELR 439, 439–40 (2009).

260 These constraints are to be distinguished from statutes of limitations (or prescription) of a *substantive* character that foreclose prosecution in cases when the prescribed period of time for bringing a criminal action, if any, has passed as measured against the date of the underlying crime or its discovery (discussed *supra*).

host State evidently is of paramount importance. For instance, in 1977, a Paris Court of Appeals found no criminal issue with Abu Daoud, a Palestinian alleged to have participated in the 1972 massacre of Israeli Olympic athletes in Munich, after a cursory twenty-minute proceeding only four days after his arrest, and so instead ordered his expulsion to Algeria, thereby thwarting West Germany's extradition request on the grounds that it had not yet been verified via diplomatic channels.[261]

Second, extradition can be denied where a pursuing State fails to meet a treaty-based submission deadline,[262] or takes excessive time post-indictment to invoke an extradition treaty and seek the fugitive's return, at least where a pursuing State is aware of the fugitive's whereabouts. The logic underlying this latter refusal is that it would be unjust and oppressive vis-à-vis the fugitive to delay progress on extradition once a decision has been made to charge him with a crime.[263]

For example, in June 2001, Spain denied a U.S. extradition request for a former U.S. automobile industry executive for misappropriating trade secrets, in part due to "the fact that the United States took seven years to formulate the extradition request."[264] This dynamic applies *a fortiori* in instances where (i) the fugitive has asked to be returned,[265] or (ii) a pursuing State fails to formally seek extradition after the host State has effected the provisional arrest of a fugitive on a pursuing

261 *See* Liskofsky, *supra* n.76 (adding that Algeria received Daoud with a hero's welcome" and that Israel had also sought his extradition but was denied for other suspect reasons). Notably, the chambre d'accusation did not elaborate on why it felt the case needed to be disposed of so promptly and was unwilling to wait perhaps a few extra days for the West German Government to confirm its official request. *Id.*

262 In other cases, the failure to meet a filing deadline can prove inconsequential. *See, e.g.*, *Geldof v. Meulemeester & Steffen*, Court of Cassation, Belg., Feb. 20, 1961, [1961] *Pasicrise belge* 674 [French text], *reprinted in* 31 ILR 385 (E. Lauterpacht ed. 1966) (the Netherlands Government extradited the subject despite Belgium's extradition request submitted two days after the deadline set by the governing treaty).

263 A post-indictment delay in seeking extradition is an equitable consideration. *Platko*, 213 F. Supp.2d at 1234. Interestingly, although the Sixth Amendment to the U.S. Constitution grants to criminal defendants the right to a speedy *trial*, no such right exists to a speedy *extradition hearing* under either that Amendment or the due process clause of the Fifth Amendment. SUSAN N. HERMAN, THE RIGHT TO A SPEEDY AND PUBLIC TRIAL: A REFERENCE GUIDE TO THE UNITED STATES CONSTITUTION 221 (2006).

264 "Madrid Court Rejects Extradition in GM Case," *Wall St. J.*, June 20, 2001, at A15.

265 For example, in *United States v. McConahy*, a U.S. appellate court found that a five-year delay in filing a request for extradition was unjustifiably long where the fugitive was known to be in a foreign prison and his return had not been requested. 505 F.2d 770, 773–74 (7th Cir. 1974).

State's behalf, as the individual should not be held any longer than can be reasonably justified.[266]

Third, even when an extradition request is timely filed with the host State, it still can be refused to the extent that sufficient evidence supporting that request is not presented within a prescribed or other reasonable period of time.[267] A variant on that theme is when the host State is unwilling to entertain a pursuing State request for additional time to collect, prepare, or produce supplemental evidence, which sometimes occurs when the host State wishes to dispose of a case quickly to avoid potential political embarrassment. For example, in the *Eisler* case, the British magistrate released Gerhart Eisler after only two weeks in custody in May 1949 while rejecting a U.S. request for more time to arrange for additional documentation to be submitted in support of his extradition.[268]

Fourth, host State domestic law may require a fugitive's release if he is held beyond a certain maximum time period pending an extradition determination, regardless of the number of court appeals and their repeated failure.[269] Finally, once the host State has determined that a fugitive is to be extradited, should a pursuing State fail to arrange for his return within a specified time or without undue delay, the fugitive can request and may obtain release from detention under some municipal legal systems.[270]

Non-compliance with Host State Domestic Law. Finally, at times the host State will deny an extradition request strictly because certain of its domestic criminal laws or protocols were not followed apart from those related to filing, paperwork, and timing. For example, where a pursuing State has taken liberties in terms of collecting case-related information or

266 Stanbrook & Stanbrook, *supra* n.12, at 144–45.

267 *Id.*; for example, in November 2010, Spain released fugitive Carlos Vielman, who was alleged to have participated in the extrajudicial killing of prisoners in Guatemalan jails, when Guatemala failed to timely supply a supporting document in connection with its extradition request. Bruce Zagaris, *Spain Releases Former Minister After Guatemala Fails to Meet Deadline*, 27 IELR 558 (2011).

268 *Eisler*, 170 F.2d 273; George A. Finch, Editorial Comment, *The Eisler Extradition Case*, 43 AJIL 487, 490 (1949).

269 *E.g.*, Jack Ewing, "Financier, Free Again, Comes to Rest on Home Turf," *INYT*, Aug. 4, 2014, at 1, 16 (discussing the case of German financier Florian Homm, who was released from prison in Pisa, Italy, in June 2014, despite a succession of failed appeals, but where his attorneys exploited a loophole in the Italian legal system regarding the maximum period of detention pending extradition).

270 *E.g.*, 18 U.S.C. § 3188 (2012) ("Time of Commitment Pending Extradition").

surveilling or interrogating a fugitive on host State territory without the knowledge or participation of local law enforcement authorities, the host State may determine that a violation of its local criminal law has occurred, and consequently choose to reject an extradition request. This occurred in February 2014 when the Court of Justice in Curaçao denied the U.S. extradition request for three individuals on drug trafficking charges because it found that the United States had breached Dutch criminal laws in the manner in which the United States had undertaken its in-country investigation of the suspects without the knowledge or involvement of the Public Prosecutor.[271]

* * * * *

This chapter has examined the first set of impediments to extradition with a focus on legal standards and governmental factors. The next chapter will identify and assess impediments arising out of the fugitive's individual status and circumstances.

[271] *See* Bruce Zagaris, *Curacao Denies U.S. Extradition Request for 3 Persons Accused of Narcotics Offenses*, 30 IELR 173 (2014).

6

Impediments II

Individual Status and Circumstances

This chapter focuses exclusively on impediments to extradition arising out of a fugitive's individual status or circumstances, and consists of the following four sections: (i) nationality or residency bars; (ii) immunities; (iii) special relationships; and (iv) personal circumstances.

a Nationality or Residency Bars

An individual's status[1] in a given State could be as a national, whether born or naturalized, and whether maintaining one or plural nationalities.[2] Alternatively, an individual could be a permanent or temporary resident alien,[3] an illegal (or prohibited) alien,[4]

[1] Cases exist when an individual's nationality or citizenship status is factually indeterminate. *E.g., Levinge v. Director of Custodial Services, et al.*, N.S.W. Ct. of App., July 23, 1987, 9 N.S.W. L. Rep. 546, 549 ("The determination of whether or not the appellant was and is a citizen of the United States or Mexico is impossible to make on the materials before this Court.").

[2] *See* n.5 in the Introduction for a definition of the terms "nationals" and "nationality."

[3] "The term 'resident alien' is generally understood as referring to an alien who has been admitted to and has resided in the territory of a State for a period of time in accordance with the relevant national laws." UNGA, *Expulsion of Aliens*, U.N. Doc. A/CN.4/565, July 10, 2006, at 99 [hereinafter *Expulsion of Aliens*]. A *temporary* resident alien is a non-national whose presence in that State has been authorized via a work, tourist, or student visa and is limited in time. Under U.S. law, "[i]n return for the U.S. granting temporary residence, these aliens owe 'temporary allegiance' to the United States. Temporary allegiance involves obeying all U.S. laws while within the U.S., implied consent to U.S. court jurisdiction for alleged violation of tort and commercial laws, and submission to the court system's power of subpoena." Rights, Privileges, and Duties of Aliens," Legal Info. Inst. website, *available at* www.law.cornell.edu/wex/alien (last visited on May 9, 2016). In the United States, a *permanent* resident alien (now known as a lawful permanent resident, or LPR) enjoys more rights and privileges than a temporary resident alien, including the right to reside permanently in the United States, the opportunity to apply for U.S. citizenship, and the right to attend public schools and universities.

[4] "The term 'illegal alien' is generally understood as referring to an alien whose status is illegal as a result of failing to comply with the relevant national laws of the territorial State

a refugee,[5] or an asylee.[6] Although customary international law, in principle, imposes no restrictions on the extradition of a host State national, a pursuing State national, or a third State national,[7] a number of States have chosen not to extradite their own *nationals*[8] or, less commonly, their *residents*. In addition to analyzing these two scenarios, this section examines concerns raised by *third States* when their nationals are the subject of (typically non-treaty-based) extraditions between other States.

Perhaps the single most common barrier to extradition[9] is the unwillingness on the part of many States, particularly those with a civil law

concerning the admission, the continuing presence, the permitted activities or the residence of aliens." *Expulsion of Aliens, supra* n.3, at 98. This defintion would encompass any aliens lacking proper documentation.

[5] "Refugees within the mandate of UNHCR, and therefore eligible for protection and assistance by the international community, include not only those who can, on a case-by-case basis, be determined to have a well-founded fear of persecution on certain grounds (so-called 'statutory refugees'); but also other often large groups of persons who can be determined or presumed to be without, or unable to avail themselves of, the protection of the government of their State of origin (now often referred to as 'displaced persons' or 'persons of concern'). In each case, it is essential that the persons in question should have crossed an international frontier and that, in the case of the latter group, the reasons for flight should be traceable to conflicts, or radical political, social, or economic changes in their own country. With fundamental human rights at issue, the key remains violence, or the risk or threat of violence, but only in certain cases; those who move because of pure economic motivation, pure personal convenience or criminal intent are excluded." GUY S. GOODWIN-GILL, THE REFUGEE IN INTERNATIONAL LAW 29 (2d ed. 1996) (citation omitted).

[6] "A person enjoying asylum may be referred to as an 'asylee'. He may or may not be a refugee in accordance with an accepted definition in international or municipal law." Atle Grahl-Madsen, *Territorial Asylum, in* 1 ENCYCLOPEDIA OF PUBLIC INTERNATIONAL LAW 283–84 (Rudolf Bernhardt ed. 1992). *See also* n.99 in Chapter 5.

[7] SIR ROBERT JENNINGS & SIR ARTHUR WATTS, EDS., 1 OPPENHEIM'S INTERNATIONAL LAW 955 (9th ed. 1992).

[8] By contrast, this impediment generally does not apply to the surrender of fugitives to international criminal tribunals. HELEN DUFFY, THE 'WAR ON TERROR' AND THE FRAMEWORK OF INTERNATIONAL LAW 110 (2005). For an exception, *see* Const. of the Repub. of Poland, Apr. 2, 1997, art. 55, *as published in* Dziennik Utsaw No. 78, Item 483 ("Poland need not surrender a Polish citizen to an international judicial body in connection with genocide, crimes against humanity, war crimes or crimes of aggression").

[9] Neil Boister, *The Trend to 'Universal Extradition' over Subsidiary Universal Jurisdiction in the Suppression of Transnat'l Crime*, 2003 ACTA JURIDICA 287, 299 (2003). Some extradition treaties, however, expressly prohibit this ground for refusal. *E.g.*, Treaty on Extradition, U.S.-Rom., Sept. 10, 2007, S. Treaty Doc. 110–11, 2 CTIA 351, 364 (2007) ("Extradition shall not be refused based on citizenship of the person sought.").

tradition,[10] to extradite their own nationals to other States. This concept, which is based on a "strong notion of [a State's] exclusive criminal jurisdiction over its own nationals,"[11] effectively creates a safe haven for persons committing crimes overseas who manage to return to their State of nationality before being arrested (at least to the extent the State in question itself chooses not to prosecute him).[12]

[10] *See* Boister, *supra* n.9, at 299 (citing German and Austrian law as examples); Michael Abbell, Extradition to and from the United States 79 (2010) (most post-1960s U.S. extradition treaties with civil law countries "[p]rovid[e] power to exercise discretion in extradition of (one's) own nationals"). By contrast, common law States generally have maintained a policy of not denying extradition requests on nationality grounds. Melanie M. Laflin, Note, *Kidnapped Terrorists: Bringing Int'l Criminals to Justice Through Irregular Rendition and Other Quasi-Legal Options*, 26 J. Legis. 315, 317–18 (2000); Jennings & Watts, *supra* n.7, at 956 (the United Kingdom does not distinguish between its own and other nationals in making extradition decisions); *Sayne v. Shipley*, 418 F.2d 679 (5th Cir. 1969) (absent treaty provisions to the contrary, U.S. practice has been to extradite its nationals). The flexibility of the U.S. stance on this matter is exemplified by 18 U.S.C. § 3196 (2012) (incorporated under the Int'l Narcotics Control Act of 1990, Nov. 21, 1990, § 11(a), Pub. L. 101-623, Nov. 21, 1990, § 11(a)) ("If the applicable treaty or convention does not obligate the United States to extradite its citizens to a foreign country, the Secretary of State may, nevertheless, order the surrender to that country of a United States citizen whose extradition has been requested by that country if the other requirements of that treaty or convention have been met.").

[11] Boister, *supra* n.9, at 299. *Accord* Beverly Izes, *Drawing Lines in the Sand: When State-Sanctioned Abduction of War Criminals Should be Permitted*, 31 Colum. J. L. & Soc. Probs. 1, 5 (1997–98); Geoff Gilbert, *Extradition, in* The Harvard Research in International Law: Contemporary Analysis and Appraisal 264 (John P. Grant & J. Craig Barker eds. 2007); Zsuzsanna Deen-Racsmány, *Modernizing the Nationality Exception: Is the Non-extradition of Residents a Better Rule?*, 75 Nordic J. Int'l L. 29, 29–30 (2006) [hereinafter Deen-Racsmány, *Nationality Exception*] (noting that it is "disadvantageous to be tried in a foreign language, separated from friends, resources and character witnesses"); *e.g.*, *In re Arevalo*, Sup. Ct., Colom., Apr. 30, 1942, *reprinted in* 10 Ann. Dig. & Rep. Pub. Int'l L. Cases 329, 330 (No. 99) (H. Lauterpacht ed. 1945) (expressing concern about the "grave dangers" to Colombian nationals in trials in other States and indicating a statutory intention to prosecute such nationals in Colombian courts). This practice dates back to medieval times and is rooted in the notion that feudal subjects were "entitled not to be withdrawn from the jurisdiction of local courts (*ius de non evocando*)." Laflin, *supra* n.10, at 317–18. In States that do not bar extradition on nationality grounds, this protection is arguably offset by the *prima facie* or probable cause evidence requirement. *See* Ivor Stanbrook & Clive Stanbrook, Extradition: Law and Practice 133 (2d ed. 2000).

[12] In addition to possibly contributing to impunity, a State's refusal to extradite its own nationals or otherwise prosecute such cases could well have evidentiary, diplomatic, and human rights implications. *See* Laflin, *supra* n.10, at 333 (noting that the State where the crime occurred generally has a stronger interest in prosecution); *Bonnechaux v. Switzerland*, Appl. No. 8224/78, Eur. Comm'n of Hum. Rts., 18 D.R. 100, Dec. 5, 1979 (concerned about a French national's release and his likely flight to France, a nearly three-year pre-trial detention of a 74-year-old was upheld). But although the purpose is to

This issue is less straightforward than it may first appear because States apply different domestic law definitions and forms to nationality; the legal source for the non-extradition of nationals may be constitutional or statutory;[13] the nature of this practice can be applied in absolute terms or with exceptions, and in some instances can even be waived by the individual;[14] and the domestic law on this matter across many States has changed in recent years. These dimensions warrant closer examination.

The *constitutions* of some States, such as Honduras,[15] Russia,[16] and Venezuela,[17] contain blanket prohibitions regarding the extradition of their own nationals, assuming they can prove their nationality.[18] Other

ensure a fair trial for the accused, it can prove "overprotective" in instances where the underlying crime is particularly horrific, such as genocide, in which case there is a more compelling need for accountability than insulation. Izes, *supra* n.11, at 6. For its first thirty years of statehood, Israel had a policy of extraditing its nationals, but in 1978 it shifted gears and adopted the civil law approach of the non-extradition of nationals; by the mid-1990s, however, Israel recognized it was becoming a safe haven for Jewish criminals, so by 1999 it reverted to a policy of extraditing its nationals but with a caveat for those resident in Israel at the time the extradition request is lodged, such that they need to serve any imposed sentence in Israel. Abraham Abramovsky & Jonathan I. Edelstein, *The Post-Sheinbein Israeli Extradition Law: Has It Solved the Extradition Problems Between Israel and the United States or Has It Merely Shifted the Battleground?*, 35 VAND. J. TRANSNAT'L L. 1, 2–3 (2002). *See also infra* n.46.

13 DUFFY, *supra* n.8, at 110; Richard Downing, Recent Development, *The Domestic and Int'l Legal Implications of the Abduction of Criminals from Foreign Soil*, 26 STAN. J. INT'L L. 573, 576 (1989–90).

14 Such a waiver was invoked, for instance, by then-IMF President Dominque Strauss-Kahn, a French national, as a condition of obtaining bail so as to avoid pre-trial confinement in New York in connection with his arrest on sexual assault charges. "Dominique Strauss-Kahn Waives His Extradition Rights," *The Telegraph* (London), May 19, 2011.

15 Const. of Honduras, Jan. 11, 1982, art. 102, *as amended* ("No Honduran may be expatriated nor delivered by the authorities to a foreign State.").

16 Const. of the Russian Federation, Dec. 12. 1993, art. 61(1) ("A citizen of the Russian Federation may not be deported out of Russia or extradited to another State.").

17 Const. of the Bolivarian Repub. of Venezuela, Dec. 15, 1999, art. 69. Prior to 1999, Venezuela had only a statutory bar in place. U.S. Department of State, *Third Report on Int'l Extradition Pursuant to Section 3203 of the Emergency Supplemental Act, 2000, as Enacted in Public Law 106–246 Relating to Plan Colombia* (2002) [hereinafter *Third Report on Int'l Extradition*].

18 Where an accused cannot prove he is a national, he is not generally protected against extradition on nationality grounds under a State's constitution. *E.g., In re Vasquez*, Sup. Ct., El Salvador, July 4, 1938, [1938] 43 *Revista Judicial* 304 [Spanish text]. Incidentally, in July 2000, El Salvador voted to amend its constitution to permit the extradition of its nationals. Bruce Zagaris, *El Salvadoran Legislature Approves Constitutional Amendment to Allow Extradition of Nationals*, 16 IELR 901, 901 (2000).

national constitutions provide significant, albeit not categorical, extradition-related protection to their own nationals; for example:

- the current Constitution of Brazil insulates all Brazilian-born nationals from extradition, but would permit the extradition of its *naturalized* citizens in two specified instances;[19]
- the Constitution of Colombia authorizes extradition of its "native-born" nationals but only in connection with crimes committed after December 17, 1997 (the effective date of the amendment), and only for offenses calling for a minimum prison sentence of four years;[20]
- the Constitution of Cyprus permits the extradition of Cypriot nationals to States operating under the Council Framework Decision of 2002, but otherwise only for crimes committed before July 26, 2006 (the effective date of the amendment);[21]

[19] Const. of Braz., Oct. 5, 1988, art. 5, *as amended* ("No Brazilian shall be extradited, except the naturalized ones in the case of a common crime committed before naturalization, or in the case there is sufficient evidence of participation in the illicit traffic of narcotics and related drugs, under the terms of the law"). This constitutional provision expressly supersedes the U.S.-Brazil Extradition Treaty that entered into force in 1964, which allows for the extradition of anyone accused or convicted of a crime carrying a sentence of one year or more. Treaty on Extradition, U.S.-Braz., Jan. 13, 1961, 15 U.S.T. 2093, T.I.A.S. No. 5691.

[20] Const. of Colombia, July 4, 1991, art. 35. This constitution was amended on December 17, 1997, to allow for extradition of its native-born nationals but only under the two identified conditions, thereby effectively barring the extradition of a number of drug cartel leaders for earlier committed crimes, and authorizing extradition only for a limited scope of offenses. *Third Report on Int'l Extradition, supra* n.17. In 1999, Colombia extradited a home-grown drug lord for the first time in nine years, Bruce Zagaris, *Colombia Extradites Suspected Drug Lord to the U.S.*, 16 IELR 556 (2000), and since then several native-born Colombians have been extradited to the United States, including members of the FARC. Gilbert, *supra* n.11, at 268. Relatedly, in December 1986, the Colombian Supreme Court found the 1979 U.S.-Colombia Extradition Treaty, which had allowed the transfer of nationals to the United States, to be invalid on the ground that the Treaty's enabling legislation was defective; this occurred after a campaign of terror by the *extraditables*, drug traffickers subject to extradition. Corrective enabling legislation, signed by President Barco, resolved matters for a brief interlude, until February 17, 1987, when the Supreme Court refused to rule on extradition, given that there was no treaty in force. Notwithstanding that constraint, for the next decade Colombia extradited some non-native-born fugitives to the United States under executive decree. Boister, *supra* n.9, at 299 n.70; *Third Report on Int'l Extradition, supra* n.17; Igor I. Kavass, *Colombia: Supreme Court Decision on Law Concerning the Extradition Treaty Between Colombia and the United States*, June 25, 1987, *reprinted in* 27 ILM 492 (1988).

[21] Cyprus, National Procedures for Extradition, CoE website, *available at* www.coe.int/t/dghl/standardsetting/pc-oc/Country_information1_en_files/CYPRUS%20%20national%20procedures%20for%20extradition.pdf (last visited on May 9, 2016).

- the Constitution of Germany allows the extradition of its nationals to only two types of destinations;[22] and
- the Constitutions of Georgia, Italy, and Lithuania bar the extradition of their nationals unless an international treaty prescribes otherwise.[23]

In addition, many States have expressed through *national legislation* a policy to refuse the extradition of their own nationals, either wholesale, in principle, or only under specified circumstances. Examples of absolute prohibition include Libya,[24] Morocco,[25] Namibia,[26]

[22] Germany, Basic Law for the F.R.G., May 8, 1949, art. 16(2), *published as revised* in the Fed. Law Gazette Part III, classification number 100–1, *last amended* by the Act of 21 July 2010 (Fed. Law Gazette I p. 944) ("No German may be extradited to a foreign country. The law can provide otherwise for extraditions to a member state of the European Union or to an international court of justice as long as the rule of law is upheld."). The German Constitution was amended in 2006 to implement the Rome Statute of the ICC and the EAW to allow for the extradition of German nationals under certain conditions. Michael Plachta, *Polish Parliament Amends Constitution to Accommodate European Arrest Warrant*, 23 IELR 48, 49 (2007). An earlier iteration of Germany's Constitution, which afforded no exception under art. 16(2), was interpreted to prohibit Germany from handing back a German citizen "to the country from which he had come in order that his extradition might be accomplished through the territory of a country other than Germany." *Extradition (Germany) Case*, Fed. Const. Ct., FRG, Oct. 20, 1959, 10 BVerfGE 136, *reprinted in* 28 ILR 319, 319–20 (1963). When Florian Homm, a German financier wanted by the United States for defrauding investors, was released from prison in Pisa, Italy, in June 2014, he immediately took a train to Florence, where, upon arrival, he contacted his lawyers who arranged for a car to "whisk him to Germany," where he reportedly "let out a whoop of joy," given Germany's unwillingness to extradite one of its own nationals under the circumstances at play. Jack Ewing, "Financier, Free Again, Comes to Rest on Home Turf," *INYT*, Aug. 4, 2014, at 1.

[23] Const. of Georgia, Aug. 24, 1995, art. 13(4), *as amended*; Const. of the Repub. of Italy, Const. of the Repub. of Lithuania, Oct. 25, 1992, art. 13; Dec. 22, 1947, art. 26(1), *as amended* (Italian nationals can be extradited where "expressly envisaged by international conventions.").

[24] Article 493 of the Libyan Code of Crim. Proc. provides that Libya may extradite offenders insofar as "the extradition does not relate to a Libyan citizen." Donna E. Arzt, *The Lockerbie 'Extradition by Analogy' Agreement: 'Exceptional Measure' or Template for Transnat'l Criminal Justice?*, 18 Am. U. Int'l L. Rev. 163, 174 (2002); *Letter from the Perm. Rep. of the Libyan Arab Jamahiriya, to the Pres. of the UNSC*, U.N. Doc. S/23441, Jan. 18, 1992.

[25] Middle East and North Africa Financial Action Task Force (MENAFATF), *Mutual Evaluation Report of The Kingdom of Morocco on Anti-Money Laundering and Combating Financing of Terrorism*, Nov. 6, 2007, ¶¶ 394–95, *available at* www.menafatf.org/images/UploadFiles/MENAFATF.5.07.E.P6.R1_02-01-08_.pdf (last visited on May 28, 2016).

[26] Namibia, Extradition Act 11 of 1996, July 1, 1996, § 2(1).

Nicaragua,[27] the PRC,[28] and Sweden.[29] Instances of qualified bars can be found in:

- the Dominican Republic – authorizing "the extradition of [D.R.] nationals only for [serious] charges, including murder, kidnapping, sexual abuse of minors, as well as other [including narcotics] offenses";[30]
- Japan – adopting a policy not to extradite Japanese nationals in all cases unless an extradition treaty provides otherwise;[31] and
- Switzerland – maintaining the right of refusal in principle not to extradite Swiss nationals, but may do so with an individual's written consent.[32]

Naturalized citizens nearly always receive the same preferential treatment as born citizens do in States that refuse to extradite their nationals.[33] Accordingly, where an actual or accused offender can obtain naturalized citizenship in a State that has a firm policy of protecting its own nationals from exposure to foreign legal systems, extradition can be thwarted. For example, in 1949, Herbertus Bikker, a Dutch national, was given a life sentence by Dutch courts for committing war crimes in the Netherlands while acting as a German SS officer during World War II; in

[27] Nicaragua, Code of Crim. Proc., Nov. 13, 2001, art. 349, *reprinted in available at* www.oas.org/juridico/mla/fr/nic/fr_nic-ext-gen-process.doc – 02/06/2008 (last visited on May 9, 2016) ("Nicaraguans may not be extradited from the national territory.").

[28] PRC, Extradition Law, Order of the President No. 42, adopted at the 19th Meeting of the Standing Comm. of the Ninth National People's Congress, Dec. 28, 2000, art. 8 [hereinafter PRC Extradition Law] (the PRC may refuse extradition request from a foreign State if: "(1) the person sought is a national of the People's Republic of China under the laws of the People's Republic of China").

[29] Sweden, Extradition for Crim. Offences (1957:668), Dec. 6, 1957, § 2, *as amended* ("A Swedish national may not be extradited under this Act.").

[30] *See* Joshua H. Warmund, *Removing Drug Lords and Street Pushers: The Extradition of Nationals in Colombia and the Dominican Republic*, 22 Fordham Int'l L.J. 2373, 2422–24 (1999) (discussing Dominican Republic's Ley No. 278–98 of July 29, 1998, and noting how the D.R.'s prior law, Ley No. 489-69 (1969), had eliminated any discretion on the part of its executive branch in terms of extraditing nationals and thereby had created a safe haven for D.R. nationals committing crimes abroad).

[31] Japanese Ministry of Justice, Law of Extradition, Law No. 68 of 1953, art. 2(9), *as amended*. As noted above, Japan refused the extradition to Peru of former Peruvian President Alberto Fujimori, partly on the grounds that he is a Japanese national. Tetsuya Morimoto, *First Japanese Denial of U.S. Extradition Request: Economic Espionage Case*, 20 IELR 288 (2004).

[32] Switz., Federal Act on Int'l Mutual Assistance in Crim. Matters [IMAC], Mar. 20, 1981, art. 7(1)&(2), *as amended, reprinted in* 20 ILM 1339 (1981).

[33] An exception can be seen in the Constitution of Brazil, *supra* n.19.

1952 he managed to escape from prison and flee to West Germany, where, based on his SS membership, he was granted German citizenship. For years, Germany refused to extradite this naturalized citizen back to the Netherlands under its strict "non-extradition of nationals" law.[34]

In 1933, a Greek court refused extradition to Bulgaria where a Bulgarian citizen had acquired Greek nationality *after* the offense that was the subject of the extradition, but where the governing Greek statute categorically rejected the transfer of any Greek national to a foreign power.[35] In addition, at times it appears that some States with such nationality-based exclusionary policies have intentionally expedited the naturalization process or otherwise promptly conferred citizenship to help shield certain persons from extradition.[36]

When determining how to reconcile domestic laws with competing provisions found in bilateral extradition treaties with respect to the non-extradition of nationals, the more restrictive legal authority, generally prevails, and in practice can obstruct the extradition of nationals even involving egregious offenses.[37] Even when such laws or

[34] Zsuzsanna Deen-Racsmány, *A New Passport to Impunity?: Non-Extradition of Naturalized Citizens versus Criminal Justice*, 2 J. INT'L CRIM. JUST. 761, 761–62 (2004) [hereinafter Deen-Racsmány, *Passport to Impunity*]; Gilbert, *supra* n.11, at 265 & n.68.

[35] *In re D.G.D.*, Ct. of Thrace (Chambre du Conseil), Greece, [1933] 46 *Thémis* 291, *reprinted in* 7 ANN. DIG. & REP. INT'L LAW CASES 335, 335 [1933–1934] (No. 141) (H. Lauterpacht ed.) (1940).

[36] *E.g.*, Deen-Racsmány, *Passport to Impunity, supra* n.34, at 762 (in November 2003, Russian Jew Leonid Nevzlin was granted Israeli citizenship with extraordinary speed; concerns spread that friendly Israeli officials may have expedited his naturalization to shield him from prosecution in Russia where he had been a close associate of Mikhail Khodorkovsky, former head of the Russian oil company Yukos, who was under pre-trial arrest in Moscow for charges of fraud and tax evasion); George Ginsburgs, *Russia's Practice of Extraditing Political Offenders to Azerbaijan: Rendition Refused*, 16 CRIM. L.F. 303, 312–13 (2005) (discussing the expedited nationality granted to Abdurakhman Vezirov, former First Secretary of the Central Committee of the Communist Party of Azerbaijan, by Russia, thereby immunizing him from extradition on charges of abuse of power and official position); Bruce Zagaris, *Iceland Grants Bobby Fischer Citizenship and Japan Deports Him to Iceland*, 21 IELR 186, 186–88 (2005) (in March 2005, Iceland's Parliament in short order granted U.S. national and chess champion Bobby Fischer citizenship, resulting in Japan's decision to release him from detention and deport him to Iceland rather than send him to the United States, which had requested his extradition on charges that he had violated economic sanctions against Yugoslavia by accepting payment to play an exhibition chess match there in 1992).

[37] *See* Arnd Düker, *The Extradition of Nationals: Comments on the Extradition Request for Alberto Fujimori*, 4 GERMAN L.J. 1165, 1170–73 (2003) (discussing Peru's request for the extradition of former Peruvian President Alberto Fujimori, who was accused of murder

policies that militate against the extradition of one's own nationals do not operate to outright prevent the physical transfer of a fugitive into another's State's custody or control, they can sometimes result in delays through additional legal process and/or potentially mitigate the severity of a national's punishment.[38] In addition, at least one extradition treaty stipulates that extradition may be conditioned on a pursuing State's assurance that if the fugitive is a host State national and is extradited, tried, and convicted, he must be returned to the host State to serve out any assigned sentence.[39]

States desiring not to extradite their own nationals can additionally rely on domestic laws that broadly define nationality status for extradition purposes.[40] Such laws can expansively encompass, or can be judicially construed to include, for example, other States' nationals,[41] persons sharing an ethnic bond,[42] or those having children who are nationals of the host State.[43] The other major way the term "national" tends to become subject to

and torture); Robert Cryer, et al., An Introduction to International Criminal Law and Procedure 79 (2d ed. 2010).

38 For example, a few months after fleeing North Carolina, U.S. Marine Cpl. Cesar Laurean, the prime suspect in the murder of a pregnant Marine in that state, was arrested in Mexico where he also held citizenship. That status entitled him under Mexican law to receive an extradition hearing and expressly removed the prospect of the death penalty as a condition of extradition under Mexican law. "DA Expects Captured Marine Back in U.S. Quickly," *CNN*, Apr. 11, 2008, *available at* www.cnn.com/2008/CRIME/04/11/missing.marine/index.html?eref=ib_topstories (last visited on May 28, 2016). Dual citizenship can play out in different ways. The U.S.-Jamaica extradition treaty, for example, is explicit that dual U.S.-Jamaican citizens may not be withheld from extradition on the basis of nationality. Treaty on Extradition, U.S.-Jam., June 14, 1983, art. VII(2).

39 *See* Prot. between the Gov't of the United States of America and the Gov't of the State of Israel Amending the Conv. on Extradition of December 10, 1962, July 6, 2005, art. IV(2), S. Treaty Doc. No. 109-3 (2005).

40 Stanbrook & Stanbrook, *supra* n.11, at 134.

41 *See* Ilias Bantekas & Susan Nash, International Criminal Law 179, 190 (2d ed. 2003); *e.g.*, Sweden, Citizenship Act (2001:82), Mar. 1, 2001, sections § 16 and 20 (Sweden defines its nationals under certain circumstances to include nationals of Denmark, Finland, Iceland, and Norway domiciled in its territory), although such a broad-gauged definition of nationals does not apply for purposes of intra-E.U. extradition. *Explanatory Report to Conv. Relating to Extradition between the Member States of the E.U.*, May 26, 1997, art. 7, *reprinted in O.J.C.* 191 (June 23, 1997).

42 *E.g.*, *In re Del Porto*, Trib. Féd. Suisse, Mar. 6, 1931, *reprinted in* 6 Ann. Dig. Pub. Int'l L. Cases 307 (No. 167) (H. Lauterpacht ed. 1938) (discussing how a Greek court refused to extradite to Albania an Albanian national who was of Hellenic ethnicity on the grounds that such persons qualified as Greek nationals who could not be extradited).

43 In Brazil, until 1980, domestic law prohibited the extradition of fugitives who were neither born nor naturalized citizens, but who had merely fathered a Brazilian child. Brazil, Immigration Law, Law 6.815, Aug. 19, 1980, *as amended*; *e.g.*, "Brazilian Court

legal review is to determine when a person's naturalization took effect.[44] A treaty or other multilateral scheme might indicate that a person's nationality shall be set as of the date of: (i) the underlying act for which extradition is being sought, (ii) the extradition request,[45] (iii) the extradition decision,[46] or even (iv) the custodial transfer itself. When no legal guidance is supplied for identifying the event to which nationality is material, domestic courts by default generally side with granting such protection by construing the language prohibiting the extradition of nationals at any point in time, even as late as the extradition act itself.[47]

Some States, including Denmark, Finland, and Sweden, extend the application of this nationality exception to specified nationals domiciled (*i.e.*, permanent resident aliens) within their territory.[48] The logic undergirding this approach is that, as the world increasingly adopts a rehabilitative (versus punitive) perspective on crime, residents as much as citizens would benefit from post-sentence reintegration into their community by virtue of non-extradition coupled with prosecution at home.[49] This practice is well illustrated by the London Scheme for the Extradition within the Commonwealth in which permanent residents are treated synonymously with nationals for purposes of non-extradition.[50]

Won't Extradite 'Great Train Robbery' Fugitive," *N.Y. Times*, Nov. 13, 1997 (Brazil rejected a U.K. request for the extradition of robbery convict and prison escapee, Ronnie Biggs, because he had fathered a son with his Brazilian girlfriend).

44 Israel, which pursuant to its Law of Return, may confer citizenship on any legally Jewish person, calculates whether one of its nationals *was resident in Israel* at the time the extradition request was submitted; if so, it will insist that the extradition be contingent on the person's return, if convicted, to serve any sentence in Israeli prisons. Abramovsky & Edelstein, *supra* n.12, at 3–4. The Israeli Knesset recognized in this distinction that a significant proportion of Israeli nationals do not have strong connections to Israel because, for example, they are recent arrivals. *Id.* at 59.

45 *E.g.*, London Scheme for Extradition within the Commonwealth, Nov. 2002, art. 15(3)(c), LMM (90)32 [hereinafter London Scheme]. Where treaties so dictate, States parties must suspend naturalization proceedings pending a decision on an extradition request. *E.g.*, Treaty on Extradition, U.S.-Costa Rica, Dec. 4, 1982, art. 8(2) (as discussed in *United States v. Anderson*, 472 F.2d 662, 666–67 (9th Cir. 2006)).

46 *E.g.*, Eur. Conv. on Extradition, Dec. 13, 1957, art. 6(1)(c), E.T.S. No. 24.

47 Jennings & Watts, *supra* n.7, at 956 n.2 (citing *In re A*, Ct. of App. of Aix, Fr., Mar. 15, 1951, *reprinted in* 18 ILR 324 (1951)).

48 *See supra* n.41.

49 Deen-Racsmány, *Nationality Exception, supra* n.11, at 30.

50 London Scheme, *supra* n.45, art. 15(3)(a) ("A request for extradition may be refused on the basis that the person sought is a national *or permanent resident* of the requested country.") (emphasis supplied).

Finally, nationality may surface as an issue not only when one's own nationals (or permanent residents) are the subject of an extradition request, but also when a *third State's* nationals are contemplated for an extradition between two other States, particularly in cases where less formal means are employed. Under those circumstances, third State governments may protest such transfers of custody on the ground that criminal procedural and human rights protections ordinarily found in treaties are otherwise bypassed.[51] This dynamic is more likely to occur these days due to the increasing incidence of dual (or plural) nationals.

In such cases, the host State may feel politically pressured by the third State, may be influenced by diplomatic or trade incentives or disincentives, or may simply find the logic of the protesting State's arguments compelling. Under any of these conditions, the host State may reconsider its decision to extradite and stand down. Significantly, however, States generally do not appear to pay deference to whether a given pursuing State also has a nationality claim or to whether a third State's nationality claim is stronger than that of the host State.[52]

b Immunities

This section addresses the extent to which the individual at issue is shielded, wholly or in part, from extradition on account of a legally recognized immunity by virtue of his office, position, or status. In that regard, this section examines the various types of immunities that are potentially applicable to sovereigns, heads of State, and heads of government; diplomatic and consular officers; legislators; armed forces personnel; and international organization personnel. Because a convicted person or a criminal defendant may secure the functional equivalent of immunity from extradition by virtue of being granted amnesty or

[51] For example, in November 1962, the United Kingdom protested when Briton Greville Wynne was informally extradited from Hungary to the Soviet Union. JENNINGS & WATTS, *supra* n.7, at 952 & n.11.

[52] Stefan Oeter, *Effect of Nationality and Dual Nationality on Judicial Cooperation, Including Treaty Regimes Such as Extradition*, *in* RIGHTS AND DUTIES OF DUAL NATIONALS: EVOLUTION AND PROSPECTS 59 (David A. Martin & Kay Hailbronner eds. 2003) ("The other nationality is not taken in perspective; the dual national is treated simply as a national, with a blind eye toward all other nationalities. Questions of the dominant or effective nationality have never been raised internationally in cases of extradition, it seems.").

a pardon, or by entering into a "plea bargain" with host State prosecutors, respectively, such arrangements are evaluated as well.

Sovereigns and Heads of State/Government.[53] As a general rule,[54] *while serving in office*, a *de jure* monarch, other head of State (*e.g.*, a president in a non-parliamentary system), or head of government (*e.g.*, a prime minister or premier) enjoys "absolute" (versus "relative") immunity[55] from arrest or prosecution[56] in another State,[57] regardless of the severity of the offense.[58] This international legal protection that attaches to the person, known as *immunity ratione personae*,[59] even extends to the individual's family

[53] Immunity conferred on individual sovereigns or heads of State should not be confused with the related but distinct "Act of State" doctrine under U.S. law, "which presents no jurisdictional question but instead addresses the Court's permissible scope of inquiry into certain governmental acts. It is more properly understood as an issue preclusion device than an immunity prohibiting prosecution." *United States v. Noriega*, 746 F. Supp. 1506, 1521 (S.D. Fla. 1990), *aff'd*, 117 F.3d 1206 (11th Cir. 1997).

[54] It must be stressed that [t]he scope of this immunity is in an amorphous and undeveloped state." *In re Doe*, 860 F.2d 40, 44 (2d Cir. 1988).

[55] STANBROOK & STANBROOK, *supra* n.11, at 124 & n.76.

[56] Such persons also are immune to civil lawsuits, ALUN JONES & ANAND DOOBAY, JONES AND DOOBAY ON EXTRADITION AND MUTUAL ASSISTANCE 113 (2005), but such litigation lies outside the scope of this inquiry.

[57] The present analysis involving law enforcement action by States is to be distinguished from that undertaken by international criminal tribunals, which, based on statute and practice, do not recognize head of State immunity. *E.g.*, Statute of the Int'l Crim. Tribunal for the Former Yugoslavia, adopted May 25, 1993, art. 7(2), *as amended*, U.N. Doc. S/25704, Annex ("The official position of any accused person, whether as Head of State or Government, or as a responsible Government official, shall not relieve such person of criminal responsibility or mitigate punishment."). The ICTY indicted Slobodan Milošević in 1999 while he was still head of State, as President of the Federal Republic of Yugoslavia (FRY), citing the SCSL decision denying immunity to Charles Taylor, the former Liberian President. Micaela Frulli, *A Turning Point in Int'l Efforts to Apprehend War Criminals: The U.N. Mandates Taylor's Arrest in Liberia*, 4 J. INT'L CRIM. JUST. 351, 352 (2006). The ICTY has held that the principle that individuals are personally responsible for acts of *torture*, whatever their official position, is indisputably declaratory of customary international law. *Prosecutor v. Furundzija*, No. IT-95-17/1-T, Judgment, ICTY Tr. Ch., Dec. 10, 1998, ¶ 140. *See also Prosecutor v. Taylor*, Case No. SCSL-2003-01-I, App.Ch., Decision on Immunity from Jurisdiction, May 31, 2004 (rejecting the immunity claim by former Liberian President Charles Taylor for war crimes, crimes against humanity, and other serious violations committed while he was a sitting head of State).

[58] *E.g.*, *Gaddafi*, Case No. 1414, Arrêt de la Cour de Cassation, Fr., Mar. 13, 2001, *reprinted in* 125 ILR 490 (applying absolute immunity to Moammar Gaddafi, as head of State in Libya, in a case where he was indicted for complicity in an airplane explosion over Nigeria in 1989).

[59] *See* ILC, *Second Report on Immunity of State Officials from Foreign Criminal Jurisdiction* (Roman Anatolevich Kolodkin, Special Rapporteur), U.N. Doc. A/CN.4/631, June 10, 2010, ¶ 94(i) [hereinafter ILC, *State Official Immunity*] ("Immunity *ratione personae*,

members and private servants who are regarded as part of his/her household.[60] "The rationale behind the doctrine is to promote international comity and respect among sovereign nations by ensuring that leaders are free to perform their governmental duties without being subject to detention, arrest, or embarrassment in a foreign country's legal system."[61] Such treatment possibly applies to sitting ministerial-level individuals as well.[62] As this immunity protects such a person from arrest or detention while in a foreign State, by logical extension, that (host) State would not be at liberty to extradite him either.

Once a monarch, head of State, or head of government, however, is *no longer in office and no longer recognized as the legitimate ruler*[63] – for example, a deposed or exiled king or a president who has resigned or been replaced – he retains only partial protection from law enforcement action against him in another State, to the extent of the "official acts he performed in the exercise of his functions," known as *immunity ratione materiae*.[64] Under this type of "relative" immunity, he may not be arrested or prosecuted in another State for any conduct (acts or omissions) performed in his

which is enjoyed by a narrow circle of high-ranking State officials, extends to illegal acts performed by an official both in an official and in a private capacity, including prior to taking office. This is what is known as absolute immunity"); *id.* ¶ 94(j) ("Being linked to a defined high office, personal immunity is temporary in character and ceases when a person leaves office. Immunity *ratione personae* is affected neither by the fact that acts in connection with which jurisdiction is being exercised were performed outside the scope of the functions of an official, nor by the nature of his stay abroad, including in the territory of the State exercising jurisdiction").

60 Jones & Doobay, *supra* n.56, at 113.

61 *Noriega*, 746 F. Supp. at 1519.

62 *E.g., Case Concerning the Arrest Warrant of 11 April 2000* (D.R.C. v. Belg.) [2002] I.C.J. Rep. 3 (Feb. 14) [hereinafter *Arrest Warrant Case*] (involving charges against the sitting Foreign Minister of the D.R.C., Abdulaye Yerodia Ndombasi).

63 Depending on the circumstances, it could be that a *de jure* sovereign *in exile* enjoys immunity even while located abroad. Jones & Doobay, *supra* n.56, at 113. *E.g., Lafontante v. Aristide*, 844 F. Supp. 128 (E.D.N.Y. 1994) (adhering to U.S. Department of State policy recognizing Jean-Bertrand Aristide as the legitimate President of Haiti and therefore eligible for head of State immunity despite his having been living in exile for more than two years).

64 Virpi Koivu, *Head-of-State Immunity v. Individual Criminal Responsibility under Int'l Law*, 12 Finn. Y.B. Int'l L. 305, 312 (2001); *id.* at 313–14 ("According to Lord Hope of Craighead [in the U.K. House of Lords' Judgment of March 24, 1999, in the *Pinochet case*] ... 'the fact that acts done for the state have involved conduct which is criminal does not remove the immunity. Indeed, the whole purpose of the residual *immunity ratione materiae* is to protect the former head of state against allegations of such conduct after he has left office.'"); Jones & Doobay, *supra* n.56, at 113.

official capacity while in office,[65] even involving allegedly criminal conduct,[66] except possibly *jus cogens*[67] or customary international law violations,[68] although case law is concededly scarce on this matter.[69] That

[65] ILC, *State Official Immunity, supra* n.59, ¶ 94(b) ("State officials enjoy immunity *ratione materiae* from foreign criminal jurisdiction, i.e. immunity in respect of acts performed in an official capacity, since these acts are acts of the State which they serve itself"); *cf. id.* ¶ 94(g) ("Immunity *ratione materiae* does not extend to acts which were performed by an official prior to his taking up office").

[66] *See id.* ¶ 94(f) ("Immunity *ratione materiae* extends to *ultra vires* acts of officials and to their illegal acts."). *Compare R. v. Bow Street Metropolitan Magistrate and Others, ex parte Pinochet Ugarte (No. 3)* [2001] 1 A.C. 147 (H.L.), 3 WLR 1456, 1457 (while the 1964 Diplomatic Privileges Act conferred former head of State immunity from criminal jurisdiction on Gen. Auguste Pinochet for official acts he performed while serving as Chile's head of State, "the crimes of torture and hostage-taking fell outside what international law would regard as functions of a head of state" and so was not so immunized from extradition proceedings regarding those crimes committed after the date of the United Kingdom's ratification of the CAT) *with Arrest Warrant Case, supra* n.62 (Foreign Minister of Congo's jurisdictional immunity not removed in the face of a Belgian warrant for his arrest in connection with charges including crimes against humanity and breaches of the Geneva Conventions of 1949 with respect to official acts committed while in office).

[67] *Jus cogens* norms are preeminent customary international law norms that are universal, peremptory, and nonderogable; and cannot be preempted by treaty but rather only by an emergent norm of equal status. *Committee of U.S. Citizens Living in Nicaragua v. Reagan*, 859 F.2d 929, 939–40 (D.C. Cir. 1988).

[68] The reasoning of the *Pinochet* court was divided into three camps. In the 6–1 House of Lords judgment ultimately authorizing the U.K. Home Secretary to extradite Pinochet to Spain (which was subsequently declined on humanitarian grounds) for acts of torture he had committed after December 8, 1988 (the date on which U.K. law came into effect recognizing torture committed outside its territory a crime), two of the Lords held that Pinochet forfeited his claim to immunity on account of customary international law, given the crime of torture, while three other Lords held that such immunity was stripped due to the United Kingdom's ratification of the Torture Convention. BETH VAN SCHAACK & RONALD C. SLYE, INTERNATIONAL CRIMINAL LAW AND ITS ENFORCEMENT 872 (2007). Lord Hope of Craighead alone held that former head of State immunity was forfeited due to the fact that the conduct in question violated a *jus cogens* norm. Koivu, *supra* n.64, at 314.

[69] *See* Andrea Bianchi, *Immunity versus Human Rights: The Pinochet Case*, 10 EUR. J. INT'L L. 237, 255 (1999) ("As rightly noted, [former head of State immunity] is an area of the law 'which is in many respects still unsettled, and on which limited state practice casts an uneven light.'") (quoting Arthur Watts, "The Legal Position in Int'l Law of Heads of States, Heads of Governments and Foreign Ministers," 247 *Rec. des Cours* 9, 21 (1994)). Even when there is an example, it can be shrouded in controversy. For example, in late 2011, the Tunisian Prime Minister decided to extradite Al-Baghdadi Ali al-Mahmoudi, the former Libyan Prime Minister under Moammar Gaddafi (2006–11) to face charges arising out of the Libyan civil war. Andrew Baskin, *Tunisia Will Extradite Gaddafi's Prime Minister to Libya*, 28 IELR 21 (2012). Notably, some months later, Tunisian President Moncef Marzouki criticized that decision based ostensibly on human rights treatment concerns if al-Baghdadi were sent back to Libya, and indicated he might raise the case with the Tunisian Constitutional Assembly. Bruce Zagaris, *Tunisia President Rebukes*

determination tends to turn on whether his conduct took place "under the color of law or in the ostensible exercise of public authority,"[70] also known as *acta jure imperii*. Any other conduct, including offenses of a personal or private character (*acta jure gestionis*), such as rape or embezzlement, could be subject to criminal accountability.[71] Under such circumstances, therefore, such a person could be arrested and extradited.

Such immunity, to the extent it applies, however, does not necessarily equate with *impunity* as the State the individual serves could, on its own initiative, still choose to prosecute him[72] or, alternatively, waive his immunity where another State otherwise was willing to prosecute him.[73] Besides, a critical prerequisite to this type of immunity is that the former government official in question must be *recognized* as a sovereign or head of State by the executive branch of the State in whose custody he finds himself.[74] Thus, for example, while Gen. Manuel Noriega was Commandante of the Panamanian Defense Forces and the country's *de facto* leader, the United States continued to recognize Eric Delvalle as the legitimate leader of Panama for most of the time Gen. Noriega was in power and consequently did not accord Gen.

Prime Minister for Extraditing a Former Libyan Official to Libya, 28 IELR 330, 330–31 (2012). Al-Mahmoudi was extradited to Libya in June 2012. Ali Shuaib, "Gaddafi's PM Al-Baghdadi Ali al-Mahmoudi Is Extradited," *The Independent* (U.K.), June 25, 2012.

70 Jones & Doobay, *supra* n.56, at 113 (quoting Sir Arthur Watts). *See also* ILC, *State Official Immunity, supra* n.59, ¶ 94(d) ("Classification of the conduct of an official as official conduct does not depend on the motives of the person or the substance of the conduct. The determining factor is that the official is acting in a capacity as such. The concept of an 'act of an official as such,' i.e. of an 'official act,' must be differentiated from the concept of an 'act falling within official functions.' The first is broader and includes the second.").

71 For example, in October 2008, absent any discussion of immunity, the Mexican Government extradited former Guatemalan President Alfonso Antonio Portillo Cabrera (Portillo) to Guatemala on embezzlement charges (US $15 million). Bruce Zagaris, *Mexico Extradites Former Guatemalan President to Guatemala*, 24 IELR 478, 478 (2008). *Contra Arrest Warrant Case, supra* n.62 (adopting an absolutist view by drawing no distinction between official and private acts committed by ministers of foreign affairs during their terms in office). Commercial acts are not necessarily of a private nature. *See* ILC, *State Official Immunity, supra* n.59, ¶ 94(e) ("An official performing an act of a commercial nature enjoys immunity from foreign criminal jurisdiction *if this act is attributed to the State*") (emphasis supplied).

72 *See Arrest Warrant Case, supra* n.62; Van Schaack & Slye, *supra* n.68, at 872 (discussing how, upon Gen. Pinochet's return to Chile following the U.K. Home Secretary's decision not to extradite him to Spain to face torture charges, the Supreme Court of Chile stripped Gen. Pinochet of his immunity and he was placed under house arrest).

73 *See Noriega*, 746 F. Supp. at 1519–20 (noting that the "grant of immunity is a privilege which the [conferring State] may withhold from any claimant").

74 *Kadic v. Karadžić*, 70 F.3d 232, 248 (2d Cir. 1995).

Noriega immunity from criminal prosecution.[75] This suggests, by implication, that the United States would have felt no immunity-related restriction about extraditing him back to Panama had law enforcement authorities found Gen. Noriega on U.S. territory, Panama had sought his return for criminal violations, and U.S. prosecutorial priorities had been different.

Diplomatic Officers. The 1961 Vienna Convention on Diplomatic Relations (VCDR) with near universal State membership,[76] together with customary international law, governs the issue of diplomatic immunity.[77] A diplomatic agent, who is "the head of the mission or a member of the diplomatic staff of the mission,"[78] may not be arrested or detained and "shall enjoy immunity from the criminal jurisdiction of the receiving State"[79] (including offenses against the receiving State itself[80]), unless expressly waived by the sending State.[81]

[75] Downing, *supra* n.13, at 587.

[76] The VCDR has 190 member States to date. U.N. Treaty Collection website, *available at* https://treaties.un.org/Pages/ViewDetails.aspx?src=TREATY&mtdsg_no=III-3&chapter=3&lang=en (last visited on May 10, 2016).

[77] To the extent that issues are not expressly addressed in the VCDR itself, the Convention defers to customary international law for clarification. Vienna Conv. on Diplomatic Relations, Apr. 18, 1961, Preamble, ¶ 6, 23 U.S.T. 3227, T.I.A.S. No. 7502, 500 U.N.T.S. 95 [hereinafter VCDR]. Non-parties to the VCDR would not be bound by its terms except to the extent such provisions constitute customary international law.

[78] *Id.*, art. 1(e). Those persons employed by the United Nations but not representing their home State would not fall within the ambit of this definition. *See, e.g., People v. Leo*, 407 N.Y.S.2d 941, 942 (N.Y.S. 1978) (a Tanzanian national was found to be a U.N. employee in New York, but was not eligible for diplomatic immunity where he held no position on behalf of the Government of Tanzania, had not been issued a diplomatic passport, and resided in the United States on a G-4 visa issued to international civil servants of the United Nations). In such cases, *U.N.* diplomatic immunities would apply. *See* discussion *infra*.

[79] VCDR, *supra* n.77, arts. 29 and 31(1). Notably, such immunity, however, "does not exempt him from the jurisdiction of the sending State." *Id.*, art. 31(4). The "receiving State" in this context refers to *the State to which the diplomat is officially posted or assigned*; the "sending State" refers to *the State of which he is a national and on whose behalf he has been dispatched for official representation purposes.*

[80] *E.g., United States v. Kostadinov*, 734 F.2d 905 (2d Cir. 1984), *cert. denied*, 469 U.S. 881 (1985); *United States v. Enger*, 472 F. Supp. 490 (D.N.J. 1978) (espionage cases).

[81] VCDR, *supra* n.77, art. 32(1) and (2). Significantly in such matters, immunity rests with the sending State – not with the diplomat himself. If the sending State chooses to waive its immunity over a particular diplomat, it must be express – silence is not sufficient and the waiver may not be invoked on a blanket basis. The sending State has no obligation to waive immunity, however, even for a serious crime, and may instead recall the diplomat. If the sending State chooses neither to waive immunity nor recall him, the receiving State can choose to declare him *persona non grata* (*PNG*) and ask for his recall. If he is declared *PNG* and not recalled, the receiving State may deny him diplomatic immunities. B.J.

The rationale for extending this immunity derives from three sources: (i) the diplomatic agent is the representative of the sovereign or State and should be treated accordingly; (ii) he is operating in space within receiving State territory regarded as a diplomatic enclave of the sending State; and (iii) the immunity is essential to the effective performance of the diplomat's functions.[82] To enjoy this immunity, a diplomat must be duly notified to, and accredited by, the receiving State.[83] Mere possession of a diplomatic passport (or an A-2 visa) does not confer diplomatic status,[84] which instead generally requires the receiving government to accept that individual as a member of a foreign diplomatic mission, include him on a diplomatic register, issue him a diplomatic identity card, or satisfy other similar indicia of accreditation.[85]

This form of immunity takes effect from the moment a protected person enters the receiving State's territory (or if already on the territory, from the moment his appointment is notified to the appropriate government ministry) and ceases when he leaves the country (or within a reasonable period after his functions have come to an end).[86] "The members of the family of a diplomatic agent forming part of his household" and "[m]embers of the administrative and technical staff of the mission, together with members of their families forming part of their respective households," shall, "if they are not nationals of the receiving State," enjoy immunity from arrest, detention, and criminal jurisdiction

George Jr., *Immunities and Exceptions, in* 1 International Criminal Law: Crimes 114–15 (2d ed. M. Cherif Bassiouni ed. 1999).

[82] *Id.* at 107–08.

[83] Jones & Doobay, *supra* n.56, at 121; *e.g., R. v. Governor of Pentonville Prison, ex parte Teja* [1971] 2 QB 274, [1971] 2 All E.R. 11 (where the U.K. Secretary of State issued a letter stating that an Indian fugitive was not accredited to the Court of St. James, despite having been issued a diplomatic passport and possessing a letter designating him an economic adviser to the Government of India, he was found to lack diplomatic immunity); *United States v. Kuznetsov*, 442 F. Supp.2d 102, 107–08 (S.D.N.Y. 2006) (holding that a U.N. employee indicted for conspiracy to commit money laundering was not entitled to diplomatic immunity even though he was a career Russian diplomat and a Russian delegate to a U.N. working group on budget issues, as he he had not been accredited to the U.S. Department of State as a member of a mission, was on leave without pay from his post with the Russian Ministry of Foreign Affairs, and his U.N. assignment required that he not accept any instructions from a government).

[84] *E.g., Kostadinov*, 734 F.2d 905 (an assistant commercial counselor in Bulgaria's New York trade office, even with an A-2 visa and working in an office co-located with the Bulgarian Embassy, did not qualify him as a member of the foreign mission entitled to diplomatic immunity from prosecution for an espionage charge).

[85] *Noriega*, 746 F. Supp. at 1523–25.

[86] VCDR, *supra* n.77, art. 39(1) and (2).

by the host State.[87] Retired diplomatic agents retain their immunity only with respect to official acts undertaken while representing their State abroad but such immunity lasts indefinitely.[88]

For an example of how diplomatic immunity may thwart, lawfully or pretextually, a request for a provisional arrest, let alone for extradition, consider the case of the infamous 1985 hijacking of the Italian cruise ship *Achille Lauro* that also entailed the targeted murder of an invalid American Jew, Leon Klinghoffer. After the hijacking, Mohammed Abbas, a member of the Palestine Liberation Organization (PLO) Executive Committee and the hijacking's suspected mastermind, fled to Italy. The United States sought his provisional arrest subject to a formal extradition request, but the Italian authorities claimed they had insufficient evidence to detain him and, besides, he was entitled to diplomatic immunity as the official representative of the PLO (based on a *non-State* diplomatic passport he held in an *assumed name*). Abbas then flew to Yugoslavia. The United States again sought his provisional arrest until an extradition request could be prepared and submitted. Like the Italian Government, the Yugoslavs denied that request on diplomatic immunity grounds, claiming that Abbas was a member of the PLO Executive Committee, and Yugoslavia recognized the PLO as the only legitimate representative of the Palestinian people.[89]

Consular Officers. The 1963 Vienna Convention on Consular Relations (VCCR),[90] along with customary international law, controls the extent to which consular officers are entitled to immunity.[91] The criminal law-related immunity provisions of the VCCR are substantially similar to those of the VCDR. Consular officers, who include all persons with responsibility for exercising consular functions within

87 *Id.*, art. 37(1) and (2). More limited immunities also apply to the members of the mission's service staff and private servants of the members of the mission, to the extent they are not nationals or permanent residents of the receiving State. *Id.*, art. 37(3) and (4).

88 Jones & Doobay, *supra* n.56, at 121; George, *supra* n.81, at 116.

89 Jordan J. Paust, *Extradition and United States Prosecution of the* Achille Lauro *Hostage-Takers: Navigating the Hazards*, 20 Vand. J. Transnat'l L. 235, 236 (1987); "Extradition Request Denied by Belgrade," *Wash. Post*, Oct. 18, 1985, at A33.

90 Like the VDCR, the VCCR is one of the most subscribed treaties in the world today with 178 member States to date. U.N. Treaty Collection website, *available at* https://treaties.un.org/pages/ViewDetails.aspx?src=TREATY&mtdsg_no=III-6&chapter=3&lang=en (last visited on May 10, 2016).

91 Vienna Conv. on Consular Relations, Apr. 24, 1963, Preamble, ¶ 6, 21 U.S.T. 77, 596 U.N.T.S. 261 [hereinafter VCCR]. Consular officers are not entitled to invoke individual rights under the VCCR to support a private damage action. *Gandara v. Bennett*, 528 F.3d 823 (11th Cir. 2008).

a foreign mission,[92] may not be arrested or detained before a trial, *except* for grave crimes (*i.e.*, felonies) when determined by a competent judicial body.[93] The head of the consular post must be designated by the sending State and accredited by the receiving State before any such immunity can attach.[94]

In addition, consular officers, as well as consular employees (*i.e.*, those responsible for administrative or technical services at a consular post[95]), are "not amenable to the jurisdiction of judicial or administrative authorities of the receiving State in respect of acts performed in the exercise of consular functions,"[96] unless the sending State waives such immunity.[97] Family members of a consular post member forming part of his household and members of private staff receive the same protection as consular officers.[98] The applicable time frame and post-service provisions for consular immunity are the same as for those subject to diplomatic immunity under the VCDR.[99]

In sum, consular officers do not enjoy the same high degree of arrest and detention immunity as diplomatic officers and, therefore, it is conceivable that, at least in the instance of a felony charge following

[92] VCCR, *supra* n.91, art. 1(d).

[93] *Id.*, art. 41.

[94] *Id.*, art. 10(1). In May 2009, a former U.S. consular officer assigned to the U.S. Consulate in Milan filed a lawsuit against the U.S. State Department, contending that it had failed to invoke consular immunity on her behalf in connection with the Italian indictment against her for participating in the CIA-organized "extraordinary rendition" of Abu Omar, a radical Muslim cleric, in February 2003. Some have speculated that the State Department's reluctance to invoke the immunity is because it is limited to "acts performed in the exercise of consular functions" of which the alleged rendition would not qualify. Bruce Zagaris, *Former U.S. Gov't Employee Sues for Immunity in CIA Rendition Case*, 25 IELR 275, 275–77 (2009). More recently, after Aruba arrested Hugo Carvajal, a former chief of Venezuela's military intelligence, despite his having been named Venezuela's consul-general in Aruba, an Aruban judge ruled that the arrest was valid as Carvajal did not yet enjoy consular immunity because the Dutch Government had yet to accredit him to that post. After Venezuela's naval ships approached Aruba and Curaçao and threatened to sever its commercial links with Aruba and Caraçao and withdraw a critical oil refinery contract with Caraçao, the Aruban prosecutor overrode the judicial ruling, announced that Carvajal in fact had immunity, and released him on *PNG* status. Juan Forero & Dan Molinski, "Venezuelan in Aruba is Freed on Immunity," *Wall St. J.*, July 28, 2014, at A14; Kejal Vyas & José Cordoba, "Aruba Says Venezuela Raised Military Pressure on It," *Wall St. J.*, July 28, 2014.

[95] VCCR, *supra* n.91, art. 1(e).

[96] *Id.*, art. 43.

[97] *Id.*, art. 45.

[98] *Id.*, art. 53(2).

[99] *Id.*, art. 53(2)–(4).

a warrant granted by a competent judicial authority from the receiving State, a consular officer could be arrested[100] and extradited to a third State. Most typically, the sending State would simply recall the officer with the aim of prosecuting him rather than seek his extradition. The sending State also could choose to waive any immunity accorded the consular officer in the receiving State to allow for his arrest on a misdemeanor charge.

Legislators. Unlike the case with diplomats and consular officers whose immunity is based primarily on broadly subscribed international conventions, national parliamentarians or legislators derive their jurisdictional immunity from their home State municipal law.[101] The purpose of such immunity is to protect lawmakers from having their votes or views influenced by the threat of prosecution and from distracting them from their work while engaged in litigation. Accordingly, to the extent an individual can attain legislator status, he may be immunized from extradition by his *home* State to face charges abroad. For example, Shmuel Flatto-Sharon, who was wanted for embezzling US $60 million, fled from France to Israel in 1975, where he promptly sought a seat in the Knesset (Israel's parliament) in the hope, (at least in part), of escaping extradition to France on account of legislative immunity; as it happened, he won election and consequently was not extradited.[102]

Armed Forces Personnel. Immunity from prosecution sometimes attaches to armed forces personnel (and their dependents) deployed abroad via Status of Forces Agreements (SOFAs), Visiting Forces Agreements (VFAs), or other military exchange treaties. In such instances, extradition as a means to secure the custody of a serviceman

[100] U.S. Dep't of State, Office of Foreign Missions, *Diplomatic and Consular Immunity: Guidance for Law Enforcement and Judicial Authorities*, June 2015, at 11, 40 [hereinafter *Office of Foreign Missions Guidance*].

[101] This type of prosecutorial immunity by another State must be distinguished from parliamentary action conferring *amnesty* on legislators to preclude any *in-country* criminal liability. In perhaps the best-known example of legislative amnesty, former Chilean President Augusto Pinochet, who retired with the title "Senator for Life," ensured that the legislature, over which his military junta exercised enormous influence, passed amnesty laws during his tenure granting lifetime immunity to all members of parliament, including himself. Chile, however, "rejected General Pinochet's defense of amnesty in proceedings brought against him after he was returned from the United Kingdom in 2002." Van Schaack & Slye, *supra* n.68, at 874.

[102] "Israel Court Orders Candidate to Begin a Bribery Jail Term," *N.Y. Times*, June 28, 1984. Subsequently, however, he was convicted in Israel for election pay-offs in his successful 1977 campaign and sentenced to a three-month term in prison. *Id.*

(or eligible dependent) who has committed a crime within its territory but has since fled that territory, at least to the extent covered by the immunity, becomes effectively moot not because extradition itself is off-limits, but because its *end purpose* – criminal prosecution – is barred. Examples include:

(i) the South Korea-Kyrgyzstan SOFA grants total immunity from criminal prosecution to South Korean servicemen by Kyrgyz authorities for any crime;[103]
(i) the 2007 Trinidad & Tobago (T&T) Visiting Forces Act confers on visiting South Korean forces full immunity from the criminal jurisdiction of T&T with regard "to acts taken in the course of their official duties";[104] and
(ii) under Article 10 of the 1996 U.S.-Mongolia Agreement on Military Exchanges and Visits, Mongolia has no criminal jurisdiction over acts by U.S. military personnel within Mongolian territory, although, at the discretion of the United States, it can consider a Mongolian request to waive jurisdiction with respect to offenses unrelated to official duty.[105]

Beyond such agreements, there are also circumstances in which crew members of warships docked in foreign harbors or ports commit crimes within that State's territory. In such cases, such individuals generally enjoy immunity from host State criminal jurisdiction to the extent that their offenses were committed in the course of their official duties.[106] Extradition as to such individuals would prove meaningless unless the applicable military exchange treaty allowed for prosecution or the offenses allegedly committed fell outside the scope of the prosecution immunity.

International Organization Personnel. The Convention on the Privileges and Immunities of the United Nations (1946) governs immunity from legal process for three sets of personnel: U.N. officials,[107] U.N. member representatives (whether to principal or subsidiary organs of the

103 CSIS, Scott Snyder, "A Call to Justice and the U.S.-ROK Alliance," PacNet, No. 53A, Pacific Forum CSIS (Honolulu, HI), Dec. 18, 2002.
104 Trinidad & Tobago, Visiting Forces Act, Act No. 8 of 2007, Mar. 23, 2007, art. 5(1).
105 R. Chuck Mason, *Status of Forces Agreement (SOFA): What Is It, and How Has It Been Utilized?*, C.R.S. Report to Congress, Dec. 1, 2008, at 4.
106 Stanbrook & Stanbrook, *supra* n.11, at 132.
107 U.N. officials are designated by the U.N. Secretary-General and do not include employees who lack diplomatic status. *United States v. Enger*, 472 F Supp. 490 (D.N.J. 1978).

United Nations), and experts on missions on behalf of the United Nations.[108] In all three cases, such personnel are immune from legal process of every kind with regard to all acts performed by them in their official capacities.[109] In addition, the representatives of members and any experts on missions are immune from arrest or detention, whether in the exercise of their functions or while traveling to or from a meeting.[110]

Because such immunities are accorded to ensure their independence while working for the U.N., they are not intended for the benefit of the individuals themselves, and therefore member States have a duty to waive such immunity in the case of representatives (and the U.N. Secretary-General has a duty to waive such immunity regarding U.N. officials or experts on missions), where such immunity is believed to "impede the course of justice."[111]

Representatives and officials of *non-U.N.* international organizations, such as the North Atlantic Treaty Organization (NATO), the Organization of American States (OAS), the Asia Pacific Economic Cooperation Forum (APEC), and the Organization for Economic Cooperation and Development (OECD), may also enjoy immunity from States' legal processes as set forth in their constituitive documents or establishment agreements, headquarters or host country agreements,

[108] Conv. on the Privileges and Immunities of the U.N., Feb. 13, 1946, arts. 4, 5, and 6, 21 U.S.T. 1418, 1 U.N.T.S. 16 [hereinafter Privileges and Immunities Conv.]. *See also* Charter of the United Nations, June 26, 1945, art. 105(2) ("Representatives of the Members of the United Nations and officials of the Organization shall similarly [as Members] enjoy such privileges and immunities as are necessary for the independent exercise of their functions in connection with the Organization.").

[109] Privileges and Immunities Conv., *supra* n.108, arts. 11(a), 18(a), and 22(b). Accordingly, where the criminal act at issue is of an entirely private or personal nature, such as resisting arrest at a location away from the U.N. office, no such immunity attaches. *People v. Leo*, 407 N.Y.S.2d at 943. Likewise, espionage is an example of conduct that lies outside the scope of official duties. *E.g., Enger*, 472 F. Supp. at 502.

[110] Privileges and Immunities Conv., *supra* n.108, arts. 11 and 22; *e.g., Difference Relating to Immunity From Legal Process of a Special Rapporteur of the Commission on Human Rights*, Adv'y Op., 1999 I.C.J. 62, ¶ 56 (Apr. 29) ("the Court is of the opinion that the [U.N.] Secretary-General correctly found that Mr. [Dato' Param] Cumaraswamy [a Malaysian jurist, as the Commission's Special Rapporteur on the Independence of Judges and Lawyers], in speaking the words quoted in the article in *International Commercial Litigation*, was acting in the course of the performance of his mission as Special Rapporteur of the Commission. Consequently, Article VI, Section 22(b) of the General Convention [*i.e.*, the Privileges and Immunities Conv.] is applicable to him in the present case and affords Mr. Cumaraswamy immunity from legal process of every kind.").

[111] Privileges and Immunities Conv., *supra* n.108, arts. 14, 20, and 23.

and/or domestic implementing legislation.[112] For example, Article 134 of the OAS Charter (1948) reads: "The representatives of the Member States on the organs of the Organization, the personnel of their delegations as well as the Secretary General and the Assistant Secretary General, shall enjoy the privileges and immunities corresponding to their position and necessary for the independent performance of their duties."[113] This tracks the nature and extent of immunity enjoyed by "diplomatic agents" discussed above, and has since been elaborated upon in a 1949 multilateral agreement as well as in a series of bilateral agreements with OAS member States.[114]

In sum, although diplomatic-level staff of missions to international organizations may not be arrested or detained, *support staff* of those missions and international organization staff may be, even though they all remain subject to official acts immunity for prosecution purposes in the receiving State.[115] Thus, given the nature and scope of this immunity, all but diplomatic-level staff of missions to international organizations could be arrested and extradited, and even the diplomatic-level staff themselves could be arrested and extradited were their immunity waived.

In addition, members of *Special Missions*[116] under the 1969 Convention on Special Missions (at least with respect to those States parties) are treated on par with international organization staff in the sense that their

[112] George, *supra* n.81, at 134. A distinction must be drawn between *organizational* immunity and immunity conferred on *individual* officers, employees, or representatives of that organization operating in an official capacity. *Broadbent v. OAS*, 628 F.2d 27, 35 (1980).

[113] Charter of Organization of American States (OAS), Apr. 30, 1948, art. 134, 2 U.S.T. 2394, T.I.A.S. No. 2361, *as amended* by the Prot. of Buenos Aires, Feb. 27, 1967, 21 U.S.T. 607, T.I.A.S. No. 6847.

[114] William M. Berenson, *Immunity for Int'l Organizations? Squaring the Concept of Immunity with the Fundamental Right to a Fair Trial: The Case of the OAS*, OAS website, at 5–6, *available at* www.oas.org/legal/english/IMMUNITY_WB_111110.doc – 12/10/2010 (last visited on May 11, 2016). The OAS immunity provision was implicated in October 2010, when the Prosecutor General's Office of Colombia requested the OAS to revoke the immunity of staff from the Inter-Am. Inst. for Cooperation on Agriculture (IICA), a component of the OAS, for alleged criminal negligence in allowing wealthy landowning candidates proposed by the Colombian Ministry of Agriculture to receive government agricultural subsidies when the subsidy program was designed to help small-scale farmers. Linda Azodi, "Colombia asks OAS to Waive Diplomatic Immunity," *Colombia Reports*, Oct. 27, 2010.

[115] *Office of Foreign Missions Guidance, supra* n.100.

[116] A Special Mission is defined as "a temporary mission, representing the State, which is sent by one State to another State with the consent of the latter for the purpose of dealing with it on specific questions or of performing in relation to it a specific task," Conv. on Special Missions (CSM), Dec. 18, 1969, art. 1(a), 1400 U.N.T.S. 231, No. 23431, and the "Members of the Special Mission" are defined to include "the head of the special mission,

immunity is limited to not being subject to the criminal jurisdiction of the receiving State,[117] and accordingly they could be arrested or detained (although not tried) and subsequently to a third State.

Amnesty and Pardon Grantees. Persons who have been granted legislative amnesty or a presidential pardon by the host State are effectively immunized from any legal process, including extradition, arising out of the underlying criminal conduct. "Amnesty is usually granted *before* prosecution or conviction, and in that respect it resembles a statute of limitations, while pardon is usually granted *after* a person is found guilty."[118] Some bilateral extradition treaties expressly proscribe extradition in cases of a presidential pardon,[119] and certain domestic legislation treats any such impediment to prosecution or punishment likewise as a bar to extradition.[120]

The discretion to grant amnesty, however, does not appear to be unfettered, such as in cases of significant human rights violations, war crimes, or crimes against humanity.[121] In any event, "[a] state that has afforded amnesty to an individual may find it politically impossible to extradite that individual to another state, even notwithstanding an international obligation to do so under an extradition treaty."[122] An example of a presidential pardon occurred when, in April 2013, Italian President Giorgio Napolitano pardoned U.S. Air Force Col. Joseph Romano, who

the representatives of the sending State in the special mission and the members of the staff of the special mission." *Id.*, art. 1(f).

117 *Id.*, art. 31.1.

118 M. Cherif Bassiouni, International Extradition: United States Law and Practice 796 (6th ed. 2014) [hereinafter Bassiouni, U.S. Extradition] (emphasis supplied).

119 *E.g.*, Treaty on Extradition, U.S.-Austl., May 14, 1974, art. VII, *reprinted in* Igor I. Kavass, 1 Extradition Laws and Treaties: United States (2000 & Supp. 2004) (no extradition is granted when a person of interest has been pardoned in the host State for an offense for which extradition is sought).

120 Bassiouni, U.S. Extradition, *supra* n.118, at 1078 (citing by example the U.K. and Turkey).

121 For example, the Inter-American Court found the Peruvian amnesty law that protected individuals involved in human rights abuses in that country between 1980 and 1995 violated provisions of the Am. Conv. on Human Rights (ACHR). *Barrios Altos v. Peru (Merits)*, Inter-Am. C.H.R. OEA/ser. C, Mar. 14, 2001 Judgment, May 14, 2001, *reprinted in* 41 ILM 93 (2002). *See also* Bruce Zagaris, *Interpol Issues 'Red Notice' against Former Liberian President*, 20 IELR 53 (2004) (the issuance in December 2003 of an INTERPOL Red Notice in the Charles Taylor case, despite Nigeria's conferral of amnesty, signaled that no amnesty is recognized for war crimes or crimes against humanity).

122 Andreas O'Shea, Amnesty for Crime in International Law and Practice 99 (2002).

had been convicted by Italian courts in connection with the alleged extraordinary rendition by U.S. Government officials of Abu Omar from Milan in 2009.[123]

Subjects of Plea Bargains. Sometimes, admitted criminals negotiate with host State prosecutors to shield themselves from extradition (or even to avoid certain kinds of punishment in the host State itself) in exchange for their cooperation in identifying and testifying against other (usually more senior) perpetrators and/or serving as an informant about important criminal organizations or their operations through so-called "plea bargains."[124] In a recent example, in February 2012, an Indian court authorized prosecutors to indict David Coleman Headley, a U.S. citizen who had confessed in a U.S. court to "playing a major role in the [2008] Mumbai attacks, which killed at least 163 people."[125] U.S. prosecutors, however, had effectively immunized Headley from extradition to India (and from imposition of the death penalty in the United States) in exchange for information about Lashkar-e-Taiba (LeT), an Islamist terrorist organization operating in South Asia, of which he was an operative, and about other extremists, and for his ongoing role as an informant for the DEA.[126]

[123] "Italy Abu Omar Rendition: Col. Romano Pardoned in CIA Case," *BBC News Europe*, Apr. 6, 2013, *available at* www.bbc.com/news/world-europe-22048932 (last visited on May 28, 2016) (citing several reasons for his decision, including the fact that it was unprecedented for Italy to prosecute a U.S. military officer for acts committed in Italy).

[124] *See* DoJ, *U.S. Attorneys' Manual*, § 9–15.800 (2d ed. 2007–3 Supp.) ("Persons who are cooperating with a prosecutor may try to include a 'no extradition' clause in their plea agreements. Such agreements, whether formal or informal, may be given effect by the courts."); *e.g.*, *Petition of Geiser*, 627 F.2d 745 (5th Cir. 1980). In addition, "[i]f the relator had negotiated a plea of guilty with respect to conduct which is the same or substantially the same as the one giving rise to the criminal charge for which extradition is requested, the United States cannot grant extradition without vacating the plea and any judgment entered." Bassiouni, U.S. Extradition, *supra* n.118, at 787. However, when the State agrees to immunize an individual from *prosecution* in exchange for testimonial cooperation, the effect is not to clean the slate in terms of criminality but rather only to bar prosecution; therefore, while the State could not share information collected under such an agreement with a pursuing State, such immunity from prosecution would *not* impede to that pursuing State. *Id.*

[125] Vikas Bajaj & Hari Kumar, "India Allows Prosecutors to Charge U.S. Citizen," *IHT*, Feb. 20, 2012, at 3.

[126] *Id.* In lieu of extradition, the United States prosecuted Headley and the court sentenced him to thirty-five years in prison in January 2013, accounting for his past and future anticipated cooperation in sharing intelligence information with U.S. Government authorities. U.S. DoJ, "David Coleman Headley Sentenced to 35 Years in Prison for Role in India and Denmark Terror Plots," Press Release, Jan. 24, 2013.

c Special Relationships

This section now turns to a type of discretionary legal or political consideration that can result in the refusal to grant extradition, namely, when the host State wishes to protect and/or nurture a special relationship with the subject of an extradition request. Such relationships include individuals who are former political leaders; intelligence officers or agents; prisoners of war (POWs); asylees or refugees; those in receipt of witness protection; and prominent or locally popular figures.

Former Political Leaders. Former heads of State or government, while still enjoying *immunity ratione materiae*, might still be prosecutable in their home States for non-official-related felonies or misdemeanors.[127] Ex-leaders fearing such prosecution, therefore, may seek refuge in other States. Notwithstanding the capacity of the former leader's State to satisfy all substantive and procedural requirements for extradition, the host State may choose to deny a request on discretionary grounds[128] – sometimes expressly available by statute[129] – although the host State may suffer political, diplomatic, or economic consequences for that decision. A State's executive may opt to exercise such discretion, say, as an expression of courtesy toward a former foreign leader who maintained supportive and cooperative relations with the host State during his service in office, or with whom it shares a political ideology, or because he has contributed economically to the host State since his arrival.[130]

For example, after being ousted from power in December 1990, Hissène Habré, Chad's leader since June 1982, settled into a new life in Dakar, Senegal, which effectively treated him as a "guest of the State."[131] There he invested in real estate and other business ventures for a decade without legal problems until a Dakar regional court indicted him

[127] *See* pp. 245–48.

[128] Aimée J. Buckland, *Offending Officials: Former Gov't Actors and the Political Offense Exception to Extradition*, 94 Cal. L. Rev. 423, 439 (2006).

[129] *E.g.*, 18 U.S.C. § 3186 (2012) (providing the subject of an extradition the opportunity to petition the U.S. Secretary of State for a stay of execution).

[130] This treatment assumes the host State has chosen not to grant asylum to the former political leader; if it has, *see* discussion on asylees *infra*.

[131] Stephen P. Marks, *The Hissène Habré Case: The Law and Politics of Universal Jurisdiction*, *in* Universal Jurisdiction: National Courts and the Prosecution of Serious Crimes under International Law 135, 140 (Stephen Macedo ed. 2004). According to the International Court of Justice (ICJ), Habré successfully sought "political asylum" in Senegal following a brief period in Cameroon. *Questions Relating to the Obligation to Prosecute or Extradite* (Belg. v. Sen.), [2012] I.C.J. Rep. 422, ¶ 16 (July 20) [hereinafter *ICJ Case, Belg. v. Sen.*].

in February 2000 as an accomplice to torture and he was placed under house arrest. Later, Chad requested his extradition for alleged crimes he committed in the 1980s, including killing of thousands of his own people, but Senegal suspended the extradition at the eleventh hour ostensibly out of concern that his human rights would be violated if returned.[132]

Intelligence Officers or Agents. Numerous instances exist in which host States have been unwilling to extradite their own current (or former) intelligence officers or the agents they run (or ran) to face prosecution elsewhere. Such reluctance typically stems from a concern about the potential disclosure of sensitive intelligence information that could compromise existing sources and methods of collection or otherwise expose historical espionage operations that could engender distrust or trigger the breakdown of inter-State relations. Such unwillingness to extradite one's intelligence personnel or assets also may derive from a sense of loyalty to such individuals and an appreciation for the personal risks they undertook on behalf of the State. Prominent examples include:

- In May 2007, Russia refused to extradite former KGB agent Andrei Lugovoi who was charged in the United Kingdom with the November 2006 murder in London by radioactive poisoning (via Polonium 210) of Alexander Litvinenko, a former KGB agent and vocal critic of Russian President Vladimir Putin.[133]
- In February 2007, the U.S. State Department legal adviser announced that the U.S. Government would not entertain a prospective request by the Italians for the extradition of 25 CIA operatives (and a U.S. Air Force officer) who were indicted nearly two weeks earlier for the alleged "extraordinary rendition" of Abu Omar, a radical Muslim cleric, from Milan in 2003.[134]

[132] Marks, *supra* n.132, at 140; AP, "Senegal Calls Off Extradition of Hissène Habré to Chad," *France24 Int'l News*, Nov. 7, 2011, *available at* www.france24.com/en/20110710-habre-chad-senegal-extradition-un-human-rights (last visited on May 28, 2016). In July 2012, however, the ICJ issued a decision requiring Senegal to either prosecute or extradite Habré. *ICJ Case, Belg. v. Sen.*, *supra* n.131, ¶ 122(6). Subsequently, under the new leadership of Senegal President Macky Sall, a special tribunal was established to prosecute Habré and, in June 2013, the Senegalese police arrested Habré. Adam Nossiter, "Senegal Detains Ex-President of Chad, Accused in the Deaths of Opponents," *N.Y. Times*, June 30, 2013.

[133] "Spy Death: Russia Blocks Extradition," *CNN*, May 22, 2007, *available at* www.cnn.com/2007/WORLD/europe/05/22/uk.spy/ (last visited on May 28, 2016).

[134] Bruce Zagaris, *State Department Legal Adviser Says U.S. Will Not Extradite CIA Defendants to Italy*, 23 IELR 181 (2007). Presumaby on the basis of the U.S. State Department legal adviser's public statement, German authorities announced they were

- For years, the United States has refused to extradite Luis Posada Carriles to Venezuela, which has charged him with various terrorist attacks, including the bombing of a Cuban airliner in 1976, presumably at least in part because of his reported affiliation with the CIA, including participation in the failed 1961 "Bay of Pigs" invasion.[135]
- It has long been alleged that the U.S. Government failed to pursue the extradition and prosecution of former Nazi war criminals in part because it had recruited suspected war criminals, including Klaus Barbie, as intelligence agents at the outset of the Cold War.[136]

POWs. The Geneva Convention Relative to the Treatment of Prisoners of War of August 12, 1949, more commonly known as Geneva Convention III (GC III), governs how POWs are to be treated during and after periods of an international armed conflict (IAC).[137] While some provisions spell out clear obligations expected of member States, some ambiguity remains regarding how a POW is to be handled when more than one State seeks to hold him criminally accountable for actions unrelated to the armed conflict itself but while he continues to enjoy post-conflict POW status.

Among the germane provisions that need to be reconciled are: Article 118 ("Prisoners of war shall be released and repatriated without delay after the cessation of active hostilities");[138] Article 115 ("Prisoners of war detained in connection with a judicial prosecution or conviction and who are designated for repatriation or accommodation in a neutral country, may [be released] before the end of the proceedings or the completion of

unlikely to make a formal extradition request to the United States on arrest warrants issued for thirteen alleged CIA operatives claimed to be linked to the December 2003 "extraordinary rendition" of a German citizen in Macedonia (El-Masri). *Id.*

135 Kevin Jon Heller, "The Strange Case of Luis Posada Carriles," *Opinio Juris*, Feb. 9, 2006, *available at* http://opiniojuris.org/2006/02/09/the-strange-case-of-luis-posada-carriles/ (last visited on May 11, 2016); Bruce Zagaris, *U.S. Court Frees Alleged Anti-Castro Terrorist as CARICOM Calls for Prosecution*, 23 IELR 262 (2007).

136 James W. Moeller, *United States Treatment of Alleged Nazi War Criminals: Int'l Law, Immigration Law, and the Need for Int'l Cooperation*, 25 Va. J. Int'l L. 793, 796–97 & n.16 (1985).

137 Article 3 of GC III is the sole exception, as it applies specifically to "case[s] of armed conflict not of an international character," Geneva Conv. Relative to the Treatment of Prisoners of War, Aug. 12, 1949, art. 3, 6 U.S.T. 3316, T.I.A.S. No. 3364, 75 U.N.T.S. 135 [hereinafter GC III], *i.e.*, to non-international armed conflicts (NIACs), such as civil wars, at least those in which no other State is engaged in support of the militia fighting against government forces.

138 *Id.*, art. 118.

the punishment, *if the Detaining Power consents*"[139]); and Article 12 ("Prisoners of war may only be transferred by the Detaining Power to a Power which is a party to the Convention and after the Detaining Power has satisfied itself of the willingness and ability of such transferee Power to apply the Convention").[140]

The case that brought this particular issue to the fore involved Gen. Manuel Noriega, former *de facto* leader of Panama, who, from 1992, had been serving a lengthy criminal sentence in the United States for narcotics trafficking and conspiracy.[141] France sought his extradition from the United States, pursuant to an *in absentia* money laundering conviction, upon his completion of the U.S. sentence, but Gen. Noriega's lawyers had contended that their client was entitled to repatriation under Article 118 and that the United States had not complied with its obligations under Article 12.[142] In April 2010, however, following seventeen years in a federal penitentiary and another two and half years behind bars while battling to avoid extradition, the United States decided not to repatriate him, but rather to extradite him to France.[143] This case helped clarify States' legal obligations under such scenarios, but POW status could still conceivably be treated as an impediment to extradition under different circumstances.

Asylees and Refugees. The 1951 Convention Relating to the Status of Refugees and its 1967 Protocol define a "refugee" as one who:

139 *Id.*, art. 115 (emphasis supplied).

140 *Id.*, art. 12.

141 Apart from the question of extradition, as a POW (confirmed in *United States v. Noriega*, 808 F. Supp. 791 (S.D. Fla. 1992)), Gen. Noriega was entitled to certain privileges compared with other inmates, including a very large cell with a study, the opportunity to exercise in private, and a sentence reduced from forty to thirty years. Bruce Zagaris, *U.S. Announces Parole Date for Noriega, Does Not Respond to Panama Extradition Request*, 21 IELR 484 (2005).

142 Elena Papangelopoulou, *U.S. District Court Judge Cites Geneva Conv. to Stay Noriega's Extradition*, 24 IELR 135, 135–36 (2008).

143 Rich Phillips, "Noriega Extradited to France," *CNN*, Apr. 26, 2010, *available at* www.cnn.com/2010/CRIME/04/26/noriega.extradition/ (last visited on May 28, 2016). Although he had received a seven-year sentence upon a new trial for laundering drug profits into French banks in the late 1980s, and had served only some months in French jail, France chose to extradite him in December 2011 to his native Panama, which sought his custody based on an *in absentia* conviction and a twenty-year sentence for offenses committed while he was in power, including for the murder of political opponents. "Manuel Noriega Extradited to Panama to Serve Jail Terms," *BBC News*, Dec. 12, 2011, *available at* www.bbc.com/news/world-latin-america-16129630 (last visited on May 28, 2016).

> owing to a well-founded fear of being persecuted for reasons of race, religion, nationality, membership of a particular social group or political opinion, is outside the country of his nationality and is unable or, owing to such fear, is unwilling to avail himself of the protection of that country; or who, not having a nationality and being outside the country of his former habitual residence is unable or, owing to such fear, is unwilling to return to it.[144]

A bedrock principle of refugee law known as *non-refoulement*, as articulated in the 1951 Refugee Convention, holds that:

> No Contracting State shall expel or return ('refouler') a refugee *in any manner whatsoever* to the frontiers of territories where his life or freedom would be threatened on account of his race, religion, nationality, membership of a particular social group or political opinion.[145]

Because this principle, which implicates extradition, is recognized under customary international law as well, it applies to *all States*, even if they are not parties to the 1951 Convention or the 1967 Protocol.[146] The principle applies not only to refugees but also to *political asylees* (who are legally equivalent to refugees but who have requested and secured protection, once located on host State territory rather than from abroad, based on fear specifically of political persecution)[147] and *asylum-seekers* (whose

[144] Conv. Relating to the Status of Refugees, July 28, 1951, art. 1(A)(2), 19 U.S.T. 6259, T.I.A.S. No. 6577, 189 U.N.T.S. 150 [hereinafter Refugee Conv.]; Prot. to the Conv. Relating to the Status of Refugees, Jan. 31, 1967, art. 1, 19 U.S.T. 6223, T.I.A.S. No. 6577, 606 U.N.T.S. 267. A refugee also must not already be receiving protection per Article 1D or be expressly excluded from protection (due to his having committed certain serious crimes or acts per Article 1F).

[145] Refugee Conv., *supra* n.144, art. 33(1) (emphasis supplied). *Accord Decl. on Territorial Asylum*, Dec. 14, 1967, art. 3(1), UNGA Res. 2312 (XXII), 22 U.N. GAOR Supp. (No. 16) at 81, U.N. Doc. A/6716 (1967) (no person seeking asylum from persecution "shall be subjected to measures such as rejection at the frontier or, if he has already entered the territory in which he seeks asylum, expulsion or compulsory return to any State where he may be subjected to persecution.").

[146] Sibylle Kapferer, Dep't of Int'l Protection, U.N. High Comm'r for Refugees, Legal and Protection Policy Research Series, *The Interface Between Extradition and Asylum*, PPLA/2003/05, Nov. 2003, ¶ 218; *UNHCR Note on the Principle of Non-Refoulement*, UNHCR website, Nov. 1997, *available at* www.refworld.org/docid/438c6d972.html (last visited on May 11, 2016).

[147] Asylum can be permanent or temporary. An example of the latter can be seen in the case of Edward Snowden, a former U.S. Government contractor who leaked U.S. intelligence information related to an NSA surveillance program and who was granted asylum by Russia for one year only. Steven Lee Myers & Andrew E. Kramer, "Defiant Russia Grants Snowden Year's Asylum," *N.Y. Times*, Aug. 1, 2013. (Snowden was subsequently granted permission to reside in Russia for an additional three years, until 2017, but *not* as a political asylee. "Snowden is Granted Permit to Reside in Russia for 3 Years," *INYT*,

status has yet to be formally determined).[148] For example, where a U.S. federal appeals court suspected the Government of Panama, which sought the extradition of a former Panamanian minister against whom it might hold a political vendetta, the court remanded the case for a factual determination as to whether the subject had a well-founded fear of persecution if he were extradited to Panama.[149]

There is, however, an exception with respect to a refugee "whom there are reasonable grounds for regarding as a danger to the security of the country in which he is, or who, having been convicted by a final judgment of a particularly serious crime, constitutes a danger to the community of that country."[150] That exception, however, must be "interpreted restrictively"[151] and in no instance may be invoked to return a person who is likely to face torture or inhuman or degrading treatment or punishment;[152] the OAU's 1969 Refugee Convention, in particular, treats *non-refoulement* as an absolute prohibition.[153] The principle of not extraditing a refugee or political asylee is now broadly embedded in domestic law. In a few States, this principle is manifested in national constitutions, such as those of Algeria

Aug. 8, 2014, at 4.) A variant of temporary asylum is sometimes known as "parole," in which an individual is allowed to stay in the host State for a temporary period on a discretionary basis usually because of emergency humanitarian conditions or other compelling reasons of public interest, but such designation is not tantamount to an admission of an alien. *E.g.*, 8 U.S.C. § 1182(d)(5)(a) (2012).

148 Kapferer, *supra* n.146, ¶ 217. *Diplomatic* asylees are similar to political asylees, except that in the former case their request for protection must occur in a legation (*i.e.*, a diplomatic mission, a residence of the Chief of Mission, or dedicated premises for asylees), a military camp, war vessel, or aircraft of the State in question. *E.g.*, OAS Conv. on Diplomatic Asylum, Mar. 28, 1954, art. I, OAS T.S. No. 18.

149 *Nicosia v Wall*, 442 F.2d 1005 (5th Cir. 1971). In addition, the United States provides for another category known as "restriction on removal," which, by contrast with asylum, does not discretionarily authorize an individual to remain permanently in the granting State, yet does bar his return to a State where he fears persecution. 8 U.S.C. § 241(b)(3) (2012).

150 Refugee Conv., *supra* n.144, art. 33(2). *Accord Decl. on Territorial Asylum, supra* n.145, art. 3(2) ("Exception may be made to the foregoing principle [*non-refoulement*] only for overriding reasons of national security or in order to safeguard the population, as in the case of a mass influx of persons.").

151 *The Exclusion Clauses: Guidelines on Their Application*, UNHCR, Dec. 1996, ¶ 8, *available at* www.refworld.org/docid/3ae6b31d9f.html (last visited on May 11, 2016).

152 *See* Kapferer, *supra* n.146, ¶¶ 220 and 221 & n.398 (the Convention characterizes the return to face torture or inhuman or degrading treatment or punishment as a *jus cogens* or peremptory norm).

153 OAU Conv. Governing the Specific Aspects of Refugee Problems in Africa, Sept. 10, 1969, art. II(3).

and Switzerland, although in most cases it can be found in statutory or judicial law.[154]

Once such refugee or political asylee status is conferred, extradition is almost always thwarted;[155] indeed, asylum and extradition operate in direct opposition to one another.[156] For example, the Government of Panama announced that it would not extradite to Iran overthrown Iranian leader Mohammad Reza Shah Pahlavi who had been conferred political asylum for humanitarian reasons, given that capital charges had been leveled against him.[157] Similarly, in the fall of 2003, the United Kingdom granted political asylum to Boris Berezovsky, a prominent Russian businessman with investment interests in the media, mining, and oil industries, as well as a vocal political opponent of Russian President Vladimir Putin; the granting of political asylum to Berezovsky promptly led to the dismissal of extradition proceedings against him.[158]

Likewse, in 2008, Russia refused to extradite to Serbia on charges of cigarette smuggling the widow (Mirjana Marković) and son (Marko) of former Serbian leader Slobodan Milosević, to whom Russia had granted refugee status.[159] In yet another case, in 2012, Niger was unwilling to extradite Saadi Gaddafi, son of slain Libyan leader Moammar Gaddafi, wanted by Libya for having "taken goods by force and intimidation when he led the Libyan football federation," but whose political asylee status "on humanitarian grounds" persisted despite his having violated its conditions by "predicting an imminent uprising in Libya" during a TV interview.[160]

[154] Kapferer, *supra* n.146, ¶¶ 226–28 & nn.401–06 (identifying specific provisions in a wide variety of States).

[155] If asylum is granted *before* an extradition request, the asylum signals to a pursuing State that its request is likely to be denied, although the host State can always withdraw its grant of asylum; if asylum is granted *after* an extradition request has been issued, the host State can deny the request on political offense grounds or as an exercise of executive discretion. Bassiouni, U.S. Extradition, *supra* n.118, at 184.

[156] *See id.* at 167 (discussing "competing international duties").

[157] "Panamanian Foreign Minister Says Shah of Iran Will Not Be Extradited," U.S. Dep't of State Cable, Panama 141355, Jan. 14, 1980 (declassified).

[158] Bruce Zagaris, *English Court Denies Russian Extradition Request for Chechen Official*, 20 IELR 12, 13 (2004).

[159] "We will not extradite them. They were granted refugee status in Russia," the Federal Migration Service's press secretary Konstantin Poltoranin was quoted as saying by Interfax. "Serbia Demands Extradition of Milosevic Widow, Son," *Reuters*, Feb. 28, 2008.

[160] "Niger Will Not Extradite Kadhafi Son," *AFP*, Feb. 12, 2012. By March 2014, however, evidence that Saadi had not complied with Niger's conditions and had tried to destabilize neighboring Libya had mounted, ultimately leading to Niger extraditing Saadi to Libya from his house arrest status in the Nigerian capital of Niamey. David D. Kirkpatrick,

While the host State's determination as to refugee status is still pending, it generally will not honor an extradition request for that individual.[161] At the same time, however, a decision regarding an asylum application may be suspended pending resolution of an extradition proceeding.[162]

Those Accorded Witness Protection. What about an instance in which a fugitive has been granted witness protection in one State but is wanted for a crime in another?[163] This situation was addressed in a rare 1976 case in which the U.S. Court of Appeals for the Fourth Circuit found that a witness protection agreement with the U.S. Department of Justice to protect him from "underworld assassins" did not bar him from extradition to Sweden to face criminal prosecution, given that the agreement was not intended to protect him from criminal law proceedings abroad.[164] That said, it is conceivable that such an agreement could yield an extradition denial under other State laws and/or different circumstances.

Prominent or Popular Figures. At times, a State will choose to protect an individual from extradition simply because of his stature, local popularity, or the contributions he has made to the economic welfare of the host State. In one example, Jacob "Kobi" Alexander, former chief executive officer of Comverse Technology, invested in or contributed substantially to the Namibian economy and consequently was widely appreciated and protected on that basis evidently from extradition.[165] Likewise, Jamaican Prime Minister Bruce Golding "authorized the retention of a U.S. law firm – for a hundred thousand dollars per quarter – to lobby officials in Washington" to oppose a U.S. extradition request for Christopher (Dudus) Coke, "known as the country's most powerful 'don'" as the leader of a "garrison

"Niger Extradites a Son of Qaddafi to Libya, Saying He Didn't 'Stay Quiet,'" *N.Y. Times*, Mar. 7, 2014, at A6.

161 *E.g.*, Bruce Zagaris, *Brazil Helps Convicted Former Bolivian Opposition Leader to Escape from Brazilian Embassy to Brazil, Igniting Demands from Bolivia for his Return*, 29 IELR 405 (2013) (the Brazilian Ministry of Justice stated that former Bolivian opposition leader Roger Pinto would neither be extradited nor deported until a decision on his refugee status was rendered by the National Committee for Refugees (CONARE).

162 *E.g., Barapind v. Reno*, 225 F.3d 1100, 1114 (9th Cir. 2000).

163 Since the 1990s, witness protection programs have become increasingly critical in combating organized crime and terrorism in Europe. Parliamentary Ass'y of the CoE, Comm. on Legal Affairs and Hum. Rts., *Witness Protection as an Indispensable Tool in the Fight against Organized Crime and Terrorism in Europe*, Doc. No. 13647, Dec. 9, 2014, ¶ 41, (Arcadio Diaz Tejera, Rapporteur).

164 *Peroff v. Hylton*, 542 F.2d 1247, 1249 (4th Cir. 1976) (per curiam), *cert. denied*, 429 U.S. 1062 (1977).

165 Bruce Zagaris, *Alexander Requests Dismissal of Presiding Officer of Namibian Extradition Proceeding*, 23 IELR 378 (2007).

community" known as Tivoli Gardens in West Kingston, on narcotics and firearms trafficking charges.[166] In another instance, for years the military junta in Bolivia protected Klaus Barbie, the "Butcher of Lyon," from extradition while he assisted Bolivian officials reportedly with repressive techniques.[167] And in July 2010, the Swiss Justice Minister defended the denial of a U.S. extradition request for famed film director Roman Polanski in part on the grounds that he had been traveling to Switzerland in good faith for years.[168]

d Personal Circumstances

The host State also may recommend that an extradition request be withdrawn or postponed or deny it outright under either express domestic law or via political discretion for humanitarian reasons in cases where an individual is of advanced age, suffering from poor health, or facing other challenging personal or family circumstances.[169] The underlying rationale for such exceptional treatment varies and could include that: (i) certain physically or mentally disabled individuals could be unfit for trial,[170] (ii) some could

[166] Mattathais Schwartz, *A Reporter at Large: A Massacre in Jamaica*, THE NEW YORKER, Dec. 12, 2011, at 62 (implying the "campaign against the extradition" stemmed from "Coke's dangerously high standing with the Jamaican government").

[167] It was only Bolivia's transition to a civilian government under President Siles Zuazo in October 1982 that finally enabled France to secure Barbie's transfer through deportation. Tracy Wilkinson, "Bolivia Expels Fugitive to Face Death Sentence," *The Bryan Times* [Ohio], Feb. 5, 1983, at 3; Wash. Post Service, "Barbie Case May Open Old Wounds in France," *The Milwaukee Journal*, Feb. 9, 1983, at 9; Richard Bernstein, "As the Trial of Barbie Begins, France Also Is Being Judged," *N.Y. Times*, May 11, 1987.

[168] Bruce Zagaris, *Swiss Gov't Denies U.S. Extradition Request for Roman Polanski*, 26 IELR 354 (2010).

[169] ABBELL, *supra* n.10, at 129–30.

[170] Under section 25 of the U.K.'s Extradition Act of 2003, the test is not actually whether one is suffering from a mental illness, as he or she could presumably be properly cared for elsewhere under such a circumstance, but whether the individual is psychologically "unfit," say, because he stands a high risk of suicide. *A Review of the United Kingdom's Extradition Arrangements*, Sept. 30, 2011, at 406–07 (citing *Jasons v. Riga Dist. Ct., Latvia* [2009] EWHC 1845 (Admin)). Beginning in 2011 with the conviction of John Demjanjuk for his accessory role in the murder of tens of thousands at the Sobibor Concentration Camp in Nazi-controlled Poland, Germany renewed its interest after years of dormancy in seeking the extradition of Nazi criminals in the United States, but at this point many of those perpetrators are quite old, and this ignited a controversy over whether they should be prosecuted and imprisoned at such an advanced stage of life, notwithstanding the gravity of their crimes. Eric Lichtblau, "A Retiree, 89, Is Held in Deaths at Auschwitz," *N.Y. Times*, June 18, 2014 (discussing the conviction of an 89-year-old Philadelphia resident Johann Breyer for his role seven decades earlier as a "Death's Head" guard at Auschwitz Concentration Camp in aiding and abetting murder).

not physically manage the geographical transition between States, (iii) others could suffer disproportionately or would present a strong suicide risk due to their age or fragile state if convicted and sentenced,[171] and (iv) in some instances *third parties* might be incidentally injured by an extradition or its timing.[172]

Many domestic laws allow for the consideration of humanitarian factors in connection with States' extradition determinations.[173] In one case, France postponed the extradition of Helmet Elsner to Austria until February 2007 to allow the seventy-one-year-old former director-general of Ban für Arbeit und Wirtscht (Bawag) indicted on charges of fraud, false accounting, and breach of trust, to undergo multiple treatments for a heart condition.[174] In June 1987, an Israeli judge opined that the extradition of William Nakash to France on murder charges should be delayed for up to a year to permit Nakash to obtain a divorce and thereby keep his wife from becoming a "deserted woman," a highly disreputable status under Jewish and Israeli law.[175]

More recently, in January 2014, the Belizean Minister of Justice denied a U.S. request for the extradition of Belize national Rhett Fuller for his

[171] *See, e.g.*, "Gary McKinnon Extradition to U.S. Blocked by Theresa May," *BBC News*, Oct. 16, 2012, *available at* www.bbc.com/news/uk-19957138 (last visited on May 28, 2016) (summarizing the U.K. Home Secretary's decision to deny the extradition of a hacker of sensitive U.S. Government computers on account of his having Asperger's syndrome, a form of autism, and the related human rights concerns that he could commit suicide if locked away in a U.S. prison for as long as sixty years if convicted).

[172] Examples can be found at nn.175 and 176 and accompanying text *infra*.

[173] *E.g.*, Slovak Repub., Crim. Procedure Act, Act No. 141/1961, Nov. 29, 1961, art. 403(2), *as amended* (the Minister of Justice may refuse extradition if: "(c) taking into account the age and personal circumstances of the person whose extradition is sought, he would most likely be inadequately severely punished by extradition in proportion to the level of gravity of the criminal offence he allegedly committed."); PRC Extradition Law, *supra* n.28, art. 9(2) (an extradition request may be denied if "extradition is incompatible with humanitarian considerations in view of the age, health or other conditions of the person sought."); N.Z. Extradition Act Pub. Act 55 of 1999, May 20, 1999, § 7(f) & (g), *as amended* (barring extradition if a person has a mental disability or intellectual incapacity).

[174] Bruce Zagaris, *France Extradites Former Bank Head to Austria*, 23 IELR 133, 133–34 (2007). Sometimes, however, extradition proceeds notwithstanding a fugitive's medical condition. For example, Guatemala extradited its former President Alfonso Portillo "from a medical hospital where he was receiving treatment for liver and heart problems and put on an air ambulance, where he was taken to New York to respond to an indictment for conspiring to launder money derived from corrupt payments." Bruce Zagaris, *Guatemala Extradites Former President to U.S. on Money Laundering Charges*, 29 IELR 282 (2013).

[175] Naomi Hillel, *A Digest of Selected Judgments of the Supreme Court of Israel*, 23 Isr. L. Rev. 506, 509 (1989).

alleged participation in the 1990 murder of a U.S. national in South Beach, Florida, noting as an important factor the adverse impact extradition would have on the Fuller family, as the subject is the father of an autistic child.[176] The United States is something of an exception in this regard, with no federal appellate court to date having denied extradition on humanitarian grounds,[177] based on an elevated legal standard requiring that the anticipated punishment or procedure awaiting a returned fugitive must be "antipathetic to a federal court's sense of decency."[178]

Heads of State or designated ministers often have the final say and can overturn a favorable extradition decision on by a domestic court humanitarian grounds.[179] In January 2000, for example, the British Home Secretary exercised his discretion not to extradite Gen. Augusto Pinochet, former President of Chile, to Spain for charges related to crimes against humanity committed against Spanish citizens in Chile during his rule, finding that Pinochet's poor physical health made him unfit to stand trial.[180] Similarly, in October 2008, French President Nicolas Sarkozy refused to follow a French court order to extradite to Italy Marina Petrella, who had been convicted of murder and other violent crimes while part of the Red Brigades terrorist group from 1977 to 1982, on the grounds that she had stopped eating and her overall health had deteriorated to the point where there was concern she would die if extradited.[181]

* * * * *

This chapter has evaluated the category of impediments to extradition related to individual status and circumstances. The next chapter will focus on the third and final category, which addresses inter-State relations and sensitivities.

176 Glenn Tillett, "Long-standing U.S. Extradition Request Finally Denied by Belize," *Caribbean News Now!*, Jan. 17, 2014.

177 Andrew J. Parmenter, *Death by Non-Inquiry: The Ninth Circuit Permits the Extradition of a U.S. Citizen Facing the Death Penalty for a Non-Violent Drug Offense [*Prasoprat v. Benov, *421 F.3d 1009 (9th Cir. 2005)]*, 45 Washburn L.J. 657, 658, 666 & n.92 (2006) (collecting cases through 2006, including *Prasoprat* in which a U.S. national was extradited to Thailand to face the death penalty for a non-violent drug offense).

178 *Gallina v Fraser*, 278 F.2d 77, 79 (2d Cir.), *cert. denied*, 364 U.S. 851 (1960).

179 *See* pp. 163–64 in Chapter 4 regarding the U.S. Secretary of State's role.

180 Stanbrook & Stanbrook, *supra* n.11, at 131.

181 Bruce Zagaris, *French Refuse Italian Extradition Request of Ex-Member of Red Brigades on Humanitarian Grounds*, 24 IELR 477, 477–78 (2008).

7

Impediments III

Inter-State Relations and Sensitivities

In this chapter, the discussion of impediments to extradition continues with a focus on inter-State relations and sensitivities. Specifically, the following grounds for denial will be addressed: (i) lack of an operative extradition treaty; (ii) political tensions, agendas, and motives; (iii) justice system interplay restrictions; (iv) competing jurisdictional claims; (v) international human rights concerns; and (vi) conflict resolution and national security considerations.

a Lack of an Operative Extradition Treaty

Some States, particularly those with a common law tradition,[1] refuse to extradite fugitives absent an effective extradition treaty of which the pursuing State at issue is a party.[2] That means that, absent such an extradition treaty, the host State applying such a law or practice generally will not entertain an extradition request even on the basis of reciprocity or comity.[3]

[1] David Freestone, *Int'l Cooperation against Terrorism and the Development of Int'l Law Principles of Jurisdiction, in* Terrorism and International Law 46 (Rosalyn Higgins & Maurice Flory eds. 1997); Thomas F. Muther, Jr., *Extradition of Int'l Criminals: A Changing Perspective*, 24 Denv. J. Int'l L. & Pol'y 221, 223 n.16 (1995).

[2] M. Cherif Bassiouni, *Unlawful Seizures and Irregular Rendition Devices as Alternatives to Extradition*, 7 Vand. J. Transnat'l L. 25, 63–64 (1973) [hereinafter Bassiouni, *Unlawful Seizures*]. In other cases, a State may require at least a surrogate provision found in another bilateral or multilateral agreement or some enabling municipal legislation, as discussed in Chapter 4.c. *See, e.g.*, India, The Extradition Act, Act No. 34 of 1962, Sept. 15, 1962, § 3(4), *as amended* [hereinafter India Extradition Act] ("Where there is no extradition treaty made by India with any foreign State, the Central Government may, by notified order, treat any Convention to which India and a foreign State are parties, as an extradition treaty made by India with that foreign State providing for extradition in respect of the offences specified in that Convention.").

[3] *E.g.*, Bruce Zagaris, *Uganda Tries to Obtain Custody of Former Minister on Bribery Charges*, 24 IELR 93 (2008) (the United States denied Uganda's request for the extradition of Zoe Bakoko Bakoru, former Ugandan Minister of Gender, Labor and Social Development, on charges of abuse of office and bribery, because no extradition treaty existed between the

The United States, for example, has maintained such a restrictive domestic law, almost without deviation,[4] throughout most of its history.[5] Even today, with a single exception authorized in the mid-1990s,[6] the U.S. criminal code provisions governing extradition maintain that they "shall continue in force" regarding the transfer of "persons who have committed crimes in foreign countries"[7] "*only during the existence of any treaty of*

United States and Uganda). At the same time, however, the lack of a bilateral extradition treaty would not necessarily invalidate an *arrest and detention* effected pursuant to an extradition request. *See* Bruce Zagaris, *Accused Croatian War Criminal Loses Effort to Block Australian Extradition Hearing*, 23 IELR 54, 55 (2007).

4 A rare exception can be found during the U.S. Civil War in 1864, when, despite the absence of a bilateral treaty between the United States and Spain, U.S. President Abraham Lincoln's Secretary of State authorized the extradition of a Cuban military official and accused slave trader, Col. Don Jose Augustin Arguelles, to Spain on the basis of comity. BARBARA M. YARNOLD, INTERNATIONAL FUGITIVES: A NEW ROLE FOR THE INTERNATIONAL COURT OF JUSTICE 14–15 (1991); CHRISTOPHER H. PYLE, EXTRADITION, POLITICS, AND HUMAN RIGHTS 267 (2001); Louis Klarevas, *The Surrender of Alleged War Criminals to Int'l Tribunals: Examining the Constitutionality of Extradition Via Congressional-Executive Agreement*, 8 UCLA J. INT'L L. & FOR. AFF. 77, 106 (2003).

5 *United States v. Rauscher*, 119 U.S. 407 (1886); *Factor v. Laubenheimer*, 290 U.S. 276 (1933); *United States v. Fernandez-Morris*, 99 F. Supp.2d 1358 (S.D. Fla. 1999). In a celebrated case in January 1947, the Soviet Union requested that the United States turn over Kirill Alekseev, a former Soviet Trade Representative in Mexico, on the charge of embezzling public funds, should he be found on U.S. soil. The U.S. Government responded by stating that the executive branch had no authority to extradite an individual absent an applicable treaty or other legislative authority, neither of which then existed. "Request for Extradition of Former Soviet Trade Representative Denied," 16 *Dep't of State Bull.* 212, 212 (1947) (as reflected in a Letter from Thompson, Eastern Eur. Affairs Div. Chief, U.S. Dep't of State, to Tarassenko, Counsellor, Soviet Emb. in Wash., D.C., Jan. 20, 1947).

6 *See* 18 U.S.C. § 3181(b) (2012) (incorporated under the Antiterrorism and Effective Death Penalty Act of 1996, Pub. L. 140–132, Apr. 24, 1996, § 443(a), (identifying an exception when persons other than U.S. citizens or permanent residents "have committed crimes of violence against nationals of the United States in foreign countries without regard to the existence of any treaty of extradition with such foreign Government if the Attorney General certifies, in writing, that (1) evidence has been presented by the foreign government that indicates that had the offense been committed in the United States, they would constitute crimes of violence as defined under section 16 of this title; and (2) the offenses charges are not of a political nature.").

7 *Id.* § 3181(a). No extradition treaty is required, however, to extradite a fugitive who actually or allegedly committed one or more crimes in "any foreign country or territory, or any part thereof . . . occupied by or under the control of the United States," who then fled to the United States and is the subject of a request for his return by the "military governor or other chief executive officer in control of such foreign country or territory." *Id.* § 3185 (2012). Even when an operative extradition treaty exists, however, extradition may not be authorized when the fugitive is sought *from* U.S.-occupied territory, *Neely v. Henkel*, 180 U.S. 109, 120 (1901), or when the fugitive is alleged to have committed a crime on foreign-occupied territory that has since reverted to original possession by the pursuing State at issue. *United States v. Icardi*, 140 F. Supp. 383 (D.D.C. 1956) (involving

extradition"[8] with such foreign government.[9] Other States that insist on the existence of an operative treaty to authorize an extradition include, by way of example, Canada[10] and Singapore.[11] Some other States (*e.g.*, Colombia[12] and Trinidad & Tobago[13]) maintain a general but less absolutist approach to this extradition treaty requirement.

Whether based on national law, principle, or pretext, it is not uncommon for States to deny extradition on the basis that no treaty exists recognizing or contemplating extradition between the host State and a given pursuing State. For example:

- In December 1974, the Bolivian Supreme Court rejected a French request for the extradition of Klaus Barbie, a former Gestapo official, on the ground that there was no extradition treaty between Bolivia and France.[14]

a charge of murder on Italian territory while it had been under wartime German occupation).

[8] 18 U.S.C. § 3181(a) (2012) (emphasis supplied). It should be noted, however, that U.S. federal courts have recognized so-called congressional-executive agreements as tantamount to treaties and as a sufficient basis for extradition. Such treaties call for the concurrence of a simple majority of both chambers of the U.S. Congress (*i.e.*, the Senate and House of Representatives) rather than the traditional, Constitution-based two-thirds supermajority "consent" of the U.S. Senate alone. Frederic L. Kirgis, "Int'l Agreements and U.S. Law," *ASIL Insights*, May 27, 1997, *available at* www.asil.org/insights/volume/2/issue/5/international-agreements-and-us-law (last visited on May 28, 2016); *e.g., Williams v. Rogers*, 449 F.2d 513, 521 (8th Cir. 1971), *cert. denied*, 405 U.S. 926 (1972).

[9] This law does not preclude the United States from seeking extradition from other States with which it lacks an extradition treaty. Christopher L. Blakesley, *Extradition Between France and the United States: An Exercise in Comparative and Int'l Law*, 13 VAND. J. TRANSNAT'L L. 653, 661–62 (1980); Alona E. Evans, *Acquisition of Custody over the Int'l Fugitive Offender—Alternatives to Extradition: A Survey of United States Practice*, 40 B.Y.B.I.L. 77, 79 (1964) ("[M]any instances can be cited of requests by the United States for extradition on grounds of comity, but usually with the understanding that reciprocity in similar circumstances should not be expected.").

[10] Extradition Act of Canada, Royal Statutes of Canada (R.S.C.) June 17, 1999, § 3(1), *as amended* [hereinafter Canada Extradition Act] ("A person may be extradited from Canada in accordance with this Act and a relevant extradition agreement on the request of an extradition partner").

[11] Singapore, Extradition Act, Act. 14 of 1968, Aug. 1, 1968, § 4(1), *as amended.*

[12] *E.g., In re Bachnofer*, Sup. Ct. of Justice, Colom. Nov. 13, 1959, *reprinted in* 28 ILR 322 (1963).

[13] Trinidad & Tobago, Extradition (Commonwealth and Foreign Territories) Act, Jan. 31, 1986, § 4(1) (an extradition treaty is required for an extradition to foreign versus Commonwealth States).

[14] E.J. Dionne, Jr., "Ex-Gestapo Aide is Taken to France," *N.Y. Times*, Feb. 6, 1983, at 3; *Altmann (Barbie) v. France*, Appl. No. 10689/83, Eur. Comm'n of Hum. Rts., 37 D.R. at R

- After terrorists sought refuge in Lebanon following their hijacking of TWA Flight 847 in June 1985, their extradition was expressly rejected because no extradition treaty existed between the United States (the pursuing State at issue) and Lebanon (the host State).[15]
- Because no extradition treaty existed between Israel and Venezuela, the latter refused to extradite to Israel Mahmoud El-Abed Ahmad (a/k/a Mahmoud Abed Atta) after he fled Palestine for Venezuela following his attack on a West Bank bus carrying Israeli settlers in April 1986.[16]
- In April 1990, Austria denied an extradition request from Bulgaria where their bilateral legal cooperation treaty did not provide for assistance in criminal cases.[17]
- In July 1994, Pakistan refused to extradite Agha Hasan Abedi to Abu Dhabi because no extradition treaty existed between Pakistan and the United Arab Emirates (UAE).[18]

States may not have executed an extradition treaty for any number of reasons; it may have been the practice of one or both States not to rely on such legal instruments;[19] or perhaps there had been no historical need for such a treaty, given little or no criminal intersection or movement between their populations;[20] or it may be a function of their simply

225, July 4, 1984; Jean-Olivier Viout, *The Klaus Barbie Trial and Crimes Against Humanity*, 3 Hofstra L. & Pol'y Symp. 155, 156–57 (1999).

[15] Brandon S. Chabner, Comment, *The Omnibus Diplomatic Security and Antiterrorism Act of 1986: Prescribing and Enforcing United States Law against Terrorist Violence Overseas*, 37 UCLA L. Rev. 985, 1002 n.75 (1990).

[16] Andreas F. Lowenfeld, *Ahmad: Profile of an Extradition Case*, 23 N.Y.U. J. Int'l L. & Pol. 723, 723–24 (1991).

[17] *Stoichkov v. Bulgaria*, Appl. No. 9808/02, 44 EHRR, ¶ 19, Mar. 24, 2005 [hereinafter *Stoichkov Case*].

[18] Geoff Gilbert, Transnational Fugitive Offenders in International Law 47 n.95 (1998).

[19] *See* Tetsuya Morimoto, *First Japanese Denial of U.S. Extradition Request: Economic Espionage Case*, 20 IELR 288 (2004) (as of July 2004, Japan had only two extradition treaties in effect, one with the United States and the other with South Korea); "Japan, China to Meet Wednesday on Extradition Treaty for First Time in Five Years," *The Japan Times*, June 1, 2015 (confirming that to date Japan has entered into only two extradition treaties, but is engaging with the PRC in a second round of talks toward a third such treaty).

[20] *E.g.*, Richard Downing, Recent Development, *The Domestic and Int'l Legal Implications of the Abduction of Criminals from Foreign Soil*, 26 Stan. J. Int'l L. 573, 576 (1989–90) (the United States and Brazil did not execute an extradition treaty for about fifty years until 1964).

being on unfriendly terms,[21] suspicious about one another's motivations, or an alternative satisfactory approach to fugitive transfers has been relied upon by one or both States.[22] Such absence also may stem from one State perceiving such a treaty relationship to be largely one-sided and therefore disproportionately onerous.[23]

In other instances, a bilateral extradition treaty may technically exist, but is not regarded by the host State as in effect for such reasons as:

(i) the treaty has been ruled unconstitutional or unenforceable by the host State's judiciary;[24]
(ii) as a newly independent or successor State, the host State inherited an extradition treaty that it views as suspect or no longer binding;[25] or
(iii) the treaty was entered into decades ago and, given the vast changes to extradition law and practice in the interim, the host State does not regard it as legitimate any longer.[26]

[21] *E.g.*, Bruce Zagaris, *U.S. Court Frees Alleged Anti-Castro Terrorist as CARICOM Calls for Prosecution*, 23 IELR 262, 263 (2007) (historical enmity between the United States and Cuba has prevented the conclusion of an extradition treaty between them).

[22] *See* Evans, *supra* n.9, at 93–94 ("[I]t was surmised in the [U.S.] Department of State in 1931, that Greek reliance upon the convenience of rendition by deportation was proving to be a deterrent to the conclusion of an extradition treaty with that country.").

[23] *See* AP, "Singapore Opposes Indonesia on Extradition," *Wall St. J.*, Feb. 14, 2005, at A15 (Indonesia has long sought an extradition treaty with Singapore to obtain custody of and prosecute Indonesian business tycoons who allegedly violated Indonesian law and brought their assets to Singapore; Singapore does not want to become Indonesia's law enforcer and so has consistently refused such a request).

[24] For example, in December 1986, the Colombian Supreme Court ruled the 1979 U.S.-Colombia Extradition Treaty (that entered into force in 1982) unenforceable because its domestic enabling legislation was invalid. Bruce Zagaris, *Colombian Supreme Court Inquires About Potential U.S. Violations of Extradition Terms*, 21 IELR 222 (2005).

[25] *E.g.*, *Heeralall v. Comm'r of Prisons*, Sup. Ct., Mauritius, Mar. 30, 1992, 1992 MAURITIUS REP. 70, 72–73 *reprinted in* 107 ILR 169 (E. Lauterpacht, *et al.*, eds. 1997) [*hereinafter Heeralall Case*] (the Mauritian Supreme Court ruled the extradition treaty between the United Kingdom and France as no longer binding on Mauritius after it gained independence from the United Kingdom in 1968 based on: (i) Mauritius' express intention for the treaty to lapse two years hence unless considered still in effect under the rules of customary international law; and (ii) France evidently regarded the treaty as no longer in force between them). In *Artukovic v Boyle*, 107 F. Supp. 11, 33 (S.D. Cal. 1952), the trial court determined that the U.S. Government, following the surrender of the Central Powers in World War I and the repartitioning of Europe, regarded all previous treaties with those countries as no longer in force, but that judgment was reversed by the appeals court, which concluded that "open recognition" of the treaty on the part of both the United States and Yugoslavia had in fact continued. *Ivancevic v. Artukovic*, 211 F.2d 565, 574 (9th Cir. 1954).

[26] *E.g.*, "MP Faces U.S. Judge," *Modern Ghana News*, Nov. 23, 2007 (Ghana had denied recent extradition requests under an outdated and suspect extradition treaty between the

A mere change of national leadership or to the form of government by one of the contracting parties, however, is not considered sufficient under international law to render an otherwise operative extradition treaty no longer in force.[27] Alternatively, a bilateral extradition treaty may once have existed, but has since lapsed[28] or been suspended due to the passage of time, a break in diplomatic relations,[29] a current state of armed conflict,[30] or because one State may be struggling to re-establish a functioning government.[31]

The absence of an extradition treaty between host and pursuing States may not only operate to scuttle an extradition request, but also can create vulnerabilities, as criminals may be able to exploit such legal

United Kingdom and the United States dating from December 1931 and extended to Ghana after British colonial rule in June 1935). Along these lines, Nigeria's Extradition Act of 1966 ANN. VOL. L. FED. REP. NIG. A375 (1966), was promulgated to supplant all British colonial-era legislation related to extradition. Momodu Kassim-Momodu, *Extradition of Fugitives by Nigeria*, 35 INT'L & COMP. L.Q. 512, 514 (1986).

27 *Perlin v. Superintendent of Prisons*, Sup. Ct., Palestine, Nov. 16, 1942, 9 LAW REPORTS OF PALESTINE 683 (1942), *reprinted in* 10 ANN. DIG. & REP. PUB. INT'L L. CASES 328, 329 (H. Lauterpacht ed. 1945). *See also* pp.172–73 in Chapter 4.

28 South Africa's "withdrawal from the Commonwealth in 1961 resulted in the lapse of many of its extradition treaties with other Commonwealth States." *Harksen v. President of the Repub. of So. Afr. and Others*, Case CCT 41/99, Const. Ct., So. Afr., Mar. 30, 2000, [2000] (2) SA 825, *reprinted in* 132 ILR 529, 557, ¶ 3 (E. Lauterpacht, *et al.*, eds. 2008). In addition, the extradition treaty between the United Kingdom and Rhodesia [now Zambia and Zimbabwe] dating to December 23, 1963, lapsed in the late 1970s. ALUN JONES & ANAND DOOBAY, JONES AND DOOBAY ON EXTRADITION AND MUTUAL ASSISTANCE 88 (2005).

29 *E.g.*, Evans, *supra* n.9, at 96 ("During the period of the revolution following the downfall of the Madero regime in 1913, the United States did not maintain diplomatic relations with Mexico and considered that the Extradition Treaty was suspended.").

30 For example, during World War II a number of States abrogated or suspended their extradition treaties with Germany. Whether such treaties were reactivated after hostilities ended amounts to a question of fact in which courts looked to the political and diplomatic actions of the States, such as an exchange of notes. *Argento v. Horn*, 241 F.2d 258 (6th Cir. 1957). As a general rule, however, "it is now well settled that the outbreak of war does not necessarily abrogate treaties or treaty provisions. The test seems to be whether the treaty by its nature is so incompatible with a state of war as to be voided by the commencement of hostilities." *In re Extradition of D'Amico*, 177 F. Supp. 648, 653 (S.D.N.Y. 1959) (finding that the U.S.-Italy Extradition Treaty relating to the extradition of non-political criminals was not voided by the outbreak of war between the two States).

31 *See* Michael H. Cardozo, *When Extradition Fails, is Abduction the Solution?*, 55 AJIL 127, 133 (1961) ("In the *Ker* case, a private detective from the United States, while in Peru, received duly executed extradition papers from the U.S. Government, conforming to the requirements of the extradition treaty between the United States and Peru. He did not use them, however, because he had no access to the proper Government of Peru, which was disorganized as a result of military occupation of the capital city by Chilean forces.").

requirements by identifying "safe havens" to which to flee.[32] While the host and pursuing States, in principle, could agree to an extradition outside the terms of a treaty framework, some States insist on strict reciprocity and will refuse to extradite absent such a commitment by a pursuing State.[33]

b Political Tensions, Agendas, and Motives

Even where an operative extradition treaty is recognized to exist between two States, their bilateral relations with one another; the host State's pursuit of political, ideological, reputational, or foreign policy objectives; or its interest in making a political "statement" or in protecting information or officials, could complicate or postpone, if not quash, an extradition request as shown in the following scenarios:

(i) the host State is non-receptive to providing any form of international criminal law enforcement cooperation to the pursuing State at issue, given the strained political, diplomatic, or economic relations that then exist between them;[34]

(ii) the host State has an extremist agenda that involves material support to terrorists or the like and is therefore less inclined to care about or honor its international legal commitments;[35]

[32] *See* Bassiouni, *Unlawful Seizures, supra* n.2, at 63–64. Namibia has been cited as an example of a fugitive-friendly destination, which has few extradition treaties and where extradition requests are infrequently granted, documents go missing, technicalities prevail, and corruption is widespread. Robyn Dixon, "Africa's Land of Sand and Fugitives," *L.A. Times*, Dec. 8, 2006 (where such fugitives as Jacob "Kobi" Alexander, Hans-Jürgen Koch, Wesley Snipes, and Vito Bigione all sought refuge from foreign prosecutors). Namibia has been compared to the "remote desert planet of Tatooine [in the film series *Star Wars*], hangout for aliens, bounty hunters and dodgy fugitives from intergalactic justice." *Id.*

[33] *See* discussion on reciprocity on pp. 151–52 in Chapter 4.

[34] *See, e.g.*, Vikas Bajaj & Hari Kumar, "India Allows Prosecutors to Charge U.S. Citizen," *IHT*, Feb. 20, 2012, at 3 (noting that "Pakistan has previously refused to hand over people whom India has accused of plotting the [2008] attacks" in Mumbai that killed at least 163 persons, as India has accused Pakistan, its neighbor and regional rival of complicity in the attacks).

[35] *See* Jackson Nyomuya Maogoto, Battling Terrorism: Legal Perspectives on the Use of Force and the War on Terror 65 (2005) (a requested State that "directs its agents or allied entities to attack diplomats abroad or to take hostages within its own borders obviously will not order the extradition or prosecution of these perpetrators.").

(iii) the host State chooses to "pay back" the pursuing State treaty partner for its denial of an important extradition request issued by the host State;[36]
(iv) the host State has determined that aggressive actions by a particular pursuing State to recover a fugitive in breach of a third State's territory suggest a lack of respect for sovereignty and international cooperation;[37]
(v) the host State feels under political pressure from other States, typically from within its geographical region, not to cooperate with a specific pursuing State regarding extradition where the prevailing view is that the fugitive in question warrants protection, not prosecution or punishment, for his actions.[38]
(vi) the host State is apprehensive that extraditing a government official of its own could lead to the identification of more senior officials involved in the offense and greater attendant foreign policy exposure when that official defends himself at trial;[39]

[36] *See* Erika de Wet & Jure Vidmar, eds., Hierarchy in International Law: The Place of Human Rights 148 (2012) ("If the [requested state] decides to refuse the extradition request . . . it will elicit the wrath of the requesting state that may choose to retaliate in kind by denying extradition in similar situations.").

[37] *See* Michael Abbell, Extradition to and from the United States 377–78 (2010) (in the mid-1990s, the Costa Rican Supreme Court declared that its 1991 extradition treaty with the United States was unenforceable due to perceived overreaching on the part of the United States in seizing Humberto Álvarez-Machaín from Mexico, followed by the U.S. Supreme Court's assertion of personal jurisdiction over him).

[38] *Cf.* Tom McCarthy, "Edward Snowden Praises E.U. Parliament Vote against U.S. Extradition," *The Guardian*, Oct. 29, 2015 (describing how the European "parliament voted 285–281 to pass a largely symbolic measure, a resolution that called on European Union member states to 'drop any criminal charges against Edward Snowden, grant him protection and consequently prevent extradition or rendition by third parties, in recognition of his status as whistleblower and international human rights defender.'").

[39] *See, e.g.*, Paul Lewis, "Sanctions on Libya Begin to Take Hold as Deadline Passes; U.N. Seeks Full Isolation," *N.Y. Times*, Apr. 15, 1992, at A1, A6 ("Diplomats assume Libya does not want to have its two officers tried for the explosion of the Pan Am 103 aircraft because the suspects might defend themselves by implicating other more senior government officials in the bombing"). But, interestingly, extradition itself may be desired precisely on the same self-protective rationale, as outsourcing justice can keep the local population in the dark regarding "wrongdoing against their own countrymen." "Extradition in Latin America: How to Handle a Drug Gang," *The Economist*, Nov. 21, 2015, at 36 (adding by way of example that "[i]n 2008 Mr. [Álvaro] Uribe [President of Colombia] sent 14 members of right-wing paramilitary groups to the United States on drug charges just as Colombian investigators were examining their alleged human-rights violations and potential ties to the government. Many of their records were sealed, causing the president's opponents to accuse him of using extradition as part of a cover-up.").

(vii) the host State has reservations about extraditing a non-national who maintains a shared political ideology or worldview or like-minded abhorrence toward the alleged victims;[40]

(viii) the host State is concerned that an individual (outside of the State apparatus[41]) with extensive insider knowledge about that State's military or intelligence secrets, if extradited, potentially could disclose such information in the course of criminal proceedings in another State;[42]

(ix) the host State recognizes that by seeking the extradition of a former leader of one's government, where many of that individual's ministers or other senior political staff remain in power, the current State's abuses could become exposed at trial as well;[43]

(x) the host State is concerned about potential foreign policy backlash or adverse publicity that could arise by extraditing a fugitive to, and thereby demonstrating law enforcement cooperation with, a particular State that has become a foreign policy target for others;[44]

[40] For example, for years after World War II, many South American States adopted a protective posture vis-a-vis Nazi war criminals. Josef Mengele, known as the "Angel of Death" for his ghoulish medical experiments at Auschwitz, spent most of his post-war life in Argentina, while dying in Brazil in 1979; and Edward Roschmann, the so-called "Butcher of Riga," died in Paraguay in 1977. Monte Reel, "In South America, a 'Last Chance' to Hunt Down Nazi War Criminals," *Wash. Post*, Dec. 6, 2007, at A20. As referenced in Chapter 5.d, in 2005, Argentina finally acknowledged and repealed a secret order that prohibited Jews fleeing the Holocaust from entering the country. *Id.*

[41] A State's own military and intelligence officials are discussed in Chapter 6.c.

[42] For example, Russia, as a third party, applied pressure both on (i) the Thai Government not to extradite Viktor Bout, a Russian arms trafficking suspect, to the United States, and (ii) the U.S. Government not to pursue the extradition of Bout by threatening non-cooperation on arms control and the war in Afghanistan; some believe Russia was concerned that through interrogation, the United States could learn what Bout knew about sensitive Russian military or intelligence secrets. AP, "Suspected Arms Trafficker Flown to NYC," *CBS New York*, Nov. 17, 2010, *available at* http://newyork.cbslocal.com/2010/11/17/suspected-arms-trafficker-flown-from-bangkok-to-nyc/ (last visited on May 28, 2016).

[43] For example, Chadian Justice Minister Mahamat announced in January 1998 the intention of Chad to formally request the extradition of Hissène "Habré under the 1960 justice cooperation convention with Senegal to face charges in Chad ranging from graft to murder"; but no formal request was made, it is speculated, because at least three of Habré's ministers served in his successor's (Idriss Déby) cabinet, and the Déby government had a record of its own abuses it sought to protect from public exposure. Stephen P. Marks, *The Hissène Habré Case: The Law and Politics of Universal Jurisdiction*, *in* Universal Jurisdiction: National Courts and the Prosecution of Serious Crimes under International Law 136–37 (Stephen Macedo ed. 2004).

[44] *E.g.*, Melanie M. Laflin, Note, *Kidnapped Terrorists: Bringing Int'l Criminals to Justice Through Irregular Rendition and Other Quasi-Legal Options*, 26 J. Legis. 315, 326–27 (2000) ("Due to unstable political conditions and the spread of Islamic fundamentalism,

(xi) the host State is unwilling to contribute to a particular pursuing State's propaganda efforts where extradition is perceived to be a vehicle to that end;[45]

(xii) the host State views domestic incarceration of a given high-profile or "trophy" perpetrator "as a matter of national dignity," as opposed to "outsourcing justice" via extradition to a pursuing State;[46] or

(xiii) the host State insists on deferring to a broad-based political body, such as a regional organization, the decision whether to seek extradition, or how to respond to an extradition request.[47]

Whether in communicating its extradition denial the host State chooses to express the true reason or provide a pretextual but plausible alternative ground drawn from the treaty provisions will depend on the specific circumstances involved and the host State's predominant interests (*e.g.*, in fostering harmonious relations or in underscoring its displeasure).

In addition, host State courts or executive branch officials can deny extradition requests that are regarded as having an underlying political

some countries do not want to be viewed as a U.S. partner in bringing terrorists to justice; they can ill afford the publicity and attention that a formal extradition process would create.").

45 *E.g.*, Matthew Lippman, *The Pursuit of Nazi War Criminals in the United States and in Other Anglo-American Legal Systems*, 29 Cal. W. Int'l J. 1, 15 (1998) (attributing the United Kingdom's refusal to extradite a number of alleged Nazi war criminals to the Soviet Union during the post-war period out of concern that such allegations were driven by propagandist interests).

46 *E.g., The Economist, supra* n.39, at 35 (discussing Mexico's handling of Joaquín ("El Chapo") Guzmán, a notorious narcotics trafficker, whom the United States sought for extradition); Joshua Partlow, "Hurdle Cleared on 'El Chapo': Mexico Grants Extradition to U.S.," *Wash. Post*, May 21, 2016, at A1 ("After his first recapture in 2014, Mexican authorities rejected U.S. pressure and vowed to force Guzmán to face justice on his home soil, making it a point of pride that they could hold him secure, extract intelligence from him and successfully convict him").

47 For example, in November 2005, Senegal Foreign Minister Cheik Tidiane Gadio announced that former Chadian leader Hissène Habré, who was wanted for crimes against humanity, war crimes, and torture, would be allowed to remain in Senegal until the African Union (AU) ruled on the Belgian extradition request in 2006; Gadio believed it was the responsibility of the African continent to issue a collective ruling on demands that Habré be brought to account for his crimes. Bruce Zagaris, *Senegal Allows Habre to Stay Pending African Union Decision*, 22 IELR 59, 59 (2006). As it turned out, in July 2006, the AU's Assembly of heads of State and government mandated that Senegal move to prosecute Habré. *Questions Relating to the Obligation to Prosecute or Extradite* (Belg. v. Sen.), [2012] I. C. J. Rep. 422, ¶ 23 (July 20) [hereinafter *ICJ Case, Belg. v. Sen.*].

motive,[48] and therefore are being used improperly as a tool, for example, to exert undue pressure on a government,[49] to remove an influential individual from the political scene,[50] or for other ulterior reasons. This type of determination is to be distinguished both from an extradition denial based on the political offense exclusion (*see* Chapter 5.a.iii), where the underlying crime is deemed to have a political complexion, and from an extradition denial emanating from a concern that the individual will be subject to unfair treatment at trial due to political discrimination (*see* sub-section e.i. *infra*), although not infrequently concerns about politically motivated extraditions and discriminatory treatment at trial go hand-in-hand.

c Justice System Interplay Restrictions

Apart from how States relate to each other politically, there are three basic reasons why an extradition request may be denied or subsequently

[48] *See, e.g.*, Treaty on Extradition, U.S.-Lux., Oct. 1, 1996, art. 4(3), S. Rep. 105–10 ("Notwithstanding the terms of paragraph 2 of this Article [defining what constitutes a political offense], extradition shall not be granted if the executive authority of the Requested State determines that the request was politically motivated."); Treaty on Extradition, U.S.-U.K., Mar. 31, 2003, art. 3(a) ("Notwithstanding any other provision of this Supplementary Treaty, extradition shall not occur if the person sought establishes to the satisfaction of the competent judicial authority by a preponderance of the evidence that the request for extradition has in fact been made with a view to try . . . him on account of his . . . political opinions").

[49] *See, e.g.*, Alan Cullison and Nicole Lundeen, "Austrian Court Denies U.S. Request to Extradite Dmytro Firtash, *Wall St. J.*, May 1, 2015 (discussing an Austrian court's denial of a U.S. extradition request for a Ukrainian billionaire aligned with the recently ousted pro-Moscow President of Ukraine, Viktor Yanukovych, regarding a charge that the billionaire, Dmytro Firtash, conspired to bribe Indian officials to expand his titanium interests there and in doing so routed some of the payments through U.S. banks; "Mr. Firtash's lawyers argued that the U.S. used the Indian case to pressure Mr. Firtash and, in turn, Ukraine's leaders, as they considered whether to pursue closer relations to Moscow or the West. The contest between Moscow and Washington for influence in Ukraine sharpened in the past two years, as Kiev considered rival offers from Moscow and the European Union to sign economic cooperation agreements.").

[50] *E.g.*, M. Cherif Bassiouni, *The Political Offense Exception in Extradition Law and Practice*, *in* International Terrorism and Political Crimes 416 (M. Cherif Bassiouni ed. 1975) (citing the 1908 *Rudewitz* case in which the U.S. Secretary of State determined that the charges of murder, arson, burglary, and larceny brought by the Czarist government against a Russian revolutionary were political in nature and therefore refused to issue a transfer warrant); *cf.* Editorial, "Let Mr. Erdogan Fight His Own Battles," *N.Y. Times*, May 31, 2014, at A16 (opining that Turkish Prime Minister Tayyip Erdogan appeared to be seeking the return from the United States of Fethullah Gülen, an influential Islamic preacher living in Pennsylvania, based on resentment of Gülen due to his outspoken criticism of the Turkish Government).

withdrawn arising out of the interaction between their criminal justice systems: (i) double jeopardy (alternatively referred to as *non bis in idem* or the *autrefois* rule); (ii) specialty (or speciality, as it is called in some European and British Commonwealth States); and (iii) pending or anticipated criminal proceedings by the host State of the same individual for the same offense.

i Double Jeopardy

In the international extradition context (versus under the narrower international human rights law[51] or U.S. Constitutional law standard[52]), the

[51] International human rights treaties prohibit prosecution twice for the same offense *but only by the same State. See* Christine van den Wyngaert, *Applying the European Conv. on Human Rights to Extradition: Opening Pandora's Box?, in* INTERNATIONAL CRIMINAL LAW AND PROCEDURE 233 n.99 (John Dugard & Christine van den Wyngaert 1996) ("[I]nternational human rights instruments are silent on [whether] States [are obligated] to accept judgments rendered in third States; . . . they provide only a domestic *non bis in idem* rule, without mentioning that this rule should apply *erga omnes*. For example, the Human Rights Committee has declared any communication by a person who had been twice condemned for the same facts inadmissible because Art. 14(7) of the Covenant does not guarantee *non bis in idem* with regard to jurisdictions of two or more States . . . this provision prohibits double jeopardy only with regard to an offence adjudicated in a given State") (citation omitted); *e.g., A.R.J. v. Australia*, Commc'n No. 692/1996, U.N. Doc. CCPR/C/60/D/692/1996, Feb. 6, 1996; *A.P. v. Italy*, Commc'n. No. 204/1986, U.N. Doc. CCPR/C/31/D/204/1986, Nov. 2, 1987.

[52] The double jeopardy principle under the U.S. Constitution, as found in the Fifth Amendment, does not apply across two States, but rather only with respect to prosecutions within the same State. *See United States v. Rashed*, 234 F.3d 1280, 1282 (D.C. Cir. 2000) (the double jeopardy clause of the Fifth Amendment to the U.S. Constitution "forecloses multiple prosecutions for the same offense by the same sovereign, but not ones by different sovereigns . . . The exception for dual sovereignty flows from the understanding that every sovereign has the authority to punish infractions of its own laws."), *cert. denied*, 533 U.S. 924 (2001). The Amanda Knox case almost presented a novel question regarding the applicability of the U.S. Constitution's double jeopardy prohibition, as also arguably reflected in Article VI of the U.S.-Italy Extradition Treaty, to thwart a potential extradition request by Italy for Knox's return from the United States. She and her Italian boyfriend, Raffaele Sollecito, were first convicted in 2009 of the 2007 murder of Knox's roommate, Meredith Kercher, in Perugia, Italy, and after spending four years in prison, that conviction was reversed on appeal in 2011, at which point she returned to her home town of Seattle, Washington. In March 2013, however, Italy's highest court reversed that appellate ruling and called for a retrial, which yielded guilty verdicts by the appeals court in Florence of twenty-eight and half and twenty-five years for the two defendants, respectively, in January 2014. Had this latter conviction been upheld by the Italian Court of Cassation in Rome, *and* Italy had sought Knox's extradition, *and* the United States had been politically persuaded or otherwise inclined to grant the request, the double jeopardy issue likely would have turned on the status of her prosecution under the Italian judicial system, namely,

principle of double jeopardy operates to prevent two States from each prosecuting or otherwise exposing a person to the risk of punishment for the same offense (or, more rarely, for the same *acts*).[53] In practice, that means that extradition[54] generally will be *denied* to the extent that a "final judgment" has been issued (whether via acquittal and discharge or conviction with or without an accompanying sanction),[55] possibly where there has been an out-of-court settlement,[56] or amnesty or a pardon has been granted.[57] Even where double jeopardy does not operate ultimately to thwart an extradition, its invocation can significantly prolong proceedings.[58]

whether the original appeals court ruling was final or was simply a phase of the same drawn-out legal proceeding. *See* Merry Neal, "The Amanda Knox Case and the Politics of Extradition Law," *LegalWeek*, Feb. 10, 2014, *available at* www.legalweek.com/legal-week/blog-post/2327968/the-amanda-knox-case-and-the-politics-of-extradition-law (last visited on May 12, 2016).

53 Since World War II, U.S. extradition treaties generally contain provisions prohibiting extradition in instances in which the "same offense" is at issue, but a few call for the "same acts." ABBELL, *supra* n.37, at 109

54 Some courts have drawn a distinction between the extradition itself (which would lead to a foreign trial) and a hearing to consider the merits of extradition, finding the former, but not the latter, barred by the double jeopardy principle. Courts in the United Kingdom, for example, have considered that the principle does not apply to the extradition hearing itself. *E.g., Rees v. Sec'y of State for the Home Dep't* [1986] 1 A.C. 937 (H.L.), [1986] 2 All E.R. 321.

55 Int'l Covenant on Civil and Political Rights (ICCPR), Dec. 16, 1966, art. 14(7), UNGA Res. 2200, U.N. GAOR, 21st Sess., Supp. No. 21, U.N. Doc. A/6316 (1967); IVOR STANBROOK & CLIVE STANBROOK, EXTRADITION: LAW AND PRACTICE 137 (2d ed. 2000); HELEN DUFFY, THE 'WAR ON TERROR' AND THE FRAMEWORK OF INTERNATIONAL LAW 109 (2005); Clive Nicholls, *The Rule of Non-Inquiry in Extradition Cases*, paper presented to the Oxford Conf. on Int'l Co-operation in Crim. Matters, Aug. 24–28, 1998, at 72–74.

56 *See* Bert (A.H.J.) Swart, *Refusal of Extradition and the United Nations Model Treaty on Extradition*, 23 NETH. Y.B. INT'L L. 175, 209 (1992) ("Prosecution [after a case has been settled out of court] would be irreconcilable with the idea of *ne bis in idem*. It seems only fair not to extradite the person claimed in such cases. However, as yet most extradition laws and treaties contain no explicit provisions with respect to this method of terminating proceedings, and neither does the U.N. Model [Treaty on Extradition].").

57 ROBERT CRYER, ET AL., AN INTRODUCTION TO INTERNATIONAL CRIMINAL LAW AND PROCEDURE 79 (2d ed. 2010).

58 In a high-profile example from 2007, the United States sought the extradition of Mario Villanueva Madrid, former Governor of the Mexican state of Quintana Roo, on charges of drug trafficking, money laundering, and racketeering, but as he had just served six years for money laundering in a Mexican prison, his attorney fought extradition under the double jeopardy principle, which tied up proceedings for several years. Bruce Zagaris, *Mexico Arrests Former Governor on U.S. Extradition Warrant*, 23 IELR 365, 365–66 (2007).

As a well-established international legal concept, the double jeopardy principle is broadly captured in such diverse legal instruments as the U.N. Model Treaty on Extradition,[59] regional extradition conventions,[60] domestic extradition-related legislation,[61] and bilateral extradition treaties,[62] and is implicitly interpreted where it is not expressly written.[63]

For double jeopardy to obtain, a genuine risk of punishment must exist. Accordingly, double jeopardy would not be implicated under such circumstances as a prosecution that was terminated because of a legal technicality, thereby foreclosing a judgment on the merits,[64] or a prosecution that was discontinued.[65] Notably, in a May 2014 preliminary ruling, the European Court of Justice (ECJ) found that, in the context of the Convention Implementing the Schengen Agreement (CISA), the

[59] U.N. Model Treaty on Extradition, Dec. 14, 1991, art. 3(d) & (e), UNGA Res. 45/116, Annex, 45 U.N. GAOR Supp. (No. 49A), at 212, U.N. Doc. A/45/49 (1990) [hereinafter U.N. Model Extradition Treaty] (extradition shall not be granted if "there has been a final judgment rendered against the person in the requested State in respect of the offense for which the person's extradition is requested; [or i]f the person whose extradition is requested has, under the law of either Party, become immune from ... punishment for any reason, including ... amnesty.").

[60] *E.g.*, Eur. Conv. on Extradition, Dec. 13, 1957, art. 9, CoE, E.T.S. No. 24; Inter-Am. Conv. on Extradition, Feb. 25, 1981, art. 4(1), OAS T.S. No. 60, *reprinted in* 20 ILM 723 (1981) (no extradition permitted "[w]hen the person sought has completed his punishment or has been granted amnesty, pardon or grace for the offense for which extradition is sought, or when he has been acquitted or the case against him for the same offense has been dismissed with prejudice.").

[61] *E.g.*, PRC Extradition Law, Order of the President No. 42, adopted at the 19th Mtg. of the Standing Comm. of the Ninth National People's Congress, Dec. 28, 2000, art. 8(2) [hereinafter PRC Extradition Law] (extradition request shall be rejected if "at the time the request is received, [a] judicial organ of the People's Republic of China has rendered an effective judgment or terminated the criminal proceedings in respect of the offence indicated in the request for extradition").

[62] *See, e.g.*, Treaty on Extradition, U.S.-Austl., May 14, 1974, art. VII(a), *reprinted in* Igor I. Kavass, 1 Extradition Laws and Treaties: United States (2000 & Supp. 2004) (extradition shall not be granted "when the person whose extradition is requested ... has been tried and discharged or punished, or has been pardoned, in the territory of the requested State for the offense for which his extradition is requested").

[63] Stanbrook & Stanbrook, *supra* n.55, at 137.

[64] *Id.* at 139.

[65] *E.g.*, Treaty on Extradition, U.S.-Jam., June 14, 1983, art. IV ("Extradition shall not be precluded by the fact that the competent authorities in the Requested State ... have decided to discontinue any criminal proceedings which have been initiated against the person sought."). While extradition may be refused when the host State has made a considered decision not to institute criminal proceedings at all with respect to the same underlying offense, *e.g.*, Eur. Conv. on Extradition, *supra* n.60, art. 9, that refusal would not be a function of double jeopardy as such, but rather of the *aut dedere aut judicare* principle (discussed in Chapter 9.c).

double jeopardy principle did not bar Germany from prosecuting Zoran Spasić, a Serbian national for fraud, even though he had earlier been convicted of the same crime in Italy but had only paid the required fine and not yet served the one-year custodial sentence.[66]

In any event, the burden of proof lies with the accused to show that he had been exposed to a prosecution or other deliberative process that met the double jeopardy standard.[67] Applicable prior legal proceedings undertaken by a *third* State also may bar extradition between two other States, although this might well fall to a discretionary call on the part of the host State.[68]

ii Specialty

The rule of specialty[69] presents another way in which extradition[70] can be stymied, although in this case typically by insisting on its subsequent withdrawal rather than by denying it in advance.[71] Specialty, a rule premised on international comity[72] and one often raised in tandem with the principle of dual criminality,[73] stands for the proposition that a pursuing State may not detain, try, or punish a fugitive for any offense

66 *Preliminary Ruling in Case of Zoran Spasic*, Case No. C-129/14, ECJ, Gr. Ch., May 27, 2014 (applying the CISA standard for *ne bis in idem* where the imposed penalty has been enforced, is in the process of being enforced, or cannot be imposed under the laws of the sentencing State).

67 Stanbrook & Stanbrook, *supra* n.55, at 140.

68 *See* Abbell, *supra* n.37, at 111 *cf.* Addt'l Prot. to the Eur. Conv. on Extradition, Oct. 15, 1975, art. 2, E.T.S. No. 86 (amending original art. 9) (identifying situations in which extradition would be refused on the basis of double jeopardy where a final judgment were issued by a third State).

69 The term derives etymologically from the French "specialitie," meaning particularity.

70 Specialty applies strictly in cases of extradition versus other forms of international law enforcement cooperation. *E.g., United States v. Trujillo*, 871 F. Supp. 215, 219 (D. Del. 1994).

71 Specialty is a rule of personal jurisdiction (discussed in Chapter 13.a.i) – *not* subject matter jurisdiction (as addressed in Chapter 2.c). *United States v. Vreeken*, 803 F.2d 1085, 1089 (10th Cir. 1986), *cert. denied*, 107 S. Ct. 955 (1987).

72 *United States v. Najohn*, 785 F.2d 1420, 1422 (9th Cir.) (per curiam), *cert. denied*, 479 U.S. 1009 (1986).

73 To avoid conceptual confusion between these two rules, consider that while dual criminality requires correspondence between the *laws* of the host and pursuing States, specialty calls for a correspondence between the *charges* in the indictment and the offenses set forth in the extradition order. Christopher L. Blakesley, Terrorism, Drugs, International Law, and the Protection of Human Liberty: A Comparative Study of International Law, Its Nature, Role, and Impact in Matters of Terrorism, Drug Trafficking, War, and Extradition 250 (1992) [hereinafter Blakesley, Comparative Study].

committed *before* his extradition,[74] except any specifically that were the subject of the extradition request and approval[75] (consistent with the provisions of any applicable extradition treaty[76]), unless the transferor State lends its agreement[77] or a lesser included offense arose out of the same underlying facts.[78] The rule of specialty has emerged as customary international law[79] and today has almost universal application[80] in extradition-related treaties,[81] national legislation,[82] and judicial practice alike, including in non-treaty-based extraditions.[83]

The purpose of specialty is both to safeguard the integrity of the judicial process of the transferor State after it has conceded its jurisdictional control over a fugitive *and* to protect the individual extraditee from potential abuse at the hands of the transferee State when tried for an offense that was not the basis for the extradition.[84] Accordingly, specialty

[74] ABBELL, *supra* n.37, at 88–89; STANBROOK & STANBROOK, *supra* n.55, at 50 (distinguishing offenses committed after extradition has been effected); *e.g., In re Albrand*, Ct. of Cassation, Fr., Dec. 22, 1969, *reprinted in* 51 ILR 269 (1978).

[75] *See In re Dilasser*, Fed. and Cassation Ct., Venez., July 30, 1952, *reprinted in* 19 ILR 377 (1957) (refusing to allow France to prosecute an individual for a crime for which he had not been properly extradited by Venezuela); *cf. Collier v. Vaccaro*, 51 F.2d 17, 21 (4th Cir. 1931) ("We cannot assume that a friendly government [Canada], in violation of [a bilateral extradition treaty] would try the accused on any other charge than that for which he was surrendered to be tried.").

[76] SIR ROBERT JENNINGS & SIR ARTHUR WATTS, EDS., 1 OPPENHEIM'S INTERNATIONAL LAW 961 (9th ed. 1992). For a rare exception, *see* STANBROOK & STANBROOK, *supra* n.55, at 51 n.22 (citing a case involving the prosecution of former Nigerian Government ministers in February 1989, where the 1966 Nigerian extradition order was trumped by a subsequent Nigerian decree "empowering a special military tribunal to try public officials accused of any offense notwithstanding anything to the contrary in any other enactment," and thereby defeating the principle of specialty operating pursuant to the extradition treaty).

[77] Eur. Conv. on Extradition, *supra* n.60, art. 14(1)(a); ABBELL, *supra* n.37, at 89–90; BLAKESLEY, COMPARATIVE STUDY, *supra* n.73, at 253; STANBROOK & STANBROOK, *supra* n.55, at 50; *e.g., United States ex rel. Donnelly v. Mulligan*, 74 F.2d 220 (2d Cir. 1934).

[78] ABBELL, *supra* n.37, at 90; Yvonne G. Grassie, Note, *Federally Sponsored Int'l Kidnapping: An Acceptable Alternative to Extradition?*, 64 WASH. U.L.Q. 1205, 1206–07 n.11 (1986).

[79] ILIAS BANTEKAS & SUSAN NASH, INTERNATIONAL CRIMINAL LAW 184 (2d ed. 2003).

[80] BLAKESLEY, COMPARATIVE STUDY, *supra* n.73, at 250; STANBROOK & STANBROOK, *supra* n.55, at 47, 50.

[81] JENNINGS & WATTS, *supra* n.76, at 961 (most extradition treaties contain a specialty provision); *e.g.*, U.N. Model Extradition Treaty, *supra* n.59, art. 14.

[82] *E.g.*, Thailand Extradition Act 2551 (C.E. 2008), § 11.

[83] *E.g., United States v. Evans*, 667 F. Supp. 974 (S.D.N.Y. 1987).

[84] STANBROOK & STANBROOK, *supra* n.55, at 47–48; BANTEKAS & NASH, *supra* n.79, at 184; *Fiocconi v. United States*, 462 F.2d 475, 481 (2d Cir.) ("The 'principle of specialty' reflects a fundamental concern of governments that persons who are surrendered should not be

is a right conferred on the transferor State, which can be invoked by diplomatic protest[85] or waived at its discretion (possibly through acquiescence).[86] That right does not preclude the extradition subject from consenting to additional charges announced or contemplated by the pursuing State,[87] or effecting the same outcome by simply waiving the formalities of extradition,[88] and in some jurisdictions might even be allowed to raise a specialty claim on his own in the context of criminal proceedings.[89] In any event, however, an individual cannot invoke the

subject to indiscriminate prosecution by the receiving government, especially for political crimes."), *cert. denied*, 409 U.S. 509 (1972).

85 Jennings & Watts, *supra* n.76, at 961.

86 *See United States v. Najohn*, 785 F.2d 1420, 1422–23 (9th Cir.) (per curiam) (finding that the Swiss Government waived specialty under its bilateral extradition treaty with the United States, thereby allowing the United States to prosecute the appellant under a new set of charges), *cert. denied*, 479 U.S. 1009 (1986); *Fiocconi*, 462 F.2d at 479–82 (although the narcotics charge was brought by the United States after the fugitives were extradited from Italy, they were not released on the ground that the Government of Italy had not affirmatively protested). *But see United States v. Lehder-Rivas*, 668 F. Supp. 1523, 1525 (M.D. Fla. 1987) ("When the extraditing country does not expressly state an objection to a prosecution, as in this case, the Court must inquire whether the surrendering state would regard the prosecution at issue as a breach.") (internal quotations omitted).

87 *See* Stanbrook & Stanbrook, *supra* n.55, at 53–54 (noting that an individual may be anxious to have all charges against him handled at the same time so as to clear his name once and for all); Scheme Relating to the Rendition of Fugitive Offenders within the Commonwealth, May 3, 1966, ¶ 15(5), *as amended in* 1990 and then renamed as London Scheme for Extradition within the Commonwealth in Nov. 2002, LMM (90)32 [hereinafter London Scheme]; *e.g., In re Arietto*, Crim. Ct. of Cassation, Italy Feb. 7, 1933, 26 *Rivista di Diritto Int'l* 267 (1934), *reprinted in* 7 Ann. Dig. & Rep. Int'l Law Cases 334, 334 [1933–1934] (No. 140) (H. Lauterpacht ed. 1940) (pursuant to the Italy-France Extradition Treaty, which permitted additional charges to be brought upon the express and voluntary consent of the accused, the court found that the trial on the additional charges was proper where the accused consented thereto).

88 *See, e.g., In re Tirptiz*, Ct. of Cassation, Belg., Feb. 8, 1937, *reprinted in* [1938–40] 9 Ann. Dig. & Rep. Pub. Int'l L. Cases 401, 401 (No. 149) (H. Lauterpacht ed. 1942) (finding that the appellant, by "declar[ing] to the French authorities that he wished to waive all the formalities and guarantees provided for in his favour in connection with extradition," had "expressly consented to be tried for offences other than those for which his extradition was granted.").

89 *See United States v. Abello-Silva*, 948 F.2d 1168 (10th Cir. 1991) (noting disagreement among legal authorities regarding whether a criminal defendant may raise a specialty claim absent an objection by the extraditing State, but finding that he may do so), *cert. denied*, 506 U.S. 835 (1992); *United States v. Martonak*, 187 F. Supp.2d 117, 121–22 (S.D.N.Y. 2002) (observing "divided authority" on whether an individual has standing, noting that some courts have held that "the extradited individual may raise whatever objections the asylum state might have had," and concluding that the defendant in this case had standing to argue specialty absent any official declaration by the host State that

specialty principle as a means of preventing or limiting the *admissibility* of evidence against him at trial.[90]

Traditionally, the rule of specialty has been strictly applied,[91] and even the particular designation of the charge is not determinative of whether the specialty rule will be triggered.[92] When the specialty rule is violated, an extradition can be nullified *ex post facto* and the subject released prior to or during criminal proceedings, or a criminal conviction in a pursuing State can be vacated. For example, in a 1993 case, the U.S. Court of Appeals for the Ninth Circuit ruled that while Pakistan expressly agreed to extradite on one count of a U.S. superseding indictment related to conspiracy to import narcotics into the United States, Pakistan's extradition documents were silent as to a second count, and the failure to ascertain unambiguous agreement as to that second charge proved fatal to the prosecution on specialty grounds.[93] Likewise, in 1934, Spain's Supreme Court discharged a prisoner on a specialty challenge where the extradition request made of Portugal sought him for "falsification of a private document as a means of swindling" but where Spain tried and convicted him for the crime of "falsification of a mercantile document which did not cause property loss to anyone."[94]

A final caveat is in order. Many extradition treaties and domestic laws require States to provide fugitives the opportunity to leave their territory within a specified number of days following conditional or final release from detention before they will prosecute those individuals under any offense that was not the subject of an approved extradition.[95] By the same token, if such

no specialty issue existed). This individual standing issue is discussed further in Chapter 13.a.ii.

90 *E.g., Alvarez-Moreno*, 874 F.2d 1402 (11th Cir. 1989), *cert. denied*, 494 U.S. 1032 (1990).

91 *But see United States v. Jetter*, 722 F.2d 371, 373 (8th Cir. 1983) (in light of all circumstances, finding that Costa Rica intended to extradite for a conspiracy charge, in addition to substantive offenses, despite the fact that a reference to conspiracy was omitted from the judicial order).

92 Stanbrook & Stanbrook, *supra* n.55, at 52; *e.g., United States v. Sensi*, 879 F.2d 888, 894–95 (D.C. Cir. 1989); *R. v. Corrigan* [1931] 1 KB 527, *reprinted in* 6 Ann. Dig. & Rep. Int'l L. Cases 319 (No. 177) (H. Lauterpacht ed. 1938).

93 *United States v. Khan*, 993 F.2d 1368, 1373–75 (9th Cir. 1993). *Accord United States v. Rauscher*, 119 U.S. 407 (1886) (no prosecution allowed where the individual was extradited for murder but was tried on the offense of cruelty under the same facts).

94 *Fiscal v. Samper*, Sup. Ct., Spain, June 22, 1934, 130 *Jurisprudencia Criminal* 694 (1934), *reprinted in* [1938–40] 9 Ann. Dig. & Rep. Pub. Int'l L. Cases 402, 403–05 (No. 152) (H. Lauterpacht ed. 1942) (finding the two charges were to be punished differently).

95 *E.g.*, Eur. Conv. on Extradition, *supra* n.60, art. 14(1)(b) (1957) (an individual has forty-five days to leave); Thailand Extradition Act, *supra* n.82, § 11(2) (allowing 45 days to leave

an individual fails to take advantage of that window of time or, alternatively, if he leaves transferee State territory but then returns or is returned, legal proceedings can be brought against him for charges that were not within the scope of the original transferor State's extradition authorization.[96]

iii Concurrent Proceedings

In addition, when the host State is in the midst of a criminal proceeding against an individual, or is seriously contemplating or planning to undertake such a proceeding, his requested extradition by a pursuing State for the same or different offenses may be denied or postponed pending final disposition of the host State case.[97] In such a circumstance the host State is forced to choose in the first instance between: (i) granting an extradition request by a pursuing State, or (ii) prosecuting a fugitive under its own criminal justice system for a violation of its domestic law (possibly under an applicable *aut dedere aut judicare* provision, as discussed in Chapter 9.c).

The European Conv. on Extradition, at Article 8, frames the standard in representative terms regarding proceedings on the *same* offense: "The requested Party may refuse to extradite the person claimed if the competent authorities of such Party are proceeding against him in respect of the offence or offences for which extradition is requested."[98] Bilateral extradition treaties frequently speak to the issue of concurrent proceedings,[99] and domestic laws in such States as the PRC and Japan

the requesting State's territory "after being free to do so"); Switz., Int'l Mutual Assistance in Crim. Matters, art. 38(2) [hereinafter Swiss IMAC] (allowing forty-five days after conditional or final release).

96 Abbell, *supra* n.37, at 88; Swiss IMAC, *supra* n.95, art. 38(2)(b); *e.g.*, *Novic v. Public Prosecutor of the Canton of Basel-Stadt*, Ct. of Cassation, Switz., Oct. 27, 1955, *reprinted in* 22 ILR 515 (1955).

97 Bantekas & Nash, *supra* n.79, at 190. This assumes, of course, that the fugitive has not already been arrested on charges by an occupying power in the host State; for example, U.S. troops had detained Turkish Islamists Burhan Kus and Sadettin Aktas at Baghdad's Abu Ghraib prison on unrelated charges compared with Turkey's underlying request for their extradition for a 2003 terrorist attack in Istanbul. Bruce Zagaris, *Turkey Requests Iraqi Extradition of Two Islamists for 2003 Attack*, 21 IELR 356, 356–57 (2005).

98 Eur. Conv. on Extradition, *supra* n.60, art. 8.

99 *See, e.g.*, Treaty on Extradition, U.S.-Braz., Jan. 13, 1961, art. V(2), 15 U.S.T. 2093, T.I.A.S. No. 5691 (extradition shall be denied "[w]hen the person whose surrender is sought . . . is at the time of the request being prosecuted in the requested State for the crime or offense for which his extradition is requested."); U.S.-Austl. Extradition Treaty, *supra* n.62, art. VII (no extradition is permitted if the person is being proceeded against by the host State).

contain such provisions,[100] while others, like the United States, have more permissive provisions that allow deference to foreign extradition requests, assuming double jeopardy does not attach.[101]

An example of such a concurrent proceeding clash arose in the case of Egyptian jihadist Abu Hamza al-Masri, the first person detained under the 2003 amended U.S.-U.K. Extradition Treaty. After al-Masri was arrested in the United Kingdom in May 2004, the United States sought his extradition on eleven terrorist-related charges, but the United Kingdom decided to postpone a decision until it first prosecuted al-Masri for incitement and racial hatred offenses in violation of its own domestic law.[102] In cases such as this, however, it generally takes years to conclude criminal proceedings and for the subject to serve out any assigned prison term in the host State before he potentially would be available for extradition.[103]

d Competing Jurisdictional Claims

Closely related to, but distinct from, concurrent proceeding scenarios between the host and a pursuing State is the situation in which two or more pursuing States simultaneously seek the extradition of a fugitive for alleged or actual violations of their respective domestic laws,[104] and the

[100] PRC Extradition Law, *supra* n.61, art. 9(1) (extradition may be rejected where the PRC has jurisdiction and "criminal proceedings are being instituted against the person or preparations are being made for such proceedings"); Japan Law of Extradition, Law No. 68 of 1953, art. 2(7), *as amended.*

[101] Under U.S. law, absent an issue presented by double jeopardy, federal or state prosecutors may dismiss the present charges in favor of those brought by a pursuing State. Abbell, *supra* n.37, at 110–11.

[102] *See, e.g.*, Bruce Zagaris, *U.K. Court Rules Abu Hamza al-Masri can be Extradited to the U.S.*, 24 IELR 1, 1–2 (2008) (al-Masri was sentenced to serve seven years in the United Kingdom).

[103] *Cf.* Bruce Zagaris, *Mexico Arrests El Chapo with Help from the United States*, 30 IELR 175, 177 (2014) ("Mexican authorities increasingly want people who commit crimes in Mexico to serve their time in Mexican prisons before they are sent to the U.S., so that Mexican authorities have full access to the intelligence generated from suspects and can show that the Mexican judicial system can reliably hold top criminals.").

[104] In federalist States, such as the United States, there may be more than one state or province, or more than one federal jurisdiction, which has lodged criminal charges against a given fugitive. In such an instance, the competing authorities (in the case of sub-national entities) or the national justice minister (in the case of federal jurisdictions) from the pursuing State would need to internally resolve which one takes priority. *See, e.g.*, Joshua Partlow, "Hurdle Cleared on 'El Chapo': Mexico Grants Extradition to U.S.," *Wash. Post*, May 21, 2016, at A1, A6 (discussing how the U.S. Attorney General would need to determine whether the Western District of Texas or the Southern District of

host State is interested neither in prosecution nor in entertaining asylum for the fugitive. In such instances, the host State may choose only one pursuing State for initial extradition.[105]

There is no customary international law that guarantees one State automatic priority over another based on the nature of their subject matter jurisdictional claims.[106] Most treaties likewise do not establish a hierarchy of claims,[107] leaving host States frequently to make a discretionary call.[108] In such cases, States generally make their determination based on a totality of the circumstances,[109] although some bilateral treaties and municipal laws identify criteria to help guide decision-making.[110] Such criteria typically include, at a minimum, the

California "could generate a case covering most, if not all, of the alleged criminal conduct" relevant to Joaquín 'El Chapo' Guzmán, head of the Sinaloa drug cartel).

105 A variation on this scenario can occur when the host State has no plans to prosecute an individual and must choose between, on the one hand, a State seeking extradition for an alleged or actual crime and, on the other hand, the State of the individual's nationality aiming to shield him from prosecution or punishment. This fact pattern played out in July 2013, when Panama chose to return to the United States Robert Seldon Lady, an alleged former CIA officer convicted *in absentia* of involvement in the seizure of Abu Omar from Milan in 2003, rather than extradite him to Italy to face prosecution. Javier Cordoba & Deb Riechmann, "Panama Opts to Send ex-CIA Agent to U.S.," *Phila. Inquirer*, July 20, 2013, at A3.

106 *See* pp. 96–98 in Chapter 2.

107 *See* Joseph J. Lambert, Terrorism and Hostages in International Law 164 (1990) (no priority of jurisdiction established under the 1979 Hostage Convention; nor can such priority be implied from the language of Article 5, or from any other provision of the Convention, or from its *travaux preparatoires*). *But see* Abbell, *supra* n.37, at 93 (noting that the earliest U.S. bilateral treaties, up to the 1950s, assigned priority to the first one received).

108 *E.g.*, U.N. Model Extradition Treaty, *supra* n.59, art. 16 ("If a Party receives requests for extradition for the same person from both the other Party and a third State it shall, at its discretion, determine to which of those States the person is to be extradited."); Treaty on Extradition, U.S.-Mex., May 4, 1978, art. 16, 31 U.S.T. 5059, T.I.A.S. 9656, *reprinted in* 17 ILM 1058 (1978) (where there is more than one request for extradition of the same person, whether for the same or different offenses, the host State has the right to decide which request it will grant).

109 *See* Abbell, *supra* n.37, at 93 (observing that most post-1960 U.S. extradition treaties assign priority based on such factors as the place of commission of the offense, the relative gravity of offenses, the nationality of the requested person, the possibility of re-extradition, the order of receipt of the requests, and the provisions of the applicable treaties); *e.g.*, India Extradition Act, *supra* n.2, § 30 ("[T]he Central Government may, having regard to the circumstances of the case, surrender the fugitive criminal to such State or country as that Government thinks fit.") (emphasis in original).

110 *E.g.*, Inter-Am. Conv. on Extradition, *supra* n.60, art. 15 (requiring the requested State to give priority to the territorial State where there are two or more requests for the extradition of a person for the same offense; if two or more requests for extradition

relative dates on which the requests were made, the nationality of the fugitive, and the seriousness of the offenses at issue.[111] The host State may insist that as a condition of extradition to one State (State A), the individual must be extradited to the other (State B) after prosecution and any related punishment in State A have occurred.[112]

The decision regarding which State's jurisdictional claim takes priority matters, at least in part, because the State(s) *not* selected may not ultimately obtain custody at all. This could occur if, for example, the fugitive dies while serving a sentence in the chosen State, or is not eligible for re-extradition (discussed in Chapter 8.c) by the chosen State on account of such factors as a nationality or time bar. Even if another State does eventually obtain custody, there may be a lengthy wait while he serves out his initial sentence(s); the prosecution's case against him may be compromised by dwindling witnesses or lost physical evidence; and the punishment may prove to be abbreviated if, say, his physical health has deteriorated by the time he is transferred and a maximum term of incarceration can no longer be justified on humanitarian grounds.

To illustrate how competing jurisdictional claims can play out, including how they may be manipulated to political ends, consider the following example. In October 2005, the Swiss Justice Ministry decided to extradite Yevgeny Adamov, a Russian nuclear physicist, to the United States to face charges for financial crimes arising out of his alleged

but for different offenses, extradition is granted to the State that seeks an offender for the crime punishable by the most severe penalty; if offenses are of equal gravity, priority is determined by the order in which the requests were received); Swiss IMAC, *supra* n.95, art. 40 (where the same offence is at issue, priority is given to the State where the "offence was committed or principally committed; where different offences are at issue, "the decision shall be made having due regard to all circumstances, especially the seriousness of the offences, the place of commission, the chronological order in which the requests were received, the nationality of the person pursued, the better prospect of social rehabilitation and the possibility of extradition to another State."); Thailand Extradition Act, *supra* n.82, § 26 (relevant factors for determining to which State extradition shall be made include: "(1) whether or not the Requesting State has an extradition treaty with Thailand; (2) the place where each offense was committed; (3) the severity of offense which affects Requesting State and penalty; (4) the order of request received from Requesting State; (5) the nationality of the offender; (6) the interest and readiness of prosecution; (7) other reasons with respect to international relation[s] according to the opinion given by the Ministry of Foreign Affairs.").

111 *See supra* n.110.

112 *E.g.*, Sweden, Extradition for Crim. Offences Act (1957:668), Dec. 6, 1957, § 13, *as amended* ("Where the requests relate to different offences, it may be stipulated that the person to be extradited to one state shall subsequently be extradited to another state, subject to conditions to be determined in accordance with Section 12.").

diversion of US $9 million in program funds into his personal bank account while directing a U.S. Government-funded nuclear research institute in the 1990s. Adamov was arrested in response to a U.S. warrant, but promptly following his apprehension, Russia indicted him for fraud and abuse committed during his service as Minister of Atomic Energy of the Russian Federation (MinAtom) between 1998 and 2001, although many saw this move primarily motivated by concern that his prosecution in the United States potentially could reveal Russian state secrets.[113]

In December 2005, the Swiss Federal Court reversed the Justice Ministry's decision and ruled that he be extradited to Russia. Although once extradited to Russia, given his nationality, he could not later be extradited to the United States (*see* chapter 6.a), the Swiss court favored the Russian petition because its extradition request had arrived first, Adamov was a Russian national, his alleged offenses had occurred in Russia, and Russian prosecutors agreed to investigate the U.S. charges against him.[114] Tellingly, while later convicted in a Russian court to a five-and-a-half-year prison term, his sentence was vacated less than two months later and he was set free.[115]

e International Human Rights Concerns

The host State's decision not to extradite also may turn on human rights concerns it may harbor regarding the record or reputation of a particular pursuing State's criminal justice system, notably including its political independence or impartiality, available or preferred punishment options, the potential for abusive or discriminatory treatment, and/or actual or perceived degree of procedural fairness.[116] Over the past quarter-century, human rights considerations have increasingly influenced extradition determinations, primarily building upon such seminal conventions as the 1966 International Covenant on Civil and Political Rights (ICCPR), the 1984 Convention against Torture and All Forms of Cruel, Inhuman or Degrading Treatment or Punishment (CAT), and the 1950 European

113 Peter Finn, "Swiss Court Extradites Former Nuclear Head Back to Russia," *Wash. Post*, Dec. 29, 2005.

114 *Id.*; Bruce Zagaris, *Swiss Appellate Court Extradites Former Russian Official to Russia Rather than to U.S.*, 22 IELR 98 (2006).

115 "Adamov Given Suspended Sentence," *The Moscow Times*, Apr. 18, 2008, Issue 3886.

116 Other human rights-related concerns are addressed by such provisions as those prohibiting extradition on the basis of political offenses (*see* Chapter 5.a.iii), double jeopardy, and specialty (discussed *supra*).

Convention for Human Rights and Fundamental Freedoms (ECHR),[117] as well as counterpart provisions found in domestic legislation.[118]

This section first examines substantive legal areas of concern – namely, abusive treatment, unfair trials, and excessive or discriminatory punishment – as these are frequently cited as grounds for precluding extradition. The examination considers not only States' courts but also international and regional human rights bodies, as fugitive defendants sometimes appeal to such bodies as the European Court of Human Rights or the Committee against Torture to enjoin a domestically authorized extradition from proceeding. This section next focuses on two procedural aspects in connection with evaluating the propriety of extradition determinations, on human rights grounds, specifically, the rule of non-inquiry and diplomatic assurances.

i Substantive Issues

1 Abusive Treatment

A common concern for States contemplating extradition is whether a given pursuing State will torture or otherwise mistreat the subject individual once he is in its custody[119] (or, alternatively, re-extradite the individual to a third State where such abuse is likely to occur[120]). A pursuing State could, after all, request extradition as a pretext to arbitrarily punish or intimidate a person, make an example of him (possibly accompanied by a "show" trial) to dissuade others from acting similarly,[121] or extract information or a confession through extreme

[117] "While doubtful there is any rule of international law requiring extradition procedures to take account of general principles of human rights, in practice, many treaties impose procedural protections if surrender would lead to gross human rights violations." Bantekas & Nash, *supra* n.79, at 205–06. Although since World War II, human rights has played a role in limiting extradition in individual cases on a discretionary basis, its role has become markedly more prominent since 1989 with the European Court of Human Rights' case of *Soering v. U.K.*, Appl. No. 14038/88, 11 EHRR 439, July 7, 1989 [hereinafter *Soering Case*]. Stanbrook & Stanbrook, *supra* n.55, at 16.

[118] States tend to look to the text of human rights conventions for such guidance. John Dugard & Christine van den Wyngaert, *Reconciling Extradition with Human Rights*, 92 AJIL 187, 205–06 (1998).

[119] *See, e.g.*, PRC Extradition Law, *supra* n.61, art. 8 (a request must be rejected if: "(7) the person sought has been or will probably be subjected to torture or other cruel, inhuman or humiliating treatment or punishment in the Requesting State").

[120] *See* n.126 *infra*.

[121] *See* section b *supra*.

coercive treatment once he is in its custody.[122] Under such circumstances, the authorized host State official generally must make a discretionary decision whether to permit or deny extradition or to grant it conditionally;[123] and an affirmative call at times can be brought into question and overridden by an international or regional human rights body acting to prevent such abusive treatment from occurring under the terms of a corresponding treaty.[124]

The leading international legal instrument prohibiting extradition in the face of torture is the CAT.[125] Its operative provision reads: "No State party shall expel, return (*refouler*) or extradite a person to another State where there are substantial grounds for believing that he would be in danger of being subjected to torture."[126] For purposes of the CAT, "torture" is defined as "any act by which severe pain or suffering, whether physical or mental, is intentionally inflicted on a person" for such reasons as extracting information or a confession, punishment, intimidation or coercion, or discrimination.[127]

When determining whether such grounds exist, the host State "shall take into account all relevant considerations[128] including, where applicable, the

[122] *E.g., Núñez Chipana v. Venezuela*, Commc'n No. 110/1998, U.N. Doc. CAT/C/21/D/110/1998 ¶ 6.4, Nov. 10, 1998 ("... the Committee [against Torture] received numerous allegations from reliable sources concerning the use of torture by [Peruvian] law enforcement officials in connection with the investigation of the offences of terrorism and treason with a view to obtaining information or a confession.").

[123] *E.g.*, 22 C.F.R. § 95.3(b) (discussing the U.S. Secretary of State's options).

[124] *E.g.*, ICCPR, *supra* n.55, art. 7; Eur. Conv. for the Protection of Human Rights and Fundamental Freedoms, Nov. 4, 1950, art. 3, 213 U.N.T.S. 262, T.S. No. 71 (1953) [hereinafter ECHR] ("No one shall be subjected to torture or to inhuman or degrading treatment or punishment.").

[125] U.N. Conv. against Torture and Other Cruel, Inhuman or Degrading Treatment or Punishment, Dec. 10, 1984, UNGA Res. 39/46 Annex, U.N. GAOR, 39th Sess., Supp. No. 51, U.N. Doc. E/CN.4/1984/72, Annex (1984), 1465 U.N.T.S. 85, *reprinted in* 23 ILM 1027 [hereinafter CAT]. Notably, by contrast, extradition treaties do not specifically proscribe extradition in the event torture appears likely. Abbell, *supra* n.37, at 130.

[126] CAT, *supra* n.125, art. 3(1). In its interpretation of this article, the Committee against Torture has indicated that the phrase "another State" refers not only to the State to which the person is being extradited or returned, but also to a State to which he may subsequently be extradited or returned (*i.e.*, the process known as re-extradition). Comm. Against Torture, CAT Gen. Cmt. 1, *Communications Concerning the Return of a Person to a State Where There may be Grounds he would be Subjected to Torture (Article 3 in the Context of Article 22)* U.N. Doc. A/53/44, Annex IX, ¶ 2, Nov. 21, 1997. [hereinafter CAT Gen. Cmt. 1].

[127] CAT, *supra* n.125, art. 1(1). The ECtHR has adopted this definition for its purposive element. *Salman v. Turkey*, Appl. No. 21986/93, 34 EHRR, ¶ 114, June 27, 2000.

[128] *See, e.g., Ismail Alan v. Switzerland*, Commc'n No. 21/1995, U.N. Doc. CAT/C/16/D/21/1995, ¶ 11.3, May 8, 1996 ("In the instant case, the Committee [against Torture]

existence in the State concerned of a consistent pattern of gross, flagrant, or mass violations of human rights."[129] The "substantial grounds" phrase has been construed to entail a risk that exceeds "mere theory or suspicion" but need not "meet the test of being highly probable."[130] The complainant must establish a "personal, present and foreseeable risk" of being tortured or otherwise mistreated should he be returned.[131]

To date, the treaty has broad global support with 159 States as parties,[132] but because its proscription against torture has assumed customary international law,[133] if not *jus cogens*, status,[134] non-States parties

considers that the author's ethnic background, his alleged political affiliation, his history of detention, and his internal exile should all be taken into account when determining whether he would be in danger of being subjected to torture upon his return.").

[129] CAT, *supra* n.125, art. 3(2). This criterion refers only to "violations by or at the instigation of or with the consent or acquiescence of a public official or other person acting in an official capacity." CAT Gen. Cmt. 1, *supra* n.126, ¶ 3. In addition, "the existence of a pattern of this nature does not in itself constitute a sufficient reason for deciding whether the person in question is in danger of being subjected to torture on her return to this country; there must be specific reasons for believing that the person concerned is personally in danger. Similarly, the absence of this pattern does not mean that a person is not in danger of being subjected to torture in her specific case." *Núñez Chipana*, *supra* n.122, ¶ 6.3.

[130] CAT Gen. Cmt. 1, *supra* n.126, ¶ 6. *See also* U.S. regulations incorporating the CAT, 22 C.F.R. § 95.1(c) & 95.2(b) (construing "substantial grounds" to mean "more likely than not").

[131] *Cf. Khalsa, et al. v. Switzerland*, Commc'n No. 336/2008, U.N. Doc. CAT/C/46/D/336/2008, ¶ 11.8, May 26, 2011, (finding the deportation of the complainant from Switzerland to India would violate Article 3 of the CAT).

[132] U.N. Treaty Collection website, *available at* https://treaties.un.org/Pages/ViewDetails.aspx?src=IND&mtdsg_no=IV-9&chapter=4&lang=en (last visited on May 12, 2016).

[133] The prohibition of torture is absolute and applies even during times of armed conflict or when national security is threatened. CAT, *supra* n.125, art. 2 (no exceptional circumstances whatsoever may be invoked as a justification of torture). *See also* American Law Inst., RESTATEMENT (THIRD) OF THE FOREIGN RELATIONS LAW OF THE UNITED STATES, May 14, 1986 (1987), § 702(d) [hereinafter RESTATEMENT (THIRD)]; Silvia Borelli, *The Rendition of Terrorist Suspects to the United States: Human Rights and the Limits of Int'l Cooperation, in* ENFORCING INTERNATIONAL LAW NORMS AGAINST TERRORISM 343 (Andrea Bianchi ed. 2004) ("no state publicly supports torture or opposes its eradication"); *Filártiga v. Pena-Irala*, 630 F.2d 876 (2d Cir. 1980) (recognizing as a customary international law norm the prohibition of government torture).

[134] *See ICJ Case, Belg. v. Sen.*, *supra* n.47, ¶ 99 ("In the Court's opinion, the prohibition of torture ... has become a peremptory norm (*jus cogens*)."); RESTATEMENT (THIRD), *supra* n.133, § 702 cmt. n; *Siderman de Blake v. Repub. of Arg.*, 965 F.2d 699, 717 (9th Cir. 1992) (concluding "that the right to be free from official torture is fundamental and universal, a right deserving of the highest status under international law, a norm of *jus cogens*."), *cert. denied*, 507 U.S. 1017 (1993); *Al-Adsani v. Gov't of Kuwait and Others (No. 2)* [1996] 2 LRC 333 (CA), *reprinted in* 107 ILR 536 (1996); HRC, Gen.

as well are expected to satisfy its legal obligations. The Committee against Torture, which is responsible for implementing the CAT, has prevented authorized host State extraditions from proceeding on the ground that doing so would violate Article 3 of that Treaty.

In a case released in July 2011, for instance, the Committee found that Morocco's planned extradition of Djamel Ktiti to Algeria was prohibited because, *inter alia*, the Committee had received "many serious allegations" regarding "cases of torture and ill-treatment inflicted on detainees by [Algerian] law-enforcement officers"; an informant "underwent severe torture while in police custody in Algeria" to extract Djamel Ktiti's name "as the leader of the drug-trafficking ring in question"; and Mr. Ktiti was secretly sentenced to life imprisonment *in absentia* based on that forced testimony.[135]

Other international and regional human rights treaties and adjudicatory bodies likewise espouse the fundamental tenet that extradition must be barred when the individual at stake likely would be the subject of torture, persecution, or other serious mistreatment in a given pursuing State.[136] Mistreatment short of torture could include harsh interrogation

Cmt. No. 24 (52), *General Comment on Issues Relating to Reservations made upon Ratification or Accession to the Covenant or the Optional Protocols thereto, or in Relation to Declarations under Article 41 of the Covenant*, Nov. 2, 1994, U.N. Doc. CCPR/C/21/Rev.1/Add.6 (1994).

135 *Yousri Ktiti v. Morocco*, Commc'n No. 419/2010, July 5, 2011, ¶¶ 8.5–8.6, U.N. Doc. CAT/C/46/D/419/2010 (the complainant, Yousri, sought relief on behalf of his brother Djamel).

136 *E.g.*, Charter of Fundamental Rights of the European Union, Dec. 18, 2000, art. 19(2), 2000/C 364/01 [hereinafter E.U. Charter] ("No one may be removed, expelled or extradited to a State where there is a serious risk that he or she would be subjected to . . . torture or other inhuman or degrading treatment or punishment."); *Hilal v. U.K.*, Appl. No. 45276/99, 33 EHRR 2, Mar. 6, 2001 (final issued on June 6, 2001) (parties to the ECHR are obligated to refuse a request for extradition where there are substantial grounds for believing a person would face a real risk of being subjected to torture or ill treatment in the receiving State); Am. Conv. on Human Rights, Nov. 22, 1969, art. 5(2), OAS Official Records Serv. XVI/1.1 Doc. 65, Rev. 1, Corr. 1 (Jan. 1, 1970), 1144 U.N.T.S. 123 [hereinafter ACHR] ("No one shall be subjected to torture or to cruel, inhuman, or degrading punishment or treatment."); Inter-Am. Conv. to Prevent and Punish Torture, Dec. 9, 1985, art. 13, OAS T.S. No. 67, *reprinted in* 25 ILM 519 (1986) ("Extradition shall not be granted nor shall the person sought be returned when there are grounds to believe that his life is in danger [or] that he will be subjected to torture or to cruel, inhuman or degrading treatment"). The two inter-American conventions, however, lack specific implementation mechanisms, so there is no applicable case law.

techniques,[137] public flogging, female genital mutilation (FGM), and inhumane incarceration or execution methods. Noteworthy cases from the Human Rights Committee (HRC) (which interprets and enforces the provisions of ICCPR) and the European Court of Human Rights (ECtHR) (applying the provisions of the ECHR) in which extradition was challenged on the basis of incarceration or execution methods include:

- *Shamayov and Others v. Georgia and Russia.* Were Georgia to extradite Ruslan Gelogayev, a Chechen rebel, to Russia it would violate Article 3 of the ECHR, given the documented treatment of other Chechen rebels by Russian authorities, including solitary confinement, no contact with lawyers, and no information regarding their location to family members, as well as the persecution of Chechens lodging applications with the European Court.[138]
- *Soering v. United Kingdom.* The ECtHR found that if Jens Soering were extradited to Virginia for his role in a double murder, it was foreseeable that he would be convicted, sentenced, and committed to "death row," which would most likely entail a lengthy detention in physically challenging conditions coupled with the constant specter of death hanging over him; the Court unanimously (18–0) ruled that such circumstances in combination, dubbed the "death row phenomenon," amounted to inhuman treatment in violation of Article 3.[139]
- *Ahmad and Others v. United Kingdom.* The ECtHR found that if the five alleged terrorists at issue were extradited to the United States to face terrorism-related charges, and were incarcerated in a so-called "supermax" prison with maximum security conditions without parole, such detention conditions and the length of sentences would *not*

[137] *See* Conclusion and Recommendations of the Committee against Torture: Israel, May 9, 1997, ¶ 5, U.N. Doc. CAT/C/SR.297/Add. 1 (1997) (recognizing that particularly harsh methods of pre-trial interrogation can constitute cruel and inhuman treatment); *Ireland v. U.K.*, Appl. No. 5310/71, 2 EHRR, ¶ 90, Jan. 18, 1978 (intimidatory interrogation techniques could be inhuman and degrading); Borelli, *supra* n.133, at 345 (the use of the so-called "truth serum" [sodium pentothal] could even possibly constitute a violation of an individual's right to be free from degrading treatment).

[138] *Shamayev and Others v. Georgia and Russia*, Appl. No. 36378/02, 44 EHRR, ¶ 362–68, Apr. 12, 2005 (final issued on Oct. 12, 2005).

[139] Soering *Case*, *supra* n.117, at 462–78. Soering ultimately was extradited after the Virginia state prosecutors gave assurances that they would not seek the death penalty upon conviction, and he received two life sentences. Dwight Aarons, *Can Inordinate Delay Between a Death Sentence and Execution Constitute Cruel and Unusual Punishment?*, 29 SETON HALL L. REV. 147, 202 n.219 (1998).

amount to ill treatment under Article 3 (inhuman and degrading treatment or punishment);[140] *however*, because of the severity of defendant Haroon Aswat's mental condition, the Court found there was a real risk that the more hostile prison environment (but not the prospective length of incarceration) in a different country would result in a significant deterioration of his mental and physical health and thereby violate Article 3.[141]

- *Ng v. Canada*. The HRC found that Canada's planned extradition to the United States of an individual who, if sentenced to death, would foreseeably face gas asphyxiation, a method of execution held to produce "prolonged suffering and agony," as it is not "carried out in such a way as to cause the least possible physical and mental suffering,"[142] would constitute a violation of Article 7 of the ICCPR.[143]

Concerns about torture and other maltreatment of extraditees, however, are not the exclusive domain of international and regional tribunals; domestic courts also may rule unfavorably on extradition requests based on human rights concerns deriving from their own national laws or human rights sensibilities. For example, in 1990, the Supreme Court of Ireland denied the extradition of Dermot Finucane and James Pius Clarke, two Irish Republican Army (IRA) militants wanted by the United Kingdom on weapons possession charges, partly out of a belief

140 *See* Alan Cowell & John F. Burns, "Britain Is Allowed to Send 5 Terror Suspects to U.S.," *IHT*, Apr. 11, 2012, at 6. Maximum security conditions include "concrete furniture, timed showers, tiny cell windows and no outside communications." *Id.* Inadequate prison conditions nevertheless can be grounds for an extradition denial. *See, e.g.*, "European Arrest Warrant—Germany—Alternatives to Extradition," *Presseportal fur Pressemitteilungen und Nachrichten*, Jan. 24, 2015 (during interview with German Defence Counsel Dr. Martin Rademacher, he remarked that in 2014 the "higher Regional Court in Bremen rejected a plea for extradition to Bulgaria, because the conditions of the prisons in Bulgaria do not meet the minimal standards set by international law.").

141 *Aswat v. United Kingdom*, Appl. No. 17299/12, Apr. 16, 2013, ECtHR, ¶¶ 55–57 (this case originally was part of *Ahmad and Others v. United Kingdom*). Following this judgment, the United States provided diplomatic assurances that Aswat would be held instead in a psychiatric referral center and examined by doctors, and the extradition was approved. Steven Erlanger, "Mentally Ill Terrorism Suspect, Long Sought by the U.S., is Extradited," *N.Y. Times*, Oct. 22, 2014, at A11.

142 HRC, Gen. Cmt. No. 20, *Article 7 (Prohibition of Torture, or Other Cruel, Inhuman or Degrading Treatment or Punishment)*, U.N. Doc. HRI/GEN/1/Rev.1 at 30 (1994), ¶ 6, Mar. 10, 1992.

143 *Ng v. Canada*, Commc'n No. 469/1991, U.N. Doc. CCPR/C/49/D/469/1991, ¶ 16.2–16.4, Nov. 5, 1993.

that Finucane "probably would be beaten by prison guards if returned to the jail from which he escaped in 1983."[144]

Likewise, in 2012, a U.K. court reversed a decision to extradite U.S. national Shawn Sullivan because the United States had not guaranteed that he would not have to participate in a "civil commitment" program for sex offenders[145] in Minnesota, as such a commitment, if required, would amount to a violation of Article 5 of the ECHR, which prohibits the deprivation of liberty except under circumstances inapplicable to this case.[146] More recently, in October 2015, a Polish court rejected a U.S. request for the extradition of Roman Polanski, a famed filmmaker and French-Polish dual national wanted for a 1977 statutory rape conviction; the court justified its ruling in part on the grounds that California prisons would be "unlikely to provide humane living conditions" for the 82-year-old fugitive.[147]

2 Unfair Trials

The host State also may refuse to extradite a fugitive premised on how a pursuing State, upon his delivery, would be expected to adjudicate.

[144] John Quigley, *The Rule of Non-Inquiry and the Impact of Human Rights on Extradition Law*, 15 N.C. J. INT'L L. & COMM. REG. 401, 423 (1990); "Irish High Court Bars Extraditing 2 in I.R.A.," *N.Y. Times*, Mar. 15, 1990, at A3; AP, "Escaped IRA Gunman Savors Liberty in Dublin," *L.A. Times*, June 24, 1990.

[145] *See, e.g.*, Washington State, Dep't of Corrections, "Civil Commitment of Sexually Violent Predators," 2012, *available at* www.doc.wa.gov/community/sexoffenders/civilcommitment.asp (last visited on May 12, 2016) ("Offenders, including those who pose a greater risk of harm to the community, cannot be held in confinement after they have served their court-ordered sentence for a criminal offense. But civil commitment laws allow a judge or jury to determine whether a sex offender who appears to meet the definition of a sexually violent predator should be released to the community following their confinement period or whether they should be placed in a secure [Department of Social and Health services]-operated facility for control, care, and treatment. Prior to release from state confinement, the [End of Sentence Review Committee] will request a forensic psychological evaluation to determine whether those offenders who appear to meet the definition of a sexually violent predator do in fact meet criteria for civil commitment.").

[146] Bruce Zagaris, *U.K. Court Rejects U.S. Extradition Request Due to Restrictive Treatment Program for Sex Offenders*, 28 IELR 331, 331–32 (2012).

[147] Michal Kolanko & Michael Cieply, "Polish Judge Rejects Extradition of Roman Polanski," *N.Y. Times*, Oct. 30, 2015. Along those lines, a U.K. court rejected Italy's request for the extradition of Domenico Rancadore, who was convicted in 1999 of being a "man of honour" in the Sicilian mafia and collecting bribes, on the grounds that the judge "could not accept assurances from the Italian authorities that prison conditions [particularly overcrowding] in the country would not breach Rancadore's human rights." Josh Halliday, "Fugitive Mafia Boss Domenico Rancadore Wins Extradition Fight," *The Guardian*, Mar. 17, 2014.

Consider the following four scenarios: (i) reliance on *in absentia* judgments; (ii) the use of special or extraordinary courts; (iii) the lack of fundamental trial rights, such as the unavailability of a public hearing and no presumption of innocence; and (iv) the prospect of prosecutorial discrimination or prejudicial influence. Some host State tribunals presume that the pursuing State court system must be able to provide a fair trial or logically the two States would not have entered into a bilateral extradition treaty in the first place.[148]

***In Absentia* Judgments.** As a general matter, an *in absentia* judgment occurs when a criminal court holds proceedings resulting in a guilty verdict on one or more counts and then sentences a defendant who has not been effectively able to put forward his case either because he was not physically present in the courtroom or at least was not represented by legal counsel.[149] This is true *unless* the defendant voluntarily waived (explicitly or tacitly) his right to be present at trial, having been served with a summons, given ample opportunity to attend, and yet chose not to appear or ask counsel to represent him.[150] (As to waiver, it "must be established in an unequivocal manner and be attended by minimum safeguards commensurate with its importance."[151] Moreover, it cannot "be inferred merely from his status as a 'fugitive' (latitante) . . . that he had waived his right to appear at trial and defend himself."[152])

148 *See, e.g.*, Bruce Zagaris, *Spain Orders Mubarak Crony and Son Extradited to Egypt on Corruption Charges*, 28 IELR 165, 165–67 (2012) (Spain's National Court presumed that the Egyptian court system was capable of dispensing justice, given that they had concluded a bilateral extradition treaty).

149 *See* Robert Iraola, *Foreign Extraditions and* In Absentia *Convictions*, 39 Seton Hall L. Rev. 843, 848–56 (2009).

150 *See Crosby v. United States*, 506 U.S. 255, 260 (1993) ("where the offense is not capital and the accused is not in custody, . . . if, after the trial has begun in his presence, he voluntarily absents himself, this does not nullify what has been done or prevent the completion of the trial, but, on the contrary, operates as a waiver of his right to be present and leaves the court free to proceed with the trial in like manner and with like effect as if he were present") (quoting *Diaz v. United States*, 223 U.S. 442, 455 (1912)); *Stoichkov Case, supra* n.17, ¶¶ 51–59 (ruling that as the defendant was convicted *in absentia* on rape charges and never waived his right to appear and defend himself, it would violate the principle embedded in Article 6(3)(c) (affording individual defendants the right to defend themselves in person or through legal counsel) if he were not granted a retrial in his presence on the merits; the fact that the Bulgarian Supreme Court of Cassation contended that the case file from the original proceedings had been destroyed a few years earlier did not remedy that defect or alter the legal requirement).

151 *Sejdovic v. Italy*, Appl. No. 56581/00, Gr. Ch., 42 EHRR 17, ¶ 86, Mar. 1, 2006 [hereinafter *Sejdovic Case*].

152 *Id.* ¶ 87.

Civil law (versus common law) States more typically rely on *in absentia* trials,[153] and tend to hold them to help ensure that criminal proceedings take place while physical evidence can still be garnered and while witnesses remain alive, can be located, and their memories are largely intact. If States wait until the defendant is captured and returned to face trial, which may take many years, if it is possible at all, they fear their chances of a successful prosecution will be hampered.[154]

At the same time, however, *in absentia* trials can be perceived as disadvantageous to the accused,[155] who was not present to work with counsel on litigation strategy, make a positive impression on the judge and/or jurors, help counsel verify and respond to factual testimony,[156] or possibly take the stand himself. This matter is compounded in the extradition context to the extent that the host State is not necessarily familiar with the trial procedures used by the pursuing State at issue and the extradition subject may well be unaware of the nature and severity of the extant conviction.[157] The concern here is that, upon his return, the fugitive could be punished based on a compromised trial at which he was not afforded full and fair representation.[158]

Today, in the interest of fairness, many treaties (*e.g.*, the Second Additional Protocol to the European Convention on Extradition[159]), international arrangements (*e.g.*, the Council Framework Decision on

[153] Clive Nicholls, et al., eds., The Law of Extradition and Mutual Assistance 17 (2d ed. 2007).

[154] Matthew W. Henning, Note, *Extradition Controversies: How Enthusiastic Prosecutions Can Lead to Int'l Incidents*, 22 B.C. Int'l & Comp. L. Rev. 347, 369 (1999).

[155] It is for precisely this reason that *in absentia* trials are not allowed by the ICTY or ICTR. The Tribunals' Rules of Procedure and Evidence (RPEs), however, permit war crimes victims to be heard in proceedings in which the suspects are not present, but in such events, the purpose is to create a public record and no guilt or punishment is imposed. Brian T. Hildreth, Comment, *Hunting the Hunters: The United Nations Unleashes Its Latest Weapon in the Fight against Fugitive War Crimes Suspects – Rule 61*, 6 Tul. J. Int'l & Comp. L. 499, 501–02 (1998).

[156] *See, e.g., Sejdovic Case, supra* n.151, ¶ 92 (discussing the "need to verify the accuracy of [the defendant's] statements and compare them with those of the victim . . . and of the witnesses.").

[157] Jennings & Watts, *supra* n.76, at 948 n.10.

[158] In practice, "[t]his defense [against *in absentia* trials] is not recognized in those states whose legal systems permit such trials, while it may be a defense in those legal systems that do not permit such trials." M. Cherif Bassiouni, International Extradition: United States Law and Practice 797 (6th ed. 2014).

[159] Mar. 17, 1978, art. 3, E.T.S. No. 98 (in the context of an *in absentia* conviction, "the requested Party may refuse to extradite for this purpose if, in its opinion, the proceedings leading to the judgment did not satisfy the minimum rights of defence recognized as due to everyone charged with criminal offence. However, extradition shall be granted if the

the European Arrest Warrant[160]), and municipal laws (*e.g.*, the PRC extradition statute[161]) grant extradition on the condition that, where an *in absentia* conviction has occurred, the verdict and sentence be set aside and the individual be given an opportunity to appear at a fresh trial (or at least provided a review or appeal amounting to a retrial) upon his return.[162] As a result, a large number of initially denied extraditions on account of *in absentia* trials are ultimately reversed based on diplomatic assurances (discussed in sub-section e.ii) regarding the willingness to offer the defendant a new trial.[163]

Nevertheless, extraditions may be refused or prohibited where a pursuing State is unable or unwilling to retry the convicted individual,[164] or if for any

requesting Party gives an assurance considered sufficient to guarantee to the person claimed the right to a retrial which safeguards the rights of defence.").

160 June 13, 2002, art. 5(1), 2002/584/JHA, OJEC 1–20, L190/1 of July 18, 2002 ("where the European arrest warrant has been issued for the purposes of executing a sentence or a detention order imposed by a decision rendered in absentia and if the person concerned has not been summoned in person or otherwise informed of the date and place of the hearing which led to the decision rendered *in absentia*, surrender may be subject to the condition that the issuing judicial authority gives an assurance deemed adequate to guarantee the person who is the subject of the European arrest warrant that he or she will have an opportunity to apply for a retrial of the case in the issuing Member State and to be present at the judgment").

161 PRC Extradition Law, *supra* n.61, art. 8 (an extradition request must be rejected where: "(8) the request is made by the Requesting State on the basis of a judgement rendered by default, unless the Requesting State undertakes that the person sought has the opportunity to have the case retried under conditions of his presence.").

162 *See* Stanbrook & Stanbrook, *supra* n.55, at 150–51; *e.g.*, *Sejdovic Case*, *supra* n.151, ¶ 82 ("a denial of justice . . . occurs where a person convicted in absentia is unable subsequently to obtain from a court which has heard him a fresh determination of the merits of the charge, in respect of both law and fact, where it has not been established that he has waived his right to appear and to defend himself.").

163 *E.g.*, *In re D'Amico*, 177 F. Supp. 648 (S.D.N.Y. 1959); Bruce Zagaris, *Canada Deports Anibalzinho to Mozambique on Murder Charges*, 21 IELR 93 (2005) (the Mozambican Supreme Court decision to allow retrial, following an *in absentia* conviction with a twenty-eight-year sentence, was critical to the Canadian immigration board determination to transfer Anibal dos Santos, better known as Anibalzinho, to Mozambique to stand trial for his part in murder of an investigative journalist) (deportation case). But not all States follow this practice. For example, U.S. courts tend to treat *in absentia* convictions as tantamount to an indictment, Restatement (Third), *supra* n.133, § 475 cmt. h (1987), although to the extent a petitioner through evidence can cast doubt upon the fundamental fairness of the proceedings that led to the conviction, a court may well deny extradition. *Esposito v. I.N.S.*, 936 F.2d 911, 914 (7th Cir. 1991).

164 For instance, in May 1979, the Indictment Division of the Limoges Court of Appeal in France disallowed the extradition of Italian national Lorenzo Bozano to Italy, where the Assize Court of Appeal in Italy had convicted and sentenced him *in absentia* to life imprisonment for the abduction and murder of a Swiss girl in Genoa and the attempt at

reason a retrial itself were deemed inadequate. For example, applicable domestic law may not provide for retrials under the specific circumstances at play;[165] the case files from the original proceedings may have become lost or destroyed in the interim;[166] or the prospect of a retrial would be regarded as unjust, given the difficulty in resurrecting evidence and witnesses due to the passage of time and/or the commission of alleged offenses during a period of civil war.[167]

Special or Extraordinary Courts. A number of treaties and domestic laws make extradition expressly conditional upon a pursuing State *not* trying the individual in a special or extraordinary court.[168] Such

extortion for her return, as well as to four years' imprisonment for indecent assault with violence against four women, given that the lack of adversarial proceedings were regarded as "incompatible with French public policy (*ordre public*)" and Italy did not provide for an obligatory retrial. *Bozano v. France*, Appl. No. 9990/82, 9 EHRR 297, ¶ 12–18, Dec. 2, 1987.

[165] *E.g.*, *Sejdovic Case*, *supra* n.151, ¶¶ 102–05 (concluding that neither remedy available to the individual under Italy's Code of Criminal Procedure (CCP) – whether based on procedural irregularities leading to the judgment or a legal precondition for leave to appeal – would afford him "the opportunity to obtain a fresh determination of the merits of the charge against him"); Steven Levy, "Getting Away With It," *Newsweek*, Dec. 15. 1997, at 58 (discussing France's initial rejection of a U.S. extradition request for Ira Einhorn, an American fugitive wanted for murder, despite his having voluntarily waived his right to be present at trial and receiving a full trial with effective assistance of counsel, where Pennsylvania state law did not permit new trials under such circumstances). The Pennsylvania legislature, however, later passed a law to specifically allow for such retrials, but faced steep opposition that questioned the bill's constitutionality to the extent it allowed the legislature to overrule a court judgment in violation of the separation of powers doctrine, which enabled Einhorn's extradition in 2001. Jacqueline Soteropolous, "Einhorn Requests a Ruling from Pa.; The Former Fugitive Wants the State's High Court to Take Charge of His Case; He Also Formally Sought a New Trial," *Philly.com*, Sept. 13, 2001, *available at* http://articles.philly.com/2001-09-13/news/25314032_1_buffy-hall-ira-einhorn-holly-maddux (last visited on May 12, 2016).

[166] *E.g.*, *Stoichkov Case*, *supra* n.17, ¶¶ 57–58 (discussing the impossibility of a retrial due to a destroyed original case file, although not in the extradition context).

[167] *E.g.*, Drago Hedl & Anna McTaggart, "British Refusal to Extradite Serb Angers Croatia," *Balkan Insight*, Mar. 30, 2007, *available at* http://publicinternationallawandpolicygroup.org/wp-content/uploads/2011/04/wcpw_vol02issue16.html (last visited on May 28, 2016) (discussing a British judge's refusal to grant extradition to Croatia of Milan Spanović, a Serb convicted in 1993 in a mass *in absentia* trial for war crimes against civilians during the conflict in Croatia from 1991–95, arising out of a concern about reconstructing facts based on the difficulty of finding evidence and witnesses from sixteen years ago in the midst of a civil armed conflict).

[168] *E.g.*, Inter-Am. Conv. on Extradition, *supra* n.60, art. 4(3) (extradition to be denied "[w]hen the person sought has been tried or sentenced or is to be tried before an extraordinary or ad hoc tribunal of the requesting State."); Inter-Am. Conv. to Prevent and Punish Torture, *supra* n.136, art. 13 (proscribes extradition where individual will be tried by special or *ad hoc* courts); Swiss IMAC, *supra* n.95, art. 38(1)(c)

reasoning derives from the fundamental human rights concern that a court must be genuinely independent[169] – and such special or extraordinary courts, by their very nature, tend to lack that attribute compared with their established judicial counterparts.[170] Special or extraordinary courts, by and large, are erected on an *ad hoc* basis by the executive typically without legislative vetting or oversight, and their empanelled judges do not necessarily have the substantive knowledge or experience of evaluating complex legal matters, and they may even have been selected precisely because of their ideological leanings.[171]

In November 2001, Spain announced that it would not extradite to the United States eight alleged Islamic extremists implicated in the attacks of September 11, 2001, unless they were subject to trial by a civilian court. Spain was reportedly concerned that if the adjudication were held before one of the newly established Military Commissions (distinct from ordinary military courts) envisioned by President George W. Bush pursuant to his Order of November 13, 2001, the defendants would be unable to choose their own counsel, the hearings would be held in secret, and the military officers who sat as judges could be biased.[172]

(prohibiting requesting State from bringing an extraditee "before an extraordinary court"); Treaty on Extradition, U.S.-Braz., *supra* n.99, art. V(4) (no extradition is to be allowed "[w]hen the person sought would have to appear, in the requesting State, before an extraordinary tribunal or court.").

169 *See Basic Principles on the Independence of the Judiciary*, Principle 5, U.N. Doc. A/CONF 121/22/Rev 1, adopted at the 1985 Milan conference and approved by UNGA Res. 40/32 (Nov. 29, 1985) and UNGA Res. 40/146 (Dec. 13, 1985) ("Everyone shall have the right to be tried by ordinary courts or tribunals using established legal procedures. Tribunals that do not use the duly established procedures of the legal process shall not be created to displace the jurisdiction belonging to the ordinary courts or judicial tribunals.").

170 Notably, States are not generally concerned with the fairness of *ordinary military courts*. *See, e.g.*, Montevideo Conv. on Extradition, Dec. 26, 1933, art. 3(d), 49 Stat. 3111, *reprinted in* 28 AJIL 65 (1934). *But see* Lowenfeld, *supra* n.16, at 743–44 (first a U.S. magistrate judge issued a denial and later a U.S. district court judge called for a hearing with respect to the requested extradition to Israel of alleged Palestinian terrorist Mahmoud El-Abed Ahmad (a/k/a Mahmoud Abed Atta), given that he would face trial there before a military court).

171 *See* Amnesty Int'l, "State Injustice: Unfair Trials in the Middle East and North Africa," Apr. 15, 1998, AI Index MDE 01/002/98, at 54, *available at* www.amnesty.org/en/documents/mde01/002/1998/en/ (last visited on May 28, 2016).

172 Sam Dillon with Donald G. McNeil Jr., "Spain Sets Hurdle for Extraditions; Tells U.S. That Terror Suspects Must Receive Civilian Trials," *N.Y. Times*, Nov. 24, 2001, at A1, B4; Duffy, *supra* n.55, at 140. More recently, even following Military Commission reforms, "[a] number of countries have indicated that they will not cooperate with the United

To overcome such concerns, a pursuing State may give diplomatic assurances that no special or extraordinary court will be engaged to adjudicate charges against the fugitive defendant. In January 2003, for example, in connection with the U.S. request for the extradition from Germany of Sheik Mohammed Ali Hassan Moayad, adviser to the Yemeni Minister for Religious Foundations, the U.S. Government "assured Germany that he would not be tried by military tribunal or any other extraordinary court" in order to satisfy Germany's Constitutional Court that Moayad would receive a fair trial.[173]

Lack of Fundamental Trial Rights. Extradition treaties and domestic laws often make a fugitive defendant's receipt of fundamental trial rights protections in the transferee State a condition for authorizing extradition.[174] The U.N. Model Treaty on Extradition, for example, prohibits extradition "if the person has not received or would not receive the minimum guarantees in criminal proceedings, as contained in [ICCPR], article 14."[175] Among the most important of these include the guarantees:

States in certain counterterrorism efforts – for instance, in providing evidence or extraditing suspects – if [it] intends to use that cooperation in pursuit of a military commission prosecution." Eric Holder, *Remarks by U.S. Attorney General on National Security Law*, Northwestern Univ. School of Law, Chicago, *Lawfare* blog, Mar. 5, 2012, *available at* www.lawfareblog.com/text-attorney-generals-national-security-speech (last visited on May 12, 2016).

173 Eva Wagner, *German Federal Constitutional Court Approves Extradition of Yemeni Citizen*, 20 IELR 14 (2004).

174 *See, e.g., Al-Moayad v. Germany*, Appl. No. 35865/03, Decision on Admissibility, 44 EHRR, ¶ 101, Feb. 20, 2007 ("In the [ECtHR's] view, the right to a fair trial in criminal proceedings, as embodied in Article 6, holds a prominent place in a democratic society ... A flagrant denial of a fair trial, and thereby a denial of justice, undoubtedly occurs where a person is detained because of suspicions that he has been planning or has committed a criminal offence without having any access to an independent and impartial tribunal to have the legality of his or her detention reviewed and, if the suspicions do not prove to be well-founded, to obtain release."); Agreement between the United States of America and the Gov't of Hong Kong for the Surrender of Fugitive Offenders, Dec. 20, 1996, art. 6(3)(c), T.I.A.S. 98-121; *Heeralall, Case, supra* n.25, at 74 ("[I]f a question is raised as to whether a person who is proposed to be extradited by the courts in Mauritius would be deprived of the guarantees against forced interrogation and his right to silence, then our courts would be bound by the provisions of our Constitution not to extradite him since our courts would not be in a position to protect that person or to ensure that those guarantees are made available to him.").

175 U.N. Model Extradition Treaty, *supra* n.59, art. 3(f).

(i) to receive "a fair and public hearing"[176] presided over by a "competent, independent, and impartial tribunal established by law,"
(ii) "to be presumed innocent until proved guilty according to law,"
(iii) to "have adequate time and facilities for the preparation of his defence,"
(iv) to "be tried without undue delay,"
(v) to have "legal assistance of his own choosing" or, where the defendant does not have sufficient financial means, to "have legal assistance assigned to him,"
(vi) "[n]ot to be compelled to testify against himself," and
(vii) to have any conviction and sentence "reviewed by a higher tribunal according to law."[177]

Many of these rights are widely regarded as non-derogable even during states of national emergency.[178] These rights also tend to encompass a prohibition of summary trial proceedings as they would almost necessarily compromise the fair trial rights of defendants[179] as well as to criminal proceedings premised on *ex post facto* legislation in a transferee State court.[180]

In a number of cases, extraditions have been denied out of concern for a lack of specific fundamental trial rights. For example, courts in France,[181]

176 It would contravene the principle of a "fair" trial, for instance, if "potentially influential material" were withheld from the defendant during his prosecution by a transferee State. *E.g.*, *Ramda v. Sec'y of State for the Home Dep't* [2002] EWHC 1278 ¶ 25 (Admin).

177 ICCPR, *supra* n.55, art. 14. *Accord* ECHR, *supra* n.124, art. 6; ACHR, *supra* n.136, art. 8.

178 HRC, Gen. Cmt. No. 29, *States of Emergency (Article 4)*, U.N. Doc. CCPR/C/21/Rev.1/Add.11, Aug. 31, 2001 ("States Parties may in no circumstances invoke article 4 of the Covenant as justification for acting in violation of humanitarian law or peremptory norms of international law, for instance by taking hostages ... or by deviating from fundamental principles of fair trial, including the presumption of innocence."); *id.* ¶ 15 ("It is inherent in the protection of rights explicitly recognized as non-derogable in article 4(2), that they must be secured by procedural guarantees, including, often, judicial guarantees."); *Gonzalez del Rio v. Peru*, Commc'n No. 263/1987, U.N. Doc. CCPR/C/46/D/263/1987, ¶ 5.1, Nov. 2, 1992 (maintaining that the right to be tried by an independent and impartial tribunal is absolute and subject to no exceptions).

179 *E.g.*, *Bader & Kanbor v. Sweden*, Appl. No. 13284/04, 46 EHRR, ¶ 47, Nov. 8, 2005 (summary proceedings in Syria in which no oral evidence was taken, only the prosecutor's evidence was submitted, and neither the defendant nor his counsel was present "must be regarded as a flagrant denial of a fair trial").

180 *E.g.*, *In re Croissant*, Conseil d'État, Fr., July 7, 1978, *reprinted in* 74 ILR 505.

181 *Case of Bivugarabago*, File No. 2008/00029, N662, Ct. of App. of Toulouse, Fr., Oct. 23, 2008.

Finland,[182] Germany,[183] Switzerland,[184] and the United Kingdom[185] each rejected extradition requests by the Rwandan Government regarding charges of genocide and crimes against humanity in connection with its 1994 civil war because of concerns that the Rwandan courts would be unable to adequately protect defendants' fair trial rights, particularly their ability to call, examine, and protect supporting witnesses.[186]

Prosecutorial Discrimination/Prejudicial Influence. Fair trial rights also entail the absence of any prosecutorial discrimination toward a defendant on account of his race, religion, nationality, political opinion, or other such factors, as well as a lack of pre-judgment due either to deep-seated ideological differences between the individual and the pursuing State at issue or to widespread media coverage that can adversely influence a judge and/or jury's mindset.

Domestic courts tend to prohibit extradition where evidence reveals a discriminatory prosecutorial motive. For example, in 1960, a U.S. judge denied an extradition to Greece upon finding that charges had been pretextually political against a Greek national residing in Alabama after being convicted *in absentia* of embezzlement, where despite full knowledge of his decision to move to the United States, no one contested the move; he was not informed of the trial proceedings and was not represented by counsel; and he had led the City Council on behalf of the Anti-Communist

182 *E.g.*, "Finns Reject Rwandan Extradition," *BBC News*, Feb. 20, 2009, *available at* http://news.bbc.co.uk/2/mobile/europe/7901693.stm (last visited on May 28, 2016) (the Government of Finland denied an extradition request by Rwanda for François Bazaramba, who was wanted for genocide, crimes against humanity, and membership in a criminal organization, on the grounds that he was unlikely to receive a fair trial in Rwanda).

183 *E.g., Cases of Callixte Mbarushimana and Onesphore Rwabukombe*, 2 Ausl. A 106/08 Oberlandesgericht Frankfurt am main Beschluss, Ger., Nov. 6, 2008.

184 *E.g.*, Bruce Zagaris, *Switzerland Denies Rwandan Extradition Request of Former Minister on Genocide Charges*, 25 IELR 364 (2009) (adding that the facts stated in the extradition request were not sufficiently detailed).

185 *E.g., Brown and Others v. Gov't of Rwanda and Sec'y of State of the Home Dep't*, Case No. CO/8862/2008, [2009] EWHC 770 (Admin), ¶ 121.

186 "Until the International Criminal [Tribunal for] Rwanda wound down, countries denied extradition requests to Rwanda because of concerns about its due process. However, Rwanda has made improvements and countries have found that suspects can receive fair treatment in Rwanda." Bruce Zagaris, *Netherlands Arrest Genocide Suspect for Extradition to Rwanda*, 30 IELR 186, 187 (2014) (noting that "in January 2014, Freed Teeven, the Dutch Minister for Migration, Security and Justice promised his country was ready to extradite or deport some genocide suspects to Rwanda within the next 18 months.").

Party for two years just prior to his departure and the next year the Communist Party came into power and its leaders lodged the claims against him.[187]

During the Cold War, Western States were often disinclined to extradite to Soviet bloc States individuals who either embraced Western ideology or otherwise exhibited views or interests antithetical to those of the U.S.S.R. and its satellites because of a concern about discriminatory prosecution.[188] Even since the Cold War ended, certain residual ideological tensions can give a Western State pause to transfer an individual to an oppositional State, as in the case of the United States to Cuba, although U.S.-Cuba political relations now appear to be thawing.

Concerns about adverse media attention, whether national or local, particularly involving a high-profile defendant's identity or affiliation, or a widely despised alleged crime, can contribute to a wave of influential public opinion that can potentially render a trial unfair to the accused, and that prospect can sabotage an extradition request, when the case is to be heard before a jury of peers. For example, reservations were raised about the negative media impact on a prospective criminal trial in the United Kingdom of Joseph Magee, a member of the Irish National Liberation Army (INLA) who had killed an Army sergeant in cold blood in Northern Ireland in 1993, influencing the Irish High Court the following year to dismiss the extradition request.[189] Similarly, in June 2004, a Bahaman court granted a *habeas corpus* petition to Samuel Knowles, and thereby refused extradition to the United States, on the grounds that the broad publicity surrounding his U.S. presidential designation as a "narcotics kingpin" likely would predetermine his guilt among Florida jurors.[190]

[187] *In re Mylonas*, 187 F. Supp. 716 (N.D. Ala. 1960).

[188] Lyal S. Sunga, The Emerging System of International Criminal Law: Developments in Codification and Implementation 261 (1997).

[189] *Magee v. O'Dea*, Sup. Ct., Ir., [1994] I.R. 500, ¶ 510–13 (finding a "serious risk" existed that the "quality and extent of the media publicity" surrounding the accused would lead to an unfair trial). In a similar case in 1988, the Attorney General of Ireland would not authorize an extradition where the fugitive was alleged to have supplied weapons to the IRA in Northern Ireland as there was concern about finding neutral jurors to hear the case. Robin Oakley & Jamie Dettmer, "Ryan Decision 'a Great Insult' Says Thatcher," *The Times* (London), Dec. 14, 1988, at 1.

[190] Bruce Zagaris, *Bahamas Court Denies U.S. Extradition Request for Narcotics Kingpin Due to Fair Trial Considerations*, 20 IELR 377, 377–78 (2004).

3 Excessive or Discriminatory Punishment

This section turns from the trial proceedings to the punishment phase following a criminal conviction; it examines three types of potentially applied sanctions in a pursuing State that have given many host States pause when contemplating whether to grant an extradition request: (i) the death penalty, (ii) a life sentence, and (iii) discriminatory punishment based on the defendant's race, religion, nationality, political opinion, or possibly other criteria such as age, gender, or sexual orientation.[191]

Death Penalty. Most States around the world have abolished capital punishment as a constitutional, legislative, or *de facto* matter.[192] As a general rule, those "abolitionist" States negotiate provisions in their human rights treaties consistent with that sentiment. Protocol 13 to the European Convention for the Protection of Human Rights and Fundamental Freedoms (2002), which boasts forty-four States parties to date, provides for an *absolute* prohibition of condemning or executing anyone under the death penalty (*i.e.*, no derogation or reservation is permitted).[193] Likewise,

[191] Two additional categories arguably exist: (i) excessive recidivism laws, such as California's "three strikes" legislation in which, *inter alia*, upon conviction of any felony (including a so-called "wobbler" that lies in the gray area between a felony and a misdemeanor) following two serious or violent felony convictions over any stretch of time, one must receive a minimum sentence of twenty-five years to life; such laws may conflict with international human rights standards governing arbitrary detention and inhuman or degrading punishment, as set forth in leading international instruments, and thereby could result in extradition denials, *see* Anne Goldin, *The California Three Strikes Law: A Violation of Int'l Law and a Possible Impediment to Extradition*, 15 Sw. J. Int'l L. 327 (2009); and (ii) comparatively excessive punishment if convicted; for example, the Federal Supreme Court of Brazil rejected an extradition request by Hong Kong on the grounds that the return of individuals immediately before the agreed date on which sovereignty transferred from the United Kingdom to the PRC (July 1, 1997) would subject them to a stiffer Chinese-based criminal justice system than warranted (*i.e.*, the so-called "Hong Kong defense"). Dugard & van den Wyngaert, *supra* n.118, at 194.

[192] *See* Hands Off Cain, *The Death Penalty Worldwide: 2015 Report, available at* www.handsoffcain.info/bancadati/index.php?tipotema=arg&idtema=20000712 (last visited on May 12, 2016) (identifying as of June 30, 2015, 103 fully abolitionist States, six abolitionist States for ordinary crimes, 46 *de facto* abolitionist States (*i.e.*, those that have not executed anyone for at least ten years or that have a binding obligation against its use), six retentionist States that have imposed an ongoing moratorium on executions, and thirty-seven fully retentionist States, including in this last group some democratic ones, such as the United States, Japan, and India, a number which has dropped from forty-two in 2010 and from fifty-four in 2005 (note: the list includes several entities or territories that do not qualify as U.N. member States, including the Cook Islands, Bermuda, and Taiwan).

[193] Prot. 13 to the ECHR, *Concerning the Abolition of the Death Penalty*, May 3, 2002, art. 2(2), E.T.S. No. 187. *Accord* E.U. Charter, *supra* n.136, art. 2(2) ("No one shall be condemned to the death penalty, or executed.").

the Protocol to the American Convention on Human Rights (1990) to Abolish the Death Penalty, to which twelve States have ratified or acceded to date, prohibits the application of the death penalty in all but one narrow circumstance.[194]

Because the death penalty is not currently regarded as a *per se* violation of international law,[195] fully or *de facto* abolitionist States tend to incorporate provisions in their domestic laws militating against extradition to States where the death penalty could be imposed[196] and advocate for such provisions when negotiating multilateral agreements or arrangements,[197] as well as in their bilateral extradition treaties[198] with "retentionist" States. Consequently, absent diplomatic assurances that, upon conviction, no death penalty will be imposed, ministry officials or municipal courts from abolitionist States frequently deny extradition requests to retentionist States.[199] Abolitionist State courts have been known to invalidate grants of extradition *after* a fugitive was turned over to a retentionist State where the transferor State belatedly discovered that it had not obtained the necessary assurances that the death penalty would not be imposed.[200]

194 Prot. to the Am. Conv. on Human Rights (ACHR) to Abolish the Death Penalty, June 8, 1990, art. 2, OAS T.S. No. 73 (the single exception is when, upon ratification or accession, a State Party reserves use of the death penalty in wartime with respect to "extremely serious crimes of a military nature.").

195 Geoff Gilbert, *Extradition*, *in* The Harvard Research in International Law: Contemporary Analysis and Appraisal 270 (John P. Grant & J. Craig Barker eds. 2007); *United States v. Burns*, Sup. Ct., Can., Feb. 15, 2001, [2001] 1 S.C.R. 283, ¶ 89 (there is not as yet an "international law norm against the death penalty").

196 *E.g.*, N.Z. Extradition Act Pub. Act 55 of 1999, May 20, 1999, § 30(3) (the Foreign Minister may refuse to extradite if he determines that the individual of interest may be or has been sentenced to death and there are insufficient assurances that he will not be so sentenced or that capital punishment will not be imposed).

197 *E.g.*, E.U. Charter, *supra* n.136, art. 19(2) ("No one may be removed, expelled or extradited to a State where there is a serious risk that he or she would be subjected to the death penalty."); London Scheme, *supra* n.87, art. 15(2)(a) (permitting a refusal to extradite if the "person is likely to suffer the death penalty for the extradition offence and that offence is not punishable by death in the requested country").

198 *E.g.*, U.S.-Jam. Extradition Treaty, *supra* n.65, art. V (where the requested State is abolitionist but the requesting State is retentionist, the requested State may refuse to grant extradition on account of the death penalty but in such cases the requested State will give due consideration to assurances that the death penalty will not be imposed).

199 Duffy, *supra* n.55, at 111.

200 *Cf.* James Finstein, *Extradition or Execution? Policy Constraints in the United States' War on Terror*, 77 S. Cal. L. Rev. 835, 861–62 (2004) (the South African Constitutional Court found that al-Qaida operative Khalfan Khamis Mohamed had been extradited to the United States in violation of his constitutional rights because South Africa had not

In 1990, the Supreme Court of the Netherlands denied a U.S. extradition request for an American military officer, Sgt. Charles Donald Short, who, while stationed with a U.S. unit at a Dutch air force base, allegedly murdered his Turkish wife and cut her body into pieces. The court opined that the State's international human rights commitments superseded its obligation to extradite, and consequently made extradition conditional on assurances that the accused would not be tried for a capital offense.[201] Likewise, in November 1997, Mexican officials announced they would not extradite Jose Luis De Toro, a twenty-one-year-old American national, to the United States to face murder charges in connection with the slaying of a mother of quadruplets in Sarasota, Florida, unless state prosecutors were committed to not pursuing the death penalty.[202]

Retentionist States at times reflect contingency arrangements in their municipal laws to accommodate such demands,[203] and more often than not are forthcoming about providing such assurances to the extent they prove necessary to bring fugitives to justice.[204] That said, retentionist

secured proper assurances that, upon conviction, he would not face the death penalty for his participation in the bombing of the U.S. Embassy in Tanzania in 1998).

201 *The Netherlands v. Short*, Sup. Ct., Neth., Mar. 30, 1990, *reprinted in* 29 ILM 1375; Kellee A. Brown & Sophia A. Muirhead, *Extradition: Divergent Trends in Int'l Cooperation*, 33 Harv. Int'l L.J. 223 (1992).

202 AP, "Mexico Refusing to Extradite Suspect in Killing of Mother," *L.A. Times*, Nov. 29, 1997. *See also* Andrea Bianchi, *Int'l Decision:* Venezia v. Ministero di Grazia e Giustizia, Const. Ct., Italy, June 27, 1996, 79 *Rivista di Diritto Int'l* 825, *reprinted in* 91 AJIL 727 (1997) (discussing the *Venezia* case in which an Italian court in June 1996 ruled unconstitutional a Ministry of Justice decision to extradite Pietro Venezia to the United States to face murder charges in Dade County, Florida, claiming that the Italian Constitution's ban on the death penalty prohibits extradition for a capital crime absent satisfactory assurances that the death penalty will not be applied).

203 *E.g.*, India Extradition Act, *supra* n.2, § 34C ("where a fugitive criminal, who has committed an extradition offence punishable with death in India, is surrendered or returned by a foreign State on the request of the Central Government and the laws of that foreign State do not provide for a death penalty for such an offence, such fugitive criminal shall be liable for punishment of imprisonment for life only for that offence.").

204 For example, the U.S. Government agreed not to seek the death penalty in order to permit the extradition from Germany of Mohammed Ali Hamadei, who had been arrested in Frankfurt and identified as one of two terrorists who had hijacked a TWA jet on June 14, 1985, between Athens and Rome, diverted it to Beirut, and killed U.S. Navy diver Robert Stethem. Philip Shenon, "U.S. Will Not Seek Death in Hijacking; Agrees to a Term Set by Bonn for Extraditing a Lebanese Arrested in Frankfurt," *N.Y. Times*, Jan. 19, 1987, at A5. Likewise, in 2006, the Government of Rwanda agreed not to impose the death penalty on four men accused of participating in the 1994 Rwanda genocide if they were extradited from the United Kingdom and later convicted, in order to meet U.K. extradition requirements. Bruce Zagaris, *U.K. Arrests Four Rwanda Genocide Suspects for Potential Extradition*, 23 IELR 89 (2007).

States may choose not to pursue extradition in certain egregious cases when they are unwilling to compromise their justice standards and accept something less than the worst-case punishment.[205] In other instances, a State's laws may simply not provide for the death penalty to be forsaken under certain circumstances, even if necessary to secure a fugitive's custody through extradition.[206]

Life Sentence. Capital punishment is not the only type of prospective criminal sentence that can prompt a State to refuse an extradition request. In some instances, States have expressed concern about the imposition of life sentences[207] that, like the death penalty, can be viewed as cruel, extreme, or inhumane.[208] Sometimes, this manifests itself as a constitutional prohibition; for example, the Constitutions of Brazil, El Salvador, and Portugal expressly ban the extradition of anyone to a State, where, if convicted, he could be subjected to life imprisonment, unless binding assurances are provided that no such penalty will be imposed.[209] In other instances it appears as a statutory provision.[210] In still others, it can be issued as a domestic judicial ruling, as occurred with the Mexican Supreme Court in October 2001 when it held life imprisonment to be

205 For example, the U.S. Government decided not to seek the extradition of Moroccan national Mounir Motassadeq, who was charged with over 3,000 counts of accessory to murder in connection with the attacks on U.S. soil on September 11, 2001, because of fear that any such request would be rejected by a firmly abolitionist Germany and where the United States would definitely have wanted to seek the death penalty. Finstein, *supra* n.200, at 835–37.

206 *See* Bruce Zagaris, *South Africa Denies Two Botswana Extradition Requests Due to Failure to Give Undertaking on the Death Penalty*, 27 IELR 1001, 1001–02 (2011) (discussing Botswanan law).

207 Sometimes this sentence is described as a life sentence *without the possibility of parole*. In an added twist, in May 2009, the Rwandan lower house of parliament approved a bill that would require anyone convicted of a genocide crime to face a life sentence in *solitary confinement*. Bruce Zagaris, *Swedish Supreme Court Finds Extraditable to Rwanda Genocide and Crimes Against Humanity Suspect as Rwandan House Approves Law to Impose Solitary on Killers*, 25 IELR 317, 318 (2009).

208 A State may insist on a maximum imposed length of punishment short of life imprisonment. *See, e.g.*, *Benitez v. Garcia*, 449 F.3d 971 (9th Cir. 2006) (per curiam) (unanimously holding that a California Superior Court has to honor a Venezuelan grant of extradition under the U.S.-Venezuela Extradition Treaty that Cristobal Rodriguez Benitez, a Mexican national, was to receive a punishment not exceeding thirty years, and consequently struck down an indefinite sentence of fifteen years to life imprisonment).

209 Rodrigo Labardini, *Extradition from Mexico Allowed with Assurances that Life Imprisonment Will Not Be Imposed*, 18 IELR 404, 411 (2002).

210 *E.g.*, Namibia, Extradition Act 11 of 1996, July 1, 1996, art. 5(a) (open-endedly proscribing any type of punishment that is not likewise applied in Namibia, including life sentences, absent assurances that they will not be imposed).

a form of "unusual or extreme" punishment, and therefore a violation of Article 22 of the Mexican Constitution.[211]

This restriction is frequently embedded in multilateral[212] or bilateral[213] treaty provisions and is enforced by human rights courts. In July 2010, partly on the grounds that Abu Hamza al-Masri, an Egyptian jihadist who allegedly attempted to help establish a terrorist training camp in Oregon and provided support to al-Qaida, could face life imprisonment without the possibility of parole if extradited from the United Kingdom to the United States, the ECtHR temporarily barred his extradition.[214] More recently, in September 2014, the ECtHR ruled that Belgium was not permitted under Article 3 of the ECHR to extradite Nizar Trabelsi, a Tunisian national wanted for four acts of terrorism, to the United States where he could end up serving life imprisonment without the possibility of parole.[215]

It is not uncommon in such circumstances for pursuing States to accommodate treaty requirements by agreeing not to impose a life sentence on persons convicted following extradition;[216] however, not only can this additional step cause processing delays, but also may render the problem irremediable, such as when the prosecution is unwilling to

211 Labardini, *supra* n.209, at 404 (citing 14 S.J.F. 13 (9a época 2001)). That prohibition lasted only until late November 2005. Duncan Hollis, "Is Life Imprisonment an 'Unusual' Punishment?," *Opinio Juris*, Dec. 2, 2005, *available at* http://lawofnations.blogspot.it/2005/12/is-life-imprisonment-unusual.html (last visited on May 13, 2016).

212 *E.g.*, Inter-Am. Conv. on Extradition, *supra* n.60, art. 9.

213 *E.g.*, Treaty of Extradition, U.S.-Venez., Jan. 19 and 22, 1922, art. IV, 43 Stat. 1698, T.S. 675, 49 L.N.T.S. 435.

214 John F. Burns, "Court Delays Muslim Cleric's Extradition to U.S.," *N.Y. Times*, July 8, 2010. By September 2012, however, the Court had changed its mind and removed its ban on al-Masri's extradition to the United States. Dominic Casciani, "Abu Hamza: What Happens Next?," *BBC News* (U.K.), Sept. 25, 2012, *available at* www.bbc.com/news/uk-19715309 (last visited on May 28, 2016).

215 *Trabelsi v. Belgium*, Appl. No. 140/10, [2014] ECHR 893, Sept. 4, 2014 (citing to *Vinter and Others v. U.K.* [2013] ECHR 645, July 9, 2013.)

216 *E.g.*, Bruce Zagaris, *Colombia Extradites Rebel Woman Commander to the U.S. as Extraditions Since 1977 Reach 239*, 21 IELR 185, 185–86 (2005) [hereinafter Zagaris, *Rebel Woman Commander*] (in February 2005, the U.S. Government signed a new diplomatic note to the effect that it would not impose a life sentence on any persons extradited from Colombia); Jonathan Gilbert, "Argentina Agrees to Extradite American Who Sought Asylum," *N.Y. Times*, Jan. 3, 2015, at A8 (discussing an Argentine Supreme Court ruling that Kurt Sonnenfeld, a former Federal Emergency Management Agency (FEMA) spokesperson, could be extradited to the United States to face murder charges, based on the assurance provided by the Denver District Attorney's Office, that if extradited, prosecuted, and convicted, he would not be sentenced to life in prison without the possibility of parole in contravention of Argentina's Constitution).

downgrade to charges that carry reduced sentences or that allow for parole.[217]

Discriminatory Punishment. Various agreements proscribe the transfer of fugitives to pursuing States where evidence supports that an extraditee is likely to be punished specifically on account of his race, religion, nationality, political opinion, or possibly other grounds such as ethnic origin, color, mental or physical disability, gender, or sexual orientation. Under the London Scheme for Extradition within the Commonwealth, extradition is barred if it appears that the person at issue may be "punished ... by reason of race, religion, sex, nationality or political opinions."[218] Some multilateral crime suppression treaties[219] and domestic extradition laws of many States, including those as varied as Canada,[220] Dominica,[221] and Malaysia,[222] echo this standard. In an example of this principle, a U.S. trial court found (although it was later overturned on appeal) that a PIRA fugitive's extradition to Northern Ireland would run afoul of the U.S.-U.K. Supplementary Extradition Treaty of 1986, as he likely would be punished because of his religion and political opinions both upon his return to prison and his later release into the population at large.[223]

ii Procedural Matters

Along with substantive human rights law, two procedural matters[224] are relevant when assessing the prospect of an extradition denial in the

217 For example, in the case of Juan Manuel Casillas Jr., a Mexican national who was alleged to have murdered two teenage girls, the Los Angeles extraditions unit insisted on seeking an appropriately harsh penalty that in their judgment required, at a minimum, life imprisonment. Vanessa Maaskamp, *Extradition and Life Imprisonment*, 25 Loy. L.A. Int'l & Comp. L. Rev. 741, 752 (2003).

218 London Scheme, *supra* n.87, art. 13(a)(ii).

219 *E.g.*, Eur. Conv. on the Suppression of Terrorism, Jan. 27, 1977, art. 5, E.T.S. No. 90 ("Nothing in this Convention shall be interpreted as imposing an obligation to extradite if the requested State has substantial grounds for believing that the request for extradition for an offence mentioned in Article 1 or 2 has been made for the purpose of ... punishing a person on account of his race, religion, nationality or political opinion").

220 Canada Extradition Act, *supra* n.10, § 44(b).

221 Dominica Extradition Act, Act No. 6 of 1981, Feb. 19, 1981, art. 7(1)(c).

222 Malaysia Extradition Act, Act No. 479 of 1992, Feb. 21, 1992, § 8(c).

223 *In re Requested Extradition of Smyth*, 863 F. Supp. 1127 (N.D. Cal. 1994), *rev'd*, 61 F.3d 711 (9th Cir.), *amended*, 73 F.3d 887 (9th Cir. 1995), *cert. denied*, 518 U.S. 1022 (1996).

224 Technically, a third procedural matter involves individual standing, as a judge or magistrate may allow a fugitive in custody to contend that his prospective extradition to a given pursuing State would violate his human rights. Individuals may exercise the right to petition directly before certain supranational courts or supervisory bodies for

human rights context; these consist of the rule of non-inquiry and diplomatic assurances. While both militate *in favor of* extradition – and therefore are not "impediments" as such – their application is addressed herein because, as is shown below, the rule of non-inquiry is on the retreat these days and diplomatic assurances are replete with loopholes.

Rule of Non-Inquiry. When the host State operates under the rule of non-inquiry in the present context,[225] one of its courts evaluates an extradition request by refraining from any close examination of a pursuing State's good faith or motivation for seeking physical custody of the fugitive,[226] its judicial standards and procedures for prosecution, its likely treatment of the individual while in detention, or the fairness of

prospective (or past) injuries due to an alleged human rights treaty breach. Borelli, *supra* n.133, at 339; *e.g.*, First Optional Prot. to the ICCPR, Dec. 19, 1966, art. 1, 999 U.N.T.S. 302 (recogniz[ing] the competence of the [Human Rights] Committee to receive and consider communications from individuals subject to its jurisdiction who claim to be victims of a violation by that State Party of any of the rights set forth in the Covenant."); ACHR, *supra* n.136, art. 44 ("Any person ... may lodge petitions with the [Inter-Am. Comm'n on Human Rights] containing denunciations or complaints of violation of this Convention by a State Party."); Int'l Conv. on the Elimination of All Forms of Racial Discrimination (CERD), Dec. 21, 1965, art. 14, UNGA Res. 2106 (XX), 660 U.N.T.S. 195 (same). In addition, some States even now allow individuals to cite to human rights treaty provisions in their domestic courts, including in extradition proceedings, in order to avoid being transferred. Borelli, *supra* n.133, at 339; Dugard & van den Wyngaert, *supra* n.118, at 191 (citing courts in Germany, the Netherlands, and Switzerland). One effect of international human rights law to empower individuals to challenge the propriety of extradition on human rights grounds is to impede extraditions. The issue of individual standing will be addressed in the post-return context in Chapter 13.a.ii.

225 The rule of non-inquiry surfaces in public international law in two distinct situations but the term is seldom distinguished. The rule of non-inquiry at issue here arises in the extradition context, is applied by the host State court, and is forward-looking, *i.e.*, how a pursuing State is likely to manage or treat the subject individual once the transfer has been effected. The other scenario occurs when a State seizes an individual from another State's territory and returns him to face prosecution (*see* Chapter 13.a.i); in that instance, a heretofore *pursuing State* court may apply the rule of non-inquiry, *outside* of the extradition context and *retrospectively*, to determine whether it properly possesses personal jurisdiction to proceed with the case. *See* Patrick M. Haggan, Note, *Gov't Sponsored Extraterritorial Abductions in the New World Order: The Unclear Role of Int'l Law in United States Courts and Foreign Policy*, 17 SUFFOLK TRANSNAT'L L. REV. 438, 445 & n.33 (1994); William C. Birkett, Comment, *Cracks in the Foundation of Extraterritorial Law Enforcement – A Challenge to Basic Judicial Doctrines*, 15 S. ILL. U. L.J. 599, 609–10 (1991).

226 Aimée J. Buckland, *Offending Officials: Former Gov't Actors and the Political Offense Exception to Extradition*, 94 CAL. L. REV. 423, 435 (2006); *In re Extradition of Sacirbegovic*, 2005 U.S. Dist. LEXIS 707 (S.D.N.Y. Jan. 19, 2005).

any punishment that could be imposed upon conviction.[227] While the host State court still would ensure, for example, that the crime was extraditable, that the dual criminality requirement was satisfied, and that no double jeopardy attached, the court, by and large, would leave such matters as the existence of any political motivation behind the request or human rights-related conditions of the pursuing State's judicial system to the discretion of the executive branch.[228]

The logic underlying this rule is essentially five-fold: (i) to avoid impugning or impinging upon a pursuing State's sovereignty;[229] (ii) to extend good will and respect to another State, especially given that an applicable bilateral extradition treaty is presumed to be based on mutual recognition as to procedural fairness;[230] (iii) to help ensure criminals are brought to justice;[231] (iv) to avoid reciprocal scrutiny regarding one's own judicial proceedings and record of human rights compliance;[232] and (v) in recognition that "there is another branch of government [*i.e.*, the executive branch], which has both final say and greater discretion in [extradition] proceedings, to whom these questions are more properly addressed."[233]

[227] Tracey Hughes, Note, *Extradition Reform: The Role of the Judiciary in Protecting the Rights of a Requested Individual*, 9 B.C. Int'l & Comp. L. Rev. 293, 310 (1986); Neil Boister, *The Trend to 'Universal Extradition' over Subsidiary Universal Jurisdiction in the Suppression of Transnat'l Crime*, 2003 Acta Juridica 287, 304 & n.108 (2003); Bantekas & Nash, *supra* n.79, at 189–91 (noting that this rule reflects the traditional approach of State courts); Dugard & van den Wyngaert, *supra* n.118, at 189; *e.g.*, *Jhirad v. Ferrandina*, 536 F.2d 478 (2d Cir. 1976). An exception to this rule in U.S. jurisprudence can be found when an individual has been accused of an arguably political offense. Restatement (Third), *supra* n.133, § 476(2); *e.g.*, *Quinn v. Robinson*, 783 F.2d 776 (9th Cir. 1984), *cert. denied*, 479 U.S. 882 (1986).

[228] Hughes, *supra* n.227, at 303; *Eain v. Wilkes*, 641 F.2d 504, 516 (7th Cir.) ("the evaluations of the motivation behind a request for extradition so clearly implicate the conduct of this country's foreign relations as to be a matter better left to the Executive's discretion."), *cert. denied*, 454 U.S. 894 (1981).

[229] Andrew J. Parmenter, *Death by Non-Inquiry: The Ninth Circuit Permits the Extradition of a U.S. Citizen Facing the Death Penalty for a Non-Violent Drug Offense* [Prasoprat v. Benov, *421 F.3d 1009 (9th Cir. 2005)*], 45 Washburn L.J. 657, 665 (2006).

[230] Hughes, *supra* n.227, at 305; Bantekas & Nash, *supra* n.79, at 191.

[231] Parmenter, *supra* n.229, at 665.

[232] Stephen Dycus, et al., Counterterrorism Law 515 (2007); Bruce Zagaris, *Proposed France-China Extradition Treaty Raises Human Rights Issues*, 23 IELR 96 (2007).

[233] *United States v. Kin-Hong*, 110 F.3d 103, 111 (1st Cir. 1997). Another way to express this point is that a court is not as well-suited as a foreign affairs ministry to determine the conditions a fugitive likely would face upon return to another country. Parmenter, *supra* n.229, at 665. In Japan, both the judiciary and executive branches are competent to inquire into the position of human rights in a given pursuing State, but the Tokyo High

With the ascendancy of international human rights law, however, this traditional rule, which had once facilitated extraditions, has eroded.[234] As noted above, many States are obligated under various treaties not to extradite where substantial grounds exist for believing that an individual's human rights potentially could be in jeopardy.[235] In recent years, even courts in States like the United Kingdom and the United States, where the rule has long been applied,[236] *at times* have adopted a posture that is more actively protective of human rights,[237] although two particular departures are noteworthy.[238]

Court has held that it is more appropriate for the executive to make determinations related to predicting future events. Dugard & van den Wyngaert, *supra* n.118, at 191.

234 *See* DUFFY, *supra* n.55, at 111–12. Exceptionally, in the United States, the rule of non-inquiry experienced something of a shock wave when in a 1960 case, the U.S. Court of Appeals for the Second Circuit expressed "some disquiet" over the rule's application. *See Gallina*, 278 F.2d at 78–79 ("We can imagine situations where the relator, upon extradition, would be subject to procedures or punishment so antipathetic to a federal court's sense of decency as to require reexamination of the [non-inquiry] principle").

235 *See, e.g.*, Inter-Am. Conv. to Prevent and Punish Torture, *supra* n.136, art. 13(4) ("Extradition shall not be granted nor shall the person sought be returned when there are grounds to believe that his life is in danger, that he will be subjected to torture or to cruel, inhuman or degrading treatment, or that he will be tried by special or ad hoc courts in the requesting State."); Conv. Relating to the Status of Refugees, July 28, 1951, art. 33(1), 19 U.S.T. 6259, T.I.A.S. No. 6577, 189 U.N.T.S. 150 ("No Contracting State shall expel or return ('refouler') a refugee in any manner whatsoever to the frontiers of territories where his life or freedom would be threatened on account of his race, religion, nationality, membership of a particular social group or political opinion.").

236 *See, e.g.*, *Neely v. Henkel*, 180 U.S. 109 (1901); *In re Extradition of Ryan*, 360 F. Supp. 270, 274 (E.D.N.Y. 1973).

237 *See* Quigley, *supra* n.144, at 418; John T. Parry, *Int'l Extradition, the Rule of Non-Inquiry, and the Problem of Sovereignty*, 90 BOSTON U. L. REV. 1973 (2010) (noting an exception from the standard application at least when the political offense exclusion is at issue and in unusual penal or procedural circumstances); *Ahmad v. Wigen*, 726 F. Supp. 389, 405 (E.D.N.Y. 1989), *aff'd*, 910 F.2d 1063 (2d Cir.), *stay denied*, 111 S. Ct. 23 (1990). But such treatment is far from uniform. *See Hoxha v. Levi*, 465 F.3d 554, 563 (3d Cir. 2006) ("such humanitarian considerations [*i.e.*, whether the petitioner would face torture and possibly be murdered if extradited to Albania] are within the purview of the executive branch and generally should not be addressed by the courts in deciding whether petitioner is extraditable."); *Arronategui v. Nat'l High Ct. of Spain* [2012] EWHC 1170 (Admin), [2012] All E.R. (D) 81 (finding on appeal that the district judge should not have addressed whether the appellant could be convicted in Spain of an attempted assassination charge). B.U. L. Rev.

238 First, both the U.S. Courts of Appeals for the Fourth and Ninth Circuits have ruled that a 1998 federal statutory provision – *i.e.*, § 2242 of the Foreign Affairs Reform and Restructuring Act (FARRA) – precludes federal courts from reviewing a decision rendered by the U.S. Secretary of State to extradite a fugitive, despite claims that the subject likely will be tortured in the pursuing State. *Mironescu v. Costner*, 480 F.3d 664 (4th Cir. 2007); *Trinidad y Garcia v. Thomas*, 683 F.3d 952, 957 (9th Cir. 2012). Second, while

Courts in States that have not traditionally subscribed to the rule of non-inquiry often continue to probe for human rights concerns in connection with a contemplated extradition.[239] Furthermore, courts or bodies enforcing or applying the provisions of human rights treaties like the ECHR,[240] the ICCPR,[241] and the Refugee Convention of 1951[242] have added pressure to States parties by insisting that they factor into their decisions an assessment of prospective procedures, treatment, and punishment in the pursuing State prior to granting extradition.

Diplomatic Assurances. As indicated above, the purpose of diplomatic assurances is to persuade the host State that the subject of extradition (or deportation or expulsion, as the case may be) will be treated in compliance with applicable legal standards.[243] As Judge Johannes Silvis of the ECtHR commented in May 2014, diplomatic assurances, whether

Article 3 of the U.S.-U.K. Extradition Treaty of 1985 expressly called for U.S. judicial scrutiny of treatment of suspected terrorists in Northern Ireland courts (the so-called "Diplock Courts"), which were then perceived as procedurally unjust as they allowed "violently coerced confessions in court," lent heavy weight to "uncorroborated testimony of paid informants," and provided defendants with only "minimal access to lawyers," Matthew Murchison, Note, *Extradition's Paradox: Duty, Discretion, and Rights in the World of Non-Inquiry*, 43 STAN. J. INT'L L. 295, 303 (2007) (citing to U.S. Senate hearings in July 1986 based on then-Sen. John Kerry's testimony), the 2003 U.S.-U.K. Extradition Treaty ratified by the U.S. Senate in September 2006, did not contain that express exception to the non-inquiry rule. *Id.* at 303 n.62.

239 *E.g., In re Lujambio-Galdeano*, Conseil d'Etat, Assemblé Fr., Sept. 26, 1984, J.C.P. II No. 20346 (1985) [French text] (in a case involving the requested extradition from France to Spain of Basque separatists, the Conseil d'État found, as a prerequisite to extradition, that the Spanish judicial system respected individual rights and liberties).

240 *E.g., Drodz and Janousek v. France and Spain*, Appl. No. 12747/87, 14 EHRR, ¶ 110, June 26, 1992 *Soering Case, supra* n.117 (refusing to extradite because of anticipated cruel conditions of incarceration); *Kaboulov v. Ukraine*, Appl. No. 41015/04, 50 EHRR, Nov. 19, 2009 (finding an extradition to Kazakhstan would violate Article 3 of the ECHR because of the prospect of human rights violations in that country).

241 *E.g.*, HRC, *Concluding Observations of the Human Rights Committee: Sweden*, Apr. 24, 2002, U.N. Doc. CCPR/CO/74/SWE (2002).

242 *E.g., Sindona v. Grant*, 619 F.2d 167 (2d Cir.), *rev'd on other grounds*, 619 F.2d 167 (2d Cir. 1980).

243 For example, in November 2006, the Queen's Bench Division Court in the United Kingdom ruled that, absent strong contrary evidence, U.S. diplomatic assurances that alleged terrorists would neither be tried before a military commission nor designated as enemy combatants were sufficient to protect the appellants' human rights. Bruce Zagaris, *U.K. Appellate Court Affirms Reliance on U.S. Diplomatic Note in Extradition Case*, 23 IELR 85 (2007).

issued via the exchange of aide-mémoires or written MOUs, are to be treated as binding instruments of international law.[244] Such assurances most typically are sought in the following instances: (i) the pursuing State prosecutors will not seek or impose the death penalty (or a life sentence) in the event of conviction, (ii) the State authorities will not subject the individual to torture (or cruel, inhuman, or degrading treatment or punishment) while in its custody, (iii) the State will afford the individual a retrial in the event of an *in absentia* conviction, and (iv) the State will ensure the individual receives a fair trial in a regularly established court with a full set of procedural guarantees.[245]

Diplomatic assurances are far from a panacea, however, and in many instances this vehicle may not yield the desired result, leading to a denied extradition.[246] To begin, a diplomatic assurance must be conveyed by an authorized government official,[247] as opposed to, say, legal counsel, in order to carry the proper diplomatic authority.[248] Along these lines, some assurances may not pass legal muster, if, for instance, they are provided by a prosecutor who makes a promise that lies within the prerogative of a judge, and where because the executive and judicial branches are independent, the delivery of such an assurance cannot be guaranteed.[249]

244 Johannes Silvis, *Extradition and Human Rights – Diplomatic Assurances and Human Rights in the Extradition Context*, COE website, May 20, 2014, *available at* www.coe.int/t/dghl/standardsetting/pc-oc/PCOC_documents/Documents%202014/Special%20session%20Extradition%20-%20Extradition%20and%20human%20rights%20-%20Silvis.pdf (last visited on May 13, 2016).

245 Stanbrook & Stanbrook, *supra* n.55, at 153; *e.g., R. v. Governor of Brixton Prison, ex parte Armah* [1968] A.C. 192 (H. L.).

246 In the United States, the Secretary of State's determination as to whether diplomatic assurances are satisfactory is not reviewable. Abbell, *supra* n.37, at 130

247 In federalist systems, this may require assurances by state or provincial prosecutors, at least in those cases where the charges were lodged at the state or provincial level, even if domestic law requires that such assurances be transmitted between governments at the federal level.

248 *E.g., Ex parte Armah, supra* n.245.

249 For example, in the case of Jesus Amezcua, an infamous amphetamines trafficker, a trial court in Mexico found inadequate a U.S. diplomatic note assuring that prosecutors would not seek a life sentence, given that the executive and judicial branches are independent, leaving the judge to decide on a sentence notwithstanding prosecutor representations. Maaskamp, *supra* n.217, at 751. *But see* David Zapp, "Extradited Defendant Gets Life Sentence Despite Government's Promise," Legal Publications in Spanish, Vol. 1, No. 4, Mar. 19, 2007, at 1–2 (discussing how in 2002 Alex Restrepo was extradited to the United States to face life imprisonment notwithstanding diplomatic assurances by the S.D.N.Y prosecutor that he would not seek that penalty and, if the court nevertheless imposed it, the prosecutor would take action to have the sentence commuted to a term of years).

Some States are unwilling to provide the required assurances[250] as, for example, reverting charges for a capital offense to a life sentence with the possibility of parole.[251] Furthermore, an assurance may not be regarded as credible in cases where the pursuing State promises, say, not to engage in a certain objectionable practice but has a long record that cannot easily be discounted.[252] Moreover, under certain arrangements treaties, a transferee State may have an ongoing obligation to monitor implementation of the promised conduct with the understanding that, should it fall short, the extradition could be recalled.[253]

f Conflict Resolution and National Security Considerations

States also at times refuse an extradition request for any number of reasons related to the peaceful resolution of a conflict or national security concerns.

Conflict Resolution. In favor of restoring peace in its own or a neighboring country, a State may decide to at least temporarily suspend certain extraditions, albeit typically accompanied by conditions. For

[250] For example, in connection with the proposed extradition of Botswana national Jerry Ofense Pitsoe (Phale), a letter dated in Feb. 2010 "addressed to the National Prosecuting Authority of South Africa, the Deputy Director of Public Prosecutions in Botswana intimated that no assurance that the death penalty will not be imposed by the President of Botswana, would be forthcoming." *Tsebe and Another v. Minister of Home Affairs and Others*, Case Nos. 27682/10, 51010/10, So. Gauteng High Ct., Johannesburg, So. Afr., Sept. 22, 2011, 1 All SA 83, ¶ 48. *See also supra* n.208.

[251] *E.g.*, *In re Fidan*, Conseil d'État, Fr., Feb. 27, 1987, 1987 *Receuil Dalloz-Sirey (D.S.) Jur.* 261, 305 [French text] (barring an extradition where Turkey failed to agree not to impose the death penalty in a case involving the murder of a Turkish national residing in France).

[252] *E.g.*, *Suresh v. Canada (Minister of Citizenship and Immigration)*, Sup. Ct., Can., [2002] 1 S.C.R. 3 (the Canadian Supreme Court was unwilling to deport Chinese smuggling kingpin Lai Cheong Sing a/k/a Lai Changxing and his wife to the PRC despite a diplomatic note assuring Canada that they would not be tortured or executed upon their return to the PRC); *Ismoilov and Others v. Russia*, Appl. No. 2947/06, 49 EHRR, ¶ 127, Apr. 24, 2008 ("In its judgment in the Chahal case the Court cautioned against reliance on diplomatic assurances against torture from a State where torture is endemic or persistent."). After all, it should be noted that diplomatic assurances are not always honored. *See, e.g.*, James Brooke, "Canada's Haven: For Notorious Fugitives, Too?," *N.Y. Times*, Dec. 29, 2000 (noting how in January 2000, Canada deported Chinese national Yang Fong to the PRC on computer fraud charges involving US $130,000, for which the PRC had assured Canada the maximum penalty would be a ten-year prison sentence, and yet he was executed); Owen Bowcott, "U.K. Extradition Procedures May Breach Human Rights, Say Peers," *The Guardian*, Mar. 10, 2015 (reporting a concern voiced by the U.K. House of Lords Select Committee on Extradition Law that changes to prison conditions promised in such countries as Lithuania, Poland, and Trinidad & Tobago had not occurred).

[253] Duffy, *supra* n.55, at 114 (citing by way of example *Chahal v U.K.*, Appl. No. 22411/93, 23 EHRR 413, ¶ 80, Nov. 15, 1996.

example, in 2003, to secure peace with domestic paramilitary forces, the Gov't of Colombia extended a deal known as "Justicia y Paz" (Justice and Peace), pledging no extraditions and reduced prison sentences in exchange for their leaders surrendering, laying down their arms, and discontinuing any further criminal activity, such as narcotics trafficking, money laundering, and terrorist financing.[254] Although the program ultimately broke down by 2008, President Álvaro Uribe effectively halted extraditions of paramilitary individuals during that five-year period.[255]

In another case, as part of a peace plan to end violence in Liberia, Nigerian President Olusegun Obasanjo agreed, with the support of Western allies, to extend political asylum to then-Liberian President Charles Taylor despite an outstanding request for his surrender issued by the Special Court of Sierra Leone (SCSL). The political asylum was granted on a few conditions, namely, that Taylor relinquish control of the Liberian Government, leave the country, and not interfere in its domestic affairs, while understanding that he would be returned if and when Liberia wished to prosecute him for alleged crimes he committed in connection with Liberia's eleven-year civil war.[256] While Taylor was eventually sent to Liberia – as he was found to be meddling in Liberia's domestic affairs and Liberia's new President requested his extradition[257] – and, in turn, to the SCSL at The Hague to undergo prosecution, the political asylum kept him from being brought to justice for three years (2003–2006).[258]

[254] *See* Anne Kelsey, *Colombian Paramilitary Leader to be Extradited to the U.S.*, 24 IELR 217 (2008) (distinguishing the May 2008 Colombian extradition of paramilitary leader Carlos Jimenez (a/k/a Macaco) on the grounds of his continuing involvement in paramilitary activities from his prison cell).

[255] Anne Kelsey, *Colombia Extradites Paramilitary Leaders to the U.S.*, 24 IELR 272, 272–73 (2008). More than a decade earlier, Colombia President César Gaviria Trujillo "assured drug rings in that country that traffickers will not be extradited if they turn themselves in and confess to at least one drug crime. Two major drug ring figures, Jorge Luis Ochoa and his brother, Fabio Ochoa, have turned themselves in under that plan." David Johnston, "F.B.I. Arrests 2 Drug Suspects on High Seas," *N.Y. Times*, Feb. 22, 1991, at A16. The Bolivian Government followed suit a few months later, announcing that it would not extradite to the United States any drug traffickers if they surrendered in the next four months and agreed not to engage any longer in the cocaine trade. Michael Isikoff, "Bolivia Offers No-Extradition Deal to Traffickers," *Wash. Post*, July 19, 1991, at A13.

[256] Jason McClurg, *Pressure Mounts on Nigeria to Extradite Warlord Charles Taylor*, 21 IELR 272 (2005).

[257] *Id.* at 272–74.

[258] Hans Nichols and Lydia Polgreen, "Liberia Ex-Leader Faces War-Crimes Court," *N.Y. Times*, Apr. 4, 2006 (noting the venue transfer from Sierra Leone to The Hague on

National Security. The host State might well refuse (or perhaps postpone) an extradition for various security-related reasons, such as fear of retaliation by terrorists or drug cartels, as a bargaining chip for the release of hostages, to afford an opportunity to interrogate an individual about foreign intelligence, or to set an example for crime suppression with the local population by holding the criminal proceedings at home.

Examples of States dodging an extradition request out of terrorist intimidation or retribution concerns include the following:

(i) largely out of fear that terrorism would be directed upon French citizens, the *Chambre d'Accusation* of the Paris Court of Appeals in January 1977 rebuffed both West German and Israeli requests for the extradition of Mohammad Daoud Oudeh (Abu Daoud), the Palestinian terrorist leader behind the seizing and slaying of eleven Israeli athletes during the 1972 Munich Olympics, and arranged for his release on questionable procedural technicalities;[259]

(ii) in 1985, fearing a violent PLO backlash, Italy refused to cooperate with an incipient U.S. extradition request for the PLO terrorists who had hijacked the *Achille Lauro* cruise ship, and even evidently helped Mohammed Abu Abbas, its alleged mastermind, escape to Yugoslavia;[260] and

(iii) in April 1990, the day after "12 Colombian police officers were murdered, another eight were wounded, and a Colombian senator was kidnapped by cartel assassins," President Virgilio Barco declared that Colombia would not proceed with the extradition of any Medellín drug cartel leaders, including the notorious Pablo Escobar, despite the fact that only seven months earlier,

account of concerns about instability in Sierra Leone, given the recent departure of the last of the U.N. peacekeepers).

259 *See* Sidney Liskofsky, *The Abu Daoud Case: Law or Politics*, 7 Isr. Y.B. Hum. Rts. 66 (1977); D. Cameron Findlay, *Abducting Terrorists Overseas for Trial in the United States: Issues of Int'l and Domestic Law*, 23 Tex. Int'l L.J. 1, 10 (1988). In another example of European hesitance in the face of potential PLO retribution, despite outstanding arrest warrants, neither France nor Switzerland extradited, let alone apprehended, Palestinian terrorists George Habash (PFLP) or Ahmed Jibril (PFLP-General Command) when they visited those countries, respectively, for medical treatment in 1992. Charles Fenyvesi, ed., "Affaire célèbre, Washington Whispers," *U.S.N.& W.R.*, Feb. 24, 1992, at 26; Douglas Kash, *Abducting Terrorists under PDD-39: Much Ado About Nothing New*, 13 Am. Univ. Int'l L. Rev. 139, 147 (1997–98).

260 Laflin, *supra* n.44, at 318; Findlay, *supra* n.259, at 10; John Walcott, *et al.*, "Getting Even," *Newsweek*, Oct. 21, 1985, at 25–26.

> Colombia had extradited fifteen alleged drug traffickers to the United States.[261]

States also may be prone to forgo extradition where doing so is viewed as the leverage needed to help release citizens taken hostage.[262] For example, in January 1987, West German authorities in Frankfurt arrested Mohammed Ali Hamadei, who, in June 1985, along with fellow terrorists, had hijacked TWA Flight 847, forced the plane down in Beirut, murdered U.S. Navy diver Robert Stethem, and held thirty-nine passengers and crew hostage; within eight days, two German citizens were kidnapped in Beirut, and West Germany was told that the hostages would be released partly on the condition that Hamadei was not extradited to the United States, which was then busily preparing its official request. Due to concern about the safety of the German hostages, Chancellor Helmut Kohl ultimately decided not to extradite Hamadei but rather to prosecute him in a German court on the charge of kidnapping, and the hostages were released.[263]

Likewise, in December 2004, Colombian President Álvaro Uribe announced that he was prepared to halt the extradition of FARC leader Ricardo Palmera (alias Simón Trinidad) to the United States in exchange for the leftist paramilitary group's release of sixty-three hostages, including three U.S. Department of Defense (DoD) contractors. While the FARC did not accept those terms, the proposed bargain reflects how non-extradition can be used as leverage to manage hostage situations.[264]

A State also may believe a person in its custody has valuable intelligence –whether about a foreign State or an organized criminal enterprise, and whether about activities, policies, plans, resources, or networks – that could be extracted through effective interrogation. That State may therefore decide not to extradite (or at least postpone any transfer) in favor of exploiting this intelligence-gathering opportunity. For example, despite

[261] "World in Brief: Colombia: Barco Makes Offer to Drug Cartel Chief," *L.A. Times*, Apr. 5, 1990, at 1; Michael R. Pontoni, *Authority of the United States to Extraterritorially Apprehend and Lawfully Prosecute Int'l Drug Traffickers and Other Fugitives*, 21 CAL. W. INT'L L.J. 215, 216 (1990–91). *See also* Laflin, *supra* n.44, at 319 (in 1986, the Colombian Supreme Court voided the law that enabled the U.S.-Colombian Extradition Treaty; most believe that decision was the result of fear and intimidation arising out of the narco-terrorist response to extraditions to the United States).

[262] Bassiouni, *Unlawful Seizures, supra* n.2, at 63–64.

[263] Findlay, *supra* n.259, at 10–11; David M. Kennedy, *et al.*, *The Extradition of Mohammed Hamadei*, 31 HARV. INT'L L.J. 5, 5–11 (1990).

[264] Bruce Zagaris, *Colombia Extradites FARC Leader*, 21 IELR 52 (2005); Zagaris, *Rebel Woman Commander, supra* n.216, at 186.

a February 2002 U.S. request for the extradition of Ahmed Omar Saeed Sheikh, the chief suspect behind the kidnapping and murder of American journalist Daniel Pearl, Pakistani law enforcement denied that request, reportedly at least in part to question Ahmed Omar about his terrorist ties.[265]

Another national security-related rationale provided for the denied extradition of Ahmed Omar Saeed Sheikh came from Pakistan President Pervez Musharraf himself: to ensure that "their punishment at home could serve as an example to those defying his crackdown on terrorism."[266]

* * * * *

The last four chapters focused on extradition and its diverse array of impediments. The next chapter, which alone comprises Part III of this book, analyzes which measures a pursuing State can take collaterally or remedially to secure a fugitive's custody through extradition when a request has been denied or its prospects, without something more, look dim.

[265] "Pakistan Refuses to Extradite Pearl Murder Suspect," *China Daily*, Feb. 28, 2002.
[266] AP, "Pakistan Resists U.S. Extradition," *Wall St. J.*, May 6, 2002, at A18.

PART III

Remedial or Collateral Means to Secure Extradition

8

Initiatives, Inducements, and Interventions

When the host State has denied a request for extradition, it has signaled a reluctance to grant extradition, or an apparent impediment to extradition otherwise exists, what recourse, if any, does a pursuing State have to secure the custody of a fugitive short of exploring alternatives to extradition? There are, in fact, various means and methods available to a pursuing State *via extradition* either by lodging a challenge, revamping its approach, applying conditions or leverage, or seeking external engagement. These may be bundled into three categories as follows: (i) those based on unilateral activity, (ii) those involving bilateral diplomacy, and (iii) those entailing a third-party role.

a Options Based on Unilateral Activity

Appeal the Decision Denying Extradition. Where permitted under domestic law or the applicable extradition treaty, the pursuing State at interest may try to appeal an extradition denial. Although uncommon, it is possible that a higher-level court (or arbitration panel, as the case may be[1]) could overturn a judicial or executive branch decision that refused an extradition request.[2] In the United States, this is especially difficult because extradition orders are generally not appealable under

[1] *E.g.*, Charles Cheney Hyde, *The Extradition Case of Samuel Insull Sr. in Relation to Greece*, 28 AJIL 307, 312 (1934) (discussing an arbitration appeal under the U.S.-Greece Extradition Treaty in the case of Samuel Insull Sr.).

[2] Although ultimately unsuccessful, the United States sought a review by Portugal's Supreme Court after it had denied the U.S. request for the extradition of American national George Wright. Bruce Zagaris, *Portuguese Supreme Court Rejects U.S. Appeal on George Wright's Extradition*, 28 IELR 91, 92 (2012). The United States also sought an appeal of an Austrian court's denial of an extradition request for Ukrainian billionaire Dmytro Firtash on bribery charges. Alan Cullison and Nicole Lundeen, "Austrian Court Denies U.S. Request to Extradite Dmytro Firtash," *Wall St. J.*, May 1, 2015.

long-established law,[3] and can only be challenged via a *habeas corpus* petition.[4]

Nevertheless, an example of a successful appeal occurred in a case implicating the 1985 Supplementary U.S.-U.K. Extradition Treaty that authorized a specific exception to the rule against extradition appeals.[5] James Joseph Smyth, an IRA member sentenced to twenty years for the murder of an off-duty prison official in 1978, managed to escape from Northern Ireland's Maze maximum security prison in 1983 and fled to the United States, where, upon his arrest for use of a fraudulent passport in 1992, the United Kingdom sought his extradition to serve out the remainder of his term.[6] While Smyth's argument convinced the trial court judge that his return to the United Kingdom would expose him to disproportionate punishment because of his political views and based on his prior treatment both in and out of prison, the U.S. Court of Appeals for the Ninth Circuit reversed that ruling, finding that he was unable to support his claim by a preponderance of the evidence, and ordered that he be extradited.[7]

Modify the Charges to Ensure Extraditability. To the extent that the host State does not recognize a particular charge as extraditable under its own law or denies extradition with respect to a specific offense (*e.g.*, a lack of dual criminality), pursuing State prosecutors can reconsider their charges,[8] even if they may not yield as significant a criminal penalty, so as to ensure at

[3] *See* p. 162 in Chapter 4.

[4] *In re Metzger*, 46 U.S. (5 How.) 176, 191 (1847); *In re Mackin*, 668 F.2d 122, 125–30 (2d Cir. 1981).

[5] Supplementary Treaty Concerning the Extradition Treaty between the Gov't of the United States of America and the Gov't of the United Kingdom of Great Britain and Northern Ireland Signed at London on 8 June 1972, June 25, 1985, art. 3(b), 24 ILM 1105 (1985), *reprinted in* S. Exec. Rep. No. 17, 99th Cong., 2d Sess. (1986) (a grant of extradition shall be immediately appealable "if the person sought establishes to the satisfaction of the competent judicial authority by a preponderance of the evidence that the request for extradition has in fact been made with a view to try or punish him on account of his race, religion, nationality, or political opinions, or that he would, if surrendered, be prejudiced at his trial or punished, detained or restricted in his personal liberty by reason of his race, religion, nationality or political opinions.").

[6] *In re Requested Extradition of Smyth*, 863 F. Supp. 1127 (N.D. Cal. 1994), *rev'd*, 61 F.3d 711 (9th Cir.), *amended*, 73 F.3d 887 (9th Cir. 1995), *cert. denied*, 116 S. Ct. 2258 (1996).

[7] *Id.*, 61 F.3d at 720.

[8] Many extradition treaties stipulate that once a request for an individual's extradition has been denied, a subsequent request is not allowed *for the same offense. E.g.*, Treaty on Extradition, U.S.-Arg., Jan. 21, 1972, art. 20, 23 T.I.A.S 7510 (1972). *But see* Montevideo Conv. on Extradition, Dec. 26, 1933, art. 12, 49 Stat. 3111, reprinted in 28 AJIL 65 (1934) (no extradition application is permitted following a denial for "the same alleged *act*") (emphasis supplied).

a minimum that extradition (and eventually prosecution on some ground) can occur. For example, when Germany sought the extradition of Uri Brodsky, a suspected Israeli intelligence officer, for involvement in the assassination of a Hamas leader in Dubai in January 2010, and Poland was unwilling to extradite him on espionage charges because Poland did not regard espionage against Germany as punishable under Polish law, Germany reframed the request to seek Brodsky's extradition for passport fraud in connection with the assassination.[9]

b Options Involving Bilateral Diplomacy

Negotiate and Enter Into a Bilateral Extradition Treaty or Functionally Equivalent Agreement. In some instances, the host State will refuse to extradite absent an operative extradition arrangement with a particular pursuing State.[10] In such circumstances, one option is to expeditiously undertake to negotiate, execute, and (as necessary) ratify[11] a bilateral extradition treaty or other law enforcement cooperation agreement authorizing the transfer of physical custody of a fugitive between the parties for prosecution or punishment purposes. Although that exercise normally can take months or even years to achieve, with sufficient political will it could occur more quickly and, once in effect, such a legal instrument could be relied upon to formally effect extradition.

For example, in April 2004, promptly following high-level political discussions between Equatorial Guinea (E.G.) and Zimbabwe, the latter's President, Robert Mugabe, initially agreed to change his nation's extradition policy and execute a bilateral extradition treaty with E.G. in order to legally accommodate the transfer of seventy suspected mercenaries then in Zimbabwe charged with conspiring to overthrow the E.G. Government.[12]

[9] Bruce Zagaris, *Polish Court Approves Extradition of Israeli Suspect to Germany for Role in Hamas Assassination*, 26 IELR 353 (2010). The change in tactics paid off: Brodsky was extradited in August 2010 to Germany on the passport fraud charge. AP, "Poland Extradites 'Uri Brodsky' to Germany," *Ynetnews.com*, Aug. 12, 2010, *available at* www.ynetnews.com/articles/0,7340,L-3935278,00.html (last visited on May 16, 2016).

[10] *See* Chapter 7.a.

[11] The ratification step would only be required for dualist States that do not treat the execution of an international treaty as becoming incorporated immediately and verbatim into its domestic law, as would be the case for monist States. *See generally* Malcolm N. Shaw, Public International Law 131–32 (6th ed. 2008).

[12] *See* "Zimbabwe Issues Extradition Agreement with Equatorial Guinea," *Voice of America*, Apr. 28, 2004. Notably, however, a few months later, President Mugabe rejected the

Sometimes, States may already be in the midst of extradition treaty negotiations and a pending case triggers its rapid conclusion, as illustrated by the *Najim* case. Although U.S. intelligence knew the whereabouts of Eyad Ismail Najim, the alleged driver of the van carrying the explosives that were detonated in the underground parking lot of New York City's World Trade Center in February 1993, his extradition from Jordan could not be effected until an extradition treaty could be concluded between the two States. As a result, the United States and Jordan quickly finalized their ongoing negotiations, and within days of its completion, Najim was transferred aboard a U.S. Government plane from Amman.[13]

Renegotiate the Treaty Provisions Governing Bilateral Extradition to Address Impediments to Implementation. Where a pursuing State suffers repeated denials of its extradition requests from the host State, the former may choose to renegotiate the terms of the applicable treaty via the execution of a treaty addendum or protocol. Alternatively, a pursuing State could prompt the host state to enter into a separate but related treaty that rectifies the problematic provision(s) or fills in the gap(s) responsible for the denials, possibly by pledging to abstain from certain conduct deemed objectionable to the other State.

For example, in 1994, after it was discovered that neither the U.S.-Mexico Extradition Treaty of 1978 nor any other treaty between those two States specifically addressed cross-border seizures – and that such a practice had become a bone of contention and the basis for extradition denials – the United States and Mexico negotiated and signed a Treaty to Prohibit Transborder Abductions, which in exchange for the United States agreeing to discontinue any practice of State-sponsored abductions [*i.e.*, SDOs], Mexico would be more amenable to extraditing its own nationals to the United States.[14]

extradition request on the grounds that no extradition treaty was in effect with E.G. at the time of the arrest in March 2004. Andrew Meldrum, "Mugabe Refuses Extradition," *The Guardian*, Aug. 23, 2004.

[13] Robin Wright & Ronald J. Ostrow, "Bomb Suspect Extradited to the U.S. from Jordan," *L.A. Times*, Aug. 3, 1995. In March 1994, Najim was convicted and sentenced to 240 years in prison. *Id.*

[14] Treaty to Prohibit Transborder Abductions, U.S.-Mex., Nov. 23, 1994, 31 U.S.T. 5059, *reprinted in* 5 Michael Abbell & Bruno A. Ristau, International Judicial Assistance: Criminal A-676.3 to 676.6 (1990 & 1995 Supp.); *see also* Melanie M. Laflin, Note, *Kidnapped Terrorists: Bringing Int'l Criminals to Justice Through Irregular Rendition and Other Quasi-Legal Options*, 26 J. Legis. 315, 330 (2000). That Treaty, however, was never submitted to the U.S. Senate and therefore has yet to be ratified. Steven W. Bender, Run for the Border: Vice and Virtue in U.S.-Mexico Border Crossings 25 (2012).

Propose that as a Condition of Extradition any Assigned Criminal Sentence of a Host State National Shall Occur in the Host State. Some domestic laws require that any time a State extradites one of its own nationals for prosecution purposes, that individual must be returned to face any assigned punishment in its own criminal justice system.[15] This practice also is recognized in the Convention on the Transfer of Sentenced Persons.[16] Given the apparent appeal of this approach, in a particular circumstance, and especially where its laws are so amenable, the host State might be persuaded to extradite one of its nationals on the condition that he serve any imposed criminal sentence in his own country.[17]

Offer Positive or Negative Inducements or Apply Diplomatic Pressure to Enhance Extradition Prospects.[18] There are also a host of diplomatic "carrots" and "sticks" a pursuing State can employ to encourage the host State to extradite a given fugitive. A pursuing State could, for example, propose to increase its foreign aid appropriation or offer debt relief to the host State in exchange for a favorable decision on an extradition request.[19] A pursuing State also could agree to limit the

[15] *See* Abraham Abramovsky & Jonathan I. Edelstein, *The Post-Sheinbein Israeli Extradition Law: Has It Solved the Extradition Problems Between Israel and the United States or Has It Merely Shifted the Battleground?*, 35 VAND. J. TRANSNAT'L L. 1 (2002) (discussing Israeli law with respect to Israeli residents at the time the extradition request is issued); Const. of the Kingdom of the Netherlands 2008, art. 2(3).

[16] Conv. on the Transfer of Sentenced Persons, Mar. 21, 1983, art. 2(2), E.T.S. 112 ("A person sentenced in the territory of a Party may be transferred to the territory of another Party, in accordance with the provisions of this Convention, in order to serve the sentence imposed on him.").

[17] *See* ABA, "Overcoming Legal Challenges in Extradition," Charles A. Caruso, Asia Law Initiative (undated), at 7, *available at* http://www.americanbar.org/content/dam/aba/directories/roli/raca/asia_raca_charlescaruso_overcoming.authcheckdam.pdf (last visited on May 16, 2016) (referring to such measures as "conditional extradition").

[18] Sometimes, diplomatic pressure by one country can be so powerful that it elicits an immediate political response in another. This occurred, for example, in January 2012, when "[w]ithin 24 hours of [Honduran] President Porfirio Lobo's meeting with U.S. officials in Miami ... the Honduran Congress passed a constitutional reform to allow in principle the extradition of Honduran nationals charged with certain crimes." Hannah Stone, "With Extradition Law, Honduras Outsources Justice to U.S.," *Insightcrime.org*, Jan. 30, 2012, *available at* http://www.insightcrime.org/news-analysis/with-extradition-law-honduras-outsources-justice-to-us (last visited on May 16, 2016) (noting that "[t]he move to allow extradition seems likely to have been influenced by U.S. pressure ... and it will probably be used primarily to send suspects [sic] to the U.S.").

[19] *Cf.* Jovan Kovacic, "U.S. Envoy Warns Serb President to Aid Tribunal," *Boston Globe*, Nov. 8, 1996, at A2 (in November 1996, the U.S. Asst. Sec'y of State for Human Rights indicated to Serbian President Slobodan Milosević, who was then facing a war-ravaged economy, that international financial assistance depended on far more cooperation with the ICTY) (hybrid

maximum prison sentence upon conviction for a fugitive to a level no higher than what could be imposed by the host State for the same offense.[20] In the broader context of normalizing political relations with Cuba in the spring of 2015, and in particular removing Cuba from the list of countries considered to be State sponsors of terrorism, the United States expressly hoped to find Cuba more amenable to returning Americans who have sought refuge from U.S. justice in the Caribbean island.[21]

More often, however, pursuing States rely on *disincentives*, such as threats to impose economic sanctions on the host State; raise import tariffs on its goods; discontinue foreign development assistance or loans;[22] reduce or cease law enforcement cooperation of one kind or another;[23] or apply greater travel restrictions on its nationals to pursuing

court example); Rodney D. Sieh, "Obama Ties Debt Relief to Taylor Handover," *Nigeria/Africa Masterweb News Report*, June 22, 2005, *available at* http://www.africamasterweb.com/AdSense/ObamaTiesDebtReliefTaylorHandover.html (last visited on May 16, 2016) (as U.S. Senator from Illinois, Barack Obama urged that any debt relief for Nigeria must be conditioned on the Nigerian Government's surrender of former Liberian dictator Charles Taylor to the Special Court for Sierra Leone (SCSL) (hybrid court example). Sometimes, however, the dynamic operates in the opposite direction; a State sweetens the pot in order to *dissuade* a pursuing State from continuing to seek extradition. For example, in 1934, the U.S. Government proposed to Mexico that the United States would return a fugitive named López to Mexico, who had been seized by bounty-hunters Hernandez and Villareal and brought to the United States, in exchange for Mexico dropping its extradition request for Hernandez on kidnapping charges. M. CHERIF BASSIOUNI, INTERNATIONAL EXTRADITION AND WORLD PUBLIC ORDER 141 n.42 (1974).

20 *See, e.g.*, Bruce Zagaris, *Brazil Extradites Alleged Colombian Cocaine Capo to the U.S.*, 24 IELR 432 (2008) (U.S. officials were willing to limit Juan Carlos Ramirez-Abadia's maximum prison term to thirty years if convicted, the same level to which he had been sentenced earlier by Brazil for money laundering and other offenses, in order to encourage his extradition from Brazil). This type of inducement also could be made directly to the fugitive; such discussions are addressed in Chapter 12.b.i.

21 *See* Theodore Schleifer, "U.S. Eyes Extradition of Fugitives Living in Cuba," *CNN*, Apr. 16, 2015, *available at* www.cnn.com/2015/04/15/politics/cuba-extradition-fugitives / (last visited on May 28, 2016)

22 *See, e.g.*, Peter Finn, "Serb Leaders Hand Over Milosevic for Trial by War Crimes Tribunal; Tribunal Lives up to Its Promise," *Wash. Post*, June 29, 2001, at A1 (discussing "pressure from western governments to [extradite Milosević] or forgo development aid") (international criminal tribunal example).

23 For example, it was reported that "Russian Foreign Minister Sergei Lavrov warned U.S. Secretary of State Hillary Rodham Clinton that Russia's cooperation on anti-narcotics efforts in Afghanistan might be curtailed unless [arms smuggler Viktor] Bout was freed." AP, "Suspected Arms Trafficker Flown to NYC," *CBS New York*, Nov. 17, 2010.

State territory. In addition, in the event the fugitive were a passenger on a flagged vessel at sea, a pursuing State could advise the master of the ship that failure to produce the fugitive would result in a forfeiture action against the ship for aiding and abetting the escape of an actual or alleged offender.[24]

In July 1999, in an effort to goad Afghanistan's Taliban leadership into ceasing refuge for and turning over Usama Bin Laden in connection with the August 1998 bombings of the U.S. Embassies in Kenya and Tanzania that killed twelve Americans and nearly 300 Africans while injuring thousands more, U.S. President Bill Clinton issued an Executive Order freezing all Taliban assets held in the United States, barring all U.S. imports of Afghan products, and prohibiting the export of all U.S. goods and services to Afghanistan (except for humanitarian purposes).[25] Likewise, in September 1972, after a Paraguayan court denied extradition to the United States of Auguste Joseph Ricord, a Corsican drug trafficker and a principal member of the "French Connection," for conspiracy to smuggle narcotics into the United States, a high-level U.S. State Department envoy threatened to cut off millions of dollars in U.S. foreign aid and American support for international development banks loans to Paraguay to encourage Paraguay to extradite Ricord; perhaps coincidentally, a Paraguayan Court of Appeals granted the extradition a week later.[26]

Such diplomatic overtures need not be confined to economic, commercial, or financial pressures; they also can threaten or undertake to create a foreign policy embarrassment for the host State or otherwise humiliate its government officials for their complicity in crimes or for other questionable conduct. For example, in the late 1980s, prior to his seizure by U.S. agents in 1988, "U.S. authorities reportedly threatened to name Honduran military officers tied to the drug trade in order to motivate Honduras to surrender Juan Ramón Matta-Ballesteros, one of most notorious drug traffickers in the world."[27]

[24] *E.g.*, Clifton Daniel, "Seizure of Eisler Assailed in London by Polish Embassy," *N.Y. Times*, May 16, 1949, at 1, 3 (describing how such threats were communicated by the U.S. to the master of the Polish liner *Batory*).

[25] U.S. Exec. Order No. 13,129, 64 Fed. Reg. 36,759 (1999); *see also* John Lancaster, "Clinton Bans Trading with Taliban Militia; Afghanistan Rulers Accused of Giving Terrorist Refuge," *Wash. Post*, July 7, 1999, at A15.

[26] Ethan A. Nadelmann, *The Evolution of United States Involvement in the Int'l Rendition of Fugitive Criminals*, 25 N.Y.U. J. Int'l L. & Pol. 813, 862–64 (1993).

[27] Paul Lieberman, "Camarena Case Spotlight Shifts to L.A. Unit's Tactics," *L.A. Times*, May 7, 1990, at A1, A23.

In June 2007, to spur the U.K. Government into extraditing Boris Berezovsky, a Russian billionaire, critic of Russian President Vladimir Putin, and U.K. political asylee, on fraud charges, Russia's Federal Security Service (FSB) opened a criminal investigation into allegations that Berezovsky and murdered ex-KGB agent Alexander Litvinenko were British spies.[28] In a similar vein, there was speculation in 1998 that Russia might be willing to extradite Shakhin Musaev, former chief of the General Staff of the Armed Forces of Azerbaijan charged with being an agent of the GRU and plotting attacks against Azerbaijani President Heidar Aliyev, as a *quid pro quo* for Azerbaijan not publicly exposing illegal Russian arms shipments to Armenia, a major source of embarrassment and sensitivity in their bilateral relations.[29]

Dispatch a Government Official or Prosecutor to Engage Host State Officials in Discussions. To prompt host State officials to reconsider their resistance to extradition, or to encourage more cooperation generally in the delivery of fugitives, a senior government official or prosecutor from the pursuing State could travel to the host State and try to engage its counterpart officials in a dialogue to find a possible way forward.[30] In March 2015, Wang Qishan, who "heads the ruling [Chinese] Communist party's graft watchdog, the Central Commission for Discipline Inspection," was planning a visit to the United States to explore ways of recovering Chinese criminals who had fled overseas.[31] Such an approach also was undertaken by Queens, New York, District Attorney John J. Santucci, together with U.S. DoJ officials, in connection with seeking the extradition, over Italian Government objections, of Anthony Sciacca, a twenty-seven-year-old living in Sicily accused of killing a restaurant owner in Queens a decade earlier.[32] A DoJ spokesperson noted "it was 'not unprecedented' for a local prosecutor to take part in

[28] Bruce Zagaris, *Russia Opens Criminal Investigation into Alleged British Espionage*, 23 IELR 297, 297–98 (2007).

[29] George Ginsburgs, *Russia's Practice of Extraditing Political Offenders to Azerbaijan: Rendition Refused*, 16 Crim. L.F. 303, 316–17 (2005).

[30] Where a personal friendship happens to exist between senior officials in the two governments (*e.g.*, presidents, attorneys general, or foreign ministers), that relationship also can prove useful in advancing the agenda toward greater extradition cooperation.

[31] Tom Mitchell, "China Graft Tsar Plans U.S. Visit Amid Drive to Extradite Fugitives," *Financial Times*, Mar. 17, 2015.

[32] Joseph P. Fried, "Santucci to Go to Italy in Battle over a Slaying," *N.Y. Times*, July 14, 1990, at 24.

discussions abroad about disputed matters involving fugitives fleeing criminal charges in the prosecutor's jurisdiction."[33]

c Options Entailing a Third-Party Role

Request the Re-extradition of a Fugitive. A pursuing State (State C) can seek to have a fugitive transferred into its physical custody after he has first been extradited from the original transferor State (State A) to the original transferee State, which, upon securing custody, becomes the new host State (State B)[34] with respect to offenses at issue prior to the initial extradition. Despite a surprising paucity of provisions governing re-extradition in multilateral and bilateral extradition treaties and in domestic extradition law itself, the general rule is that before State B re-extradites the fugitive to State C, State B must first obtain the consent of State A (or at least offer it the opportunity to have the fugitive instead),[35] given that re-extradition is viewed as an exception to the specialty rule designed to protect the interests of the original transferor State and the rights of the fugitive alike.[36]

Departures from the general rule requiring State A's consent may apply, however, such as when a fugitive fails to leave State B's territory

33 *Id.*

34 Re-extradition to State C is not permitted in instances where State B obtained physical custody of the fugitive via transfer from the ICC. Clive Nicholls, et al., eds., The Law of Extradition and Mutual Assistance 58 (2d ed. 2007).

35 *See* Ivor Stanbrook & Clive Stanbrook, Extradition: Law and Practice 61 (2d ed. 2000); *e.g.*, Eur. Conv. on Extradition, Dec. 13, 1957, art. 15, E.T.S. No. 24; Portugal, Int'l Judicial Co-operation in Crim. Matters, Law No. 144/99, Aug. 31, 1999, art. 34 *as amended*, (translated text) (allowing re-extradition where Portugal consents and the transfer operates under the same terms established for an extradition request to Portugal). The United States can re-extradite only with the consent of State A *unless* another exception to the specialty rule under the applicable treaty would permit State C to prosecute or punish the individual of interest for an offense other than that for which he was originally extradited. Michael Abbell, Extradition to and from the United States 91–92 (2010); *United States ex rel. Donnelly v. Mulligan*, 74 F.2d 220 (2d Cir. 1934); American Law Inst., Restatement (Third) of the Foreign Relations Law of the United States, May 14, 1986 (1987), § 478.

36 *See* CoE, *Extradition: European Standards – Explanatory Notes and Minimum Standards*, Dec. 2006, at 38, *available at* www.coe.int/t/dghl/standardsetting/pc-oc/978-92-8716076-8.pdf (last visited on May 16, 2016) [hereinafter *European Standards*] (additionally noting the importance of seeking the individual's view of the matter). Re-extradition can create problems since State C would not be bound by the bilateral extradition treaty, including any particular conditions, under which the original extradition took place. Sir Robert Jennings & Sir Arthur Watts, eds., 1 Oppenheim's International Law 960 n.4 (9th ed. 1992).

within a specified time frame after his discharge,[37] when he voluntarily returns to State B's territory after leaving it,[38] or when the fugitive volunteers to be re-extradited.[39] Should concurrent requests for extradition be submitted by two States (B and C), State A ought to indicate whether it disapproves of re-extradition to State C when making its extradition decision to State B,[40] or else it will be deemed to have forfeited any such right of control.

Re-extradition may be possible to State C even when State B finds no criminal culpability in the extradited individual following prosecution. For example, in a 1999 case, an English Divisional Court upheld the United Kingdom's re-extradition of a fugitive named Johnson to Australia (State C) on a charge of conspiracy to defraud, based on a request by Australia submitted during U.K. criminal proceedings and the confirmed re-extradition consent by Austria (State A), notwithstanding the fact that the United Kingdom (State B) ultimately acquitted Johnson on similar fraud charges.[41]

Seek an Independent Ruling that the Fugitive in Question is Not a Host State National in the Hope of Foreclosing an Extradition Denial on the Basis of Nationality. Where the fugitive's nationality is the host State's exclusive or even principal basis for denying extradition, but where such nationality remains ambiguous, a pursuing State could seek an outside, neutral mechanism to render a favorable determination. For example, Japan denied Peru's extradition request since July 2001 for Alberto Fujimori, former President of Peru, on the grounds that he was a Japanese national, and Japanese law bars the extradition of its nationals.[42] Although Peru never actually challenged that decision, it

37 *E.g., Donnelly*, 74 F.2d at 223 (ruling that the prisoner has one month after gaining his liberty to return to France, which had extradited him to the United States, or else the United States would be free to consider extraditing him to Canada based on its pending request).

38 *See* discussion pertaining to specialty in Chapter 7.c.ii.

39 *E.g.*, Eur. Conv. on Extradition, *supra* n.35, art. 15; Framework Decision on the European Arrest Warrant & the Surrender Procedures Between Member States, June 13, 2002, art. 28(2), 2002/584/JHA, OJEC 1–20, L190/1 of July 18, 2002 [hereinafter Framework Decision on the EAW].

40 *European Standards, supra* n.36, at 38. Under the EAW, a member State may notify the General Secretariat of the CoE that it has given its *a priori* open-ended consent to designated member States for re-extradition. Framework Decision on the EAW, *supra* n.39, art. 28(1).

41 *R. v. Sec'y of State for the Home Dep't, ex parte Johnson* [1999] QB 1174, [1999] 2 WLR 932.

42 *See* Renee Dopplick, "International Laws Aid Fujimori's Extradition," *Inside Justice* (blog), Oct. 15, 2006, *available at* www.insidejustice.com/author/renee/page/21/ (last

did consider this tactic,[43] as it was plausible that an alternative dispute resolution panel might have ruled that Fujimori was *not* a Japanese national.

Invite a Third-Party Mediator to Resolve Differences over a Requested Extradition. When the host State and a pursuing State are at an impasse over whether it would be proper to extradite a fugitive under the governing authorities, including an applicable extradition treaty, any other relevant agreements, and domestic laws, the States could seek the intervention of a neutral third party, as appropriate, such as the United Nations, a regional body (*e.g.*, the E.U. or the OAS), or another reputable institution or individual with international standing, to mediate the dispute. Such third-party mediation was contemplated by the United States and Jamaican Governments when the latter was trying to determine whether Christopher "Dudus" Coke, a Jamaican national, should be extradited to the United States on narcotics and firearms trafficking charges.[44] "Such mediation would determine the legitimacy of the U.S. assertions that it acted in accordance with the spirit and intent of the Extradition Treaty and the Memorandum of Understanding."[45]

Dispatch a Local Lobbyist to Bring Pressure to Bear on the Host State. This tack involves a pursuing State hiring a well-placed and influential lobbying firm in the host State's capital to help advocate for a favorable executive branch disposition.[46]

Ask the ICTY or ICTR to Direct the Host State to Extradite a Fugitive. Under a 2006 amendment to Rule 11 *bis* of their Rules of

visited on May 16, 2016) (noting two other grounds for Japan's denial: the absence of a Japan-Peru Extradition Treaty and the lack of sufficient evidence in Peru's extradition request).

43 "Peru to Seek International Mediation for Fujimori's Extradition," *China Daily*, July 5, 2001 ("'We could argue that Fujimori is Peruvian and not Japanese. Then, what should we do? We could resort to international mediation to determine what nationality Fujimori has,' said the Peruvian ambassador to Japan.").

44 Desmond Allen, "'Dudus' Dispute Heading to U.N.?," *Jamaica Observer*, Mar. 14, 2010 (indicating that both governments were mulling over expert advice that they submit their dispute to mediation, possibly with the United Nations).

45 *Id.*

46 In a counter-example, in early 2010, Jamaican Prime Minister Bruce Golding hired a Washington, D.C.-based firm to influence the United States to back off its extradition request for Christopher "Dudus" Coke on narcotics and arms trafficking charges. Bruce Zagaris, *Jamaica PM Approves Extradition After Admission of Hiring U.S. Lobbyist to Oppose U.S. Extradition of Coke*, 26 IELR 268 (2010). Golding's admission led to calls for his resignation.

Procedure and Evidence (RPE), the UNSC-established ICTY and ICTR may

> direct a State which harbours an accused to extradite that person to another State, regardless of whether that accused is or has been in the custody of the Tribunal or whether he or she is a national of the requesting or requested State. This direction can be supplemented by an arrest warrant, and under Article 29 of the ICTY Statute and Article 28 of the ICTR Statute all U.N. Member States are obliged to comply with such an order, on pain of sanctions by the Security Council.[47]

This approach would be limited, however, to those fugitives wanted by one of the two international criminal tribunals and only for the finite remaining period in which they continue to operate.

Request a Ruling by the International Court of Justice. When (i) a pursuing State has had one or more extradition requests turned down by the host State, (ii) the host State has failed to indict the individual at issue or to pursue criminal prosecution in good faith based on any charges levied, (iii) a dispute has "crystallized" [48] between the host and pursuing States over the transfer of a particular fugitive; and (iv) both States recognize the competence of the International Court of Justice (ICJ),[49] a pursuing State could seek to resolve such an impasse with the intervention of the U.N.'s highest judicial body.[50] A pursuing State may be particularly motivated in cases where enough time has elapsed that it has become concerned that potential victims and witnesses may no longer be available and/or has doubts about the host State's genuine intentions to bring the individual to justice.

This situation arose with respect to Hissène Habré, the former President of Chad, who allegedly killed up to 40,000 opponents and tortured many others, including Belgians, during his rule between June 1982 and December 1990. Impatient with Senegal's failure to prosecute (after more than ten years) or extradite (denying or ignoring several of its requests since 2005), Belgium filed a request in

[47] Colin Warbrick, *Current Developments in Public Int'l Law*, 55 INT'L & COMP. L.Q. 219, 222 (2006).

[48] Robert Kolb, *The Scope* Ratione Materiae *of the Compulsory Jurisdiction of the ICJ, in* U.N. GENOCIDE CONVENTION: A COMMENTARY 447 (Paola Gaeta ed. 2009) ("[T]he dispute must in principle be crystallized at the time of the seizing of the ICJ. The filing of the request against another state does not *ipso facto* create a dispute").

[49] Statute of the ICJ, Apr. 18, 1946, art. 36.

[50] The host State likewise may engage the ICJ to seek declaratory relief that its unwillingness to extradite is in compliance with its international legal obligations. This arose in the *Lockerbie* case, discussed *infra*.

February 2009[51] for an ICJ decision to compel Senegal either to submit the matter for prosecution or to extradite him.[52] In July 2012, the ICJ (by a 14–2 vote) found Senegal to have violated its obligations under the CAT both by failing to immediately undertake a "preliminary inquiry into the facts" once Senegal had reason to believe that Habré, who was then within its territory, was responsible for acts of torture (under Article 6(2)), and by not submitting the case to its competent authorities once it had decided not to extradite Habré (under Article 7(1)); the Court consequently ordered Senegal either to extradite or submit the case for prosecution without further delay.[53]

In other instances, a pursuing State may merely *threaten* to bring its claim to the ICJ for adjudication in the hope of prompting the host State to extradite a wanted fugitive. In June 2011, for example, after Brazil's Supreme Court affirmed a decision not to extradite Cesare Battisti, who thirty years earlier had escaped from an Italian prison while awaiting trial on four counts of murder allegedly committed while he belonged to the Armed Proletarians for Communism, the Italian Foreign Minister threatened to seek action against Brazil before the ICJ.[54] In addition, reportedly in April 2005, "Peru had been planning to file suit against Japan before the International Court of Justice at the Hague to force the extradition of Fujimori from Japan."[55] In neither case was the threat actualized.

Seek U.N. Security Council Intervention. When the U.N. Security Council (UNSC) determines that "a threat to the peace, breach of the peace, or act of aggression" exists,[56] it is authorized under Chapter VII of

[51] Belgium requested and Senegal agreed that Habré remain within Senegalese territory during the pendency of the case. *Questions Relating to the Obligation to Prosecute or Extradite* (Belg. v. Sen.) [2012] I.C.J. Rep. 422, ¶ 33 (July 20) [hereinafter "*I.C.J. Case, Belg. v. Sen.*].

[52] Marlise Simons, "Tug of War over Trial for Ex-President of Chad," *IHT*, Mar. 14, 2012, at 5. This request implicates the legal concept known as *aut dedere aut judicare*, which is discussed in Chapter 9.c.

[53] *I.C.J. Case, Belg. v. Sen., supra* n.51, ¶¶ 88, 121, 122(6). The I.C.J. incidentally ruled that Senegal could not rely on a decision by the ECOWAS Court of Justice or its own purported financial difficulties to vitiate the African State's obligations under the CAT. *Id.* ¶¶ 111, 112. Notably, in a separate ICJ case in February 2002 related to Belgium's circulated arrest warrant for the D.R.C.'s Minister of Foreign Affairs, the Court found that, based on the subject's entitled immunity to jurisdiction, Belgium had overstepped its authority and no extradition was mandated. *Arrest Warrant of 11 April 2000* (D.R.C. v. Belg.) [2002] I. C. J. Rep. 3 (Feb. 14).

[54] Bruce Zagaris, *Brazilian Supreme Court Upholds Denial of Extradition to Italy and Italy Plans to Bring Action in ICJ*, 27 IELR 829, 829–30 (2011).

[55] Dopplick, *supra* n.42.

[56] Charter of the United Nations, June 26, 1945, art. 39.

the U.N. Charter (as an express exception to the prohibition against U.N. intervention "in matters which are essentially within the domestic jurisdiction of any state"[57]) to address that situation either with measures "not involving the use of armed force"[58] or with the use of force "as may be necessary to maintain or restore international peace and security."[59] Such extraordinary situations are unlikely to arise in the extradition context; however, there may be circumstances that call for UNSC intervention, such as in the celebrated *Lockerbie* case (discussed *infra*), where the host State was deemed unworthy of *bona fide* cooperation, given its presumed complicity in, or interest to conceal, an underlying heinous offense and/or because of a concern that more such unlawful conduct could occur absent a rapid law enforcement effort to net the alleged perpetrators.

On November 14, 1991, the United States and the United Kingdom independently charged two Libyan intelligence officers with responsibility for the explosion of Pan Am Flight 103 while it was *en route* over Lockerbie, Scotland, on December 21, 1988, resulting in the deaths of 270 airline crew, passengers, and villagers on the ground.[60] A week later, the U.S. and U.K. Governments requested extradition from Libya of the two alleged offenders, an admission of Libyan responsibility, payment of compensation, and access to evidence and witnesses. Pursuant to the *aut dedere* provision (Article 7) of the governing "Montreal Convention,"[61] Libya chose not to extradite, but rather to try the two alleged offenders, consistent with its domestic legal prohibition against extraditing its own nationals.

The Libyan magistrate judge ordered the two men be taken into custody, allowed U.S. and U.K. observers in the courtroom, and invited

57 *Id.*, art. 2(7).

58 *Id.*, art. 41 (citing several examples, including "complete or partial interruption of economic relations").

59 *Id*, art. 42.

60 This brief case study is based on multiple sources, including principally M. Cherif Bassiouni & Edward M. Wise, Aut Dedere aut Judicare: *The Duty to Extradite or Prosecute, in* International Law 58–67 (1995); Neil Boister, *The Trend to 'Universal Extradition' over Subsidiary Universal Jurisdiction in the Suppression of Transnat'l Crime,* 2003 Acta Juridica 287, 309–10 (2003); Laflin, *supra* n.14, at 333–34; and Donna E. Arzt, *The Lockerbie 'Extradition by Analogy' Agreement: 'Exceptional Measure' or Template for Transnat'l Criminal Justice?*, 18 Am. U. Int'l L. Rev. 163 (2002).

61 Conv. for the Suppression of Unlawful Acts against the Safety of Civil Aviation, Sept. 23, 1971, U.N. Doc. A/C.6/418/Corr.2, Annex III, 974 U.N.T.S. 177, 24 U.S.T. 564, *reprinted in* 10 ILM 1151.

American and British Government assistance in the investigation. Nevertheless, mistrusting Libyan intentions and doubting an impartial proceeding – and with the active support of France which by now had its own suspicions about Libyan Government involvement in an airplane incident over Niger in 1989 – the United States and the United Kingdom secured adoption of UNSC Resolution 731, which exhorted Libya "to provide a full and effective response" to the outstanding requests.[62]

On March 3, 1992, Libya engaged the ICJ by seeking declaratory relief that it was in full compliance with its duties under the Montreal Convention and that the United States and the United Kingdom, which were also parties to that Convention, were improperly interfering with Libya's treaty prerogatives. Libya also requested provisional measures[63] to keep the United States and the United Kingdom from any further efforts to secure the release of the two accused. After ICJ hearings but before it had issued a ruling, the UNSC adopted Resolution 748,[64] claiming Libya's resistance to extradition constituted a threat to international peace and security, favoring extradition over domestic prosecution, and imposing sanctions (versus the threat or use of force) pending compliance. Those sanctions included various restrictions on (i) international flights by, and the overseas office operations of, Libyan Airlines (its national flag carrier); (ii) the sale of aircraft, arms, and spare parts to Libya; and (iii) the movement of Libyan diplomats, in addition to limiting the size of Libyan Embassy personnel.[65]

On April 14, 1992, the ICJ rejected the Libyan request for provisional measures on the grounds that, although under the U.N. Charter, the Court was not authorized to evaluate the UNSC resolution for its validity, the resolution nevertheless trumped any obligations under an international treaty and therefore proved dispositive, and such provisional measures "would be likely to impair the rights which appear prima

[62] UNSC Res. 731, U.N. SCOR, 47th Sess., 3033d mtg., U.N. Doc. S/23574 (1992), *reprinted in* 31 ILM 731 (1992).

[63] Provisional measures, which are sometimes referred to as "emergency measures" or "interim measures," are intended to "preserve the respective rights of either party" pending a decision on the merits of a case without, at the same time, prejudging that decision. Statute of the ICJ, *supra* n.49, art. 41.

[64] UNSC Res. 748, U.N. SCOR, 47th Sess., 3063d mtg., U.N. Doc. S/RES/748 (1992), *reprinted in* 31 ILM 749 (1992).

[65] Paul Lewis, "Sanctions on Libya Begin to Take Hold as Deadline Passes; U.N. Seeks Full Isolation," *N.Y. Times*, Apr. 15, 1992, at A1.

facie to be enjoyed by the United States by virtue of Security Council resolution 748."[66]

Ultimately, after years of stalemate, Libya agreed to submit the two alleged offenders to a trial in a special court subject to Scottish criminal law on neutral territory in a facility outside of The Hague. One of the men was found guilty and sentenced to life imprisonment; the other was found not guilty by reason of insufficient evidence. Some, however, have criticized the role of the UNSC in this regard, contending in essence that "[t]he preference of the United Kingdom and the United States for coercion over negotiation, cooperation, and judicial settlement, against the backdrop of Libya's stated willingness to cooperate with foreign criminal investigators and its pledge to prosecute the two suspects in its custody, indicates how easily some of the more influential States may be provoked into shortsighted overreaction."[67]

Significantly, the *Lockerbie* case represented the first, but not the last, time the UNSC exercised its Chapter VII authorities to try to prod a State into extraditing fugitives to face prosecution elsewhere.[68] In January 1996, the UNSC issued Resolution 1044, "[c]all[ing] upon the Government of the Sudan to comply with the requests of the Organization of African Unity [OAU] without further delay to: (a) Undertake immediate action to extradite to Ethiopia for prosecution the three suspects shelter[ed] in the Sudan and wanted in connection with the assassination attempt [on the President of Egypt in June 1995 while visiting Addis Ababa] on the basis of the 1964 Extradition Treaty between Ethiopia and the Sudan."[69] Nearly three months later, via Resolution 1054, and with express reference to its Chapter VII authorities, the UNSC mandated that:

> all States shall: (a) Significantly reduce the number and the level of the staff at Sudanese diplomatic missions and consular posts and restrict or control the movement within their territory of all such staff who remain; and (b) Take steps to restrict the entry into or transit through their territory of members

[66] *Case Concerning Questions of Interpretation and Application of 1971 Montreal Conv. Arising from the Aerial Incident at Lockerbie*, (Libyan Arab Jamahiriya v. U.K.), *Provisional Measures*, Order [1992] I.C.J. Rep. 114, ¶ 44 (Apr. 14).

[67] Lyal S. Sunga, The Emerging System of International Criminal Law: Developments in Codification and Implementation 274–75 (1997).

[68] Arzt, *supra* n.60, at 168. One author, Michael Plachta, has coined a variant on this concept – *aut dedere aut transfere* – to denote that rare circumstance when the UNSC mandates a State to transfer a fugitive to a third State to undergo prosecution. Boister, *supra* n.60, at 310.

[69] UNSC Res. 1044, Jan. 31, 1996, ¶ 4, U.N. Doc. S/RES/1044 (1996).

> of the Government of Sudan, officials of that Government and members of the Sudanese armed forces; [while] ... 5. [c]all[ing] upon all States, including States not members of the United Nations and the United Nations specialized agencies to act strictly in conformity with this resolution.[70]

In addition, in May 1996 the UNSC issued a statement in which it "deplore[d] the failure to date of the Federal Republic of Yugoslavia to execute the arrest warrants issued by the [ICTY] against [certain] individuals ... and call[ed] for the execution of those arrest warrants without delay."[71] In November 1998, the UNSC followed up with a resolution that "[c] ondemn[ed] the failure to date of the Federal Republic of Yugoslavia to execute the arrest warrants issued by the Tribunal ... and demand[ed] the immediate and unconditional execution of those arrest warrants, including the transfer to the custody of the Tribunal of those individuals."[72] Although the UNSC went no further, it could have done so, and thereby at least implicitly invited foreign forces to take action to address the fact that the FRY had not executed any arrest warrants.[73]

In yet another instance, in October 1999, pursuant to its Chapter VII authorities, the UNSC adopted Resolution 1267, calling for Afghanistan to turn over Usama Bin Laden, the leader of al-Qaida, within a specified time frame to the appropriate authorities of a State that could bring him to justice, or else the UNSC would impose a sanctions regime on Afghanistan that included denying landing rights to all Taliban-operated aircraft and freezing all Taliban assets abroad.[74]

* * * * *

[70] UNSC Res. 1054, Apr. 26, 1996, ¶¶ 3–5, U.N. Doc. S/RES/1054 (1996). The sanctions ceased when it was discovered that the three suspected assassins were not present in the Sudan.

[71] *Statement of the President of the Security Council*, U.N. Doc. S/PRST/1996/23, May 8, 1996.

[72] UNSC Res. 1207, Nov. 17, 1998, ¶ 3, U.N. Doc. S/RES/1207 (1998).

[73] Indeed, presumably acting consistent with the spirit of the UNSC resolutions, "NATO troops reportedly secretly entered the FRY in April 2000 and snatched former Bosnian Serb prison camp commander Dragan Nikolic from his home ... just outside of Belgrade." Michael P. Scharf, *Jurisdiction with Respect to Crime: Universal Jurisdiction and the Harvard Research*, *in* The Harvard Research in International Law: Contemporary Analysis and Appraisal 965 (John P. Grant & J. Craig Barker eds. 2007) (international criminal tribunal example).

[74] UNSC Res. 1267, Oct. 15, 1999, ¶ 2, *reprinted in* 39 ILM 235 (2000). On a related note, in November 2005, the UNSC unanimously adopted Resolution 1638 under its Chapter VII powers to authorize U.N. Mission in Liberia (UNMIL) personnel to arrest Charles Taylor to the extent he is returned to Liberia and to facilitate his transfer to the Special Court for Sierra Leone (SCSL). UNSC Res. 1638, Nov. 11, 2005, ¶ 1, U.N. Doc. S/RES/1638 (2005) (hybrid court example).

This Part has sought to identify a number of remedial or collateral means a pursuing State may undertake to secure a fugitive's custody *via* extradition even if the host State has already denied such a request or is presumptively or demonstrably predisposed to do so. Each of these approaches is generally in compliance with international law standards, although the intervention of the U.N. Security Council has been contested by some due to the controversial invocation of Chapter VII powers in such circumstances. Part IV begins an examination of *alternatives to extradition* when extradition, including remedial or collateral means to attain it, has proven infeasible or is deemed undesirable.

PART IV

Fallback Alternatives to Extradition

9

Partial or Redirected Alternatives

Having examined extradition, its operation and impediments, as well as various means available for securing a fugitive's custody by extradition as a remedial or collateral matter, we now turn to *alternatives* to extradition. This treatment identifies two types: fallback alternatives and full-scale alternatives. The first is addressed in this part; the second will be discussed in Part V.

"Fallback alternatives to extradition" are defined herein as *those partial or redirected means of bringing a fugitive to justice other than by extradition that, by virtue of a pursuing State's inability to meet the functional end result of extradition – namely, securing the physical custody of a fugitive and prosecuting or punishing him under its own judicial system – reflects a second-order preference.* More specifically, those alternatives consist of: (i) preliminary independent initiatives designed strictly to facilitate a fugitive's eventual capture or return; (ii) efforts that call upon host State or third-party support solely to locate or arrest a fugitive overseas; and (iii) actions that result in the delivery of a fugitive to another State court or international criminal tribunal to face justice, rather than to a particular pursuing State's own judicial system. This part will catalogue all available fallback alternatives, illustrate how they work, and evaluate the extent of their lawfulness.[1]

[1] Other options for coping with fugitives abroad may not ultimately intend to prosecute or punish them, but instead seek to extract intelligence from them, retaliate against them, or simply neutralize them to minimize any further damage or harm they can wreak. Examples include: (i) undertaking a "targeted killing" (this amounts to a "premeditated act[] of lethal force employed by states in times of peace or during armed conflict to eliminate specific individuals outside their custody." Council on Foreign Relations, Jonathan Masters, *Targeted Killings*, Nov. 7, 2011 (citing a U.N. Special Report)); (ii) perpetrating a "disappearance" (this term appears to have originated in Argentina during the so-called "Dirty War" between 1976 and 1983 when non-returning family members were labeled "los desaparecidos" (the disappeared ones), and is defined as "when a person is secretly abducted or imprisoned by a State or political organization or by a third party with the authorization, support,

a Independent Measures to Facilitate a Fugitive's Capture or Return[2]

The following approaches can be undertaken independently by a pursuing State on a preliminary basis to facilitate either (i) a fugitive's eventual capture by host State authorities or (ii) his ultimate delivery to pursuing State territory, custody, or control.

Arrange for a Sealed (or Secret) Indictment. By sealing an indictment, the fugitive is less likely to discover that a pursuing State has a law enforcement interest in him and therefore may prove less circumspect about his travel (particularly to overseas destinations), communications, and business dealings, and thus he may more readily come to the attention of law enforcement authorities, including through surveillance or undercover operations.[3] Furthermore, he may invest less time and effort

or acquiescence of a State or political organization, followed by a refusal to acknowledge the person's fate and whereabouts, with the intent of placing the victim outside the protection of the law." JEAN-MARIE HENCKAERTS & LOUISE DOSWALD-BECK, CUSTOMARY INTERNATIONAL HUMANITARIAN LAW: RULES 342 (ICRC 2005)); (iii) placing a bounty on the fugitive's head (this occurred, for example, in February 1989 in connection with Iran Supreme Leader Ayatollah Ruhollah Khomeini's issuance of a *fatwa* (Islamic legal opinion or order) over Tehran Radio that Salman Rushdie, the Indian-born, award-winning author then living in London, must die for blaspheming Islam and its Prophet Mohammed in his fourth novel, *The Satanic Verses*, published in 1988; some days later, the government announced that a bounty on Rushdie's head was set at US $2.6 million if Rushdie were killed by an Iranian and US $1 million otherwise; *see* William E. Smith, "Hunted by an Angry Faith: Salman Rushdie's Novel Cracks Open a Fault Line Between East and West," *Time*, Feb. 27, 1989, at 28–31; "Ayatollah Khomeini Personally Issued the Fatwa on Salman Rushdie," *Iran Press Service*, Apr. 29, 2002)); or (iv) engage in an "extraordinary rendition" (*see* definition in Chapter 1.d). These options are not regarded as *bona fide* alternatives to extradition; as such, they lie beyond the ambit of this study.

2 Three standard independent measures that need no elaboration are when a pursuing State: (i) conducts surveillance of the fugitive to determine his whereabouts, daily or weekly routines, or intended travel plans or destinations, through human or electronic intelligence under its own auspices; (ii) pays informants to report on the fugitive's associates, movements, and vulnerabilities; and (iii) invests greater domestic financial resources in tracking fugitives, such as when in March 2012 a U.S. Senator introduced a bill in Congress that would direct US $1–3 million each year to the Fugitive Extradition and Apprehension Trust Fund, whose aim would be to improve fugitive apprehension efforts. The funds would derive from forfeited bail and appearance bonds and would fund the U.S. Marshal's Service, the U.S. Attorneys' Offices (*i.e.*, federal prosecutors), and the Justice Department's Office of International Affairs. Gary Marx & David Jackson, "Durbin Pushes Reforms to Help Capture Fugitives," *Chi. Trib.*, Mar. 12, 2012.

3 *See* Colette Retif, *By What Means Justice? The Acceptance of Secret Indictments in the United States and in Int'l Law*, 13 PACE INT'L L. REV. 233, 234 (2001) (characterizing as "common sense" that public indictments can tip off fugitives); *United States v. Davis*, 598

in developing a physical disguise,[4] establishing an assumed name, cultivating a new persona, and/or keeping a low profile. As a result, he could be more easily identified and captured. This represents a lawful measure.[5]

In August 1995, for example, a sealed indictment was filed against Eyad Ismail Najim, a Jordanian national believed to be the driver of the bomb-laden van that entered the underground parking lot of the World Trade Center in February 1993 and whose explosion killed six persons and injured over 1,000 others.[6] "The indictment had been sealed to ensure that Najim would not learn that he had been identified and try to flee again."[7] Another example can be found in the case of Baz Mohammad (a/k/a Haji Baz Mohammad), one of the world's most wanted drug kingpins and allegedly linked to the Taliban; in December 2003, a sealed indictment in the United States was returned against him, and by January 2005, U.S. and Afghan authorities had succeeded in arresting him.[8]

F. Supp. 453, 456 (S.D.N.Y. 1984) ("The Government also reasonably believed that if [co-defendant] Lee learned that he had been indicted by a grand jury here, he would be more likely to keep to ground in Ireland.").

4 For example, when Christopher "Dudus" Coke, a Jamaican national charged with gun and drug smuggling, was captured at a motor vehicle checkpoint in June 2010, he had shaved his beard and was wearing a woman's wig. Bruce Zagaris, *Coke Waives Extradition to the U.S. after Jamaica Arrests Him*, 26 IELR 352 (2010).

5 U.S. Fed. R. Crim. Pr. 6(e)(4), Title III; *United States v. Richard*, 943 F.2d 115 (1st Cir. 1991); *United States v. Smaldone*, 484 F.2d 311 (10th Cir. 1973); Agreement for the Prosecution and Punishment of the Major War Criminals of the European Axis [London Charter], Aug. 8, 1945, art. 16, 59 Stat. 1544, 82 U.N.T.S. 279, *reprinted in* 39 AJIL 1945, Supp. 257 (1945); Int'l Tribunal for the Prosecution of Persons Responsible for Serious Violations of Int'l Humanitarian Law Committed in the Territory of the Former Yugoslavia since 1991 (ICTY), Rules of Procedure and Evidence (RPE), arts. 17–19, U.N. Doc. IT/32/Rev.7 (1996), *amendments adopted* Jan. 8, 1996.

6 Robin Wright & Ronald J. Ostrow, "Bomb Suspect Extradited to the U.S. from Jordan," *L.A. Times*, Aug. 3, 1995.

7 *Id.*

8 Bruce Zagaris, *Afghanistan Extradites Alleged Heroin Kingpin to the U.S.*, 22 IELR 36, 36–38 (2006). Likewise, in August 1999, based on the ICTY prosecutor's sealed indictment, Gen. Momir Talić, Chief of Staff of the Army of Republika Srpska, who was charged with committing crimes against humanity in connection with the war in the Balkans, was evidently less cautious about attending a military conference of the National Defense Academy in Vienna, where he was arrested by undercover Austrian police. As was observed, "[by] keeping the indictment sealed, [t]he Chief Prosecutor believe[d] she had a better chance of arresting those it accuse[d]." Inst. for War & Peace Reporting (IWPR), "Arrest of General Talic," Aug. 28, 1999, *available at* iwpr.net/global-voices/arrest-general-talic (last visited on May 16, 2016); Marlise Simons, "Top Bosnian Serb Officer Arrested

Issue a "Silent Parole" to Permit an Unwitting Fugitive Temporary Entry into Pursuing State Territory. Where the fugitive is unaware that a pursuing State has indicted him and where he has attempted to travel to pursuing State territory but his entry has been impeded on account of a visa problem (*e.g.*, he overstayed his last visit), pursuing State officials can issue a "silent parole" by which he would be granted a waiver and allowed temporary entry. This would amount to a subterfuge to facilitate his return to or arrival in pursuing State territory.

This tactic was employed by the Multnomah County District Attorney in Oregon to secure the custody of Deniz Aydiner, a Turkish national charged with the 2001 sexual assault and murder of a college student in Portland.[9] The deception was ruled lawful by the Court of Appeals of the State of Oregon, because the Court found that the tactic did not violate the U.S.-Turkey Extradition Treaty (which did not explicitly prohibit such methods), extradition was understood not to constitute the exclusive means available for securing an individual's custody from the other party to that Treaty, and there was no violation of due process rights found, as it was deemed improper to inquire as to how the defendant came before the Court.[10]

Although many may take exception to this state court's reasoning, and others might find such a subterfuge to be *per se* unacceptable, merely enabling a fugitive who voluntarily wishes to enter pursuing State territory constitutes as minimal and passive a law enforcement deception as one can imagine and does not appear facially anathema to international legal standards.

Revoke a Fugitive's Passport or Validate it Solely for Return to a Particular Pursuing State. To the extent that the fugitive is a pursuing State national, the State of nationality could revoke his passport. Such a tactic can render that individual's presence in another State unlawful and consequently compel or generate pressure toward his deportation.[11] At a minimum, however, this method can limit a fugitive's mobility and thereby facilitate law enforcement efforts to

for U.N. Tribunal," *N.Y. Times*, Aug. 26, 1999, at A10 (international criminal tribunal example).

[9] *State v. Aydiner*, 208 P.3d 515 (Or. Ct. App. 2009).

[10] *Id.* (relying heavily on the 1992 U.S. Supreme Court opinion in *Álvarez-Machaín*).

[11] *E.g.*, "Turkey Revokes Passport of Cleric Based in the U.S.," *INYT*, Feb. 5, 2015, at 5 (in its pursuit of Fethullah Gülen, an influential cleric in self-imposed exile in Pennsylvania, who is accused of undermining the Turkish Government by establishing a "parallel structure," Turkey revoked his passport "in a push for his deportation.").

locate and arrest him.[12] After all, any time the fugitive tried to travel to another State, he would be discovered holding an invalid travel document.

This scenario played out in December 2003, when the United States revoked chess champion Bobby Fischer's passport in order to prompt Japan to remove him to his country of nationality to stand trial for violations of U.S. economic sanctions imposed on the former Yugoslavia when he played a twenty-year anniversary exhibition match there in 1992. Thus, in August 2004, when Fischer attempted to fly from Tokyo to Manila, Japanese authorities detained him for trying to depart Japan without a valid travel document.[13] More recently, in June 2013, the United States revoked former NSA contractor Edward Snowden's passport after he had publicly disclosed classified U.S. Government information and had fled abroad.[14] Some States, however, are reluctant to revoke their nationals' passports, as they view them as more than travel documents and as "fundamental to an individual's identity."[15]

[12] Notably, however, such a tactic does not affect the individual's citizenship status.

[13] Audrey McAvoy, "Fischer Tries New Moves in Effort to Avoid Charges," *Wash. Post*, Aug. 17, 2004, at A10. Nevertheless, after months of detention, in March 2005 and despite pressure for his removal to the United States, Japan "paid due attention[] to the foreign national's intention," Gov't of Japan, MoJ, Immigration Procedures Guidebook, Deportation and Departure Order System, § 2(a) (Destinations of Deportation), and opted to deport him to Iceland, the site of his historic 1972 match against then-Soviet chess champion Boris Spassky, once Fischer was offered and accepted its parliament's offer of citizenship. AP, "Bobby Fischer Lands in Iceland," *CBS News*, Mar. 25, 2005, *available at* www.cbsnews.com/news/bobby-fischer-lands-in-iceland/ (last visited on May 28, 2016). In June 2005, Iceland's parliament voted 40-0-2 to grant Fischer citizenship and, within days of its decision, planned to issue him an Icelandic passport. "Iceland Approves Bobby Fischer Citizenship," *UPI*, Mar. 21, 2005. Fischer's renunciation of U.S. citizenship did not immunize him from prosecution for crimes under U.S. law. Sarah Lyall, "Iceland Granting Citizenship to Bobby Fischer, Held in Japan," *N.Y. Times*, Mar. 22, 2005 (citing a State Department spokesperson). He lived the next three years in Reykjavik as a fugitive from U.S. justice until his death. Bruce Weber, "Bobby Fischer, Chess Master, Dies at 64," *N.Y. Times*, Jan. 18, 2008.

[14] David Trifunov, "U.S. Revokes Edward Snowden's Passport, Urges Russia to Expel Whistleblower," *Globalpost*, June 24, 2013, *available at* www.globalpost.com/dispatch/news/politics/130623/us-revokes-edward-snowdens-passport-focuses-anger-putins-russia (last visited on May 16, 2016) (according to State Department representative Jen Psaki: "Persons wanted on felony charges, such as Mr. Snowden, should not be allowed to proceed in any further international travel, other than is necessary to return him to the United States").

[15] David P. Warner, *Bringing White-Collar Criminals to Justice—Fugitive Apprehension and Return and Obtaining Evidence Abroad*, 11 U.S.-Mex. L.J. 171, 172 (2003) (discussing this perspective).

A variant of this tactic, when the opportunity arises, is to validate a fugitive's passport exclusively for return to the State of his nationality. This approach, in effect, "stacks the deck" in a given pursuing State's favor by precluding the alien fugitive's admission to another State.[16]

Seize or Freeze a Fugitive's Financial Assets. Where substantial financial assets of a fugitive happen to be held in accounts located in a pursuing State, and domestic law permitting, a pursuing State could confiscate or freeze all or some portion of those assets while he remains at large. In addition to isolating the fugitive and effectively penalizing him, this approach could encourage the fugitive to turn himself in[17] or, more likely, to increase his exposure to law enforcement officials tracking him down. That is because some fugitives rely on such assets to pay for their security details, private jets, and/or safe houses.[18] Without access to such funds, some fugitives could become more vulnerable to capture,[19] especially those engaged in money laundering.[20]

For example, the Swiss Government froze millions of euros' worth of German financier Florian Homm's assets after "compil[ing] a thick dossier of testimony from former employees and associates of Mr. Homm or the hedge fund he founded" regarding his efforts to defraud investors and then hide those monies.[21] One surprising downside risk of this approach is that the host State's taxpayers may need to

16 Alona E. Evans, *Acquisition of Custody over the Int'l Fugitive Offender—Alternatives to Extradition: A Survey of United States Practice*, 40 B.Y.B.I.L. 77, 87 & n.2 (1964).

17 Marshall Freeman Harris, et al., Making Justice Work 50 (1998).

18 *See* Michael P. Scharf, *The Tools for Enforcing Int'l Criminal Justice in the New Millennium: Lessons from the Yugoslavia Tribunal*, 49 DePaul L. Rev. 925, 945 (2000) (citing by way of example Radovan Karadzić, who was "said to be protected by a small mercenary force which he pays for through funds on deposit in Cyprus"). There may be an alternative or perhaps complementary, explanation, however, for Karadzic's capture. *See* "Serbian Paper Says U.S. Paid $5mln Award for Karadzic Capture," *Sputnik News*, Aug. 6, 2008, *available at* http://sputniknews.com/world/20080806/115844745.html (last visited on May 28, 2016) ("The U.S. State Department paid $5 million as a reward to an anonymous recipient for assistance in the capture of former Bosnian Serb leader Radovan Karadzic, Serbian newspaper Press said.").

19 A variant on this approach would be to urge other States to join this effort in instances where the fugitive had multiple overseas accounts, but then this approach would be more properly categorized under one of the other sections of this chapter.

20 Keith R. Fisher, In Rem *Alternatives to Extradition for Money Laundering*, 25 Loy. L.A. Int'l & Comp. L. Rev. 409, 427 *et seq.* (2003).

21 Jack Ewing, "Financier, Free Again, Comes to Rest on Home Turf," *INYT*, Aug. 4, 2014, at 1, 16.

pick up the legal defense fees used to challenge extradition where an individual is left with insufficient assets, even if he is otherwise in essence extremely wealthy.[22]

b Reliance on Others to Locate or Arrest a Fugitive Abroad

Beyond independent initiatives, a pursuing State may undertake various measures that are designed to locate or otherwise lead to the arrest of a fugitive but that depend on the support or engagement of either the host State or a third party.

i Assistance From or Coordination with the Host State

Encourage the Host State to Assign Greater Priority to Locating or Arresting a Fugitive. Where the host State appears reluctant to actively seek out or apprehend a fugitive, a pursuing State can try to persuade its counterpart through diplomatic channels or otherwise provide incentives or disincentives to encourage the host State to invest greater resources, or to take a more serious interest, in tracking down a given fugitive. In February 1985, for example, in a "Sense of the Congress" statement, the U.S. legislature urged Paraguay to step up its efforts in the search for Dr. Josef Mengele, a Nazi physician at the Auschwitz Concentration Camp and generally referred to by his victims as the "Angel of Death."[23] Although this approach did not eventually yield Mengele's capture, it could prove beneficial in other contexts.

Such encouragement also can be sought in the context of high-level political visits or in bilateral or regional law enforcement cooperation forums, including in instances where no extradition treaty exists between the concerned States. For example, in recent years, despite the absence of a bilateral extradition treaty, PRC officials have held discussions with

[22] *E.g.*, "Hound of Hounslow Granted Legal Aid to Fight his Extradition: Asset Freeze by the U.S. Means British Taxpayers are Forced to Pick Up Lawyers' Bill," *Daily Mail Reporter*, May 13, 2015 (thirty-six-year-old British securities trader Navinder Singh Sarao, reported to be worth £27 million, was indicted by the United States for wire fraud, commodities fraud, market manipulation, and "spoofing" in connection with the 2010 "Flash Crash" in which the Dow Jones Industrial Average dropped more than 700 points in a single day and he capitalized on the market fluctuation to the order of £500,000; because his assets were frozen, the United Kingdom was forced to cover his legal fees to challenge his extradition).

[23] U.S. S. Conc. Res. 14 – Relating to Josef Mengele, 99th Cong., 1st Sess, 131 Cong. Rec. S1444 (daily ed. Feb. 19, 1985).

their U.S. counterparts in such venues as the U.S.-China Joint Liaison Group on Law Enforcement Cooperation and the APEC Network of Anti-Corruption Authorities and Law Enforcement Agencies (ACT-NET) to explore ways to bring greater law enforcement resources to bear on Chinese fugitives who came to the United States between 2003 and 2012, allegedly with stolen assets worth billions of dollars.[24]

Request the Host State to Cancel a Fugitive's Travel Authorization. A pursuing State can ask the host State to terminate an active visa or cancel a border-crossing card (as applicable in the U.S.-Mexico context) held by a fugitive.[25] This tactic can be helpful in tracking down and arresting a fugitive by effectively limiting his travel opportunities, operating along the same logic as the mirror-image passport revocation option discussed *supra*. This approach has its challenges, however, as the border officials must possess updated information about each individual's visa status.[26]

Share Intelligence Leads, Critical Information, Computer Software, Tracking Devices, or Surveillance Technology to Increase Host State Capacity to Locate a Fugitive. If a fugitive is known to be in a certain State's jurisdiction at a given time, even while he is in transit, supplying the host State government with criminal intelligence[27] could facilitate its capacity to arrest him.[28] For example, in January 1987, West German

[24] Alexandra Viers, "Should the United States Extradite Chinese Fugitives or Protect Them from an Unfair Justice System Back Home?," *Int'l Affairs Review* (Geo. Wash. Univ. Elliott School of Int'l Affairs), Mar. 12, 2015.

[25] *E.g.*, 22 C.F.R. § 41.122 (2003) (Revocation of Visas). *See also* David P. Warner, *Challenges to Int'l Law Enforcement Cooperation for the U.S. in the Middle East and North Africa: Extradition and Its Alternatives*, 50 Vill. L. Rev. 479, 493–96 (2005) (discussing visa revocation as a law enforcement tool).

[26] To underscore this point, consider that one of the college students (although not then a fugitive, let alone a suspect) arrested in the 2013 Boston Marathon bombing had been allowed to re-enter the United States from Kazakhstan, despite the fact that his student visa was no longer valid and he was no longer in school. "Official: Arrested Student Azamat Tazhayakov Entered U.S. without Visa," *wcvb.com* (Boston), May 1, 2013, *available at* www.wcvb.com/news/local/metro/official-arrested-student-azamat-tazhayakov-entered-us-without-visa/19974038 (last visited on May 17, 2016).

[27] Intelligence is information that "has been processed and given meaning," Combating Serious Crimes in Postconflict Societies: A Handbook for Policymakers and Practitioners 114 (Colette Rausch, ed. 2006), and while it "can be used as a tool to collect evidence," often it "cannot be used in court, either because it is insufficiently reliable or detailed or because it comes from sensitive sources." *Id.* at 117.

[28] *See* Ethan A. Nadelmann, Cops Across Borders: The Internationalization of U.S. Criminal Law Enforcement 436 (1993) (U.S. Government officials "have provided foreign authorities with the tactical intelligence needed to find and arrest fugitives on their territory."). Under U.S. law, the provision of "information to a foreign functionary is

police greeted Mohammed Ali Hamadei – a Lebanese citizen and Hezbollah terrorist who had participated in the June 1985 hijacking of TWA Flight 847 – at Frankfurt Airport while traveling on a false passport and carrying liquid explosives in his suitcase, "based on intelligence probably provided by the U.S. Government."[29]

Similarly, in April 1985, acting on a U.S. DEA tip, Costa Rican authorities located on the outskirts of San Jose Rafael Caro-Quintero, a major Guadalajara-based drug trafficker and the primary suspect in the kidnapping and murder of DEA Special Agent Enrique Camarena Salazar and his Mexican pilot, Alfredo Zavala Avelar.[30] In another case, in January 2012, most likely based on "high alert" information provided by the U.S. Government in December 2011, Thai authorities arrested a Swedish-Lebanese terrorist suspect, Hussein Atris, believed to belong to the Shiite Muslim organization, Hezbollah, in connection with feared attacks against places in Bangkok popular with Americans and Israelis.[31]

A pursuing State also can provide the host State with critical information, such as "DNA profiles, dactyloscopic data [fingerprinting][32] and

not sufficient involvement for the Government to be considered a participant in acts the foreign functionary takes based on that information." *United States v. Marzano*, 537 F.2d 257, 270 (7th Cir. 1976).

[29] David M. Kennedy, *et al.*, *The Extradition of Mohammed Hamadei*, 31 HARV. INT'L L.J. 5, 8 (1990). Hamadei served nineteen years in a German prison for smuggling explosives into the country; although originally sentenced to life, "Conviction of Mohammad Hamadei," *Cong. Rec.*, May 17, 1989, at S4563, he was released in 2005. The U.S. continues to seek his custody for the 1985 hijacking of TWA Flight 847 and the murder of U.S. Navy diver Robert Stethem. "FBI, State Dept. Dangle $5 Million Rewards in Hunt for Top Terrorists," *FoxNews.com*, Feb. 13, 2007, *available at* www.foxnews.com /story/2007/02/13/fbi-state-dept-dangle-5-million-rewards-in-hunt-for-top-terrorists.html (last visited on May 17, 2016).

[30] *See* Isaac A. Levi, "Reputed Mexican Drug Baron Arraigned," *AP News Wire*, Apr. 9, 1985. In August 2013, after serving twenty-eight years in prison, Caro-Quintero was promptly released from his forty-year sentence on the ground that he had been improperly prosecuted in federal court when they had been in fact state offenses. Adriana Gomez Licon & Mark Stevenson, "Mexico Releases Drug Kingpin Rafael Caro Quintero," *AP*, Aug. 9, 2013.

[31] "Thailand Arrests Suspect Amid Terror Warning," *CNN.com*, Jan. 13, 2012; "U.S. 'Wants to Question Suspect,'" *Bangkok Post*, Jan. 19, 2012, at 3. The suspect, Atris Hussein, was later arrested, tried, convicted, and sentenced to two years and eight months for possessing explosive material. Reuters, "Swedish-Lebanese Man Accused of Hezbollah Ties Jailed by Thai Court for Bomb Materials," *Jerusalem Post*, Sept. 18, 2013.

[32] Sometimes, a fugitive's fingerprints are elicited by ruse so as not to divulge the real law enforcement interest in him. *E.g.*, Greg Pallone, "'Shawshank' Fugitive on Lam Since 1959 now Fighting Extradition," *Bay News 9* [Brevard County, Fla.], May 14, 2015, *available at* www.baynews9.com/content/news/baynews9/news/article.html/content/news/articles/cf

certain national vehicle registration data,"[33] as well as computer software that can facilitate the identification of wanted individuals when they cross international boundaries. For example, the U.S. Department of State's Terrorist Interdiction Program (TIP), which began in 2002, "helps foreign governments improve their border control capability through software for creating an automated terrorist screening system with [a] fusion of names and relevant data. A benefit of TIP is that it provides immigration officials in selected countries with a computer-based, real-time system to verify the identities of travelers presenting themselves at border crossings."[34]

In addition, supplying host State law enforcement officers with location-tracking equipment like GPS devices may assist them in pinpointing the whereabouts of a fugitive.[35] Another way to increase host State capacity to locate fugitives is to provide it with electronic surveillance equipment or, more ambitiously, to jointly establish an electronic monitoring center within host State territory.[36]

Ask the Host State to Conduct Surveillance or Intercept Communications of a Fugitive and/or Provide the Fruits of Such

n/2015/5/14/shawshank_fugitive_fl.html (last visited on May 27, 2016) (discussing the case of Frank Freshwater, alias William Cox, who had escaped in 1959 from the Ohio State Reformatory (the site of the 1994 prison escape film, *The Shawshank Redemption*), but was arrested by a Brevard County, Florida, deputy sheriff following fingerprinting via a ruse).

33 *See* Bruce Zagaris, *E.U. Justice and Home Affairs Progresses on Illegal Aliens, Cooperation to Prevent and Investigate Criminal Offenses, and Environmental Crimes*, 24 IELR 330, 331 (2008). In June 2007, the Justice and Home Affairs Council of the E.U. agreed to the so-called Prüm decision to "improve the exchange of information between authorities responsible for the prevention and investigation of criminal offenses," including on the "conditions and procedure for the automated transfer" of key biodata and other identifying information. *Id.*

34 Raphael F. Perl, *Int'l Terrorism: Threat, Policy, and Response*, C.R.S. Report to Congress, updated Jan. 3, 2007, at 25.

35 *E.g.*, "GPS Aids in Tracking Fugitive to Mosier Rest Area," *The Dalles Chronicle* [Oregon], Oct. 19, 2013 (describing how Oregon Police troopers tracked a man who had fled a traffic crash scene and later stole a construction company's truck by relying on the GPS device in the company vehicle) (municipal case example).

36 *See* U.S. Dep't of State, 2014 International Narcotics Control Strategy Report (INCSR), Country Report on El Salvador (undated), *available at* www.state.gov/j/inl/rls/nrcrpt/2014/ (last visited on May 17, 2016) ("The United States has collaborated with El Salvador since 2010 to establish a National Electronic Monitoring Center (NEMC), which began operations in June 2012. The center allows Salvadoran law enforcement with judicial warrants to intercept electronic communications in furtherance of investigations of drug trafficking transnational criminal organizations. NEMC operations in 2013 resulted in 82 arrests from 10 separate investigations.")

Law Enforcement Activities. The host State, upon request, may be willing to conduct physical surveillance or signals/electronic interception of a fugitive that might yield information about his location, plans, schedules, haunts, associates, and the like, facilitating his capture once an arrest warrant has been issued. For example, the Colombian National Police, albeit on its own initiative rather than at a pursuing State's request, "obtained a court order to place a wiretap on [U.S. drug trafficker and prison escapee Harold] Rosenthal's phone" in connection with an investigation into possible cocaine smuggling operations.[37]

The host State also may be willing to share audio or video recordings, photographic images, or detailed physical descriptions, as well as the fruits of any signals or electronic interception, with pursuing State officials, which can help track down and pinpoint the location of a fugitive or the individuals with whom he is in regular contact. This occurred, for instance, via a secret agreement between the U.S. DEA and the Jamaican Ministry of National Security, when the latter allowed the former to listen in on the intercepted phone calls of Christopher "Dudus" Coke, a powerful head of a garrisoned community in Jamaica who faced narcotics trafficking charges in the United States.[38]

Request Authorization to Collect Supplementary Factual Information or Criminal Evidence within Host State Territory. To pinpoint the whereabouts of a fugitive and help construct a more compelling case for host State cooperation in his arrest, a pursuing State might choose to collect tangible evidence, interview witnesses, obtain judicial records, or undertake other investigatory measures within host State territory.[39]

[37] *United States v. Rosenthal*, 793 F.2d 1214, 1225 (11th Cir.) ("During one conversation, Rosenthal discussed murdering the Colombian Minister of Justice. Thereafter, the Colombian government became interested in expelling Rosenthal back to the United States."), *cert. denied*, 480 U.S. 919 (1986).

[38] "This led eventually to the [U.S.] extradition request [in August 2009]." Mattathais Schwartz, *A Report At Large: A Massacre in Jamaica*, The New Yorker, Dec. 2011, at 66. After months of wrangling over the extradition request, Coke was ultimately extradited by Jamaica to the United States where he was convicted and sentenced. "Jamaica Drug Kingpin 'Dudus' Coke Jailed for 23 Years," *BBC News*, June 8, 2012, *available at* www.bbc.com/news/world-us-canada-18371383 (last visited on May 28, 2016).

[39] *See, e.g.*, Agreement between the United States of America and El Salvador on Narcotic Drugs, Mar. 31, 2000, *as extended on* Aug. 20–21, 2014, T.I.A.S. 14–821 (concerning U.S. "Access to and Use of Facilities at the International Airport of El Salvador for Aerial Counter-Narcotics Activities").

Sometimes these activities are authorized pursuant to a bilateral[40] or multilateral[41] Mutual Legal Assistance Treaty (MLAT) or Mutual Legal Assistance Agreement (MLAA),[42] which, as a rule, however, do not apply to arrests, the enforcement of verdicts, or purely military offenses.[43] Absent an MLAT or MLAA, a pursuing State may request host State permission through the customary approach known as Letters Rogatory,[44] but such correspondence can often take a year or more to process.[45] Host State authorization of some kind is required, as it is a *prima facie* rule of international law (*see* Chapter 2.a) that a State may not engage in police activities on another State's territory absent its consent.

A fascinating application of such cooperation occurred prior to 1984, when the Republic of South Africa and the governments of Transkei and Ciskei (although not "independent" entities and therefore not recognized as States) reportedly entered into a secret reciprocal arrangement by which they agreed to permit one another's police forces free rein to cross their common border to follow up on suspected criminal activity.[46]

40 *E.g.*, Treaty on Mutual Legal Assistance in Crim. Matters, U.S.-Braz., Oct. 14, 1997, art. 1, U.S. Sen. Treaty No. 105–42, T.I.A.S. 12889.

41 *E.g.*, Eur. Conv. on Mutual Assistance in Crim. Matters, Apr. 20, 1959, art. 1, E.T.S. No. 30 [hereinafter Eur. MLAT Conv.] ("Contracting Parties undertake to afford each other . . . the widest measure of mutual assistance in proceedings in respect of [criminal] offences"); Draft Int'l Agreement on Illicit Payments, May 25, 1979, art. 10(1), U.N. Doc. E/1979/104, *reprinted in* 18 ILM 1025 (1979) ("Contracting States shall afford one another the greatest possible measure of assistance in connexion with criminal investigations and proceedings brought in respect of any of the offences [referenced in Article 1].").

42 Since the 1960s, the trend has been toward executing bilateral versus multilateral MLATs. M. CHERIF BASSIOUNI, INTRODUCTION TO INTERNATIONAL CRIMINAL LAW 353 & n.84 (2003) [hereinafter BASSIOUNI, INTRODUCTION]. MLATs, like extradition treaties, may contain exclusions, exceptions, and defenses, and are substantively similar to their extradition treaty counterparts. *Id.* at 353.

43 *E.g.*, Eur. MLAT Conv., *supra* n.41, art. 1.

44 This practice, which is premised on comity versus treaty law, and operates mainly in the civil versus criminal law context, occurs when a court in one State seeks the assistance of a court in another State for the purpose of collecting evidence. BASSIOUNI, INTRODUCTION, *supra* n.42, at 352. In the United States, the relevant statute can be found at 28 U.S.C. §§ 1696 and 1782 (2012). Letters Rogatory were issued, for example, by Belgium to Senegal and Chad in September and October 2001, respectively, for the purpose of seeking judicial cooperation in connection with bringing former Chadian leader Hissène Habré to justice. *See Questions Relating to the Obligation to Prosecute or Extradite* (Belg. v. Sen.), Judgment [2012] I.C.J. Rep. 422, ¶ 20 (July 20) [hereinafter *ICJ Case, Belg. v. Sen.*].

45 DoJ, *U.S. Attorneys' Manual*, Title 9, CRM 275 (2d ed. 2007–3 Supp.) [hereinafter *U.S. Attorneys' Manual*].

46 *See* Johannes T. Schoombee, *A Licence for Unlawful Arrests Across the Border?*, 101 S. AFR. L.J. 713 (1984) (arguing that such an arrangement was unlawful under South African municipal law).

Coordinate on or Undertake Joint Investigations. A pursuing State also can coordinate with the host State (or even with the assistance of a third party[47]) in detective work or to carry out a joint investigation, which can ultimately lead to a fugitive's location and arrest. For example, in 2005, Hong Kong and Singapore worked together to investigate a man wanted by Hong Kong on charges of theft who was also traveling to Singapore on multiple passports; he was eventually arrested at Singapore's Changi Airport and extradited to Hong Kong.[48] In another case, in 2004, a Diplomatic Security Special Agent assigned to the U.S. Embassy in Belize worked closely with Belizean police to locate in Belize City Reinaldo Silvestre, a Cuban national wanted on multiple counts in connection with performing unlicensed surgeries resulting in the permanent disfigurement of his patients.[49]

A more generalized version of this approach is for a law enforcement agency from one State to establish an office in another State and then work closely together to investigate crimes or criminal organizations of common concern.[50]

Participate in Joint Sting/Arrest Operations. Pursuing States can go even further by conducting joint "sting operations" in which agents of pursuing and host States combine forces to capture a fugitive through an "undercover or hidden police officer or surrogate, or some other form of deception."[51] The sting could be set in motion unilaterally by undercover pursuing State agents.[52]

47 For example, EUROJUST is credited with having effectively coordinated the arrest operation undertaken by Dutch Special Forces and the Italian Carabinieri of a fugitive A.D., nicknamed "Zio," who was connected to a Naples-based organized crime group in July 2011. Bruce Zagaris, *Dutch Arrest Fugitive Italian Mafia Boss with Use of New E.U. Mechanisms*, 27 IELR 975, 975–76 (2011).

48 Bruce Zagaris, *Singapore Arrests and Extradites Theft Fugitive to Hong Kong*, 21 IELR 225 (2005).

49 Bruce Zagaris, *Belize Arrests Miami Beach Fugitive Posing as Physician*, 21 IELR 11 (2005).

50 *See* Abraham Abramovsky, *Partners against Crime: Joint Prosecutions of Israeli Organized Crime Figures by U.S. and Israeli Authorities*, 19 FORDHAM INT'L L.J. 1903, 1918–19 (1996) (reporting that the FBI had opened offices in Moscow and Italy to operate jointly with their counterparts on investigations).

51 Graeme R. Newman with Kelly Socia, *Sting Operations*: Response Guide No. 6, Center for Problem-Oriented Policing, 2007, *available at* www.popcenter.org/responses/sting_operations/ (last visited on May 28, 2016).

52 For example, a U.S. DEA undercover agent posing as a cocaine buyer arranged for cocaine suppliers, a pilot, and someone to help transport the cocaine, and then when they all met in Panama City for the payment to be made, the DEA agent identified all the others to Panamanian law enforcement authorities as drug dealers, who were then arrested. *United States v. Cordero*, 668 F.2d 32, 35 (1st Cir. 1981).

Alternatively, it could be the product of a coordinated effort by agents of the pursuing and host States. For example, in March 2008, U.S. and Thai anti-narcotics officials joined together to lead a successful sting operation to snag Viktor Bout, a major global arms trafficker, which led ultimately to his extradition to the United States in November 2010.[53] Similarly, in January 2004, a U.S.-Panamanian joint operation resulted in the arrest and eventual extradition of Arcangel de Jesus Henao Montoya, an alleged Colombian cocaine trafficker, to the United States.[54] In addition, in October 1999, a coordinated operation between the U.S. FBI and South African police yielded the arrest in Cape Town of Khalfan Khamis Mohamed, who had been indicted in the United States for murder and conspiracy in the August 1988 bombings of the U.S. Embassies in Kenya and Tanzania.[55]

In March 2011, a Foreign-Deployed Advisory Support Team (FAST), "a special commando-style squad[ ] that [the U.S. DEA] has been quietly deploying for the past several years to Western Hemisphere nations, including Haiti, Honduras, the Dominican Republic, Guatemala, and Belize, to battle violent, transnational drug cartels," "assisted Guatemalan forces in [the] arrest of Juan Alberto Ortiz-Lopez, a top cocaine smuggler for the Sinaloa cartel."[56] Furthermore, in June 1997, U.S. officials acknowledged they had "negotiated an extraordinary diplomatic arrangement with another country" that needed to "remain secret to facilitate future law enforcement operations" in connection with the arrest of Mir Aimal Kasi, accused of murdering two CIA employees and injuring three others at its suburban Virginia Headquarters entrance in 1993.[57]

Sting operations, while generally upheld as a legitimate law enforcement technique,[58] risk violating international (and possibly municipal)

[53] AP, "Suspected Arms Trafficker Flown to NYC," *CBS New York*, Nov. 17, 2010, *available at* http://newyork.cbslocal.com/2010/11/17/suspected-arms-trafficker-flown-from-bangkok-to-nyc/ (last visited on May 28, 2016).

[54] Bruce Zagaris, *Panama Extradites Alleged Colombia Drug Lord to the U.S.*, 20 IELR 89, 89–90 (2004).

[55] Lynne Duke, "Ninth Suspect Charged in Embassy Bombings; Tanzanian Man Arrested in S. Africa," *Wash. Post*, Oct. 9, 1999, at A2.

[56] Charlie Savage, "Quietly, Special U.S. Squads Help Fight Drug Cartels," *IHT*, Nov. 8, 2011, at 5.

[57] Pierre Thomas & Roberto Suro, "Going Global to Get Their Man: Halfway Around the World, Lure of Reward Triggered FBI Undercover Effort to Capture CIA Suspect," *Wash. Post*, June 19, 1997, at A1, A10, A11.

[58] *E.g.*, "Briton to Be Extradited Within 10 Days Over Alleged Arms Exports to Iran," *The Guardian*, Feb. 13, 2012 (discussing the ECtHR's rejection of a retired British businessman's entrapment defense in connection with a U.S. Government sting

legal standards in one or more of three principal ways: (i) when government conduct is regarded as outrageous and thereby violates due process or principles of fundamental fairness;[59] (ii) when foreign officials directly participate in an arrest (although they can generally mentor and train domestic officers and even physically accompany them on the operation);[60] and (iii) when government conduct in devising enticements overreaches to the point of unlawful "entrapment".[61]

operation that revealed his attempt to sell controlled items to Iran in violation of trade sanctions); *Aniruddha Bahal v. State*, Crt. M.C. 2793/2009, High Ct., New Delhi, India, Sept. 24, 2010 (upholding the lawfulness of sting operations under Indian law).

59 This occurred, for example, when U.S. Customs Service (USCS) and U.S. DEA officials requested that Belize police plant 45 kilograms of cocaine on a Belize Air flight from Belize to Miami in April 1991 as part of an investigation into narcotics shipments between Belize and the United States. When the plane made an unscheduled stopover in Honduras, and drug-sniffing dogs detected the cocaine, the crew and passengers were detained "under abusive conditions" for almost a week. USCS and DEA agents had failed to coordinate this operation with the flight crew, the Honduran police, or the U.S. Embassy in Honduras. The U.S. Court of Appeals for the Eleventh Circuit affirmed a lower court ruling, finding the U.S. Government liable under the Federal Tort Claims Act (FTCA) for "injurious negligence and incompetence." *Couzada v. United States*, 105 F.3d 1389 (11th Cir. 1997). For other States' legal standards, *see, e.g., R. v. Latif* [1996] 1 WLR 104 (H.L.), [1996] 2 Cr. App. R. 92 (U.K. law authorizes a judge "in the exercise of his discretion to decide whether there has been an abuse of process, which amounts to an affront to the public conscience and requires the criminal proceedings to be stayed.") (finding that the trial judge did not err in refusing to stay the proceedings); DON STUART, CANADIAN CRIMINAL LAW: A TREATISE 612 (5th ed. 2007) (quoting *R. v. Young*, Ontario Ct. of App., [1984] 40 O.R. (2d) 520) (Canadian law permits stays of proceedings when "compelling an accused to stand trial would violate those fundamental principles of justice which underlie the community's sense of fair play and decency" or where the proceedings are "oppressive or vexatious.")).

60 Savage, *supra* n.56, at 5. Under U.S. law, pursuant to the so-called Mansfield Amendment, "[n]o officer or employee of the United States may directly effect an arrest in any foreign country as part of any foreign police action with respect to narcotics control efforts, notwithstanding any other provision of law." 22 U.S.C. § 2291(c) (2012) (international narcotics trafficking).

61 As one author explained the limits of lawful entrapment in the aftermath of the 1992 U.S. Supreme Court's *Jacobson* decision, 503 U.S. 540 (1992), "agents may not be able to become so involved in the criminal enterprise that they, in essence, operate it. Officers may not be able to plant the idea of crime in the mind of the citizen and then ensure its fruition by a process of detailed instructions to that citizen. Moreover, the government may not be permitted to conduct an operation in which the individual is targeted over a very long period of time and then only solicited to commit a crime at the end of the extensive investigation." Paul Marcus, *Presenting, Back From the [Almost] Dead, the Entrapment Defense*, College of William & Mary Law School Faculty Publications, 1995, *available at* http://scholarship.law.wm.edu/cgi/viewcontent.cgi?article=1612&context=facpubs (last visited on May 17, 2016). The major factor in determining entrapment under U.S. law is whether criminal intent originated with the defendant or the government agents. *United States v. Nations*, 764 F.2d 1073, 1079 (5th Cir. 1985). Significantly,

ii Third-Party Support

Press Third States, Individuals Close to the Fugitive, and/or INTERPOL to Supply Law Enforcement or Intelligence Leads. It could prove helpful for a pursuing State to obtain information about a fugitive from States where he has family members, has resided or been imprisoned, or otherwise one that has taken a law enforcement interest in his activities. Such information, on its own or when combined with other pieces of intelligence, could assist a pursuing State to locate a fugitive for use in requesting his arrest.

A related approach is to ask individuals close to the fugitive, *e.g.*, parents, siblings, ex-romantic partners, or former business associates, for any information they may be able to supply that could help determine the fugitive's whereabouts, reveal his daily routines or travel plans, or identify his aides, among other types of tips. Such solicitations can rely on monetary payments, appeals to patriotism, or perhaps an exchange of favors. For example, shortly after Edward Snowden was identified as the person responsible for leaking classified U.S. intelligence information to journalists, FBI agents sought intervention by his father, Lon Snowden, an ex-U.S. Coast Guard officer, to help coax his son home, but he was unwilling to travel to Moscow on such a mission once he learned his son was being viewed as a traitor.[62]

A pursuing State also could request assistance from INTERPOL, via issuance of a so-called "blue notice," to solicit reports on locational or other information about a named fugitive from law enforcement agencies worldwide.[63]

Ask a Third State to Arrest a Fugitive Upon Entering or Before Leaving Its Territory. To the extent that: (i) intelligence concerning a fugitive reveals that he may plan on his own to travel from a "safe haven" State to the territory of a third State more amenable to bringing him to justice,[64]

neither the United Kingdom nor Canada recognizes entrapment *per se* as a defense. *See also* n.211 and accompanying text in Chapter 5.

62 Greg Miller, "U.S. Officials Scrambled to Nab Snowden, Hoping He Would Take a Wrong Step. He Didn't.," *WashingtonPost.com*, June 14, 2014, *available at* www.washingtonpost.com/world/national-security/us-officials-scrambling-to-nab-snowden-hoped-he-would-take-a-wrong-step-he-didnt/2014/06/14/057a1ed2-f1ae-11e3-bf76-447a5df6411f_story.html (last visited on May 17, 2016).

63 INTERPOL website, Notices, "Blue Notice," *available at* www.interpol.int/INTERPOL-expertise/Notices (last visited on May 17, 2016) (intended "to solicit additional information about a person's identity, location or activities in relation to a crime").

64 For example, after Brazil was unsuccessful in winning the extradition of Italian citizen Salvatore Cacciola, a highly sought-after white-collar criminal in connection with bank

(ii) the fugitive is being lured to such a third State (labeled herein as a "tactical" lure and capture operation[65]), or (iii) it is learned that the ship or aircraft on which a fugitive is a passenger (including while the subject of deportation) has a scheduled destination or stopover in such a third State (or will be making or has just made an *un*scheduled layover there), a pursuing State could request that authorities in that third State apprehend the fugitive once he enters (or at least before he leaves) their jurisdiction,[66] most likely pursuant to an INTERPOL Red Notice[67] or a Provisional Arrest Warrant (PAW).[68]

Ultimately, the aim of this approach is to seek the fugitive's onward extradition, deportation, or other transfer to the pursuing State at issue. This is a reasonably common method of arresting a fugitive who otherwise is non-extraditable from a "safe haven" State, although not all such cross-border movements prove consequential from a law enforcement perspective.[69] Successful examples abound, including the following:

fraud charges and who had taken refuge in Italy after skipping bail, he was arrested when he carelessly crossed into Monaco, whose courts eventually approved his extradition to Brazil in July 2008. Bruce Zagaris, *Monaco Will Extradite Alleged Bank Defrauder to Brazil*, 24 IELR 357, 357 (2008).

65 This designation is intended to distinguish this type of lure and capture operation (LCO) from one in which the destination of a lure operation is *pursuing State territory or elsewhere within pursuing State custody or control*, and, if so, is labeled herein as a "strategic" LCO. *See* Chapter 1.h. The lawfulness of tactical LCOs is examined in Chapter 12.c.i.

66 *See U.S. Attorneys' Manual, supra* n.45, § 9–15.620 ("If the fugitive travels outside the country from which he or she is not extraditable, it may be possible to request his or her extradition from another country. This method is often used for fugitives who are citizens in their country of refuge.").

67 *See* n.73 in the Introduction.

68 For instance, while he remained in Belgium, the United States was unable to proceed against Belgian national Wilfried Van Cauwenberghe for fraudulently inducing an American citizen to invest in a real estate partnership in Kansas City, but as soon as U.S. authorities learned that he was traveling on a short business trip to Geneva, the United States requested issuance of a PAW from Swiss authorities in November 1984, followed by submission of an extradition request four months later in March 1985. *United States v. Van Cauwenberghe*, 827 F.2d 424, 424–25 (9th Cir. 1987).

69 For example, in the case of Hollywood film director Roman Polanski, after skipping bail in California and fleeing to France, which refused his extradition to the United States on child sex abuse charges for over thirty years, in 2009 Polanski traveled to Zurich to receive an award at a film festival and was arrested by Swiss authorities, but Switzerland declined to extradite him, citing doubts about the conduct of the judge in the original trial. Nick Cumming-Bruce & Michael Cieply, "Swiss Reject U.S. Request to Extradite Polanski," *N.Y. Times*, July 12, 2010 (noting that Polanski was under house arrest in his chalet in Gstaad during the ten-month proceedings). Pursuant to a U.S. extradition request to the

- In May 1949, British law enforcement officers arrested Gerhardt Eisler, a German-born U.S. Communist who had jumped bail during U.S. appellate proceedings and stowed away on a merchant ship flying under the Polish flag, while anchored in Southampton, in British territorial waters; the United States, which sought his extradition on charges of contempt of Congress and false statements, had learned of his departure and wired to the British Government asking for its assistance in his recovery.[70]
- In January 1985, the Australian Federal Police requested that the U.S. FBI help secure the arrest of Walter Alexander Levinge, who was wanted for a large number of "crimes of dishonesty," during one of his regular ventures across the Mexican border into San Diego, California.[71]
- In March 1995, after twenty years of failed attempts to win extradition from the United States (due to constitutional "freedom of speech" objections) of Gary Lauck, a U.S. citizen residing in Nebraska and known as the "Farm Belt Führer" for his publishing and dissemination of anti-Semitic and other Neo-Nazi literature, Germany obtained his custody when he traveled to Hundige, Denmark, and was arrested by Danish authorities and turned over to Germany via an INTERPOL Red Notice.[72]

Polish Government in January 2015, new court proceedings were held in Krakow, where Polanski was shooting a film on the Dreyfus Affair. Given Polanski's revered status in Poland (where he is also a national), coupled with the Polish Government's agreement not to extradite him to the United States as a condition of his filming in Krakow, it came as no surprise when Poland refused his extradition. *See* Matthew Day, "Roman Polanksi U.S. Extradition Case Adjourned by Polish Court," *The Telegraph* (U.K.), May 22, 2015; Michal Kolanko & Michael Cieply, "Polish Judge Rejects Extradition of Roman Polanski," *N.Y. Times*, Oct. 30, 2015.

70 *See* R.Y. Jennings, *The Eisler Case*, 26 B.Y.B.I.L. 468, 468 (1949) (The Polish Government protested the arrest on the ground that Eisler was protected as a political asylee, but the British rebutted that "[t]he absence of any right to grant asylum on board merchant ships sprang from a universally recognized principle of international law that a merchant ship in the ports or roadsteads of another country falls under the jurisdiction of the coastal State."); George A. Finch, Edit. Cmt., *The Eisler Extradition Case*, 43 AJIL 487, 487 (1949).

71 *Levinge v. Director of Custodial Services, et al.*, N.S.W. Ct. of App., July 23, 1987, 9 N.S.W. L. Rep. 546 ("'[I]t is considered probable by the FBI agents that he commutes regularly across the Mexican border through Tijuana into San Diego where he is known to have a number of associates and therefore a decision has been taken at this time to allow inquiries to proceed along the present lines of attempting to secure ... [his] arrest in the United States.'") (quoting Australia Federal Police cable).

72 Thomas F. Muther, Jr., *The Extradition of Int'l Criminals: A Changing Perspective*, 24 Denv. J. Int'l L. & Pol'y 221, 221–22 & n.8 (1995).

- In December 1995, at the request of the United Kingdom, acting on behalf of its Crown colony Hong Kong, U.S. authorities detained Lui Kin-Hong when he deplaned in Boston during a business trip and held him on a PAW pending extradition proceedings.[73]
- In December 2007, on the authority of an outstanding arrest warrant, Trinidadian police arrested Jorge Hernan Ospina-Zuluaga, a fugitive from U.S. justice for thirteen years, based on an indictment for conspiracy to launder drug-trafficking revenues, when he traveled to Trinidad from Colombia, which did not then recognize the charged offense under its domestic law and so had been unwilling to extradite him.[74]
- In March 2013, when German financier Florian Homm, who was aware of U.S. and Swiss law enforcement interest in him for defrauding investors and had consequently lived "incognito in Colombia [beginning in 2007] before resurfacing in 2012," left Germany "to visit his ex-wife and son in Florence," where he was monitored by "U.S. and Italian law enforcement authorities and arrested at the Uffizi Gallery."[75]

As far as such LCO scenarios are concerned, the third State is not necessarily involved in the *lure* portion of the operation, but rather tends to cooperate with a pursuing State during the *capture* portion. Some examples are illustrative.

- In February 1977, a U.S. DEA agent induced a fugitive, who had escaped from prison after only serving the first few years of his ten-year sentence for the interstate transportation of stolen securities, to fly to Panama City, where he was held for seven days before being put on an aircraft bound for Miami.[76]
- After the Netherlands refused to arrest one of its nationals, Stuart Artie Van Sichem, pending an extradition request to face drug charges in New York, the United States "arranged for him to be enticed into

[73] *United States v. Kin-Hong*, 110 F.3d 103, 107 (1st Cir. 1997) (notably, Kin-Hong, who was charged in Hong Kong with conspiracy to receive and receiving bribes, was aware of Hong Kong's law enforcement interest in him and consequently had not returned there since April 1994).

[74] Bruce Zagaris, *Trinidad Extradites Colombian to the U.S. on Money Laundering Charges*, 24 IELR 266 (2008).

[75] Jack Ewing, "Financier, Free Again, Comes to Rest on Home Turf," *INYT*, Aug. 4, 2014, at 1, 16.

[76] *Di Lorenzo v. United States*, 496 F. Supp. 79 (S.D.N.Y. 1980).

Belgium by an informant" and from there he was extradited to the United States.[77]

- In 1982, former CIA agent Edwin Wilson, who had been charged with smuggling munitions to Muammar Qaddafi, "was duped by [undercover] agents of the government [the U.S. Marshal's Service] who persuaded him to travel [from his safe haven in Libya] to the Dominican Republic. With the cooperation of [police] authorities there Wilson was placed on a commercial aircraft bound for the United States," during which he was arrested.[78]
- In January 2003, following a successful lure from Yemen to Germany on the promise of meeting a potential donor in Frankfurt am Main, Sheik Mohammed Ali Hassan Moayad, adviser to Yemeni Minister for Religious Foundations who was suspected of providing material support to al-Qaida and Hamas, was arrested together with his secretary; subsequently, the United States requested his extradition, which was granted after challenges were denied.[79]

This scenario also can play out where a pursuing State seeks the arrest and detention by a cooperative third State within whose territory the ship or aircraft on which the fugitive is a passenger is directed, most commonly in connection with an alien fugitive's deportation. Accordingly, where the host State is prepared to deport a fugitive to a third (destination) State, which, in turn, is to cooperate with the pursuing State at issue in bringing the fugitive to justice, the fugitive could be the subject of a PAW directed at that third State to be effected upon his arrival. For example, William Robb, a British national, was deported from the Philippines and placed on a KLM flight *en route* to the United Kingdom first via Dubai (where he was not allowed to de-plane) and later via Amsterdam, where the DEA had arranged for him to be detained and later extradited by the Netherlands to the United States.[80]

[77] Philip B. Heymann & Ian Heath Gershengorn, *Pursuing Justice, Respecting the Law, in* PRINCIPLES AND PROCEDURES FOR A NEW TRANSNATIONAL CRIMINAL LAW: DOCUMENTATION OF AN INTERNATIONAL WORKSHOP IN FREIBURG, MAY 1991, at 146 (Albin Eser & Otto Lagodny eds. 1992).

[78] *United States v. Wilson*, 732 F.2d 404, 411 (5th Cir.), *cert. denied*, 469 U.S. 1099 (1984); *see also* Michael Wines, "U.S. Cites Right to Seize Fugitives Abroad," *N.Y. Times*, Oct. 14, 1989, at 6.

[79] Eva Wagner, *German Federal Constitutional Court Approves Extradition of Yemeni Citizen*, 20 IELR 14 (2004).

[80] Howard Marks, "Extradition, U.S. Drug Policy, and the Erosion of Individual Liberties," Int'l Substance Use Library, *DrugText.org* website, Dec. 12, 1999, *available at* www.drugtext.org/Law-and-treaties/extradition-us-drug-policy-and-the-erosion-of-individual-liberties.html (last visited on May 17, 2016).

Alternatively, where the deportation route consists of a scheduled stopover or there happens to be an emergency layover in a cooperative third State, and the pursuing State at issue is able to closely monitor the deported individual's movements once he leaves the host State,[81] a pursuing State could transmit a PAW to that third State or, better yet, have arranged in advance via INTERPOL for the issuance of a Red Notice for that fugitive's arrest. For example, in 1963, in an effort to secure the custody of OAS leader Captain Jean-Marie Curutchet, France arranged for his passport and paid for his flight from Switzerland to Uruguay, and when the airplane made a scheduled stop at Dakar, "he was arrested by Senegalese personnel under the command of a French officer [and] taken to France."[82]

Request the Cooperation of Third States Working Together to Precipitate an Unscheduled Stopover and, if Necessary, Enforce Their Sovereign Rights by Conducting an Aircraft Interception. One aggressive approach is to arrange with a regional bloc of cooperative third States to restrict use of their airspace to aircraft suspected of carrying a fugitive of interest and thereby circumstantially force an unscheduled stopover (for refueling purposes) in a State ideally willing to help bring that fugitive to justice. This tactic was well illustrated by a recent aircraft operation that might best be characterized as a "*passive interception.*"[83]

France, Portugal, and Spain all barred a private Bolivian aircraft carrying President Evo Morales from flying over its airspace on July 2, 2013, effectively forcing it to land in Vienna, Austria, to refuel. At the request of the United States, these European allies agreed to restrict the aircraft's passing through their sovereign space because it was suspected that Edward Snowden, the NSA contractor who had leaked volumes of classified U.S. intelligence, was on board. [84] When the aircraft was being refueled, it was searched, but Snowden was not found and, because Morales was not charged with a crime, no one was arrested. The French Government later apologized to Bolivia for having delayed the President's journey by forcing it to divert its scheduled route and having

81 Such monitoring can be effected, for example, through the use of paid informants, hired investigators, or photographic devices.

82 "Kidnapping Incidents," 32 *Bull. of the Int'l Comm'n of Jurists* 24, 28 (Dec. 1967).

83 "Passive interception" is defined herein as *a State's verbal admonition, that its territory, including sovereign waters and airspace, as appropriate, are restricted from use or passage by specified aircraft, vessels, or vehicles suspected of carrying a fugitive.*

84 Jonathan Watts & Dan Roberts, "Bolivian President Leaves Austria as Diplomatic Row Erupts Over Diversion," *The Guardian*, July 3, 2013.

to refuel in order to complete the trip.[85] More aggressive yet would be to encourage those cooperating States to enforce any failure to adhere to such no-flyover warnings by carrying out an (active) interception operation.[86]

Seek the Cooperation of One or More Third States to Exclude Refuge or Territorial Admission to an Alien Fugitive. Rather than ask a third State to *arrest* a fugitive on its behalf, a pursuing State could request at least the denial of refuge in or admission to its territory. The logic behind this approach is to foreclose potential destinations for an alien removed by another State, and thereby ensure that he, ultimately or by default, arrives in pursuing State or sympathetic third State territory. In the *Soblen Case*, for example, the United States reportedly exhorted both Greece and the United Kingdom to exclude Robert Soblen's admission, as cities in those States constituted interim scheduled stops by the Israeli airliner transporting him to the United States.[87]

Similarly, to help compel Samuel Insull's return from Greece to the United States, American authorities requested States neighboring Greece to exclude his admission.[88] In another instance, the United States reportedly asked Tunisia and Greece to disallow an aircraft carrying the four Palestinian hijackers of the *Achille Lauro* cruise ship, as well as Abu Abbas and another PLO leader, from landing in their territory after the hijackers had departed Egypt in the hope of reaching a "safe haven."[89]

[85] Samantha Stainburn, "France Apologizes to Bolivia for Blocking President's Plane; Bolivia Calls It 'Virtual Kidnapping,'" *Globalpost*, July 4, 2013, *available at* www.globalpost.com/dispatch/news/regions/americas/130704/france-apologizes-bolivia-blocking-president-s-plane (last visited on May 17, 2016).

[86] Aircraft interception operations are discussed in Chapter 12.b.iv in the context of a unilateral full-scale alternative to extradition, as that is the manner in which they have generally manifested. The lawfulness of aircraft interception operations is addressed in Chapter 12.c.iii.

[87] "A Spy Waiting for Death; Dr. Robert A. Soblen Family Scattered," *N.Y. Times*, July 2, 1962, at 1.

[88] Evans, *supra* n.16, at 84.

[89] *See* Jonathan Broder, "U.S. Enters New Phase against Terrorism," *Chi. Trib.*, Oct. 13, 1985 ("The cooperation of Greece and Tunisia in refusing landing rights to the Egyptian plane also helped, the experts said. They suggested, however, that Greece's anti-American posture and Tunisia's anger over U.S. support for Israel's Oct. 1 air strike on PLO headquarters in Tunis made their decision a question of realpolitik, not moral considerations.").

Offer a Monetary Reward for the Capture of a Fugitive or for Information Leading to His Arrest. When pursuing States have reason to believe private individuals could be motivated through sizable monetary payments to furnish valuable information regarding the whereabouts of a fugitive, governments may well choose to adopt a rewards program.[90] Examples include:

- In May 1985, several million dollars, including US $1 million from the Government of Israel and the World Zionist Organization, were offered for the capture of Dr. Josef Mengele, the Auschwitz Concentration Camp physician.[91]
- In July 1985, the United States posted a reward of US $100,000 for information leading to the arrest of those responsible for killing six Americans in El Salvador.[92]
- In June 1997, the United States offered US $2 million for information leading to the capture of Mir Aimal Kasi, wanted for his shooting spree outside of the CIA Headquarters entrance in 1993 that killed two and injured three persons.[93]
- In 2007, a collective bounty of over €300,000 was made available by the German and Austrian Governments, together with the Los Angeles-based Wiesenthal Center, for the capture of Aribert Heim, a Nazi physician at the Mauthausen Concentration Camp in Austria who was alleged to have killed hundreds of prisoners in operations without anesthesia.[94]
- Also in 2007, the U.S. Department of State, under its Narcotics Rewards Program, offered to pay up to US $5 million for the capture of Diego León Montoyo Sánchez, a Colombian narcotics boss who

[90] *See* Perl, C.R.S. Report, *supra* n.34, at 18 ("Rewards for information have been instrumental in Italy in destroying the Red Brigades and in Colombia in apprehending drug cartel leaders. A State Department program is in place, supplemented by the aviation industry, usually offering rewards of up to $5 million to anyone providing information that would prevent or resolve an act of international terrorism against U.S. citizens or U.S. property, or that leads to the arrest or conviction of terrorist criminals involved in such acts.").

[91] "Israel to Reward Mengele's Captor," *N.Y. Times*, May 8, 1985.

[92] Bernard Gwertzman, "U.S. Offers $100,000 for Killers of 6 Americans in San Salvador," *N.Y. Times*, July 20, 1985, at 1.

[93] Thomas & Suro, *supra* n.57, at A1, A11 (the reward reportedly "played a significant part in motivating those who helped identify and locate [him]").

[94] Monte Reel, "In South America, a 'Last Chance' to Hunt Down Nazi War Criminals," *Wash. Post*, Dec. 6, 2007, at A20.

appeared on the U.S. Department of Treasury's Specially Designated National List.[95]

A potential wrinkle can occur, however, where the individual or group responsible for handing over the fugitive does not itself have "clean hands" and yet is otherwise entitled to the bounty. For example, when Seleka, a rebel group operating in the Central African Republic (CAR), sought the US $5 million bounty offered for information leading to the capture of Dominic Ongwen, a senior commander of the Lord's Resistance Army (LRA) wanted by the ICC, after Seleka had captured and turned over Ongwen to the United States, the United States was placed in an awkward posture, given that it had earlier blamed Seleka for other atrocities, including killing civilians.[96]

Circulate Photographs or Other Images of a Fugitive Through the Media. Sometimes arrests are made possible by virtue of members of the public seeing photographs, artistic sketches, or other images of a fugitive displayed on posters, in magazines, on television shows, and on Internet websites who then might contact law enforcement officers regarding the location of the fugitive or his residence or office or commercial establishments he frequents, or the names of individuals with whom he socializes. An example of this occurred in November 1988, when after escaping custody a decade earlier from Tennessee for two counts of rape and murder as well as aggravated assault of a police officer, Joseph Alan Shepherd fled to Ontario, Canada, under the assumed name James Joseph Tripp, but was identified by a neighbor who saw his photograph on a U.S. television program called "Unsolved Mysteries" that featured individuals on the FBI's "Most Wanted" List.[97] In another instance, Julian Tzolov, a former Wall Street broker accused of securities fraud and who was believed to have fled to Spain's Costa del Sol in May 2009, was discovered, despite his use of false identities and bodyguards, after an international search that included Spain's National Police circulating his photograph.[98]

[95] Bruce Zagaris, *Colombia Arrests Alleged Head of Drug Cartel and Prepares to Extradite*, 23 IELR 441 (2007) (Montoyo was eventually arrested by the Colombian Army by a special forces unit in September 2007).

[96] Craig Whitlock, "Militia Commander's Surrender Has a Catch," *Wash. Post*, Jan. 14, 2015, at A7.

[97] *In re Shepherd and Minister of Employment & Immigration*, Ontario Ct. of App., [1989] 70 O.R. (2d) 765 (his identity was verified by fingerprinting).

[98] Bruce Zagaris, *Spain Arrests Fugitive New York Banker*, 25 IELR 372, 372–73 (2009).

c Avenues of Recourse Under Another's Judicial System

The final type of fallback alternative to extradition available to a pursuing State is to ensure that prosecution of some kind proceeds against a fugitive, even if it does not take place in its own domestic judicial system.[99] This approach tends to be followed in instances where a pursuing State has been or strongly fears it will be rebuffed regarding an extradition request[100] and has therefore lost faith it will ever obtain physical custody of the fugitive, while, at the same time, believing that another forum – whether the host State, a third State, or an international criminal tribunal – would be able to satisfactorily prosecute the fugitive. Alternatively, a pursuing State may choose to support a prosecution elsewhere by offering to share material evidence or fact or expert witnesses.

Such *redirection* is generally a second-order preference because a pursuing State cannot be certain (i) that an arrested fugitive will necessarily be prosecuted elsewhere, (ii) even if he is, that the most serious or all available charges will be lodged; (iii) even if they are, that he will be prosecuted zealously; (iv) even if he is, that he will be convicted; (v) even if so, that he will receive an appropriately long, rather than a diminished, prison sentence; and (vi) even if he does, that he will not ultimately obtain a suspended sentence, an early parole, or be the beneficiary of a pardon, amnesty, or a prisoner exchange by another State.[101]

Request the Host State Itself to Prosecute a Fugitive. Where the host State is faced with a choice between extradition and domestic prosecution, and where it is legally prohibited from extraditing a given fugitive (or even where extradition is otherwise regarded as undesirable for political, human rights, or practical reasons[102]), a pursuing State could

[99] This fallback alternative to extradition relates only to prosecution, not punishment, as the operational aim.

[100] Curiously, at times, if an extradition request is denied, a pursuing State and the host State may each elect to undertake criminal proceedings (the former in an *in absentia* posture) against the subject individual in parallel, which not only is an inefficient use of judicial resources but also can complicate the availability of witnesses and evidence for use in court. *See* Bruce Zagaris, *U.S. Senator Introduces Legislation to Track Foreign Fugitives*, 28 IELR 164, 165 (2012) (discussing how Mozambique and South Africa undertook concurrent legal proceedings against the same alleged criminal (Mozambique national Chakoma Machaba) for the same offense (for his role in an attack on two individuals in South Africa)).

[101] *See generally* Heymann & Gershengorn, *supra* n.77, at 140–42.

[102] In such circumstances, domestic prosecution can at times be a more effective means of ensuring a fugitive is appropriately punished, such as when the choice is to extradite him

press the host State to undertake domestic prosecution, as that approach may hold out the best prospect of the fugitive being brought to justice at all. It is also possible that the host State will opt to prosecute on its own initiative[103] under a recognized jurisdictional principle,[104] or may be required to satisfy an express treaty obligation under the principle known as *aut dedere aut judicare* (abbreviated herein as *aut dedere* and introduced in Chapter 2.c.ii).[105]

Host States occasionally prosecute fugitives in lieu of extradition. For example, beginning in September 2009, after refusing to extradite François Bazaramba, a former Rwandan pastor, to face genocide and murder charges in Rwanda, the Finnish Government prosecuted him in its own courts, ultimately finding him guilty of genocide and murder of or the incitement to murder at least five persons.[106] In another case, in 2007, the United States decided to prosecute Mexico's former Deputy Attorney General Mario Ruiz Massieu, who had fled to the United States in 1999 after being implicated in drug-related corruption and money laundering, despite Mexico's attempt to have him extradited or

to a State in the throes of political chaos or where there is a substantial risk that a particular pursuing State government will change hands and, given its anticipated political or ideological sympathies, the person may not remain in jail for very long. For example, in January 2003 when an alleged human rights abuser, Carl Dorélien, was deported back to his native Haiti and imprisoned there, he was released shortly thereafter in 2004 by anti-President Aristide insurgents who had by then regained power. Simona Agnolucci, *Deportation of Human Rights Abusers: Toward Achieving Accountability, Not Fostering Impunity*, 30 Hastings Int'l & Comp. L. Rev. 347, 356–58, 364 (2007).

103 *Cf.* Meeting of the Justice and Interior Ministers of The Eight (G-8), Dec. 9–10, 1997, Communiqué, Wash., D.C., Dec. 10, 1997 [hereinafter G-8 Communiqué] (in 1997 Justice and Interior Ministers of the G-8 countries committed to conduct "effective domestic prosecutions in lieu thereof" where the extradition of nationals was not possible).

104 *See* Chapter 2.c.

105 Even apart from any applicable treaty obligations, it has been argued that an additional duty to prosecute may exist under the principle of legality. Otto Lagodny, *Legally Protected Interests of the Abducted Alleged Offender*, 27 Isr. L. Rev. 339, 342 n.13 (1993). The "principle of legality" has been defined as follows: "In its broadest sense, [it] encompasses the following in respect of criminal provisions: (1) the principle of non-retroactivity . . .; (2) the prohibition against analogy . . .; (3) the principle of certainty . . .; and (4) the prohibition against uncodified, i.e. unwritten, or judge-made criminal provisions . . . In sum, this means that an act can be punished only if, at the time of its commission, the act was the object of a valid, sufficiently precise, written criminal law to which a sufficiently certain sanction was attached." Claus Kreß, *Nulla poena nullum crimen sine lege*, Max Planck Encyclopedia of Public International Law, at 1.

106 *See Ahorugeze v. Sweden*, Appl. No. 37075/09, 55 EHRR, ¶ 65–66, Oct. 27, 2011 (final issued on June 4, 2012) (Bazaramba case discussed therein).

deported.[107] Similarly, although the Government of the Netherlands was unwilling to extradite one of its nationals, Stuart Artie Van Sichem, to the United States to face drug charges, it was prepared to prosecute him under its own domestic laws.[108]

As one of the most commonly cited examples of an extradition alternative in the literature, *aut dedere* warrants a reasonably detailed examination.[109] The purpose of this principle is to suppress crime[110] and hold perpetrators accountable by presenting the host State[111] with a binary choice: *either extradite the individual to a pursuing State*[112] *or*

[107] Bruce Zagaris, *U.S. Arrests Mexican Fugitive on Drug Charges*, 23 IELR 352 (2007). This decision to prosecute was driven by the fact that the U.S. Magistrate Judge (in Newark, N.J.) ruled that he would not allow Massieu to be extradited to Mexico because, as he stated: "In all good conscience, I cannot [grant extradition]. I find to be incredible and unreliable all of the statements taken from witnesses in this case. I will not sign a certificate to send a man to a country which has admittedly practiced torture in the questioning of suspects." Robert L. Jackson & Juanita Darling, "U.S. Judge Won't Extradite Former Mexico Official," *L.A. Times*, June 23, 1995.

[108] Heymann & Gershengorn, *supra* n.77, at 146.

[109] *Aut dedere* is not an "alternative to extradition" in the strict sense that one possible end result of its application is in fact extradition itself. It follows, then, that the true alternative to extradition in this context would be good faith measures undertaken by the host State toward prosecution in its own courts. This is why *aut dedere* is not identified herein as an alternative to extradition *per se*. It is also noteworthy that, by contrast with many of the other "fallback alternatives" described, which are fully accessible to a *pursuing State*, this particular mechanism lies within the exclusive control of the *host State*. The leading ICJ case today on *aut dedere* is *Questions Relating to the Obligation to Prosecute or Extradite* (Belg. v. Sen.), *supra* n.44.

[110] M. Cherif Bassiouni & Edward M. Wise, Aut Dedere aut Judicare: The Duty to Extradite or Prosecute in International Law 3 (1995). The *aut dedere* principle derives from the general interest of States in "upholding each other's criminal laws whenever these laws' protected social interests are the same." Bassiouni, Introduction, *supra* n.42, at 336.

[111] To be subject to the obligation of *aut dedere*, all conventions invariably require that the alleged offender be in the territory of the custodial (or host) State (*judex deprehensionis*). Robert Kolb, *The Exercise of Criminal Jurisdiction over Int'l Terrorists, in* Enforcing International Law Norms against Terrorism 268 (Andrea Bianchi ed. 2004).

[112] A 2006 treaty containing an *aut dedere* provision allowed, for the first time, for the physical transfer to another State in accordance with its international obligations or to *an international criminal tribunal it recognizes.* Int'l Conv. for the Protection of All Persons from Enforced Disappearance, UNGA Res. 61/177, Dec. 20, 2006, art. 9(2), U.N. Doc. A/61/448. An apparent conflict would seem to exist under all other conventions between an obligation to "extradite" and "surrendering" a fugitive at the request of an international criminal tribunal. *See* Chapter 2.c.iv. In such a circumstance, there would be no issue with those courts like the ICTY and ICTR possessing concurrent jurisdiction as they have primacy, but with courts like the ICC that have complementary jurisdiction, it remains unclear. Claire Mitchell, *The Scope and Operate of the Obligation*

take good faith measures toward prosecution under its own judicial system. More pointedly, to the extent a State decides not to extradite and consequently is obliged under the language of most formulations to "submit the case to competent authorities in view of prosecution,"[113] it is decidedly not a *requirement* to prosecute *per se* but rather to turn the case over to the appropriate domestic law enforcement agencies to determine in good faith whether prosecution is warranted.[114] This phraseology recognizes the separation of governmental powers by preserving the prerogatives of the executive branch.[115]

The term itself, while useful, is concededly inexact: (i) *dedere* means to surrender or deliver (the verb *extradere* did not exist in classical or medieval Latin, first appearing in the eighteenth century in French and in the nineteenth century in English[116]); and (ii) *judicare* means to judge (by way of trial), even though the conventional requirement is only to take steps toward prosecution, so no full trial necessarily results and therefore the term *prosequi* (meaning to pursue or prosecute) arguably is more precise.[117] Notably, the "dedere" option, as understood today, does not contemplate deportation or informal transfers, as the former would not always result in the fugitive's prosecution or punishment, while the latter would not ensure the fugitive obtained certain human rights safeguards (such as specialty) afforded under extradition.[118]

Prevailing legal authority suggests that *aut dedere* has yet to emerge as an affirmative obligation under customary international law; rather, its

(Part 2) of Aut Dedere, aut Judicare: *The Extradite or Prosecute Clause in Int'l Law*, IHEID, Graduate Inst. Publications Online, 2009, ¶¶ 5–7, *available at* http://books.openedition.org/iheid/249 (last visited on May 17, 2016). *See also* n.280 and accompanying text in Chapter 2.

113 *E.g.*, Conv. for the Suppression of Unlawful Acts against the Safety of Civil Aviation, Sept. 23, 1971, art. 7, U.N. Doc. A/C.6/418/Corr.2, Annex III, 974 U.N.T.S. 177, 24 U.S.T. 564, *reprinted in* 10 ILM 1151 [hereinafter Montreal Conv.].

114 This formulation first appeared in the 1970 "Hague Hijacking Convention," more formally known as the Conv. for the Suppression of Unlawful Seizure of Aircraft, Dec. 16, 1970, U.N. Doc. A/C.6/418/Corr.1, Annex II, 860 U.N.T.S. 105, 22 U.S.T. 1641, *reprinted in* 10 ILM 133 (1971), and has proven to be a model for such a provision in almost all international and regional treaties since then. Mitchell, *supra* n.112, ¶ 2.

115 Bart DeSchutter, *Problems of Jurisdiction in the Int'l Control and Repression of Terrorism*, *in* International Terrorism and Political Crimes 386 (M. Cherif Bassiouni ed. 1975).

116 Bassiouni & Wise, *supra* n.110, at 4 n.7.

117 *Id.* at 4 & n.5; Kolb, *supra* n.111, at 263.

118 Chatham House, Miša Zgonec-Rožej and Joanne Foakes, *Int'l Criminals: Extradite or Prosecute?*, Chatham House Briefing Paper, IL BP 2013/01, July 2013, at 10 [hereinafter Chatham House Briefing Paper].

status as a duty remains contingent upon express treaty ratification.[119] Despite the large number of international conventions that incorporate some *aut dedere* formulation,[120] many significant conventions lack such a provision[121] while the existing provisions are devoid of uniform phraseology.[122] Moreover, States continue to prize their sovereign right

119 *See* Neil Boister, *The Trend to 'Universal Extradition' over Subsidiary Universal Jurisdiction in the Suppression of Transnat'l Crime*, 2003 ACTA JURIDICA 287, 305 (2003); D. Cameron Findlay, *Abducting Terrorists Overseas for Trial in the United States: Issues of Int'l and Domestic Law*, 23 TEX. INT'L L.J. 1, 9 (1988); LYAL S. SUNGA, THE EMERGING SYSTEM OF INTERNATIONAL CRIMINAL LAW: DEVELOPMENTS IN CODIFICATION AND IMPLEMENTATION 254–56 (1997); SIR ROBERT JENNINGS & SIR ARTHUR WATTS, EDS., 1 OPPENHEIM'S INTERNATIONAL LAW 950 n.9 (9th ed. 1992); *ICJ Case, Belg. v. Sen., supra* n.44, at 476–80 (Abraham, J., Sep. Op.); *In re Tribble*, Fed. Ct., Venez., May 26, 1953, *reprinted in* 20 ILR 366 (1957); *State of Japan v. Mitsuyo Kono & Takao Kono*, Tokyo High Ct., Japan, Mar. 30, 1971, *reprinted in* 59 ILR 472 (1971). *Contra Janes, et al. Claim* (U.S. v. Mex.), Gen. Claims Comm'n, 4 RIAA 82, 94 n.1 (1925) ("If the offender has escaped and returned to his mother country, the sovereign must be asked to do justice, and since that sovereign must not allow his subjects to molest or wrong the subjects of another sovereign and, much less, boldly offend the foreign powers, he must compel the offender to make amends for the damage or insult, if it can be done, or subject him to exemplary punishment, or according to circumstances deliver him up to the offended state for the proper administration of justice") (quoting as translated in PAUL PRADIER-FODÉRÉ, 1 TRAITÉ DE DROIT INTERNATIONAL PUBLIC 616 (1885)).

120 *See* Mitchell, *supra* n.112, ¶¶ 2, 11–13 (cataloguing at least thirty multilateral conventions and eighteen regional treaties, including multilateral extradition treaties that contain some version of the *aut dedere* principle); Chatham House Briefing Paper, *supra* n.118, at 3 (noting the existence of "over 60 multilateral treaties combining extradition and prosecution as alternative courses of action in order to bring suspects to justice."). Professor Bassiouni has characterized *aut dedere* as the "cornerstone" of domestic law enforcement of international crimes today. BASSIOUNI, INTRODUCTION, *supra* n.42, at 334.

121 *See* Mitchell, *supra* n.112, ¶ 10 (identifying by way of example the 1993 Chemical Weapons Convention, the 1948 Genocide Convention, and the 1973 Apartheid Convention). In addition, in the significant U.N. Convention against Corruption (UNCAC), *aut dedere* applies only optionally: "[A] State Party whose law so permits *may* grant the extradition of a person for any of the offences covered by this Convention that are not punishable under its own domestic law." UNCAC, Oct. 31, 2003, art. 44(2), Annex to UNGA Res. 58/4, U.N. Doc. A/58/422 (emphasis supplied). It is also noteworthy that no reference exists to *aut dedere* in AP I to the Geneva Conventions of 1949. Addt'l Prot. to the Geneva Convs. of August 12, 1949, and Relating to the Protection of Victims of Int'l Armed Conflicts of June 8, 1977, arts. 88 and 89, U.N. Doc. A/32/144 (1977) Annex I, *reprinted in* 16 ILM 1391. Indeed, "[t]here is … no treaty-based obligation *aut dedere aut judicare* for genocide, crimes against humanity and, except in the case of grave breaches, for serious violations of the laws and customs applicable in armed conflicts of an international or non-international character." Chatham House Briefing Paper, *supra* n.118, at 3.

122 *Compare* Conv. on Offences and Certain Other Acts Committed on Board Aircraft, Sept. 14, 1963, art. 16(2), U.N. Doc. A/C.6/418/Corr.1, Annex II, 704 U.N.T.S. 219, 20 U.S.T.

to grant asylum,[123] and resistance is still strong in practice among many States regarding whether to proceed with prosecution when extradition has been denied and jurisdictional grounds exist to prosecute.[124]

In short, the requisite State practice and *opinio juris*[125] to constitute customary international law appear to be deficient.[126] That said, there is

2941, ICAO Doc. 8364, *reprinted in* 2 ILM 1042 (1963) ("nothing in this Convention shall be deemed to create an obligation to grant extradition") *and id.*, art. 9 ("The aircraft commander may deliver to the competent authorities of any Contracting State in the territory of which the aircraft lands any person who he has reasonable grounds to believe has committed on board the aircraft an act which, in his opinion, is a serious offence according to the penal law of the State of registration of the aircraft.") *with* Conv. on Combating Bribery of Foreign Public Officials in Int'l Business Transactions, Dec. 18, 1997, art. 10(3), *reprinted in* 37 ILM 1 (1998) [hereinafter Combating Bribery Conv.] ("A Party which declines a request to extradite a person for bribery of a public official solely on the ground that the person is its national shall submit the case to its competent authorities for the purpose of prosecution.") *with* Int'l Conv. for the Suppression of the Financing of Terrorism, Dec. 9, 1999, art. 10(1), U.N. Doc. A/Res/54/109 (1999), *reprinted in* 39 ILM 270 (2000) [hereinafter Anti-Terrorism Financing Conv.] ("The State Party in the territory of which the alleged offender is present shall, in cases to which article 7 applies, if it does not extradite that person, be obliged, without exception whatsoever and whether or not the offence was committed in its territory, to submit the case without undue delay to its competent authorities for the purpose of prosecution, through proceedings in accordance with the laws of that State. Those authorities shall take their decision in the same manner as in the case of any other offence of a grave nature under the law of that State.").

123 *See* Common Eur. Asylum System, EC website, Aug. 13, 2014, *available at* http://ec.europa.eu/dgs/home-affairs/e-library/docs/ceas-fact-sheets/ceas_factsheet_en.pdf (last visited on May 17, 2016) ("Asylum is a fundamental right; granting it is an international obligation, first recognised in the 1951 Geneva Convention on the protection of refugees."); *id.* ("Since 1999, the E.U. has been working to create a Common European Asylum System (CEAS) and improve the current legislative framework."); Juan Forero, "Latin American Leaders Assert Right to Offer Asylum," *Wash. Post*, July 13, 2013, at A8 (noting that, in the context of seeking the capture of Edward Snowden by diverting Bolivian President Evo Morales' plane in July 2013, the Mercosur members, including Argentina, Brazil, Paraguay, Uruguay, and Venezuela, strongly affirmed their right to confer political asylum).

124 Boister, *supra* n.119, at 309 & n.132 (citing by example the United Kingdom's refusal to prosecute Gen. Augusto Pinochet after refusing to extradite him in 2000); Kolb, *supra* n.111, at 261–62.

125 *Opinio juris* is a subjective element required to constitute customary international law; it calls for States to adopt a particular practice out of a genuine sense of legal obligation versus on account of convenience, courtesy, political motivation, or otherwise. *See* Statute of the ICJ, Apr. 18, 1946, art. 38(1)(b); *North Sea Continental Shelf Cases* (F.R.G v. Den., F.R.G v. Neth.) [1969] I.C.J. Rep. 3, 44 (Feb. 20).

126 *See* Mitchell, *supra* n.112, ¶¶ 64–85 (no general *aut dedere* obligation yet exists regarding international crimes *writ large*); Chatham House Briefing Paper, *supra* n.118, at 5–6 ("The state practice described above demonstrates that there is no clear answer to the question whether the obligation to extradite or prosecute for core crimes under

a small chorus of voices that would label the concept an emerging principle of customary international law[127] – and therefore one that would apply notwithstanding any treaty obligation – and even some that would already denominate it a *jus cogens* norm,[128] given its increasingly popular use.

As indicated above, the nature and strength of *aut dedere* provisions found in international and regional crime suppression treaties vary to some extent.[129] In some, the focus is entirely on establishing a duty "to submit the case to its competent authorities," but only where extradition of a fugitive is barred on account of his being a national of that State.[130] In some pre–World War II treaties, domestic prosecution by the host State depends on two factors; first, that extradition is unavailable for reasons unrelated to the offense (which is a broad category that could include, for example, human rights concerns regarding prospective treatment by the pursuing State); and second, that the host State generally recognizes extraterritorial jurisdiction.[131]

international law has become part of customary international law. States' implementation of this obligation seems to be primarily based on treaties to which they are parties. It is thus questionable whether state practice beyond treaties is sufficient to meet the requirements prescribed for the formation of customary international law.").

[127] *E.g.*, Bassiouni & Wise, *supra* n.110, at 5; *Fourth Report on the Obligation to Extradite or Prosecute* (aut dedere aut judicare), Zdzislaw Galicki, Special Rapporteur, ILC, 63d Sess., 2011, U.N. Doc. A/CN.4/648, May 31, 2011 (discussing the trend toward recognition of *aut dedere* as a norm of customary international law).

[128] *See* Kenneth S. Gallant, *Securing the Presence of Defendants before the Int'l Tribunal for the Former Yugoslavia: Breaking with Extradition*, 5 Crim. L.F. 557, 567–68 & n.28 (1994) (*aut dedere* is a *jus cogens* norm based on the plethora of multilateral conventions that recognize it, including by ICJ Judge Weeramantry in his dissenting opinion in the *Lockerbie* case partly in reliance on Professor Bassiouni).

[129] For one classification of treaty provision types, *see* Bassiouni & Wise, *supra* n.110, at 11–19 (segregating out extradition treaties according to three formulae modeled on the Counterfeiting Convention (1929), the Geneva Conventions of 1949, and the Hague Hijacking Convention (1970)).

[130] *E.g.*, Combating Bribery Conv., *supra* n.122, art. 10(3); Eur. Conv. on Extradition, Dec. 13, 1957, art. 6(2), E.T.S. No. 24; Montevideo Conv. on Extradition, Dec. 26, 1933, art. 2, 49 Stat. 3111, *reprinted in* 28 AJIL 65 (1934). A contemporary example in which domestic prosecution occurred because extradition was barred on account of the nationality of the individual of interest can be found in the case of Samuel Sheinbein. *See* David Sharrock, "Israel Refuses to Hand Murder Suspect to U.S.," *The Guardian*, Feb. 26, 1999, at 18. An historical example can be found in *In re Korosi*, Crim. Ct. of Cassation, Italy, Jan. 23, 1925, *reprinted in* [1925–26] Ann. Dig. 309, 3 ILR 309 (1929).

[131] *E.g.*, Conv. for the Suppression of Illicit Traffic in Dangerous Drugs, June 26, art. 8, 1936, 198 L.N.T.S. 299 (1939); Int'l Conv. for the Suppression of Counterfeiting Currency, Apr. 20, 1929, 112 L.N.T.S. 371 (1931).

In still others, the host State is under no obligation to extradite but if the fugitive returns voluntarily or involuntarily to his State of nationality, then that State is required to prosecute him.[132] In the vast majority of contemporary treaties, however, the *aut dedere* principle employs unconditional terms requiring the host State either to extradite or, alternatively, to take steps toward prosecution or at least to assert criminal jurisdiction,[133] regardless of the circumstances involved.[134] And in some it is additionally mandated, explicitly or implicitly, that there be no undue delay in proceeding with prosecution[135] and/or that the investigation and proceedings shall be conducted as if the same offense had been

[132] *E.g.*, Conv. for the Suppression of the Traffic in Persons and of the Exploitation of the Prostitution of Others, Mar. 21, 1950, art. 9, 96 U.N.T.S. 271.

[133] *E.g.*, Inter-Am. Conv. to Prevent and Punish Torture, Dec. 9, 1985, art. 14, OAS T.S. No. 67, *reprinted in* 25 ILM 519 (1986); Prot. for the Suppression of Unlawful Acts against the Safety of Fixed Platforms Located on the Continental Shelf, Mar. 10, 1988, art. 3(4), IMO Doc. Sua/Con/16/Rev.1, *reprinted in* 27 ILM 685 [hereinafter Fixed Platforms Prot.]; Conv. for the Suppression of Unlawful Acts against the Safety of Maritime Navigation, Mar. 10, 1988, art. 6(4), IMO Doc. Sua/Con/15/Rev.1, *reprinted in* 27 ILM 668, 676 (1988) [hereinafter Maritime Navigation Conv.]. In one exceptional agreement, an *aut dedere* provision expressly calls for the person sent back "to be tried" while exempting cases of minor offenses. Exchange of Notes Constituting an Agreement Relating to Hijacking of Aircraft and Vessels and Other Offenses (with MOU), U.S.-Cuba, Feb. 15, 1973 T.S. No. 13067, 916 U.N.T.S. 85.

[134] *E.g.*, Montreal Conv., *supra* n.113, art. 7 ("The Contracting State in the territory of which the alleged offender is found, if it does not extradite him, is obliged, *without exception whatsoever* and whether or not the offence was committed in its territory, to submit the case to its competent authorities for the purpose of prosecution.") (emphasis supplied); Int'l Conv. against the Taking of Hostages, Dec. 17, 1979, art. 8(1), UNGA Res. 34/146 (XXXIV), 34 U.N. GAOR Supp. (No. 46), at 245, U.N. Doc. A/34/46 (1979), 1316 U.N.T.S. 205, T.I.A.S. No. 11081, *reprinted in* 18 ILM 1456 [hereinafter New York Conv.].

[135] *E.g.*, Conv. on the Prevention and Punishment of Crimes against Int'lly Protected Persons, Including Diplomatic Agents, Dec. 14, 1973, art. 7, UNGA Res. 3166 (XXVIII), 28 U.N. GAOR Supp. (No. 30), at 146, U.N. Doc. A/9030 (1974), 28 U.S.T. 1975, 1035 U.N.T.S. 167, T.I.A.S. No. 8532, *reprinted in* 13 ILM 41 (1977) ("The State Party in whose territory the alleged offender is present shall, if it does not extradite him, submit, without exception whatsoever and *without undue delay*, the case to its competent authorities for the purpose of prosecution, through proceedings in accordance with the laws of that State.") (emphasis supplied); Anti-Terrorism Financing Conv., *supra* n.122, art. 10(1) ("without undue delay"); *ICJ Case, Belg. v. Sen.*, *supra* n.44, ¶¶ 114–15 (finding it "necessarily implicit in the text" of the Convention against Torture that the obligation to submit the case for prosecution under Article 7(1) must be implemented "without delay," "consistent with the object and purpose of the Convention.").

committed in its own territory,[136] thereby ensuring that it not be assigned an unduly low priority.

Examining the term itself, it is reasonable to inquire whether States parties to international treaties generally tend to ascribe precedence to extradition *or* to prosecution by the host State's courts, or whether the two alternatives are placed on an equal footing. In the vast majority of provisions, due to logical sequencing, States are called upon to pursue prosecution if extradition is unavailable,[137] but in a few other instances, States may elect to extradite in lieu of domestic prosecution.[138]

While arguments can be advanced in favor of each position – for example, as a teleological matter, the purpose of crime suppression treaties ultimately is to prosecute and punish offenders, but as

[136] *E.g.*, Anti-Terrorism Financing Conv., *supra* n.122, art. 10(1) ("Those authorities shall take their decision in the same manner as in the case of any other offence of a grave nature under the law of that State."); Conv. on Cybercrime, Nov. 23, 2001, art. 24(6), E.T.S. No. 185; Conv. to Prevent and Punish the Acts of Terrorism Taking the Form of Crimes against Persons and Related Extortion that are of Int'l Significance, Feb. 2, 1971, art. 5, OAS Doc. A6/Doc.88 rev.1, corr.1, 27 U.S.T. 3949, T.I.A.S. No. 8413 (1976), *reprinted in* 10 ILM 255, 256.

[137] *E.g.*, U.N. Conv. against Torture and Other Cruel, Inhuman or Degrading Treatment or Punishment [CAT], Dec. 10, 1984, art. 7(1), UNGA Res. 39/46 Annex, U.N. GAOR, 39th Sess., Supp. No. 51, U.N. Doc. E/CN.4/1984/72, Annex (1984), 1465 U.N.T.S. 85, *reprinted in* 23 ILM 1027 [hereinafter CAT] ("The State Party in the territory under whose jurisdiction a person alleged to have committed an offence referred to in article 4 is found shall in the cases contemplated in article 5, if it does not extradite him, submit the case to its competent authorities for the purpose of prosecution").

[138] *E.g.*, Geneva Conv. for the Amelioration of the Condition of the Wounded and Sick in Armed Forces in the Field, Aug. 12, 1949, art. 49, 6 U.S.T. 3114, T.I.A.S. No. 3362, 75 U.N.T.S. 31 [GC I]; Geneva Conv. for the Amelioration of the Condition of the Wounded, Sick and Shipwrecked Members of Armed Forces at Sea, Aug. 12, 1949, art. 50, 6 U.S.T. 3217, T.I.A.S. No. 3363, 75 U.N.T.S. 85 [GC II]; Geneva Conv. Relative to the Treatment of Prisoners of War, Aug. 12, 1949, art. 129, 6 U.S.T. 3316, T.I.A.S. No. 3364, 75 U.N.T.S. 135 [GC III]; Geneva Conv. Relative to the Protection of Civilian Persons in Time of War, Aug. 12, 1949, art. 146, 6 U.S.T. 3516, T.I.A.S. No. 3365, 75 U.N.T.S. 287 [GC IV] ("Each High Contracting Party shall be under the obligation to search for persons alleged to have committed, or to have ordered to be committed, such grave breaches, and shall bring such persons, regardless of their nationality, before its own courts. It may also, if it prefers, and in accordance with the provisions of its own legislation, hand such persons over for trial to another high Contracting Party concerned, provided such High Contracting Party has made out a *prima facie* case."). There is some question whether the *aut dedere* principle that appears in the Geneva Conventions of 1949 without express reference to the word extradition is suggesting that deportation would be a permissible method of turning a person over. Gallant, *supra* n.128, at 354. However, only extradition for trial would satisfy the conventional requirement, as removal would not ensure that prosecution ultimately occurred. Kolb, *supra* n.111, at 258.

a function of pragmatism, the State in which the offense allegedly occurred (typically a pursuing State) is more likely to succeed in that prosecution, thereby supporting extradition[139] – it seems that they are postured as equally acceptable counterparts,[140] at least in the international (versus regional) legal context.[141] In any event, the key impetus behind these provisions is to encourage concrete action *of some kind* toward bringing a fugitive to justice, although as a general practice, States often act more in line with *realpolitik* than out of high-minded principle.

Operational aspects of *aut dedere* also must be considered. To begin, neither the principle itself nor crime suppression treaty provisions articulating it tend to supply much in the way of meaningful implementation criteria.[142] Indeed, the provisions are spare and appear to accept without question or caveat that any extradition or domestic prosecution will be handled according to proper and reasonable standards.[143] Some limited exceptions exist, such as the requirement that a person may not be handed over to another State under any of the four Geneva

[139] *Id.* at 257–60.

[140] *Id.* at 257; Bassiouni & Wise, *supra* n.110, at xii (the order in which the terms appear is not meant to assign priority to extradition over prosecution); Mitchell, *supra* n.112, ¶¶ 15–16 (discussing a variety of formulations with some wording suggesting extradition and others indicating prosecution as the default). At the same time, however, "[m]ost of the treaties concerned impose an obligation to prosecute whenever the alleged offender is present in the territory of the state: the obligation arises as soon as that presence is discovered, regardless of any request for extradition. It is only when such a request is made that the alternative course of action – extradition – becomes available to the state." Chatham House Briefing Paper, *supra* n.118, at 6. *See also ICJ Case, Belg. v. Sen., supra* n.44, ¶ 95 ("[I]f the State in whose territory the suspect is present has received a request for extradition in any of the cases envisaged in the provisions of the Convention [against Torture], it can relieve itself of its obligation to prosecute by acceding to that requirement. It follows that the choice between extradition or submission for prosecution, pursuant to the Convention, does not mean that the two alternatives are to be given the same weight. Extradition is an option offered to the State by the Convention, whereas prosecution is an international obligation under the Convention the violation of which is a wrongful act engaging the responsibility of the State.").

[141] Under *regional* extradition treaties, there appears to be a preference for extradition over prosecution. Kolb, *supra* n.111, at 257.

[142] Case law, however, supplies some guidance on this score. *See ICJ Case, Belg. v. Sen., supra* n.44 (discussing the application of the *aut dedere* principle in the context of the Convention against Torture (CAT), including with respect to the requirement of a member State to undertake a preliminary inquiry to determine if torture was committed by a fugitive within its territory, that the decision to prosecute or extradite be taken without delay, and that national legal or financial considerations do not supersede this international legal obligation).

[143] Bassiouni, Introduction, *supra* n.42, at 344.

Conventions of 1949 unless it is a High Contracting Party[144] that has made out a *prima facie* case for criminal liability for a grave breach.[145] Furthermore, little if any instruction is provided on how a State is expected to resolve conflicts that may arise out of its exercise of *aut dedere* (*e.g.*, when two or more States concurrently request extradition from the host State) beyond generally applying the principle of "good faith" in meeting State obligations.[146]

Most crime suppression treaties with *aut dedere* provisions consist of language such as "the authorities shall take their decision in the same manner as in the case of any other offence of a grave nature under *the law of that State*."[147] That text is tantamount to a "national treatment" standard[148] as opposed to an "international minimum" standard,[149] thereby allowing States, say, to "rely on different factors in deciding whether to prosecute for a 'political' offence, rather than an 'ordinary' offence."[150] As that duty arises out of a treaty binding the interests of States to one another, rather than from language found in purely domestic legislation, arguably a State must additionally exercise due diligence to ensure there is no interference by the State's political bodies to compromise its genuine consideration.[151] In any event, however, such decisions

[144] Examples of other treaties specifying that an accused can be extradited only to States parties are the Fixed Platforms Prot., *supra* n.133, art. 3(4); and Maritime Navigation Conv., *supra* n.133, art. 6(4). To the extent that a treaty fails to specify whether the *aut dedere* provision applies to States parties only or to any State, such a provision should be construed as applying to any State. Kolb, *supra* n.111, at 259 (noting that such important limitations cannot be presumed).

[145] GC I, GC II, GC III, and GC IV, *supra* n.138.

[146] Bassiouni, Introduction, *supra* n.42, at 344.

[147] *E.g.*, Int'l Conv. against the Recruitment, Use, Financing and Training of Mercenaries, Dec. 4, 1989, art. 12, *reprinted in* 29 ILM 91 (1990) (emphasis supplied); *accord* New York Conv., *supra* n.134, art. 8(1). Sometimes, however, the duty to prosecute appears under slightly different phraseology as "in the same manner as in case of any ordinary offence of a serious nature *under municipal law*." *E.g.*, CAT, *supra* n.137, art. 7(1) (emphasis supplied).

[148] This position was reflected in a G-8 Communiqué in 1997, when the justice and interior ministers stated: "Those of us that conduct domestic prosecution of our nationals in lieu of extradition agree to pursue such extraditions with the same commitment of time, personnel and financial resources as are devoted to the prosecution of serious crimes committed within our own territory." G-8 Communiqué, *supra* n.103.

[149] Kolb, *supra* n.111, at 261.

[150] Mitchell, *supra* n.112, ¶ 3.

[151] Kolb, *supra* n.111, at 262; Melanie M. Laflin, Note, *Kidnapped Terrorists: Bringing Int'l Criminals to Justice Through Irregular Rendition and Other Quasi-Legal Options*, 26 J. Legis. 315, 317 (2000) (noting that customary international law imposes a duty of due diligence and citing the General Claims Commission's finding in the *Jane's Case* that Mexico was liable for the failure to exercise due diligence).

ultimately rely on prosecutorial discretion, which, in turn, typically accounts for such factors as the weight of evidence, the likelihood of conviction, the significance of the charges, the time and resources estimated to secure a conviction, and the opportunity cost of not pursuing other criminal cases.

For all of its positive features, however, *aut dedere* suffers from several drawbacks. First, its scope of application is limited, as only States that are parties to treaties containing *aut dedere* provisions are expected in good faith to apply that principle in specific agreed contexts,[152] and only after any ratified treaty has entered into force with respect to that State,[153] and only to the extent that any announced declarations, reservations, objections, or notifications do not further constrain that application.[154]

Second, the *aut dedere* principle can be rendered ineffectual to the extent a State does not take seriously the antecedent responsibility to locate and arrest a fugitive within its territory, let alone if it actively assists the fugitive in evading capture.[155]

Third, *aut dedere* does not guarantee that if extradition is denied or otherwise unavailable, the host State will necessarily prosecute the alleged offender. After all, the host State need only review the charges and evidence against the individual with an eye toward making a prosecution determination, while any number of factors may militate

152 *See* Antonio Cassese, *The Int'l Community's 'Legal' Response to Terrorism*, 38 Int'l & Comp. L.Q. 589, 593 (1989) ("we have seen how the hijackers of a Kuwaiti aircraft have been allowed to escape owing to the fact that Algeria was not a party to the relevant [terrorism suppression] treaties and, accordingly, could not be compelled to 'extradite or punish' them."). *See also* discussion at pp. 374–77 regarding how *aut dedere* has not yet ascended to customary international law status.

153 *See ICJ Case, Belg. v. Sen., supra* n.44, ¶ 100 ("The Court notes that nothing in the Convention against Torture reveals an intention to require a State party to criminalize, under Article 4, acts of torture that took place prior to its entry into force for that State, or to establish its jurisdiction over such acts in accordance with Article 5. Consequently, in view of the Court, the obligation to prosecute, under Article 7, paragraph 1, of the Convention does not apply to such acts."). In that case, although Belgium had sought the prosecution of crimes by Hissène Habré during his tenure as Chad's leader from June 1982 to December 1990, because the applicable convention (the CAT) had not entered into force vis-á-vis Senegal, the host State, until June 1987, any acts Habré may have committed before then were not under consideration. *Id.* ¶¶ 19, 100.

154 *See* Amnesty Int'l, *The Int'l Law Commission: The Obligation to Extradite or Prosecute* (Aut Dedere Aut Judicare), 2009, Annex II, at 60–72 (cataloguing all "Reservations and Declarations to Treaties Relating to *Aut Dedere Aut Judicare*").

155 Cassese, *supra* n.15, at 595.

against moving forward.[156] For instance, a State may choose to: (i) offer the fugitive amnesty in order to elicit cooperation in connection with a truth and reconciliation commission inquiry;[157] (ii) protect sensitive national security information from possible public disclosure at trial;[158] (iii) shield parties who, while allegedly perpetrating crime, incidentally provide certain critical social services to the population;[159] or (iv) enter into a bargain where the subject is exchanged for hostages or prisoners[160] or where he is freed from culpability by turning State's evidence against more senior members of a criminal organization.[161] In practice, State court judges are "careful not to impinge with their decisions on their governments' international policies and interests."[162]

156 *See* Findlay, *supra* n.119, at 10 (noting how the formalities of the process afford a number of opportunities for interested groups to bring political pressure to bear on the decision-maker).

157 It is unsettled law whether an amnesty or pardon is consistent with the *aut dedere* concept. On the one hand, a State should be allowed to exercise such authority under its own domestic law; on the other hand, an amnesty or pardon would seem to run counter to the notion of criminal accountability that lies at the heart of such a provision. *See* Mitchell, *supra* n.112, ¶ 4 (noting the lack of State practice on this score while stressing how the "good faith" principle can be used to ensure proper reconciliation between these competing interests) (citing Kolb, *supra* n.111, at 264–65)). *See also* Draft Prot. to the Statute of the Int'l Criminal Court on the Proper Limitations to Municipal Amnesties, *promulgated in* ANDREAS O'SHEA, AMNESTY FOR CRIME IN INTERNATIONAL LAW AND PRACTICE 330–36 (2004).

158 *See* Stefano Betti, *The Duty to Bring Terrorists to Justice and Discretionary Prosecution*, 4 J. INT'L CRIM. JUST. 1104, 1113–14 (2006). A possible example involves alleged terrorist Luis Posada Carriles, who was arrested in the United States on an immigration violation but his indictment was dismissed in May 2007. Since then, both Venezuela and Cuba have sought his extradition for his alleged role in the 1976 bombing of an *Air Cubana* plane that resulted in the death of seventy-three persons. To date, the United States has refused to grant either request due to concerns about his receiving a fair trial and treatment in those countries. At the same time, the United States has not undertaken a domestic prosecution of Carriles under the *aut dedere* principle reportedly in part due to his association with the CIA in the 1960s and 1970s (based on declassified documents) as well as his involvement in the 1986 Iran-Contra scandal. Bruce Zagaris, *U.S. Court Frees Alleged Anti-Castro Terrorist as CARICOM Calls for Prosecution*, 23 IELR 262 (2007).

159 *See* Betti, *supra* n.158, at 1113 (citing the protection of those associated with Hezbollah for the beneficial social services the terrorist organization furnishes the local population).

160 *E.g.*, New York Conv., *supra* n.134, art. 3 (a State may release a kidnapper in exchange for the release of hostages).

161 *See* Betti, *supra* n.158, at 1114–15 (citing the example of Germany releasing Shadi Abdalla, a Jordanian extremist, because he provided critical information on al-Qaida).

162 *See* Eyal Benvenisti, *Judicial Misgivings Regarding the Application of Int'l Law: An Analysis of Attitudes of Nat'l Courts*, 4 EUR. J. INT'L L. 159, 161 (1993) (noting that this phenomenon occurs at three stages: (i) courts interpret narrowly those articles of

Fourth, even when prosecution proceedings are initiated, the case often will need to overcome a number of logistical, financial, and evidentiary hurdles. Victims and witnesses, who generally are found in the State where the crime was committed, will need to be transferred to the host State to testify. Their travel and accommodation can prove difficult and costly, and they may well encounter language barriers.[163] Plus, the admissibility or weight accorded evidence across States' courts may vary considerably. In addition, at times multiple-count cases can be carved up in such a way that more than one court will adjudicate the charges, thereby complicating the availability of witnesses and physical evidence at trial.[164]

Fifth, it is not always clear that host State judicial systems have the will and capacity to prosecute and punish an offender adequately.[165] This concern has led particularly more powerful States to distrust the domestic prosecution option under *aut dedere* as exercised by others, especially those that are autocratic, have a reputation for political or judicial abuse, care little about a specific case, or have an interest in protecting an accused with powerful contacts or an association with the host State government.[166]

their national constitutions that import international law into the local legal systems; (ii) they then interpret international rules so as not to upset their government's interests, sometimes actually seeking guidance from the executive for interpreting treaties; and (iii) they use a variety of avoidance doctrines, like the Act of State doctrine, or standing or justiciability in ways that give their own governments an effective shield against judicial review).

163 Mary Lee Warren, Dep. Asst. Att. Gen., Crim. Div. Dep't of Justice, *The Importance of Extradition in Int'l Crime Control*, Testimony Before the Criminal Justice, Drug Policy and Human Resources Subcomm. of the House Gov't Reform Comm., May 13, 1999.

164 *See* Rodrigo Labardini, *Domestic Prosecution in Lieu of Extradition from Mexico*, 22 IELR 33, 35 (2006) (identifying this as one reason among many why the U.S. Government is not generally satisfied with domestic prosecution in lieu of extradition); Boister, *supra* n.119, at 308 & n.128.

165 Host States are generally more inclined to take such prosecutions more seriously when the crime victims are among its nationals. *See, e.g.*, Bruce Zagaris, *U.S. and Ecuador at Odds Over U.S. Effort to Obtain Custody over Murder Suspect*, 27 IELR 782, 782–83 (2011) (discussing the case of Luis A. Guaman who was charged in the United States with murdering two Ecuadorians, but Ecuador, the host State, was willing to undertake the prosecution).

166 *See* Boister, *supra* n.119, at 312; *id.* at 307–08 & n.127 (the U.S. Government has often been disappointed with the manner and speed of the Mexican judicial process); Gallant, *supra* n.128, at 569–70 (crimes may have been committed by persons working on behalf of the State).

For example, instead of granting the U.S. request for the extradition of Pedro Miguel González-Pinzón for the first-degree murder of a U.S. Army sergeant and the attempted murder of another in an assault in Panama in June 1992, the Panamanian Government held a trial in 1997, acquitting him of all charges.[167] Notably, González-Pinchón had well-placed political contacts, as he was the son of a founding member of a leading political party in Panama who was also a friend of the father of the then-President of Panama.[168] Even when sentences are imposed, they can later be commuted or the convict otherwise released early,[169] as occurred in the case of Palestinian Omar Rezaq, who was freed after only seven years of a twenty-five-year prison sentence by Malta ostensibly for "good behavior" but allegedly due to Libyan Government pressure.[170]

The *Lockerbie* case profiled in Chapter 8.c presents another example. While Libya contended it was fully justified in its straightforward application of the *aut dedere* provision in the Montreal Convention, the case points out a major deficiency in that principle's operation. Where, as there, the host State (Libya), which was then despotic and not known for an impartial judicial system, wished to prosecute two of its own government agents, the United States and the United Kingdom had a reasonable basis for objection in the interest of justice. Whether the use of the UNSC as a vehicle to overcome the conventional obligation to pursue domestic

[167] Bruce Zagaris, *Election of Panamanian Accused of Murdering U.S. Soldiers Clouds Prospects for Ratification of FTA*, 23 IELR 419, 419–20 (2007).

[168] *Id.* When the verdict was announced, the U.S. Government expressed doubts about the legitimacy of the court proceedings, although it has yet been able to prove any underlying corruption. *Id.* It is equally the case that when a criminal defendant is taken outside of his home country, and he is bereft of his power and influence, there is a greater likelihood of obtaining real justice. Accordingly, one of the most potent weapons the United States and Colombia have in their battle against the Medellín cartel for cocaine trafficking into the United States is to remove cartel members from their "untouchable" position in Colombia and place them on trial in the United States, where their wealth and political power have less influence, especially given how the cartel has corrupted and incapacitated the Colombian judiciary, and the Colombian people in general have no desire to pursue, capture, and place traffickers on trial because of what this process will cost them and their homeland. Steven Y. Otera, *Int'l Extradition and the Medellín Cocaine Cartel: Surgical Removal of Colombian Cocaine Traffickers for Trial in the United States*, 13 Loy. L.A. Int'l & Comp. L.J. 955, 1007 (1991).

[169] Douglas Kash, *Abducting Terrorists under PDD-39: Much Ado About Nothing New*, 13 Am. U. Int'l L. Rev. 139, 141 (1997–98).

[170] "Terrorism in the Sky: Hijacking of Egypt Air Flight 648," *India TV News*, Feb. 22, 2013, *available at* http://m.indiatvnews.com/crime/news/terrorism-in-the-sky-hijacking-of-egypt-air-flight-648-2713.html (last visited on May 17, 2016).

prosecution was appropriate can be debated, but we must not overlook this Achilles' heel of inadequate or unfair judicial systems when assessing the net utility of the *aut dedere* option.

Promote Transfer of a Fugitive to a Suitable Third State or International Criminal Tribunal for Prosecution. Where host State A is not permitted or is unwilling to extradite a fugitive to pursuing State B, and where State A's domestic prosecution machinery or system is deemed unsophisticated or unreliable, pursuing State B may choose to advocate, or serve as an intermediary, for the agreed transfer of the fugitive to State C or to an appropriate international criminal tribunal instead. This amounts to a contingency option that would seek to maximize the likelihood that the fugitive would be brought to justice somewhere.

For example, in the *Lockerbie* case, after it was clear that Libya would not extradite its accused intelligence officers to either the United States or the United Kingdom, the pursuing States agreed to have the two Libyan Government defendants transferred initially to the Netherlands and then onward to Scottish custody to territory temporarily assigned to Scotland at Camp Zeist (a former NATO airbase) under a specialized U.K.-Netherlands agreement.[171] Similarly, in March 2006, pursuant to Liberian President Ellen Sirleaf Johnson's request for the extradition from Nigeria of the exiled former President of Sierra Leone, Charles Taylor, who was indicted by the Special Court of Sierra Leone (SCSL) in 2003 for war crimes and crimes against humanity during Sierra Leone's civil war, Nigeria "transferred" him to Liberia, which promptly turned him over to the custody of the U.N. Mission in Liberia (UNMIL) and then to Sierra Leone and ultimately to The Hague, where he was put on trial before the SCSL.[172]

[171] Agreement Concerning a Scottish Trial in the Netherlands, Neth.-U.K., Sept. 18, 1998, *reprinted in* 38 ILM 926 (1999); Donna E. Arzt, *The Lockerbie 'Extradition by Analogy' Agreement: 'Exceptional Measure' or Template for Transnat'l Criminal Justice?*, 18 Am. U. Int'l L. Rev. 163, 177 (2002). This arrangement should be distinguished from re-extradition in which prosecution or punishment occurs first and then the individual is forwarded to the next State. *See* treatment on re-extradition in Chapter 8.c.

[172] "The Prosecutor v. Charles Ghankay Taylor," SCSL Cases, *SCSL* website, *available at* www.rscsl.org/Documents/Decisions/Contempt/2012-01/SCSL-12-01-T-012.PDF (last visited on May 17, 2016) (noting that in May 2012 Taylor was sentenced to a fifty-year prison term); Chris Morris, "Charles Taylor War Crimes Convictions Upheld," *BBC News*, Sept. 26, 2013, *available at* www.bbc.com/news/world-africa-24279323 (last visited on May 28, 2016) (his conviction and sentence were upheld on appeal).

Provide Collateral Support to the Prosecuting State or an International Criminal Tribunal. Apart from promoting or facilitating the *transfer* of a fugitive to another forum to face prosecution, a pursuing State could opt to *assist* that forum, whether a State court or an international tribunal, through the provision of material evidence or witnesses in the furtherance of justice. Thus, for example, after Greek Prime Minister Constantine Mitsotakis overturned a Greek Supreme Court ruling that had authorized the extradition to the United States of Mohammed Rashid, a Palestinian charged with planting a bomb on a U.S. commercial aircraft in 1982, and Greece decided to prosecute domestically, the United States supplied both a key fact witness (a Rashid accomplice shielded under the Witness Protection Program (WPP)) and three expert witnesses (from the FBI) that proved instrumental in reaching a murder conviction.[173]

In another instance, in the spring of 2011, after Luis A. Guaman, an Ecuadorian national, fled from Massachusetts to Ecuador after being suspected of the murder of his housemate and her two-year-old son, Ecuador offered to prosecute Guaman, as its constitution prohibited the extradition of its own nationals, and asked Massachusetts authorities to provide supporting evidence so that Ecuador could bring murder charges against him.[174]

* * * * *

This chapter has evaluated what are termed herein as "fallback" alternatives to extradition. Seeking preliminary steps toward the location, arrest, or delivery of a fugitive ("partial" approach) or enabling another judicial system to undertake prosecution ("redirected" approach) constitute *bona fide* alternatives to extradition, yet in general they are not entirely satisfactory or complete from a pursuing State's standpoint. Part V comprehensively explores those that meet *all* the key functional indicia of extradition.

[173] Ethan A. Nadelmann, *The Evolution of United States Involvement in the Int'l Rendition of Fugitive Criminals*, 25 N.Y.U. J. Int'l L. & Pol. 813, 879 (1993).

[174] Bruce Zagaris, *U.S. and Ecuador at Odds Over U.S. Effort to Obtain Custody over Murder Suspect*, 27 IELR 782, 782–83 (2011).

PART V

Full-Scale Alternatives to Extradition

10

Alternative I

Reliance on Immigration Laws

Part V pivots from a discussion of one set of alternatives to extradition ("fallback") to the other ("full-scale"). "Full-scale alternatives to extradition" are defined herein as *those non-extradition-related means of bringing a fugitive to justice that functionally approximate the end result of extradition; namely, securing the physical custody of a fugitive and bringing him within a pursuing State's judicial system to be prosecuted or punished.* Full-scale alternatives are generally regarded as of a first-order preference as they completely satisfy the objectives of extradition.

Three types of full-scale alternatives can be discerned:[1] (i) immigration law-based approaches (discussed in this chapter), (ii) informal law enforcement cooperation (covered in Chapter 11), and (iii) unilateral measures undertaken by a pursuing State (addressed in Chapter 12).[2] Such approaches are undertaken in circumstances not only when extradition is denied, is effectively unavailable, or is regarded as

[1] It is not always clear to the public which type of extradition alternative has been employed in a given case or whether the fugitive may have even waived extradition proceedings. *E.g.*, Bruce Zagaris, *Guatemala Arrests and Returns U.S. National Wanted in Prosecution of Poker Sites*, 27 IELR 838 (2011) (noting how Ira Rubin may have waived extradition, been deported, or been subject to an informal handover between law enforcement officials).

[2] By comparison, Harvard Law Professor Philip Heymann has classified U.S. Government options to include "cooperative methods" (*e.g.*, via extradition, deportation, and other arrangements) and "unilateral methods" (by which he meant, *e.g.*, extraterritorial seizures). Philip B. Heymann & Ian Heath Gershengorn, *Pursuing Justice, Respecting the Law*, *in* PRINCIPLES AND PROCEDURES FOR A NEW TRANSNATIONAL CRIMINAL LAW: DOCUMENTATION OF AN INTERNATIONAL WORKSHOP IN FREIBURG, MAY 1991, at 136 (Albin Eser & Otto Lagodny eds. 1992).

undesirable,[3] but also when retrieval of a given fugitive tends to be of priority importance.[4]

While reliance on immigration law as a means to elicit delivery of a fugitive depends predominantly on the application of host State (*i.e.*, removing State – *see infra*) law, *pursuing State* (*i.e.*, receiving State – *see infra*) law potentially can be implicated as well; for example, to the extent a negotiated exchange of fugitive aliens is struck or an immigration action is the product of a cooperative bilateral arrangement.[5] *International* law also may come into play, say, where the receiving State is found to have perpetrated a wrongful act through collusion or otherwise[6] or with respect to how the fugitive alien is handled once in its custody or control.[7] Before analyzing its legal dimensions, this chapter will review core immigration law terminology, analyze the comparative merits of reliance on immigration law versus extradition, and describe the general nature of operations in this arena.

[3] *See* Satyadeva Bedi, Extradition: A Treatise on the Laws Relevant to the Fugitive Offenders Within and With the Commonwealth Countries 396 (2002) (States rely on alternatives "either because of breakdown of the extradition mechanism or for expediency"); M. Cherif Bassiouni, International Extradition and World Public Order 132 (1974) [hereinafter Bassiouni, World Public Order] (stressing the "length and formalism surrounding the extradition procedure as well as its exclusive dependence on the decision making process of the state of refuge").

[4] *See* Heymann & Gershengorn, *supra* n.2, at 130 (noting that typically the circumstances consist of "a high-profile criminal or crime").

[5] When a removing State arranges to deport a fugitive to a specific destination, the receiving State must concur and may even impose conditions. For example, when King Hussein agreed to allow Mousa Mohammed Abu Marzook, the political leader of Hamas, into Jordan, he insisted that Marzook abide by Jordanian law "under a deal worked out with United States authorities." "Militant Ejected by U.S. Meets with Jordan King," *N.Y. Times*, May 14, 1997, at A11.

[6] To the extent collusion is involved, a receiving State potentially could be liable for aiding or assisting the removing State in the commission of an internationally wrongful act. *See* ILC, *Responsibility of States for Int'lly Wrongful Acts with Commentaries* (Draft), Dec. 12, 2001, arts. 16 and 17, Annex to UNGA Res. 56/83, U.N. GAOR, 56th Sess., Supp. No. 10, at 43, U.N. Doc. A/56/10 (2001); *e.g.*, *R. v. Mullen* [1999] 2 Cr. App. R. 143 (CA), [1999] WLR 777 [hereinafter *Mullen Case*] (holding the United Kingdom culpable where "British authorities had initiated and procured the appellant's deportation from Zimbabwe by unlawful means for the purposes of putting him on trial. By so doing, they had encouraged unlawful conduct in Zimbabwe and had acted in breach of public international law.").

[7] Minimum international legal standards for detainee treatment would apply; these are discussed in Chapter 13.a.i.

a Immigration Law

States possess an inherent right to control the admission of aliens[8] (*i.e.*, non-nationals[9]) into their territory;[10] to extend visitor or residency

[8] *See* GUY S. GOODWIN-GILL, INTERNATIONAL LAW AND THE MOVEMENT OF PERSONS BETWEEN STATES 201 (1978); *Fong Yue Ting v. United States*, 149 U.S. 698, 711 (1893). *Nationals*, by contrast, have a broadly established right under international law to enter and leave their country of nationality. *See* Universal Decl. of Human Rights, Dec. 10, 1948, art. 13, UNGA Res. 217A (III), U.N. Doc. A/810 (1948) [hereinafter UDHR]; Int'l Covenant on Civil and Political Rights (ICCPR), Dec. 16, 1966, art. 12(2), UNGA Res. 2200, U.N. GAOR, 21st Sess., Supp. No. 21, U.N. Doc. A/6316 (1967); *id.*, art. 12(4) ("no one shall be arbitrarily deprived of the right to enter his own country"); Fourth Prot. to the Eur. Conv. for the Protection of Human Rights and Fundamental Freedoms (ECHR), Sept. 16, 1963, art. 3, *as amended by* Prot. No. 11 [hereinafter Fourth Prot. to the ECHR]; Am. Conv. on Human Rights, Nov. 22, 1969, art. 22(5), OAS Official Records Serv. XVI/1.1 Doc. 65, Rev. 1, Corr. 1 (Jan. 1, 1970), 1144 U.N.T.S. 123 [hereinafter ACHR]; OAU, AFRICAN CHARTER ON HUMAN AND PEOPLES' RIGHTS, June 27, 1981, art. 12(2), CAB/LEG/67/3 rev. 5, *reprinted in* 21 ILM 58 (1982) [hereinafter BANJUL CHARTER]; League of Arab States, ARAB CHARTER ON HUMAN RIGHTS, May 22, 2004, art. 27, *reprinted in* 12 IHRR 893 (2005).

The deportation of a born or naturalized citizen is called "banishment" or "exile," and is rather uncommon in contemporary practice. IVAN A. SHEARER, EXTRADITION IN INTERNATIONAL LAW 76 (1971). Indeed, under U.S. law, if a criminal is a naturalized citizen, he must be denaturalized before he can be subjected to deportation proceedings, *Schneiderman v. United States*, 320 U.S. 118 (1943), but this tends to occur only in serious instances of fraud or misrepresentation in connection with the naturalization process. Robert A. Cohen, Note, *United States Exclusion and Deportation of Nazi War Criminals: The Act of October 30, 1978*, 13 N.Y.U. J. INT'L L. & POL. 101, 129 (1980); James W. Moeller, *United States Treatment of Alleged Nazi War Criminals: Int'l Law, Immigration Law, and the Need for Int'l Cooperation*, 25 VA. J. INT'L L. 793, 814 (1985). Denaturalization proceedings in the United States are governed by the Federal Rules of Civil Procedure, as the loss of nationality is treated as a civil penalty for violating U.S. immigration laws, and therefore is not accompanied by a right to a jury trial (*United States v. Walus*, 453 F. Supp. 699, 702–03 (N.D. Ill. 1978), *rev'd on other grounds*, 616 F.2d 283 (7th Cir. 1980)), and yet the consequence in some instances can be as serious as a criminal penalty. Moeller, *supra*, at 818–19; *e.g.*, *Bensayah v. Bosnia & Herzegovina*, Case No. CH/02/9499, Decision on Admissibility and Merits, H.R. Ch. for Bosn. & Herz. Apr. 4, 2003, ¶ 38 [hereinafter *Bensayah Case*] (B&H revoked an alien's citizenship in November 2001 on the grounds that, when he applied for it, "he had had hidden intentions to violate the Constitution and laws of the Federation"; he was exiled two months later).

[9] An "alien" is essentially defined as a non-national. *See, e.g.*, U.K. Legislation, British Nationality Act 1981, Oct. 30, § 51(4) (an alien is a "person who is neither a Commonwealth citizen nor a British protected person nor a citizen of the Republic of Ireland"); 8 U.S.C. § 1101(a)(3) (2012); Austrian Aliens Act, June 1997, BGBI (Fed. Law Gazette) I Nr. 75/1997, *as amended by* BGBI I 126/2002. These definitions exclude from their scope Stateless persons. Moreover, an alien must be a "natural person." UNGA, *Expulsion of Aliens*, U.N. Doc. A/CN.4/565, July 10, 2006, at 23.

[10] This rule applies even to returning, long-term resident aliens. BASSIOUNI, WORLD PUBLIC ORDER, *supra* n.3, at 134 n.29 (citing by way of example *Shaughnessy v. Mezei*, 345 U.S.

privileges; and to expel[11] or remove them, as desired,[12] subject to any limiting international legal obligations they may have undertaken.[13] The main factors a State considers when deciding whether to deny an

206 (1953), in which a twenty-five-year U.S. resident who had left the United States temporarily to visit his mother was permissibly excluded from returning, even without a hearing).

11 "Expulsion" is defined as "the exercise of State power which secures the removal, either 'voluntarily', under threat of forcible removal, or forcibly, of an alien from the territory of a State." GOODWIN-GILL, *supra* n.8 at 201.

12 *See* Louis B. Sohn & Thomas Buergenthal (eds.), *The Movement of Persons Across Borders*, ASIL, STUDS. IN TRANSNAT'L LEG. POL'Y, No. 23, at 89 (1992) ("Such a right is essential for the protection of the State and for the maintenance of its public order, morality and public health."); *e.g.*, Zambia Immigration and Deportation Act, No. 18 of 2010, Apr. 13, 2010, § 17(1). Authority exists for the proposition that while States "possess[] the general right of expulsion," such a practice must: (i) "only be resorted to in extreme instances," (ii) "be accomplished in the manner least injurious to the person affected," and (iii) entail an adequate justification for the expulsion "when occasion demands." *Boffolo Case* (Italy v. Venez.), Claims Comm'n, 10 RIAA 528, 537 (1903). On this last point, *see* SIR ROBERT JENNINGS & SIR ARTHUR WATTS, OPPENHEIM'S INTERNATIONAL LAW 943–44 (9th ed., 1992) ("While the failure of a state to advance any reason for the expulsion may not itself be a breach of any international legal obligation, the refusal to give reasons may lend support to a finding of arbitrariness in the expulsion.") (citations omitted); GOODWIN-GILL, *supra* n.8, at 231 ("Expulsion is a drastic measure which, by its very nature, presupposes substantial justification."); *id.* at 233 (good faith requires justification or reasonable cause for State removal of alien). Because "many municipal systems provide that the authorities of a country may deport aliens without reasons having to be stated," the customary international law on whether a State must provide a justifiable basis for an expulsion remains in conflict. MALCOLM N. SHAW, PUBLIC INTERNATIONAL LAW 826 (6th ed. 2008). Reference to applicable treaty law is therefore the most useful legal guidance available.

13 *See* GOODWIN-GILL, *supra* n.8, at v; BEDI, *supra* n.3, at 400 (deportation and expulsion are inherent rights that cannot be challenged unless a State has limited its liberty through a treaty obligation); *Chahal v U.K.*, Appl. No. 22411/93, 23 EHRR 413, ¶ 73, Nov. 15, 1996 [hereinafter *Chahal Case*]; Treaty Between Denmark, Finland, Iceland, Norway and Sweden on the Conveyance in Transit of Deported Persons, Dec. 3, 1965, 572 U.N.T.S. 105 (1966); Eur. Conv. on Establishment, Dec. 13, 1955, art. 3, E.T.S. No. 019 (mandating, *inter alia*, that "[e]xcept where imperative considerations of national security otherwise require, a national of any Contracting Party who has been so lawfully residing for more than two years in the territory of any other Party shall not be expelled without first being allowed to submit reasons against his expulsion and to appeal to, and be represented for the purpose before, a competent authority or a person or persons specially designated by the competent authority."); JEAN S. PICTET, ED., COMMENTARY ON GENEVA CONVENTION RELATIVE TO THE PROTECTION OF CIVILIAN PERSONS IN TIME OF WAR 235 n.1 and 266 (ICRC 1958) (under GC IV, international humanitarian law recognizes the right of expulsion on national security grounds, but prohibits the forced repatriation against the will of an alien during an international armed conflict) (citations omitted)).

individual alien[14] access, extend his visitor or residency status, or remove him from its territory include[15] whether:

- he was found to have entered the host State illegally across a border area without a checkpoint or otherwise;[16]
- his passport was forged (possibly including the use of an alias), is out of date, or was revoked by the issuing State;[17]
- his visa or residency permit was falsified, he has overstayed the allowable period under the visa or permit,[18] or failed to meet any other

[14] Although collective or mass expulsions or removal operations lie outside the scope of this analysis, they are generally regarded as inconsistent with international human rights standards governing removal operations as they cannot realistically take proper account of individual circumstances. *See* Comm. on the Elimination of Racial Discrimination, Gen. Recom. No. 30, *Discrimination against Non Citizens*, Oct. 1, 2004, ¶ 26; Fourth Prot. to the ECHR, *supra* n.8, art. 4; ACHR, *supra* n.8, art. 22(9). An example can be found in December 2009 when the "[G]overnment of Thailand forcibly repatriated to Laos about 4,000 Lao Hmong from Huay Nam Khao camp in Phetchabun, as well as 158 Lao Hmong detained in the Nong Khai Immigration Detention Centre since November 2006," despite the fact that "[i]n recent years, forcibly repatriated Lao Hmong have been subject to disappearance, imprisonment, forced re-education, and physical and sexual assault." APRRN, *Joint Statement on the Principle of Non-Refoulement and the Recent Forced Deportations of the Uighurs from Cambodia and the Lao Hmong from Thailand*, Jan. 14, 2010, APRRN website, *available at* http://aprrn.info/joint-statement-on-the-principle-of-non-refoulement-and-the-recent-forced-deportations-of-the-uighurs-from-cambodia-and-the-lao-hmong-from-thailand/ (last visited on May 19, 2016) [hereinafter *Forced Deportations*]. *See also* Richard Plender, "The Ugandan Crisis and the Right of Expulsion under International Law," 9 *The Review: Int'l Comm'n of Jurists* 19, 27–28 (Dec. 1972).

[15] This list is not intended to be exhaustive, as States frequently prohibit entry or authorize removal on a variety of other grounds. For example, Zimbabwe's Immigration law, Immigration Act, Chapter 4:02, June 1, 1979, *as amended*, denominates "prohibited persons" to include "any person who at the time of his entry into Zimbabwe is likely to become a public charge," *id.*, art. 14(1)(b); "any person is deaf and dumb, or deaf and blind, or dumb and blind, or otherwise physically incapacitated," *id.*, art. 14(1)(c)(ii); or "any person who is a prostitute or homosexual." *Id.*, art. 14(1)(f)(i).

[16] In a rather dramatic case, Colton Harris-Moore, better known as the "Barefoot Bandit," was deported to the United States after pleading guilty to crash-landing a stolen aircraft in Bahamian territorial waters. Bruce Zagaris, *Bahamas Deports Barefoot Bandit after He Pleads Guilty*, 26 IELR 351 (2010).

[17] *E.g.*, DoJ, *U.S. Attorneys' Manual*, § 9-15.640 (2d ed. 2007–3 Supp.) ("Revocation of the passport can result in loss of the fugitive's lawful residence status, which may lead to his or her deportation.").

[18] For example, in January 2008, the U.S. Immigration and Customs Enforcement (ICE) agency announced the removal of Carlos Alberto Fernandez-Mena, a Costa Rican citizen and former police officer, who had entered the United States as a visitor in February 2004 and illegally remained in the country; he was apprehended based on an international arrest warrant for murder charges issued in October 2007. Bruce Zagaris, *U.S. Surrenders to Costa Rica a Former Police Officer Wanted for Murder*, 24 IELR 134, 134–35 (2008).

specified conditions under the visa or permit (assuming the illegal alien has not been granted amnesty *ex post facto*[19]);

- his citizenship application was forged or contains material omissions or misrepresentations;[20]
- prior to admission, he was convicted of or charged with a crime of moral turpitude[21] or even possibly any intentional crime,[22] or INTERPOL has issued a Red Notice for his arrest;
- once admitted, he commits certain kinds of crimes, poses a national security threat, engages in subversive activities, or his continued presence otherwise is deemed harmful or undesirable;[23] or
- he has just completed a domestic prison sentence.[24]

[19] For example, in April 1974, the United Kingdom granted amnesty to illegal aliens who had arrived in the country before January 1, 1973, to allow them to remain indefinitely in the U.K. "Illegal Aliens Get Amnesty," *The Virgin Islands Daily News*, Apr. 23, 1974, at 5.

[20] This is an all too common occurrence with fugitives, who are keen on their visa applications to conceal their true identity and/or their previous conviction of a crime.

[21] *E.g.*, 8 U.S.C. § 1182(a)(2)(A)(i)) (2012). This provision has been extended a number of times under U.S. law with respect to specific types of individuals to authorize their inadmissibility or removal, including: (i) 8 U.S.C. § 1182(a)(3)(E)(i)) (2012) (related to individuals who participated in Nazi persecution via the so-called Holtzman amendment of 1978) named for Rep. Elizabeth Holtzman (D-N.Y.); (ii) 8 U.S.C. § 1182(a)(3)(E)(ii) (2012) (related to aliens who had engaged in genocidal conduct); (iii) 8 U.S.C. § 1227(a) (related to those who committed, ordered, incited, arrested, or otherwise participated in the commission of torture or extrajudicial killing abroad under the color of law); and (iv) 8 U.S.C. § 1182(a) (2012) (related to foreign government officials who committed particularly severe violations of religious freedom).

[22] *See, e.g.*, Ivan Richard, "Federal Judge Orders Cesare Battisti's Deportation to Mexico or France," *EBC Agencia Brasil*, Mar. 3, 2015 (a lower court ruling that a former Italian activist was not eligible for permanent residency in Brazil, as under its Immigration Law, Law 6.815, Aug. 19, 1980, *as amended*, no alien may be granted a visa if he has been charged with or convicted of an intentional crime in another State).

[23] *See* Bedi, *supra* n.3, at 399; Cohen, *supra* n.8, at 103; 8 U.S.C. § 1227(a)(2) (2005); *Bugajewitz v. Adams*, 228 U.S. 585 (1913); Maïa de la Baume, "Top French Court Backs Move to Strip Citizenship," *INYT*, Jan. 24–25, 2015, at 5 (France's Constitutional Council ruled that Ahmed Sahnouni, a Moroccan national who also became a French citizen in 2003, could be stripped of his French citizenship where, as here, he was convicted on terrorism charges within fifteen years of acquiring French citizenship).

[24] *E.g.*, Zambia Immigration and Deportation Act, *supra* n.12, § 39 (deportation occurs, *inter alia*, "at expiration of the [prison] sentence"). It is also possible that *extradition* can follow a prison term, for example, as occurred in the case of Gen. Manuel Noriega when, after completing his prison term in the United States, he was extradited to France to face retrial based on an *in absentia* conviction for money-laundering charges in 1999. Haroon Siddique, "U.S. Judge Approves Noriega Extradition," *The Guardian*, Aug. 28, 2007.

The two[25] primary types of immigration actions relied on by States to manage illegal or unwanted aliens are exclusions and deportations. An "exclusion" can be defined as the *ejection of an alien by a State on account of security or other significant concerns*[26] *when he is seeking admission or asylum at a border or other port of entry.*[27] It is sometimes hard to distinguish whether an individual has entered a State's territory as a legal versus a factual matter;[28] in such cases domestic immigration law

[25] A third immigration law method, known as "reconduction à la frontière" (or "droit de renvoi"), also exists under some national laws. "The practice of some states may also be distinguished, whereby destitute aliens, foreign vagabonds, suspicious aliens without identity papers, alien criminals who have served their punishment, and the like, are, without any formalities, arrested by the police and reconducted to the frontier. But although such reconduction ... is materially not much different from expulsion, it nevertheless differs much from it in form, since expulsion is an order to leave the country, whereas reconduction is forcible conveying away of foreigners." JENNINGS & WATTS, *supra* n.12, at 940 n.1. In addition, States may deny or withdraw a residency permit from an alien, in an act sometimes known as "refus de séjour," as a precursor step to deportation, but because the act itself does not remove an individual from the host State, and because in many instances those aliens are afforded an opportunity to *voluntarily* depart from the State within a reasonable time period, such a mechanism is of little applicability to this inquiry. *See* GOODWIN-GILL, *supra* n.8, at 253–54 (1978) ("Both the French and German systems employ the 'refus de séjour' as an intermediate stage between lawful residence and expulsion. The alien whose residence permit is refused or withdrawn comes under a duty to leave with due dispatch, although he is not at that time generally subject to police measures"). In addition, a State also can opt to punish directly an individual for violating its immigration laws other than through deportation. For example, Botswana convicted John K. Modise, a founder in 1978 of the Botswana National Front opposition party, and sentenced him to ten months' imprisonment for unlawful entry and being a prohibited immigrant, notwithstanding the fact that his father was a Botswanan citizen. *Modise v. Botswana*, Commc'n No. 97/93, (2000) AHRLR 25, ¶ 4, Nov. 6, 2000 [hereinafter *Modise Case*].

[26] *See* Cohen, *supra* n.8, at 103 (citing reasons for exclusion as including intentional misrepresentation of material facts, convictions of a crime of moral turpitude, and membership in a totalitarian party).

[27] *See* Alona E. Evans, *Acquisition of Custody over the Int'l Fugitive Offender—Alternatives to Extradition: A Survey of United States Practice*, 40 B.Y.B.I.L. 77, 77 n.1 (1964); BEDI, *supra* n.3, at 399 (noting non-access at border has no effect on an individual's liberty to travel elsewhere); *e.g.*, *Öcalan v. Turkey (Merits)*, Appl. No. 46221/99, Gr. Ch., 41 EHRR 45, ¶ 14–15, May 12, 2005 (in October 1998, when Turkish national and Kurdish separatist leader Abdullah Öcalan was expelled from Syria where he had been living for many years, he tried to win admission to Greece, but was rebuffed at the border and within two hours was asked to leave and his application for political asylum was denied).

[28] *See* Brandon S. Chabner, Comment, *The Omnibus Diplomatic Security and Antiterrorism Act of 1986: Prescribing and Enforcing United States Law against Terrorist Violence Overseas*, 37 UCLA L. REV. 985, 1011 n.123 (1990) (citing as an example when the person has crossed a border but has not yet reported to a border station); *Expulsion of Aliens*, *supra* n.9, at 65 ("There are two categories of aliens who

tends to be determinative.[29] Similar to, yet distinct from, exclusion, "deportation" can be defined as *the execution of an expulsion order by a State from its sovereign territory of an alien, even if only having been temporarily admitted, on the ground that he violated its immigration laws upon entering the territory, is otherwise illegally within the territory, or while present has proven to be a public menace or security threat.*[30]

Both exclusions and deportations[31] can be labeled more broadly a form of "removal."[32] As a matter of nomenclature in the present discourse, States that exclude or deport an alien under their immigration laws are called "removing States,"[33] while those accepting such

may be in such a position: (1) passengers who arrive by airplane or ship at an international transportation facility located in the territory of the State (other than transit passengers) and are denied admission; or (2) aliens who have crossed the border and entered the State without complying with the requirements for admission under its national immigration law.").

29 *Expulsion of Aliens, supra* n.9, at 47.

30 *See* Bedi, *supra* n.3, at 399; Shearer, *supra* n.8, at 76; Clive Nicholls, et al., eds., The Law of Extradition and Mutual Assistance 3 (2d ed. 2007); Karl Doehring, *Aliens, Expulsion and Deportation, in* 1 Encyclopedia of Public International Law 109, 111 (Rudolf Bernhardt ed. 1992) ("[E]xpulsion means the prohibition to remain inside the territory of the ordering State; deportation is the factual execution of the expulsion order."); *Bensayah Case, supra* n.8, ¶ 112. *Cf. Expulsion of Aliens, supra* n.9, at 50–52 (although a vessel is generally treated as "floating territory" of the flagged State, the mandated departure of an alien from a foreign-flagged ship to a host State ship in the latter's territorial waters most likely would not technically qualify as an "expulsion," and accordingly would not be governed by international law related to the expulsion of aliens but rather by international maritime law). Deportation in this context when handling aliens is to be distinguished from deportation in the domestic resettling context or in the international criminal law context when used in reference to "the forced displacement of persons by expulsion or other coercive acts from the area in which they are lawfully present, without grounds permitted under international law." Robert Cryer, et al., An Introduction to International Criminal Law and Procedure 249 (2d ed. 2010) (citing to ICTY Statute, art. 7(2)(d) as a type of crime against humanity).

31 Some national laws refer to one or both of these processes as "*refoulement.*" *E.g.*, Honduras, Immigration Act, Decreto 208–2003, Mar. 3, 2004, art. 3(23), *reprinted in La Gaceta* (term used as the functional equivalent of exclusion); Madagascar, Immigration Law, June 6, 1962, arts. 12 and 17, *as amended* [French text] (term used as the functional equivalent of deportation).

32 In 1996, the U.S. Congress passed legislation eliminating the distinction between exclusion and deportation and replaced them jointly with the single term, "removal." Illegal Immigration Reform and Responsibility Act (IIRRA), Pub. L. 104–208, Sept. 30, 1996, § 301 *et seq.* "Removal" is defined herein *as a State's exercise of immigration power through either exclusion or deportation and that can be effected directly, indirectly (with the assistance of a third State intermediary), or via a negotiated arrangement.*

33 A "removing State" is defined as *a State that is in the process of removing or has removed an alien from its sovereign territory.*

aliens are called "receiving States."[34] Exclusions and deportations share common traits, mainly that the State's chief concern in both instances is to ensure the alien is prohibited from being within its sovereign territory.[35]

But key differences between exclusions and deportations exist as well: (i) in exclusions the alien is at the gateway to State territory while with deportations he is already within the territory;[36] (ii) exclusion decisions are necessarily based on conduct that occurred in other States whereas with deportations it is frequently about the alien's behavior within the host State's territory; (iii) unlike exclusions, which deprive aliens of a *prospective* benefit, deportations deprive aliens of an *existing* one;[37] (iv) under international humanitarian law, deportations alone are expressly proscribed with respect to militarily occupied territory;[38] and (v) aliens may be accorded certain procedural and substantive protections in a deportation hearing that are not afforded in an exclusion hearing.[39]

Deportations, which are far more applicable to the present inquiry, can be classified into one of three types: formal, informal, and voluntary. A "formal deportation" is *involuntary and undertaken through officially established channels while complying with the applicable conditions*

[34] A "receiving State" is defined in the *immigration* law (versus the diplomatic) context as *a State that is accepting or has accepted into its sovereign territory an alien removed by another State.*

[35] SHEARER, *supra* n.8, at 90; Silvia Borelli, *The Rendition of Terrorist Suspects to the United States: Human Rights and the Limits of Int'l Cooperation, in* ENFORCING INTERNATIONAL LAW NORMS AGAINST TERRORISM 338 n.27 (Andrea Bianchi ed. 2004).

[36] SHEARER, *supra* n.8, at 76; Chabner, *supra* n.28, at 1011.

[37] Cohen, *supra* n.8, at 103. A deportation could effectively divest the alien of certain acquired rights earned on account of his residence in the host State. *Expulsion of Foreign National (Germany) Case*, Admin. Ct. App., Nord-Rhein-Westfalen, 1961, *reprinted in* 32 ILR 255 (1961).

[38] Geneva Conv. Relative to the Protection of Civilian Persons in Time of War, Aug. 12, 1949, art. 49, 6 U.S.T. 3516, T.I.A.S. No. 3365, 75 U.N.T.S. 287 [hereinafter GC IV]; and Addt'l Prot. to the Geneva Convs. of August 12, 1949, and Relating to the Protection of Victims of Int'l Armed Conflicts of June 8, 1977 (AP I), art. 85(4)(a), U.N. Doc. A/32/144 (1977), Annex I, *reprinted in* 16 ILM 1391. Both provisions prohibit expulsions from occupied territory – *not* from one's own territory.

[39] For example, under U.S. law, in deportation hearings, an alien is entitled to seven days' notice of the charges against him, which is not so with exclusion hearings; and in a deportation, if the I.N.S. prevails, the alien may seek review from a U.S. court of appeals whereas an alien can challenge an order of exclusion only via a petition for a *writ of habeas corpus. Landon v. Plasencia*, 459 U.S. 21, 26 (1982). In addition, at exclusion hearings alone the alien bears the burden of establishing his admissibility. JOHN F. MURPHY, PUNISHING INTERNATIONAL TERRORISTS: THE LEGAL FRAMEWORK FOR POLICY INITIATIVES 85 (1985) (citing to U.S. law).

and requirements of a removing State's laws.[40] (A State legislature could even seek to amend its immigration laws to accommodate a particular deportation.[41]) An "informal deportation" is also *involuntary, undertaken through casual arrangements, and typically handled on an expedited basis.*[42] A "voluntary deportation" *occurs when an alien freely consents to be deported to his home or a third State prior to a deportation determination by the host State.*[43] An alien may volunteer for any number of reasons, including a wish to avoid protracted removal hearings for which he is unlikely to prevail, a desire to be reunited without undue delay with his family or friends, and/or avoidance of punishment that may arise from any liability found under the removing State's criminal laws.[44]

[40] The case of Fyodor Fedorenko, the Ukrainian-born naturalized U.S. citizen who collaborated with the Nazis during World War II as a guard at the Treblinka death camp in Poland, is illustrative. *See* Robert Gillette, "Fedorenko, Deported From U.S., Doomed by Soviets as War Criminal," *L.A. Times*, June 20, 1986 (after stripping him of his citizenship in 1979, based on finding in a civil lawsuit that he had obtained U.S. citizenship by omitting reference to his position as a concentration camp guard, the U.S. Government deported him to the Soviet Union in December 1984 after lengthy proceedings). Three years after he was deported, Russia executed him. Felicity Barringer, "Soviet Reports It Executed Nazi Guard U.S. Extradited," *N.Y. Times*, July 28, 1987, at A3.

[41] *E.g.*, R. Stuart Phillips, *The Political Offence Exception and Terrorism: Its Place in the Current Extradition Scheme and Proposal for Its Future*, 15 Dickinson J. Int'l L. 337, 345 (1997) (citing to the case of former pro-Nazi Croatian Government Minister Andrija Artuković, whose extradition to Yugoslavia was denied by a U.S. court out of concern over potential political persecution; as a result, the U.S. Congress amended its immigration laws in 1978 to allow for his deportation to stand trial for his complicity in executing some 200,000 Serbian prisoners).

[42] *See* Michael Abbell, Extradition to and from the United States 379 (2010) (noting the absence of a resort to formal procedures, the frequent use in narcotics cases, and the likelihood of occurring where a "close working relationship" exists between law enforcement officers of the two States involved). For example, in May 1979, Thai immigration authorities informally deported Steven Paul Valot to the United States by bringing him to the transit lounge of Bangkok's International Airport and handing him over to DEA officials who took him on board a flight to Hawaii, where he was wanted for falsifying statements in his passport application. *United States v. Valot*, 625 F.2d 308 (9th Cir. 1980).

[43] *E.g.*, U.S. Dep't of State, *Foreign Affairs Manual*, Vol. 7 – Consular Affairs, Other Extradition Matters, 7 FAM 1643.b., *updated* Feb. 18, 2011 ("In most cases, the person whose deportation is sought has the choice of voluntarily departing the United States (presumably for a country other than the one in which the person is charged with or convicted of a crime) before the adjudication of deportability.").

[44] *See* M.G. Cowling, *Unmasking 'Disguised' Extradition—Some Glimmer of Hope*, 109 S. Afr. L.J. 241, 243 (1992); *R. v. Ayu* [1958] 3 All E.R. 636, [1959] 1 W.L.R. 1246. For the rules governing voluntary departures during a time of international armed conflict, *see* GC IV, *supra* n.38, art. 35 ("All protected persons who may desire to leave the territory

The destination of a removed alien is determined by municipal law, which varies considerably:

> National legislation may allow the alien to choose the State of destination, but may require that the latter be willing to grant the alien entry, or that the selection be limited to those States where the alien's entry would be legal. A State may grant this choice as the primary option, an alternative primary option, or an alternative secondary option for selecting the State of destination. A State may place conditions on the choice of a contiguous or adjacent State, or select a State of destination if the alien's choice is not made promptly or would prejudice the expelling State's interests.[45]

In principle, removing States should have little or no interest in the alien's destination; the overriding purpose of removal, after all, is merely to keep unwanted or dangerous individuals outside of its territory.[46] By and large, State statutes tend to assign default priority to the alien's home State or the State from which he last embarked for the host State,[47] and international law obligates the State of his nationality to avail itself as a receiving State.[48] As noted above, the alien's preference is generally honored[49] so long as the designated State is willing to receive the alien,[50] *refoulement* is not at issue,

at the outset of, or during a conflict, shall be entitled to do so, unless their departure is contrary to the national interests of the State.").

45 *Expulsion of Aliens, supra* n.9, at 314 (citations omitted).

46 *See* Nicholls, *supra* n.30, at 4 (the purpose of deportation is achieved when an alien leaves the State's territory; unlike extradition, the destination of the deportee is irrelevant to the purpose of deportation). *But see* 4 Digest of Int'l Law 30 (Green H. Hackworth ed. 1942) (while fully acknowledging this purposive distinction, the then-U.S. State Department Legal Adviser Green Hackworth acknowledged that "requests are sometimes made by governments for the deportation by other governments of fugitives from justice, and occasionally steps are taken – especially in the absence of an extradition treaty – to deport such persons.").

47 Shearer, *supra* n.8, at 77–78; D. Cameron Findlay, *Abducting Terrorists Overseas for Trial in the United States: Issues of Int'l and Domestic Law*, 23 Tex. Int'l L.J. 1, 7 (1988). The destination need not be a State with a shared land border. *E.g., Wallace v. State of the Netherlands*, Sup. Ct., Neth., Sept. 13, 1963, *reprinted in* Neth. Int'l L. Rev., Vol. XI (1964) 303, 304 [hereinafter *Wallace Case*].

48 Shaw, *supra* n.12, at 827.

49 *See* Doehring, *supra* n.30, at 111 ("A duty of the expelling State to give the individual the possibility of choosing a receiving country is not recognized although this opportunity may be, and often is, granted."); HRC, Gen. Cmt. No. 15, *The Position of Aliens Under the Covenant*, U.N. Doc. HRI/GEN/1/Rev.1 at 18 (1994), ¶ 9, Apr. 11, 1986 ("Normally an alien who is expelled must be allowed to leave for any country that agrees to take him"); Christopher H. Pyle, Extradition, Politics, and Human Rights 208 (2001) ("Under U.S. law, aliens who have entered the country illegally have traditionally been able to choose the country of their deportation.") (citing, *inter alia*, 8 U.S.C. § 1253 (2012)); *e.g., Landon*, 459 U.S. 21 (1982).

50 Moeller, *supra* n.8, at 814.

and doing so would not be antithetical to the removing State's national interests.[51]

However, candidate States may refuse receipt for the same concerns that prompt host States to call for removal in the first instance,[52] and, indeed, it is not unprecedented for a removing State to not obtain the consent of a receiving State before a removal.[53] In any event, a removing State retains the ultimate discretion to choose the country destination.[54] Once the destination is finalized, the alien is moved usually via commercial airline or chartered aircraft (for longer distances), via ground transportation (when crossing borders or for shorter distances),[55] or via ship (if traveling across smaller bodies of water or if otherwise it is the most convenient means of passage).

b Removal v. Extradition

What are the major distinctions between removals and extraditions,[56] and what are their respective advantages and disadvantages as vehicles?

51 Abbell, *supra* n.42, at 307–08; 8 U.S.C. 1253(a) (2012); 8 U.S.C. § 1253(h) (2012). An example of national interests scuttling an alien's choice of destination for deportation can be found in *R. v. Governor of Brixton Prison, ex parte Soblen* [1963] 2 QB 243, 3 WLR 1154 [hereinafter *Soblen Case*] (the United Kingdom rejected Soblen's request to be deported to Czechoslovakia, a State willing to take him, because Czechoslovakia was then a Soviet satellite country and Soblen had been convicted and sentenced to life imprisonment in the United States as a Soviet spy in 1960 at the height of the Cold War).

52 Shearer, *supra* n.8, at 77 (citing by way of example *In re Guerreiro*, (1955) SCR (1) 1284, Sup. Ct., Arg., Nov. 27, 1951, *reprinted in* 18 ILR 315 (1951)).

53 *E.g., Jama v. ICE*, 543 U.S. 335 (2005) (approving the decision by U.S. immigration authorities to remove Keyse Jama, a Somali national, to his country of birth, even though Somalia then had no capacity, as a failed State, to consent to receive him; such consent is required only when an alien is to be removed to a country other than the one of his choice, one in which he is a citizen, or one in which he has a lesser connection).

54 *E.g., Muller v. Superintendent, Presidency Jail, Calcutta & Others*, (1995) SCR (1) 1284, Sup. Ct., India, Feb. 23, 1955, (1955) SCR (1) 1284, *reprinted in* 22 ILR 497, 499 (1958) [hereinafter *Muller Case*] ("In the case of expulsion . . . if a person is prepared to leave voluntarily he can ordinarily go as and when he pleases. But he has no *right* in that regard. Under Indian law, the matter is left to the unfettered discretion of the Union Government and that Government can prescribe the route and the port or place of departure and can place him on a particular ship or plane") (emphasis in original).

55 Bruce Zagaris, *U.S. Congress Holds Hearings on Deportees in Latin America and the Caribbean*, 23 IELR 392 (2007) (citing the head of the Deportation and Removal Office (DRO), part of the Department of Homeland Security's (DHS's) Bureau of Immigration and Customs Enforcement (ICE)).

56 Regrettably, the terms "expulsion" or "deportation" (immigration law terms) and "extradition" (a law enforcement term) are often used interchangeably in the media, case law,

Differences. A number of key differences exist between removals and extraditions, including the following:

- With removals, the State's executive branch (in the guise of its immigration authorities) is generally the sole decision-maker,[57] while with extraditions it can be and often is a mix between the executive branch (the foreign affairs ministry and/or justice ministry) and the judiciary that determines the outcome.[58]
- In the case of removals, the non-host (receiving) State is typically a passive participant, whereas with extraditions, the non-host (pursuing) State is in almost all cases an active, if not the initiating, participant.[59]
- Removals generally deport or exclude only aliens (including denaturalized nationals), while extraditions, unless a specific domestic legal or treaty prohibition applies, may involve host State nationals.[60]
- The main objective of removals is to safeguard a State's own citizens, while the primary aim of extraditions is to transfer the individual to another State to help it achieve a law enforcement purpose.[61]

and government reports alike. *E.g.*, *Giry v. Dominican Repub.*, Commc'n No. 193/1985, U.N. Doc. CCPR/C/39/D/193/1985 ¶ 5.5, July 20, 1990 ("The State Party initially submitted that the author was *deported* from Dominican territory on the basis of an *extradition* treaty between the Dominican Republic and the United States of America.") (emphasis supplied).

57 *See* David Freestone, *Int'l Cooperation against Terrorism and the Development of Int'l Law Principles of Jurisdiction*, *in* Terrorism and International Law 47 (Rosalyn Higgins & Maurice Flory eds. 1997). In the United States, the executive branch immigration law authorities include administrative law judges who hold hearings on admissibility, but they are not part of the federal judiciary, and have broad discretion when admitting and evaluating evidence, as they do not follow the Federal Rules of Evidence (FRE). Rules of Practice for Admin. Law Judge Proceedings, 20 C.F.R. § 655.425. Under German immigration law, by contrast, deportation remains entirely within the province of the executive, *except* when a violation of constitutional rights is alleged, in which case the matter falls within the jurisdiction of the Federal Constitutional Court. Shearer, *supra* n.8, at 83.

58 *See* pp. 153–54 in Chapter 4 (discussing extradition decision-making).

59 *See* n.82 and accompanying text in Chapter 1. By contrast with extraditions, the Deportation with Assurances (DWA) MOUs (discussed *infra*) sponsored by the United Kingdom call for a State to request the partner State to *receive* (versus transfer) a given individual under stipulated conditions. *See also* nn.224–26 and accompanying text *infra*.

60 *See* Chapter 6.a; *e.g.*, *Linnas v. I.N.S.*, 790 F.2d 1024, 1031 (2d Cir. 1986).

61 Doehring, *supra* n.30, at 110; Moeller, *supra* n.8, at 814; Bedi, *supra* n.3, at 399–400.

- In the case of removals, the individual typically leaves the host State as a free person,[62] whereas with extraditions the subject necessarily departs in the physical custody of government officials.[63]
- Extraditees generally are entitled to certain "formalities," including access to counsel and the right to challenge an extradition order, compared with those ordered for removal where such rights often are subject to strict limitations.[64]
- Extradition treaties may contain a re-extradition provision restricting an individual's transfer to a third State without the prior approval of the original host State; no such provision attends removal orders.[65]

Comparative Advantages of Extradition. Assuming a particular alien is a candidate for either removal or extradition by the host

[62] In a recent exceptional instance, Kenya claimed to have nominally "deported" 45 Taiwanese nationals for violating their visas, but those individuals, "suspected of being part of a criminal syndicate in Nairobi" targeting citizens in China, appear to have been seized by Chinese law enforcement officers and "forcibly taken to China, in two flights on April 8 and April 12, some in hoods and handcuffs." Editorial, "China's Seizures in Kenya: The Nabbing of Taiwanese in Nairobi Looks Like Another Example of Beijing's Overreach Abroad," *Wash. Post*, Apr. 16, 2016, at A14.

[63] *See Muller Case*, *supra* n.54, at 1300–01 (although an alien subject to a deportation order "may be conducted to the frontier under detention he must be permitted to leave a free man and cannot be handed over under arrest. In a case of extradition, he does not leave a free man. He remains under arrest throughout and is merely handed over by one set of police to the next."); Shearer, *supra* n.8, at 87–88; Evans, *supra* n.27, at 94. As a practical matter, however, this distinction can be nullified, for example, by merely placing the removed alien on a flagged ship or plane of the State with a law enforcement interest in him, thereby allowing that State's officials to promptly effect his arrest, or, alternatively, bringing him in custody to an international border crossing and then once he has passed to the other side, pursuing State officials are there to apprehend him. The lawfulness of such tactics is explored *infra*.

[64] *See Muller Case*, *supra* n.54, at 1299; ICCPR, *supra* n.8, art. 13; Prot. 7 to the Eur. Conv. for the Protection of Human Rights and Fundamental Freedoms (ECHR), art. 1, *as amended by* Prot. No. 11, Nov. 22, 1984, E.T.S. No. 155 [hereinafter Seventh Prot.].

[65] *See* Cryer, *supra* n.30, at 84–85 (recognizing that re-extradition requirements can be circumvented by deporting fugitives under immigration laws) (citing to *Bozano v France*, Appl. No. 9990/82, 9 EHRR 297, Dec. 2, 1987 [hereinafter *Bozano Case*]. In *Ahmad v. Wigen*, once Venezuela deported Ahmad to the United States (his country of nationality), U.S. authorities were then in a position to extradite him to Israel to face criminal charges there, without complaint by Venezuela, despite the absence of an extradition treaty between Venezuela and Israel that had precluded a direct transfer in the first instance. 726 F. Supp. 389, 394 (E.D.N.Y. 1989), *aff'd*, 910 F.2d 1063 (2d Cir.), *stay denied*, 111 S. Ct. 23 (1990).

State,[66] in rendering a decision between the two options, the factors weighing in favor of extradition from the *host State's perspective* might well include: (i) assisting the international community in suppressing crime; (ii) winning the appreciation of, and potential reciprocity from, a particular pursuing State in bringing a fugitive to justice; (iii) avoiding the need to first denaturalize a national where its laws otherwise prohibit the removal of nationals;[67] and (iv) helping the pursuing State to avert any "premature exposure" of its criminal case against the alien fugitive in the course of holding immigration proceedings.[68]

Other extradition advantages that inure directly to the *individual's* benefit, but which may nevertheless influence the decisions of some host States, include the fact that extradition generally affords individuals judicial review in addition to executive branch discretion;[69] and an individual likely would receive such standard protections as the specialty rule,[70] the prohibition against double jeopardy,[71] and application of the political offense exclusion.[72]

Comparative Advantages of Removal. The host State conversely may opt for a removal operation over extradition for one of several reasons. Apart from circumstances where extradition may simply be unavailable

66 For example, in April 2014, U.S. law enforcement authorities arrested Albanian national and U.S. permanent national Altin Hasani, pursuant to an extradition request by Albania for the 1990 stabbing of a man that resulted in his death and for which Hasani had been sentenced *in absentia* in 1999 to twenty years in prison. At the same time, Hasani had never disclosed that conviction in connection with the receipt of any of his immigration benefits and so could be a legitimate subject of deportation. U.S. Immigration and Customs Enforcement (ICE), "International Fugitive Arrested Following Extradition Request," Apr. 28, 2014, *available at* www.ice.gov/news/releases/international-fugitive-arrested-following-extradition-request (last visited on May 22, 2016).

67 *See supra* n.8; ABBELL, *supra* n.42, at 307 & n.569 (discussing U.S. law).

68 David P. Warner, *Challenges to Int'l Law Enforcement Cooperation for the U.S. in the Middle East and North Africa: Extradition and Its Alternatives*, 50 VILL. L. REV. 479, 497 (2005).

69 Freestone, *supra* n.57, at 47.

70 ABBELL, *supra* n.42, at 380 (deportees receive no protection under the specialty rule unless a separate promise was negotiated); SHEARER, *supra* n.8, at 88; Paul O'Higgins, *Disguised Extradition: The Soblen Case*, 27 MOD. L. REV. 521, 525 (1964) (deportation lacks judicial hearings of extradition and smacks of a Star Chamber) (quoting H.G. Reuschlein, *Provisional Arrest and Detention in Int'l Extradition: A Survey of Practice and Procedure*, GEO. L.J. 37, 77–78 (1934)).

71 *See* ABBELL, *supra* n.42, at 380–381 (noting the lack of protection against double jeopardy once an individual has been deported, based on a conviction in the removing State, including under the ICCPR, *supra* n.8, art. 14(7)).

72 *See, e.g.*, SHEARER, *supra* n.8, at 88 & 89 n.1 (citing the *Greville Wynne* case in which Hungary deported a British subject to the Soviet Union to face political charges).

as an option, say, because of a lack of an extraditable offense[73] or the prospect of human rights abuse in the pursuing State, removal might be favored because the host State has a political conflict directly or indirectly with a particular pursuing State and so would rather exercise its deportation option so as not to appear as diplomatically accommodating.[74] In addition, removal is widely viewed as, and in fact often constitutes, the more expeditious and cheaper alternative compared with extradition.[75]

c Application

Having viewed removal from the standpoint of the *host* State, we now turn the analysis on its head and consider how removal would look from the perspective of a given *pursuing* State, and more specifically how it might proactively seek removal as a full-scale alternative to extradition. This approach, however, offers no guarantee of success, as the host State might elect not to deport for any number of reasons and, of course, deportation presumes that the fugitive at issue were an alien or a denaturalized citizen, rather than a national of the host State. In addition to assessing its operational facets, this section also briefly explores various factors that weigh for or against removal as a means for securing the custody of a fugitive.

[73] *See, e.g.*, Bruce Zagaris, *Iceland Grants Bobby Fischer Citizenship and Japan Deports Him to Iceland*, 21 IELR 186, 186–88 (2005) (discussing how after the U.S. Government was unable to have former world chess champion Bobby Fischer extradited from Japan because Japan did not recognize a violation of economic sanctions as an extraditable offense, the United States attempted to have him deported on the ground that he was traveling on false documents).

[74] *See* nn.38 and 44 and accompanying text in Chapter 7.

[75] *See* Shearer, *supra* n.8, at 86 (States generally "choose deportation as the more convenient and practical choice"); Isidoro Zanotti, Extradition in Multilateral Treaties and Conventions xi (2006) (noting the speed of deportation compared with "cumbersome extradition procedures"); Geoff Gilbert, Responding to International Crime 12–13 (2006) (quoting Alona E. Evans, panel moderator, *International Procedures for the Apprehension and Rendition of Fugitive Offenders*, Apr. 18, 1980, 74 ASIL Proc. 274, 276 (1980) (in a study of 231 instances of rendition of persons charged with international terrorist offenses, only six of eighty-seven extradition requests were granted while 144 terrorists were removed by 28 States). *But see* Simona Agnolucci, *Deportation of Human Rights Abusers: Toward Achieving Accountability, Not Fostering Impunity*, 30 Hastings Int'l & Comp. L. Rev. 347, 364 (2007) (the removal process itself can often be onerous and time-consuming, cases sometimes taking six–seven years of litigation once the individual has been apprehended and individuals may pursue repeated appeals to avoid deportation).

i How Removal Operates

Removal operations manifest in one of three ways: direct, indirect, or via some kind of negotiated arrangement. The *direct* route is by far the most common and consists of a pursuing State requesting or expressing interest in the removal to its territory of an alien, most typically in cases where the alien is one of its own nationals, and generally via diplomatic channels.[76] That option may be preceded by the revocation of the fugitive's passport and notification of the same to the host State, as most States treat the absence of a valid travel document as a violation of their immigration laws, and therefore as grounds to remove an alien from their territory.[77] Direct removals also have taken place in contravention of the host State's own constitutional or statutory law or a domestic judicial order, presumably in order to curry political favor with a particular pursuing State.[78]

An example of direct removal can be found when Romania removed to the United States, at the latter's request, U.S. citizen Michael Harvey, who had fled in 1999 after being charged with multiple counts of sexual offenses with minors in three California counties.[79] The U.S. request was made only after California prosecutors were advised that extradition was not feasible under the then-applicable 1924 U.S.-Rumania Extradition Treaty, which treated rape and "carnal knowledge of children under 12 years of age" as the only sexually-related extraditable crimes,[80] thereby leaving rape offenses against Harvey's teenage victims outside its ambit. Consequently, with FBI assistance, California state prosecutors initially sought a federal warrant based on a federal crime

[76] *E.g., U.S. Attorneys' Manual, supra* n.17, § 9–15.610. This scenario can be distinguished from those deportations described in Chapter 9 (*see* pp. 366–67, 368) as this one is directly between a pursuing-cum-receiving State and the removing State, whereas those from the last chapter involved the cooperation of third States.

[77] *See* pp. 350–52 in Chapter 9.

[78] For example, Malawi authorities deported to the United States (into CIA custody) alleged members of al-Qaida suspected of financing terrorism, overriding its own constitutional law and despite pending judicial proceedings. Int'l Comm'n of Jurists, Center on the Independence of Judges and Lawyers, "U.S. and Malawi: Rule of Law Compromised in Fight against Terrorism," ICJ website, July 1, 2003, *available at* www.icj.org/us-and-malawi-rule-of-law-compromised-in-fight-against-terrorism/ (last visited on May 22, 2016).

[79] *Garvey v. U.S. Dep't of Justice*, 2007 U.S. Dist. LEXIS 15245 (E.D. Cal. Mar. 5, 2007).

[80] Treaty on Extradition, U.S.-Rumania, July 23, 1924, art. II(3) T.S. No. 713. In September 2007, the United States and Romania updated their extradition treaty. Treaty on Extradition, U.S.-Rom., Sept. 10, 2007, S. Treaty Doc. 110–11, 2 CTIA 351 (2007).

known as unlawful flight to avoid prosecution (UFAP),[81] which sequentially triggered revocation of Harvey's passport by the U.S. Department of State, his arrest for violation of Romania's immigration laws, and finally his deportation.[82]

One variant of the direct approach is for a pursuing State to arrange in advance with the removing State the placement of an alien fugitive on a ship or airplane destined for a receiving State but routed through that pursuing State's territory as a scheduled layover. For example, in 2006, after being acquitted on drug possession charges in Ecuador, Iranian national Mehrzad Arbane was deported to Iran but routed through Houston, Texas, where, during that intermediate stop, U.S. authorities arrested him on a charge of unlawful importation of cocaine and later federally removed him to Florida to face prosecution.[83]

The *indirect* approach to removal requires a cooperating third-party role. Here, a pursuing State obtains the fugitive's custody, either through extradition, removal, or a simple transfer from an intermediary State, which is legally postured to receive the fugitive initially by removal from the original host State. For example, due to the lack of a bilateral extradition treaty between them, Venezuela was unwilling to extradite to Israel Mahmoud El-Abed Ahmad for his alleged role in attacking a civilian bus in the West Bank. In considering its options for bringing Ahmad to justice, Israel turned to the United States as a potential intermediary State, given that Ahmad was a dual Palestinian-American national. In May 1987, the United States arranged to have Ahmad deported to its territory in response to his violating Venezuelan immigration laws and then, in turn, extradited him to Israel to face criminal prosecution there.[84]

[81] "If the fugitive is wanted on [U.S.] state charges only, it will be necessary to obtain a warrant on a UFAP complaint because the Department of State is only authorized to revoke the passports of persons named in *federal* warrants." *U.S. Attorneys' Manual, supra* n.17, § 9-15.640 (emphasis supplied).

[82] *Garvey Case, supra* n.79.

[83] *United States v. Arbane*, 446 F.3d 1223, 1225 (11th Cir. 2006). (the court judgment remains unclear as to whether or not this amounted to a coordinated plan between the Ecuadorian and U.S. Governments). An intended receiving State must be prepared, however, when the same interventionist tactics are used against it by a pursuing State. *See* Abbell, *supra* n.42, at 380 n.39 (many flights land in third countries *en route* to the United States, thereby requiring cooperation between U.S. authorities and the authorities of those transit countries).

[84] Ethan A. Nadelmann, *The Evolution of United States Involvement in the Int'l Rendition of Fugitive Criminals*, 25 N.Y.U. J. Int'l L. & Pol. 813, 879 (1993) [hereinafter Nadelmann, *Int'l Rendition*].

A pursuing State also can enter into a *bargained arrangement* with the host State whereby the two agree to simultaneously or sequentially "exchange prisoners by deportation, a procedure which may subject those exchanged to criminal proceedings in their respective States of origin. The U.S. Department of State explicitly recognized this situation in 1941, in arranging for the deportation to the Soviet Union of Mikhail Gorin, [who was] convicted of espionage and later pardoned [by the U.S. Government] in anticipation of his being exchanged for two American nationals held by Soviet authorities."[85] (This arrangement is to be distinguished from both: (i) the inter-State transfer of sentenced persons as a form of international cooperation to ensure their fair treatment and social rehabilitation;[86] and (ii) non-prisoner "officer swaps" intended for each government to retrieve its own valued but captured military, intelligence, or political officers,[87] neither of which would involve deportation.)

In another example, in December 1989, "the DEA was contacted by Mexican federal judicial police [MFJP] to discuss the possible exchange of prisoners" involving, among others, Humberto Álvarez-Machaín, a medical doctor from Guadalajara charged with participating in the torture and murder of a DEA agent.[88] Specifically, for its part, the United States was expected to deport Isaac Naredo-Moreno, who "was wanted for stealing $500 million from Mexican politicians," and the DEA even proceeded to arrest and hold Naredo-Moreno in a safe house, but ultimately was unwilling to meet the advance payment demands (US $50,000) of the MFJP commandante and his associates, so the deal broke down.[89] More recently, in 2003, there were press reports, denied by

[85] Evans, *supra* n.27, at 88 ("In so far as Mr. Gorin personally is concerned, we are inclined to the belief that in view of his carelessness in permitting incriminating documents to fall into the hands of the American authorities, he will receive after his return to the Soviet Union punishment at least as severe as the serving of his full sentence in the United States") (citing 1 *Foreign Relations*, 1941, at 937 (1958)).

[86] *E.g.*, U.N. Model Agreement on the Transfer of Foreign Prisoners and Recommendations on the Treatment of Foreign Prisoners, Nov. 29, 1985, U.N. Doc. A/CONF.121/22/Rev.1 (1986); U.N. Conv. on Transnational Organized Crime, Nov. 15, 2000, art. 17, U.N. GAOR, 55th Sess., 62d Plen. Mtg., Annex I, U.N. Doc. A/RES/55/25.

[87] This famously occurred when Soviet Col. Rudolf Abel, who had been convicted in the United States for espionage, was traded for U-2 pilot Francis Gary Powers, also convicted of espionage for his overflight of Soviet territory in May 1961. Tom Wicker, "Powers is Freed by Soviet in an Exchange for Abel; U-2 Pilot on Way to U.S.," *N.Y. Times*, Feb. 10, 1962, at 1.

[88] Heymann & Gershengorn, *supra* n.2, at 133.

[89] Pyle, *supra* n.49, at 282.

Iran, that it was willing to deport al-Qaida detainees wanted by the United States in exchange for "U.S.-held Iranian opposition figures."[90]

A variant of this approach would be to remove one or more individuals to another State as part of a swap for economic or trade benefits, a decision to drop an extradition request, or other desired ends. For example, in December 2009, two days after Cambodia deported twenty ethnic Uighur asylum seekers to the PRC, the receiving State extended fourteen commercial deals to Cambodia valued in the aggregate at US $1 billion, conceivably as a *quid pro quo*.[91] Such deals are not typically publicized or acknowledged as such, and therefore are difficult to challenge on legal grounds.

ii Factors Militating for and against Removal

When no applicable extradition treaty exists and the host State's law prohibits extradition absent such a treaty,[92] or when extradition has been denied[93] or is regarded as a highly unlikely prospect, a pursuing State may choose to seek removal of the fugitive alien from the host State as a contingency option.[94] In some instances, a State simply may be politically or pragmatically unwilling to wait for expected lengthy extradition proceedings to play out and want to bring a fugitive to justice without undue delay. Removal proceedings, which can sometimes take years to

90 "Iran Won't Hand Over Al Qaeda Suspects to U.S.," *AP*, Aug. 4, 2003.

91 *Forced Deportations*, *supra* n.14.

92 *See* Evans, *supra* n.27, at 93 ("Exclusion or expulsion of the alien offender from the United States has been used pending the conclusion of an extradition treaty with the requesting State").

93 As an example, after eight years, once U.S. federal courts determined that Joseph Doherty, an IRA guerrilla who had been convicted in Northern Ireland for the murder of a British soldier, could not be extradited on the grounds that his offense was determined to be "political," he was deported to Northern Ireland into British custody. James Barron, "I.R.A. Fugitive Sent to Belfast from U.S. Jail," *N.Y. Times*, Feb. 20, 1992, at A1. Notably, the British authorities refused to grant him "credit" for time served in U.S. prisons. "Stiff Term for IRA Man," *Wash. Post*, Aug. 4, 1992, at A6.

94 For example, although the United States and Cuba do not have an extradition treaty, Cuba has demonstrated a willingness to cooperate with the United States through removal operations regarding specific violations where the two States share an interest in law enforcement. *See* Bruce Zagaris, *Cuba Deports American Fugitive Wanted for Sexual Crimes against a Minor*, 24 IELR 315, 315 (2008) (Cuba, citing the grave character of the crimes at issue, arrested and deported Leonard Auerbach, a mortgage specialist from California, to the United States, which had charged him with "sexually abusing a Costa Rican girl and possessing child pornography").

complete,[95] generally are shorter and quicker than those for extraditions.[96]

Relatedly, the longer extradition proceedings persist, the greater is the opportunity for a wealthy and/or well-connected fugitive (who has been denied bail) to bribe his way out of prison, or (if granted bail) to flee to a "safe haven" State. This concern was evident, for instance, in April 1985, when notwithstanding the existence of an extradition treaty between Costa Rica and Mexico, the United States urged Costa Rica to deport to Mexico Rafael Caro-Quintero, a Guadalajara-based drug lord wanted in Mexico for the kidnapping and murder of a DEA agent, ostensibly because it was feared he could buy his way out of jail, as he had done once before.[97]

It is also possible that, while extradition is technically available, a pursuing State may find it to be undesirable (or at least relatively *less* desirable than removal) based, for example, on a high evidentiary threshold set by the host State,[98] and in such cases extradition might be pursued as a second-best option.[99]

There may be reasons, however, such as concerns about perceived political bias or motivation, for a pursuing State on its own initiative to

[95] For example, Léon Mugesera, who was charged with inciting the 1994 Rwandan genocide by encouraging fellow Hutus to kill Tutsis and by calling them "cockroaches" and "scum" during a political speech in 1992, fought his deportation from Canada to Rwanda for sixteen years. "Canada to Deport Alleged Rwandan War Criminal Despite U.N.," *CBC News*, Jan. 11, 2012, *available at* www.cbc.ca/news/canada/montreal/canada-to-deport-alleged-rwandan-war-criminal-despite-un-1.1128980 (last visited on May 29, 2016).

[96] *See supra* n.75.

[97] Abraham Abramovsky, *Extraterritorial Abductions: America's 'Catch and Snatch' Policy Run Amok*, 31 VA. J. INT'L L. 151, 161–62 (1991).

[98] *See generally* M. CHERIF BASSIOUNI, INTERNATIONAL EXTRADITION: UNITED STATES LAW AND PRACTICE 216 (6th ed. 2014) (there exists an opportunity for "law enforcement and prosecutorial officials to exploit the gap between [extradition and removal as processes] and the differences between their norms and evidentiary standards.").

[99] For instance, in February 2002, appreciating the difficulty of obtaining extradition from the Namibian Government (notorious for corruption and denials) of German citizen Hans-Jürgen Koch, wanted for fraud, tax evasion, and falsifying documents in connection with his business activities in Germany between 1987 and 2000, Germany initially sought his deportation. *See* Bruce Zagaris, *German Fraud Suspect Fights Extradition from Namibia*, 21 IELR 9 (2005) (when deportation was denied, extradition was pursued). Likewise, when the United States sought custody of several Algerian-origin Bosnian citizens believed to have participated in the World Trade Center attack of September 11, 2001, it opted against extradition in favor of requesting that the Bosnian Government deport them, following their being stripped of citizenship. Ian Fisher, "Qaeda Suspect's Bosnian Wife Says He's No Terrorist," *N.Y. Times*, Jan. 28, 2002, at A3.

forgo attempts at seeking removal despite its legal availability and prospect of success. For example, between January 2008 and October 2009, the Government of Uganda sought the custody of Zoe Bakoko Bakoru, its former Minister of Gender, Labor and Social Development, on counts of abuse of office and taking bribes in connection with her approval of a joint venture between a private company and the National Social Security Fund that resulted in a substantial financial loss for the workers' pension scheme. Although the Ugandan Government retained the option of revoking her passport and requesting her deportation from the United States (possibly because extradition was foreclosed absent a bilateral extradition treaty), any such move could have raised suspicions that Uganda was simply singling her out as a political target because of her ex-ministerial portfolio.[100]

Pursuing States also may anticipate or encounter roadblocks in connection with seeking another State's removal of a fugitive from its territory.[101] Removal requires, for example, that the individual of interest violated the removing State's immigration laws.[102] During World War I, German officer Werner von Horn planted a bomb on a Canadian railroad from still-neutral U.S. territory. He was later arrested in Maine, pled guilty, and was sent to a federal detention center in Atlanta. In 1917, the U.S. Department of Justice first contemplated deporting him to Canada, which sought his custody, but von Horn had not violated U.S. immigration laws, having entered the country lawfully. As a result, von Horn was not deported, but rather eventually *extradited* to Canada in 1918.[103]

In other instances, there may be political pressures or special relationships that thwart a removal. The case of Orlando Bosch is illustrative. Bosch was a militantly anti-Castro Cuban exile who was implicated in dozens of terrorist attacks in New York, Miami, and in Latin America in the late 1960s and 1970s.[104] In 1988, he entered Florida illegally, was

[100] Edward Anyoli, "IGG Drops Charges on Bakoko Bakoru," New Vision website, Oct. 13, 2009, *available at* www.newvision.co.ug/new_vision/news/1203741/igg-drops-charges-bakoko-bakoru (last visited on May 23, 2016); Bruce Zagaris, *Uganda Tries to Obtain Custody of Former Minister on Bribery Charges*, 24 IELR 93 (2008).

[101] This sub-section addresses only non-human rights-related considerations; a human rights analysis follows in section (d).

[102] Evans, *supra* n.27, at 86.

[103] Grant W. Grams, *Karl Respa and German Espionage in Canada During World War One*, 8 J. Mil. & Strat. Stud., Fall 2005, Issue 1, at 3.

[104] In one instance, in 1968, he was convicted in the United States of firing a bazooka at a Havana-bound Polish freighter while docked in the Miami harbor, and sentenced to

detained for an earlier parole violation, and subjected to a deportation order. The U.S. Department of Justice claimed to have reached out to thirty-one States, each of which refused to accept him, presumably given his lengthy criminal record. The United States, however, refused to deport (or extradite) him to Cuba, where he was also wanted, ostensibly due to fair trial concerns. Some believe that the actual or an additional reason was politically driven. In July 1990, under pressure from his son Jeb, who had close ties with the Cuban exile community in Florida, and possibly because of Bosch's reported affiliation with the CIA, U.S. President (and former CIA Director) George H.W. Bush pardoned Bosch rather than continue to have him detained pending deportation.[105]

d Human Rights Law Protections

A removal operation potentially implicates a number of internationally recognized human rights, which can serve as significant barriers to its use.[106] These are organized into three categories: (i) human rights protections to which the subject is entitled arising out of the *removing* State's conduct, such as the non-discrimination principle, procedural safeguards, private and family life concerns, and international humanitarian law-related considerations;[107] (ii) human rights protections relevant to treatment by the *receiving* State, including, *inter alia*, prospective concerns about abusive treatment, fair trial rights, and proper detention authority; and (iii)

ten years in prison. While on parole, he fled to Latin America, but was arrested by Venezuela in 1976 for his alleged role that year in the bombing of Cubana Air Flight 455 that killed seventy-three persons. After his conviction was reversed on appeal, he was released, but only after having spent eleven years in prison. Michael Carlson, "Orlando Bosch: CIA-Backed Cuban Exile Implicated in Numerous Anti-Castro Terrorist Operations," *The Independent* (U.K.), June 30, 2011; Pyle, *supra* n.49, at 216.

105 Carlson, *supra* n.104; Pyle, *supra* n.49, at 216; "Orlando Bosch Dies at 84; Cuban Militant Acquitted of 1976 Bombing of Jet," *L.A. Times*, Apr. 29, 2011. Similarly, Iceland, a country passionate about chess, extended citizenship to Bobby Fischer, a former world chess champion and U.S. fugitive, AP, "Bobby Fischer Lands in Iceland," *CBS News*, Mar. 25, 2005, *available at* www.cbsnews.com/news/bobby-fischer-lands-in-iceland/ (last visited on May 29, 2016), thereby effectively eliminating the possibility of his deportation to the United States from Japan, where he had been residing.

106 *See generally* Sean D. Murphy, *The Expulsion of Aliens and Other Topics: The Sixty-Fourth Sess. of the Int'l Law Comm'n*, 107 AJIL 164 (2013) (discussing the ILC draft articles concerning the expulsion of aliens).

107 International human rights law continues to apply even during international armed conflicts unless expressly derogated. *Legal Consequences of the Construction of the Wall in the Occupied Palestinian Territory*, Adv'y Op., [2004] I.C.J. Rep. 136, ¶ 106 (July 9).

human rights protections related to the *method* of removal. Together with the follow-on examination of "disguised extradition," these two discussions analyze the propriety of the immigration law alternative to extradition from an international law perspective.

i Law Relevant to Removing State Conduct

Non-Discrimination. A removing State is generally obligated to treat an alien as an equal before the law and not to unfairly or arbitrarily discriminate[108] against him either in the enactment of facially discriminatory laws or in the discriminatory implementation of valid laws.[109] The non-discrimination principle has been enunciated in the provisions of a number of human rights treaties, in General Comments by human rights implementing bodies, and in judgments by human rights tribunals, as well as in the U.N. Charter itself.[110] The International Court of Justice has even characterized non-discrimination as such a basic right that it gives rise to an obligation *erga omnes* extended by all States.[111]

The ICCPR states: "[T]he law shall prohibit any discrimination and guarantee to all persons equal and effective protection against discrimination on any ground such as race, colour . . . national or social origin . . . or other status."[112] In its General Comment No. 15, the Human Rights Committee (HRC) addressed the rights of *aliens* against discrimination more specifically: "[T]he *general* rule is that each one of the rights of the Covenant must be guaranteed without discrimination between citizens and aliens," and that even though in principle States choose who may

[108] "Discrimination is not synonymous with differential treatment. The concept of discrimination, as employed in international law, connotes distinctions which are unfair, unjustifiable, or arbitrary." GOODWIN-GILL, *supra* n.8, at 78. "Distinctions are reasonable if they pursue a legitimate aim and have an objective justification, and a reasonable relationship of proportionality exists between the aim sought to be realized and the means employed. These criteria will usually be satisfied if the particular measures can reasonably be interpreted as being in the public interest as a whole and do not arbitrarily single out individuals or groups for invidious treatment." WARWICK MACKEAN, EQUALITY AND DISCRIMINATION UNDER INTERNATIONAL LAW 287 (1983).

[109] Sohn & Buergenthal, *supra* n.12, at 17–18.

[110] CHARTER OF THE UNITED NATIONS, June 26, 1945, art. 1(3) (identifying as a purpose "promoting and encouraging respect for human rights and for fundamental freedoms for all without distinction as to race, sex, language, or religion"); *id.*, art. 55(c) (U.N. "shall promote universal respect for, and observance of, human rights and fundamental freedoms for all without distinction as to race, sex, language, or religion.").

[111] *See Barcelona Traction, Light & Power Co.* (Belg. v. Spain), Second Phase [1970] I.C.J. Rep. 3, ¶¶ 33–34 (Feb. 5).

[112] ICCPR, *supra* n.8, art. 26.

enter and reside within their territory, "*in certain circumstances* an alien may enjoy the protection of the Covenant even in relation to entry or residence, for example, when considerations of non-discrimination … arise."[113]

At the same time, however, in principle, the HRC plausibly could justify distinctions between citizens and aliens on grounds such as national security and public order (so long as legitimate aims and proportionate means were employed);[114] and in fact has separately carved out citizen-specific political rights[115] and has differentiated between citizens and at least illegal aliens with respect to the freedom of movement.[116]

Consistent with this principle, the Committee on the Elimination of Racial Discrimination has recommended that States parties additionally adopt measures to "[e]nsure that laws concerning deportation or other forms of removal of non-citizens from [their] jurisdiction … do not discriminate in purpose or effect among non-citizens on the basis of race, colour, or ethnic or national origin."[117] The Committee, however, has recognized differential treatment based on "citizenship or immigration status" where the purpose of the discrimination is consistent with the objectives of the Convention, the methods are proportional to achieving those objectives, and do not run afoul of any special measures set forth under Article 1(4).[118]

[113] HRC, Gen. Cmt. No. 15, *supra* n.49, ¶¶ 2, 5 (emphasis supplied).

[114] *See* limitations clauses in ICCPR, *supra* n.8, arts. 18(3) (freedom of religion), 19(3)(b) (freedom of expression), and 22(2) (freedom of association). *See generally* U.N. OHCHR, *The Rights of Non-Citizens*, HR/PUB/06/11, 2006, at 7; Joan Fitzpatrick, Conf. Paper, "The Human Rights of Migrants," Conference on Int'l Legal Norms and Migration, Geneva, May 23–25, 2002, at 3, *available at* www.baliprocess.net/files/conferencedocumentation/the%20human%20rights%20of%20migrants_%202002.pdf (last visited on May 23, 2016).

[115] *E.g.*, ICCPR, *supra* n.8, art. 25 (only citizens have the right to vote or to "take part in the conduct of public affairs"); ACHR, *supra* n.8, art. 23(1) (same); Eur. Conv. for the Protection of Human Rights and Fundamental Freedoms, Nov. 4, 1950, art. 16, 213 U.N.T.S. 262, T.S. No. 71 (1953) [hereinafter ECHR] (High Contracting Parties may impose restrictions on "the political activity of aliens"). *See also Rights of Non-Citizens*, *supra* n.114, at 8.

[116] *E.g.*, ICCPR, *supra* n.8, art. 12 ("Everyone *lawfully* within the territory of a State, within that territory, have [sic] the right to liberty of movement") (emphasis supplied); ACHR, *supra* n.8, art. 22(1).

[117] Comm. on the Elimination of Racial Discrimination, Gen. Recom. No. 30, *Discrimination against Non-Citizens*, Oct. 1, 2004, ¶ 25 [hereinafter CERD, Gen. Recom. 30].

[118] *Id.* ¶ 4.

This principle was the subject of a 1996 case involving a Moroccan citizen who had resided in Belgium for thirty years, but who had twice been criminally convicted and sentenced and was now the subject of a deportation order for "seriously prejudic[ing] public order."[119] The ECtHR ruled that he was *not* a "victim of discrimination on the grounds of nationality and race" under Article 14 of the ECHR (the non-discrimination provision), as he had alleged.[120] Rather, his deportation, which "amounted to less favourable treatment than was accorded to criminals who [were] nationals of a member State of the European Union," was "based on an objective and reasonable justification, given that the member States of the European Union form a special legal order, which has, in addition, established its own citizenship."[121]

Procedural Safeguards. Procedural protections ensure that aliens obtain due process to contest a decision to remove them[122] before a competent national authority "in accordance with law"[123] (*i.e.*, the practice must be consistent with host State domestic law *and* not incompatible with applicable treaty provisions[124]). The point is to ensure that no arbitrary decision is made regarding their status, not only with respect to adhering to the law itself (*e.g.*, not deporting a national), but also with respect to ensuring that the law is both accessible and foreseeable.[125] A robust formulation of such protections can be found at Article 13 of the ICCPR, which provides that:

[119] *C. v. Belgium*, Appl. No. 21794/93, 32 EHRR, ¶¶ 6, 7, 10, 11, 14, 15, Aug. 7, 1996.

[120] *Id.* ¶ 37.

[121] *Id.* ¶¶ 37–38.

[122] *See* Fitzpatrick, *supra* n.114, at 9 ("The right to challenge an expulsion is vital to the right to seek asylum and to the human rights bars to *refoulement*, as well as to fundamental fairness.").

[123] The notion of "in accordance with law," which applies to all types of written and unwritten laws, whether constitutional, statutory, or administrative, *Malone v. U.K.*, Appl. No. 8691/79, 7 EHRR, Aug. 2, 1984, serves as the modern-day equivalent for the customary international law principle of "prohibition against arbitrariness." *See* Jennings & Watts, *supra* n.12, at 940; HRC, Gen. Cmt. No. 15, *supra* n.49, ¶ 10 (the purpose of requiring a removal order to be "in accordance with law" is "to prevent arbitrary expulsions").

[124] *Maroufidou v. Sweden*, Commc'n No. 58/1979, U.N. Doc. CCPR/C/12/D/58/1979, ¶ 9.3, Apr. 9, 1981 [hereinafter *Maroufidou Case*].

[125] *See Sunday Times v. U.K.*, Appl. No. 6538/74, 2 EHRR 245, ¶ 49, Apr. 26, 1979 (defining the synonymous term "prescribed by law" as requiring these two elements; the first to ensure individuals are aware of the applicable law, and the second to ensure that it is precise enough to help individuals conform their conduct accordingly).

> An alien *lawfully in the territory* of a State Party to the present Convention may be expelled therefrom only in pursuance of a decision reached in accordance with law and shall, *except where compelling reasons of national security otherwise require*, be allowed to submit the reasons against his expulsion and to have his case reviewed by, and be represented for the purpose before, the competent authority or a person or persons especially designated by the competent authority.[126]

Notably, these safeguards, which include the right to counsel and the right of consular notification and access,[127] do not apply to illegal aliens, and are, in any event, subject to a national security exception. That said, a "good faith" requirement exists both for a State: (i) to weigh the competing equities of ensuring public order against an individual's various rights and interests[128] in determining whether to remove an alien, and (ii) to implement a removal order with propriety.[129] Deportation decisions, however, have not yet been found applicable to "the determination of an applicant's civil rights or obligations or of a criminal charge against [a fugitive]," as set forth in the fair trial provisions of the ICCPR (Article 14) and the ECHR (Article 6).[130]

The HRC found a violation under Article 13 of the ICCPR in the case of Pierre Giry, a French citizen who, in February 1985, after spending two days in the Dominican Republic (D.R.), went to the airport to purchase a ticket to Saint-Barthélemy, was taken by D.R. authorities to an airport office where he was thoroughly searched, and then forcibly boarded on

126 ICCPR, *supra* n.8, art. 13 (emphasis supplied).

127 *See* Vienna Conv. on Consular Relations (VCCR), Apr. 24, 1963, arts. 5, 36, 37, 21 U.S.T. 77, 596 U.N.T.S. 261; *LaGrand Case* (Ger. v. U.S.) [2001] I.C.J. Rep. 466 (June 27); *The Right to Information on Consular Assistance in the Framework of the Guarantee of the Due Process of Law*, Adv'y Op., OC-16/99, Oct. 1, 1999, Inter-Am. C.H.R. (ser. A) No. 16 (1999).

128 Goodwin-Gill, *supra* n.8, at 262.

129 *See Čonka v. Belgium*, Appl. No. 51564/99, 34 EHRR, ¶ 42, Feb. 5, 2002 [hereinafter *Čonka Case*] ("even as regards overstayers, a conscious decision by the authorities to facilitate or improve the effectiveness of a planned operation for the expulsion of aliens by misleading them about the purpose of a notice so as to make it easier to deprive them of their liberty is not compatible with Article 5 [of the ECHR].").

130 *Maaouia v. France*, Appl. No. 39652/98, 33 EHRR, ¶ 40, Oct. 5, 2000 (reasoning limited to an interpretation of Article 6(1) of the ECHR). *See also* Jennifer Tooze, *Deportation With Assurances: The Approach of the U.K. Courts*, [Apr. 2010] Pub. L. (U.K.) 362, 365 ("Deportation proceedings are public (not civil) law proceedings and the ECtHR has repeatedly found that Article 6 of the Convention (fair trial) does not apply to them because they do not determine any civil right even where a person's Article 8 family rights are indirectly affected by the deportation decision."); *Ahani v. Canada*, Commc'n No. 1051/2002, U.N. Doc. CCPR/C/80/D/1051/2002, ¶ 10.9, Mar. 29, 2004 (not applying Article 14 to expulsion proceedings) [hereinafter *Ahani Case*].

a flight bound for Puerto Rico, whereupon "he was arrested and charged with conspiracy and attempt to smuggle drugs into the United States."[131] While the D.R. invoked the national security exception to Article 13 of the ICCPR by noting Giry's involvement in drug trafficking, the Committee ruled that the D.R. had failed to demonstrate that its removal decision was reached "in accordance with law" (despite several solicitations, the D.R. was unable to supply the text of a removal decision) and that the "author was not afforded an opportunity ... to submit the reasons against his expulsion or to have his case reviewed by a competent authority."[132]

Other substantially similar procedural provisions contained in legal instruments include: (i) Protocol 7 to the ECHR at Article 1;[133] (ii) the Arab Charter on Human Rights at Article 26(2);[134] and (iii) the UNGA Declaration A/RES/40/144 at Article 7.[135] In addition, while not providing as strongly worded a set of protections as those cited above, both the American Convention on Human Rights (ACHR) and the African Charter of Human and Peoples' Rights (ACHPR) require that any alien lawfully within a State Party's territory can be expelled only if based on a decision taken in "accordance with the law."[136]

Domestic legislation or regulations, *inter alia*, characteristically identify eligible or prioritized destinations to which an alien may be sent following a removal order, although they almost always provide for return in principle to the alien's country of citizenship, which, as it happens, is frequently the very State with a law enforcement interest in that individual.[137] Accordingly, where a host State that genuinely but

[131] *Giry, supra*, n.56, ¶¶ 1, 3.1.

[132] *Id.* ¶¶ 4.3–4.4, 5.5.

[133] Seventh Prot., *supra* n.64, art. 1; *e.g., Lupsa v. Romania*, Appl. No. 10337/04, 46 EHRR, ¶ 59, June 8, 2006 ("the authorities failed to provide the applicant with the slightest indication of the offence of which he was suspected and that the public prosecutor's office did not send him the order issued against him until the day of the one hearing before the Court of Appeal ... [and] the Court of Appeal dismissed all requests for an adjournment, thus preventing the applicant's lawyer from studying the aforementioned order and producing evidence in support of her application for judicial review of it.").

[134] Arab Charter on Human Rights, *supra* n.8, art. 26(2).

[135] UNGA, *Decl. on the Human Rights of Individuals Who are Not Nationals of the Country in Which They Live*, Dec. 13, 1985, art. 7, U.N. Doc. A/RES/40/144.

[136] ACHR, *supra* n.8, art. 22(6); Banjul Charter, *supra* n.8, art. 12(4).

[137] *See Expulsion of Aliens, supra* n.9, at 320 ("The State of nationality appears to be the most common destination for nationals who have been expelled from the territory of other States.").

unsuccessfully has sought to locate another State willing to accept the alien, leaving no choice for a deportation destination apart from the State with an express law enforcement interest in the individual, domestic law ought to treat that as reasonable under the circumstances.[138]

Effective Remedy. Closely related to, but distinct from, procedural safeguards is the right to an effective remedy. Whereas procedural protections focus on the underlying removal proceedings, an effective remedy concerns itself with an opportunity to repair a breach of a convention, which typically amounts in the immigration context to an appeal of a removal order. For example, per a recommendation by the Committee on the Elimination of Racial Discrimination, aliens must "have equal access to effective remedies, including the right to challenge expulsion orders, and [must be] allowed effectively to pursue such remedies."[139] As interpreted by the ECtHR, the term "effective" "does not depend on the certainty of a favourable outcome for the applicant," need not be pursued in every instance through a *judicial* authority, and the remedy afforded must be "effective in practice as well as in law."[140] Furthermore, in ECtHR cases implicating national security information, an effective remedy requires the following minimum elements:

> [T]he competent independent appeals authority must be informed of the reasons grounding the deportation decision, even if such reasons are not publicly available. The authority must be competent to reject the executive's assertion that there is some threat to national security where it finds it arbitrary and unreasonable. There must be some form of adversarial proceedings, if need be through a special representative after a security clearance.[141]

The ICCPR at Article 2(3) provides that each State party undertakes to "ensure that any person whose rights or freedoms as herein recognized are violated shall have an effective remedy, notwithstanding that the violation has been committed by persons acting in an official capacity," that any such claim for a remedy shall be determined by a "competent authority," and that the competent authority shall enforce any conferred

[138] *See* Shearer, *supra* n.8, at 90–91 (outlining "reasonable" principles to guide an immigration authority to include removal *in lieu* of or following a denial of extradition so long as the alien is found to be removable under domestic law and "it is believed upon reasonable grounds that no State other than the requesting State will accept the alien.").

[139] CERD, Gen. Recom. 30, *supra* n.117, ¶ 25.

[140] *Al-Nashif v. Bulgaria*, Appl. No. 50963/99, 36 EHRR, ¶¶ 132, 136, June 20, 2002, [2002] ECHR 497.

[141] *Id.* ¶ 137.

remedy.[142] In a 2003 case, the HRC found that Canada had violated Article 2(3) regarding its decision to deport U.S. citizen Roger Judge to face the death penalty for murder in Pennsylvania without first affording him an opportunity to exercise his right of appeal, given the government's acknowledgment that the Court of Appeal could have reviewed the Superior Court's judgment on the merits and that the government did not have to suddenly remove him "within hours" of the lower court ruling.[143]

Similarly, the Committee against Torture found a violation of Article 3 (the *non-refoulement* provision) in the case of Ahmed Agiza, an Egyptian citizen, who was removed by Sweden to Egypt in December 2001.[144] Initially, the Committee had to wrestle with the fact that Article 3 is silent as to a remedy; it reasoned that the article contains an *implied* remedy for a breach, which otherwise would leave its protections "largely illusory."[145] The Committee then defined the appropriate remedy in this context as requiring "an opportunity for effective, independent and impartial review of the decision to expel or remove."[146] The Committee next observed that the ordinary mechanisms for reviewing a decision to expel, through operation of the Migration Board and the Aliens Appeals Board, were forsaken due to national security concerns, but as Article 3 allows for no exceptions, some form of effective, independent, and impartial review was warranted, even if adjusted to accommodate national security concerns, and yet none was provided.[147]

The right to an effective remedy also has been honored under the African Charter on Human and Peoples' Rights (ACHPR). Article 7(1) specifically calls for "[t]he right to an appeal to competent national organs against acts of violating his fundamental rights as recognized and guaranteed by conventions, laws, regulations and customs in force."[148] Unlike other conventions, the ACHPR does not strictly limit application of such a provision to criminal defendants. The African Commission has read this article broadly to include even cases involving deportation. For example, in a 1996 case brought by a Senegalese-based

142 ICCPR, *supra* n.8, art. 2(3).

143 *Judge v. Canada*, Commc'n No. 829/1998, U.N. Doc. CCPR/C/78/D/829/1998, ¶ 10.8, Oct. 20, 2003 [hereinafter *Judge Case*].

144 *Agiza v. Sweden*, Commc'n No. 233/2003, U.N. Doc. CAT/C/34/D/233/2003, ¶ 1.1, May 20, 2005.

145 *Id.* ¶ 13.6.

146 *Id.* ¶ 13.7.

147 *Id.* ¶ 13.8.

148 BANJUL CHARTER, *supra* n.8, art. 7(1)(a).

NGO on behalf of 517 illegal West African aliens expelled from Zambia in February 1992, the Commission pointed out that "none of the deportees had the opportunity to seize the Zambian courts to challenge their detention or deportation, thereby constituting a breach of Article 7."[149]

Private Life. Another legal basis for potentially barring a government-authorized removal operation arises from the deference paid by a variety of human rights conventions and implementing bodies to an alien's private life. Although not an absolute right,[150] it is accorded considerable weight in determining whether a given removal order is permissible. Article 17 of the ICCPR, for instance, states: "No one shall be subjected to arbitrary or unlawful interference with his privacy,"[151] and "[e]veryone has the right to the protection of the law against such interference."[152] The American Convention on Human Rights (ACHR) provides for virtually the same rights and protections as the ICCPR.[153] The European Convention, at Article 8, likewise recognizes the general right "to respect for private ... life,"[154] but exceptionally allows for interference when "it is in accordance with the law and is necessary in a democratic society in the interests of national security, public safety or the economic well-being of the country, for the prevention of disorder or crime, for the protection of health or morals, or for the protection of the rights and freedoms of others."[155]

An example of how private rights are addressed can be seen in the 2001 ECtHR case of Abdel Bensaid, an Algerian national who in September 1996, after a five-week visit to his home country, sought to re-enter the United Kingdom as a resident, based on his marriage to a U.K. citizen since 1993 and the government's May 1995 grant of leave for him to remain in the United Kingdom as a foreign spouse.[156] After the

149 *Rencontre Africaine pour la Defense des Droits de l'Homme (RADDHO) v. Zambia*, Commc'n No. 71/92, (2000) AHRLR 321, ¶¶ 1, 30, Oct. 1996.

150 Alexandra Rengel, Privacy in the 21st Century 108 (2013).

151 ICCPR, *supra* n.8, art. 17(1).

152 *Id.*, art. 17(2). The HRC has construed this provision to mean that any such interference must be "envisaged by the law," must be "reasonable in the particular circumstances," and must "comply with the provisions, aims and objectives of the Covenant." HRC, Gen. Cmt. No. 16, *The Right to Respect of Privacy, Family, Home and Correspondence, and Protection of Honour and Reputation (Art. 17)*, U.N. Doc. HRI/GEN/1/Rev.1 at 21 (1994), ¶¶ 3, 4, Apr. 8, 1988.

153 ACHR, *supra* n.8, art. 11(2) & (3).

154 ECHR, *supra* n.115, art. 8(1).

155 *Id.*, art. 8(2). Both the ECHR and ACHR have been described as sources of customary international law. *Filártiga v. Pena-Irala*, 630 F.2d 876, 883–84 (2d Cir. 1980).

156 *Bensaid v. U.K.*, Appl. No. 44599/98, 33 EHRR, ¶¶ 1, 9–10, Feb. 6, 2001, [2001] ECHR 82 [hereinafter *Bensaid Case*].

government determined that his marriage was a fraud and gave him a notice of removal, Bensaid sought review on the basis that he suffered from schizophrenia and that his return to Algeria would cause a relapse of this serious mental health condition otherwise generally held in check through medication.[157]

The European Court found no government violation, reasoning that while such matters as gender identification, sexual orientation, and even mental health when associated with moral integrity are all parts of private life protected in principle under Article 8, Bensaid's removal to Algeria was not anticipated to significantly affect his moral integrity and, in any event, the United Kingdom had acted in full compliance with Article 8's exceptions.[158] While the ECtHR jurisprudence has recognized a possible breach "where there are sufficiently adverse effects on physical and moral integrity,"[159] "it has so far not found any violation of [A]rticle 8 on the sole ground that the person will face a severe interference with his or her private life."[160]

Family Life. Linked to the right to private life and, indeed, often addressed under the same convention provision, is the well-established right to family life, which is concerned with family integrity and particularly the right of spouses, as well as parents and their children, to live together and associate as a family unit.[161] As early as 1948, the Universal Declaration of Human Rights (UDHR) expressed: "The family is the natural and fundamental group unit of society and is entitled to protection by society and the State,"[162] and "[n]o one shall be subjected to arbitrary interference with his . . . family."[163] Although this unanimously adopted UNGA declaration does not qualify as a treaty, its provisions broadly have been accorded customary international law status, which

[157] *Id.* ¶¶ 10–21.
[158] *Id.* ¶¶ 47–48.
[159] *Id.* ¶ 46.
[160] UNHCHR, *Expulsions of Aliens in Int'l Human Rights Law*, OHCHR Discussion Paper, Sept. 2006, at 8 [hereinafter OHCHR Discussion Paper].
[161] "The concept of 'family unity', which has been adopted by major legal systems of the world, has found expression in numerous instruments concerning international protection of human rights. These instruments vary, however, in determining which categories of persons are to be considered members of the family. While there can be no doubt that a person's spouse and minor children are to be so regarded, the practice is not uniform as regards the status of minor children of a spouse by a previous marriage, illegitimate children, aged parents and dependent relatives." Sohn & Buergenthal, *supra* n.12, at 65.
[162] UDHR, *supra* n.8, art. 23(1).
[163] *Id.*, art. 17(1).

binds even non-signatory States.[164] The nearly universal ICCPR, which aimed to codify the UDHR's civil and political rights, reiterates these provisions verbatim, adding only that family interference must also not be "unlawful."[165] Along these lines, the Committee on the Elimination of Racial Discrimination has advised that States parties to the CERD must "[a]void expulsions of *non-citizens*, especially of long-term residents, that would result in disproportionate interference with the right to family life."[166]

Regional human rights treaties likewise have recognized this principle. The ECHR, at Article 8, provides that "[e]veryone has the right to respect for his ... family life" but, as described above in the private life context, carves out exceptions for interference when "it is in accordance with the law and is necessary in a democratic society" in the furtherance of certain compelling State interests, such as public safety.[167] The ACHR, at Articles 11 and 17(1), express almost identical rights and protections as the ICCPR; and the Inter-American Commission on Human Rights, which adjudicates claimed breaches of the ACHR, has held that the right to family life "is a right so basic to the Convention that it is considered to be non-derogable even in extreme circumstances."[168]

In examining the case law arising from the ECtHR, it is apparent that these adjudicatory bodies insist, first, that the removal order be based on a legal process that is authorized by formal law, that the law itself is not arbitrary or unreasonable, and is characterized by procedural regularity, including notice, an opportunity to be heard, and the chance to present and challenge evidence at a hearing. But the right must also be evaluated

164 *See* Restatement (Third) of the Foreign Relations Law of the United States, § 701, rep. note 6 (1987) ("[T]he Declaration has become the accepted general articulation of recognized rights."). A judge in a 1989 ICJ advisory opinion also recognized the right to family life's customary law standing:

> The integrity of a person's family and family life is a basic human right protected by prevailing principles of international law which derive not only from conventional international law or customary international law but from general principles of law recognized by civilized nations.

Applicability of Article VI, Section 22, of the Conv. on the Privileges and Immunities of the U.N., Adv'y Op., [1989] I.C.J. Rep. 177, 210–11 (Dec. 15) (Evensen, J., Sep. Op.) (internal quotation omitted).

165 ICCPR, *supra* n.8, art. 17.

166 CERD, Gen. Recom. 30, *supra* n.117, ¶ 28 (emphasis supplied).

167 ECHR, *supra* n.115, art. 8(2).

168 *X & Y v. Argentina*, Case 10.506, Inter-Am. C.H.R., OEA/ser. L/V/II.95, Doc. 7 rev. at 50, ¶ 96, Oct. 15, 1996.

according to the principle of proportionality, in which the removing State's public interest in interfering with an alien's genuine family ties via a removal order must outweigh the hardship that interference imposes upon the alien and his family integrity.[169]

The ECtHR conducted this balancing test in the case of Mohand Beldjoudi, an Algerian national residing in France who was ordered to be deported in November 1979 "on the ground that his presence on French territory was a threat to public order (*ordre public*)."[170] Beldjoudi, who had been convicted and sentenced six times between 1969 and 1986 for such offenses as assault and battery, aggravated theft, and acquisition and possession of controlled weapons or ammunition, challenged the order for years under domestic law and ultimately claimed a breach of Article 8 under the ECHR as the deportation order "constitute[d] an excessive interference with his family life."[171] In its judgment, the European Court found that France had acted in accordance with its domestic law and its aim was legitimate in seeking to prevent crime or disorder, so the focus of its analysis lay with whether the deportation order was truly "necessary in a democratic society."[172]

To that end, the ECtHR examined Beldjoudi's family links to France: he was born in France of parents who were French; while a minor he lost his French citizenship when his parents neglected to make the necessary declaration affirming their French citizenship under the Évian Accords once Algeria gained its independence from France in 1963, but then sought to remedy that oversight; he was declared fit for French military service; married a Frenchwoman; was educated in French (rather than Arabic); his parents and four siblings resided in France; he had no apparent links with Algeria apart from his nationality; he had lived his entire life (over 40 years) in France; and his deportation would entail his wife's as well, which would cause a raft of transitional problems for her culturally and linguistically, but also potentially jeopardize their marital status.[173] On balance, the Court concluded that deporting Beldjoudi

[169] Shayana Kadidal, *'Federalizing' Immigration Law: Int'l Law as a Limitation on Congress's Power to Legislate in the Field of Immigration*, 77 Fordham L. Rev. 501, 515, 518–19 (2008).

[170] *Beldjoudi v. France*, Appl. No. 12083/86, 14 EHRR, ¶¶ 9, 15, Mar. 26, 1992, [1992] ECHR 42.

[171] *Id.* ¶¶ 12–13, 16, 27.

[172] *Id.* ¶¶ 68–80.

[173] *Id.* ¶¶ 77–78.

would be disproportionate to the aim pursued and therefore the deportation order violated Article 8.[174]

In 2001, the HRC ruled on a family life claim brought by Hendrik Winata and So Lan Li, both formerly Indonesian nationals (now Stateless) on their own behalf as a *de facto* married couple and that of their son, an Australian national by virtue of his birth there, to challenge an Australian Government order for the parents' removal to Indonesia on account of their overstaying the allowable limits under a visitor and student visa, respectively.[175] The HRC concluded that Australia was in violation of its obligations under Articles 17(1) and 23 with respect to all three Winatas because of the "arbitrariness" of "a simple enforcement of its immigration law" in light of the fact that the subjects had been in Australia for fourteen years and, particularly, that their son who had been there for thirteen years since birth, "attending Australian schools as an ordinary child would and developing the social relationships inherent in that."[176] This case underscores that, even when a State's immigration law has been clearly breached, the right to family life and the premium accorded to family integrity can trump to prevent removal, especially when a child's interests are at stake.

IHL-Related Human Rights Considerations. "Article 49 of Geneva Convention IV categorically bars transfers of protected persons out of occupied territory, and Article 147 makes such transfers a grave breach of the Convention. Individuals who are not covered by these protections set out in Geneva Conventions III and IV must nonetheless be protected against transfer to a situation in which the fundamental guarantees set out in Article 75 of Additional Protocol I to the Geneva Conventions, which reflects customary international law, would be violated."[177]

[174] *Id.* ¶ 79. Other cases have followed suit. *E.g., Boultif v. Switzerland*, Appl. No. 54273/00, 22 EHRR, Aug. 2, 2001, [2001] ECHR 493 (concluding that an Algerian alien's conviction for a "ruthless and brutal" robbery and the State's corresponding concern about maintaining public order were not compelling enough to justify his removal from Switzerland, given that his Swiss wife of eight years, who had never lived in Algeria and had no ties to that country, could not be expected to follow her husband there).

[175] *Winata v. Australia*, Commc'n No. 930/2000, U.N. Doc. CCPR/C/72/D/930/2000, ¶¶ 1, 2.1, July 26, 2001.

[176] *Id.* ¶ 7.3.

[177] Margaret L. Satterthwaite, *The Legal Regime Governing the Transfer of Persons in the Fight against Terrorism*, N.Y.U. Public Law and Legal Theory Working Papers, Paper 192, May 1, 2010, at 26.

In addition, pursuant to a High Contracting Party's (HCP's) obligation to "respect and ensure respect"[178] for the Fourth Geneva Convention of 1949 (GC IV),[179] which includes specific civilian safeguards in the context of *non*-international armed conflicts (NIACs),[180] must an HCP provide temporary refuge to an alien who is otherwise subject to deportation until the NIAC in his homeland ceases or he is otherwise resettled to a third State? One unambiguous answer to this query was provided in 1989 by a federal trial court in California in *American Baptist Churches in the U.S.A. v. Meese*[181] in connection with the planned deportation of Salvadoran and Guatemalan aliens to their home countries then embroiled in internal armed conflicts. The U.S. federal court found that Article 1 of GC IV confers no rights upon private parties, nor does it "impose any specific obligations on the signatory nations [or] ... provide any intelligible guidelines for judicial enforcement,"[182] and therefore held that the Convention grants no right of temporary refuge to aliens who would be removed to countries facing civil war.[183]

ii Law Relevant to Receiving State Conduct[184]

Prospective Abusive Treatment. *Non-refoulement* is an international legal principle that aims to protect individuals from being returned, transferred, or otherwise *refouled* (*i.e.*, "turned back") to States where their rights to life, liberty, and security of person, particularly including the freedom from extrajudicial killing (EJK), enforced disappearance, torture, and other abusive treatment, are believed to be

[178] GC IV, *supra* n.38, art. 1, which also appears as Article 1 of GC I, II, and III, and therefore is known as Common Article 1.

[179] GC IV pertains to the protection of civilians during armed conflict.

[180] *Id.*, art. 3 (prohibiting "violence to life and person" and "humiliating and degrading treatment," among others); as this provision appears verbatim in all four Geneva Conventions, it is known as Common Article 3.

[181] 712 F. Supp. 756 (N.D. Cal. 1989).

[182] *Id.* at 770.

[183] *Id.*

[184] Although international law proscribes removal action by the *removing* State, where the underlying conduct of concern would occur at the hands of the *receiving* State, such matters are treated in this sub-section. In addition to the legal standards enumerated in this sub-section, a removing State must be reasonably satisfied that the receiving State will not expel or otherwise transfer the alien to a *third State* where he could be at risk of torture; cruel, inhuman, or degrading treatment or punishment; an unfair trial; or the death penalty. *E.g.*, CoE, Comm. of Ministers, *Twenty Guidelines on Forced Return*, Guideline 2(3), Sept. 2005 [hereinafter *Twenty Guidelines*] (citing the inadmissibility decision of *T.I. v. U.K.*, [2000] INLR 211, Mar. 7, 2000).

threatened.[185] A large number of international and regional human rights instruments (either express in their text or as interpreted by their implementing bodies), as well as many domestic constitutions and statutes, have embraced this principle; these include, *inter alia*, the CAT,[186] the ICCPR,[187] the ECHR,[188] the ACHR,[189] the African Charter of Human and Peoples' Rights (ACHPR),[190] the CERD,[191] and the relatively new International Convention for the Protection of All Persons from Enforced Disappearance (ICPPED);[192] the Constitutions

185 *See* n.134 in Chapter 5.

186 U.N. Conv. against Torture and Other Cruel, Inhuman or Degrading Treatment or Punishment, Dec. 10, 1984, art. 3, UNGA Res. 39/46 Annex, U.N. GAOR, 39th Sess., Supp. No. 51, U.N. Doc. E/CN.4/1984/72, Annex (1984), 1465 U.N.T.S. 85, *reprinted in* 23 ILM 1027 [hereinafter CAT] ("No State Party shall expel, return ('refouler') or extradite a person to another State where there are substantial grounds for believing that he or she would be in danger of being subjected to torture.").

187 ICCPR, *supra* n.8, art. 7; *see also* HRC, Gen. Cmt. No. 20, *Article 7 (Prohibition of Torture, or Other Cruel, Inhuman or Degrading Treatment or Punishment)*, U.N. Doc. HRI/GEN/1/Rev.1 at 30 (1994), ¶ 8, Mar. 10, 1992 ("In the view of the Committee, States parties must not expose individuals to the danger of torture or cruel, inhuman or degrading treatment or punishment upon return to another country by way of their extradition, expulsion or refoulement."). This view has been fortified by a General Comment construing States Parties' Article 2 obligation to respect and ensure ICCPR rights for all persons within their territory to include that they do not return or remove a person from their territory where substantial grounds exist that there is a real risk of irreparable damage in the receiving State or any other State from which the person may later be removed. HRC, Gen. Cmt. No. 31 [80], *Nature of the General Legal Obligation Imposed on States Parties to the Covenant,* U.N. Doc. CCPR/C/21/Rev.1/Add.13, ¶ 12, Mar. 29, 2004.

188 ECHR, *supra* n.115, art. 3.

189 ACHR, *supra* n.8, art. 22(8). But note that the Inter-American Convention to Prevent and Punish Torture appears to be confined to *extraditions* in its *non-refoulement* provision with respect to torture or cruel, inhuman, or degrading treatment or punishment. Inter-Am. Conv. to Prevent and Punish Torture, Dec. 9, 1985, art. 13, OAS T.S. No. 67, *reprinted in* 25 ILM 519 (1986).

190 The African Commission on Human and Peoples' Rights has interpreted Article 5 of the ACHPR, which prohibits torture and cruel, inhuman, or degrading treatment or punishment, to encompass a bar on returning a person to a country where he would face torture or cruel, inhuman or degrading punishment or treatment. *Modise Case, supra* n.25, ¶ 31.

191 CERD, Gen. Recom. 30, *supra* n.117, ¶ 27 ("Ensure that non-citizens are not returned or removed to a country or territory where they are at risk of being subject to serious human rights abuses, including torture and cruel, inhuman or degrading treatment or punishment").

192 Int'l Conv. for the Protection of All Persons from Enforced Disappearance, UNGA Res. 61/177, Dec. 20, 2006, art. 16, U.N. Doc. A/61/448 ("No State Party shall expel, return ('refouler'), surrender or extradite a person to another State where there are substantial grounds for believing that he or she would be in danger of being subjected to enforced disappearance.").

of Switzerland,[193] Costa Rica,[194] and Mexico;[195] and the immigration legislation of Italy,[196] Guatemala,[197] and Sweden.[198] In addition, the concept is found in Geneva Conventions III and IV of 1949 governing prisoners of war (POWs) and civilians, respectively, in times of international armed conflict.[199]

Because of its broad-ranging acceptance as a normative legal rule, the U.N. High Commissioner for Refugees (UNHCR) and some scholars maintain that *non-refoulement* has achieved customary international law status.[200] Were that the case, then even non-States parties to treaties with *non-refoulement* provisions would be obligated to honor this principle; the supporting evidence for this proposition is more extensive in the jurisprudence of supranational tribunals than in individual State removal decisions.[201] In addition, the very term,

[193] Fed. Const. of Swiss Confed., Apr. 18, 1999, art. 25(3) ("No one may be deported to a state in which they face the threat of torture or any other form of cruel or inhumane treatment or punishment.").

[194] Const. of the Repub. of Costa Rica, Nov. 7, 1949, art. 31, *as amended.*

[195] Const. of Mexico, Jan. 31, 1917, art. 15, *as amended.*

[196] Testo Unico sull'Immigrazione, Legis. Decree No. 286/98, July 25, 1998, art. 19(1), *as amended by* Law 189/02 (2002).

[197] Guatemala, Ley de Migración (Immigration Statute), Decreto Número 95–98, Nov. 26, 1998, art. 26.

[198] Sweden, Act Concerning Special Control in Respect of Aliens (1991:572), May 30, 1991, § 1.

[199] Geneva Conv. Relative to the Treatment of Prisoners of War, Aug. 12, 1949, art. 12, 6 U.S.T. 3316, T.I.A.S. No. 3364, 75 U.N.T.S. 135 [GC III]; GC IV, *supra* n.38, art. 45(4) ("In no circumstances shall a protected person be transferred to a country where he or she may have reason to fear persecution for his or her political opinions or religious beliefs.").

[200] UNHCR, *Note on the Principle of Non-Refoulement*, Nov. 1997 ("This view is based on a consistent State practice combined with a recognition on the part of States that the principle has a normative character. [T]he principle has been incorporated in international treaties adopted at the universal and regional levels to which a large number of States have now become parties. Moreover, the principle has also been systematically reaffirmed in Conclusions of the Executive Committee and in resolutions adopted by the General Assembly, thus demonstrating international consensus in this respect and providing important guidelines for the interpretation of the aforementioned provisions."); Guy Goodwin-Gill, *Non-refoulement and the New Asylum Seekers, in* THE NEW ASYLUM SEEKERS: REFUGEE LAW IN THE 1980S, at 103 (David A. Martin ed. 1986).

[201] Despite the robust *non-refoulement* perspective adopted by the international and regional human rights bodies and tribunals, decisions by individual *State courts* have sometimes reflected a contrary inclination. For example, in 1978, the U.S. Congress amended the Immigration Act of 1952, which had barred deportation of any person believed to face threatened persecution upon his return, to specifically exempt from that rule U.S. aliens associated with any Nazi government operating between March 1933

while often described in undifferentiated terms, is in fact a concept with inherent variability. Sometimes, the principle is accompanied by express exceptions[202] or the feared result must be based on one of several specified forms of persecution;[203] and in still other instances it is applied unconditionally.[204] An examination of specific cases can prove instructive to appreciate how this principle has been applied.

In the seminal 1996 case of Karamjit Singh Chahal, a Sikh from India's Punjab region who had immigrated to the United Kingdom in 1971, the ECtHR found that the August 1990 U.K. Home Secretary's decision to deport him back to India would constitute a violation of ECHR Article 3,[205] which prohibits a removed person from being "subjected to torture or to inhuman or degrading treatment or punishment."[206]

and May 1945 who had persecuted people because of their race, religion, national origin, or political opinion. Immigration and Naturalization Act-Nazi Germany, Pub. L. 95–549, 92 Stat. 2065 (1978), *codified at* 8 U.S.C. §§ 1182(a)(33), 1182(d)(3), 1251 (a)(10), 1253(h), and 1254(e). As a direct result, Nazi war criminals living illegally in the United States became eligible for deportation back to States even where they had a reasonable fear of persecution. This included Andrija Artuković, a Croatian known as the "Himmler of the Balkans" during World War II, who had entered the United States illegally in 1948 and avoided deportation since 1951 partly on the ground that if returned to Yugoslavia, he would face persecution. Moeller, *supra* n.8, at 810, 838. *Contra Spring v. Switz.*, Jan. 21, 2000, ¶ 4(c)(bb), Fed. Sup. Ct., Bündesgericht, Ct. Rep. 126 II 145 (holding that *non-refoulement* embodies "an inalienable human right" under current law); Erika de Wet, Jus Cogens *and Obligations* Erga Omnes, *in* THE OXFORD HANDBOOK OF INTERNATIONAL HUMAN RIGHTS LAW 548 n.43 (Dinah Shelton ed. 2013) ("The Swiss Federal Supreme Court has asserted that *non-refoulement* in itself constitutes *jus cogens*").

202 *E.g.*, Conv. Relating to the Status of Refugees, July 28, 1951, art. 33(2), 19 U.S.T. 6259, T.I.A.S. No. 6577, 189 U.N.T.S. 150 ("The benefit of the present provision may not, however, be claimed by a refugee whom there are reasonable grounds for regarding as a danger to the security of the country in which he is, or who, having been convicted by a final judgment of a particularly serious crime, constitutes a danger to the community of that country.").

203 *E.g.*, ACHR, *supra* n.8, art. 22(8) ("In no case may an alien be deported or returned to a country, regardless of whether or not it is his country of origin, if in that country his right to life or personal freedom is in danger of being violated because of his race, nationality, religion, social status or political opinions.").

204 *E.g.*, ICCPR, *supra* n.8, art. 7, as interpreted by the HRC in *Ahani Case, supra* n.130, ¶ 10.10 ("the prohibition on torture, including as expressed in article 7 of the Covenant, is an absolute one that is not subject to countervailing considerations.").

205 *Chahal Case, supra* n.13, ¶¶ 12, 25, 107.

206 ECHR, *supra* n.115, art. 3. The ECtHR has provided some guidance as to what constitutes such prohibited treatment under Article 3: it must attain "a minimum level of severity and involve actual bodily injury or intense physical or mental suffering" and "the suffering which flows from naturally occurring illness, physical or mental, may be covered by article 3, where it is, or risks being, exacerbated by treatment, whether

The U.K. decision was based on a concern that Chahal's "continued presence in the United Kingdom was unconducive to the public good for reasons of national security and other reasons of a political nature, namely the international fight against terrorism."[207] As an activist leader in the U.K.'s Sikh community, Chahal had been detained twice as a suspect in politically-motivated murder conspiracies to advance the Sikh separatist cause in the Punjab, and had been convicted (although later acquitted) on assault charges.

Chahal contended, however, that, if returned to India, he faced a "real risk" of being subjected to torture and other persecution at the hands of the Indian authorities.[208] Chahal claimed to have been beaten to unconsciousness, electrocuted, and subjected to a mock execution by the Punjabi police in the spring of 1984 during a return trip to India, and evidence existed of human rights abuses by the Indian security forces.[209] Rejecting the U.K. Government's argument that Article 3 contained an implicit national security-based limitation, the ECtHR held that the Article 3 prohibition is *absolute* – making no provision for exception regardless of how "undesirable or dangerous" the alien may be[210] or for derogation even when a public emergency threatens the life of the nation[211] – and fully applies in instances of deportation, given the Court's well-established jurisprudence in closely related expulsion cases.[212]

flowing from conditions of detention, expulsion or other measures, for which the authorities can be held responsible." *Pretty v. U.K.*, Appl. No. 2346/02, 35 EHRR 1, ¶ 52, Apr. 29, 2002 (final issued on July 29, 2002).

207 *Chahal Case, supra* n.13, ¶ 25.

208 *Id.* ¶¶ 23, 24, 72.

209 *Id.* ¶¶ 16, 18

210 *Id.* ¶ 80.

211 This is in noteworthy contrast with the *non-refoulement* provision under the ACHR, which allows for derogation "in times of war or other public emergencies that threaten the independence and security of the State party." ACHR, *supra* n.8, art. 22.

212 *Chahal Case, supra* n.13, ¶¶ 76–81. Likewise, the European court ruled that Turkey had not "meaningfully assess[ed]" the alleged risk that Mrs. Hoda Jabari, an Iranian national who had committed adultery, could be stoned, flogged, or whipped upon her authorized return to Iran. *Jabari v. Turkey*, Appl. No. 40035/98, ECtHR, 9 BHRC 1, ¶ 40, July 11, 2000 (in light of the absolute nature of Article 3, States must undertake a "rigorous scrutiny of claims" that expulsion to a third country will expose that person to treatment prohibited by Article 3). *See also Saadi v. Italy*, Appl. No. 37201/06, 49 EHRR, ¶¶ 124–49, Feb. 28, 2008 (ruling that the deportation of Nassim Saadi, an accused terrorist from Italy to Tunisia would violate Article 3, given Tunisia's documented record of torture and ill-treatment toward other accused terrorists).

The Committee against Torture, which construes the provisions of the CAT, has taken a similar position. Consider the 1999 case of Sadiq Shek Elmi, a Somali national and a member of the small and unarmed Shikal clan, who arrived in Australia in October 1997 without valid travel documents.[213] When the Government of Australia ruled in favor of his expulsion and after he effectively exhausted his domestic remedies,[214] Elmi sought review under Article 3 of the CAT, which prohibits the expulsion or *refoulement* of an individual to a State where substantial grounds exist for believing he personally could be subjected to torture.[215]

The Committee found evidence, in fact, that Somalia had committed "gross, flagrant, and mass violations of human rights,"[216] and that the area of Mogadishu to which Elmi would be returned was under the quasi-governmental control of the Hawiye clan[217] that had previously targeted Elmi's Shikal family (killing his father and brother, raping his sister, and forcing the others to flee) for refusing to provide "financial support and fighters for the Hawiye militia."[218] Additionally factoring in the publicity of his case that could result in his being "accused of damaging the reputation of the Hawiye," the Committee concluded that his forcible

213 *Elmi v. Australia*, Commc'n. No. 120/1998, U.N. Doc. CAT/C/22/D/120/1998, ¶¶ 1, 2.4–2.6, Nov. 17, 1998 [hereinafter *Elmi Case*].

214 *Id.* ¶ 2.7.

215 CAT, *supra* n.192, art. 3. The U.S. Senate ratified the non-self-executing CAT, subject to the understanding that the phrase "substantial grounds" would be interpreted to mean "if it is more likely than not that he would be tortured." 136 Cong. Rec. 36 (Oct. 27, 1990) (incorporating Article 3 into U.S. law by § 2242 of the 1998 Foreign Affairs Reform and Restructuring Act (FARRA), Pub. L. 105–277, 1999 U.S.C.C.A.N. (112 Stat. 2681) 871, *codified at* 8 U.S.C. § 1231 *et seq.* (2012).). As a result, under U.S. law, Article 3 of the CAT forbids the United States from deporting an alien if he can show "a chance greater than fifty percent that he will be tortured if removed." *Hamoui v. Ashcroft*, 389 F.3d 821, 827 (9th Cir. 2004).

216 *Elmi Case, supra* n.213, ¶ 6.6.

217 Under the CAT, torture is specifically defined as being committed by or with the consent of public authorities, CAT, *supra* n.192, art. 1; therefore, it is essential that the author of a Communication under the CAT fear torture from public authorities rather than, say, private gangs or organized criminal syndicates.

218 *Elmi Case, supra* n.213, ¶¶ 2.2, 6.7, 6.8. Factors that the Committee examines in such cases include the human rights record of the State to which the individual is being returned and any recent changes thereto, whether the author has been the victim of torture or abusive treatment in the recent past and any corroborating physical or medical evidence for such treatment, whether the individual has continued his political or other activities, and his credibility, including any inconsistencies in his claims. CAT, Gen. Cmt. No. 1, *Communications Regarding the Return of a Person to a State Where There May be Grounds he Would be Subjected to Torture (Article 3 in the context of Article 22)*, U.N. Doc. A/53/44, Annex IX, at 52 (1998), ¶ 8, Nov. 21, 1997.

removal "to Somalia or to any other country where he runs a risk of being expelled or returned to Somalia" would violate Australia's obligations under Article 3.[219]

This judgment is significant for at least three reasons: (i) it did *not* try to balance Australia's immigration law equities against its Convention obligations – rather, it solely examined the record to determine whether an adequate prospective case of torture against the author could be established; (ii) it did *not* require establishing a nexus, such as race or religion, for the underlying cause of the torture; and (iii) it ruled out any *indirect* deportation scenario to Somalia via a third State.[220]

The jurisprudence regarding *non-refoulement* emanating from the international and regional human rights tribunals is not limited, however, to concerns about torture; the case law and implementing body commentary also have focused on inhuman or degrading treatment or punishment. Below are some indicative examples:

- In 1997, the African Commission on Human and Peoples' Rights found Botswana to be in breach of its obligation under Article 5 of the African Charter (prohibiting "cruel, inhuman or degrading punishment and treatment") when it deported Stateless John Modise, a leader of the Botswana National Front opposition party, to South Africa, where he was forced to live for eight years in the Bophuthatswana "homeland" followed by another seven years in a "no-man's land" between Bophuthatswana and Botswana and away from his family, thereby exposing him to personal suffering and "inhuman and degrading treatment."[221]
- In the same year, the ECtHR ruled that a St. Kitts native, who had just completed a prison sentence for illegally importing narcotics into the United Kingdom but who in the interim had been diagnosed as being HIV-positive and a victim of AIDS, could not be deported to his home country without violating Article 3 of the ECHR (prohibiting inhuman or degrading treatment or punishment), given that his life expectancy in light of this terminal illness would be substantially curtailed on account of a lack of proper medication and hospital facilities in

219 *Elmi Case, supra* n.213, ¶¶ 6.8, 7.

220 In another example, in May 2011, the Committee found that "the complainants have established a personal, present and foreseeable risk of being tortured if they were to be returned to India" and so their deportation would have constituted a violation of Article 3 of the CAT. *Khalsa, et al. v. Switzerland*, Commc'n No. 336/2008, CAT/C/46/D/336/2008, ¶ 11.8, May 26, 2011.

221 *Modise Case, supra* n.25.

St. Kitts, and that he would be left to spend his final days in pain and suffering away from close family and any moral or social support they could provide.[222]

- In 2001, the HRC, in its report on compliance by the Netherlands with its obligations under the ICCPR, advised that States that returned women to countries where they were likely to be subjected to Female Genital Mutilation (FGM) would violate Article 7 of the Covenant (prohibiting cruel, inhuman, or degrading treatment or punishment).[223]

Consistent with such standards, since 2005, the United Kingdom has executed a series of Memoranda of Understanding (MOUs) with such States as Ethiopia, Jordan, Lebanon, and Libya to encourage the deportation of terrorists (or those who pose a threat of terrorism) to the State of their nationality, pursuant to domestic immigration laws and subject to a host of assurances that they are to be treated in accordance with international human rights law standards.[224] These so-called Deportation with Assurances (DWA) MOUs call for a host State party to request a partner State to *receive* a given individual under stipulated conditions and with foreknowledge regarding the receiving State's prosecutorial or punishment intentions.[225]

To implement this policy, the U.K.'s Special Immigration Appeals Commission (SIAC) has adopted a general four-part test to ensure compliance with Article 3 of the ECHR: (i) the terms must indicate that the individual will not be subjected to treatment contrary to Article 3; (ii)

[222] *D. v. U.K.*, Appl. No. 30240/96, 24 EHRR 425, May 2, 1997. The ECtHR, however, did *not* find a violation of Article 3 in the case of an Algerian man suffering from schizophrenia, as critical medication for this long-term mental illness would be available to him in Algeria, the risk of relapse was possible whether he was removed or remained in the United Kingdom, and concerns regarding inadequate family support or care in Algeria were largely speculative. *Bensaid Case, supra* n.156, ¶¶ 32–41 (case discussed at nn.156–159 and accompanying text *supra*).

[223] HRC, *Concluding Observations on the Netherlands*, U.N. Doc. CCPR/CO/72/NET, ¶ 11, Aug. 27, 2001.

[224] Columbia Law School Human Rights Inst., *Promises to Keep: Diplomatic Assurances against Torture in U.S. Terrorism Transfers*, Dec. 2010, at 126–40, *available at* http://web.law.columbia.edu/sites/default/files/microsites/human-rights-institute/files/PromisestoKeep.pdf (last visited on May 29, 2016) (containing copies of four such MOUs).

[225] *E.g.*, MOU, U.K.-Jordan, Regarding Provision of Undertakings in Respect of Specified Persons Prior to Deportation, Aug. 10, 2005, *available at* www.gov.uk/government/uploads/system/uploads/attachment_data/file/226968/UNC_Jordan_-_MOU.pdf (last visited on May 23, 2016).

assurances must be given in good faith; (iii) there must exist a sound objective basis for believing the assurances will be followed; and (iv) the assurances as followed must be capable of being verified.[226]

Prospective Unfair Trials. By its actions, a removing State may not contribute to an alien's exposure to an anticipated unfair trial in the receiving State, pursuant to any applicable removing State obligations under such international human rights instruments as the ICCPR,[227] ECHR,[228] ACHR,[229] ACHPR,[230] and the Arab Charter on Human Rights.[231] Accordingly, for example, if an alien were deported to a State that had convicted and sentenced him *in absentia* and was willing to provide diplomatic assurances of a retrial, but only under a special or *ad hoc* court[232] or largely based on secret evidence unavailable to the defendant and his counsel,[233] the removing State most likely would violate the applicable convention's fair trial provisions.

Such a case arose in January 2012, when the ECtHR overturned a U.K. House of Lords decision to deport Omar Othman, better known as Abu

226 Tooze, *supra* n.130, at 379.

227 ICCPR, *supra* n.8, art. 14.

228 ECHR, *supra* n.115, art. 6.

229 ACHR, *supra* n.8, art. 8.

230 Banjul Charter, *supra* n.8, art. 7.

231 Arab Charter on Human Rights, *supra* n.8, arts. 6, 7, 14, 16.

232 In February 2012, Malaysia deported to his home country Hamza Kashgari, a young Saudi journalist who was picked up in Malaysia while *en route* to New Zealand (to seek asylum) after posting on Twitter some allegedly blasphemous comments about the Islamic Prophet Mohammed. That deportation was carried out despite the prospect of his facing an unfair trial in Saudi Arabia based on concerns about a lack of presumed innocence coupled with a trial in a non-civilian court – "a committee of top clerics branded him an 'infidel' and demanded he be tried in an Islamic court" – and possibly receiving the death penalty. M. Jegathesan, "Malaysia Deports Saudi Journalist," *AFP*, Feb. 12, 2012. As it happened, however, Kashgari never actually stood trial in Saudi Arabia, even though he was detained some twenty months. "Freedom House Welcomes Release of Saudi Writer Hamza Kashgari," Freedom House website, Oct. 29, 2013, *available at* https://freedomhouse.org/article/freedom-house-welcomes-release-saudi-writer-hamza-kashgari (last visited on May 23, 2016).

233 In this vein, the U.S. Congress established a mechanism known as the Alien Terrorist Removal Court (ATRC), which, although not yet used, authorizes the *removal* of a non-permanent resident alien suspected of terrorist activities on the basis of secret evidence of which he has no access except for a court-approved unclassified summary thereof. Antiterrorism and Effective Death Penalty Act of 1996, Pub. L. 104–132, Apr. 24, 1996, § 443(a), *codified at* 8 U.S.C. §§ 1531–37 (2012). The use of secret evidence is a controversial practice and, in fact, a U.S. bill was introduced in September 2001 that sought to render its use unconstitutional in immigration proceedings. Stephen Franklin & Ken Armstrong, "Secret Evidence Bill Raises Concerns," *Chi. Trib.*, Sept. 30, 2001.

Qatada, an influential jihadist cleric, to his birth country, Jordan. (The deportation order was based on the fact that Abu Qatada had entered the United Kingdom on a forged passport in 1993.[234]) While the Court found that Jordan's diplomatic assurances pursuant to the 2005 U.K.-Jordan DWA MOU (discussed *supra*) provided an adequate safeguard from potential human rights abuse in Jordan (he allegedly had been tortured twice by Jordanian authorities),[235] the Court concluded there was a "real risk" that, upon his return, he would be retried[236] based on witness evidence extracted through torture and that such evidence would be "of considerable, perhaps decisive, importance," which would constitute a "flagrant denial of justice" in contravention of Article 6 of the ECHR.[237] This ruling forced Jordan to accept the condition of furnishing diplomatic assurances to the extent that any evidence obtained through torture would not be used in a retrial against Abu Qatada.[238] In July 2013, after the United Kingdom became satisfied with Jordan's assurances, it agreed to deport Abu Qatada to face terrorism charges there.[239]

Courts evaluate the prospect of an unfair trial using a variety of criteria and their rulings do not uniformly prohibit removal. For instance, an Iranian citizen, who as a crew member on an Iranian Government-owned ship sold cannabis to an undercover Australian customs agent and was arrested on narcotics-related charges, applied for refugee status, contending that upon his return to Iran he would not receive a fair trial (and possibly be killed). In that case, the HRC found no violation of ICCPR Article 14(1) and (3) because he would have an opportunity to challenge his alleged violations in Iran, he would be allowed legal representation, the Iranian courts were deemed competent to examine his case, and any

[234] *Othman (Abu Qatada) v. U.K.*, Appl. No. 8139/09, 55 EHRR, Jan. 17, 2012 (final issued on May 9, 2012) [hereinafter *Othman Case*].

[235] *Id.* ¶¶ 190–207.

[236] He had previously been convicted and sentenced to life imprisonment *in absentia* for his role in two terrorist plots, one against Amman hotels in 1998 and the other in connection with the Millennium celebrations planned in Jordan. Duncan Gardham, "Abu Qatada Cannot be Deported to Jordan, European Judges Rule," *The Telegraph* (U.K.), Jan. 17, 2012.

[237] *Othman Case*, *supra* n.234, ¶¶ 281–82.

[238] "Abu Qatada Wins Jordan Deportation Appeal," *BBC News*, Jan. 17, 2012; Robert Chesney, "European Court: U.K. Cannot Deport Abu Qatada to Jordan," *Lawfare*, Jan. 17, 2012, *available at* www.lawfareblog.com/european-court-uk-cannot-deport-abu-qatada-jordan (last visited on May 23, 2016).

[239] "Abu Qatada Deported from U.K. to Stand Trial in Jordan," *BBC News*, July 7, 2013, *available at* www.bbc.com/news/uk-23213740 (last visited on May 29, 2016).

conviction and sentence received would be entitled to review by a higher court.[240]

Prospective Death Penalty Imposition. Many States have abolished the death penalty and obligated themselves through international or regional treaties not to put a person at serious risk of being subjected to the death penalty by another State. As the HRC has explained, even if a State does not itself impose the death penalty on an individual, "by deporting him to a country where he was under sentence of death, [a State] established the crucial link in the causal chain that would make possible the execution of the author."[241] For those abolitionist States, the removal of a person to a State where the death penalty appears plausible upon his return, absent diplomatic assurances to the contrary, typically will be barred either by domestic courts themselves or upon review by a supranational human rights tribunal under a "right-to-life" standard.

An example can be found in the September 2011 South African court judgment concerning the proposed deportation to his home country of a Botswanan citizen named Jerry Ofense Pitsoe ("Phale").[242] Raising concerns about Botswana's record of death penalty implementation,[243] citing to several domestic and overseas cases in which extradition was barred on account of prospective death penalty imposition,[244] and not finding a meaningful distinction in the present case between extradition and deportation,[245] the South Gauteng High Court in Johannesburg ruled that South African authorities were prohibited from deporting Phale "unless and until the Government of the Republic of Botswana provides a written assurance . . . that the applicant will not be subject to the death penalty in Botswana under any circumstances."[246]

In 2003, the HRC found a violation of the ICCPR's "right to life" provision (Article 6) in connection with Canada's deportation to the United States of Roger Judge, a U.S. citizen who had been convicted

240 *A.R.J. v. Australia*, Commc'n No. 692/1996, U.N. Doc. CCPR/C/60/D/692/1996, ¶ 6.15, Feb. 6, 1996.

241 *Judge Case, supra* n.143, ¶ 10.6.

242 This litigation consolidated two actions with largely similar claims and counter-claims; the plaintiff in the other action was named Emmanuel Tsebe, also a Botswanan citizen but who died in November 2010 prior to the High Court's hearing. *Tsebe and Another v. Minister of Home Affairs and Others*, Case Nos. 27682/10, 51010/10, So. Gauteng High Ct., Johannesburg, So. Afr., Sept. 22, 2011, 1 All SA 83, ¶¶ 1–2, 12.

243 *Id.* ¶¶ 61–68.

244 *Id.* ¶¶ 115–17.

245 *Id.* ¶¶ 87–98.

246 *Id.* ¶ 130.

and sentenced to death in Pennsylvania for two counts of first-degree murder, but who upon escaping from prison, fled to Canada, was convicted there of two robberies and was ordered to be deported once he had served out his sentence.[247] As to this violation, which arose out of Canada's failure to seek assurances from the United States that the death penalty would not be imposed,[248] the HRC concluded:

> For countries [like Canada] that have abolished the death penalty, there is an obligation not to expose a person to the real risk of its application. Thus, they may not remove [including by deportation] individuals from their jurisdiction if it may be reasonably anticipated that they will be sentenced to death, without ensuring that the death sentence would not be carried out.[249]

Similarly, in 2005, the ECtHR ruled that Sweden's approved deportation back to Syria of Kamal Bader Muhammad Kurdi ("Bader"), a Syrian national for whom an *in absentia* conviction and death sentence had been imposed in 2003 for alleged complicity in a murder, would violate

[247] *Judge Case, supra* n.143, ¶¶ 1, 2.1–2.4.

[248] *Id.* ¶ 5.2.

[249] *Id.* ¶ 10.4. In November 2005, but only after this decision was rendered, Canada ratified the ICCPR's Second Optional Protocol, which abolishes the death penalty in all circumstances with the single possible exception, that must be invoked upon ratification or accession, for "a most serious crime of a military nature committed during wartime." Second Optional Prot. to the ICCPR, Aiming at the Abolition of the Death Penalty, Dec. 15, 1989, arts. 1, 2.1, UNGA Res. 44/128, U.N. Doc. A/44/49 (1989). The *Judge Case* marked a substantial departure from *Kindler v. Canada* issued in July 1993, in which the HRC had found that the transfer of an individual from an abolitionist State to a retentionist State (*i.e.*, one that has retained the death penalty) was not a *per se* violation of Article 6. *Kindler v. Canada*, Commc'n No. 470/1991, U.N. Doc. CCPR/C/48/D/470/1991, ¶ 14.6, July 30, 1993. In distinguishing the jurisprudence, the HRC observed that over the prior decade there had been a "broadening international consensus in favour of abolition of the death penalty" and that the ICCPR "should be interpreted as a living instrument and the rights protected under it should be applied in context and in the light of present-day conditions." *Judge Case, supra* n.143, ¶ 10.3. Accordingly, municipal deportation decisions in the 1980s in the face of capital punishment effectively lost their precedential value. For example, in a Canadian deportation case involving an American citizen who had been convicted of murder by a U.S. court and where the jury had recommended the death penalty, and where a provision of the extradition treaty between the United States and Canada permitted Canada to deny extradition on the basis of prospective capital punishment in the United States, an Ontario Court of Appeal opined: "[C]ourts should not in a case such as this take into account other possible consequences of deportation, such as the possibility of capital punishment for the respondent." *MacDonald v. Kindler* Fed. Ct., Can., [1987] 41 D.L.R. (4th) 78, 84–5. *Accord In re Shepherd and Minister of Employment & Immigration*, Ontario Ct. of App., [1989] 70 O.R. (2d) 765 [hereinafter *Shepherd Case*].

Article 2 of the ECHR (the "right to life" provision) to the extent that the death sentence, even if still permitted in principle, followed a summary criminal proceeding (in which only prosecutorial evidence was examined, no oral evidence was taken, and neither the defendant nor his counsel was present), which would constitute an arbitrary deprivation of life.[250] The Court observed that because "the death sentence for serious crimes is enforced in Syria," and the Swedish Government had received no assurance that Syrian authorities would reopen his trial and that the death penalty would not be sought or imposed, he faced a real risk of being executed if deported to Syria.[251]

Unclear Grounds or Improper Motive for Detention. A related human rights concern arises when the removing State fails to seek and obtain information regarding the express legal basis for the receiving State's prospective detention of an alien. Failure to know the ground on which an individual is to be detained can constitute a breach of a removing State's obligations to protect that individual against arbitrary detention by a foreign government under such provisions as Article 9(1) of the ICCPR, Article 5(1) of the ECHR, and Article 7(3) of the ACHR (all concerning the right to liberty and security of person). For example, in January 2002 the Human Rights Chamber for Bosnia and Herzegovina (B&H) found precisely such a violation of ECHR Article 5(1) in connection with the handover by B&H to U.S. forces of Belkasem Bensayah, who was believed to be a member of a terrorist cell that had attacked the U.S. Embassy in Sarajevo.[252]

A deportation also can be denied under various multilateral conventions when a fugitive's removal is sought for improper reasons, such as to coerce him into a confession. For instance, in 2000, the Committee against Torture ruled that it was impermissible for France to remove Josu Arkauz Arana, a Spaniard of Basque origin, to Spain where the removal was sought not based on an indictment or to serve out an outstanding sentence, but rather evidently to be tortured or to extract a confession related to ETA crimes.[253]

[250] *Bader & Kanbor v. Sweden*, Appl. No. 13284/04, 46 EHRR, ¶¶ 1, 17, 42, 47, Nov. 8, 2005.

[251] *Id.* ¶¶ 44, 45, 48. Although Sweden already had ratified Protocol 13 to the ECHR, which abolished the death penalty in all circumstances, the Court did not deem it necessary to reach a decision regarding the possible violation under this Protocol as it had already found a violation under Article 2. *Id.* ¶ 49.

[252] *Bensayah Case, supra* n.8, ¶¶ 167–73.

[253] *Arana v. France*, Commc'n No. 63/1997, U.N. Doc. CAT/C/23/D/63/1997, June 5, 2000 [hereinafter *Arana Case*].

iii Law Relevant to the Removal Method

Although human rights treaties do not expressly address removal methods,[254] general standards of treatment nevertheless apply and have been interpreted in case law and expounded upon by secondary legal sources. The main areas that have been addressed in this regard are whether: (i) an alien's self-respect and sense of dignity have not been protected; (ii) disproportionate physical force and treatment has been exercised upon an alien; and (iii) deceptive tactics have been used to lure an alien to immigration authorities.[255]

Lack of Respect or Dignity for the Alien. In connection with the method of removal, the former U.N. Special Rapporteur on Human Rights of Migrants stated: "the expulsion, deportation or repatriation of undocumented migrants should be carried out with respect and dignity."[256] The Council of Europe also has underscored the importance of protecting the dignity of the removed individual, while coupling it with safety considerations for those involved in his transport.[257] Therefore, however the removal operation is designed and implemented, it should not show disrespect toward or otherwise humiliate the alien. In one illustrative application of this principle, the European Court of Justice (ECJ) recently opined that "any detention of third-country nationals ending their removal must, as a rule, take place in a specialised facility and can take place only on an exceptional basis in prison accommodation, the Member State then having to ensure that the third-country national is kept separated from ordinary prisoners."[258]

[254] OHCHR Discussion Paper, *supra* n.160, at 17.

[255] In addition to the factors enumerated, notification of the removal order itself should meet certain basic conditions, including that it should be provided in a language the alien understands, establish the legal and factual grounds on which the order is based, identify any available remedies and their corresponding deadlines, and indicate the consequences of non-compliance. *Twenty Guidelines, supra* n.184, Guideline 4. Removing States also should ensure that any aliens removed are medically fit to travel. *Id.*, Guideline 16. Furthermore, satisfactory conditions of pre-removal detention include clean and adequate accommodations and recreational opportunities; trained custodial staff; no co-location with prisoners; access to doctors, lawyers, and family members, and the right to file complaints. *Id.*, Guideline 10.

[256] Comm'n on Human Rights, Gabriela Rodríguez Pizarro, *Report of the Special Rapporteur on the Human Rights of Migrants: Migrant Workers*, E/CN.4/2005/85, ¶ 75, Dec. 27, 2004 [French text] [hereinafter *Migrant Workers Report*].

[257] *Twenty Guidelines, supra* n.184, Guideline 17.

[258] *Bero v. Kassel, Bouzalmate v. Kleve, and Pham v. Schweinfurt*, Joined Case Nos. C-473/13, C-514/13, and C-474/13, ECJ, July 17, 2014, Press Release No. 105/14.

Undue Physical Force and Treatment. Perhaps the most commonly expressed concern about the method of removal arises out of how the alien is physically treated and the extent to which force may have been unnecessary, restraints were excessive, or liberties were taken with respect to such measures as the administering of sedatives or the withholding of food and water while in transit. International law insists on certain minimum standards that do not tolerate unnecessary or disproportionate force or physical mistreatment.[259] For example, as the HRC observed regarding Belgium's treatment of aliens, "[p]rocedures used in the repatriation of some asylum seekers, in particular the placing of a cushion on the face of an individual in order to overcome resistance, entails a risk of life. The recent case of a Nigerian national who died in such a manner illustrates the need to re-examine the whole procedure of forcible deportations."[260]

In September 2005, the CoE's Committee of Ministers adopted a document entitled "Twenty Guidelines on Forced Return," which was intended to provide guidance to municipal governments. Guideline 19 addresses "means of restraint" and stipulates, in part, as follows: (i) restraints must be "strictly proportionate responses to the actual or reasonably anticipated resistance of the returnee with a view to controlling him"; (ii) "restraints partially or wholly obstructing the airways are prohibited because they risk asphyxia"; and (iii) "medication is only to be administered on the basis of a case-by-case medical decision."[261] A related claim sometimes invoked by aliens subject to removal is that the physical transfer itself will aggravate their state of health. The Committee against Torture, however, repeatedly has held that such aggravation arguments do not amount to cruel,

[259] *See Migrant Workers Report, supra* n.256, ¶¶ 221–28 (discussing the treatment of Gilbert Kouam Tamo during his forced repatriation at the Zurich Airport in August 2003 to Cameroon; allegations of mistreatment included physical abuse, injections with a sedative, and food and water deprivation, but these were rejected by the Swiss authorities, who claimed a proportional response regarding his physical treatment and denied the other claims); Charlotte Granville-Chapman, *et al.*, "Harm on Removal: Excessive Force against Failed Asylum Seekers," Freedom From Torture website (2004), at 18–32, *available at* www.freedomfromtorture.org/sites/default/files/documents/Harm%20on%20Removal%20-%20final2_0.pdf (last visited on May 23, 2016).

[260] HRC Concluding Observations on Belgium, U.N. Doc. CCPR/C/79/Add.99, ¶ 15. Nov.19, 1998. *See also* HRC Concluding Observations on Belgium, U.N. Doc. CCPR/CO/81/BEL, ¶ 14, Aug. 12, 2004 [French text].

[261] *Twenty Guidelines, supra* n.184, Guideline 19.

inhuman, or degrading treatment or punishment as envisioned by CAT Article 16.[262]

Certain Deceptive Practices. Immigration officials may try to lure aliens subject to deportation to a police station on the pretense of questioning them on an unrelated charge but in reality with the objective of bringing them in for deportation. While not technically a removal method itself, such a lure operation qualifies as a preliminary step thereof. When such cases have been brought before the ECtHR, a violation of Article 5(1) (the right to liberty and security) has been found. As one judgment stated: a "conscious decision by the authorities to facilitate or improve the effectiveness of a planned operation for the expulsion of aliens by misleading them about the purpose of a notice so as to make it easier to deprive them of their liberty is not compatible with article 5."[263]

e "Disguised Extradition"

Even if a fugitive can be justifiably removed in reliance on the host State's immigration laws, including by overcoming the vast array of human rights barriers discussed above, there may still be a legal impediment[264] to such an operation to the extent it is viewed as constituting "disguised extradition."[265] As noted in Chapter 1.f, "disguised extradition" entails a *purposeful circumvention of extradition law or an applicable treaty by the host State to deliver a fugitive directly or indirectly to a State with a law enforcement interest in him,*

[262] *E.g., G.R.B. v. Sweden,* Commc'n No. 83/1997, U.N. Doc. CAT/C/20/D/83/1997, ¶ 6.7, May 15, 1998; *S.S.S. v. Canada,* Commc'n No. 245/2004, U.N. Doc. CAT/C/35/D/245/2004, ¶ 7.3, Nov. 16, 2005.

[263] *Čonka Case, supra* n.129, ¶ 42.

[264] *See R. v. Governor of Brixton Prison, ex parte Sarno* [1916] 2 KB 742, 749 (misuse of deportation powers would be grounds for invalidating an immigration order).

[265] Disguised extradition often overlaps with informal law enforcement cooperation (discussed in Chapter 11). Where the host State expressly denominates the transfer of custody to another State as a *removal operation,* this study will treat it as such, notwithstanding the fact that it also may otherwise possess attributes of informal law enforcement cooperation, such as when the custody of an alien fugitive is passed to pursuing State agents while still in host State territory or along a shared territorial border. For example, in the early 1970s, U.S. drug enforcement agents worked closely with special police units in Latin America to apprehend and "expel" more than fifty major drug traffickers to the United States without resort to formal extradition procedures under so-called "Operation Springboard." Nadelmann, *Int'l Rendition, supra* n.84, at 861.

most often via the exercise of immigration laws.[266] As this definition suggests, the mere fact of removing an alien to a State expressly prepared to prosecute or enforce a prior punishment, *without some indicia of its intentionally bypassing extradition*, is unlikely to be found to constitute "disguised extradition."[267] This sub-section addresses how courts have evaluated "disguised extradition" claims, including to what extent State treaty obligations have been found to be unmet or individual rights have been breached in the process.[268]

Mixed Record of Lawfulness. Various national laws expressly prohibit "disguised extradition,"[269] a customary "good faith" obligation presumably exists not to expel an alien from State territory for ulterior

[266] *See Residence Prohibition Order Case (2)*, Super. Admin. Ct., Münster, F.R.G, Oct. 1, 1968, *reprinted in* 61 ILR 433, 435 (1968) ("[E]xpulsion may not be ordered as a means of evading this prohibition against extradition. However, such expulsion is deemed inadmissible only where it has become evident that the intention of the authorities was to avoid the restrictive regulations on extradition."); *Shepherd Case, supra* n.249, at 775–76 (maintaining that to succeed in a challenge on "disguised extradition" grounds a party would need to show that the Immigration Minister "did not genuinely consider it in the public interest to expel the person in question" but rather that the purpose was "to surrender the person as a fugitive criminal to a state because it asked for him").

[267] It is noteworthy from an empirical standpoint that over nearly a five-year period beginning on October 1, 2009, the U.S. Immigration and Customs Enforcement's (ICE's) Enforcement and Removal Operations (ERO), whose job is to identify, apprehend, and remove U.S. illegal aliens, removed more than 720 foreign fugitives from the United States wanted in their native countries for serious crimes. *ICE Repatriates Accused Mexican Cop Killer Captured in Los Angeles*, ICE website, Aug. 19, 2015, *available at* https://www.ice.gov/news/releases/ice-repatriates-accused-mexican-cop-killer-captured-los-angeles (last visited on May 23, 2016).

[268] A *receiving* State's conduct also may be reviewed to determine compliance with its domestic law. The European Commission on Human Rights addressed this very issue in *Altmann (Barbie) v. France*, Appl. No. 10689/83, Eur. Comm'n of Hum. Rgts., 37 D.R. 225, 230, July 4, 1984 [hereinafter *Barbie Case/Eur. Comm'n*], finding no arbitrariness in the French court ruling that the former Nazi Klaus Barbie had been detained lawfully, despite evidence of collusion between Bolivia (the removing State) and France (the receiving State) in effecting his removal in *lieu* of extradition.

[269] *See* Findlay, *supra* n.47, at 7 (noting that Austria, Belgium, Brazil, France, Germany, and Italy have laws that prohibit the use of deportation or exclusion in order to deliver fugitives to another State); *e.g., Barton v. Commw. of Australia*, High Ct., Austl., May 20, 1974, 131 C.L.R. 477, 483–84, 3 A.L.R. 70 (1974) [hereinafter *Barton Case*] ("It is an unsatisfactory practice, from an international as well as a domestic point of view, to employ a power of expulsion as such a substitute [for extradition]. Further, an executive, being bound by statute as to the occasions for and purposes of expulsion, cannot validly agree to employ that power as a general equivalent to a power to extradite, however much on occasions the expulsion may serve as an extradition in an individual case because of its circumstances.").

motives,[270] and some legal commentary maintains that the practice is unlawful.[271] Nevertheless, determining the lawfulness of "disguised extradition" is not straightforward; its record is mixed with some, but not all, national courts treating particular variables as dispositive. Indeed, although many court judgments pay lip service to the unlawfulness of "disguised extradition," their holdings at times fail to cite to specific international legal sources or standards to justify its illegality, thereby adopting an essentially conclusory logic.[272] The legal analysis is further complicated when failed States or other extreme political circumstances are involved, or when a reviewing tribunal is limited to finding a violation of a provision in a particular treaty.[273] Moreover, State courts apply varying standards of review – some stricter, others looser – when second-guessing a removal decision.

The essence of "disguised extradition" is when removal is undertaken in the face of an extant extradition treaty, and thereby potentially deprives the individual concerned of substantive, extradition-specific protections.[274] The consequences could include that the alien fugitive

[270] James Crawford, Brownlie's Principles of Public International Law 609 (8th ed. 2012); Goodwin-Gill, *supra* n.8, at 307–08. Ulterior motives for removal might include, for example, the confiscation of alien property, persecution, or circumvention of extradition.

[271] *See Expulsion of Aliens, supra* n.9, at 280 ("In certain instances, criminals have been expelled to a country which might otherwise have made a request for extradition, but that such expulsion procedure is arbitrary and therefore unsatisfactory.") (quoting CoE, Parliamentary Assembly, Recom. 950 (1982) on Extradition of Criminals, Oct. 1, 1982, ¶ 8); Christopher L. Blakesley, Terrorism, Drugs, International Law, and the Protection of Human Liberty: A Comparative Study of International Law, Its Nature, Role, and Impact in Matters of Terrorism, Drug Trafficking, War, and Extradition 278–79 (1992) (it is "improper for one State to request another to deport or expel an individual as a means of circumventing extradition procedures").

[272] *E.g., Barton Case, supra* n.269, at 483–84 ("There are obvious objections to the use of immigration or expulsive powers as a substitute for extradition") (citing legal scholars but no treaty, statutory, or case law).

[273] *E.g., Barbie Case/Eur. Comm'n, supra* n.268, 37 D.R. at 233 ("It follows that, even if the applicant's expulsion could be described as a disguised extradition, this would not, as such, constitute a breach of the [European] Convention.").

[274] *See* Paul O'Higgins, *supra* n.69, at 539 ("an evasion of the special statutory procedures laid down for extradition . . . ought to be unlawful."); ILA, *Report of the Comm. on Extradition and Human Rights, in* ILA, Report of the Sixty-Sixth Conference 142, 164 (1994); Bedi, *supra* n.3, at 402 ("If a deportation order is made with improper intentions – not only to get rid of the asylum seeker but to assist a friendly country in procuring its fugitive offender thru disguised extradition – it is unlawful because while extradition provides for judicial hearings, deportation procedure lacks such safeguards and smacks of the Star Chamber, so courts are authorized to upset the deportation order.").

would be: (i) subject to new criminal charges, absent the removing State's consent, other than those contained in the extradition request; (ii) tried for crimes unrecognized by, or for which the statute of limitations has already run in, the removing State, and would thus have been foreclosed per the provisions of an extradition treaty;[275] and/or (iii) prosecuted for political offenses that otherwise would have been barred under the terms of an extradition treaty.[276]

Indicia Favoring Unlawfulness. "Disguised extradition" is most commonly found in the following three types of circumstances: (i) instigation or collusion, (ii) a flagrant violation of domestic or international law undertaken to suggest an intent to enable or facilitate removal as a substitute, and (iii) the treatment of the alien fugitive more as a criminal than as a deportee.

Instigation or Collusion. Because "disguised extradition" may involve an aggressive pursuing State, that practice can sometimes entail: (i) *instigation* (*i.e.*, the provocation or incitement of the host State to arrest and transfer the alien fugitive);[277] or (ii) *collusion* (*i.e.*, when pursuing State officials enter into a secret agreement or understanding with their host State counterparts in violation of the law or to the detriment of the alien fugitive). Although such roles are not an essential

275 For example, when Mexican officials located convicted murderer Ernesto Lopez who had escaped from a Texas prison in 1962 and had been living in Mexico for thirty-five years, they deported him back to the United States – via a hand-off to Texas prison officials along the Rio Grande border crossing – for entering the country illegally, but only after a failed attempt at extradition due to the fact that the statute of limitations for murder in Mexico had run and so dual criminality could not be established. AP, "Murderer Convicted of 1956 Crime Back in Texas After Escape," *Lubbock Avalanche-Journal*, June 27, 1987, *available at* http://lubbockonline.com/news/062897/murderer.htm (last visited on May 29, 2016).

276 This occurred in 1882 when, acting under the broad legal discretion afforded by Gibraltar's Aliens Order in Council (1873), a magistrate judge ruled that three Cuban ex-officers who had escaped from a prison in Cadiz, Spain, were to be deported back to Spain at its request, despite the fact that the 1878 Anglo-Spanish Extradition Treaty (governing Gibraltar as a British overseas territory) would have prohibited such a transfer under the political offense exclusion as they had been imprisoned for leading uprisings against Spain. O'Higgins, *supra* n.69, at 522–23. *See also Soblen Case, supra* n.51 (the U.K. Home Secretary was allowed to place the fugitive on a non-stop flight to the United States via a removal order despite the fact that the U.S.-U.K. Extradition Treaty would have barred his return to the United States on political offense grounds due to his espionage conviction).

277 In the case of France, the issuance of an extradition request by the receiving State at all has been found sufficient to invalidate the removal to that State. *E.g., In re López de la Calle Gauna*, Case No. 234005, Conseil d'État, Fr., Apr. 10, 2002.

ingredient of "disguised extradition," when such activity occurs, some courts have found a violation of law expressly on such grounds.

In a 1998 case, Norwegian border police inquired with their British counterparts about the status of two individuals traveling from the United Kingdom with forged and stolen documents and learned merely that they "were wanted in connection with criminal activities in England." In that instance, applying the relevant legal standard, a U.K. court concluded that British authorities had not "procured, influenced or colluded in the decisions to deport the applicants" and that therefore no abuse of process or violation of law had occurred.[278] Likewise, in a 1982 case, in finding no violation on "disguised extradition" grounds, the High Court of England ruled: "[T]here is no ground whatever for supposing the police have tried to persuade the United States' authorities to deport this applicant so that they could arrest him in this country and thus circumvent the provisions of the extradition treaty between the two countries."[279]

However, in the 1999 *Mullen Case*, the U.K. Court of Appeal found that the British Secret Intelligence Service (SIS) "took active steps to persuade the CIO [Zimbabwe's Central Intelligence Organisation] that there existed grounds for deportation and provided evidence, including crucially, evidence of previous convictions, as well as draft documents recommending grounds for deportation"; and out of concern that if the appellant had an opportunity to challenge the deportation order in court or to express a preference to be sent to Ireland (his country of nationality), "the SIS recognized the need for stage-management of the timing of his detention by reference to an immediately available flight to London . . . and specifically considered and suggested to the CIO how to deal with any last-minute claim by the appellant to be deported to Ireland."[280] The Court held that by "initiat[ing] and subsequently assist-[ing] in and procur[ing] the deportation of the appellant, by unlawful

[278] *R. v. Staines Magistrates' Court, ex parte Westfallen* [1998] 4 All E.R. 210, [1998] 1 WLR 652, 652–53.

[279] *R. v. Guildford Magistrates' Court, ex parte Healy* [1983] 1 WLR 108, *reprinted in* 77 ILR 345, 348. *Accord Stevenson v. United States*, 381 F.2d 142, 144 (9th Cir. 1967) (in a case where Mexican immigration officials transported two Americans to the U.S. border and turned them over to Arizona sheriff's deputies, "the evidence shows that the removal of the appellants from Mexico was not initiated by the United States," that the arresting Mexican police officer was unaware that an extradition request had ever been made by the United States, and that "it was the Mexican authorities who first contacted American officials with regard to the appellants.").

[280] *Mullen Case, supra* n.6, 2 Cr. App. R. at 249–50.

means, in circumstances in which there were specific extradition facilities between [the two States], "they were not only encouraging unlawful conduct in Zimbabwe, but they were also acting in breach of public international law."[281]

Flagrant Law Violation Suggesting Bypass Intent. Another basis for a court finding removal unlawful as a function of "disguised extradition" is when a State violates domestic and/or international law in such a flagrant way as to suggest an intent to enable or facilitate removal as a substitute for extradition. An example in the domestic law arena can be found in May 2001, when the South African Constitutional Court ruled in a case involving Khalfan Khamis Mohamed, a Tanzanian national who: (i) based on a false passport and an assumed name, was issued a temporary residence permit in South Africa in the fall of 1998; (ii) was indicted in December 1998 by the United States for murder and other charges related to the August 1998 bombing of the U.S. Embassy in Dar es Salaam, Tanzania; (iii) was arrested for immigration violations in October 1999 by the Republic of South Africa (RSA) in a joint operation with the FBI; and (iv) within two days was transferred into FBI custody in Cape Town and then removed to New York by a dedicated plane to stand trial for capital offenses.[282]

The Court found Mohamed's deportation violative of two South African laws. First, the deportation was made under so-called Regulation 23 that identified all eligible destinations to which an alien could be removed, strictly limiting the options to States where the alien held a passport, was a citizen, or had the right to domicile (in Stateless instances), and found that his deportation as a Tanzanian national to the United States, therefore, was impermissible as it did not qualify under these criteria.[283] Second, South African authorities were obligated under the RSA Constitutional Bill of Rights – which promotes and protects the

[281] *Id.* at 2050. *Accord R. v. Bow Street Magistrates' Court, ex parte Mackeson*, (1981), 75 Cr. App. R. 24 (D.C.), *reprinted in* 77 ILR 336 (finding that through collusion between Zimbabwe-Rhodesia (Z-R) and British officials – although not with any conscious wrongdoing on the part of the British police officer who had merely informed the authorities in Z-R of Britain's law enforcement interest in him – Z-R unlawfully deported a U.K. citizen wanted for fraud in what was characterized as "extradition by the back door," given that his extradition was unavailable on account of a lapsed extradition treaty).

[282] *Mohamed v. The President of the Repub. of So. Afr.*, Case CCT 17/01, Const. Ct., So. Afr., May 28, 2001, [2001] (3) SA 893, 898, 901, 906 [hereinafter *Mohamed Case*].

[283] *Id.* at 906–09.

rights to life, human dignity, and a prohibition on cruel, inhuman, or degrading treatment or punishment – to seek pre-removal assurance from the United States that it would not impose a death sentence on Mohamed in the event of a conviction, which it failed to do.[284] Although a government's violation of its immigration laws is not tantamount to "disguised extradition," when coupled with the State's reliance on removal in these circumstances, it appeared that a purposeful circumvention of extradition had occurred.[285]

International or regional courts or monitoring bodies also would be unlikely to allow removals to proceed after extradition already has been refused on human rights grounds,[286] such as prospective concerns about torture,[287] the death penalty being imposed,[288] unfair judicial proceedings,[289] or the denial of access to a judicial hearing.[290] Such a removal could well be viewed as evidence of a violation of international law suggestive of purposeful circumvention of extradition. The key permissible conditions in such instances are that there must be a valid basis in law for the removal and that all individual rights set forth in the applicable treaty are respected.[291]

Treatment as a Criminal versus a Deportee. Another way in which removal has been found unlawful as a function of "disguised extradition" is where the alien fugitive was transferred to the receiving State more in

284 *Id.* at 909–17. Notably, the *Mohamed* Court did not address the death penalty provision in the then-executed but not yet ratified extradition treaty between the United States and RSA, which provided that "the Requested State may refuse extradition unless the Requesting State provides assurances that the death penalty will not be imposed, or if imposed, will not be carried out." *United States v. Bin Laden*, 156 F. Supp.2d 359, 365 & n.10 (S.D.N.Y. 2001) (quoting Extradition Treaty, U.S.-RSA, Sept. 16, 1999) [hereinafter *Bin Laden Case*]. The then-prevailing extradition treaty did not allow for such a conditionality. Treaty of Extradition, U.S.-RSA, Dec. 18, 1947, 2 U.S.T. 884.

285 After Mohamed's conviction, but before the U.S. trial's penalty phase, although the court did not preclude the prosecution from seeking the death penalty, it did allow Mohamed to submit a summary of the RSA Constitutional Court's decision to serve as a mitigating factor. *Bin Laden Case, supra* n.284, at 371. Although "[t]here is no way to gauge the significance that the jury attached ... to the decision of the Constitutional Court," the jury was unable to reach a unanimous verdict on the death penalty. *Id.*

286 CoE Comm. of Experts on the Operation of Eur. Convs. on Co-operation in Crim. Matters, *Note on the Relationship Between Extradition and Deportation/Expulsion (Disguised Extradition)*, PC-OC (2012) 08 rev2, Nov. 15, 2012, at 3.

287 *E.g., Arana Case, supra* n.253.

288 *E.g., Mohamed Case, supra* n.282.

289 *E.g., Bozano Case, supra* n.65.

290 *E.g., Mullen Case, supra* n.6.

291 *Id.* at 4.

the guise of a criminal than as a deportee. This may occur in an instance where the alien is not allowed to leave the removing State's territory as a "free man," but rather in handcuffs or under other physical restraint and/or within the custody or armed escort of receiving State officials. Such conduct implicates the rights to liberty and security of person, which are protected under such broadly subscribed multilateral conventions as the ICCPR,[292] the ECHR,[293] and the ACHR.[294]

A number of courts have issued "disguised extradition" rulings, and thereby denied deportations, on this basis, including the Supreme Court of India,[295] the Supreme Court of Brazil,[296] the European Court of Human Rights,[297] and the Human Rights Chamber for Bosnia and Herzegovina.[298] At the same time, however, this notion of departure as a "free man" is fraught with significant logistical limitations, as the freedom experienced may be only momentary or otherwise short-lived, depending on the circumstances under which the alien physically leaves removing State's territory and any foreknowledge a pursuing State has as to the routing of his outbound journey.[299]

292 ICCPR, *supra* n.8, art. 9.

293 ECHR, *supra* n.115, art. 5.

294 ACHR, *supra* n.8, art. 7.

295 *E.g., Muller Case, supra* n.54, at 1300–01 (while an alien "may be conducted to the frontier under detention he must be permitted to leave a free man, and cannot be handed over under arrest.").

296 *See In re Esposito*, Fed. Sup. Ct., Braz., July 25, 1932, III *Revista de Direito* 73, *reprinted in* [1933–34] 7 ANN. DIG. & REP. PUB. INT'L L. CASES 332 (H. Lauterpacht ed. 1940)("If the petitioner, outside of our territory, were not left at liberty but were to be sent to Italy [where he was likely to be prosecuted for political offenses], there would really be carried out a true extradition which the Italian Government has not requested and which the Brazilian Government has not decided to grant.").

297 *E.g., Bozano Case, supra* n.65, ¶¶ 23–26, 60 (finding a violation of ECHR art. 5(1)(f) as the alien was transported out of France in an unmarked car, wearing handcuffs, and flanked between two police officers).

298 *E.g., Bensayah Case, supra* n.8, ¶¶ 50, 171–73 (finding a violation of ECHR, art. 5(1) where the alien was handed off to U.S. forces at Butmir Base in Sarajevo, with the full knowledge that the alien was to be kept detained in U.S. custody on B&H territory until he was transported (the following day) to Guantánamo Bay, Cuba).

299 *See Muller Case, supra* n.54, at 1300 ("It is true [the removed alien] may be apprehended the moment he leaves, by some other power and consequently, in some cases this would be small consolation to him, but in most cases the distinction is substantial, for the right of a foreign power to arrest except in its own territory and on its own boats is not unlimited."); *R. v. Sec'y of State for Home Affairs, ex parte Duke of Chateau Thierry* [1917] 1 KB 922, 937 (finding the deportation order lawful so long as it specified which ship the alien was to board rather than a designated country).

Indicia Favoring Lawfulness. The most popular bases for undermining an allegation of "disguised extradition" appear to be when: (i) no operative extradition treaty exists between the removing and receiving States; (ii) extradition protections are nevertheless preserved in the removal context; and (iii) a removing State has conducted due diligence to explore other potential destinations for the removal.

No Extradition Treaty Exists. Not surprisingly, in instances where no extradition treaty exists, courts seem less concerned about any evidence of apparent inter-State collusion in connection with delivering a fugitive for a pursuing State's benefit. For example, in the *Barbie* Case, France's Court of Cassation held that Bolivia and France's joint effort in February 1983 to return the former Nazi to France by way of indirect removal[300] (via French Guyana) was permissible because France could lawfully secure the custody of a fugitive beyond reliance merely on voluntary return or extradition arrangements, and that any collusion by State authorities was inconsequential given that no extradition treaty was circumvented.[301]

Extradition Protections Preserved. Removal in the face of an active extradition treaty need not bypass the protections guaranteed under that legal instrument, either because of the specific circumstances involved; or the receiving State's courts may insist on such protections, as in the *Barbie Case* cited above, where, following his deportation, Barbie was entitled to a full set of rights and due process as a defendant in the course of his judicial proceedings;[302] or because the States agree to cooperate by ensuring that such protections are still honored. An example of the last of these can be found in 1917, when the United Kingdom issued a deportation order for the so-called Duke of Chateau Thierry, who was wanted in France for military desertion. As recounted by British legal scholar Paul O'Higgins, in this case "it was admitted on behalf of the states concerned that the principles of specialty and non-surrender of political offenders should apply. The states themselves

[300] His deportation was premised on a violation of Bolivian immigration law arising out of his use of a false identity to obtain Bolivian citizenship. *Fédération Nationale des Déportés et Internés Résistants et Patriotes and Others v. Barbie*, Ct. of Cassation (Crim. Ch.), Fr., Oct. 6, 1983, *reprinted in* 78 ILR 125, 125 (1988).

[301] *Id.* at 128.

[302] *Id.* at 131. At the same time, however, the Court allowed new charges related to crimes against humanity to be brought against Barbie absent any applicable rule of specialty (or statute of limitations for such offenses). *Id.* at 132–47 (discussing Court of Cassation judgments dated Jan. 26, 1984, and Dec. 20, 1985).

treated the surrender as a special form of extradition to which the general rules governing extradition should be applied."[303]

Other Removal Destinations Considered. When contemplating removal, a State is generally expected to exercise due diligence in considering potential removal destinations for an alien, especially when no other State volunteers or can be identified by the alien himself.[304] Such measures tend to negate any concern about "disguised extradition." As a Dutch court reasoned: "[T]here was no question of veiled extradition, because there had been no evidence that the State had influenced West Germany's decision to withdraw the request for extradition, and the State reasonably felt obliged to hand over the West German to the West German border police since only West Germany was bound to admit him, and the State was justified in assuming that no other country would be willing to admit him since he had no valid travel document."[305]

Threshold for Review. Even if an extradition treaty is in fact bypassed in favor of removal, however, some States maintain that such a practice should not be challenged except in extraordinary instances of abuse, given that the two approaches – extradition and removal – are complementary and neither has *a priori* supremacy.[306] Indeed, case law stands for the proposition that a State should be given due deference in exercising its immigration authorities and that where a removal order is valid on its face, a reviewing court should not second-guess its motives unless the order were conspicuously a "sham."[307] This derives from the concept that

[303] O'Higgins, *supra* n.69, at 528 (although using this example to argue, conversely, that States recognize that disguised extradition is improper).

[304] *E.g., Wallace Case, supra* n.47, at 305 (finding no evidence of improper intent on the part of Dutch immigration authorities in deporting Wallace to the United States while notably indicating that the alien was unable to identify any other State willing to receive him); *Linnas*, 790 F.2d at 1031 (noting the defendant's "own failure to designate a country of deportation [after such an opportunity was granted him] lends credence to the immigration judge's finding that no country other than the Soviet Union would accept him").

[305] *Lülf v. State of the Netherlands*, Ct. of App. of The Hague, Neth., June 17, 1976, *reprinted in* 74 ILR 424.

[306] Sohn & Buergenthal, *supra* n.12, at 95.

[307] *R. v. Superintendent of Chiswick Police Station, ex parte Sacksteder* [1918] 1 KB 578 (ruling in favor of the Home Secretary's reliance on a deportation order to effect the return of military deserters to France); *see also Sitaram v. Superintendent Rangoon Central Jail*, High Ct., Burma, Feb. 15, 1957, [1957] BURMA L. REP. 190, *reprinted in* 28 ILR 313 (1963) (holding that Burmese courts need not examine the executive's decision to rely on deportation instead of extradition and the executive need not provide any justification for its decision).

governments generally should be accorded a "margin of appreciation" or broad discretion in such decisions,[308] as they tend to be driven by legitimate policy concerns about national security and the public welfare. Accordingly, courts are generally loath to scrutinize the claimed justifications for removal decisions, unless there is some facially powerful reason to do so.[309]

Furthermore, where a pursuing State expresses interest in securing the custody of a fugitive for law enforcement purposes, it appears there is no compelling reason in principle why the host State could not choose to remove an alien under its immigration laws rather than rely on an existing extradition treaty.

> [Extradition treaties] tend to facilitate cooperation among States rather than to give additional rights to an accused person. It would be difficult to conclude from a treaty on extradition that a person who could be lawfully expelled to a certain country would be exempt from expulsion once the

[308] GOODWIN-GILL, *supra* n.8, at 262 ("In determining whether its interests are adversely affected by the continuing presence of the alien, or whether there is a threat to 'ordre public,' the expelling State enjoys under international law a fairly wide margin of appreciation."); *id.* at 275 ("A full appeal on the merits, or even some special administrative tribunal which hears representations, may not be demanded, especially in political and security matters where the executive enjoys the widest margin of appreciation."); *Maroufidou Case, supra* n.124, ¶ 10.1 ("It is not within the powers or functions of the Committee to evaluate whether the competent authorities of the State party in question have interpreted and applied the domestic law correctly . . . under the Optional Protocol, unless it is established that they have not interpreted and applied in good faith or that it is evident that there has been an abuse of power.") (articulating the eponymous "Maroufidou formula"); *Barbie Case/ Eur. Comm'n, supra* n.268, 37 D.R. at 234 ("[T]he Commission has always considered that, in cases where the Convention refers to domestic law, it is primarily the responsibility of the national authorities to interpret and apply this law, but at the same time the Commission retains a limited power of control over the manner in which the national authorities have performed this task [to ensure it has not been arbitrary].").

[309] "If [a removing State] does give reasons, any scrutiny of them, and the evidence supporting them, is (unless it is a question of establishing that specific conditions laid down by treaty have been met) probably to be limited to establishing that they are *prima facie* sufficient to negate any presumption of arbitrariness: particularly where interests of national security are concerned, a meticulous scrutiny of the reasons for a state's decision would be inappropriate." JENNINGS & WATTS, *supra* n.12, at 943–44. *See also R. v. Home Sec'y, ex parte Hosenball* [1977] 3 All E.R. 452, [1977] 1 WLR 766 ("In my judgment, there being no allegation that the Secretary of State acted in bad faith, we are bound to accept that he is the person who must decide whether particular matters are fit for disclosure or not when national security is involved.").

> State of destination makes a request in view of submitting the same person to criminal proceedings.[310]

The U.S. Supreme Court has gone a step farther, maintaining that "unless an extradition treaty contains an explicit provision making the treaty the exclusive means by which a defendant's presence may be secured, extra-treaty seizures are permitted."[311] In almost every instance, extradition treaties do not expressly claim to be the only available mechanism by which a fugitive can be returned to a pursuing State, and therefore its provisions and even demonstrable circumvention would be of no consequence for courts holding such a view in evaluating the lawfulness of "disguised extradition."

In a similarly styled ruling, the European Commission on Human Rights found no breach of the ECHR despite evidence of circumvented extradition on the ground that "the Convention contains no provisions either on the conditions under which extradition may be granted or on the procedure to be applied before the extradition may be granted."[312] Furthermore, as a practical matter, State decision-making on alien removals is difficult to challenge because, even if a court decides to peer behind the veil of a removing State's decision-making calculus, there is a heavy burden of proof to show that the removal was primarily pretextual.[313] "[T]he principle of good faith in international law is advantageously presumptive, and it will never be very easy to establish *mala fides* on the part of the expelling State."[314]

At the same time, however, other courts have adopted a principled view that they have no power to inquire into the circumstances that brought a fugitive into its jurisdiction, and therefore have been unwilling to consider whether collusion over deportation, let alone forceful or fraudulent seizures, have occurred, and if so whether such conduct has breached international law. That Roman maxim, known as *male captus*

310 Giorgio Gaja, *Expulsion of Aliens: Some Old and New Issues in Int'l Law*, 3 Cursos Euromediterráneos Bancaja de Derecho Internacional 283, 299–300 (1999).

311 *United States v. Álvarez-Machaín*, 504 U.S. 655, 664 (1992), *on remand*, 971 F.2d 310 (9th Cir. 1992), *reprinted in* 31 ILM 902.

312 *Barbie Case/Eur. Comm'n*, *supra* n.268, 37 D.R. at 233.

313 *See* Shearer, *supra* n.8, at 84 (overall, where the case is a *prima facie de facto* extradition rather than blatant "disguised extradition," attempts to have the order upset are likely to fail as the onus falls to an extent on the applicant to show that discretion was improperly exercised, if any judicial review can be obtained at all); *e.g.*, *Shepherd Case*, *supra* n.249, at 775–76 (indicating that a "heavy onus" is imposed on the party alleging that the removing government unlawfully exercised its power).

314 Goodwin-Gill, *supra* n.8, at 206.

bene detentus (Latin for "an unlawful apprehension may nevertheless give rise to lawful detention and prosecution"),[315] maintains that the means by which a fugitive reached the courtroom is not relevant to whether the court has proper personal jurisdiction over the individual. This doctrine will be discussed more extensively in Chapter 13.a.i, but for present purposes, it is worth noting that the maxim has been applied in "disguised extradition" cases.

In 1985, a U.K. court was unwilling to entertain allegations of "collusion" on *male captus* grounds in *R. v. Plymouth Magistrates' Court, and Others ex parte Driver*,[316] where U.K. police had informed Turkish officials that, if it was within their legal authority to deport a U.K. citizen wanted for murder, that would be helpful. Shortly thereafter, Turkey deported him by placing him on a plane headed for London and, upon his arrival, he was promptly arrested and charged.[317] Similarly, in *United States v Cordero*, notwithstanding the existence of an extradition treaty between the United States and Panama, the U.S. Court of Appeals for the First Circuit found no difficulty asserting personal jurisdiction over the defendants – Josephine Cordero and her pilot William Sorren, who were suspected of smuggling cocaine from Panama into the United States – where DEA officials simply requested assistance from a friendly government (Panama) to seize them, subject them to an expulsion order, and put them on a plane to an intermediate destination (Venezuela) whose cooperation had also been obtained.[318]

* * * * *

This chapter has explored the operational and legal dimensions of the first of the three types of full-scale alternatives to extradition: reliance on domestic immigration laws. We now shift in Chapter 11 to the second type of full-scale alternative: informal law enforcement cooperation.

[315] This term occasionally has been referred to alternatively as "*male captus, bene judicatus*," meaning essentially "wrongly captured but properly adjudicated." *E.g.*, Tineke Poort, Male Captus, Bene Judicatus: *Disguised Extradition and Other Practices*, 1 LEIDEN J. INT'L L. 65 (1988).

[316] [1985] 2 All E.R. 681 (QB).

[317] *Id.*

[318] PYLE, *supra* n.49, at 271–72.

11

Alternative II

Informal Law Enforcement Cooperation

This study now turns from immigration laws to bilateral cooperation, where the physical custody of a fugitive is transferred not pursuant to municipal statutes but through informal arrangements. This chapter, which will address the second of the three full-scale alternatives to extradition, begins by discussing the nature and scope of informal law enforcement cooperation, then evaluates host State motivation to engage in such cooperation followed by host State participation and acquiescence – its two forms of application. Next, this chapter will consider the extent to which this full-scale alternative to extradition is lawful by examining general principles and specific legal grounds implicated by such scenarios, as well as by taking a close look at the landmark *Öcalan* case.

a Definition, Nature, and Scope

In this analysis, "informal law enforcement cooperation" is defined as *a form of inter-State cooperation handled through casual or other less conventional procedures or channels between law enforcement authorities (or other government officials acting in support of law enforcement) resulting in the direct or indirect rendition of a fugitive.* Let us consider the various elements and dynamics integral to this concept.

- The law enforcement or other authorities must be current officers operating under the color of law and conceivably may include military, customs, or intelligence officials serving in a law enforcement support function; accordingly, they must *not* be: (i) private individuals,[1] (ii) law

[1] To the extent private individuals, such as bounty hunters or private detectives, are engaged on the pursuing end, such an operation would more accurately constitute a "silver platter" scenario (*see* Chapter 3.b). An example of this can be found in the famous U.S. Supreme Court case, *Ker v. Illinois*, 119 U.S. 436 (1886). "In the *Ker* case, a private detective from the United States, while in Peru, received duly executed extradition papers from the U.S.

enforcement or other types of government officers acting in their personal capacity, or *ultra vires*, or (iii) immigration officials.

- The host State must be aware of the operation and, in one official form or another and on one level of government or another, actively support or otherwise approve of it.[2]
- The transfer of custody must be via non-conventional procedures, such that it does not emanate from an extradition treaty or other written agreement such as a SOFA; would not operate under formal extradition procedures, including a transfer authorized via comity or reciprocity; and the fugitive would not be provided any kind of legal process.
- The transfer of custody between the authorities of the two States may operate either directly or indirectly, including with the intervention of a third State (either as an intermediary destination or as an agent on behalf of pursuing State's authorities[3]), and does not depend on whether an extradition treaty is in effect between the pursuing and host States.
- Informal law enforcement cooperation would stand regardless of whether the host State publicly conceals or denies its role in any such transfer of custody of a fugitive;[4] hence, the host State's *ex post facto*

Government, conforming to the requirements of the extradition treaty between the United States and Peru. He did not use them, however, because he had no access to the proper Government of Peru, which was disorganized as a result of military occupation of the capital city by Chilean forces. The latter assisted the American officers in forcing Ker to board a U.S. vessel." Michael H. Cardozo, *When Extradition Fails, is Abduction the Solution?*, 55 AJIL 127, 133 (1961).

2 If the host State has no foreknowledge of the operation or does not play any role or authorize it in some way, it would be more properly classified as a *unilateral* measure (discussed in Chapter 12.a and b). To the extent the host State only discovers the operation after the fact, its failure to protest at that juncture likely would qualify as acquiescence, but the underlying action nevertheless would be classified as a unilateral operation. If the host State mistakenly transfers the fugitive, even if based on an unintentional misrepresentation by a pursuing State, it would fall within the scope of a "silver platter" scenario (*see* Chapter 3.c).

3 For example, "following the First World War there was apparently some thought of bringing Grover C. Bergdoll back to the United States for trial on a charge of evading military service by having him forcibly removed from Germany by British agents." Alona E. Evans, *Acquisition of Custody over the Int'l Fugitive Offender—Alternatives to Extradition: A Survey of United States Practice*, 40 B.Y.B.I.L. 77, 92 (1964).

4 Given political sensitivities, especially if the subject individual is a host State national, many States wish to maintain a low profile and/or deny any involvement with respect to helping pursuing States bring, say, terrorists or narcotics offenders to justice. *See* Ethan A. Nadelmann, *The Evolution of United States Involvement in the Int'l Rendition of Fugitive Criminals*, 25 N.Y.U. J. Int'l L. & Pol. 813, 865 (1993) [hereinafter Nadelmann, *Int'l*

repudiation or protestation of an operation that resulted in the fugitive's transfer out of its territory would not negate the fact that such cooperation had occurred.[5]

b Application

This section examines the two forms of informal law enforcement cooperation by the host State government – participation and acquiescence[6] – but first briefly explores the motivation of host State officials to offer their services or extend their consent.

In many cases, the host State shares a law enforcement interest in the particular fugitive's capture and removal.[7] In addition or alternatively, the host State may be willing to participate in or acquiesce to an operation on its territory as a political favor or as a *quid pro quo* for something of comparable value, such as preferred trade treatment, political support on a key issue in a certain international or regional forum, or cooperation on a reciprocal law enforcement matter extended by a particular pursuing State.

At other times, particularly when only selected individuals or offices within a given State's government are made aware of a planned cooperation,

Rendition] (a DEA agent who had been prominently involved in Operation Springboard told Nadelmann that the Uruguayan Interior Minister had approved an irregular rendition plan only on condition that his consent would not be publicly revealed if anything went wrong); *e.g., United States v. Caro-Quintero et al.*, 745 F. Supp. 599, 602 (C.D. Cal. 1990) (initially when the DEA approached Mexican officials about apprehending Dr. Humberto Álvarez-Machaín, who was suspected of involvement in the torture and death of a DEA agent operating in Mexico, the Mexican officials reportedly wanted the arrangements to be made "under the table" to avoid upsetting Mexican citizens, but the deal broke down over the DEA's unwillingness to pay them US $50,000 in advance for "transportation expenses"), *aff'd sub nom. United States v. Álvarez-Machaín*, 946 F.2d 1466 (9th Cir. 1991), *rev'd*, 504 U.S. 655 (1992).

5 An example of how such denials can play out in public once cooperation comes to light can be found in connection with U.S. anti-narcotics smuggling efforts in the Bahamas that implicated Bahaman Government officials. Reginald Stuart, "U.S.-Bahamian Relations are Straining Under Drug Investigations," *N.Y. Times*, Sept. 28, 1983, at A21.

6 *See* Paul Michell, *English-Speaking Justice: Evolving Responses to Transnat'l Forcible Abduction after* Alvarez-Machain, 29 Cornell Int'l L.J. 383, 421 (1996) (noting that abduction [SDOs] can occur either through the "active participation" or "tacit assistance" of the host State (citing to the *Valot, Lira, Cotton, Sobell, Insull,* and *Karoly* cases).

7 Such common interest may be reflected in a bilateral or multilateral treaty. *See, e.g.*, Inter-Am. Conv. against Terrorism, June 3, 2002, art. 8, OAS Res. 1840 (XII-O/02), OAS No. A-66 ("The states parties shall work closely with one another, consistent with their respective domestic legal and administrative systems, to enhance the effectiveness of law enforcement action to combat the offenses established in the international instruments listed in article 2.").

given the sensitivities involved (such as the prospect of a tip-off to officials sympathetic to the fugitive; concerns about foreign policy, international politics, or popular backlash; and/or the controversial character of the planned tactics[8]), informal law enforcement cooperation may occur strictly at the local level. There, the motive to willingly assist or "turn a blind eye" may arise out of a personal friendship established over years of working together, a "professional understanding," or even simple bribery, most typically in the guise of cash or ammunition.[9] It is also possible that the host State may be willing to cooperate when "induced by fraud or deception on the part of the [pursuing] state agents to facilitate the surrender of the fugitive offenders."[10]

i Host State Participation

A host State may engage in informal law enforcement cooperation through active participation, either by: (i) engaging in a seizure/arrest/detention followed by fugitive delivery exclusively or principally under its own auspices via a physical handover or by means of deceptive practice; (ii) the onward delivery of a fugitive as or to a cooperating transit or intermediary State;[11] or (iii) carrying out a joint SDO with pursuing State

[8] *See* Ethan A. Nadelmann, Cops Across Borders: The Internationalization of U.S. Criminal Law Enforcement 442–43 (1993) [hereinafter Nadelmann, Cops].

[9] *Id.* at 444. *See also* Pete Axthelm with Anthony Marro, "The Drug Vigilantes," *Newsweek*, Aug. 16, 1976, at 56 (quoting a U.S. federal agent as saying: "Clearly we have paid for some of these people. It might not have been a specific 'quid pro quo' but we would give x dollars or x cases of ammunition to officials who helped get these people on planes."); *id.* (DEA payoffs made to Senegalese police allegedly prompted their cooperation in the seizure and deportation to the United States of Dominique Orsini, discussed at n.11 *infra*).

[10] Satyadeva Bedi, Extradition: A Treatise on the Laws Relevant to the Fugitive Offenders Within and With the Commonwealth Countries 396 (2002). This might occur, for instance, as a result of deliberately faulty or fabricated information provided by pursuing State officials. Such a situation, however, would present grounds for protest, whether publicly or privately communicated, as a function of bad faith at a minimum.

[11] During the time a fugitive is located within the geographical boundaries of a given State, even temporarily during transit, *that* State qualifies as the host State. *See* definition of "host State" in Chapter 1.b. For example, in August 1975, while his flight between Buenos Aires and Nice stopped briefly for refueling in Dakar, Senegal, Dominique Orsini, who was wanted on narcotics conspiracy charges in the United States, was arrested and detained by the Senegalese police at the behest of the DEA and then deported to the United States. *United States v. Orsini*, 424 F. Supp. 229 (E.D.N.Y. 1976), *aff'd without opinion*, 559 F.2d 1206 (2d Cir. 1977), *cert. denied*, 434 U.S. 997 (1977); Nadelmann, *Int'l Rendition, supra* n.4, at 443, 866; Kyle M. Medley, Note, *The Widening of the Atlantic: Extradition Practices Between the United States and Europe*, 68 Brook. L. Rev. 1213, 1238 (2002–03).

authorities or otherwise accepting their material, on-the-ground operational support.

Physical Handovers and Deceptive Practices. When host State officials undertake an operation on their own with the intention of delivering a fugitive to their pursuing State counterparts, and do so directly, the handover tends to occur along their common land or water border (if neighboring States), on a ship, or at an international airport, and is effected absent any kind of legal proceedings or the fugitive's access to an attorney.[12] For example, in January 1934, in Nuevo Laredo, Mexico, four men (including at least two positively identified as Mexicans) seized a U.S. citizen named López, who was then transported by car to the Rio Grande (the river dividing Mexico and the United States) and forced to hold on to a tub while two of the men towed him across the river to the U.S. side, where he was arrested by a U.S. marshal.[13] The process of physically pushing fugitives across a border, sometimes literally under a fence, into the waiting arms of pursuing State authorities, has been dubbed "extradition Mexican-style" because this practice has occurred with notorious frequency between the United States and Mexico.[14]

Such cross-border cases can be found beyond North America as well. Until 1965, when the Irish Supreme Court ceased the practice, once informed about a fugitive on Irish territory, the local police would locate and arrest the individual, take him to a place near the border without any legal process, and physically thrust him over the frontier to U.K. law enforcement officers.[15] In July 1988, a fugitive named Beahan "was taken by members of the Botswana Police Force from Botswana and was handed to members of the Zimbabwe Republic Police" at the border where he was detained.[16] In August 1994, Nepali police informally transferred custody of Yakub Memon, who was the chief suspect in the

[12] In or about January 1956, Mexican law enforcement officers seized Emil Wentz, a U.S. citizen, in Mexico City and transported him by auto to Laredo, Texas, where he was transferred into the custody of U.S. agents. *Wentz v. United States*, 244 F.2d 172, 176 (9th Cir.), *cert. denied*, 355 U.S. 806 (1957).

[13] *Ex parte López*, 6 F. Supp. 342, 344 (S.D. Tex. 1934).

[14] *See* Nadelmann, Cops, *supra* n.8, at 437.

[15] Ivan A. Shearer, Extradition in International Law 75 (1971). In 1965, the Supreme Court of Ireland "declared such actions a contempt of court because it deprived the subject of his constitutional right to seek habeas corpus" and regular extradition procedures were thereby restored. *Id.* (adverting to *The State (Quinn) v. Ryan*, Sup. Ct., Ir., [1965] I.R. 70).

[16] *State v. Beahan*, Sup. Ct., Zimb., Sept. 4, 1991, [1991] 2 Zimb. L.R. 98, *reprinted in* 103 ILR 203, 206 (finding no violation of international law as there was no affront to Botswana's sovereignty).

Bombay bombings that killed 260 persons in March 1993, to their Indian counterparts along the border with Bihar.[17]

Consider also the following examples in which a physical hand-over was effected in a non-border location, such as at a seaport or airport. In March 1934, after failed attempts to win the extradition (and later deportation) from Greece of Samuel Insull, a Chicago financier who had perpetrated a major fraud, the United States sought the intervention of the Turkish police to seize him while his Greek-flagged steamship was anchored in the Bosporus straits (Turkish territorial waters) to stock up on provisions. The Turkish police prevented the ship's departure, boarded the ship, and removed him to Istanbul and onward to Smyrna, where he was then taken on to the U.S.-owned *S.S. Exilona* and delivered to a U.S. Government agent who took him into custody and sailed back to the United States.[18] Likewise, in a February 1911 case, after Vinayak Damodar Savarkar, a Hindu revolutionary who was in transit from England to India to face criminal charges, escaped while his ship was docked in Marseilles, a French port police officer, while on French-controlled territory, handed Savarkar over to the Indian Army military police guard responsible for escorting him.[19]

In July 1993, at the request of the FBI and upon his orchestrated transfer from Ghana, Nigerian Government officials denied the admission of Omar Mohammod Ali Rezaq, a Palestinian who had killed an American airline passenger during a hijacking in 1985, and turned him over at the Lagos Airport to FBI agents (who took him on a charter flight back to the United States)[20] at a time when such an activity would be easily overlooked during a period of political chaos in Nigeria.[21] And in July 2014, after U.S. State Department and FBI officers located Neil Stammer, who had been on the lam since 2000 on a charge of unlawful flight to avoid prosecution (UFAP) and living under a false name and

[17] John F. Burns, "India Presses Bombing Case against Pakistan," *N.Y. Times*, Aug. 11, 1994; Sheela Bhatt, "The Strange Case of Yakub Memon," *Rediff.com*, Aug. 7, 2007, *available at* www.rediff.com/news/2007/aug/07sheela.htm (last visited on May 23, 2016).

[18] *United States v. Insull*, 8 F. Supp. 310, 311 (N.D. Ill. 1934); Nadelmann, Cops, *supra* n.8, at 438.

[19] *Savarkar Case* (Fr. v. Gr. Br.), PCA Award, Hague Ct. Rep. (Scott) 276, Feb. 24, 1911.

[20] This is an example of a two-step operation consisting initially of an immigration law action (here, an exclusion) followed by informal law enforcement cooperation.

[21] Douglas Kash, *Abducting Terrorists under PDD-39: Much Ado About Nothing New*, 13 Am. U. Int'l L. Rev. 139, 141 (1997–98); Stephen Dycus, et al., Counterterrorism Law 522 (2007).

passport in Nepal, Nepali authorities informally turned him over to their American counterparts, which escorted him from Nepal to New Mexico.[22]

Host State officials also can engineer the delivery of a fugitive *directly* to a pursuing State's territory (including one of its flagged vessels) by deceptive means, including through the use of lures or other inducements,[23] rather than through physical force or manhandling. For example, in the case of the former Kurdish separatist leader Abdullah Öcalan (discussed more extensively *infra*), the Kenyan Minister of Foreign Affairs had misinformed the Greek Ambassador in Ankara (with whom Öcalan had been staying) that Öcalan would be put on a plane to the Netherlands, which had reportedly agreed to grant him political asylum, but instead placed him on a Turkish-registered aircraft where he was promptly arrested.[24] That exercise qualified as a "surrogate" lure and capture operation (LCO) because it was carried out solely by host State authorities on behalf of a particular pursuing State, to distinguish it from other LCO varieties.[25]

Onward Delivery as or to a Cooperating Transit State. In other instances, the host State can facilitate a pursuing State to secure custody of a fugitive by directly transferring him, upon receipt, to pursuing State territory. Specifically, when an airplane or ship carrying a fugitive arrives in a State's territory, whether on a scheduled visit (including under a lure scenario) or for maintenance, refueling, or emergency stopover purposes,

[22] Bruce Zagaris, *Nepal Arrests and Returns Fugitive to New Mexico*, 30 IELR 417, 418 (2014).

[23] *See also* next sub-section, which addresses lure operations as a preliminary measure. To the extent deceptive techniques are used by a pursuing State to lure a fugitive to a cooperating third State as a final destination, that practice would qualify as a *fallback alternative to extradition*. Where the LCO is used to bring a fugitive to third State territory as a preliminary step with the ultimate aim of delivering him back to pursuing State territory, that would constitute an *intermediate rendition/operation*.

[24] *See* Melanie M. Laflin, Note, *Kidnapped Terrorists: Bringing Int'l Criminals to Justice Through Irregular Rendition and Other Quasi-Legal Options*, 26 J. Legis. 315, 321 (2000) (characterizing his boarding the Turkish aircraft as an act of trickery). For another example, *see Blankenship v. Peyton*, 295 F. Supp. 16 (W.D. Va. 1969) (describing how in November 1962, Jimmie Blankenship alleged he had been tricked into waiving his right to an extradition hearing in West Virginia, apparently after a conversation with a [host state] West Virginia judge, and consequently agreed to accompany a Virginia state officer across the border into Virginia [the pursuing state]) (municipal case example).

[25] The other types, as defined in Chapter 1.h, are unilateral, consensual, and joint. As the lawfulness analysis of LCOs is essentially uniform, regardless of type, it will be presented altogether in Chapter 12.c.i.

the (new/temporary) host State has been known to exercise its jurisdiction to place him on another vessel bound for pursuing State territory.

For instance, in February 1977, after an undercover DEA agent induced securities violation convict and prison escapee Anthony DiLorenzo to fly to Panama City, he was held there for a week before Panamanian officials placed him on an aircraft headed to Miami.[26] Likewise, in June 1981, after former CIA agent Edwin Wilson, who had been charged with illegal arms shipments to Libya, was lured out of Libya to the Democratic Republic (D.R.), upon his arrival at the airport, local police detained him on the pretext that his customs papers were not in order and then proceeded to board him on a U.S. aircraft to New York, during which flight a U.S. marshal arrested him.[27] In another example, in November 1973, after being lured from Argentina to Bolivia by a DEA informant, Julio Lujan, an Argentine pilot charged with heroin trafficking, was shortly thereafter placed on an aircraft bound for the United States without ever having been charged under Bolivian law.[28]

Sometimes, the host State attempts to effect a fugitive's transfer to a pursuing State via a cooperating third State, that is, one willing to extradite, deport, or otherwise forward on the fugitive to that pursuing State once he reaches the cooperating third State's territory. In this type of operation, the initial host State sets the two-stage travel arrangements in motion rather than serving as the intermediate-cum-host State that receives the fugitive after the first stage of travel and then forwards him on to pursuing State territory, as discussed above.

For example, in the 1920s, a Hungarian national accused of embezzlement fled from Hungary to Egypt, where, absent an extradition treaty between the two States, the Hungarian Consul in Cairo requested the Egyptian police to seize the accused in Alexandria and transport him to Trieste, Italy, from where he could be extradited back to Budapest pursuant to an Hungary-Italy Extradition Treaty.[29]

Similarly, in July 1993, after completing a lengthy criminal sentence in Malta for an unrelated crime, Omar Mohammod Ali Rezaq, who had

[26] *Di Lorenzo v. United States*, 496 F. Supp. 79 (S.D.N.Y. 1980).

[27] *United States v. Wilson*, 565 F. Supp. 1416, 1421–22 (S.D.N.Y. 1983), *aff'd*, 750 F.2d 7 (2d Cir. 1984).

[28] *United States ex rel. Lujan v. Gengler*, 510 F.2d 62 (2d Cir. 1975), *cert. denied*, 421 U.S. 1001 (1975).

[29] *In re Károly R.*, No. B XXX, 2138/1925, Royal Hungarian Crim. Ct. at Budapest, Jan. 26, 1928, *reprinted in* [1927–28] 4 Ann. Dig. Pub. Int'l L. Cases 345, 345 (No. 236) (A.D. McNair & H. Lauterpacht eds. 1931).

murdered a U.S. national in the course of an airplane hijacking in 1985, fled to Ghana. The FBI arranged with Ghanian law enforcement authorities to have him shipped to Nigeria, as that State was willing to cooperate in returning him to the United States under cover of a "political upheaval."[30] In another example, Italian law enforcement authorities requested the arrest of D.R. permanent resident and fraud indictee Camillo Caltagirone by their D.R. counterparts, which put him on a plane headed for Spain, where, at the Italians' behest, Spanish officials then routed him on another plane to Italy.[31]

Undertaking a Joint SDO or Accepting a Pursuing State's Operational Support. By contrast with the types of independently executed measures described above, in many instances, host State authorities may choose to engage in a joint SDO or otherwise allow their pursuing State counterparts (or agents) to provide material, on-the-ground operational support with the aim of capturing and transferring a fugitive to a pursuing State's territory (or to one of its facilities or flagged vessels). Such exercises are labeled herein joint seizure and delivery operations (SDOs) to distinguish them from the unilateral, surrogate, or consensual varieties outlined in Chapter 1.i.

For example, in early 1988, "DEA and U.S. Marshal's Service agents worked discreetly with selected Honduran officials to devise a plan"[32] whereby they could quickly seize and remove from Tegucigalpa, Honduras, Juan Ramón Matta-Ballesteros, "a cocaine chemist and intermediary in the Medellin cartel, [who] was wanted, among other things, for ordering [DEA Agent Enrique] Camareno's murder, but who was shielded not only by Honduras' Constitution that prohibited the extradition of its nationals but also by powerful allies in the government."[33] In April 1988, an "elite force" of sixty Honduran military police (known as the Cobras) seized Matta-Ballesteros when he returned to his home one morning and delivered him to U.S. marshals, who then handcuffed and hooded him and forced him into a Land Cruiser van driven by a U.S. marshal and was taken to the

[30] Kash, *supra* n.21, at 141.

[31] M. Cherif Bassiouni, International Extradition: United States Law and Practice 286 (6th ed. 2014).

[32] Nadelmann, Cops, *supra* n.8, at 448.

[33] Christopher H. Pyle, Extradition, Politics, and Human Rights 282 (2001) (adding that the "DEA had tried several times before without success to kidnap [Matta-Ballesteros] before turning to the Honduran military for help").

airport "while two Honduran soldiers with stun guns guarded the prisoner."[34]

Similarly, in February 1995, FBI agents and State Department Diplomatic Security officers, working discretely together with Pakistani officials, arrested Ramzi Ahmed Yousef, who was suspected of involvement in the 1993 New York City World Trade Center bombing, and then the Pakistani officials turned him over to U.S. agents in Islamabad and he was transported to the United States the following day.[35] In November 1985, the DEA, working in concert with Guatemalan non-uniformed security officers, seized Angel John Zabeneh, a Belizean who had traveled to Guatemala City to pick up goods for his family's fruit plantation. He was strip-searched, placed in a room in the airport overnight, and then put on an aircraft headed for Houston, where he was formally arrested on marijuana smuggling charges, despite the existence of a U.S.-Belize Extradition Treaty.[36]

ii Host State Acquiescence

Apart from active participation (whether related to the investigation, seizure/arrest, or transfer of a fugitive), the other major way in which the host State can assist a pursuing State to secure a fugitive through informal law enforcement cooperation is by consenting or

[34] *Id. See also Matta-Ballesteros ex rel. Stolar v. Henman*, 697 F. Supp. 1040, 1042 (S.D. Ill. 1988) (adding how Matta-Ballesteros' "van was surrounded by many military men with weapons in front of his home after returning from a visit to his lawyer" and how "among those present at his house were some Americans in civilian clothing"), *aff'd*, 896 F.2d 255 (7th Cir.), *cert. denied*, 498 U.S. 878 (1990). The United States first tried to fly him to the D.R. but he was turned away because he lacked a passport, so U.S. authorities placed him on a commercial U.S. plane bound for Puerto Rico, at which point he was taken into U.S. custody. Bill McAllister, "Trap Set as Honduran Suspect Jogged; Americans Joined Raid at Home of Reputed Drug Czar, Lawyer Says," *Wash. Post*, Apr. 7, 1988, at A8. In another such case, "U.S. and Mexican officials working together forcibly seized and ejected [Campbell] from Mexico into the custody of a U.S. Marshal," after Campbell had jumped bail. *Ex parte Campbell*, 1 F. Supp. 899 (S.D. Tex. 1932).

[35] Laflin, *supra* n.24, at 326. Typically, such operations are undertaken in the hope that they will not be publicly disclosed due to political sensitivities. *See id.* (noting that Pakistan did not want to publicize the fact that it had contributed to suspected terrorist Ramzi Ahmed Yousef's rendition to the United States).

[36] Jim Schachter, "Long Arm of Law Bends the Rules," *L.A. Times*, July 17, 1986, at 4. It is not clear whether this was a cooperative operation between States' law enforcement agencies or a unilateral operation in which Guatemalan agents working in their private capacity were engaged to assist.

acquiescing[37] (often discretely) to law enforcement activities to be undertaken by the pursuing State within host State territory. Sometimes host State law enforcement officers will provide minimal logistical support or other backstopping but the thrust of the operation under this approach is carried out by pursuing State officials or agents and, to the extent their operation succeeds, they maintain physical custody of the fugitive from the moment he is caught. In any event, such consent or affirmation must be made with foreknowledge; otherwise, the operation would properly constitute a *unilateral* measure (*see* Chapter 12). Such exercises are referred to herein as *consensual* renditions, as opposed to joint, surrogate, or unilateral ones.

Such consent is typically signaled by "a wink and a nod" or other form of informal agreement[38] rather than by any kind of diplomatic or formal correspondence. The point is to allow the activity to occur within host State territory without drawing attention to such consent or so that any host State acquiescence has plausible deniability, as there are often countervailing domestic, regional, or international political pressures to the alternatives of extradition or prosecution.[39] Such acquiescence means that the host State does not interfere with the planned operation either before or during its execution, but the host State often will feel compelled to repudiate or protest the operation *ex post facto* to the extent the operation is made public in order to "save face" with the relevant political constituencies.[40]

[37] *See* Ian C. MacGibbon, *The Scope of Acquiescence in Int'l Law*, 31 B.Y.B.I.L. 143, 182 (1954) ("Acquiescence is equivalent to tacit or implied consent. It takes the form of silence or absence of protest in circumstances which, according to the practice of States and the weight of authority, demand a positive reaction in order to preserve a right ... Acquiescence may furnish an indication of an intention to abandon a right previously enjoyed or a claim previously asserted.").

[38] *See* Bruce Zagaris, *U.S. Tries Extraordinary Rendition in Libya and Somalia with Mixed Results*, 29 IELR 439, 442 (2013) (discussing the U.S. commando seizure of Abu Anas al-Libi, an alleged al-Qaida operative, in October 2013 in Libya in which U.S. Secretary of State John Kerry acknowledged that the Libyan Government was aware of the operation).

[39] *See* Michael John Garcia, *Renditions: Constraints Imposed by Laws on Torture*, C.R.S., Report No. 7-5700, Sept. 8, 2009 ("In some instances, a significant factor in a decision to allow rendition is a desire of the country with physical jurisdiction over the suspect to avoid any domestic political fallout or possible terrorist retaliation which may result from public extradition proceedings or domestic prosecution of the suspect.").

[40] *See* Abraham D. Sofaer, Letter to the Editor, "The Case For and against Abducting Terrorists," *N.Y. Times*, Jan. 28, 1986, at A24 (observing that extraordinary cases may arise that entail "the host nation overtly objecting but silently cooperating or acquiescing in the endeavor").

A high-profile example of the host State waiving its rights to a foreign sovereign conducting a law enforcement operation on its soil can be found in the *Kasi* case. Pakistani national Mir Aimal Kasi was responsible for murdering two CIA employees and wounding three others one morning in January 1993 outside the CIA Headquarters compound in Langley, Virginia, at an intersection while they sat in their cars waiting for the light to turn green. After an extended manhunt for the perpetrator, in June 1997, four FBI agents located and seized the perpetrator from his hotel room in Pakistan. The U.S. agents applied physical restraints, immediately took him into U.S. custody, and, while "never [leaving] his presence," confined him for two days in a Pakistani "holding facility" where they presumably interrogated him.[41] Afterward, they flew him back to the United States to face criminal charges. Although the White House was unwilling to disclose specifics regarding the operation,[42] "many believe that the United States negotiated a highly unusual diplomatic agreement with Pakistan and thus enabled U.S. agents to enter its territory and abduct the Pakistani national."[43]

An arguable variant of a consensual SDO would arise where the host State agrees that pursuing State authorities may exercise the so-called "right of hot pursuit" within its sovereign territory.[44] It is permissible

41 *Kasi v. Commw. of Virginia*, 508 S.E.2d 57, 60–61 (Va. 1998), *cert. denied*, 527 U.S. 1038 (1999).

42 While Pakistan allowed the FBI to help with the investigation on its territory, when the first public announcements were made about Kasi's arrest, neither the U.S. nor Pakistani Government made any reference to where the arrest had occurred, both "to protect the people who handed him over from possible vengeance of his kinsmen" and as a "matter of considerable political sensitivity in Muslim Pakistan to allow delivery of one of its citizens into the hands of the United States." Thomas W. Lippman, "2 Governments Cloak Details of the Capture," *Wash. Post*, June 19, 1997, at A10.

43 Kash, *supra* n.21, at 141.

44 *See* Mark Brkljacic, Note, *The Dangers of State Sponsored and Court Ratified Abduction*, 5 J. Int'l L. & Prac. 117, 129–30 (1996) (acknowledging the permissibility of seizing a fugitive through the exercise of hot pursuit). This doctrine can manifest in treaty form as well. For example, in May 2009, the United States and Canada entered into a framework agreement on integrated cross-border maritime law enforcement operations that provides, *inter alia*, for designated officers in urgent and exceptional situations to continue law enforcement operations on land adjacent to shared waterways, including to prevent "the immediate and unlawful flight of persons liable to detention or arrest." Framework Agreement on Integrated Cross-Border Maritime Law Enforcement Operations, U.S.-Canada, May 26, 2009, arts. 3(3) and 4. For an historical example, *see* Nicholas M. Poulantzas, The Right of Hot Pursuit in International Law 12–13 (2d ed. 2002) (citing the Treaty between the Free City of Danzig and Poland, Nov. 9, 1920, art. 106(1), 6 L.N.T.S. 191 (1920), which provides: "The police officers and the members of the security services are permitted in case of imminent danger to pursue fugitive

under international law for State law enforcement officials to continue their uninterrupted pursuit of an escaped convict or bail-jumping indictee,[45] while "hot on his trail" into another State's territory, whether on land or in sea or air, so long there is express agreement by the State whose territory is at issue.[46] This situation would arise, say, where pursuing State officials were closely monitoring a fugitive's movements or they received a timely intelligence tip.

While such a circumstance would not be expected to occur with any regularity,[47] and logically is not the kind of approach one can plan out in advance, it does represent one possible means of securing the physical custody of a fugitive through law enforcement consent or acquiescence. States are highly protective of their sovereign territory, so, unless an agreement has been entered into, States tend to be sensitive about others taking such liberties. For example, Kurdish and Iraqi officials have complained about Turkish ground forces chasing Kurdish separatists across the border into Iraqi territory, a practice that occurred in October 2011;[48] in August 1986, Mexico rejected a U.S. request to fly aircraft across the Mexican border when in hot pursuit of drug traffickers;[49] and in August 1974, the Canadian Government protested U.S. officials pursuing a U.S. Army deserter across the border into Canadian territory and the United States agreed to return him.[50]

offenders – immediately after the commission of a crime, or immediately after the offenders have been surprised – from their territory and up to eight kilometres within the other territory and apprehend them.") (translation provided by Poulantzas)).

45 While the doctrine likewise applies to a criminal suspect during an ongoing crime, that scenario lies outside the scope of this inquiry.

46 *See id.* at 346.

47 One example occurred in August 1999 when an anonymous caller informed the Tribal Police Department that Kenneth Lazore, a fugitive for five years since failing to report to federal prison for a gun-running offense, was present on the American side of the Akwesasne Reservation that is bisected by the U.S.-Canadian border. A police officer walked toward his truck and called out his name, prompting Lazore to flee toward the border; eventually, the officer tackled and pinned down Lazore on the Canadian side of the border, arrested him, and transported him back to the U.S. side. *United States v. Lazore*, 90 F. Supp.2d 202, 203 (N.D.N.Y. 2000). To this author's knowledge, the Canadian Government never protested this cross-border incident.

48 Sebnem Arsu, "'Hot Pursuit' of Attackers near Iraq, Turkey Vows," *IHT*, Oct. 20, 2011, at 6.

49 AP, "De la Madrid Rejects U.S. 'Hot Pursuit' by Aircraft," *L.A. Times*, Aug. 15, 1986, at 17.

50 *See* Brief for the Gov't of Canada as *Amicus Curiae* in Support of Respondent, *United States v. Alvarez-Machain, reprinted in* 31 ILM 919 (1992) and 60 U.S.L.W. 4523 (U.S. June 15, 1992) (No. 91–712) (describing the case of James Anderson who, after being identified as an Army deserter at a U.S.-Canadian border crossing ran back across the

Finally, it is possible that the host State will allow pursuing State law enforcement officers to arrest a fugitive within its sovereign territory, but then have doubts about its decision and seek to have the fugitive returned into its own custody. That scenario occurred, for example, in the 1863 *Aunis* incident in which the prefect of Genoa, Italy, requested permission from the French consul in Genoa to board a French ship lying in the Genoa harbor and apprehend five suspected fugitives. The French consul assented and the fugitives were arrested and removed from the ship. The next day, the French consul changed his mind and sought the fugitives' return, but the Italian Government refused on the ground that the arrest was effected pursuant to French consent and therefore was consistent with international law.[51]

c Lawfulness Analysis

Having reviewed the types of informal law enforcement cooperation, this study now examines various general principles and specific grounds under *international law*[52] to ascertain whether and to what extent such cooperation can be considered lawful.[53] With rare exception, the courts hearing allegations of legal violation tend to be those located in the

border into Canada, where he was pursued by U.S. officials, arrested, forcibly taken back across the border, and turned over to the FBI).

51 "State Responsibility," 2 Y.B. INT'L L. COMM'N, A/CN.4/SER.A/1979/Add.l (Part 1), U.N. Doc. A/CN.4/318 and Add.1–4 (1979), at 33–34. The Italian position comports with international law. *See also* discussion of mistaken returns in Chapter 3.c.

52 Some cases have found *domestic* legal violations in such cooperative scenarios. *See, e.g., The State (Quinn) v. Ryan, supra* n.15 (declaring that the cross-border handover of fugitives amounted to a contempt of court as it deprived the individual of his domestic constitutional right to seek *habeas corpus* relief); BEDI, *supra* n.10, at 396; 6 BRITISH DIGEST OF INT'L LAW 480–81 (Clive Parry ed. 1965) (noting a violation of municipal law when local policemen helped U.S. law enforcement agents return a fugitive from Liverpool, England, in the *Townsend* case). Notably, in such cases American courts find *no* constitutional violation under the Fourth Amendment's "search and seizure" clause on the grounds that the constitution is not construed as applying to U.S. Government actions against aliens on foreign territory or in international waters. *Kasi*, 508 S.E.2d at 63.

53 Whether or not cooperating State agents treated the fugitive outrageously during arrest, detention, or transfer is but a collateral consideration to the lawfulness of the underlying cooperative means of securing his custody. Nevertheless, sometimes a fugitive will plead such abusive treatment when challenging the court's jurisdiction or seeking relief through *habeas corpus*. For example, Juan Ramón Matta-Ballesteros claimed that during his trip to the Tegucigalpa airport, he was repeatedly shocked and burned with a "double pronged electric" and on the first leg of his flight to the United States, he was beaten on his head and shocked on his testicles and feet. *Matta-Ballesteros*, 697 F. Supp. at 1042. Despite a medical exam consistent with his claims, the U.S. federal court refused to divest itself of

pursuing State, as the nature and timing of such informal rendition operations do not generally provide the subject individual the opportunity to pursue legal recourse in the host State,[54] and few such cases reach international or regional tribunals.[55] When they do, substantively relevant multilateral conventions do not necessarily apply, as participating States may not be subject to them.[56]

i General Principles[57]

No Presumed Restriction on States' Freedom of Action. The seminal *Lotus* case[58] may be said to stand for the proposition that States may exercise their freedom of action unless a specific rule of international law prohibits as much, rather than requiring that they conform their conduct only to those actions expressly authorized under international law. The PCIJ reasoned in that case as follows:

> International law governs relations between independent States. The rules of law binding upon States therefore emanate from their own free will as expressed in conventions or by usages generally accepted as expressing

jurisdiction on the basis of his treatment, which was not deemed sufficiently egregious. *Id.* This issue is discussed more extensively in Chapter 13.a.i.

54 Indeed, it bears noting that the European Court of Justice (ECJ) recently ruled that "judicial authorities cannot refuse to execute a European arrest warrant [EAW] issued for the purposes of conducting a criminal prosecution on the ground that the requested person was not heard in the issuing Member State before that arrest warrant was issued." *In re Radu*, Case C-396/11, ECJ, Gr. Ch., ¶ 43 Jan. 29, 2013.

55 One prominent example of a regional court adjudication is the *Öcalan* case, profiled *infra*. In addition, as Dr. Rutsel Martha, a former General Counsel of INTERPOL, has observed, the *Savarkar* case before the PCA "is probably the only case where a tribunal established under international law was called upon to settle an inter-State dispute concerning police cooperation." Rutsel Silvestre J. Martha, The Legal Foundations of INTERPOL 16 (2010).

56 For example, when Illich Ramírez Sánchez (a/k/a Carlos the Jackal) claimed that he had been abducted, tied up, drugged, and hooded by the Sudanese police before being turned over to French officials who boarded him on a French military aircraft, the European Commission opined that it was not competent to assess the circumstances of his treatment by Sudan as that State is not a member party of the ECHR. *Ramirez Sánchez v. France*, Appl. No. 28780/95, Eur. Comm'n of Hum. Rts., 86 D.R. 155, June 24, 1996; Francesco de Sanctis, *The Practice of Nat'l and Int'l Courts on Transnat'l Seizure: Is a Fair Balance Between Human Rights and Accountability Possible?*, 22 Neth. Q. Hum. Rts. 529, 550 (2004).

57 Much of this discussion of general principles tracks the structure found in Martha, *supra* n.55, at 18–38.

58 *SS "Lotus"* (Fr. v. Turk.) 1927 P.C.I.J. (ser. A) No. 10 (Sept. 7, 1927), *reprinted in* Ann. Dig. Pub. Int'l L. Cases 153 (No. 98) (H. Lauterpacht ed. 1938) [hereinafter *Lotus Case*].

> principles of law and established in order to regulate the relations between these co-existing independent communities with a view to the achievement of common aims. Restrictions upon the independence of States cannot therefore be presumed.[59]

Accordingly, States at least in principle are free to operate in cooperation with one another on law enforcement matters of mutual concern so long as no international law restricts such conduct; and its corollary holds that, if one challenges that conduct, one would have to bear the burden of proof that a specific law had been violated.[60]

Flexible Form of International Agreements. As Dr. Rutsel Martha maintains: "States must be presumed to be free to choose any form they would like for establishing international agreements, unless a rule of international law prescribes otherwise. Accordingly, it is generally accepted that international law itself prescribes neither form nor procedure for the making of international undertakings."[61] He then adverts to a series of examples in which "international legal acts [have taken] the form of oral communications, a telegram, a radio announcement, a telephonic communication, a symbolic act, tacitly, joint communiqués, minutes (*procès-verbal*) of a meeting, and in modern days, of course, e-mails."[62] It is noteworthy that "[c]ooperation is virtually unregulated

[59] *Id.* at 18. The notion that international law permits what it does not prohibit was echoed by the U.S. Supreme Court in *Álvarez-Machaín*, 504 U.S. 655 (1992), to the extent that the most conspicuously pertinent convention, the U.S.-Mexico Extradition Treaty, did not expressly forbid extraterritorial seizures. Sherri L. Burr, *From Noriega to Pinochet: Is There an Int'l Moral and Legal Right to Kidnap Individuals Accused of Gross Human Rights Violations?*, 29 Denv. J. Int'l L. & Pol'y 101, 102 (2001). But note that inter-State law enforcement cooperation over the apprehension and return of a fugitive is *not* precisely comparable to one State asserting criminal jurisdiction over another State's nationals as was the case in *Lotus*, and even within that distinct and arguably more open-ended criminal jurisdictional context, in which the Court stated, "every State remains free to adopt the principles which it regards as best and most suitable," *Lotus Case, supra* n.58, at 19, the passage in which this proposition is found has been the subject of criticism and subsequent Court deviation. *See* Malcolm N. Shaw, Public International Law 301 (6th ed. 2008) (citing, *inter alia, Nottebohm Case* (Liech. v Guat.), Second Phase, Judgment [1955] I.C.J. Rep. 4 (Apr. 6)).

[60] Martha, *supra* n.55, at 19.

[61] *Id.* at 20 (citing Arnold McNair, The Law of Treaties 6 (1961)).

[62] *Id.* (citations omitted). *Cf. Case Concerning the Temple of Preah Vihear* (Camb. v. Thai.), Merits [1962] I.C.J. Rep. 15, 35 (June 15) (finding the inter-State frontier line as set forth by a stand-alone map relied upon by Thailand and Cambodia, although later confirmed to be erroneous, as determinative of the basis for their understood border, trumping the watershed line contained in a 1904 bilateral treaty).

by international convention."[63] Therefore, an exchange of notes or other less formal (even oral) type of agreement between the respective law enforcement officials of two cooperating States would not itself appear to invalidate the transfer of a fugitive's custody between them.

Attribution of Acts by a Domestic Police Officer to a State. It has been contended, including by France in the *Savarkar* case, that the acts of domestic police officers performing their official law enforcement duties on the international scene cannot be imputed to their States, but rather that when they act in a bilateral cooperation context, they act in their personal capacity. There is little merit to this argument, as the police officer is unequivocally an agent of the State when carrying out his official functions.[64] Indeed, the Permanent Court of Arbitration (PCA) found that the French *gendarmerie* was acting on behalf of France in *Savarkar*, and the State – not the individual officers – consistently has been held accountable based on its officer's actions.[65] Therefore, any agreement reached between individual police officers operating under the color of law is attributable to the States on whose behalf they acted.

Non-exclusivity of International Cooperation Arrangements. Some legal authorities maintain that if an extradition treaty exists between two States, no alternative means of transferring the custody of a fugitive can lawfully occur, as the specifically agreed terms and conditions of extradition set forth the exclusive set of possibilities.[66] But as Dr. Martha

[63] Edmund S. McAlister, Note, *The Hydraulic Pressure of Vengeance:* United States v. Alvarez-Machain *and the Case for a Justifiable Abduction*, 43 DePaul L. Rev. 449, 474 (1994).

[64] Even *ultra vires* acts by a State officer are attributable to the State on whose behalf he has acted. ILC, *Responsibility of States for Int'lly Wrongful Acts with Commentaries* (Draft), Dec. 12, 2001, art. 7, Annex to UNGA Res. 56/83, U.N. GAOR, 56th Sess., Supp. No. 10, at 43, U.N. Doc. A/56/10 (2001) [hereinafter ILC, *State Responsibility*] ("The conduct of an organ of a State or of a person or entity empowered to exercise elements of the governmental authority shall be considered an act of the State under international law if the organ, person or entity acts in that capacity, *even if it exceeds its authority or contravenes instructions.*") (emphasis supplied).

[65] Martha, *supra* n.55, at 22 & nn.29–30 (citing *Suárez de Guerrero v. Colombia*, Commc'n No. R.11/45, U.N. Doc. A/37/40, Supp. No. 40 at 137, Feb. 5, 1979 and *Church of Scientology in the Netherlands Foundation et al. v. (1) Herold and (2) Heinrich Bauer Verlag*, Dist. Ct. of Amsterdam, Neth., June 4, 1980, NJ 1981 No. 501).

[66] *See generally* Michael Abbell, *The Need for U.S. Legislation to Curb State-Sponsored Kidnapping, in* The Alleged Transnational Criminal: The Second Biennial International Criminal Law Seminar 89 (Richard D. Atkins ed. 1993) (quoting author's congressional testimony on July 29, 1992) ("It cannot be emphasized too strongly that treaties are not negotiated in a vacuum. They are negotiated in the context of generally accepted principles and tenets of international law ... One of the most

explains, "in the absence of any mandatory rule of international law or a previous legal undertaking . . . it is for each State to determine in every individual case whether to assist [on law enforcement matters], and if so, on the nature of that assistance."[67] This position was upheld by the U.S. Supreme Court in the *Álvarez-Machaín* case:

> [T]o imply from the terms of this [U.S.-Mexico Extradition Treaty] that it prohibits obtaining the presence of an individual by means outside of the procedures the Treaty establishes requires a much larger inferential leap, with only the most general of international law principles to support it.[68]

As Dr. Martha maintains, "[w]hat was true in 1910 in the case of Savarkar about the need for speedy, flexible and operationally oriented arrangements is still valid and perhaps even more relevant today."[69] Furthermore, there is ample experience historically with such international law enforcement cooperation in the face of extradition treaties that States parties ought to be able to anticipate and foreclose such operations, as desired, via negotiated text.

Wrongfulness Precluded by Voluntariness, Acquiescence, or Consent. When States mutually choose to deviate from the procedures set forth in a bilateral extradition treaty and voluntarily coordinate on the transfer of a fugitive from one State to the other, international law recognizes no violation of either State's rights.[70] Like voluntariness, acquiescence gives rise to the same vitiation of any potential unlawfulness, as expressed by the famous Harvard Research in International Law report of the mid-1930s:

> It only remains to be emphasized that by no means every irregularity in the recovery of a fugitive from criminal justice is a "recourse to measures in violation of international law or international convention." If the State in which the fugitive is found acquiesces or agrees, through its officers or

fundamental of those principles ... is that every nation must respect the territorial integrity of every other nation with which it is at peace.").

67 Martha, *supra* n.55, at 24.

68 *Álvarez-Machaín*, 504 U.S. at 669. Other U.S. federal and state courts have spoken with the same voice. *E.g., Ex parte Campbell*, 1 F. Supp. 899; *Kasi*, 508 S.E.2d at 60–61. *Accord* John M. Rogers, International Law and United States Law 180–81 (1999).

69 Martha, *supra* n.55, at 25 (citing by way of example the advent of cybercrimes).

70 *See* Kathryn Selleck, Note, *Jurisdiction after Int'l Kidnapping: A Comparative Study*, 8 B.C. Int'l & Comp. L. Rev. 237, 255 (1985) (citing *Geldof v. Meulemeester & Steffen*, Ct. of Cassation, Belg., Feb. 20, 1961, [1961] *Pasicrise belge* 674 [French text], *reprinted in* 31 ILR 385 (E. Lauterpacht ed. 1966)).

> agents, to a surrender accomplished even in the most informal and expeditious way, there is no element of illegality.[71]

The same principle applies to consent: "Valid consent by a State to the commission of a given act by another State precludes the wrongfulness of the act in relation to the former State to the extent that the act remains within the limits of that consent."[72] It follows, then, that when States, through their officials acting on their behalf, agree to cooperate, or when the host State consents or acquiesces to an informal arrangement to effect a fugitive's transfer to pursuing State custody or control, international law poses no principled objection.

Due Diligence is Expected of the Cooperating States. Consistent with fundamental human rights principles, cooperation between the host and pursuing States (assuming their respective judiciaries are functional) should be based on a reasonable degree of pre-delivery scrutiny, such that any arrest or transfer of the fugitive has occurred only after: (i) the host State has duly considered whether a particular pursuing State has a legitimate basis for his requested prosecution or punishment, that his rights to a fair trial and other procedural protections will be honored upon delivery, and that no genuine risk of *refoulement*[73] will attend the transfer;[74] *and* (ii) a pursuing State has properly evaluated whether the host State, in carrying out the transfer, may be in violation of certain human rights obligations it owes the fugitive, as a pursuing State otherwise could be derivatively liable for facilitating his transfer.[75] Apart from an obligation to assess any

[71] Harvard Research in Int'l Law, "Comment to Article 16 to Draft Extradition Treaty," 29 AJIL 631 (Supp. 1935) (interior citations omitted). "There may be, however, some precedent in international law for the argument that complicity of asylum [host] state officials in the abduction robs the asylum [host] state's protest of its import under international law." DoJ, *Extraterritorial Apprehension by the Federal Bureau of Investigation*, 4B Op. Off. Legal Counsel 543, 549.

[72] ILC, *State Responsibility, supra* n.64, art. 20. This includes the commission of sovereign acts of a State or its agents in the territory of another State, including the arrest of a fugitive. S.P. Jagota, *State Responsibility: Circumstances Precluding Wrongfulness*, 16 Neth. Y.B. Int'l L. 249, 255 (1985).

[73] Margaret L. Satterthwaite, *The Legal Regime Governing Transfer of Persons in the Fight against Terrorism*, N.Y.U. Public Law and Legal Theory Working Papers, Paper 192, May 1, 2010, at 20 (discussing the various applications of this principle to include: "torture or ill-treatment; persecution; enforced disappearance; and arbitrary deprivation of life").

[74] *Id.* at 16.

[75] *Id.* (citing to ILC, *State Responsibility, supra* n.64, art. 16: "A State which aids or assists another State in the commission of an internationally wrongful act by the latter is internationally responsible for doing so if (a) That State does so with knowledge of the circumstances of the internationally wrongful act . . .").

refoulement concerns, however, this standard is premised on soft law, and therefore any meaningful enforceability is far from assured.

ii Specific Grounds

Violation of Territorial Sovereignty. "It is a rule of international law that a State must not perform acts of sovereignty on the territory of another State. Hence the arrest of a fugitive criminal by the officials of one State in the territory of another is *prima facie* a breach of international law. But if the State of asylum [the host State] *acquiesces in the arrest*, as when officials of that State participate in the irregular apprehension, there is no breach of international law."[76] U.S. Attorney General Eric Holder, who served under President Barack Obama, echoed this principle when he remarked: "[T]he use of force in foreign territory would be consistent with ... international legal principles if conducted, for example, with the consent of the nation involved."[77]

Ordinarily, then, a cooperative law enforcement activity is not regarded as a violation of territorial sovereignty, as the cooperating host State is viewed as voluntarily handing over the fugitive. This perspective is reinforced by the fact that the host State rarely objects to the engagement of pursuing State agents on its territory – and indeed often is not positioned to do so even if it wished[78] – and thus it is justified under

[76] Paul O'Higgins, *Unlawful Seizure and Irregular Extradition*, 36 B.Y.B.I.L. 279, 280 (1960) (emphasis supplied). *Accord* Cardozo, *supra* n.1, at 132 ("One consistent thread runs through ... all [abduction cases]: an abduction on foreign soil by officers of another government is a violation of international law, unless the government in control of the asylum country expressly or impliedly gives its consent."); American Law Inst., RESTATEMENT (THIRD) OF THE FOREIGN RELATIONS LAW OF THE UNITED STATES, May 14, 1986 (1987), § 432(2) ("A state's law enforcement officers may exercise their functions in the territory of another state only with the consent of the other state, given by officials authorized to do so."); Mary Alice Kovac, *Apprehension of War Crimes Indictees: Should the U.N. Outsource Private Actors to Catch Them?*, 51 CATH. U. L. REV. 619, 642 n.153 (2002) ("if a competent asylum [host] state official partakes in the arrest, even if this arrest is illegal under asylum [host] state law, this involvement is sufficient to constitute consent and to preclude any assertion of responsibility by the asylum [host] state"). *See also* discussion of territorial sovereignty in Chapter 12.c.ii.

[77] Eric Holder, Remarks by U.S. Att'y Gen. on National Security Law, NWU School of Law, Chicago, Mar. 5, 2012, *available at* www.justice.gov/opa/speech/attorney-general-eric-holder-speaks-northwestern-university-school-law (last visited on May 24, 2016).

[78] *See* Terry Richard Kane, *Prosecuting Int'l Terrorists in United States Courts: Gaining the Jurisdictional Threshold*, 12 YALE J. INT'L L. 294, 333 (1987) (noting that evident collaboration of host State police "deprive[s]" that State "of any basis for complaint, even if it had wanted to raise an objection.").

international law as a case of sovereign consent. For example, after news broke of the transfer into U.S. custody of Honduran national Juan Ramón Matta-Ballesteros, who was locally popular, a mob gathered around and set fire to the U.S. Embassy in Tegucigalpa and a few congressmen issued a disapproving statement, but neither the president, the foreign ministry, nor the legislature of Honduras officially protested, thereby strongly suggesting that the Honduran Government had in fact fully cooperated with U.S. law enforcement officers.[79]

To the extent that host State agents physically transfer a fugitive to a pursuing State's registered aircraft sitting in an international zone of a host State airport, as was the case in the *Öcalan* case, that, too, has been found to be permissible, as the aircraft would be subject to the jurisdiction of the State of the flagged aircraft, rather than to the host State.[80] In other cases, the question of a territorial breach is dismissed as one better left to governments to resolve through diplomacy rather than for courts to rule on as a legal matter.[81] At bottom, this author is not aware of a single case in which an international, regional, or domestic tribunal has ruled that such informal bilateral cooperation has been deemed a violation of territorial sovereignty.

Arbitrary Arrest and Detention. The ICCPR provides that: "No one shall be subjected to arbitrary arrest or detention. No one shall be deprived of his liberty except on such grounds and in accordance with such procedure as are established by law."[82] In evaluating a claimed violation of this provision, the Human Rights Committee (HRC) examines whether there were any procedural irregularities found in the application of domestic law. Notably, the HRC found that a joint operation between the Uruguayan police and DEA agents to arrest Colombian national Edgar A. Cañón Garcia on drug trafficking charges from a hotel lobby in Uruguay and return him to the United States in July 1987 violated Article 9(1).

The HRC observed that Garcia's arrest and detention had been "arbitrary," given the "administrative and procedural irregularities" conceded by the host State government, which led to the fugitive's maltreatment (*e.g.*, he was held locked to a table and chair overnight without even

[79] Nadelmann, Cops, *supra* n.8, at 448.

[80] *Öcalan v. Turkey (Merits)*, Appl. No. 46221/99, Gr. Ch., 41 EHRR 45, May 12, 2005 [hereinafter *Öcalan Case*].

[81] *E.g., Ex parte López*, 6 F. Supp. at 344.

[82] Int'l Covenant on Civil and Political Rights (ICCPR), Dec. 16, 1966, art. 9(1), UNGA Res. 2200, U.N. GAOR, 21st Sess., Supp. No. 21, U.N. Doc. A/6316 (1967).

a glass of water) and was denied requests for access to an attorney or the Colombian consulate after his *Miranda* rights were read to him (which expressly include the right to an attorney).[83] The host State also could be found liable under international treaty law for holding a fugitive under administrative detention for an unreasonably long period prior to the delivery itself.[84]

In such informal cooperation cases, however, the fugitive almost never receives any meaningful procedural due process by the host State, as he is transferred away quickly. This would seem to raise a potential claim that such fundamental rights were violated, but such allegations lodged before *pursuing* State courts in any case generally fall on deaf ears. Some courts deem it inappropriate to probe into the domestic matters of other States, while other courts simply see any such failure to provide adequate domestic procedural safeguards as outside their purview. For example, in *Wentz v. United States*, the U.S. Court of Appeals for the Ninth Circuit expressed no concern when an American national alleged that he had been detained by Mexican authorities in Mexico City and denied access to an attorney and any court proceedings there before being transferred to the United States.[85]

The *Wentz* case is probably more representative than the *Cañón Garcia* case in terms of how such claims tend to be adjudicated. Had Ecuador not overreached and, instead, acted more faithfully with its own "established law" in *Cañón Garcia*, no violation of Article 9 likely would have been found. The violation appears to have been a function much more of excessive treatment under the circumstances than a repudiation of informal law enforcement cooperation as an extradition alternative itself.

Bribery. Informal law enforcement cooperation often can implicate bribery. Where law enforcement agents of a pursuing State pay bribes to their host State counterparts to win their assistance in securing the custody, directly or indirectly, of a wanted fugitive, there appears to be no *international* legal prohibition for such conduct, although domestic law might well proscribe it. Perhaps the closest applicable international

[83] *Cañón Garcia v. Ecuador*, Commc'n No. 319/1988, U.N. Doc. CCPR/C/43/D/319/1988, ¶¶ 1, 2.2, 2.4, 4.1, 6.1, Nov. 5, 1991.

[84] *See* Satterthwaite, *supra* n.73, at 19 & n.97 ("Regarding the permissible duration of detention prior to transfer, although there is not a great deal of jurisprudence on the issue, existing norms suggest that an individual can only be held for a reasonable period needed to effect the transfer; detention in excess of this period or when transfer becomes impossible becomes arbitrary.") (citing U.N. and ECtHR sources).

[85] 244 F.2d 172, 176 (9th Cir.), *cert. denied*, 355 U.S. 806 (1957).

authority is the OECD's Convention on Combating Bribery of Foreign Public Officials in International Business Transactions,[86] but that treaty's express scope would not encompass bribes made in connection with State-to-State law enforcement cooperation.[87] The host State, however, might collaterally use evidence of the bribery of individuals to contend on a *prima facie* basis that the host State government itself was not aware of an operation, and therefore had not positively sanctioned its execution, although testimonial evidence might prove otherwise.

Vicarious Liability. One incidental circumstance that can arise out of informal law enforcement cooperation is that host State police might have sole custody of the fugitive for a period of time before he is transferred to pursuing State authorities. In such a case, should the fugitive suffer maltreatment while in such custody, the fugitive is unlikely to prevail under a claim of vicarious liability against the pursuing State officials or their agents for having "created the opportunity" for such physical abuse. This notion was tested in *Di Lorenzo v. United States*, when although a DEA agent induced Anthony DiLorenzo to fly to Panama City and arranged for his arrest by Panamanian authorities, any maltreatment during his seven days in Panamanian custody prior to his deportation to the United States could not be imputed to the United States for merely having set this plan in motion.[88]

Others. In addition, a number of international legal violations potentially could be found in connection with informal law enforcement cooperation, most notably including:

- *disguised extradition*, say, to the extent that a tribunal concluded that the pursuing and host States had colluded in order to circumvent extradition and the application of its attendant procedural protections;[89]
- *noncompliance with an extradition treaty obligation*, at least for those courts that interpret bilateral extradition treaties as setting forth the

86 OECD Conv. on Combating Bribery of Foreign Public Officials in Int'l Business Transactions, Dec. 18, 1997, *reprinted in* 37 ILM 1.

87 *Id.*, art. 1(1) (bribery must be for the purpose of "obtain[ing] or retain[ing] business or other improper advantage in the conduct of international business.").

88 *Di Lorenzo*, 496 F. Supp. 79.

89 *E.g.*, *Bennett, Petitioner*, High Ct., Scot. [1994] SCCR 902, [1995] S.L.T. 510; *R. v. Hartley*, Ct. of App., N.Z. (Wellington), Aug. 5, 1977, [1978] 2 NZLR 199 (finding that New Zealand police had sought to bypass extradition procedures by telephoning their Melbourne (Australia) counterparts to ask if a fugitive (Bennett – no relationship to the Scottish case of the same name cited above) could be placed on the next flight to New Zealand, notwithstanding the absence of a warrant for his extradition).

full universe of means available for the transfer of fugitives between them;

- *lack of security of the person*, as found in such international instruments as the ICCPR (Article 3) and the Universal Declaration of Human Rights (UDHR) (Article 3) in the sense that the State has an obligation to protect the physical integrity of its citizens from abuse by its official authorities; and
- *the opportunity to challenge in advance a transfer to pursuing State territory* on *non-refoulement* grounds before an "independent decision-maker with the power to suspend the transfer during the pendency of review"[90] and to insist on certain core requirements in the event diplomatic assurances are provided to justify the transfer.[91]

Given the paucity of court judgments to date regarding fugitive transfers via informal law enforcement cooperation, however, it is difficult to draw any meaningful generalized conclusions about this body of law. To provide some additional insight, a concentrated look at one celebrated case can be instructive.

iii Case Study: Öcalan v. Turkey[92]

Abdullah Öcalan is a Turkish national and former leader of the Kurdistan Workers' Party (PKK). The PKK's original objective was to create an independent Kurdish State but it later sought co-existence for Kurds as a free people within Turkey. To pursue its objectives, beginning in 1978, the PKK wrought violence in Turkey through thousands of armed attacks, kidnappings, and targeted bombings. As a result, Turkey viewed Öcalan as a terrorist, charging him with trying to undermine the territorial integrity of Turkey and perpetrate serious crimes. Turkey's courts issued multiple warrants for his arrest and secured an INTERPOL Red

[90] Satterthwaite, *supra* n.73, at 28–29 (citing CAT, ICCPR, and ECtHR sources).

[91] *Id.* at 29-31 (referencing in particular the CAT standard: "(1) Assurances must be obtained using 'clear' and established procedures; (2) Assurances must be subject to judicial review; and (3) Assurances must be followed by effective post-return monitoring of the treatment of the individual returned subject to assurances.") (citations omitted).

[92] Sources for this section include, *inter alia, Öcalan Case, supra* n.80; de Sanctis, *supra* n.56, at 550–51; ILIAS BANTEKAS & SUSAN NASH, INTERNATIONAL CRIMINAL LAW 221–22 (2d ed. 2003); and ALUN JONES & ANAND DOOBAY, JONES AND DOOBAY ON EXTRADITION AND MUTUAL ASSISTANCE 99–100 (2005). This case study arguably also could fall within the scope of a removal operation (*see* Chapter 10.c.i), as Öcalan had violated Kenya's immigration law, but as it more fundamentally implicates informal law enforcement cooperation, it has been selected for discussion in the present chapter.

Notice. For many years, he resided in Syria, but after he was expelled in October 1998, he spent the next few months in search of a place to live; he unsuccessfully sought refuge in Greece (twice), Russia (twice), and Italy.

Eventually, on February 2, 1999, he arrived at the airport in Nairobi, Kenya, most likely accompanied by Greek security service agents, and was greeted by Greek Embassy officials and put up at the Greek Ambassador's home. The Kenyan Ministry of Foreign Affairs later announced that it had learned of Öcalan's secret arrival in which he had not gone through passport control while being escorted by Greek officials. Upset about the Greek Ambassador's role, the security risk he had imposed upon Kenya, and his initial denials that the subject individual was in fact Öcalan, the Kenyans sought the Ambassador's immediate recall.

A day before the recall request, the Kenyan Minister of Foreign Affairs had informed the Greek Ambassador that Öcalan was free to leave Kenya to the destination of his choice and that the Netherlands had agreed to admit him. On February 15, 1999, Kenyan officials retrieved Öcalan from the Greek Embassy to take him to the airport but would not allow the Greek Ambassador to join him. The Kenyan official driving the car deviated from the convoy and took Öcalan to the airport's international zone where a Turkish-registered aircraft together with Turkish officials were waiting for him. Upon boarding the aircraft, he was arrested and then flown to Turkey, where he was prosecuted and sentenced. Kenya and Turkey had misled Öcalan and the Greek Embassy.

After exhausting domestic remedies for his claimed mistreatment in Turkey, Öcalan engaged the European Court of Human Rights, which issued a judgment in March 2003. His principal claims, apart from denying that he was a terrorist, included: (i) the arrest procedures did not comply with international or national standards and as a result he was unlawfully denied his liberty and security of person under Article 5(1) of the ECHR; (ii) Turkish officials had no jurisdiction to operate abroad and had violated Kenya's territorial sovereignty; and (iii) he had not been made subject to extradition proceedings and therefore had been denied all substantive and procedural protections that ordinarily accompany such a transfer.

Turkey responded by arguing that: (i) Öcalan had been arrested and detained according to prescribed legal procedure, including by properly issued arrest warrants; (ii) Turkish officials had not breached Kenya's sovereignty, as Öcalan had been arrested by Kenyan authorities and handed over to Turkish officials cooperatively on non-Kenyan territory; and (iii) no extradition treaty existed between Kenya and Turkey and it was not "disguised extradition" because Kenya simply transferred him into their custody as he had been found to have entered Kenya illegally with false identity papers.

The ECtHR found no violation. It reasoned that Öcalan's arrest had been valid. Not only had Turkish officials complied with domestic criminal procedure, acting on seven warrants for Öcalan's arrest and an INTERPOL Red Notice, but he had been arrested by Turkish officials on a Turkish-registered aircraft while sitting in an international zone of the Nairobi airport and therefore was clearly within Turkish jurisdiction for purposes of Article 1 of the ECHR. In addition, the Court found that the Kenyans had decided on their own volition to hand over Öcalan to the Turks and that the transfer of his custody was therefore cooperative; significantly, it did not lead to any claims for redress or return by the Kenyans or any erosion of Kenyan-Turkish diplomatic relations, and so there was no ground for addressing a violation of territorial sovereignty.

In addition, the complainant was unable to show that the Turkish authorities had acted in a manner inconsistent with Kenya's sovereignty. Moreover, the Court noted that the ECHR does not prohibit States from cooperating to remove fugitive offenders so long as the cooperative procedures employed do not violate any rights specifically protected by the Convention, and "disguised extradition" for the purpose of removal, as here, did not qualify as such a violation.[93] Finally, because there was no extradition treaty in effect, one could not contend that its terms and conditions had not been followed.

Significantly, there are two key factors that, had either been different, may have led to the opposite court judgment. First, as it turns out, the Kenyan authorities were conveniently able to rely on their immigration laws to justify Öcalan's removal, but had he not entered Kenyan territory unlawfully, there is a chance the Court would have found his handover to the Turkish authorities impermissible. Second, had the Turks been less cautious about maintaining their registered aircraft in the airport's international zone or not patiently waited for Öcalan to be brought into the plane (*i.e.*, into Turkish constructive territory) but rather met him in the

[93] As characterized by N.Y.U. Law Professor Margaret Satterthwaite, "the European Court of Human Rights has accepted informal transfers in the counter-terrorism context when they are carried out with the consent of the host state and in conformity with the transferring state's domestic law." Satterthwaite, *supra* n.73, at 14.

airport itself, the Court might have been less inclined to treat this transfer as lawful. In sum, courts tend to take a large number of factors into account in determining whether or not to find an instance of informal law enforcement cooperation lawful – and the specific circumstances matter.

* * * * *

This chapter has explored the second type of full-scale alternative to extradition specifically related to informal law enforcement cooperation. We now turn to the third, final, and most controversial of these alternatives, which addresses unilateral measures a pursuing State can take to obtain the custody of a fugitive abroad.

12

Alternative III

Unilateral Measures

This chapter focuses on the final type of full-scale alternative to extradition: unilateral measures. Chapters 10 and 11 examined various approaches to retrieving fugitives by way of some form of involvement or acquiescence on the part of host State officials or their agents. This chapter, by contrast, explores means undertaken exclusively by pursuing State officials or agents without the knowledge, let alone the participation or consent, of the host State, in what many would label "self-help" measures. The chapter looks first at the nature, scope, and impetus behind such unilateral approaches, then describes and assesses the various applications, and finally considers the lawfulness of each of those options.

a Nature, Scope, and Impetus

The key ingredient comprising a "unilateral measure," in addition, of course, to it being for the purpose of prosecution or punishment,[1] is that it must be only pursuing State officials or agents involved in its execution. There can be no host State officials or agents – at least in their official capacity – participating in, cooperating with, or consenting to, the operation, nor can there be private volunteers, unless acting as agents of the pursuing State.[2] While generally such measures have an extraterritorial

[1] This point is stressed because, at times, extraterritorial seizures occur that are unrelated to criminal law enforcement. For example, in July 1952, Dr. Walter Linse, director of the Economic Department of the Investigation Committee of Free Jurists, whose job was "to collect economic information from underground workers throughout East Germany, was kidnapped from his home in West Berlin and taken into the Soviet Zone. He was not a wanted criminal but rather an important source of intelligence." *See* "Anti-Red Abducted After Gun Battle in Western Berlin," *N.Y. Times*, July 9, 1952, at 1.

[2] To the extent there is any host State complicity, such an operation would be more properly classified under the label of informal law enforcement cooperation (*see* Chapter 11), and to the extent private volunteers alone were engaged, it would qualify as a "silver platter" scenario (*see* Chapter 3.b).

dimension and entail some form of overseas physical incapacitation of the fugitive, whether characterized as a seizure, capture, or arrest, these are not required features.

Four varieties of unilateral measures can be discerned: (i) negotiations with the fugitive for his return;[3] (ii) unilateral lure and capture operations (LCOs),[4] (iii) unilateral seizure and delivery operations (SDOs) (whether staged during peacetime or wartime),[5] and (iv) interception operations. The last three of these are referred to herein as "operational" measures or as types of renditions.[6]

As a preliminary note, it need not be *law enforcement* officers from the pursuing State at issue who are involved in the operation; there conceivably could be military or intelligence officers instead, although they may not have the authority to effect an arrest *per se*. Further, the fact that a pursuing State may rely on its military to lure, seize, and/or help escort a fugitive from foreign territory does not imply that there is a military conflict underway; they could be discharged with such support duties in peacetime.[7] In some States, like the United States, there is a longstanding presumption against the military conducting law enforcement work,[8] as

3 Where deception is involved in a negotiated arrangement between a government official or agent and a fugitive to entice him to return to pursuing State territory, custody, or control, that measure would more properly be characterized as a unilateral LCO.

4 While a unilateral LCO is typically followed by the physical delivery of the fugitive to pursuing State territory, that is not always the case. Further, to the extent the subject is ill-treated by pursuing State officials or agents during post-capture delivery, any incidental violations of international law should be treated as independent of the LCO itself.

5 LCOs and SDOs are defined in Chapter 1.h and 1.i, respectively.

6 In addition, certain extreme forms of unilateral operations also could be undertaken, but they will not be examined herein because they are so improbable, and would clearly violate international law. A pursuing State, for example, could threaten to detonate high-impact explosives in the host State's capital city if it failed to turn over a wanted fugitive. Another possibility might involve a pursuing State forcefully appropriating the host State *territory* where the individual of interest is located; in that way, the individual would no longer need to be transferred, as he would now be found within the pursuing State's newly acquired sovereign, if hotly disputed, territory.

7 Military involvement may be sought to provide supplemental security when dealing with a particularly dangerous individual or someone who is part of a violent or well-armed organization. For example, "Army commandos helped escort Ricardo Palmera, the highest-ranking leader of the Revolutionary Armed Forces of Colombia (FARC), to a U.S. government plane near Bogotá when he was extradited to the United States." Bruce Zagaris, *Colombia Extradites FARC Leader*, 21 IELR 52 (2005).

8 *See* Christopher A. Donesa, Note, *Protecting National Interests: The Legal Status of Extraterritorial Law Enforcement by the Military*, 41 Duke L.J. 867, 869 (1991) (noting the purpose of "protect[ing] the rights and civil liberties of citizens"); *e.g., United States v. Walden*, 490 F.2d 372 (4th Cir.) (a military officer may not serve as an undercover agent in civil operations), *cert. denied*, 416 U.S. 983 (1974).

reflected in the Posse Comitatus Act,[9] but some exceptions apply[10] and in a few instances the collateral involvement of U.S. military personnel in unilateral operations to recover fugitives has been upheld.[11]

Why would a State be inclined to undertake a *unilateral* operation to retrieve a fugitive? Several possible reasons exist, but typically such conduct derives from the lack of viable or desirable alternatives, and therefore is often, but not always, viewed as a last resort. Standard retrieval options, such as extradition and removal, would be regarded as hopeless or unavailable;[12] the host State would not be expected to prosecute the fugitive in good faith or to the fullest extent of the law; and informal law enforcement cooperation would be rejected either because of strained political relations between the pursuing and host States[13] or

[9] Act of June 18, 1878, ch. 263, 20 Stat. 152, *codified at* 18 U.S.C. § 1835 (2012). This Act expressly prohibits the Army and Air Force (the latter added in 1956 legislation) to enforce the law "except in cases and under circumstances expressly authorized by the Constitution or Act of Congress." This term was "[n]amed after a practice under which county sheriffs could impress citizens to aid in enforcement of civil authority." Donesa, *supra* n.8, at 871. Although the statutory text does not apply to the Navy or the Marine Corps, "both services have adhered to its provisions as a matter of administrative interpretation and amendments have applied directly to those military branches, but no prohibition applies to the Coast Guard." *Id.* at 872; *see also Walden*, 490 F.2d at 374–75. Under the Act, as amended, the military services may share information and intelligence, loan equipment, and provide training in connection with law enforcement operations. Donesa, *supra* n.8, at 872 n.33.

[10] The U.S. President may employ the military to enforce the law in times of national crisis or emergency, 10 U.S.C. §§ 332, 333 (2012) (Use of Militia and Armed Forces to Enforce Federal Authority), and may allow an indirect or passive military role in law enforcement. *United States v. Red Feather*, 392 F. Supp. 916, 921 (D.S.D. 1975). In addition, a December 1989 U.S. DoJ opinion appears to support the view that the Posse Comitatus Act should *not* apply to an extraterritorial law enforcement action. Peter M. Sanchez, *The 'Drug War': The U.S. Military and National Security*, 34 A.F. L. Rev. 109, 133 (1991); Michael Isikoff & Patrick E. Tyler, "U.S. Military Given Foreign Arrest Powers," *Wash. Post*, Dec. 16, 1989, at A1, A10.

[11] *See, e.g.*, *United States v. Hartley*, 796 F.2d 112 (5th Cir.) (holding that the U.S. military may use its assets to track a fugitive's plane on behalf of a civilian law enforcement authority), *cert. denied*, 479 U.S. 839 (1986); *United States v. Yunis*, 924 F.2d 1086, 1093–94 (D.C. Cir. 1991) (finding no violation of the Act when Navy vessels and aircraft were used in connection with the apprehension of a Palestinian terrorist on the high seas).

[12] *See* Philip B. Heymann & Ian Heath Gershengorn, *Pursuing Justice, Respecting the Law, in* Principles and Procedures for a New Transnational Criminal Law: Documentation of an International Workshop in Freiburg, May 1991, at 123 (Albin Eser & Otto Lagodny eds. 1992) (noting by way of example lacunae in extradition treaties, time delays, executive branch discretion, and the political offense exclusion).

[13] Beverly Izes, *Drawing Lines in the Sand: When State-Sanctioned Abduction of War Criminals Should be Permitted*, 31 Colum. J. L. & Soc. Probs. 1, 9–10 (1997–98); Heymann & Gershengorn, *supra* n.12, at 137.

because of concerns about corrupt host State officials potentially tipping off the fugitive or otherwise protecting him.[14] Additionally, a pursuing State may wish to extract a fugitive as quickly as possible so as to deny him additional opportunity to wreak havoc or to seek legal recourse from the host State[15] where, depending on his influence and public image, he might be expected to obtain special treatment.

Because of the risks frequently involved in the exercise of unilateral operational measures,[16] a pursuing State is unlikely to elect such an approach unless the fugitive is of particularly high law enforcement priority.[17] Despite recent developments on the international law enforcement cooperation front that have eroded the impetus for unilateral operations,[18] where no

[14] *See* Stephen Dycus, et al., Counterterrorism Law 526 (2007) (citing tip-offs to the fugitive and potential defects with *aut dedere*); Douglas Kash, *Abducting Terrorists under PDD-39: Much Ado About Nothing New*, 13 Am. U. Int'l L. Rev. 139, 153 (1997–98) [hereinafter Kash, *PDD-39*]; Christopher H. Pyle, Extradition, Politics, and Human Rights 281–82 (2001) (noting concerns about corrupt police, military, and government officers protecting those responsible for torturing and murdering DEA Agent Enrique Camarena-Salazar and his pilot, Alfredo Zavala-Avelar, in Mexico and how the DEA spent US $2.7 million on informants alone).

[15] Satyadeva Bedi, Extradition: A Treatise on the Laws Relevant to the Fugitive Offenders Within and With the Commonwealth Countries 393 (2002).

[16] *See* Douglas Kash, *Abduction of Terrorists in Int'l Airspace and on the High Seas*, 8 Fla. J. Int'l L. 65, 85 (1993) [hereinafter Kash, *Airspace*] (noting that "forms of self-help" should be used "sparingly," given the negative political implications and strong public reactions, such as the mass riots in Egypt that ensued following the U.S. interception of the *Achille Lauro* hijackers aboard an Egyptian aircraft).

[17] Not surprisingly, unilateral operations can take a toll on foreign relations. In 1983, to avoid jeopardizing U.S.-Bahamian relations, the U.S. Ambassador to the Bahamas vetoed a planned unilateral LCO by FBI and DEA agents to move Bahamian Cabinet Minister and suspected drug money launderer Kendal Nottage to the United States. Reginald Stuart, "U.S.-Bahamian Relations are Straining Under Drug Investigations," *N.Y. Times*, Sept. 28, 1983, at A21. In 1971, when the Panamanian chief of air traffic control, Joaquim Him Gonzalez, was lured into the Panama Canal Zone to play in a softball game, without the knowledge of the local U.S. Ambassador, and was arrested there by U.S. police and shortly thereafter flown to the United States, Evert Clark & Nicholas Horrock, Contrabandista! 193–98 (1973), U.S.-Panamanian relations became tense for some time. Ethan A. Nadelmann, Cops Across Borders: The Internationalization of U.S. Criminal Law Enforcement 445 (1993) [hereinafter Nadelmann, Cops].

[18] There is an uptick in agreements on law enforcement and judicial cooperation; moreover, conventions increasingly are treating terrorist acts as either expressly extraditable or at least not subject to the political offense exclusion; and new extradition or law enforcement cooperation conventions customarily include an *aut dedere* provision, which, at least in principle, should ensure some form of criminal accountability Silvia Borelli, *The Rendition of Terrorist Suspects to the United States: Human Rights and the Limits of Int'l Cooperation, in* Enforcing International Law Norms against Terrorism 362–63 (Andrea Bianchi ed. 2004). *See also* Chapter 4.f.

other alternatives can be found for reining in hardened terrorists or narcotics traffickers[19] or to "relieve pent-up frustration that might otherwise provoke truly rash action,"[20] States still may be motivated to pursue this course of action.[21]

b Application

i Negotiations for the Fugitive's Return

To the extent a pursuing State can locate a fugitive abroad and arrange for direct or indirect communication with him,[22] it can try to influence his voluntary decision to return to its territory through the use of "carrots" or "sticks," thereby bypassing the need to cooperate with the host (or any other) State. In short, the idea is to induce a fugitive to return through offered incentives or disincentives, rather than through any form of deception or via involvement by host State authorities. Such an approach offers little promise, on average, in part, because fugitives tend to be distrustful of pursuing State's intentions and in part because the inducements are unlikely to be of a character sufficient to prompt the fugitive to leave the relative comfort and safety of the host State and risk arrest and punishment.

[19] *See* Heymann & Gershengorn, *supra* n.12, at 124 (citing U.S. Sen. Arlen Specter); Kash, *PDD-39, supra* n.14, at 153 (unilateral measures "may be the only method to effectuate an arrest and bring the suspect to court.").

[20] Heymann & Gershengorn, *supra* n.12, at 124 (citing a *N.Y. Times* editorial).

[21] In addition to helping bring fugitives to justice, such unilateral operations can have the added benefit of deterring cross-border movements by others who are similarly situated and who worry about being captured. *See* Steven Emerson, "Should We Extradite Sheik Obeid?; Despite Legal Precedent Bush Is Slow to Act," *Wash. Post*, Aug. 6, 1989, at B2 ("Following the arrest of [Lebanese hijacker Fawaz] Yunis [discussed in sub-section b.ii *infra*], American intelligence detected that international terrorists restricted their movements abroad."). Another potential benefit can be to secure a detainee who can be traded for the release of individuals of one's own interest to the pursuing State. *Cf.* David Halevy & Neil C. Livingstone, "Hostages: Lessons Learned: Short-Term Thinking May Hurt Israel," *Wash. Post*, Aug. 6, 1989, at B1 (it has been surmised that "the overriding reason for [Israel's seizure of Sheik Abdul Karim Obeid from Lebanon in September 1989] was to win release of three Israeli POWs.").

[22] On high-profile cases, a pursuing State may be able to communicate its willingness to negotiate through newsworthy statements made at public events. For example, in January 2014, U.S. Attorney General Eric Holder indicated at an event held at the University of Virginia that if Edward Snowden, the former NSA contractor who disclosed classified information about U.S. surveillance operations, were to plead guilty, the United States "would engage with his lawyers" to discuss the handling of his criminal prosecution. Steve Kenny, "U.S. Willing to Hold Talks if Snowden Pleads Guilty," *INYT*, Jan. 25–26, 2014, at 5.

That said, a pursuing State could promise a fugitive that, if he returns to its territory or custody, certain counts in the indictment would be dropped,[23] a lesser punishment pursued,[24] or certain advantages conferred such as a reduced bail threshold[25] or not being held in a maximum security prison;[26] that upon his return he would retain all rights otherwise accorded under the applicable extradition treaty;[27] or that, under certain equitable doctrines that bar a fugitive from taking advantage of the judicial system while he remains a fugitive,[28] once he has abandoned

[23] A pursuing State could, for instance, try to negotiate a settlement agreement over bank, insurance, or securities fraud charges with that fugitive. To the extent such an agreement promised to relieve a fugitive of major outstanding charges against him, it might make him more inclined to return to a pursuing State to face any remaining charges. In addition, this approach might incidentally help restore injured parties and ensure the fugitive's return of ill-gotten gains.

[24] Such inducements can sometimes take the form of reduced sentences in exchange not only for physically returning, but also for providing sought-after criminal intelligence. *Cf.* Bruce Zagaris, *Brazil Extradites Alleged Colombian Cocaine Capo to the U.S.*, 24 IELR 432, 432 (2008) (Juan Carlos Ramírez-Abadía, the alleged leader of a Brazilian drug cartel known as Norte del Valle (NVC), was reportedly enthusiastic about the prospect of being extradited to the United States rather than serving prison time in Brazil, where he would have faced a thirty-year sentence, as he was believed to see a chance for a reduced sentence in the United States based on information he could supply to American authorities).

[25] *E.g.*, James Quinn, "NatWest Three's David Bermingham Tells Flash Crash Trader: Don't Fight Extradition," *The Telegraph* (U.K.), Apr. 23, 2015 (a former extraditee, based on his actions related to Enron's collapse, advised Navinder Singh Sarao, the so-called "flash crash" trader, not to resist extradition because "[a]ll holding out does is make things worse" and "[i]f you agree to waive your right to an extradition hearing, you can hope to achieve some form of bail when you arrive in the U.S., and possibly even be allowed to return to the U.K. until your case is heard.").

[26] *E.g.*, AP, "Drug Lord Wants to Be Sent to U.S., Attorney Says: 'El Chapo' Claims Guards at Mexican Prison Don't Let Him Sleep," *Wash. Post*, Mar. 3, 2016 (drug lord instructed his attorney to "negotiate with U.S. authorities for a lighter sentence and confinement at a medium-security prison" in order to be relieved of being awakened every four hours at night for a head count under the special security measures of the Altiplano maximum security prison in Mexico).

[27] *Cf.* Linda Friedman Ramirez, *District Court Finds Violation of Dual Criminality in Case of Extradition from India*, 24 IELR 434, 434–35 (2008) (Stefan Wahne, an Icelandic national, agreed to return voluntarily to the United States on the conditions that all rights otherwise covered under the bilateral U.S.-India Extradition Treaty would continue to apply).

[28] Under U.S. law, the fugitive disentitlement doctrine (*e.g.*, 28 U.S.C. § 2466) generally provides that a fugitive from justice may not seek relief from the judicial system whose authority he or she evades. The rationale for this doctrine includes the difficulty of enforcement against one not willing to subject himself to the court's authority, the inequity of allowing that fugitive to use the resources of the courts only if the outcome is an aid to him, to avoid prejudice to the non-fugitive party, and to discourage flights from justice. *Molinaro v. New Jersey*, 396 U.S. 365, 366 (1970) (per curiam). This doctrine was upheld in a case brought by a Canadian fugitive in which the Inter-American

his fugitive status, he would be able to lodge a civil suit that could be of considerable potential value to him. A pursuing State also could choose not to promise anything concrete at all, but merely the opportunity to negotiate freely in good faith with the fugitive or his lawyers.[29]

Alternatively, a fugitive could be threatened with the revocation of his passport[30] or the pursuit of extradition,[31] or be advised that an award to which he otherwise would be entitled would not be granted unless and until he returns. On this final point, for example, in October 2011, the Basque Regional Government (within Spain) announced that, while Joseba Sarrionandia, a talented Basque essayist who had been convicted due to his membership in the separatist organization Euskadi Ta Askatasuna (ETA) and been at large for twenty-five years since escaping from a San Sebastian prison, had won a top Basque language literary prize worth £15,500, it would not be conferred upon him until he turned himself in and "regularize[d] his legal situation."[32]

Such cited motivators do not raise international or even domestic law concerns; however, a pursuing State would appear to be prohibited from blackmailing or extorting a fugitive into repatriating by threatening, say, that his non-return would proximately result in the death, physical injury, or imprisonment of a family member or close friend or in the lodging of fabricated criminal charges.[33] In August 2015, it was reported

Commission on Human Rights denied admissibility of his claims on account of his unwillingness to return to the United States in order to first exhaust domestic judicial remedies. *Walker v. United States*, Case No. 12.049, Inter-Am. C.H.R., OEA/ser. L/V/ II.118, Doc. 70 rev. 2 at 550, Oct. 10, 2003 [hereinafter *Walker Case*].

29 For an example, *see supra* n.22.

30 *See* pp. 350–52 in Chapter 9.

31 Remarkably, in recent years the mere threat of extradition has prompted more than twenty Japanese executives and employees in auto parts cartels to plead guilty and serve time in the United States, despite the low probability of extradition success. *See* Yoshiya Usami, *Why Did They Cross the Pacific? Extradition: A Real Threat to Cartelists?*, Am. Antitrust Inst. (AAI) Working Paper No. 14–01, Mar. 20, 2014 (hypothesizing the causes as: (i) the uncertainty regarding extradition and the comparatively lower stakes involved under a plea agreement; (ii) "the assurance to travel freely for business activities in the U.S. after they completed their terms of imprisonment"; and (iii) "there could be arrangements, formally or informally, between companies and individuals that the companies would allow individuals who decided to serve prison terms in the U.S. to return to their previous companies, or, at least, related companies when they finish their terms of imprisonment").

32 "Wanted Man Wins Literary Prize," *The Independent* (U.K.), Oct. 3, 2011.

33 *Cf.* Alona E. Evans, Panel Moderator, *Int'l Procedures for the Apprehension and Rendition of Fugitive Offenders*, Apr. 18, 1980, 74 ASIL Proc. 274, 277 (1980) (citing as a "[l]ess obvious" form of "irregular rendition" the "resort to a repatriation program designed to [induce] (or blackmail) an individual to return to the country from which he has fled").

that "young Chinese agents, operating undercover, have been dispatched to a number of countries to induce the alleged fugitives to return to China, sometimes with threats against relatives at home."[34] Although no treaty or case law on point appears to exist, such extortion or threats by public officials would exceed the bounds of reasonableness and proportionality even where law enforcement, rather than personal gain, is the objective.[35]

ii Unilateral Lure and Capture Operations

Unilateral lure and capture operations (LCOs), which like other LCOs involve deceptive means of enticing fugitives to a particular location with the aim of apprehension, are to be distinguished from those that take place either: (i) with the sole participation of host State officials or agents at the behest of a pursuing State ("surrogate" LCOs), (ii) by pursuing State officials or agents with the acquiescence of the host State ("consensual" LCOs); or (iii) by host State and pursuing State officials or agents working together ("joint" LCOs).[36] Unilateral LCOs are conducted entirely by pursuing State officials or agents (including possibly with the assistance of paid police officers or military officials from the host State acting in their private capacity or *ultra vires*[37]) but without the official knowledge or consent of the host State itself.

34 Karen DeYoung, "Obama Warns China about Using Secret Operatives in the U.S." *Wash. Post*, Aug. 17, 2015, at A2. The White House reminded the PRC via diplomatic channels that any such repatriation attempts "should be conducted through proper U.S. legal channels." *Id.*

35 *See Code of Conduct for Law Enforcement Officials*, UNGA Res. 34/169, art. 2, 34 U.N. GAOR Supp. (No. 46), U.N. Doc. A/34/46 (1980), Dec. 17, 1979 (law enforcement officials must "respect and protect human dignity and maintain and uphold the human rights of all persons"); *id.*, art. 3 (law enforcement officials may "use force only when strictly necessary and to the extent required for the performance of their duty").

36 *See* discussion of these terms in Chapter 1.h.

37 State responsibility is based on the actual or apparent conduct of its officials, even if acting *ultra vires*, that is, beyond the scope of their competence or in disobedience of instructions or protocols. ILC, *Responsibility of States for Int'lly Wrongful Acts with Commentaries* (Draft), Dec. 12, 2001, art. 7, Annex to UNGA Res. 56/83, U.N. GAOR, 56th Sess., Supp. No. 10, at 43, U.N. Doc. A/56/10 (2001) [hereinafter ILC, *State Responsibility*]. Accordingly, if an official acts "within the actual capacity of a State organ" or "under cover of its official character," or while "cloaked with governmental authority," the conduct would be attributable to the State. Kimberley N. Trapp, State Responsibility for International Terrorism 35 (2011) (citations omitted). By contrast, when acts are undertaken in a "purely private capacity," they are not regarded as the responsibility of the State to which the official otherwise serves. That

Unilateral LCOs are made to pursuing State territory or otherwise to pursuing State custody or control ("strategic" LCOs) or, alternatively, either to some intermediary destination, including international waters or zones[38] or other locations within the host State or to third States (but in any event without their participation or acquiescence) ("tactical" LCOs).[39] Unilateral LCOs can be effected from beyond host State territory via telephone, fax, or over the Internet,[40] and then carried out through the use of a wide variety of vehicles, including train; bus; truck; automobile; or commercial, official, chartered, or private aircraft, even possibly flown by the fugitive himself to the extent he is a licensed pilot.[41]

said, the imputation of State responsibility on account of the fact that its rogue officials acted under cover of official character at the time, does not, by extension, impute foreknowledge of or consent by the State itself regarding the acts for which they are to be held responsible. Therefore, acts for which State responsibility may be attributed *ex post* does not alter the fact that those acts were carried out as a unilateral LCO. *See* n.44 in Chapter 3.

[38] *E.g.*, David Johnston, "F.B.I. Arrests 2 Drug Suspects on High Seas," *N.Y. Times*, Feb. 22, 1991, at A16 (recounting an FBI lure operation of a private yacht to international waters off the South American coastline of two suspected money launderers from Colombia who were then transferred to a U.S.CG cutter and taken to Puerto Rico and eventually to Los Angeles for trial).

[39] An example of a unilateral LCO to a third State but without its apparent participation or acquiescence involved Mordechai Vanunu, the Israeli technician who shared information about Israel's nuclear capability to the *London Times*. It has been reported that in September 1986 "he was tricked by a woman Mossad agent into traveling [on holiday from London] to [Rome,] Italy, where he was drugged and taken covertly to Israel ... [where] he was convicted and sentenced to 18 years in prison [for treason and espionage]." Alun Jones & Anand Doobay, Jones and Doobay on Extradition and Mutual Assistance 90 (2005); *see also AFP*, "How Israel's Mossad Captured Nuclear Whistleblower Vanunu," Apr. 18, 2004. Italy seems to have had no knowledge of the operation, as it subsequently launched an investigation into allegations that he had been unlawfully smuggled out of its territory. "Italian Judge Opens Inquiry into Charges of Israeli Abduction," *N.Y. Times*, Dec. 25, 1986.

[40] Michael P. Scharf, *The Tools for Enforcing Int'l Criminal Justice in the New Millennium: Lessons from the Yugoslavia Tribunal*, 49 DePaul L. Rev. 925, 970 (2000). In fact, "[t]he lure scenario may be as simple as initiating a telephone call, sending an e-mail or transmitting a page." David P. Warner, *Challenges to Int'l Law Enforcement Cooperation for the U.S. in the Middle East and North Africa: Extradition and Its Alternatives*, 50 Vill. L. Rev. 479, 501 & n.103 (2005).

[41] For example, in October 1973, Julio Lujan, a licensed Argentine pilot accused of heroin trafficking, was approached by a DEA informant about flying him to Bolivia to transact mining business there; upon his arrival, Lujan was seized by local police officers acting as paid agents without their government's knowledge or authority, and about a week later flown to the United States to face charges. *Lujan v Gengler*, 510 F.2d 62, 63 (2d Cir.), *cert. denied*, 421 U.S. 1001 (1975) [hereinafter *Lujan Case*].

LCOs in general often rely on confidential informants or agents who are known to, if not trusted by, the individual of interest.[42] LCOs are frequently accompanied by sealed indictments so that the individual of interest is not put on notice that he may be arrested if he leaves the safety of the host State.[43] All LCOs, including those of a unilateral character, can be classified into one of three main categories based on the general nature of the deception: (i) law enforcement-related; (ii) commercial, professional, or non-law enforcement-related governmental activity; and (iii) social, personal, or recreational.

Law Enforcement-Related Activity. The first category includes those related to a law enforcement deceit of some kind, whether or not connected to the fugitive's actual or alleged underlying offense, such as a ruse to support a law enforcement activity or criminal prosecution; where the fugitive is made to believe he is a suspect in a criminal case and is given an opportunity to exculpate himself; or where he is afforded an opportunity to minimize his law enforcement exposure, including by a promise of political asylum, whether by a pursuing or third State. Notably, for purposes of this typology, the *object* of the ruse is determinative; therefore, where a procedural guarantee of safe passage is offered, there also must be a law enforcement-related end to the deceit, such as the fugitive's providing testimony in another prosecution or lending assistance to a criminal investigation.

An example of a scenario fitting this category can be found in the case of Norbert Schmidt, a German national accused of importing cannabis into Germany, who was lured from Ireland by a police officer in England, who falsely represented over the phone to Schmidt and his solicitor that he, the police officer, was investigating a check fraud. The officer invited Schmidt to come to England to be interviewed in order to clear his name but that, if he refused, his name would be circulated as that of a suspect and he likely would be arrested the next time he tried to cross the border into England. When Schmidt, convinced of the legitimacy of the threat,

[42] *E.g.*, *United States v. Yunis*, 681 F. Supp. 896 (D.D.C. 1988) (a friend of the fugitive who had been co-opted by the DEA and CIA lured Fawaz Yunis from Cyprus to a ship in the Mediterranean), *aff'd*, 924 F.2d 1086 (D.C. Cir. 1991); Eva Wagner, *German Federal Constitutional Court Approves Extradition of Yemeni Citizen*, 20 IELR 14 (2004) (a confidential informant of Yemeni citizenship lured Sheik Mohammed Ali Hassan Moayad from Yemen to Germany).

[43] Colette Retif, *By What Means Justice? The Acceptance of Secret Indictments in the United States and in Int'l Law*, 13 PACE INT'L L. REV. 233, 234 (2001).

arrived in London in November 1992 to meet the officer, he was promptly arrested.[44]

A variant of such a law enforcement-related LCO occurs when the fugitive is induced to "waive extradition" and voluntarily travel to pursuing State territory. There may be instances in which the fugitive's whereabouts are known, and while extradition is either unavailable or undesirable between the pursuing and host States, the fugitive (presumably unaided by counsel) may not be aware that he is residing in a safe haven or otherwise appreciate the nature and extent of any extradition rights for which he is eligible. A pursuing State official could approach the fugitive; claim that extradition papers have been filed; explain that such proceedings would be likely to succeed but prove protracted and expensive; and it would be in the fugitive's self-interest simply to voluntarily return with or without the accompaniment of a pursuing State official or agent, at pursuing State expense.[45]

This category also captures LCO scenarios in which the fugitive's job is of a law enforcement nature, such as serving as a police officer or customs official, and he is tricked into performing an activity that falls within the scope of his official duties. For example, in a case arising a remarkable four and a half centuries ago (1569) and thereby underscoring the long-established practice of LCOs, British law enforcement agents enticed Dr. John Story, who was suspected of plotting against the Queen, to come aboard an English ship in then-Spanish-controlled Antwerp, where he served as a customs officer checking ships for sacrilegious English goods, on the pretext that some blasphemous books had been found. Once Story went on board, the ship immediately headed off for England.[46]

Commercial, Professional, and non-Law Enforcement-Related Government Activity. The second category covers those deceits in which a fugitive is lured into engaging in or undertaking a commercial, professional, or non-law enforcement-related government activity. Such activities can be seemingly innocuous, such as attending an industry

[44] *In re Schmidt* [1995] 1 A.C. 339 (H.L.), [1994] 3 WLR 229 ("*Schmidt II*").

[45] A similar LCO would involve a law enforcement officer deliberately misinforming a fugitive that he is not wanted for an offense or that the offense for which he *is* wanted is not extraditable and consequently coaxing the fugitive to return to pursuing State territory.

[46] Paul O'Higgins, *Unlawful Seizure and Irregular Extradition*, 36 B.Y.B.I.L. 279, 281–82 (1960).

conference, delivering a lecture, advising as an expert on a film,[47] or paying a ceremonial government visit.

For example, in 1967 the Egyptian Government invited a dozen members of the Yemeni Government, including its Prime Minister, on "an official visit" to Cairo, where they were then arrested.[48] In another case, a former CIA officer's acquaintance pretended to be a representative of the U.S. National Security Council (NSC) and expressed an interest in consulting with the fugitive in the Democratic Republic, where he was assured he would be safe.[49] In December 1992, U.S. national Joseph Garfield Brown was lured from the Philippines to Virginia for espionage charges on the promise of a tae kwon do teaching contract at the CIA.[50] In 1924, a German police officer invited a French police officer named Schneabele to attend a conference on border issues and promised him safe passage, but he was arrested upon his arrival.[51]

Such LCOs may exploit an offender's predisposition to participate in a particular type of illegal conduct. For example, in May 1999, undercover FBI agents, posing as foreign government spies, lured from Bangkok Jean-Philippe Wispeleare, a former Australian Defense Intelligence Organization official who had stolen classified documents and was trying to earn money by selling them to an interested government; he was arrested upon his arrival at the Dulles International Airport in Virginia.[52] Similarly, in October 1987, an undercover DEA agent lured from Mexico Raul Lopez Alvarez, a former Mexican police officer who had boasted of helping to torture DEA agent Camarena, by posing as someone who wanted a U.S. Customs agent killed for US $10,000; Alvarez was arrested at a restaurant in California.[53] In

[47] This scenario occurred in October 2013, when "alleged Somali pirate Mohamed 'Afweyene' Abdi Hassan arrived at the Brussels airport, believing he would advise as an expert in a film project on maritime piracy, only to be immediately arrest[ed] on kidnapping and hijacking charges." Bruce Zagaris, *Belgium Lures and then Arrests Somali Pirate Mastermind*, 30 IELR 20 (2014).

[48] "Kidnapping Incidents," 32 *Bull. of the Int'l Comm'n of Jurists* 24, 27 (Dec. 1967) [hereinafter *ICJ Bull.*] (noting, however, that they were later returned).

[49] *United States v. Wilson*, 721 F.2d 967, 972 (4th Cir. 1983).

[50] Robert O'Harrow, Jr., "Man Stepping Off Plane at Dulles Is Arrested on Espionage Charges," *Wash. Post*, Dec. 29, 1992, at B1.

[51] Lawrence Preuss, *Kidnaping of Fugitives from Justice on Foreign Territory*, 29 AJIL 502, 507 (1935); Kathryn Selleck, Note, *Jurisdiction after Int'l Kidnapping: A Comparative Study*, 8 B.C. Int'l & Comp. L. Rev. 237, 257 (1985).

[52] David Johnston, "U.S. Arrests an Australian in Spying Case," *N.Y. Times*, May 18, 1999 (the undercover agents offered him US $120,000 for over 700 classified documents).

[53] Paul Lieberman, "Camarena Case Spotlight Shifts to L.A. Unit's Tactics," *L.A. Times*, May 7, 1990, at A1, A23.

another instance, in April 1985, a former Belize Cabinet minister, Eligio Briceno, who was wanted for conspiracy to import marijuana into the United States, was lured and arrested by undercover DEA agents under the guise that he would receive a US $35,000 payout for helping to "arrange the smuggling of 5,000 pounds of marijuana a month by plane into the coastal area of North Carolina."[54]

Social, Personal, and Recreational Activity. The third category involves LCOs of a social, personal (including self-promotional), or recreational nature. These can consist of such varying pretexts as an invitation to participate in an athletic competition, attend a party, engage in a romantic interlude (a/k/a a "honey pot" or "honey trap"), enjoy an all-expense-paid trip to the fugitive's home country, or publish a book about his life or be the subject of a film. For example, in 1971, the Panamanian chief of air traffic control, Joaquim Him Gonzalez, was lured into the Panama Canal Zone to play in a softball game.[55] In September 1986, Mordechai Vanunu, an Israeli nuclear technician who had publicly disclosed information about Israel's nuclear capability, was enticed by an undercover female Israeli intelligence (Mossad) agent to travel from London to Rome on a holiday trip together.[56]

iii Unilateral Seizure and Delivery Operations

Just as the case with LCOs, seizure and delivery operations (SDOs) come in a variety of forms. Unilateral SDOs must be distinguished from their surrogate, consensual, and joint counterparts. The key attribute of a unilateral SDO is that the capture and subsequent delivery of a fugitive to pursuing State territory, custody, or control is undertaken by a pursuing State without reliance on an intermediary third State or on a participating or acquiescing host State; *i.e.*, it acts alone, although possibly with the assistance of private actors, including even host or third State officials operating *ultra vires* or in their *personal* capacity.[57]

[54] Jon Nordheimer, "U.S. Accuses Ex-Minister from Belize in Plot to Import Marijuana," *N.Y. Times*, Apr. 9, 1985, at A15.

[55] Clark & Horrock, *supra* n.17, at 193–98.

[56] *See supra* n.39.

[57] An example of an SDO carried out by host State officials acting in their private capacity can be found in January 2005, when the Colombian Government "admitted that it had paid an unspecified reward to bounty hunters to capture Rodrigo Granda, a leader of the [FARC from a subway station in Caracas, Venezuela], and take him across the border to the Colombian city of Cucuta." Juan Forero, "Venezuela: Ambassador to Colombia Recalled over Captured Rebel," *N.Y. Times*, Jan. 14, 2005, at A12. Venezuela detained

Unilateral SDOs, by and large, are "strategic" (versus "tactical") in terms of destination.

Standard Operation. By far, the most popular manifestation of a unilateral SDO is a clandestine operation in which the fugitive is physically taken off the street, from a railroad platform,[58] or from a home, office, or hotel, whether in broad daylight or under cover of darkness, and escorted by foot across a national border, or brought to an automobile, sea-going vessel, or aircraft waiting to whisk him away from host State territory,[59] sometimes following initial questioning in a safe house or other secure location. The seizure component of a unilateral SDO also can occur on board a flagged vessel on the high seas,[60] in the host State's contiguous zone, or in its territorial waters.

Many examples exist, although arguably the two cases that have elicited the greatest volume of legal commentary involve: (i) Adolf Eichmann, who masterminded the systematic Nazi deportation and execution of six million Jews from Eastern Europe in the late 1930s and early 1940s known as the Holocaust, and (ii) Humberto Álvarez-Machaín, a Guadalajaran medical doctor accused of keeping DEA Agent Enrique Camarena Salazar alive while he was tortured for information about DEA plans and operations in Mexico.[61]

five of its own National Guardsmen and three police officers on suspicion of participation. *Id.; see also supra* n.37 for a discussion of *ultra vires* conduct.

58 For instance, in April 1935, German officials, arriving by train, seized Joseph Lampersberger, a German political refugee, from Czechoslovakia while he was waiting for a train at the Eisenstein Station, and then carried him across the border into Germany. Preuss, *supra* n.51, at 504.

59 Variations on this score are also possible. For example, in November 1964, Egyptian agents tried to return Moroccan-born Mordechai Luk, reportedly a double intelligence agent for the Egyptians and Israelis, to Egypt by packing and shipping him in a trunk, although it is unclear whether Egypt had charged him with any crime. AP, "Italy Balks Air Abduction of Man in a Trunk," *N.Y. Times*, Nov. 18, 1964, at 1.

60 To the extent a fugitive is seized from an *unflagged or dual-flagged* vessel on the high seas (*see* n.156 and accompanying text *infra*), it would amount to an SDO in the guise of an international arrest, rather than a unilateral SDO. *See* Chapter 1.h.

61 Although Eichmann was ultimately tried, convicted, sentenced to death, and hanged (in 1962), by contrast in the case of Álvarez-Machaín, ultimately a federal judge found the evidence arrayed against the defendant to be based on "hunches" and the "wildest speculation" such that it did not support the charges, thereby clearing him of any wrongdoing. Seth Mydans, "Judge Clears Mexican in Agent's Killing," *N.Y. Times*, Dec. 15, 1992, at A20. At the same time, however, Álvarez-Machaín's civil action for damages against the U.S. Government and the individuals who participated in the SDO was dismissed. *Sosa v. Álvarez-Machaín*, 542 U.S. 692 (2004).

In May 1960, after learning of Eichmann's whereabouts in Buenos Aires (where he had been living under the pseudonym Richard Klement for a decade), Israeli Mossad officials stalked him and then plotted to seize him from a residential street during his daily office commute home from a neighborhood bus stop. After seizing him, confirming his identity, and interrogating him at a "safe house," the Mossad agents transported him back to Israel on an El Al aircraft that had flown an Israeli delegation to celebrate Argentina's 150th anniversary celebration.[62]

With respect to Álvarez-Machaín, in April 1990, the so-called "Wild Geese," a group cobbled together by a DEA informant and consisting of "former military police officers, civilians, and at least two current policemen," while "wearing federal police uniforms broke into Álvarez-Machaín's medical office, put a gun to his head, locked his secretary and a maid in a closet, and hustled the doctor away to a house in Guadalajara."[63] The next day, he was flown to El Paso, Texas, in a private plane where the DEA took custody of him.[64]

Peacetime Military Raids or Expeditions. A second type of unilateral SDO, albeit far less common, occurs when pursuing State personnel conduct *peacetime* military raids (whether or not in secret) or lead expeditionary forces to capture and retrieve one or more fugitives.

For example, in February 1973, members of the Israeli Defense Force (IDF) launched an open raid to seize and bring back to Israel from a refugee camp 100 miles inside neighboring Lebanon to face criminal prosecution eleven suspected Palestinian militants – including twenty-three-year-old Turkish national Falik Bulut – in large measure because of their organizational affiliation with al-Fatah.[65] Likewise, in July 1989,

[62] *Attorney General of the Gov't of Israel v. Eichmann*, Crim. Case No. 40/61, Dist. Ct. of Jerusalem, Isr., Dec. 12, 1961, *reprinted in* 36 ILR 5, *aff'd sub nom., Eichmann v. Attorney General of the Gov't of Israel,*, Sup. Ct., Isr., May 29, 1962, *reprinted in* 36 ILR 277 (E. Lauterpacht ed. 1968); Scott S. Evans, Note, *Int'l Kidnapping in a Violent World: Where the United States Ought to Draw the Line*, 137 Mil. L. Rev. 187, 200 (1992); Izes, *supra* n.13, at 16; "Israel, Argentina Declare Nazi Case a Closed Incident," *N.Y. Times*, Aug. 4, 1960, at 1.

[63] Pyle, *supra* n.14, at 282–83.

[64] Jones & Doobay, *supra* n.39, at 91.

[65] Note, *Extraterritorial Jurisdiction and Jurisdiction Following Forcible Abduction: A New Israeli Precedent in Int'l Law*, 72 Mich. L. Rev. 1087, 1087–88 (1974) [hereinafter Note, *Israeli Precedent*]; M. Cherif Bassiouni, International Extradition and World Public Order 124 & 125 n.8 (1974) [hereinafter Bassiouni, World Public Order]. Israel carried out a similar raid into Lebanon in September 1972 in which it seized and delivered ten Arab guerrilla suspects for being members of unlawful organizations and possessing arms and explosives with the intent to harm Israel. "Captured Arabs Tried in Israel," *N.Y. Times*, July 24, 1973, at 6.

twelve Israeli commandos, arriving in helicopters, swooped in to Jibchit, Lebanon, and seized and delivered to Israel Sheik Abdul Karim Obeid, the spiritual leader of the pro-Iranian Party of God (Hezbollah), who was alleged to have harbored terrorists as well as incited, planned, and materially supported terrorist attacks against Israel and its population.[66]

In addition, in December 1989, an hour before a military invasion was scheduled to launch to seize Commander-in-Chief of the Panama Defense Forces (PDF) and *de facto* Panamanian leader Gen. Manuel Noriega from Panama and return him to the United States (*see* discussion *infra*), "a snatch squad of Delta Force commandos raided one of his haunts, only to find that [he and his advisors] had just left."[67] More recently, in October 2013, U.S. Special Forces launched a military raid into Tripoli, Libya, to capture Nazih Abdul-Hamed al-Ruqai, better known by his *nom de guerre* Abu Anas al-Liby, off the streets of Tripoli, for his alleged involvement in the 1998 bombings of the U.S. Embassies in Kenya and Tanzania.[68]

Wartime Invasion. A third type of a unilateral SDO, but one that is particularly rare, occurs when a fugitive, whether a civilian, combatant, or even a political or military leader of the host State, is captured in the course of an international armed conflict precipitated at least in part to retrieve that fugitive.[69] The latter scenario likely would only take place if the targeted fugitive was of critical law enforcement significance and no other means of his capture and retrieval were deemed feasible.[70] The only

66 Robert J. Beck & Anthony Clark Arend, *Don't Tread on Us: Int'l Law and Forcible State Responses to Terrorism*, 12 Wis. Int'l L.J. 153, 177–78 (1994); Joel Brinkley, "Israeli Commandos Seize Leader of a Pro-Iran Group in Lebanon," *N.Y. Times*, July 29, 1989, at 1.

67 Pyle, *supra* n.14, at 278. Had that surgical military raid succeeded, it might well have obviated the need for the large-scale invasion. In another example of a failed attempt at a unilateral SDO, in 1916, U.S. Brigadier General Jack Pershing led an expeditionary force into Mexico to capture and bring to justice Francisco ("Pancho") Villa, who was a leader in a revolution-wrought and political dysfunctional Mexico and who had, among other things, robbed U.S. banks and murdered American citizens. Nadelmann, Cops, *supra* n.17, at 456; Pyle, *supra* n.14, at 266.

68 Carlotta Gall, *et al.*, "Libya Seeks Answer After U.S. Capture of Militant," *IHT*, Oct. 7, 2013, at 1.

69 As this part of the book is concerned with full-scale alternatives to extradition, it examines only measures that pursuing States may undertake to retrieve fugitives, rather than circumstances, such as warfare, that might arise incidentally and which then can be exploited for law enforcement ends, including in instances of military occupation (*e.g.*, *Chandler Case* discussed at nn.168 and 300 and accompanying text *infra*).

70 As a *de facto* leader of Panama, it was "almost inconceivable that [Gen. Noriega] would be brought to trial while he held power" to account for the crimes for which he had been

modern example[71] of such a unilateral operation involved Gen. Manuel Noriega, who ruled Panama from 1983 to 1989 and was wanted on narcotics trafficking, money laundering, and related charges in connection with protecting the Medellín cartel and their cocaine shipments to the United States.[72]

The U.S. Government seized Gen. Noriega in early January 1990 after launching a military attack on Panama with approximately 25,000 troops[73] in late December 1989 (called "Operation Just Cause") with one of its express aims (if not its primary mission[74]) to recover Gen. Noriega in order to criminally prosecute him in the United States.[75] General Noriega managed initially to evade capture before seeking refuge in the Papal Nunciate (the Embassy of the Holy See in Panama City), after ten days of which the Vatican envoy to Panama announced that Gen. Noriega's refuge would expire and he had to choose between giving

indicted by two grand juries in February 1988. Heymann & Gershengorn, *supra* n.12, at 131. "Panamanian judges would have found [Gen. Noriega] immune from extradition both as their de facto head of state and as a Panamanian national (Panama's constitution frowned on the surrender of its nationals); plus, a number of charges against him would not satisfy the rule of double criminality (racketeering charges, in particular, had no counterpart in Panamanian law)." Pyle, *supra* n.14, at 277. This case represented the first time a *de jure* or *de facto* leader of a sovereign State was the subject of a unilateral SDO to the United States to face criminal charges.

71 "No close precedent exists for the manner and circumstances in which Noriega was apprehended and brought to trial in the United States." Nadelmann, Cops, *supra* n.17, at 457. From an historical perspective, there is at least one *approximate* precedent. *See* Pyle, *supra* n.14, at 267 ("The U.S. military conquest of [Spanish-controlled] East Florida in 1817 was triggered, in part, because the Mikasuki Seminoles refused to allow U.S. troops to recover fugitive slaves from their territory" who had escaped by the hundreds and were "stag[ing] cross-border raids, plundering white settlements and encouraging other slaves to join them").

72 Another national leader indicted by the United States while in office was Norman Saunders of the Turks & Caicos Islands (for narcotics-related charges for which he was convicted in 1985). Richard L. Berke, "Noriega Arraigned in Miami in a Drug-Trafficking Case; He Refuses to Enter a Plea; Claims of Coercion; He Surrendered for Fear of Losing Sanctuary, Lawyer Maintains," *N.Y. Times*, Jan. 5, 1990, at A1, A10.

73 *See* Pyle, *supra* n.14, at 278 ("approximately 24,000 troops"); Nadelmann, Cops, *supra* n.17, at 455 (U.S. military force consisted of "more than 25,000 troops"); Frances Y.F. Ma, *Noriega's Abduction from Panama: Is Military Invasion an Appropriate Substitute for Int'l Extradition?*, 13 Loy. L.A. Int'l & Comp. L.J. 925, 925 n.3 (1991) (citing a *UPI* article).

74 Pyle, *supra* n.14, at 278.

75 Some legal experts have compared the U.S. operation to capture Noriega with "when the ancient Romans brought back in chains leaders of conquered lands." Neil A. Lewis, "Scholars Say Arrest of Noriega Has Little Justification in Law," *N.Y. Times*, Jan. 10, 1990, at A12.

himself up to U.S. forces or to the Panamanian people.[76] Although Gen. Noriega was received into the hands of a U.S. military general, he immediately was transported to a U.S. AFB in Panama, where DEA officials arrested him and flew him to Florida.[77]

iv Interception Operations

Another means by which a pursuing State can unilaterally retrieve a fugitive overseas is by intercepting an aircraft, although also conceivably it could be a ship, automobile, or other vehicle in which the fugitive is believed to be aboard. An "interception operation" is one that, *through either force or the threat of force exerted from the* <u>*outside*</u> *of a transport vessel or vehicle, directs its movement to a location where the identity of any suspected fugitives on board can be safely confirmed and, if so, apprehended.*[78] Some examples can help illustrate this dynamic.

In chronological order, there are five well-documented instances of international aircraft interceptions,[79] all of which occurred over a three-decade period between 1956 and 1986, two perpetrated by Israel, and one

[76] Andrew Rosenthal, "Vatican Issues an Ultimatum," *N.Y. Times*, Jan. 5, 1990, at A1.

[77] *See* Sanchez, *supra* n.10, at 134; Ma, *supra* n.73, at 934. This has been accurately described as the "most ambitious snatch operation in history," given the number of troops involved and the fact that "26 Americans and more than 700 Panamanians, mostly civilians, died, and that property damage exceeded 1.5 billion dollars." Pyle, *supra* n.14, at 278.

[78] By contrast, a "commandeering operation" can be understood herein as one that, *through force or the threat of force exerted from the* <u>*inside*</u> *of a transport vessel or vehicle, seizes control with the aim of reaching a destination where the identity of any suspected fugitives on board can be safely confirmed and, if so, apprehended.* While there are no known examples of a commandeering operation, as defined above, in the open literature, such an operation theoretically could occur, and therefore should not be discounted from this analysis. It could occur with or without casualties, but in any event absent the knowledge or consent of the owner and "pilot" of the aircraft, vessel, or vehicle involved. Such an operation could be challenging to execute in the sense that the transport vessel or vehicle in question might be well guarded and those carrying it out could face resistance during the seizure of control and/or at the point of destination. An illustrative example of commandeering in a non-law enforcement context can be seen in the manner by which the hijackers of the Achille Lauro took control of the Italian cruise ship in 1985 not after boarding from another ship but from already being on the cruise ship itself. Antonio Cassese, *The Int'l Community's 'Legal' Response to Terrorism*, 38 Int'l & Comp. L.Q. 589, 603 (1989) [hereinafter Cassese, *Legal Response*].

[79] In addition to actually executed interceptions, others were considered by pursuing States. In the ICC context, for example, prosecutors reportedly "contemplated a mid-air interception [within the air space of a State Party] if Seif al-Islam el-Qaddafi, son of [Libyan] Col. Muammar el-Qaddafi and one-time heir apparent, tries to flee by plane to an African safe haven." J. David Goodman, "Prosecutor Says Qaddafi Son May Turn Himself In," *IHT*, Oct. 29–30, 2011, at 5. The United States also reportedly considered interdicting

each by France, the United States, and Yemen. In the first of these, in October 1956, France forced down a civilian aircraft in then-French-controlled Algeria while flying over international waters *en route* between Tunisia and Morocco, in order to secure the custody of Ahmed Ben Bella (who later became President of Algeria) and fellow Front de Libération Nationale (Algerian Liberation Movement, or FLN) leaders who were passengers on that flight. He and his associates were then arrested, taken to France, and imprisoned.[80]

In the second instance, in August 1973, two Israeli fighter jets intercepted a civilian airliner (owned by Middle East Airlines but chartered to Iraqi Airways) carrying seventy-four passengers and seven crew members shortly after it took off from Beirut (but still over Lebanese territory) *en route* to Baghdad. The aircraft was forced to land on an Israeli military base and then everyone on board was instructed to disembark and subjected to questioning. After about two hours of detention, the passengers and crew were permitted to proceed on their airliner's scheduled route. The purpose of the interception was to capture Dr. George Habash, leader of the Popular Front for the Liberation of Palestine (PFLP) and other Palestinian militants who were suspected of being on board. It turned out, however, that the Israelis confused flight 006 (which reportedly was carrying the individuals of interest) with flight 006A (which was the one intercepted), both of which coincidentally had a Beirut-to-Baghdad flight plan and departed at about the same time of day.[81]

The third case, in October 1985, originated when four Palestine Liberation Front (PLF)[82] gunmen hijacked an Italian cruise ship (the *Achille Lauro*) carrying 545 passengers and crew twenty-seven nautical miles outside of Port Said, Egypt, and killed one disabled Jewish American passenger (Leon Klinghoffer). After being denied admission in a Syrian port, the hijackers negotiated a deal with the Egyptian

Panamanian strongman Gen. Manuel Noriega's aircraft over the high seas. PYLE, *supra* n.14, at 277.

[80] *ICJ Bull.*, *supra* n.48, at 29–30; "Ahmed Ben Bella," Obituary, *The Telegraph* (U.K.), Apr. 12, 2012.

[81] Terence Smith, "Israeli Jets Over Lebanon Force Down Arab Airliner; Military Says it Diverted Wrong Plane in Search for Palestinian Guerrillas—81 are Freed after 2 Hours," *N.Y. Times*, Aug. 11, 1973, at 1, 6; Cassese, *Legal Response, supra* n.78, at 601; Beck & Arend, *supra* n.66, at 174–75; Kash, *Airspace, supra* n.16, at 91; George M. Borkowski, Recent Developments, *Use of Force: Interception of Aircraft*, 27 HARV. INT'L L.J. 761, 764 n.35 (1986); Note, *Israeli Precedent, supra* n.65, at 1088 n.4.

[82] The PLF was then a faction of the PLO.

Government through a PLO intermediary (Abu Abbas) to allow them safe passage to Tunis, the site of the PLO Headquarters, on an Egyptian Government aircraft that carried the four gunmen, Abu Abbas, another PLO leader, five Egyptian diplomats, and ten armed guards.

The aircraft, however, was denied admission by Tunisia and (later) Greece (probably at the request of the United States) and, while returning to Egypt and upon U.S. President Ronald Reagan's order (but without the knowledge of Egypt or Italy), four U.S. fighter jets from an aircraft carrier based in southern Europe intercepted the Egyptian plane above international waters near Crete and forced it to land at the Italian-NATO air base in Sigonella, Sicily. A fifty-member U.S. Special Forces team, which had been tasked with putting the hijackers and PLO representatives on two U.S. transport aircraft that had landed about the same time and returning them to the United States, surrounded the Egyptian plane but they, in turn, were encircled by Italian troops. After tense discussions, and with the support of Egypt, Italy agreed to prosecute the hijackers if the United States would stand down; as a result, Italy took custody of the hijackers and the PLO representatives.[83]

In the fourth episode, in February 1986, two Israeli military aircraft intercepted a Libyan executive jet carrying a Syrian Government delegation, two Lebanese militia officials, and three crew members on a trip from Tripoli (Libya) to Damascus (Syria). The interception occurred over the Mediterranean Sea east of Cyprus in international air space and the plane was forced to land in a northern Israeli airfield. As in the 1973 case, Israel mistakenly believed that those alleged criminals it sought to retrieve – in this instance, most likely Syrian-based Ahmed Jabril, leader of the PFLP–General Command (PFLP-GC), or Dr. George Habash (*see supra*) – were aboard and, just as before, allowed the passengers and crew to carry on to their destination after being detained for a period of hours.[84]

[83] Stuart Taylor Jr., "Plane Diversion Raises Legal Issues," *N.Y. Times*, Oct. 11, 1985, at A11; Pyle, *supra* n.14, at 273–74; Antonio Cassese, Violence and Law in the Modern Age 62–63 (1988) (translated into English by S.J.K. Greenleaves) [hereinafter Cassese, Violence]; Borkowski, *supra* n.81, at 761; Kash, *Airspace, supra* n.16, at 88–89; Beck & Arend, *supra* n.66, at 175–76.

[84] Judith Miller, "Qaddafi Orders His Jets to Intercept Israeli Airliners," *N.Y. Times*, Feb. 8, 1986, at A3; Cassese, *Legal Response, supra* n.78, at 603; Borkowski, supra n.81, at 761; Michael J. Bazyler, *Capturing Terrorists in the 'Wild Blue Yonder': Int'l Law and the* Achille Lauro *and Libyan Aircraft Incidents*, 8 Whittier L. Rev. 685, 694 & n.65 (1987); Kash, *Airspace, supra* n.16, at 90–91; Beck & Arend, *supra* n.66, at 176–77.

In the fifth instance, in August 1986, "two South Yemeni MIG fighters intercepted a Djibouti commercial airliner over the Red Sea and forced it to land at Aden airport in South Yemen. In Aden, the guards made the fifty-nine passengers disembark and kept the Boeing 720 jet on the ground for four hours while they searched for political opponents, particularly supporters of deposed South Yemeni President Ali Nasser Hasani."[85] Although initially the South Yemenis tried to detain one Hasani associate found on the aircraft, they ultimately "relented and allowed all the passengers . . . to depart."[86]

c Lawfulness Analysis

This section examines each of the three aforementioned unilateral operational types for their lawfulness, beginning with LCOs (including its other varieties), followed by SDOs, and then interception operations. Afterward, a number of cross-cutting justifications will be discussed.

i Lure and Capture Operations (All Kinds)

Whether unilateral, surrogate, consensual, or joint in terms of the configuration of party involvement – and whether strategic or tactical with regard to intended destination – LCOs tend to be uniformly evaluated for their lawfulness. That is, the legal standard does not vary depending on such factors,[87] and accordingly all kinds of LCOs are evaluated for their lawfulness together in this section.

This lawfulness analysis focuses strictly on the substantive legality of carrying out an LCO by a government official or agent[88] and is

[85] Bazyler, *supra* n.81, at 695.

[86] *Id.*

[87] At the same time, however, when the host State has participated or acquiesced in the operation, or the host State is not the fugitive's State of nationality, States are less likely to mount a protest after the fact. *E.g.*, *United States v. Reed*, 639 F.2d 896, 902 (2d Cir. 1981) (the Government of the Bahamas "made no attempt to seek [Reed's] return [after he had been lured by U.S. agents out of the Bahamas to the Florida coast] or to make any protest (probably in part because Reed was a U.S. citizen)").

[88] The legality of lure and capture operations carried out pursuant to governmental powers must be distinguished from those undertaken privately by individual citizens, in which case such an operation typically is treated as a domestic criminal offense. *E.g.*, Swiss Crim. Code, Dec. 21, 1937, art. 271(2), *as amended* ("Any person who abducts another by using violence, *false pretences* or threats and takes him abroad in order to hand him over to a foreign authority, party or other organisation or to expose him to a danger to life or limb is liable to a custodial sentence of not less than one year.") (emphasis supplied).

independent of other related variables that courts often take into account when reviewing such cases, including whether undue force or outrageous treatment was inflicted upon the fugitive incidental to the lure or capture,[89] whether domestic constitutional guarantees apply to the fugitive in a given instance,[90] whether the fugitive has standing to bring a claim alleging a violation of international law,[91] or whether a fugitive's asserted defenses at trial ultimately prove successful.[92] (Personal jurisdiction and individual standing will be addressed in Chapter 13 *infra* as judicial process considerations.)

Indicia of Unlawfulness. Many States, tribunals, and legal experts find such deceptive practices to be a violation of international and/or municipal law whether as a constitutional or procedural matter.[93] The International Penal Law Association (IPLA) adopted a resolution that "enticing a person under false pretenses to come voluntarily from another country in order to subject such a person to arrest and criminal prosecution is contrary to public international law and should not be

89 *E.g.*, Stephanie Carter, Note, *Forcible Abduction of Fugitive in Foreign Country Does Not Violate Due Process*, United States v. Reed, *639 F.2d 896 (2d Cir. 1981)*, 6 Suffolk Transnat'l L.J. 357, 364 (1981–82) ("In defining what was necessary and reasonable in an ordinary arrest [following a lure operation] the *Reed* court [negatively] sanctioned the use of both physical and psychological force to some extent" [including holding a gun to the fugitive's head]).

90 *Cf. Yunis*, 681 F. Supp. at 917–18 (noting the preliminary question as to whether U.S. constitutional protections even apply to non-nationals overseas).

91 *E.g., Wilson*, 721 F.2d at 972 (holding that the defendant had no standing to raise a violation of international law "absent such protest or objection by the offended sovereign"); *United States v. Cordero*, 668 F.2d 32, 37 (1st Cir. 1981).

92 For example, during his prosecution, a fugitive arrested following an LCO potentially could assert the affirmative defense of entrapment. However, "[i]nternationally, there is limited interest in the entrapment defense. Until very recently, the entrapment defense was available only in the United States; it was not a feature in English common law, and no other industrialized nations traditionally recognized it. Entrapment's absence from these other legal traditions is due partly to other devices in their legal systems for regulating police activity, such as outright criminal liability for government agents who overreach. A second possible factor is the cultural difference regarding privacy expectations, as Europeans seem to have a greater tolerance for more invasive government surveillance. Although some countries have begun to recognize the entrapment defense for the first time, they are generally far less judicious than U.S. courts in awarding the entrapment defense." Paul W. Valentine, *To Catch an Entrapper: The Inadequacy of the Entrapment Defense Globally and the Need to Reevaluate Our Current Legal Rubric*, Pace Int'l L. Rev. Online Companion, Aug. 2009, at 22, 23, *available at* http://digitalcommons.pace.edu/cgi/viewcontent.cgi?article=1001&context=pilronline (last visited on May 29, 2016).

93 Some States treat LCOs as no less unlawful than SDOs. Jordan J. Paust, '*Such a Narrow Approach' Indeed*, 29 Va. J. Int'l L. 413, 443–46 (1989); Dycus, *supra* n.14, at 523.

tolerated."[94] Along those lines, the *U.S. Attorneys' Manual*, which is intended for use by federal prosecutors, states:

> [S]ome countries will not extradite a person to the United States if the person's presence in that country was obtained through the use of a lure or other ruse. In addition, some countries may view a lure of a person from its territory as an infringement on its sovereignty.[95]

It also has been maintained that luring is a breach of the general principle of good faith to the extent it erodes or undermines cooperation, friendship, and trust between States; and/or violates existing treaty and other international obligations that insist on good faith.[96]

In July 1982, in the *Case of X*, the Swiss Federal Court refused to authorize the extradition of a Belgian national to Germany on the grounds that he had arrived on Swiss territory after being lured by German authorities from Belgium.[97] In September 1987, after Lebanese national Fawaz Younis[98] was lured from Cyprus into international waters and apprehended by the United States, the Lebanese Minister of Justice vilified such conduct as "an act close to piracy" and an "aggression against the dignity of Lebanon."[99] In 1924, France demanded the return of German national Schnaebele after he had been enticed out of French territory across the German border by a German police official who had invited the fugitive to attend a meeting with safe passage.[100] Such cases can involve host States complaining about nationals or non-nationals lured out of their

[94] *Mutual Assistance in Crim. Matters: XVth Congress of Int'l Penal Law Ass'n Adopts Resolutions, reprinted in* 10 IELR 383, 387 (1994).

[95] DoJ, *U.S. Attorneys' Manual*, § 9-15.630 (2d ed. 2007–3 Supp.).

[96] Brief for the Gov't of Canada as *Amicus Curiae* in Support of Respondent, *United States v. Álvarez-Machaín, reprinted in* 31 ILM 919 (1992) and 60 U.S.L.W. 4523 (U.S. June 15, 1992) (No. 91–712) [hereinafter Canada *Amicus Curiae*]. *See generally* Vienna Conv. on the Law of Treaties (VCLT), May 23, 1969, art. 26, 1155 U.N.T.S. 332, *reprinted in* 8 ILM 679 ("Every treaty in force is binding upon the parties to it and must be performed by them in good faith.").

[97] Otto Lagodny, *Legally Protected Interests of the Abducted Alleged Offender*, 27 Isr. L. Rev. 339, 341 n.8 (1993).

[98] The actual spelling of his name is Younis, although the U.S. federal court labeled the case *United States v. Yunis*.

[99] AP, "Berri Says U.S. Arrest of Accused Hijacker 'Close to Piracy,'" *AP News Archive*, Sept. 19, 1987, *available at* www.apnewsarchive.com/1987/Berri-Says-U-S-Arrest-of-Accused-Hijacker-Close-To-Piracy-/id-1d1834b93db27fbb33b98576515c12d1 (last visited on May 29, 2016); *cf.* Beck & Arend, *supra* n.66, at 174 n.100 (noting that the LCO "engendered little other international reaction," although it is also the case that no other States had strong national interests in the matter).

[100] Selleck, *supra* n.51, at 257 (Germany's Prince Bismarck agreed to return him to France).

territory or third States contesting lures of their nationals out of another's territory.

In addition, in a rare instance of a reported international arbitration case addressing the lawfulness of a lure operation, in 1933 the United States-Panama Claims Commission ruled that US $500 in compensatory damages were owed by the United States (even after the fugitive's mandated return) when one of its police officers assigned to the Panama Canal Zone had deceived Guillermo Colunje, a Panamanian citizen, to enter the Zone for a softball game in order to arrest him.[101] Pursuant to a claim by the Government of Panama, the Arbitration Commission reasoned as follows:

> It is evident that the police agent of the Zone by inducing Colunje by false pretenses to come with him to the Zone with the intent of arresting him there unduly exercised authority within the jurisdiction of the Republic of Panamas to the prejudice of a Panamanian citizen, who, as a result thereof, suffered the humiliation incident to a criminal proceeding. For this act of a police agent in the performance of his functions, the United States of America should be held liable.[102]

Lawfulness Rationale. At the same time, LCOs are not prohibited *per se* under any international convention or even as a function of customary international law.[103] In addition, a number of courts have held LCOs to be permissible because they are viewed as fundamentally voluntary on the part of the fugitive, rather than coerced.[104] A U.K. court in 1990 plainly set forth the rationale on voluntariness as follows:

> In the present case the appellant [and his associate] came to Hong Kong of their own free will to collect, as they thought, the illicit profits of their heroin trade. They were present in Hong Kong not because of any

[101] *Colunje Claim*, U.S.-Panama Claims Comm'n, June 27, 1933, 6 RIAA 342 (1933), *reprinted in* Annual Digest and Reports of Int'l Law Cases 1933–34 (No. 96) at 250–51, U.S. Dep't of State Arbitration Series, No. 6, at 733–49 (1934).

[102] *Id.*

[103] Indeed, as a general rule, domestic police forces are authorized to carry out deceptive practices, including undercover or sting operations, in order to capture suspected criminals, and there is a compelling international interest in bringing criminals to justice.

[104] Some lure operations, of course, are more coercive than others. For example, in *Schmidt*, the U.K. House of Lords assessed a claim by the petitioner who had been lured into the United Kingdom on the false pretense that if he did not cooperate by traveling to the United Kingdom as requested, he would face the severe consequence of being arrested the next time he tried to enter the country. One judge found this particular type of lure objectionable on that ground. *In re Schmidt* [1995] 1 A.C. 339, 358 (H.L.), [1994] 3 WLR 229 ("*Schmidt II*") (Lord Sedley).

unlawful conduct of the authorities but because of their own criminality and greed.[105]

This rationale was also followed by the European Court of Human Rights in the *Stocké* case in which the Court found no violation of Article 5(1) (right to liberty and security of person) where, even though the German prosecuting authorities had arranged with an informant to lure Stocké from France to Germany on the pretext of a flight to Luxembourg, the cooperation did not amount to an unlawful activity such as returning him "against his will."[106] Furthermore, some courts, including the U.S. Court of Appeals for the Fifth Circuit, in characterizing LCOs as nothing more than "a nonviolent trick,"[107] have stressed the fact that, absent force or violence, it would be unfair or unreasonable to regard such government conduct as overstepping legal bounds.[108]

Violation of Territorial Sovereignty? One upshot of such voluntary, non-forcible departure from host State territory is that LCOs generally are not regarded as infringing on or interfering with territorial sovereignty.[109] For example, Slavko Dokmanović, a Croatian Serb and Mayor of Vukovar

105 *Liangsiriprasert v. United States* [1991] 1 A.C. 225 (P.C.), [1990] 2 All E.R. 866.

106 *Stocké v. F.R.G.*, Appl. No. 11755/85, 13 EHRR 839, ¶ 51, Mar. 19, 1991 [hereinafter *Stocké Case*].

107 *United States v. Wilson*, 732 F.2d 404, 411 (5th Cir.), *cert. denied*, 469 U.S. 1099 (1984).

108 *See, e.g., Walker Case, supra* n.28, ¶ 28, (the U.S. Customs Service unilaterally lured Kenneth Walker, a Canadian businessman and commodity trader, by providing him at the last minute with a purchased airline ticket from Toronto to the Bahamas, which included a stopover in New York City; "the Ontario Court of Appeal found that Mr. Walker had voluntarily cleared U.S. Customs and Immigration before boarding the plane to The Bahamas of his own free will, and that he only had to look at his plane ticket to realize he would be stopping in New York."); *Prosecutor v. Dokmanović*, Case No. IT-95-13a-PT, Tr. Ch. II, Decision on the Motion for Release by the Accused, Oct. 22, 1997, [hereinafter *Dokmanović Case*] (rejecting the defense claim that a lure operation, which tricked Slavko Dokmanović into entering a vehicle in Serbia that then carried him into U.N.-controlled territory in Croatia where he was arrested, was tantamount to "a forcible abduction or kidnapping") (international criminal tribunal example).

109 While not usually explicit in court reasoning, LCOs are not directed at the host State but rather at an individual, and the operation does not infringe on the host State's territorial integrity or political independence, as its reliance on sovereign territory to effect the deceit tends to be incidental at most. Notable exceptions to this viewpoint include Germany and Switzerland. *See* Neil Boister, An Introduction to Transnational Criminal Law 233 (2012) (discussing *Yemeni Citizens Extradition Case*, 2 BvR 1506/03, Ger., Nov. 5, 2003); *Case of X, Belgian Citizen v. Swiss Justice and Police Dept*, Trib. Féd. Suisse, July 15, 1982, 10 Europaische Grundrechte-Zeitschrift (EuGRZ) 435 (1983) (denying extradition to Germany based in part on the conclusion that Germany had violated Belgium's territorial sovereignty when a Belgian national was lured to Switzerland.

indicted for his complicity in a hospital massacre in Eastern Croatia in November 1991, claimed in 1997 that U.N. officials had violated Serbian sovereignty when he was lured into Croatia under what he believed to be a promise of safe conduct to attend a meeting with the Transitional Administrator of Eastern Slavonia Baranja and Western Sirmium ostensibly to arrange to compensate Dokmanović for property he had been forced to abandon. He voluntarily crossed the border and entered a UNTAES vehicle in eastern Croatia, where he was driven to the town of Erdut, then arrested, read his rights, put on a UNTAES plane to The Hague, and surrendered to the ICTY for prosecution.[110] Dokmanović's claim was rejected by the ICTY, as the operation was found to have neither violated international law nor the Federal Republic of Yugoslavia's (FRY's) sovereignty.[111]

Some legal commentators have corroborated that view when assessing the lawfulness, for example, of the United States' LCO of Lebanese national Fawaz Younis from Cyprus to international waters (*i.e.*, beyond the twelve-nautical-mile point marking the end of a coastal State's territorial sea) by finding that, absent any physical force or abduction, no valid claim can be made out for a breach of territorial sovereignty under such facts.[112] A minority of commentators, however, focus instead on the fact that LCOs take place to some extent, however superficially or fleetingly, on host State territory[113] and for them it arguably follows that the host State's interests suffer on account of a deprivation of the fugitive's legal rights.[114]

Some courts have found that, in balancing the equities, LCOs have been neither too extreme in nature nor disproportionate vis-à-vis the

110 *Dokmanović Case, supra* n.108 (international criminal tribunal example); Scharf, *supra* n.40, at 970–71.

111 *Dokmanović Case, supra* n.108.

112 *E.g.*, Nadelmann, Cops, *supra* n.17, at 454 (no infringement of Cypriot sovereignty found in the *Yunis* case); Melanie M. Laflin, Note, *Kidnapped Terrorists: Bringing Int'l Criminals to Justice Through Irregular Rendition and Other Quasi-Legal Options*, 26 J. Legis. 315, 324, 326 (2000) (no sovereignty was violated in the *Yunis* case because the subject voluntarily embarked).

113 *E.g.*, Edwin M. Borchard, *The Factor Extradition Case*, 28 AJIL 742 (1934) (noting that the deceit involved is "consummated" in host State territory).

114 *See* Frederick A. Mann, *Reflections on the Prosecution of Persons Abducted in Breach of Int'l Law, in* International Law at a Time of Perplexity: Essays in Honour of Shabtai Rosenne 408–09 (Yoram Dinstein ed. 1989) (international law violation occurs where "the State or its agent … induces him by fraud or other illegal means to leave the country of refuge and proceed to some other country where he is apprehended … In such circumstances … the wrong is committed in the foreign state [the host State], because the illegal means are used or have their effect there. A State, being sovereign, is not expected to tolerate acts that involve generally recognized illegality, though they are not performed by force. It is not necessarily the use of force, but the illegality, that constitutes the wrong done to the sovereignty of the State.").

underlying crime as to warrant case dismissal. For example, in a case involving an undercover U.K. customs official who, in connection with an LCO, physically imported heroin into the United Kingdom after being handed a package during a drug deal with a suspected Pakistan-based narcotics smuggler – in order to establish evidence of criminal conduct and to set him up for an arrest when he was later invited to the United Kingdom by another customs official who had secured an entry visa for him – the House of Lords found the conduct of the customs officer who imported the heroin "not so unworthy or shameful that it was an affront to the public conscience."[115] Similarly, in November 2003, "the German Federal Constitutional Court rejected a challenge by two Yemenis to their extradition to the U.S. to face terrorism charges, who had been lured to Germany by an undercover U.S. agent, on the [partial] basis that . . . the sovereignty violation of the state from which they were lured was *proportional* to the serious nature of the offences involved."[116]

Finally, to the extent that host State law enforcement agents raid another State's flagged vessel anchored in the host State's territorial waters in order to seize a fugitive, its lawfulness, absent evidence of consent, tends to turn on whether the vessel was merely passing through (illegal) or was proceeding from or to the host State's internal waters (legal).[117]

Circumvention of Extradition Treaty? The international legal community remains divided on the extent to which an LCO can or should be considered unlawful *where an operative extradition treaty was ignored by the pursuing State*. The difference of opinion generally turns on one's view as to the underlying purpose of the extradition treaty. For some, an extradition treaty is regarded as a means simply to protect a State's territorial sovereignty from infringement; accordingly, an LCO, which entails no use or threat of force, nor is it directed against a State itself,

[115] *R. v. Latif* [1996] 1 WLR 104 (H.L.), [1996] 2 Cr. App. R. 92.

[116] Boister, *supra* n.109, at 233 (discussing *Yemeni Citizens Extradition Case*, *supra* n.109, ¶¶ 53–62) (emphasis supplied)).

[117] *See* Conv. on the Territorial Sea and the Contiguous Zone, Apr. 29, 1958, art. 19(2) and (5), 15 U.S.T. 1606, 516 U.N.T.S. 205 (the host/coastal State may only take steps to arrest a fugitive on board a flagged vessel while in territorial waters if that vessel has come from or is going into the host State's internal waters); *cf.* Bart DeSchutter, *Problems of Jurisdiction in the Int'l Control and Repression of Terrorism, in* International Terrorism and Political Crimes 382 n.10 (M. Cherif Bassiouni ed. 1975). Although the *Samuel Insull* case (1934) follows these facts, it occurred two decades before the controlling treaty standard in effect today.

would not generally be treated as a circumvention of that treaty.[118] For others, an extradition treaty is recognized implicitly as the exclusive method by which fugitives are to be returned between States; an LCO, therefore, may well be seen as an abrogation of that understanding.[119] This divide is complicated by the fact that, sometimes, the host State will not grant an extradition request for political reasons, but nevertheless consent *sub rosa* to a fugitive's departure from its territory by other means, including via deception.

Summary. In the end, there appears to be no clear consensus under international law regarding the legality of LCOs. Although no express prohibition exists in treaty law and there is no customary practice at variance with its use (particularly in light of States' not infrequent reliance on this method), there is considerable opposition to the use of LCOs among some States and legal authorities. In many instances, host States cooperate at some level on pursuing State-led LCOs, but in unilateral scenarios, offended States may choose to protest after the fact and in doing so seek to have the fugitive returned. It would be constructive for the international community to fashion a clear and reasonable legal standard governing such operations, possibly around the perfidy notion found in the law of war (*see* sub-section c in the Conclusion).

ii Unilateral Seizure and Delivery Operations

When assessing the lawfulness of unilateral SDOs,[120] there are a number of potential violations of international law[121] to consider; most notably including: (i) a breach of territorial sovereignty, (ii) non-compliance with an extradition or other type of applicable treaty; and (iii) the failure to observe certain international human rights standards. SDOs may implicate international law at any one of three phases: the physical apprehension, the

[118] *E.g.*, Laflin, *supra* n.112, at 326 (discussing the *Yunis* case).

[119] *E.g.*, Manuel R. Garcia-Mora, *Criminal Jurisdiction of a State over Fugitives Brought from a Foreign Country by Force or Fraud: A Comparative Study*, 32 Ind. L.J. 427, 429 (1957).

[120] Those SDOs that specifically involve the participation or acquiescence of the host State are discussed in Chapter 11.b.

[121] In addition, a State's domestic legislation may prohibit its law enforcement officers from effecting an arrest overseas. *See, e.g.*, U.S. Pub. L. 94–329, 90 Stat. 729, 22 U.S.C. § 2291(c)(1) (2012) (known as the "Mansfield Amendment" named after Mike Mansfield (D-MT), U.S. Senate Majority Leader, 1961–77) ("No officer or employee of the United States may directly effect an arrest in any foreign country as part of any foreign police action with respect to narcotics control efforts, notwithstanding any other provision of law.").

departure from host State territory, or the treatment of the fugitive once in pursuing State custody.[122] This section will review the applicability and limits by violation type,[123] and a later section will gauge the merits of various justifications postulated for conducting such unilateral SDOs notwithstanding a *prima facie* violation of international law.[124]

122 It is worth noting on a preliminary basis that the United States, which arguably has been the world's most active contemporary exponent of unilateral SDOs, for much of its history did not view such operations as lawful – and indeed publicly rebuked or protested against them. *See* Pyle, *supra* n.14, at 267 ("Until the 1970s abductions [SDOs] were rare and those that came to the attention of the U.S. courts usually were carried out by private persons or local police. The reason is plain: federal executive did not believe that kidnapping [SDOs] was a legal or necessary law-enforcement measure."). "During the Cold War, American officials were infuriated by abductions carried out by East German secret police in the American sector of Berlin. The United States also objected when Soviet officials in New York tried to force two asylum-seeking teachers to return home." *Id.; see also* "Anti-Red Abducted After Gun Battle in Western Berlin," *N.Y. Times*, July 9, 1952, at 1; "U.S. Rejects Soviet Charges Concerning Refusal of Two Russian Teachers to Return to Soviet Union," 19 *Dep't of State Bull.* 251 (1948); Selleck, *supra* n.51, at 247 (citing to the *Kasenkina* case in which, after the Soviet Union attempted to seize a Soviet citizen from New York State in August 1948, the U.S. Government declared that no police power exercised by a foreign power would be allowed). *But see In re State of Vermont v. Brewster*, 7 Vt. 118 Vt. Sup. Ct. (1835) (SDO case); "A Primer on U.S. Extradition Law," Free Existence website, Apr. 2009, *available at* www.freeexistence.org/us_extradition.html (last visited on May 25, 2016) (an early SDO in "United States history was that of John Surratt, a conspirator in a plot to kidnap President Lincoln, and believed to be a conspirator in his assassination. Surratt fled to Canada, followed by England, Italy, and later Egypt. Surratt was recognized in Alexandria, Egypt, and [seized] by United States agents in Alexandria, Egypt, in 1866 and returned to the United States for trial (he was later acquitted).").

123 Although the UNGA has considered whether to request the ICJ to render an advisory opinion regarding the legality of forcible unilateral measures in securing the custody of an individual on foreign sovereign territory no such request ever has materialized. Virginia Morris & M.-Christiane Bourloyannis-Vrailas, "Request for an Advisory Opinion from the Int'l Court of Justice (item 148)," *The Work of the Sixth Committee at the Forty-eighth Sess. of the U.N. General Assembly*, 88 AJIL 343, 357–58 (Apr. 1994).

124 From time to time, the lawfulness of an SDO will not reach a court for judgment as the fugitive-cum-criminal defendant and the prosecutor will reach a deal, often known as a "plea agreement," that precludes any legal analysis. For example, in *Prosecutor v. Simić*, Case No. IT-95-9-T, Tr. Ch., Oct. 17, 2003, co-defendant Stevan Todorović, who was indicted for the murder and rape of Croatian and Muslim civilians in Bosnia, alleged that a British Air Service team had seized him from Serbia and transported him to Bosnia in September 1998 and then turned him over to Stabilization Forces in Bosnia and Herzegovina (SFOR), Tom Walker, "SAS Carried Out Serb Raid," *The Times* (London), Nov. 11, 1998, at 15, and subsequently to ICTY officials, but when the Trial Chamber asked SFOR to provide documents and materials relating to his arrest, a plea agreement preempted the disclosure. Francesco de Sanctis, *The Practice of National and Int'l Courts on Transnat'l Seizure: Is a Fair Balance Between Human Rights and Accountability*

1 Territorial Sovereignty Analysis

The chief argument advanced for the unlawfulness of a unilateral SDO relates to a violation of the host State's territorial sovereignty. This analysis first examines the general rule and then looks at more complex geographical scenarios, including failed State territory, militarily occupied territory, and non-sovereign territory/international space.[125]

General Rule. It is well-established under international law that a pursuing State may not violate the territorial sovereignty of the host State in connection with an extraterritorial law enforcement action:

> In public international law, territorial jurisdiction is one of the basic attributes of sovereignty. 'By territorial jurisdiction is meant the jurisdiction of the State over individuals living on its territory, over things which are on this territory and over facts which occur there.' In a normal situation – or more precisely in a classical situation – the territorial jurisdiction is exclusive and complete. This has two consequences: the positive aspect implies the exclusive right to exercise all state activities, and the negative explicitly excludes any other state jurisdiction within a given territory.[126]

Possible?, 22 NETH. Q. HUM. RTS. 529, 543 (2004) (international criminal tribunal example).

[125] It is also theoretically possible that an SDO could occur on territory that is the subject of disputed ownership or control. This author is not aware of any case law related to such an instance. Such matters presumably would be resolved based on the specific facts at play.

[126] SERGE LAZAREFF, STATUS OF MILITARY FORCES UNDER CURRENT INTERNATIONAL LAW 7 (1971) (quoting ROUSSEAU, DROIT INTERNATIONAL PUBLIC, ed. 1953, no. 250) (interior quotation omitted)). *See also* Michael Akehurst, *Jurisdiction in Int'l Law*, 46 B.Y.B.I.L. 145, 148 (1972–73) ("There is abundant authority for the proposition that it is a breach of international law for the agents of one State to seize an individual . . . in the territory of another State," provided the purpose was to "giv[e] effect to the sovereign powers of the seizing State."); *id.* at 148–49 (simply because "[i]ndividuals who have been seized in the territory of another State are not usually allowed to plead this fact as a bar to their prosecution . . . does not mean that the seizure is lawful under international law; the seizure is illegal"). This proposition was proffered as early as 1773 by the distinguished jurist Emmerich de Vattel: "We should not only refrain from usurping the territory of others; we should also respect, and abstain from every act contrary to the rights of the sovereign; for, a foreign nation can claim no right in it. We cannot, then, without doing an injury to a state, enter its territories with force and arms in pursuit of a criminal, and take him from thence. This would at once be a violation of the safety of the state, and a trespass on the rights of empire or supreme authority vested in the sovereign." EMMERICH DE VATTEL, THE LAW OF NATIONS OR THE PRINCIPLES OF NATURAL LAW GOVERNING THE BEHAVIOUR AND PRACTICE OF STATES § 93 (1773). *See also* discussion on the possible violation of territorial sovereignty in Chapter 11.c.ii.

International treaty law strongly supports this proposition. Several provisions of the U.N. Charter,[127] the OAS Charter,[128] the Inter-American Treaty of Reciprocal Assistance (better known as the "Rio Treaty"),[129] and the U.N. Convention against Illicit Traffic in Narcotic Drugs and Psychotropic Substances,[130] embrace this principle. Beyond international treaties, a number of UNGA and UNSC resolutions also have upheld this precept, most notably including the Declaration on the Inadmissibility of Intervention in the Domestic Affairs of States and the Protection of their Independence and Sovereignty (1965);[131] the Declaration on Principles of Int'l Law Concerning Friendly Relations

[127] Charter of the United Nations, June 26, 1945, art. 1(2) and (3) (among the purposes of the United Nations are to "develop friendly relations among nations" and to "achieve international cooperation in solving international problems"); art. 2(1) ("The Organization is based on the principle of the sovereign equality of all its Members."); art. 2(4) (among the U.N. principles to be subscribed to include that all members shall "refrain in their international relations from the threat or use of force against the territorial integrity or political independence of any state, or in any other manner inconsistent with the Purposes of the United Nations."); and art. 2(7) (enunciating the non-intervention principle).

[128] Charter of Organization of American States (OAS), Apr. 30, 1948, art. 5(b), 2 U.S.T. 2394, T.I.A.S. No. 2361, *as amended* by the Prot. of Buenos Aires, Feb. 27, 1967, 21 U.S.T. 607, T.I.A.S. No. 6847 [hereinafter OAS Charter] ("International order consists essentially of respect for the personality, sovereignty and independence of States, and the faithful fulfillment of obligations derived from treaties and other sources of international law"); *id.*, art. 15 ("No State ... has the right to intervene, directly or indirectly, for any reason whatever, in the internal or external affairs of any other State. The foregoing principle prohibits not only armed force but also any other form of interference or attempted threat against the personality of the State or against its political, economic, and cultural elements"); *id.*, art. 17 ("The territory of a State is inviolable; it may not be the object, even temporarily, of military occupation or of other measures of force taken by another State, directly or indirectly, on any grounds whatever"); *id.*, art. 21 ("No territorial acquisitions or special advantages obtained either by force or by other means of coercion shall be recognized").

[129] Inter-Am. Treaty of Reciprocal Assistance [Rio Treaty], Sept. 2, 1947, art. 1, 62 Stat. 1681, T.I.A.S. No. 1838, 21 U.N.T.S. 77 (condemning the use or threat of force "in any manner inconsistent with the provisions of the Charter of the United Nations.").

[130] U.N. Conv. against Illicit Traffic in Narcotic Drugs and Psychotropic Substances, Dec. 20, 1988, art. 2(2), U.N. Doc. E/CONF/82/15 (1988), *reprinted in* 28 ILM 493 (1989) ("The Parties shall carry out their obligations under this Convention in a manner consistent with the principles of sovereign equality and territorial integrity of States and that of non-intervention in the domestic affairs of other States"); *id.*, art. 2(3) ("A Party shall not undertake in the territory of another Party the exercise of jurisdiction and performance of functions which are exclusively reserved for the authorities of that other Party by its domestic law.").

[131] UNGA Res. 2131, Dec. 21, 1965, U.N. GAOR, 20th Sess., Supp. No. 14, U.N. Doc. A/RES/20/2131 (1965).

and Cooperation Among States in Accordance with the Charter of the United Nations (1970);[132] UNSC Resolution 138 regarding the seizure of Adolf Eichmann by Israel from Buenos Aires (1960);[133] UNSC Resolution 579 condemning hostage-taking and abductions following a spate of such incidents (1985);[134] and UNSC Resolution 638 relating to the seizure of Sheik Obeid by Israel from Beirut (1989).[135]

Customary international law also lends support to this principle, as widespread and largely uniform evidence exists for such State practice specifically when taken out of a sense of legal obligation. Of particular note,

> Canada undertook a survey of the policies and laws of some countries on the question of extraterritorial abduction [SDOs] by law enforcement officers. The 1992 survey received replies from Australia, Austria, Britain, Finland, Germany, The Netherlands, Norway, New Zealand, Sweden, and Switzerland. All countries indicated that that they would regard such abductions as a violation of their sovereignty and of international law. There was a clear acceptance of the principle that abducted persons must be returned to a nation when it protests the infringement of its sovereignty.[136]

[132] UNGA Res. 2625, Oct. 24, 1970, U.N. GAOR, 25th Sess. (Supp. No. 28), U.N. Doc. A/8028 (1971), *reprinted in* 9 ILM 1292 (1970).

[133] *Question Relating to the Case of Adolf Eichmann*, UNSC Res. 138, June 23, 1960, S/RES/138 (1960), 15 U.N. SCOR (868th mtg.), U.N. Doc. S/INF/15/Rev.1/1960) ("Considering that the violation of the sovereignty of a Member State is incompatible with the Charter of the United Nations . . . [and n]oting that the repetition of acts such as that giving rise to this situation would involve a breach of the principles upon which international order is founded creating an atmosphere of insecurity and distrust incompatible with the preservation of peace . . . [the UNSC requests] the Government of Israel to make appropriate reparation in accordance with the Charter of the United Nations and the rules of international law.").

[134] UNSC Res. 579, Dec. 18, 1985, U.N. SCOR, U.N. Doc. S/RES/579 (1985), *reprinted in* 25 ILM 243 (1986).

[135] UNSC Res. 638, July 31, 1989, U.N. SCOR, U.N. Doc. S/RES/638 (condemning "all acts of hostage-taking and abduction as offenses of grave concern to all States and serious violations of international law" and demanding "the immediate safe release of all hostages and abducted persons, wherever and by whomever they are being held."). While the phraseology of the UNSC resolutions relating to specific cases is characteristically hedged – indeed, in the case of Sheik Obeid neither his name nor the role played by Israel is even mentioned – this can reasonably be viewed as a function of the political compromise required to reach unanimity rather than necessarily attributable to any reservations held by the UNSC as to the merit of this principle.

[136] Hermann F. Woltring & Joanne Greig, *State-Sponsored Kidnapping of Fugitives: An Alternative to Extradition?, in* THE ALLEGED TRANSNATIONAL CRIMINAL: THE SECOND BIENNIAL INTERNATIONAL CRIMINAL LAW SEMINAR 119 (Richard D. Atkins ed. 1993).

In addition, the Governments of Mexico and Canada each submitted *amicus curiae* briefs to the U.S. Supreme Court in connection with its adjudication of the *Álvarez-Machaín Case* in 1992, asserting this principle.[137] Furthermore, States like Israel,[138] Germany,[139] and the United States,[140] when they have resorted to SDOs, discussed their possibility, or examined the extent of their lawfulness, have rhetorically extended support to the principle, in effect, through denials or exceptions.[141] Moreover, several domestic courts have found SDOs to be unlawful and/or insisted that fugitives be returned to the host State from which they were seized on account of territorial infringements,

[137] Canada *Amicus Curiae, supra* n.96; Brief for the United Mexican States as *Amicus Curiae* in Support of the Affirmance, *United States v. Álvarez-Machaín, reprinted in* 31 ILM 934 (1992) and 60 U.S.L.W. 4523 (U.S. June 15, 1992) (No. 91-712).

[138] In 1960, Israel evidently recognized that the SDO of Adolf Eichmann was unlawful (or at least would elicit broad international criticism), as they initially denied identifying where the apprehension had occurred and further claimed that the operation had been undertaken by independent volunteers. *See* Gary J. Bass, *The Adolf Eichmann Case: Universal and National Jurisdiction, in* UNIVERSAL JURISDICTION: NATIONAL COURTS AND THE PROSECUTION OF SERIOUS CRIMES UNDER INTERNATIONAL LAW 86 (Stephen Macedo ed. 2004).

[139] "Following the West German Government's offer of a $25,000 reward for the recovery of Martin Bormann, a government official was reported to have pointed out that if Bormann were recovered by kidnapping, 'the reward would be paid only if the country of hiding later gave its approval.'" Alona E. Evans, *Acquisition of Custody over the Int'l Fugitive Offender—Alternatives to Extradition: A Survey of United States Practice*, 40 B.Y.B.I.L. 77, 89 n.3 (1964) (quoting UPI, "Bonn Offers $25,000 for Bormann's Capture," *N.Y. Times*, Nov. 24, 1964, at 12).

[140] In June 1989, U.S. DoJ's Office of Legal Counsel (OLC) issued an advisory opinion to the effect that the FBI could arrest an individual on foreign soil for a violation of U.S. law without the host State's consent. The opinion reversed a position taken by the same office nine years earlier on the same issue. The thrust of the 1989 opinion was that the U.S. President was permitted under the U.S. constitutional system to take or direct actions in the national interest that departed from customary international law (CIL), and thereby recognized the underlying CIL status of this principle. Richard Pregent, *Presidential Authority to Displace Customary Int'l Law*, 129 MIL. L. REV. 77 (1990) (although the 1989 opinion was not publicly disclosed, Asst. AG William Barr testified about it before the Subcomm. on Civil and Constitutional Rights of the Judiciary Comm. of the U.S. House of Reps. on Nov. 8, 1989).

[141] As the ICJ has stated: "If a State acts in a way prima facie incompatible with a recognized rule, but defends its conduct by appealing to exceptions or justifications contained within the rule itself, then whether or not the State's conduct is in fact justifiable on that basis, the significance of that attitude is to confirm rather than to weaken the rule." *Military and Paramilitary Activities in and against Nicaragua* (Nicar. v. U.S.), Merits [1986] I.C.J. Rep. 14, 98 (June 27) [hereinafter *Nicaragua Case*].

including *In re Jolis* (France),[142] *State v. Ebrahim* (South Africa),[143] and *Bennett Case* (U.K.).[144]

International jurisprudence advancing this principle can be found, for example, in such cases as the *Lotus Case* (PCIJ, 1927),[145] the *Corfu Channel Case* (ICJ, 1949),[146] and the *Nicaragua Case* (ICJ, 1986).[147] Soft law and other sources include the Sixth Committee (Legal Questions) of UNGA at its 48th Session;[148] the Restatement (Third) of U.S. Foreign Relations Law;[149] the Harvard Draft Convention on Jurisdiction With Respect to Crime;[150] Principle VI of the CSCE/Helsinki

[142] *In re Jolis*, Tribunal Correctionnel de'Avesnes, Fr., July 22, 1933, *reprinted in* [1933–34] 7 ANN. DIG. & REP. PUB. INT'L L. CASES 191 (No. 77) (H. Lauterpacht, ed., 1940) (finding unlawful the apprehension of a Belgian national on Belgian territory by French constables and therefore ordering the release of the accused at the request of the Belgian Government).

[143] *State v. Ebrahim*, Sup. Ct. (App. Div.), So. Afr., Feb. 26, 1991, 2 S. A. REP. 553 [Afrikaans text], *reprinted and translated in* 31 ILM 888 (1992).

[144] *R. v. Horseferry Road Magistrates' Court, ex parte Bennett* [1994] 1 A.C. 42 (H.L.) [1993] 3 All E.R. 138, *reprinted in* 95 ILR 355.

[145] *SS "Lotus"* (Fr. v. Turk.) 1927 P.C.I.J. (ser. A) No. 10 at 18 (Sept. 7, 1927), *reprinted in* ANN. DIG. 153 (No. 98) (H. Lauterpacht ed. 1938) ("[T]he first and foremost restriction imposed by international law upon a State is that – failing the existence of a permissive rule to the contrary – it may not exercise its powers in any form in the territory of another State.").

[146] *Corfu Channel Case* (U.K. v. Alb.) [1949] I.C.J. Rep. 4, 35 (Apr. 9).

[147] *Nicaragua Case, supra* n.141, at 106 ("the principle of non-intervention involves the right of every sovereign State to conduct its affairs without outside interference; though examples of trespass against this principle are not infrequent, the Court considers it part and parcel of customary international law.").

[148] The Committee generally agreed that: (1) "international law prohibits a state from exercising its criminal jurisdiction beyond its territory as contrary to the sovereign equality and territorial integrity of states, unless the other state concerned has given its consent; (2) the use of unilateral measures, such as the abduction of a suspected criminal from another state for trial before the national courts of the abducting state, undermines existing mechanisms for international cooperation in the apprehension and prosecution of criminal offenders, as well as treaty obligations to prosecute or extradite such offenders." Morris & Bourloyannis-Vrailas, *supra* n.123, at 357–58.

[149] American Law Inst., RESTATEMENT (THIRD) OF THE FOREIGN RELATIONS LAW OF THE UNITED STATES (1987) & 2008 Ann. Supp., § 102 [hereinafter RESTATEMENT (THIRD)] (States may not exercise sovereign functions in the territorial jurisdiction of other states); *id.* § 432(2) ("[A] state's law enforcement officers may exercise their functions in the territory of another state only with the consent of the other state given by duly authorized officials of that state.").

[150] Draft Conv. on Research in Int'l Law of the Harvard Law School, "Jurisdiction with Respect to Crime," art. 16, *reprinted in* 29 AJIL 435 (Supp. 1935) (not formally adopted by States).

Accords;[151] and the Inter-American Juridical Committee (IAJC) of the Permanent Council of the OAS.[152]

The principle applies in general regardless of which form sovereign territory (actual or constructive) takes, including not only land territory within recognized borders, but also territorial seas, warships on the high seas,[153] diplomatic or consular missions, or authorized military bases on foreign soil.[154] Vessels sailing on the high seas are not "subject to interference" – and are therefore protected against an SDO[155] – *unless* the

[151] OSCE, Conference on Security and Co-operation in Europe: Final Act ("Helsinki Accords"), Aug. 1, 1975, 73 *Dep't of State Bull.* 323, *reprinted in* 14 ILM 1292 (1975).

[152] *Legal Opinion on the Decision of the Sup. Ct. of the United States in the* Álvarez-Machaín *Case*, OAS Res. CJI/Res.II-15/92, Inter-Am. Juridical Comm., OEA/ser. G/CI, Doc.No. 2302/92, ¶ 9, Sept. 1, 1992, *reprinted in* 13 HUM. RTS. L.J. 395 (1992) [hereinafter *OAS Legal Op.*] ("[T]he [Inter-American Juridical] Committee considers that it cannot be disputed or is not in doubt that the abduction in question [of Álvarez-Machaín by the DEA] was a serious violation of public international law since it was a transgression of the territorial sovereignty of Mexico.").

[153] *See* Third U.N. Conv. on the Law of the Sea, Dec. 10, 1982, art. 95, U.N. Doc. A/CONF.62/122 & Corr.1–8, 1833 U.N.T.S. 3, *reprinted in* 21 ILM 1261–1354 [hereinafter Law of the Sea Conv.] (warships on the high seas are completely immune from the jurisdiction of any State except the flag State); SIR ROBERT JENNINGS & SIR ARTHUR WATTS, EDS., 1 OPPENHEIM'S INTERNATIONAL LAW 1167–69 (9th ed. 1992) (citations omitted) ("A warship with all persons and goods on board, remains under the jurisdiction of her flag-state even during her stay in foreign waters . . . No official of the littoral state is allowed to board the vessel without special permission of the commander . . . Even individuals *who do not belong to the crew* but who, after having committed a crime on the territory of the littoral state, have taken refuge on board, cannot be forcibly taken off the vessel; if the commander refuses their surrender, it can be obtained only by diplomatic means from his home state. As in other cases of jurisdictional immunity, the flag state of the warship may waive its privileges so as to allow the exercise of jurisdiction by the littoral state.") (emphasis supplied). Where, however, an "auxiliary ship of the Uruguayan Navy was serving in a commercial or merchant capacity, it was not entitled to sovereign immunity as [a] warship and so law enforcement authorities were permitted to board the ship." Legal Memorandum, Office of the Legal Adviser, U.S. Dep't of State, July 13, 1989, *reprinted in* DIGEST OF U.S. PRACTICE IN INTERNATIONAL LAW 1 (1989–90) (analyzing the immunities accorded the Uruguayan ship named the *Presidente Rivera*).

[154] "The military base or other premises of the members of the armed forces of a State in the territory of another State may be inviolable. In time of peace, the armed forces of a State may be present in the territory of another State on a temporary or long-term basis with the consent of the receiving State. The presence of the armed forces is usually governed by an agreement between the States concerned. The exercise of jurisdiction by the sending or receiving State with respect to military or civilian aliens who are present in the territory of the receiving State, including on a military base under the authority of the sending State, is usually governed by the terms of the agreement between the States concerned." UNGA, *Expulsion of Aliens*, July 10, 2006, U.N. Doc. A/CN.4/565, at 52–53.

[155] *E.g.*, *United States v. Crews*, 445 U.S. 463 (1979).

ship: "(1) is engaged in piracy, slave trade, or unauthorized broadcasting; (2) is without nationality [*i.e.*, is unflagged, bears two or more State flags, or is not otherwise registered with a State[156]]; or (3) though flying a foreign flag or refusing to show its flag, is in fact of the same nationality as the warship or law enforcement ship."[157] The law is more equivocal in instances where a flagged vessel is in a pursuing State's territorial waters,[158] or even in a pursuing State's maritime contiguous zone (*i.e.*, between twelve and twenty-four nautical miles from shore) to the extent the fugitive is accused of having violated the pursuing State's "customs, fiscal, immigration or sanitary laws and regulations."[159]

Failed State Territory. Would an SDO be lawful in terms of territorial sovereignty when executed specifically on failed State territory? A "failed State" is a controversial concept and no consensus definition exists. For the purposes of this discussion, the oft-cited Fund for Peace concept has been adopted:

> A state that is failing has several attributes. One of the most common is the loss of physical control of its territory or a monopoly on the legitimate use of force. Other attributes of state failure include the erosion of legitimate authority to make collective decisions, an inability to provide reasonable public services, and the inability to interact with other states as a full member of the international community.[160]

156 Patrick Sorek, Note, *Jurisdiction over Drug Smuggling on the High Seas: It's A Small World After All:* United States v. Marino-Garcia, 44 U. Pitt. L. Rev. 1105, 1106 (1983); *cf.* Paul Michell, *English-Speaking Justice: Evolving Responses to Transnat'l Forcible Abduction after* Alvarez-Machain, 29 Cornell Int'l L.J. 383, 421 n.195 (1996).

157 Restatement (Third), *supra* n.149, § 522(2). This legal standard would largely apply to an analysis of whether an SDO complied or failed to comply with maritime treaties restricting interference, such as the 1958 Convention on the High Seas, the 1958 Convention on the Territorial Sea and the Contiguous Zone, or the 1982 Third U.N. Convention on the Law of the Sea. To avoid redundancy, therefore, these treaties are not reviewed in the next sub-section on treaty compliance.

158 *See supra* n.117 and accompanying text.

159 *See* Iain A. Cameron, The Protective Principle of International Criminal Jurisdiction 94 (1994); Conv. on the Territorial Sea and the Contiguous Zone, Apr. 29, 1958, art. 24, 15 U.S.T. 1606, 516 U.N.T.S. 205; *e.g.*, *United States v. Best*, 172 F. Supp.2d 656 (D.V.I. 2001) (finding it impermissible for the USCG to seize individuals from a Brazilian-flagged ship sixteen nautical miles from St. Croix without having sought or received the ship captain's or the Brazilian Government's consent, where there was insufficient evidence to show that the individuals at issue had violated U.S. immigration laws for conspiracy to bring aliens into the United States), *rev'd on other grounds*, 304 F.3d 308 (D.V.I. 2002).

160 Blake Hounshell, 2009 *Failed State Index – FAQ and Methodology* (based on collaboration between Fund for Peace and *Foreign Policy* magazine), *Foreign Policy* website, June 22, 2009, *available at* http://foreignpolicy.com/2009/06/22/2009-failed-states-index-faq-methodology/ (last visited on May 25, 2016).

In any event, a "failed State" is to be distinguished from a government that simply poorly serves its population through misguided policies or ineptitude.

In the case of a "failed State," "conventional notions of sovereignty and territorial integrity do not apply."[161] No offense, in effect, has occurred against a sovereign, no consent or protest can be issued, and by default no responsibility is attributable to a pursuing State when it undertakes an SDO on that territory.[162] For example, in the early 1980s, Lebanon was "divided into several tiny fiefdoms each controlled by a different armed force. The nominal Government of Lebanon actually control[ed] only a tiny portion of the nation's territory; most of the country [was] either occupied by Syrian or Israeli troops or controlled by the Phalange, Amal, Hezbollah, or Druze militias. Lebanon ha[d] no control over persons or things within its jurisdiction."[163] Therefore, an SDO in Lebanon at that time in all likelihood would not have breached territorial "sovereignty."[164]

Militarily Occupied Territory. There is ample authority for the proposition that when a State occupies foreign territory during war or through an armistice,[165] the occupying power effectively has control over the territory for purposes of SDOs and may, from a legal perspective, treat such operations as an internal matter.[166] The Allied occupation after

[161] D. Cameron Findlay, *Abducting Terrorists Overseas for Trial in the United States: Issues of Int'l and Domestic Law*, 23 Tex. Int'l L.J. 1, 17 (1988).

[162] *See* Michell, *supra* n.156, at 421 n.195 (citing as supporting case law *Ker, Tokyo Rose, Gillars, Chandler, Noriega*, and *Afouneh*).

[163] *Id.*

[164] The State of which the seized individual is a national, however, could protest on the fugitive's behalf, and the fugitive himself might be allowed to challenge a pursuing State court's personal jurisdiction on the grounds that his human rights had been violated in the process of his seizure and delivery. *See* discussion on individual standing in Chapter 13.a.ii.

[165] "The war occupation, or *occupatio bellica*, is an occupation of an enemy territory during hostilities. It is primarily a factual situation but subject to the rules of war. It is essentially a provisional situation although its duration may be unlimited. It also confers on the occupying State very extensive powers but the sovereignty of the occupied State survives. The occupation could also be conventional, that is derived from a legal act (generally an armistice) defining the respective powers of the occupying authorities and of the authorities of the occupied State." Lazareff, *supra* n.126, at 8. There are two divergent schools of thought on jurisdiction with respect to peaceful military occupation: (i) the "'law of the flag,' that gives extensive jurisdictional powers to the [external] force" and (ii) the sharing of jurisdictional power between the receiving [occupied] and the sending [occupying] State. "In fact, there is no example of full territorial sovereignty, that is of forces fully subject to all the laws of the receiving State." *Id.* at 9.

[166] *See* Evans, *supra* n.139, at 88 (observing that, under such circumstances, "any irregularity in the acquisition of custody of the accused is obviated.").

World War II illustrates this point. "The Nuremberg and Tokyo trials were conducted in territory occupied by the Allies, who were entitled to occupy Germany and Japan pursuant to terms of unconditional surrender; thus, the Allies were in a position to apprehend and prosecute the offenders on the spot through the tribunals themselves or through thousands of subsequent trials in the occupied zones."[167]

During the post-war U.S. occupation of Germany, U.S. military forces seized Douglas Chandler, a U.S. citizen charged with treason for broadcasting anti-U.S. propaganda during the war, and returned him to the United States to face trial. As Germany had no effective control over its territory, there was no violation of its territorial sovereignty.[168] Indeed, under the laws of war, "[t]he authority of the legitimate power having in fact passed into the hands of the occupant,"[169] the military governor becomes the competent authority to arrest or turn over a fugitive found in the occupied territory.[170]

Non-Sovereign Territory/International Space. As referenced in the Introduction, the notion of non-sovereign territory/international space comprises any geographical space not currently belonging to an individual State, including the high seas, unclaimed islands outside of territorial waters, and Antarctica.[171] Logically it follows, then, that an SDO conducted in such space would not implicate territorial sovereignty,[172] *except* generally in the case of a properly flagged or registered foreign vessel on the high seas or a flagged aircraft in superadjacent airspace, as discussed above, on account of constructive territory.

[167] Lyal S. Sunga, The Emerging System of International Criminal Law: Developments in Codification and Implementation 300 (1997).

[168] *Chandler v. United States*, 171 F.2d 921 (1st Cir. 1948), *cert. denied*, 336 U.S. 918 (1949); Findlay, *supra* n.161, at 17; Michael H. Cardozo, *When Extradition Fails, is Abduction the Solution?*, 55 AJIL 127, 133 (1961). *Accord Gillars v. United States*, 182 F.2d 962 (D.C. Cir. 1950) (the U.S. Army in the American Zone of Occupation in Germany could properly seize and deliver fugitives to the United States for trial); *Best*, 76 F. Supp. 138 (rejecting the defendant's argument that U.S. military occupation after World War II did not authorize U.S. officers to seize and deliver the fugitive to the United States to face trial).

[169] Hague Regulations Respecting the Laws and Customs of War on Land and Its Annex, Oct. 18, 1907, art. 43, *reprinted in* The Laws of Armed Conflicts: A Collection of Conventions, Resolutions and Other Documents 60–87 (Dietrich Schindler & Jirf Toman eds. 2004).

[170] *See* Charles Fairman, Comment, Ker v. Illinois *Revisited*, 47 AJIL 678, 685 (1953).

[171] *See* n.48 in the Introduction.

[172] Mark Brkljacic, Note, *The Dangers of State Sponsored and Court Ratified Abduction*, 5 J. Int'l L. & Prac. 117, 120–21 (1996); Kash, *Airspace, supra* n.16, at 83.

Exceptions to the exceptions above – and hence where SDOs would *not* breach territorial sovereignty – would include the following instances: (i) consent by the captain of the flagged vessel or by the State where the vessel is registered (*see* discussion *infra*); (ii) where the aircraft or ship were reasonably believed to be a pirate vessel, as "pirates are considered *hostes humani generis* – enemies of all mankind, and all states have universal jurisdiction to capture and punish them anywhere in the world,"[173] or a slave vessel or one conducting unauthorized broadcasting;[174] or (iii) arguably where a fugitive is being provided safe passage on an aircraft or vessel by a State that is in a common criminal enterprise with the fugitive and thereby not acting responsibly with respect to bringing him to justice (discussed *infra*).

2 Treaty Compliance Analysis[175]

The lawfulness of SDOs also may be challenged on the ground of non-compliance with applicable international treaties. Although the principal type of treaty invoked in this context is the bilateral or multilateral extradition treaty that operates between the host and pursuing States, other treaties can be implicated, depending on the circumstances at play or the particular status of the fugitive, including notably treaties prohibiting the use or threat of force and those safeguarding internationally protected persons and premises.[176]

Extradition Treaties. To the extent a valid extradition treaty exists between the host and pursuing States, the question arises whether reliance on a unilateral SDO by a pursuing State will necessarily circumvent

[173] Kash, *Airspace*, *supra* n.16, at 83–84. *Accord* Findlay, *supra* n.161, at 18.

[174] *See supra* n.157 and accompanying text.

[175] Only those States that are parties to specific treaties are obligated to follow their provisions. *E.g.*, *Ramirez Sánchez v. France*, Appl. No. 28780/95, Eur. Comm'n of Hum. Rts., 86 D.R. 155, 161-62, June 24, 1996 (the Commission found it was not competent to address alleged unlawful activities perpetrated by Sudanese officials in connection with seizing and turning over "Carlos the Jackal" to France because Sudan was not a party to the ECHR). Further, States parties are only so obligated insofar as they did not introduce applicable reservations or understandings at the time of ratification. Non-parties, then, have no such duty unless and only to the extent that the treaty is (or pertinent provisions are) deemed to constitute customary international law. Where treaty law does not govern in a given situation, by default, the States involved most likely would apply their domestic law, customary international law, and general principles of international law.

[176] This analysis does not purport to be comprehensive in scope, but rather to represent significant types of treaties relevant to SDOs. To avoid redundancy, human rights treaties are addressed in the SDO human rights analysis, and treaties requiring that disputes be resolved by peaceful means are covered under the lawfulness analysis on interceptions *infra*.

or breach that treaty. This query can be rephrased as whether absent (i) an express provision in an extradition treaty prohibiting SDOs; (ii) an explicit understanding to that effect based on party statements made in connection with the treaty's signature or ratification; and (iii) an articulated purpose set forth in the treaty preamble that it would exclusively govern all forms of renditions, the treaty should be construed implicitly to bar the use of SDOs, and thus, at a minimum, extradition-related protections should continue to apply in operational contexts other than extradition. Although there is much international opinion in support of this proposition, there is no clear consensus and one can reasonably discern logic on both sides.

This is concededly one of the most contentious issues in this field, as reflected by the strong dissenting opinions and critical international reactions to the U.S. Supreme Court's 1992 ruling in the landmark *Álvarez-Machaín* case. The Supreme Court majority (6-3) ruled that the terms of the 1978 U.S.-Mexico Extradition Treaty should not be interpreted as governing procedures for securing the personal jurisdiction of a fugitive by any means other than extradition, and that to do so would entail a considerable "inferential leap."[177] The dissent observed that the majority had disregarded the purpose of the extradition treaty,[178] applicable general principles of international law,[179] and fundamental

[177] *United States v. Álvarez-Machaín*, 504 U.S. 655, 669 (1992), *on remand*, 971 F.2d 310 (9th Cir. 1992), *reprinted in* 31 ILM 902 (1992) [hereinafter *Álvarez-Machaín Case*]. *Accord* Michael J. Glennon, *Agora: Int'l Kidnapping: State-Sponsored Abduction: A Comment on* United States v. Alvarez-Machain, 86 AJIL 746, 748 (1992) ("Extradition treaties were never intended to serve as catalogues of every right and obligation that exists between two states in all of customary and conventional law"). *See also* discussion at pp. 470–71.

[178] *Álvarez-Machaín Case*, *supra* n.177, at 673–74 (Stevens, J., dissenting op.) ("From the preamble, through the description of the parties' obligations with respect to offenses committed within as well as beyond the territory of a requesting party, the delineation of the procedures and evidentiary requirements for extradition, the special provisions for political offenses and capital punishment and other details, the Treaty appears to have been designed to cover the *entire subject* of extradition.") (emphasis supplied). *Accord* *Report of the Working Group on Arbitrary Detention*, U.N. Comm'n of Hum. Rts., 50th Sess., Agenda Item 10, U.N. Doc. E/CN.4/1994/27, at 138 (1993) [hereinafter *Working Group Rep.*] (finding that, despite the 1978 U.S.-Mexico Extradition Treaty's failure to expressly prohibit abductions [SDOs], "the object and purpose of the Treaty [which was intended to improve law enforcement cooperation], and an analysis of the context, lead to the unquestionable conclusion that abduction for the purpose of bringing someone in Mexico or in the United States before a court of the requesting party is a breach of the 1978 Treaty.").

[179] *OAS Legal Op.*, *supra* n.152, ¶ 12(c) ("By interpreting the U.S.-Mexico extradition treaty to the effect that it is not an impediment to the abduction of persons, the United States

safeguards for fugitives that would be forfeited to the extent the extradition treaty were not honored.[180]

States, however, need not rely on such implicitness, as express terms or understandings regarding exclusive aims are always available as an option, particularly in light of the well-established empirical record to date concerning SDOs. An historical example of an explicit understanding occurred in 1881, when U.S. Secretary of State James Blaine, in commenting on the then-U.S.-Mexico Extradition Treaty, observed that it "prescribes the forms for carrying it into effect, and does not authorize either party, for any case, to deviate from those forms or arbitrarily abduct from the territory of one party a person charged with crime, for trial within the jurisdiction of the other."[181] A more recent instance can be found in the aftermath of the *Álvarez-Machaín* decision, where Mexico insisted on a transborder abduction prohibition treaty,[182] which makes clear that SDOs are not to be tolerated as a means of obtaining the physical custody over fugitives on the other's territory.[183]

In short, in executing an extradition treaty, States are free to specify that its aim is to exclusively govern all means for bringing fugitives to justice. Not only does no rule or principle of international law preclude the introduction of such a condition, but even if one State party initially resisted such an express provision at the suggestion of the other, it would reveal their respective understandings, could be the subject of a negotiated

fails to consider the precept by which treaties must be interpreted . . . in relation to the applicable rules and principles of international law.").

180 *Álvarez-Machaín Case, supra* n.177, at 673. *Accord Ex parte Bennett, supra* n.144, 3 All E.R. at 139 ("It was an abuse of power for a person to be forcibly brought within the jurisdiction in *disregard of extradition procedures available* for the return of an accused person to the United Kingdom") (emphasis supplied); Woltring & Greig, *supra* n.136, at 123 ("[E]xtradition treaties contain certain safeguards for the individual, which are nullified by forced abductions. The *ne bis in idem,* specialty and dual criminality rules are prime examples."); *cf. Collier v. Vaccaro*, 51 F.2d 17, 19 (4th Cir. 1931) (in connection with an SDO by U.S. Government agents of R.A. Price from Canada to the United States, the court ruled that "[a] person may be carried out of the country to answer for crime . . . only by the authority of the highest executive officials and *in accordance with treaty provisions governing extradition*") (emphasis supplied).

181 Statement of Prof. Ralph G. Steinhardt before the Subcomm. on Civil and Constitutional Rights of the Comm. on the Judiciary, U.S. House of Reps., *reprinted in* 4 Crim. L. Forum 137 (1993).

182 While concluded in 1994, it has yet to be forwarded to and ratified by the U.S. Senate. Treaty to Prohibit Transborder Abductions, U.S.-Mex., Nov. 23, 1994, 31 U.S.T. 5059, *reprinted in* 5 Michael Abbell & Bruno A. Ristau, International Judicial Assistance: Criminal § 13-4-1, at A-676.3 to 676.6 (1990 & 1995 Supp.).

183 *Id.*

compromise, and would in any event leave a record for later interpretation in the *travaux preparatoires* of the treaty.[184]

Treaties Prohibiting the Use of Force. Two of the chief treaties prohibiting the use of force by States are the U.N. Charter and the OAS Charter. Article 2(4) of the U.N. Charter calls upon all Members "to refrain in their international relations from the threat or use of force against the territorial integrity or political independence of any state, or in any other manner inconsistent with the Purposes of the United Nations."[185] Article 19 of the OAS Charter provides: "No State or group of States has the right to intervene, directly or indirectly, for any reason whatever, in the internal or external affairs of any other State. The foregoing principle prohibits not only armed force but also any other form of interference or attempted threat against the personality of the State or against its political, economic, and cultural elements."[186] Article 22 of the OAS Charter further states: "The American States bind themselves in their international relations not to have recourse to the use of force, except in the case of self-defense in accordance with existing treaties or in fulfillment thereof."[187]

Standard Operations and Peacetime Military Raids. In assessing the lawfulness of an SDO under such treaties, one must first consider that these treaties focus on force in the specific context of *inter-State* relations. They are concerned, therefore, with measures that would challenge or undermine another State's political or economic independence, rather than whether a specific individual has been targeted for seizure. As Ian Brownlie, law professor emeritus at Oxford University, observed more than a half-century ago, "actions specifically directed *against individuals* within the territory of a state do not violate the territorial integrity or political independence of that state."[188] A forceful limited seizure of a fugitive within another's territory, after all, is not force directed against the State itself as much as against private rights.[189]

184 This issue is referenced in the Recommendation section of the Conclusion.

185 U.N. CHARTER, *supra* n.127, art. 2(4).

186 OAS CHARTER, *supra* n.128, art. 19.

187 *Id.*, art. 22.

188 IAN BROWNLIE, INTERNATIONAL LAW AND THE USE OF FORCE BY STATES 56 (1963) (emphasis supplied). *Accord* Kash, *PDD-39, supra* n.14, at 146 ("[T]he actions of espionage or law enforcement agents within a nation's territory have never been considered a use of force under international law") (citing DEREK W. BOWETT, SELF-DEFENCE IN INTERNATIONAL LAW 25 (1958)).

189 *United States v. Noriega*, 746 F. Supp. 1506, 1533–34 (S.D. Fla. 1990), *aff'd*, 117 F.3d 1206 (11th Cir. 1997).

A second consideration is how the use of "force" is defined in the international context. Given that it is broadly understood to mean strictly *armed force*, as opposed to political, economic, or other physical force short of military means,[190] a surgical operation that does not employ the use of armed force, such as one that physically manhandles a fugitive off the street or from his home, would not seem to violate the use of force prohibition.[191]

Wartime Military Invasions. Regarding a military invasion scenario with the intention of seizing and delivering a fugitive, the use of force treaties are of more direct significance. To begin, consider the long-held rule as articulated by Professor Michael Akehurst: "Entry of armed forces into the territory of another State without the latter's permission is a clear breach of international law."[192] This rule is reinforced by UNGA Resolution 3314 in which States are to refrain from all acts of aggression,[193] defined to include the "invasion or attack by the armed forces of a State of the territory of another State"[194] and which qualify as a "crime against international peace"[195] and that "[n]o consideration of whatever nature, whether political, economic, military or otherwise, may serve as a justification for aggression."[196]

On that score, it is worth reviewing the official U.S. justification for invading Panama to help evaluate the potential lawfulness of such operations: "In conjunction with the 13,000 U.S. forces already present, military operations were initiated on December 20, 1989, to protect American lives, to defend democracy in Panama, to apprehend Noriega and bring him to trial on the drug-related charges for which he was indicted in 1988, and to ensure the integrity of the Panama Canal Treaties."[197]

190 *See* BRUNO SIMMA, THE CHARTER OF THE UNITED NATIONS: A COMMENTARY 112 (1994).

191 *See* OLIVIER CORTEN, THE LAW AGAINST WAR: THE PROHIBITION ON THE USE OF FORCE IN CONTEMPORARY INTERNATIONAL LAW 52–65 (2010) (distinguishing between "military force" and "police measures" based on the key criteria of the gravity of force and the intention behind its use).

192 Akehurst, *supra* n.126, at 149.

193 *Definition of Aggression*, UNGA Res. 3314 (XXIX), Dec. 14, 1974, ¶ 3, 2319th Plenary Sess., U.N. Doc. A/RES/3314 (XXIX).

194 *Id.*, Annex, art. 3(a).

195 *Id.*, Annex, art. 5(2).

196 *Id.*, Annex, art. 5(1).

197 Letter from U.S. Pres. George H.W. Bush to U.S. House Speaker Thomas Foley, Dec. 21, 1989, *Communication from the President of the United States Transmitting a Report on the Development Concerning the Deployment of United States Forces to Panama on December 20, 1989, reprinted in* H.R. Doc. No. 127, 101st Cong., 2d Sess. (1990).

The first asserted ground was to "protect American lives." This appears to be a reformulation of a State's customary right to self-defense, *i.e.*, to exercise force "to protect the lives or property of nationals," in addition to defending against an attack by another State.[198] While some have made a case for such conduct under international law based on Article 51 of the U.N. Charter[199] (and by extension Article 21 of the OAS Charter[200]) and the underlying policy rationale,[201] the better view is that Article 51 does not currently support that proposition. For one thing, there are legitimate policy concerns about the potential for abuse and pretextual interventions under such a rule.[202]

Besides, as a factual matter, an attack against a particular pursuing State's nationals abroad would have to be tantamount to an attack against the State itself to fall within the scope of Article 51.[203] The White House claimed it was justified in attacking Panama in self-defense because of a "pattern of aggression" by Gen. Noriega's government that included a declaration of war and the killing of a U.S. soldier.[204] But the precipitating events – a declaration of war by Panama unaccompanied by any actual military preparations and a single, low-level incident involving one Marine death, another wounded, and a third beaten, while not trivial,

198 Kash, *Airspace, supra* n.16, at 84–85 (citing Prof. Derek Bowett).

199 "Nothing in the present Charter shall impair the inherent right of individual or collective self-defense if an armed attack occurs against a Member of the United Nations, until the Security Council has taken measures necessary to maintain international peace and security." U.N. CHARTER, *supra* n.127, art. 51.

200 "The American States bind themselves in their international relations not to have recourse to the use of force, except in the case of self-defense in accordance with existing treaties or in fulfillment thereof." OAS CHARTER, *supra* n.128, art. 22 (in effect mimicking the U.N. Charter standard).

201 *See* Derek W. Bowett, *The Use of Force for the Protection of Nationals Abroad, in* THE CURRENT LEGAL REGULATION OF THE USE OF FORCE 40–46 (Antonio Cassese ed. 1986).

202 *See* Int'l Dev. Research Centre, *The Responsibility to Protect: Research, Bibliography, Background*, Dec. 2001, Supplementary Volume to the Report of the Int'l Comm'n on Intervention and State Sovereignty (surveying ten "episodes of nonconsensual military intervention that were conducted for claimed humanitarian purposes or that resulted in clear humanitarian benefits during the Cold War period, 1945–1989," including the U.S. invasion of Panama, and "document[ing] why controversy surrounds" those episodes); CHRISTINE GRAY, INTERNATIONAL LAW AND THE USE OF FORCE 78 (2d ed. 2004) ("The U.S. interventions clearly went beyond the protection of nationals that was claimed as one of the justifications for the intervention and the invitation was not enough to legitimate the intervention as far as a majority of states were concerned.").

203 STANIMIR A. ALEXANDROV, SELF-DEFENSE AGAINST THE USE OF FORCE IN INTERNATIONAL LAW 188–204 (1996).

204 NADELMANN, COPS, *supra* n.17, at 455.

hardly rise to the level of aggression justifying an armed attack.[205] Moreover, under the circumstances, no colorable argument can be made to invoke the anticipatory self-defense doctrine,[206] as there was no evidence of an imminent assault by the PDF and, in any event, the Bush Administration did not rely on such logic.

Even if such a use of force were permissible, it is clear it would need to be exercised under customary international law as a last resort and be undertaken on a limited and temporary basis to satisfy the elements of necessity and proportionality.[207] The U.S. military invasion of Panama almost certainly did not meet those criteria; more precisely, while one U.S. Marine officer had been killed, diplomatic options to resolve inter-State differences had not been exhausted, the military invasion was disproportionate to the ends sought,[208] and the United States remained in Panama long after the hostilities had ended.[209] That said, a military invasion launched to safeguard the lives of nationals could conceivably do so,[210] but only in the particularly narrow instance in which those lives

[205] Although there is no clearly defined set of criteria to trigger an "armed attack" under *jus ad bellum*, certainly more than a low-level of intensity, as here, is required. "The International Court of Justice (ICJ) in the *Nicaragua Case* established that a certain level of 'gravity' was required, effectively ruling out 'low-level warfare'. While its ruling made clear that the mere provision of weapons, frontier incidents, the boarding of flagged vessels, or the equivalent would not qualify as an 'armed attack' (as required to trigger the right of self-defense), the Court's opinion left some room for interpretation and, in any event, has been the subject of considerable criticism." David A. Sadoff, *Striking a Sensible Balance on the Legality of Defensive First Strikes*, 42 VAND. J. TRANSNAT'L L. 441, 471 n.139 (2009) [hereinafter Sadoff, *Sensible Balance*](citing *Nicaragua Case, supra* n.141, at 543 (Jennings, J., dissenting op.) (observing that the provision of arms coupled with other kinds of involvement could amount to "armed conflict"). *Contra* Chatham House, Elizabeth Wilmshurst, *Principles of Int'l Law on the Use of Force by States in Self-Defence* 6 (2005) ("An armed attack means any use of force, and does not need to cross some threshold of intensity.").

[206] While subject to ongoing debate, there are reasonably compelling grounds to doubt that Article 51 of the U.N. Charter countenances anticipatory self-defense. *See* BROWNLIE, *supra* n.188, at 278.

[207] *See* Ved P. Nanda, *et al.*, *Agora: U.S. Forces in Panama: Defenders, Aggressors, or Human Rights Activists?*, 84 AJIL 494, 496 (1990); ALEXANDROV, *supra* n.203, at 202 (citing Waldock's three-part test: "(i) an imminent threat of injury to nationals, (ii) a failure or inability on the part of the territorial sovereign to protect them, and (iii) measures of protection strictly confined to the object to protecting them against injury").

[208] *See* Ma, *supra* n.73, at 939–40 (describing the number of troops employed, the sophistication of the weaponry used, the number of Panamanian deaths (3,000–4,000), the extent of property damage (an estimated 18,000 civilian homes destroyed), and the number of displaced civilians (over 50,000)).

[209] *Id.* at 933 & n.67.

[210] Tom Farer, *Agora: Panama: Beyond the Charter Paradigm*, 84 AJIL 503, 512–13 (1990).

endangered could not be readily evacuated or otherwise safeguarded,[211] the number of forces was not disproportionately large, and the length of time spent on foreign soil was strictly limited to the protective mission,[212] and even then this argument would be a close call at best.

The other asserted grounds by the U.S. Government to defend the lawfulness of the military invasion of Panama are even more tenuous.[213] As University of Denver Law Professor Ved Nanda has pointed out, "[n]o international legal instrument permits intervention to maintain or impose a democratic form of government in another State,"[214] there was "no evidence that the [Panama] Canal or its operation faced any threat from Noriega's forces requiring action to protect it,"[215] and apprehending criminals does not warrant the use of force against another State under international law.[216] In sum, although an SDO that entailed a military invasion as in Panama is difficult to square with international law,[217] theoretically, such an invasion could pass legal muster but *only* under an expansive definition of self-defense and then solely if applied as a last resort and in a strictly limited way.

Treaties Shielding Internationally Protected Persons and Premises. Some treaties expressly safeguard the rights of Internationally Protected Persons (IPPs) in connection with their apprehension by a pursuing State in host State territory. An IPP is defined as:

> (a) a Head of State, including any member of a collegial body performing the functions of a Head of State under the constitution of the State concerned, a Head of Government or a Minister for Foreign Affairs,

211 Louis Henkin, *The Invasion of Panama Under Int'l Law: A Gross Violation*, 29 Colum. J. Transnat'l L. 293, 296–97 (1991).

212 At the same time, there still could be a valid claim that a State has the inherent sovereign right to protect its nationals *outside* the self-defense context, and indeed States that have sought to protect their nationals have not always invoked the self-defense ground. Alexandrov, *supra* n.203, at 204.

213 The occasional citation to Article 3 of the Geneva Conventions of 1949 as a basis for the invasion's unlawfulness insofar as it prohibits "violence to life and person" and "outrages upon personal dignity," for example, Geneva Conv. Relative to the Treatment of POWs, Aug. 12, 1949, art. 3, 6 U.S.T. 3316, T.I.A.S. No. 3364, 75 U.N.T.S. 135 (GC III), is misplaced, as Article 3 is limited to non-international armed conflicts (NIACs), and not to international armed conflicts (IACs) between States, as here.

214 Nanda, *supra* n.207, at 498.

215 *Id.* at 501.

216 *Id.* at 502.

217 The invasion was roundly viewed by the international community as a violation of international law and of the non-intervention principle. *See* Nadelmann, Cops, *supra* n.17, at 455 (citing the seminal UNGA and OAS resolutions).

> whenever any such person is in a foreign State, as well as members of his family who accompany him; (b) any representative or official of a State or any official or other agent of an international organization of an intergovernmental character who, at the time when and in the place where a crime against him, his official premises, his private accommodation or his means of transport is committed, *is entitled pursuant to international law to special protection from any attack on his person, freedom or dignity*, as well as members of his family forming part of his household.[218]

The Vienna Conventions on Diplomatic[219] and Consular[220] Relations dated 1961 and 1963, respectively, reinforce this type of protection. International privileges and immunities accorded by various treaties generally immunize from apprehension and legal process not only diplomats and consular officials, but also members of *ad hoc* or special diplomatic missions,[221] international civil servants (including U.N. officials), and military officers and multinational forces stationed abroad.[222]

In addition, to the extent that individuals seek refuge in "inviolable" premises within host State territory, such as diplomatic missions,[223] consular premises,[224] special missions,[225] and intergovernmental organization premises,[226] obtaining their custody for delivery purposes

218 Conv. on the Prevention and Punishment of Crimes against Int'lly Protected Persons, Including Diplomatic Agents [IPP Conv.], Dec. 14, 1973, art. 1(1), UNGA Res. 3166 (XXVIII), 28 U.N. GAOR Supp. (No. 30) at 146, U.N. Doc. A/9030 (1974), 28 U.S.T. 1975, 1035 U.N.T.S. 167, T.I.A.S. No. 8532, *reprinted in* 13 ILM 41 (emphasis supplied).

219 Vienna Conv. on Diplomatic Relations, Apr. 18, 1961, art. 29, 23 U.S.T. 3227, T.I.A.S. No. 7502, 500 U.N.T.S. 95 [hereinafter VCDR] ("The person of a diplomatic agent shall be inviolable. He shall not be liable to any form of arrest or detention. The receiving State shall treat him with due respect and shall take all appropriate steps to prevent any attack on his person, freedom or dignity.").

220 Vienna Conv. on Consular Relations, Apr. 24, 1963, art. 35(5), 21 U.S.T. 77, 596 U.N.T.S. 261 [hereinafter VCCR] ("In the performance of his functions [the Consular Officer] shall be protected by the receiving State. He shall enjoy personal inviolability and shall not be liable to any form of arrest or detention.").

221 *Cf. United States v. Sissoko*, 995 F. Supp. 1469, 1471 (S.D. Fla. 1997) (denying immunity to a special advisor to a special mission in the United States after he pled guilty to a charge of bribery).

222 UNGA, *Expulsion of Aliens, supra* n.165, at 26–33. *See also* the discussion of immunities in Chapter 6.b.

223 VCDR, *supra* n.219, art. 22(1).

224 VCCR, *supra* n.220, art. 31(1)–(2).

225 Conv. on Special Missions (CSM), Dec. 18, 1969, art. 25(1), 1400 U.N.T.S. 231, No. 23431. It is noteworthy that this Convention only has thirty-eight parties to date and has not been found to reflect customary international law by a U.S. court.

226 Agreement between the United Nations and the United States Regarding the Headquarters of the United Nations, June 26, 1947, § 9(a)–(b), 11 U.N.T.S. 11, No. 147.

likewise could be stymied. For example, more than a century ago, in a case where three German deserters from the French Foreign Legion under the protection of the German consul were arrested by French soldiers while being transferred to a ship by a German official, the arbitral tribunal held that it "was wrong for the French military authorities not to respect, as far as possible, the actual protection being granted to these deserters in the name of the German consulate."[227]

3 Human Rights Analysis

The three international human rights standards most likely to be implicated by SDOs[228] are: (i) the prohibition against arbitrary arrest and detention (which can be seen as falling within the scope of the right to liberty and security of person); (ii) the prohibition against torture, physical abuse, or degrading treatment; and (iii) procedural due process to which detainees are entitled.[229]

[227] *Deserters of Casablanca* (Fr. v. Ger.), PCA Award, Hague Ct. Rep. (Scott) 110, May 22, 1909 (translated from French).

[228] It may appear that "false imprisonment" should be treated as another legal ground, but this is a domestic law concept – not one recognized under international law. *ICJ Bull., supra* n.48, at 24. Post-return treatment, including respect for one's judicial rights, will be addressed in Chapter 13.a. In addition, the protection of "personal integrity" is referenced in various international human rights treaties, such as the ACHR, but that right has been construed as effectively falling within the scope of the other human rights standards addressed in this sub-section, *see* Daniel W. Hill, Jr., *The Concept of Personal Integrity Rights in Empirical Research*, Fla. State Univ. (FSU) website, Aug. 13, 2013, at 6, *available at* http://myweb.fsu.edu/dwh06c/pages/documents/pi_concept13Aug13.pdf (last visited on May 29, 2016) (describing a breach of personal integrity as the application of force that either violates due process or causes severe bodily or psychological pain or discomfort), so it is not separately analyzed. Finally, the ICCPR, among other legal authorities, recognizes the right to freedom of movement, but it is not directly apposite here. That general right includes the right to move freely within a State and choose one's place of residence there; the right to cross an international border, which amounts to the right to leave a State; and the right to return to a State. Jane McAdam, *An Intellectual History of Freedom of Movement in Int'l Law: The Right to Leave as a Personal Liberty*, 12 MELB. J. INT'L L. 1, 4–5 (2011). While one could argue that this right is violated to the extent that an SDO has denied an individual the right to choose one's place of residence, State-sanctioned detention is more germane to the right to personal liberty, and where the two sets of rights intersect (*e.g.*, Articles 9 and 12 of the ICCPR), the examples cited by the U.N. Human Rights Committee (HRC) address situations of extended banishment – quite distinct from the scenario at issue. HRC, Gen. Cmt. No. 27, *Art. 12 (Freedom of Movement)*, U.N. Doc. CCPR/C/21/Rev.1/Add.9, ¶ 7, Nov. 2, 1999.

[229] *See* Robert J. Currie, *Abducted Fugitives Before the Int'l Criminal Court: Problems and Prospects*, 18 CRIM. L.F. 349, 354 (2007) (SDOs "will tend to violate international human rights norms, particularly those dealing with due process and security of person.").

Prohibition against Arbitrary Arrest and Detention. Perhaps remarkably, no stand-alone anti-kidnapping or anti-abduction treaty (other than one pertaining to children[230]) exists under international law.[231] Instead, the international community relies on restrictions against "arbitrary arrest and detention," such as Article 9(1) of the ICCPR,[232] which states: "Everyone has the right to liberty and security of person. No one shall be subjected to arbitrary arrest or detention. No one shall be deprived of his liberty except on such grounds and in accordance with such procedure as are established by law."[233] Similarly, Article 9 of the Universal Declaration of Human Rights (UDHR)[234] provides: "No one

[230] Hague Conv. on the Civil Aspects of Int'l Child Abduction, Oct. 25, 1980, T.I.A.S. No. 11670, 1343 U.N.T.S. 89.

[231] *See* RESTATEMENT (THIRD), *supra* n.149, § 432, Rep. Note 1 ("None of the international human rights conventions to date ... provides that forcible abduction or irregular extradition is a violation of international human rights law.").

[232] When the U.S. Government ratified the Int'l Covenant on Civil and Political Rights (ICCPR) in 1992, it did so with five reservations, including one that the treaty would not be self-executing. Thus, until the U.S. Congress passes a law incorporating it as a U.S. statute, and to date it has not, no private right of action may arise out of this treaty. Accordingly, the U.S. Supreme Court found no basis under domestic law for Álvarez-Machaín's claim that he had been arbitrarily arrested and detained by U.S. Government officials. *Sosa v. Álvarez-Machaín*, 542 U.S. 692 (2004). To be clear, that ruling only relates to *U.S. domestic* law; the United States is still bound by its ratification to the ICCPR under *international* law, at least to the extent of its reservations, understandings, and declarations.

[233] ICCPR, art. 9(1), UNGA Res. 2200, U.N. GAOR, 21st Sess., Supp. No. 21, U.N. Doc. A/6316 (1967) [hereinafter ICCPR]. *See* closely related provisions regarding the "right to liberty and security of person" in the African Charter on Human and Peoples' Rights [ACHPR or BANJUL CHARTER], June 27, 1981, art. 6, CAB/LEG/67/3 rev. 5, *reprinted in* 21 ILM 58 (1982) and the Eur. Conv. for the Protection of Human Rights and Fundamental Freedoms, Nov. 4, 1950, art. 5(1), 213 U.N.T.S. 262, T.S. No. 71 (1953) [hereinafter ECHR]. Notably, Art. 5(1)(f) of the ECHR, which provides an exception for instances in which "action is being taken with a view to deportation or extradition," while still requiring the arrest or detention be lawful, does not require that the deportation or extradition be so, Stefan Trechsel, *The Right to Liberty and Security of the Person – Article 5 of the Eur. Conv. on Human Rights in the Strasbourg Case-Law*, 1 HUM. RTS. L.J. 88, 123–24 (1980), although courts nevertheless tend to examine whether "the proceedings [were] not conducted with the requisite diligence or if the detention result[ed] from some misuse of authority." *Lynas v. Switzerland*, Appl. No. 7317/75, Eur. Comm'n of Hum. Rts., 6 D.R. 141, Oct. 6, 1976.

[234] Although the UDHR is not a treaty, its content is widely regarded as reflecting customary international law, and to that extent all States are obligated to comply with its provisions. Vojin Dimitrijevic, "Customary Law as an Instrument for the Protection of Human Rights," Programma Diritti Umani, *Istituto Per Gli Studi Di Politica Internazionale*, Working Paper 7 (2006), *available at* www.ispionline.it/it/documents/wp_7_2006.pdf (last visited on May 25, 2016).

shall be subjected to arbitrary arrest, detention or exile."[235] The U.N. General Assembly also passed a resolution in December 1988 along these lines that specifically provides: "Arrest, detention or imprisonment shall only be carried out strictly in accordance with the provisions of the law and by competent officials or persons authorized for that purpose."[236]

A U.N. working group on arbitrary detention in 1993 cited each of these authorities in finding that the U.S. deprivation of Humberto Álvarez-Machaín's liberty between April 2, 1990, when he was seized in Mexico, and December 14, 1992, when he was acquitted of all charges, had been "arbitrary" by contravening Article 9 of the ICCPR.[237] The working group specifically pointed out that the "deprivation of liberty took place without the order of any authority whatsoever," as under any of the applicable legal authorities the deprivation of liberty required compliance with *procedures established by law*.[238]

In addition, the Human Rights Committee (HRC), a body of independent experts that monitors implementation of the ICCPR, has found that SDOs violate Article 9 of the ICCPR. For example, the HRC ruled that it was a violation of Article 9(1) of the ICCPR when, in November 1978, Uruguayan Government agents working with two Brazilian police officials[239] seized four individuals, including Lilian Celiberti de Casariego, in Brazil and returned them by car across the Uruguayan border where they remained in detention.[240]

235 UDHR, Dec. 10, 1948, art. 9, UNGA Res. 217A (III), U.N. Doc. A/810 (1948).

236 UNGA, *Body of Principles for the Protection of All Persons under Any Form of Detention or Imprisonment*, Dec. 9, 1988, Annex, Principle 2, U.N. Doc. A/RES/43/173, 76th plenary mtg. [hereinafter UNGA, *Body of Principles*].

237 *Working Group Rep.*, *supra* n.178, at 139–40. *Contra Sosa*, 542 U.S. 692 (finding no arbitrary arrest in *Álvarez-Machaín* in part because the UDHR does not impose a legal obligation on States and a rule as broad as the ICCPR's Article 9 cannot properly be treated as binding customary law).

238 *Working Group Rep.*, *supra* n.178, at 139 (emphasis supplied).

239 It is unclear from the reported facts whether the Uruguayan police officers were operating in an official or private capacity, and therefore whether this was, strictly speaking, a unilateral SDO, but the human rights analysis would remain the same under either scenario.

240 *Celiberti de Casariego v. Uruguay*, Commc'n No. 56/1979, U.N. Doc. [hereinafter *Casariego Case*]. Notably, the HRC confirmed that there was no jurisdictional bar to its hearing the case under either Article 2(1) of the ICCPR or Article 1 of the Optional Prot. to the ICCPR (Dec. 19, 1966, 999 U.N.T.S. 171) whose scope *ratione loci* specifies that States parties are responsible for "all individuals within its territory and subject to its jurisdiction" and that the Court has competence to hear communications from "individuals subject to its jurisdiction," respectively. The Court observed that Article 2(1) "does not imply that the State party concerned cannot be held accountable for violations of

The European Court of Human Rights has made clear by implication that it, too, would find unlawful a unilateral SDO. In the *Stocké* case, the Court reasoned that luring Stocké to enter Germany where he was arrested was not violation of Article 5 of the ECHR, by contrast with by contrast with "unlawful activities abroad such as [returning] the applicant against his will from France to the Federal Republic of Germany."[241] The Court, therefore, distinguished between lawful LCOs and unlawful SDOs based on the fact that the former is essentially voluntary while the latter is not.

Likewise, in the *Öcalan* case, the Court stated: "An arrest made by the authorities of one State on the territory of another State, without the consent of the latter, affects the person concerned's individual rights to security under Article 5 § 1."[242] While the Court declined to conclude that the arrest itself was arbitrary, because "the applicant [could] not adduce[ ] evidence enabling concordant inferences . . . to be drawn that Turkey failed to respect Kenyan sovereignty or to comply with international law,"[243] had this operation been a unilateral SDO, rather than a cooperative enforcement or domestic immigration law exercise, the Court might well have found a breach of Article 5(1).[244]

Prohibition against Torture or Inhuman or Degrading Treatment. To the extent that a unilateral SDO entails drugging or beating an individual or otherwise transporting him in cramped quarters, applying

rights under the Covenant which its agents commit upon the territory of another State, whether with the acquiescence of the Government of that State or in opposition to it." *Casariego Case, supra*, ¶ 10.3. And the reference to Article 1 of the Optional Protocol "is not to the place where the violation occurred, but rather to the relationship between the individual and the State in relation to a violation of any of the rights set forth in the Covenant, wherever they occurred." *Id.* ¶ 10.2.

241 *Stocké Case, supra* n.106, ¶ 51.

242 *Öcalan v. Turkey* (*Merits*), Appl. No. 46221/99, Gr. Ch., 41 EHRR 45, ¶ 85, May 12, 2005.

243 *Id.* ¶ 98.

244 As a practical matter, even if a human rights treaty violation were found in principle, however, the absence of customary international law on this point could thwart enforcement under certain circumstances. *See* Alberto Costi, *Problems with Current Int'l and Nat'l Practices Concerning Extraterritorial Abductions*, 8 NZACL Y.B. 57 (2002) ("International human rights treaties suffer from many limitations. First, if the state carrying out an abduction [SDO] is not party to a treaty, it will not be bound by its provisions. Second, only the European Convention gives the right to all persons who have suffered an alleged violation of a right contained therein to lodge a complaint against a state party to the Convention. In the other cases, the right of individuals to bring petitions against a state depends on the consent of the state. Third, the application might be rejected on the basis of a procedural defect. Finally, some of the international bodies may only make remarks and their views lack binding force.").

electric prods to his body, depriving him of sleep, denying him food or water, exposing him to extremely hot or cold temperatures, or the like, such pursuing State conduct potentially could violate applicable treaty obligations. Article 7 of the ICCPR states: "No one shall be subjected to torture or to cruel, inhuman or degrading treatment or punishment."[245] Article 5(2) of the ACHR, Article 3 of the ECHR, and Article 5 of the ACHPR provide substantially similar protections. Accordingly, the HRC found a violation of Article 7 of the ICCPR in the 1981 *Lopez Burgos* case (*supra*) where, in connection with the subject's seizure from Buenos Aires by Uruguayan officers and his later detention in Uruguay, Sergio Euben Lopez Burgos was tortured and, *inter alia*, endured a broken jawbone and perforated eardrums.[246]

A related human rights treaty provision that also could be implicated by a unilateral SDO is one that calls for a State to treat an individual deprived of his liberty with humanity and dignity. Article 10(1) of the ICCPR is representative: "All persons deprived of their liberty shall be treated with humanity and with respect for the inherent dignity of the human person."[247] For example, in the 1984 *Casariego* case (*supra*), the HRC concluded that Uruguay had violated Article 10(1) when, as part of the subject's detention following her seizure from Argentina and delivery to Uruguay, she was held incommunicado for four months.[248]

Procedural Due Process. The Inter-American Juridical Committee has observed "the incompatibility of the practice of abduction [SDOs] with the right of due process to which every person is entitled, no matter how serious the crime they are accused of, a right protected by international law."[249] In the context of SDOs, a captured fugitive's procedural due process rights can be foreclosed in such ways as the following: (i) denial to notify family members and a consular officer of one's arrest and detention;[250] (ii) failure to "be promptly informed of any charges against

[245] ICCPR, *supra* n.233, art. 7.

[246] *Lopez Burgos v. Uruguay*, Commc'n No. R.12/52, U.N. Doc. A/36/40, Supp. No. 40 at 176, July 29, 1981.

[247] ICCPR, *supra* n.233, art. 10(1).

[248] *Casariego Case, supra* n.240, ¶ 11. *See generally* HRC Gen. Cmts. 9 and 21; *cf. Nenova, et al. v. Libya*, Commc'n No. 1880/2009, U.N. Doc. CCPR/C/104/D/1880/2009, May 2, 2012, ¶¶ 3.6, 7.5-7.7 (acknowledging the authors had been denied requisite contact with family members while in confinement, the HRC did not need to reach Article 10 as it found other overarching violations, including torture).

[249] *OAS Legal Op., supra* n.152, ¶ 13.

[250] *E.g., LaGrand Case* (Ger. v. U.S.) [2001] I.C.J. Rep. 466 (June 27) (discussing the right to notify a consular officer); UNGA, *Body of Principles, supra* n.236, Principle 16 (everyone

him";[251] and (iii) prevented from seeking relief from a court without undue delay regarding the lawfulness of a criminal arrest or detention.[252] The failure of a State to ensure any of these basic rights in carrying out an SDO could potentially lead to a finding of a legal violation, assuming a court is willing to hear such a challenge (*see* Chapter 13.a.i). The right to counsel is not as strong a claim, as it tends to apply in connection strictly with extradition proceedings.[253]

A related issue arises with regard to how long a State can carry out interrogations, absent the presence of defense counsel, of an indicted individual seized extraterritorially and believed to possess actionable intelligence. According to current U.S. practice, terrorist suspects may be first detained and interrogated for intelligence collection purposes, pursuant to U.S. military authorities and the law of war, while in military custody often aboard a Navy vessel at sea.[254] The length of such an interrogation can vary depending on a number of factors, including, *inter alia*, how much fresh intelligence the individual is believed to possess, how forthcoming he is, and the state of his health.

He is then turned over to a new set of government personnel, including federal investigators, now operating under civilian laws who proceed to effect his criminal arrest, thereby triggering the requirement that he be

who is arrested, detained, or imprisoned has the right to inform, or have the authorities notify, their family or friends).

251 *E.g.*, ICCPR, *supra* n.233, art. 9(2) ("Anyone who is arrested shall be informed, at the time of arrest, of the reasons for his arrest and shall be promptly informed of any charges against him.").

252 *E.g.*, *id.*, art. 9(4) ("Anyone who is deprived of his liberty by arrest or detention shall be entitled to take proceedings before a court, in order that that court may decide without delay on the lawfulness of his detention and order his release if the detention is not lawful."). *See also* ECHR, *supra* n.233, art. 5(3); John Quigley, *Gov't Vigilantes at Large: The Danger to Human Rights from Kidnapping of Suspected Terrorists*, 10 Hum. Rts. Q. 193, 198–205 (1988).

253 *See, e.g.*, Switz., Federal Office of Justice (FOJ), *Description of Extradition Procedures in Switzerland related to Article 17*, IMAC, Dec. 1, 2012 ("You have the right to appoint a trial attorney of choice to act on your behalf," but that appointment "is only valid for the extradition procedure before the FOJ"); *cf.* Third Addt'l Prot. to the Eur. Conv. on Extradition, Nov. 10, 2010, art. 4(2) (an individual's consent to extradition or renunciation of his entitlement to the rule of specialty must be "expressed voluntarily and in full awareness of the legal consequences" and to that end the individual has the right to appoint legal counsel and the assistance of an interpreter, as appropriate).

254 *See* Council on Foreign Relations, "How Obama Brings Terrorists to Justice," Interview between Jonathan Masters (Interviewer) and Stephen I. Vladeck (Interviewee), website, Oct. 9, 2013, *available at* www.cfr.org/terrorism-and-the-law/obama-brings-terrorists-justice/p31597 (last visited on May 25, 2016).

read his *Miranda* rights[255] and be supplied a lawyer (upon request), as well as the onset of the "speedy trial" clock. Under U.S. law, nothing uttered by the subject during interrogation prior to receiving his *Miranda* rights will be deemed admissible at his criminal trial.[256]

In one such instance, a U.S. federal court found no violation when Nazih Abdul-Hamed al-Ruqai (a/k/a Anas al-Libi), who had been charged with involvement in the 1998 bombings of the U.S. Embassies in Kenya and Tanzania, was interrogated aboard a Navy vessel in the Mediterranean Sea without access to counsel following his seizure in Libya.[257] The Court's reasoning relied on the fact that no right to counsel can be triggered unless and until the suspect has been criminally arrested,[258] suggesting that, in principle, initial military-custody interrogation may potentially last without temporal restriction. Others have contended that more than a short-term interrogation period (say, over six weeks) could present legal problems,[259] in part because a person's psychology and will could be irremediably influenced by pre-*Miranda* questioning.[260]

255 In 1966, in a landmark decision, the U.S. Supreme Court found that a criminal defendant's constitutional rights under the Fifth and Sixth Amendments (*i.e.*, the privilege against self-incrimination and the right to counsel, respectively) had been violated in connection with his arrest, and as a corrective measure required henceforth as follows: "Prior to any questioning, the person must be warned that he has a right to remain silent, that any statement he does make may be used as evidence against him, and that he has a right to the presence of an attorney, either retained or appointed. The defendant may waive effectuation of these rights, provided the waiver is made voluntarily, knowingly and intelligently. If, however, he indicates in any manner and at any stage of the process that he wishes to consult with an attorney before speaking there can be no questioning. Likewise, if the individual is alone and indicates in any manner that he does not wish to be interrogated, the police may not question him. The mere fact that he may have answered some questions or volunteered some statements on his own does not deprive him of the right to refrain from answering any further inquiries until he has consulted with an attorney and thereafter consents to be questioned." *Miranda v. Arizona*, 384 U.S. 436, 444–45 (1966).

256 Ken Dilanian, "U.S. Delays Miranda Rights for Captured Al Qaeda Operative," *L.A. Times*, Oct. 9, 2013.

257 Benjamin Weiser, "Request to Appoint Lawyer for Terror Suspect is Denied," *N.Y. Times*, Oct. 11, 2013.

258 *Id.*

259 Council on Foreign Relations, *supra* n.254 (expressing the views of interviewee Vladeck).

260 *See* Dilanian, *supra* n.256 (citing to New York criminal defense attorney Lee Ginsburg, who represented one such defendant, an al-Qaida operative named Ahmed Abdulkadir Warsame). More recently, defense counsel claimed due process violations in connection with a peacetime military raid south of Benghazi, Libya, in June 2014, which resulted in the seizure of their client Abu Khattala, a Libyan terrorism suspect, "and his interrogation for twelve days aboard a U.S. Navy ship without a lawyer present," despite his request for one. Spencer S. Hsu, "U.S. Defends Handling of Benghazi Suspect," *Wash. Post*, Sept. 4, 2015, at A2.

iii Interception Operations

Interception operations implicate some of the same international legal standards covered in the LCO and SDO contexts, particularly violations of territorial sovereignty and breaches of international treaty provisions.[261]

1 Territorial Sovereignty Analysis

Under international law, a violation of territorial sovereignty could be found in any of the following three ways: (i) by intercepting an aircraft over another's sovereign territory (versus over one's own territory or non-sovereign territory/international space); (ii) by intercepting a vessel in another State's territorial waters (or in its contiguous zone for violations specifically of immigration, fiscal, and other laws within its territory or its territorial seas); or (iii) by "commandeering" another State's flagged aircraft or vessel[262] anywhere.[263]

To circumvent such potential legal liability, to date, all but one of such operations have followed the same pattern: *interception* of aircraft over the *high seas*. In that way, territorial sovereignty is not arguably violated, as no pursuing State official or agent actually ever has to enter either sovereign airspace or the flagged aircraft itself. Indeed, when U.S. fighters intercepted the Egyptian airliner carrying the Palestinian hijackers of the *Achille Lauro* cruise ship in 1985, the United States defended its action in part by noting that the operation had occurred over international waters.[264]

2 Treaty Compliance Analysis

The major types of treaty laws, apart from extradition treaties (*see* discussion *supra*), which ostensibly could be breached on account of an interception operation include: (i) treaties prohibiting the unauthorized

[261] The human rights analysis relevant to these operations closely tracks that applicable to SDOs and so is dispensed with in this sub-section.

[262] Commandeering operations are defined at *supra* n.78. Flagged ships are treated here as a form of constructive State territory. *See* pp. 71–72 in Chapter 2.

[263] A fourth possibility theoretically could occur to the extent that such an operation forced down a plane into a third State's territory, either because of the need for an emergency landing or pilot navigational error, in which case that State might claim a breach of territorial sovereignty for an unauthorized landing and that likely would be compounded, political relations considerations aside, if pursuing State officials began to interrogate the crew and passengers aboard once in that territory.

[264] Borkowski, *supra* n.81, at 762.

use or threat of force; (ii) treaties requiring that disputes should be resolved through means not endangering peace and security; (iii) aviation treaties; and (iv) hijacking and piracy suppression treaties. As referenced earlier, not all States are subject to the same obligations under a treaty; it will depend on whether they are parties to a particular treaty (or are otherwise subject to the provisions via customary international law) and, even if they are parties, whether they ratified a given treaty with express reservations or understandings.

Treaties Prohibiting the Use or Threat of Force. As discussed above, the U.N. Charter and OAS Charter are prime examples of treaties prohibiting the use or threat of force. It is unquestionable that an interception operation could be effected only through the use or threat of armed force[265] in order to compel a plane to land. It is less clear, however, that such an operation would have the effect of violating the flagged State's territorial sovereignty or political independence – which is also a required element of such legal standards. After all, the aircraft or vessel itself could remain intact (in the event of threat, anyway) and the purpose of the operation would not be to seize territory, undermine the integrity or independence of the State, or even take measures against the State itself.[266]

In addition, to determine the lawfulness of such an operation, the merit of available defenses must be evaluated. Consider first Article 51 of the U.N. Charter, which represents the principal[267] cognizable basis for justifiable self-defense under conventional international law.[268] Under that article, a pursuing State possesses "the inherent right of

[265] Although the U.S. Government sought in part to justify its interception of the Egyptian airliner carrying the *Achille Lauro* hijackers by noting that no shots were fired, *id.*, U.S. officials did not, and could not, deny that the interception required the *threat* of force to succeed.

[266] *See* discussion at pp. 522–23.

[267] Other types of lawful self-defense a State may exercise under conventional law include via an authorized U.N. peacekeeping mission, *see* U.N. CHARTER, *supra* n.127, arts. 42 and 43, or a collective self-defense treaty. *E.g.*, North Atlantic Treaty [NATO Charter], Apr. 4, 1949, 34 U.N.T.S. 243.

[268] Notably, self-defense provisions found elsewhere in U.N. documents or in other sources typically either expressly cite to or otherwise rely on the phraseology found in Article 51 of the U.N. Charter. *E.g.*, UNGA, *Declaration on the Enhancement of the Effectiveness of the Principle of Refraining from the Threat or Use of Force in Int'l Relations*, ¶ 13, Res. 42/22, U.N. Doc. A/RES/42/22, Nov. 18, 1987 ("States have the inherent right of individual or collective self-defence if an armed attack occurs, as set forth in the Charter."); ILC, *State Responsibility, supra* n.37, art. 21("The wrongfulness of an act of a State is precluded if the act constitutes a lawful measure of self-defence taken in conformity with the Charter of the United Nations").

individual ... self-defence if an armed attack occurs against" that member State.[269] When applied, the U.N. Security Council voted unanimously to condemn Israel's interception of a Middle East Airlines flight in August 1973, thereby rejecting Israel's self-defense plea invoked to protect its nationals from prospective terrorist attacks.[270]

Suppose, however, that State P (a pursuing State) had been the target of an armed attack by State H (the host State), and that the head of State, the head of government, or a senior military official of State H were on board an aircraft and that individual incidentally were the subject of an indictment issued by State P, one could see how the threat of force against such an aircraft in order to simultaneously meet self-defense and law enforcement needs could be justified. That is concededly a very narrow case. But here is another: State P might reasonably contend that an aircraft interception was lawful under a self-defense rationale where agents or proxies of State H were known to be aboard a State H-flagged aircraft and where State H was known to be sponsoring and financing a series of terrorist "pinprick" (low-intensity) attacks[271] against the pursuing State's nationals and installations around the world through such agents or proxies, who, as a result, were wanted by law enforcement for violation of domestic antiterrorism statutes.[272] The point here is we must not be categorical in our judgments about the unlawfulness of aircraft interception operations.

Furthermore, the prevailing notions of anticipatory self-defense would not apply so well mainly because of the requisite element of imminence.[273]

269 U.N. Charter, *supra* n.127, art. 51.

270 Cassese, *Legal Response, supra* n.78, at 601; Beck & Arend, *supra* n.66, at 175; Brandon S. Chabner, Comment, *The Omnibus Diplomatic Security and Antiterrorism Act of 1986: Prescribing and Enforcing United States Law against Terrorist Violence Overseas*, 37 UCLA L. Rev. 985, 1018–19 (1990) ("The United Nations hardly could have intended Article 51 on self-defense to justify unilateral law enforcement efforts by one nation in another's territories, and the United Nations itself has never endorsed such counterterrorism tactics.").

271 *See* Yoram Dinstein, War, Aggression and Self-Defence 202 (4th ed. 2005). ("A persuasive argument can be made that, should a distinctive pattern of behaviour emerge, a series of pin-prick assaults might be weighed in its totality and count as an armed attack"); Sadoff, *Sensible Balance, supra* n.205, at 472 n.143; *cf.* Natalino Ronzitti, *The Expanding Law of Self-Defence*, 11 J. Conflict & Sec. L. 343, 351 (2006) (leaving open-ended the question whether a string of frontier incidents might cumulatively qualify as an "armed attack").

272 *See* Kash, *Airspace, supra* n.16, at 92 (discussing Israel's interception of a Libyan aircraft in Feb. 1986).

273 *See* Robert Y. Jennings, *The* Caroline *and* McLeod *Cases*, 32 AJIL 82, 89 (1938) (quoting the so-called *Caroline* standard enunciated by then-U.S. Secretary of State Daniel Webster as requiring "necessity of self-defence, instant, overwhelming, leaving no choice

Although anticipatory self-defense remains a controversial concept and its lawfulness fundamentally indeterminate, "there appears to be a developing, but not yet fully accepted, international legal standard permitting States to launch anticipatory self-defensive strikes in inter-State conflicts."[274] "Under the emerging norm, the more compelling the evidence of an imminent attack, the more complete the expected destruction, the more tailored the response, and the more dedicated the efforts made at averting armed conflict, the more likely an anticipatory strike taken in self-defense would be treated as lawful."[275] Under that standard – although, again, such a fugitive-capture scenario would be extremely unlikely to ever occur – an aircraft interception plausibly could be justified under international law where it was carrying the leader of a State who reasonably was believed to be poised imminently to launch a military strike against the pursuing State at issue, and that individual was also charged with one or more crimes (such as drug trafficking or money laundering) by the pursuing State.

Treaties Requiring that Disputes Be Resolved by Peaceful Means. Article 2(3) of the U.N. Charter provides that: "All Members shall settle their international disputes by peaceful means in such a manner that international peace and security, and justice, are not endangered."[276] One potential problem with interception operations is that, even where the threat, rather than the use, of force is exercised, and where no weapons have been fired or lives lost, international peace and security could still be jeopardized if the aircraft pilot or sea captain were to fail to comply with an instruction or even potentially if there were a miscommunication or other error incident to the operation.

The counter-argument would stress that the law enforcement effort at issue is focused on a single individual, and therefore no underlying inter-State conflict exists to even trigger this provision; however, the unwillingness to engage constructively on a State-to-State basis (as an initial matter or following denied cooperation) for the delivery of the fugitive

of means, and no moment of deliberation."). The fact that a given interception operation exhibited the attributes of necessity and proportionality alone, based on a targeted attack against known perpetrators in which innocent civilians were left unharmed, would not be sufficient in and of itself to legally justify such a preemptive strike, although the U.S. Government did note these as mitigating factors when explaining its legal rationale for intercepting an Egyptian aircraft in 1985. Borkowski, *supra* n.84, at 762.

[274] David A. Sadoff, *A Question of Determinancy: The Legal Status of Anticipatory Self-Defense*, 40 Geo. J. Int'l L. 523, 583 (Winter 2009).

[275] *Id.*

[276] U.N. Charter, *supra* n.127, art. 2(3).

could be viewed as reflecting an underlying difference or tension, and consequently an interception operation could be seen as a non-peaceful means of resolving it.

Aviation Treaties. Several conventions govern international aviation matters and they, too, can be implicated by an aircraft interception operation. The 1944 Convention on International Civil Aviation (the "Chicago Convention"), for example, expressly proscribes interceptions of "civil aircraft" rather than "State aircraft," the latter defined to include military and police usage.[277] In the cases of both the U.S. interception in October 1985 of the Egyptian aircraft, as it was being used for a government purpose, and the Israeli interception in February 1986 of the Libyan "State" aircraft, the prohibition against interceptions of civilian aircraft, therefore, would not apply. However, in the cases of the Israeli interception of the Middle East Airways civilian aircraft in August 1973 and in the Yemeni interception in August 1986 of a Djibouti commercial airliner, such treaties would appear to have been violated.

The 1963 Convention on Offences and Certain Other Acts Committed on Board Aircraft (the "Tokyo Convention") also requires that, in the event an aircraft is forced to land, the passengers and crew be allowed to continue their journey as soon as practicable and the aircraft and its cargo be returned to those lawfully entitled to possession.[278] Each of the interceptions described in this chapter seem to have satisfied that particular requirement, but that need not always be the case.

A third applicable aviation-related treaty is the 1971 Convention for the Suppression of Unlawful Acts against the Safety of Civil Aviation (the "Montreal Convention"), which treats as an offense any act or attempted act of violence against a person on board an aircraft in flight, if that act is likely to endanger the safety of that aircraft.[279] But as in the other conventions, State aircraft are not covered, and so while interceptions would

[277] Conv. on Int'l Civil Aviation [Chicago Conv.], Dec. 7, 1944, arts. 3, 5, 10 (1994) 15 U.N.T.S. 295. In addition, the 1963 Convention on Offenses and Certain Other Acts Committed on Board Aircraft denominates as an offense an act where the safety of a civilian aircraft used for law enforcement purposes or persons or property on the aircraft are jeopardized, but excludes from its scope of application *State* aircraft used for law enforcement purposes. Conv. on Offences and Certain Other Acts Committed on Board Aircraft, Sept. 14, 1963, art. 1(b), U.N. Doc. A/C.6/418/Corr.1, Annex II, 704 U.N.T.S. 219, 20 U.S.T. 2941, ICAO Doc. 8364, *reprinted in* 2 ILM 1042.

[278] *Id.*, art. 11(2).

[279] Conv. for the Suppression of Unlawful Acts against the Safety of Civil Aviation [Montreal Conv.], Sept. 23, 1971, art. 1, U.N. Doc. A/C.6/418/Corr.2, Annex III, 974 U.N.T.S. 177, 24 U.S.T. 564, *reprinted in* 10 ILM 1151.

ordinarily constitute a violation because of the threat of force involved, in three of the interception cases reviewed, as well as the "passive interception" operation described above,[280] no violation would be found.

Hijacking or Piracy Suppression Treaties. When U.S. fighters intercepted the Egyptian aircraft transporting the Palestinian terrorists in connection with the *Achille Lauro* incident, Iran, Poland, and the PLO criticized the act as aerial piracy or hijacking.[281] A year later, during the U.N. Security Council debate following the Israeli interception of the Libyan executive jet in February 1986, 10 of 15 members voted affirmatively condemning Israel for aerial hijacking and piracy, with four members abstaining and only one permanent member (the United States) exercising its veto power.[282] Under international law, however, hijacking and interception are mutually exclusive concepts.

According to the 1970 Convention for the Suppression of Unlawful Seizure of Aircraft, "hijacking" is defined as the "unlawful seizure, by force or threat of force or any other form of intimidation, of an aircraft, *committed while on board an aircraft in flight*."[283] Therefore, an interception, which takes place wholly outside an aircraft (as opposed to a commandeering operation, at least as defined herein), cannot constitute a hijacking *per se*. Likewise, such interception operations, by definition, cannot possibly qualify as piracy, as piracy must be undertaken by "a private ship or a private aircraft" and "for private ends,"[284] which would

280 *See* nn.83–86 and accompanying text in Chapter 9. At the same time, as in this particular instance a head of State (the President of Bolivia) was involved, as an IPP, "his official premises, his private accommodation or his means of transport . . . is entitled pursuant to international law to special protection from any attack on his person, freedom or dignity," and therefore there could well have been a violation of the IPP Convention of 1973, as the United States and the other States involved are all parties to that Convention. *See* pp. 526–27 in this chapter.

281 Borkowski, *supra* n.81, at 763.

282 Henry Kamm, "Rabin Defends Air Interception: Vows More 'Unconventional' Acts," *N.Y. Times*, Feb. 6, 1986, at A10; Judith Miller, "Qaddafi Orders His Jets to Intercept Israeli Airliners," *N.Y. Times*, Feb. 8, 1986, at A3.

283 Conv. for the Suppression of Unlawful Seizure of Aircraft [Hague Hijacking Conv.], Dec. 16, 1970, art. 1, U.N. Doc. A/C.6/418/Corr.1, Annex II, 860 U.N.T.S. 105, 22 U.S.T. 1641, *reprinted in* 10 ILM 133 (1971) (emphasis supplied). In addition, under this Convention, hijacking cannot occur against a State aircraft, but only a commercial or civil one. *Id.*, art. 3.

284 Law of the Sea Conv., *supra* n.153, art. 101 (defining "piracy" as: "(a) any illegal acts of violence or detention, or any act of depredation, committed for private ends by the crew or the passengers of a private ship or a private aircraft, and directed: (i) on the high seas, against another ship or aircraft, or against persons or property on board such ship or aircraft; (ii) against a ship, aircraft, persons or property in a place outside the jurisdiction of any State; (b) any act of voluntary participation in the operation of a ship or of an

not occur in connection with a law enforcement operation undertaken as an official matter by a pursuing State intended to capture fugitives and bring them to justice.

iv Cross-Cutting Justifications

A number of justifications have been advanced to defend the lawfulness of some or all of the unilateral operations at issue and, as such, may be characterized as "cross-cutting." These include instances where: (i) the rendered State and/or the State of the fugitive's nationality[285] expresses consent or otherwise acquiesces after public revelation of a unilateral operation; (ii) the rendered State is unable or unwilling to address a recognized threat or, more seriously, is demonstrably in league with a criminal enterprise; (iii) a imperative exists, as there is no viable alternative to deal with a fugitive; and (iv) the underlying crime is particularly heinous or loathsome.

1 Consent or Silence

The rendered State or the State of which the fugitive is a national may react *ex post facto* to a unilateral operation in terms of a violation of treaty law or of the fugitive's human rights by express consent or silence, rather than by protest.[286] In addition, the rendered State can provide *ex post facto* consent or remain silent regarding a violation of its territorial sovereignty.[287] This sub-section examines the legal effect of consent or silence.[288]

aircraft with knowledge of facts making it a pirate ship or aircraft; (c) any act inciting or of intentionally facilitating an act described in sub-paragraph (a) or (b).").

285 The State of which the fugitive is a national could of course also choose to lodge a formal protest against the State carrying out an SDO. *Cf.* Michell, *supra* n.156, at 421 n.195 (discussing seizure operations from Stateless vessels on the high seas on the grounds of diplomatic protection).

286 Given his German nationality, when Adolf Eichmann was seized from Argentina in May 1960, Germany could have complained on his behalf. But "far from advancing any such claims, the German Government even refused to accede to the requests made by the Defence to give protection to Eichmann in any form. Moreover, the German authorities actively assisted Israel in the examination of trial witnesses in Germany. Thus, by acquiescence or approbation, Germany waived whatever claim in tort she might have had against Israel." Georg Schwarzenberger, International Law and Order 241–42 (1971).

287 This principle applies even in international waters, where an SDO is authorized with the consent of the State in whose name the vessel is registered. *E.g., United States v. Perlaza*, 439 F.3d 1149 (9th Cir. 2006) (U.S. agents intercepted a Colombian-flagged fishing boat off the South American coast and, with Colombia's consent, seized those aboard and took them to the United States to face prosecution).

288 Chapter 13.b.i considers the significance of an official protest.

Consent. Consent is a multi-faceted concept. Consent can be communicated or conveyed formally, informally,[289] or tacitly; it can be made in advance of or following a law enforcement operation; it can be provided on a blanket, contextual,[290] or *ad hoc* basis; and it can occur purposefully, accidentally, under coercion, or via fraud.[291] International law recognizes that wrongfulness by a pursuing State that otherwise perpetrated a police action on the host State's sovereign territory may be precluded by express, valid,[292] and prior (or contemporaneous) consent granted by the host State to the pursuing State and where the police action did not exceed the limits of that consent.[293] Where such consent is provided in advance, a reversal of consent *ex post facto* does not affect the lawfulness of the operation.[294] Where consent is only provided *ex post facto*, however, it does not render the operation lawful, but rather effectively waives the right of the consenting State to seek reparations for the wrongful

[289] *See* Prepared Statement of William P. Barr, Asst. AG, Office of Legal Counsel, DOJ, *FBI Authority to Seize Suspects Abroad: Hearing Before the Subcommittee on Civil and Constitutional Rights of the Committee on the Judiciary, U.S. House of Representatives*, No. H521-45, 101st Cong., 1st Sess., at 20 (Nov. 8, 1989) ("There may also be occasions when we are permitted to perform an extraterritorial law enforcement operation with the informal cooperation of representatives or departments of a foreign government while the government publicly withholds its formal consent.") [hereinafter AG Barr Statement].

[290] An example of contextual consent occurred when the "British Royal Navy arrested four Russian fugitives from a Danish ship intercepted on the high seas and brought them to a British port to be searched for contraband under an agreement with Denmark to avoid danger and inconvenience of such a search being conducted on the high seas. The court did not treat this incident as though they had been arrested on the high seas or forcibly removed from a neutral vessel, but rather that they were arrested in a British port so no foreign sovereignty was violated; neither Denmark nor Russia objected." O'Higgins, *supra* n.46, at 287.

[291] Jordan J. Paust, *After* Alvarez-Machain*: Abduction, Standing, Denials of Justice, and Unaddressed Human Rights Claims*, 67 St. John's L. Rev. 551, 569 n.65 (1993).

[292] The consent must not be subject to fraud or coercion. ILC, *State Responsibility, supra* n.37, art. 20. Mistaken consent, however, is still valid. *Id.; Savarkar Case* (Fr. v. Gr. Br.), PCA Award, Hague Ct. Rep. (Scott) 276, Feb. 24, 1911; *Gov't of Jamaica v. United States*, 770 F. Supp. 627 (M.D. Fla. 1991). Validity likewise is not compromised if made by local officials on an *ultra vires* basis. ILC, *State Responsibility, supra* n.37, art. 20; *Ben Barka* Case, (1966), *reprinted in* Ann. Fr. de Droit Int'l 899 [French text].

[293] ILC, *State Responsibility, supra* n.37, art. 20; Michell, *supra* n.156, at 420.

[294] Michell, *supra* n.156, at 421 n.194; "State Responsibility," 2 Y.B. Int'l L. Comm'n, A/CN.4/SER.A/1979/Add.l (Part 1), U.N. Doc. A/CN.4/318 and Add.1-4 (1979), at 33-34 (discussing the 1863 incident case in which France had second thoughts after consenting to allow the Italian police to board a French vessel named *Aunis* docked in the Genoa harbor and seize five fugitives).

act.[295] As applied to unilateral operations, then, *ex post facto* consent alone would not render an otherwise unlawful LCO, SDO, or interception lawful *per se*, but would minimize any legal consequences arising therefrom.

Silence. Absent express consent or protest, the question arises whether the international community should treat silence functionally as implied or tacit consent. Although there is a difference of view on this score, the preponderance of opinion appears to be that consent or acquiescence may *not* be implied by silence. This position is maintained not only by the Int'l Law Commission (ILC), which makes clear that consent must be express,[296] but also by Professor Frederick Mann who posited: "if the State does or says nothing, the illegality remains. It is impossible to infer consent from silence or inactivity. Even if the State declares that it does not require the return of the abducted person, it is at least arguable that it waives the remedy rather than the wrong."[297]

Professor Mann further suggests that the rendering State at issue should bear the burden of proving that the rendered State (from which the fugitive was seized) had given its consent.[298] The contrary view is maintained by States, like the United States, which treat the failure to protest or object as acquiescence.[299] Sometimes, a State is not able to

[295] Michell, *supra* n.156, at 421. *Contra Lujan Case, supra* n.41, 510 F.2d at 67 ("Thus the failure of Bolivia or Argentina to object to Lujan's abduction [SDO] would seem to preclude any violation of international law which might otherwise have occurred").

[296] *See* ILC, *State Responsibility, supra* n.37, art. 20 cmt. 6 ("[Consent] must be actually expressed by the State rather than merely presumed on the basis that the State would have consented if it had been asked."). Consent could be implied, however, if a State had a legal duty to express its view in the face of an ostensible legal violation and then chose to remain silent. *See Case Concerning the Temple of Preah Vihear* (Camb. v. Thai.), Merits [1962] I.C.J. Rep. 6, 23 (June 15) ("[I]t is clear that the circumstances were such as called for some reaction, within a reasonable period, on the part of the Siamese authorities, if they wished to disagree with the map or had any serious question to raise in regard to it. They did not do so, either then or for many years, and thereby must be held to have acquiesced.").

[297] Mann, *supra* n.114, at 409; *accord* Michell, *supra* n.156, at 422 & n.197; *cf.* Andreas F. Lowenfeld, *U.S. Law Enforcement Abroad: The Constitution and Int'l Law, Continued*, 84 AJIL 444, 489 (1990) (observing how difficult it is to tell when silence can legitimately be construed as consent).

[298] Mann, *supra* n.114, at 409.

[299] *E.g., Lujan Case, supra* n.41, 510 F.2d 62; *United States v. Unverzagt*, 299 F. 1015, 1017 (W.D. Wash. 1924) (finding no violation when U.S. officials forcibly transferred a U.S. citizen from Vancouver to Washington state, noting "Canada is not making any application to this court in his behalf or its behalf, because of any unlawful acts charged, and if Canada or British Columbia desires to protest, the question undoubtedly is a political matter, which must be conducted through diplomatic channels."). This

register a protest, even if it might wish to, because it is operating under military occupation by a foreign power,[300] or simply is constrained in doing so due to foreign policy or diplomatic pressures.[301] In any event, consistent with the consent analysis above, when the rendered State is silent, its failure to protest should be viewed as a waiver of any relief or redress from a rendering State, rather than as a basis for precluding wrongfulness.[302]

2 The Rendered State Is Unable or Unwilling to Address a Recognized Threat or Is in Complicit with a Criminal Enterprise

Since the late 1980s, senior U.S. officials and classified U.S. policy, under both Democratic and Republican administrations, have held that, pursuant to international law, a pursuing State could be justified in exercising force or engaging in a law enforcement operation on another's sovereign territory to the extent that the host State were either not addressing a recognized threat or, worse yet, affirmatively protecting, harboring, or supporting an individual fugitive or group of fugitives. As recently as March 2012, U.S. Attorney General Eric Holder announced: "[T]he use of force in foreign territory would be consistent with ... international legal principles if conducted, for example ... after a determination that the nation is unable or unwilling to deal effectively with a threat to the United States."[303]

position is reinforced by some legal commentators who view implied or tacit consent as precluding wrongfulness based on State practice. *E.g.*, Jonathan A. Gluck, *The Customary Int'l Law of State-Sponsored Int'l Abduction and United States Courts*, 44 Duke L.J. 612, 622–24 (1994); Mary Alice Kovac, *Apprehension of War Crimes Indictees: Should the U.N. Outsource Private Actors to Catch Them?*, 51 Cath. U. L. Rev. 619, 642 n.153 (2002).

300 For example, Peru was not able to object to the seizure of Frederick Ker by a private U.S. agent with the assistance of occupying Chilean forces. Cardozo, *supra* n.168, at 133. Similarly, due to its then-U.S.-occupied status, Germany did not protest when the United States seized Douglas Chandler from German territory following World War II. M. Cherif Bassiouni, *Kidnapping and Hostage Taking*, *in* 1 International Criminal Law: Crimes 416–17 (2d ed. M. Cherif Bassiouni ed. 1999).

301 *See generally* Lowenfeld, *supra* n.297, at 489 ("For one thing, the states that do not protest tend to be, if not client states, at any rate states that have various reasons not to make formal protests.").

302 Bassiouni, World Public Order, *supra* n.65, at 174–75; Kovac, *supra* n.299, at 641 & n.145 (citing the *Ker, Argoud*, and *Ndhlovu* cases); Michell, *supra* n.156, at 422 & n.198.

303 Eric Holder, Remarks by U.S Att'y Gen. on National Security Law, NWU School of Law, Chicago, Mar. 5, 2012, *available at* www.justice.gov/opa/speech/attorney-general-eric-holder-speaks-northwestern-university-school-law (last visited on May 26, 2016).

In addition, at the end of the 1980s, U.S. Assistant Attorney General William Barr testified before a congressional subcommittee as follows: "[I]n appropriate circumstances we may have a sound basis under international law to take [law enforcement] action against large-scale drug traffickers being given safe haven by a government acting in complicity with their criminal enterprise."[304] Furthermore, in June 1995, in what was intended as a classified U.S. policy document known as Presidential Decision Directive 39 (or PDD-39) addressing counterterrorism, the United States adopted the position that "[i]f we do not receive adequate cooperation from a state that harbors a terrorist whose extradition we are seeking, we shall take appropriate measures to induce cooperation. Return of suspects by force may be effected without the cooperation of the host government, consistent with the procedures outlined in NSD-77, which shall remain in effect."[305] Or, as one legal commentator, put it:

> If a plane from country X is carrying terrorists who have committed, or organized and planned, an act of terrorism, then country X is assisting such terrorists in escaping and evading detection, abduction and/or prosecution, all nations, even those not victimized by the act of terrorism committed by those on board, may seize the aircraft and arrest its occupants.[306]

There is, however, no international treaty law to support this justification. To find any cognizable international legal basis, one would have to turn to either the customary practice of self-defense (as arguably preserved within the context of Article 51 of the U.N. Charter) or the legitimate but narrowly confined measure known as "countermeasures" as a means of self-help.[307] As a commentator opined with regard to the self-defense rationale:

[304] AG Barr Statement, *supra* n.289, at 20.

[305] Dycus, *supra* n.14, at 527 (quoting classified but unpublished part of PDD-39) (National Security Directive-77, or NSD-77, remains classified); *see also* Murali Jasti, *Extraditing Terrorists Hits a Death Penalty Kibosh*, 22 Wis. Int'l L.J. 163, 184 & n.121 (2004); Borelli, *supra* n.18, at 351–53.

[306] Kash, *Airspace, supra* n.16, at 84.

[307] A third arguable basis could be the Friendly Relations Declaration, which, *inter alia*, provides: "Every State has the duty to fulfil in good faith its obligations under the generally recognized principles and rules of international law ... Every State has the duty to fulfil in good faith its obligations under international agreements valid under the generally recognized principles and rules of international law." *Decl. on Principles of Int'l Law Concerning Friendly Relations and Co-operation Among States in Accordance with the Charter of the United Nations*, UNGA Res. 2625, U.N. GAOR, 25th Sess. (Supp. No. 28), U.N. Doc. A/8028 (1971), Oct. 24, 1970, *reprinted in* 9 ILM 1292 (1970). Such obligations presumably include identifying, locating, and arresting known or alleged criminals and certainly not sheltering or supporting them.

> [S]tates practicing self-help contend that a state which gives terrorists sanctuary and refuses to apprehend or prosecute them itself violates international law, not only by assisting the alleged criminal to evade prosecution, but also by encouraging similar terrorist attacks in the future. Therefore, states that disregard their international obligations should not be able to invoke territorial sovereignty to frustrate efforts by offended states to exact retribution for attacks on their citizens.[308]

Another wrote: "a state's authorities may justifiably engage in an unconsented apprehension in another state against terrorists which pose a continuing threat and which are being given sanctuary in the latter state. To the extent indicted war criminals located in the FRY or Croatia constitute a threat to the NATO or United Nations troops lawfully stationed in the territory of the former Yugoslavia, this could provide justification for abducting individuals from the FRY or Croatia for purposes of arrest."[309] The self-defense argument, as applied to Israel's interception of the Libyan aircraft in February 1986, would require that Israel be able to show the following elements: "(1) that possible future acts of the terrorists sought could be properly attributable to Libya; [and] (2) the peril created by the future terrorism must be both grave and imminent."[310] This is a highly controversial concept and would be difficult to prove.

The legal standard governing countermeasures, or non-forceful reprisals, allows a State to undertake such a measure against another State responsible for an internationally wrongful act in order to induce that State to comply with its obligations, but not to punish. A countermeasure must be limited to the non-performance for the time being of international obligations; can be undertaken only if all other peaceful means of dispute resolution have been exhausted; shall be taken as far as possible to permit the resumption of performance of the obligations in question; shall not affect a State's obligation to refrain from the threat or use of force, the protection of fundamental human rights, reprisals, or peremptory norms of general international law; and must be proportionate with the injury suffered, provide advance notice, and cease as soon as the wrongful act has ceased.[311] As countermeasures must not involve the use or threat of force, aircraft interceptions would not appear to pass muster under this justification.

[308] Chabner, *supra* n.270, at 1018.
[309] Scharf, *supra* n.40, at 965 (supranational criminal law context).
[310] Kash, *Airspace, supra* n.16, at 92.
[311] ILC, *State Responsibility, supra* n.37, arts. 22, 49–53.

A variant on this theme is the so-called "Efficient Breach Justification," which builds on law and economics principles, offers a means of crisis management, and factors in cost-benefit logic.[312] The argument here is that a unilateral operation should be treated as legally tenable where a combination of certain factors exist: "(1) the [security] threat appears imminent and the opportunity for [a given unilateral operation] is fleeting; (2) the target nation is unwilling to extradite or prosecute; (3) the operation involves minimal threat to bystanders; (4) the territorial infringement is reasonably limited; and (5) the accused will receive humane treatment and a fair trial."[313] While such an operation would be unlawful in principle, the international community's reaction could be muted and the operation effectively excused depending on the specific facts at play, particularly the nature and imminence of the threat posed by the subject and the extent to which the rendered State's territorial sovereignty were breached.

3 No Viable Law Enforcement Alternative Exists

Some have contended that where there is a law enforcement imperative to apprehend a particular fugitive but no feasible alternative exists, a unilateral operation can be justified under the doctrine of necessity, which is related to, but distinct from, the ground discussed immediately above. Under international law, necessity is a means to preclude wrongfulness when it is the only way for a pursuing State to safeguard an essential interest against a grave and imminent peril; a pursuing State cannot seriously impair an essential interest of the host State or another to which an obligation exists; and a pursuing State cannot have contributed to the situation of necessity.[314] Necessity derives in part from the challenge posed by the host State's assistance furnished to certain fugitives, which renders it "virtually impossible" to secure their custody "using traditional means."[315]

For example, when Israel wanted to secure the custody of Adolf Eichmann from Argentina, Israel had to consider the reality that: (i) the two States had no extradition treaty between them; (ii) even if they had such a treaty, any extradition request might have tipped him off (by a sympathizer within the Argentine Government, much like had occurred with Josef

[312] Andrew J. Calica, *Self-Help is the Best Kind: The Efficient Breach Justification for Forcible Abduction of Terrorists*, 37 Cornell Int'l L.J. 389, 414 (2004); Richard Morrison, *Efficient Breach of Int'l Agreements*, 23 Denv. J. Int'l L. & Pol'y 183 (1994).

[313] Calica, *supra* n.312, at 415.

[314] ILC, *State Responsibility, supra* n.37, art. 25.

[315] Kash, *Airspace, supra* n.16, at 85 (relying on the example of terrorism).

Mengele, who disappeared from Buenos Aires after an extradition request was issued for him in 1959 and he resurfaced safely in Paraguay); (iii) Eichmann had been living in Argentina for ten years and the host State had made no effort to bring him to justice and it had failed to deport or extradite any other Nazi war criminals; and (iv) neither Germany nor Hungary had sought to exercise subject matter jurisdiction over him.[316] Such a last resort approach has the added feature of imposing an effective deterrent against fugitives seeking a safe harbor in States unwilling to prosecute or extradite them.[317]

At bottom, however, necessity requires that a "grave and imminent peril" exist. In the case with Adolf Eichmann, for all of his monstrous acts in furtherance of the so-called "Final Solution," he no longer posed any danger to Israel, imminent or otherwise. Therefore, this justification would fall short under these circumstances; however, were a different set of facts to apply, particularly one involving a fugitive who still actively posed a threat to a particular pursuing State, it is conceivable that such a justification could pass legal muster.

4 Heinousness of the Underlying Crime

Finally, it is tempting for a rendering State to try to have its unilateral operation viewed within a larger ethical context by arguing that, however improper its conduct may have been, it does not compare in severity with the underlying crime committed by the fugitive and thus is justifiable in morally relativistic terms. Such attempts at justifications tend to surface in such extreme cases as major war crimes, mass murder, piracy, or slave trade, in which the crime is regarded as *hostis humani generis* (an enemy of all mankind)[318] or otherwise as being so heinous in nature so as to excuse a rendering State for having taken law enforcement liberties that technically violated international law standards. This concept was recognized by a U.K. court in 1999 when it stated:

> In arriving at this conclusion we strongly emphasize that nothing in this judgment should be taken to suggest that there may not be cases, such as *Latif*, in which the seriousness of the crime is so great relative to the nature of the abuse of process that it would be a proper exercise of judicial discretion to permit a prosecution to proceed or to allow a conviction to

[316] Bass, *supra* n.138, at 86–87; Izes, *supra* n.13, at 18.

[317] Izes, *supra* n.13, at 24.

[318] Borkowski, *supra* n.81, at 770 (in such instances any State may capture and punish a criminal in the interest of and on behalf of all States).

> stand notwithstanding an abuse of process in relation to the defendant's presence within the jurisdiction. In each case, it is a matter of discretionary balance, to be approached with regard to the particular conduct complained of and the particular offence charged.[319]

This is sometimes labeled the "Eichmann exception" in reference to that former Nazi's unconscionable conduct in orchestrating the Holocaust. In conducting its SDO operation in Buenos Aires in 1960 to bring Adolf Eichmann to justice, Israeli President David Ben Gurion "did not deny that Israel had violated Argentine sovereignty but apologized and asked the Argentine government to consider the wider moral context."[320] As one legal commentator astutely observed: "The U.N. took no punitive action against Israel for abduction. It was noteworthy because it could have taken this opportunity to set a powerful example concerning repercussions of state-sanctioned abductions. It almost tacitly approved Israel's conduct by its weak response."[321]

A particularly good example is piracy *jure gentium*, as that crime holds a special place in international law, as codified in the 1982 Law of the Sea Convention, given that it affords any State the privilege of arresting and prosecuting an individual for acts of piracy that occurred on the high seas.[322] It is essential to recognize, however, that piracy has a limited definitional scope: (i) pirates must have seized goods or property for private ends (rather than acting with political motivations) (ii) from another vessel (not from one on which they are already aboard) and (iii) while on the high seas (versus from territorial or archipelagic waters[323]).[324] International law is likely to be more permissive – and the international community's reaction probably less critical – with respect to a pursuing State's unilateral operation targeted against a pirate, and thereby mitigate any unlawfulness found against a rendering State.

Consider, for instance, the reaction to the U.S. interception in October 1985 of the Egyptian aircraft carrying the PLO terrorists involved in the *Achille Lauro* hijacking. Most of the negative reaction emanated from Middle Eastern States, especially Egypt and Iran, but the

319 *R. v. Mullen* [1999] 2 Cr. App. R. 143 (CA), [1999] WLR 777.

320 Bass, *supra* n.138, at 86.

321 Izes, *supra* n.13, at 17.

322 Cassese, Violence, *supra* n.83, at 68. This is a fine example of an *erga omnes* norm.

323 Since 2005, however, at least in Asia a regional anti-piracy treaty now extends to acts occurring even in territorial and archipelagic waters. Regional Cooperation Agreement on Combating Piracy and Armed Robbery against Ships in Asia (ReCAAP), Nov. 11, 2004, *reprinted in* 44 ILM 829 (2005).

324 Law of the Sea Conv., *supra* n.153, art. 101.

criticism was notably muted, with Jordan and Syria declining to make any official comment on the incident and with Sudan characterizing the incident as "not productive" and "conflict[ing] with international norms and charters."[325] The chorus from Western and Eastern European States alike was generally supportive and, while some editorial commentators opined that the interception violated international law, they nevertheless assessed the action as being either necessary or morally justified.[326] As one legal writer observed: "The effect of an incident on legal norms is ultimately a function of what relevant elites are willing to accept as legitimate."[327] But other examples exist, such as the case of Humberto Álvarez-Machaín, of allegedly horrific conduct[328] that did not elicit such forgiveness or understanding from the international community.[329]

* * * * *

This chapter has examined the third and final type of full-scale alternatives to extradition: unilateral measures. Part VI addresses the full range of implications – judicial, diplomatic, and policy – when a pursuing State undertakes a full-scale operational alternative.

325 Gregory V. Gooding, *Fighting Terrorism in the 1980's: The Interception of the* Achille Lauro *Hijackers*, 12 Yale J. Int'l L. 158, 170–71 (1987) (quoting the Sudanese Government spokesperson).

326 *Id.* at 172–73.

327 *Id.* at 172.

328 Dr. Humberto Álvarez-Machaín allegedly was responsible for prolonging the life of a captured DEA officer through the infusion of drugs in order to elicit additional information about DEA operations in Mexico through torture. *Álvarez-Machaín Case, supra* n.177, at 657.

329 Mark S. Zaid, *Military Might Versus Sovereign Right: The Kidnapping of Dr. Humberto Alvarez-Machain and the Resulting Fallout*, 19 Hous. J. Int'l L. 829 (1997).

PART VI

Post-Delivery Review, Recourse, and Impact

13

Judicial, Diplomatic, and Policy Dimensions

This final part explores what may occur on account of a fugitive being brought back for prosecution or punishment through the use of one of the full-scale operational alternatives to extradition examined in Chapters 10–12. More specifically, it assesses the operational delivery of the fugitive from three vantage points: (i) whether, and if so how, a judiciary evaluates claims of pursuing State unlawfulness; (ii) which diplomatic options, including legal remedies, are available to States from which a fugitive was rendered or to States of which the fugitive is a national; and (iii) which world public order and bilateral policy implications may arise out of the exercise of such alternatives to extradition. These considerations address the full range of consequences – judicial, diplomatic, and policy – in connection with a fugitive being brought to face justice via such alternative means.

a Judicial Considerations

When a fugitive is delivered to pursuing State territory and a claim is brought by the former host State, the State of the fugitive's nationality, or by the fugitive himself based on the manner in which his custody was secured (and possibly by the way in which he was treated during capture and/or in transit), a court must consider whether it has *personal* jurisdiction over the fugitive to hear the claim and, even if it does, whether it might elect not to exercise that jurisdiction. This section examines first how courts make such jurisdictional determinations and next embarks on a discussion of individual standing, as either matter could prove dispositive with respect to a court's ruling.[1]

[1] Apart from personal jurisdiction and individual standing, another factor bearing on the judgment of a court hearing criminal charges is the *applicable law*. Many States rely heavily in their case analysis on domestic law and doctrine at the expense of international law and

i Personal Jurisdiction

As discussed in Chapter 2.b, personal jurisdiction is a required element, along with subject matter jurisdiction, to enforce a State's laws in court against any individual defendant. Although *physical custody* by a pursuing State is not essential – for example, the individual could be held by another State's law enforcement authorities on a pursuing State's behalf – it is by far the most common means by which personal jurisdiction is established. A major issue facing a domestic criminal court in cases in which a fugitive's physical custody is obtained through a full-scale operational alternative to extradition is whether personal jurisdiction may be vitiated on account of an abuse of process by the executive branch or, alternatively, whether the court may choose not to exercise that jurisdiction as a discretionary matter, thereby resulting in a stay of proceedings.[2]

To probe this jurisdictional element, we begin with the "rule of non-inquiry,"[3] popularly known in this context by the Roman maxim *male captus bene detentus* (defined below), and then consider its scope, justification, and significance; the extent of its application (or non-application) by States' courts, including recognized exceptions to the

standards. *See* Gregory S. McNeal & Brian J. Field, *Snatch-and-Grab Ops: Justifying Extraterritorial Abduction*, 16 J. Transnat'l L. & Contemp. Probs. 491, 519 (2007) (domestic courts addressing seizures abroad tend to base their decisions not on international law but rather on their own nation's traditions and laws); Yvonne G. Grassie, Note, *Federally Sponsored Int'l Kidnapping: An Acceptable Alternative to Extradition?*, 64 Wash. U.L.Q. 1205, 1215 (1986) ("American courts, although recognizing constitutional due process guarantees in international kidnapping cases, largely overlook internationally protected human rights.").

2 Another independent basis for which personal jurisdiction can be challenged is diplomatic or consular immunity. For one notable case in this regard, *see In re Grand Jury Proceedings*, 817 F.2d 1108 (4th Cir.), *cert. denied*, 484 U.S. 965 (1987), in which a U.S. appellate court did not grant Ferdinand Marcos, former head of State of the Philippines, immunity from criminal prosecution because the immunity issue was deemed to be unsettled under U.S. case law and because immunity is founded on the respect for sovereignty of other nations and should only apply when it serves those goals, and therefore because Corazon Aquino, the new head of State of the Philippines, did not want Marcos to be treated with immunity, the U.S. Government had no reason to grant it. Peter M. Sanchez, *The 'Drug War': The U.S. Military and National Security*, 34 A.F. L. Rev. 109, 135 (1991).

3 The term "rule of non-inquiry" in this particular context is defined as follows: *a State's judiciary does not regard it as proper to query how a criminal defendant came before it, and therefore is willing to assert personal jurisdiction regardless of the circumstances surrounding his capture and transfer. See also* n.281 and accompanying text in Chapter 2; n.187 and accompanying text in Chapter 5; and nn.225–42 and accompanying text in Chapter 7.

rule and modern trend lines; as well as the way in which the maxim's typical application – a stay of proceedings – operates.

1 *Male Captus Bene Detentus*

Under this traditional legal maxim, a domestic criminal court may not divest itself of personal jurisdiction over the fugitive defendant so long as he is physically within the territorial jurisdiction of the court, regardless of the means or circumstances by which the State's executive branch may have secured his presence.[4] The term, which effectively translates from Latin into "*an unlawful apprehension may nevertheless give rise to lawful detention and prosecution*," stands for the proposition that *a court must treat as immaterial for personal jurisdictional purposes how a criminal defendant came before it*.[5] Stated otherwise, it is not the court's business to inquire into the alleged irregularity by which a fugitive was delivered to the pursuing State.[6] When viewed as a choice between honoring the rights of other States and of the fugitives themselves versus permitting the prosecution of alleged crimes against one's own State, this maxim favors the latter.[7]

Scope. Examples of executive branch conduct that would not prevent a domestic criminal court from exercising personal jurisdiction under this rule, at least as it has been applied in *absolute terms*,[8] include where: (i) a fugitive was the subject of a unilateral SDO,[9] informal law

[4] Ilias Bantekas & Susan Nash, International Criminal Law 218 (2d ed. 2003); Frederick A. Mann, *Reflections on the Prosecution of Persons Abducted in Breach of Int'l Law*, *in* International Law at a Time of Perplexity: Essays in Honour of Shabtai Rosenne 414 (Yoram Dinstein ed. 1989); Douglas Kash, *Abducting Terrorists under PDD-39: Much Ado About Nothing New*, 13 Am. U. Int'l L. Rev. 139, 150 (1997–98).

[5] Gerhard von Glahn, Law Among Nations 315 (6th ed. 1992).

[6] Michael R. Pontoni, *Authority of the United States to Extraterritorially Apprehend and Lawfully Prosecute Int'l Drug Traffickers and Other Fugitives*, 21 Cal. W. Int'l L.J. 215, 237 (1990–91); *United States v. Sobell*, 142 F. Supp. 515 (S.D.N.Y. 1956), *aff'd*, 244 F.2d 520 (2d Cir.), *cert. denied*, 355 U.S. 873 (1957), *reh'g denied*, 355 U.S. 920 (1958).

[7] Mark Brkljacic, Note, *The Dangers of State Sponsored and Court Ratified Abduction*, 5 J. Int'l L. & Prac. 117, 117 (1996).

[8] Kathryn Selleck, Note, *Jurisdiction after Int'l Kidnapping: A Comparative Study*, 8 B.C. Int'l & Comp. L. Rev. 237, 264–65 (1985); Note, *The Effect of Illegal Abductions by Law Enforcement Officials on Personal Jurisdiction*, 35 Md. L. Rev. 147, 153–56 (1975) [hereinafter Note, *Illegal Abductions*] (discussing a variety of scenarios and citing applicable U.S. case law).

[9] *E.g.*, *United States v. Álvarez-Machaín*, 504 U.S. 655 (1992), *on remand*, 971 F.2d 310 (9th Cir. 1992), *reprinted in* 31 ILM 902 (1992).

enforcement cooperation,[10] a fraudulent lure or inducement to waive extradition,[11] or disguised extradition;[12] (ii) the transferor State or a third State protested a physical transfer on legal grounds;[13] (iii) the fugitive was arrested without a warrant;[14] (iv) the fugitive was delivered to pursuing State territory following physical maltreatment or unlawful confinement;[15] (v) the fugitive was denied an extradition hearing or legal counsel to challenge his treatment in the transferor State;[16] (vi) the means of delivering the fugitive expressly breached municipal legislation;[17] or (vii) the delivery of a fugitive was effected outside the context of an effective bilateral extradition treaty.[18]

Justification. A variety of justifications have been advanced in support of the *male captus* principle. Courts claim with some strength of logic that the rule is sensible because: (i) executive branch liberties or irregularities in bringing a fugitive to pursuing State territory should not cancel out the underlying criminal offense perpetrated by the fugitive for which accountability is warranted; (ii) the court has an obligation to try criminal cases that come before it;[19] and (iii) the judiciary should not meddle in

[10] *E.g., Wentz v. United States*, 244 F.2d 172 (9th Cir.), *cert. denied*, 355 U.S. 806 (1957).

[11] *E.g., Blankenship v. Peyton*, 295 F. Supp. 16 (W.D. Va. 1969) (municipal case example).

[12] *E.g., Sitaram v. Superintendent Rangoon Central Jail*, High Ct., Burma, Feb. 15, 1957, [1957] Burma L. Rep. 190, *reprinted in* 28 ILR 313 (1963).

[13] *E.g., Attorney General of the Gov't of Israel v. Eichmann*, Crim. Case No. 40/61, Dist. Ct. of Jerusalem, Isr., Dec. 12, 1961, *reprinted in* 36 ILR 5, *aff'd sub nom., Eichmann v. Attorney General of the Gov't of Israel*, Sup. Ct., Isr., May 29, 1962, *reprinted in* 36 ILR 277 (E. Lauterpacht ed. 1968) (Argentina protested); *Gov't of Jamaica v. United States*, 770 F. Supp. 627 (M.D. Fla. 1991) (Jamaica lodged an official protest on the grounds that the U.S. Government had carried out an extradition prematurely in violation of its municipal law and, by extension, Article 8 of their bilateral extradition treaty, where the defendant had filed an appeal that had not been acted upon only because it had been misfiled; the U.S. court held that any such protest should be handled via diplomatic channels).

[14] *E.g., United States v. Washington*, 253 F.2d 913, 916 (7th Cir. 1958).

[15] *E.g., United States v. Yunis*, 924 F.2d 1086 (D.C. Cir. 1991) (the subject's wrists were broken during the take-down).

[16] *E.g., Wentz*, 244 F.2d 172.

[17] *E.g., United States v. Cotten*, 471 F.2d 744, 749 (9th Cir.) (discussing 18 U.S.C. § 1385 (2012) related to the Posse Comitatus Act), *cert. denied*, 411 U.S. 936 (1973); *People v. Pratt*, 78 Cal. 345 (Cal. Sup. Ct. 1889) (en banc) (personal jurisdiction was not defeated when the California Governor arranged for the return of a fugitive from Japan absent a U.S.-Japan extradition treaty, even though an extradition treaty was required under U.S. law).

[18] *E.g., United States v. Cordero*, 668 F.2d 32 (1st Cir. 1981) (Panama and Venezuela); *United States v. Stevenson*, 381 F.2d 142 (9th Cir. 1967) (Mexico).

[19] *R. v. Horseferry Road Magistrates' Court, ex parte Bennett* [1994] 1 A.C. 42 (H.L.) [1993] 3 All E.R. 138, *reprinted in* 95 ILR 355 (Lord Oliver, dissenting op.).

political disputes between States that should be resolved by their executive branches on a diplomatic plane.[20]

Weaker rationales include that individuals are merely *objects* of inter-State relations, agreements, and proceedings, and that fugitives, therefore, have no stand-alone rights to assert, but as discussed below, individuals are protected under international human rights treaties and also may well have rights arising out of an extradition treaty under domestic law (*e.g.*, application of the specialty principle, entitlement to an extradition hearing).[21] In addition, the maxim has been rationalized on the basis that courts are not authorized to second-guess the manner in which the executive branch brought a fugitive before it, but courts in many States, including the United States, regularly exclude from proceedings evidence illegally seized by law enforcement officers,[22] and deny personal jurisdiction altogether in *civil* cases where evidence exists that a person or property has been obtained via force or fraud.[23]

The chief criticisms aimed at the rule are that it appears to condone unlawful conduct, and thereby not only undermines the court's integrity and reputation as it effectively serves as a kind of accomplice, but also encourages States to operate outside the law (including the extradition

[20] *E.g.*, *Ex parte López*, 6 F. Supp. 342 (S.D. Tex. 1934). This defense, however, has been challenged by one legal commentator as follows: "Although it must be readily conceded that the courts should not invade the province of the political department of the government, it cannot reasonably be doubted that matters relating to the abduction of fugitives in foreign countries are of a strictly legal nature and, thus, there is no justifiable reason why such questions should be transferred from the regulatory province of the law to the discretionary domain of politics." Manuel R. Garcia-Mora, *Criminal Jurisdiction of a State over Fugitives Brought from a Foreign Country by Force or Fraud: A Comparative Study*, 32 IND. L.J. 427, 438 (1957).

[21] This difference of opinion reflects to an extent the respective historical views of those embracing "positive law" versus "natural law." Positivists maintained that individuals are but objects of international law and therefore only derive rights therefrom if States confer such rights on individuals, even if they somehow are incidental beneficiaries. Those adopting a natural law perspective held that individuals are subjects of international law due to its being a part of natural law and therefore derive enforceable rights from it. Kenneth E. Levitt, Note, *Int'l Extradition, The Principle of Specialty and Effective Treaty Enforcement*, 76 MINN. L. REV. 1017, 1021–22 (1992).

[22] *See* ANDREW L.-T. CHOO, ABUSE OF PROCESS AND JUDICIAL STAYS OF CRIMINAL PROCEEDINGS 86 (1993) [hereinafter CHOO, JUDICIAL STAYS] (discussing the "fruit of the poisonous tree" concept); *e.g.*, *Abel v. Smith*, 151 Va. 568 (Va. Sup. Ct. 1928).

[23] Note, *Illegal Abductions*, *supra* n.8, at 153–56; Paul Michell, *English-Speaking Justice: Evolving Responses to Transnat'l Forcible Abduction after* Alvarez-Machain, 29 CORNELL INT'L L.J. 383, 390 n.23 (1996); *In re Johnson*, 167 U.S. 120 (1897) ("The law will not permit a person to be kidnapped or decoyed within the jurisdiction for the purpose of being compelled to answer to a mere private claim.").

regime), confident that their unlawful conduct will not be a ground for setting aside the underlying prosecution.[24]

Significance. To better appreciate its significance, the *male captus* principle can be further evaluated according to three key indices: (i) whether it has any status under *international law*, (ii) to what extent its invocation reflects ratification by pursuing State courts in the underlying conduct of its executive branch officials, and (iii) how it stands up to a competing Roman legal maxim.

As to the first index, domestic courts have never characterized the *male captus* principle as mandated by international law; in fact, it has always been treated as a domestic legal rule applicable mainly in terms of distinguishing the respective roles of the judicial and executive branches of government.[25] Although adopted by a large number of States, the principle has not yet been accorded customary international law status, as there is no evident *opinio juris* (*i.e.*, a sense of legal obligation) supporting that practice and, increasingly, domestic courts are even deviating from its application (discussed *infra*).

With regard to the second index, it must be stressed that in choosing to exercise jurisdiction over the fugitive and to carry out criminal proceedings against him, a domestic court has neither necessarily approved nor disapproved of the underlying executive's conduct, but rather has approached the matter indifferently and as outside of its authority.[26] In short, it adopts an agnostic posture, and its

[24] American Law Inst., RESTATEMENT (THIRD) OF THE FOREIGN RELATIONS LAW OF THE UNITED STATES, May 14, 1986, § 432 rep. note 2 [hereinafter RESTATEMENT (THIRD)]; Philip B. Heymann & Ian Heath Gershengorn, *Pursuing Justice, Respecting the Law, in* PRINCIPLES AND PROCEDURES FOR A NEW TRANSNATIONAL CRIMINAL LAW: DOCUMENTATION OF AN INTERNATIONAL WORKSHOP IN FREIBURG, MAY 1991, at 122 (Albin Eser & Otto Lagodny eds. 1992); Mann, *supra* n.4, at 419 (rewarding extraterritorial seizures with prosecution "amounts to an invitation to commit similar illegalities in the wrongdoing state").

[25] Silvia Borelli, *The Rendition of Terrorist Suspects to the United States: Human Rights and the Limits of Int'l Cooperation, in* ENFORCING INTERNATIONAL LAW NORMS AGAINST TERRORISM 354 n.92 (Andrea Bianchi ed. 2004).

[26] Some scholars have drawn a "ratification" analogy to the situation where a State to whom a fugitive is delivered by a private individual chooses not to return the fugitive to the State from which he was taken, meaning the fortuitously acquiring State has in effect ratified the underlying act. This analogy is inapposite for several reasons. First, there is a material difference between (a) the judicial branch second-guessing the conduct of the executive branch within a given State and (b) decisions taken entirely within a single branch. Second, in the case of alleged "judicial ratification," the court relies on a long-established principle, the "rule of non-inquiry," while in the case of the executive branch not returning a fortuitously acquired fugitive, no attendant principle

jurisdictional determination should not be confused with ratification or validation by the court, as a branch of the pursuing State's government, of the lawfulness of the underlying executive branch conduct.[27] The U.S. Supreme Court's opinion in the *Álvarez-Machaín* case addressed this distinction clearly when it observed that the SDO used to bring the fugitive to the United States "may be in violation of general international law principles"[28] while, at the same time, finding no basis to reject personal jurisdiction.[29]

The third index queries the validity of the *male captus* rule by positing a countervailing law maxim:[30] *ex injuria ius non oritur*, which in essence means that a lawful result cannot arise from an unlawful act. This maxim, which adopts a "clean hands" logic, militates in favor of precluding a State's courts from asserting personal jurisdiction, and thereby not hearing the underlying charges against a fugitive defendant, in a case where his presence was obtained by a legal violation in the process, such as by

exists. Third, courts alone continue to carry out their chief function (*i.e.*, adjudicating the underlying criminal charges) without any abdication of their responsibility, while still leaving open for the executive branch the possibility of negotiating through diplomatic channels the fugitive's delivery.

27 Satyadeva Bedi, Extradition: A Treatise on the Laws Relevant to the Fugitive Offenders Within and With the Commonwealth Countries 394–95 & nn.16–17 (2002); *Matta-Ballesteros v. Henman*, 896 F.2d 255, 263 (7th Cir.) ("we do not condone government misconduct such as [the fugitive defendant] alleges"), *aff'd*, 896 F.2d 255 (7th Cir.), *cert. denied*, 498 U.S. 878 (1990). *Cf. Walker v. United States*, Case No. 12.049, Inter-Am. C.H.R., OEA/ser. L/V/II.118, Doc. 70 rev. 2 at 550, ¶ 51, Oct. 10 2003 [hereinafter *Walker Case*] ("The Commission also wishes to note that its determination as to the admissibility of Mr. Walker's claims should not be interpreted as condoning or otherwise passing judgment upon the propriety of the alleged actions of U.S. officials in the circumstances of Mr. Walker's arrest and detention [*i.e.*, a unilateral LCO from Canada to the United States]."). *But see* discussion of inherent supervisory powers in sub-section a.i.

28 *Álvarez-Machaín*, 504 U.S. at 669.

29 *Id.*

30 Emeritus DePaul University Law Professor M. Cherif Bassiouni introduces a second competing maxim known as *nunquam decurritur ad extraordinarium sed ubi deficit ordinarium* (*i.e.*, never resort to the extraordinary until the ordinary fails), contending in effect that the *male captus* rule is extraordinary, and therefore that all ordinary procedural means must first be exhausted. M. Cherif Bassiouni, International Extradition and World Public Order 143–44 (1974) [hereinafter Bassiouni, World Public Order]. The application of this otherwise reasonable maxim in the abstract is less persuasive, however, in the specific context of how courts determine personal jurisdiction, as it is at least debatable whether *male captus*, a manifestation of the long-established rule of non-inquiry, constitutes an extraordinary rule in the first place, as courts are, in a very real sense, simply executing their mandate to adjudicate alleged underlying offenses.

breaching another State's sovereignty.[31] In effect, it is contended that no personal jurisdiction should be found in such a circumstance, much like the exclusionary rule operates to treat as inadmissible evidence gathered unlawfully by law enforcement officers, or like a vessel seized at sea in violation of treaty law should not be subject to a court's legal process.[32] There is merit to this maxim, but *male captus* clearly appears to be the *lex specialis* in this instance, and therefore should take precedence.[33]

2 State Practice

The *male captus* principle took hold nearly two centuries ago in Britain[34] and the United States,[35] and eventually gained wide application throughout the world. As the American Law Institute commented in 1987: "Nearly all states have followed the rule that, absent protest from other states, they will try persons brought before their courts through irregular means, even through an abduction from another state in violation of international law."[36] This had been true not only of the British Commonwealth States,[37] but also of States with civil law systems such as

31 Margaret L. Satterthwaite, *The Legal Regime Governing Transfer of Persons in the Fight against Terrorism*, N.Y.U. Public Law and Legal Theory Working Papers, Paper 192, May 1, 2010, at 12.

32 Bassiouni, World Public Order, *supra* n.30, at 144–45; Garcia-Mora, *supra* n.20, at 446–47; Edwin D. Dickinson, *Jurisdiction Following Seizure or Arrest in Violation of Int'l Law*, 28 AJIL 231, 236 (1934); *e.g., Abel*, 151 Va. 568. When a fugitive defendant contended that his "body" should be excluded as evidence under the Fourth Amendment to the U.S. Constitution, however, a U.S. appeals court outright rejected it. *Matta-Ballesteros*, 896 F.2d at 262–63.

33 *Cf.* Natasha Balendra, *Int'l Human Rights Law and Int'l Humanitarian Law: Alternative Frameworks for Interaction, in* The New International Law: An Anthology 117–18 (Christopher C. Eriksen & Marius Emberland eds. 2010) ("Under the *lex specialis* maxim, when two laws contemporaneously apply to the same situation, the more specific or more 'special' law takes precedence over the other.") (discussing the interplay in application between international human rights law and international humanitarian law in the context of an international armed conflict).

34 *Ex parte Scott* [1829] 9 B. & C. 446.

35 *In re State of Vermont v. Brewster*, 7 Vt. 118 (Vt. Sup. Ct. 1835).

36 Restatement (Third), *supra* n.24, § 432.

37 For example, relevant case law in Canada includes *In re Walton*, Ontario High Ct. of Justice, [1905] 11 O.L.R. 94, *Re Hudson and the Queen*, Ontario High Ct. of Justice, Sept. 20, 1973, [1974] 1 O.R. (2d) 206; and *Halm v. Canada (Minister of Employment & Immigration)* Fed. Ct., Can., [1995] 2 F.C. 331 (T.D.). *See also* India: *Rudolf Stallmann alias Rudolph von Konig*, High Ct. of Calcutta, India, Aug. 21, 1911, *reprinted in* [1911] 12 Cr. L.J. 505, and Palestine: *Afouneh v. Attorney General*, Sup. Ct., Palestine, Feb. 11, 1942, *reprinted in* [1941–42] 10 Ann. Dig. & Rep. Pub. Int'l L. Cases 327 (H. Lauterpacht ed. 1945). Other Commonwealth States are discussed *infra*.

Hungary[38] and Belgium.[39] Over the past few decades,[40] however, increasing skepticism about the rationale underlying the rule has been expressed[41] and court opinions setting aside the traditional principle have been issued, which will presently be explored.

United States. The seminal U.S. court case cited in support of the *male captus* rule is *Ker v. Illinois*, a Supreme Court case dating to 1886.[42] In that case, a private (Pinkerton Company) detective named Henry Julian was tasked by a Chicago bank to bring back Frederick Ker, a former bank clerk who had fled Illinois to Lima, Peru, to evade larceny charges. Although Julian had obtained extradition papers in advance, the Peruvian Government was then in such disarray on account of its military occupation by Chile that extradition proved infeasible. As a result, with the cooperation of the Chilean military but not with U.S. Government authorization, Julian arranged to forcibly seize Ker and bring him back to Illinois. After his return, Ker challenged the Illinois trial court's jurisdiction on the ground that both his rights under the specialty provision of the U.S.-Peru Extradition Treaty (as the charge had since been changed to embezzlement) and his due process rights had been violated.

38 *In re Károly R.*, No. B XXX, 2138/1925, Royal Hungarian Crim. Ct. at Budapest, Jan. 26, 1928, *reprinted in* [1927–28] 4 Ann. Dig. Pub. Int'l L. Cases 345 (No. 236) (A.D. McNair & H. Lauterpacht eds. 1931) ("There is no rule of public international law according to which courts of a State have no right to conduct criminal proceedings against an accused who returned from abroad by any means other than extradition. The fact that the accused had been brought home otherwise than in the course of regular extradition proceedings can have no influence on the prosecution of the crime.").

39 *Geldof v. Meulemeester & Steffen*, Ct. of Cassation, Belg., Feb. 20, 1961, [1961] *Pasicrise belge* 674 [French text], *reprinted in* 31 ILR 385 (E. Lauterpacht ed. 1966).

40 Even a half-century earlier, notably the Draft Convention on Jurisdiction with Respect to Crime proposed by the Harvard Research in International Law saw no basis for the *male captus* rule when it wrote in 1935: "In exercising jurisdiction under this Convention, no State shall prosecute or punish any person who has been brought within its territory or a place subject to its authority by recourse to measures in violation of international law or international convention without first obtaining the consent of the State or States whose rights have been violated by such measures." Draft Conv. on Research in Int'l Law of the Harvard Law School, "Jurisdiction with Respect to Crime," 29 AJIL 435, 442, art. 16 (Supp. 1935).

41 *E.g.*, Restatement (Third), *supra* n.24, Rep. Note 2; Borelli, *supra* n.25, at 354.

42 *Ker v. Illinois*, 119 U.S. 436 (1886). Judges and legal commentators often refer to the so-called *Ker-Frisbie* doctrine; the second case is in reference to *Frisbie v. Collins*, 342 U.S. 519 (1952), which was an *intra-state* seizure case between Michigan and Illinois that occurred more than six decades after *Ker* but that stands for the same general proposition.

The U.S. Supreme Court denied both claims, holding that since his transfer had not been effected as an extradition, no extradition treaty rights (including specialty) were implicated, and that so long as he was properly indicted and prosecuted in accordance with his constitutional rights, no due process violation had occurred. The trial court therefore could assert personal jurisdiction over Ker and hear the criminal charge of embezzlement against him.[43] At the same time, the Supreme Court acknowledged that Peru could seek Julian's extradition on kidnapping charges and that the proper remedy for any alleged breach of international law against Peru would be via diplomatic channels.[44] Significantly, Peru never protested the SDO, but this may well have been due to the fact that its government was then not operating normally, with Chilean forces in control.

Since *Ker*, U.S. courts consistently have upheld the *male captus* rule,[45] including the 1992 U.S. Supreme Court case of *Álvarez-Machaín*, despite a number of material factual differences with the *Ker* case that potentially could have proven legally consequential. A case comparison is therefore instructive. Humberto Álvarez-Machaín, a Mexican national and medical doctor, was charged by the United States with crimes in connection with the torture and murder of DEA agent Enrique Camarena-Salazar and his in-country driver in 1985. In April 1990, under the leadership of the DEA, a team of five or six armed men were dispatched to Guadalajara, seized Álvarez-Machaín from his medical office, placed him on a private plane, and flew him to El Paso, Texas, where he was

[43] *Ker*, 119 U.S. at 444.

[44] *Id.* For commentary on this point, *see* Scott S. Evans, Note, *Int'l Kidnapping in a Violent World: Where the United States Ought to Draw the Line*, 137 MIL. L. REV. 187, 203–04 (1992); Thomas L. Horan, Note, *Extradition-Int'l Law—The United States Ninth Circuit Court of Appeals Holds Gov't Sponsored Abduction Abroad is Not a Lawful Alternative to Extradition.* United States v. Verdugo-Urquidez, *939 F.2d 1341 (9th Cir. 1991)*, 21 GA. J. INT'L & COMP. L. 525, 527 n.11 (1991); ALUN JONES & ANAND DOOBAY, JONES AND DOOBAY ON EXTRADITION AND MUTUAL ASSISTANCE 80–81 (2005).

[45] *E.g., Sobell*, 142 F. Supp. 515. In one marked departure from this standard, *see United States v. Verdugo-Urquidez*, 856 F.2d 1214 (9th Cir. 1988), *rev'd*, 494 U.S. 259 (1990) ("Verdugo I"). U.S. state courts have followed in step with the federal courts. *E.g., Pratt*, 78 Cal. 345.

arrested and then transferred to Los Angeles to face prosecution.[46] The case drew extensive international criticism as well as a vocal protest from Mexico.[47]

Key differences between the two cases include: (i) while the Peruvian Government did not protest, the Mexican Government did – repeatedly and vehemently between April and July 1990; (ii) while the extradition treaty could not realistically have been invoked with the Peruvian Government at the time to bring back Ker, nothing prevented the U.S. Government in principle from requesting extradition from the Mexicans to obtain custody over Álvarez-Machaín; (iii) while the Pinkerton detective in *Ker* operated on his own, the armed gunmen in *Álvarez-Machaín* were tasked by the U.S. Government; and (iv) a special history existed between the United States and Mexico in which over the course of more than 100 years a strong opposition to SDOs from their respective territories had been expressed.[48]

The U.S. Supreme Court found that one relevant difference between the cases was the involvement of the U.S. Government in the SDO of Álvarez-Machaín, and concluded that so long as there was no express or implied term in the extradition treaty prohibiting an SDO (whether based on the language of the treaty, the history of treaty negotiations, or the States' practice under the treaty), then the *Ker* standard applied, and as no such term existed, the rest of the treaty was of no moment since extradition was not followed.[49] Although the Court recognized that the cases differed on account of Mexico's registered protest, the Court found that such matters

[46] *See* nn.63–64 and accompanying text in Chapter 12. For a more detailed commentary on the *Álvarez-Machaín* court decision, *see* Rosemary Rayfuse, *Int'l Abduction and the United States Supreme Court: The Law of the Jungle Reigns, in* International Criminal Law and Procedure 269–71 (John Dugard & Christine van den Wyngaert eds. 1996); Jones & Doobay, *supra* n.44, at 91–92; Christopher H. Pyle, Extradition, Politics, and Human Rights 286–92 (2001).

[47] *See* Mark S. Zaid, *Military Might Versus Sovereign Right: The Kidnapping of Dr. Humberto Alvarez-Machain and the Resulting Fallout*, 19 Hous. J. Int'l L. 829 (1997) (collecting statements from over twenty governments expressing outrage, criticism, or disagreement with the Court's opinion).

[48] In 1881, U.S. Secretary of State Blaine informed the Governor of Texas that the U.S.-Mexico Extradition Treaty did not allow either party to abduct persons charged with crimes from the other's territory. In 1887, U.S. Secretary of State Bayard protested as kidnapping the removal from Texas to Mexico of Francisco Arresures by three Texas deputy sheriffs in collusion with a Mexican policeman. In addition, in 1987 and 1989, the United States and Mexico reaffirmed their opposition to abduction in treaties providing for mutual assistance and drug law enforcement. Pyle, *supra* n.46, at 293.

[49] *Álvarez-Machaín*, 504 U.S. at 662–66.

are properly managed as a political, not a judicial, matter.[50] The Court also rejected Álvarez-Machaín's due process argument, finding that all of his constitutionally guaranteed safeguards related to a fair trial had been observed.[51] In addition, the Court did not believe customary international law principles prohibiting breaches of territorial sovereignty were specific enough to apply in that case.[52]

While alive and well in the United States, the *male captus* principle is not categorical in its application, but rather is subject to two recognized, yet narrow, exceptions. First, as seen in Chapter 12.c.ii, to the extent a treaty proscribes SDOs (or equivalent conduct) as a means of securing the custody of a fugitive from a treaty partner's territory, or otherwise specifically[53] prohibits other behavior (*e.g.*, no breach of diplomatic immunity),[54] a U.S. court should take cognizance of such a provision. Even then, however, courts may choose to assert jurisdiction while regarding the treaty breach as a political matter for the executive branches to resolve.[55]

Second, under the 1974 *United States v. Toscanino*[56] standard, as refined a year later by *Lujan v. Gengler*[57] and by subsequent appellate courts, a trial court must divest itself of personal jurisdiction when the means of seizure and delivery were of "a most shocking, and outrageous character,"[58] or "would shock the conscience of the court."[59] Such instances are limited to torture, brutality, and similar outrageous conduct, and must be perpetrated directly by paid officials or agents of

[50] *Id.* at 667–70.

[51] "[D]ue process of law is satisfied when one present in court is convicted of crime after . . . a fair trial in accordance with constitutional procedural safeguards." *Id.* at 661–62. *Accord United States v. Marzano*, 537 F.2d 257, 271 (7th Cir. 1976) ("It has long been held that due process has been satisfied when a person is apprised of the charges against him and is given a fair trial. The power of a court to try a person is not affected by the impropriety of the method used to bring the defendant under the jurisdiction of the court.").

[52] *Álvarez-Machaín*, 504 U.S. at 666–67.

[53] U.S. courts are generally disinclined to imply a provision that would defeat its jurisdiction. *E.g., United States v. Najohn*, 785 F.2d 1420 (9th Cir.) (per curiam), *cert. denied*, 479 U.S. 1009 (1986).

[54] *E.g., Cook v. United States*, 288 U.S. 102 (1932); *Ford v. United States*, 273 U.S. 593 (1927); *United States v. Rauscher*, 119 U.S. 407 (1886).

[55] *E.g., Sobell*, 142 F. Supp. 515; *United States v. Insull*, 8 F. Supp. 310 (N.D. Ill. 1934); *United States v. Lopez*, 542 F.2d 283 (5th Cir, 1976).

[56] *United States v. Toscanino*, 500 F.2d 267 (2d Cir.), *reh'g denied*, 504 F.2d 1830 (1974), *motion to dismiss denied on remand*, 398 F. Supp. 916 (E.D.N.Y. 1975).

[57] *United States ex rel. Lujan v. Gengler*, 510 F.2d 62 (2d Cir.), *cert. denied*, 421 U.S. 1001 (1975).

[58] *Id.* at 65.

[59] *Cordero*, 668 F.2d at 37.

the U.S. Government,[60] such that the treatment would be regarded as a violation of the fugitive's fundamental due process rights. To date, however, no U.S. federal court has ever found a set of facts that met this exceptionally high threshold.[61]

Great Britain/U.K. England has a long history with the *male captus* rule dating to *Ex parte Scott*.[62] In that 1829 case, a British police constable traveled to Brussels to seize Susannah Scott, who was wanted on the charge of perjury. The police officer had a warrant for her arrest and possibly effected her apprehension with the cooperation of the Belgian authorities. In any event, he succeeded in returning her to England, but rather than argue lack of personal jurisdiction, Scott sought release under England's *habeas corpus* statute. Precedent existed for no inquiry in felony cases but for an inquiry in civil actions, and perjury qualified somewhere in between as a misdemeanor. The court decided to treat her misdemeanor crime akin to a felony and thereby determine only whether the warrant was valid without examining the lawfulness of the underlying seizure.[63]

For about the next 150 years, until 1981, including the *Elliott* case (1949),[64] in which British officers escorted an army corporal charged with

60 *See United States v. Lara*, 539 F.2d 495, 495 (5th Cir. 1976) (per curiam) (where U.S. Government agents were found to have played no direct role in the torture allegedly administered by Panamanian authorities and there was no proof that U.S. agents were even present at the time, the *Toscanino* exception was inapplicable); *United States v. Lira*, 515 F.2d 68, 70–71 (2d Cir.) (rejecting application of the *Toscanino* exception where no evidence existed that the U.S. representatives "participated or acquiesced in the alleged misconduct of the Chilean officials" or that "Chilean police were acting as agents of the United States in arresting or mistreating Mellafe or that United States representatives were aware of such misconduct."), *cert. denied*, 423 U.S. 847 (1975); *United States v. Fielding*, 645 F.2d 719, 723–24 (9th Cir. 1981) (even outrageous treatment by foreign officials while in their custody where U.S. officials knew about it would not vitiate the rule's application).

61 *See United States v. Yunis*, 681 F. Supp. 909, 919 (D.D.C. 1988) ("Although most circuits have acknowledged the exception carved out by *Toscanino*, it is highly significant that *no* court has ever applied it to dismiss an indictment.") (emphasis in original); Jonathan A. Bush, *How Did We Get Here?: Forcible Abduction after* Alvarez-Machain, 45 STAN. L. REV. 939, 961 (1993) ("No claimant has ever prevailed under the *Toscanino* exception"); Daniel L. Pines, *Rendition Operations: Does U.S. Law Impose any Restrictions?*, 42 LOYOLA UNIV. CHICAGO L.J. 523, 545 n.128 (2011) (no one has yet prevailed under the *Toscanino* standard).

62 *See supra* n.34.

63 PYLE, *supra* n.46, at 265; JONES & DOOBAY, *supra* n.44, at 79–80; Selleck, *supra* n.8, at 249–50.

64 *R. v. Officer Commanding, Depot Battalion, RASC, Colchester, ex parte Elliott* [1949] 1 All E.R. 373 (KB).

desertion from Belgium to a British army base in Germany in a manner contrary to Belgian law,[65] Britain continued to adhere without variation to the *male captus* rule. With *Ex parte Mackeson*[66] and *Ex parte Healy*,[67] two "disguised extradition" cases, the British courts changed course temporarily and inquired into whether there had been any pre-trial police irregularity in effecting the fugitive defendants return to the United Kingdom. An abrupt reversal back to the no-inquiry rule, however, occurred in 1985 with another "disguised extradition" case known as *Ex parte Driver*.[68] The jurisprudential conflict between *Mackeson* and *Driver* remained unresolved until 1993[69] with the House of Lords' judgment in *Ex parte Bennett*.[70]

In *Bennett*, British police tracked to South Africa a New Zealand national who had fraudulently purchased a helicopter in the United Kingdom in 1989. Although no extradition treaty then existed between the United Kingdom and South Africa, under U.K. statutory law, "special extradition arrangements" could have been sought.[71] Instead, on the pretense of deporting Bennett to New Zealand, South African authorities arranged with the connivance of their British counterparts to route his flight through London, where he was arrested.[72] Overruling *Driver*, the *Bennett* court reasoned through the Lords' collective opinions that the court must serve a supervisory role to foster the rule of law and human rights, that abuses of process must not be permitted, and that if illegally confiscated evidence is not admissible, by analogy, nor should unlawfully seized individuals.[73]

65 Jones & Doobay, *supra* n.44, at 83–84; Note, *Extraterritorial Jurisdiction and Jurisdiction Following Forcible Abduction: A New Israeli Precedent in Int'l Law*, 72 Mich. L. Rev. 1087, 1106 n.104 (1974) [hereinafter Note, *Israeli Precedent*]. Such pure military offenses as desertion, however, generally fall outside the scope of extradition. *See* Chapter 5.a.iii.

66 *R. v. Bow Street Magistrates' Court, ex parte Mackeson* (1981) 75 Cr. App. R. 24 (D.C.), *reprinted in* 77 ILR 336.

67 *R. v. Guildford Magistrates' Court, ex parte Healy* [1983] 1 WLR 108, *reprinted in* 77 ILR 345.

68 *R. v. Plymouth Magistrates' Court and Others, ex parte Driver* [1985] 2 All E.R. 681 (QB).

69 Courts during this interim period were evidently reluctant to break this impasse. *E.g., R. v. Bateman & Cooper*, [1989] Crim. L. Rev. 590 (CA) (expressly declining to resolve).

70 *Ex parte Bennett*, *supra* n.19.

71 *Id.* at 51.

72 *Id.* at 51–52; *see also* Jones & Doobay, *supra* n.44, at 93–95; Andrew L.-T. Choo, *Int'l Kidnapping, Disguised Extradition and Abuse of Process*, 57 Mod. L. Rev. 626, 626 (1994) [hereinafter Choo, *Int'l Kidnapping*].

73 *Ex parte Bennett*, *supra* n.19.

As one legal commentator summed it up: "Under authority of *Bennett*, British courts have the discretion to refuse jurisdiction in any case of collusion or connivance by British authorities in the abduction of a fugitive aimed at circumventing established extradition procedures and nullifying the guarantees those procedures accord to the fugitive."[74] Although it was not immediately clear in the aftermath of *Bennett* whether the remedy of imposing a stay of proceedings (discussed *infra*) was compulsory or discretionary in such instances,[75] U.K. case law has evolved to the point where, at present, courts effectively undertake a balancing test, as articulated by the *Latif* court (1996):

> [I]t is possible to say that in a case such as the present the judge must weigh in the balance the public interest in ensuring that those that are charged with grave crimes should be tried and the competing public interest in not conveying the impression that the court will adopt the approach that the end justifies the means.[76]

Other States. As for other States' domestic courts, there is a broad range of practice. At one extreme, joining the United States in its tenacious allegiance to the *male captus* rule, are judiciaries in States like Scotland[77] and Israel.[78] At the other end of the spectrum are courts in States like Spain[79] and Switzerland that believe there must be no personal jurisdiction in such cases, whether because the underlying executive's conduct has vitiated it or as a function of judicial discretion. With respect to

74 Francesco de Sanctis, *The Practice of Nat'l and Int'l Courts on Transnat'l Seizure: Is a Fair Balance Between Human Rights and Accountability Possible?*, 22 NETH. Q. HUM. RTS. 529, 535 (2004).

75 Andrew L.-T. Choo, Ex Parte Bennett*: The Demise of the* Male Captus, Bene Detentus *Doctrine in England?*, 5 CRIM. L.F. 165, 179 (1994).

76 *R. v. Latif* [1996] 1 WLR 104 (H.L.), [1996] 2 Cr. App. R. 92 [hereinafter *Latif Case*] (concerning an LCO).

77 *E.g.*, *Sinclair v. H.M. Advocate*, High Ct., Scot., Mar. 20, 1890, 17 R. (J) 38, 41(1890); *H.M. Advocate v. Vervuren*, High Ct., Scot., [2002] SCCR 481, 2002 S.L.T. 555 (2002).

78 *Attorney General of the Gov't of Israel v. Eichmann*, Crim. Case No. 40/61, Dist. Ct. of Jerusalem, Isr., Dec. 12, 1961, 36 ILR 5, *aff'd sub nom.*, *Eichmann v. Attorney General of the Gov't of Israel*, Sup. Ct., Isr., May 29, 1962, 36 ILR 277 (E. Lauterpacht ed. 1968) (recognizing the sole exception of specialty); Stephen Franklin, "Israeli Faces Treason Sentence," *Chi. Trib.*, Mar. 25, 1988 (discussing how the three-judge panel, in a trial not open to the public, convicted Mordechai Vanunu of "revealing state secrets and aiding Israel's enemies" despite his having been lured on to a yacht and captured by Israeli Government agents).

79 *E.g.*, *Fiscal v. Samper*, Sup. Ct., Spain, June 22, 1934, 130 *Jurisprudencia Criminal* 694, *reprinted in* [1938–40] 9 ANN. DIG. & REP. PUB. INT'L L. CASES 402 (No. 152) (H. Lauterpacht ed. 1942) (recognizing an individual's right to protection afforded by a State in which a fugitive has sought refuge).

Switzerland, in 1982, where German officials had seized a Belgian national from Belgium and brought him to Switzerland and from which Germany sought his extradition, the Swiss court declined the request on the ground that the fugitive's presence had been secured via a violation of Belgian sovereignty and the Swiss court did not want in effect to be an accessory to wrongful conduct.[80]

Along this continuum lie German courts, which have adopted the *male captus* rule in general, but with the important exception that if the State from which the fugitive was taken or removed complains and seeks restitution, the German courts need to stay proceedings;[81] and the courts of Zimbabwe, which recognize the *male captus* rule unless there is evidence that pursuing State agents violated the sovereign territory of the rendered State.[82]

Significantly, beginning in the late 1970s and extending into the 1980s and 1990s, many States that had once embraced the *male captus* rule began to question its merit and became amenable in principle to staying proceedings against, and releasing, fugitive defendants.[83] This trend began in essence with the 1978 New Zealand case called *Regina v. Hartley*.[84] In that case, the court found that the fugitive, charged with manslaughter, had been forcibly seized in Australia and transferred by plane to New Zealand with the cooperation of N.Z. law enforcement authorities, and the court reasoned that it had the inherent power to determine if an abuse of process had been perpetrated.[85]

In neighboring Australia, in two cases arising in the late 1980s, courts asserted the right to stay proceedings where they found an abuse of process, such as an illegal extradition.[86] South African jurisprudence represents another example of significant transition from a well-established *male captus* posture, as found in the *Abrahams* case

[80] *Case of X, Belgian Citizen v. Swiss Justice and Police Dept*, Trib. Féd. Suisse, July 15, 1982, 10 Europaische Grundrechte-Zeitschrift (EuGRZ) 435 (1983).

[81] *E.g., Stocké v. F.R.G.*, Fed. Sup. Ct., F.R.G., 1984, NStZ 563.

[82] *E.g., State v. Beahan*, Sup. Ct., Zimb., Sept. 4, 1991, [1991] 2 Zimb. L.R. 98, *reprinted in* 103 ILR 203, 203–04 (1996).

[83] de Sanctis, *supra* n.74, at 538.

[84] Ct. of App. (Wellington), Aug. 5, 1977, 2 NZLR 199 (1978).

[85] *Id.* Notably, only two years later, Judge Richmond, who had sat on the *Hartley* appeal, switched his position, raising doubts about the "abuse of process" doctrine in staying proceedings based on executive branch conduct. *See Moevao v Dep't of Labor*, Ct. of App., N.Z (Wellington), [1980] 1 NZLR 464.

[86] *Levinge v. Director of Custodial Services, et al.*, N.S.W. Ct. of App., July 23, 1987, 9 N.S.W.L. Rep. 546 [hereinafter *Levinge Case*]; *R. v. Fan*, N.S.W. Sup. Ct., July 1, 1989, 98 F.L.R. 119.

(1963),[87] to a failure to find personal jurisdiction in *Ebrahim* (1991).[88] One noteworthy anomaly in this regard appears to be France, where for decades its courts had refused to exercise personal jurisdiction in cases in which French officials had violated international law in securing custody of a fugitive, but later embraced the *male captus* doctrine in *Argoud* (1964).[89]

Another counter-trend arguably can be found in the jurisprudence of the ICTY,[90] namely, in its 2003 *Nikolić case*,[91] in which the fugitive was forcibly seized by unidentified persons in Serbia & Montenegro and

[87] *Abrahams v. Minister of Justice and Others*, Cape Provincial Div., So. Afr., [1963] 4 S.A. L. REP. 542, 543 ("Once a person is in lawful custody within the jurisdiction of a court, the Court will not enquire, and in fact has no power to enquire, into the circumstances in which he came to find himself there.").

[88] *State v. Ebrahim*, Sup. Ct. (App. Div.), So. Afr., Feb. 26, 1991, 2 S.A. REP. 553 [Afrikaans text], *reprinted and translated* in 31 ILM 888 (1992) [hereinafter *Ebrahim Case*] (stressing that the court has a duty, not just the discretion, to inquire into the lawfulness of executive branch conduct).

[89] *Compare Case of Nollet*, Ct. of App. of Douai, Fr., 1891, *reprinted in* 18 JOURNAL DU DROIT INTERNATIONAL 1188 (forgoing jurisdiction in a seizure case as the fugitive defendant would not be before the court but for a violation of Belgium's sovereign territory by French Government officials) *and In re Jolis*, Tribunal Correctionnel de'Avesnes, Fr., July 22, 1933, *reprinted in* [1933–34] 7 ANN. DIG. & REP. PUB. INT'L L. CASES 191 (No. 77) (H. Lauterpacht, ed., 1940) [hereinafter *Jolis Case*] (forgoing jurisdiction because all proceedings that followed the unlawful seizure were null and void) *with In re Argoud*, Ct. of Cassation (Crim. Ch.), Fr., June 4, 1964, *reprinted in* 45 ILR 90 (1972) [hereinafter *Argoud Case*] ("[T]he circumstances in which an accused person who is the subject of a lawful prosecution and has been apprehended on a lawful warrant for arrest and handed over to justice, even if they constituted an infringement of the criminal law or the traditional principles of our law, are not of a character – however deplorable they may appear – to entail of themselves the nullity of the prosecution.").

[90] There is little point in reviewing the case law of the human rights bodies, such as the HRC and ECtHR, as their function is narrowly to "adjudge whether a particular prosecution undertaken in spite of abduction or illegal rendition was itself a violation of its constitutive human rights instrument, or at least whether the mode of apprehension itself was offensive." Robert J. Currie, *Abducted Fugitives Before the Int'l Criminal Court: Problems and Prospects*, 18 CRIM. L.F. 349, 360 (2007); *see id.* at 362 (noting, however, that in the *Öcalan* case, discussed in Chapter 11.c.iii, the ECtHR confirmed that, for an arrest to be illegal, there must be either a violation of territorial sovereignty or a breach of an extradition or other agreed transfer arrangement).

[91] *Prosecutor v. Nikolić*, Case No. IT-94-2-AR73, Decision on Interlocutory Appeal Concerning Legality of Arrest, App. Ch., June 5, 2003 [hereinafter *Nikolić Case*]. Pre-*Nikolić* ICTY or ICTR jurisprudence provides only peripheral insight regarding this proposition. In *Prosecutor v. Dokmanović*, Case No. IT-95-13a-PT, Tr. Ch. II, Decision on the Motion for Release by the Accused, Oct. 22, 1997, *reprinted in* 111 ILR 458 (1997), the ICTY expressed no concern about the LCO used to bring the defendant into the Tribunal's jurisdiction, but noted that case dismissal could occur in the event of a forcible abduction. *Id.* ¶ 77. And in *Prosecutor v. Barayagwiza*, Case No. ICTR-97-19-AR72, App.

taken to Bosnia & Herzegovina, where SFOR arrested and transferred him to The Hague to face prosecution. The ICTY's appellate chamber was presented with the question of whether the trial chamber should have been permitted to exercise personal jurisdiction under the circumstances. After analyzing domestic case law involving similar facts, the appellate chamber applied the following standards: (i) in instances where universally condemned crimes, such as genocide and crimes against humanity, are at stake, these should outweigh in seriousness any limited territorial intrusion to secure the fugitive's custody, and therefore jurisdiction should stand or it would disserve international justice; but (ii) in cases in which other, lesser crimes are at issue, jurisdiction should be dispensed with if either the fugitive's human rights have been violated to an egregious extent (*i.e.*, most likely one shocking to the public conscience and on par with the *Toscanino* standard[92]) or if a State complains that its sovereign territory has been breached.[93]

At bottom, there is no consistent practice of States, but a general trend line can be discerned toward domestic courts declining to assert personal jurisdiction where the underlying circumstances reflect demonstrably unlawful action.[94] At the same time, however, that emerging approach cannot be said to have transformed yet into customary international law,[95] given both the variability that continues across national jurisprudence and courts' frequent reliance on domestic legal principles (versus international law) in reaching their judgments.[96] Plus, it may well be that the balancing-act *Nikolić* opinion comes to be relied upon as persuasive authority by or serve as a model for domestic courts in adjudicating such matters going forward.

Ch., Nov. 3, 1999, the ICTR indicated a willingness to dismiss a case where violations were serious enough to raise questions about the Tribunal's "integrity." *Id.* ¶ 74.

92 Susan Lamb, *Illegal Arrest and the Jurisdiction of the ICTY, in* ESSAYS ON ICTY PROCEDURE AND EVIDENCE IN HONOUR OF GABRIELLE KIRK MCDONALD 34 & n.31 (Richard May, *et al.* eds. 2001); *Nikolić Case, supra* n.91, ¶¶ 29 (citing *Toscanino*).

93 *Nikolić Case, supra* n.91, ¶¶ 24–31.

94 Selleck, *supra* n.8, at 251 (citing the *Hartley* and *Mackeson* cases).

95 Currie, *supra* n.90, at 359. Likewise, the *male captus* maxim itself does not qualify as customary international law. Abdul Ghafur Hamid, *Jurisdiction over a Person Abducted from a Foreign Country: Alvarez-Machain Case Revisited*, 31 J. MALAYSIAN AND COMP. L. 69 (2004).

96 For example, in the *Ebrahim* opinion, the Supreme Court of South Africa expressly referenced Roman-Dutch law as a principal source. *See generally* de Sanctis, *supra* n.74, at 537–38 (observing courts' reliance on national rules and principles); Borelli, *supra* n.25, at 358 (same).

3 Abuse of Process and Inherent Supervisory Powers

Following the discussion of *what* the legal standard is and State practice to date, we now examine *how* courts have evolved doctrinally on this score. Traditionally, most domestic judiciaries believed they were not at liberty to second-guess the actions of their respective executive branches, that any such matters offending inter-State relations lay outside their purview, and that their job was simply to hear the underlying criminal suit against the fugitive defendant. Over time, however, courts have fashioned mechanisms for empowering or asserting themselves as a check against executive branch excesses, finding grounds to justify an absence or the non-exercise of personal jurisdiction, and determining the means, where appropriate, by which proceedings could be stayed or charges dismissed altogether.

There are essentially two judicial doctrines or vehicles through which domestic criminal courts have sought to address perceived over-reaching executive branch conduct in connection with a full-scale operational alternative to extradition. The first is the determination that an executive branch "abuse of process" has occurred, and in the interest of *rule of law*, the court should be deprived of personal jurisdiction, which leads to a stay of the proceedings and which ultimately may yield a dismissal of the indictment.[97] The second is the exercise of a court's own "inherent supervisory powers," which allows a court at its discretion and in the interest of *judicial integrity* not to invoke personal jurisdiction; such cases generally lead to a dismissal of the charges, an end to the prosecution, and the physical release of the fugitive defendant.[98]

Abuse of Process Doctrine. In examining this doctrine, it is essential as an initial matter to distinguish between: (a) due process concerns with regard to how a fugitive was treated by the executive branch in connection with his apprehension, detention, and transfer to a pursuing State's court jurisdiction, and (b) due process rights in the judicial "fair trial" sense consisting, for example, of assistance of counsel, evidentiary

[97] While a stay is not legally equivalent to an acquittal, as a practical matter, it can ultimately yield the same result. CHOO, JUDICIAL STAYS, *supra* n.22, at 7. For an example of how the two could vary in effect, consider the case of *Toscanino* in which the appellate court issued a stay and later remanded the case to the trial court for an evidentiary hearing at which the defendant had the burden of showing credible evidence that the actions alleged had been taken by or at the direction of U.S. Government officials. *Toscanino*, 500 F.2d at 281.

[98] *See* MICHAEL ABBELL, EXTRADITION TO AND FROM THE UNITED STATES 381 (2010) (defendants may challenge prosecution on one or both of these grounds).

standards, and an independent and impartial tribunal.[99] The former (executive branch) type, which is of interest in this context, can vitiate personal jurisdiction, while the latter (judicial branch) type cannot, although a defendant nevertheless can be set free if such procedural trial violations are sufficiently serious.

In the 1974 case of *United States v. Toscanino*, the U.S. Court of Appeals for the Second Circuit held that: "a court [must] divest itself of jurisdiction over the person of the defendant where it has been acquired as the result of the government's deliberate, unnecessary and unreasonable invasion of the accused's constitutional rights."[100] Courts elsewhere likewise have established elevated thresholds for finding such abuse.[101] Many courts also factor into their judgment whether an abuse of process has occurred based on the egregiousness of executive branch conduct in comparison with the gravity of the underlying criminal offense charged,[102] or the practical need for and utility of clever or aggressive law enforcement techniques in combating crimes of an international character.[103]

[99] *See* John G. Kester, *Some Myths of United States Extradition Law*, 76 GEO. L.J. 1441, 1450 & n.51 (1998); Gary J. Bass, *The Adolf Eichmann Case: Universal and Nat'l Jurisdiction, in* UNIVERSAL JURISDICTION: NATIONAL COURTS AND THE PROSECUTION OF SERIOUS CRIMES UNDER INTERNATIONAL LAW 89 (Stephen Macedo ed. 2004).

[100] 500 F.2d at 275. This standard was applied in the 1992 case of *Álvarez-Machaín*, 504 U.S. 655, wherein the Supreme Court found no abuse of process despite allegations that the defendant had been punched in the stomach, forced to lie face down in a car, shocked with an electric prod, and injected with a drug during the seizure operation).

[101] *E.g., Levinge Case, supra* n.86.

[102] *E.g., R. v. Mullen* [1999] 2 Cr. App. R. 143 (CA), [1999] WLR 777; *Latif Case, supra* n.76; *Levinge Case, supra* n.86, at 565 ("[C]onduct which might be regarded as constituting an abuse of process in respect of a comparatively minor charge may not have the same character in respect of a serious matter."). *Cf.* ROSALYN HIGGINS, PROBLEMS AND PROCESS: INTERNATIONAL LAW AND HOW WE USE IT 72–73 (1994) (arguing for an exception to the "abuse of process" doctrine in cases like *Eichmann* where universally condemned offenses are at issue).

[103] *E.g., Liangsiriprasert v. United States* [1991] 1 A.C. 225 (P.C.), [1990] 2 All E.R. 866, 871–72 ("As to the suggestion that it was oppressive or an abuse of process [to lure a Thai heroin smuggler to Hong Kong in order to have him extradited from there], the short answer is that international crime has to be fought by international co-operation between law enforcement agencies. It is notoriously difficult to apprehend those at the centre of the drug trade; it is only their couriers who are usually caught. If the courts were to regard the penetration of a drug dealing organisation by the agents of a law enforcement agency and a plan to tempt the criminals into a jurisdiction from which they could be extradited as an abuse of process it would indeed be a red-letter day for the drug barons."); *Latif Case, supra* n.76 (sometimes deception has to be used "otherwise the courts will not get to try this sort of offense [drug smuggling] against people who are seriously involved in it").

A number of domestic courts have found abuse of process in SDO, LCO, and deportation cases, such as *Hartley* (New Zealand), *Bennett* (United Kingdom), and *Ebrahim* (South Africa), but LCO cases, as a general rule, have been treated as less legally objectionable. For example, in the 1994 case involving Norbert Schmidt, the U.K. House of Lords found that the false story concocted by a Metropolitan police officer to entice a German national out of Ireland on the pretext that he had an opportunity to clear his name in a check fraud investigation was "not so grave or serious to have warranted intervention of the High Court on the grounds of abuse of process."[104] In addition, in *Yunis*, the federal district court for the District of Columbia found nothing suggesting the "sort of intentional, outrageous government conduct" needed to divest it of jurisdiction, even though the lure operation and related apprehension and delivery were decidedly not "picture perfect," and involved the breaking of the fugitive's wrists during his arrest, placing him in metal leg irons, tranquilizing him, and putting him at sea incommunicado for several days.[105]

Although in the United States the standard for staying a criminal proceeding on the grounds of "abuse of process" is markedly high, in many other States, including the United Kingdom, Australia, and Canada, courts tend to engage in a balancing test. Among those elements considered are: (i) whether the rendition means employed featured significant rights violations or physical violence and the extent to which they were undertaken in bad faith (if so, this would favor a stay); (ii) whether the pursuing State's law enforcement officials or agents were operating under exigent circumstances, such as to arrest someone planning a terrorist attack (if so, this would disfavor a stay); and (iii) the seriousness of the offense charged against the fugitive defendant (the more severe, the less likely it would favor a stay).[106] At the other extreme, were stays to be deemed mandatory in instances of "abuse of process," such a rule would not properly account for defendants like Adolf Eichmann who committed heinous crimes, or those persons posing ongoing national security threats to the adjudicating State.[107]

Inherent Supervisory Powers. Apart from finding an abuse of process and calling for a stay of proceedings, a domestic criminal court also can dismiss a prosecution under its inherent supervisory powers, to the

[104] *In re Schmidt* [1995] 1 A.C. 339 (H.L.), [1994] 3 WLR 229 *("Schmidt II")*.
[105] *Yunis*, 681 F. Supp. at 912–13.
[106] Choo, *Int'l Kidnapping, supra* n.72, at 631.
[107] Choo, Judicial Stays, *supra* n.22, at 111–18.

extent such powers are recognized under its jurisprudence. A court would invoke such powers where it does not want to foster serious misconduct on the part of the executive branch in bringing the fugitive to the court's jurisdiction, while hoping to preserve judicial integrity by not validating or signaling support for any unlawful activity.[108] Because this mechanism can result in a court dismissing a criminal case, it tends to be used only sparingly and under strict conditions.[109]

Under U.S. law, for example, a criminal trial court can exercise this power for one of only three possible purposes: (i) to remedy violations of recognized rights; (ii) to shield judicial integrity "by ensuring that a conviction rests on appropriate considerations validly before the jury"; and (iii) to discourage unlawful law enforcement conduct.[110] This doctrine "is designed and invoked *primarily* to preserve the integrity of the judicial system" "to prevent the federal courts from becoming accomplices to government misconduct."[111] "If, for example, [the court] were confronted with a pure law enforcement effort in which government agents deliberately killed and tortured individuals for the sole purpose of discovering a fugitive's whereabouts in order to secure his arrest, the Court would face a situation which properly calls for invocation of its supervisory powers."[112]

Underlying Rationale. What is the logic followed by those courts that have chosen to divest themselves of, or otherwise not exercise, personal jurisdiction in cases where a fugitive's delivery to pursuing State territory was conducted under unlawful or objectionable means? Although the rationale varies from court to court, in the aggregate it breaks down roughly into the following three types: (i) promoting healthy *inter-State relations* by respecting one another's sovereign territory and treaty obligations and by not encouraging unlawful activity against others by

[108] *See Connelly v. Director of Public Prosecutions* [1964] 2 A.C. 1254 (H.L.) (holding that the court has discretion to stay criminal proceedings where a prosecution would threaten the moral integrity of the judicial process itself).

[109] *E.g., United States v. Noriega*, 746 F. Supp. 1506, 1535 (S.D. Fla. 1990), *aff'd*, 117 F.3d 1206 (11th Cir. 1997).

[110] *United States v. Hasting*, 461 U.S. 499, 505 (1983). *Accord United States v. Matta-Ballesteros*, 71 F.3d 754, 763 (9th Cir. 1995) (applying the *Hasting* standard and finding that despite "disturbing" circumstances surrounding the fugitive's seizure, none of the grounds were satisfied).

[111] *United States v. Omni Int'l Corp.*, 634 F. Supp. 1414, 1438 (D. Md. 1986) (emphasis supplied) (quoting *United States v. Payner*, 447 U.S. 727, 744 (1980) (Marshall, J., dissenting op.)).

[112] *Noriega*, 746 F. Supp. at 1536.

virtue of holding its own executive accountable; (ii) protecting the *rights of fugitives* not to be physically maltreated and ensuring they have access to procedural benefits available to them under extradition treaties and to safeguards afforded by "safe haven" State laws; and (iii) ensuring the *sound administration of justice,*[113] by insisting on the prosecuting State having "clean hands" and by fostering the integrity and dignity of the judicial system so it does not become viewed as an accessory to the executive in perpetrating unlawful conduct.[114] The consequence of divestiture generally is custodial release of the fugitive defendant; if the divestiture is made *without* prejudice, then the court can hear the criminal case again if the fugitive is later rendered to a particular pursuing State.

ii Individual Standing

In addition to determining its posture whether to exercise personal jurisdiction involving a fugitive defendant who has been returned via a full-scale operational alternative to extradition, a domestic criminal court often will have to consider whether the fugitive defendant has standing (*locus standi*) to raise legal issues or claims on his own behalf, including to defeat the court's personal jurisdiction.[115] Individual standing has three essential components under many domestic legal systems, as reflected by the U.S. standard: (i) "a party seeking relief must allege a sufficient personal interest in the controversy to ensure concrete adverseness in the presentation of the issues"; (ii) "the complainant must be within the zone of interests sought to be protected by the law in question"; and (iii) "there must be a logical nexus between status asserted and the claim sought to be adjudicated to ensure that the litigant is the proper party to represent the interests involved."[116]

[113] As U.S. Supreme Court Justice Felix Frankfurter stated: the rule of law "inescapably imposes upon [the] court an exercise of judgment upon the whole course of the proceedings in order to ascertain whether they offend those canons of decency and fairness which express the notion of justice of English speaking peoples even toward those charged with the most heinous offenses." *Malinski v. New York,* 324 U.S. 401, 416–17 (1944).

[114] Choo, *Int'l Kidnapping, supra* n.72, at 629.

[115] Standing to challenge as unlawful an action by the rendering State against the fugitive defendant must be distinguished from his standing to file a *private* claim against government officials or agents for violating his civil rights. *E.g., United States v. Di Lorenzo,* 496 F. Supp. 79, 82 (S.D.N.Y. 1980).

[116] *Diggs v. Schultz,* 470 F.2d 461, 464 (D.C. Cir. 1972).

In the post-delivery context, regardless of the means by which a fugitive defendant is brought before a domestic criminal court, the traditional rule on standing has been that an individual was regarded not as a *subject*, but only as an *object*, of international law, and consequently lacked standing to independently assert a claim alleging a State violation of a treaty obligation to his detriment.[117] The essential logic undergirding this rule is that States are the sole parties to a treaty and therefore they alone are conferred enforceable rights and benefits under it,[118] even if their actions happen to have "a direct bearing on [an individual fugitive's] personal liberty."[119]

As a result, by virtue of the traditional rule, a fugitive defendant has no standing on his own to raise a substantive claim[120] against a State under a treaty[121] absent either: (i) an express treaty provision to that effect,[122] or

[117] MALCOLM N. SHAW, PUBLIC INTERNATIONAL LAW 258 (6th ed. 2008); John Dugard & Christine van den Wyngaert, *Reconciling Extradition with Human Rights*, 92 AJIL 187, 189 (1998).

[118] *See Argoud Case, supra* n.89, 45 ILR at 96 ("Individuals have no capacity to plead in judicial proceedings a contravention of international law. The putting in issue of international responsibilities concerns only the relations between State and State, without individuals being entitled to claim to intervene."). *See generally* Mitchell J. Matorin, *Unchaining the Law: The Legality of Extraterritorial Abduction in Lieu of Extradition*, 41 DUKE L.J. 907, 923 (1992) (treaties "originated as way for sovereign nations to order their relationship with each other").

[119] CHRISTOPHER L. BLAKESLEY, TERRORISM, DRUGS, INTERNATIONAL LAW, AND THE PROTECTION OF HUMAN LIBERTY: A COMPARATIVE STUDY OF INTERNATIONAL LAW, ITS NATURE, ROLE, AND IMPACT IN MATTERS OF TERRORISM, DRUG TRAFFICKING, WAR, AND EXTRADITION 274 (1992).

[120] Likewise, individuals have no standing to lodge *procedural* claims against a State party to a treaty. *See, e.g., U.S. v. Antonakeas*, 255 F.3d 714, 720 (9th Cir. 2001) ("the appellant has no standing to raise in district court an alleged missed extradition deadline after Germany determined that the treaty provisions were fulfilled and extradition was proper.").

[121] For an individual to have standing under a treaty, it must be either a self-executing treaty or one that has been incorporated into the domestic law. Rayfuse, *supra* n.46, at 275. But even that alone may not be sufficient, as a self-executing treaty would not confer standing on a defendant to enforce its terms if, for example, the specialty provision expressly required the consent of the transferor State for the defendant to assert it. Mary-Rose Papandrea, Note, *Standing to Allege Violations of the Doctrine of Specialty: An Examination of the Relationship Between the Individual and the Sovereign*, 62 U. CHI. L. REV. 1187, 1201–02 (1995).

[122] *See Extradition (Jurisdiction) Case*, Sup. Ct. of the Reich (in Crim. Matters), Aug. 13, 1936, *reprinted in* [1935–37] 8 ANN. DIG. & REP. PUB. INT'L L. CASES 348, 349–50 (No. 165) (H. Lauterpacht ed. 1941) [hereinafter *Germany Extradition Case*] ("Extradited persons, being objects of extradition, cannot claim rights under extradition conventions nor contest the legality of their extradition, unless such a right has been expressly conceded to them by treaty."); SHAW, *supra* n.117, at 258 (States also "may

(ii) an official protest by one of the contracting State parties to the applicable treaty,[123] and then his standing would be only on a derivative basis, anyway.[124] This rule generally applies no less with respect to alleged violations of an extradition treaty[125] as it does to a complained-of breach of territorial sovereignty under the U.N. Charter, the OAS Charter, or any other multilateral convention.[126]

agree to confer particular rights on individuals which will be enforceable under international law, independently of municipal law," as when five Central American States established the Central American Court of Justice in 1907 and allowed individuals to bring cases directly before it); Eur. Conv. for the Protection of Human Rights and Fundamental Freedoms (ECHR), Nov. 4, 1950, art. 34, 213 U.N.T.S. 262, T.S. No. 71 (1953) (granting individuals standing to bring suits against States parties).

[123] Anthony D'Amato, *Nat'l Prosecution for Int'l Crimes, in* 3 INTERNATIONAL CRIMINAL LAW: ENFORCEMENT 219 (2d ed. M. Cherif Bassiouni ed. 1999); RESTATEMENT (THIRD), *supra* n.24, § 902 cmt a; *Reed*, 639 F.2d at 902 ("[A]bsent protest or objection by the offended sovereign [the appellant] has no standing to raise violation of international law as an issue"); *Yunis*, 681 F. Supp. at 916 (absent an objection by either Lebanon or Cyprus to the circumstances under which Younis was arrested, Younis was precluded from raising his objections); *Matta-Ballesteros*, 697 F. Supp. at 1044 ("Absent the fact of an official protest, petitioner is without standing to assert the violation of any extradition treaty as grounds for the relief he seeks.") (finding no official protest by the Honduran Government based merely on a declaration submitted to the National Congress by seven congressmen, with no vote or approval by congress or adoption by the executive branch), *aff'd*, 896 F.2d at 260 ("Were we to conclude that Honduras protested Matta's arrest in the absence of word from the Honduran government, we would be denying the sovereignty of the Republic of Honduras."). More so, no *non-contracting party* may invoke that treaty to protest its unlawful application. *See, e.g., United States v. Trujillo*, 871 F. Supp. 215, 221 (D. Del. 1994) (Colombia has no standing to complain about provisions of the U.S.-U.K. extradition treaty).

[124] RESTATEMENT (THIRD), *supra* n.24, § 477 cmt b; Brandon S. Chabner, Cmt., *The Omnibus Diplomatic Security and Antiterrorism Act of 1986: Prescribing and Enforcing United States Law against Terrorist Violence Overseas*, 37 UCLA L. REV. 985, 1019–20 (1990); *Leighnor v. Turner*, 884 F.2d 385 (8th Cir. 1989). The logic here is that if the affected State acquiesces by failing to protest, then any breach is effectively "cured" or waived, and the fugitive defendant would have no violation about which to complain. Selleck, *supra* n.8, at 247–48. An example where a State's protest opened the door to individual standing can be found in *United States v. Caro-Quintero, et al.*, 745 F. Supp. 599 (C.D. Cal. 1990) (the Embassy of Mexico presented three diplomatic notes to the U.S. State Department protesting the arrest and prosecution of Humberto Álvarez-Machaín), *aff'd sub nom. United States v. Álvarez-Machaín*, 946 F.2d 1466 (9th Cir. 1991), *rev'd on other grounds*, 504 U.S. 655 (1992).

[125] *See Yunis*, 681 F. Supp. at 916 (recognizing as a rule of public international law that "only sovereign nations have the authority to complain about violations of extradition treaties.").

[126] *See* Beverly Izes, *Drawing Lines in the Sand: When State-Sanctioned Abduction of War Criminals Should be Permitted*, 31 COLUM. J. L & SOC. PROBS. 1, 33 (1997–98) (observing that Panama's new government had lodged no complaint concerning Gen. Noriega's

Two possible exceptions to the traditional rule, each controversial, warrant mention.[127] The first exception takes the form of the specialty rule, discussed in Chapter 7.c.ii.[128] That rule's central objective is to ensure that a fugitive is not prosecuted for a crime for which he was not specifically extradited. It serves the interests of both the fugitive and the transferor State, as each would be injured by non-compliance.[129] There is a division among the U.S. Courts of Appeals (a so-called "circuit split") regarding whether standing should be conferred upon an individual defendant to contest a specialty rule violation.[130] The circuit courts favoring independent conferral point out that, but for the fugitive defendant raising the issue, the transferor State might not come to know about the violation or, if it ever did, it might be too late for that State to seek any recourse. In effect, then, the individual defendant acts as an agent or surrogate of the transferor State.[131]

seizure from Panama in January 1990, and absent a claim by an offended state that its sovereign territory has been violated, an individual cannot vicariously assert sovereign rights; therefore, Gen. Noriega could not raise claims regarding Panama's sovereignty); *Argoud Case, supra* n.89, 45 ILR at 97 ("[E]ven accepting that Argoud had been abducted on the territory of the Federal Republic of Germany in violation of the rights of that country and of its sovereignty, it would be for the Government of the injured State alone to complain and demand reparation. The accused has no capacity to plead a contravention of the rules of public international law").

127 In addition, where customary international law arguably has been violated, some have contended that, to the extent it is a constituent part of domestic law, an individual defendant should be entitled to plead such rights, quite independent of whether or not treaty law has been breached. Rayfuse, *supra* n.46, at 275–76.

128 *E.g., United States v. Vreeken*, 803 F.2d 1085, 1088 (10th Cir. 1986) *cert. denied*, 107 S. Ct. 955 (1987).

129 The transferor State has an interest in ensuring that it act faithfully with regard to its own criminal legal standards and values, and "not be induced to return an individual under false pretenses," Levitt, *supra* n.21, at 1025, while it would be unfair to a fugitive defendant if he is tried on offenses not recognized by the transferor State. Note, *Israeli Precedent, supra* n.65, at 1109.

130 *See* Matorin, *supra* n.118, at 924–25 (noting how the Second, Fifth, and Sixth Circuits require State protest while the Eighth, Ninth, and Eleventh Circuits confer standing absent State protest).

131 Evans, *supra* n.44, at 211 & n.158; *e.g., Antonakeas*, 255 F.3d at 720 ("once the person sought has been turned over to the requesting country for specified offenses, the requested country has no recourse if the offenses ultimately charged are different from the offenses upon which the extradition was allowed. For this reason, it is necessary to allow the person extradited to raise this type of treaty violation"). *But see Germany Extradition Case, supra* n.122, at 349–50 ("Even if extradition takes place in respect of a crime which is not provided for by the treaty, the extradited person is not entitled to object. It is the task of the authorities of the extraditing State, not that of the German courts, to watch over the correct application of foreign extradition law.").

Under the second exception, some courts do not require that a State *expressly* protest to concede an individual defendant's standing so long as, in the court's judgment, the former host State *might have raised* an objection consistent with an interest it demonstrated or signaled in another context. Accordingly, as the U.S. Supreme Court reasoned as far back as 1886, although Great Britain had not protested fugitive William Rauscher's prosecution for a lesser crime that had not been the subject of the U.S. extradition request, Great Britain's disapproval could be inferred based on its previous refusal to transfer the fugitive absent a guarantee that the specialty rule would apply.[132] As the U.S. Court of Appeals for the Ninth Circuit expressed this sentiment a century later: "the person extradited may raise whatever objections the rendering country might have."[133]

Furthermore, a number of legal commentators have questioned the merit of reliance on a State's protest to confer standing upon a fugitive defendant to challenge a court's jurisdiction. As one asserted: "There are simply too many reasons why a state may decline to assert the rights of an accused before the courts of another country to make the observance of international law in practice depend on such assertion."[134] A State's decision not to protest could be influenced by politics as opposed to law or principle;[135] States may have colluded with one another so the transferor State would have no incentive to protest; in other cases, the former host State may not even realize that a fugitive has vacated its territory;[136] and even if a State chooses to protest, it may do so by seeking a remedy other than restitution (*e.g.*, Argentina in the *Eichmann* case).

b Diplomatic Remedies

This section now turns from judicial to diplomatic matters. More specifically, it explores which types of diplomatic recourse, including legally sanctioned remedies, are available to an injured State,[137] following the

132 *Rauscher*, 119 U.S. 407.

133 *Najohn*, 785 F.2d at 1422. *Accord United States v. Puentes*, 50 F.3d 1567, 1572 (11th Cir. 1995).

134 Andreas F. Lowenfeld, *Ahmad: Profile of an Extradition Case*, 23 N.Y.U. J. Int'l L. & Pol. 723, 743 (1991).

135 Dugard & van den Wyngaert, *supra* n.117, at 201; Evans, *supra* n.44, at 217.

136 Michell, *supra* n.23, at 437.

137 An "injured State" is defined herein as *the former host State or the State of a fugitive's nationality that has suffered harm arising out of acts or omissions by a pursuing State, typically via a full-scale alternative to extradition.* Although fortuitously acquired States

rendition of a fugitive. Outside the scope of this analysis lie options that can be pursued by the injured State on its own, *i.e.*, without any inter-State communication or intervention, such as financially compensating the families of the fugitive or any other collaterally injured parties;[138] calling for an investigation or inquiry to understand exactly what happened and to avoid such situations arising in the future;[139] or exacting punishment on anyone within its jurisdiction believed to have participated in or otherwise facilitated the subject operation.[140]

In broad terms, three forms of diplomatic recourse may be undertaken either in isolation or, more commonly, in combination: (i) demands, (ii) retaliation, and (iii) engagement. Any diplomatic recourse typically would follow a registered protest[141] of the offensive conduct issued via one or more diplomatic notes (*e.g.*, a *note verbale*) conveyed between one State's ministry of foreign affairs and the other State's embassy. In any event, such protests must be issued by the executive branch of the injured State – not by a surrogate State or entity or even by the host State's legislature.[142] Injured States are less inclined to protest "more routine treaty violations" because of their tendency to "create or heighten political tensions between the countries."[143]

have not perpetrated any injury on another State as such, their decision to prosecute or punish an obtained individual, rather than to return him upon the request of the former host State, could yield consequences not unlike those to which rendering States are subject. Nevertheless, the thrust of this discussion centers on rendering States, and accordingly reference is made solely to them as the injuring parties. *See* n.39 in Chapter 1.

138 *See* Paul O'Higgins, *Unlawful Seizure and Irregular Extradition*, 36 B.Y.B.I.L. 279, 293–94 (1960) (When in 1807 the British ship *Leopard* attacked an American frigate, the *Chesapeake*, in order to search for and arrest deserters from the Royal Navy, the British Government eventually agreed to . . . pay money compensation to those injured in the brief encounter").

139 *E.g.*, "Israel, Argentina Declare Nazi Case a Closed Incident," *N.Y. Times*, Aug. 4, 1960, at 1 [hereinafter Closed Case article].

140 *See* O'Higgins, *supra* n.138, at 293–94 (discussing the 1807 *Leopard-Chesapeake* incident in which the British Government eventually took "disciplinary measures against the captain of the *Leopard*").

141 In its protest letter to the United States in the *Verdugo-Urquidez* case, Mexico did not seek the fugitive's repatriation. Horan, *supra* n.44, at 536. Some protests are issued for symbolic significance only. Mary Alice Kovac, *Apprehension of War Crimes Indictees: Should the U.N. Outsource Private Actors to Catch Them?*, 51 Cath. U. L. Rev. 619, 642 (2002).

142 Michell, *supra* n.23, at 424.

143 Levitt, *supra* n.21, at 1038 n.96.

i Demands

A demand by an injured State is directed toward the rendering State and requests some specific action on its part. The four major types of demands include: (i) satisfaction, (ii) repatriation of the rendered fugitive, (iii) extradition of any perpetrators, and (iv) monetary compensation or other reparation.[144] A rendering State's failure to meet an injured State's demands can result in retaliation or other negative consequences.[145]

It is possible that one demand can be bargained away for another, as when in 1935, the United States offered to return to Mexico a seized fugitive (López) in exchange for Mexico dropping its extradition request for Hernandez, one of the two government agents who had carried out López's seizure.[146] In addition, a demand may not always be necessary to yield the desired response, as a rendering State may reconsider its action *sua sponte* and volunteer to make reparations, as occurred in 1967, when after South Korea had seized seventeen of its own nationals from German territory, the South Korean Government issued an official apology to the F.R.G and offered to facilitate the return of those Koreans who had been taken against their will and who wished to return.[147]

Satisfaction. An injured State may demand the issuance of a formal apology, an expression of regret, or at least a public acknowledgment that the subject rendition was in breach of international law.[148] Such a request ultimately was made by Argentina of Israel following the SDO of Adolf Eichmann from Buenos Aires in 1960.[149] Israel's apology to Argentina

[144] "It is a principle of international law that the breach of engagement involves an obligation to make reparation in an adequate form." *Chorzów Factory*, Jurisdiction (Ger. v. Pol.) (Ger. v Pol.), 1927 P.C.I.J. at 21 (ser. A) No. 9 (July 26, 1927).

[145] For example, in 1989, then-U.S. State Department Legal Adviser Abraham Sofaer recognized that the U.S. Government's unwillingness to extradite its agents involved in an authorized mission to secure a given fugitive "could lead the foreign country to cease extradition cooperation with us. Moreover, our agents would be vulnerable to extradition from third countries they visit." Statement of Abraham Sofaer, *The Int'l Law and Foreign Policy Implications of Nonconsensual Extraterritorial Law Enforcement Activities*, Hearings Before the Subcomm. on Civil and Constitutional Rights of the House Judiciary Comm., 101st Cong., 1st Sess., at 14–15 (1989) [hereinafter Sofaer Testimony].

[146] *Villareal & Hernandez v. Hammond*, 74 F.2d 503 (5th Cir. 1934).

[147] "Kidnapping Incidents," 32 *Bull. of the Int'l Comm'n of Jurists* 24, 25 (Dec. 1967).

[148] ILC, *Responsibility of States for Int'lly Wrongful Acts with Commentaries* (Draft), Dec. 12, 2001, art. 37(2), Annex to UNGA Res. 56/83, U.N. GAOR, 56th Sess., Supp. No. 10, at 43, U.N. Doc. A/56/10 (2001).

[149] Argentina originally sought Eichmann's repatriation from Israel, but eventually dropped that demand and sought only international censure and an apology. Michell, *supra* n.23, at 423–24.

took the form of a joint communiqué in which Israel acknowledged that it had "infringed fundamental rights of the state of Argentina."[150] Although an apology may be appropriate and sufficient in some instances, in others where, say, an individual "has been subjected to prolonged detention or convicted and sentenced to severe penalties,"[151] it may not.

Repatriation of the Fugitive. It is a precept of State responsibility that when a State has violated its international obligations, reparations should seek to the greatest extent possible to restore the *status quo ante*, which in the case of a rendered fugitive require his repatriation.[152] At the same time, however, an injured State must specifically request the fugitive's repatriation or return in its protest letter(s), as repatriation is not always desired[153] and will not necessarily be assumed.[154] Broad customary international law authority supports the proposition that when an injured State calls for the repatriation of a fugitive, the rendering State is expected to return him.[155] Examples from various jurisdictions include: Denmark (*The Red Crusader* case);[156] France (*In re Jolis* case);[157] Germany (*Jacob-Salomon* case);[158] Italy (*Mantovani*

[150] Closed Case article, *supra* n.139, at 1.

[151] *LaGrand Case* (Germ. v. U.S.) [2001] I.C.J. Rep. 466, ¶ 125 (June 27).

[152] *See Chorzów Factory*, Indemnity (Ger. v. Pol.), 1928 P.C.I.J. at 47 (ser. A) No. 17 (Sept. 13, 1928) ("reparation must, as far as possible, wipe out all the consequences of the illegal act and reestablish the situation which would, in all probability, have existed if that act had not been committed."); *Legal Opinion on the Decision of the Sup. Ct. of the United States in the* Alvarez-Machain *Case*, OAS Res. CJI/Res.II-15/92, Inter-Am. Juridical Comm., OEA/ser. G/CI, Doc. No. 2302/92, ¶ 10, Sept. 1, 1992, *reprinted in* 13 Hum. Rts. L.J. 395 (1992).

[153] *See, e.g.*, Brief for the Gov't of Canada as *Amicus Curiae* in Support of Respondent, *United States v. Alvarez-Machain*, at 12–13, *reprinted in* 31 ILM 919 (1992) and 60 U.S.L.W. 4523 (U.S. June 15, 1992) (No. 91-712) (asking only for Canada's intentions, not for the fugitive's return, after Canadian law enforcement officials arrested Derrick Hills about 200 yards [meters] within U.S. territory along the U.S-Canadian border near Detroit, Michigan, in January 1991).

[154] Restatement (Third), *supra* n.24, § 432 cmt c; Matorin, *supra* n.118, at 928 (distinguishing between a "protest" and a "demand"); *Verdugo-Urquidez* Case, 939 F.2d 1341, ¶ 88 (9th Cir. 1991) *("Verdugo II")* ("Mexico's silence after a treaty violation will be construed as a waiver of its rights.") (Browning, J., dissenting op.).

[155] Michell, *supra* n.23, at 427.

[156] *The Red Crusader*, Comm'n of Enquiry (Den. v. U.K.), Mar. 23, 1962, 35 ILR 485 (1967).

[157] *Jolis Case, supra* n.89.

[158] *See* Lawrence Preuss, *Settlement of the Jacob Kidnaping Case (Switzerland-Germany)*, 30 AJIL 123 (1936) (discussing how Berthold Jacob-Salomon, a Jew, was seized by the Nazis in Switzerland and brought back to Germany, only to be later repatriated to Switzerland).

case);[159] South Africa (*Higgs* case);[160] and the United States (*Jaffe* case),[161] with the United Kingdom falling generally in line as well.[162] This does not always occur, however, as *the Eichmann* case demonstrates, despite initial Argentine demands for his repatriation.

Extradition of the Perpetrators. An injured State may request that the rendering State deliver those individuals who participated in a unilateral rendition on a charge such as kidnapping or fraud. Mexico, for example, has sought such perpetrators from the United States on multiple occasions, including in 1934 when it sought the extradition of Villareal and Hernandez for their role in seizing López (discussed *supra*), in 1992 when it requested the extradition of two DEA agents who were believed to have organized the SDO to bring Humberto Álverez-Machaín to the United States,[163] and in 2003 when it called for the extradition of three bounty hunters for their role in seizing from Mexican territory a U.S. national previously convicted of raping three women.[164] While it is highly unlikely that a rendering State would turn over its officials or agents involved in an "authorized mission,"[165] a State likely would have little reluctance

[159] *See* Charles Rousseau, "Chronique des faits internationaux," 69 Rev. Generale de Droit Int'l Public 761, 834–35 (1965) (discussing how following Switzerland's protest of Italy's seizure of an Italian national from Lugano, Switzerland, the fugitive was returned into Swiss custody).

[160] *See* Alona E. Evans, *Acquisition of Custody over the Int'l Fugitive Offender—Alternatives to Extradition: A Survey of United States Practice*, 40 B.Y.B.I.L. 77, 90 n.1 (1964) (quoting *N.Y. Times*, Sept. 3, 1964, at 3) ("In kidnapping of Dennis Higgs from Northern Rhodesia to the Union of South Africa in August 1964, the South African Government, which wanted him on charges of participation in a bomb explosion, agreed to return him to Northern Rhodesia in view of the 'unusual circumstances of the case.'").

[161] *Jaffe v. Boyles*, 616 F. Supp. 1371 (W.D.N.Y. 1985); Brkljacic, *supra* n.7, at 125 n.53 (upon Canada's demand that Sydney Jaffe, a Canadian citizen, be repatriated, and with the support of the U.S. State and Justice Departments, he was released back to Canada by the state of Florida). One can view the *Jaffe* case as an exception to general U.S. Government practice, however, as that SDO was undertaken by a private party - not by the U.S. Government itself. By contrast, when the U.S. Government has mounted a unilateral SDO, it is has been far less inclined to return the subject individual. *E.g., Álvarez-Machaín*, 504 U.S. 655.

[162] *See* O'Higgins, *supra* n.138, at 293–94 ("British practice is in accordance with the principle that in case of apprehension in violation of international law there is an obligation upon the arresting State to restore the person arrested.").

[163] Tod Robberson, "Mexico Seeks DEA Agents on Charges of Kidnapping," *Wash. Post*, Dec. 16, 1992, at A10.

[164] David Carr, "Bounty Hunter Held on Charges Involving '03 Capture in Mexico," *N.Y. Times*, Sept. 15, 2006, at A18.

[165] Sofaer Testimony *supra* n.145, at 14–15.

to transfer to an injured State for trial individuals like bounty hunters who operated without government authorization.[166]

Monetary Compensation or Other Reparation. In principle, an injured State could also request monetary or other forms of reparation to compensate for a suffered injury.[167] According to one legal commentator, "the concept of monetary reparations has been indirectly proposed by the U.N. in previous disputes . . . and has been endorsed by the Restatement (Third) of Foreign Relations Law."[168] Such forms of reparation are rare, however, as reflected by the following observation:

> There seems to have been no case in which the United Kingdom has granted monetary compensation to the aggrieved State in addition to restoring to it the person unlawfully seized. Money compensation paid in the *Chesapeake* case was in respect of death and physical injury to the crew as a result of the unlawful attack.[169]

That said, in one reported case almost 100 years ago decided by an arbitral tribunal, US $500 in damages was awarded to Panama regarding the unlawful seizure of a man named Colunje from Panamanian territory who was lured to the U.S.-controlled Panama Canal Zone where he was prosecuted, but notably even there the reparation was not based on a demand by one State of the other.[170] It is difficult to uncover other examples of monetary compensation in this context, but *conceivably* an injured State could request other kinds of "reparation" that might include, by way of illustration, most favored trade status, increased

[166] *See, e.g.*, Andrew Seymour, "Bounty Hunters Plead Guilty," *Ottawa Sun*, Nov. 24, 2004 (noting how Daniel Kear, the bounty hunter responsible for seizing Sidney Jaffe in Toronto and bringing him back to Florida to face land fraud charges, was later extradited by the United States to Canada and convicted of kidnapping).

[167] *See* Michell, *supra* n.23, at 422 & n.199 (noting the possibility of financial compensation).

[168] Pontoni, *supra* n.6, at 241 (referencing Restatement (Third) § 432 and the *Eichmann* case when the UNSC called for Israel to make "appropriate reparations").

[169] O'Higgins, *supra* n.138, at 296–97.

[170] *Id. See also* nn.101–02 and accompanying text in Chapter 12. Monetary compensation is more common and appropriate when awarded to individuals than to States. In one such case, a financial sum was awarded to the widow of Col. Amekrane as part of a settlement arising out of the European Commission of Human Rights' ruling, following an SDO carried out between Moroccan and Gibraltar authorities that led to his killing once he was brought back to Morocco, which had imposed the death penalty on him for his rebellious activities. *Amekrane v. U.K.*, Appl. No. 5961/72, Eur. Comm'n of Hum. Rgts., 44 C.D. 101, Oct. 11, 1973.

development aid, or support for its membership in a regional body such as the European Union.[171]

ii Retaliation

A second option available to an injured State in the aftermath of a full-scale operational alternative to extradition is retaliation. Retaliation can manifest itself in any number of ways, including denial, disengagement, reciprocity, and active hostility.

An injured State may seek to retaliate by cutting off diplomatic relations with the rendering State. This can occur by recalling one's ambassador from that State and/or by expelling the rendering State's ambassador from one's own capital. An example of this practice can be found in connection with the Eichmann seizure (discussed *supra*) from Argentina. An injured State also may elect to withdraw from cooperation with the rendering State by disengaging from economic, trade, or law enforcement cooperation,[172] including by not attending scheduled summits or conferences.[173] Another approach would be for an injured State (or one otherwise allied with or sympathetic to it) to refuse to satisfy the rendering State's requests for extradition in the future,[174] including in a related case,[175] or to suspend a bilateral treaty, most likely an extradition treaty, with that State.

[171] Another form of reparation found to be appropriate under ICJ jurisprudence, at least when an individual's consular rights have been violated, is for the violating State to "provide, by means of its own choosing, review and reconsideration of the convictions and sentences" of the defendants involved. *Avena and Other Mexican Nationals* (Mex. v. U.S.), [2004] I.C.J. Rep. 12, ¶ 153(9) (Mar. 31).

[172] For example, in 1807, U.S. President Thomas Jefferson ordered a trade embargo on Great Britain after a British ship, the *HMS Leopard*, attacked the *USS Chesapeake*, and seized sailors from her crew, many of whom were sailors who had deserted from the British Navy and could expect courts-martial upon their return. Pyle, *supra* n.46, at 265.

[173] Such disengagement need not be limited to the injured State; it also can be effected by third States offended by the rendering or fugitive-acquiring State's underlying conduct or subsequent reaction. For example, in protest for U.S. military intervention in Panama in 1989, Peru opted, *inter alia*, not to attend a drug summit scheduled in February 1990 in Colombia. "Colombia Decries Intervention; Peru Recalls Envoy; Guerrillas Ask for Role," *Wash. Post*, Dec. 22, 1989, at A33.

[174] *See* Michael Abbell, *The Need for U.S. Legislation to Curb State-Sponsored Kidnapping, in* The Alleged Transnational Criminal: The Second Biennial International Criminal Law Seminar 87 (Richard D. Atkins ed. 1993) (quoting Abbell's congressional testimony on July 29, 1992) [hereinafter *State-Sponsored Kidnapping*] (citing by way of example Costa Rica's refusal to extradite to the United States in the wake of the *Álvarez-Machaín* ruling involving Mexico in 1992).

[175] *See Walker Case*, *supra* n.27, ¶ 18 (discussing how after the United States lured a Canadian businessman from Toronto to New York and arrested him; he later entered

An injured State also can retaliate by taking reciprocal action, namely, by rendering a fugitive of its own from the territory of the rendering State possibly by the same means perpetrated against it (*e.g.*, via an LCO or SDO). For example, to retaliate against Israel's 1986 interception of a Libyan aircraft, Libyan President Muammar Qaddafi threatened that any Israeli civilian aircraft detected flying in Libyan airspace would be forced down and its passengers searched for "Israeli terrorists."[176] An extreme but unlawful application would be to launch a retaliatory military strike. In 1861, during the U.S. Civil War, in reaction to a Union warship intercepting a British ship in international waters and removing two Confederate commissioners, Great Britain ordered the deployment of 8,000 troops to Canada in preparation for war,[177] although no attack materialized.

iii Engagement

Alternatively, an injured State might choose to: (i) engage the rendering State to deter such incidents from recurring by amending applicable bilateral treaty provisions, (ii) seek resolution or satisfaction through third-party intervention, and/or (iii) pursue longer-term improvements to the extradition regime through multilateral dialogue.

Bilateral Treaty Relations. An injured State could try to renegotiate the terms of an operative bilateral extradition treaty with the rendering State or otherwise enter into a protocol effectively amending the extradition treaty to avoid its future offensive application. In 1988, a year after bounty hunters seized Sidney Jaffe from Toronto and returned him to Florida, Canada and the United States agreed to a protocol to their extradition treaty, the impetus of which was to ensure U.S. cooperation in preventing future bounty hunter-led SDOs

into a plea agreement but, upon his return to Canada, reneged on that agreement; then when the United States sought his extradition as a fugitive a second time, the Canadian Government balked, citing the underlying LCO).

176 Judith Miller, "Qaddafi Orders His Jets to Intercept Israeli Airliners," *N.Y. Times*, Feb. 8, 1986, at A3. This threat, however, was never actualized.

177 Pyle, *supra* n.46, at 266 (adding that, in response, the United States agreed to release the two men).

in Canada.[178] Similarly, in November 1994, shortly following the 1992 U.S. Supreme Court decision in *Álvarez-Machaín*, and at Mexico's behest, the two States concluded a Treaty to Prohibit Transborder Abductions as a protocol to their extradition treaty,[179] although to date the U.S. Senate has not ratified the protocol.

Third-Party Intervention. An injured State also could try to engage a third party, such as an arbitral panel, the UNSC, or the ICJ, to win leverage toward, or to obtain, reparations or otherwise to seek satisfaction through a vote of condemnation or a declaratory judgment. Although rare, such approaches are not unprecedented. For example, in 1935, after German agents had seized a German national living in Switzerland, and the Swiss Government objected, the two States agreed to submit their dispute to arbitration, although before the tribunal could convene and presumably facing low prospects of success, the German Government decided to repatriate the German national to Switzerland.[180] In addition, in 1960, after Adolf Eichmann was spirited out of Buenos Aires with the help of an Israeli intelligence squad, Argentina successfully sought a UNSC resolution condemning Israel for its violation of Argentina's territorial sovereignty.[181]

Multilateral Dialogue. While not directly related to a given incident, an injured State nevertheless may find it constructive to engage with other States to address the conditions that gave rise to an objectionable rendition. States could discuss ways to streamline extradition procedures,[182] establish specialized international criminal tribunals that would not be subject to many of the impediments that can thwart inter-State extradition[183] (*see* the Recommendations section in the Conclusion), develop ways to "stigmatize" those States that provide "safe havens" for criminals,[184] fashion liberalized regimes for transferring fugitives modeled on the European Arrest Warrant, and so forth.

[178] Prot. Amending the Treaty on Extradition Between the United States of America and Canada, December 3, 1971, *as amended* by an Exchange of Notes on June 28 and July 9, 1974, signed on Jan. 11, 1988, CTS 1991 No. 37.

[179] Treaty to Prohibit Transborder Abductions, U.S.-Mex., Nov. 23, 1994, 31 U.S.T. 5059, *reprinted in* 5 Michael Abbell & Bruno A. Ristau, International Judicial Assistance: Criminal § 13-4-1, at A-676.3 to 676.6 (1990 & 1995 Supp.).

[180] Preuss, *supra* n.158 (discussing the case of Berthold Jacob-Salomon).

[181] *Question Relating to the Case of Adolf Eichmann*, UNSC Res. 138, S/RES/138 (1960), 15 U.N. SCOR (868th mtg.), U.N. Doc. S/INF/15/Rev.1/1960), June 23, 1960.

[182] Kovac, *supra* n.141, at 644 n.164.

[183] Faiza Patel, *Crime Without Frontiers: A Proposal for an Int'l Narcotics Court*, 22 N.Y.U. J. Int'l L. & Pol. 709, 746 (1990).

[184] Pontoni, *supra* n.6, at 242.

c Policy Implications

Putting aside the law enforcement benefit of bringing fugitives to justice, when States pursue full-scale operational alternatives to extradition, especially when in such circumstances their courts exercise personal jurisdiction over fugitive defendants,[185] various adverse consequences for world public order[186] and bilateral relations reasonably can be expected, most notably the following: (i) promoting disrespect for international law, (ii) fostering retribution and reciprocity, and (iii) undermining the extradition regime and international law enforcement cooperation more generally.

Disrespect for International Law. The failure to comply with established international legal norms, standards, and procedures by breaching treaty provisions, violating territorial sovereignty, and/or trespassing on recognized human rights in order to bring an offender to justice demonstrates a lack of respect for international law.[187] As the South African Supreme Court remarked: "Society is the ultimate loser when, in order to convict the guilty, it uses methods that lead to decreased respect for the law."[188] When States flout international law, they undercut the long, hard work it has taken to lay those foundations and to create a stable, predictable, and trust-based system for inter-State relations. If States choose to ignore the law, that only "breeds contempt for the law," "invites anarchy,"[189] and increases tensions. The more States that act without regard to the law and choose to circumvent it, the fewer remain with any credibility to insist on its proper operation.[190]

Retribution and Reciprocity. As discussed above in the context of diplomatic recourse, injured States, as well as others offended by the way in which a fugitive was rendered, may choose to wreak vengeance on the rendering State either by reciprocating or by taking other

[185] *See* Note, *Israeli Precedent, supra* n.65, at 1110 (observing that a court's asserting jurisdiction after a "forcible abduction may encourage internationally illegal abductions").

[186] *See* Bassiouni, World Public Order, *supra* n.30; Evans, *supra* n.44, at 198–200. For more on the concept of "world public order," *see* Myres S. McDougal & Florentino P. Feliciano, Law and Minimum World Public Order: The Legal Regulation of International Coercion (1961).

[187] Mann, *supra* n.4, at 420.

[188] *Ebrahim Case, supra* n.88, 31 ILM at 898.

[189] *Olmstead v. United States*, 277 U.S. 438, 485 (1928) (Brandeis, J., dissenting op.).

[190] *State-Sponsored Kidnapping, supra* n.174, at 90 (quoting Abbell's congressional testimony on July 29, 1992).

retaliatory measures to express their disapproval. A number of courts and commentators have warned about such a reaction.[191] As U.S. Supreme Court Justice Louis Brandeis expressed: "To declare that in the administration of the criminal law the end justifies the means – to declare that the government may commit crimes in order to secure the conviction of a private criminal – would bring terrible retribution."[192] A U.S. Congressional Research Service Report stated that the United States conducting SDO-type operations "raises prospects of other nations using similar tactics against U.S. citizens."[193] This is not just a theoretical possibility. For example, following the U.S. military intervention in Panama in December 1989, "the Sandinista government ordered troops and tanks to surround the U.S. embassy" in Managua; and "[t]wo well-trained guerrilla movements – Colombia's nationalist M-19 and Chile's Manual Rodriguez Patriotic Front – offered to come to the aid of Panamanian forces or by attacking American interests outside the country."[194]

The Extradition Regime and International Law Enforcement Cooperation Undermined. For all of its imperfections, the extradition regime is critical to the international community's efforts to combat crime. It is only through cooperation that States can hope to bring fugitives to justice, as no single State or small group of States possess the jurisdictional authority, intelligence, and wherewithal to tackle this enormous task through unilateral measures alone.[195] The extradition regime is not only essential for practical and efficiency reasons, but also because it reflects certain significant shared values and safeguards important human rights, both substantive and procedural.[196]

The extradition regime is undermined by the incidence of the more aggressive full-scale alternatives,[197] because of the distrust it evidences in terms of the utility of existing treaties and procedures, as well as the need to negotiate new treaties or bring into force those that have been signed

[191] Mann, *supra* n.4, at 419 (noting that abductions [SDOs] could trigger reciprocal conduct).

[192] *Olmstead*, 277 U.S. at 485.

[193] Raphael F. Perl, *Int'l Terrorism: Threat, Policy, and Response*, C.R.S. Report to Congress, updated Jan. 3, 2007, at 17.

[194] "Colombia Decries Intervention; Peru Recalls Envoy; Guerrillas Ask for Role," *Wash. Post*, Dec. 22, 1989, at A33.

[195] *See State-Sponsored Kidnapping, supra* n.174, at 90–91.

[196] Note, *Israeli Precedent, supra* n.65, at 1112.

[197] Mann, *supra* n.4, at 420.

but not yet ratified.[198] And it is not only the extradition regime itself that will suffer, but also international law enforcement cooperation more generally. As Yale Law Professor Ruth Wedgwood explained: "It's hard to have your cake and eat it too. If you are going to ask people to cooperate with you in enforcing criminal law, and at the same time stick your finger in their eye by intruding on their territory, that's not going to last."[199]

[198] *State-Sponsored Kidnapping, supra* n.174, at 87 and 91 (quoting the author's congressional testimony on July 29, 1992).

[199] Sharon LaFraniere, "Baker Offers Reassurances After Court Kidnap Ruling; Foreign Governments Condemn U.S. Abduction Decision," *Wash. Post*, June 17, 1992, at A2 (quoting Prof. Wedgwood).

Conclusion

This book has attempted to erect a new analytical framework, complete with a refreshed vernacular and a series of typologies, for understanding the panoply of operational means available to a State desiring to bring an international fugitive to justice, as well as to evaluate the lawfulness and implications of those means. This Conclusion is divided into three parts. First, it sets forth a summary of the content; second, it posits several general observations about jurisdiction, extradition, and its alternatives; and third, it proffers a number of constructive recommendations to address, resolve, or mitigate particular problem areas.

a Summary

This study began with core terminology, some new and others simply clarified and updated. It then discussed the concept of subject matter jurisdiction, which is central to criminal law, and in particular focused on the notion of extraterritorial jurisdiction, a critical component in bringing an overseas fugitive to justice. Next, it attempted to isolate from the analysis of extradition and its alternatives those instances in which a fugitive finds his way to pursuing State jurisdiction, custody, or control by sheer fortuity (so-called "silver platter" scenarios), such as by error or misunderstanding, a voluntary return unrelated to law enforcement pressures, or the involuntary delivery on the part of private/non-State actors or government officials acting *ultra vires*. Those cases are not generally problematic from a legal standpoint, but represent only a small fraction of the fugitive population. The vast majority of fugitives, to the contrary, actively seek out safe havens and adopt pseudonyms or new nationalities, and for those who can afford it, pay off corrupt politicians or law enforcement officers and surround themselves with bodyguards. The remainder of the study addressed what affirmative steps States can take to secure the custody of fugitives and evaluated their legal and policy significance.

Extradition remains, at least in principle, the single most widely recognized and (positively) sanctioned mechanism worldwide for bringing fugitives to justice. For all of its strengths, adaptable features, and ongoing liberalization, however, extradition is replete with impediments, which were set forth herein by way of a comprehensive typology. Those impediments may derive from legal standards or governmental factors, individual status or circumstances, or inter-State relations or sensitivities. Extradition may be barred based merely on a fugitive's nationality, advanced age, or frail health, and can entail a protracted and expensive process as well as an uncertain outcome. Moreover, political factors cannot readily be separated from or discounted in extradition decision-making. Nevertheless, it may still be possible to secure the extradition of a fugitive, even if at first rejected, via any number of remedial or collateral means, which were then discussed, ranging from revamped charges to financial inducements to third-party intervention.

Because of the many formidable obstacles facing extradition, a State ultimately may choose to pursue an alternative means to extradition for securing a fugitive's custody. Just as extradition has a long history, so too do its alternatives,[1] which have been used with "unexpected frequency."[2] Given their close contextual relationship, alternatives to extradition cannot be critically assessed without reference to extradition itself, much like the "death row phenomenon"[3] cannot be properly evaluated divorced from the underlying context of capital punishment.[4]

The alternatives to extradition are highly varied; some – those referred to herein as "fallback" alternatives – have the limited objective either to

[1] "[C]ircumventing extradition . . . is as old as extradition itself and will probably continue to exist as long as courts persist in their current refusal to consider the issue." Christine van den Wyngaert, *Applying the Eur. Conv. of Human Rights to Extradition: Opening Pandora's Box*, 39 Int'l & Comp. L.Q. 757, 778 (1990).

[2] Kandy G. Webb, Note, *Constitutional and Int'l Law – Int'l Kidnapping – Gov't Illegality as a Challenge to Jurisdiction*, 50 Tul. L. Rev. 169, 170 (1975–76).

[3] "The 'death row phenomenon' is a legal – not a clinical – term perhaps best generally defined as a 'combination of circumstances to which a prisoner would be exposed if he were sentenced to death' and placed on death row. The two key circumstances underpinning the phenomenon are the harsh, dehumanizing conditions of confinement and the prolonged period of detention an inmate may endure on death row." David A. Sadoff, *Int'l Law and the Mortal Precipice: A legal Policy Critique of the Death Row Phenomenon*, 17 Tul. J. Int'l & Comp. L. 77, 81–82 (2008) (internal citation omitted.) *See also* n.137 in Chapter 7.

[4] *See id.* at 81 ("The death row phenomenon cannot realistically be detached from the death penalty itself; logically they are inseparable.").

adopt independent measures to facilitate the capture of a fugitive, rely on others to locate and arrest a fugitive, or seek the prosecution of a fugitive in another judicial system. Others specifically seek the physical custody of a fugitive with the intent of prosecuting or punishing him in its own judicial system. The latter set, denominated herein as "full-scale" alternatives, are diverse, and may rely on the host State's immigration laws, entail informal law enforcement cooperation, or constitute unilateral options. Unilateral means include negotiated returns, lure and capture operations (LCOs), seizure and delivery operations (SDOs), and interception operations. Because of their more controversial legal status, the operational full-scale alternatives give rise to a number of post-return judicial, diplomatic, and public policy implications, including personal jurisdiction, individual standing, injured State demands and retaliation, and the health of the extradition regime and international law enforcement coordination more generally, each of which was examined.

b General Observations

This section covers three sets of broad observations about this field: (i) the need for greater terminological and conceptual clarity; (ii) the nature of ongoing developments related to jurisdiction and extradition; and (iii) some significant outstanding issues.

Terminological and Conceptual Clarity. The existing terminology in this field can be a source of confusion, prove misleading, and even adversely influence how one assesses the lawfulness of certain actions. As reflected in Chapter 1, fundamental terms, such as "fugitive," "extradition," "surrender," and "disguised extradition," do not have uniform definitions and their conventional usage is to some extent imprecise. In addition, while at times underlying facts remain publicly unknown, far too often even when information is fully adequate, deportations are mislabeled as extraditions. Notably, such confusion can skew lawfulness determinations to the extent that they are subject to an erroneous legal standard. Likewise, certain terms like "rendition," "lure," and "seizure" tend to be applied generically when each can, and should, be differentiated for maximum clarity according to their destination (tactical versus strategic) and the participatory status of the operation itself (unilateral versus consensual versus cooperative versus joint).

In addition, use of the terms "asylum State" and "forum State" can lead to misunderstanding when relied on to denote the States involved in a given operation to secure or transfer a fugitive's custody. Those terms *may* prove helpful but only in specific contexts or circumstances. By contrast, the terms "host State" and "pursuing State," respectively, lend greater precision to the discourse. Furthermore, terms like "abduction" and "kidnapping," by definition, tend to prejudge the unlawfulness of certain conduct, whereas the proposed term "seizure and delivery operation" more accurately describes the activity at issue, which may or may not ultimately prove to be a violation of international (or domestic) law.

Linked to the absence of terminological clarity is a lack of conceptual clarity. Frequently courts and legal commentators alike treat the *male captus bene detentus* rule, which is a neutral rule of non-inquiry, as if its application were tantamount to a court's blessing the underlying law enforcement action that brought a fugitive within the court's jurisdiction. It is *not*; rather, it simply stands for the proposition that the court should carry out its role in adjudicating criminal charges when it has personal jurisdiction over a fugitive defendant as the court does not believe it is its business to review inherently political matters that are more properly handled by executive branch officials or agents.

It is also complicating that this field of law has two different types of due process, two separate rules of non-inquiry, two varieties of concurrent jurisdiction, two forms of jurisdiction in general (subject matter and personal), two applications of conditional release, and two types of individual standing (pre-rendition and post-rendition) that are not always adequately distinguished. Likewise, two closely related but distinct concepts, such as extraditable offenses and dual criminality, or concurrent jurisdiction and competing jurisdictional claims, are often treated as synonymous when they are not. Other conceptual issues include the fact that "silver platter" scenarios, collateral or remedial means to secure extradition, "extraordinary renditions" and even *aut dedere aut judicare* are often regarded as genuine extradition *alternatives* when none strictly qualifies. Moreover, conceptual clarity is lacking with respect to how cases are categorized and evaluated; for instance, many lump all "lure" cases together regardless of the participants involved, informal law enforcement operations may be classified as deportations, and some SDOs may be regarded as a form of informal law enforcement cooperation despite the fact that host State officials were acting in their personal capacity.

Recent Developments. As a field, international criminal procedure and law enforcement cooperation have experienced a number of striking changes in the past few decades. With regard to *subject matter* jurisdiction, the United States, among others, has sought since the 1980s to extend its extraterritorial reach especially over terrorists and narco-traffickers, mainly by liberalizing the use of the passive personality principle to crimes committed against American nationals abroad. With respect to *personal* jurisdiction, there is a discernible inclination on the part of a number of States' courts away from a strict *male captus* posture, at least to the extent that the gravest crimes are not involved and where either a State has complained that its sovereignty has been breached or evidence exists that police conduct was such that it would shock the conscience. Relatedly, States' courts increasingly are granting individual standing to fugitive defendants to challenge criminal charges on specialty grounds.

As far as extradition is concerned, recent years have witnessed a number of States that which traditionally did not rely on extradition treaties now entering into new treaty arrangements for the recovery of fugitives. We also have seen domestic legislation or constitutional amendments introduced with the intention of facilitating extradition (including the elimination of nationality bars and simpler ways to satisfy the dual criminality standard) and States now granting extradition under circumstances that previously would have yielded denials. In addition to an overall uptick in the usage of extradition worldwide and the advent of creative yet formal inter-State surrogates for extradition treaties, we also have observed new and improved mechanisms for regional extradition cooperation, most notably the European Arrest Warrant (EAW).

Outstanding Issues. For all the recent positive developments outlined, a number of significant unresolved issues remain. In short, *geography matters.*[5] States vary considerably not only in their overall common or civil law complexion, but also in their extraterritorial jurisdictional reach, their faith in the extradition regime, their willingness to grant asylum or serve as a "safe haven" for fugitives, their handling of extradition requests, their predisposition to consider alternatives to extradition to secure the custody of fugitives, their tendency to rely on political versus legal bases for decision-making, and their inclination to exercise

[5] *Timing* also matters, as there may well be, as reflected in examples seen herein, strong political pressures based on recent or pending circumstances (*e.g.*, terrorist threats, extradition cooperation or failure to respect territorial sovereignty by a pursuing State, or the compelling need for trade or development opportunities) that may help drive a certain decision. Timing also relates to how new or old an applicable extradition treaty is, as treaties of newer vintage tend to be more progressive, on average, than historical ones.

personal jurisdiction even in the face of an apparent abuse of process. Accordingly, the lack of consistent treatment renders certain States more extradition-friendly or -hostile than others, and therefore tends to influence where fugitives choose to reside or flee, and where a fugitive is located may ultimately dictate the disposition of a given case.[6]

Key issues that continue to divide the international community include whether and how to treat political offenses as an extradition exclusion, whether States should exempt their own nationals from extradition, how to detect "disguised extradition" and how to handle such cases, whether or to what extent an LCO should be considered unlawful when an operative extradition treaty was not invoked by a pursuing State, whether courts should assert or decline personal jurisdiction in the face of unlawful pursuing State police conduct, and whether courts should regard unilateral means of securing a fugitive's custody as falling outside the scope of an extradition treaty where no provision or other relevant communication expressly indicates that extradition is intended to be the exclusive means of securing a fugitive's custody.

Indeed, the overall record of lawfulness of the full-scale operational alternatives to extradition can be inconsistent and some law remains unsettled. While certainly fundamental international law plays an integral role in this arena, many court opinions appear to be dictated mainly by domestic law and political considerations, and consequently it is often difficult to ascertain much by way of clear legal guidance of general applicability.

c Recommendations

Mindful of the above observations, the most successful or promising extradition-related developments in recent years, and the international community's overall interests, the following recommendations are proffered. Their objectives are to: (i) increase the use and effectiveness of

[6] *Cf.* Am. Bar Ass'n, "Overcoming Legal Challenges in Extradition," Charles A. Caruso, ABA ROLI website, Asia Law Initiative, undated, *available at* www.americanbar.org/content/dam/aba/directories/roli/raca/asia_raca_charlescaruso_overcoming.authcheckdam.pdf (last visited on May 26, 2016) ("[M]uch of the legal regimen that now surrounds extradition is the result of the significance given to various recurring legal themes by the individual national judiciaries. Thus in discussing overcoming legal challenges in extradition, as with all things left to the disparate national judiciaries, we find differences as well as similarities between jurisdictions."). To compound matters, some States maintain internally inconsistent case law in this arena, such as the United States.

extradition; (ii) render full-scale operational alternatives to extradition less *necessary*; (iii) render full-scale operational alternatives to extradition less *desirable*;[7] and (iv) diminish the prospect of retaliation or reciprocity by an injured State in the event a full-scale operational alternative to extradition is undertaken.

i Increase the Use and Effectiveness of Extradition

1 Promote the Execution of Bilateral Extradition Treaties or Functionally Equivalent Arrangements. Many States today have entered into only a modest number of bilateral extradition treaties. As a result, there is a significant opportunity for the execution of more such instruments. For those States less inclined to follow the bilateral extradition treaty route, they could be encouraged to explore and consider *ad hoc* arrangements, non-treaty-based cooperative schemes, or the promulgation of domestic laws that would at least authorize extradition in ways not currently available. One way to precipitate such movement could be to hold a regularly scheduled international criminal law cooperation conference, perhaps sponsored by UNODC and/or INTERPOL. Reliance on the U.N. Model Treaty on Extradition[8] also could be more aggressively promoted.

2 Update Existing Bilateral or Multilateral Extradition Treaty Provisions. States should seek to draft, ratify, and enforce bilateral or multilateral extradition treaties that contain more up-to-date, progressive, and cooperative provisions that do not bar extradition except in fully justifiable instances. Such treaties should, for example, be more forgiving with submission time limits and not require evidence greater than probable cause to trigger a denied extradition request. For States parties so inclined, such treaties should indicate in the text or the *travaux preparatoires* whether or not they intend to operate *exclusively* of all other means of obtaining extraterritorial custody over a fugitive.

3 Conclude More Regional or Sub-Regional Extradition Treaties. Regional or sub-regional extradition treaties, such as the Inter-American

[7] Consistent with this view, Prof. M. Cherif Bassiouni has expressed a distinct preference for streamlining the extradition system as opposed to relying on alternative means. M. Cherif Bassiouni, International Extradition and World Public Order 184 (1974).

[8] Dec. 14, 1991, UNGA Res. 45/116, Annex, 45 U.N. GAOR Supp. (No. 49A), at 212, U.N. Doc. A/45/49 (1990), *reprinted in* 30 ILM 1407.

Convention and that which exists among the Benelux countries, provide effective models for other regions or sub-regions to adopt, particularly in sub-Saharan Africa, North Africa and the Middle East, the Baltic States, and Southeast Asia. Such multilateral treaties have the distinct advantage of introducing a greater degree of uniformity and standardization of provisions compared with bilateral treaties, not to mention increased efficiency.[9] Ideally, those treaties could be streamlined to allow for less impeded transfers along the lines of the EAW system, but to ensure that no abuse occurs, arrest warrants should only be issued when there is clear and convincing evidence against the fugitive and only when a speedy trial and proper legal representation can be guaranteed for the fugitive upon delivery to the transferee State.[10]

ii Render Full-Scale Operational Alternatives to Extradition Less Necessary

4 Encourage Reliance on Fallback Alternatives to Extradition. Chapter 9 sets forth an array of options that could be employed short of a full-scale approach to securing a fugitive's custody and prosecution under one's own judicial system. Examples include seizing or freezing the fugitive's financial assets; cancelling his passport or requesting the host State to revoke his travel authorization; and requesting a third State to arrest him upon arrival or to exclude him at a port of entry. In certain circumstances, these options may well satisfy a pursuing State's essential objectives without, at the same time, risking international censure, foreign policy fallout, and possible retaliation that may accompany the employment of more aggressive full-scale alternatives.

5 Agree to Adopt *Aut Dedere Aut Judicare* as the General Rule. *Aut dedere* is already mandatory under a large number of international crime suppression treaties and is arguably close to becoming customary international law.[11] States parties to those international conventions that do not currently make *aut dedere* compulsory could seek respective

[9] *Cf.* M. Cherif Bassiouni, International Extradition: United States Law and Practice 42 (6th ed. 2014) (describing bilateral extradition treaties as "the most cumbersome form that can be relied upon").

[10] *See* Duncan Campbell, "European Law's Blunt Instrument," *The Guardian*, June 22, 2010.

[11] *Fourth Report on the Obligation to Extradite or Prosecute* (aut dedere aut judicare), Zdzislaw Galicki, Special Rapporteur, ILC, 63d Sess., U.N. Doc. A/CN.4/648, May 31, 2011.

protocols to employ *aut dedere* in all cases in which host States that choose not to extend asylum, grant amnesty, or extradite a specific fugitive pursuant to a legitimate extradition request would be obligated to make a good faith effort to explore prosecution.[12]

To ensure each such U.N. convention's effectiveness, the accompanying protocols could contain enforcement provisions that call upon the UNSC to insist on compliance under the threat of economic sanctions, at least where its Chapter VII authorities so allowed. To sweeten the deal, States parties could be asked to make annual contributions into a collective pot that could be used to assist the less well financially endowed among them in carrying out any prosecution in such circumstances. Such an agreement would additionally help beneficiary States eliminate any reputation they have established, fairly or unfairly, as "safe havens" for fugitives.

6 Establish a Permanent U.N.-Based Tribunal for Prosecuting Selected Cases. Certain kinds of cases tend to be less prone to extradition approval. Among them are those in which the political offense exclusion can be invoked in otherwise terrorism-related crimes,[13] cases in which the host State is concerned about human rights treatment in a pursuing State, and cases where host States refuse to extradite their own nationals.[14] A permanent (versus temporary or *ad hoc*) U.N. tribunal, modeled as appropriate on the concurrent jurisdiction of the ICTY and ICTR, could be established to handle such prosecutions.

Such a court would ensure that criminals were brought to justice while overcoming many of the obstacles now encountered in the existing extradition regime and by providing a politically neutral forum with fair trial procedures. Such an approach may meet with resistance from those States that opposed the stand-up of the International Criminal Court (ICC) and/or that remain skeptical regarding such a forum's capacity for political even-handedness. In addition, experience with the ICTY and ICTR has not been altogether positive; many question their

[12] *Id.* ¶ 39 ("[I]t seems that the duty to cooperate in the fight against impunity may be realized in the best and most effective way by the application of the principle of *aut dedere aut judicare.*").

[13] *See* Andrew L. Liput, Note, *An Analysis of the Achille Lauro Affair: Towards an Effective and Legal Method of Bringing Int'l Terrorists to Justice*, 9 Fordham Int'l L.J. 328, 369–70 (1986) (recommending a U.N.-based tribunal to prosecute terrorist-related crimes). For such a tribunal to prove effective, some consensus regarding a definition of "terrorism" almost certainly would be required.

[14] Faiza Patel, *Crime Without Frontiers: A Proposal for an Int'l Narcotics Court*, 22 N.Y.U. J. Int'l L. & Pol. 709 (1990).

relative benefit in light of the high costs incurred, and "tribunal fatigue" may discourage others from this approach.

iii Render Full-Scale Operational Alternatives to Extradition Less Desirable

7 Stay Criminal Proceedings in Discretionary Circumstances. As discussed in Chapter 13.a.i, some domestic courts will stay proceedings for lack of personal jurisdiction in instances where an abuse of process has been found, while others decline to do so. The former has been referred to as the "due process" model while the latter as the "crime control" model.[15] One middle-ground approach would be to stay proceedings on a discretionary basis where the nature of the rendition of the fugitive has been egregious (but not at the ultra-high threshold applied by States adhering to the *male captus* principle), *unless* the underlying crime itself was particularly grave, such as torture or slavery.[16] If this approach were adopted by State judiciaries, their respective executive branches might well be less inclined to undertake certain full-scale alternatives to extradition, particularly unilateral SDOs, knowing that the proceedings might be stayed and the fugitive defendant released due to the means used to secure his custody.

8 Permit Fugitive Defendants to Challenge Rights Violations. With rare exception, fugitive defendants are not presently conferred individual standing to challenge a court's personal jurisdiction based on rights violations they allegedly experienced. A few courts permit a fugitive defendant to raise a specialty claim on his own, absent the former host State's protest, and others have recognized individual standing with respect to ill-treatment in connection with how he was physically transferred to the court's jurisdiction. Were fugitive defendants allowed to raise such specialty and human rights claims that are

[15] Andrew L.-T. Choo, Abuse of Process and Judicial Stays of Criminal Proceedings 87 (1993). Some legal commentators have proposed applying the logic of a court declining jurisdiction over unlawfully seized individuals just as is done with illegally seized evidence. *E.g.*, Manuel R. Garcia-Mora, *Criminal Jurisdiction of a State over Fugitives Brought from a Foreign Country by Force or Fraud: A Comparative Study*, 32 Ind. L.J. 427, 442 & n.84 (1957). This proposal would fall within the "due process" model and would, in this author's judgment, go too far.

[16] *See* Rosalyn Higgins, Problems and Process: International Law and How we Use It 72–73 (1994). Alternatively, instead of staying proceedings, courts could adopt new sentencing guidelines where the length of prison terms is reduced based on the underlying harm caused.

directly relevant to them (versus claims based on a violation of territorial sovereignty or a breach of an extradition treaty that are fundamentally a State's concern), this would seem not only fair to a potentially injured party, but also acknowledge that States must "recognize that sovereigns should represent the interests of their people"[17] – not just the sovereign rights of other States. Furthermore, the prospect of such challenges ought to have a sobering influence on States contemplating an aggressive full-scale alternative to extradition.

9 Delineate Clearly the Permissible Exercise of an LCO by Analogy to Ruses Used during War. The lawfulness of deceptive practices to bring fugitives to justice today is largely uncertain and therefore susceptible to exploitation. One constructive approach would be to gauge its permissibility by consulting international humanitarian law (IHL) standards by analogy. Ruses of war are expressly permissible[18] and include "acts which are intended to mislead an adversary or to induce him to act recklessly, but which infringe no rule of international law applicable in armed conflict and which are not perfidious because they do not invite the confidence of an adversary with respect to protection under that law."[19] Cited examples include "the use of camouflage, decoys, mock operations and misinformation."[20] Unlawful acts of perfidy, by contrast, would include, by way of illustration: "(a) the feigning of an intent to negotiate under a flag of truce or of a surrender; (b) the feigning of an incapacitation by wounds or sickness; [or] (c) the feigning of civilian, non-combatant status."[21]

[17] Mary-Rose Papandrea, Note, *Standing to Allege Violations of the Doctrine of Specialty: An Examination of the Relationship Between the Individual and the Sovereign*, 62 U. Chi. L. Rev. 1187, 1213 (1995).

[18] *See* Jean-Marie Henckaerts & Louise Doswald-Beck, Customary International Humanitarian Law 203 (ICRC 2005) ("Rule 57. Ruses of war are not prohibited as long as they do not infringe a rule of international humanitarian law.").

[19] Addt'l Prot. to the Geneva Convs. of August 12, 1949, and Relating to the Protection of Victims of Int'l Armed Conflicts of June 8, 1977, art. 37(2), U.N. Doc. A/32/144 (1977) Annex I, *reprinted in* 16 ILM 1391 [hereinafter AP I]. To the extent this Protocol contains customary international law, even non-ratifying States like the United States, are expected to abide by such provisions, and this general rule is regarded as constituting customary international law. *See* Henckaerts & Doswald-Beck, *supra* n.18, at 203 ("This is a long-standing rule of customary international law already recognised in the Lieber Code and the Brussels Declaration, and codified in the Hague Regulations ... The rule permitting ruses of war is stated in numerous military manuals. It is supported by several official statements and other practice.").

[20] AP I, *supra* n.19, art. 37(2).

[21] *Id.*, art. 37(1).

Were this analogy to apply, the only LCO scenario that arguably ought to be proscribed is where government officials induce a fugitive to assist with a law enforcement matter, including any incidental promise of safe passage, because doing so would operate much like perfidy in unfairly inviting, and then betraying, confidence with respect to the very set of laws erected to ensure protection. Although such an analogy can be challenged on the ground that wartime and peacetime conduct should not be assessed against the same legal standards, wartime conduct and international criminal law enforcement actions are comparable to the extent that both involve oppositional forces and may entail violent methods, and therefore each calls for careful line-drawing as significant consequences hang in the balance.

10 Erect a Specific, High-Threshold Legal Standard for the Exercise of an SDO. Evaluating the lawfulness of an SDO bears some similarity to appraising the legality of an anticipatory self-defensive strike.[22] Both sets of actions basically lie outside the international legal framework but both have been introduced into State practice out of a sense of practical necessity and at least under highly restricted circumstances arguably could pass legal muster. Both also rely on either soupy or disaggregated international legal standards. There is some merit in constructing a clear, sensible, and balanced legal standard that could apply to SDOs that would not only guide the character of SDOs themselves, but also help the international community assess a given operation's compliance with international law.

Such a standard ought to set a high threshold and presumably could consist of such illustrative elements as the following:

(i) the underlying crime should be significant and of an international character;
(ii) there should be strong, if not compelling, evidence of the underlying crime;
(iii) the pursuing State should have unequivocal extraterritorial jurisdiction under its domestic law to conduct the operation;
(iv) (a) the host State should have demonstrated an unwillingness or inability either to prosecute or extradite the fugitive or otherwise has exposed him to a sham trial, (b) based on the historical record and current political realities, the host State would be extremely unlikely to

[22] *See* David A. Sadoff, *Striking a Sensible Balance on the Legality of Defensive First Strikes*, 42 Vand. J. Transnat'l L. 441 (2009) (proposing a novel legal standard for anticipatory self-defense).

extradite or prosecute, *or* (c) no feasible alternative otherwise exists to obtain custody of the fugitive ("necessity");

(v) there should be limited infringement of territorial sovereignty, consistent with strictly meeting the operational objective, while posing a minimal risk of collateral damage or injury ("proportionality");

(vi) all practicable and reasonable efforts have been taken to protect and respect the fugitive's human rights in the manner in which he was apprehended and transferred, including an opportunity for him to contact his family and consulate; and

(vii) the host State has reported the action, together with salient operational details, to the UNSC within a reasonable time after the operation occurred.

iv Diminish the Risk of Retaliation Following Unilateral Operations

11 Promote Greater Reliance on Binding Arbitration to Resolve Disputes. Contemporary extradition treaties and other agreements tend not to provide dispute settlement clauses, but, as we have seen, unilateral operations can trigger inter-State tension and result in retaliation or reciprocal actions. States should enter into agreements that, to the extent conflicts arise regarding the exercise of unilateral extraterritorial enforcement actions, they will submit to binding arbitration to resolve the dispute.[23] Binding arbitration would be preferable to the existing systemic reliance on domestic courts (which may not inquire into the underlying executive branch actions), human rights bodies (which review claims based strictly on compliance with their constituitive documents), or even the ICJ (which has its own jurisdictional constraints).[24] The arbitrators would operate without binding precedent but could draw freely upon judgments as persuasive authority from other tribunals as they saw fit.

Arbitration is a proven mechanism, and has been used successfully in extradition alternative cases, including by the Permanent Court of

[23] *E.g., United States v. Insull*, 8 F. Supp. 310 (N.D. Ill. 1934); Charles Cheney Hyde, *The Extradition Case of Samuel Insull Sr. in Relation to Greece*, 28 AJIL 307 (1934).

[24] Notably, Article 28 of Harvard Research suggested that the Permanent Court of Arbitration (PCA) be the default tribunal where pre-existing mechanisms were not in place to resolve inter-State differences arising out of extraterritorial enforcement actions. Draft Conv. on Research in Int'l Law of the Harvard Law School, "Jurisdiction with Respect to Crime," 29 AJIL 435 (Supp. 1935).

Arbitration (PCA) and pursuant to bilateral treaties. One need only look to the increasing trend of "arbitralization" of the ICJ[25] to confirm that States are amenable to this form of dispute resolution. Particularly muscular or weak States might be more reluctant to enter into such an arrangement, there could be an issue of enforcing rulings, there would not necessarily be an opportunity to appeal an unfavorable judgment, and "[t]here is little, if anything, to support the primacy of *restitutio in integrum* in international arbitral practice."[26] Nevertheless, this approach holds promise, and would help defuse tensions, while offering a constructive means to resolve post-delivery differences by avoiding outright hostility.

* * * * *

Crime, like death and taxes, is an inevitable feature of our world. Those who commit, or are alleged to have committed, crimes may be located, whether by choice or happenstance, in territory other than that of a State that has charged or convicted them of a crime. In such instances, the challenge posed to individual States and to the international community at large is to find reasonable and appropriate ways to bring those individuals to justice (and, in the process, deter others from committing offenses) without, at the same time, compromising our cherished principles and values, including the rule of law, human rights, due process, territorial sovereignty, and the integrity of the judicial system itself. It is, in a fundamental sense, a matter of striking a delicate balance. In undertaking this exercise, it is clear that States must not stoop to the level of those they themselves find repugnant and seek to prosecute or punish. As U.S. Supreme Court Justice Oliver Wendell Holmes wrote nearly a century ago: "I think it a less evil that some criminals should escape than that the Government should play an ignoble part."[27]

[25] Georges Abi-Saab, *The Int'l Court as a World Court, in* FIFTY YEARS OF THE INTERNATIONAL COURT OF JUSTICE (Vaughan Lowe & Malgosia Fitzmaurice eds. 1996).

[26] CHRISTINE D. GRAY, JUDICIAL REMEDIES IN INTERNATIONAL LAW 13 (1987). The term *restitutio in integrum* means the "re-establishment of the situation which would in all probability have existed if the illegal act had not been committed. That is, it does not expressly involve an order for specific performance, and it goes further than specific performance in that it may involve the rectification of harm already caused by the illegal act." *Id.* at 12–13

[27] *Olmstead v. United States*, 277 U.S. 438, 470 (1928) (Holmes, J., separate op.).

GLOSSARY[1]

Active Extradition the extradition process undertaken by, and from the perspective of, a *pursuing* State, commencing with the submission of an extradition request. (Compare with *Passive Extradition*)

Alternatives to Extradition refers expansively to all measures, methods, and mechanisms, whether ultimately regarded as lawful or unlawful, that: (i) fall outside the extradition regime; (ii) aim to bring a fugitive to justice fully or partially, directly or indirectly; and (iii) do not entail a fugitive's delivery as a function of sheer fortuity. (See *Full-Scale Alternatives to Extradition* and *Fallback Alternatives to Extradition*)

Aut dedere aut judicare (Latin) stands for the legal principle under which the host State is contractually obligated either to extradite a fugitive to a pursuing State or to undertake good faith measures toward adjudicating the fugitive under its own judicial system. (Sometimes referred to by the functionally synonymous terms ***aut dedere aut punire*** and ***aut dedere aut prosequi***)

Bring to Justice a law enforcement action with the end result of: (i) prosecuting an individual for a charged crime; or (ii) punishing an individual whose guilt has been established but has yet to pay his debt to society, whether by incarceration, re-incarceration (in the event of a prison escape), or other legally sanctioned means.

Commandeering Operation an operation that, through force or the threat of force exerted from the inside of a transport vessel or vehicle, seizes control with the aim of reaching a destination where the identity of any suspected fugitives on board can be safely confirmed and, if so, apprehended. (Compare with *Interception Operation*)

[1] Some of the definitions that appear herein, such as "commandeering operation," "host State," and "silver platter scenario," are tailored to the subject of this book and may well have broader or alternative definitions when used in other contexts.

Conditional Extradition the host State's agreement to extradite a fugitive to a pursuing State only on one or more stipulated conditions (*e.g.*, that he be retried in the event of a prior *in absentia* conviction or that a host State national serve any imposed sentence in his own country).

Conditional Release (i) a variant of *summary extradition* in which an individual in host State custody, or confinement is transferred to a pursuing State on the condition that he be returned to the host State for its own law enforcement purposes as soon as the adjudicatory proceedings and any resulting sentence have concluded; or (ii) the circumstance in which a State temporarily releases a criminal defendant from detention pending an extradition decision.

Consensual Operation the carrying out of a fugitive recovery activity on host State territory exclusively by pursuing State officials or agents with the prior consent of the host State, typically via "a wink and a nod." (Compare with *Consensual Rendition*)

Consensual Rendition the physical transfer of an individual from host State territory to pursuing State territory when conducted exclusively by pursuing State officials or agents with the prior consent of the host State, typically via "a wink and a nod." (Compare with *Consensual Rendition*)

De Facto Extradition a State's formal or informal exercise of non-extradition-related laws, authorities, or administrative procedures that yields the delivery of a fugitive directly or indirectly to a State with a law enforcement interest in him. (Compare with *Disguised Extradition* and *Extradition*)

Deportation the execution of an expulsion order by a State from its sovereign territory of an alien, even if only having been temporarily admitted, on the ground that he violated its immigration laws upon entering the territory, is otherwise illegally within the territory, or while present has proven to be a public menace or security threat. (Compare with *Exclusion* and *Expulsion*)

Disguised Extradition a subset of *de facto extradition* that entails a purposeful circumvention of extradition laws or treaties by the host State to deliver a fugitive directly or indirectly to a State with a law enforcement interest in him, most commonly via the exercise of immigration laws. (Compare with *De Facto Extradition*)

Exclusion the ejection of an alien by a State on account of security or other significant concerns when he is seeking admission or asylum at a border or other port of entry. (Compare with *Deportation* and *Expulsion*)

Expulsion "the exercise of State power which secures the removal, either 'voluntarily', under threat of forcible removal, or forcibly, of an alien from the territory of a State."[2] (Compare with *Deportation* and *Exclusion*)

Extradition (or *De Jure Extradition*) a cooperative law enforcement process by which the physical custody of a person: (i) charged with committing a crime or (ii) convicted of a crime whose punishment has not yet been determined or fully served, is formally transferred, directly or indirectly, by authorities of one State to those of another at the request of the latter for the purpose of prosecution or punishment, respectively.[3] (Compare with *De Facto Extradition* and *Surrender*)

Extraordinary Rendition "the extra-judicial transfer of persons from one jurisdiction or State to another, for the purposes of detention and interrogation outside the normal legal system, where there [is] a real risk of torture or cruel, inhuman or degrading treatment."[4] (Compare with *Rendition and International Rendition*)

Failed State "A state that is failing has several attributes. One of the most common is the loss of physical control of its territory or a monopoly on the legitimate use of force. Other attributes of state failure include the erosion of legitimate authority to make collective decisions, an inability to provide reasonable public services, and the inability to interact with other states as a full member of the international community."[5]

Fallback Alternatives to Extradition the partial or redirected means of bringing a fugitive to justice other than by extradition that, by virtue of a pursuing State's inability to meet the functional end result of extradition – namely, securing the physical custody of a fugitive and prosecuting

[2] Guy S. Goodwin-Gill, International Law and the Movement of Persons Between States 201 (1978).

[3] This definition applies specifically to *international* (inter-State) versus *domestic* (intra-State) extradition.

[4] *Ahmad and Others v. U.K.*, Appl. Nos. 24027/07, 11949/08, 36742/08, 66911/09, and 67354/09, 56 EHRR, Apr. 10, 2012 (final issued on Sept. 24, 2012).

[5] Blake Hounshell, 2009 *Failed State Index – FAQ and Methodology* (based on collaboration between Fund for Peace and *Foreign Policy* magazine), *Foreign Policy* website, June 22, 2009, *available at* http://foreignpolicy.com/2009/06/22/2009-failed-states-index-faq-methodology/ (last visited on May 25, 2016).

or punishing him under its own judicial system – reflects a second-order preference. (Compare with *Full-Scale Alternatives to Extradition*)

Formal Deportation an involuntary deportation undertaken through officially established channels in compliance with the applicable conditions and requirements of a removing State's laws. (Compare with *Informal Deportation*)

Formal Rendition any rendition carried out pursuant to a formal written agreement between States or between a State and an international criminal tribunal. (Compare with *Informal Rendition* and *Semi-formal Rendition*)

Fortuitously Acquiring State a pursuing State to which a fugitive: (i) is delivered by serendipity or at the initiative of the host State or an international criminal tribunal or by a private party, including one or more government officials operating in a non-official capacity or *ultra vires*, or (ii) arrives on his own volition, even if acting upon innocently mistaken information or representations. (Compare with *Transferee State*, *Rendering State*, and *Receiving State* and see *Silver Platter Scenarios*)

Fugitive see *International Fugitive from Justice*

Full-scale Alternatives to Extradition any non-extradition-related means of bringing a fugitive to justice that functionally approximate the end result of extradition; namely, securing the physical custody of a fugitive and bringing him within a pursuing State's judicial system to be prosecuted or punished. (Compare with *Fallback Alternatives to Extradition*)

Host State the State, other than that of a pursuing State, within whose territory a particular fugitive is currently located, however temporarily, whether within or outside the extradition context. (Compare with *Pursuing State*)

Indirect Extradition an extradition between States that lack diplomatic relations with one another, and therefore all related communications and the physical transfer itself occur via an intermediary party.

Informal Deportation an involuntary deportation undertaken through casual arrangements and typically handled on an expedited basis. (Compare with *Formal Deportation*)

Informal Law Enforcement Cooperation a form of inter-State cooperation handled through casual or other less conventional procedures or channels between law enforcement authorities (or other government officials acting in support of law enforcement) resulting in the direct or indirect rendition of a fugitive.

Informal Rendition any rendition handled absent any legal process. (Compare with *Formal Rendition* and *Semi-Formal Rendition*)

Injured State the former host State or the State of a fugitive's nationality that has suffered harm arising out of acts or omissions by a pursuing State, typically via a full-scale alternative to extradition.

Interception Operation an operation that, through either force or the threat of force exerted from the outside of a transport vessel or vehicle, directs its movement to a location where the identity of any suspected fugitives on board can be safely confirmed and, if so, apprehended. (Compare with *Commandeering Operation* and *Passive Interception*)

Intermediate Rendition the initial and temporary physical transfer of a fugitive to third State territory, custody, or control, where the aim is subsequently to transfer him to pursuing State territory, custody, or control. (Compare with *Tactical Rendition*)

International Arrest the apprehension of a fugitive by pursuing State authorities carried out on non-sovereign territory/international space.

International Extradition see *Extradition*

International Fugitive from Justice a person formally charged with a crime, or a convicted criminal whose punishment has not yet been determined or fully served, who is currently outside the territorial jurisdiction and beyond the custody or control of the State (or of the custody or control of the international criminal tribunal) pursuing him.

International Rendition the involuntary physical transfer of an individual of interest between two States for any law enforcement, military, or intelligence purpose, or between a State and an international criminal tribunal. (Compare with *Rendition and Extraordinary Rendition*)

Joint Operation the carrying out of a fugitive recovery activity within host State territory when conducted by pursuing and host State officials or agents working together.

Joint Rendition the physical transfer of an individual from host State territory to pursuing State territory when conducted by pursuing and host State officials or agents working together.

Lure and Capture Operation (LCO) a deceptive activity in which pursuing State and/or host State officials or agents entice a fugitive to travel to another location or jurisdiction with the consequential intention of apprehending him.

Male captus bene detentus (Latin) in translation it means "an unlawful apprehension may nevertheless give rise to lawful detention and prosecution," and stands for the proposition that a court must treat as immaterial for personal jurisdiction purposes how a criminal defendant came before it. (Compare with *Rule of Non-Inquiry*)

Non-refoulement (French) an international legal principle that prohibits individuals from being returned, removed, transferred, or otherwise *refouled* (*i.e.*, "turned back") to States where their rights to life, liberty, and security of person, particularly including the freedom from extrajudicial killing, enforced disappearance, torture or other abusive treatment, or imprisonment on improper grounds, are believed to be threatened.

Non-Sovereign Territory/International Space any territory or space not recognized by the international community as currently subject to sovereign ownership or control.

Passive Extradition the extradition process undertaken by, and from the perspective of, the *host* State, commencing with the receipt of an extradition request. (Compare with *Active Extradition*)

Passive Interception a State's verbal admonition, that its territory, including sovereign waters and airspace, as appropriate, are restricted from use or passage by specified aircraft, vessels, or vehicles suspected of carrying a fugitive. (Compare with *Interception Operation*)

Provisional Arrest the temporary arrest of a fugitive made on an emergency basis at the behest of a pursuing State (or international criminal tribunal) prior to but in anticipation of an extradition (or surrender) request.

Pursuing State a State that seeks the prosecution or punishment of a fugitive, prior to any delivery into its own territory, custody, or control, whether within or outside the extradition context. (Compare with *Host State*)

Receiving State in the immigration law context, a State that is accepting or has accepted into its sovereign territory an alien removed by another State (compare with *Removal* and *Removing State*); or in the diplomatic context, a State to which a foreign diplomatic or consular officer is officially posted or assigned. (Compare with *Sending State*)

Removal a State's exercise of immigration power through either exclusion or deportation and that can be effected directly, indirectly (with the assistance of a third State intermediary), or via a negotiated arrangement.

Removing State a State that is in the process of removing or has removed an alien from its sovereign territory. (Compare with *Receiving State*)

Rendered State the former host State from whose territory a pursuing State unilaterally is transferring or has transferred a fugitive into its own territory, custody, or control. (Compare with *Rendering State* and *Injured State*)

Rendering State a pursuing State that unilaterally is transferring or has transferred a fugitive from host State territory into its own territory, custody, or control. (Compare with *Rendered State*)

Rendition the involuntary physical transfer of an individual of interest by officials or agents of a State from one location or jurisdiction to another for any law enforcement, military, or intelligence purpose. (Compare with *International Rendition* and *Extraordinary Rendition*)

Requested State the State with jurisdiction over a fugitive and from which his physical custody is sought via an extradition request. (Compare with *Requesting State*)

Requesting State the State that seeks physical custody over a fugitive from the State with jurisdiction over him and submits a request for his extradition to that end. (Compare with *Requested State*)

Rule of Non-Inquiry the principle in which: (i) a State's executive deems it inappropriate to ascertain the motive behind another State's request for the custodial transfer of a fugitive and/or to examine another State's legal standards or procedures for handling a fugitive post-delivery, and therefore is prepared to transfer a fugitive without scrutiny; or (ii) a State's judiciary does not regard it as proper to query how a criminal defendant came before it, and therefore is willing to assert personal jurisdiction regardless of the circumstances surrounding his capture and transfer. (Compare with *Male Captus Bene Detentus*)

Safe Haven a State that provides legal protection to individuals or groups residing within its jurisdictional control while they carry out unlawful operations and/or evade the reach of overseas law enforcement.

Seizure and Delivery Operation (SDO) the capture or arrest of a fugitive effected in territory other than that of a pursuing State carried out by pursuing State and/or host State officials or agents with the intended subsequent delivery of that fugitive to pursuing State territory, custody, or control.

Semi-formal Rendition any rendition handled through an *ad hoc*, non-treaty-based arrangement that nevertheless involves some legal process. (Compare with *Formal Rendition* and *Informal Rendition*)

Sending State the State that dispatches a diplomatic or consular officer to another State for official representation purposes. (Compare with *Receiving State*)

Silver Platter Scenarios situations in which a fugitive returns, is returned, or his return is substantially facilitated to pursuing State territory, custody, or control by sheer fortuity. More specifically, such scenarios may occur: (i) based on an error or misunderstanding by the fugitive or by host State or international tribunal officials or agents, (ii) intentionally by the fugitive but in reliance on personal motivations unrelated to law enforcement measures or pressures, (iii) purposefully by the host State pursuant to its immigration laws when unaware of receiving State law enforcement interest in the fugitive or in reversing an initial extradition denial when prompted by external, non-law enforcement-related factors, or (iv) by private actors, including government officials acting in their personal capacity or *ultra vires*, regardless of motivation.

Specialty a rule of customary international law applied in the extradition context in which a pursuing State may not detain, try, or punish a fugitive for any offense committed before his extradition, except those that were the subject of the extradition request and approval, unless the host State lends its agreement or a lesser included offense arose out of the same underlying facts.

State Agents any non-State officials contracted on behalf of a national government to undertake a specific task, project, or mission whose conduct during such time is attributable to that State; such persons could include paid or unpaid private citizens or even State Officials of another government while acting in their personal capacity.

State Officials any national government employees, *i.e.*, bureaucrats.

Strategic Rendition the rendition of an individual to pursuing State territory, custody, or control. (Compare with *Tactical Rendition*)

Summary Extradition an expedited or abbreviated extradition, which may be formally or informally executed.

Surrender the transfer of physical custody of a fugitive from a State 'vertically' to an international criminal tribunal, such as the ICTY or ICC, as opposed to 'horizontally' to another State. (Compare with *Extradition*)

Surrogate Operation the carrying out of a fugitive recovery activity on host State territory when conducted exclusively by host State officials or agents at a pursuing State's behest.

Surrogate Rendition the physical transfer of an individual from host State territory to pursuing State territory, custody, or control when conducted exclusively by host State officials or agents at a pursuing State's behest.

Tactical Rendition the rendition of an individual to non-pursuing State territory, custody, or control, whether on an intermediate basis or as a final destination. (Compare with *Intermediate Rendition* and *Strategic Rendition*)

Territorial State the State in which the actual or alleged crime by the fugitive in question was committed, regardless of where the fugitive is presently located.

Transferee State the State into whose territory, custody, or control a fugitive is being or has been cooperatively delivered by another State or an international criminal tribunal for law enforcement purposes. (Compare with *Transferor State, Receiving State, Rendering State,* and *Fortuitously Acquiring State*)

Transferee Tribunal the international criminal tribunal into whose custody or control a fugitive is being or has been cooperatively surrendered by any means for law enforcement purposes. (Compare with *Transferor Tribunal*)

Transferor State the State that is effecting or has effected the cooperative law enforcement delivery of a fugitive by any means into the jurisdiction, custody, or control of another State or an international criminal tribunal. (Compare with *Transferee State*, *Removing State*, and *Rendered State*)

Transferor Tribunal the international criminal tribunal that is effecting or has effected the cooperative law enforcement delivery of a fugitive into the territory, custody, or control of a State. (Compare with *Transferee Tribunal*)

Unilateral Operation the carrying out of a fugitive recovery activity on host State territory when conducted by pursuing State officials or agents without the participation, knowledge, or consent of the host State.

Unilateral Rendition the physical transfer of an individual from host State territory to pursuing State territory when conducted by pursuing State officials or agents without the participation, knowledge, or consent of the host State.

Voluntary Deportation a deportation in which an alien freely consents to be deported to his home or a third State prior to a deportation determination by the host State.

SELECTED BIBLIOGRAPHY

I Books and Chapters

ABBELL, MICHAEL, EXTRADITION TO AND FROM THE UNITED STATES (2010).

BANTEKAS, ILIAS & SUSAN NASH, INTERNATIONAL CRIMINAL LAW (2d ed. 2003).

BASSIOUNI, M. CHERIF, 2 INTERNATIONAL CRIMINAL LAW: MULTILATERAL AND BILATERAL ENFORCEMENT MECHANISMS (3d ed. 2008).

BASSIOUNI, M. CHERIF, INTERNATIONAL EXTRADITION AND WORLD PUBLIC ORDER (1974).

BASSIOUNI, M. CHERIF, INTERNATIONAL EXTRADITION: UNITED STATES LAW AND PRACTICE (6th ed. 2014).

BASSIOUNI, M. CHERIF & EDWARD M. WISE, AUT DEDERE AUT JUDICARE: THE DUTY TO EXTRADITE OR PROSECUTE IN INTERNATIONAL LAW (1995).

BEDI, SATYADEVA, EXTRADITION: A TREATISE ON THE LAWS RELEVANT TO THE FUGITIVE OFFENDERS WITHIN AND WITH THE COMMONWEALTH COUNTRIES (2002).

Blakesley, Christopher L., *Extraterritorial Jurisdiction, in* 2 INTERNATIONAL CRIMINAL LAW: PROCEDURE AND ENFORCEMENT MECHANISMS (2d ed. M. Cherif Bassiouni ed. 1999).

BOISTER, NEIL, AN INTRODUCTION TO TRANSNATIONAL CRIMINAL LAW (2012).

Borelli, Silvia, *The Rendition of Terrorist Suspects to the United States: Human Rights and the Limits of International Cooperation, in* ENFORCING INTERNATIONAL LAW NORMS AGAINST TERRORISM (Andrea Bianchi ed. 2004).

CAMERON, IAIN A., THE PROTECTIVE PRINCIPLE OF INTERNATIONAL CRIMINAL JURISDICTION (1994).

CHOO, ANDREW L.-T., ABUSE OF PROCESS AND JUDICIAL STAYS OF CRIMINAL PROCEEDINGS (1993).

D'Amato, Anthony, *National Prosecution for International Crimes, in* 3 INTERNATIONAL CRIMINAL LAW: ENFORCEMENT (2d ed. M. Cherif Bassiouni ed. 1999).

Evans, Alona E., *The Apprehension and Prosecution of Offenders: Some Current Problems, in* LEGAL ASPECTS OF INTERNATIONAL TERRORISM (Alona E. Evans & John F. Murphy eds. 1978).

Evans, Alona E., *Extradition and Rendition: Problems of Choice, in* INTERNATIONAL ASPECTS OF CRIMINAL LAW: ENFORCING UNITED STATES LAW IN THE WORLD COMMUNITY (Richard B. Lillich ed. 1981).

FORDE, MICHAEL & KIERAN KELLY, EXTRADITION LAW AND TRANSNATIONAL CRIMINAL PROCEDURE (4th ed. 2012).

GILBERT, GEOFF, RESPONDING TO INTERNATIONAL CRIME (2006).

GOODWIN-GILL, GUY S., INTERNATIONAL LAW AND THE MOVEMENT OF PERSONS BETWEEN STATES (1978).

Heymann, Philip B. & Ian Heath Gershengorn, *Pursuing Justice, Respecting the Law, in* PRINCIPLES AND PROCEDURES FOR A NEW TRANSNATIONAL CRIMINAL LAW: DOCUMENTATION OF AN INTERNATIONAL WORKSHOP IN FREIBURG, MAY 1991 (Albin Eser & Otto Lagodny eds. 1992).

Higdon, Paul, *Interpol's Role in International Police Cooperation, in* INTERNATIONAL POLICE COOPERATION: A WORLD PERSPECTIVE (Daniel J. Koenig & Dilip K. Das eds. 2001).

JONES, ALUN & ANAND DOOBAY, JONES AND DOOBAY ON EXTRADITION AND MUTUAL ASSISTANCE (2005).

Kolb, Robert, *The Exercise of Criminal Jurisdiction over International Terrorists, in* ENFORCING INTERNATIONAL LAW NORMS AGAINST TERRORISM (Andrea Bianchi ed. 2004).

Labayle, Henri, *Terrorism and Extradition: A French Perspective, in* TERRORISM AND INTERNATIONAL LAW (Rosalyn Higgins & Maurice Flory eds. 1997).

Lamb, Susan, *Illegal Arrest and the Jurisdiction of the ICTY, in* ESSAYS ON ICTY PROCEDURE AND EVIDENCE IN HONOUR OF GABRIELLE KIRK MCDONALD (Richard May, *et al.* eds. 2001).

Mann, Frederick A., *Reflections on the Prosecution of Persons Abducted in Breach of International Law, in* INTERNATIONAL LAW AT A TIME OF PERPLEXITY: ESSAYS IN HONOUR OF SHABTAI ROSENNE (Yoram Dinstein ed. 1989).

MARTHA, RUTSEL SILVESTRE J., THE LEGAL FOUNDATIONS OF INTERPOL (2010).

Muir, Matthew A., *A Guide to the Law and Practice of International Extradition, in* 4 A MODERN LEGAL SYSTEMS CYCLOPEDIA (Kenneth Robert Redden ed. 1989).

NADELMANN, ETHAN A., COPS ACROSS BORDERS: THE INTERNATIONALIZATION OF U.S. CRIMINAL LAW ENFORCEMENT (1993).

NICHOLLS, CLIVE, ET AL., EDS., THE LAW OF EXTRADITION AND MUTUAL ASSISTANCE (2d ed. 2007).

O'Shea, Sheila, *Interaction Between International Criminal Tribunals and National Legal Systems, in* INTERNATIONAL LAW DECISIONS IN NATIONAL COURTS (Thomas M. Franck & Gregory H. Fox eds. 1996).

PALMER, EDITH, THE AUSTRIAN LAW ON EXTRADITION AND MUTUAL ASSISTANCE IN CRIMINAL MATTERS (1983).

PIGGOTT, FRANCIS, EXTRADITION: A TREATISE ON THE LAW RELATING TO FUGITIVE OFFENDERS (1910).

PYLE, CHRISTOPHER H., EXTRADITION, POLITICS, AND HUMAN RIGHTS (2001).

Rayfuse, Rosemary, *International Abduction and the United States Supreme Court: The Law of the Jungle Reigns, in* INTERNATIONAL CRIMINAL LAW AND PROCEDURE (John Dugard & Christine van den Wyngaert eds. 1996).

SAMBEI, ARVINDER & JOHN R.W.D. JONES, EXTRADITION LAW HANDBOOK (2005).

SHEARER, IVAN A., EXTRADITION IN INTERNATIONAL LAW (1971).

STANBROOK, IVOR & CLIVE STANBROOK, EXTRADITION: LAW AND PRACTICE (2d ed. 2000).

Swart, Bert, *Extradition, in* INTERNATIONAL CRIMINAL LAW IN THE NETHERLANDS (Bert Swart & Andre Klip eds. 1997).

van den Wyngaert, Christine, *Applying the European Convention on Human Rights to Extradition: Opening Pandora's Box?, in* INTERNATIONAL CRIMINAL LAW AND PROCEDURE (John Dugard & Christine van den Wyngaert eds. 1996).

VAN DEN WYNGAERT, CHRISTINE, THE POLITICAL OFFENCE EXCEPTION TO EXTRADITION: THE DELICATE PROBLEM OF BALANCING THE RIGHTS OF THE INDIVIDUAL AND THE INTERNATIONAL PUBLIC ORDER (1980).

Vogler, Theo, *Perspectives on Extradition and Terrorism, in* INTERNATIONAL TERRORISM AND POLITICAL CRIMES (M. Cherif Bassiouni ed. 1975).

WHITEMAN, MARJORIE M., 6 DIGEST OF INTERNATIONAL LAW (1968).

Wise, Edward M., Aut Dedere Aut Judicare: *The Duty to Prosecute or Extradite, in* 2 INTERNATIONAL CRIMINAL LAW: PROCEDURAL AND ENFORCEMENT MECHANISMS (M. Cherif Bassiouni ed. 1999).

Woltring, Hermann F. & Joanne Greig, *State-Sponsored Kidnapping of Fugitives: An Alternative to Extradition?, in* THE ALLEGED TRANSNATIONAL CRIMINAL: THE SECOND BIENNIAL INTERNATIONAL CRIMINAL LAW SEMINAR (Richard D. Atkins ed. 1993).

YARNOLD, BARBARA M., INTERNATIONAL FUGITIVES: A NEW ROLE FOR THE INTERNATIONAL COURT OF JUSTICE (1991).

ZANOTTI, ISIDORO, EXTRADITION IN MULTILATERAL TREATIES AND CONVENTIONS (2006).

II Scholarly Articles

Abramovsky, Abraham, *Extraterritorial Abductions: America's 'Catch and Snatch' Policy Run Amok*, 31 VA. J. INT'L L. 151 (1991).

Arzt, Donna E., *The Lockerbie 'Extradition by Analogy' Agreement: 'Exceptional Measure' or Template for Transnational Criminal Justice?*, 18 AM. U. INT'L L. REV. 163 (2002).

Bassiouni, M. Cherif, *Unlawful Seizures and Irregular Rendition Devices as Alternatives to Extradition*, 7 VAND. J. TRANSNAT'L L. 25 (1973).

Blakesley, Christopher L., *A Conceptual Framework for Extradition and Jurisdiction over Extraterritorial Crime*, 1984 UTAH L. REV. 685 (1984).

Brkljacic, Mark, Note, *The Dangers of State Sponsored and Court Ratified Abduction*, 5 J. INT'L L. & PRAC. 117 (1996).

Brown, Kellee A. & Sophia A. Muirhead, *Extradition: Divergent Trends in International Cooperation*, 33 HARV. INT'L L.J. 223 (1992).

Bush, Jonathan A., *How Did We Get Here?: Forcible Abduction after Alvarez-Machain*, 45 STAN. L. REV. 939 (1993).

Calica, Andrew J., *Self-Help is the Best Kind: The Efficient Breach Justification for Forcible Abduction of Terrorists*, 37 CORNELL INT'L L.J. 389 (2004).

Campbell, Andrew B., Note, *The* Ker-Frisbie *Doctrine: A Jurisdictional Weapon in the War on Drugs*, 23 VAND. J. TRANSNAT'L L. 385 (1990).

Cardozo, Michael H., *When Extradition Fails, Is Abduction the Solution?*, 55 AM. J. INT'L L. 127 (1961).

Cassese, Antonio, *The International Community's 'Legal' Response to Terrorism*, 38 INT'L & COMP. L.Q. 589 (1989).

Choo, Andrew L.-T., *International Kidnapping, Disguised Extradition and Abuse of Process*, 57 MOD. L. REV. 626 (1994).

Costi, Alberto, *Problems with Current International and National Practices Concerning Extraterritorial Abductions*, 8 NZACL Y.B. 57 (2002).

D'Amato, Anthony, *Agora: The Invasion of Panama Was a Lawful Response to Tyranny*, 84 AM. J. INT'L L. 516 (1990).

de Sanctis, Francesco, *The Practice of National and International Courts on Transnational Seizure: Is a Fair Balance Between Human Rights and Accountability Possible?*, 22 NETH. Q. HUM. RTS. 529 (2004).

Deen-Racsmány, Zsuzsanna, *Modernizing the Nationality Exception: Is the Non-extradition of Residents a Better Rule?*, 75 NORDIC J. INT'L L. 29 (2006).

Dickinson, Edwin D., *Jurisdiction Following Seizure or Arrest in Violation of International Law*, 28 AM. J. INT'L L. 231 (1934).

Dinstein, Yoram, *Some Reflections on Extradition*, 36 GER. Y.B. INT'L L. 46 (1993).

Downing, Richard, Recent Development, *The Domestic and International Legal Implications of the Abduction of Criminals from Foreign Soil*, 26 STAN. J. INT'L L. 573 (1989–90).

Dugard, John & Christine van den Wyngaert, *Reconciling Extradition with Human Rights*, 92 AM. J. INT'L L. 187 (1998).

Epps, Valerie, *The Development of the Conceptual Framework Supporting International Extradition*, 25 LOY. L.A. INT'L & COMP. L. REV. 369 (2003).

Evans, Alona E., *Acquisition of Custody over the International Fugitive Offender—Alternatives to Extradition: A Survey of United States Practice*, 40 Brit. Y.B. Int'l L. 77 (1964).

Evans, Scott S., Note, *International Kidnapping in a Violent World: Where the United States Ought to Draw the Line*, 137 Mil. L. Rev. 187 (1992).

Fawcett, J.E.S., *The Eichmann Case*, 38 Brit. Y.B. Int'l L. 181 (1964).

Findlay, D. Cameron, *Abducting Terrorists Overseas for Trial in the United States: Issues of International and Domestic Law*, 23 Tex. Int'l L.J. 1 (1988).

Gallant, Kenneth S., *Securing the Presence of Defendants before the International Tribunal for the Former Yugoslavia: Breaking with Extradition*, 5 Crim. L.F. 557 (1994).

Glennon, Michael J., *Agora: International Kidnapping: State-Sponsored Abduction: A Comment on United States v. Alvarez-Machain*, 86 Am. J. Int'l L. 746 (1992).

Gluck, Jonathan A., *The Customary International Law of State-Sponsored International Abduction and United States Courts*, 44 Duke L.J. 612 (1994).

Griffith, Gavan QC, & Claire Harris, *Recent Developments in the Law of Extradition*, 6 Melb. J. Int'l L. 33 (2005).

Harrington, Joanna, *The Role for Human Rights Obligations in Canadian Extradition Law*, 43 Can. Y.B. Int'l L. 45 (2005).

Henkin, Louis, *The Invasion of Panama Under International Law: A Gross Violation*, 29 Colum. J. Transnat'l L. 293 (1991).

Henning, Matthew W., Note, *Extradition Controversies: How Enthusiastic Prosecutions Can Lead to International Incidents*, 22 B.C. Int'l & Comp. L. Rev. 347 (1999).

Iraola, Robert, *Foreign Extraditions and In Absentia Convictions*, 39 Seton Hall L. Rev. 843 (2009).

Izes, Beverly, *Drawing Lines in the Sand: When State-Sanctioned Abduction of War Criminals Should be Permitted*, 31 Colum. J. L & Soc. Probs. 1 (1997–98).

Jennings, R.Y., *The Eisler Case*, 26 Brit. Y.B. Int'l L. 468 (1949).

Joyner, Christopher C., *International Extradition and Global Terrorism: Bringing International Criminals to Justice*, 25 Loy. L.A. Int'l & Comp. L. Rev. 493 (2003).

Kane, Terry Richard, *Prosecuting International Terrorists in United States Courts: Gaining the Jurisdictional Threshold*, 12 Yale J. Int'l L. 294 (1987).

Kash, Douglas, *Abduction of Terrorists in International Airspace and on the High Seas*, 8 Fla. J. Int'l L. 65 (1993).

Kasirer, Nicholas, *Defenses, Exceptions and Exemptions to Extradition*, 62 Int'l Rev. Penal L. 91 (1991).

Kassim-Momodu, Momodu, *Extradition of Fugitives by Nigeria*, 35 Int'l & Comp. L.Q. 512 (1986).

Kennedy, David M., *et al.*, *The Extradition of Mohammed Hamadei*, 31 Harv. Int'l L.J. 5 (1990).

Kester, John G., *Some Myths of United States Extradition Law*, 76 Geo. L.J. 1441 (1998).

Khan, Andy N., *Trial Without Extradition—Abuse of Court's Process*, 1986 N.Z.L.J. 123 (Apr. 1986).

Koivu, Virpi, *Head-of-State Immunity v. Individual Criminal Responsibility under International Law*, 12 Finn. Y.B. Int'l L. 305 (2001).

Kolb, Robert, *Universal Criminal Jurisdiction in Matters of International Terrorism: Some Reflections on Status and Trends in Contemporary International Law*, 50 Revue Hellénique de Droit Int'l 43 (1997).

Laflin, Melanie M., Note, *Kidnapped Terrorists: Bringing International Criminals to Justice Through Irregular Rendition and Other Quasi-Legal Options*, 26 J. Legis. 315 (2000).

Lanham, David, *Informal Extradition in Australian Law*, 11 Crim. L.J. 3 (Feb. 1987).

Levitt, Kenneth E., Note, *International Extradition, The Principle of Specialty and Effective Treaty Enforcement*, 76 Minn. L. Rev. 1017 (1992).

Liskofsky, Sidney, *The Abu Daoud Case: Law or Politics*, 7 Isr. Y.B. Hum. Rts. 66 (1977).

Lowenfeld, Andreas F., *Ahmad: Profile of an Extradition Case*, 23 N.Y.U. J. Int'l L. & Pol. 723 (1991).

McCarthy, John G., Note, *The Passive Personality Principle and Its Use in Combatting International Terrorism*, 13 Fordham Int'l L.J. 298 (1989–90).

McNair, Arnold, *Extradition and Exterritorial Asylum*, 28 Brit. Y.B. Int'l L. 172 (1951).

McNeal, Gregory S. & Brian J. Field, *Snatch-and-Grab Ops: Justifying Extraterritorial Abduction*, 16 J. Transnat'l L. & Contemp. Probs. 491 (2007).

Mackarel, Mark, *The European Arrest Warrant – the Early Years: Implementing and Using the Warrant*, 15 Eur. J. Crime, Crim. L. & Crim. Just. 37 (2007).

Matorin, Mitchell J., *Unchaining the Law: The Legality of Extraterritorial Abduction in Lieu of Extradition*, 41 Duke L.J. 907 (1992).

Medley, Kyle M., Note, *The Widening of the Atlantic: Extradition Practices Between the United States and Europe*, 68 Brook. L. Rev. 1213 (2002–03).

Michell, Paul, *English-Speaking Justice: Evolving Responses to Transnational Forcible Abduction after Alvarez-Machain*, 29 Cornell Int'l L.J. 383 (1996).

Mitra, N.L., *Extradition: Policy and Practice in India*, 62 Int'l Rev. Penal L. 607 (1991).

Mohit, Abraham, *The Customary Law of International Abductions: Limits and Boundaries*, 11 Asian Y.B. Int'l L. 123 (2003–04).

Morgenstern, Felice, *Jurisdiction in Seizures Effected in Violation of International Law*, 29 Brit. Y.B. Int'l L. 265 (1952).

Murchison, Matthew, *Note, Extradition's Paradox: Duty, Discretion, and Rights in the World of Non-Inquiry*, 43 Stan. J. Int'l L. 295 (2007).

Murphy, Sean D., *The Expulsion of Aliens and Other Topics: The Sixty-Fourth Session of the International Law Commission*, 107 Am. J. Int'l L. 164 (2013).

Muther, Jr., Thomas F., *The Extradition of International Criminals: A Changing Perspective*, 24 Denv. J. Int'l L. & Pol'y 221 (1995).

Nadelmann, Ethan A., *The Evolution of United States Involvement in the International Rendition of Fugitive Criminals*, 25 N.Y.U. J. Int'l L. & Pol. 813 (1993).

Nanda, Ved P., *Bases for Refusing International Extradition Requests – Capital Punishment and Torture*, 23 Fordham Int'l L.J. 1369 (1999).

O'Higgins, Paul, *Unlawful Seizure and Irregular Extradition*, 36 Brit. Y.B. Int'l L. 279 (1960).

Papandrea, Mary-Rose, *Note, Standing to Allege Violations of the Doctrine of Specialty: An Examination of the Relationship Between the Individual and the Sovereign*, 62 U. Chi. L. Rev. 1187 (1995).

Paust, Jordan J., *After Alvarez-Machain: Abduction, Standing, Denials of Justice, and Unaddressed Human Rights Claims*, 67 St. John's L. Rev. 551 (1993).

Paust, Jordan J., *Responding Lawfully to International Terrorism: The Use of Force Abroad*, 8 Whittier L. Rev. 711 (1986).

Plachta, Michael, *European Arrest Warrant: Revolution in Extradition?*, 11 Eur. J. Crime, Crim. L. and Crim. J. 178 (2003).

Plachta, Michael, *The Lockerbie Case: The Role of the Security Council in Enforcing the Principle Aut Dedere Aut Judicare*, 12 Eur. J. Int'l L. 125 (2001).

Pontoni, Michael R., *Authority of the United States to Extraterritorially Apprehend and Lawfully Prosecute International Drug Traffickers and Other Fugitives*, 21 Cal. W. Int'l L.J. 215 (1990–91).

Poort, Tineke, *Male Captus, Bene Judicatus: Disguised Extradition and Other Practices*, 1 Leiden J. Int'l L. 65 (1988).

Preuss, Lawrence, *Kidnaping of Fugitives from Justice on Foreign Territory*, 29 Am. J. Int'l L. 502 (1935).

Satterthwaite, Margaret L., *The Legal Regime Governing Transfer of Persons in the Fight against Terrorism*, N.Y.U. Public Law and Legal Theory Working Papers, Paper 192 (2010).

Seaman, Perry John, Note, *International Bountyhunting: A Question of State Responsibility*, 15 Cal. W. Int'l L.J. 397 (1985).

Shea, Michael P., *Expanding Judicial Scrutiny of Human Rights in Extradition Cases after Soering*, 17 Yale J. Int'l L. 85 (1992).

Stein, Torsten, *Rendition of Terrorists: Extradition Versus Deportation*, 19 Isr. Y.B. Hum. Rts. 281 (1989).

Topiel, Michael S., Note, *The Doctrine of Non-Inquiry and the Preservation of Human Rights: Is There Room for Reconciliation?*, 9 Cardozo J. Int'l & Comp. L. 389 (2001).

van den Wyngaert, Christine, *The Political Offence Exception to Extradition: How to Plug the Terrorist Loophole Without Departing From Fundamental Human Rights*, 62 Int'l Rev. of Penal L. 291 (1991).

Warbrick, Colin, *Judicial Jurisdiction and Abuse of Process*, 49 Int'l & Comp. L.Q. 489 (2000).

Warbrick, Colin, *Recent Developments in U.K. Extradition Law*, 56 Int'l & Comp. L.Q. 199 (2007).

Warner, David P., *Challenges to International Law Enforcement Cooperation for the U.S. in the Middle East and North Africa: Extradition and Its Alternatives*, 50 Vill. L. Rev. 479 (2005).

Wedgwood, Ruth, *The Argument against International Abduction of Criminal Defendants, Amicus Curiae Brief Filed by the Lawyers Committee for Human Rights in United States v. Humberto Alvarez-Machain*, 6 Am. U. J. Int'l L. & Pol'y 537 (1991).

Wilkitski, Peter, *Defences, Exceptions and Exemptions in the Extradition Law and Practice and the Criminal Policy of the Federal Republic of Germany (Excluding the Political Offence Defence)*, 62 Int'l Rev. Penal L. 281 (1991).

Williams, Andrew S., *The Interception of Civil Aircraft over the High Seas in the Global War on Terror*, 59 A.F.L. Rev. 73 (2007).

Williams, Sharon A., *Human Rights Safeguards and International Cooperation in Extradition: Striking the Balance*, 3 Crim. L.F. 191 (1992).

NAME INDEX

SUBJECT INDEX